Eighth International Joint Conference on Natural Language Processing (IJCNLP 2017)

Short Papers

Taipei, Taiwan
1 December 2017

ISBN: 978-1-5108-5293-8

IJCNLP 2017

The Eighth International Joint Conference on Natural Language Processing

Proceedings of the Conference, Vol. 2 (Short Papers)

November 27 - December 1, 2017
Taipei, Taiwan

Preface

Welcome to the 8th International Joint Conference on Natural Language Processing (IJCNLP). IJCNLP was initiated in 2004 by the Asian Federation of Natural Language Processing (AFNLP) with the major goal to provide a platform for researchers and professionals around the world to share their experiences related to natural language processing and computational linguistics. In the past years, IJCNLPs were held in 7 different places: Hainan Island (2004), Jeju Island (2005), Hyderabad (2008), Singapore (2009), Chiang Mai (2011), Nagoya (2013) and Beijing (2015). This year the 8th IJCNLP is held in Taipei Nangang Exhibition Hall on November 27-December 1, 2017.

We are confident that you will find IJCNLP 2017 to be technically stimulating. The conference covers a broad spectrum of technical areas related to natural language processing and computation. Besides main conference, the program includes 3 keynote speeches, 6 tutorials, 17 demonstrations, 5 workshops, and 5 shared tasks (new event).

Before closing this brief welcome, we would like to thank the entire organizing committee for their long efforts to create and event that we hope will be memorable for you. Program chairs Greg Kondrak and Taro Watanabe coordinate the review process allowing for top quality papers to be presented at the conference. Workshop chairs Min Zhang and Yue Zhang organize 5 nice pre-conference and post-conference workshops. Tutorial chairs Sadao Kurohashi and Michael Strube select 6 very good tutorials. Demo chairs Seong-Bae Park and Thepchai Supnithi recommend 17 demonstrations. Shared Task chairs Chao-Hong Liu, Preslav Nakov and Nianwen Xue choose 5 interesting shared tasks. Sponsorship chairs Youngkil Kim, Tong Xiao, Kazuhide Yamamoto and Jui-Feng Yeh design sponsor packages and find financial supports. We thank all the sponsors. Publicity chairs Pushpak Bhattacharya, Xuanjing Huang, Gina-Anne Levow, Chi Mai Loung and Sebastian Stüker help circulate the conference information and promote the conference. We would like to express our special thanks to publication chairs Lung-Hao Lee and Derek F. Wong. After the hard work, they deliver an excellent proceeding to the participants.

Finally, we would like to thank all authors for submitting high quality research this year. We hope all of you enjoy the conference program, and your stay at this beautiful city of Taipei.

General Chair

Chengqing Zong, Institute of Automation, Chinese Academy of Sciences, China

Organization Co-Chairs

Hsin-Hsi Chen, National Taiwan University, Taiwan
Yuen-Hsien Tseng, National Taiwan Normal University, Taiwan
Chung-Hsien Wu, National Cheng Kung University, Taiwan
Liang-Chih Yu, Yuan Ze University, Taiwan

Message from the Program Co-Chairs

Welcome to the 8th International Joint Conference on Natural Language Processing (IJCNLP 2017) organized by National Taiwan Normal University and the Association for Computational Linguistics and Chinese Language Processing (ACLCLP) and hosted by The Asian Federation of Natural Language Processing (AFNLP).

Since the first meeting in 2004, IJCNLP has established itself as a major NLP conference. This year, we received 580 submissions (337 long and 243 short), which is by far the largest number ever for a stand-alone IJCNLP conference. From these, 179 papers (103 long and 76 short) were accepted to appear at the conference, which represents an acceptance rate of 31%. In particular, approximately 46% of the accepted papers are from Asia Pacific, 30% from North America, and 20% from Europe.

Our objective is to keep the conference to three parallel sessions at any one time. 86 long papers and 21 short papers are scheduled as oral presentations, while 17 long papers and 55 short papers will be presented as posters.

We are also very pleased to announce three exciting keynote talks by the renowned NLP researchers: Rada Mihalcea (University of Michigan), Trevor Cohn (University of Melbourne) and Jason Eisner (Johns Hopkins University).

The conference will conclude with the award presentation ceremony. The Best Paper Award goes to Nikolaos Pappas and Andrei Popescu-Belis for their paper "Multilingual Hierarchical Attention Networks for Document Classification." The Best Student Paper award goes to "Roles and Success in Wikipedia Talk Pages: Identifying Latent Patterns of Behavior" by Keith Maki, Michael Yoder, Yohan Jo and Carolyn Rosé.

We would like to thank everyone who has helped make IJCNLP 2017 a success. In particular, the area chairs (who are listed in the Program Committee section) worked hard on recruiting reviewers, managing reviews, leading discussions, and making recommendations. The quality of the technical program reflects the expertise of our 536 reviewers. All submissions were reviewed by at least three reviewers. The review process for the conference was double-blind, and included an author response period, as well as subsequent discussions.

We would like to acknowledge the help and advice from the General Chair Chengqing Zong, and the Local Arrangements Committee headed by Liang-Chih Yu. We thank the Publication Chairs Lung-Hao Lee and Derek F. Wong for putting together the conference proceedings and handbook, and all the other committee chairs for their great work.

We hope you will enjoy IJCNLP 2017!

IJCNLP 2017 Program Co-Chairs

Greg Kondrak, University of Alberta
Taro Watanabe, Google

Organizing Committee

Conference Chair

Chengqing Zong, Institute of Automation, Chinese Academy of Sciences

Program Committee Co-Chairs

Greg Kondrak, University of Alberta
Taro Watanabe, Google

Workshop Co-Chairs

Min Zhang, Soochow University
Yue Zhang, Singapore University of Technology and Design

Tutorial Co-Chairs

Sadao Kurohashi, Kyoto University
Michael Strube, Heidelberg Institute for Theoretical Studies

Demo Co-Chairs

Seong-Bae Park, Kyungpook National University
Thepchai Supnithi, National Electronics and Computer Technology Center (NECTEC) of Thailand

Shared Task Workshop Co-Chairs

Chao-Hong Liu, ADAPT Centre, Dublin City University
Preslav Nakov, Qatar Computing Research Institute
Nianwen Xue, Brandies University

Publication Co-Chairs

Lung-Hao Lee, National Taiwan Normal University
Derek F. Wong, University of Macau

Sponsorship Co-Chairs

Youngkil Kim, ETRI
Tong Xiao, Northeast University
Kazuhide Yamamoto, Nagaoka University of Technology
Jui-Feng Yeh, National Chiayi University

Publicity Co-Chairs

Pushpak Bhattacharya, IITB
Xuanjing Huang, Fudan University
Gina-Anne Levow, University of Washington
Chi Mai Loung, Institute of Information Technology
Sebastian Stüker, Karlsruhe Institute of Technology

Financial Chair

Lun-Wei Ku, Institute of Information Sciences, Academia Sinica

Local Co-Chairs

Hsin-Hsi Chen, National Taiwan University
Yuen-Hsien Tseng, National Taiwan Normal University
Chung-Hsien Wu, National Cheng Kung University
Liang-Chih Yu, Yuan Ze University

Program Committee

Program Committee Co-Chairs

Greg Kondrak, University of Alberta
Taro Watanabe, Google

Area Chairs

Mausam (Information Extraction and Text Mining Area)
Asli Celikyilmaz (Semantics Area)
Wenliang Chen (Syntax and Parsing Area)
Colin Cherry (Machine Translation Area)
Jackie Chi Kit Cheung (Summarization and Generation Area)
Monojit Choudhury (Resources and Tools Area)
Kevin Duh (Semantics Area)
Micha Elsner (Discourse, Dialogue, Pragmatics Area)
Manaal Faruqui (Machine Learning Area)
Jianfeng Gao (Information Retrieval and Question Answering Area)
Yvette Graham (Machine Translation Area)
Gholamreza Haffari (Machine Learning Area)
Liang Huang (Syntax and Parsing Area)
Minlie Huang (Sentiment Analysis and Opinion Mining Area)
Mans Hulden (Morphology, Segmentation and Tagging Area)
Nancy Ide (Resources and Tools Area)
Jing Jiang (Sentiment Analysis and Opinion Mining Area)
Daisuke Kawahara (Semantics Area)
Mamoru Komachi (NLP Applications Area)
Fei Liu (Web and Social Media Area)
Zhiyuan Liu (Web and Social Media Area)
Wei Lu (Information Extraction and Text Mining Area)
Ryo Nagata (NLP Applications Area) Mikio Nakano (Discourse, Dialogue, Pragmatics Area)
Jong-Hoon Oh (Information Retrieval and Question Answering Area)
Thamar Solorio (Sentiment Analysis and Opinion Mining Area)
Xu Sun (Morphology, Segmentation and Tagging Area)
Jun Suzuki (Machine Learning Area)
Xiaojun Wan (Summarization and Generation Area)
Tiejun Zhao (Machine Translation Area)

Reviewers

Alan Akbik, Chris Alberti, Enrique Alfonseca, David Alvarez-Melis, Silvio Amir, Daniel Andrade, Marianna Apidianaki, Jun Araki, Yuki Arase, Yoav Artzi, Kristjan Arumae, Wilker Aziz
Niranjan Balasubramanian, Timothy Baldwin, Kalika Bali, Rafael E. Banchs, Srinivas Bangalore, Timo Baumann, Kedar Bellare, Anja Belz, Steven Bethard, Chandra Bhagavatula, Suma Bhat, Joachim Bingel, Or Biran, Yonatan Bisk, Johannes Bjerva, Dasha Bogdanova, Bernd Bohnet, Danushka Bollegala, Florian Boudin, Chris Brockett, Julian Brooke, William Bryce, Paul Buitelaar, Jill Burstein, Stephan Busemann, Miriam Butt
José G. C. de Souza, Deng Cai, Burcu Can, Ziqiang Cao, Daniel Cer, Kai-Wei Chang, Ming-Wei Chang, Baobao Chang, Wanxiang Che, Xinchi Chen, Tao Chen, Danqi Chen, Kuang-hua Chen, John Chen, Boxing Chen, Pu-Jen Cheng, Hai Leong Chieu, laura chiticariu, KEY-SUN CHOI,

Shamil Chollampatt, Christos Christodoulopoulos, Jennifer Chu-Carroll, Miriam Connor, John Conroy, Matthieu Constant, Danish Contractor, Anna Corazza, Mark Core, Benoit Crabbé, Danilo Croce, Paul Crook, Heriberto Cuayahuitl

Raj Dabre, Bharath Dandala, Kareem Darwish, Gerard de Melo, Luciano Del Corro, Leon Derczynski, Nina Dethlefs, Lipika Dey, Bhuwan Dhingra, Giuseppe Di Fabbrizio, Marco Dinarelli, Daxiang Dong, Li Dong, Doug Downey, Lan Du, Nadir Durrani

Richard Eckart de Castilho, Steffen Eger, Yo Ehara, Patrick Ehlen, Vladimir Eidelman, Akiko Eriguchi, Tomaž Erjavec, Ramy Eskander, Miquel Esplà-Gomis

Licheng Fang, Geli Fei, Chong Feng, Oliver Ferschke, Andrew Finch, Orhan Firat, Margaret Fleck, Markus Forsberg, George Foster, Dayne Freitag, Atsushi Fujii, Fumiyo Fukumoto, Kotaro Funakoshi

Matt Gardner, Tao Ge, Kallirroi Georgila, Pablo Gervás, Alfio Gliozzo, Dan Goldwasser, Kyle Gorman, Isao Goto, Jiatao Gu, Camille Guinaudeau

Thanh-Le Ha, Christian Hadiwinoto, Masato Hagiwara, Dilek Hakkani-Tur, William L. Hamilton, Chung-Wei Hang, Kazi Saidul Hasan, Sadid A. Hasan, Kazuma Hashimoto, Eva Hasler, Matthew Hatem, Katsuhiko Hayashi, Luheng He, Matthew Henderson, Aurélie Herbelot, Ryuichiro Higashinaka, Cong Duy Vu Hoang, Chris Hokamp, Yu Hong, Kai Hong, Baotian Hu, Yuheng Hu, Xuanjing Huang, Po-Sen Huang, Jen-Wei Huang

Michimasa Inaba, Kentaro Inui, Hitoshi Isahara

Guoliang Ji, Yangfeng Ji, Sittichai Jiampojamarn, Wenbin Jiang, Zhanming Jie, Melvin Johnson Premkumar

Nobuhiro Kaji, Tomoyuki Kajiwara, Arzoo Katiyar, David Kauchak, Anna Kazantseva, Hideto Kazawa, Casey Kennington, Sunghwan Mac Kim, Jung-Jae Kim, Norihide Kitaoka, Julien Kloetzer, Mamoru Komachi, Kazunori Komatani, Parisa Kordjamshidi, Zornitsa Kozareva, Julia Kreutzer, Jayant Krishnamurthy, Lun-Wei Ku, Shankar Kumar, Jonathan K. Kummerfeld, Tsung-Ting Kuo

Sobha Lalitha Devi, Wai Lam, Man Lan, Ni Lao, Guy Lapalme, Carolin Lawrence, Joseph Le Roux, Logan Lebanoff, John Lee, Hung-yi Lee, Kenton Lee, Lung-Hao Lee, Sungjin Lee, Els Lefever, Gina-Anne Levow, Shaohua Li, Haibo Li, Haizhou Li, Sujian Li, Qing Li, Lishuang Li, Yaliang Li, Sheng Li, Chenliang Li, Kexin Liao, Xiao Ling, Pierre Lison, Qun Liu, Shulin Liu, Shujie Liu, Jiangming Liu, Yang Liu, Lemao Liu, Xiaohua Liu, Nikola Ljubešić, Chi-kiu Lo, Oier Lopez de Lacalle, Annie Louis, Stephanie Lukin, Jiaming Luo, Franco M. Luque, Anh Tuan Luu

Xuezhe Ma, Tengfei Ma, Wei-Yun Ma, Wolfgang Macherey, Andreas Maletti, Benjamin Marie, Yuichiroh Matsubayashi, Yuji Matsumoto, Takuya Matsuzaki, Diana McCarthy, Tara McIntosh, Susan McRoy, Sameep Mehta, Edgar Meij, Arul Menezes, Helen Meng, Adam Meyers, Bonan Min, Koji Mineshima, Amita Misra, Teruhisa Misu, Makoto Miwa, Daichi Mochihashi, Marie-Francine Moens, Samaneh Moghaddam, Karo Moilanen, Luis Gerardo Mojica de la Vega, Manuel Montes, Taesun Moon, Glyn Morrill, Alessandro Moschitti, Lili Mou, Aldrian Obaja Muis, Yugo Murawaki

Seung-Hoon Na, Preslav Nakov, Courtney Napoles, Jason Naradowsky, Shashi Narayan, Alexis Nasr, Mark-Jan Nederhof, Graham Neubig, Guenter Neumann, Vincent Ng, Dong Nguyen, Jian-Yun NIE, Hiroshi Noji, Scott Nowson

Diarmuid Ó Séaghdha, Yusuke Oda, Stephan Oepen, Tim O'Gorman, Jong-Hoon Oh, Kiyonori Ohtake, Hidekazu Oiwa, Naoaki Okazaki, Manabu Okumura, Naho Orita, Petya Osenova, Hiroki Ouchi

Inkit Padhi, Sebastian Padó, Hamid Palangi, Aasish Pappu, Peyman Passban, Adam Pease, Nanyun Peng, Gerald Penn, Juan Antonio Pérez-Ortiz, Peter Phandi, Karl Pichotta, Massimo Poesio, Maja Popović, Soujanya Poria, Daniel Preoţiuc-Pietro, Matthew Purver

Ashequl Qadir, Xian Qian

Dinesh Raghu, Afshin Rahimi, A Ramanathan, Sudha Rao, Pushpendre Rastogi, Georg Rehm, Martin Riedl, German Rigau, Brian Roark, Michael Roth, Alla Rozovskaya, Rachel Rudinger, Attapol Rutherford

Ashish Sabharwal, Kugatsu Sadamitsu, Markus Saers, Keisuke Sakaguchi, Germán Sanchis-Trilles, Ryohei Sasano, Carolina Scarton, David Schlangen, Eva Schlinger, Allen Schmaltz, Djamé Seddah, Satoshi Sekine, Lei Sha, Kashif Shah, Ehsan Shareghi, Shiqi Shen, Shuming Shi, Tomohide Shibata, Sayaka Shiota, Prasha Shrestha, Maryam Siahbani, Avirup Sil, Miikka Silfverberg, Patrick Simianer, Sameer Singh, Sunayana Sitaram, Jan Šnajder, Wei Song, Yang Song, Sa-kwang Song, Virach Sornlertlamvanich, Matthias Sperber, Caroline Sporleder, Vivek Srikumar, Manfred Stede, Mark Steedman, Pontus Stenetorp, Svetlana Stoyanchev, Karl Stratos, Kristina Striegnitz, L V Subramaniam, Katsuhito Sudoh, Hiroaki Sugiyama, Huan Sun

Sho Takase, David Talbot, Liling Tan, Jiwei Tan, Niket Tandon, Takehiro Tazoe, Joel Tetreault, Ran Tian, Takenobu Tokunaga, Gaurav Singh Tomar, Sara Tonelli, Fatemeh Torabi Asr, Ming-Feng Tsai, Richard Tzong-Han Tsai, Masashi Tsubaki, Jun'ichi Tsujii, Yulia Tsvetkov, Zhaopeng Tu, Cunchao Tu, Francis Tyers

Kiyotaka Uchimoto, Masao Utiyama

Tim Van de Cruys, Keith VanderLinden, Lucy Vanderwende, Vasudeva Varma, Eva Maria Vecchi, sriram venkatapathy, Marc Verhagen, David Vilar, David Vilares, Martin Villalba, Svitlana Volkova, Ivan Vulić

Xuancong Wang, Longyue Wang, Pidong Wang, Wei Wang, Rui Wang, Baoxun Wang, William Yang Wang, Mingxuan Wang, Leo Wanner, Bonnie Webber, Ingmar Weber, Julie Weeds, Furu Wei, Aaron Steven White, Jason D Williams, Tak-Lam Wong, Kam-Fai Wong, Derek F. Wong, Fangzhao Wu, Shih-Hung Wu, Joern Wuebker

Tong Xiao, Xinyan Xiao, Deyi Xiong, Wenduan Xu, Ruifeng Xu, Ying Xu

Bishan Yang, Yi Yang, Cheng Yang, Helen Yannakoudakis, Wenpeng Yin, Anssi Yli-Jyrä, Yuya Yoshikawa, Naoki Yoshinaga, Koichiro Yoshino, Dianhai Yu, Mo Yu, Bei Yu, Jianfei Yu

Fabio Massimo Zanzotto, Sina Zarrieß, Xiaodong Zeng, Feifei Zhai, Min Zhang, Sheng Zhang, Wei-Nan Zhang, Jian Zhang, Longtu Zhang, Hao Zhang, Meishan Zhang, Jiajun Zhang, Jian ZHANG, Meishan Zhang, Lei Zhang, Chengzhi Zhang, Dongyan Zhao, Jun Zhao, Hai Zhao, Alisa Zhila, Guangyou Zhou, Muhua Zhu, Heike Zinsmeister, Pierre Zweigenbaum

Invited Talk: Words and People

Rada Mihalcea

University of Michigan

Abstract

What do the words we use say about us and about how we view the world surrounding us? And what do we - as speakers of those words with our own defining attributes, imply about the words we utter? In this talk, I will explore the relation between words and people and show how we can develop cross-cultural word models to identify words with cultural bias – i.e., words that are used in significantly different ways by speakers from different cultures. Further, I will also show how we can effectively use information about the speakers of a word (i.e., their gender, culture) to build better word models.

Biography

Rada Mihalcea is a Professor in the Computer Science and Engineering department at the University of Michigan. Her research interests are in computational linguistics, with a focus on lexical semantics, multilingual natural language processing, and computational social sciences. She serves or has served on the editorial boards of the Journals of Computational Linguistics, Language Resources and Evaluations, Natural Language Engineering, Research in Language in Computation, IEEE Transactions on Affective Computing, and Transactions of the Association for Computational Linguistics. She was a program co-chair for the Conference of the Association for Computational Linguistics (2011) and the Conference on Empirical Methods in Natural Language Processing (2009), and a general chair for the Conference of the North American Chapter of the Association for Computational Linguistics (2015). She is the recipient of a National Science Foundation CAREER award (2008) and a Presidential Early Career Award for Scientists and Engineers awarded by President Obama (2009). In 2013, she was made an honorary citizen of her hometown of Cluj-Napoca, Romania.

Invited Talk: Learning Large and Small: How to Transfer NLP Successes to Low-resource Languages

Trevor Cohn

University of Melbourne

Abstract

Recent advances in NLP have predominantly been based upon supervised learning over large corpora, where rich expressive models, such as deep learning methods, can perform exceptionally well. However, these state of the art approaches tend to be very data hungry, and consequently do not elegantly scale down to smaller corpora, which are more typical in many NLP applications.

In this talk, I will describe the importance of small data in our field, drawing particular attention to so-called "low-" or "under-resourced" languages, for which corpora are scarce, and linguistic annotations scarcer yet. One of the key problems for our field is how to translate successes on the few high-resource languages to practical technologies for the remaining majority of the world's languages. I will cover several research problems in this space, including transfer learning between high- and low-resource languages, active learning for selecting text for annotation, and speech processing in a low-resource setting, namely learning to translate audio inputs without transcriptions. I will finish by discussing open problems in natural language processing that will be critical in porting highly successful NLP work to the myriad of less-well-studied languages.

Biography

Trevor Cohn is an Associate Professor and ARC Future Fellow at the University of Melbourne, in the School of Computing and Information Systems. He received Bachelor degrees in Software Engineering and Commerce, and a PhD degree in Engineering from the University of Melbourne. He was previously based at the University of Sheffield, and before this worked as a Research Fellow at the University of Edinburgh. His research interests focus on probabilistic and statistical machine learning for natural language processing, with applications in several areas including machine translation, parsing and grammar induction. Current projects include translating diverse and noisy text sources, deep learning of semantics in translation, rumour diffusion over social media, and algorithmic approaches for scaling to massive corpora. Dr. Cohn's research has been recognised by several best paper awards, including best short paper at EMNLP in 2016. He will be jointly organising ACL 2018 in Melbourne.

Invited Talk: Strategies for Discovering Underlying Linguistic Structure

Jason Eisner

Johns Hopkins University

Abstract

A goal of computational linguistics is to automate the kind of reasoning that linguists do. Given text in a new language, can we determine the underlying morphemes and the grammar rules that arrange and modify them?

The Bayesian strategy is to devise a joint probabilistic model that is capable of generating the descriptions of new languages. Given data from a particular new language, we can then seek explanatory descriptions that have high prior probability. This strategy leads to fascinating and successful algorithms in the case of morphology.

Yet the Bayesian approach has been less successful for syntax. It is limited in practice by our ability to (1) design accurate models and (2) solve the computational problem of posterior inference. I will demonstrate some remedies: build only a partial (conditional) model, and use synthetic data to train a neural network that simulates correct posterior inference.

Biography

Jason Eisner is Professor of Computer Science at Johns Hopkins University, where he is also affiliated with the Center for Language and Speech Processing, the Machine Learning Group, the Cognitive Science Department, and the national Center of Excellence in Human Language Technology. His goal is to develop the probabilistic modeling, inference, and learning techniques needed for a unified model of all kinds of linguistic structure. His 100+ papers have presented various algorithms for parsing, machine translation, and weighted finite-state machines; formalizations, algorithms, theorems, and empirical results in computational phonology; and unsupervised or semi-supervised learning methods for syntax, morphology, and word-sense disambiguation. He is also the lead designer of Dyna, a new declarative programming language that provides an infrastructure for AI research. He has received two school-wide awards for excellence in teaching.

Table of Contents

Conference Program

Tuesday, November 28, 2017

11:50–12:00 Machine Translation 1

11:50–12:00 *CKY-based Convolutional Attention for Neural Machine Translation*
Taiki Watanabe, Akihiro Tamura and Takashi Ninomiya

Tuesday, November 28, 2017

11:50–12:00 Syntax and Parsing

11:50–12:00 *Supervised Attention for Sequence-to-Sequence Constituency Parsing*
Hidetaka Kamigaito, Katsuhiko Hayashi, Tsutomu Hirao, Hiroya Takamura, Manabu Okumura and Masaaki Nagata

Tuesday, November 28, 2017

11:50–12:00 Semantics 1

11:50–12:00 *Transferring Semantic Roles Using Translation and Syntactic Information*
Maryam Aminian, Mohammad Sadegh Rasooli and Mona Diab

Tuesday, November 28, 2017

Tuesday, November 28, 2017 (continued)

CVBed: Structuring CVs usingWord Embeddings
Shweta Garg, Sudhanshu S Singh, Abhijit Mishra and Kuntal Dey

Leveraging Diverse Lexical Chains to Construct Essays for Chinese College Entrance Examination
Liunian Li, Xiaojun Wan, Jin-ge Yao and Siming Yan

Draw and Tell: Multimodal Descriptions Outperform Verbal- or Sketch-Only Descriptions in an Image Retrieval Task
Ting Han and David Schlangen

Wednesday, November 29, 2017

11:50–12:00   Machine Learning 1

11:50–12:00   *Grammatical Error Correction with Neural Reinforcement Learning*
Keisuke Sakaguchi, Matt Post and Benjamin Van Durme

Wednesday, November 29, 2017

11:50–12:00   Discourse 1

11:50–12:00   *Coreference Resolution on Math Problem Text in Japanese*
Takumi Ito, Takuya Matsuzaki and Satoshi Sato

Thursday, November 30, 2017

11:50–12:00   Summarization

11:50–12:00   *Towards Abstractive Multi-Document Summarization Using Submodular Function-Based Framework, Sentence Compression and Merging*
Yllias Chali, Moin Tanvee and Mir Tafseer Nayeem

Thursday, November 30, 2017

11:50–12:00   Information Extraction

11:50–12:00   *Domain Adaptation for Relation Extraction with Domain Adversarial Neural Network*
Lisheng Fu, Thien Huu Nguyen, Bonan Min and Ralph Grishman

Thursday, November 30, 2017

11:50–12:00   NLP Application

11:50–12:00   *Lexical Simplification with the Deep Structured Similarity Model*
Lis Pereira, Xiaodong Liu and John Lee

Thursday, November 30, 2017

CKY-based Convolutional Attention for Neural Machine Translation

Taiki Watanabe and **Akihiro Tamura** and **Takashi Ninomiya**
Ehime University
3 Bunkyo-cho, Matsuyama, Ehime, JAPAN
{t_watanabe@ai.cs, tamura@cs, ninomiya@cs}.ehime-u.ac.jp

Abstract

This paper proposes a new attention mechanism for neural machine translation (NMT) based on convolutional neural networks (CNNs), which is inspired by the CKY algorithm. The proposed attention represents every possible combination of source words (e.g., phrases and structures) through CNNs, which imitates the CKY table in the algorithm. NMT, incorporating the proposed attention, decodes a target sentence on the basis of the attention scores of the hidden states of CNNs. The proposed attention enables NMT to capture alignments from underlying structures of a source sentence without sentence parsing. The evaluations on the Asian Scientific Paper Excerpt Corpus (ASPEC) English-Japanese translation task show that the proposed attention gains 0.66 points in BLEU.

1 Introduction

Recently, neural machine translation (NMT) based on neural networks (NNs) is known to provide both high-precision and human-like translation through its simple architecture. In NMT, the encoder-decoder model, which is intensively studied, converts a source-language sentence into a fixed-length vector and then generates a target-language sentence from the vector by using recurrent NNs (RNNs) with gated recurrent units (GRUs) (Cho et al., 2014a) or long short-term memory (LSTM) (Hochreiter and Schmidhuber, 1997; Gers et al., 2000; Sutskever et al., 2014). An attention-based NMT (ANMT) is one of the state-of-the-art technologies for MT, which is an extension of the encoder-decoder model and provides highly accurate translation (Luong et al., 2015; Dzmitry et al., 2015). ANMT is a method of translation in which the decoder generates a target-language sentence, referring to the history of the encoder's hidden layer state.

The encoder-decoder model has also been extended to syntax-based NMT, which utilizes structures of source sentences, target sentences, or both. In particular, Eriguchi et al. (2016b) have shown that a source-side structure (i.e., constituent trees of source sentences) are useful for NMT on the English-Japanese translation. However, syntax-based NMT requires sentence parsing in advance.

This paper proposes a new attention mechanism for NMT based on convolutional neural networks (CNNs) to leverage the structures of source sentences in NMT without parsing. In the parsing field, the CKY algorithm (Kasami, 1965; Younger, 1967) parses a sentence in a bottom-up manner through the CKY table, which efficiently considers all possible combinations of words and represents the structure of the sentence through dynamic programming. Inspired by the algorithm, we incorporate CNNs that imitate the CKY table into the attention mechanism of ANMT. In particular, the proposed attention constructs CNNs in the same order as the calculation procedures in the CKY table, and then ANMT decodes a target sentence by referring to each state of the hidden layers of CNNs, which corresponds to each cell in the CKY table. The proposed attention enables the ANMT model to capture underlying structures of a source sentence that are useful for a prediction of each target word, without sentence parsing in advance.

The evaluations on the ASPEC English-Japanese translation task (Nakazawa et al., 2016) show that the proposed attention gains 0.66 points in BLEU. Furthermore, they show that our attention can capture structural alignments (e.g., align-

Proceedings of the The 8th International Joint Conference on Natural Language Processing, pages 1–6,
Taipei, Taiwan, November 27 – December 1, 2017 ©2017 AFNLP

ment to a case structure), which is not a word-level alignment.

There are several previous studies on NMT using CNNs (Kalchbrenner and Blunsom, 2013; Cho et al., 2014b; Lamb and Xie, 2016; Kalchbrenner et al., 2016). Their models consist of serially connected multi-layer CNNs for encoders or decoders, similar to image recognition CNNs for 1D image processing. Therefore, their models do not have any direct mechanisms for dealing with the connections between phrases/words in long distance. Our model adopts CKY-based connections between multi-layer CNNs, which enables the NMT to calculate direct connections between phrases/words in encoders, and the attention mechanism enables the NMT to capture structural alignment between decoders and encoders[1].

2 Attention-based NMT (ANMT)

ANMT (Luong et al., 2015; Dzmitry et al., 2015) is an extension of the encoder-decoder model (Sutskever et al., 2014; Cho et al., 2014a). The model uses its RNN encoder to convert a source-language sentence into a fixed-length vector and then uses its RNN decoder to generate a target-language sentence from the vector.

We used a bi-directional two-layer LSTM network as the encoder. Given a source-language sentence $\mathbf{x} = x_1, x_2, \cdots, x_T$, the encoder represents the i-th word, x_i, as a d-dimensional vector, v_i, by a word embedding layer. The encoder then computes the hidden state of v_i, h_i, as follows:

$$\overrightarrow{h_i^{(1)}} = LSTM^{(1)}(v_i), \qquad (1)$$

$$\overleftarrow{h_i^{(1)}} = LSTM^{(1)}(v_i), \qquad (2)$$

$$\overrightarrow{h_i^{(2)}} = LSTM^{(2)}(\overrightarrow{h_i^{(1)}}) + \overrightarrow{h_i^{(1)}}, \qquad (3)$$

$$\overleftarrow{h_i^{(2)}} = LSTM^{(2)}(\overleftarrow{h_i^{(1)}}) + \overleftarrow{h_i^{(1)}}, \qquad (4)$$

$$h_i = \overrightarrow{h_i^{(2)}} + \overleftarrow{h_i^{(2)}}, \qquad (5)$$

where $\rightarrow$ and $\leftarrow$ indicate the forward direction (i.e., from the beginning to the end of a sentence) and the reverse direction, respectively. $LSTM^{(1)}$ and $LSTM^{(2)}$ represent the first- and second-layer LSTM encoders, respectively. The dimensions of $\overrightarrow{h_i^{(1)}}$, $\overleftarrow{h_i^{(1)}}$, $\overrightarrow{h_i^{(2)}}$, $\overleftarrow{h_i^{(2)}}$, and h_i are d.

In ANMT, the decoder generates a target-language sentence, referring to the hidden layer's states of the LSTM encoder, h_i. The attention mechanism explained below is called *global attention (dot)* (Luong et al., 2015). We used a two-layer LSTM network as the decoder. The initial states of the first- and second-layer LSTM decoders are initialized as the states of the first- and second-layer LSTM encoders in the reverse direction, respectively.

Each state of the hidden layers of LSTM decoders, $s_j^{(1)}$ and $s_j^{(2)}$, is calculated by

$$s_j^{(1)} = LSTM^{(1)}([w_{j-1}; \hat{s}_{j-1}]), \qquad (6)$$

$$s_j^{(2)} = LSTM^{(2)}(s_j^{(1)}), \qquad (7)$$

where w_{j-1} indicates word embedding of the output word y_{j-1}, ';' represents a concatenation of matrices, and $\hat{s}_{j-1}$ is an attentional vector used for generating the output word y_{j-1}, which is explained below[2].

The dimensions of w_{j-1} and $\hat{s}_{j-1}$ are d. The attention score $\alpha_j(i)$ is calculated as follows:

$$\alpha_j(i) = \frac{exp(h_i \cdot s_j^{(2)})}{\sum_{k=1}^{T} exp(h_k \cdot s_j^{(2)})}. \qquad (8)$$

The context vector c_j for generating a target-language sentence is calculated by

$$c_j = \sum_{i=1}^{T} \alpha_j(i) h_i. \qquad (9)$$

The attentional vector $\hat{s}_j$ is calculated by using the context vector as follows:

$$\hat{s}_j = tanh(W_c[s_j^{(2)}; c_j]), \qquad (10)$$

and then using the state of this hidden layer, the probability of the output word y_j is given by

$$p(y_j|y_{<j}, \mathbf{x}) = softmax(W_s \hat{s}_j), \qquad (11)$$

where W_c and W_s represent weight matrices[3].

3 NMT with CKY-based Convolutional Attention

Figure 1 shows the overall structure of the proposed attention. In the proposed attention, a gen-

---

[1] In a preliminary experiment, we directly applied a CNN to the encoder of the encoder-decoder model. However, the method (BLEU: 25.91) does not outperform our proposed method (BLEU: 26.75).

[2] Providing an attentional vector as inputs to the LSTM in the next time step is called input feeding (Luong et al., 2015).

[3] In our experiments, target sentences are generated by the greedy algorithm on the basis of output probabilities.

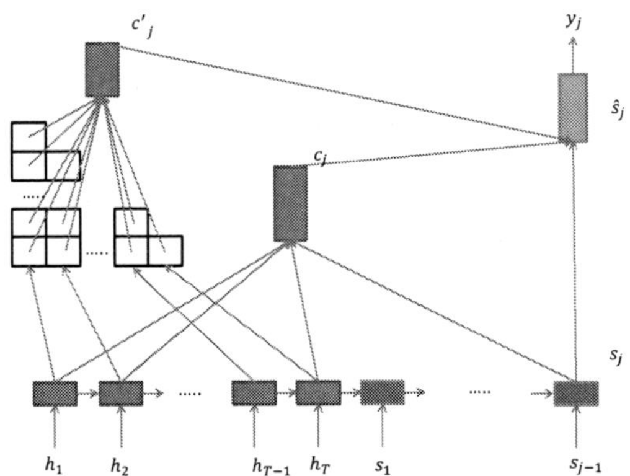

Figure 1: Overall View of CKY-based Attention

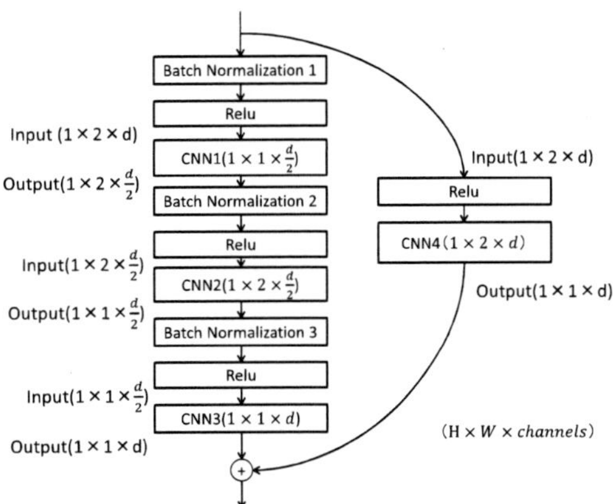

Figure 2: Deduction Unit in CKY-based Attention

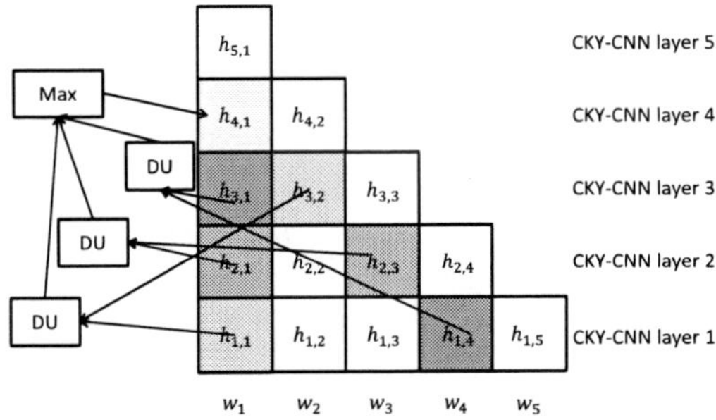

Figure 3: An Example of Max-pooling with CKY-CNN

erative rule in the CKY algorithm is imitated by the network structure shown in Figure 2. We call the network as the *Deduction Unit (DU)*. In a DU, four types of CNNs are connected by a residual connection[4]. In Figure 2, the size of filters and the number of output channels for each CNN are shown in a parenthesis. In particular, the filter sizes of CNN1, CNN2, CNN3, and CNN4, are 1×1, 1×2, 1×1, and 1×2, and their channel numbers are $\frac{d}{2}$, $\frac{d}{2}$, d, and d, respectively. Each DU receives d-dimensional vectors (states) of two cells in a CKY table and computes a d-dimensional vector for an upper-level cell, which corresponds to a generation rule in the CKY algorithm. By using DUs, the state of each cell in a CKY table is induced by folding the states of lower-level cells in the same order as the calculation procedures in the CKY algorithm. We call the network for this overall procedure as the *CKY-CNN*. We hereafter denote the state of the j-th cell in the i-th CKY-CNN layer as $h_{i,j}^{(cky)}$. Note that the states of the first-layer of the CKY-CNN (i.e., $\mathbf{h_1^{(cky)}} = (h_{1,1}^{(cky)}, ..., h_{1,T}^{(cky)})$) are set to the states of the LSTM encoder (i.e., $\mathbf{h} = (h_1, ..., h_T)$). In the CKY-CNN, the state of a cell is induced from multiple candidates of outputs from DUs, similar to the CKY algorithm. Specifically, the state of a cell is set to the output vector with the highest sum of values of all dimensions as follows:

$$h_{i,j}^{(cky)} = Max_{1 \le k \le i-1} DU(h_{k,j}^{(cky)}, h_{i-k,j+k}^{(cky)}) \tag{12}$$

---

[4]Through a preliminary experiment, we confirmed that a simple DU composed of one type of CNN did not work well. Therefore, we have improved the DU in reference to (He et al., 2016).

Figure 3 shows an example of convolutions in the CKY-CNN, highlighting the process of generating the state of the yellow cell. In this process, three DUs generate vectors based on the states of the two blue cells, those of the two red cells, and those of the two green cells, respectively. The vector with the highest sum of vector elements is then set to the state of the yellow cell. Through the CKY-CNN, the states of the cells in a CKY table ($\mathbf{h}^{(cky)}$) are obtained.

NMT with the CKY-based convolutional attention decodes a target sentence by referring to the states of the hidden layers of the CKY-CNN in addition to the states of the hidden layer of the LSTM encoder. The alignment scores are calculated as follows:

$$\alpha'(i,j)$$
$$= \frac{exp(h_i \cdot s_j^{(2)})}{\sum_{k=1}^{T} exp(h_k \cdot s_j^{(2)}) + \sum_{k=1}^{T} \sum_{l=1}^{T-k+1} exp(h_{k,l}^{(cky)} \cdot s_j^{(2)})}, \tag{13}$$

3

$$\alpha''(i_1, i_2, j)$$

$$= \frac{exp(h_{i_1,i_2}^{(cky)} \cdot s_j^{(2)})}{\sum_{k=1}^{T} exp(h_k \cdot s_j^{(2)}) + \sum_{k=1}^{T} \sum_{l=1}^{T-k+1} exp(h_{k,l}^{(cky)} \cdot s_j^{(2)})}. \tag{14}$$

Note that $s_j^{(2)}$ is the hidden layer's state of the second-layer LSTM encoder (see Section 2). The context vector c_j' for CKY-CNN is calculated by

$$c_j' = \sum_{k=1}^{T} \alpha'(k, j)h_k + \sum_{k=1}^{T} \sum_{l=1}^{T-k+1} \alpha''(k, l, j)h_{k,l}^{(cky)}. \tag{15}$$

$\hat{s}_j$ is calculated on the basis of the context vector of the LSTM encoder (c_j), which is defined in Section 2, and that of the CKY-CNN (c_j') as follows:

$$\hat{s}_j = tanh(\hat{W}[s_j^{(2)}; c_j; c_j']), \tag{16}$$

where $\hat{W} \in R^{d \times 3d}$ is a weight matrix. By applying the softmax function to the $\hat{s}_j$ in the same way as in the conventional ANMT (see Section 2), the encoder predicts the j-th target word.

4 Experiments

4.1 Settings

We used Asian Scientific Paper Excerpt Corpus (ASPEC)'s English-Japanese corpus[5] in this experiment. We used the Moses decoder for word segmentation of the English corpus and Kytea (Neubig et al., 2011) for the Japanese corpus. For each corpus, all characters are lowercased. We used the first 100,000 sentences ($<$ 50 words) for training, 1,790 sentences for parameter tuning, and 1,812 sentences for testing. The words that appeared less than twice in the training data were replaced with the special symbol UNK.

The number of dimensions of word vectors and hidden layers was 256. Adam (Kingsma and Ba, 2014) was used for learning each parameter, and the initial values of the parameters were set to $\alpha = 0.01$, $\beta_1 = 0.9$, and $\beta_2 = 0.99$. The learning rate was halved after 9 and 12 epochs. A gradient clipping technique was used with a clipping value of 3.0, following (Eriguchi et al., 2016a). We used dropout (Srivastava et al., 2014) and weight decay to prevent over-fitting. The dropout ratio for LSTMs was 0.2, that for the CNN was 0.3, and the weight decay coefficient was 10^{-6}.

Table 1: Evaluation Results

	BLEU (%)
Baseline Model	26.09
Proposed Model	26.75

4.2 Results

We compared the NMT with the CKY-based convolutional attention (see Section 3) with the NMT with the conventional attention (see Section 2) to confirm the effectiveness of the proposed CKY-based attention. The only difference between the baseline and the proposed model is their attention mechanisms. Table 1 shows the translation performance by BLEU (Papineni et al., 2002). For reference, we obtained a 18.69% BLEU score using the Moses phrase-based statistical machine translation system (Koehn et al., 2007) with the default settings.

Table 1 shows that the proposed model outperforms the baseline model, which indicates that the proposed attention is useful for NMT.

Figure 4 shows the attention scores of an instance in the test data. The deeper color of a cell represents a higher attention score. The vertical axis represents a source sentence. In Figure 4, the test sentence is "finally, this paper describes the recent trend and problems in this field .". The horizontal axis indicates the depth of the CKY-CNN. Note that an attention score of the first layer of the CKY-CNN corresponds to an attention score of the hidden layer of the LSTM. Figure 4 shows that for the words whose alignments are clearly defined such as content words (e.g., "最後 (finally)", "分野 (field)", "述べ (describe)"), high alignment scores are located in the first layer. On the other hand, for the words whose alignments are not clearly defined such as function words (e.g., "に", "け", "る"), high alignment scores are located at a deeper layer. The Japanese word "に" shows a case structure, and "け" and "る" are parts of the Japanese preposition "おける (in)". This indicates that while the conventional attention finds word-level alignments, the proposed attention captures structural alignments.

---

[5] http://orchid.kuee.kyoto-u.ac.jp /WAT/WAT2015/index.html

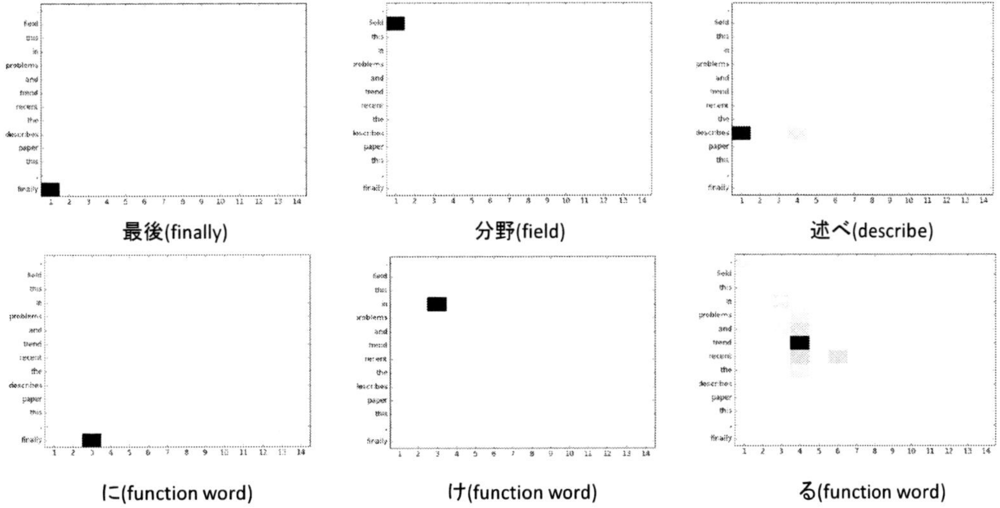

Figure 4: Examples of Attention Scores

5 Conclusions

This paper proposed an attention mechanism for NMT based on CNNs, which imitates the CKY algorithm. The evaluations on the ASPEC English-Japanese translation task showed that the proposed attention gained 0.66 points in BLEU and captured structural alignments, which could not be captured by a conventional attention mechanism. The proposed model consumes excessive amounts of memory because the proposed model keeps hidden states of all cells in a CKY table. In future, we would like to improve the proposed attention in terms of memory consumption, and then verify the effectiveness of the proposed attention for larger datasets.

Acknowledgements

This work was supported by JSPS Grants-in-Aid for Scientific Research Grant Number 25280084. We are grateful to Shinsuke Mori, Kazuma Hashimoto, and Akiko Eriguchi for their technical advice to this work.

References

Kyunghyun Cho, Bart van Merrienboer, Caglar Gulcehre, Dzmitry Bahdanau, Fethi Bougares, Holger Schwenk, and Yoshua Bengio. 2014a. Learning phrase representations using rnn encoder–decoder for statistical machine translation. In *Proceedings of the 2014 Conference on Empirical Methods in Natural Language Processing*, pages 1724–1734.

Kyunghyun Cho, Bart Van Merriënboer, Dzmitry Bahdanau, and Yoshua Bengio. 2014b. On the properties of neural machine translation: Encoder-decoder approaches. *arXiv preprint arXiv:1409.1259*.

Bahdanau Dzmitry, Cho KyungHyun, and Bengio Yoshua. 2015. Neural machine translation by jointly learning to align and translate. In *Proceedings of the 3rd International Conference on Learning Representations*.

Akiko Eriguchi, Kazuma Hashimoto, and Yoshimasa Tsuruoka. 2016a. Character-based decoding in tree-to-sequence attention-based neural machine translation. In *Proceedings of the 3rd workshop on Asian Translation*, pages 175–183.

Akiko Eriguchi, Kazuma Hashimoto, and Yoshimasa Tsuruoka. 2016b. Tree-to-sequence attentional neural machine translation. In *Proceedings of the 54th Annual Meeting of the Association for Computational Linguistics*, pages 823–833.

Felix A Gers, Jürgen Schmidhuber, and Fred Cummins. 2000. Learning to forget: Continual prediction with lstm. *Neural computation*, 12(10):2451–2471.

Kaiming He, Xiangyu Zhang, Shaoqing Ren, and Jian Sun. 2016. Deep residual learning for image recognition. In *Proceedings of the IEEE conference on computer vision and pattern recognition*, pages 770–778.

Sepp Hochreiter and Jürgen Schmidhuber. 1997. Long short-term memory. *Neural computation*, 9(8):1735–1780.

Nal Kalchbrenner and Phil Blunsom. 2013. Recurrent continuous translation models. In *Proceedings of the 2013 Conference on Empirical Methods in Natural Language Processing*, page 413.

Nal Kalchbrenner, Lasse Espeholt, Karen Simonyan, Aaron van den Oord, Alex Graves, and Koray Kavukcuoglu. 2016. Neural machine translation in linear time. *arXiv preprint arXiv:1610.10099*.

Tadao Kasami. 1965. An efficient recognition and syntax algorithm for context-free languages. Technical Report AFCRL-65-758.

Diederik Kingsma and Jimmy Ba. 2014. Adam: A method for stochastic optimization. In *5th International Conference on Learning Representations*.

Philipp Koehn, Hieu Hoang, Alexandra Birch, Chris Callison-Burch, Marcello Federico, Nicola Bertoldi, Brooke Cowan, Wade Shen, Christine Moran, Richard Zens, et al. 2007. Moses: Open source toolkit for statistical machine translation. In *Proceedings of the 45th annual meeting of the Association for Computational Linguistics on interactive poster and demonstration sessions*, pages 177–180.

Andrew Lamb and Michael Xie. 2016. Convolutional encoders for neural machine translation. *arXiv preprint arXiv:1611.02344*.

Thang Luong, Hieu Pham, and Christopher D. Manning. 2015. Effective approaches to attention-based neural machine translation. In *Proceedings of the 2015 Conference on Empirical Methods in Natural Language Processing*, pages 1412–1421.

Toshiaki Nakazawa, Manabu Yaguchi, Kiyotaka Uchimoto, Masao Utiyama, Eiichiro Sumita, Sadao Kurohashi, and Hitoshi Isahara. 2016. Aspec: Asian scientific paper excerpt corpus. In *Proceedings of the Ninth International Conference on Language Resources and Evaluation*, pages 2204–2208.

Graham Neubig, Yosuke Nakata, and Shinsuke Mori. 2011. Pointwise prediction for robust, adaptable japanese morphological analysis. In *Proceedings of the 49th Annual Meeting of the Association for Computational Linguistics*, pages 529–533.

Kishore Papineni, Salam Roukos, Todd Ward, and Wei-Jing Zhu. 2002. Bleu: a method for automatic evaluation of machine translation. In *Proceedings of the 40th Annual Meeting of the Association for Computational Linguistics*, pages 311–318.

Nitish Srivastava, Geoffrey E Hinton, Alex Krizhevsky, Ilya Sutskever, and Ruslan Salakhutdinov. 2014. Dropout: a simple way to prevent neural networks from overfitting. *Journal of Machine Learning Research*, 15(1):1929–1958.

Ilya Sutskever, Oriol Vinyals, and Quoc V Le. 2014. Sequence to sequence learning with neural networks. In *Advances in neural information processing systems*, pages 3104–3112.

Daniel H. Younger. 1967. Recognition and parsing of context-free languages in time n^3. *Information and Control*, 2(10):189–208.

Supervised Attention for Sequence-to-Sequence Constituency Parsing

Hidetaka Kamigaito†, Katsuhiko Hayashi,
Tsutomu Hirao and Masaaki Nagata
NTT Communication Science Laboratories, NTT Corporation
2-4 Hikaridai, Seika-cho, Soraku-gun, Kyoto, 619-0237, Japan
†kamigaito.hidetaka@lab.ntt.co.jp

Hiroya Takamura and Manabu Okumura
Tokyo Institute of Technology, Yokohama, Kanagawa 226-8503, Japan

Abstract

The sequence-to-sequence (Seq2Seq) model has been successfully applied to machine translation (MT). Recently, MT performances were improved by incorporating supervised attention into the model. In this paper, we introduce supervised attention to constituency parsing that can be regarded as another translation task. Evaluation results on the PTB corpus showed that the bracketing F-measure was improved by supervised attention.

1 Introduction

The sequence-to-sequence (Seq2Seq) model has been successfully used in natural language generation tasks such as machine translation (MT) (Bahdanau et al., 2014) and text summarization (Rush et al., 2015). In the Seq2Seq model, attention, which encodes an input sentence by generating an alignment between output and input words, plays an important role. Without the attention mechanism, the performance of the Seq2Seq model degrades significantly (Bahdanau et al., 2014). To improve the alignment quality, Mi et al. (2016), Liu et al. (2016), and Chen et al. (2016) proposed a method that learns attention with the given alignments in a supervised manner, which is called supervised attention. By utilizing supervised attention, the translation quality of MT is improved.

The Seq2Seq model can also be applied to other NLP tasks. We can regard parsing as a translation task from a sentence to an S-expression, and Vinyals et al. (2015) proposed a constituent parsing method based on the Seq2Seq model. Their method achieved the state-of-the-art performance.

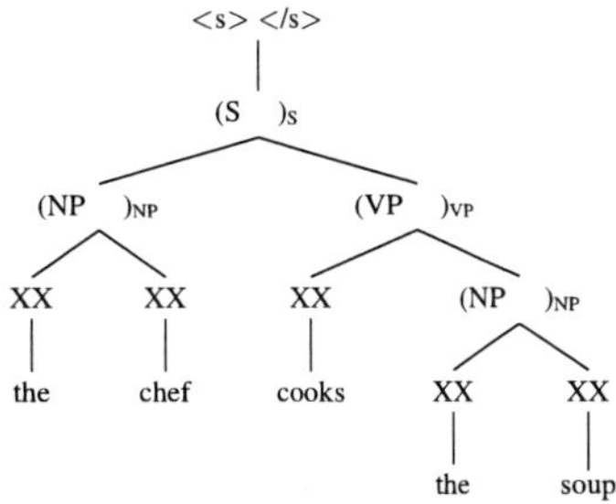

Figure 1: S-expression format for Vinyals et al. (2015)'s Seq2seq constituency parser. The Seq2seq model employs "<s> (S (NP XX XX)NP (VP XX (NP XX XX)NP)VP)S </s>" as output tokens. <s> and </s> are start and end of sentence symbols, respectively.

In their method, based on the alignment between a nonterminal and input words, the attention mechanism has also an important role. However, since the attention is learned in an unsupervised manner, the alignment quality might not be optimal. If we can raise the quality of the alignments, the parsing performance will be improved. Unlike MT, however, the definition of a gold standard alignment is not clear for the parsing tasks.

In this paper, we define several linguistically-motivated annotations between surface words and nonterminals as "gold standard alignments" to enhance the attention mechanism of the constituency parser (Vinyals et al., 2015) by supervised attention. The PTB corpus results showed that our method outperformed Vinyals et al. (2015) by over 1 point in the bracketing F-measure.

Proceedings of the The 8th International Joint Conference on Natural Language Processing, pages 7–12,
Taipei, Taiwan, November 27 – December 1, 2017 ©2017 AFNLP

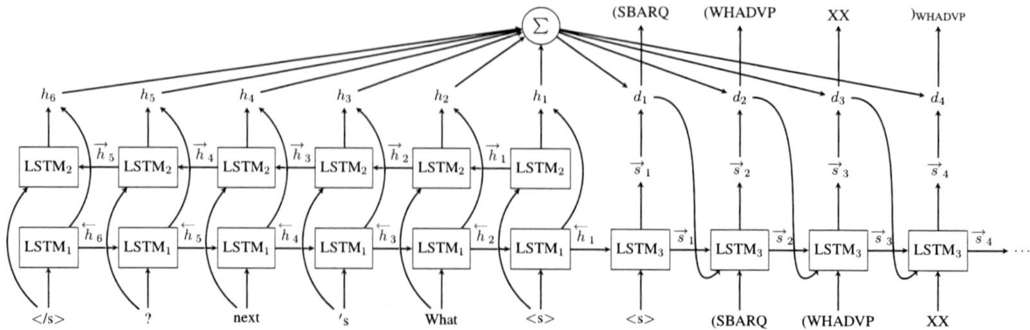

Figure 2: Network structure of our sequence-to-sequence model.

2 Sequence-to-Sequence based Constituency Parser on Supervised Attention Framework

The Seq2Seq constituency parser (Vinyals et al., 2015) predicts nonterminal labels $\mathbf{y} = (y_1, ..., y_m)$, for input words $\mathbf{x} = (x_1, ..., x_n)$, where m and n are respectively the lengths of the word and the label sequences. As shown in Fig. 1, we use normalized labels (Vinyals et al., 2015) in our Seq2Seq model, which consists of encoder and decoder parts. Its overall structure is shown in Fig. 2.

The encoder part employs a 3-layer stacked bidirectional Long Short-Term Memory (LSTM) to encode input sentence $\mathbf{x}$ into a sequence of hidden states $\mathbf{h} = (h_1, ..., h_n)$. Each h_i is a concatenation of forward hidden layer $\overrightarrow{h}_i$ and backward hidden layer $\overleftarrow{h}_i$. $\overleftarrow{h}_1$ is inherited by the decoder as an initial state.

The decoder part employs a 3-layer stacked forward LSTM to encode previously predicted label y_{t-1} into hidden state s_t.

For each time t, with a 2-layer feed-forward neural network r, encoder and decoder hidden layers $\mathbf{h}$ and $\overrightarrow{s}_t$ are used to calculate the attention weight:

$$\alpha_t^i = \frac{exp(r(h_i, \overrightarrow{s}_t))}{\sum_{i'=1}^{n} exp(r(h_{i'}, \overrightarrow{s}_t))}.$$

Using attention weight α_t^i and 1-layer feed-forward neural network u, label probabilities are calculated as follows:

$$P(y_t \mid y_{t-1}, ..., y_1) = \frac{exp(u(d_t)_{v=y_t})}{\sum_{v=1}^{V} exp(u(d_t)_v)},$$

$$d_t = [\sum_{i=1}^{n} \alpha_i^t \cdot h_i, \overrightarrow{s}_t],$$

where V is the label size. Note that d_t and the embedding of label y_t are concatenated and fed to the decoder at time $t + 1$.

In a supervised attention framework, attentions are learned from the given alignments. We denote a link on an alignment between y_t and x_i as $a_t^i = 1$ ($a_t^i = 0$ denotes that y_t and x_i are not linked.). Following a previous work (Liu et al., 2016), we adopt a soft constraint to the objective function:

$$-\sum_{t=1}^{n} logP(y_t \mid y_{t-1}, ..., y_0, \mathbf{x})$$

$$-\lambda \times \sum_{i=1}^{n} \sum_{t=1}^{m} a_t^i \times log\alpha_t^i,$$

to jointly learn the attention and output distributions. All our alignments are represented by one-to-many links between input words $\mathbf{x}$ and nonterminals $\mathbf{y}$.

3 Design of our Alignments

In the traditional parsing framework (Hall et al., 2014; Durrett and Klein, 2015), lexical features have been proven to be useful in improving parsing performance. Inspired by previous work, we enhance the attention mechanism utilizing the linguistically-motivated annotations between surface words and nonterminals by supervised attention.

In this paper, we define four types of alignments for supervised attention. The first three methods use the monolexical properties of heads without incurring any inferential costs of lexicalized annotations. Although the last needs manually constructed annotation schemes, it can capture bilexical relationships along dependency arcs. The followings are the details:

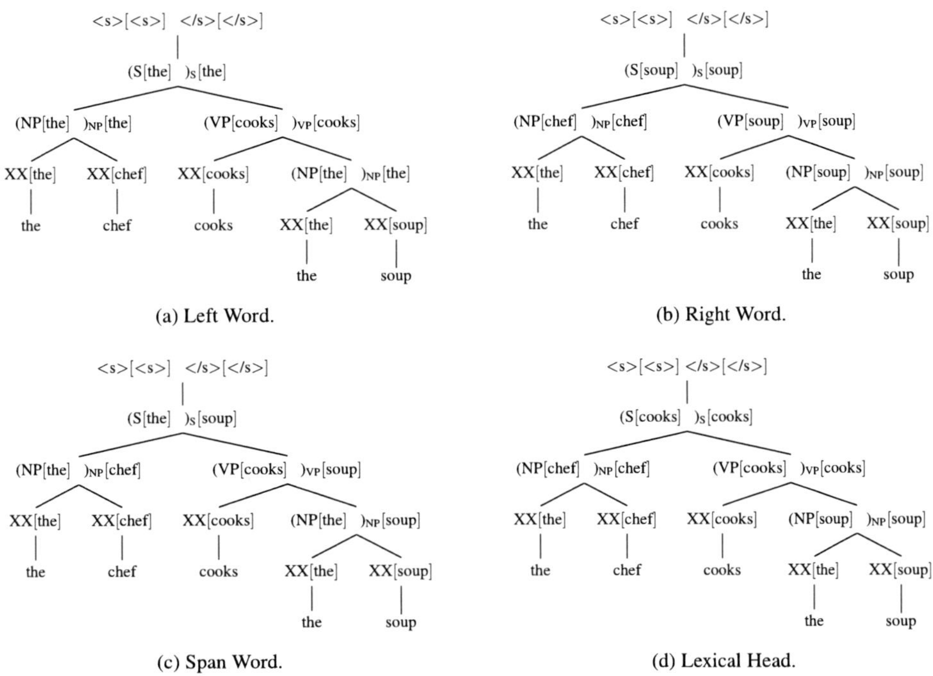

Figure 3: Example of our alignments. The word in [ ] is linked to each output token.

- **Left word**: In English, the syntactic head of a verb phrase is typically at the beginning of the span. Based on this notion, this method uses the identity of the starting word of a nonterminal span. Figure 3a shows an alignment example where an output token is linked to its leftmost word of the span.

- **Right word**: On the contrary, the syntactic head of a simple English noun phrase is often at the end of the span. The alignment example in Fig. 3b is produced by this method, where an output token is linked to the rightmost word of the span.

- **Span word**: Here, we unify the above two methods. All output tokens are linked to their leftmost word, except the ending bracket tokens, which are linked to their rightmost word. Figure 3c shows an alignment example produced by this method.

- **Lexical head**: Lexicalization (Eisner, 1996; Collins, 1997), which annotates grammar nonterminals with their head words, is useful for resolving the syntactic ambiguities involved by such linguistic phenomena as co-ordination and PP attachment. As shown in Fig. 3d, this method produces alignments by linking an output token and its head word[1].

4 Experimental Evaluation

4.1 Evaluation Settings

We experimentally evaluated our methods on the English Penn Treebank corpus (PTB), and split the data into three parts: The Wall Street Journal (WSJ) sections 02-21 for training, section 22 for development and section 23 for testing.

In our models, the dimensions of the input word embeddings, the fed label embeddings, the hidden layers, and an attention vector were respectively set to 150, 30, 200, and 200. The LSTM depth was set to 3. Label set L_{con} had a size of 61. The input vocabulary size of PTB was set to 42393. Supervised attention rate λ was set to 1.0. To use entire words as a vocabulary, we integrated word dropout (Iyyer et al., 2015) into our models with smoothing rate 0.8375 (Cross and Huang, 2016). We used dropout layers (Srivastava et al., 2014) to

---

[1] For head annotations, we used ptbconv 3.0 tool (Yamada and Matsumoto, 2003), which is available from http://www.jaist.ac.jp/h-yamada/.

Setting	WSJ Section 22				WSJ Section 23			
	P	**R**	**F$_1$**	**AER**	**P**	**R**	**F$_1$**	**AER**
Seq2Seq	88.1	88.0	88.1	–	88.3	87.6	88.0	–
Seq2Seq+random	67.1	66.3	66.7	96.3	66.5	65.5	66.0	96.3
Seq2Seq+first	70.3	69.7	70.0	0.0	69.6	68.7	69.2	0.0
Seq2Seq+last	66.7	66.1	66.4	0.0	66.1	64.8	65.4	0.0
Seq2Seq+head	89.2	88.9	89.1	6.9	89.2	88.1	88.6	6.9
Seq2Seq+left	**89.6**	**89.4**	**89.5**	1.8	89.4	**88.7**	89.0	1.7
Seq2Seq+right	89.2	88.9	89.0	4.7	**89.5**	88.6	**89.1**	4.7
Seq2Seq+span	89.3	89.1	89.2	1.6	89.2	88.4	88.8	1.6
Vinyals et al. (2015) w att†	–	–	88.7	–	–	–	88.3	–
Vinyals et al. (2015) w/o att†	–	–	< 70	–	–	–	< 70	–
Seq2Seq+beam	89.0	88.7	88.8	–	89.1	88.3	88.7	–
Seq2Seq+beam+random	71.0	69.9	70.4	96.3	69.4	68.1	68.7	96.3
Seq2Seq+beam+first	73.9	73.0	73.5	0.0	73.2	71.8	72.5	0.0
Seq2Seq+beam+last	70.5	69.6	70.0	0.0	69.7	68.1	68.9	0.0
Seq2Seq+beam+head	89.6	89.2	89.4	6.9	89.6	88.4	89.0	6.9
Seq2Seq+beam+left	**89.9**	**89.6**	**89.8**	1.8	89.8	**89.0**	89.4	1.7
Seq2Seq+beam+right	89.6	89.2	89.4	4.7	89.7	88.9	89.3	4.7
Seq2Seq+beam+span	89.6	89.4	89.5	1.6	**90.0**	**89.0**	**89.5**	1.6
Seq2Seq+ens(base)	90.5	90.1	90.3	–	90.6	89.6	90.1	–
Seq2Seq+ens(feat)	**91.3**	**90.7**	**91.0**	–	**91.5**	**90.5**	**91.0**	–
Vinyals et al. (2015) w att+ens†	–	–	90.7	–	–	–	90.5	–
Seq2Seq+beam+ens(base)	91.4	90.9	91.1	–	91.5	90.5	91.0	–
Seq2Seq+beam+ens(feat)	**91.9**	**91.4**	**91.7**	–	**92.1**	**91.0**	**91.5**	–

Table 1: Results of parsing evaluation: **Seq2Seq** indicates the Seq2Seq model on a single model with greedy decoding. +beam shows the beam decoding results. +lex, +left, +right and +span respectively show the results on our proposed *lexical head*, *left word*, *right word*, and *span word* alignments. +random, +first, and +last respectively show the results on the alignment of baselines *random*, *first word*, and *last word*. +ens(base) shows the ensemble results of five Seq2Seq models without the given alignments. +ens(feat) shows the ensemble results of a Seq2Seq model without a given alignment and Seq2Seq models with *lexical head*, *left word*, *right word* and *span word* alignments. † denotes the scores reported in the paper.

each LSTM input layer (Vinyals et al., 2015) with a dropout rate of 0.3.

The stochastic gradient descent (SGD) was used to train models on 100 epochs. SGD's learning rate was set to 1.0 in the first 50 epochs. After the first 50 epochs, the learning rate was halved after every 5th epoch. All gradients were averaged in each mini-batch. The maximum mini-batch size was set to 16. The mini-batch order was shuffled at the end of every epoch. The clipping threshold of the gradient was set to 1.0.

We used greedy and beam searches for the decoding. The beam size was set to ten. The decoding was performed on both a single model and five-model ensembles. We used the products of the output probabilities for the ensemble.

All models were written in C++ on Dynet (Neubig et al., 2017).

We compared Seq2Seq models with and with-

out our alignments. To investigate the influence of the supervised attention method itself, we also compared our alignments to the following alignments:

- **Random**: Based on uniform distribution, each output token was randomly linked to at most one input token.

- **First word**: All output tokens were linked to the start of the sentence tokens in the input sentence.

- **Last word**: All output tokens were linked to the end of the sentence tokens in the input sentence.

We evaluated the compared methods using bracketing Precision, Recall and F-measure. We used evalb[2] as a parsing evaluation. We also eval-

---

[2] http://nlp.cs.nyu.edu/evalb/

uated the learned attention using alignment error rate (AER) (Och and Ney, 2003) on their alignments. Following a previous work (Luong et al., 2015), attention evaluation was conducted on gold output.

4.2 Results

Table 1 shows the results. All our *lexical head*, *left word*, *right word* and *span word* alignments improved bracket F-measure of baseline on every setting. From the +random, +first, and +last results, only supervised attention itself did not improve the parsing performances. Furthermore, each AER indicates that the alignments were correctly learned. These results support our expectation that our alignments improve the parsing performance with Seq2Seq models.

5 Discussion

All of the baseline alignments *random*, *first word* and *last word*, largely degraded the parsing performances. *random* prevented the learning of attention distributions, and *first word* and *last word* fixed the attention distributions. These resemble disable the attention mechanism. Vinyals et al. (2015) reported that the bracket F-measure of Seq2Seq without an attention mechanism is less than 70. Our evaluation results, which are consistent with their score, and it supports our expectation that the attention mechanism is critical for Seq2Seq constituency parsing.

Comparing the results of our proposed alignments in Table 1, even though the bracket F-measure of the *lexical head* is lower than that of the *left word*, *right word* and *span word*, the *lexical head* is the most intuitive alignment. Except for *random*, the AER of *lexical head* is the highest in all the alignments. This means that *lexical head* is difficult to learn on attention distribution. The prediction difficulty may degrade the parsing performances. Our analysis indicates that an alignment which can be easily predicted is suitable for the supervised attention of Seq2Seq constituency parsing.

6 Conclusion

We proposed methods that use traditional parsing features as alignments for the sequence-to-sequence based constituency parser in the supervised attention framework. In our evaluation, the proposed methods improved the bracketing scores on the English Penn Treebank against the baseline methods. These results emphasize, the effectiveness of our alignments in parsing performances.

Acknowledgement

We thank the anonymous reviewers for their careful reading and useful comments.

References

Dzmitry Bahdanau, Kyunghyun Cho, and Yoshua Bengio. 2014. Neural machine translation by jointly learning to align and translate. *CoRR*, abs/1409.0473.

Wenhu Chen, Evgeny Matusov, Shahram Khadivi, and Jan-Thorsten Peter. 2016. Guided alignment training for topic-aware neural machine translation. *CoRR*, abs/1607.01628.

Michael Collins. 1997. Three generative, lexicalised models for statistical parsing. In *Proceedings of the 8th European chapter of the Association for Computational Linguistics*, pages 16–23. Association for Computational Linguistics.

James Cross and Liang Huang. 2016. Span-based constituency parsing with a structure-label system and provably optimal dynamic oracles. In *Proceedings of the 2016 Conference on Empirical Methods in Natural Language Processing*, pages 1–11, Austin, Texas. Association for Computational Linguistics.

Greg Durrett and Dan Klein. 2015. Neural crf parsing. In *Proceedings of the 53rd Annual Meeting of the Association for Computational Linguistics and the 7th International Joint Conference on Natural Language Processing (Volume 1: Long Papers)*, pages 302–312, Beijing, China. Association for Computational Linguistics.

Jason M Eisner. 1996. Three new probabilistic models for dependency parsing: An exploration. In *Proceedings of the 16th conference on Computational linguistics-Volume 1*, pages 340–345. Association for Computational Linguistics.

David Hall, Greg Durrett, and Dan Klein. 2014. Less grammar, more features. In *Proceedings of the 52nd Annual Meeting of the Association for Computational Linguistics (Volume 1: Long Papers)*, pages 228–237, Baltimore, Maryland. Association for Computational Linguistics.

Mohit Iyyer, Varun Manjunatha, Jordan Boyd-Graber, and Hal Daumé III. 2015. Deep unordered composition rivals syntactic methods for text classification. In *Proceedings of the 53rd Annual Meeting of the Association for Computational Linguistics and the 7th International Joint Conference on Natural Language Processing (Volume 1: Long Papers)*, pages 1681–1691, Beijing, China. Association for Computational Linguistics.

Lemao Liu, Masao Utiyama, Andrew Finch, and Eiichiro Sumita. 2016. Neural machine translation with supervised attention. In *Proceedings of COLING 2016, the 26th International Conference on Computational Linguistics: Technical Papers*, pages 3093–3102, Osaka, Japan. The COLING 2016 Organizing Committee.

Thang Luong, Hieu Pham, and Christopher D. Manning. 2015. Effective approaches to attention-based neural machine translation. In *Proceedings of the 2015 Conference on Empirical Methods in Natural Language Processing*, pages 1412–1421, Lisbon, Portugal. Association for Computational Linguistics.

Haitao Mi, Zhiguo Wang, and Abe Ittycheriah. 2016. Supervised attentions for neural machine translation. In *Proceedings of the 2016 Conference on Empirical Methods in Natural Language Processing*, pages 2283–2288, Austin, Texas. Association for Computational Linguistics.

Graham Neubig, Chris Dyer, Yoav Goldberg, Austin Matthews, Waleed Ammar, Antonios Anastasopoulos, Miguel Ballesteros, David Chiang, Daniel Clothiaux, Trevor Cohn, et al. 2017. Dynet: The dynamic neural network toolkit. *arXiv preprint arXiv:1701.03980*.

Franz Josef Och and Hermann Ney. 2003. A systematic comparison of various statistical alignment models. *Computational linguistics*, 29(1):19–51.

Alexander M. Rush, Sumit Chopra, and Jason Weston. 2015. A neural attention model for abstractive sentence summarization. In *Proceedings of the 2015 Conference on Empirical Methods in Natural Language Processing*, pages 379–389, Lisbon, Portugal. Association for Computational Linguistics.

Nitish Srivastava, Geoffrey Hinton, Alex Krizhevsky, Ilya Sutskever, and Ruslan Salakhutdinov. 2014. Dropout: A simple way to prevent neural networks from overfitting. *The Journal of Machine Learning Research*, 15(1):1929–1958.

Oriol Vinyals, Ł ukasz Kaiser, Terry Koo, Slav Petrov, Ilya Sutskever, and Geoffrey Hinton. 2015. Grammar as a foreign language. In C. Cortes, N. D. Lawrence, D. D. Lee, M. Sugiyama, and R. Garnett, editors, *Advances in Neural Information Processing Systems 28*, pages 2773–2781. Curran Associates, Inc.

Hiroyasu Yamada and Yuji Matsumoto. 2003. Statistical dependency analysis with support vector machines. In *Proceedings of IWPT*, volume 3, pages 195–206.

Transferring Semantic Roles Using Translation and Syntactic Information

Maryam Aminian[1], Mohammad Sadegh Rasooli[2], Mona Diab[1]
[1]Department of Computer Science, The George Washington University, Washington
[2]Department of Computer Science, Columbia University, New York
[1]{aminian,mtdiab}@gwu.edu
[2]rasooli@cs.columbia.edu

Abstract

Our paper addresses the problem of annotation projection for semantic role labeling for resource-poor languages using supervised annotations from a resource-rich language through parallel data. We propose a transfer method that employs information from source and target syntactic dependencies as well as word alignment density to improve the quality of an iterative bootstrapping method. Our experiments yield a 3.5 absolute labeled F-score improvement over a standard annotation projection method.

1 Introduction

Semantic role labeling (SRL) is the task of automatically labeling predicates and arguments of a sentence with shallow semantic labels characterizing "Who did What to Whom, How, When and Where?" (Palmer et al., 2010). These rich semantic representations are useful in many applications such as question answering (Shen and Lapata, 2007) and information extraction (Christensen et al., 2011), hence gaining a lot of attention in recent years (Zhou and Xu, 2015; Täckström et al., 2015; Roth and Lapata, 2016; Marcheggiani et al., 2017). Since the process of creating annotated resources needs significant manual effort, SRL resources are available for a relative small number of languages such as English (Palmer et al., 2005), German (Erk et al., 2003), Arabic (Zaghouani et al., 2010) and Hindi (Vaidya et al., 2011). However, most languages still lack SRL systems. There have been some efforts to use information from a resource-rich language to develop SRL systems for resource-poor languages. *Transfer* methods address this problem by transferring information from a resource-rich language

(e.g. English) to a resource-poor language.

Annotation projection is a popular transfer method that transfers supervised annotations from a *source* language to a *target* language through parallel data. Unfortunately this technique is not as straightforward as it seems, e.g. *translation shifts* lead to erroneous projections and accordingly affecting the performance of the SRL system trained on these projections. Translation shifts are typically a result of the differences in word order and the semantic divergences between the source and target languages. In addition to translation shifts, there are errors that occur in translations, automatic word alignments as well as automatic semantic roles, hence we observe a cascade of error effect.

In this paper, we introduce a new approach for a *dependency-based SRL* system based on annotation projection without any semantically annotated data for a target language. We primarily focus on improving the quality of annotation projection by using translation cues automatically discovered from word alignments. We show that exclusively relying on partially projected data does not yield good performance. We improve over the baseline by filtering irrelevant projections, iterative bootstrapping with relabeling, and weighting each projection instance differently with data-dependent cost-sensitive training.

In short, contributions of this paper can be summarized as follows; We introduce a weighting algorithm to improve annotation projection based on cues obtained from syntactic and translation information. In other words, instead of utilizing manually-defined rules to filter projections, we define and use a customized cost function to train over noisy projected instances. This newly defined cost function helps the system weight some projections over other instances. We then utilize this algorithm in a bootstrapping framework. Un-

Proceedings of the The 8th International Joint Conference on Natural Language Processing, pages 13–19,
Taipei, Taiwan, November 27 – December 1, 2017 ©2017 AFNLP

like traditional bootstrapping, ours relabels every training instance (including labeled data) in every self-training round. Our final model on transferring from English to German yields a 3.5 absolute improvement labeled F-score over a standard annotation projection method.

2 Our Approach

We aim to develop a dependency-based SRL system which makes use of training instances projected from a source language (SLang) onto a target language (TLang) through parallel data. Our SRL system is formed as a pipeline of classifiers consisting of a predicate identification and disambiguation module, an argument identification module, and an argument classification module. In particular, we use our re-implementation of the greedy (local) model of Björkelund et al. (2009) except that we use an averaged perceptron algorithm (Freund and Schapire, 1999) as the learning algorithm.

2.1 Baseline Model

As our baseline, we apply automatic word alignment on parallel data and preserve the intersected alignments from the source-to-target and target-to-source directions. As our next step, we define a *projection density criteria* to filter some of the projected sentences. Given a target sentence from TLang with w words where f words have alignments ($f \leq w$), if the source sentence from SLang has p predicates for which p' of them are projected ($p' \leq p$), we define projection density as $(p' \times f)/(p \times w)$ and prune out sentences with a density value less than a certain threshold. The threshold value is empirically determined during tuning experiments performed on the development data. In this criteria, the denominator shows the maximum number of training instances that could be obtained by projection and the nominator shows the actual number of relevant instances that are used in our model. In addition to speeding up the training process, filtering sparse alignments helps remove sentence pairs with a significant translation shifts. Thereafter, a supervised model is trained directly on the projected data.

2.2 Model Improvements

As already mentioned, the quality of projected roles is highly dependent on different factors including translation shifts, errors in automatic word alignments and the SLang supervised SRL system. In order to address these problems, we apply the following techniques to improve learning from partial and noisy projections, thereby enhancing the performance of our model:

- Bootstrapping to make use of unlabeled data;

- Determining the quality of a particular projected semantic dependency based on two factors: 1) source-target syntactic correspondence; and, 2) projection completeness degree. We utilize the above constraints in the form of a data-dependent cost-sensitive training objective. This way the classifier would be able to learn translation shifts and erroneous instances in the projected data, hence enhancing the overall performance of the system.

Bootstrapping Bootstrapping (or self-training) is a simple but very useful technique that makes use of unlabeled data. A traditional self-training method (McClosky et al., 2006) labels unlabeled data (in our case, fill in missing SRL decisions) and adds that data to the labeled data for further training. We report results for this setting in §3.1 as *fill–in*. Although fill–in method is shown to be very useful in previous work (Akbik et al., 2015), empirically, we find that it is better to *relabel* **all** training instances (including the already labeled data) instead of only labeling unlabeled raw data. Therefore, the classifier is empowered to discover outliers (resulting from erroneous projections) and change their labels during the training process. Figure 1 illustrates our algorithm. It starts with training on the labeled data and uses the trained model to label the unlabeled data and relabel the already labeled data. This process repeats for a certain number of epochs until the model converges, i.e., reaches its maximum performance.

Data-dependent cost-sensitive training In our baseline approach, we use the standard perceptron training. In other words, whenever the algorithm sees a training instance x_i with its corresponding label y_i, it updates the weight vector θ for iteration t based on the difference between the feature vector $\phi(x_i, y_i)$ of the gold label and the feature vector $\phi(x_i, y_i^*)$ of the predicted label y_i^* (Eq. 1).

$$\theta^t = \theta^{t-1} + \phi(x_i, y_i) - \phi(x_i, y_i^*) \qquad (1)$$

In Eq. 1, the algorithm assumes that every data point x_i in the training data $\{x_1, \cdots, x_n\}$ has the

Inputs: 1) Projected data $\mathcal{D} = \mathcal{D}^{\mathcal{L}} \cup \mathcal{D}^{\mathcal{U}}$ where $\mathcal{D}^{\mathcal{L}}$ and $\mathcal{D}^{\mathcal{U}}$ indicate labeled and unlabeled instances in the projected data; 2) Number of self-training iterations m.

Algorithm:
 Train model θ^0 on $\mathcal{D}^{\mathcal{L}}$
 for $i = 1$ to m **do**
  $\mathcal{D}^{\mathcal{U}} \leftarrow$ Label data $\mathcal{D}^{\mathcal{U}}$ with model θ^{i-1}.
  $\mathcal{D}^{\mathcal{L}} \leftarrow$ Relabel data $\mathcal{D}^{\mathcal{L}}$ with model θ^{i-1}.
  Train model θ^i on $\mathcal{D}^{\mathcal{L}} \cup \mathcal{D}^{\mathcal{U}}$
Output: The model parameters θ^m.

Figure 1: The iterative bootstrapping algorithm for training SRL on partially projected data.

same importance and the cost of wrongly predicting the best label for each training instance is uniform. We believe this uniform update is problematic especially for the transfer task in which different projected instances have different qualities. To mitigate this issue, we propose a simple modification, we introduce a cost $\lambda_i \in [0, 1]$ for each training instance x_i. Therefore, Eq. 1 is modified as follows in Eq. 2.

$$\theta^t = \theta^{t-1} + \lambda_i \left(\phi(x_i, y_i) - \phi(x_i, y_i^*) \right) \quad (2)$$

In other words, the penalty of making a mistake by the classifier for each training instance depends on the importance of that instance defined by a certain cost. The main challenge is to define an effective cost function, especially in our framework where we don't have supervision. Accordingly, we experiment with the following cost definitions:

- **Projection completeness**: Our observation shows that the density of projection is a very important indicator of projection quality. We view it as a rough indicator of translation shifts: the more alignments from source to target, the less we have a chance of having translation shifts. As an example, consider the sentence pair extracted from English–German Europarl corpus: *"I sit here between a rock and a hard place"* and its German translation *"Zwei Herzen wohnen ach in meiner Brust"* which literally reads as *"Two hearts dwell in my chest"*. The only words that are aligned (based on the output of Giza++) are the English word *"between"* and the German word *"in"*. In fact, the German sentence is an idiomatic translation of the English sentence. Consequently predicate–argument structure of these sentences vary

tremendously; The word *"sit"* is predicate of the English sentence while *"wohnen (dwell)"* is the predicate of the German sentence.

We use the definition of *completeness* from Akbik et al. (2015) to define the sparsity cost (λ^{comp}): this definition deals with the proportion of a verb or direct dependents of verbs in a sentence that are labeled.

- **Source-target syntactic dependency match**: We observe that when the dependency label of a target word is different from its aligned source word, there is a higher chance of a projection mistake. However, given the high frequency of source-target dependency mismatches, it is harmful to prune those projections that have dependency mismatch; instead, we define a different cost if we see a training instance with a dependency mismatch. For an argument x_i that is projected from source argument s_{x_i}, we define the cost λ_i^{dep} according to the dependency of the source and target words $dep(x_i)$ and $dep(s_{x_i})$ as Eq. 3.

$$\lambda_i^{dep} = \begin{cases} 1 & \text{if } dep(x_i) = dep(s_{x_i}) \\ 0.5 & \text{otherwise} \end{cases} \quad (3)$$

As an example, consider Fig. 2 that demonstrates an English-German sentence pair from EuroParl *"I would urge you to endorse this"* with its German translation that literally reads as *"I ask for your approval"*. As we can see, there is a shift in translation of English clausal complement *"to endorse this"* into German equivalent *"um Zustimmung (your approaval)"* which leads the difference in the syntactic structure of source and target sentences. Therefore, neither the predicate label of English verb *"endorse"* nor the argument *"A2"* should not be projected to the German noun *"Zustimmung"*. Dashed edges between sentences show intersected word alignments. Here, projecting semantic role of *"endorse"* (A2) to to the word *"Zustimmmung"* through alignment will lead to the wrong semantic role for this word.

- **Completeness + syntactic match**: We employ the average of λ^{dep} and λ^{comp} values as defined above. This way, we simultaneously encode both the completeness and syntactic similarity information.

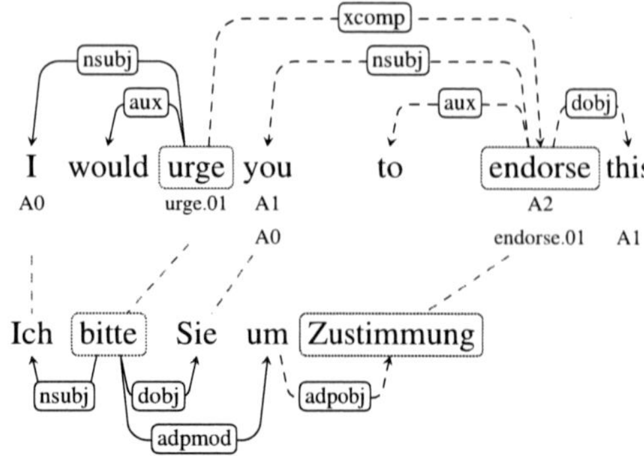

Figure 2: Example of English-German sentences from Europarl with dependency structure. Different dependencies are shown with dashed arcs. Predicate–argument structure of the English sentence is shown bellow each word.

3 Experiments

Data and Setting We use English as the source and German as the target language. In our setting, we assume to have supervised part-of-speech tagging and dependency parsing models for both the source (SLang) and target (TLang) languages. We use the Universal part-of-speech tagset of Petrov et al. (2011) and the Google Universal Treebank (McDonald et al., 2013). We ignore the projection of the *AM* roles to German since this particular role does not appear in the German dataset.

We use the standard data splits in the CoNLL shared task on SRL (Hajič et al., 2009) for evaluation. We replace the POS and dependency information with the predictions from the Yara parser (Rasooli and Tetreault, 2015) trained on the Google Universal Treebank.[1] We use the parallel Europarl corpus (Koehn, 2005) and Giza++ (Och and Ney, 2003) for extracting word alignments. Since predicate senses are projected from English to German, comparing projected senses with the gold German predicate sense is impossible. To address this, all evaluations are conducted using the Gold predicate sense.

After filtering projections with density criteria of §2.1, 29417 of the sentences are preserved. The number of preserved sentences after filtering sparse alignments is roughly one percent of the

---

[1]Our ideal setting is to transfer to more languages but because of the semantic label inconsistency across CoNLL datasets, we find it impossible to evaluate our model on more languages. Future work should work on defining a reliable conversion scheme to unify the annotations in different datasets.

Model	Cost	Lab. F1
Baseline	×	60.3
Bootstrap–fill-in	×	61.6
Bootstrap–relabel	×	62.4
Bootstrap–relabel	comp.	$63.0_{(+1.0)}$
Bootstrap–relabel	dep.	$63.4_{(+1.8)}$
Bootstrap–relabel	comp.+dep.	$\mathbf{63.8}_{(+1.3)}$
Supervised	–	79.5

Table 1: Labeled F-score for different models in SRL transfer from English to German using gold predicates. Cost columns shows the use of cost-sensitive training using projection completeness ("comp."), source-target dependency match ("dep.") and both ("comp.+dep."). The numbers in parenthesis show the absolute improvement over the Bootstrap-fill-in method.

original parallel data (29K sentences out of 2.2M sentences). Density threshold is set to 0.4 determined based on our tuning experiments on development data.

3.1 Results and Discussion

Table 1 shows the results of different models on the German evaluation data. As we can see in the table, bootstrapping outperforms the baseline. Interestingly, relabelling all training instances (Bootstrap–relabel) gives us 0.8 absolute improvement in F-score compared to when we just predict over instances without a projected label (Bootstrap–fill-in). Here, the fill-in approach would label only the German word "um" in Fig. 2 that does not have any projected label from the English side. While the relabeling method will overwrite all projected labels with less noisy predicted labels.

We additionally observe that the combination of the two cost functions improves the quality further. Overall, the best model yields 3.5 absolute improvement F-score over the baseline. As expected, none of the approaches improves over supervised performance. We further analyzed the effects of relabeling approach on identification and classification of non–root semantic dependencies. Figure 3 shows precision, recall and F–score of the two most frequent semantic dependencies (predicate pos + argument label): VERB+A0, VERB+A1 throughout relabeling iterations. As demonstrated in the graph, both precision and recall improve by cost-sensitive re-

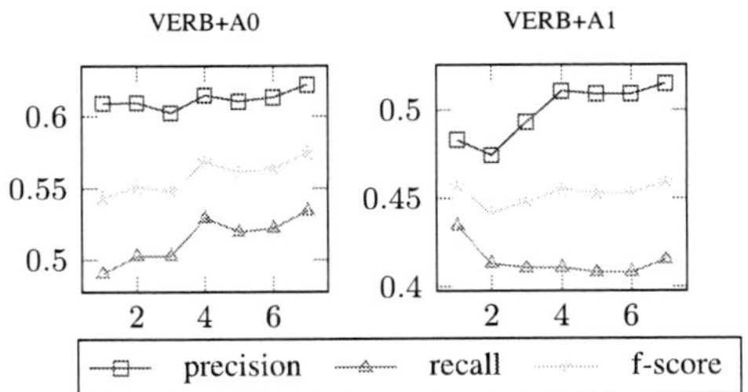

Figure 3: Precision, recall and F–score of VERB+A0 and VERB+A1 during relabeling iterations on the German development data. Horizontal axis shows the number of iterations and vertical axis shows values of precision, recall and F–score.

labeling for VERB+A0. In fact, cost-sensitive training helps the system refine irrelevant projections at each iteration and assigns more weight on less noisy projections, hence enhancing precision. Our analysis on VERB+A0 instances shows that source–target dependency match percentage also increases during iterations leading to increase the recall. In other words, weighting projection instances based on dependency match helps classifier label some of the instances which were dismissed during projection, thereby will increase the recall. While similar improvement in precision is observed for VERB+A1, Figure 3 shows that the recall is almost descending by relabeling. Our analysis shows that unlike VERB+A0, percentage of source–target dependency match remains almost steady for VERB+A1. This means that cost-sensitive relabeling for this particular semantic dependency has not been very successful in labeling unlabeled data.

4   Related Work

There have been several studies on transferring SRL systems (Padó and Lapata, 2005, 2009; Mukund et al., 2010; van der Plas et al., 2011, 2014; Kozhevnikov and Titov, 2013; Akbik et al., 2015). Padó and Lapata (2005), as one of the earliest studies on annotation projection for SRL using parallel resources, apply different heuristics and techniques to improve the quality of their model by focusing on having better word and constituent alignments. van der Plas et al. (2011) improve an annotation projection model by jointly training a transfer system for parsing and SRL. They solely focus on fully projected annotations and train only on verbs. In this work, we train on all predicates

as well as exploit partial annotation. Kozhevnikov and Titov (2013) define shared feature representations between the source and target languages in annotation projection. The benefit of using shared representations is complementary to our work encouraging us to use it in future work.

Akbik et al. (2015) introduce an iterative self-training approach using different types of linguistic heuristics and alignment filters to improve the quality of projected roles. Unlike our work that does not use any external resources, Akbik et al. (2015) make use of bilingual dictionaries. Our work also leverages self-training but with a different approach: first of all, ours does not apply any heuristics to filter out projections. Second, it trains and relabels all projected instances, either labeled or unlabeled, at every epoch and does not gradually introduce new unlabeled data. Instead, we find it more useful to let the target language SRL system rule out noisy projections via relabeling.

5   Conclusion

We described a method to improve the performance of annotation projection in the dependency-based SRL task utilizing a data-dependent cost-sensitive training. Unlinke previous studies that use manually-defined rules to filter projections, we benefit from information obtained from projection sparsity and syntactic similarity to weigh projections. We utilize a bootstrapping algorithm to train a SRL system over projections. We showed that we can get better results if we relabel the entire train data in each iteration as opposed to only labeling instances without projections.

For the future work, we consider experimenting with newly published Universal Proposition Bank (Wang et al., 2017) that provides a unified labeling scheme for all languages. Given the recent success in SRL systems with neural networks (Marcheggiani et al., 2017; Marcheggiani and Titov, 2017), we plan to use them for further improvement. We expect a similar trend by applying the same ideas in a neural SRL system.

Acknowledgments

This work has been partly funded by DARPA LORELEI Grant and generous support by Leidos Corp. for the 1st and 3rd authors. We would like to acknowledge the useful comments by three anonymous reviewers who helped in making this publication more concise and better presented.

References

Alan Akbik, laura chiticariu, Marina Danilevsky, Yunyao Li, Shivakumar Vaithyanathan, and Huaiyu Zhu. 2015. Generating high quality proposition banks for multilingual semantic role labeling. In *Proceedings of the 53rd Annual Meeting of the Association for Computational Linguistics and the 7th International Joint Conference on Natural Language Processing (Volume 1: Long Papers)*, pages 397–407. Association for Computational Linguistics.

Anders Björkelund, Love Hafdell, and Pierre Nugues. 2009. *Proceedings of the Thirteenth Conference on Computational Natural Language Learning (CoNLL 2009): Shared Task*, chapter Multilingual Semantic Role Labeling. Association for Computational Linguistics.

Janara Christensen, Mausam, Stephen Soderland, and Oren Etzioni. 2011. An analysis of open information extraction based on semantic role labeling. In *Proceedings of the Sixth International Conference on Knowledge Capture*, K-CAP '11, pages 113–120, New York, NY, USA. ACM.

Katrin Erk, Andrea Kowalski, Sebastian Padó, and Manfred Pinkal. 2003. Towards a resource for lexical semantics: A large german corpus with extensive semantic annotation. In *Proceedings of the 41st Annual Meeting of the Association for Computational Linguistics*, pages 537–544, Sapporo, Japan. Association for Computational Linguistics.

Yoav Freund and Robert E. Schapire. 1999. Large margin classification using the perceptron algorithm. *Machine Learning*, 37(3):277–296.

Jan Hajič, Massimiliano Ciaramita, Richard Johansson, Daisuke Kawahara, Antònia Maria Martí, Lluís Màrquez, Adam Meyers, Joakim Nivre, Sebastian Padó, Jan Štepánek, Pavel Straňák, Mihai Surdeanu, Nianwen Xue, and Yi Zhang. 2009. *Proceedings of the Thirteenth Conference on Computational Natural Language Learning (CoNLL 2009): Shared Task*, chapter The CoNLL-2009 Shared Task: Syntactic and Semantic Dependencies in Multiple Languages. Association for Computational Linguistics.

Philipp Koehn. 2005. Europarl: A parallel corpus for statistical machine translation. In *MT summit*, volume 5, pages 79–86.

Mikhail Kozhevnikov and Ivan Titov. 2013. Cross-lingual transfer of semantic role labeling models. In *Proceedings of the 51st Annual Meeting of the Association for Computational Linguistics (Volume 1: Long Papers)*, pages 1190–1200. Association for Computational Linguistics.

Diego Marcheggiani, Anton Frolov, and Ivan Titov. 2017. A simple and accurate syntax-agnostic neural model for dependency-based semantic role labeling. In *Proceedings of the 21st Conference on Computational Natural Language Learning (CoNLL 2017)*, pages 411–420. Association for Computational Linguistics.

Diego Marcheggiani and Ivan Titov. 2017. Encoding sentences with graph convolutional networks for semantic role labeling. In *Proceedings of the 2017 Conference on Empirical Methods in Natural Language Processing*, pages 1507–1516. Association for Computational Linguistics.

David McClosky, Eugene Charniak, and Mark Johnson. 2006. Effective self-training for parsing. In *Proceedings of the Human Language Technology Conference of the NAACL, Main Conference.*

Ryan McDonald, Joakim Nivre, Yvonne Quirmbach-Brundage, Yoav Goldberg, Dipanjan Das, Kuzman Ganchev, Keith Hall, Slav Petrov, Hao Zhang, Oscar Täckström, Claudia Bedini, Núria Bertomeu Castelló, and Jungmee Lee. 2013. Universal dependency annotation for multilingual parsing. In *Proceedings of the 51st Annual Meeting of the Association for Computational Linguistics (Volume 2: Short Papers)*, pages 92–97, Sofia, Bulgaria. Association for Computational Linguistics.

Smruthi Mukund, Debanjan Ghosh, and Rohini Srihari. 2010. Using cross-lingual projections to generate semantic role labeled annotated corpus for urdu - a resource poor language. In *Proceedings of the 23rd International Conference on Computational Linguistics (Coling 2010)*, pages 797–805. Coling 2010 Organizing Committee.

Franz Josef Och and Hermann Ney. 2003. A systematic comparison of various statistical alignment models. *Computational Linguistics*, 29(1).

Sebastian Padó and Mirella Lapata. 2005. Cross-lingual bootstrapping of semantic lexicons: The case of framenet. In *Proceedings of the National Conference on Artificial Intelligence*, volume 20, pages 1087–1092.

Sebastian Padó and Mirella Lapata. 2009. Cross-lingual annotation projection for semantic roles. *Journal of Artificial Intelligence Research*, 36(1):307–340.

Martha Palmer, Daniel Gildea, and Paul Kingsbury. 2005. The proposition bank: An annotated corpus of semantic roles. *Computational Linguistics, Volume 31, Number 1, March 2005.*

Martha Palmer, Daniel Gildea, and Nianwen Xue. 2010. Semantic role labeling. *Synthesis Lectures on Human Language Technologies*, 3(1):1–103.

Slav Petrov, Dipanjan Das, and Ryan McDonald. 2011. A universal part-of-speech tagset. *arXiv preprint arXiv:1104.2086.*

Lonneke van der Plas, Marianna Apidianaki, and Chenhua Chen. 2014. Global methods for cross-lingual semantic role and predicate labelling. In *Proceedings of COLING 2014, the 25th International Conference on Computational Linguistics: Technical Papers*, pages 1279–1290. Dublin City University and Association for Computational Linguistics.

Lonneke van der Plas, Paola Merlo, and James Henderson. 2011. Scaling up automatic cross-lingual semantic role annotation. In *Proceedings of the 49th Annual Meeting of the Association for Computational Linguistics: Human Language Technologies*, pages 299–304. Association for Computational Linguistics.

Mohammad Sadegh Rasooli and Joel Tetreault. 2015. Yara parser: A fast and accurate dependency parser. *arXiv preprint arXiv:1503.06733*.

Michael Roth and Mirella Lapata. 2016. Neural semantic role labeling with dependency path embeddings. In *Proceedings of the 54th Annual Meeting of the Association for Computational Linguistics (Volume 1: Long Papers)*, pages 1192–1202. Association for Computational Linguistics.

Dan Shen and Mirella Lapata. 2007. Using semantic roles to improve question answering. In *Proceedings of the 2007 Joint Conference on Empirical Methods in Natural Language Processing and Computational Natural Language Learning (EMNLP-CoNLL)*, pages 12–21, Prague, Czech Republic. Association for Computational Linguistics.

Oscar Täckström, Kuzman Ganchev, and Dipanjan Das. 2015. Efficient inference and structured learning for semantic role labeling. *Transactions of the Association of Computational Linguistics*, 3:29–41.

Ashwini Vaidya, Jinho Choi, Martha Palmer, and Bhuvana Narasimhan. 2011. Analysis of the hindi proposition bank using dependency structure. In *Proceedings of the 5th Linguistic Annotation Workshop*, pages 21–29, Portland, Oregon, USA. Association for Computational Linguistics.

Chenguang Wang, Alan Akbik, laura chiticariu, Yunyao Li, Fei Xia, and Anbang Xu. 2017. Crowd-in-the-loop: A hybrid approach for annotating semantic roles. In *Proceedings of the 2017 Conference on Empirical Methods in Natural Language Processing*, pages 1914–1923, Copenhagen, Denmark. Association for Computational Linguistics.

Wajdi Zaghouani, Mona Diab, Aous Mansouri, Sameer Pradhan, and Martha Palmer. 2010. The revised arabic propbank. In *Proceedings of the Fourth Linguistic Annotation Workshop*, pages 222–226, Uppsala, Sweden. Association for Computational Linguistics.

Jie Zhou and Wei Xu. 2015. End-to-end learning of semantic role labeling using recurrent neural networks. In *Proceedings of the 53rd Annual Meeting of the Association for Computational Linguistics and the 7th International Joint Conference on Natural Language Processing (Volume 1: Long Papers)*, pages 1127–1137. Association for Computational Linguistics.

Neural Lattice Search for Domain Adaptation in Machine Translation

Huda Khayrallah[†] **Gaurav Kumar**[†] **Kevin Duh**[‡] **Matt Post**[‡] **Philipp Koehn**[†]
[†]Center for Language and Speech Processing
[‡]Human Language Technology Center of Excellence
Johns Hopkins University
{huda, gkumar, kevinduh, post, phi}@cs.jhu.edu

Abstract

Domain adaptation is a major challenge for neural machine translation (NMT). Given unknown words or new domains, NMT systems tend to generate fluent translations at the expense of adequacy. We present a stack-based lattice search algorithm for NMT and show that constraining its search space with lattices generated by phrase-based machine translation (PBMT) improves robustness. We report consistent BLEU score gains across four diverse domain adaptation tasks involving medical, IT, Koran, or subtitles texts.

1 Introduction

Domain adaptation is a major challenge for neural machine translation (NMT). Although impressive improvements have been achieved in recent years (c.f. Bojar et al. (2016)), NMT systems require a large amount of training data and thus perform poorly relative to phrase-based machine translation (PBMT) systems in low resource and domain adaptation scenarios (Koehn and Knowles, 2017). In such situations, neural systems often produce fluent output that unfortunately contains words not licensed by the unfamiliar source sentence (Arthur et al., 2016; Tu et al., 2016). Phrase-based systems, in contrast, explicitly model the translation of all source words via coverage vectors, and tend to produce translations that are adequate but less fluent. This situation is depicted in Table 1, which contains examples of PBMT and NMT systems trained on WMT training sets which are then applied to IT texts.

We present an approach that combines the best of both worlds by using the lattice output of PBMT to constrain the search space available to an NMT decoder, thereby bringing together the *adequacy*

src	Versionsinformationen ausgeben und beenden
ref	output version information and exit
PBMT	Spend version information and end
NMT	Spend and end versionary information
NMT$_l$	Print version information and exit

Table 1: Translations of sentence #925 from the IT corpus with systems trained on WMT data. The NMT$_l$ line was produced by a WMT-trained NMT search over a WMT-trained PBMT lattice.

and the *fluency* properties of PBMT and NMT systems. The final line of Table 1 demonstrates the improvement this can bring. Our contributions are (1) a simple stack-based lattice search algorithm for NMT,[1] and (2) a set of domain adaptation experiments showing that PBMT lattice constraints are effective in achieving robust results compared to NMT decoding with standard beam search.

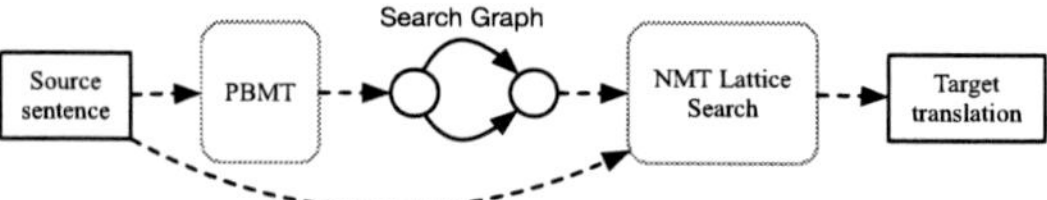

Figure 1: NMT lattice search over a PBMT-generated lattice.

2 Stack-based Neural Lattice Search

Figure 1 demonstrates our system; given an input sentence, the PBMT system generates a lattice, which is then used as input to the neural lattice search algorithm. We would like to score every path in the lattice with the NMT system and then search. However, this is generally prohibitively expensive because the RNN architectures in NMT

---

[1] github.com/khayrallah/
nematus-lattice-search

Proceedings of the The 8th International Joint Conference on Natural Language Processing, pages 20–25,
Taipei, Taiwan, November 27 – December 1, 2017 ©2017 AFNLP

do not permit recombination of hypotheses on the lattice, since NMT states encode the entire sentence history. This explodes the search lattice into an exponentially sized tree. To address this problem, we use a *stack decoding* algorithm that groups hypotheses by the number of target words, extending items from each stack in order of score, and adding them to later stacks.[2] This strategy allows us to group together roughly equivalent intermediate nodes, allowing for pruning.

Algorithm 1: Stack decoding over a lattice

Data: lattice root N, NMT init state I, beam size b

Result: output string s

1   goalStack = []; stacks = []
2   heappush(stacks[0], (0.0, N, I, null, 0))
3   **for** $i = 0$; $i <len(stacks)$; i++ **do**
4   **for** b_i in $1 \ldots b$ **do**
5   score, node, state, _, len = heappop(stacks[i])
6   **for** *arc in node.arcs()* **do**
7   newState, cost = scorer(state, arc)
8   newScore = score + cost
9   newLen = len + arc.len
10   **if** *isFinalState(node)* **then**
11   stack = goalStack
12   **else**
13   stack = stack[newLen]
14   heappush(stack, (newScore, arc.head, newState, arc, newLen))
15   return extractBest(heappop(goalStack))

The pseudocode is in Algorithm 1, and a graphical depiction in Figure 2. In the lattice (Figure 2(a)), arcs are annotated with phrases of one or more words indicating the target sides of phrases that were applied during PBMT decoding. Nodes represent recombined states in the PBMT search space (i.e., states that have identical source coverage vectors and language model states). The search nodes contain the cumulative score, the current lattice node, the current neural state, the incoming arc, and the target length along this path. After initialization, the outer loop (line 3) proceeds over stacks, starting at stack 1, and

continuing through the longest path through the lattice (subject to pruning). Upon visiting each stack, it considers the top b items (line 4). It pops each of them in turn and retrieves its node in the underlying lattice and the associated neural state (line 5). It then considers all of the node's outgoing arcs (line 6). The neural scorer is used to score each of them (line 7), returning a new neural state that is stored with a new item (line 14) on the appropriate stack.

Figure 2 depicts this process, but without pruning or sorting. A beam of size 2 would prune off one item from stack 2, along with all of its descendants, thus culling the exponentially sized tree.

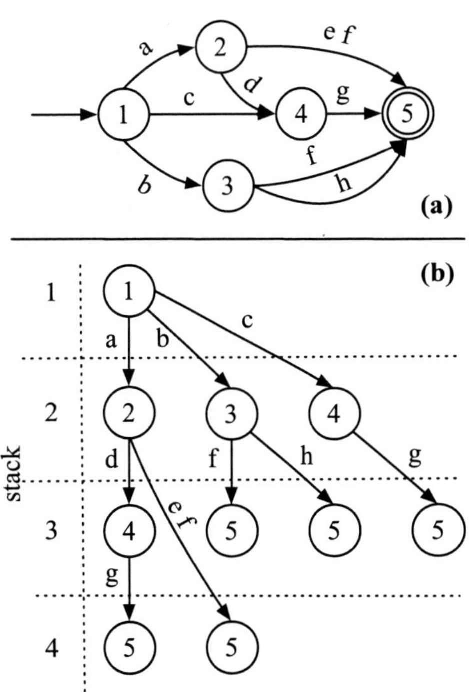

Figure 2: (a) A PBMT search lattice and (b) stack-based decoding over that lattice. Each letter represents a word.

In (b), the exponential expansion of the lattice in (a) is apparent, since states that had recombined in (a) due to identical n-gram history do not recombine in (b). This figure does not demonstrate pruning, descendants of items that fall off the beam would not be explored.

---

[2] This is similar to PBMT stack decoding. However, in PBMT stack decoding, stacks are grouped by the number of translated source words, which is not possible in NMT, since the translation of individual source words is not tracked.

Corpus	Words	Sentences	W/S
Medical	14,301,472	1,104,752	13
IT	3,041,677	337,817	9
Koran	9,848,539	480,421	21
Subtitles	114,371,754	13,873,398	8
WMT	113,165,079	4,562,102	25

Table 2: Size of the training data for each domain

3 Experiment Setup

Our German-to-English evaluation consists of a large out-of-domain bitext (WMT2016 (Bojar et al., 2016), news/parliamentary text) and four distinct in-domain bitexts from OPUS (Tiedemann, 2009, 2012): Medical (EMEA), IT (GNOME, KDE, PHP, Ubuntu, and OpenOffice), Koran (Tanzil), and Subtitles (OpenSubtitles[3]).

The in-domain corpora use the same train/tune/test splits as Koehn and Knowles (2017), and for each in-domain training set we build PBMT and NMT models, termed $PBMT_{in}$ and NMT_{in}. We also build PBMT and NMT models on the out-of-domain WMT bitext, termed $PBMT_{out}$ and NMT_{out}. For each **in-domain test set**, we consider four configurations:

1. $PBMT_{out} \times NMT_{out}$: the unsupervised domain adaptation setting where no training data is available for the domain of interest.

2. $PBMT_{in} \times NMT_{in}$: the matched domain setting where the training data matches the test data in terms of domain, but the training data is not large (relative to WMT).

3. $PBMT_{in} \times NMT_{out}$: PBMT is trained on small in-domain data while NMT is trained on larger out-of-domain data.

4. $PBMT_{out} \times NMT_{in}$: NMT is trained on small in-domain data while PBMT is trained on larger out-of-domain data.

For each training configuration, we are interested in seeing how our proposed NMT lattice search compares to standard NMT beam search. Additionally, we compare the results of PBMT 1-best decoding and PBMT N-best lists rescoring (N=500) using the same NMT model.

The PBMT models are trained with Moses (Koehn et al., 2007). The $PBMT_{out}$ models

include German specific processing and Neural Network Joint Models (Devlin et al., 2014), replicating Ding et al. (2016). The $PBMT_{in}$ models are Moses models with standard settings, replicating Koehn and Knowles (2017). The NMT models are trained with Nematus (Sennrich et al., 2017). The NMT_{out} models replicate Sennrich et al. (2016);[4] the NMT_{in} models replicate Koehn and Knowles (2017). We use Marian (Junczys-Dowmunt et al., 2016a) to rescore N-best lists.

The search graphs are pre-processed by converting them to the OpenFST format (Allauzen et al., 2007) and applying operations to remove epsilon arcs, determinize, minimize and topsort. Since the search graphs may be prohibitively large in size, we prune them with a threshold.[5] We perform 5-fold cross-validation over pruning thresholds (.1, .25, .5) and lattice search beamsizes (1, 10, 100).

Very aggressive pruning with a small beam limits the search to be very similar to the PBMT output. In contrast, a very deep lattice with a large beam begins to approach the unconstrained search space of standard decoding in NMT.

4 Results

Table 3 summarizes the BLEU results on each test domain. Note that PBMT 1-best results are equivalent for $PBMT_{in} \times NMT_{in}$ and $PBMT_{in} \times NMT_{out}$ since the same PBMT model is used and NMT is not relevant. For both PBMT 1-best and NMT Standard Search, there are two sets of equivalent results among the four training configurations.

We want to highlight the fact that the PBMT 1-best in-domain models outperform the out of domain ones, despite being much simpler models. Additionally, the BLEU scores for NMT standard search are higher for the in-domain models, despite the smaller amount of training data. This emphasizes the importance of the domain of the training corpora.

In cross-validation for our domains, smaller beams and aggressive pruning tend to perform well. This follows from the fact that PBMT 1-best outperforms NMT standard search. We want to strongly limit the search space given to NMT in such a scenario. However, these parameters need to be tuned to a specific domain and language.

---

[3]opensubtitles.org

[4]github.com/rsennrich/wmt16-scripts

[5]Pruning removes arcs that do not appear on a lattice path whose score is within than $t \otimes w$, where w is the weight of the FST's shortest path, and t is the pruning threshold.

Test Domain	Training Configuration	PBMT 1-best	NMT Standard Search	N-best Rescoring	NMT Lattice Search
IT	$\text{PBMT}_{out} \times \text{NMT}_{out}$	25.1 (-0.3)	22.5 (-2.9)	22.2 (-3.2)	25.4
	$\text{PBMT}_{in} \times \text{NMT}_{in}$	47.4 (-4.2)	34.2 (-17.4)	47.6 (-4.0)	51.6
	$\text{PBMT}_{in} \times \text{NMT}_{out}$	47.4 (-5.2)	22.5 (-30.1)	47.6 (-5.0)	**52.6***
	$\text{PBMT}_{out} \times \text{NMT}_{in}$	25.1 (-2.2)	34.2 (6.9)	22.4 (-4.9)	27.3
Medical	$\text{PBMT}_{out} \times \text{NMT}_{out}$	33.3 (-0.9)	32.9 (-1.3)	30.8 (-3.4)	34.2
	$\text{PBMT}_{in} \times \text{NMT}_{in}$	47.4 (-0.7)	37.8 (-10.3)	40.2 (-7.9)	**48.1***
	$\text{PBMT}_{in} \times \text{NMT}_{out}$	47.4 (-0.4)	32.9 (-14.9)	39.7 (-8.1)	**47.8**
	$\text{PBMT}_{out} \times \text{NMT}_{in}$	33.3 (-2.7)	37.8 (1.8)	31.2 (-4.8)	36.0
Koran	$\text{PBMT}_{out} \times \text{NMT}_{out}$	14.7 (-0.2)	10.8 (-4.1)	13.9 (-1.0)	14.9
	$\text{PBMT}_{in} \times \text{NMT}_{in}$	**20.6 (-0.1)**	15.9 (-4.8)	19.3 (-1.4)	**20.7**
	$\text{PBMT}_{in} \times \text{NMT}_{out}$	**20.6 (-0.2)**	10.8 (-10.0)	19.4 (-1.4)	**20.8***
	$\text{PBMT}_{out} \times \text{NMT}_{in}$	14.7 (-1.4)	15.9 (-0.2)	13.9 (-2.2)	16.1
Subtitle	$\text{PBMT}_{out} \times \text{NMT}_{out}$	26.6 (-0.9)	25.3 (-2.2)	19.7 (-7.8)	27.5
	$\text{PBMT}_{in} \times \text{NMT}_{in}$	26.8 (-1.1)	24.9 (-3.0)	17.8 (-10.1)	**27.9**
	$\text{PBMT}_{in} \times \text{NMT}_{out}$	26.8 (-1.6)	25.3 (-3.1)	17.1 (-11.3)	**28.4***
	$\text{PBMT}_{out} \times \text{NMT}_{in}$	26.6 (-1.0)	24.9 (-2.7)	19.8 (-7.8)	27.6

Table 3: Results across test domains and training configurations. For each system, we show the BLEU score and its difference with NMT Lattice Search under the same training configuration (same row) in parentheses. E.g. in the last row, NMT Lattice Search achieves 27.6 BLEU and is better than PBMT 1-best by 1.0 BLEU, and better than NMT Standard Search by 2.7 BLEU. For each test domain we mark the best score among all systems and training configurations with an asterisk, and bold any score with less than a 0.5 BLEU difference.

Our research questions are as follows:

Does lattice search perform best across training configurations? As observed across each row in Table 3, lattice search typically outperforms the three other systems. Importantly, the BLEU gains against standard beam search in NMT and N-best rescoring of PBMT with NMT are noticeable regardless of training configuration. E.g., in the Subtitles task the gains range from 2.2 to 3.1 BLEU. There are also consistent gains compared to PBMT 1-best (e.g. 0.9-1.6 BLEU gain), which forms the basis of the search space; this implies that PBMT and NMT can serve as effective hybrid systems, where the former provides the potential translation candidates and the latter scores them.

Given the choice, which training configuration is best for domain adaptation? While the answer depends on the amount of in-domain and out-of-domain data, we find that $\text{PBMT}_{in} \times \text{NMT}_{in}$ and $\text{PBMT}_{in} \times \text{NMT}_{out}$ perform the best. This supports previous findings (Koehn and Knowles, 2017) that PBMT_{in} is robust when training data is insufficient. In conclusion, we recommend using lattice search with search graphs from PBMT_{in}, and NMT models can be trained on either in-domain or out-of-domain corpora.

5 Related Work

Previous work on domain adaptation in NMT focuses on training methods such as transfer learning or fine-tuning (Luong and Manning, 2015; Freitag and Al-Onaizan, 2016; Chu et al., 2017). This strategy begins with a strong model trained on a large out-of-domain corpus and then continuesx training on an in-domain corpus. Our approach is orthogonal in that we focus on search. Conceivably, advances in training methods might be incorporated to improve our individual NMT_{in} models.

Our lattice search algorithm is related to previous work in hybrid NMT/PBMT systems, which can be visualized on a spectrum depending on how tightly integrated the two systems are. On one end, NMT can easily be used to rerank N-best lists output by PBMT; on the other, NMT can be incorporated as features in PBMT (Junczys-Dowmunt et al., 2016b). In the middle of the spectrum is NMT search (or re-scoring) based on constraints from PBMT.

Our algorithm is conceptually very similar to Stahlberg et al. (2016), who rescore a WFSA reformulation of the Hiero formalism. Their algorithm is a breadth-first search over all the nodes of the lattice, capped by a beam. Other hybrid methods include: constraining the output vocabulary of NMT on a per-sentence basis, using bilingual information provided by PBMT (Mi et al., 2016), Minimum Bayes Risk decoding with PBMT n-gram posteriors (Stahlberg et al., 2017), and incorporating PBMT hypotheses as additional input in a modified NMT architecture (Wang et al., 2017).

Related works in lattice search/re-scoring with RNNs (without NMT encoder-decoders) (Ladhak et al., 2016; Deoras et al., 2011; Hori et al., 2014) may serve as other interesting comparisons. Specifically, Auli et al. (2013) and Liu et al. (2016) provide alternatives to our approach to the problem of recombination. The former work allows the splitting of previously recombined decoder states (thresholded) while the latter clusters RNN states based on their n-gram context.

6   Conclusion

We present a stack-based lattice search algorithm for NMT, and show that constraining decoding to candidate translations in a PBMT search graph leads to robust improvements for domain adaptation. Our method can be viewed as as simple yet effective way to combine the *adequacy* advantages of PBMT, which stems from explicit models of coverage, with the *fluency* advantages of NMT. When presented with a domain adaptation problem we recommend using lattice search with search graphs from PBMT$_{in}$, with NMT models either trained on either in-domain or out-of-domain corpora.

Future work includes interpolation of the NMT and PBMT scores in the lattice search, which requires additional tuning but may further improve results.

Acknowledgments

This material is based upon work supported in part by the Defense Advanced Research Projects Agency (DARPA) under Contract No. HR0011-15-C-0113. Any opinions, findings and conclusions or recommendations expressed in this material are those of the authors and do not necessarily reflect the views of DARPA.

References

Cyril Allauzen, Michael Riley, Johan Schalkwyk, Wojciech Skut, and Mehryar Mohri. 2007. OpenFst: A General and Efficient Weighted Finite-State Transducer Library. In *Proceedings of the Ninth International Conference on Implementation and Application of Automata, (CIAA 2007)*, volume 4783 of *Lecture Notes in Computer Science*. Springer. http://www.openfst.org.

Philip Arthur, Graham Neubig, and Satoshi Nakamura. 2016. Incorporating Discrete Translation Lexicons into Neural Machine Translation. In *Proceedings of the 2016 Conference on Empirical Methods in Natural Language Processing*, Austin, Texas. Association for Computational Linguistics.

Michael Auli, Michel Galley, Chris Quirk, and Geoffrey Zweig. 2013. Joint Language and Translation Modeling with Recurrent Neural Networks. In *Proceedings of the 2013 Conference on Empirical Methods in Natural Language Processing*, Seattle, Washington, USA. Association for Computational Linguistics.

Ondřej Bojar, Rajen Chatterjee, Christian Federmann, Yvette Graham, Barry Haddow, Matthias Huck, Antonio Jimeno Yepes, Philipp Koehn, Varvara Logacheva, Christof Monz, Matteo Negri, Aurelie Neveol, Mariana Neves, Martin Popel, Matt Post, Raphael Rubino, Carolina Scarton, Lucia Specia, Marco Turchi, Karin Verspoor, and Marcos Zampieri. 2016. Findings of the 2016 Conference on Machine Translation. In *Proceedings of the First Conference on Machine Translation*, Berlin, Germany. Association for Computational Linguistics.

Chenhui Chu, Raj Dabre, and Sadao Kurohashi. 2017. An Empirical Comparison of Simple Domain Adaptation Methods for Neural Machine Translation. *CoRR*, abs/1701.03214.

Anoop Deoras, Tomáš Mikolov, and Kenneth Church. 2011. A fast re-scoring strategy to capture long-distance dependencies. In *Proceedings of the Conference on Empirical Methods in Natural Language Processing*, EMNLP, Stroudsburg, PA, USA. Association for Computational Linguistics.

Jacob Devlin, Rabih Zbib, Zhongqiang Huang, Thomas Lamar, Richard Schwartz, and John Makhoul. 2014. Fast and Robust Neural Network Joint Models for Statistical Machine Translation. In *Proceedings of the 52nd Annual Meeting of the Association for Computational Linguistics*, Baltimore, Maryland. Association for Computational Linguistics.

Shuoyang Ding, Kevin Duh, Huda Khayrallah, Philipp Koehn, and Matt Post. 2016. The JHU Machine Translation Systems for WMT 2016. In *Proceedings of the First Conference on Machine Translation*, Berlin, Germany. Association for Computational Linguistics.

Markus Freitag and Yaser Al-Onaizan. 2016. Fast Domain Adaptation for Neural Machine Translation. *CoRR*, abs/1612.06897.

Takaaki Hori, Yotaro Kubo, and Atsushi Nakamura. 2014. Real-time one-pass decoding with recurrent neural network language model for speech recognition. In *2014 IEEE International Conference on Acoustics, Speech and Signal Processing (ICASSP)*.

Marcin Junczys-Dowmunt, Tomasz Dwojak, and Hieu Hoang. 2016a. Is Neural Machine Translation Ready for Deployment? A Case Study on 30 Translation Directions. In *Proceedings of the 9th International Workshop on Spoken Language Translation (IWSLT)*, Seattle, WA.

Marcin Junczys-Dowmunt, Tomasz Dwojak, and Rico Sennrich. 2016b. The AMU-UEDIN Submission to the WMT16 News Translation Task: Attention-based NMT Models as Feature Functions in Phrase-based SMT. In *Proceedings of the First Conference on Machine Translation*, Berlin, Germany. Association for Computational Linguistics.

Philipp Koehn, Hieu Hoang, Alexandra Birch, Chris Callison-Burch, Marcello Federico, Nicola Bertoldi, Brooke Cowan, Wade Shen, Christine Moran, Richard Zens, Chris Dyer, Ondrej Bojar, Alexandra Constantin, and Evan Herbst. 2007. Moses: Open Source Toolkit for Statistical Machine Translation. In *Proceedings of the 45th Annual Meeting of the Association for Computational Linguistics Companion Volume Proceedings of the Demo and Poster Sessions*, Prague, Czech Republic. Association for Computational Linguistics.

Philipp Koehn and Rebecca Knowles. 2017. Six Challenges for Neural Machine Translation. In *Proceedings of the 1st Workshop on Neural Machine Translation (and Generation) at ACL*. Association for Computational Linguistics.

Faisal Ladhak, Ankur Gandhe, Markus Dreyer, Lambert Mathias, Ariya Rastrow, and Björn Hoffmeister. 2016. LATTICERNN: Recurrent Neural Networks over Lattices. In *Interspeech*.

Xunying Liu, Xie Chen, Yongqiang Wang, Mark J. F. Gales, and Philip C. Woodland. 2016. Two Efficient Lattice Rescoring Methods Using Recurrent Neural Network Language Models. *IEEE/ACM Trans. Audio, Speech and Lang. Proc.*, 24(8).

Minh-Thang Luong and Christopher D. Manning. 2015. Stanford Neural Machine Translation Systems for Spoken Language Domain. In *International Workshop on Spoken Language Translation*, Da Nang, Vietnam.

Haitao Mi, Zhiguo Wang, and Abe Ittycheriah. 2016. Vocabulary Manipulation for Neural Machine Translation. In *Proceedings of the 54th Annual Meeting of the Association for Computational Linguistics*, Berlin, Germany. Association for Computational Linguistics.

Rico Sennrich, Orhan Firat, Kyunghyun Cho, Alexandra Birch, Barry Haddow, Julian Hitschler, Marcin Junczys-Dowmunt, Samuel Läubli, Antonio Valerio Miceli Barone, Jozef Mokry, and Maria Nadejde. 2017. Nematus: a Toolkit for Neural Machine Translation. In *Proceedings of the Software Demonstrations of the 15th Conference of the European Chapter of the Association for Computational Linguistics*, Valencia, Spain. Association for Computational Linguistics.

Rico Sennrich, Barry Haddow, and Alexandra Birch. 2016. Edinburgh Neural Machine Translation Systems for WMT 16. In *Proceedings of the First Conference on Machine Translation*, Berlin, Germany. Association for Computational Linguistics.

Felix Stahlberg, Adrià de Gispert, Eva Hasler, and Bill Byrne. 2017. Neural Machine Translation by Minimising the Bayes-risk with Respect to Syntactic Translation Lattices. In *Proceedings of the 15th Conference of the European Chapter of the Association for Computational Linguistics*, Valencia, Spain. Association for Computational Linguistics.

Felix Stahlberg, Eva Hasler, Aurelien Waite, and Bill Byrne. 2016. Syntactically Guided Neural Machine Translation. In *Proceedings of the 54th Annual Meeting of the Association for Computational Linguistics*, Berlin, Germany. Association for Computational Linguistics.

Jörg Tiedemann. 2009. News from OPUS - A collection of multilingual parallel corpora with tools and interfaces. In N. Nicolov, K. Bontcheva, G. Angelova, and R. Mitkov, editors, *Recent Advances in Natural Language Processing*, volume V. John Benjamins, Amsterdam/Philadelphia, Borovets, Bulgaria.

Jörg Tiedemann. 2012. Parallel Data, Tools and Interfaces in OPUS. In *Proceedings of the 8th International Conference on Language Resources and Evaluation*.

Zhaopeng Tu, Zhengdong Lu, Yang Liu, Xiaohua Liu, and Hang Li. 2016. Modeling Coverage for Neural Machine Translation. In *Proceedings of the 54th Annual Meeting of the Association for Computational Linguistics*, Berlin, Germany. Association for Computational Linguistics.

Xing Wang, Zhengdong Lu, Zhaopeng Tu, Hang Li, Deyi Xiong, and Min Zhang. 2017. Neural Machine Translation Advised by Statistical Machine Translation.

Analyzing Well-Formedness of Syllables in Japanese Sign Language

Satoshi Yawata[*] **Makoto Miwa** **Yutaka Sasaki** **Daisuke Hara**

Toyota Technological Institute

2-12-1 Hisakata, Tempaku-ku, Nagoya, Aichi, 468-8511, Japan

yawata@nsk.com

{makoto-miwa,yutaka.sasaki,daisuke.hara}@toyota-ti.ac.jp

Abstract

This paper tackles a problem of analyzing the well-formedness of syllables in Japanese Sign Language (JSL). We formulate the problem as a classification problem that classifies syllables into well-formed or ill-formed. We build a data set that contains hand-coded syllables and their well-formedness. We define a fine-grained feature set based on the hand-coded syllables and train a logistic regression classifier on labeled syllables, expecting to find the discriminative features from the trained classifier. We also perform pseudo active learning to investigate the applicability of active learning in analyzing syllables. In the experiments, the best classifier with our combinatorial features achieved the accuracy of 87.0%. The pseudo active learning is also shown to be effective showing that it could reduce about 84% of training instances to achieve the accuracy of 82.0% when compared to the model without active learning.

1 Introduction

Japanese Sign Language (JSL) is a widely-used natural language different from Japanese. JSL vocabulary needs to be expanded because JSL vocabulary seems much smaller than Japanese one (Tokuda and Okumura, 1998) and JSL words for new concepts are always required (Japanese Federation of the Deaf, 2011). Many JSL words and syllables, which are basic units that compose words, are newly coined to meet these requirements, e.g., (Japanese Federation of the Deaf, 2011). However, some of the syllables are *ill-formed*, or unnatural for JSL natives, since

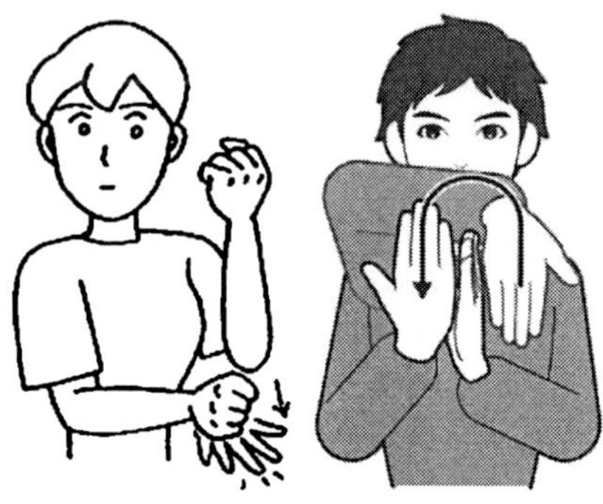

Figure 1: Examples of well-formed (left) and ill-formed (right) JSL syllables. They are also mono-syllable words: the left syllable means "basis" and the right syllable means "avocado" (Yonekawa, 1997; Japanese Federation of the Deaf, 2011).

these new syllables are often coined by non-natives (Hara, 2016a). This ill-formedness is problematic since this can cause miscommunication and also erroneous learning for JSL non-natives. Figure 1 illustrates the examples of well-formed and ill-formed JSL syllables (monosyllable words): "basis"[1] and "avocado"[2].

The phonology and phonotactics of JSL have not been well studied and the causes for this ill-formedness have not been revealed. Natives can distinguish such syllables, but they cannot clearly explain the causes since the ill-formedness stems from their intuition. It is thus difficult to distinguish ill-formed syllables from well-formed ones without the help of natives. A practical approach is required to analyze and understand the ill-formedness of syllables objectively to exclude

---

[*]Currently at NSK Ltd.

[1]Stand up the left elbow, touch the closed right hand and open it downwards.

[2]Put the right little finger to the back of the left hand standing up and move the right hand to cut it towards the palm of the left hand

Proceedings of the The 8th International Joint Conference on Natural Language Processing, pages 26–30,
Taipei, Taiwan, November 27 – December 1, 2017 ©2017 AFNLP

the ill-formed syllables and avoid producing them with little burden on native signers.

In this paper, we describe an approach to model the well-formedness of syllables in JSL as a classification problem and analyze the cause of the well-formedness. We build a data set that contains 2,891 hand-coded syllables with their well-formedness. Based on the data set, we train an L1-regularized logistic regression classifier using a fine-grained feature set to investigate the applicability of machine learning (ML) approaches and to find the differences between well-formed and ill-formed syllables. We also apply pseudo active learning (Settles, 2009) to the data to investigate the possibility in reducing the annotation costs.

As far as we know, this is the first approach that tackles the well-formedness of JSL syllables with ML. We got the following insights from our experiments. First, the syllables can be classified into well-formed or not in the accuracy of 87.0% with the simple classifier on sparse fine-grained features. Second, we disclosed features that are useful for the classification. Third, we show that active learning can reduce the annotation costs. We will make the annotated data available upon request[3].

2   Method

This section explains how we define and tackle the classification problem to analyze the well-formedness of JSL syllables. We first define the representation of syllables. We then explain the classification and pseudo active learning methods.

2.1   Syllable representation

JSL is a visual language, and the syllables are expressed visually. To avoid the difficulty in dealing with the visual language[4], we decide to hand-code syllables. JSL syllables are usually composed of three elements: handshapes, movements, and locations (Kimira et al., 2011).

We hand-code JSL syllables with the encoding scheme by Hara (2016b), which is extended from Hara (2003). Each syllable is represented with seven components in this coding: `types`, `handshapes`, `locations`, `movements`, `contacts`, `directions of palms`, and `directions of wrists`. We

---

[3]Please contact the last author for data related inquiry.

[4]We left the automatic coding of visually-expressed syllables as future work.

here briefly explain these components: `Types` denote the number of hands used and, if two hands are involved, the information about whether both hands have the identical or different handshapes, and whether both hands move together or not. `Handshapes` represent the handshape types. `Locations` correspond to 28 locations of hands on or around the body such as the eye, the shoulder, neutral space, i.e., space in front of the signer, and so on. `Movements` are the movement types of hands such as path movement, orientation change movement, and handsape change movement, and their relationships such as synchronous movement and alternating movement. `Contacts` indicate whether and when both hands have contact in the syllable execution. `Directions of palms` show which direction the palm faces. `Directions of wrists` denote directions to which the tip of the metacarpal bones point.

Syllables have little overlap in this coding and it is impossible to find the discriminative characteristics between well-formed syllables and ill-formed ones, so we decompose the components in the coding into a set of fine-grained binary features, aiming that the features are shared among syllables without losing the original information. `Types` are represented with nine binary features, e.g., whether both hands are used, whether both hand movements are symmetric, etc. `Handshapes` are decomposed into 208 binary features to represent whether each finger in hands is used and whether each finger joint in hands is stretched, loosely bent, or bent. Similarly, we define 98 binary features for `locations`, 398 for `movements`, 171 for `contacts`, and 62 for `directions of palms`, and 62 for `directions of wrists`. With this decomposition, we define 1,017 binary features in total.

2.2   Well-formedness classification

We employ an L1-regularized logistic regression classifier to classify well-formed and ill-formed syllables. Training instances are not so many and it is unknown how ML approaches work on this problem, so we decide to employ this simple classifier as the first step toward this problem. We use the L1 penalty to encourage the model to be sparse, expecting that we can make the finding of discriminative features easier. We also consider adding the **combinatorial features** of two binary

	Accuracy	F1
most frequent	0.826	–
binary features	0.837	0.533
+ combinatorial features	0.870	0.613

Table 1: Classification results

features so that we can get more descriptive features.

2.3 Pseudo active learning

There are plenty of JSL syllables in practice, and it is infeasible to manually annotate these syllables[5]. We apply pseudo active learning to the data set and investigate the possibility of reducing the annotation cost. We employ two strategies: an **uncertainty** sampling strategy that chooses the least confident instances (Lewis and Catlett, 1994) and a **certainty**-based strategy that chooses most negative (ill-formed) instances, which was shown to be effective for imbalanced data sets (Fu and Lee, 2013; Miwa et al., 2014).

3 Evaluation

3.1 Experimental settings

Data sets: We employed 25 JSL natives to hand-code 2,891 syllables and annotate their well-formedness. The syllables are taken from Yonekawa (1997) and the book series of "Our Sign Language", e.g., (Japanese Federation of the Deaf, 2011). We split the syllables into training and test data sets. The training data set contained 2,053 well-formed (positive) syllables and 538 ill-formed (negative) syllables. The test data set contained 238 positive and 52 negative syllables.

Well-formedness classification: We employed the L1-regularized logistic regression classifier in scikit-learn[6]. We evaluated the classification performance by using both the classification accuracy and F1 score on negative, ill-formed syllables as the evaluation metrics. We also compared two models to check whether the combinatorial features help: one uses binary features and the other uses combinatorial features of two binary features. We tuned the regularization parameter by a 20-fold cross validation (CV) on the training data.

Pseudo active learning: Using the classification accuracy as the evaluation metric, we compared

three models: random baseline with binary features (random), active learning with binary features (active), and active learning with binary and combinatorial features (active(combi)). We also compared the two active learning strategies using binary and combinatorial features. We built the initial classifier by training the classifier on 20 instances consisting of 10 well-formed and 10 ill-formed syllables. We added labeled instances one by one in active learning. We tuned the regularization parameter using the 20-fold CV each time 50 instances are added by active learning.

3.2 Results

We first examined the number of features that appeared in the data set. For binary features, 849 out of 1,017 features appeared in the data set. This shows there are some features that rarely or never appear in JSL syllables. Similarly, not all combinatorial features appeared in the data set, and 174,986 out of 359,976 (*i.e.* $\binom{849}{2}$=849×848/2) features appeared. This is mainly because some binary features are disjunctive and their combinations are physically impossible.

Next, we evaluated the classification performance on the test data set (Table 1). Our classifiers produced better accuracy than did the most frequent baseline that always predicted syllables as well-formed. These high accuracies show that our classifiers can detect relatively few ill-formed syllables. The F1 scores are still low, which indicates that we need to investigate how to alleviate the data imbalance problem. This table also shows that the combinatorial features are useful for improving the performance.

Table 2 lists up some contributing features in the model. Among the top 20 features, 9 and 11 features were related to dominant and non-dominant features respectively for binary features, whereas 7, 2, and 11 features were related to dominant, non-dominant, and both hands respectively for combinatorial features. These differences and the performance difference between the features indicate that the relation of both hands are important to decide the ill-formedness.

Figure 2 shows the learning curves of three models (random baseline, active learning, active learning with combinatorial features) explained in Section 3.1 during **active learning**. Each curve in this figure shows the average of 10 runs. This shows active learning work well compared to

---

[5]We need an established way to automatically code JSL syllables beforehand, e.g., by extending Sako et al. (2016).

[6]http://scikit-learn.org

Dominant hand
Second joints of middle and ring fingers are bent
The base of ring finger is bent and the palm direction is diagonally forward
The hand moves according to an orbital movement and the palm direction is backward.

Both hands
Movements are not symmetric and there is no contact at the end of a syllable
Different handshapes and the direction of the metacarpal bone of the dominant hand is upward
Symmetric handshapes and no contact at the beginning of a syllable

Table 2: Examples of contributing combinatorial features

the random baseline. From this figure, random baseline required 1,284 instances while the active learning 184 to achieve 82% in accuracy, so the active learning need about 14.3% of the training data compared to the random baseline. The use of combinatorial features produces slightly worse results, but the final performance is higher than one without combinatorial features which indicates that the combinatorial features work well only with enough training instances.

Lastly, we compare the two active learning strategies in Figure 3. Certainty-based method worked slightly worse than uncertainty-based method did, but the difference is small and, as a whole, both strategies work almost similarly. This result is interesting since the certainty-based strategy focuses only on ill-formed syllables.

4 Related work

Although automatic sign language analysis has been widely studied since 1990s (Starner et al., 1998; Ong et al., 2005), there are relatively few studies on computational approaches to JSL.

Kimira et al. (2011) proposed a JSL dictionary consisting of over 2,000 JSL sign[7]. Each sign is defined with handshapes, motions, and locations, and a movie is attached to the sign. They did not deal with the well-formedness of JSL syllables.

Studies on automatic recognition of JSL are also relatively few, and most of them aim at a small number of syllables or signs. Sako et al. (2016) recently proposed automatic JSL recognition using Kinect v2. They used contour-based hand-shape recognition, and they recognized hand location and motion by Hidden Markov Models and Gaussian Mixture Models. They evaluated their system on 223 JSL signs. The combination of our method with these automatic recognition methods is one of the interesting research directions.

---

[7]A sign consists of one or more syllables

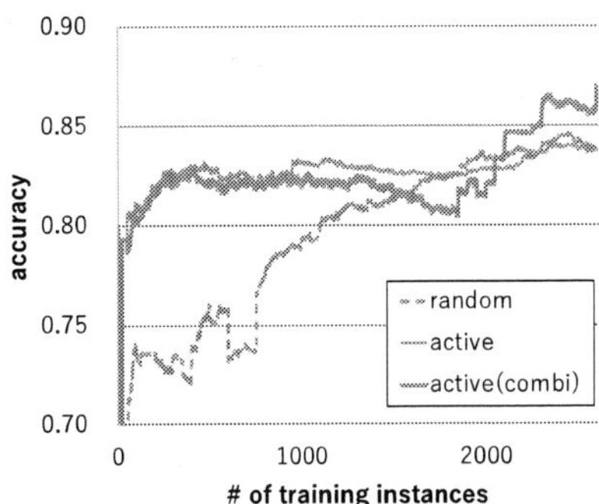

Figure 2: Learning curve with pseudo active learning

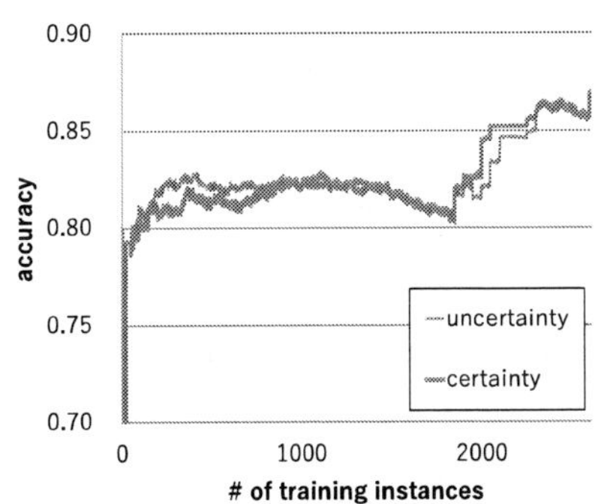

Figure 3: Comparison of pseudo active learning strategies

5 Conclusion

This paper tackled a problem of analyzing the well-formedness of JSL syllables. We created the data set consisting of 2,891 hand-coded syllables with their well-formedness. We then built and evaluated classifiers using the fine-grained binary features on the classification of syllables into well-formed or not. We also investigated the possibility of active learning on the analysis of the well-formedness. The results show that our classifier achieves 87.0% in accuracy and that the active learning can reduce the number of annotations.

As future work, we would like to incorporate more sophisticated ML approaches such as kernels and deep neural networks to consider more combinations of features. We also would like to develop a system that can code visual syllables into our features to make our method practical to support defining new syllables.

Acknowledgments

This work was supported by JSPS KAKENHI Grant Numbers JP16H03813 and JP15K02536 and DAIKO FOUNDATION.

References

JuiHsi Fu and SingLing Lee. 2013. Certainty-based active learning for sampling imbalanced datasets. *Neurocomputing*, 119:350–358.

Daisuke Hara. 2003. *A Complexity-Based Approach to the Syllable Formation in Sign Language*. Ph.D. thesis, The University of Chicago, Chicago, IL.

Daisuke Hara. 2016a. An information-based approach to the syllable formation of Japanese Sign Language. In Masahiko Minami, editor, *Handbook of Japanese Applied Linguistics*, chapter 18, pages 452–482. Gruyter Mouton, Boston, MA.

Daisuke Hara. 2016b. *New Coding Manual for Japanese Sign language*. (In Japanese).

Japanese Federation of the Deaf, editor. 2011. *Our sign language 2011: new sign language*. Japanese Federation of the Deaf, Tokyo, Japan. (In Japanese).

Tsutomu Kimira, Daisuke Hara, Kazuyuki Kanda, and Kazunari Morimoto. 2011. Expansion of the system of jsl-japanese electronic dictionary: An evaluation for the compound research system. In *Proceedings of the 2nd International Conference on Human Centered Design*, HCD'11, pages 407–416, Berlin, Heidelberg. Springer-Verlag.

David D. Lewis and Jason Catlett. 1994. Heterogeneous uncertainty sampling for supervised learning. In *Proceedings of the Eleventh International Conference on Machine Learning*, pages 148–156. Morgan Kaufmann.

Makoto Miwa, James Thomas, Alison OMara-Eves, and Sophia Ananiadou. 2014. Reducing systematic review workload through certainty-based screening. *Journal of biomedical informatics*, 51:242–253.

Sylvie CW Ong, Surendra Ranganath, et al. 2005. Automatic sign language analysis: A survey and the future beyond lexical meaning. *IEEE transactions on pattern analysis and machine intelligence*, 27(6):873–891.

Shinji Sako, Mika Hatano, and Tadashi Kitamura. 2016. *Real-Time Japanese Sign Language Recognition Based on Three Phonological Elements of Sign*. Springer International Publishing, Cham.

Burr Settles. 2009. Active learning literature survey. Computer Sciences Technical Report 1648.

Thad Starner, Joshua Weaver, and Alex Pentland. 1998. Real-time american sign language recognition using desk and wearable computer based video. *IEEE Transactions on Pattern Analysis and Machine Intelligence*, 20(12):1371–1375.

Masaaki Tokuda and Manabu Okumura. 1998. Towards automatic translation from japanese into japanese sign language. *Assistive Technology and Artificial Intelligence*, pages 97–108.

Akihiko Yonekawa. 1997. *Japanese – Japanese Sign Language Dictionary*. Japanese Federation of the Deaf, Tokyo, Japan. (In Japanese).

Towards Lower Bounds on Number of Dimensions for Word Embeddings

Kevin Patel, Pushpak Bhattacharyya
Department of Computer Science and Engineering
Indian Institute of Technology Bombay
{kevin.patel,pb}@cse.iitb.ac.in

Abstract

Word embeddings are a relatively new addition to the modern NLP researcher's toolkit. However, unlike other tools, word embeddings are used in a black box manner. There are very few studies regarding various hyperparameters. One such hyperparameter is the dimension of word embeddings. They are rather decided based on a rule of thumb: in the range 50 to 300. In this paper, we show that the dimension should instead be chosen based on corpus statistics. More specifically, we show that the number of pairwise equidistant words of the corpus vocabulary (as defined by some distance/similarity metric) gives a lower bound on the the number of dimensions , and going below this bound results in degradation of quality of learned word embeddings. Through our evaluations on standard word embedding evaluation tasks, we show that for dimensions higher than or equal to the bound, we get better results as compared to the ones below it.

1 Introduction

Word embeddings are a crucial component of modern NLP. They are learned in an unsupervised manner from large amounts of raw corpora. Bengio et al. (2003) were the first to propose neural word embeddings. Many word embedding models have been proposed since then (Collobert and Weston, 2008; Huang et al., 2012; Mikolov et al., 2013a; Levy and Goldberg, 2014).

Word vector space models can only capture differences in meaning (Sahlgren, 2006). That is, one can infer the meaning of a word by looking at its neighbors. An isolated word on its own does not mean anything in the word vector space. Thus, one needs to think of embedding algorithm's capability to capture these differences effectively, which is governed by its hyperparameters. The hyperparameters affect the information to be represented and the available degree of freedom to express it.

Most word embeddings share different design choices and hyperparameters such as context type, window size, number of dimensions of the embeddings, *etc.* However, a large portion of the research community uses word embeddings without their in-depth analysis; many proceed with default settings that come with off-the-shelf word embedding toolkits. While other hyperparameters have been studied to varying extents (see section 2), there are no rigorous studies on the number of dimensions that should be used while training word embeddings. They are usually decided via a rule of thumb (established as a side effect of other evaluations): use between 50 to 300, or by trial and error. This is a common thread across many NLP applications: Part of Speech Tagging (Collobert and Weston, 2008), Named Entity Recognition Sentence Classification (Kim, 2014), Sentiment Analysis (Liu et al., 2015), Sarcasm Detection (Joshi et al., 2016).

Depending on the corpus, its vocabulary, and the context through which the differences are elicited during training of word embedding, we are bound to obtain a certain number of words, say n, that are pairwise equidistant. Such words impose an equality constraint that the embedding algorithm has to uphold. Thus, we raise the following question:

Does n (the number of pairwise equidistant words) enforce a lower bound on the number of dimensions that should be chosen for training word embeddings on the corpus?

In this paper, we show that this seems to be true

Proceedings of the The 8th International Joint Conference on Natural Language Processing, pages 31–36,
Taipei, Taiwan, November 27 – December 1, 2017 ©2017 AFNLP

for skip gram embeddings. We show how to obtain the number of pairwise equidistant points from corpus. This number determines the lower bound. Then we show how the training algorithm of skip-gram embeddings fails to uphold the equality constraint when the number of dimensions is less than the lower bound. We show this both via analysis on toy examples as well as intrinsic evaluation on real data.

2   Background and Related Work

As mentioned earlier, the number of dimensions is often decided via the rule of thumb, or by trial and error. This holds true not only for word embedding usage but also for their evaluations.

Baroni et al. (2014) claimed that neural word embeddings are better than traditional methods such as LSA, HAL, RI (Landauer and Dumais, 1997; Lund and Burgess, 1996; Sahlgren, 2005). They experimented with different settings for the number of dimensions, but their experiments were intended to evaluate the practicality of dimensions of neural embeddings as compared to their traditional methods. However, their claim was challenged by Levy et al. (2015), who showed that **superiority of neural word embeddings is not due to the embedding algorithm, but due to certain design choices and hyperparameters optimizations**. While they investigate different hyperparameters, they keep a consistent dimension of 500 for all different embedding models that they evaluated. Many other evaluations set the number of dimensions without any justifications (Schnabel et al., 2015; Zhai et al., 2016; Ghannay et al., 2016).

Melamud et al. (2016) evaluates skip-gram word embeddings on a wide range of intrinsic and extrinsic NLP tasks. An interesting observation made by them is that while the performance for intrinsic tasks such as word pair similarity, etc. peaks at around 300 dimensions, the performance of extrinsic tasks peaked at around 50, and sometimes showed degradation for higher dimensions. This justifies the need for study of bounds for dimensions.

As is evident from the above discussion, the analysis of the number of dimensions have not received enough attention. This paper is a contribution towards that direction.

3   Motivation

Let us consider the following toy corpus of four sentences (<>is sentence separator):

<>I like cats <>I love dogs <>I hate rats <>I rate bats <>

Table 1 shows the rows of the co-occurrence matrix corresponding to the four words {like, love, hate, rate}.

word	<>	I	like	love	hate	rate	rats	cats	dogs	bats
like	0	1	0	0	0	0	0	1	0	0
love	0	1	0	0	0	0	0	0	1	0
hate	0	1	0	0	0	0	1	0	0	0
rate	0	1	0	0	0	0	0	0	0	1

Table 1: Four rows corresponding to {like, love, hate, rate} of co-occurrence matrix for toy corpus

The euclidean distance between any two words from the set {like, love, hate, rate} is $\sqrt{2}$. In other words, they form a regular tetrahedron with side length $=\sqrt{2}$. The words {cats, dogs, rats, bats} form another such set. Intuitively, we know that the space which can embed a regular tetrahedron needs at least 3 dimensions. If a word embedding learning algorithm wishes to model this information correctly, it has to strive to uphold this equality constraint. However, its success will depend on the degree of freedom which it receives in terms of the number of dimensions. If it tries to embed it in a space of dimension lower than 3, then it ends up breaking the equality constraint. We end up having (0.94, 0.94), (1.77, 0.80), and (2.63, 0.10) as the average (mean, standard deviation) for the pairwise distances for dimensions 1, 2 and 3 respectively for 5 random initializations. Figure 1 shows the results of attempting to embed the regular tetrahedron created by the four words in a 1, 2, and 3-dimensional space. One can see how the algorithm fails for dimensions 1, and 2 (very high standard deviations), but succeeds in case of 3 dimensions (low standard deviation).

To further verify the distortions due to a lower than needed dimension, we make the following hypothesis: if the learning algorithm of word embeddings does not get enough dimensions, then it will fail to uphold the equality constraint. Therefore, the standard deviation of the mean of all pairwise distances will be higher. As we increase the dimension, the algorithm will get more degrees of freedom to model the equality constraint in a better way. Thus, there will be statistically significant changes in the standard deviation. Once the lower

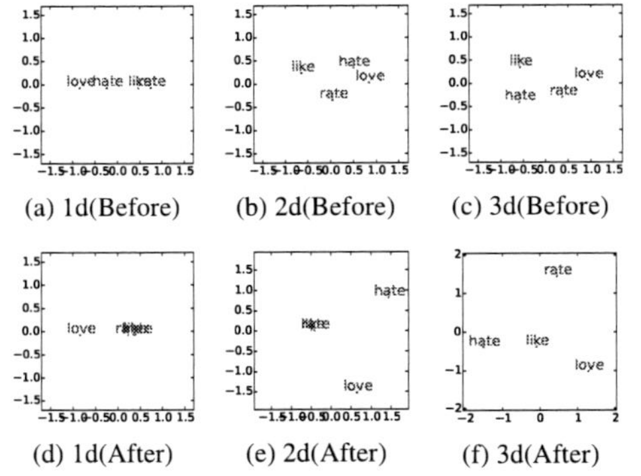

Figure 1: Trying to embed {like, love, hate, rate} in a 1,2 and 3-dimensional space. Here, *(Before)* and *(After)* indicates positions before and after training respectively. The 3 dimensional vectors in (c) and (f) are reduced to 2 dimensions using PCA for visualization purposes

bound of dimensions is reached, the algorithm gets enough degrees of freedom. Thus, from this point onwards, even if we increase dimensions, there will not be any statistically significant difference in the standard deviation.

To test this, we train word embeddings for different dimensions for an artificially created corpus with 15 pairwise equidistant words. The corpus contained sentences of the form *I $verb_i$ $noun_i$* where $1 \leq i \leq 15$. Table 2 shows the results for the same. Note how there are statistically significant reductions (p-value < 0.05) in standard deviations up until 14 ($15 - 1$). However, once the number of dimensions is higher than 14, the differences are no longer significant (p-value > 0.05). We used Welch's Unpaired t-test for testing statistical significance.

Dim	$\bar{\sigma}$	P-value	Dim	$\bar{\sigma}$	P-value
7	0.358		12	0.154	0.0058
8	0.293	0.0020	13	0.111	0.0001
9	0.273	0.0248	14	0.044	0.0001
10	0.238	0.0313	15	0.047	0.3096
11	0.189	0.0013	16	0.054	0.1659

Table 2: Avg standard deviation ($\bar{\sigma}$) for 15 pairwise equidistant words (along with two tail p-values of Welch's unpaired t-test for statistical significance)

4 Approach

We used euclidean distance in the motivation section for ease of discussion. In practice, the met-

ric used in conjunction with word vectors is cosine similarity. While the closed-form solution is available for the case of euclidean distance (Lower Bound = #Pairwise Equidistant points - 1) (Swanepoel, 2004), the same is not true for the case of cosine similarity. Instead, the relation between the number of dimensions and the maximum number of pairwise equiangular lines that can be embedded is an active area of research (Lemmens and Seidel, 1973; de Caen, 2000; Godsil and Roy, 2009; Barg and Yu, 2014). Table 3 gives the maximum number of pairwise equiangular lines E that can be embedded in a space of dimension λ (taken from (Barg and Yu, 2014)).

λ	E	λ	E
3	6	18	61
4	6	19	76
5	10	20	96
6	16	21	126
7<=n<=13	28	22	176
14	30	23	276
15	36	24<=n<=41	276
16	42	42	288
17	51	43	344

Table 3: Number of dimensions λ and the corresponding maximum number of equiangular lines E (for larger values of λ, refer (Barg and Yu, 2014))

To find the lower bound, one should follow the following approach:

1. Compute the word $\times$ word co-occurrence matrix from the corpus

2. Create the word $\times$ word cosine similarity matrix by treating the rows of co-occurrence matrix as word vectors

3. For each similarity value s_k:

   a) Create a graph, where the words are nodes. Create an edge between node i and node j if sim(i, j) = s_k

   b) Find maximum clique on this graph. The number of nodes in this clique is the maximum number of pairwise equidistant points E_k

   c) Reverse lookup E_k in table 3 to determine the corresponding number of dimension λ_k

4. The maximum λ among all λ_ks is the lower bound

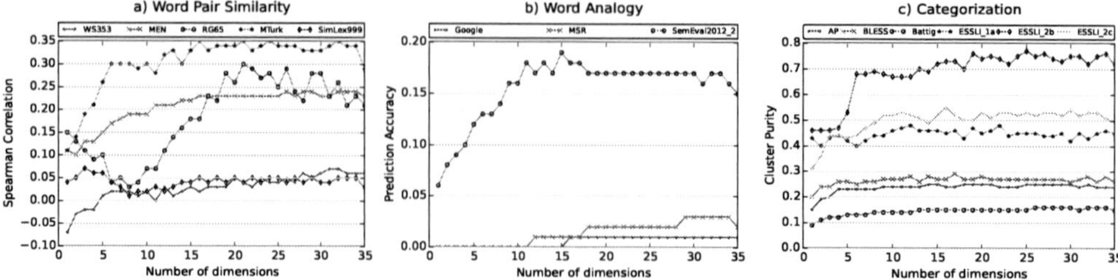

Figure 2: Performance for different tasks with respect to number of dimensions

When we applied this procedure on Brown corpus, we obtained a maximum of 62 words in step 3b), which lead to lower bound of **19 dimensions**.

A theoretical shortcoming of this approach is that finding maximum clique is NP-complete. For the Brown corpus, we obtained the maximum cliques using Parallel Maximum Clique library (PMC)(Rossi et al., 2013).

5 Experimental Setup

5.1 Word Embedding training

We train skip-gram embeddings on the Brown corpus provided with NLTK toolkit. For tokenization, we use the default tokenizer. We do not remove any stopwords. In order to control effects of randomization, we avoided it wherever possible. To this effect, we do not use negative sampling. We use hierarchical softmax to hasten the softmax computation. One word to the left and right of the input word is considered as context.

5.2 Tasks

We use the following intrinsic tasks for evaluation.

a) **Word Pair Similarity tasks** are commonly used for intrinsic evaluation of word embeddings, which involve predicting similarity between a given pair of words a and b. The evaluation involves finding cosine similarity between the embeddings of a and b, and finding the spearman correlation with human annotation. We used the WS353, MEN, RW, RG65, MTurk, and SimLex999 datasets (Faruqui and Dyer, 2014)

b) **Word Analogy tasks** are yet another commonly used tasks for intrinsic evaluation of word embeddings, which involve evaluating the accuracy of finding a missing word d in the relation: a is to b as c is to d, where (a, b)

and (c, d) have the same relation. We used the Google, MSR, and SemEval 2012 Task 2 datasets (Mikolov et al., 2013b).

c) **Categorization tasks** are yet another commonly used tasks for intrinsic evaluation of word embeddings, which involve evaluating the purity of clusters formed by word embeddings. We used the AP, BLESS, ESSLI_1a, ESSLI_2b, and ESSLI_2c datasets (Schnabel et al., 2015).

6 Results and Analysis

Figure 2 shows the effects of increasing dimensions from 1 to 35 on different tasks. One observes that each series ascends till the number of dimensions reach 19, after which it stabilizes. This is because once the lower bound is reached, the errors introduced due to the violation of equality constraint are removed. Thus, the optimal performance possible with the selected configurations is reached, and the performance stabilizes thereafter.

Note that, in some cases, the performance stabilizes before 19. This is because, for that particular dataset and task, the equality constraints that are broken at lower than 19 dimensions did not matter. But, for a realistic use case, one would be better off if they stick to the lower bound.

7 Conclusion and Future Work

We discussed the importance of deciding the number of dimensions for word embedding training by looking at the corpus. We motivated the idea using abstract examples and gave an algorithm for finding the lower bound. Our experiments showed that performance of word embeddings is poor, until the lower bound is reached. Thereafter, it stabilizes. Therefore, such bounds should be used to decide the number of dimensions, instead of trial and error.

We aim to continue the work, addressing the limitations of complexity, the validity of hypothesis in extrinsic tasks, *etc.*. We will also investigate whether the same holds for different word embedding models.

Acknowledgements

We thank Arjun Atreya, Anoop Kunchukuttan, Aditya Joshi, Abhijit Mishra and other members of the Center for Indian Language Technology (CFILT) for valuable discussions and feedback.

References

Alexander Barg and Wei-Hsuan Yu. 2014. New bounds for equiangular lines. Contemporary Mathematics 625.0:111–121.

Marco Baroni, Georgiana Dinu, and Germán Kruszewski. 2014. Don't count, predict! a systematic comparison of context-counting vs. context-predicting semantic vectors. In Proceedings of the 52nd Annual Meeting of the Association for Computational Linguistics (Volume 1: Long Papers). Association for Computational Linguistics, pages 238–247.

Yoshua Bengio, Réjean Ducharme, Pascal Vincent, and Christian Janvin. 2003. A neural probabilistic language model. Journal of Machine Learning Research 3.0:1137–1155.

Ronan Collobert and Jason Weston. 2008. A unified architecture for natural language processing: deep neural networks with multitask learning. In Machine Learning, Proceedings of the Twenty-Fifth International Conference (ICML). ACM, volume 307.0, pages 160–167.

Dominique de Caen. 2000. Large equiangular sets of lines in euclidean space. Electronic Journal of Combinatorics 7.0.

Manaal Faruqui and Chris Dyer. 2014. Community evaluation and exchange of word vectors at wordvectors.org. In Proceedings of 52nd Annual Meeting of the Association for Computational Linguistics: System Demonstrations. Association for Computational Linguistics, pages 19–24.

Sahar Ghannay, Benoit Favre, Yannick Estve, and Nathalie Camelin. 2016. Word embedding evaluation and combination. In Proceedings of the Tenth International Conference on Language Resources and Evaluation (LREC). European Language Resources Association (ELRA).

Chris Godsil and Aidan Roy. 2009. Equiangular lines, mutually unbiased bases, and spin models. European Journal of Combinatorics 30.0:246–262.

Eric Huang, Richard Socher, Christopher Manning, and Andrew Ng. 2012. Improving word representations via global context and multiple word prototypes. In Proceedings of the 50th Annual Meeting of the Association for Computational Linguistics (Volume 1: Long Papers). Association for Computational Linguistics, pages 873–882.

Aditya Joshi, Vaibhav Tripathi, Kevin Patel, Pushpak Bhattacharyya, and Mark Carman. 2016. Are word embedding-based features useful for sarcasm detection? In Proceedings of the 2016 Conference on Empirical Methods in Natural Language Processing. Association for Computational Linguistics, pages 1006–1011.

Yoon Kim. 2014. Convolutional neural networks for sentence classification. In Proceedings of the 2014 Conference on Empirical Methods in Natural Language Processing (EMNLP). Association for Computational Linguistics, pages 1746–1751.

Thomas K. Landauer and Susan T. Dumais. 1997. A solution to Plato's problem: The latent semantic analysis theory of acquisition, induction, and representation of knowledge. Psychological Review 104.0:211–240.

Petrus WH Lemmens and Johan J Seidel. 1973. Equiangular lines. Journal of Algebra 24.0:494–512.

Omer Levy and Yoav Goldberg. 2014. Dependency-based word embeddings. In Proceedings of the 52nd Annual Meeting of the Association for Computational Linguistics (Volume 2: Short Papers). Association for Computational Linguistics, pages 302–308.

Omer Levy, Yoav Goldberg, and Ido Dagan. 2015. Improving distributional similarity with lessons learned from word embeddings. Transactions of the Association of Computational Linguistics 3.0:211–225.

Pengfei Liu, Shafiq Joty, and Helen Meng. 2015. Fine-grained opinion mining with recurrent neural networks and word embeddings. In Proceedings of the 2015 Conference on Empirical Methods in Natural Language Processing. Association for Computational Linguistics, pages 1433–1443.

Kevin Lund and Curt Burgess. 1996. Producing high-dimensional semantic spaces from lexical co-occurrence. Behavior Research Methods, Instruments, & Computers 28.0:203–208.

Oren Melamud, David McClosky, Siddharth Patwardhan, and Mohit Bansal. 2016. The role of context types and dimensionality in learning word embeddings. In Proceedings of the 2016 Conference of the North American Chapter of the Association for Computational Linguistics: Human Language Technologies. Association for Computational Linguistics, pages 1030–1040.

Tomas Mikolov, Ilya Sutskever, Kai Chen, Greg S Corrado, and Jeff Dean. 2013a. Distributed representations of words and phrases and their compositionality. In Advances in Neural Information Processing Systems 26: 27th Annual Conference on Neural Information Processing Systems 2013. Proceedings of a meeting held December 5-8, 2013, Lake Tahoe, Nevada, United States.. pages 3111–3119.

Tomas Mikolov, Wen-tau Yih, and Geoffrey Zweig. 2013b. Linguistic regularities in continuous space word representations. In Proceedings of the 2013 Conference of the North American Chapter of the Association for Computational Linguistics: Human Language Technologies. Association for Computational Linguistics, pages 746–751.

Ryan A Rossi, David F Gleich, Assefaw H Gebremedhin, Mostofa A Patwary, Ryan A Rossi, David F Gleich, David F Gleich, and Ryan A Rossi. 2013. A fast parallel maximum clique algorithm for large sparse graphs and temporal strong components. arXiv preprint 1302.6256 .

Magnus Sahlgren. 2005. An introduction to random indexing. In In Methods and Applications of Semantic Indexing Workshop at the 7th International Conference on Terminology and Knowledge Engineering, (TKE).

Magnus Sahlgren. 2006. The Word-Space Model: Using Distributional Analysis to Represent Syntagmatic and Paradigmatic Relations between Words in High-Dimensional Vector Spaces. Ph.D. thesis, Stockholm University.

Tobias Schnabel, Igor Labutov, David Mimno, and Thorsten Joachims. 2015. Evaluation methods for unsupervised word embeddings. In Proceedings of the 2015 Conference on Empirical Methods in Natural Language Processing. Association for Computational Linguistics, pages 298–307.

Konrad J Swanepoel. 2004. Equilateral sets in finite-dimensional normed spaces. In Seminar of Mathematical Analysis. volume 71.0, pages 195–237.

Michael Zhai, Johnny Tan, and Jinho D. Choi. 2016. Intrinsic and extrinsic evaluations of word embeddings. In Proceedings of the Thirtieth AAAI Conference on Artificial Intelligence. AAAI Press, pages 4282–4283.

Sequence to Sequence Learning for Event Prediction

Dai Quoc Nguyen[1], Dat Quoc Nguyen[2], Cuong Xuan Chu[3],
Stefan Thater[1], Manfred Pinkal[1]

[1]Department of Computational Linguistics, Saarland University, Germany
`{daiquocn, stth, pinkal}@coli.uni-saarland.de`
[2]Department of Computing, Macquarie University, Australia
`dat.nguyen@mq.edu.au`
[3]Max Planck Institute for Informatics, Germany
`cxchu@mpi-inf.mpg.de`

Abstract

This paper presents an approach to the task of predicting an event description from a preceding sentence in a text. Our approach explores sequence-to-sequence learning using a bidirectional multi-layer recurrent neural network. Our approach substantially outperforms previous work in terms of the BLEU score on two datasets derived from WIKIHOW and DE-SCRIPT respectively. Since the BLEU score is not easy to interpret as a measure of event prediction, we complement our study with a second evaluation that exploits the rich linguistic annotation of gold paraphrase sets of events.

1 Introduction

We consider a task of event prediction which aims to generate sentences describing a predicted event from the preceding sentence in a text. The following example presents an instruction in terms of a sequence of contiguous event descriptions for the activity of baking a cake:

> Gather ingredients. Turn on oven. Combine ingredients into a bowl. Pour batter in pan. Put pan in oven. Bake for specified time.

The task is to predict event description *"Put pan in oven"* from sentence *"Pour batter in pan"*, or how to generate the continuation of the story, i.e., the event following *"Bake for specified time"*, which might be *"Remove pan from oven"*. Event prediction models an important facet of semantic expectation, and thus will contribute to text understanding as well as text generation. We propose to em-

ploy sequence-to-sequence learning (SEQ2SEQ) for this task.

SEQ2SEQ have received significant research attention, especially in machine translation (Cho et al., 2014; Sutskever et al., 2014; Bahdanau et al., 2015; Luong et al., 2015), and in other NLP tasks such as parsing (Vinyals et al., 2015; Dong and Lapata, 2016), text summarization (Nallapati et al., 2016) and multi-task learning (Luong et al., 2016). In general, SEQ2SEQ uses an *encoder* which typically is a recurrent neural network (RNN) (Elman, 1990) to encode a source sequence, and then uses another RNN which we call *decoder* to decode a target sequence. The goal of SEQ2SEQ is to estimate the conditional probability of generating the target sequence given the encoding of the source sequence. These characteristics of SEQ2SEQ allow us to approach the event prediction task. SEQ2SEQ has been applied to text prediction by Kiros et al. (2015) and Pichotta and Mooney (2016). We also use SEQ2SEQ for prediction of what comes next in a text. However, there are several key differences.

- We collect a new dataset based on the largest available resource of instructional texts, i.e., WIKIHOW[1], consisting of pairs of adjacent sentences, which typically describe contiguous members of an event chain characterizing a complex activity. We also present another dataset based on the DESCRIPT corpus—a crowdsourced corpus of event sequence descriptions (Wanzare et al., 2016). While the WIKIHOW-based dataset helps to evaluate the models in an open-domain setting, the DESCRIPT-based dataset is used to evaluate the models in a closed-domain setting.

---

[1]www.wikihow.com

37

Proceedings of the The 8th International Joint Conference on Natural Language Processing, pages 37–42,
Taipei, Taiwan, November 27 – December 1, 2017 ©2017 AFNLP

- Pichotta and Mooney (2016) use the BLEU score (Papineni et al., 2002) for evaluation (i.e., the standard evaluation metric used in machine translation), which measures surface similarity between predicted and actual sentences. We complement this evaluation by measuring prediction accuracy on the semantic level. To this purpose, we use the gold paraphrase sets of event descriptions in the DESCRIPT corpus, e.g., *"Remove cake"*, *"Remove from oven"* and *"Take the cake out of oven"* belong to the same gold paraphrase set of taking out oven. The gold paraphrase sets allow us to access the correctness of the prediction which could not be attained by using the BLEU measure.

- We explore multi-layer RNNs which have currently shown the advantage over single/shallow RNNs (Sutskever et al., 2014; Vinyals et al., 2015; Luong et al., 2015). We use a bidirectional RNN architecture for the encoder and examine the RNN decoder with or without *attention mechanism*. We achieve better results than previous work in terms of BLEU score.

2 Sequence to Sequence Learning

Given a source sequence $x_1, x_2, ..., x_m$ and a target sequence $y_1, y_2, ..., y_n$, sequence to sequence learning (SEQ2SEQ) is to estimate the conditional probability $\Pr(y_1, y_2, ..., y_n \mid x_1, x_2, ..., x_m)$ (Sutskever et al., 2014; Cho et al., 2014; Bahdanau et al., 2015; Vinyals et al., 2015; Luong et al., 2016). Typically, SEQ2SEQ consists of a RNN encoder and a RNN decoder. The RNN encoder maps the source sequence into a vector representation c which is then fed as input to the *decoder* for generating the target sequence.

We use a bidirectional RNN (BiRNN) architecture (Schuster and Paliwal, 1997) for mapping the source sequence $x_1, x_2, ..., x_m$ into the list of encoder states $s_1^e, s_2^e, ..., s_m^e$.

The RNN decoder is able to work with or without *attention mechanism*. When *not* using attention mechanism (Sutskever et al., 2014; Cho et al., 2014), the vector representation c is the last state s_m^e of the encoder, which is used to initialize the decoder. Then, at the timestep i ($1 \leq i \leq n$), the RNN decoder takes into account the hidden state s_{i-1}^d and the previous input y_{i-1} to output the hidden state s_i^d and generate the target y_i.

Attention mechanism allows the decoder to attend to different parts of the source sequence at one position of a timestep of generating the target sequence (Bahdanau et al., 2015; Luong et al., 2015; Vinyals et al., 2015). We adapt the attention mechanism proposed by Vinyals et al. (2015) to employ a concatenation of the hidden state s_i^d and the vector representation c to make predictions at the timestep i.

We use two advanced variants of RNNs that replace the cells of RNNs with the Long Sort Term Memory (LSTM) cells (Hochreiter and Schmidhuber, 1997) and the Gated Recurrent Unit (GRU) cells (Cho et al., 2014). We also use a deeper architecture of multi-layers, to model complex interactions in the context. This is different from Kiros et al. (2015) and Pichotta and Mooney (2016) where they only use a single layer. So we in fact experiment with Bidirectional-LSTM multi-layer RNN (BiLSTM) and Bidirectional-GRU multi-layer RNN (BiGRU).

3 Experiments

3.1 Datasets

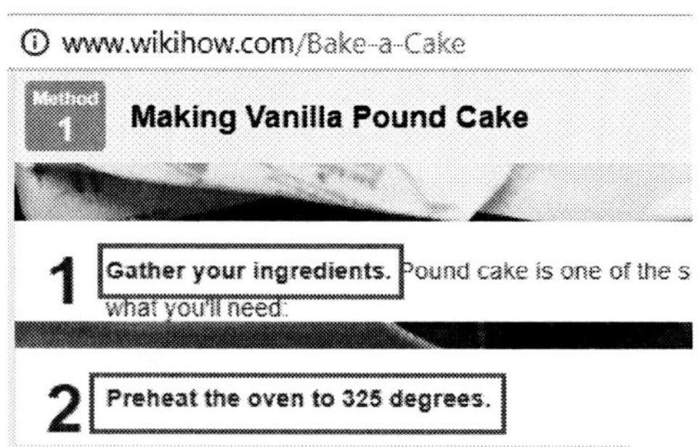

Figure 1: An WIKIHOW activity example.

WIKIHOW-based dataset: WIKIHOW is the largest collection of "how-to" tasks, created by an online community, where each task is represented by sub-tasks with detailed descriptions and pictorial illustrations, e.g., as shown in Figure 1. We collected 168K articles (e.g., *"Bake-a-Cake"*) consisting of 238K tasks (e.g., *"Making Vanilla Pound Cake"*) and approximately 1.59 millions sub-tasks (e.g., *"Gather your ingredients"*, *"Preheat the oven to 325 degrees"*), representing a wide variety of activities and events. Then we created a corpus of approximately 1.34 million pairs of subsequent sub-tasks (i.e., source and target sentences for the SEQ2SEQ model), for which we have the training set of approximately 1.28 million pairs, the development and test sets of 26,800 pairs in each. This dataset aims to evaluate the models in an open-domain setting where the predictions can go into many kinds of directions.

DESCRIPT-based dataset: The DESCRIPT corpus (Wanzare et al., 2016) is a crowdsourced corpus of event sequence descriptions on 40 different scenarios with approximately 100 event sequence descriptions per scenario. In addition, the corpus includes the gold paraphrase sets of event descriptions. From the DESCRIPT corpus, we create a new corpus of 29,150 sentence pairs of an event and its next contiguous event. Then, for each 10 sentence pairs, the 5th and 10th pairs are used for the development and test sets respectively, and 8 remaining pairs are used for the training set. Thus, each of the development and test sets has 2,915 pairs, and the training set has 23,320 pairs. This dataset helps to assess the models in a closed-domain setting where the goal is trying to achieve a reasonable accuracy.

3.2 Implementation details

The models are implemented in TensorFlow (Abadi et al., 2016) and trained with/without attention mechanism using the training sets. Then, given a source sentence describing an event as input, the trained models are used to generate a sentence describing a predicted event. We use the BLEU metric (Papineni et al., 2002) to evaluate the generated sentences against the target sentences corresponding to the source sentences. A SEQ2SEQ architecture using a single layer adapted by Pichotta and Mooney (2016) is treated as the BASELINE model.

We found vocabulary sizes of 30,000 and 5,000 most frequent words as optimal for the WIKIHOW and DESCRIPT-based datasets, respectively. Words not occurring in the vocabulary are mapped to a special token UNK. Word embeddings are initialized using the pre-trained 300-dimensional word embeddings provided by Word2Vec (Mikolov et al., 2013) and then updated during training. We use two settings of a single BiLSTM/BiGRU layer (1-LAYER-BISEQ2SEQ) and two BiLSTM/BiGRU layers (2-LAYER-BISEQ2SEQ). We use 300 hidden units for both encoder and decoder. Dropout (Srivastava et al., 2014) is applied with probability of 0.5.

The training objective is to minimize the cross-entropy loss using the Adam optimizer (Kingma and Ba, 2015) and a mini-batch size of 64. The initial learning rate for Adam is selected from $\{0.0001, 0.0005, 0.001, 0.005, 0.01\}$. We run up to 100 training epochs, and we monitor the BLEU score after each training epoch and select the best model which produces highest BLEU score on the development set.

3.3 Evaluation using BLEU score

Table 1 presents our BLEU scores with models trained on WIKIHOW and DESCRIPT-based data on the respective test sets. There are significant differences in attending to the WIKIHOW sentences and the DESCRIPT sentences. The BLEU scores between the two datasets cannot be compared because of the much larger degree of variation in WIKIHOW. The scores reported in Pichotta and Mooney (2016) on WIKIPEDIA are not comparable to our scores for the same reason.

Model	WIKIHOW		DESCRIPT	
	GRU	LSTM	GRU	LSTM
BASELINE_{NON-ATT}	1.67	1.68	4.31	4.69
1-LAYER-BISEQ2SEQ_{NON-ATT}	2.21	2.01	4.85	5.15
2-LAYER-BISEQ2SEQ_{NON-ATT}	2.53	2.69	4.98	**5.42**
BASELINE_{ATT}	1.86	2.03	4.03	4.01
1-LAYER-BISEQ2SEQ_{ATT}	2.53	2.58	4.38	4.47
2-LAYER-BISEQ2SEQ_{ATT}	**2.86**	2.81	4.76	5.29

Table 1: The BLEU scores on the DESCRIPT and WIKIHOW-based test sets. We use subscripts ATT and NON-ATT to denote models with and without using attention mechanism, respectively.

Table 1 shows that 1-LAYER-BISEQ2SEQ obtains better results than the strong BASELINE. Specifically, 1-LAYER-BISEQ2SEQ improves the baselines with 0.3+ BLEU in both cases of ATT and NON-ATT, indicating the usefulness of using bidirectional architecture. Furthermore, the two-layer architecture produces better scores than the single layer architecture. Using more layers can help to capture prominent linguistic features, that is probably the reason why deeper layers empirically work better.

As shown in Table 1, the GRU-based models obtains similar results to the LSTM-based models on the WIKIHOW-based dataset, but achieves lower scores on the DESCRIPT-based dataset. This could show that LSTM cells with memory gate may help to better remember linguistic fea-

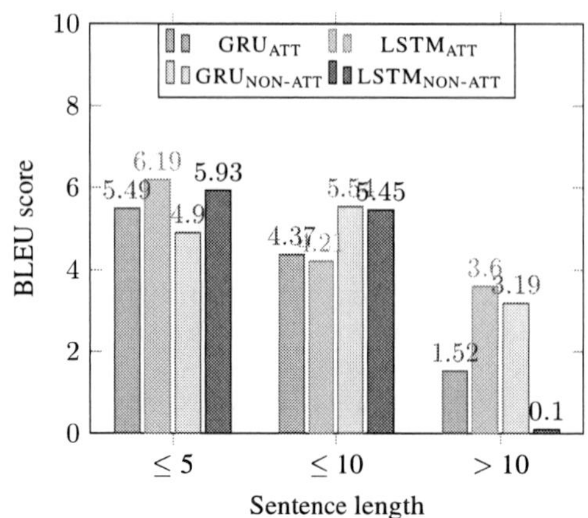

Figure 2: The BLEU scores of two-layer BiLSTM BISEQ2SEQ with/without attention on the DE-SCRIPT-based test set with respect to the source sentence lengths.

tures than GRU cells without memory gate for the closed-domain setting.

The ATT model outperforms the NON-ATT model on the WIKIHOW-based dataset, but not on the DESCRIPT-based dataset. This is probably because neighboring WIKIHOW sentences (i.e., sub-task headers) are more parallel in structure (see *"Pour batter in pan"* and *"Put pan in oven"* from the initial example), which could be related to the fact that they are in general shorter. Figure 2 shows that the ATT model actually works well for DE-SCRIPT pairs with a short source sentence, while its performance decreases with longer sentences.

3.4 Evaluation based on paraphrase sets

BLEU scores are difficult to interpret for the task: BLEU is a surface-based measure as mentioned in (Qin and Specia, 2015), while event prediction is essentially a semantic task. Table 2 shows output examples of the two-layer BILSTM SEQ2SEQ NON-ATT on the DESCRIPT-based dataset. Although the *target* and *predicted* sentences have different surface forms, they are perfect paraphrases of the same type of event.

To assess the semantic success of the prediction model, we use the gold paraphrase sets of event descriptions provided by the DESCRIPT corpus for 10 of its scenarios. We consider a subset of 682 pairs, for which gold paraphrase information is available, and check, whether a *target* event and its corresponding *predicted* event are paraphrases,

Source:	combine and mix all the ingredients as the recipe delegates
Target:	pour ingredients into a cake pan
Predicted:	put batter into baking pan
Source:	put cake into oven
Target:	wait for cake to bake
Predicted:	bake for specified time
Source:	make an appointment with your hair stylist
Target:	go to salon for appointment
Predicted:	drive to the barber shop

Table 2: Prediction examples.

Model	Accuracy (%)
BASELINE_NON-ATT	23.9
1-LAYER-BISEQ2SEQ_NON-ATT	**27.3**
2-LAYER-BISEQ2SEQ_NON-ATT	24.0
BASELINE_ATT	23.6
1-LAYER-BISEQ2SEQ_ATT	23.0
2-LAYER-BISEQ2SEQ_ATT	**25.5**

Table 3: The accuracy results of the LSTM-based models on the subset of 682 pairs.

i.e., belong to the same gold paraphrase set.

The accuracy results are given in Table 3 for the same LSTM-based models taken from Section 3.3. Accuracy is measured as the percentage of predicted sentences that occur *token-identical* in the paraphrase set of the corresponding target sentences. Our best model outperforms Pichotta and Mooney (2016)'s BASELINE by 3.4%.

Since the DeScript gold sets do not contain all possible paraphrases, an expert (computational linguist) checked cases of near misses between *Target* and *Predicted* (i.e. similar to the cases shown in Table 2) in a restrictive manner, not counting borderline cases. So we achieve a final average accuracy of about 31%, which is the sum of an average accuracy over 6 models in Table 3 (24%) and an average accuracy (7%) of checking cases of near misses (i.e, *Target* and *Predicted* are clearly event paraphrases).

The result does not look really high, but the task is difficult: on average, one out of 26 paraphrase sets (i.e., event types) per scenario has to be predicted, the random baseline is about 4% only. Also we should be aware that the task is *prediction of an unseen event*, not classification of a given event description. Continuations of a story are under-determined to some degree, which implies that the upper bound for human guessing cannot be 100 %, but must be substantially lower.

4   Conclusions

In this paper, we explore the task of event prediction, where we aim to predict a next event addressed in a text based on the description of the preceding event. We created the new open-domain and closed-domain datasets based on WIKIHOW and DESCRIPT which are available to the public at: https://github.com/daiquocnguyen/EventPrediction. We demonstrated that more advanced SEQ2SEQ models with a bidirectional and multi-layer RNN architecture substantially outperform the previous work. We also introduced an alternative evaluation method for event prediction based on gold paraphrase sets, which focuses on semantic agreement between the target and predicted sentences.

Acknowledgments

This research was funded by the German Research Foundation (DFG) as part of SFB 1102 "Information Density and Linguistic Encoding." We would like to thank Hannah Seitz for her kind help and support. We thank anonymous reviewers for their helpful comments.

References

Martín Abadi, Ashish Agarwal, Paul Barham, Eugene Brevdo, Zhifeng Chen, Craig Citro, Gregory S. Corrado, Andy Davis, Jeffrey Dean, Matthieu Devin, Sanjay Ghemawat, Ian J. Goodfellow, Andrew Harp, Geoffrey Irving, Michael Isard, Yangqing Jia, Rafal Józefowicz, Lukasz Kaiser, Manjunath Kudlur, Josh Levenberg, Dan Mané, Rajat Monga, Sherry Moore, Derek Gordon Murray, Chris Olah, Mike Schuster, Jonathon Shlens, Benoit Steiner, Ilya Sutskever, Kunal Talwar, Paul A. Tucker, Vincent Vanhoucke, Vijay Vasudevan, Fernanda B. Viégas, Oriol Vinyals, Pete Warden, Martin Wattenberg, Martin Wicke, Yuan Yu, and Xiaoqiang Zheng. 2016. Tensor-Flow: Large-Scale Machine Learning on Heterogeneous Distributed Systems. Software available from http://tensorflow.org/.

Dzmitry Bahdanau, Kyunghyun Cho, and Yoshua Bengio. 2015. Neural machine translation by jointly learning to align and translate. In *Proceedings of the 3rd International Conference on Learning Representations*.

Kyunghyun Cho, Bart van Merrienboer, Caglar Gulcehre, Dzmitry Bahdanau, Fethi Bougares, Holger Schwenk, and Yoshua Bengio. 2014. Learning Phrase Representations using RNN Encoder–Decoder for Statistical Machine Translation. In *Proceedings of the 2014 Conference on Empirical Methods in Natural Language Processing*, pages 1724–1734.

Li Dong and Mirella Lapata. 2016. Language to logical form with neural attention. In *Proceedings of the 54th Annual Meeting of the Association for Computational Linguistics (Volume 1: Long Papers)*, pages 33–43.

Jeffrey L. Elman. 1990. Finding structure in time. *Cognitive Science*, pages 179–211.

Sepp Hochreiter and Jürgen Schmidhuber. 1997. Long short-term memory. *Neural Computation*, pages 1735–1780.

Diederik P. Kingma and Jimmy Ba. 2015. Adam: A method for stochastic optimization. In *Proceedings of the 3rd International Conference on Learning Representations*.

Ryan Kiros, Yukun Zhu, Ruslan Salakhutdinov, Richard S. Zemel, Antonio Torralba, Raquel Urtasun, and Sanja Fidler. 2015. Skip-thought vectors. In *Proceedings of the 28th International Conference on Neural Information Processing Systems*, pages 3294–3302.

Minh-Thang Luong, Quoc V. Le, Ilya Sutskever, Oriol Vinyals, and Lukasz Kaiser. 2016. Multi-task sequence to sequence learning. In *Proceedings of the 4th International Conference on Learning Representations*.

Minh-Thang Luong, Hieu Pham, and Christopher D. Manning. 2015. Effective approaches to attention-based neural machine translation. In *Proceedings of the 2015 Conference on Empirical Methods in Natural Language Processing*, pages 1412–1421.

Tomas Mikolov, Ilya Sutskever, Kai Chen, Gregory S. Corrado, and Jeffrey Dean. 2013. Distributed representations of words and phrases and their compositionality. In *Advances in Neural Information Processing Systems 26: 27th Annual Conference on Neural Information Processing Systems 2013*, pages 3111–3119.

Ramesh Nallapati, Bowen Zhou, Cicero dos Santos, Caglar Gulcehre, and Bing Xiang. 2016. Abstractive Text Summarization using Sequence-to-sequence RNNs and Beyond. In *Proceedings of the 20th SIGNLL Conference on Computational Natural Language Learning*, pages 280–290.

Kishore Papineni, Salim Roukos, Todd Ward, and Wei-Jing Zhu. 2002. Bleu: A method for automatic evaluation of machine translation. In *Proceedings of the 40th Annual Meeting on Association for Computational Linguistics*, pages 311–318.

Karl Pichotta and Raymond J. Mooney. 2016. Using sentence-level lstm language models for script inference. In *Proceedings of the 54th Annual Meeting of the Association for Computational Linguistics (Volume 1: Long Papers)*, pages 279–289.

Ying Qin and Lucia Specia. 2015. Truly exploring multiple references for machine translation evaluation. In *Proceedings of the 18th Annual Conference of the European Association for Machine Translation*, pages 113–120.

M. Schuster and K.K. Paliwal. 1997. Bidirectional recurrent neural networks. *IEEE Transactions on Signal Processing*, pages 2673–2681.

Nitish Srivastava, Geoffrey Hinton, Alex Krizhevsky, Ilya Sutskever, and Ruslan Salakhutdinov. 2014. Dropout: A simple way to prevent neural networks from overfitting. *Journal of Machine Learning Research*, pages 1929–1958.

Ilya Sutskever, Oriol Vinyals, and Quoc V. Le. 2014. Sequence to sequence learning with neural networks. In *Proceedings of the 27th International Conference on Neural Information Processing Systems*, pages 3104–3112.

Oriol Vinyals, Lukasz Kaiser, Terry Koo, Slav Petrov, Ilya Sutskever, and Geoffrey Hinton. 2015. Grammar as a foreign language. In *Advances in Neural Information Processing Systems 28*, pages 2773–2781.

Lilian D. A. Wanzare, Alessandra Zarcone, Stefan Thater, and Manfred Pinkal. 2016. Descript: A crowdsourced corpus for the acquisition of high-quality script knowledge. In *Proceedings of the Tenth International Conference on Language Resources and Evaluation*, pages 3494–3501.

Input-to-Output Gate to Improve RNN Language Models

Sho Takase   **Jun Suzuki**   **Masaaki Nagata**
NTT Communication Science Laboratories
{takase.sho, suzuki.jun, nagata.masaaki}@lab.ntt.co.jp

Abstract

This paper proposes a reinforcing method that refines the output layers of existing Recurrent Neural Network (RNN) language models. We refer to our proposed method as Input-to-Output Gate (IOG)[1]. IOG has an extremely simple structure, and thus, can be easily combined with any RNN language models. Our experiments on the Penn Treebank and WikiText-2 datasets demonstrate that IOG consistently boosts the performance of several different types of current topline RNN language models.

1   Introduction

A neural language model is a central technology of recently developed neural architectures in the natural language processing (NLP) field. For example, neural encoder-decoder models, which were successfully applied to various natural language generation tasks including machine translation (Sutskever et al., 2014), summarization (Rush et al., 2015), and dialogue (Wen et al., 2015), can be interpreted as conditional neural language models. Moreover, word embedding methods, such as Skip-gram (Mikolov et al., 2013) and vLBL (Mnih and Kavukcuoglu, 2013), are also originated from neural language models that aim to handle much larger vocabulary and data sizes. Thus, language modeling is a good benchmark task for investigating the general frameworks of neural methods in the NLP field.

In this paper, we address improving the performance on the language modeling task. In particular, we focus on boosting the quality of existing Recurrent Neural Network (RNN) language models. We propose the Input-to-Output Gate (IOG) method, which incorporates an additional gate function in the output layer of the selected RNN language model to refine the output. One notable characteristic of IOG is that it can be easily incorporated in any RNN language models since it is designed to be a simple structure. Our experiments on the Penn Treebank and WikiText-2 datasets demonstrate that IOG consistently boosts the performance of several different types of current topline RNN language models. In addition, IOG achieves comparable scores to the state-of-the-art on the Penn Treebank dataset and outperforms the WikiText-2 dataset.

2   RNN Language Model

This section briefly overviews the RNN language models. Hereafter, we denote a word sequence with length T, namely, $w_1, ..., w_T$ as $w_{1:T}$ for short. Formally, a typical RNN language model computes the joint probability of word sequence $w_{1:T}$ by the product of the conditional probabilities of each timestep t:

$$p(w_{1:T}) = p(w_1) \prod_{t=1}^{T-1} p(w_{t+1}|w_{1:t}). \quad (1)$$

$p(w_1)$ is generally assumed to be 1 in this literature, that is, $p(w_1) = 1$, and thus, we can ignore the calculation of this term (See the implementation of Zaremba et al. (2014)[2], for example). To estimate the conditional probability $p(w_{t+1}|w_{1:t})$, we apply RNNs. Let V be the vocabulary size, and let $P_t \in \mathbb{R}^V$ be the probability distribution of the vocabulary at timestep t. Moreover, let D_h and D_e respectively be the dimensions of the hidden state and embedding vectors. Then, the RNN language

---

[1]Our implementation is publicly available at https://github.com/nttcslab-nlp/iog.

[2]https://github.com/wojzaremba/lstm

Proceedings of the The 8th International Joint Conference on Natural Language Processing, pages 43–48,
Taipei, Taiwan, November 27 – December 1, 2017 ©2017 AFNLP

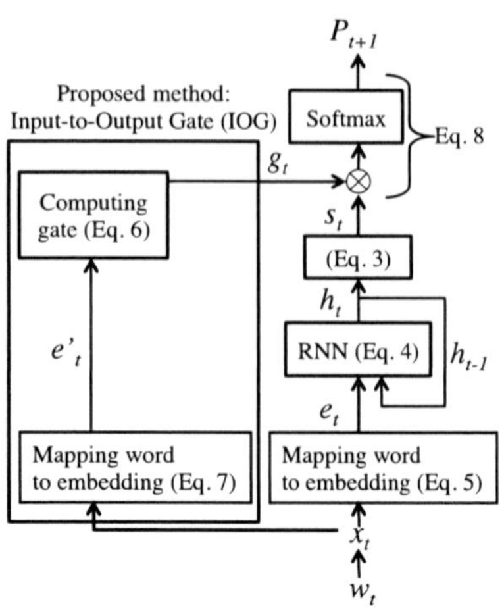

Figure 1: Overview of computing probability distribution.

models predict P_{t+1} by the following equation:

$$P_{t+1} = \text{softmax}(s_t), \qquad (2)$$
$$s_t = Wh_t + b, \qquad (3)$$
$$h_t = f(e_t, h_{t-1}), \qquad (4)$$
$$e_t = Ex_t, \qquad (5)$$

where $W \in \mathbb{R}^{V \times D_h}$ is a matrix, $b \in \mathbb{R}^V$ is a bias term, $E \in \mathbb{R}^{D_e \times V}$ is a word embedding matrix, $x_t \in \{0, 1\}^V$ is a one-hot vector representing the word at timestep t, and h_{t-1} is the hidden state at previous timestep $t - 1$. h_t at timestep $t = 0$ is defined as a zero vector, that is, $h_0 = \mathbf{0}$. Let $f(\cdot)$ represent an abstract function of an RNN, which might be the Elman network (Elman, 1990), the Long Short-Term Memory (LSTM) (Hochreiter and Schmidhuber, 1997), the Recurrent Highway Network (RHN) (Zilly et al., 2017), or any other RNN variants.

3 Input-to-Output Gate

In this section, we describe our proposed method: Input-to-Output Gate (IOG). As illustrated in Figure 1, IOG adjusts the output of an RNN language model by the gate mechanism before computing the probability of the next word. We expect that IOG will boost the probability of the word that may occur. For example, a word followed by a preposition such as 'of' is probably a noun. Therefore, if the word at timestep t is a preposition, IOG refines the output of a language model to raise the probabilities of nouns.

Hyper-parameter	Selected value
Embedding dimension D_g	300
Dropout rate	50%
Optimization method	Adam
Initial learning rate	0.001
Learning rate decay	$1/\sqrt{\text{Epoch}}$
Max epoch	5

Table 1: Hyper-parameters in training IOG.

Formally, let x_t be a one-hot vector representing w_t, IOG calculates the gate g_t by the following equations:

$$g_t = \sigma(W_g e'_t + b_g), \qquad (6)$$
$$e'_t = E_g x_t. \qquad (7)$$

Here, $W_g \in \mathbb{R}^{V \times D_g}$ is a matrix, $b_g \in \mathbb{R}^V$ is a bias term, and $E_g \in \mathbb{R}^{D_g \times V}$ is a word embedding matrix[3]. Then, we compute the probability distribution of the RNN language model by applying the above gate to the Equation (2) as follows:

$$P_{t+1} = \text{softmax}(g_t \odot s_t), \qquad (8)$$

where $\odot$ represents the element-wise multiplication of two vectors.

4 Experiments

4.1 Dataset

We conducted word-level prediction experiments on the Penn Treebank (PTB) (Marcus et al., 1993) and WikiText-2 (Merity et al., 2017b) datasets. The PTB dataset consists of 929k training words, 73k validation words, and 82k test words. The WikiText-2 dataset consists of 2,088k training words, 217k validation words, and 245k test words. Mikolov et al. (2010) and Merity et al. (2017b) respectively published pre-processed PTB[4] and WikiText-2[5] datasets. We used these pre-processed datasets for fair comparisons with previous studies.

4.2 Training Procedure

For the PTB dataset, we prepared a total of 5 RNN language models as our baseline models. First, we replicated LSTM with dropout and LSTM with variational inference based dropout, which we refer to as "LSTM" and "Variational LSTM", respectively. Following Zaremba et al. (2014) and Gal

---

[3]We prepared different embeddings from those used in an RNN language model.

[4]http://www.fit.vutbr.cz/ imikolov/rnnlm/

[5]https://einstein.ai/research/the-wikitext-long-term-dependency-language-modeling-dataset

Model	Parameters	Validation	Test
LSTM (medium) (Zaremba et al., 2014) †	20M	86.2	82.7
LSTM (medium, replication of Zaremba et al. (2014))	20M	87.1	84.0
+ IOG (proposed)	26M	84.1	81.1
LSTM (large) (Zaremba et al., 2014) †	66M	82.2	78.4
LSTM (large, replication of Zaremba et al. (2014))	66M	82.7	78.6
+ IOG (proposed)	72M	78.5	75.5
Variational LSTM (medium) (Gal and Ghahramani, 2016) †	20M	81.9 ± 0.2	79.7 ± 0.1
Variational LSTM (medium, replication of Gal and Ghahramani (2016))	20M	82.8	79.1
+ IOG (proposed)	26M	81.2	78.1
Variational LSTM (large) (Gal and Ghahramani, 2016) †	66M	77.9 ± 0.3	75.2 ± 0.2
Variational LSTM (large, replication of Gal and Ghahramani (2016))	66M	78.1	74.6
+ IOG (proposed)	72M	76.9	74.1
Variational RHN (depth 8) (Zilly et al., 2017) †	32M	71.2	68.5
Variational RHN (depth 8, replication of Zilly et al. (2017))	32M	72.1	68.9
+ IOG (proposed)	38M	69.2	66.5
Variational RHN (depth 8, replication of Zilly et al. (2017)) + WT	23M	69.2	66.3
+ IOG (proposed)	29M	67.0	64.4
Ensemble of 5 Variational RHNs	160M	66.1	63.1
+ IOG (proposed)	166M	64.7	62.0
Ensemble of 10 Variational RHNs	320M	65.2	62.3
+ IOG (proposed)	326M	64.1	61.4
Neural cache model (Grave et al., 2017) †	21M	-	72.1
Pointer Sentinel LSTM (medium) (Merity et al., 2017b) †	21M	72.4	70.9
Variational LSTM (large) + WT + AL (Inan et al., 2016) †	51M	71.1	68.5
Variational RHN (depth 10) + WT (Press and Wolf, 2017) †	24M	68.1	66.0
Neural Architecture Search with base 8 (Zoph and Le, 2017) †	32M	-	67.9
Neural Architecture Search with base 8 + WT(Zoph and Le, 2017) †	25M	-	64.0
Neural Architecture Search with base 8 + WT (Zoph and Le, 2017) †	54M	-	62.4
AWD LSTM + WT (Merity et al., 2017a) †	24M	60.0	57.3
AWD LSTM + WT (result by code of Merity et al. (2017a)[6])	24M	58.6	56.7
+ IOG (proposed)	30M	58.5	56.7
AWD LSTM + WT + cache (size = 2000) (Merity et al., 2017a) †	24M	53.9	**52.8**
AWD LSTM + WT + cache (size = 500)	24M	53.4	53.0
+ IOG (proposed)	30M	**53.3**	53.0

Table 2: Comparison between baseline models and the proposed method (represented as "+ IOG") on the Penn Treebank (PTB) dataset. † denotes results published in previous studies. The method with WT shared word embeddings (E in the Equation (5)) with the weight matrix of the final layer (W in the Equation (3)). AL denotes that the method used a previously proposed augmented loss function (Inan et al., 2016).

Model	Parameters	Validation	Test
LSTM (medium, replication of Zaremba et al. (2014))	50M	102.2	96.2
+ IOG (proposed)	70M	99.2	93.8
Variational LSTM (medium, replication of Gal and Ghahramani (2016))	50M	97.2	91.8
+ IOG (proposed)	70M	95.9	91.0
Variational LSTM (medium) + cache (size = 2000)	50M	69.6	66.1
+ IOG (proposed)	70M	69.3	65.9
Pointer Sentinel LSTM (Merity et al., 2017b) †	51M[7]	84.8	80.8
Neural cache model (size = 100) (Grave et al., 2017) †	42M	-	81.6
Neural cache model (size = 2000) (Grave et al., 2017) †	42M	-	68.9
AWD LSTM + WT (Merity et al., 2017a) †	33M	68.6	65.8
AWD LSTM + WT (result by code of Merity et al. (2017a))	33M	68.6	65.8
+ IOG (proposed)	53M	68.6	65.9
AWD LSTM + WT + cache (size = 3785) (Merity et al., 2017a) †	33M	53.8	52.0
AWD LSTM + WT + cache (size = 3785)	33M	**53.5**	**51.7**
+ IOG (proposed)	53M	53.6	**51.7**

Table 3: Comparison between baseline models and the proposed method (represented as "+ IOG") on the WikiText-2 dataset. † denotes results published in previous studies.

and Ghahramani (2016), we prepared the medium setting (2-layer LSTM with 650 dimensions for each layer), and the large setting (2-layer LSTM with 1500 dimensions for each layer) for each LSTM. We also replicated "Variational RHN" with a depth of 8 described in Zilly et al. (2017). For the WikiText-2 dataset, we prepared the medium setting standard and variational LSTMs as our baselines, which are identical as those used in Merity et al. (2017b).

After reproducing the baselines, we incorporated IOG with those models. Table 1 summarizes the hyper-parameters used for training the IOG. During training IOG, we fixed the parameters of the RNN language models to avoid over-fitting.

4.3 Results

We show the perplexities of the baselines and those combined with IOG for the PTB in Table 2, and for the WikiText-2 in Table 3. These tables, which contain both the scores reported in the previous studies and those obtained by our reproduced models, indicate that IOG reduced the perplexity. In other words, IOG boosted the performance of the baseline models. We emphasize that IOG is not restricted to a neural architecture of a language model because it improved the RHN and LSTM performances.

In addition to the comparison with the baselines, Table 2 and Table 3 contain the scores published in previous studies. Merity et al. (2017b) and Grave et al. (2017) proposed similar methods. Their methods, which are called "cache mechanism" (or 'pointer'), keep multiple hidden states at past timesteps to select words from previous sequences. Inan et al. (2016) and Press and Wolf (2017) introduced a technique that shares word embeddings with the weight matrix of the final layer (represented as 'WT' in Table 2). Inan et al. (2016) also proposed using word embeddings to augment loss function (represented as 'AL' in Table 2). Zoph and Le (2017) adopted RNNs and reinforcement learning to automatically construct a novel RNN architecture. We expect that IOG will improve these models since it can be combined with any RNN language models. In fact, Table 2 and Table 3

demonstrate that IOG enhanced the performance even when the RNN language model was combined with 'WT' or the cache mechanism.

Table 2 also shows the scores in the ensemble settings. Model ensemble techniques are widely used for further improving the performance of neural networks. In this experiment, we employed a simple ensemble technique: using the average of the output probability distributions from each model as output. We computed the probability distribution P_{t+1} on the ensemble of the M models as follows:

$$P_{t+1} = \frac{1}{M} \sum_{m=1}^{M} {}_mP_{t+1}, \qquad (9)$$

where ${}_mP_{t+1}$ represents the probability distribution predicted by the m-th model. In the ensemble setting, we applied only one IOG to the multiple models. In other words, we used the same IOG for computing the probability distributions of each language model, namely, computing the Equation (8). Table 2 describes that 5 and 10 model ensemble of Variational RHNs outperformed the single model by more than 5 in perplexity. Table 2 shows that IOG reduced the perplexity of the ensemble models. Remarkably, even though the 10 Variational RHN ensemble achieved the state-of-the-art performance on the PTB dataset, IOG improved the performance by about 1 in perplexity[8].

In addition, as additional experiments, we incorporated IOG with the latest method, which was proposed after the submission deadline of IJCNLP 2017. Merity et al. (2017a) introduced various regularization and optimization techniques such as DropConnect (Wan et al., 2013) and averaged stochastic gradient descent (Polyak and Juditsky, 1992) to the LSTM language model. They called their approach AWD LSTM, which is an abbreviation of averaged stochastic gradient descent weight-dropped LSTM. Table 2 and Table 3 indicate the results on the PTB and the WikiText-2 respectively. These tables show that IOG was not effective to AWD LSTM. Perhaps, the reason is that the perplexity of AWD LSTM is close to the best performance of the simple LSTM architecture. We also note that IOG did not have any harmful effect on the language models because it maintained the performances of AWD LSTM with 'WT' and the

---

[6]In contrast to other comparisons, we used the following implementation by the authors: https://github.com/salesforce/awd-lstm-lm

[7]The number of parameters is different from the one described in Merity et al. (2017b). We guess that they do not consider the increase of the vocabulary size.

---

[8]This result was the state-of-the-art score at the submission deadline of IJCNLP 2017, i.e., July 7, 2017, but Merity et al. (2017a) surpassed it on Aug 7, 2017. We mention the effect of IOG on their method in the following paragraph.

Model	Diff	Test
Variational RHN (replicate)	-	68.9
Variational RHN + IOG (proposed)	-	**66.5**
Variational RHN + IOG with hidden	+0.8M	75.6
Variational RHN + LSTM gate	+0.7M	68.1

Table 4: Comparison among architectures for computing the output gate on the PTB dataset. The column 'Diff' shows increase of parameters from IOG (proposed).

Input word	Top 5 weighted words
of	security, columbia, steel, irs, thrift
in	columbia, ford, order, labor, east
go	after, through, back, on, ahead
attention	was, than, ⟨eos⟩, from, to
whether	to, she, estimates, i, ual

Table 5: Top 5 weighted words for each input word on the PTB experiment.

cache mechanism. Moreover, incorporating IOG is much easier than exploring the best regularization and optimization methods for each RNN language model. Therefore, to improve the performance, we recommend combining IOG before searching for the best practice.

4.4 Discussion

Although IOG consists only of word embeddings and one weight matrix, the experimental results were surprisingly good. One might think that more sophisticated architectures can provide further improvements. To investigate this question, we examined two additional architectures to compute the output gate g_t in the Equation (6).

The first one substituted the calculation of the gate function g_t by the following g_t':

$$g_t' = \sigma(W_g'[h_t, e_t'] + b_g), \tag{10}$$

where $W_g' \in \mathbb{R}^{V \times (D_h + D_g)}$, and $[h_t, e_t']$ represents the concatenation of the hidden state h_t of RHN and embeddings e_t' used in IOG. We refer to this architecture as "+ IOG with hidden".

The second one similarly substituted g_t by the following g_t'':

$$g_t'' = \sigma(W_g h_t' + b_g), \tag{11}$$
$$h_t' = f'(e_t', h_{t-1}'), \tag{12}$$

where $f'(\cdot)$ is the 1-layer LSTM in our experiments. We set the dimension of the LSTM hidden state to 300, that is, $D_g = 300$, and the other hyperparameters remained as described in Section 4.2. We refer to the second one as "+ LSTM gate".

Table 4 shows the results of the above two architectures on the PTB dataset. IOG clearly outperformed the other more sophisticated architectures. This fact suggests that (1) incorporating additional architectures does not always improve the performance, and (2) not always become better even if it is a sophisticated architecture. We need to carefully design an architecture that can provide complementary (or orthogonal) information to the baseline RNNs.

In addition, to investigate the mechanism of IOG, we selected particular words, and listed the top 5 weighted words given each selected word as input in Table 5[9]. IOG gave high weights to nouns when the input word was a preposition: 'of' and 'in'. Moreover, IOG encouraged outputting phrasal verbs such as "go after". These observations generally match human intuition.

5 Conclusion

We proposed Input-to-Output Gate (IOG), which refines the output of an RNN language model by the gate mechanism. IOG can be incorporated in any RNN language models due to its simple structure. In fact, our experimental results demonstrated that IOG improved the performance of several different settings of RNN language models. Furthermore, the experimental results indicate that IOG can be used with other techniques such as ensemble.

Acknowledgments

We thank the anonymous reviewers for their helpful comments.

References

Jeffrey L Elman. 1990. Finding Structure in Time. *Cognitive science* 14(2):179–211.

Yarin Gal and Zoubin Ghahramani. 2016. A Theoretically Grounded Application of Dropout in Recurrent Neural Networks. In *Advances in Neural Information Processing Systems 29 (NIPS 2016)*.

Edouard Grave, Armand Joulin, and Nicolas Usunier. 2017. Improving Neural Language Models with a Continuous Cache. In *5th International Conference on Learning Representations (ICLR 2017)*.

---

[9]In this exploration, we excluded words occurring fewer than 100 times in the corpus to remove noise.

Sepp Hochreiter and Jürgen Schmidhuber. 1997. Long Short-Term Memory. *Neural Computation* 9(8):1735–1780.

Hakan Inan, Khashayar Khosravi, and Richard Socher. 2016. Tying Word Vectors and Word Classifiers: A Loss Framework for Language Modeling. In *Proceedings of the 5th International Conference on Learning Representations (ICLR 2017)*.

Mitchell P. Marcus, Mary Ann Marcinkiewicz, and Beatrice Santorini. 1993. Building a Large Annotated Corpus of English: The Penn Treebank. *Computational Linguistics* 19(2):313–330.

Stephen Merity, Nitish Shirish Keskar, and Richard Socher. 2017a. Regularizing and Optimizing LSTM Language Models. *arXiv preprint arXiv:1708.02182* .

Stephen Merity, Caiming Xiong, James Bradbury, and Richard Socher. 2017b. Pointer Sentinel Mixture Models. In *Proceedings of the 5th International Conference on Learning Representations (ICLR 2017)*.

Tomas Mikolov, Martin Karafiát, Lukás Burget, Jan Cernocký, and Sanjeev Khudanpur. 2010. Recurrent Neural Network based Language Model. In *Proceedings of the 11th Annual Conference of the International Speech Communication Association (INTERSPEECH 2010)*. pages 1045–1048.

Tomas Mikolov, Ilya Sutskever, Kai Chen, Greg S Corrado, and Jeff Dean. 2013. Distributed Representations of Words and Phrases and their Compositionality. In *Advances in Neural Information Processing Systems 26 (NIPS 2013)*, pages 3111–3119.

Andriy Mnih and Koray Kavukcuoglu. 2013. Learning Word Embeddings Efficiently with Noise-Contrastive Estimation. In *Advances in Neural Information Processing Systems 26 (NIPS 2013)*, pages 2265–2273.

Boris T Polyak and Anatoli B Juditsky. 1992. Acceleration of Stochastic Approximation by Averaging. *SIAM Journal on Control and Optimization* 30(4):838–855.

Ofir Press and Lior Wolf. 2017. Using the Output Embedding to Improve Language Models. In *Proceedings of the 15th Conference of the European Chapter of the Association for Computational Linguistics (EACL 2017)*. pages 157–163.

Alexander M. Rush, Sumit Chopra, and Jason Weston. 2015. A Neural Attention Model for Abstractive Sentence Summarization. In *Proceedings of the 2015 Conference on Empirical Methods in Natural Language Processing (EMNLP 2015)*. pages 379–389.

Ilya Sutskever, Oriol Vinyals, and Quoc V. Le. 2014. Sequence to Sequence Learning with Neural Networks. In *Advances in Neural Information Processing Systems 27 (NIPS 2014)*. pages 3104–3112.

Li Wan, Matthew Zeiler, Sixin Zhang, Yann L Cun, and Rob Fergus. 2013. Regularization of Neural Networks using DropConnect. In *Proceedings of the 30th International Conference on Machine Learning (ICML 2013)*. pages 1058–1066.

Tsung-Hsien Wen, Milica Gasic, Nikola Mrkšić, Pei-Hao Su, David Vandyke, and Steve Young. 2015. Semantically Conditioned LSTM-based Natural Language Generation for Spoken Dialogue Systems. In *Proceedings of the 2015 Conference on Empirical Methods in Natural Language Processing (EMNLP 2015)*. pages 1711–1721.

Wojciech Zaremba, Ilya Sutskever, and Oriol Vinyals. 2014. Recurrent Neural Network Regularization. In *Proceedings of the 2nd International Conference on Learning Representations (ICLR 2014)*.

Julian Georg Zilly, Rupesh Kumar Srivastava, Jan Koutník, and Jürgen Schmidhuber. 2017. Recurrent Highway Networks. *Proceedings of the 34th International Conference on Machine Learning (ICML 2017)* pages 4189–4198.

Barret Zoph and Quoc V. Le. 2017. Neural Architecture Search with Reinforcement Learning. In *Proceedings of the 5th International Conference on Learning Representations (ICLR 2017)*.

Counterfactual Language Model Adaptation for Suggesting Phrases

Kenneth C. Arnold
Harvard CS
Cambridge, MA

Kai-Wei Chang
University of California
Los Angeles, CA

Adam T. Kalai
Microsoft Research
Cambridge, MA

Abstract

Mobile devices use language models to suggest words and phrases for use in text entry. Traditional language models are based on contextual word frequency in a static corpus of text. However, certain types of phrases, when offered to writers as suggestions, may be systematically chosen more often than their frequency would predict. In this paper, we propose the task of generating suggestions that writers accept, a related but distinct task to making accurate predictions. Although this task is fundamentally interactive, we propose a counterfactual setting that permits offline training and evaluation. We find that even a simple language model can capture text characteristics that improve acceptability.

1 Introduction

Intelligent systems help us write by proactively suggesting words or phrases while we type. These systems often build on a language model that picks *most likely* phrases based on previous words in context, in an attempt to increase entry speed and accuracy. However, recent work (Arnold et al., 2016) has shown that writers appreciate suggestions that have creative wording, and can find phrases suggested based on frequency alone to be boring. For example, at the beginning of a restaurant review, "I love this place" is a reasonable *prediction*, but a review *writer* might prefer a suggestion of a much less likely phrase such as "This was truly a wonderful experience"—they may simply not have thought of this more enthusiastic phrase. Figure 1 shows another example.

We propose a new task for NLP research: generate *suggestions* for writers. Doing well at this task requires innovation in language generation but also

Figure 1: We adapt a language model to offer *suggestions* during text composition. In above example, even though the middle suggestion is predicted to be about 1,000 times more likely than the one on the right, a user prefers the right one.

interaction with people: suggestions must be evaluated by presenting them to actual writers. Since writing is a highly contextual creative process, traditional batch methods for training and evaluating human-facing systems are insufficient: asking someone whether they think something would make a good suggestion in a given context is very different from presenting them with a suggestion in a natural writing context and observing their response. But if evaluating every proposed parameter adjustment required interactive feedback from writers, research progress would be slow and limited to those with resources to run large-scale writing experiments.

In this paper we propose a hybrid approach: we maintain a natural human-centered objective, but introduce a proxy task that provides an unbiased estimate of expected performance on human evaluations. Our approach involves developing a *stochastic* baseline system (which we call the *reference policy*), logging data from how writers interact with it, then estimating the performance of candidate policies by comparing how they would behave

Proceedings of the The 8th International Joint Conference on Natural Language Processing, pages 49–54,
Taipei, Taiwan, November 27 – December 1, 2017 ©2017 AFNLP

with how the reference policy did behave in the contexts logged. As long as the behavior of the candidate policy is not too different from that of the reference policy (in a sense that we formalize), this approach replaces complex human-in-the-loop evaluation with a simple convex optimization problem.

This paper demonstrates our approach: we collected data of how humans use suggestions made by a reference policy while writing reviews of a well-known restaurant. We then used logged interaction data to optimize a simple discriminative language model, and find that even this simple model generates better suggestions than a baseline trained without interaction data. We also ran simulations to validate the estimation approach under a known model of human behavior.

Our contributions are summarized below:

- We present a new NLP task of *phrase suggestion* for writing.[1]
- We show how to use counterfactual learning for goal-directed training of language models from interaction data.
- We show that a simple discriminative language model can be trained with offline interaction data to generate better suggestions in unseen contexts.

2   Related Work

Language models have a long history and play an important role in many NLP applications (Sordoni et al., 2015; Rambow et al., 2001; Mani, 2001; Johnson et al., 2016). However, these models do not model human preferences from interactions. Existing deployed keyboards use n-gram language models (Quinn and Zhai, 2016; Kneser and Ney, 1995), or sometimes neural language models (Kim et al., 2016), trained to predict the next word given recent context. Recent advances in language modeling have increased the accuracy of these predictions by using additional context (Mikolov and Zweig, 2012). But as argued in Arnold et al. (2016), these increases in accuracy do not necessarily translate into better suggestions.

The difference between suggestion and prediction is more pronounced when showing phrases rather than just words. Prior work has extended predictive language modeling to phrase prediction (Nandi and Jagadish, 2007) and sentence comple-

tion (Bickel et al., 2005), but do not directly model human preferences. Google's "Smart Reply" email response suggestion system (Kannan et al., 2016) avoids showing a likely predicted response if it is too similar to one of the options already presented, but the approach is heuristic, based on a priori similarity. Search engine query completion also generates phrases that can function as suggestions, but is typically trained to predict what query is made (e.g., Jiang et al. (2014)).

3   Counterfactual Learning for Generating Suggestions

We consider the task of generating good words and phrases to present to writers. We choose a pragmatic quality measure: a suggestion system is good if *it generates suggestions that writers accept.* Let h denote a suggestion system, characterized by $h(y|x)$, the probability that h will suggest the word or phrase y when in context x (e.g., words typed so far).[2] We consider deploying h in an interactive interface such as Figure 1, which suggests phrases using a familiar predictive typing interface. Let δ denote a reward that a system receives from that interaction; in our case, the number of words accepted.[3] We define the overall quality of a suggestion system by its expected reward $E[\delta]$ over all contexts.

Counterfactual learning allows us to evaluate and ultimately learn models that differ from those that were deployed to collect the data, so we can deploy a single model and improve it based on the data collected (Swaminathan and Joachims, 2015). Intuitively, if we deploy a model h_0 and observe what actions it takes and what feedback it gets, we could improve the model by making it more likely to suggest the phrases that got good feedback.

Suppose we deploy a *reference model*[4] h_0 and log a dataset

$$\mathcal{D} = \{(x_1, y_1, \delta_1, p_1), \dots, (x_n, y_n, \delta_n, p_n)\}$$

of contexts (words typed so far), actions (phrases suggested), rewards, and propensities respectively, where $p_i \equiv h_0(y_i|x_i)$. Now consider deploying an alternative model h_θ (we will show an example as

---

[1]Code and data are available at `https://github.com/kcarnold/counterfactual-lm`.

[2]Our notation follows Swaminathan and Joachims (2015) but uses "reward" rather than "loss." Since $h(y|x)$ has the form of a contextual language model, we will refer to it as a "model."

[3]Our setting admits alternative rewards, such as the speed that a sentence was written, or an annotator's rating of quality.

[4]Some other literature calls h_0 a *logging policy*.

Eq. (1) below). We can obtain an unbiased estimate of the reward that h_θ would incur using importance sampling:

$$\hat{R}(h_\theta) = \frac{1}{n} \sum_{i=1}^{n} \delta_i h_\theta(y_i|x_i)/p_i.$$

However, the variance of this estimate can be unbounded because the importance weights $h_\theta(y_i|x_i)/p_i$ can be arbitrarily large for small p_i. Like Ionides (2008), we clip the importance weights to a maximum M:

$$\hat{R}^M(h) = \frac{1}{n} \sum_{i=1}^{n} \delta_i \min\{M, h_\Theta(y_i|x_i)/p_i\}.$$

The improved model can be learned by optimizing

$$\hat{h}_\theta = \operatorname{argmax}_h \hat{R}^M(h).$$

This optimization problem is convex and differentiable; we solve it with BFGS. [5]

4 Demonstration Using Discriminative Language Modeling

We now demonstrate how counterfactual learning can be used to evaluate and optimize the acceptability of suggestions made by a language model. We start with a traditional predictive language model h_0 of any form, trained by maximum likelihood on a given corpus.[6] This model can be used for generation: sampling from the model yields words or phrases that match the frequency statistics of the corpus. However, rather than offering representative samples from h_0, most deployed systems instead sample from $p(w_i) \propto h_0(w_i)^{1/\tau}$, where τ is a "temperature" parameter; $\tau = 1$ corresponds to sampling based on p_0 (soft-max), while $\tau \to 0$ corresponds to greedy maximum likelihood generation (hard-max), which many deployed keyboards use (Quinn and Zhai, 2016). The effect is to skew the sampling distribution towards more probable words. This choice is based on a heuristic assumption that writers desire more probable suggestions; what if writers instead find common phrases to be overly cliché and favor more descriptive phrases? To capture these potential effects, we add features that can emphasize various characteristics of the

---

[5]We use the BFGS implementation in SciPy.

[6]The model may take any form, but n-gram (Heafield et al., 2013) and neural language models (e.g., (Kim et al., 2016)) are common, and it may be unconditional or conditioned on some source features such as application, document, or topic context.

LM weight = 1, all other weights zero:
i didn't see a sign for; i am a huge sucker for
LM weight = 1, `long-word` bonus = 1.0:
another restaurant especially during sporting events
LM weight = 1, `POS` adjective bonus = 3.0:
great local bar and traditional southern

Table 1: Example phrases generated by the log-linear language model under various parameters. The context is the beginning-of-review token; all text is lowercased. Some phrases are not fully grammatical, but writers can accept a prefix.

generated text, then use counterfactual learning to assign weights to those features that result in suggestions that writers prefer.

We consider locally-normalized log-linear language models of the form

$$h_\theta(y|x) = \prod_{i=1}^{|y|} \frac{\exp \theta \cdot f(w_i|c, w_{[:i-1]})}{\sum_{w'} \exp \theta \cdot f(w'|c, w_{[:i-1]})}, \quad (1)$$

where y is a phrase and $f(w_i|x, w_{[:i-1]})$ is a feature vector for a candidate word w_i given its context x. ($w_{[:i-1]}$ is a shorthand for $\{w_1, w_2, \ldots w_{i-1}\}$.) Models of this form are commonly used in sequence labeling tasks, where they are called Max-Entropy Markov Models (McCallum et al., 2000). Our approach generalizes to other models such as conditional random fields (Lafferty et al., 2001).

The feature vector can include a variety of features. By changing feature weights, we obtain language models with different characteristics. To illustrate, we describe a model with three features below. The first feature (`LM`) is the log likelihood under a base 5-gram language model $p_0(w_i|c, w_{[:i-1]})$ trained on the Yelp Dataset[7] with Kneser-Ney smoothing (Heafield et al., 2013). The second and third features "bonus" two characteristics of w_i: `long-word` is a binary indicator of long word length (we arbitrarily choose ≥ 6 letters), and `POS` is a one-hot encoding of its most common POS tag. Table 1 shows examples of phrases generated with different feature weights.

Note that if we set the weight vector to zero except for a weight of $1/\tau$ on `LM`, the model reduces to sampling from the base language model with "temperature" τ. The fitted model weights of the log-linear model in our experiments is shown in supplementary material.

---

[7]`https://www.yelp.com/dataset_challenge`; we used only restaurant reviews

Reference model h_0. In counterfactual estimation, we deploy one reference model h_0 to learn another $\hat{h}$—but weight truncation will prevent $\hat{h}$ from deviating too far from h_0. So h_0 must offer a broad range of types of suggestions, but they must be of sufficiently quality that some are ultimately chosen. To balance these concerns, we use temperature sampling with a temperature $\tau = 0.5$):

$$\frac{p_0(w_i|c, w_{[:i-1]})^{1/\tau}}{\sum_w p_0(w|c, w_{[:i-1]})^{1/\tau}}.$$

We use our reference model h_0 to generate 6-word suggestions one word at a time, so p_i is the product of the conditional probabilities of each word.

4.1 Simulation Experiment

We present an illustrative model of suggestion acceptance behavior, and simulate acceptance behavior under that model to validate our methodology. Our method successfully learns a suggestion model fitting writer preference.

Desirability Model. We model the behavior of a writer using the interface in Fig. 1, which displays 3 suggestions at a time. At each timestep i they can choose to accept one of the 3 suggestions $\{s_j^i\}_{j=1}^3$, or reject the suggestions by tapping a key. Let $\{p_j^i\}_{j=1}^3$ denote the likelihood of suggestion s_j^i under a predictive model, and let $p_\emptyset^i = 1 - \sum_{j=1}^3 p_j^i$ denote the probability of any other word. Let a_j^i denote the writer's probability of choosing the corresponding suggestion, and a_j^i denote the probability of rejecting the suggestions offered. If the writer decided exactly what to write before interacting with the system and used suggestions for optimal efficiency, then a_j^i would equal p_j^i. But suppose the writer finds certain suggestions *desirable*. Let D_j^i give the desirability of a suggestion, e.g., D_j^i could be the number of long words in suggestion s_j^i. We model their behavior by adding the desirabilities to the log probabilities of each suggestion:

$$a_j^{(i)} = p_j^{(i)} \exp(D_j^{(i)})/Z^{(i)}, \; a_\emptyset^{(i)} = p_\emptyset^{(i)}/Z^{(i)}$$

where $Z^{(i)} = 1 - \sum_j p_j^{(i)}(1 - \exp(D_j^{(i)}))$. The net effect is to move probability mass from the "reject" action $a_\emptyset^i$ to suggestions that are close enough to what the writer wanted to say but desirable.

Experiment Settings and Results. We sample 10% of the reviews in the Yelp Dataset, hold them out from training h_0, and split them into an equal-sized training set and test set. We randomly sample suggestion locations from the training set. We cut off that phrase and pretend to retype it. We generate three phrases from the reference model h_0, then allow the simulated author to pick one phrase, subject to their preference as modeled by the desirability model. We learn a customized language model and then evaluate it on an additional 500 sentences from the test set.

For an illustrative example, we set the desirability D to the number of long words (≥ 6 characters) in the suggestion, multiplied by 10. Figure 3 shows that counterfactual learning quickly finds model parameters that make suggestions that are more likely to be accepted, and the counterfactual estimates are not only useful for learning but also correlate well with the actual improvement. In fact, since weight truncation (controlled by M) acts as regularization, the counterfactual estimate consistently *underestimates* the actual reward.

4.2 Experiments with Human Writers

We recruited 74 workers through MTurk to write reviews of *Chipotle Mexican Grill* using the interface in Fig 1 from Arnold et al. (2016). For the sake of simplicity, we assumed that all human writers have the same preference. Based on pilot experiments, Chipotle was chosen as a restaurant that many crowd workers had dined at. User feedback was largely positive, and users generally understood the suggestions' intent. The users' engagement with the suggestions varied greatly—some loved the suggestions and their entire review consisted of nearly only words entered with suggestions while others used very few suggestions. Several users reported that the suggestions helped them select words to write down an idea or also gave them ideas of what to write. We did not systematically enforce quality, but informally we find that most reviews written were grammatical and sensible, which indicates that participants evaluated suggestions before taking them. The dataset contains 74 restaurant reviews typed with phrase suggestions. The mean word count is 69.3, std=25.70. In total, this data comprises 5125 words, along with almost 30k suggestions made (including mid-word).

Estimated Generation Performance. We learn an improved suggestion model by the estimated expected reward ($\hat{R}^M$). We fix $M = 10$ and evaluate the performance of the learned parameters on held-i love this place. the food is good. it's a little expensive, but the food is so much more than that. and i love the people that work there. the burritos are huge and packed with flavor. i got one with chicken and beef and extra quac. it tasted fresh and i couldn't even finish it all as it was huge! i love the location and the atmosphere was great. i will definitely come back to try something different!

i hate spicy food but for some reason i love the flavor of chipotle chiles in any form, so i loooove chipotle. i have been nervous about eating here lately because of the food poisoning scandals but thankfully i have not had any problems! i alway order the burrito bowls and the portions are huge! service is just mediocre but not bad and you cant expect too much from a chain restaurant. overall i would give chipotle four stars.

Figure 2: Example reviews. A colored background indicates that the word was inserted by accepting a suggestion. Consecutive words with the same color were inserted as part of a phrase.

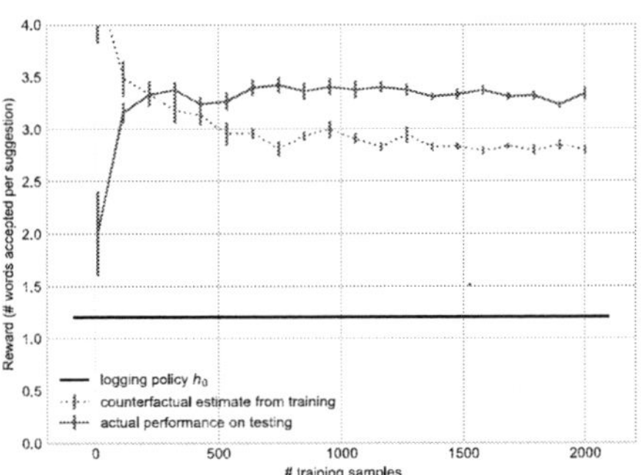

Figure 3: We simulated learning a model based on the behavior of a writer who prefers long words, then presented suggestions from that learned model to the simulated writer. The model learned to make desirable predictions by optimizing the counterfactual estimated reward. Regularization causes that estimate to be conservative; the reward actually achieved by the model exceeded the estimate.

out data using 5-fold cross-validation. Figure 4 shows that while the estimated performance of the new model does vary with the M used when estimating the expected reward, the relationships are consistent: the fitted model consistently receives the highest expected reward, followed by an ablated model that can only adjust the temperature parameter τ, and both outperform the reference model (with $\tau = 1$). The fitted model weights suggest that the workers seemed to prefer long words and pronouns, and eschewed punctuation.

5 Discussion

Our model assumed all writers have the same preferences. Modeling variations between writers, such as in style or vocabulary, could improve performance, as has been done in other domains (e.g., Lee et al. (2017)). Each review in our dataset was written by a different writer, so our dataset could be

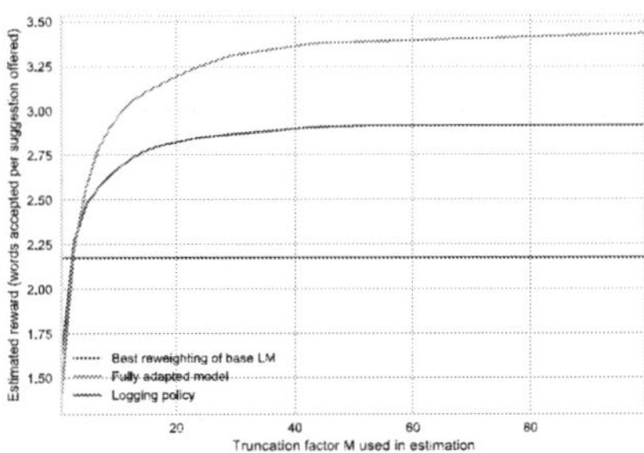

Figure 4: The customized model consistently improves expected reward over baselines (reference LM, and the best "temperature" reweighting LM) in held-out data. Although the result is an estimated using weight truncation at M, the improvement holds for all reasonable M.

used to evaluate online personalization approaches.

Our task of crowdsourced reviews of a single restaurant may not be representative of other tasks or populations of users. However, the predictive language model is a replaceable component, and a stronger model that incorporates more context (e.g., Sordoni et al. (2015)) could improve our baselines and extend our approach to other domains.

Future work can improve on the simple discriminative language model presented here to increase grammaticality and relevance, and thus acceptability, of the suggestions that the customized language models generate.

Acknowledgements Kai-Wei Chang was supported in part by National Science Foundation Grant IIS-1657193. Part of the work was done while Kai-Wei Chang and Kenneth C. Arnold visited Microsoft Research, Cambridge.

References

Kenneth C. Arnold, Krzysztof Z. Gajos, and Adam T. Kalai. 2016. On suggesting phrases vs. predicting words for mobile text composition. In *Proceedings of UIST '16*.

Steffen Bickel, Peter Haider, and Tobias Scheffer. 2005. Learning to complete sentences. In *Machine Learning: ECML 2005*, pages 497–504. Springer.

Kenneth Heafield, Ivan Pouzyrevsky, Jonathan H. Clark, and Philipp Koehn. 2013. Scalable modified Kneser-Ney language model estimation. In *Proceedings of the 51st Annual Meeting of the Association for Computational Linguistics*, pages 690–696, Sofia, Bulgaria.

Edward L Ionides. 2008. Truncated importance sampling. *Journal of Computational and Graphical Statistics*, 17(2):295–311.

Jyun-Yu Jiang, Yen-Yu Ke, Pao-Yu Chien, and Pu-Jen Cheng. 2014. Learning user reformulation behavior for query auto-completion. In *Proceedings of the 37th International ACM SIGIR Conference on Research & Development in Information Retrieval*, SIGIR '14, pages 445–454, New York, NY, USA. ACM.

Melvin Johnson, Mike Schuster, Quoc V. Le, Maxim Krikun, Yonghui Wu, Zhifeng Chen, Nikhil Thorat, Fernanda B. Viégas, Martin Wattenberg, Greg Corrado, Macduff Hughes, and Jeffrey Dean. 2016. Google's multilingual neural machine translation system: Enabling zero-shot translation. *CoRR*, abs/1611.04558.

Anjuli Kannan, Karol Kurach, Sujith Ravi, Tobias Kaufmann, Andrew Tomkins, Balint Miklos, Greg Corrado, Laszlo Lukacs, Marina Ganea, Peter Young, and Vivek Ramavajjala. 2016. Smart reply: Automated response suggestion for email. In *Proceedings of the ACM SIGKDD Conference on Knowledge Discovery and Data Mining (KDD)*.

Yoon Kim, Yacine Jernite, David Sontag, and Alexander M Rush. 2016. Character-aware neural language models. In *Proceedings of the National Conference on Artificial Intelligence (AAAI)*.

Reinhard Kneser and Hermann Ney. 1995. Improved backing-off for m-gram language modeling. In *Proceedings of the IEEE International Conference on Acoustics, Speech and Signal Processing (ICASSP)*. IEEE.

John Lafferty, Andrew McCallum, and Fernando Pereira. 2001. Conditional random fields: Probabilistic models for segmenting and labeling sequence data. In *Proceedings of the International Conference on Machine Learning (ICML)*, pages 282–289.

Hung-Yi Lee, Bo-Hsiang Tseng, Tsung-Hsien Wen, Yu Tsao, Hung-Yi Lee, Bo-Hsiang Tseng, Tsung-Hsien Wen, and Yu Tsao. 2017. Personalizing recurrent-neural-network-based language model by social network. *IEEE/ACM Trans. Audio, Speech and Lang. Proc.*, 25(3):519–530.

Inderjeet Mani. 2001. *Automatic Summarization*, volume 3 of *Natural Language Processing*. John Benjamins Publishing Company, Amsterdam/Philadelphia.

Andrew McCallum, Dayne Freitag, and Fernando Pereira. 2000. Maximum entropy Markov models for information extraction and segmentation. In *Proceedings of the International Conference on Machine Learning (ICML)*.

Tomas Mikolov and Geoffrey Zweig. 2012. Context dependent recurrent neural network language model. In *SLT*, pages 234–239.

Arnab Nandi and HV Jagadish. 2007. Effective phrase prediction. In *Proceedings of the 33rd international conference on Very large data bases*, pages 219–230. VLDB Endowment.

Philip Quinn and Shumin Zhai. 2016. A Cost-Benefit Study of Text Entry Suggestion Interaction. *Proceedings of the 2016 CHI Conference on Human Factors in Computing Systems*, pages 83–88.

Owen Rambow, Srinivas Bangalore, and Marilyn Walker. 2001. Natural language generation in dialog systems. In *Proceedings of the first international conference on Human language technology research*, pages 1–4.

Alessandro Sordoni, Michel Galley, Michael Auli, Chris Brockett, Yangfeng Ji, Margaret Mitchell, Jian-Yun Nie, Jianfeng Gao, and Bill Dolan. 2015. A neural network approach to context-sensitive generation of conversational responses. In *Proceedings of the Conference of the North American Chapter of the Association for Computational Linguistics (NAACL)*.

Adith Swaminathan and Thorsten Joachims. 2015. Counterfactual risk minimization. In *Proceedings of the 24th International Conference on World Wide Web Companion*, pages 939–941. International World Wide Web Conferences Steering Committee.

Deep Automated Multi-task Learning

Davis Liang
d1liang@ucsd.edu
University of California, San Diego

Yan Shu
yashu@ucsd.edu
University of California, San Diego

Abstract

Multi-task learning (MTL) has recently contributed to learning better representations in service of various NLP tasks. MTL aims at improving the performance of a primary task, by jointly training on a secondary task. This paper introduces automated tasks, which exploit the sequential nature of the input data, as secondary tasks in an MTL model. We explore next word prediction, next character prediction, and missing word completion as potential automated tasks. Our results show that training on a primary task in parallel with a secondary automated task improves both the convergence speed and accuracy for the primary task. We suggest two methods for augmenting an existing network with automated tasks and establish better performance in topic prediction, sentiment analysis, and hashtag recommendation. Finally, we show that the MTL models can perform well on datasets that are small and colloquial by nature.

1 Introduction

Recurrent neural networks have demonstrated formidable performance in NLP tasks ranging from speech recognition (Hinton et al., 2012) to neural machine translation (Bahdanau et al., 2014; Wu et al., 2016). In NLP, multi-task learning has been found to be beneficial for *seq2seq* learning (Luong et al., 2015; Cheng et al., 2016), text recommendation (Bansal et al., 2016), and categorization (Liu et al., 2015).

Despite the popularity of multi-task learning, there has been little work done in generalizing the application of MTL to all sequential tasks. To accomplish this goal, we use the concept of auto-mated tasks. Similar work in multi-task learning frameworks proposed in (Liu et al., 2016) and (Luong et al., 2015) are both trained on multiple labeled datasets. Though we have seen evidence of research using external unlabeled datasets in pretraining (Dai and Le, 2015) and semi-supervised multi-task frameworks (Ando and Zhang, 2005), to our knowledge there is no work dedicated to using tasks derived from the original dataset in multi-task learning with deep recurrent networks. With automated tasks, we are able to use MTL for almost any sequential task.

We present two ways of using automated multi-task learning: (1) the MRNN, a multi-tasking RNN where the tasks share an LSTM layer, and (2) the CRNN, a cascaded RNN where the network is augmented with a concatenative layer supervised by the automated task. Examples of either network are shown in Figure 1.

In summary, our main contributions are:

- We introduce the concept of automated tasks for multi-task learning with deep recurrent networks.
- We show that using the CRNN and the MRNN trained in parallel on a secondary automated task allows the network to achieve better results in sentiment analysis, topic prediction, and hashtag recommendation.

2 Automated Multi-task Learning

We generalize multi-task learning by incorporating automated tasks with our two MTL models: the CRNN and the MRNN. In the following subsections, we describe the automated tasks, the models, and their respective training methods.

2.1 Automated Tasks

The set of automated tasks we suggest include (1) next word prediction, (2) next character predic-

55

Proceedings of the The 8th International Joint Conference on Natural Language Processing, pages 55–60,
Taipei, Taiwan, November 27 – December 1, 2017 ©2017 AFNLP

in Figure 1.

The MRNN is constructed such that the primary task and automated task(s) share a body of units. This body is supervised by both the primary and automated task(s) and learns internal representations for both tasks.

2.3 CRNN

(Søgaard and Goldberg, 2016) showed that a higher-level task can benefit from making use of a shared representation learned by training on a lower-level task. Similarly, the CRNN assumes that the primary task has a hierarchical relationship with the automated task. A basic example of a CRNN is shown in Figure 1.

Specifically, we designed the CRNN to use the representations learned from an automated task as a concatenative input (Ghosh et al., 2016; Lipton et al., 2015) for the primary task. Furthermore, such a model can be supervised on an identical task at different network layers.

3 Experiments

We evaluate the performance of our models on binary sentiment analysis of the Rotten Tomato Movie Review dataset, topic prediction on the AG News dataset, and hashtag recommendation on a Twitter dataset. For each of these datasets, we compared the results from the MRNN and CRNN to a corresponding LSTM model. We separately tuned the hyper-parameters for each model with the validation sets and took the average results across the multiple runs. Note that the baseline LSTM models are 2-layered. Our MTL models and the LSTM baseline have the exact same number of parameters along the primary task stream.

In the following experiments, we use 512 LSTM cells for all models trained on the Rotten Tomato dataset and 128 LSTM cells for the AG News and Twitter datasets. Before each output layer, we have a single fully connected layer consisting of 512 hidden units for the Rotten Tomato dataset and 128 hidden units for the AG News and Twitter datasets. We use a batch size of 128 and apply gradient clipping with the norm set to 1.0 on all the parameters for all experiments.

We found that missing word completion is especially detrimental to our MTL models. We believe that removing a word from each document, which consists almost exclusively of short sequences, discards a large portion of the useful information.

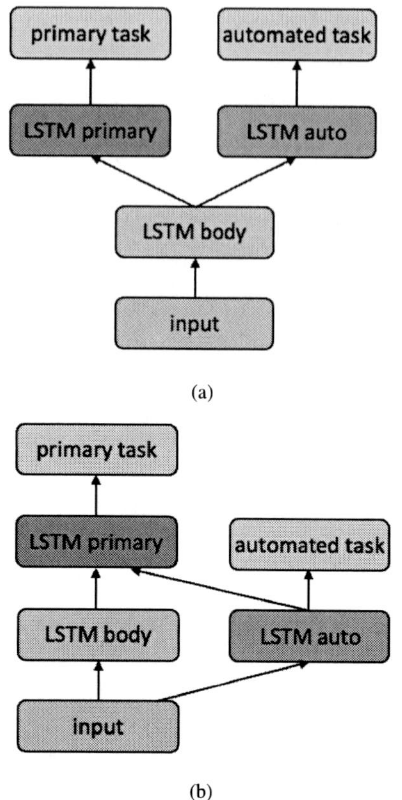

Figure 1: MRNN (a) and CRNN (b) model

tion, and (3) missing word completion.

For word and character generation, we trained a language model to predict the next word or character given the words or characters from the previous K steps. For the missing word completion task, we removed a random non-stop-word from each document and replaced it with a UNK placeholder. The removed word is fed into a word2vec model trained on Google News (Le and Mikolov, 2014) and the resulting vector is the target. We performed regression to minimize the mean squared error of predicting the missing word vector given the text. We generated predictions by finding the target word vector with the highest cosine similarity to the output vector.

2.2 MRNN

The multi-tasking RNN, MRNN, is an MTL model that we use to train our primary and automated tasks in parallel. The MRNN's initial layers are shared, and the later layers branch out to separate tasks. A basic example of an MRNN is shown

Dataset	Doc. Count	Categories	Avg. WC
RTMR	10662	2	20
AGNews	127600	4	34
Twitter	5964	71	70*

Table 1: Dataset statistics. (*character count)

Thus, the quantitative results of the missing word completion experiments have been omitted from this paper. We hypothesize that missing word completion is more useful for datasets with longer documents where discarding individual words will not have a major effect on each document.

3.1 Data

The Rotten Tomato Movie Review (RTMR)[1] (Pang and Lee, 2005) dataset consists of 5331 positive and 5331 negative review snippets. The task is to predict review sentiment. The dataset is randomly split into 90% for the training and validation sets and 10% for test set (Dai and Le, 2015).

The AG News[2] (Zhang et al., 2015) dataset consists of 120,000 training and 7,600 testing documents. The task is to classify the documents into one of four topics. Following (Wang and Tian, 2016), we took 18,275 documents from the training set as validation data.

The Twitter dataset consists of 5,964 tweets. The task is to predict one of the 71 hashtag labels. We collected 300,000 tweets using the Twitter API. We removed all retweets, URLs, uncommon symbols, and emojis. We lowercased all the characters in the tweets. We kept the tweets with the 71 most popular English hashtags, and removed the hashtags from the tweets. We used an 80/10/10 split of the remaining data. Although Twitter's Developer Policy prevents us from releasing the dataset, the entire data collection pipeline will be made available upon publication.

4 Rotten Tomatoes

4.1 Training Details

The primary task for the Rotten Tomatoes dataset is sentiment analysis. We used word generation as the automated task. The input is a 300-dimensional word2vec vector for each word. The primary task output consists of two softmax units, representing a positive or negative review. The automated task output is next word prediction of the word2vec representation, and hence is a 300 unit tanh layer. For LSTM we use a learning rate of

[1] cs.cornell.edu/people/pabo/movie-review-data/
[2] di.unipi.it/gulli/AG_corpus_of_news_articles.html

0.0001. For the MTL models, we need to tune the learning rate hyper-parameter of the automated task. Instead of tuning the primary and automated task hyper-parameters separately, we found an alternative method for tuning the learning rates using the following equation where lr_{actual} is the only learning rate hyper-parameter. lr_{actual} is optimized on the validation set.

$$lr_{\text{prim}}(\text{epoch}) = \text{epoch} * (\frac{lr_{\text{actual}}}{\text{total Epochs}}) \quad (1)$$
$$lr_{\text{auto}}(\text{epoch}) = lr_{\text{actual}} - lr_{\text{prim}}(\text{epoch})$$

We apply this type of learning rate modulation in order to simulate network pre-training on the automated task in the earlier epochs, learn shared representations in the intermediate epochs through multi-task learning, and train more exclusively on the primary task during the later epochs. We used an lr_{actual} of 0.01.

The MTL and LSTM models both use word-level word2vec representations trained on Google News (Le and Mikolov, 2014). The primary sentiment analysis task is trained using Adam optimizer (Kingma and Ba, 2014) on cross-entropy loss while the automated word generation task is trained using mean-squared error. We continue to use Adam optimizer in the rest of our experiments.

4.2 Results

We compare our experimental results with (1) SA-LSTM (Dai and Le, 2015), an LSTM initialized with a sequence auto-encoder, and (2) the adversarial model (Miyato et al., 2016), an LSTM-based text classification model with perturbed embeddings. We choose these two models because they are both LSTM-based and are thus comparable to our models. Non-LSTM models, such as convolutional neural networks, have been able to achieve higher accuracy on sentiment analysis with the Rotten Tomatoes dataset (Kim, 2014). All of our networks beat the variant of the SA-LSTM that does not use outside data for pre-training. However, the adversarial (Miyato et al., 2016) and SA-LSTM (Dai and Le, 2015) models, using external unlabeled datasets, outperform our MTL models. With the MRNN, we achieve a 1.5% gain in accuracy over SA-LSTM, and 1% over the vanilla LSTM network. With the CRNN, we achieve similar results compared to the vanilla LSTM network. We hypothesize that the reason the CRNN under-performs the MRNN is due to the lack of a clear hierarchy between sentiment analysis and

Dataset	Model	Accuracy
RTMR	SA-LSTM (2015)	79.7%
RTMR	SA-LSTM (2015)*	83.3%
RTMR	Adversarial (2016)*	83.4%
RTMR	LSTM	80.2%
RTMR	**CRNN**	**80.1%**
RTMR	**MRNN**	**81.2%**
AGNews	SC-LSTM-I (2016)	92.05%
AGNews	LSTM	91.59%
AGNews	**CRNN**	**92.19%**
AGNews	**MRNN**	**91.93%**
Twitter	LSTM	57.8%
Twitter	**CRNN**	**61.4%**
Twitter	**MRNN**	**62.0%**

Table 2: Experimental results. (*trained on external unlabeled dataset)

word generation. We suspect that sentiment analysis is primarily keyword based and cannot fully take advantage of the automated language model task. Additionally, we found that the MTL models can be trained with much higher learning rates than a standard LSTM, allowing for convergence in many fewer epochs. The MRNN model converged within the first 10 epochs, whereas the LSTM model required approximately 30 epochs to converge.

5 AG News

5.1 Training Details

For the AG News experiment, the primary task is topic prediction and the automated task is word generation. The input to the model is the 300-dimensional word2vec representations of the words from the documents. The primary task output uses a softmax layer with 4 units. The automated task output is represented by a tanh layer with 300 units. The learning rate for the LSTM is 0.001. For the MRNN, the learning rates undergo the same linear function as in the Rotten Tomatoes experiment where lr_{actual} is 0.01.

5.2 Results

For AG News dataset, we compare our experiment result with skip-connected LSTM (Wang and Tian, 2016), the previous state-of-the-art model on this dataset. The CRNN outperforms state-of-the-art by 0.14% and MRNN by 0.26%. We believe the CRNN beats the MRNN due to a hierarchical relationship between topic prediction and word generation. We suspect that topic prediction, which relies on a holistic understanding of a document, can effectively take advantage of the language model.

6 Twitter

We ran an experiment showing that our models can perform well in challenging environments with little data. We used a small dataset of 5,964 tweets. We performed regression on the word2vec representation of the hashtag given the tweet. We chose regression over classification of one-hot targets because our chosen hashtags are inherently non-orthogonal and can benefit from semantic representations in vector space. We trained three models: an LSTM model, the MRNN, and the CRNN.

6.1 Training Details

For the Twitter experiment, the primary task is hashtag recommendation and the automated task is character prediction. We use character prediction as the automated task due to the large amount of misspellings and colloquialisms in tweets.

The input to the model is the 66-dimensional one-hot encoding of the characters corresponding to the ASCII characters that we kept during preprocessing. The primary task output is a tanh layer with 300 units. The automated task output uses a softmax layer with 66 units. For all the models we chose a fixed learning rate of 0.001 based on our observation that different learning rates have little effect on the relative trend between the models on this particular task. A constant, equal learning rate allows us to compare the accuracy curves of each network against epochs run.

Since several of the hashtags are very similar to each other (i.e. #Capricorn and #Scorpio), we marked a prediction as correct if the predicted semantic vector's top 5% (top 4) closest cosine distance words contained the target hashtag.

6.2 Results

With the MRNN, we achieve a 4.2% gain in accuracy over the LSTM in the Twitter dataset. With the CRNN, we achieve a 3.6% gain in accuracy. Additionally, we have shown in Figure 2 that both the MRNN and CRNN models converge faster than the LSTM model; both MTL models take approximately half of the number of epochs to reach 50% accuracy using the same constant learning rate.

7 Conclusion

In this paper, we showed that automated multi-task learning models can consistently outperform the LSTM in sentiment analysis, topic prediction,

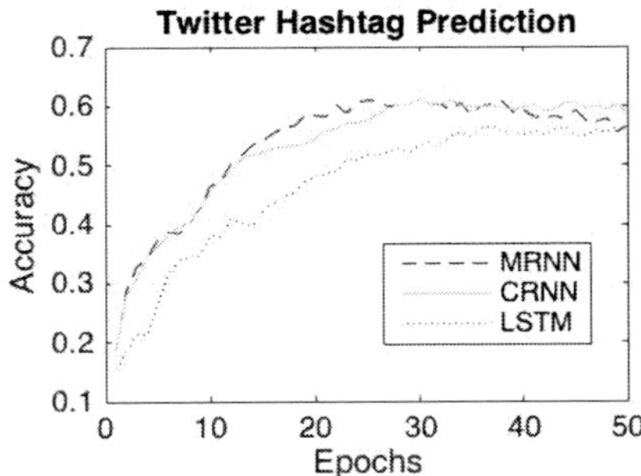

Figure 2: Hashtag prediction in Twitter.

and hashtag recommendation. Note that the concept of automated tasks can be extended to non-NLP sequence tasks such as image categorization with next row prediction as the automated task. Because automated MTL can be integrated into an existing network by adding a new branch to a pre-existing graph, we can substitute bidirectional LSTMs (Schuster and Paliwal, 1997), GRUs (Gulcehre et al., 2014), and vanilla RNNs for LSTMs in our MTL models. We will experiment on these variations in the future.

References

R. Ando and T. Zhang. 2005. A framework for learning predictive structures from multiple tasks and unlabeled data. *Journal of Machine Learning Research*.

Dzmitry Bahdanau, Kyunghyun Cho, and Yoshua Bengio. 2014. Neural machine translation by jointly learning to align and translate. *arXiv preprint arXiv:1409.0473*.

Trapit Bansal, David Belanger, and Andrew McCallum. 2016. Ask the gru: Multi-task learning for deep text recommendations. In *Proceedings of the 10th ACM Conference on Recommender Systems*, pages 107–114. ACM.

Yong Cheng, Wei Xu, Zhongjun He, Wei He, Hua Wu, Maosong Sun, and Yang Liu. 2016. Semi-supervised learning for neural machine translation. *arXiv preprint arXiv:1606.04596*.

Andrew M Dai and Quoc V Le. 2015. Semi-supervised sequence learning. In *Advances in Neural Information Processing Systems*, pages 3079–3087.

Shalini Ghosh, Oriol Vinyals, Brian Strope, Scott Roy, Tom Dean, and Larry Heck. 2016. Contextual lstm (clstm) models for large scale nlp tasks. *arXiv preprint arXiv:1602.06291*.

Caglar Gulcehre, Kyunghyun Cho, Razvan Pascanu, and Yoshua Bengio. 2014. *Learned-norm pooling for deep feedforward and recurrent neural networks*, part 1 edition, volume 8724 LNAI of *Lecture Notes in Computer Science (including subseries Lecture Notes in Artificial Intelligence and Lecture Notes in Bioinformatics)*. Springer Verlag.

Geoffrey Hinton, Li Deng, Dong Yu, George E Dahl, Abdel-rahman Mohamed, Navdeep Jaitly, Andrew Senior, Vincent Vanhoucke, Patrick Nguyen, Tara N Sainath, et al. 2012. Deep neural networks for acoustic modeling in speech recognition: The shared views of four research groups. *IEEE Signal Processing Magazine*, 29(6):82–97.

Yoon Kim. 2014. Convolutional neural networks for sentence classification. *arXiv preprint arXiv:1408.5882*.

P. Kingma and J. Ba. 2014. Adam: A method for stochastic optimization. *arXiv preprint arXiv:1412.6980*.

Quoc V Le and Tomas Mikolov. 2014. Distributed representations of sentences and documents. In *ICML*, volume 14, pages 1188–1196.

Zachary C Lipton, Sharad Vikram, and Julian McAuley. 2015. Generative concatenative nets jointly learn to write and classify reviews. *arXiv preprint arXiv:1511.03683*.

Pengfei Liu, Xipeng Qiu, and Xuanjing Huang. 2016. Deep multi-task learning with shared memory. *arXiv preprint arXiv:1609.07222*.

Xiaodong Liu, Jianfeng Gao, Xiaodong He, Li Deng, Kevin Duh, and Ye-Yi Wang. 2015. Representation learning using multi-task deep neural networks for semantic classification and information retrieval. In *HLT-NAACL*, pages 912–921.

Minh-Thang Luong, Quoc V Le, Ilya Sutskever, Oriol Vinyals, and Lukasz Kaiser. 2015. Multi-task sequence to sequence learning. *arXiv preprint arXiv:1511.06114*.

Takeru Miyato, Andrew M Dai, and Ian Goodfellow. 2016. Adversarial training methods for semi-supervised text classification. *arXiv preprint arXiv:1605.07725*.

Bo Pang and Lillian Lee. 2005. Seeing stars: Exploiting class relationships for sentiment categorization with respect to rating scales. In *Proceedings of the 43rd annual meeting on association for computational linguistics*, pages 115–124. Association for Computational Linguistics.

Mike Schuster and Kuldip K Paliwal. 1997. Bidirectional recurrent neural networks. *IEEE Transactions on Signal Processing*, 45(11):2673–2681.

Anders Søgaard and Yoav Goldberg. 2016. Deep multi-task learning with low level tasks supervised at lower layers. In *Proceedings of the 54th Annual*

Meeting of the Association for Computational Linguistics, volume 2, pages 231–235. Association for Computational Linguistics.

Yiren Wang and Fei Tian. 2016. Recurrent residual learning for sequence classification. In *Proceedings of the 2016 Conference on Empirical Methods in Natural Language Processing*, page 938943. Association for Computational Linguistics.

Yonghui Wu, Mike Schuster, Zhifeng Chen, Quoc V Le, Mohammad Norouzi, Wolfgang Macherey, Maxim Krikun, Yuan Cao, Qin Gao, Klaus Macherey, et al. 2016. Google's neural machine translation system: Bridging the gap between human and machine translation. *arXiv preprint arXiv:1609.08144*.

Xiang Zhang, Junbo Zhao, and Yann LeCun. 2015. Character-level convolutional networks for text classification. In *Advances in neural information processing systems*, pages 649–657.

Post-Processing Techniques for Improving Predictions of Multilabel Learning Approaches

Akshay Soni, Aasish Pappu, Jerry Chia-mau Ni* and Troy Chevalier

Yahoo! Research, USA

*Yahoo! Taiwan

akshaysoni, aasishkp, jerryni, troyc@oath.com

Abstract

In *Multilabel Learning* (MLL) each training instance is associated with a *set of labels* and the task is to learn a function that maps an unseen instance to its corresponding label set. In this paper, we present a suite of—MLL algorithm independent—post-processing techniques that utilize the conditional and directional label-dependences in order to make the predictions from any MLL approach more coherent and precise. We solve a constraint optimization problem over the output produced by any MLL approach and the result is a refined version of the input predicted label set. Using proposed techniques, we show absolute improvement of 3% on English News and 10% on Chinese E-commerce datasets for P@K metric.

1 Introduction

The *Multiclass Classification* problem deals with learning a function that maps an instance to its one (and only one) label from a set of possible labels while in MLL each training instance is associated with a *set of labels* and the task is to learn a function that maps an (unseen) instance to its corresponding label set. Recently, MLL has received a lot of attention because of modern applications where it is natural that instances are associated with more than one class simultaneously. For instance, MLL can be used to map news items to their corresponding topics in Yahoo News, blog posts to user generated tags in Tumblr, images to category tags in Flickr, movies to genres in Netflix, and in many other web-scale problems. Since all of the above mentioned applications are user-facing, a fast and precise mechanism for automatically labeling the instances with their multiple relevant tags is critical. This has resulted in the development of many large-scale MLL algorithms.

The most straightforward approach for MLL is *Binary Relevance* that treats each label as an independent binary classification task. This quickly becomes infeasible if either the feature dimension is large or the number of labels is huge or both. Modern approaches either reduce the label dimension, e.g., PLST, CPLST (Chen and Lin, 2012), Bayesian CS (Kapoor et al., 2012), LEML (Yu et al., 2014), RIPML (Soni and Mehdad, 2017), SLEEC (Bhatia et al., 2015), or feature dimension or both (such as WSABIE and DocTag2Vec (Chen et al., 2017)). The inference stage for all of these approaches produce a score for each potential label and then a set of top-scored labels is given as the prediction.

A potential problem with the above mentioned algorithms is that they lack the knowledge of correlation or dependency between the labels. Let us look at a toy example: our training data is such that whenever the label *mountain* is active then the label *tree* is also active. Therefore MLL algorithm should take advantage of this correlation embedded in the training data to always infer the label *tree* when *mountain* is one of the label. On the other hand, if *tree* is an active label then *mountain* may not be a label. Exploiting this directional and conditional dependency between the labels should allow us to predict a more coherent set of labels. It would—to some extend—also save the MLL algorithm from making wrong predictions since if some wrong labels (say we predict a wrong label *politics*) are predicted along with correct labels (when true labels are *tree* and *mountain*) then the overall set of predicted labels would not be coherent. Inclusion of this external knowledge about labels shows significant improvements when there is a lack of training data for some labels.

There have been many attempts (Dembszynski

61

Proceedings of the The 8th International Joint Conference on Natural Language Processing, pages 61–66,
Taipei, Taiwan, November 27 – December 1, 2017 ©2017 AFNLP

et al., 2010) of using label-hierarchies or label-correlation information as part of the MLL training process. For instance, the label-correlation in training data is used in (Tsoumakas et al., 2009); (Guo and Gu, 2011) uses conditional dependencies among labels via graphical models. Some of the other relevant works that use this information as part of the training are (Huang and Zhou, 2012; Kong et al., 2013; Younes et al., 2008) and references therein. Since these approaches use label dependency information as part of the training stage, we foresee following issues:

- Using pre-trained model: In some cases we want to use a pre-trained MLL model that did not use the label-dependency information during training and retraining a new model is not an option. The use of pre-trained models has become very common since not everyone has the hardware capability to train complex models using large amounts of data.

- Label-dependency information not available during training or else one may want to use updated or new label-dependency information after the model is trained.

- Expensive training and inference: Almost all algorithms that utilize the label-dependence as side-information are either expensive during training, or inference, or both.

In this paper, we present a suite of post-processing techniques that utilize the conditional and directional label-dependences in order to make the predictions from any MLL approach more coherent and precise. It is to be noted that the proposed techniques are algorithm independent and can even be applied over the predictions produced by approaches that use this or any other label-dependency information as part of the training. Our techniques involve solving simple constraint optimization problems over the outputs produced by any MLL approach and the result is a refined version of the input prediction by removing spurious labels and reordering the labels by utilizing the additional label-dependency side information. We show benefits of our approach on Chinese e-commerce and English news datasets.

2 Problem Description and Approaches

MLL is the problem of learning a function $f : \mathcal{I} \rightarrow 2^{\mathcal{L}}$ that maps an instance in $\mathcal{I}$ to one of the sets in the power set $2^{\mathcal{L}}$ where $\mathcal{L}$ is the set of all possible labels. For a specific instance, MLL predicts a subset $S \subset \mathcal{L}$. Our goal is to learn a subset $L \subset S$ such that L is a refined version of S.

Given a set of constraints on input labels, one can define an objective function that would potentially minimize inconsistencies between the final set of labels. Intuitively, labels may be interdependent, thus certain subsets are more coherent than the others. Label dependency can manifest either through human-curated label taxonomy or conditional probabilities. We propose two post-processing techniques in this paper to improve predicted outputs of any MLL algorithm. In the following subsections, we present details of each technique.

2.1 Steiner Tree Approximation

We formulate label coherence problem as a Steiner Tree Approximation problem (Gilbert and Pollak, 1968). Consider the following: input is a set of predicted labels $S = R \cup O$, where R is a set of coherent (required) labels and O is a set of incoherent (optional) labels. Labels are connected by directed weighted edges, thus form a graph G. The goal is to find a tree $T = (L, E, W)$ where L is a set of labels $R \subset L \subset S$ that includes all of the coherent labels and may include some of the optional labels O, E is the set of directed edges connecting nodes in L and W is set of weights assigned to the edges. For faster and approximate solutions, one can reduce Steiner tree problem to directed minimum spanning tree (MST) (Mehlhorn, 1988) and can be solved using Edmond's algorithm (Edmonds, 1967). MST has been applied in several previous works on document summarization (Varadarajan and Hristidis, 2006), text detection in natural images (Pan et al., 2011), and dependency parsing (McDonald et al., 2005). In this work, we first construct a directed graph of labels and then apply MST to obtain a tree of coherent labels. On applying MST, we choose vertices with top-K edge weights. Our goal is to find a tree that minimizes the following objective function:

$$\mathrm{cost}_d(T) := \sum_{(u,v)\in E} d(u,v),$$

where u and v are nodes, $d(u,v) = 1 - W(u,v)$. The edge weights W are determined by the conditional probabilities of co-occurrence of labels. Directionality of the edges are determined by the following criterion:

$$\begin{cases} L_i \rightarrow L_j, & \Pr(L_i|L_j) \leq \Pr(L_i|L_j) \\ L_i \leftarrow L_j, & \text{otherwise,} \end{cases}$$

where $\Pr(L_i|L_j)$ is the probability that label L_i is active given label L_j is active.

Once the directed graph is constructed based on above criterion, Edmond's algorithm recursively eliminates edges between a root node and one of the other nodes with minimum edge weights. In case of cycles, the edges are eliminated randomly. In essence, this algorithm selects highest-value connected-component in the directed graph. Thus, we are left with coherent labels.

2.2 0-1 Knapsack

Assigning labels to an instance with a budget can be considered as a resource allocation problem. `0-1` Knapsack is a popular resource allocation problem where capacity of the knapsack is limited and it can be filled with only a few valuable items. Items are added to the knapsack by maximizing the overall value of the knapsack subject to the combined weight of the items under budget. Many previous works in NLP have used Knapsack formulation, particularly in summarization (Lin and Bilmes, 2010; Ji et al., 2013; Hirao et al., 2013; McDonald, 2007). We formulate label assignment problem as a resource allocation problem, where we maximize total value of assigned labels. We determine individual value of a label based on the log likelihood of the label and its dependent labels. Intuitively, a label is included in the knapsack only when its dependent labels increase the overall log-likelihood.

$$\text{maximize} \quad \sum_{k \in S} \sum_{i \in D_k} \log(\Pr(L_k|L_i))$$

$$\text{s.t.} \quad \sum_{k \in S} |D_k| \leq C,$$

where $D_k \subset S - L_k$ is a subset of input labels S that are conditionally dependent on label L_k i.e. $\Pr(L_k|L_i) > 0$ for $i \in D_k$. To include a label L_k in the knapsack (i.e., in L), we optimize the total sum of the log conditional probabilities of labels L_k under the constraint that the total number of dependent labels are within the budget C—total number of permissible labels. The problem can be understood as a maximization of values of assigned labels. This problem is solved using a dynamic programming algorithm that runs in polynomial time (Andonov et al., 2000).

3 Experiments

The goal of this section is to emphasize on the fact that our post-processing techniques are MLL algorithm independent. For that we apply our approaches over the predictions from multiple MLL algorithms for two datasets: Yahoo News dataset in English and Chinese E-commerce dataset. Since MLL is generally used in applications where precision of predictions are important, we use Precision@K for $K = 1, 2$ and 3 as our metric.

3.1 Datasets

- **Yahoo News MLL Dataset (English)[1]**: This is one of the few publicly available large scale datasets for MLL. It contains 38968 Yahoo News articles in English for training and 10000 for testing. These are manually labeled with their corresponding category labels; overall, there are 413 possible labels.

- **Chinese E-commerce MLL dataset:** This is a propriety dataset that contains product descriptions of 230364 e-commerce products in Chinese for training and 49689 for testing. Each product is tagged with labels about the product categories; overall there are 240 tags.

3.2 MLL Approaches

Since our post-processing techniques are MLL algorithm independent, we picked three MLL approaches to apply our post-processing techniques: Naive Bayes, CNN, and DocTag2Vec. From our perspective, we can treat these approaches as black-box that for a given instance generate the set of predicted labels $S \subset \mathcal{L}$.

- **Naive Bayes (NB) MLL**: Given a sequence of words, the probability of a tag is evaluated by multiplying the prior probability of the tag and the probabilities of observing the words given the tag, pre-computed from the training data.

- **CNN MLL** (Kim, 2014): Originally designed for text classification tasks, the model views sequence of word embeddings as a matrix and applies two sequential operations: *convolution* and *max-pooling*. First, features

---

[1]available publicly via Webscope: https://webscope.sandbox.yahoo.com/catalog.php?datatype=l&did=84

Dataset	MLL Approach	P@K	Default	Highest Priors Baseline-1	Greedy Baseline-2	MST	Knapsack
Yahoo News	DocTag2Vec	1	0.6821	0.6277	0.5927	0.6942	**0.6976** (+1.5%)
		2	0.6461	0.6132	0.5836	**0.6689** (+2.2%)	0.6568
		3	0.6218	0.6052	0.5750	**0.6485** (+2.6%)	0.6203
Chinese Ecom	DocTag2Vec	1	0.5309	**0.5718** (+4.0%)	0.5563	0.5510	0.5331
		2	0.5454	**0.5748** (+2.9%)	0.5664	0.5716	0.5442
		3	0.4813	0.4928	0.5802	**0.5820** (+10%)	0.4884
Chinese Ecom	CNN	1	**0.8554**	0.7658	0.6898	0.8483	0.8479
		2	0.7387	0.7164	0.6545	**0.7814** (+4.2%)	0.7450
		3	0.6095	0.5921	0.6646	**0.7249** (+11.5%)	0.6287
Chinese Ecom	NB	1	0.8752	0.8526	0.7545	0.8982	**0.9057** (+3.0%)
		2	0.8481	0.8167	0.6738	0.8456	**0.8538** (+0.5%)
		3	0.7913	0.7519	0.7129	**0.8101** (+1.8%)	0.7385

Table 1: P@K for various values of K for the two datasets considered and for different MLL algorithms. Here default means not using a coherence stage. In brackets are shown the improvements in precision over default by the best performing coherence approach.

are extracted by a convolution layer with several filters of different window size. Then the model applies a max-over-time pooling operation over the extracted features. The features are then passed through a fully connected layer with dropout and sigmoid activations where each output node indicates the probability of a tag.

ail

- **DocTag2Vec** (Chen et al., 2017): Recently proposed DocTag2Vec embeds instances (documents in this case), tags, and words simultaneously into a low-dimensional space such that the documents and the tags associated with them are embedded close to each other. Inference is done via a SGD step to embed a new document, followed by k-nearest neighbors to find the closed tags in the space.

3.3 Post-Processing Techniques

- **Highest Priors** (Baseline-1): Given the training data, compute the prior probabilities of each label and re-rank labels in S according to the decreasing order of these prior probabilities to produce the new set L.

- **Greedy** (Baseline-2): Given the pairwise conditional probabilities among the output labels, select most probable pairs above certain threshold τ; we experimented with values in range [0.01, 0.1] and used $\tau = 0.06$ in the final experiments.

- **MST**: Steiner Tree Approximation via MST. The edge weights are computed via the conditional co-occurrence of the labels in the training data and the directionality is enforced via the criterion described in Section 2.1.

- **0-1 Knapsack**: We set $C = 15$ and solve the optimization problem described in Section 2.2.

3.4 Results

The P@K values are shown in Table 1 for the two datasets and for various coherency algorithms applied over multiple MLL approaches. The two baselines—highest priors and greedy—work reasonably well but the best performing approaches are MST and Knapsack. For most of the cases MST works well and even in the scenarios where Knapsack beats MST, they both are close in performance. By using a post-processing step for coherency we generally see a lift of around $2 - 4\%$ in most of the cases and sometimes a lift of more than 10% is observed. We note that one can design the problem with more deeper conditions i.e., $P(L_1|L_2, L_3 \ldots L_k)$ but only single label dependency has been used in our experiments. With deeper dependencies, more training data is required to reliably learn prior probabilities. Also as the number of labels increase, the number of conditionals increases, thus the inference becomes computationally expensive.

Table 2: Example tags for various Yahoo News articles. Tags highlighted in red did not appear in true labels. Superscripts on the tags denote following D: Output from DocTag2Vec system (Default in Table 1), Knap: Output from Knapsack, MST: Output from Steiner Tree Approximation. Tags without superscript were not predicted at inference.

Doc 1	telecommunication^{D,MST},company-legal-&-law-matters^{D,Knap,MST}, mergers,-acquisitions-&-takeovers laws-and-regulations,entertainment^{D}, handheld-&-connected-devices^{D,MST}
Doc 2	fashion^{D,MST},clothes-&-apparel,hollywood^{D,MST} celebrity^{D,MST,Knap},entertainment^{D,MST,Knap},music^{D,MST},contests-&-giveaways^{D}
Doc 3	handheld-&-connected-devices^{D,MST,Knap},telecommunication^{D,MST,Knap},money investment-&-company-information,investment,sectors-&-industries^{D},internet-&-networking-technology^{D}
Doc 4	autos^{D,MST,Knap},strikes,financial-technical-analysis,company-earnings^{D,Knap}
Doc 5	public-transportation^{D,MST,Knap},travel-and-transportation^{D,MST,Knap} celebrity,music^{D,MST,Knap},transport-accident^{D,MST,Knap},entertainment^{D}
Doc 6	family-health^{D,MST,Knap},mental-health^{D,MST},biology,pregnancy^{D},parenting^{D,MST,Knap},tests-&-procedures^{D}
Doc 7	laws-and-regulations^{D,MST,Knap},company-legal-&-law-matters^{D,MST,Knap}, money,investment-&-company-information,investment,lighting-&-accessories^{D}

4 Discussion and Conclusion

Table 2 illustrates MLL output of sample documents from Yahoo News corpus. We observed Knapsack algorithm is more conservative at subset selection compared to MST. Tags predicted by *Default* system include tags that are related to true tags but do not appear in the true tag subset e.g., in Doc 1 *handheld-&-connected-devices* is related to *telecommunications*, similarly Doc 2 and Doc 5 has one related tag and one spurious tag — in both cases MST and KNAPSACK prune the spurious tags. In Doc 2 *music* is related/coherent and *contest-&-giveaways* is spurious/incoherent. In Doc 5 *transport-accident* is related/coherent and *entertainment* is a spurious tag.

In this paper we presented two post-processing techniques to improve precision of any MLL algorithm. In addition to experiments discussed in the paper, we conducted experiments with other combinatorial optimization algorithms as used in previous works viz., facility location (p-median) (Alguliev et al., 2011; Ma and Wan, 2010; Cheung et al., 2009; Andrews and Ramakrishnan, 2008) and other graph-based centrality methods (Wolf and Gibson, 2004; Li et al., 2006; Guinaudeau and Strube, 2013). However, we did not observe significant improvement over default (unprocessed) output. While many approaches exist that utilize the label-correlation and dependency information during training, to the best of our knowledge, this is the first work that uses this knowledge as part of a post-processing step that is independent of MLL algorithms.

Acknowledgements

We are grateful to TC Liou, Chasel Su, Yu-Ting Chang, Brook Yang for their contributions to this project. We also wish to thank Kapil Thadani, Parikshit Shah and the anonymous reviewers for their feedback.

References

Rasim M Alguliev, Ramiz M Aliguliyev, and Chingiz A Mehdiyev. 2011. psum-sade: a modified p-median problem and self-adaptive differential evolution algorithm for text summarization. *Applied Computational Intelligence and Soft Computing* 2011:11.

Rumen Andonov, Vincent Poirriez, and Sanjay Rajopadhye. 2000. Unbounded knapsack problem: Dynamic programming revisited. *European Journal of Operational Research* 123(2):394–407.

Nicholas Andrews and Naren Ramakrishnan. 2008. Seeded discovery of base relations in large corpora. In *Proceedings of the Conference on Empirical Methods in Natural Language Processing*. ACL, pages 591–599.

Kush Bhatia, Himanshu Jain, Purushottam Kar, Prateek Jain, and Manik Varma. 2015. Locally non-linear embeddings for extreme multi-label learning. *CoRR* abs/1507.02743.

Sheng Chen, Akshay Soni, Aasish Pappu, and Yashar Mehdad. 2017. Doctag2vec: An embedding based multi-label learning approach for document tagging. In *2nd Workshop on Representation Learning for NLP*.

Yao-nan Chen and Hsuan-tien Lin. 2012. Feature-aware label space dimension reduction for multi-label classification. In *Advances in NIPS 25*, pages 1529–1537.

Jackie Chi Kit Cheung, Giuseppe Carenini, and Raymond T Ng. 2009. Optimization-based content selection for opinion summarization. In *Proceedings of the 2009 Workshop on Language Generation and Summarisation*. ACL, pages 7–14.

Krzysztof Dembszynski, Willem Waegeman, Weiwei Cheng, and Eyke Hüllermeier. 2010. On label dependence in multilabel classification. In *ICML Workshop on Learning from Multi-label data*.

Jack Edmonds. 1967. Optimum branchings. *Journal of Research of the National Bureau of Standards B* 71(4):233–240.

EN Gilbert and HO Pollak. 1968. Steiner minimal trees. *SIAM Journal on Applied Mathematics* 16(1):1–29.

Camille Guinaudeau and Michael Strube. 2013. Graph-based local coherence modeling. In *ACL (1)*. pages 93–103.

Yuhong Guo and Suicheng Gu. 2011. Multi-label classification using conditional dependency networks. In *IJCAI*. volume 22, page 1300.

Tsutomu Hirao, Yasuhisa Yoshida, Masaaki Nishino, Norihito Yasuda, and Masaaki Nagata. 2013. Single-document summarization as a tree knapsack problem. In *EMNLP*. volume 13, pages 1515–1520.

Sheng-Jun Huang and Zhi-Hua Zhou. 2012. Multi-label learning by exploiting label correlations locally. In *Twenty-Sixth AAAI Conference on Artificial Intelligence*.

Heng Ji, Benoit Favre, Wen-Pin Lin, Dan Gillick, Dilek Hakkani-Tur, and Ralph Grishman. 2013. Open-domain multi-document summarization via information extraction: Challenges and prospects. In *Multi-source, Multilingual Information Extraction and Summarization*, Springer, pages 177–201.

Ashish Kapoor, Raajay Viswanathan, and Prateek Jain. 2012. Multilabel classification using bayesian compressed sensing pages 2645–2653.

Yoon Kim. 2014. Convolutional neural networks for sentence classification. *arXiv preprint arXiv:1408.5882* .

Xiangnan Kong, Michael K Ng, and Zhi-Hua Zhou. 2013. Transductive multilabel learning via label set propagation. *IEEE Transactions on Knowledge and Data Engineering* 25(3):704–719.

Wenjie Li, Mingli Wu, Qin Lu, Wei Xu, and Chunfa Yuan. 2006. Extractive summarization using inter- and intra-event relevance. In *Proceedings of the 21st International Conference on Computational Linguistics and the 44th annual meeting of the Association for Computational Linguistics*. Association for Computational Linguistics, pages 369–376.

Hui Lin and Jeff Bilmes. 2010. Multi-document summarization via budgeted maximization of submodular functions. In *Human Language Technologies: The 2010 NAACL*. ACL, pages 912–920.

Tengfei Ma and Xiaojun Wan. 2010. Multi-document summarization using minimum distortion. In *Data Mining (ICDM), 2010 IEEE 10th International Conference on*. IEEE, pages 354–363.

Ryan McDonald. 2007. A study of global inference algorithms in multi-document summarization. In *European Conference on Information Retrieval*. Springer, pages 557–564.

Ryan McDonald, Fernando Pereira, Kiril Ribarov, and Jan Hajič. 2005. Non-projective dependency parsing using spanning tree algorithms. In *Proceedings HLT and EMNLP*. ACL, pages 523–530.

Kurt Mehlhorn. 1988. A faster approximation algorithm for the steiner problem in graphs. *Information Processing Letters* 27(3):125–128.

Yi-Feng Pan, Xinwen Hou, and Cheng-Lin Liu. 2011. A hybrid approach to detect and localize texts in natural scene images. *IEEE Transactions on Image Processing* 20(3):800–813.

Akshay Soni and Yashar Mehdad. 2017. Ripml: A restricted isometry property based approach to multilabel learning. *arXiv preprint arXiv:1702.05181* .

Grigorios Tsoumakas, Anastasios Dimou, Eleftherios Spyromitros, Vasileios Mezaris, Ioannis Kompatsiaris, and Ioannis Vlahavas. 2009. Correlation-based pruning of stacked binary relevance models for multi-label learning.

Ramakrishna Varadarajan and Vagelis Hristidis. 2006. A system for query-specific document summarization. In *Proceedings of the 15th ACM international conference on Information and knowledge management*. ACM, pages 622–631.

Florian Wolf and Edward Gibson. 2004. Paragraph-, word-, and coherence-based approaches to sentence ranking: A comparison of algorithm and human performance. In *Proceedings of the 42nd ACL*. page 383.

Zoulficar Younes, Fahed Abdallah, and Thierry Denœux. 2008. Multi-label classification algorithm derived from k-nearest neighbor rule with label dependencies. In *Signal Processing Conference, 2008 16th European*. IEEE, pages 1–5.

Hsiang-Fu Yu, Prateek Jain, Purushottam Kar, and Inderjit S. Dhillon. 2014. Large-scale Multi-label Learning with Missing Labels. In *ICML*.

Learning Kernels over Strings using Gaussian Processes

Daniel Beck* Trevor Cohn
Computing and Information Systems
University of Melbourne, Australia
{d.beck, t.cohn}@unimelb.edu.au

Abstract

Non-contiguous word sequences are widely known to be important in modelling natural language. However they are not explicitly encoded in common text representations. In this work we propose a model for text processing using string kernels, capable of flexibly representing non-contiguous sequences. Specifically, we derive a vectorised version of the string kernel algorithm and their gradients, allowing efficient hyperparameter optimisation as part of a Gaussian Process framework. Experiments on synthetic data and text regression for emotion analysis show the promise of this technique.

1 Introduction

Text representations are a key component in any Natural Language Processing (NLP) task. A common approach for this is to average word vectors over a piece of text. For instance, a bag-of-words (BOW) model uses one-hot encoding as vectors and it is still a strong baseline for many tasks. More recently, approaches based on dense word representations (Turian et al., 2010; Mikolov et al., 2013) also showed to perform well.

However, averaging vectors discards any word order information from the original text, which can be fundamental for more involved NLP problems. Convolutional and recurrent neural networks (CNNs/RNNs) can keep word order but still treat a text fragment as a *contiguous* sequence of words, encoding a bias towards short- over long-distance relations between words. Some RNN models like the celebrated LSTMs (Hochreiter

and Schmidhuber, 1997) perform better in capturing these phenomena but still have limitations. Recent work (Tai et al., 2015; Eriguchi et al., 2016) showed evidence that LSTM-based models can be enhanced by adding syntactic information, which can encode relations between non-contiguous words. This line of work requires the employment of accurate syntactic parsers, restricting their applicability to specific languages and/or text domains.

In this work we propose to revisit an approach which goes beyond contiguous word representations: string kernels (SKs). Their main power comes from the ability to represent arbitrary non-contiguous word sequences through dynamic programming algorithms. Our main contribution is a model that combines SKs with Gaussian Processes (GPs) (Rasmussen and Williams, 2006), allowing us to leverage efficient gradient-based methods to learn kernel hyperparameters. The reasoning behind our approach is that by optimising hyperparameters in a fine-grained way we can guide the kernel to learn better task-specific text representations automatically.

To enable the learning procedure we redefine the SK algorithm in a vectorised form and derive its gradients. We perform experiments using synthetic data, giving evidence that the model can capture non-trivial representations. Finally, we also show how the approach fares in a real dataset and explain how the learned hyperparameters can be interpreted as text representations.

2 String Kernels

Here we give a brief intuition[1] on string kernels, based on the formulation proposed by Cancedda

---

*This work was partially done while the first author was at The University of Sheffield, United Kingdom.

[1]We give a thorough explanation of the original SK equations in the Supplementary Material, as well as a detailed derivation of our vectorised version with its hyperparameter gradients.

Proceedings of the The 8th International Joint Conference on Natural Language Processing, pages 67–73,
Taipei, Taiwan, November 27 – December 1, 2017 ©2017 AFNLP

et al. (2003). Let $|s|$ be the length of a string s, s_j the j−th symbol in s and $s_{:-1}$ the prefix containing the full string s except for the last symbol. Define $\text{sim}(a, b)$ as a similarity measure between individual symbols a and b. Given two strings s and t and a maximum n-gram length n, the string kernel $k(s, t)$ can be obtained using the recursion

$$k_0'(s, t) = 1, \text{ for all } s, t,$$
$$\text{for all } i = 1, \ldots, n - 1 :$$
$$k_i'(sa, t) = \lambda_g k_i'(s, t) + k_i''(sa, t),$$
$$k_i''(sa, tb) = \lambda_g k_i''(sa, t) + \lambda_m^2 \text{sim}(a, b)k_{i-1}'(s, t),$$
$$k_n(sa, t) = k_n(s, t)+$$
$$\lambda_m^2 \sum_{j}^{|t|} \text{sim}(a, t_j)k_{n-1}'(s, t_{:-1}),$$
$$k(s, t) = \sum_{i=1}^{n} \mu_i k_i(s, t),$$

where λ_g and λ_m are decay hyperparameters for symbol gaps and matches, respectively, and μ_i is the weight for the kernel of n-gram order i. The decay hyperparameters smooth the kernel values when sequences are very similar to each other while the n-gram weights help to tune the signal coming from different subsequence lengths.

Our goal is optimise the kernel hyperparameters in a fine-grained way using gradient-based methods. For this, we first redefine the kernel in a vectorised form. This not only eases gradient derivations but also allow our implementation to capitalise on recent advances in parallel processing and linear algebra libraries for better performance.[2] Given two strings s and t, the equations for our vectorised version are defined as

$$\mathbf{S} = \mathbf{E}_s \mathbf{E}_t^T,$$
$$\mathbf{K}_0' = \mathbf{1},$$
$$\mathbf{K}_i' = \mathbf{D}_{|s|} \mathbf{K}_i'' \mathbf{D}_{|t|},$$
$$\mathbf{K}_i'' = \lambda_m^2 (\mathbf{S} \odot \mathbf{K}_{i-1}'),$$
$$k_i = \lambda_m^2 \sum_{j,k} (\mathbf{S} \odot \mathbf{K}_i')_{j,k},$$
$$k(s, t) = \boldsymbol{\mu}^T \mathbf{k},$$

where $\mathbf{E}_s$ and $\mathbf{E}_t$ are matrices of symbol embeddings for each string, $\odot$ is the Hadamard product

and $\mathbf{D}_\ell \in \mathbb{R}^\ell \times \mathbb{R}^\ell$ is the matrix

$$\mathbf{D}_\ell = \begin{bmatrix} 0 & \lambda_g^0 & \lambda_g^1 & \ldots & \lambda_g^{|\ell|-2} \\ 0 & 0 & \lambda_g^0 & \ldots & \lambda_g^{|\ell|-3} \\ \vdots & \vdots & \vdots & \ddots & \vdots \\ 0 & 0 & 0 & \ldots & \lambda_g^0 \\ 0 & 0 & 0 & \ldots & 0 \end{bmatrix}$$

with $\ell \in \{|s|, |t|\}$ being the corresponding string length for s or t. The purpose of D is to unroll the recursion from the original kernel equations. For the matrices $\mathbf{E}$, we focus on dense word embeddings but they could also be one-hot vectors, simulating hard matching between symbols.

Given this formulation, the hyperparameter gradients can be easily derived. From the vectorised definition, we can see that gradients with respect to $\boldsymbol{\mu}$ are simply $\mathbf{k}$, the intermediate n-gram specific kernel values. For λ_g and λ_m the gradients simply follow the kernel equations in an analogous manner. Note that the gradient calculations do not affect the time or space complexity of the main kernel, and in practice they can be obtained together using a single algorithm since they share many common terms.

Finally, we incorporate the kernel into a Gaussian Process regression model (henceforth, GP-SK). We assume the label y for an input string s is sampled from a function $f(s) \sim \mathcal{GP}(0, k(s, t))$, with t iterating over all other strings in a dataset. With this, we can define the marginal likelihood as

$$\log p(\mathbf{y}|\mathbf{s}, \boldsymbol{\theta}) = \log \int_f p(\mathbf{y}|\mathbf{s}, \boldsymbol{\theta}, f)p(f),$$
$$= -\frac{\mathbf{y}^T \mathbf{G}^{-1} \mathbf{y}}{2} - \frac{\log |\mathbf{G}|}{2} - \frac{n \log 2\pi}{2},$$

where $\mathbf{G}$ is the Gram matrix with respect to the training set $\mathbf{s}$ and $\boldsymbol{\theta}$ is the set of kernel hyperparameters. By taking its derivative and plugging in the kernel gradients, we can optimise its hyperparameters using gradient-based methods.[3]

2.1 Complexity and Runtime Analysis

The original string kernel algorithm has complexity $O(n|s||s'|)$, i.e., quadratic in the size of the largest string. Our vectorised version is cubic, $O(n\ell^3)$, where $\ell = \max(|s|, |s'|)$, due to two matrix multiplications in the equations for $\mathbf{K}_i'$. Another way of reaching this result is to realise that

---

[2]Our open-source implementation is based on TensorFlow (Abadi et al., 2015).

[3]We refer the reader to Rasmussen and Williams (2006, Chap.5) for an in-depth explanation of this procedure.

$\mathbf{K}_i''$ is actually not needed anymore: all calculations can be made by updating $\mathbf{K}_i'$ only. In fact, Lodhi et al. (2002) introduced the term k'' as a way to reduce the complexity from $O(n|s||s'|^2)$ to $O(n|s||s'|)$. The complexity for the gradient calculations is also $O(n\ell^3)$.

However, even though our vectorised version has higher complexity, in practice we see large gains in runtime. We assess this empirically running the following experiment with synthetic strings:

- We employ characters as symbols with a one-hot encoding as the embedding, using all English ASCII letters, including uppercase (52 symbols in total);

- The maximum subsequence length is set to 5;

- 100 instances are generated randomly by uniformly sampling a character until reaching the desired string length.

We test our kernels with lengths ranging from 10 to 100.

Figure 1 shows wall-clock time measurements as the string lengths increase.[4] It is clear that the vectorised version is vastly faster than the original one, with up to two orders of magnitude. Comparing the CPU and GPU vectorised implementations, we see that we can reap benefits using a GPU when dealing with long sentences. GPU processing can be further enhanced by allowing portions of the Gram matrix to be calculated in batches instead of one instance at a time.

These results are intriguing because we do not expect a quadratic complexity algorithm to be outperformed by a cubic one. It is important to note that while we made efforts to optimise the code, there is no guarantee that either of our implementations is making the most of the underlying hardware. We plan to investigate these matters in more detail in the future.

3 Experiments

We assess our approach empirically with two sets of experiments using natural language sentences as inputs in a regression setting.[5] The first one

<hr>

[4]Experiments were done in a machine with an Intel Xeon E5-2687W 3.10GHz as CPU and a GTX TITAN X as GPU.

[5]Code to replicate the experiments in this section is available at https://github.com/beckdaniel/ijcnlp17_sk. This also include the performance experiments in Section 2.1.

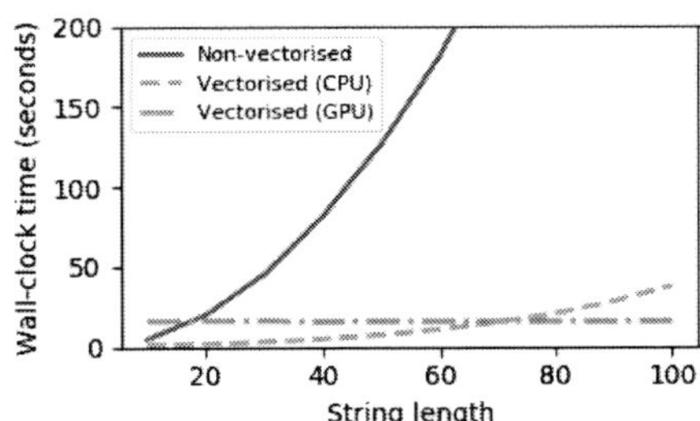

Figure 1: Wall-clock time measurements for the SK versions using different string lengths. Time is measured in seconds and correspond to the calculation of a 100×100 Gram matrix with random strings of a specific length.

uses synthetically generated response variables, providing a controlled environment to check the modelling capacities of our method. The second set uses labels from an emotion analysis dataset and serve as a proof of concept for our approach.

3.1 Synthetic Labels

Consider an ideal scenario where the data is distributed according to a GP-SK. Here we aim at answering two questions: 1) whether we can retrieve the original distribution through optimisation and 2) whether a simpler model can capture the same distribution. The first gives us evidence on how feasible is to learn such a model while the second justify the choice of a SK compared to simpler alternatives.

To answer these questions we employ the following protocol. First we define a GP-SK with the following hyperparameter values:

$\lambda_g = 0.5$	$\lambda_m = 0.2$	$\sigma^2 = 0.1$
$\mu_1 = 1.0$	$\mu_2 = 0.5$	$\mu_3 = 0.25$

where σ^2 is the label GP noise. This choice of hyperparameter values is arbitrary: our goal is simply to check if we can retrieve these values through optimisation. The same procedure could be applied for different values.

After defining the GP-SK model we calculate the its corresponding Gram matrix using a set of sentences and their respective word embeddings. This matrix contains the covariances of a multivariate Gaussian distribution with mean vector $\mathbf{0}$ and we can sample from this Gaussian to create synthetic labels. As inputs we use a random sample of sentences from the Penn Treebank (Marcus et al., 1993) and represent each word as a 100d GloVe embedding (Pennington et al., 2014).[6]

The data sampled from the procedure above is used to train another GP-SK with *randomly initialised* hyperparameters, which are then optimised. We run this procedure 20 times, using the same inputs but sampling new labels every time.

Hyperparameter stability Figure 2 shows the hyperparameter values retrieved after optimisation, for increasing training set sizes. The decay hyperparameters are the most stable ones, being retrieved with high confidence independent of the dataset size. The original noise value is also obtained but it needs more instances (1000) for that.

The n-gram coefficients are less stable compared to the other hyperparameters, although the uncertainty seems to diminish with larger datasets. A possible explanation is the presence of some level of overspecification, meaning that very different coefficient values may reach similar marginal likelihoods, which in turn corresponds to multiple plausible explanations of the data. Solutions for this include imposing bounds to the coefficients or fixing them, while freely optimising the more stable hyperparameters.

Predictive performance To evaluate if the GP-SK models can be subsumed by simpler ones, we assess the predictive performance on a disjoint test set containing 200 sentences. Test labels were sampled from the same GP-SK distribution used to generate the training labels, simulating a setting where all the data follows the same distribution.

Figure 3 shows results across different training set sizes, in Pearson's r correlation. We compare with GP baselines trained on averaged embeddings, using either a linear or a Squared Exponential (SE)[7] kernel. The SK model outperforms the baselines, showing that even a non-linear model can not capture the GP-SK distribution.

To investigate the influence of hyperparameter optimisation, we also show results in Figure 3 for a SK model with randomly initialised hyperparameter values. Clearly, optimisation helps to improve the model, even in the low data scenarios.

3.2 Emotion Analysis

As a first step towards working with real world data, we employ the proposed approach in an emo-

---

[6]nlp.stanford.edu/projects/glove. We use the version trained on Wikipedia and Gigaword.

[7]Also known as RBF kernel.

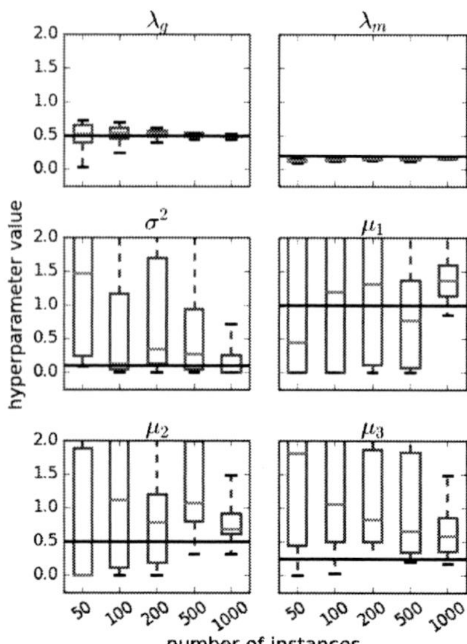

Figure 2: String kernel hyperparameter optimisation results. Original hyperparameter values are shown as black lines while each box corresponds to a specific dataset size. Red lines show the median values, while box limits correspond to the $[0.25, 0.75]$ quantiles.

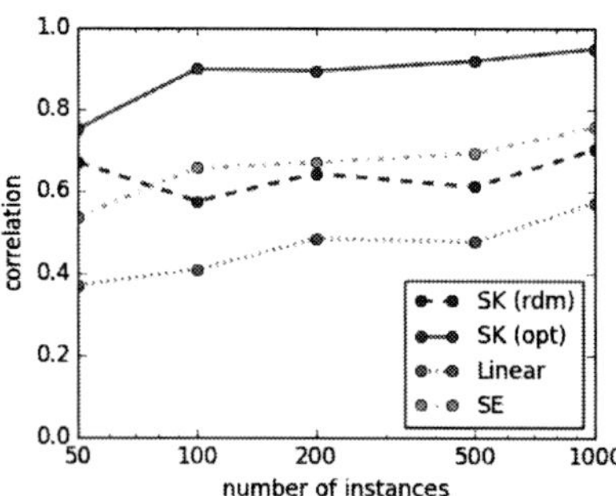

Figure 3: Prediction results, averaged over 20 runs. "SK (rdm)" corresponds to string kernel with random hyperparameter values and "SK (opt)", with optimised hyperparameters.

tion analysis setting, where the goal is to model latent emotions in text. We use the "Affective Text" dataset from the SemEval2007 shared task (Strapparava and Mihalcea, 2007), composed of 1,250 News headlines annotated with 6 scores, one per emotion. Scores are in the $[0-100]$ range and were provided by human judges. The models, baselines and embeddings are the same used in Section 3.1. Instead of using a fixed split, we perform 10-fold

	NLPD ↓	MAE ↓	r ↑
SK	4.06	10.53	0.586
Linear	4.09	11.03	0.539
SE	4.03	10.09	0.611

Table 1: Emotion analysis results, averaged over all emotions and cross-validation folds.

λ_g	7.36×10^{-7}	λ_m	0.0918		
μ_1	12.37	μ_2	33.73	μ_3	154.51
μ_4	2.58	μ_5	8.54		

Table 2: SK hyperparameter values for a single model predicting the emotion *surprise*.

cross validation and average the results.

Table 1 compares the performance of GP-SK with the baselines trained on averaged embeddings. Besides Pearson's r correlation, we also compare the models in terms of Mean Absolute Error (MAE) and Negative Log Predictive Density (NLPD), a metric that takes into account the full predictive distribution into account (Quiñonero-Candela et al., 2006). The main figure is that GP-SK outperforms the linear baseline but lags behind the SE one. This shows that non-linearities present in the data can not be captured by the GP-SK model. Since the string kernel is essentially a dot product over exponentially-sized vectors, it is not surprising that it is unable to capture non-linear behaviour. This gives us evidence that developing non-linear extensions of string kernels could be a promising avenue for future work.

Inspecting hyperparameters Probing the hyperparameters can give us insights about what kind of representation the kernel is learning. On Table 2 we show the values for one of the models that predict the emotion *surprise*. We can see that λ_g has a very low value, while the μ values show a preference for subsequences up to 3 words. This lets us conclude that the kernel learned a text representation close to *contiguous trigrams*.

4   Related Work

String kernels were originally proposed for text classification (Lodhi et al., 2002; Cancedda et al., 2003) while recent work apply them for native language identification (Ionescu et al., 2014) and sentiment analysis (Giménez-Pérez et al., 2017), with promising results. Hyperparameter optimisation in these works is done via grid search and could

potentially benefit from our proposed approach.

Gaussian Processes have been recently employed in a number of NLP tasks such as emotion analysis (Beck et al., 2014), detection of temporal patterns in microblogs (Preoiuc-Pietro and Cohn, 2013), rumour propagation in social media (Lukasik et al., 2015) and translation quality estimation (Cohn and Specia, 2013; Shah et al., 2013; Beck et al., 2016). These previous works encode text inputs as fixed-size vectors instead of working directly on the text inputs.

Among other recent work that aim at learning general structured kernels, the most similar to ours is Beck et al. (2015), who use GPs to learn tree kernels. Lei et al. (2017) unroll string kernel computations and derive equivalent neural network architectures. In contrast, our work put the learning procedure inside a GP model, inheriting the advantages of Bayesian model selection procedures. Nevertheless, many of their kernel ideas could be applied to a GP setting, which we leave for future work.

5   Conclusion

In this paper we provided the first steps in combining string kernels and Gaussian Processes for NLP tasks, allowing us to learn the text representations used by the kernels by optimising its hyperparameters in a fine-grained way. Experiments showed promising results in capturing text patterns that are not modelled by simpler baselines.

For future work, we plan to extend the model to account for non-linear representations, using approaches such as Arc-cosine kernels (Cho and Saul, 2009) and also applying the ideas from Lei et al. (2017). Another important avenue to pursue is to scale the model to larger datasets using recent advances in Sparse GPs (Titsias, 2009; Hensman et al., 2013). These in turn can enable richer kernel parameterisations not only for strings but other structures as well.

Acknowledgements

Daniel Beck was supported by funding from CNPq/Brazil (No. 237999/2012-9) and from the Australian Research Council (DP160102686). Trevor Cohn is the recipient of an Australian Research Council Future Fellowship (project number FT130101105). The authors would also like to thank the anonymous reviewers for their comments.

References

Martín Abadi, Ashish Agarwal, Paul Barham, Eugene Brevdo, Zhifeng Chen, Craig Citro, Greg S. Corrado, Andy Davis, Jeffrey Dean, Matthieu Devin, Sanjay Ghemawat, Ian Goodfellow, Andrew Harp, Geoffrey Irving, Michael Isard, Yangqing Jia, Rafael Josefowicz, Lukasz Kaiser, Manjunath Kudlur, Josh Levenberg, Dan Mané, Rajat Monga, Sherry Moore, Derek Murray, Chris Olah, Mike Schuster, Jonathon Shlens, Benoit Steiner, Ilya Sutskever, Kunal Talwar, Paul Tucker, Vincent Vanhoucke, Vijay Vasudevan, Fernanda Viégas, Oriol Vinyals, Pete Warden, Martin Wattenberg, Martin Wicke, Yuan Yu, and Xiaoqiang Zheng. 2015. TensorFlow: Large-Scale Machine Learning on Heterogeneous Distributed Systems.

Daniel Beck, Trevor Cohn, Christian Hardmeier, and Lucia Specia. 2015. Learning Structural Kernels for Natural Language Processing. *Transactions of the Association for Computational Linguistics*, 3:461–473.

Daniel Beck, Trevor Cohn, and Lucia Specia. 2014. Joint Emotion Analysis via Multi-task Gaussian Processes. In *Proceedings of EMNLP*, pages 1798–1803.

Daniel Beck, Lucia Specia, and Trevor Cohn. 2016. Exploring Prediction Uncertainty in Machine Translation Quality Estimation. In *Proceedings of CoNLL*.

Nicola Cancedda, Eric Gaussier, Cyril Goutte, and Jean-Michel Renders. 2003. Word-Sequence Kernels. *The Journal of Machine Learning Research*, 3:1059–1082.

Youngmin Cho and Lawrence K Saul. 2009. Kernel Methods for Deep Learning. In *Proceedings of NIPS*, pages 1–9.

Trevor Cohn and Lucia Specia. 2013. Modelling Annotator Bias with Multi-task Gaussian Processes: An Application to Machine Translation Quality Estimation. In *Proceedings of ACL*, pages 32–42.

Akiko Eriguchi, Kazuma Hashimoto, and Yoshimasa Tsuruoka. 2016. Tree-to-Sequence Attentional Neural Machine Translation. In *Proceedings of ACL*.

Rosa M. Giménez-Pérez, Marc Franco-Salvador, and Paolo Rosso. 2017. Single and Cross-domain Polarity Classification using String Kernels. In *Proceedings of EACL*, pages 558–563.

James Hensman, Nicolò Fusi, and Neil D. Lawrence. 2013. Gaussian Processes for Big Data. In *Proceedings of UAI*, pages 282–290.

Sepp Hochreiter and Jürgen Schmidhuber. 1997. Long Short-term Memory. *Neural Computation*, 9(8):1735–80.

Radu Tudor Ionescu, Marius Popescu, and Aoife Cahill. 2014. Can characters reveal your native language? A language-independent approach to native language identification. In *Proceedings of EMNLP*, pages 1363–1373.

Tao Lei, Wengong Jin, Regina Barzilay, and Tommi Jaakkola. 2017. Deriving Neural Architectures from Sequence and Graph Kernels. In *Proceedings of ICML*.

Huma Lodhi, Craig Saunders, John Shawe-Taylor, Nello Cristianini, and Chris Watkins. 2002. Text Classification using String Kernels. *The Journal of Machine Learning Research*, 2:419–444.

Michal Lukasik, Trevor Cohn, and Kalina Bontcheva. 2015. Point Process Modelling of Rumour Dynamics in Social Media. In *Proceedings of ACL*, pages 518–523.

Mitchell P. Marcus, Beatrice Santorini, and Mary Ann Marcinkiewicz. 1993. Building a large annotated corpus of English: The Penn Treebank. *Computational Linguistics*, 19(2):313–330.

Tomas Mikolov, Ilya Sutskever, Kai Chen, Greg Corrado, and Jeffrey Dean. 2013. Distributed Representations of Words and Phrases and their Compositionality. In *Proceedings of NIPS*, pages 1–9.

Jeffrey Pennington, Richard Socher, and Christopher D. Manning. 2014. GloVe: Global Vectors for Word Representation. In *Proceedings of EMNLP*, pages 1532–1543.

Daniel Preoiuc-Pietro and Trevor Cohn. 2013. A temporal model of text periodicities using Gaussian Processes. In *Proceedings of EMNLP*, pages 977–988.

Joaquin Quiñonero-Candela, Carl Edward Rasmussen, Fabian Sinz, Olivier Bousquet, and Bernhard Schölkopf. 2006. Evaluating Predictive Uncertainty Challenge. *MLCW 2005, Lecture Notes in Computer Science*, 3944:1–27.

Carl Edward Rasmussen and Christopher K. I. Williams. 2006. *Gaussian processes for machine learning*, volume 1. MIT Press Cambridge.

Kashif Shah, Trevor Cohn, and Lucia Specia. 2013. An Investigation on the Effectiveness of Features for Translation Quality Estimation. In *Proceedings of MT Summit XIV*.

Carlo Strapparava and Rada Mihalcea. 2007. SemEval-2007 Task 14 : Affective Text. In *Proceedings of SemEval*, pages 70–74.

Kai Sheng Tai, Richard Socher, and Christopher D. Manning. 2015. Improved semantic representations from tree-structured long short-term memory networks. In *Proceedings of ACL*.

Michalis K. Titsias. 2009. Variational Learning of Inducing Variables in Sparse Gaussian Processes. In *Proceedings of AISTATS*, volume 5, pages 567–574.

Joseph Turian, Lev Ratinov, and Yoshua Bengio. 2010. Word Representations: A Simple and General Method for Semi-supervised Learning. In *Proceedings of ACL*, pages 384–394.

Substring Frequency Features for Segmentation of Japanese Katakana Words with Unlabeled Corpora

Yoshinari Fujinuma[*]
Computer Science
University of Colorado
Boulder, CO
Yoshinari.Fujinuma@colorado.edu

Alvin C. Grissom II
Mathematics and Computer Science
Ursinus College
Collegeville, PA
agrissom@ursinus.edu

Abstract

Word segmentation is crucial in natural language processing tasks for unsegmented languages. In Japanese, many out-of-vocabulary words appear in the phonetic syllabary katakana, making segmentation more difficult due to the lack of clues found in mixed script settings. In this paper, we propose a straightforward approach based on a variant of tf-idf and apply it to the problem of word segmentation in Japanese. Even though our method uses only an unlabeled corpus, experimental results show that it achieves performance comparable to existing methods that use manually labeled corpora. Furthermore, it improves performance of simple word segmentation models trained on a manually labeled corpus.

1 Introduction

In languages without explicit segmentation, word segmentation is a crucial step of natural language processing tasks. In Japanese, this problem is less severe than in Chinese because of the existence of three different scripts: *hiragana*, *katakana*, and *kanji*, which are Chinese characters.[1] However, katakana words are known to degrade word segmentation performance because of out-of-vocabulary (OOV) words which do not appear manually segmented corpora (Nakazawa et al., 2005; Kaji and Kitsuregawa, 2011). Creation of new words is common in Japanese; around

20% of the katakana words in newspaper articles are OOV words (Breen, 2009). For example, some katakana compound loanwords are not transliterated but rather "Japanized" (e.g., ガソリンスタンド *gasorinsutando* "gasoline stand", meaning "gas station" in English) or abbreviated (e.g., スマートフォンケース *sumātofonkēsu* ("smartphone case"), which is abbreviated as スマホケース *sumahokēsu*). Abbreviations may also undergo phonetic and corresponding orthographic changes, as in the case of スマートフォン *sumātofon* ("smartphone"), which, in the abbreviated term, shortens the long vowel $\bar{a}$ to a, and replaces フォ *fo* with ホ *ho*. This change is then propagated to compound words, such as スマホケース *sumahokēsu* ("smartphone case"). Word segmentation of compound words is important for improving results in downstream tasks, such as information retrieval (Braschler and Ripplinger, 2004; Alfonseca et al., 2008), machine translation (Koehn and Knight, 2003), and information extraction from microblogs (Bansal et al., 2015).

Hagiwara and Sekine (2013) incorporated an English corpus by projecting Japanese transliterations to words from an English corpus; however, loanwords that are not transliterated (such as *sumaho* for "smartphone") cannot be segmented by the use of an English corpus alone. We investigate a more efficient use of a Japanese corpus by incorporating a variant of the well-known tf-idf weighting scheme (Salton and Buckley, 1988), which we refer to as *term frequency-inverse substring frequency* or **tf-issf**. The core idea of our approach[2] is to assign scores based on the likelihood that a given katakana substring is a word token, using only statistics from an unlabeled corpus.

---

[*]Part of the work was done while the first author was at Amazon Japan.

[1]Hiragana and katakana are the two distinct character sets representing the same Japanese sounds. These two character sets are used for different purposes, with katakana typically used for transliterations of loanwords. Kanji are typically used for nouns.

---

[2]Our code is available at https://www.github.com/akkikiki/katakana_segmentation.

Proceedings of the The 8th International Joint Conference on Natural Language Processing, pages 74–79,
Taipei, Taiwan, November 27 – December 1, 2017 ©2017 AFNLP

Our contributions are as follows:

1. We show that a word segmentation model using tf-issf alone outperforms a previously proposed frequency-based method and that it produces comparable results to various Japanese tokenizers.

2. We show that tf-issf improves the F1-score of word segmentation models trained on manually labeled data by more than 5%.

2　Proposed Method

In this section, we describe the katakana word segmentation problem and our approach to it.

2.1　Term Frequency-Inverse Substring Frequency

Let S be a sequence of katakana characters, Y be the set of all possible segmentations, $y \in Y$ be a possible segmentation, and y_i be a substring of y. Then, for instance, $y = y_1 y_2 ... y_n$ is a possible word segmentation of S with n segments.

We now propose a method to segment katakana OOV words. Our approach, *term frequency-inverse substring frequency* (**tf-issf**), is a variant of the tf-idf weighting method, which computes a score for each candidate segmentation. We calculate the score of a katakana string y_i with

$$\text{tf-issf}(y_i) = \frac{tf(y_i)}{sf(y_i)}, \tag{1}$$

where $tf(y_i)$ is the number of occurrences of y_i as a katakana term in a corpus and $sf(y_i)$ is the number of unique katakana terms that have y_i as a substring. We regard consecutive katakana characters as a single katakana term when computing tf-issf.

We compute the product of tf-issf scores over a string to score the segmentation

$$Score(y) = \prod_{y_i \in y} \text{tf-issf}(y_i), \tag{2}$$

and choose the optimal segmentation y^* with

$$y^* = \arg\max_{y \in Y} Score(y|S). \tag{3}$$

Intuitively, if a string appears frequently as a word substring, we treat it as a meaningless sequence.[3] While substrings of consecutive

---

[3] A typical example is a single character substring. However, it is possible for single-character substrings could be word tokens.

ID	Notation	Feature
1	y_i	unigram
2	y_{i-1}, y_i	bigram
3	length(y_i)	num. of characters in y_i

Table 1:　Features used for the structured perceptron.

katakana can, in principle, be a meaningful character n-gram, this rarely occurs, and tf-issf successfully penalizes the score of such sequences of characters.

Figure 1 shows an example of a word lattice for the loan compound word "smartphone case" with the desired segmentation path in bold. When building a lattice, we only create a node for a substring that appears as a term in the unlabeled corpus and does not start with a small katakana letter[4] or a prolonged sound mark "—", as such characters are rarely the first character in a word. Including terms or consecutive katakana characters from an unlabeled corpus reduces the number of OOV words.

2.2　Structured Perceptron with tf-issf

To incorporate manually labeled data and to compare with other supervised Japanese tokenizers, we use the structured perceptron (Collins, 2002). This model represents the score as

$$Score(y) = \mathbf{w} \cdot \phi(y), \tag{4}$$

where $\phi(y)$ is a feature function and $\mathbf{w}$ is a weight vector. Features used in the structured perceptron are shown in Table 1. We use the surface-level features used by Kaji and Kitsuregawa (2011) and decode with the Viterbi algorithm. We incorporate tf-issf into the structured perceptron as the initial feature weight for unigrams instead of initializing the weight vector to 0.[5] Specifically, we use $\log(\text{tf-issf}(y_i) + 1)$ for the initial weights to avoid overemphasizing the tf-issf value (Kaji and Kitsuregawa, 2011). In this way, we can directly adjust tf-issf values using a manually labeled corpus. Unlike the approach of Xiao et al. (2002), which uses tf-idf to resolve segmentation ambiguities in Chinese, we regard each katakana term as one document to compute its inverse document (substring) frequency.

---

[4] Such letters are ア *a*, イ *i*, ウ *u*, エ *e*, オ *o*, カ *ka*, ケ *ke*, ツ *tsu*, ヤ *ya*, ユ *yu*, ヨ *yo*, and ワ *wa*.

[5] We also attempt to incorporate tf-issf as an individual feature, but this does not improve the segmentation results.

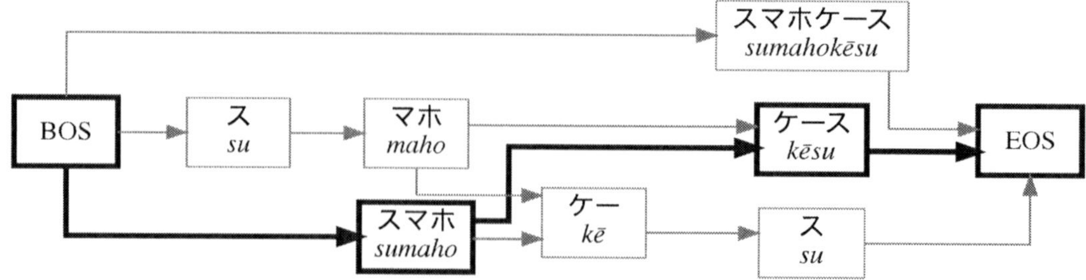

Figure 1: An example lattice for a katakana word segmentation. We use the Viterbi algorithm to find the optimal segmentation from the beginning of the string (BOS) to the end (EOS), shown by the bold edges and nodes. Only those katakana substrings which exist in the training corpus as words are considered. This example produces the correct segmentation, スマホ / ケース *sumaho / kēsu* ("smartphone case").

3 Experiments

We now describe our experiments. We run our proposed method under two different settings: 1) using only an unlabeled corpus (UNLABEL), and 2) using both an unlabeled corpus and a labeled corpus (BOTH). For the first experiment, we establish a baseline result using an approach proposed by Nakazawa et al. (2005) and compare this with using tf-issf alone. We conduct an experiment in the second setting to compare with other supervised approaches, including Japanese tokenizers.

3.1 Dataset

We compute the tf-issf value for each katakana substring using all of 2015 Japanese Wikipedia as an unlabeled training corpus. This consists of $1,937,006$ unique katakana terms.

Following Hagiwara and Sekine (2013), we test on both the general domain and on a domain with more OOV words. We use the Balanced Corpus of Contemporary Written Japanese (BCCWJ) (Maekawa et al., 2014) core data with $40,827$ katakana entries as the general domain test data. We use 3-fold cross-validation to train a structured perceptron classifier. To test on a more challenging domain with more OOV words (Saito et al., 2014) and even fewer space boundaries (Bansal et al., 2015), we also ask an annotator to label Twitter hashtags that *only* use katakana. We gather $273,711$ tweets with at least one hashtag from September 25, 2015 to October 28, 2015 using the Twitter Streaming API.[6] This provides a total of $4,863$ unique katakana hashtags, of which $1,251$ are observed in BCCWJ core

data. We filter out duplicate hashtags because the Twitter Streaming API collects a set of sample tweets that are biased compared with the overall tweet stream (Morstatter et al., 2013). We follow the BCCWJ annotation guidelines (Ogura et al., 2011) to conduct the annotation.[7]

3.2 Baselines

We follow previous work and use a frequency-based method as the baseline (Nakazawa et al., 2005; Kaji and Kitsuregawa, 2011):

$$y^* = \underset{y \in Y}{\arg\max} \frac{(\prod_{i=1}^n tf(y_i))^{\frac{1}{n}}}{\frac{C}{N^l} + \alpha} \qquad (5)$$

where l is the average length of all segmented substrings. Following Nakazawa et al. (2005) and Kaji and Kitsuregawa (2011), we set the hyperparameters to $C = 2500$, $N = 4$, and $\alpha = 0.7$. In addition, we filter out segmentations that have a segment starting with a small katakana letter or a prolonged sound mark "ー". The key difference between the baseline and tf-issf is that the length of a segmented substring is considered in the baseline method. An advantage of tf-issf over the baseline is that hyperparameters are not required.

Unsupervised segmentation (Goldwater et al., 2006; Mochihashi et al., 2009) can also be applied to katakana word segmentation; however, doing so on a large corpus is still challenging (Chen, 2013). Our work focuses on fast and scalable frequency-based methods.

We compare the performance of the word segmentation model trained with the structured per-

---

[6]https://dev.twitter.com/streaming/overview

[7]In addition, we stipulate that we always split transliterated compound words according to their spaces when they are back-transliterated to their original language.

	Method	BCCWJ				Twitter Hashtags			
		WER	P	R	F1	WER	P	R	F1
Frequency (UNLABEL)	Baseline	.174	.865	.890	.878	.576	.578	.716	.640
	tf-issf	**.119**	**.913**	**.907**	**.910**	**.312**	**.758**	**.784**	**.771**
Structured Perceptron (BOTH)	unigram	.023	.979	.984	.982	.330	.721	.767	.743
	+bigram	.023	.979	.984	.981	.316	.733	.772	.752
	tf-issf	.016	.987	.989	.988	.274	.778	.820	.798
	+bigram	**.014**	**.989**	**.990**	**.989**	.256	.793	**.827**	.810
Tokenizer	MeCab+IPADic	.155	.902	.865	.883	.424	.718	.624	.667
	MeCab+UniDic	.004*	.998*	.996*	.997*	.377	.704	.767	.734
	JUMAN	.105	.934	.908	.921	.282	**.818**	.751	.783
	Kytea	.010*	.992*	.993*	.993*	**.254**	.798	.823	**.811**
	RakutenMA	.077*	.936*	.953*	.944*	.383	.700	.752	.725

Table 2: Segmentation results for katakana words in BCCWJ and katakana Twitter hashtags. Following Hagiwara and Sekine (2013), Kytea, MeCab with UniDic (MeCab+UniDic), and RakutenMA results on BCCWJ are reported here for reference since these tokenizers use BCCWJ as a training corpus.

ceptron and tf-issf against that of state-of-the-art Japanese tokenizers JUMAN 7.01 (Kurohashi et al., 1994); MeCab 0.996 (Kudo et al., 2004) with two different dictionaries, IPADic (Asahara and Matsumoto, 2003) and UniDic (Den et al., 2007); Kytea 0.4.7 (Neubig et al., 2011); and RakutenMA (Hagiwara and Sekine, 2014).

3.3 Results

We use precision (P), recall (R), F1-score (F1), and word error rate (WER) to evaluate the performance of each method. The evaluation results are shown in Table 2.[8]

The use of tf-issf in the UNLABEL setting outperforms the other frequency-based method with statistical significance under McNemar's Test with $p < 0.01$ and yields comparable performance against supervised methods on BCCWJ. In Table 2, we show that tf-issf outperforms the frequency-based method proposed by Nakazawa et al. (2005). Although tf-issf only uses the statistics from Wikipedia, it achieves superior performance to MeCab with IPADic (MeCab+IPADic) and comparable performance to JUMAN.

The main limitation of using tf-issf alone is that it cannot completely avoid the frequency bias of the corpus. For instance, the most frequent katakana sequence occurring in Japanese Wikipedia is リンク *linku* ("link"), which is both ambiguous—potentially referring to either "rink" or "link"—and frequent, because it is the abbreviation for "hyperlinks". As a result, the tf-issf score of this string is much higher than average, which causes the word エナジードリンク *enajīdolinku* ("energy drink") to be segmented as エナジー /

ド / リンク *enajī / do / linku* ("energy / d / rink"). This problem can be ameliorated by incorporating BCCWJ to readjust the tf-issf values.

Table 2 also shows the segmentation result for Twitter hashtags. Here, the tf-issf values are readjusted using the structured perceptron and the whole of the BCCWJ core data to make a fair comparison with other tokenizers. Incorporating tf-issf into the structured perceptron improves the F1-score, from .743 to .798, when combined with unigrams. Although Kytea performs slightly better in terms of F1-score, tf-issf combined with bigrams achieves slightly higher recall because of fewer OOV words.

Table 3 shows the examples of segmentations produced for the OOV words that are not present in the BCCWJ training data. Tokenizers trained on BCCWJ except for RakutenMA fail to segment スマホケース "smartphone case" because the word スマホ "smartphone" does not appear in BCCWJ. Using tf-issf alone is also not sufficient to produce correct segmentations for all examples, and only tf-issf combined with structure perceptron successfully segments all examples.

4 Related Work

We now review relevant work on Japanese segmentation and describe the key ways in which our approach differs from previous ones.

Japanese word segmentation has an extensive history, and many Japanese tokenizers have been developed, from the rule-based tokenizer JUMAN (Kurohashi et al., 1994) to statistical tokenizers, MeCab (Kudo et al., 2004), Kytea (Neubig et al., 2011), and RakutenMA (Hagiwara and Sekine, 2014). However, these Japanese tokenizers require either manual tuning or a manually labeled corpus.

---

[8]Because the length feature only degrades the segmentation performance, we exclude the results from the tables.

Method	"Smartphone Apps"	"Ueno Daiki"	"My Number"
Gold data	スマホ / アプリ *sumaho / apuri*	ウエノ / ダイキ *ueno / daiki*	マイ / ナンバー *mai / nanbā*
Baseline	スマホ / アプリ *sumaho / apuri*	ウ/エ/ノ/ダ/イ/キ *u/e/no/da/i/ki*	マイ / ナンバー *mai / nanbā*
tf-issf (UNLABEL)	スマホ / アプリ *sumaho / apuri*	ウエノ / ダイキ *ueno / daiki*	マイナンバー *mainanbā*
tf-issf (BOTH)	スマホ / アプリ *sumaho / apuri*	ウエノ / ダイキ *ueno / daiki*	マイ / ナンバー *mai / nanbā*
MeCab+IPADic	スマホアプリ *sumahoapuri*	ウエノ / ダイキ *ueno / daiki*	マイ / ナンバー *mai / nanbā*
MeCab+UniDic	スマホアプリ *sumahoapuri*	ウエノ / ダイキ *ueno / daiki*	マイ / ナンバー *mai / nanbā*
JUMAN	スマホ / アプリ *sumaho / apuri*	ウエノダイキ *uenodaiki*	マイ / ナンバー *mai / nanbā*
Kytea	スマホアプリ *sumahoapuri*	ウエノ / ダイキ *ueno / daiki*	マイ / ナンバー *mai / nanbā*
RakutenMA	スマホ / アプリ *sumaho / apuri*	ウエノ / ダイキ *ueno / daiki*	マイナンバー *mainanbā*

Table 3: Examples of segmentation results for katakana words in Twitter hashtags using different segmentation methods. The correct segmentations are produced by tf-issf (BOTH) on these examples, while all others fail to achieve this.

4.1 Approaches Using Unlabeled Corpora

Closer to our own work, Koehn and Knight (2003) and Nakazawa et al. (2005) investigate segmenting compound words using an unlabeled corpus. These approaches do not achieve high precision on katakana words (Kaji and Kitsuregawa, 2011), however. To improve the segmentation accuracy, Kaji and Kitsuregawa (2011) incorporate a rule-based paraphrase feature (e.g., a middle dot " · ") to use an unlabeled corpus as training data without manual annotation. This method still requires manual selection of the characters used as word boundaries. Other studies use transliterations to segment katakana words using explicit word boundaries from the original English words (Kaji and Kitsuregawa, 2011; Hagiwara and Sekine, 2013). However, as not all katakana words are transliterations, it is advantageous to use a monolingual corpus.

4.2 TF-IDF-based Segmentation

Some similar work has been done on Chinese. Xiao et al. (2002) used tf-idf of context words to resolve segmentation ambiguities of Chinese words, but this approach assumes only two segmentation forms: combined and separated. This is adequate for two-character words in Chinese, which comprise the majority of Chinese words (Suen, 1986), but not for potentially very long katakana words in Japanese. In contrast to their approach, we regard each katakana term as one document and compute the inverse document frequency. The tf-issf approach also does not require context words since we compute the term frequency of each katakana term in question instead of the frequency of its context words. Thus, we need not assume that the training corpus has been automatically segmented by an existing to-kenizer, which might include segmentation errors involving context words.

In contrast to these approaches, we use a new frequency-based method, inspired by tf-idf that uses an unlabeled corpus to tackle word segmentation of character sequences of unbounded length.

5 Conclusion

In this paper, we introduce tf-issf, a simple and powerful word segmentation method for Japanese katakana words. We show that using tf-issf alone outperforms the baseline frequency-based method. Furthermore, when tf-issf is incorporated into the structured perceptron together with simple features on a manually labeled corpus, it achieves comparable performance to other state-of-the-art Japanese tokenizers, outperforming all in recall.

5.1 Future Work

While our work focuses on the peculiarities of Japanese katakana words, tf-issf may be applicable to other languages. We leave this for future work. Further research is also necessary to determine the extent to which tf-issf is dependent on the domain of the corpora, and how transferable these gains are across various domains. Investigating the phonetic and corresponding orthographic changes that occur with shortened Japanese katakana words and their transference to new compounds may also lead to further improvements in segmentation results.

Acknowledgments

We would like to thank the anonymous reviewers and Michael J. Paul for providing helpful comments.

References

Enrique Alfonseca, Slaven Bilac, and Stefan Phar-ies. 2008. Decompounding Query Keywords from Compounding Languages. In *Proceedings of ACL-HLT*, pages 253–256.

Masayuki Asahara and Yuji Matsumoto. 2003. Ipadic version 2.7.0 user's manual (in Japanese). *NAIST, Information Science Division*.

Piyush Bansal, Romil Bansal, and Vasudeva Varma. 2015. Towards Deep Semantic Analysis of Hashtags. In *Proceedings of ECIR*, pages 453–464.

Martin Braschler and Bärbel Ripplinger. 2004. How effective is stemming and decompounding for german text retrieval? *Information Retrieval*, 7(3-4):291–316.

James Breen. 2009. Identification of Neologisms in Japanese by Corpus Analysis. In *E-lexicography in the 21st century: New Challenges, New Applications*, pages 13–21.

Ruey-Cheng Chen. 2013. An Improved MDL-based Compression Algorithm for Unsupervised Word Segmentation. In *Proceedings of ACL*, pages 166–170.

Michael Collins. 2002. Discriminative Training Methods for Hidden Markov Models: Theory and Experiments with Perceptron Algorithms. In *Proceedings of EMNLP*, pages 1–8.

Yasuharu Den, Toshinobu Ogiso, Hideki Ogura, Atsushi Yamada, Nobuaki Minematsu, Kiyotaka Uchimoto, and Hanae Koiso. 2007. The Development of an Electronic Dictionary for Morphological Analysis and its Application to Japanese Corpus Linguistics (in Japanese). *Japanese Linguistics*, 22:101–123.

Sharon Goldwater, Thomas L. Griffiths, and Mark Johnson. 2006. Contextual Dependencies in Unsupervised Word Segmentation. In *Proceedings of ACL*, pages 673–680.

Masato Hagiwara and Satoshi Sekine. 2013. Accurate Word Segmentation using Transliteration and Language Model Projection. In *Proceedings of ACL*, pages 183–189.

Masato Hagiwara and Satoshi Sekine. 2014. Lightweight Client-Side Chinese/Japanese Morphological Analyzer Based on Online Learning. In *Proceedings of COLING*, pages 39–43.

Nobuhiro Kaji and Masaru Kitsuregawa. 2011. Splitting Noun Compounds via Monolingual and Bilingual Paraphrasing: A Study on Japanese Katakana Words. In *Proceedings of EMNLP*, pages 959–969.

Philipp Koehn and Kevin Knight. 2003. Empirical Methods for Compound Splitting. In *Proceedings of EACL*, pages 187–193.

Taku Kudo, Kaoru Yamamoto, and Yuji Matsumoto. 2004. Applying Conditional Random Fields to Japanese Morphological Analysis . In *Proceedings of EMNLP*, pages 230–237.

Sadao Kurohashi, Toshihisa Nakamura, Yuji Matsumoto, and Makoto Nagao. 1994. Improvements of Japanese Morphological Analyzer JUMAN. In *Proceedings of The International Workshop on Sharable Natural Language*, pages 22–28.

Kikuo Maekawa, Makoto Yamazaki, Toshinobu Ogiso, Takehiko Maruyama, Hideki Ogura, Wakako Kashino, Hanae Koiso, Masaya Yamaguchi, Makiro Tanaka, and Yasuharu Den. 2014. Balanced corpus of contemporary written Japanese. *Language Resources and Evaluation*, 48(2):345–371.

Daichi Mochihashi, Takeshi Yamada, and Naonori Ueda. 2009. Bayesian Unsupervised Word Segmentation with Nested Pitman-Yor Language Modeling. In *Proceedings of ACL-IJCNLP*, pages 100–108.

Fred Morstatter, Jürgen Pfeffer, Huan Liu, and Kathleen M. Carley. 2013. Is the Sample Good Enough? Comparing Data from Twitter's Streaming API with Twitter's Firehose. In *Proceedings of ICWSM*, pages 400–408.

Toshiaki Nakazawa, Daisuke Kawahara, and Sadao Kurohashi. 2005. Automatic Acquisition of Basic Katakana Lexicon from a Given Corpus. In *Proceedings of IJCNLP*, pages 682–693.

Graham Neubig, Yosuke Nakata, and Shinsuke Mori. 2011. Pointwise Prediction for Robust, Adaptable Japanese Morphological Analysis. In *Proceedings of ACL-HLT*, pages 529–533.

Hideki Ogura, Hanae Koiso, Yumi Fujike, Sayaka Miyauchi, and Yutaka Hara. 2011. Morphological Information Guildeline for BCCWJ: Balanced Corpus of Contemporary Written Japanese, 4th Edition (in Japanese). Research report.

Itsumi Saito, Kugatsu Sadamitsu, Hisako Asano, and Yoshihiro Matsuo. 2014. Morphological Analysis for Japanese Noisy Text based on Character-level and Word-level Normalization. In *Proceedings of COLING*, pages 1773–1782.

Gerard Salton and Christopher Buckley. 1988. Term-weighting Approaches in Automatic Text Retrieval. *Information Processing & Management*, 24(5):513–523.

Ching Y Suen. 1986. *Computational Studies of the Most Frequent Chinese Words and Sounds*, volume 3. World Scientific.

Luo Xiao, Sun Maosong, and Tsou Benjamin. 2002. Covering Ambiguity Resolution in Chinese Word Segmentation Based on Contextual Information. In *Proceedings of COLING*, pages 1–7.

MONPA: Multi-objective Named-entity and Part-of-speech Annotator for Chinese using Recurrent Neural Network

Yu-Lun Hsieh
SNHCC, TIGP, Academia Sinica, and
National Cheng Chi University, Taiwan
morphe@iis.sinica.edu.tw

Yung-Chun Chang
Graduate Institute of Data Science,
Taipei Medical University, Taiwan
changyc@tmu.edu.tw

Yi-Jie Huang, Shu-Hao Yeh, Chun-Hung Chen, and **Wen-Lian Hsu**
IIS, Academia Sinica, Taiwan
{aszx4510,night,hep_chen,hsu}@iis.sinica.edu.tw

Abstract

Part-of-speech (POS) tagging and named entity recognition (NER) are crucial steps in natural language processing. In addition, the difficulty of word segmentation places extra burden on those who deal with languages such as Chinese, and pipelined systems often suffer from error propagation. This work proposes an end-to-end model using character-based recurrent neural network (RNN) to jointly accomplish segmentation, POS tagging and NER of a Chinese sentence. Experiments on previous word segmentation and NER competition datasets show that a single joint model using the proposed architecture is comparable to those trained specifically for each task, and outperforms freely-available softwares. Moreover, we provide a web-based interface for the public to easily access this resource.

1 Introduction

Natural language processing (NLP) tasks often rely on accurate part-of-speech (POS) labels and named entity recognition (NER). Moreover, for languages that do not have an obvious word boundary such as Chinese and Japanese, segmentation is another major issue. Approaches that attempt to jointly resolve two of these tasks have received much attention in recent years. For example, Ferraro et al. (2013) proposed that joint solutions usually lead to the improvement in accuracy over pipelined systems by exploiting POS information to assist word segmentation and avoiding error propagation. Recent researches (Sun, 2011; Qian and Liu, 2012; Zheng et al., 2013; Zeng et al., 2013; Qian et al., 2015) also focus on the development of a joint model to perform Chinese word segmentation, POS tagging, and/or informal word detection.

However, to the best of our knowledge, no existing system can perform word segmentation, POS tagging, and NER simultaneously. In addition, even though there are methods that achieved high performances in previous competitions hosted by the Special Interest Group on Chinese Language Processing (SIGHAN)[1], there is no off-the-shelf NLP tools for Traditional Chinese NER but only two systems for word segmentation and POS tagging, which poses a significant obstacle for processing text in Traditional Chinese. These problems motivate us to devise a unified model that serves as a steppingstone for future Chinese NLP research.

In light of the recent success in applying neural networks to NLP tasks (Sutskever et al., 2014; Lample et al., 2016), we propose an end-to-end model that utilizes bidirectional RNNs to jointly perform segmentation, POS tagging, and NER in Chinese. This work makes the following major contributions. First, the proposed model conducts multi-objective annotation that not only handles word segmentation and POS tagging, but also can recognize named entities in a sentence simultaneously. We also show that these tasks can be effectively performed by the proposed model, achieving competitive performances to state-of-the-art methods on word segmentation and NE recognition of previous SIGHAN shared tasks. Moreover, our system not only outperforms off-the-shelf NLP tools, but also provides accurate NER results. Lastly, we provide an accessible online API[2] that has been utilized by several research groups.

---

[1] http://sighan.cs.uchicago.edu/

[2] Please visit http://monpa.iis.sinica.edu.tw:9000/chunk

Proceedings of the The 8th International Joint Conference on Natural Language Processing, pages 80–85,
Taipei, Taiwan, November 27 – December 1, 2017 ©2017 AFNLP

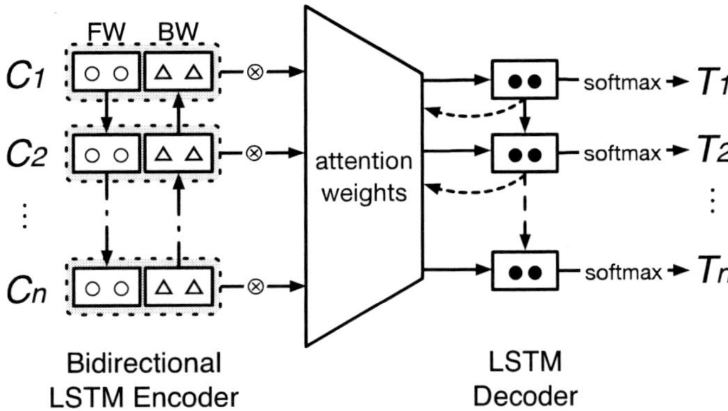

Figure 1: Overview of the encoder-decoder model with attention mechanism. Character embeddings C_1 to C_n of the input sentence is sequentially fed into the bidirectional LSTM, and the concatenated output is multiplied by attention weights and sent to the decoder for predicting the tag sequence T_1 to T_n. For simplicity, multiple layers of encoder and decoder as well as dropout layers between them are omitted.

2   Methods

Figure 1 illustrates the overview of our model, which in essence is an encoder-decoder (Sutskever et al., 2014) with attention mechanism (Luong et al., 2015). The input is a sequence of Chinese characters that may contain named entities, and the output is a sequence of POS tags and possibly NEs in the form of BIES tags. Our model mainly consists of: embedding layer, recurrent encoder layers, attention layer, and decoder layers. Detailed description of these layers are as follows.

Embedding Layer   converts characters into embeddings (Mikolov et al., 2013), which are dense, low-dimensional, and real-valued vectors. They capture syntactic and semantic information provided by its neighboring characters. In this work, we utilize pre-trained embeddings using `word2vec` and over 1 million online news articles. **Recurrent Encoder Layers** use LSTM, or Long Short-Term Memory (Hochreiter and Schmidhuber, 1997), cells which have been shown to capture long-term dependencies (Greff et al., 2017). An LSTM cell contains a "memory" cell c_t and three "gates", *i.e.*, input, forget, and output. The input gate modulates the current input and previous output. The forget gate tunes the content from previous memory to the current. Finally, the output gate regulates the output from the memory. Specifically, let x_t be the input at time t, and i_t, f_t, o_t correspond to input, forget, and output gates, respectively. c_t denotes the memory cell and h_t is the output. The learnable parameters include $W_{i,f,o,c}$ and $U_{i,f,o,c}$. They are defined as:

$$\mathbf{i}_t = \sigma(W_i\mathbf{x}_t + U_i\mathbf{h}_{t-1})$$
$$\mathbf{f}_t = \sigma(W_f\mathbf{x}_t + U_f\mathbf{h}_{t-1})$$
$$\mathbf{o}_t = \sigma(W_o\mathbf{x}_t + U_o\mathbf{h}_{t-1})$$
$$\tilde{\mathbf{c}}_t = \tanh(W_c\mathbf{x}_t + U_c\mathbf{h}_{t-1})$$
$$\mathbf{c}_t = \mathbf{f}_t \circ \mathbf{c}_{t-1} + \mathbf{i}_t \circ \tilde{\mathbf{c}}_t$$
$$\mathbf{h}_t = \mathbf{o}_t \circ \tanh(\mathbf{c}_t)$$

where "◦" denotes the element-wise product of vectors and σ represents the sigmoid function. We employ a straightforward extension named Bidirectional RNN (Graves et al., 2005), which encodes sequential information in both directions (forward and backward) and concatenate the final outputs. In this way, the output of one time step will contain information from its left and right neighbors. For tasks such as POS and NER where the label of one character can be determined by its context, bidirectional learning can be beneficial. **Attention Layer** is proposed by Luong et al. (2015) in an attempt to tackle the problem of finding corresponding words in the source and target languages when conducting machine translation. It computes a weighted average of all the output from the encoder based on the current decoded symbol, which is why it is also named "Global Attention." We consider it to be useful for the current tasks based on the same reasoning as using bidirectional encoding. Finally, **Recurrent Decoder Layers** take the sequence of output from the attention layer and project them onto a V-dimensional vector where V equals the number of possible POS and NE tags. The loss of the model is defined as the averaged cross-entropy between a output sequence and true label sequence.

3 Experiments

Test corpora from five previous SIGHAN shared tasks, which have been widely adopted for Traditional Chinese word segmentation and NER, were used to evaluate the proposed system. Besides the participating systems in the above shared tasks, we also compare with existing word segmentation toolkits Jieba and CKIP (Hsieh et al., 2012). The word segmentation datasets were taken from SIGHAN shared tasks of years 2003–2008, and NER dataset is from 2006. We follow the standard train/test split of the provided data, where 10,000 sentences of the training set are used as the validation set. Details of the word segmentation and NER datasets are shown in Table 1 and 2, respectively. Three metrics are used for evaluation: precision (P), recall (R) and F_1-score (F), defined by

$$F = \frac{2 \times P \times R}{P + R}$$

For word segmentation, a token is considered to be correct if both the left and right boundaries match those of a word in the gold standard. For the NER task, both the boundaries and the NE type must be correctly identified.

Table 1: Statistics of the word segmentation datasets (Number of words).

Year	AS		CityU	
	#Train	#Test	#Train	#Test
2003	5.8M	12K	240K	35K
2005	5.45M	122K	1.46M	41K
2006	5.5M	91K	1.6M	220K
2008	1.5M	91K	-	-

Table 2: Statistics of the 2006 NER dataset (Number of words).

#Train/Test Words		
Person	**Location**	**Organization**
36K / 8K	48K / 7K	28K / 4K

3.1 Experimental Setup

In order to obtain multi-objective labels of the training data, we first merge datasets from the 2006 SIGHAN word segmentation and NER shared tasks. Since rich context information is able to benefit deep learning-based approach, we augment the training set by collecting online news articles[3]. There are three steps for annotating the newly-created dataset. We first collect a list of NEs from Wikipedia and use it to search for NEs in the corpus, where longer NEs have higher priorities. Then, an NER tool (Wu et al., 2006) is utilized to label NEs. Finally, CKIP is utilized to segment and label the remaining words with POS tags. Three variants of the proposed model are tested, labeled as RNN_{CU06}, RNN_{YA}, and $RNN_{CU06+YA}$. RNN_{CU06} is trained using only word segmentation and NER datasets from the 2006 City University (CU) corpus; RNN_{YA} is trained using only online news corpus, and $RNN_{CU06+YA}$ is trained on a combination of the above corpora.

We implemented the RNN model using `pytorch`[4]. The maximum sentence length is set to 80, where longer sentences were truncated and shorter sentences were padded with zeros. The forward and backward RNN each has a dimension of 300, identical to that of word embeddings. There are three layers for both encoder and decoder. Dropout layers exist between each of the recurrent layers. The training lasts for at most 100 epochs or when the accuracy of the validation set starts to drop.

4 Results and Discussion

Note that since we combined external resources, performances of the compared methods are from the open track of the shared tasks. Table 3a lists the results of the RNN-based models and top-performing systems for the word segmentation subtask on the Academia Sinica (AS) dataset. First of all, RNNs exhibit consistent capabilities in handling data from different years and is comparable to the best systems in the competition. In addition, it is not surprising that the RNN_{YA} model perform better than RNN_{CU}. Nevertheless, our method can be further improved by integrating the CU06 corpus, demonstrated by the results from

---

[3]News articles are collected from the Yahoo News website and contains about 3M words.

[4]`https://github.com/pytorch/pytorch`

Table 3: Results for word segmentation on the Academia Sinica (AS) and City University (CU) datasets from different years of SIGHAN shared tasks. Bold numbers indicate the best performance in that column.

(a) AS dataset, open track

System	F-score			
	2003	2005	2006	2008
Gao et al. (2005)	95.8			
Yang et al. (2003)	90.4			
Low et al. (2005)		**95.6**		
Chen et al. (2005)		94.8		
Zhao et al. (2006)			**95.9**	
Jacobs and Wong (2006)			95.7	
Wang et al. (2006)			95.3	
Chan and Chong (2008)				**95.6**
Mao et al. (2008)				93.6
Jieba	83.0	80.9	81.3	81.8
CKIP	**96.6**	94.2	94.6	94.9
RNN$_{\text{CU06}}$	88.4	86.8	87.1	87.4
RNN$_{\text{YA}}$	94.4	92.8	93.0	93.3
RNN$_{\text{CU06+YA}}$	*94.6*	*93.2*	*93.6*	*93.8*

(b) CU dataset, open track

System	F-score		
	2003	2005	2006
Ma and Chen (2003)	**95.6**		
Gao et al. (2005)	95.4		
Peng et al. (2004)	94.6		
Yang et al. (2003)	87.9		
Low et al. (2005)		**96.2**	
Chen et al. (2005)		94.5	
Zhao et al. (2006)			**97.7**
Wang et al. (2006)			97.7
Jacobs and Wong (2006)			97.4
Jieba	80.3	81.2	82.4
CKIP	89.7	89.0	89.8
RNN$_{\text{CU06}}$	87.6	85.8	87.8
RNN$_{\text{YA}}$	88.0	87.2	88.5
RNN$_{\text{CU06+YA}}$	*91.5*	*90.1*	*91.7*

the RNN$_{\text{CU06+YA}}$ model. This indicates that RNN can easily adapt to different domains with data augmentation, which is an outstanding feature of end-to-end models. As for the CU dataset listed in Table 3b, all of the RNN models show considerable decrease in F-score. We postulate that it may be due to the training data, which is processed using an external tool focused on texts from a different linguistic context. It is also reported by (Wu et al., 2006) that segmentation criteria in AS and CU datasets are not very consistent. However, by fusing two corpora, the RNN$_{\text{CU06+YA}}$ can even surpass the performances of CKIP. Finally, comparison with Jieba validates that the RNN model can serve as a very effective toolkit for NLP researchers as well as the general public.

Table 4 lists the performances of proposed models and the only system that participated in the open track of the 2006 SIGHAN NER shared task. We can see that RNN$_{\text{CU06}}$ outperforms the model from Yu et al. (2006), confirming RNN's capability on jointly learning to segment and recognize NEs. Interestingly, RNN$_{\text{YA}}$ obtains a much lower F-score for all NE types. And RNN$_{\text{CU06+YA}}$ can only obtain a slightly better F-score for person recognition but not the overall performance of RNN$_{\text{CU06}}$, even with the combined corpus. We believe that boundary mismatch may be a major contributing factor here. We also observe that there are a large number of one-character NEs such as abbreviated country names, which can not be easily identified using solely character features.

Table 4: Results from the 2006 SIGHAN NER shared task (open track). Bold numbers indicate the best performance in that column.

System	F-score			
	PER	LOC	ORG	Overall
Yu et al. (2006)	80.98	86.04	68.01	80.51
RNN$_{\text{CU06}}$	81.13	**86.92**	**68.77**	**80.68**
RNN$_{\text{YA}}$	70.54	67.80	31.35	52.62
RNN$_{\text{CU06+YA}}$	**83.01**	82.46	54.57	75.28

5 Conclusions

We propose an end-to-end model to jointly conduct segmentation, POS and NE labeling in Chinese. Experimental results on past word segmentation and NER datasets show that the proposed model is comparable to those trained specifically for each task, and outperforms freely-available toolkits. Additionally, we implement a web interface for easy access. In the future, we will integrate existing knowledge bases, in order to provide a more advanced tool for the NLP community.

Acknowledgments

We are grateful for the constructive comments from three anonymous reviewers. This work was supported by grant MOST106-3114-E-001-002 from the Ministry of Science and Technology, Taiwan.

References

Samuel WK Chan and Mickey WC Chong. 2008. An agent-based approach to Chinese word segmentation. In *IJCNLP*. pages 112–114.

Aitao Chen, Yiping Zhou, Anne Zhang, and Gordon Sun. 2005. Unigram language model for Chinese word segmentation. In *Proceedings of the 4th SIGHAN Workshop on Chinese Language Processing*. Association for Computational Linguistics Jeju Island, Korea, pages 138–141.

Jeffrey P Ferraro, Hal Daumé III, Scott L DuVall, Wendy W Chapman, Henk Harkema, and Peter J Haug. 2013. Improving performance of natural language processing part-of-speech tagging on clinical narratives through domain adaptation. *Journal of the American Medical Informatics Association* 20(5):931–939.

Jianfeng Gao, Mu Li, Andi Wu, and Chang-Ning Huang. 2005. Chinese word segmentation and named entity recognition: A pragmatic approach. *Computational Linguistics* 31(4):531–574.

Alex Graves, Santiago Fernández, and Jürgen Schmidhuber. 2005. Bidirectional lstm networks for improved phoneme classification and recognition. *Artificial Neural Networks: Formal Models and Their Applications–ICANN 2005* pages 753–753.

Klaus Greff, Rupesh K Srivastava, Jan Koutník, Bas R Steunebrink, and Jürgen Schmidhuber. 2017. LSTM: A search space odyssey. *IEEE transactions on neural networks and learning systems* PP(99):1–11.

Sepp Hochreiter and Jürgen Schmidhuber. 1997. Lstm can solve hard long time lag problems. In *Advances in neural information processing systems*. pages 473–479.

Yu-Ming Hsieh, Ming-Hong Bai, Jason S Chang, and Keh-Jiann Chen. 2012. Improving PCFG chinese parsing with context-dependent probability reestimation. *CLP 2012* page 216.

Aaron J Jacobs and Yuk Wah Wong. 2006. Maximum entropy word segmentation of Chinese text. In *COLING* ACL 2006*. page 185.

Guillaume Lample, Miguel Ballesteros, Sandeep Subramanian, Kazuya Kawakami, and Chris Dyer. 2016. Neural architectures for named entity recognition. In *Proceedings of NAACL-HLT*. pages 260–270.

Jin Kiat Low, Hwee Tou Ng, and Wenyuan Guo. 2005. A maximum entropy approach to Chinese word segmentation. In *Proceedings of the Fourth SIGHAN Workshop on Chinese Language Processing*. volume 1612164, pages 448–455.

Thang Luong, Hieu Pham, and Christopher D. Manning. 2015. Effective approaches to attention-based neural machine translation. In *Proceedings of the 2015 Conference on Empirical Methods in Natural Language Processing*. Association for Computational Linguistics, Lisbon, Portugal, pages 1412–1421. http://aclweb.org/anthology/D15-1166.

Wei-Yun Ma and Keh-Jiann Chen. 2003. Introduction to ckip Chinese word segmentation system for the first international Chinese word segmentation bake-off. In *Proceedings of the second SIGHAN workshop on Chinese language processing-Volume 17*. Association for Computational Linguistics, pages 168–171.

Xinnian Mao, Yuan Dong, Saike He, Sencheng Bao, and Haila Wang. 2008. Chinese word segmentation and named entity recognition based on conditional random fields. In *IJCNLP*. pages 90–93.

Tomas Mikolov, Ilya Sutskever, Kai Chen, Greg S Corrado, and Jeff Dean. 2013. Distributed representations of words and phrases and their compositionality. In *Advances in neural information processing systems*. pages 3111–3119.

Fuchun Peng, Fangfang Feng, and Andrew McCallum. 2004. Chinese segmentation and new word detection using conditional random fields. In *Proceedings of the 20th international conference on Computational Linguistics*. Association for Computational Linguistics, page 562.

Tao Qian, Yue Zhang, Meishan Zhang, Yafeng Ren, and Donghong Ji. 2015. A transition-based model for joint segmentation, pos-tagging and normalization. In *Proceedings of the 2015 Conference on Empirical Methods in Natural Language Processing*. Association for Computational Linguistics, Lisbon, Portugal, pages 1837–1846. http://aclweb.org/anthology/D15-1211.

Xian Qian and Yang Liu. 2012. Joint Chinese word segmentation, pos tagging and parsing. In *Proceedings of the 2012 Joint Conference on Empirical Methods in Natural Language Processing and Computational Natural Language Learning*. Association for Computational Linguistics, Jeju Island, Korea, pages 501–511. http://www.aclweb.org/anthology/D12-1046.

Weiwei Sun. 2011. A stacked sub-word model for joint chinese word segmentation and part-of-speech tagging. In *Proceedings of the 49th Annual Meeting of the Association for Computational Linguistics: Human Language Technologies*. Association for Computational Linguistics, Portland, Oregon, USA, pages 1385–1394. http://www.aclweb.org/anthology/P11-1139.

Ilya Sutskever, Oriol Vinyals, and Quoc V Le. 2014. Sequence to sequence learning with neural networks. In *Advances in neural information processing systems*. pages 3104–3112.

Xinhao Wang, Xiaojun Lin, Dianhai Yu, Hao Tian, and Xihong Wu. 2006. Chinese word segmentation with maximum entropy and n-gram language model. In *COLING* ACL 2006*. page 138.

Chia-Wei Wu, Shyh-Yi Jan, Richard Tzong-Han Tsai, and Wen-Lian Hsu. 2006. On using ensemble methods for Chinese named entity recognition. In *Proceedings of the Fifth SIGHAN Workshop on Chinese Language Processing*. Association for Computational Linguistics, Sydney, Australia, pages 142–145. http://www.aclweb.org/anthology/W/W06/W06-0122.

Jin Yang, Jean Senellart, and Remi Zajac. 2003. Systran's Chinese word segmentation. In *Proceedings of the second SIGHAN workshop on Chinese language processing-Volume 17*. Association for Computational Linguistics, pages 180–183.

Xiaofeng Yu, Marine Carpuat, and Dekai Wu. 2006. Boosting for Chinese named entity recognition. In *Proceedings of the Fifth SIGHAN Workshop on Chinese Language Processing*. pages 150–153.

Xiaodong Zeng, Derek F. Wong, Lidia S. Chao, and Isabel Trancoso. 2013. Graph-based semi-supervised model for joint chinese word segmentation and part-of-speech tagging. In *Proceedings of the 51st Annual Meeting of the Association for Computational Linguistics (Volume 1: Long Papers)*. Association for Computational Linguistics, Sofia, Bulgaria, pages 770–779. http://www.aclweb.org/anthology/P13-1076.

Hai Zhao, Chang-Ning Huang, Mu Li, et al. 2006. An improved Chinese word segmentation system with conditional random field. In *Proceedings of the Fifth SIGHAN Workshop on Chinese Language Processing*. Sydney: July, volume 1082117.

Xiaoqing Zheng, Hanyang Chen, and Tianyu Xu. 2013. Deep learning for Chinese word segmentation and POS tagging. In *Proceedings of the 2013 Conference on Empirical Methods in Natural Language Processing*. Association for Computational Linguistics, Seattle, Washington, USA, pages 647–657. http://www.aclweb.org/anthology/D13-1061.

Recall is the Proper Evaluation Metric for Word Segmentation

Yan Shao and **Christian Hardmeier** and **Joakim Nivre**
Department of Linguistics and Philology, Uppsala University
{yan.shao, christian.hardmeier, joakim.nivre}@lingfil.uu.se

Abstract

We extensively analyse the correlations and drawbacks of conventionally employed evaluation metrics for word segmentation. Unlike in standard information retrieval, precision favours under-splitting systems and therefore can be misleading in word segmentation. Overall, based on both theoretical and experimental analysis, we propose that precision should be excluded from the standard evaluation metrics and that the evaluation score obtained by using only recall is sufficient and better correlated with the performance of word segmentation systems.

1 Introduction

Word segmentation (WS) or tokenisation can be viewed as correctly identifying valid boundaries between characters (Goldwater et al., 2007). It is the initial step for most higher level natural language processing tasks, such as part-of-speech tagging, syntactic analysis, information retrieval and machine translation. Thus, correct segmentation is crucial as segmentation errors propagate to higher level tasks.

Because only correctly segmented words are meaningful to higher level tasks, word level precision, recall and their evenly-weighted average F1-score that are customised from information retrieval (IR) (Kent et al., 1955) are conventionally used as the standard evaluation metrics for WS (Sproat and Emerson, 2003; Qiu et al., 2015).

In this paper, we thoroughly investigate precision and recall in addition to true negative rate in the scope of WS, with a special focus on the drawbacks of precision. Precision and F1-score can be misleading as an under-splitting system may obtain higher precision despite having fewer cor-

rectly segmented words. Additionally, we conduct word segmentation experiments to investigate the connections between precision and recall as well as their correlations with actual performance of segmenters. Overall, we propose that precision should be excluded and that using recall as the sole evaluation metric is more adequate.

2 Evaluation Metrics for WS

2.1 Precision and Recall

By employing word-level precision and recall, the adequacy of a word segmenter is measured via comparing to the annotated reference. The correctly segmented words are regarded as true positives (*TP*). To obtain precision, *TP* is normalised by the prediction positives (*PP*), which is equal to total number of words returned by the system. For recall, we divide *TP* by the real positives (*RP*), the total number of words in the reference. The complement of *RP* is referred to as real negatives (*RN*).

In the evaluation setup for standard IR tasks, there is no entanglement between *RP* and *RN*. For any instances i_p and i_n in *RP* and *RN*, they can be in the same output set I of an IR system as:

$$\forall i_p \in RP, \forall i_n \in RN, \exists I, \{i_p, i_n\} \subset I$$

Precision and recall are thus not directly correlated. For IR, system performance is well measured only if both precision and recall are used as it is trivial to optimise with respect to either precision or recall, but difficult to improve both. This is not the case for WS. In contrast to the situation in IR, the characters as basic elements are fixed in WS. We only predict the boundaries whereas the characters can be neither added nor deleted, which makes positives and negatives correlated.

In Table 1, the source Chinese sentence and its English translation in the form of character strings

Proceedings of the The 8th International Joint Conference on Natural Language Processing, pages 86–90,
Taipei, Taiwan, November 27 – December 1, 2017 ©2017 AFNLP

Segmenters	Source sentences: 约翰喜欢玛丽 John likes Mary Reference Segmentations: 约翰 /喜欢 /玛丽 John / likes / Mary				
	T1	T2	S1	S2	S3
Output	约 /翰 /喜 /欢 /玛 /丽	约翰喜欢玛丽	约翰 /喜欢玛丽	约翰 /喜 /欢 /玛 /丽	约翰 /喜欢 /玛 /丽
TP	0	0	1	1	2
P	0	0	1/2 = 0.5	1/5 = 0.2	2/4 = 0.5
R	0	0	1/3 = 0.33	1/3 = 0.33	2/3 = 0.67
F	0	0	0.40	0.25	0.57
TNR	1-6/18 = 0.67	1-1/18 = 0.94	1-1/18 = 0.94	1-4/18 = 0.77	1-2/18 = 0.89
Output	J/o/h/n/l/i/k/e/s/M/a/r/y	John likes Mary	John / likes Mary	John /l/i/k/e/s/M/a/r/y	John /likes /M/a/r/y
TP	0	0	1	1	2
P	0	0	1/2 = 0.5	1/10 = 0.1	2/6 = 0.33
R	0	0	1/3 = 0.33	1/3 = 0.33	2/3 = 0.67
F	0	0	0.40	0.15	0.44
TNR	1-13/88 = 0.85	1-1/88 = 0.99	1-1/88 = 0.99	1-9/88 = 0.90	1-4/88 = 0.95

Table 1: Sample sentences along with the output of two trivial segmenters (T1, T2) and three other segmenters (S1, S2, S3). True Positives (TP), Precision (P), recall (R), F1-score (F) and true negative rate (TNR) are calculated respectively.

are presented along with the outputs of five hand-crafted segmenters. In WS, a *TP* simultaneously rejects the associated true negatives (*TN*). For the English sentence in Table 1, the positive segment *John* never appears simultaneously with its associated negatives *Joh*, *Jo* or *ohn* in the output. This positively correlates precision and recall, because if we modify a boundary that optimises recall, the precision will also improve. In WS, 100% recall guarantees 100% precision and it is non-trivial to optimise one without the other.

In the most trivial case, a segmenter either predicts and returns all the possible word boundaries (T1, extremely over-splitting) or fails to identify any boundaries at all (T2, extremely under-splitting). In the example, both strategies yield zero scores for both precision and recall as both fail to return any *TP*.

Despite not being completely trivial, S1 is heavily under-splitting while S2 is the opposite. Both return one correctly segmented word for the sentences in both languages. Their corresponding recalls are therefore equal as *TP* is normalised by *RP*, which is hard-constrained by the references. However, adopting precision as the metric, S1 yields substantially higher scores as it returns much fewer *PP*. Referring to the trivial examples as well as the fact that only *TP* are meaningful to higher-level applications, S1 and S2 perform equally poorly, which is consistent with recall but not precision. Furthermore, a segmenter with less *TP* may achieve higher precision if it is drastically under-segmenting, as demonstrated by the comparison between S1 and S3.

2.2 True Negative Rate

Neither recall nor precision measure how well the system rejects the negatives. True negative rate (*TNR*) is therefore proposed by Powers (2011) as the complement. Jiang et al. (2011) show that segmenters measured by *TNR* are better correlated than precision and recall with their actual performances within IR systems. For WS, it is not straightforward to compute *TNR* by directly normalising the true negatives (*TN*) by the real negatives (*RN*). However, it can be indirectly computed via *TP*, *PP*, *RP* and the total number of possible output *TW* given a sentence. Regarding the input characters as a string, *TW* is equal to the number of substrings as $\frac{(1+N)N}{2}$, where N is the number of the characters. *RN* can then be computed by subtracting *RP*, the number of words in reference. The false negatives (*FN*) generated by the segmenter can be obtained by subtracting *TP* from *PP*, total number of words return by the segmenter. To put everything together:

$$TNR = \frac{TN}{RN} = 1 - \frac{FN}{RN} = 1 - \frac{PP - TP}{TW - RP} \quad (1)$$

When *PP* equals *TP*, we will have a *TNR* of 1, indicating that a WS system correctly rejects all *TN* if and only if all the *PP* are *TP*. Since *TW* is bounded by the input sentence length and *RP* is bounded by the reference, *TNR* is negatively correlated to *PP* as longer segmented word eliminates more *TN* and generates less *FN* in general. As shown in Table 1, *TNR* heavily favours under-splitting systems. T2 obtains the highest *TNR* in the table despite being trivial. S1 also obtains higher scores than S3, despite having lower *TP*. Overall, *TNR* is very insensitive and not always well-correlated to actual performances of segmenters.

2.3 Boundary-Based Evaluation

Instead of directly evaluating the performance in terms of *TP* at word-level, an alternative is to use boundary-based evaluation (Palmer and Burger, 1997). The drawback is that incorrectly segmented words that are not interesting to higher-level applications still contribute to the scores as long as one of the two associated boundaries is correctly detected.

3 Experiments

To further investigate the correlations and drawbacks of the metrics discussed in the previous section experimentally, we employ a neural-based word segmenter to see how they measure the segmentation performance in a real scenario. The segmenter is a simplified version of the joint segmentation and POS tagger introduced in Shao et al. (2017). It is fully character-based. The vector representations of input characters are passed to the prevalent bidirectional recurrent neural network equipped with gated recurrent unit (GRU) (Cho et al., 2014) as the basic cell. A time-wise softmax layer is added as the inference for the recurrent layers to obtain probability distribution of binary tags that indicate the boundaries of the words. Cross-entropy with respect to time step is applied as the loss function. We train the segmenter for 30 epochs and pick the weights of the best epoch that minimises the loss on the development set.

The Chinese and English sections of Universal Dependencies v2.0 are employed as the experimental data sets. We follow the conventional splits of the data sets. For Chinese, the concatenated trigram model in Shao et al. (2017) is applied. Table 2 shows the experimental results on the test sets in terms of different metrics using the standard argmax function to obtain the final output. The segmenter is relatively under-splitting for Chinese as it yields higher recall than precision, which is opposite to English. The segmenter nonetheless achieves state-of-the-art performance on both languages.[1]

[1] http://universaldependencies.org/conll17/results-words.html

	P	R	F	TNR
Chinese	92.85	93.46	93.16	99.81
English	99.33	99.09	99.21	99.99

Table 2: Evaluation scores on the test sets in precision (P), recall (R), F1-score (F) and true negative rate (TNR).

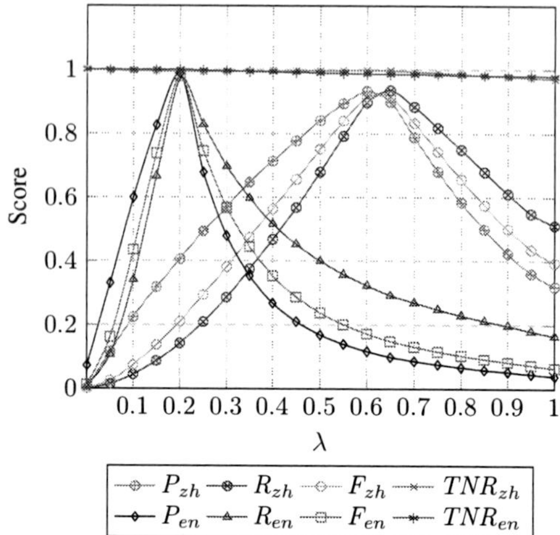

Figure 1: Evaluation scores on Chinese (zh) and English (en) in precision (P), recall (P), F1-score (F) and true negative rate (TNR) with different ratios of most probable boundaries λ.

To get a more fine-grained picture, instead of using argmax when decoding, we manually set a threshold to determine the word boundaries with respect to the scores returned by the inference layer of the neural network. All the possible output tags are ranked according to their scores of being a word boundary. For each test experiment, we accept the $\lambda * 100$ percent most probable word boundaries and regard the rest as non-word boundaries. The segmenter therefore tends towards under-splitting when λ is closer to 0 and over-splitting when λ is closer to 1. The segmenter becomes trivial when λ is equal to 0 or 1, corresponding to the extreme under-splitting and over-splitting segmenters T1 and T2 introduced in Table 1 respectively.

Figure 1 presents the evaluation scores according to the metrics under consideration with respect to different λ in the interval of 0.05. With the optimal λ_F^*, the segmenter achieves comparable F1-scores to those reported in Table 2. For Chinese, λ_F^* is around 0.6, indicating there are roughly 60% true boundaries out of all the possible segmentation points between consecutive characters. For English, λ_F^* is 0.2 as the fact that English words are relatively more coarse-grained and composed of more characters on average. In general, precision and recall are positively correlated. When λ is close to its the optimal, the values of both precision and recall increase. However, when λ is far away from both the optima and 0, precision and recall vary very substantially, clearly indicating that precision heavily favours under-splitting systems.

When λ equals 0, we obtain near-zero scores with trivial under-splitting. In contrast, the over-splitting segmenter with λ is equal to 1 yields a notable amount of true positives, due to the fact that there is a considerable amount of single-character words, especially in Chinese. This implies that actually trivial over-splitting is relatively better than under-splitting in practise, even though it is not favoured by precision.

For Chinese, the optimal λ_P^* for precision is 0.6, whereas λ_R^* for recall is 0.65. They would be different for English as well if a smaller interval of λ were adopted. λ_R^* corresponds to the system with most correctly segmented words, whereas λ_P^* is slightly biased towards under-splitting systems. The difference between λ_P^* and λ_R^* is marginal only when the segmenter performs very well as in the case of English.

Next, we investigate how the metrics behave in a learning curve experiment with ordinary argmax decoding. Instead of using the complete training set, for each test experiment, a controlled number of sentences are used for training the segmenter. The results are shown in Figure 2, in which the training set is extended gradually by 200 sentences. As expected, the segmenter is better trained and more accurate with a larger training set, which is in accordance with recall as it always increases when the training set is expanded. However, despite being closely correlated with recall in general, precision notably drops for Chinese when enlarging the train set from 800 to 1,000 as well as from 1,800 to 2,000, implying the segmenter becomes relatively over-splitting and obtains lower precision despite having more correctly segmented words. Similarly for English, the precision decreases when the training set is enlarged from 1,200 to 1,400.

The experimental results of *TNR* is also consistent with our analysis in the previous section. In WS, the values of both *RN* in the reference as well

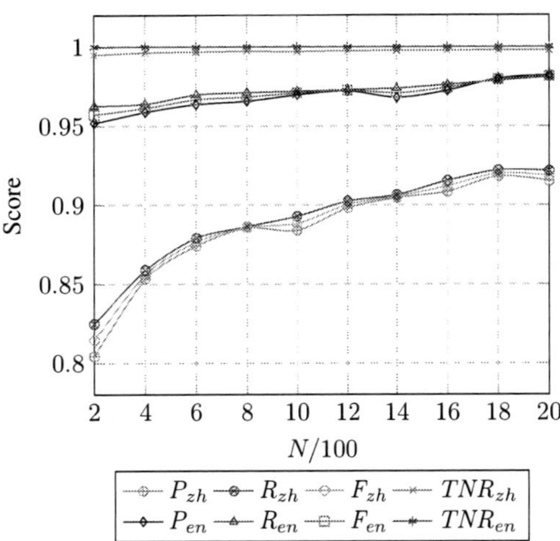

Figure 2: Evaluation scores on Chinese (zh) and English (en) in precision (P), recall (P), F1-score (F) and true negative rate (TNR) with different numbers of training instances N.

as *PN* by the system are drastically greater than the corresponding values of the positives. Thus, *TN* is high regardless of how the segmenter performs, which makes *TNR* very insensitive and inappropriate as an evaluation metric for WS.

4 Conclusion

We discuss and analyse precision, recall in addition to true negative rate (*TNR*) as the evaluation metrics for WS both theoretically and experimentally in this paper. Unlike standard evaluation for IR, all the metrics are positively correlated in general. It is non-trivial to optimise the segmenter towards either precision or recall. The difference between precision and recall is notable only if the segmenter is strongly over- or under-splitting. In either case, precision as the evaluation is misleading as it heavily favours under-splitting systems. Additionally, *TNR* is very insensitive and not suitable to evaluate WS either.

Under the circumstances, we propose that precision should be excluded from the conventional evaluation metrics. As opposed to precision, recall is hard-constrained by the reference and therefore not biased towards neither under-splitting nor over-splitting systems. It explicitly measures the correctly segmented words that are meaningful to higher level tasks. Employing recall solely is therefore sufficient and more adequate as the evaluation metric for WS.

Acknowledgments

We acknowledge the computational resources provided by CSC in Helsinki and Sigma2 in Oslo through NeIC-NLPL (www.nlpl.eu). This work is supported by the Chinese Scholarship Council (CSC) (No. 201407930015).

References

Kyunghyun Cho, Bart Van Merriënboer, Dzmitry Bahdanau, and Yoshua Bengio. 2014. On the properties of neural machine translation: Encoder-decoder approaches. *arXiv preprint arXiv:1409.1259* .

Sharon Goldwater, Thomas L Griffiths, Mark Johnson, et al. 2007. Distributional cues to word boundaries: Context is important. In *Proceedings of the 31st Annual Boston University Conference on Language Development*. pages 239–250.

Mike Tian-Jian Jiang, Cheng-Wei Shih, Richard Tzong-Han Tsai, and Wen-Lian Hsu. 2011. Evaluation via negativa of Chinese word segmentation for information retrieval. In *Proceedings of the 25th Pacific Asia Conference on Language, Information and Computation*. Institute of Digital Enhancement of Cognitive Processing, Waseda University, Singapore, pages 100–109.

Allen Kent, Madeline M Berry, Fred U Luehrs, and James W Perry. 1955. Machine literature searching VIII. operational criteria for designing information retrieval systems. *Journal of the Association for Information Science and Technology* 6(2):93–101.

David Palmer and John Burger. 1997. Chinese word segmentation and information retrieval. In *AAAI Spring Symposium on Cross-Language Text and Speech Retrieval*. pages 175–178.

David Martin Powers. 2011. Evaluation: from precision, recall and F-measure to ROC, informedness, markedness and correlation .

Xipeng Qiu, Peng Qian, Liusong Yin, Shiyu Wu, and Xuanjing Huang. 2015. Overview of the NLPCC 2015 shared task: Chinese word segmentation and POS tagging for micro-blog texts. In *National CCF Conference on Natural Language Processing and Chinese Computing*. Springer, pages 541–549.

Yan Shao, Christian Hardmeier, Jörg Tiedemann, and Joakim Nivre. 2017. Character-based joint segmentation and POS tagging for Chinese using bidirectional RNN-CRF. *arXiv preprint arXiv:1704.01314* .

Richard Sproat and Thomas Emerson. 2003. The first international Chinese word segmentation bakeoff. In *Proceedings of the second SIGHAN workshop on Chinese language processing-Volume 17*. Association for Computational Linguistics, pages 133–143.

Low-Resource Named Entity Recognition with Cross-Lingual, Character-Level Neural Conditional Random Fields

Ryan Cotterell and **Kevin Duh**
Department of Computer Science
Johns Hopkins University
Baltimore, MD 21218
`ryan.cotterell@jhu.edu`

Abstract

Low-resource named entity recognition is still an open problem in NLP. Most state-of-the-art systems require tens of thousands of annotated sentences in order to obtain high performance. However, for most of the world's languages it is unfeasible to obtain such annotation. In this paper, we present a transfer learning scheme, whereby we train character-level neural CRFs to predict named entities for both high-resource languages and low-resource languages jointly. Learning character representations for multiple related languages allows transfer among the languages, improving F_1 by up to 9.8 points over a log-linear CRF baseline.

1 Introduction

Named entity recognition (NER) presents a challenge for modern machine learning, wherein a learner must deduce which word tokens refer to people, locations and organizations (along with other possible entity types). The task demands that the learner generalize *from* limited training data and *to* novel entities, often in new domains. Traditionally, state-of-the-art NER models have relied on hand-crafted features that pick up on distributional cues as well as portions of the word forms themselves. In the past few years, however, neural approaches that jointly learn their own features have surpassed the feature-based approaches in performance. Despite their empirical success, neural networks have remarkably high sample complexity and still only outperform hand-engineered feature approaches when enough supervised training data is available, leaving effective training of neural networks in the low-resource case a challenge.

For most of the world's languages, there is a very

Sandra works for Google in Manhattan, New York.
B-PER   O   O   B-ORG   O   B-LOC   I-LOC   I-LOC

Figure 1: Example of an English sentence annotated with its typed named entities.

limited amount of training data for NER; CoNLL—the standard dataset in the field—only provides annotations for 4 languages (Tjong Kim Sang, 2002; Tjong Kim Sang and De Meulder, 2003). Creating similarly sized datasets for other languages has a prohibitive annotation cost, making the low-resource case an important scenario. To get around this barrier, we develop a cross-lingual solution: given a low-resource target language, we additionally offer large amounts of annotated data in a language that is genetically related to the target language. We show empirically that this improves the quality of the resulting model.

In terms of neural modeling, we introduce a novel neural conditional random field (CRF) for cross-lingual NER that allows for cross-lingual transfer by extracting character-level features using recurrent neural networks, shared among multiple languages and; this tying of parameters enables cross-lingual abstraction. With experiments on 15 languages, we confirm that feature-based CRFs outperform the neural methods consistently in the low-resource training scenario. However, with the addition of cross-lingual information, the tables turn and the neural methods are again on top, demonstrating that cross-lingual supervision is a viable method to reduce the training data state-of-the-art neural approaches require.

2 Neural Conditional Random Fields

Named entity recognition is typically framed as a sequence labeling task using the BIO scheme (Ramshaw and Marcus, 1995; Baldwin, 2009), i.e., given an input sentence, the goal is to assign a label

91

to each token: B if the token is the **b**eginning of an entity, or I if the token is **i**nside an entity, or O if the token is **o**utside an entity (see Fig. 1). Following convention, we focus on person (per), location (loc), organization (org), and miscellaneous (misc) entity types, resulting in 9 tags: $\{$B-ORG, I-ORG, B-PER, I-PER, B-LOC, I-LOC, B-MISC, I-MISC$\}$.

Conditional Random Fields (CRFs), first introduced in Lafferty et al. (2001), generalize the classical maximum entropy models (Berger et al., 1996) to distributions over structured objects, and are an effective tool for sequence labeling tasks like NER. We briefly overview the formalism here and then discuss its neural parameterization.

2.1 CRFs: A Cursory Overview

We start with two discrete alphabets Σ and Δ. In the case of sentence-level sequence tagging, Σ is a set of words (potentially infinite) and Δ is a set of tags (generally finite; in our case $|\Delta| = 9$). Given $\mathbf{t} = t_1 \cdots t_n \in \Delta^n$ and $\mathbf{w} = w_1 \cdots w_n \in \Sigma^n$, where n is the sentence length. A CRF is a globally normalized conditional probability distribution,

$$p_{\boldsymbol{\theta}}(\mathbf{t} \mid \mathbf{w}) = \frac{1}{Z_{\boldsymbol{\theta}}(\mathbf{w})} \prod_{i=1}^{n} \psi\left(t_{i-1}, t_i, \mathbf{w}; \boldsymbol{\theta}\right), \quad (1)$$

where $\psi\left(t_{i-1}, t_i, \mathbf{w}; \boldsymbol{\theta}\right) \geq 0$ is an arbitrary non-negative potential function[1] that we take to be a parametric function of the parameters $\boldsymbol{\theta}$ and the partition function $Z_{\boldsymbol{\theta}}(\mathbf{w})$ is the sum over all taggings of length n.

So how do we choose $\psi\left(t_{i-1}, t_i, \mathbf{w}; \boldsymbol{\theta}\right)$? We discuss two alternatives, which we will compare experimentally in §5.

2.2 Log-Linear Parameterization

Traditionally, computational linguists have stuck to a simple log-linear parameterization, i.e.,

$$\psi\left(t_{i-1}, t_i, \mathbf{w}; \boldsymbol{\theta}\right) = \exp\left(\boldsymbol{\eta}^{\top} \boldsymbol{f}\left(t_{i-1}, t_i, \mathbf{w}\right)\right), \tag{2}$$

where $\boldsymbol{\eta} \in \mathbb{R}^d$ and the user defines a feature function $\boldsymbol{f} : \Sigma \times \Sigma \times \Delta^n \to \mathbb{R}^d$ that extracts relevant information from the adjacent tags t_{i-1} and t_i and the sentence $\mathbf{w}$. In this case, the model's parameters are $\boldsymbol{\theta} = \{\boldsymbol{\eta}\}$. Common binary features include word form features, e.g., does the word at the ith position end in *-ation*?, and contextual features, e.g., is the word next to $(i-1)^{\text{th}}$ word *the*? These binary

features are conjoined with other indicator features, e.g., is the ith tag I-LOC? We refer the reader to Sha and Pereira (2003) for standard CRF feature functions employed in NER, which we use in this work. The log-linear parameterization yields a convex objective and is extremely efficient to compute as it only involves a sparse dot product, but the representational power of model depends fully on the quality of the features the user selects.

2.3 (Recurrent) Neural Parameterization

Modern CRFs, however, try to obviate the hand-selection of features through deep, non-linear parameterizations of $\psi\left(t_{i-1}, t_i, \mathbf{w}; \boldsymbol{\theta}\right)$. This idea is far from novel and there have been numerous attempts in the literature over the past decade to find effective non-linear parameterizations (Peng et al., 2009; Do and Artières, 2010; Collobert et al., 2011; Vinel et al., 2011; Fujii et al., 2012). Until recently, however, it was not clear that these non-linear parameterizations of CRFs were worth the non-convexity and the extra computational cost. Indeed, on neural CRFs, Wang and Manning (2013) find that "a nonlinear architecture offers no benefits in a high-dimensional discrete feature space."

However, recently with the application of long short-term memory (LSTM) (Hochreiter and Schmidhuber, 1997) recurrent neural networks (RNNs) (Elman, 1990) to CRFs, it has become clear that neural feature extractors are superior to the hand-crafted approaches (Huang et al., 2015; Lample et al., 2016; Ma and Hovy, 2016). As our starting point, we build upon the architecture of Lample et al. (2016), which is currently competitive with the state of the art for NER.

$$\psi\left(t_{i-1}, t_i, \mathbf{w}; \boldsymbol{\theta}\right) = \tag{3}$$
$$\exp\left(a(t_{i-1}, t_i) + \mathbf{o}(t_i)^{\top} \mathbf{W}\, \mathbf{s}(\mathbf{w})_i\right),$$

where $a(t_{i-1}, t_i)$ is the weight of transitioning from $t-1$ to t and $\mathbf{o}(t_i), \mathbf{s}(\mathbf{w})_i \in \mathbb{R}^r$ are the output tag and word embedding for the ith word, respectively. We define sentence's embeddings as the concatenation of an LSTM run forward and backward[2]

$$\mathbf{s}(\mathbf{w}) = \left[\overrightarrow{\text{LSTM}_{\boldsymbol{\theta}}}(\boldsymbol{\omega}); \overleftarrow{\text{LSTM}_{\boldsymbol{\theta}}}(\boldsymbol{\omega})\right]. \tag{4}$$

Note that the embedding for the ith word in this sentence is $\mathbf{s}(\mathbf{w})_i$. The input vector $\boldsymbol{\omega} =$

---

[1] We slightly abuse notation and use t_0 as a distinguished beginning-of-sentence symbol.

[2] We take $r = 100$ and use a two-layer LSTM with 200 hidden units, each.

$[\omega_1, \ldots, \omega_{|\mathbf{w}|}]$ to this BiLSTM is a vector of embeddings: we define

$$\omega_i = \left[\text{LSTM}_{\boldsymbol{\theta}} \left(c_1 \cdots c_{|w_i|} \right) ; \mathbf{e}(w_i) \right] , \quad (5)$$

where $c_1 \cdots c_{|w_i|}$ are the characters in word w_i. In other words, we run an LSTM over the character stream and concatenate it with a word embedding for each type. Now, the parameters $\boldsymbol{\theta}$ are the set of all the LSTM parameters and other embeddings.

3 Cross-Lingual Extensions

One of the most striking features of neural networks is their ability to abstract general representations across many words. Our question is: can neural feature-extractors abstract the notion of a named entity across similar languages? For example, if we train a character-level neural CRF on several of the highly related Romance languages, can our network learn a general representation entities in these languages?

3.1 Cross-Lingual Architecture

We now describe our novel cross-lingual architecture. Given a language label ℓ, we want to create a language-specific CRF $p_{\boldsymbol{\theta}}(\mathbf{t} \mid \mathbf{w}, \ell)$ with potential:

$$\psi\left(t_{i-1}, t_i, \mathbf{w}, \ell; \boldsymbol{\theta} \right) = \exp\left(a(t_{i-1}, t_i) + \right. \quad (6)$$
$$\left. \mathbf{u}^\top \tanh(\mathbf{W} \left[\mathbf{s}(\mathbf{w})_i ; \mathbf{l}(\ell) \right] + \mathbf{b}) \right) ,$$

where $\mathbf{l}(\ell) \in \mathbb{R}^r$ is an embedding of the language ID, itself. Importantly, we share some parameters across languages: the transitions between tags $a()$ and the character-level neural networks that discover what a form looks like. Recall $\mathbf{s}(\mathbf{w})$ is defined in Eq. 4 and Eq. 5. The part $\text{LSTM}_{\boldsymbol{\theta}} \left(c_1 \cdots c_{|w_i|} \right)$ is shared cross-lingually while $\mathbf{e}(w_i)$ is language-specific.

Now, given a low-resource target language τ and a source language σ (potentially, a set of m high-resource source languages $\{\sigma_i\}_{i=1}^m$). We consider the following training objective

$$\mathcal{L}\left(\boldsymbol{\theta} \right) = \sum_{(\mathbf{t}, \mathbf{w}) \in \mathcal{D}_\tau} \log p_{\boldsymbol{\theta}}\left(\mathbf{t} \mid \mathbf{w}, \tau \right) + \quad (7)$$
$$\mu \cdot \sum_{(\mathbf{t}, \mathbf{w}) \in \mathcal{D}_\sigma} \log p_{\boldsymbol{\theta}}\left(\mathbf{t} \mid \mathbf{w}, \sigma \right) ,$$

where μ is a trade-off parameter, $\mathcal{D}_\tau$ is the set of training examples for the target language and $\mathcal{D}_\sigma$ is the set of training data for the source language σ. In the case of multiple source languages, we add a summand to the set of source languages used, in which case set have multiple training sets $\mathcal{D}_{\sigma_i}$.

Language	Code	Family	Branch
Galician	gl	Indo-European	Romance
Catalan	cl	Indo-European	Romance
French	fr	Indo-European	Romance
Italian	it	Indo-European	Romance
Romanian	ro	Indo-European	Romance
Spanish	es	Indo-European	Romance
West Frisian	fy	Indo-European	Germanic
Dutch	nl	Indo-European	Germanic
Tagalog	tl	Austronesian	Philippine
Cebuano	ceb	Austronesian	Philippine
Ukranian	uk	Indo-European	Slavic
Russian	ru	Indo-European	Slavic
Marathi	mr	Indo-European	Indo-Aryan
Hindi	hi	Indo-European	Indo-Aryan
Urdu	ur	Indo-European	Indo-Aryan

Table 1: List of the languages used in our experiments with their ISO 639-1 codes, family and the branch in that family.

In the case of the log-linear parameterization, we simply add a language-specific atomic feature for the language-id, drawing inspiration from Daumé III (2007)'s approach for domain adaption. We then conjoin this new atomic feature with the existing feature templates, doubling the number of feature templates: the original and the new feature template conjoined with the language ID.

4 Related Work

We divide the discussion of related work topically.

Character-Level Neural Networks. In recent years, many authors have incorporated character-level information into taggers using neural networks, e.g., dos Santos and Zadrozny (2014) employed a convolutional network for part-of-speech tagging in morphologically rich languages and Ling et al. (2015) a LSTM for a myriad of different tasks. Relatedly, Chiu and Nichols (2016) approached NER with character-level LSTMs, but without using a CRF. Our work firmly builds upon on this in that we, too, compactly summarize the word form with a recurrent neural component.

Neural Transfer Schemes. Previous work has also performed transfer learning using neural networks. The novelty of our work lies in the *cross-lingual* transfer. For example, Peng and Dredze (2017) and Yang et al. (2017), similarly oriented concurrent papers, focus on domain adaptation within the same language. While this is a related problem, cross-lingual transfer is much more involved since the morphology, syntax and semantics change more radically between two languages than

	languages	low-resource ($|\mathcal{D}_\tau| = 100$)			high-resource ($|\mathcal{D}_\tau| = 10000$)		
τ	σ_i	log-linear	neural	Δ	log-linear	neural	Δ
gl	—	57.64	49.19	−8.45	87.23	89.42	+2.19
gl	es	71.46	76.40	+4.94	87.50	89.46	+1.96
gl	ca	67.32	75.40	+8.08	87.40	89.32	+1.92
gl	it	63.81	70.93	+7.12	87.34	89.50	+2.16
gl	fr	58.22	68.02	+9.80	87.92	89.38	+1.46
gl	ro	59.23	67.76	+8.44	87.24	89.19	+1.95
fy	—	62.71	58.43	−4.28	90.42	91.03	+0.61
fy	nl	68.15	72.12	+3.97	90.94	91.01	+0.07
tl	—	58.15	56.98	−1.17	74.24	79.03	+4.79
tl	ceb	75.29	81.79	+6.50	74.02	79.51	+5.48
uk	—	61.40	60.65	−0.75	85.63	87.39	+1.75
uk	ru	70.94	76.74	+5.80	86.01	87.42	+1.41
mr	—	42.76	39.02	−3.73	70.98	74.95	+4.86
mr	hi	54.25	60.92	+6.67	70.45	74.49	+4.04
mr	ur	49.32	58.92	+9.60	70.75	74.81	+4.07

Table 2: Results comparing the log-linear and neural CRFs in various settings. We compare the log-linear linear and the neural CRF in the low-resource transfer setting. The difference (Δ) is blue when positive and red when negative.

between domains.

Projection-based Transfer Schemes. Projection is a common approach to tag low-resource languages. The strategy involves annotating one side of bitext with a tagger for a high-resource language and then project the annotation the over the bilingual alignments obtained through unsupervised learning (Och and Ney, 2003). Using these projected annotations as weak supervision, one then trains a tagger in the target language. This line of research has a rich history, starting with Yarowsky and Ngai (2001). For a recent take, see Wang and Manning (2014) for projecting NER from English to Chinese. We emphasize that projection-based approaches are *incomparable to our proposed method* as they make an additional bitext assumption, which is generally not present in the case of low-resource languages.

5   Experiments

Fundamentally, we want to show that character-level neural CRFs are capable of generalizing the notion of an entity across related languages. To get at this, we compare a linear CRF (see §2.2) with standard feature templates for the task and a neural CRF (see §2.3). We further compare three training set-ups: low-resource, high-resource and

low-resource with additional cross-lingual data for transfer. Given past results in the literature, we expect linear CRF to dominate in the low-resource settings, the neural CRF to dominate in the high-resource setting. The novelty of our paper lies in the consideration of the low-resource with transfer case: we show that neural CRFs are better at transferring entity-level abstractions cross-linguistically.

5.1   Data

We experiment on 15 languages from the cross-lingual named entity dataset described in Pan et al. (2017). We focus on 5 typologically diverse[3] target languages: Galician, West Frisian, Ukranian, Marathi and Tagalog. As related source languages, we consider Spanish, Catalan, Italian, French, Romanian, Dutch, Russian, Cebuano, Hindi and Urdu. For the language code abbreviations and linguistic families, see Tab. 1. For each of the target languages, we emulate a truly low-resource condition, creating a 100 sentence split for training. We then create a 10000 sentence superset to be able to compare to a high-resource condition in those same

---

[3]While most of these languages are from the Indo-European family, they still run the gauntlet along a number of typological axes, e.g., Dutch and West Frisian have far less inflection compared to Russian and Ukranian and the Indo-Aryan languages employ postpositions (attached to the word) rather than prepositions (space separated).

languages. For the source languages, we only created a 10000 sentence split. We also create disjoint validation and test splits, of 1000 sentences each.

5.2 Results

The linear CRF is trained using L-BFGS until convergence using the CRF suite toolkit.[4] We train our neural CRF for 100 epochs using ADADELTA (Zeiler, 2012) with a learning rate of 1.0. The results are reported in Tab. 2. To understand the table, take the target language (τ) Galician. In terms of F_1, while the neural CRF outperforms the log-linear CRF the high-resource setting (89.42 vs. 87.23), it performs poorly in the low-resource setting (49.19 vs. 56.64); when we add in a source language (σ_i) such as Spanish, F_1 increases to 76.40 for the neural CRF and 71.46 for the log-linear CRF. The trend is similar for other source languages, such as Catalan (75.40) and Italian (70.93).

Overall, we observe three general trends. i) In the monolingual high-resource case, the neural CRF outperforms the log-linear CRF. ii) In the low-resource case, the log-linear CRF outperforms the neural CRF. iii) In the transfer case, the neural CRF wins, however, indicating that our character-level neural approach is truly better at generalizing cross-linguistically in the low-resource case (when we have little target language data), as we hoped. In the high-resource case (when we have a lot of target language data), the transfer learning has little to no effect. We conclude that our cross-lingual neural CRF is a viable method for the transfer of NER. However, there is a still a sizable gap between the neural CRF trained on 10000 target sentences and the transfer case (100 target and 10000 source), indicating there is still room for improvement.

6 Conclusion

We have investigated the task of cross-lingual transfer in low-resource named entity recognition using neural CRFs with experiments on 15 typologically diverse languages. Overall, we show that direct cross-lingual transfer is an option for reducing sample complexity for state-of-the-art architectures. In the future, we plan to investigate how exactly the networks manage to induce a cross-lingual entity abstraction.

---

[4] http://www.chokkan.org/software/crfsuite/

Acknowledgments

We are grateful to Heng Ji and Xiaoman Pan for sharing their dataset and providing support.

References

Breck Baldwin. 2009. Coding chunkers as taggers: IO, BIO, BMEWO, and BMEWO+. http://bit.ly/2xRo8Ni.

Adam L. Berger, Vincent J. Della Pietra, and Stephen A. Della Pietra. 1996. A maximum entropy approach to natural language processing. *Computational Linguistics*, 22(1):39–71.

Jason Chiu and Eric Nichols. 2016. Named entity recognition with bidirectional LSTM-CNNs. *Transactions of the Association of Computational Linguistics*, 4:357–370.

Ronan Collobert, Jason Weston, Léon Bottou, Michael Karlen, Koray Kavukcuoglu, and Pavel Kuksa. 2011. Natural language processing (almost) from scratch. *Journal of Machine Learning Research*, 12(Aug):2493–2537.

Hal Daumé III. 2007. Frustratingly easy domain adaptation. In *Proceedings of the 45th Annual Meeting of the Association of Computational Linguistics*, pages 256–263, Prague, Czech Republic. Association for Computational Linguistics.

Trinh-Minh-Tri Do and Thierry Artières. 2010. Neural conditional random fields. In *Proceedings of the Thirteenth International Conference on Artificial Intelligence and Statistics*, pages 177–184.

Jeffrey L. Elman. 1990. Finding structure in time. *Cognitive Science*, 14(2):179–211.

Yasuhisa Fujii, Kazumasa Yamamoto, and Seiichi Nakagawa. 2012. Deep-hidden conditional neural fields for continuous phoneme speech recognition. In *Proceedings of the International Workshop of Statistical Machine Learning for Speech Processing (IWSML)*.

Sepp Hochreiter and Jürgen Schmidhuber. 1997. Long short-term memory. *Neural Computation*, 9(8):1735–1780.

Zhiheng Huang, Wei Xu, and Kai Yu. 2015. Bidirectional LSTM-CRF models for sequence tagging. *arXiv preprint arXiv:1508.01991*.

John D. Lafferty, Andrew McCallum, and Fernando C. N. Pereira. 2001. Conditional random fields: Probabilistic models for segmenting and labeling sequence data. In *Proceedings of the Eighteenth International Conference on Machine Learning (ICML)*, pages 282–289.

Guillaume Lample, Miguel Ballesteros, Sandeep Subramanian, Kazuya Kawakami, and Chris Dyer. 2016. Neural architectures for named entity recognition.

In *Proceedings of the 2016 Conference of the North American Chapter of the Association for Computational Linguistics: Human Language Technologies*, pages 260–270, San Diego, California. Association for Computational Linguistics.

Wang Ling, Chris Dyer, Alan W. Black, Isabel Trancoso, Ramon Fermandez, Silvio Amir, Luis Marujo, and Tiago Luis. 2015. Finding function in form: Compositional character models for open vocabulary word representation. In *Proceedings of the 2015 Conference on Empirical Methods in Natural Language Processing*, pages 1520–1530, Lisbon, Portugal. Association for Computational Linguistics.

Xuezhe Ma and Eduard Hovy. 2016. End-to-end sequence labeling via bi-directional LSTM-CNNs-CRF. In *Proceedings of the 54th Annual Meeting of the Association for Computational Linguistics (Volume 1: Long Papers)*, pages 1064–1074. Association for Computational Linguistics.

Franz Josef Och and Hermann Ney. 2003. A systematic comparison of various statistical alignment models. *Computational Linguistics*, 29(1):19–51.

Xiaoman Pan, Boliang Zhang, Jonathan May, Joel Nothman, Kevin Knight, and Heng Ji. 2017. Cross-lingual name tagging and linking for 282 languages. In *Proceedings of the 55th Annual Meeting of the Association for Computational Linguistics (Volume 1: Long Papers)*, Vancouver, Canada. Association for Computational Linguistics.

Jian Peng, Liefeng Bo, and Jinbo Xu. 2009. Conditional neural fields. In *Advances in Neural Information Processing Systems (NIPS)*, pages 1419–1427.

Nanyun Peng and Mark Dredze. 2017. Multi-task domain adaptation for sequence tagging. In *Proceedings of the 2nd Workshop on Representation Learning for NLP*, Vancouver, Canada. Association for Computational Linguistics.

Lance A. Ramshaw and Mitchell P. Marcus. 1995. Text chunking using transformation-based learning. In *Proceedings of the 3rd ACL Workshop on Very Large Corpora*, pages 82–94. Association for Computational Linguistics.

Cicero Nogueira dos Santos and Bianca Zadrozny. 2014. Learning character-level representations for part-of-speech tagging. In *International Conference on Machine Learning (ICML)*, volume 32, pages 1818–1826.

Fei Sha and Fernando C. N. Pereira. 2003. Shallow parsing with conditional random fields. In *Human Language Technology Conference of the North American Chapter of the Association for Computational Linguistics, HLT-NAACL 2003*.

Erik F. Tjong Kim Sang. 2002. Introduction to the CoNLL-2002 shared task: Language-independent named entity recognition. *August*, 31:1–4.

Erik F. Tjong Kim Sang and Fien De Meulder. 2003. Introduction to the CoNLL-2003 shared task: Language-independent named entity recognition. In *Proceedings of the Seventh Conference on Natural Language Learning at HLT-NAACL 2003*, pages 142–147.

Antoine Vinel, Trinh-Minh-Tri Do, and Thierry Artières. 2011. Joint optimization of hidden conditional random fields and non linear feature extraction. In *2011 International Conference on Document Analysis and Recognition (ICDAR)*, pages 513–517. IEEE.

Mengqiu Wang and Christopher D. Manning. 2013. Effect of non-linear deep architecture in sequence labeling. In *Proceedings of the Sixth International Joint Conference on Natural Language Processing*, pages 1285–1291, Nagoya, Japan. Asian Federation of Natural Language Processing.

Mengqiu Wang and Christopher D. Manning. 2014. Cross-lingual pseudo-projected expectation regularization for weakly supervised learning. *Transactions of the Association for Computational Linguistics*.

Zhilin Yang, Ruslan Salakhutdinov, and William W3. Cohen. 2017. Transfer learning for sequence tagging with hierarchical recurrent networks. In *International Conference on Learning Representations (ICLR)*.

David Yarowsky and Grace Ngai. 2001. Inducing multilingual POS taggers and NP brackets via robust projection across aligned corpora. In *Human Language Technology Conference of the North American Chapter of the Association for Computational Linguistics, HLT-NAACL 2001*.

Matthew D. Zeiler. 2012. ADADELTA: an adaptive learning rate method. *arXiv preprint arXiv:1212.5701*.

Segment-Level Neural Conditional Random Fields for Named Entity Recognition

Motoki Sato[1,2]   **Hiroyuki Shindo**[1,2]   **Ikuya Yamada**[3]   **Yuji Matsumoto**[1,2]

[1] Nara Institute of Science and Technology
[2] RIKEN Center for Advanced Intelligence Project (AIP)
[3] Studio Ousia

{ sato.motoki.sa7, shindo, matsu }@is.naist.jp, ikuya@ousia.jp

Abstract

We present *Segment-level Neural CRF*, which combines neural networks with a linear chain CRF for *segment-level* sequence modeling tasks such as named entity recognition (NER) and syntactic chunking. Our segment-level CRF can consider higher-order label dependencies compared with conventional word-level CRF. Since it is difficult to consider all possible variable length segments, our method uses *segment lattice* constructed from the word-level tagging model to reduce the search space. Performing experiments on NER and chunking, we demonstrate that our method outperforms conventional word-level CRF with neural networks.

1 Introduction

Named entity recognition (NER) and syntactic chunking are segment-level sequence modeling tasks, which require to recognize a *segment* from a sequence of words. A segment means a sequence of words that may compose an expression as shown in Figure 1. Current high performance NER systems use the *word-level* linear chain Conditional Random Fields (CRF) (Lafferty et al., 2001) with neural networks. Especially, it has been shown that the combination of LSTMs (Hochreiter and Schmidhuber, 1997; Gers et al., 2000), convolutional neural networks (CNNs) (LeCun et al., 1989), and word-level CRF achieves the state-of-the-art performance (Ma and Hovy, 2016). Figure 1 shows an overview of the word-level CRF for NER.

However, the word-level neural CRF has two main limitations: (1) it captures only first-order word label dependencies thus it cannot capture

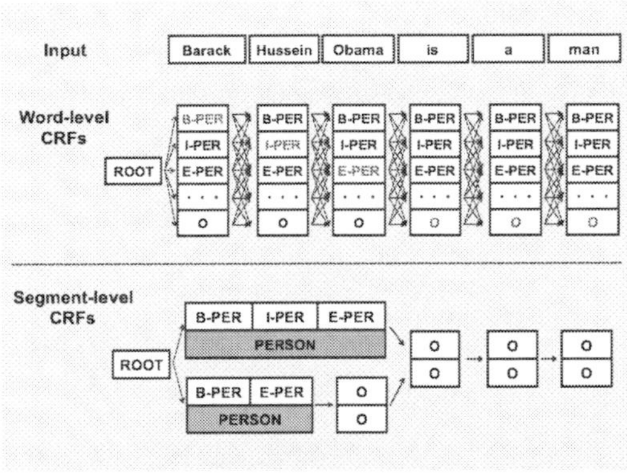

Figure 1: The difference between word-level CRF and segment-level CRF. The segment-level CRF can consider higher-order label dependencies.

segment-level information; (2) it is not easy to incorporate dictionary features directly into a word-level model since named entities and syntactic chunks consist of multiple words rather than a single word. To overcome the limitation of first-order label dependencies, previous work propose the higher-order CRF, which outperforms first-order CRF on NER task (Sarawagi and Cohen, 2005) and morphological tagging task (Mueller et al., 2013).

In this paper, we extend a neural CRF from word-level to segment-level and propose *Segment-level Neural CRF*. Our method has two main advantages: (1) *segment-level* linear chain CRF can consider higher-order word label dependencies (e.g., the relations between named entities and the other words); (2) it is easy to incorporate dictionary features into the model directly since a dictionary entry and a segment (e.g., a named entity) are in one-to-one correspondence.

Our experiments on chunking and NER demonstrate that our method outperforms conventional word-level neural CRF.

Proceedings of the The 8th International Joint Conference on Natural Language Processing, pages 97–102,
Taipei, Taiwan, November 27 – December 1, 2017 ©2017 AFNLP

2 Word-level Neural CRF

As a baseline method, we use word-level neural CRF proposed by (Ma and Hovy, 2016) since their method achieves state-of-the-art performance on NER. Specifically, they propose Bi-directional LSTM-CNN CRF (BLSTM-CNN-CRF) for sequential tagging. Here, we briefly review their BLSTM-CNN-CRF model.

Let w_t be the t-th word in an input sentence and $C_t = c_t^{(1)}, \dots, c_t^{(k)}$ be the character sequence of w_t. BLSTM-CNN-CRF uses both word-level embedding $\mathbf{w}_t \in \mathbb{R}^{d_{word}}$ and character-level embedding $\mathbf{c}_t \in \mathbb{R}^{d_{char}}$. Given a word sequence $X = w_1, \dots, w_n$, the model outputs a score vector $\mathbf{o}_t$ as follows.

$$
\begin{aligned}
\mathbf{c}_t &= \text{CNN}_{char}(C_t), \\
\mathbf{x}_t &= \mathbf{w}_t \oplus \mathbf{c}_t, \\
\mathbf{h}_t &= \text{Bi-LSTM}(\mathbf{x}_t, \mathbf{h}_{t-1}, \mathbf{h}_{t+1}) \qquad (1) \\
&= \text{LSTM}_f(\mathbf{x}_t, \mathbf{h}_{t-1}) \oplus \text{LSTM}_b(\mathbf{x}_t, \mathbf{h}_{t+1}), \\
\mathbf{o}_t &= \text{softmax}(\mathbf{W}_{TG}\mathbf{h}_t + \mathbf{b}_{TG}),
\end{aligned}
$$

where CNN_{char} is the character-level CNN function, $\oplus$ is the concatenation of two vectors, LSTM_f is the forward LSTM function, LSTM_b is the backward LSTM function, Bi-LSTM is the Bi-LSTM function, respectively. Then, $\mathbf{W}_{TG} \in \mathbb{R}^{|\mathcal{T}| \times d_{hidden}}$ is the weight matrix to learn, $\mathbf{b}_{TG} \in \mathbb{R}^{|\mathcal{T}|}$ is the bias vector to learn, $|\mathcal{T}|$ is the size of tag set $\mathcal{T}$, d_{hidden} is the size of hidden layer of Bi-LSTM, and $\mathbf{o}_t \in \mathbb{R}^{|\mathcal{T}|}$ is the score vector in which each element is the probability of a possible tag.

In BLSTM-CNN-CRF, CRF is applied to the output layer. The conditional probability of CRF is defined as follows:

$$
\begin{aligned}
\phi(y_{i-1}, y_i, o_i^{(y_i)}) &= \exp(o_i^{(y_i)} + A_{y_{i-1}, y_i}), \\
p(\mathbf{y}|\mathbf{o}; \mathbf{A}) &= \frac{\prod_{i=1}^{n} \phi(y_{i-1}, y_i, o_i^{(y_i)})}{\sum_{y' \in \mathcal{Y}} \prod_{i=1}^{n} \phi(y'_{i-1}, y'_i, o_i^{(y'_i)})},
\end{aligned}
$$

where $\phi(y_{i-1}, y_i, o_i^{(y_i)})$ is the potential function[1], $y_i \in \{0, \dots, |\mathcal{T}|-1\}$ is the index of tag, $o_i^{(j)}$ is the j-th element of the vector $\mathbf{o}_i$. Then, $\mathbf{A} \in \mathbb{R}^{|\mathcal{T}| \times |\mathcal{T}|}$ is a transition score matrix, A_{y_{i-1}, y_i} is a transition

---

[1] While (Ma and Hovy, 2016) define $\phi(y_{i-1}, y_i, o_i) = \exp(W_{y_{i-1}, y_i} o_i + A_{y_{i-1}, y_i})$ as the potential function where W is the weight vector corresponding to label pair (y_{i-1}, y_i), we use the simple potential function here.

score for jumping from tag y_{i-1} to y_i, and $\mathcal{Y}$ indicates all possible paths.

At test time, the predicted sequence is obtained by finding the highest score in a all possible paths using Viterbi algorithm as follows:

$$
\tilde{y} = \operatorname*{argmax}_{\mathbf{y} \in \mathcal{Y}} p(\mathbf{y}|\mathbf{o}_i; \mathbf{A}).
$$

3 Segment-level Neural CRF

In this section, we describe our proposed method. Our segment-level neural CRF consists of the following two steps:

(i) A *segment lattice* is constructed from a sequence of words by pruning unlikely BIO tags to reduce a search space. This is because it is difficult to consider all possible variable length segments in practice.

(ii) We use a linear chain CRF to find the highest score path on the segment lattice.

3.1 Constructing Segment Lattice

A *segment lattice* is a graph structure where each path corresponds to a candidate segmentation path as shown in the lower part of Figure 1. The segment lattice is a kind of semi-Markov model (Sarawagi and Cohen, 2005). To construct the segment lattice, we firstly give an input sentence to the word-level tagging model, then obtain the score vector $\mathbf{o}_t$ for each word that gives the probabilities of possible BIO tags. Then, we generate the candidate BIO tags whose scores are greater than the threshold T. After that, we construct the segment lattice by generating admissible segments from the candidate BIO tags. For example, we generate the *PERSON* segment from the candidate BIO tags {*B-PER, I-PER, E-PER*}.

The threshold T is a hyper-parameter for our model. We describe how to choose the threshold T in Section 4.3. While it has been shown that the CRF layer is required to achieve the state-of-the-art performance in Ma and Hovy (2016), we observe that the CRF has no significant effect on the final performance for the lattice construction. Therefore, we use BLSTM-CNN (without CRF) as the word-level tagging model in this paper.

3.2 Segment-level Vector Representation

To find the highest score path in the segment lattice, we use a standard linear chain CRF at segment-level. Since each segment has variable length, we need to obtain fixed-dimensional

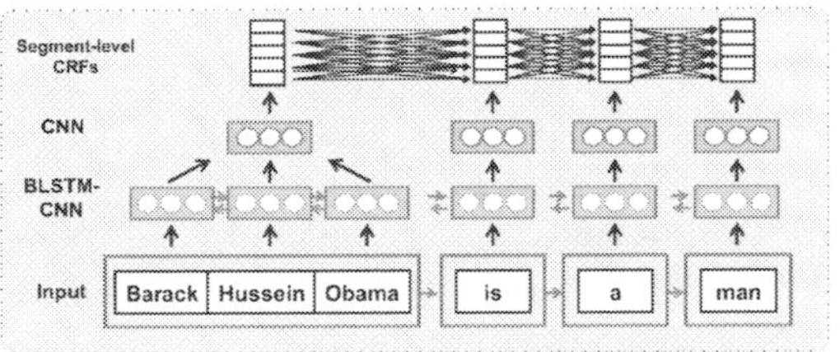

Figure 2: Details of the Segment-level Neural CRF model.

segment-level vector representation for neural networks.

Figure 2 shows the details of the segment-level neural CRF model. Let $u_i = w_b, w_{b+1}, \ldots, w_e$ be the i-th segment in a segment lattice, b is the starting word index, and e is the ending word index. To obtain the fixed-dimensional vector $\mathbf{u}_i \in \mathbb{R}^{d_{node}}$ for the segment u_i, we apply a CNN to the hidden vector sequence $\mathbf{h}_{b:e} = \mathbf{h}_b, \mathbf{h}_{b+1}, \ldots, \mathbf{h}_e$ by Eq. (1), and compute the score vector $\mathbf{z}_i$ as follows:

$$\mathbf{r}_i = \mathrm{CNN}_{node}(\mathbf{h}_{b:e}),$$
$$\mathbf{z}_i = \mathrm{softmax}(\mathbf{W}_{LS}\mathbf{r}_i + \mathbf{b}_{LS}),$$

where CNN_{node} is the CNN function for the segment vector, $\mathbf{W}_{LS} \in \mathbb{R}^{|\mathcal{N}| \times d_{node}}$ is the weight matrix to learn, $\mathbf{b}_{LS} \in \mathbb{R}^{d_{node}}$ is the bias vector to learn, $|\mathcal{N}|$ is the size of named entity type set $\mathcal{N}$, d_{node} is the size of the segment vector, and $\mathbf{z}_i \in \mathbb{R}^{|\mathcal{N}|}$ is the score vector in which each element is the probability of a possible NE type.

Finally, we apply a linear chain CRF to find the highest score path in the segment lattice as we describe in Section 2.

3.3 Dictionary Features for NER

In this subsection, we describe the use of two additional dictionary features for NER. Since an entry of named entity dictionary and the segment in our model are in one-to-one correspondence, it is easy to directly incorporate the dictionary features into our model. We use following two dictionary features on NER task.

Binary feature The binary feature $\mathbf{e}_i \in \mathbb{R}^{d_{dict}}$ indicates whether the i-th segment (e.g., a named entity) exists in the dictionary or not. We use the embedding matrix $\mathbf{W}_{dict} \in \mathbb{R}^{2 \times d_{dict}}$, where d_{dict} is the size of the feature embedding. $e \in \{0, 1\}$ is the binary index which indicates whether the segment exists in the dictionary or not. Using the index e, we extract the column vector $\mathbf{e}_i \in \mathbb{R}^{d_{dict}}$

from $\mathbf{W}_{dict}$ and concatenate the segment vector $\mathbf{r}_i$ and $\mathbf{e}_i$. The concatenated segment vector $\mathbf{r}'_i$ is defined as $\mathbf{r}'_i = \mathbf{r}_i \oplus \mathbf{e}_i$. $\mathbf{W}_{dict}$ is a randomly initialized matrix and updated in the training time. To incorporate the popularity of the Wikipedia entity into our method, we also concatenate one-dimensional vector constructed from the page view count for one month period into $\mathbf{e}_i$. The page view count is normalized by the number of candidate segments in the segment lattice. The Wikipedia dictionary is constructed by extracting the titles of all Wikipedia pages and the titles of all redirect pages from the Wikipedia Dump Data[2].

Wikipedia embedding feature Another additional feature is the Wikipedia embeddings proposed by Yamada et al. (2016). Their method maps words and entities (i.e., Wikipedia entities) into the same continuous vector space using the skip-gram model (Mikolov et al., 2013). We use only the 300 dimensional entity embeddings in this paper. Please refer to Yamada et al. (2016) for more detail.

4 Experiments

4.1 Datasets

We evaluate our method on two segment-level sequence tagging tasks: NER and text chunking[3].

For NER, we use CoNLL 2003 English NER shared task (Tjong Kim Sang and De Meulder, 2003). Following previous work (Ma and Hovy, 2016), we use BIOES tagging scheme in the word-level tagging model.

For text chunking, we use the CoNLL 2000 English text chunking shared task (Tjong Kim Sang and Buchholz, 2000). Following previous work (Søgaard and Goldberg, 2016), the section 19 of WSJ corpus is used as the development set. We use BIOES tagging scheme in the word-level tagging model and measure performance using F1 score in all experiments.

4.2 Model Settings

To generate a segment lattice, we train word-level BLSTM-CNN with the same hyper-parameters used in Ma and Hovy (2016): one layer 200 dimentional Bi-directional LSTMs for each direction, 30 filters with window size 3 in character-

---

[2]The dump data of Wikipedia is available in Wikimedia http://dumps.wikimedia.org/. We use the dump data at 2016-09-20.

[3]Our code will be available from http://xxxx

Threshold	Oracle		
	Train	Dev	Test
T=0.05	99.93	99.71	99.27
T=0.0005	99.99	99.96	99.71
T=0.00005	100.0	99.98	99.83

Table 1: Threshold T and Oracle score on NER.

	Test		
	Prec.	Recall	F1
BLSTM-CNN	89.04	90.40	89.72
BLSTM-CNN-CRF[3]	90.82	91.11	90.96
Our method	91.07	91.50	91.28
+ Binary Dict	91.05	91.69	91.37
+ WikiEmb Dict	91.29	91.58	91.44
+ Binary + WikiEmb	91.47	91.62	**91.55**
Ma and Hovy (2016)	91.35	91.06	**91.21**

Table 2: Result of CoNLL 2003 English NER.

level CNN, and 100 dimentional pre-trained word embedding of GloVe (Pennington et al., 2014). At input layer and output layer, we apply dropout (Srivastava et al., 2014) with rate at 0.5. In our model, we set 400 filters with window size 3 in CNN for segment vector. To optimize our model, we use AdaDelta (Zeiler, 2012) with batch size 10 and gradient clipping 5. We use early stopping (Caruana et al., 2001) based on performance on development sets.

4.3 How to choose threshold

The threshold T is a hyper-parameter for our model. We choose the threshold T based on how a segment lattice maintains the gold segments in the training and development sets. The threshold T and the oracle score are shown in Table 1. In our experiment, the $T = 0.00005$ is used in NER task and $T = 0.0005$ is used in chunking task.

4.4 Results and Discussions

The results of CoNLL 2003 NER is shown in Table 2. By adding a CRF layer to BLSTM-CNN, it improves the F1 score from 89.72 to 90.96. This result is consistent with the result of (Ma and Hovy, 2016). By using segment-level CRF, it further improves the F1 score from 90.96 to 91.28. Furthermore, by using the binary dictionary feature, it improves the F1 score from 91.28 to 91.37 and by using the Wikipedia embedding feature, it

	Test		
	Prec.	Recall	F1
BLSTM-CNN	90.85	91.92	91.38
BLSTM-CNN-CRF	94.67	94.43	94.55
Our method	94.55	95.12	**94.84**

Table 3: Result of CoNLL 2000 Chunking.

improves the F1 score from 91.28 to 91.44. Eventually, we achieve the F1 score 91.55 with two dictionary features.

The results of CoNLL 2000 Chunking is shown in Table 3. Similar to NER task, by adding a CRF layer to BLSTM-CNN, it improves the F1 score from 91.38 to 94.55. Furthermore, by using segment-level CRF, it improves the F1 score from 94.55 to 94.84.

In both experiments, it improves the F1 score by using segment-level CRF. On the NER experiment, the additional dictionary features help to obtain further improvement.

5 Related Work

Several different neural network methods have been proven to be effective for NER (Collobert et al., 2011; Chiu and Nichols, 2016; Lample et al., 2016; Ma and Hovy, 2016). Ma and Hovy (2016) demonstrate that combining LSTM, CNN and CRF achieves the state-of-the-art performance on NER and chunking tasks.

Mueller et al. (2013) show that higher-order CRF outperforms first-order CRF. Our work differs from their work in that it can handle segments of variable lengths and thus it is easy to incorporate dictionary features directly.

Zhuo et al. (2016) propose Gated Recursive Semi-CRF, which models a sequence of segments and automatically learns features. They combine Semi-CRF (Sarawagi and Cohen, 2005) and neural networks. However they report the F1 score 89.44% on NER and 94.73[4] on Chunking which are lower than the scores of our method.

Kong et al. (2016) propose segmental recurrent neural networks (SRNNs). SRNNs are based on Bi-LSTM feature extractor and uses dynamic programming algorithm to reduce search space.

6 Conclusion

In this paper, we propose the segment-level sequential modeling method based on a segment lat-

---

[3]This is same method in (Ma and Hovy, 2016) and this F-1 score is the result of our implementation.

[4]This is under the setting without external resource. They add Brown clusters features and report the F1 score 95.01.

tice structure. Our experimental results show that our method outperforms conventional word-level neural CRF. Furthermore, two additional dictionary features help to obtain further improvement on NER task.

Acknowledgments

Part of this work was supported by JST CREST Grant Number JPMJCR1513, Japan.

References

Rich Caruana, Steve Lawrence, and C. Lee Giles. 2001. Overfitting in neural nets: Backpropagation, conjugate gradient, and early stopping. In T. K. Leen, T. G. Dietterich, and V. Tresp, editors, *Advances in Neural Information Processing Systems 13*, MIT Press, pages 402–408.

Jason Chiu and Eric Nichols. 2016. Named entity recognition with bidirectional lstm-cnns. *Transactions of the Association for Computational Linguistics* 4:357–370.

Ronan Collobert, Jason Weston, Léon Bottou, Michael Karlen, Koray Kavukcuoglu, and Pavel Kuksa. 2011. Natural language processing (almost) from scratch. *J. Mach. Learn. Res.* 12:2493–2537.

Felix A Gers, Jürgen Schmidhuber, and Fred Cummins. 2000. Learning to forget: Continual prediction with lstm. *Neural Computation* 12(10):2451–2471.

Sepp Hochreiter and Jürgen Schmidhuber. 1997. Long short-term memory. *Neural computation* 9(8):1735–1780.

Lingpeng Kong, Chris Dyer, and Noah A Smith. 2016. Segmental recurrent neural networks. In *Proceedings of the International Conference on Learning Representations (ICLR)*.

John D. Lafferty, Andrew McCallum, and Fernando C. N. Pereira. 2001. Conditional random fields: Probabilistic models for segmenting and labeling sequence data. In *Proceedings of the Eighteenth International Conference on Machine Learning*. Morgan Kaufmann Publishers Inc., San Francisco, CA, USA, ICML '01, pages 282–289.

Guillaume Lample, Miguel Ballesteros, Sandeep Subramanian, Kazuya Kawakami, and Chris Dyer. 2016. Neural architectures for named entity recognition. In *Proceedings of the 2016 Conference of the North American Chapter of the Association for Computational Linguistics: Human Language Technologies*. Association for Computational Linguistics, San Diego, California, pages 260–270.

Yann LeCun, Bernhard Boser, John S Denker, Don nie Henderson, Richard E Howard, Wayne Hubbard, and Lawrence D Jackel. 1989. Backpropagation applied to handwritten zip code recognition. *Neural computation* 1(4):541–551.

Xuezhe Ma and Eduard Hovy. 2016. End-to-end sequence labeling via bi-directional lstm-cnns-crf. In *Proceedings of the 54th Annual Meeting of the Association for Computational Linguistics (Volume 1: Long Papers)*. Association for Computational Linguistics, Berlin, Germany, pages 1064–1074.

Tomas Mikolov, Ilya Sutskever, Kai Chen, Greg S Corrado, and Jeff Dean. 2013. Distributed representations of words and phrases and their compositionality. In *Advances in neural information processing systems*. pages 3111–3119.

Thomas Mueller, Helmut Schmid, and Hinrich Schütze. 2013. Efficient higher-order CRFs for morphological tagging. In *Proceedings of the 2013 Conference on Empirical Methods in Natural Language Processing*. Association for Computational Linguistics, Seattle, Washington, USA, pages 322–332.

Jeffrey Pennington, Richard Socher, and Christopher Manning. 2014. Glove: Global vectors for word representation. In *Proceedings of the 2014 Conference on Empirical Methods in Natural Language Processing (EMNLP)*. Association for Computational Linguistics, Doha, Qatar, pages 1532–1543.

Sunita Sarawagi and William W Cohen. 2005. Semimarkov conditional random fields for information extraction. In L. K. Saul, Y. Weiss, and L. Bottou, editors, *Advances in Neural Information Processing Systems 17*, MIT Press, pages 1185–1192.

Anders Søgaard and Yoav Goldberg. 2016. Deep multi-task learning with low level tasks supervised at lower layers. In *Proceedings of the 54th Annual Meeting of the Association for Computational Linguistics*. Association for Computational Linguistics, volume 2, pages 231–235.

Nitish Srivastava, Geoffrey Hinton, Alex Krizhevsky, Ilya Sutskever, and Ruslan Salakhutdinov. 2014. Dropout: A simple way to prevent neural networks from overfitting. *Journal of Machine Learning Research* 15:1929–1958.

Erik F Tjong Kim Sang and Sabine Buchholz. 2000. Introduction to the conll-2000 shared task: Chunking. In *Proceedings of the 2nd workshop on Learning language in logic and the 4th conference on Computational natural language learning-Volume 7*. Association for Computational Linguistics, pages 127–132.

Erik F Tjong Kim Sang and Fien De Meulder. 2003. Introduction to the conll-2003 shared task: Language-independent named entity recognition. In *Proceedings of the seventh conference on Natural language learning at HLT-NAACL 2003-Volume 4*. Association for Computational Linguistics, pages 142–147.

Ikuya Yamada, Hiroyuki Shindo, Hideaki Takeda, and Yoshiyasu Takefuji. 2016. Joint learning of the embedding of words and entities for named entity disambiguation. In *Proceedings of The 20th SIGNLL Conference on Computational Natural Language Learning*. Association for Computational Linguistics, Berlin, Germany, pages 250–259.

Matthew D Zeiler. 2012. Adadelta: an adaptive learning rate method. *arXiv preprint arXiv:1212.5701* .

Jingwei Zhuo, Yong Cao, Jun Zhu, Bo Zhang, and Zaiqing Nie. 2016. Segment-level sequence modeling using gated recursive semi-markov conditional random fields. In *Proceedings of the 54th Annual Meeting of the Association for Computational Linguistics (Volume 1: Long Papers)*. Association for Computational Linguistics, Berlin, Germany, pages 1413–1423.

Integrating Vision and Language Datasets
to Measure Word Concreteness

Gitit Kehat and **James Pustejovsky**
Department of Computer Science
Brandeis University
Waltham, MA 02453 USA
{gititkeh, jamesp}@brandeis.edu

Abstract

We present and take advantage of the inherent visualizability properties of words in visual corpora (the textual components of vision-language datasets) to compute concreteness scores for words. Our simple method does not require hand-annotated concreteness score lists for training, and yields state-of-the-art results when evaluated against concreteness scores lists and previously derived scores, as well as when used for metaphor detection.

1 Introduction

One of the most pervasive problems in cognitive science, linguistics, and AI has been establishing the semantic relationship between language and vision (Miller and Johnson-Laird, 1976; Winograd, 1972; Jackendoff, 1983; Waltz, 1993). In recent years, new datasets have emerged that enable researchers to approach this question from a new angle: that of determining both how linguistic expressions are grounded in visual images, and how features of visual images are expressible in language. To this end, large vision and language (VL) datasets have become increasingly popular, mostly used in combined VL tasks, such as visual captioning and question answering, image retrieval and more. However, *visual corpora*, the language corpora created in the service of image annotation, have properties that have yet to be exploited. Naturally, they tend to prefer concrete object labels and tangible event descriptions over abstract concepts and private or mental states (Dodge et al., 2012).

In this work, we provide further evidence that *visual corpora* are indeed less abstract than general corpora, and characterize this as a property of what we term a word's *visibility score*. We then show how this notion can be used to measure the concreteness of words, and demonstrate the usefulness of our calculated scores in solving the related problem of metaphor detection.

2 Related Work and Background

I love that crazy cat in the hat.

Figure 1: Visual Genome (top) with multiple captions, and SBU with a user-generated caption per image.

2.1 Abstractness and concreteness

A common notion for the concreteness of a word is to what extent the word represents things that can be perceived directly through the five senses (Brysbaert et al., 2014; Turney et al., 2011), such as *tiger* and *wet*. Accordingly, an abstract word

103

Proceedings of the The 8th International Joint Conference on Natural Language Processing, pages 103–108,
Taipei, Taiwan, November 27 – December 1, 2017 ©2017 AFNLP

represents a concept that is far from immediate perception, or alternatively, could be explained only by other words (as opposed to be demonstrated through image, taste, etc.), like *fun* and *truth*.

Concreteness scores are currently applied in tasks like concept visualization and image description generation, event detection in text and more. Previous methods for measuring words' concreteness used annotated datasets for training. The list by Turney et al. (2011) contains 114k pairs of words and concreteness scores, automatically generated by an algorithm trained on the MRC dataset (Coltheart, 1981). Köper and im Walde (2017) generated a huge concreteness scores list for 3M words, using 32K pairs from the list by Brysbaert et al. (2014) to train a neural network model with high correlation scores with the existed lists.

2.2 Vision and Language Datasets

VL datasets come in different formats, but they all match together visual and textual pieces of information. The visual pieces can be photos, clip-arts, paintings, etc., and the textual ones range from full texts and sentences to single words (see Figure 1). There are surprisingly few works that analyze *visual corpora* in terms of their linguistic properties. Dodge et al. (2012) found that Flickr captions have more references to physical objects. Ferraro et al. (2015) compared visual corpora using a set of linguistic criteria, including an abstract-to-concrete ratio to estimate the concreteness level of a corpus. We further discuss this task in Section 3.

3 The Concreteness Level of a Corpus

We demonstrate the differences in the concreteness level of several corpora using two concreteness ratings (or "concreteness scores") lists, each contains pairs of a word and a score, in some scale, and potentially additional meta-data regarding the annotation agreement. See Table 1 for examples.

The list of **40K concreteness ratings** by Brysbaert et al. (2014) contains ratings from 1.0 (abstract) to 5.0 (concrete) for almost 40K terms, 37K of them are unigrams[1], along with metadata like the standard deviation over the scores assigned to a term by the 30 annotators. The authors aimed to represent all English lemmas, for each they included several forms, each was scored separately (according to the definition in Section 2.1).

---

[1]The rest are bigrams, we worked with unigrams only.

	40K (1.04-5.0)	MRC (158-670)
turtle	5.0 (sd=0.0)	644
boat	4.93 (sd=0.37)	637
milk	4.92 (sd=0.39)	670
side	3.68 (sd=1.33)	394
symbol	3.11 (sd=1.37)	402
clean	3.07 (sd=1.41)	392
impossible	1.66 (sd=1.06)	198
immortality	1.52 (sd=0.87)	209
justification	1.52 (sd=0.83)	219

Table 1: Examples for words in the concreteness lists annotated as mostly concrete, in the middle, and mostly abstract.

The **MRC psycholinguistic database** (Coltheart, 1981) contains 4,295 words and concreteness scores (range from 158 to 670), given by human subjects through psychological experiments.

3.1 Descriptions of Corpora Studied

Brown corpus (Francis and Kucera, 1964). Following Ferraro et al. (2015), a representative of a non-visual "general"/"balanced" corpus.

Visual Genome (Krishna et al., 2016). The largest VL dataset to date, containing 5.4M region descriptions for more than 108K images, visual question answers and more, all created through crowd-sourcing. We used the set of all region descriptions (see Figure 1) as corpus.

SBU Captioned Photo Dataset (Ordonez et al., 2011). Another large scale dataset, containing user generated image descriptions for 1M images, created by quering Flickr. As a result, the captions are not necessarily full or accurate (see Figure 1).

Flickr 30K (Young et al., 2014). 5 captions per image for more than 31K real-world images from Flickr, created through crowd-sourcing.

Microsoft COCO (Lin et al., 2014). Includes object segmentation and 5 captions per image for more than 300K images from Flickr.

ImageNet (Deng et al., 2009). A dataset matching images and the corresponding WordNet synsets (Miller et al., 1990). We gathered all available annotated synsets as the ImageNet corpus.

We also created a set of non-visual Brown corpora by subtracting each of the corpora from the Brown corpus, to each we refer as $Brown_{NV} - VC$ in relation to some visual corpus VC.

3.2 Setup and Comparison Results

Given a corpus, we divided the words in each concreteness scores list into two non-overlapping sets (words contained in the corpus and words not

Corpus	C-list	Words-in	Words-out	Ave-in	Ave-out	Diff/Range%	Abs-ratio
Brown	40K	18191	18742	3.02	2.91	2.74%	15.24%
	MRC	3639	553	442.17	443.62	-0.28%	
Visual Genome	40K	14968	21965	3.5	2.61	22.49%	—
	MRC	3263	929	465.62	360.66	20.5%	
MSCOCO	40K	11786	25147	3.52	2.71	20.52%	12.96%
	MRC	2919	1273	469.21	380.79	17.26%	
Flickr 30k	40K	9874	27059	3.57	2.75	20.76%	14.98%
	MRC	2669	1523	471.45	391.38	15.63%	
ImageNet	40K	8397	28536	3.96	2.68	32.52%	—
	MRC	2365	1827	505.31	360.87	28.21%	
SBU	40K	20746	16187	3.3	2.55	18.85%	3.74%
	MRC	3789	403	452.67	345.41	20.94%	

Table 2: Corpus concreteness measuring using different concreteness score lists.

Corpus	D/R% 40K	D/R% MRC
$Brown_{NV} - VG$	-14.47%	-20.35%
$Brown_{NV} - MSCOCO$	-11.37%	-17.13%
$Brown_{NV} - Flickr30k$	-10.30%	-15.76%
$Brown_{NV} - ImageNet$	-12.15%	-26.21%
$Brown_{NV} - SBU$	-15.13%	-22.28%

Table 3: The Diff/Range% of the non-visual Brown corpora.

contained in the corpus), and calculated the average concreteness score of each set, as well as the difference of the two averages normalized by the score range of the list ('Diff/Range%') (see Table 2). We can see the clear differences between the concreteness level of the Brown corpus (negligible Diff/Range%) and the rest of the visual corpora (15.0% - 32%), which show nicely that the Brown corpus is indeed "balanced" in terms of concreteness. The 'Abs-ratio' column refers to previous results by Ferraro et al. (2015), who calculated an abstract-to-concrete ratio (Abs-ratio) with a fixed common-abstract-terms list, where corpus words in the list were considered as "abstract" and the rest as "concrete". The results were highly dependent on corpus size (with more words outside the fixed list ("concrete") as vocabulary grows). Accordingly, the Abs-ratios of the Brown corpus and most of the visual corpora were very similar, and large corpora such as the SBU got significantly lower ratios.

Table 3 shows the same calculations on the non-visual Brown corpora. The large negative ratios ((-26)% - (-10)%) show that these corpora are less concrete than the original Brown corpus, and are much more abstract than all the visual corpora.

4 Predicting Concreteness Scores

The leading principal here is that words contained in visual corpora tend to have significantly higher concreteness scores, and words in non-visual corpora tend to have significantly lower scores. We do not use concreteness scores lists for training, but only a visual corpus and a generic corpus to build *visibility scores* for each word, from which a concreteness score is estimated.

4.1 Visibility Scores

The *concreteness score* of a word w consists of the *concrete visibility score* and the *abstract visibility score*, both are normalized sums computed in the same manner (with only the reference corpus different, a visual for the concrete case and a non-visual for the abstract case). Each term $nei(w)$ in the set of n-best nearest neighbors of w (extracted from a model of 300-dimensional vectors for 3M terms from the Google News dataset [2]) contained in the reference corpus contributes its cosine similarity to w ($in(w) = 1.0$ if w is in the reference corpus, o/w 0.0), then the sum is normalized by the sum of all similarities:

$$ConVisEmbScore(w) = \frac{in(w) + \sum_{nei(w) \in VisCor} Sim(w, nei)}{in(w) + \sum_{nei(w)} Sim(w, nei)}, \quad (1)$$

$$AbsVisEmbScore(w) = \frac{in(w) + \sum_{nei(w) \in Brown-VisCor} Sim(w, nei)}{in(w) + \sum_{nei(w)} Sim(w, nei)}, \quad (2)$$

[2]available at https://code.google.com/archive/p/word2vec

max-sd	num-neigh	Spearman	Pearson	MSE
max(sd) =1.89	Turney	0.74	0.74	0.58
	100	0.72	0.72	0.61
	50	0.71	0.70	0.72
	10	0.63	0.62	1.11
med(sd) =1.22	Turney	0.79	0.81	0.89
	100	0.78	0.81	0.69
	50	0.77	0.79	0.78
	10	0.71	0.73	1.13
mean(sd) =1.16	Turney	0.80	0.82	0.99
	100	**0.79**	**0.82**	0.69
	50	0.78	0.81	0.78
	10	0.72	0.75	1.12

Table 4: Predicting concreteness scores.

The overall concreteness score for w is then:

$$ConcretenessScore(w) = $$
$$ConVisEmbScore(w) - AbsVisEmbScore(w) \quad (3)$$

(2) and (1) range from 0.0 (non of the neighbors is in the reference corpus) to 1.0 (all of them are). Hence, (3) ranges between -1.0 and 1.0, where a higher score means more concrete word.

Notice that no corpus-frequencies were taken into account in the above sums. This is because VL datasets are often human-focused with unrealistic high-weight for terms describing people. In addition, words in the corpora were only lowercaesd but not stemmed since we noticed it cut off too much information, leading to poorer results (due to the loss of potential discriminating concreteness features that are characteristic of many derivational suffixes). For example, 40K's scores for several unstemmed forms of the stem *woman*: woman (4.46), womanhood (2.55), womanishness (1.79), womanize (2.82), womanlike (3.14).

4.2 Results and Discussion

To best demonstrate the strength of our method, we present the results gathered by using a unified visual corpus that is both large enough to be used as a reference corpus, and has higher Diff/Range ratios. This unified corpus, which we call the **Big Visual Corpus (BVC)** consists of the Visual Genome, MSCOCO, Flickr30K, and ImageNet, and contains over 98K lowercaesd (but otherwise non-normalized) terms. Its Diff/Range%, according to the 40K and MRC lists are 25.5% and 24.53%, respectively. The generic corpus used is the Brown corpus, and respectively, the non-visual reference corpus is $Brown_{NV} - BVC$.

We follow the simple practice from Köper and im Walde (2017) and map all scores into the same interval using the following continuous function:

$$f(w) = \frac{(b - a)(x - min)}{max - min} + a, \quad (4)$$

where $[min, max]$ is the original interval and $[a, b]$ the new interval. In our case, $a = 1.04$ (the minimum unigram score in the 40K list) and $b = 5.0$. We then compute the correlation between our scores and the 40K list's scores and compare them to the correlations of the previously calculated scores by Turney et al. (2011) (see Table 4). We parameterize over both the number of neighbors (up to 100) taken into account in (1) and (2) and the maximal standard deviation (sd) of words in the 40K list we consider in computing the correlations. Using the mean sd as a threshold shows better correlations with the subset considered. Also, considering more neighbors improves all evaluation metrics.

5 Metaphor Detection

We utilize our concreteness scores to solve the task of Metaphor Detection, where a set of literal and non-literal samples is given, and the goal is to classify each into the correct class. We follow Black's (1979) observation that a metaphor is essentially an interaction between two terms, creating an implication-complex to resolve two incompatible meanings. Operationally, we follow Turney et al. and their adoption of Lakoff and Johnson's (1980) notion that metaphor is a way to move knowledge from a concrete domain to an abstract one. Hence, there should be a correlation between the "degree of abstractness in a word's context [...] with the likelihood that the word is used metaphorically." (Turney et al., 2011). We show our results on two annotated datasets:

5.1 The TSV Dataset

This dataset by Tsvetkov et al. (2014) includes several sets with instances annotated as "metaphorical" or "literal" by 5 annotators, from which we experimented with two sets. The first set, which we call TSV-AN, contains 200 adjective-noun (AN) pairs, 100 instances per class. For example, "clean conscience" is annotated as metaphorical, and "clean air" as literal. The second set, which we call TSV-SVO, contains subject-verb-object (SVO) triples or pairs (when missing 'S'/'O'), 111 for each class.

We build a logistic regression model using 10-fold cross-validation for each of the TSV-AN and

Dataset	Features	Precision	Recall	F1
TSV-AN	Linguistic	0.73	0.80	0.76
	Visual	0.60	0.91	0.73
	Multimodal	0.67	0.96	0.79
	Vis-Emb.	0.84	0.72	0.77
TSV-SVO	**Vis-Emb.**	0.83	0.80	0.81

Table 5: Results of our method (Vis-Emb.) on the dataset by Tsvetkov et al. compared to previous results by Shutova et al.

TSV-SVO sets. The feature vector for each phrase in the sets is simple, consists of our assigned concreteness score for each word in the phrase. For the second set, we divide each triple into two pairs to get 150 "literal" 'SV'/'VO' pairs and 165 "metaphorical" ones. We flipped the feature vector of the 'VO' pairs to represent scores in the form of 'OV', so that the nouns and verb would appear at consistent places in the vector. As a reference to our results, we bring previous results by Shutova et al. (2016), who used linguistic embedding model, visual embedding model, and a multimodal model that mixed the two (see Table 5).

5.2 The TroFi dataset

The dataset by Birke and Sarkar (2006) contains annotated "literal" and "non-literal" sentences from the Wall Street Journal for 50 verbs. We follow the exact same algorithm used in Turney et al. (2011) on a subset of 25 verbs, while replacing their concreteness scores with ours.

We build a 5-dimensional feature vector for each sentence, composed of the average concreteness score of words with each of the following part-of-speech tags: noun, proper noun, verb, adjective, adverb. When there are no words with a specific POS tag in the sentence, the value 0.0 is assigned to the corresponding place in the vector. The feature vectors are then used in a logistic regression classifier to build a separate model for each verb using 10-fold cross-validation. Table 6 shows our results along with the previous results by Turney et al. (and their probability-matching case).

6 Conclusion and Future Work

Even without the matching images, the captions in vision and language datasets contain useful information regarding the visibility of words appearing in them. In addition, the connection between the visibility of a word and its concreteness level is well known from psychological experiments.

Features	Accuracy	F1-score
Vis-Emb.	0.713	0.657
Turney et al.	0.734	0.639
Probability Matching	0.605	0.500

Table 6: Classifying the sentences related to 25 verbs in the TroFi dataset. Accuracy and F1-score are macro-averaged.

We exploited these properties in crafting visibility scores, based only on the occurrences of a word's neighbors (in the semantic space) in the visual corpora, and calculated a concreteness score out of them for the word. We then experimented within the related task of metaphor detection, and showed comparable results to previous works. Our method and algorithm, though relatively simple and intuitive, give surprisingly good (comparable) results, while not requiring any multimodal processing at all.

Acknowledgments

We would like to thank the three anonymous reviewers for their suggestions and comments.
This work was supported by Contract W911NF-15-C-0238 with the US Defense Advanced Research Projects Agency (DARPA) and the Army Research Office (ARO).

References

Julia Birke and Anoop Sarkar. 2006. A clustering approach for nearly unsupervised recognition of nonliteral language. In *EACL 2006, 11st Conference of the European Chapter of the Association for Computational Linguistics, Proceedings of the Conference, April 3-7, 2006, Trento, Italy.* http://aclweb.org/anthology/E/E06/E06-1042.pdf.

Max Black. 1979. More about metaphor.[in] a. ortony (ed.), metaphor and thought.

Marc Brysbaert, Amy Beth Warriner, and Victor Kuperman. 2014. Concreteness ratings for 40 thousand generally known english word lemmas. *Behavior research methods* 46(3):904–911.

Max Coltheart. 1981. The mrc psycholinguistic database. *The Quarterly Journal of Experimental Psychology Section A* 33(4):497–505. https://doi.org/10.1080/14640748108400805.

Jia Deng, Wei Dong, Richard Socher, Li-Jia Li, Kai Li, and Fei-Fei Li. 2009. Imagenet: A large-scale hierarchical image database. In *2009 IEEE Computer Society Conference on Computer Vision and Pattern Recognition (CVPR 2009), 20-25*

June 2009, Miami, Florida, USA. pages 248–255. https://doi.org/10.1109/CVPRW.2009.5206848.

Jesse Dodge, Amit Goyal, Xufeng Han, Alyssa Mensch, Margaret Mitchell, Karl Stratos, Kota Yamaguchi, Yejin Choi, III Hal Daumé, Alexander C. Berg, and Tamara L. Berg. 2012. Detecting visual text. In *Proceedings of the 2012 Conference of the North American Chapter of the Association for Computational Linguistics: Human Language Technologies*. Association for Computational Linguistics, Stroudsburg, PA, USA, NAACL HLT '12, pages 762–772. http://dl.acm.org/citation.cfm?id=2382029.2382153.

Francis Ferraro, Nasrin Mostafazadeh, Ting-Hao (Kenneth) Huang, Lucy Vanderwende, Jacob Devlin, Michel Galley, and Margaret Mitchell. 2015. A survey of current datasets for vision and language research. In *Proceedings of the 2015 Conference on Empirical Methods in Natural Language Processing, EMNLP 2015, Lisbon, Portugal, September 17-21, 2015*. pages 207–213. http://aclweb.org/anthology/D/D15/D15-1021.pdf.

W Nelson Francis and Henry Kucera. 1964. Brown corpus. *Department of Linguistics, Brown University, Providence, Rhode Island* 1. http://icame.uib.no/brown/bcm.html.

Ray Jackendoff. 1983. *Semantics and cognition*. MIT Press.

Maximilian Köper and Sabine Schulte im Walde. 2017. Improving verb metaphor detection by propagating abstractness to words, phrases and individual senses. *SENSE 2017* page 24.

Ranjay Krishna, Yuke Zhu, Oliver Groth, Justin Johnson, Kenji Hata, Joshua Kravitz, Stephanie Chen, Yannis Kalantidis, Li-Jia Li, David A. Shamma, Michael S. Bernstein, and Fei-Fei Li. 2016. Visual genome: Connecting language and vision using crowdsourced dense image annotations. *CoRR* abs/1602.07332. http://arxiv.org/abs/1602.07332.

George Lakoff and Mark Johnson. 1980. *Metaphors we live by*. University of Chicago press.

Tsung-Yi Lin, Michael Maire, Serge J. Belongie, James Hays, Pietro Perona, Deva Ramanan, Piotr Dollár, and C. Lawrence Zitnick. 2014. Microsoft COCO: common objects in context. In *Computer Vision - ECCV 2014 - 13th European Conference, Zurich, Switzerland, September 6-12, 2014, Proceedings, Part V*. pages 740–755. https://doi.org/10.1007/978-3-319-10602-1_48.

George A Miller, Richard Beckwith, Christiane Fellbaum, Derek Gross, and Katherine J Miller. 1990. Introduction to wordnet: An on-line lexical database. *International journal of lexicography* 3(4):235–244.

George A Miller and Philip N Johnson-Laird. 1976. *Language and perception.*. Belknap Press.

Vicente Ordonez, Girish Kulkarni, and Tamara L. Berg. 2011. Im2text: Describing images using 1 million captioned photographs. In *Advances in Neural Information Processing Systems 24: 25th Annual Conference on Neural Information Processing Systems 2011. Proceedings of a meeting held 12-14 December 2011, Granada, Spain.*. pages 1143–1151. http://papers.nips.cc/paper/4470-im2text-describing-images-using-1-million-captioned-photographs.

Ekaterina Shutova, Douwe Kiela, and Jean Maillard. 2016. Black holes and white rabbits: Metaphor identification with visual features. In *NAACL HLT 2016, The 2016 Conference of the North American Chapter of the Association for Computational Linguistics: Human Language Technologies, San Diego California, USA, June 12-17, 2016*. pages 160–170. http://aclweb.org/anthology/N/N16/N16-1020.pdf.

Yulia Tsvetkov, Leonid Boytsov, Anatole Gershman, Eric Nyberg, and Chris Dyer. 2014. Metaphor detection with cross-lingual model transfer. In *Proceedings of the 52nd Annual Meeting of the Association for Computational Linguistics, ACL 2014, June 22-27, 2014, Baltimore, MD, USA, Volume 1: Long Papers*. pages 248–258. http://aclweb.org/anthology/P/P14/P14-1024.pdf.

Peter D. Turney, Yair Neuman, Dan Assaf, and Yohai Cohen. 2011. Literal and metaphorical sense identification through concrete and abstract context. In *Proceedings of the 2011 Conference on Empirical Methods in Natural Language Processing, EMNLP 2011, 27-31 July 2011, John McIntyre Conference Centre, Edinburgh, UK, A meeting of SIGDAT, a Special Interest Group of the ACL*. pages 680–690. http://www.aclweb.org/anthology/D11-1063.

David L Waltz. 1993. Relating images, concepts, and words. In *Intelligent Systems*, Springer, pages 21–38.

Terry Winograd. 1972. Understanding natural language. *Cognitive psychology* 3(1):1–191.

Peter Young, Alice Lai, Micah Hodosh, and Julia Hockenmaier. 2014. From image descriptions to visual denotations: New similarity metrics for semantic inference over event descriptions. *TACL* 2:67–78. https://tacl2013.cs.columbia.edu/ojs/index.php/tacl/article/view/229.

Semantic Features Based on Word Alignments
for Estimating Quality of Text Simplification

Tomoyuki Kajiwara[†] and **Atsushi Fujita**[‡]

[†]Tokyo Metropolitan University, Tokyo, Japan
[‡]National Institute of Information and Communications Technology, Kyoto, Japan
`kajiwara-tomoyuki@ed.tmu.ac.jp, atsushi.fujita@nict.go.jp`

Abstract

This paper examines the usefulness of semantic features based on word alignments
for estimating the quality of text simplification. Specifically, we introduce seven
types of alignment-based features computed on the basis of word embeddings
and paraphrase lexicons. Through an empirical experiment using the QATS dataset
(Štajner et al., 2016b), we confirm that
we can achieve the state-of-the-art performance only with these features.

1 Introduction

Text simplification is the task of rewriting complex text into a simpler form while preserving its
meaning. Systems that automatically pursue this
task can potentially be used for assisting reading
comprehension of less language-competent people, such as learners (Petersen and Ostendorf,
2007) and children (Belder and Moens, 2010).
Such systems would also improve the performance
of other natural language processing tasks, such as
information extraction (Evans, 2011) and machine
translation (MT) (Štajner and Popović, 2016).

Similarly to other text-to-text generation tasks,
such as MT and summarization, the outputs of text
simplification systems have been evaluated sub-
jectively by humans (Wubben et al., 2012; Štajner
et al., 2014) or automatically by comparing with
handcrafted reference texts (Specia, 2010; Coster
and Kauchak, 2011; Xu et al., 2016). However, the
former is costly and not replicable, and the latter
has achieved only a low correlation with human
evaluation.

On the basis of this backdrop, Quality Estimation (QE) (Specia et al., 2010), i.e., automatic evaluation without reference, has been drawing much
attention in the research community. In the shared

Metrics	r_{length}	r_{label}
BLEU	-0.765	0.245
METEOR	-0.617	0.257
TER	0.741	-0.233
WER	0.757	-0.230

Table 1: The QATS training data shows that typical MT metrics are strongly biased by the length
difference between original and simple sentences
(r_{length}), while they are less correlated with the
manually-labeled quality (r_{label}).

task on quality assessment for text simplification
(QATS),[1] two tasks have been addressed (Štajner
et al., 2016b). One is to estimate a real-value quality score for given sentence pair, while the other
is to classify given sentence pair into one of the
three classes (*good*, *ok*, and *bad*). In the classification task of the QATS workshop, systems based
on deep neural networks (Paetzold and Specia,
2016a) and MT metrics (Štajner et al., 2016a) have
achieved the best performance. However, deep
neural networks are rather unstable because of the
difficulty of training on a limited amount of data;
for instance, the QATS dataset offers only 505 sentence pairs for training. MT metrics are incapable
of properly capturing deletions that are prevalent
in text simplification (Coster and Kauchak, 2011),
as they are originally designed to gauge semantic equivalence. In fact, as shown in Table 1,
well-known MT metrics are strongly biased by the
length difference between original and simple sentences, even though it is rather unrelated with the
quality of text simplification assessed by humans.

In order to properly account for the surface-
level inequivalency occurring in text simplification, we examine semantic similarity features
based on word embeddings and paraphrase lexicons. Unlike end-to-end training with deep neural
networks, we quantify word-level semantic corre-

---

[1]`http://qats2016.github.io/shared.html`

109

spondences using two pre-compiled external resources: (a) word embeddings learned from large-scale monolingual data and (b) a large-scale paraphrase lexicon. Using the QATS dataset, we empirically demonstrate that a supervised classifier trained upon such features achieves good performance in the classification task.

2 Semantic Features Based on Word Alignments

We bring a total of seven types of features that are proven useful for the similar task, i.e., finding corresponding sentence pairs within English Wikipedia and Simple English Wikipedia (Hwang et al., 2015; Kajiwara and Komachi, 2016). Specifically, we assume that some of these features are useful to capture inequivalency between original sentence and its simplified version introduced during simplification, such as lexical paraphrases and deletion of words and phrases.

Throughout this section, original sentence and its simplified version are referred to as x and y, respectively.

2.1 AES: Additive Embeddings Similarity

Given two sentences, x and y, AES between them is computed as follows.

$$\text{AES}(x, y) = \cos\left(\sum_{i=1}^{|x|} \vec{x}_i, \sum_{j=1}^{|y|} \vec{y}_j\right) \quad (1)$$

where each sentence is vectorized with the sum of the word embeddings of its component words, $\vec{x}_i$ and $\vec{y}_j$, assuming the additive compositionality (Mikolov et al., 2013).

2.2 AAS: Average Alignment Similarity

AAS (Song and Roth, 2015) averages the cosine similarities between all pairs of words within given two sentences, x and y, calculated over their embeddings.

$$\text{AAS}(x, y) = \frac{1}{|x||y|} \sum_{i=1}^{|x|} \sum_{j=1}^{|y|} \cos(\vec{x}_i, \vec{y}_j) \quad (2)$$

2.3 MAS: Maximum Alignment Similarity

AAS inevitably involves noise, as many word pairs are semantically irrelevant to each other. MAS (Song and Roth, 2015) reduces this kind of noise by considering only the best word alignment for each word in one sentence as follows.

$$\text{MAS}(x, y) = \frac{1}{|x|} \sum_{i=1}^{|x|} \max_{j} \cos(\vec{x}_i, \vec{y}_j) \quad (3)$$

As MAS is asymmetric, we calculate it for each direction, i.e., $\text{MAS}(x, y)$ and $\text{MAS}(y, x)$, unlike Kajiwara and Komachi (2016) who has averaged these two values.

2.4 HAS: Hungarian Alignment Similarity

AAS and MAS deal with many-to-many and one-to-many word alignments, respectively. On the other hand, HAS (Song and Roth, 2015) is based on one-to-one word alignments.

The task of identifying the best one-to-one word alignments $\mathcal{H}$ is regarded as a problem of bipartite graph matching, where the two sets of vertices respectively comprise words within each sentence x and y, and the weight of a edge between x_i and y_j is given by the cosine similarity calculated over their word embeddings. Given $\mathcal{H}$ identified using the Hungarian algorithm (Kuhn, 1955), HAS is computed by averaging the similarities between embeddings of the aligned pairs of words.

$$\text{HAS}(x, y) = \frac{1}{|\mathcal{H}|} \sum_{(i,j)\in\mathcal{H}} \cos(\vec{x}_i, \vec{y}_j) \quad (4)$$

where $|\mathcal{H}| = \min(|x|, |y|)$, as $\mathcal{H}$ contains only one-to-one word alignments.

2.5 WMD: Word Mover's Distance

WMD (Kusner et al., 2015) is a special case of the Earth Mover's Distance (Rubner et al., 1998), which solves the transportation problem of words between two sentences represented by a bipartite graph.[2] Let n be the vocabulary size of the language, WMD is computed as follows.

$$\text{WMD}(x, y) = \min \sum_{u=1}^{n} \sum_{v=1}^{n} \mathcal{A}_{uv} \text{eud}(\vec{x}_u, \vec{y}_v) \quad (5)$$

$$\text{subject to}: \sum_{v=1}^{n} \mathcal{A}_{uv} = \frac{1}{|x|} freq(x_u, x)$$

$$\sum_{u=1}^{n} \mathcal{A}_{uv} = \frac{1}{|y|} freq(y_v, y)$$

---

[2]Note that the vertices in the graph represent the word types, unlike the token-based graph for HAS.

where $\mathcal{A}_{uv}$ is a nonnegative weight matrix representing the flow from a word x_u in x to a word y_v in y, $\mathrm{eud}(\cdot, \cdot)$ the Euclidean distance between two word embeddings, and $freq(\cdot, \cdot)$ the frequency of a word in a sentence.

2.6 DWE: Difference of Word Embeddings

We also introduce the difference between sentence embeddings so as to gauge their differences in terms of meaning and simplicity. As the representation of a sentence, we used the averaged word embeddings (Adi et al., 2017).

$$\mathrm{DWE}(x, y) = \frac{1}{|x|} \sum_{i=1}^{|x|} \vec{x}_i - \frac{1}{|y|} \sum_{j=1}^{|y|} \vec{y}_j \quad (6)$$

2.7 PAS: Paraphrase Alignment Similarity

PAS (Sultan et al., 2014, 2015) is computed based on lexical paraphrases. This feature has been proven useful in the semantic textual similarity task of SemEval-2015 (Agirre et al., 2015).

$$\mathrm{PAS}(x, y) = \frac{\mathrm{PA}(x, y) + \mathrm{PA}(y, x)}{|x| + |y|} \quad (7)$$

$$\mathrm{PA}(x, y) = \sum_{i=1}^{|x|} \begin{cases} 1 & \exists j : x_i \Leftrightarrow y_j \in y \\ 0 & \text{otherwise} \end{cases}$$

where $x_i \Leftrightarrow y_j$ holds if and only if the word pair (x_i, y_j) is included in a given paraphrase lexicon.

3 Experiment

The usefulness of the above features was evaluated through an empirical experiment using the QATS dataset (Štajner et al., 2016b).

3.1 Data

The QATS dataset consists of 505 and 126 sentence pairs for training and test, respectively, where each pair is evaluated from four different aspects: **G**rammaticality, **M**eaning preservation, **S**implicity, and **O**verall quality. Evaluations are given by one of the three classes: *good*, *ok*, and *bad*.

We used two pre-compiled external resources to compute our features. One is the pre-trained 300-dimensional CBOW model[3] to compute the features based on word embeddings, while the other is PPDB 2.0 (Pavlick et al., 2015)[4] for PAS.

<hr>

[3]https://code.google.com/archive/p/word2vec/

[4]http://paraphrase.org/

3.2 Evaluation Metrics

Each system is evaluated by the three metrics as in the QATS classification task (Štajner et al., 2016b): Accuracy (A), Mean Absolute Error (E) and Weighted F-score (F). To compute Mean Absolute Error, class labels were converted into three equally distant numeric scores retaining their relation, i.e., *good* $= 1$, *ok* $= 0.5$, and *bad* $= 0$.

3.3 Baseline Systems

As the baseline, we employed four types of systems from the QATS workshop (Štajner et al., 2016b): two typical baselines and two top-ranked systems. "Majority-class" labels all the sentence pairs with the most frequent class in the training data. "MT-baseline" combines BLEU (Papineni et al., 2002), METEOR (Lavie and Denkowski, 2009), TER (Snover et al., 2006), and WER (Levenshtein, 1966), using a support vector machine (SVM) classifier.

SimpleNets (Paetzold and Specia, 2016a) has two different forms of deep neural network architectures: multi-layer perceptron (SimpleNets-MLP) and recurrent neural network (SimpleNets-RNN). SimpleNets-MLP uses seven features of each sentence: the number of characters, tokens, and word types, 5-gram language model probabilities estimated on the basis of either SUBTLEX (Brysbaert and New, 2009), SubIMDB (Paetzold and Specia, 2016b), Wikipedia, and Simple Wikipedia (Kauchak, 2013). SimpleNets-RNN, which does not require such feature engineering, uses embeddings of word N-grams.

SMH (Štajner et al., 2016a) has two types of classifiers: logistic classifier (SMH-IBk/Logistic) and random forest classifier (SMH-RandForest, SMH-RandForest-b). Both are trained relying on the automatic evaluation metrics for MT, such as BLEU, METEOR, and TER, in combination with the QE features for MT (Specia et al., 2013).

Instead of reimplementing the above baseline systems, we excerpted their performance scores from (Štajner et al., 2016b).

3.4 Systems with Proposed Features

We evaluated our proposed features in the supervised classification fashion as previous work. Specifically, we compared three types of supervised classifiers that had been also used in the above baseline systems: SVM, MLP, and Rand-Forest. Hyper-parameters of each system were de-

111

System	Grammaticality			Meaning			Simplicity			Overall		
	A ↑	E ↓	F ↑	A ↑	E ↓	F ↑	A ↑	E ↓	F ↑	A ↑	E ↓	F ↑
Majority-class	**76.2**	18.3	65.9	57.9	29.0	42.5	55.6	29.4	39.7	43.7	28.2	26.5
MT-baseline	**76.2**	18.3	65.9	66.7	20.2	62.7	50.8	26.2	48.3	38.1	41.7	37.5
SimpleNets-MLP	74.6	**17.1**	68.8	65.9	21.0	63.5	53.2	27.0	49.8	38.1	32.5	33.7
SimpleNets-RNN ($N = 2$)	75.4	18.7	65.5	57.9	27.4	51.3	50.0	27.0	47.5	52.4	25.8	46.1
SimpleNets-RNN ($N = 3$)	74.6	19.1	65.1	51.6	28.2	46.6	52.4	25.0	50.0	47.6	27.8	40.8
SMH-IBk/Logistic	70.6	19.4	71.6	**69.1**	20.2	**68.1**	50.0	28.2	51.1	47.6	28.2	47.5
SMH-RandForest	75.4	17.5	**71.8**	65.9	20.6	64.4	52.4	27.8	53.0	44.4	31.8	44.5
SMH-RandForest-b	75.4	18.3	70.0	61.9	23.8	59.7	57.1	25.4	56.4	48.4	29.0	48.6
Best score among the above	**76.2**	**17.1**	**71.8**	**69.1**	**20.2**	**68.1**	57.1	25.0	56.4	52.4	25.8	48.6
Our SVM	**76.2**	18.3	65.9	65.1	22.2	58.3	57.1	27.8	43.9	**57.9**	**23.4**	**57.7**
Our MLP	68.3	24.6	66.9	59.5	25.4	56.4	59.5	23.4	58.2	52.4	25.8	51.9
Our RandForest	**76.2**	18.3	65.9	66.7	23.0	63.2	**63.5**	**21.8**	**59.8**	51.6	26.6	48.3
Our SVM w/ MT-baseline	**76.2**	18.3	65.9	66.7	21.0	63.7	57.1	27.0	46.9	47.6	29.0	46.8
Our MLP w/ MT-baseline	63.5	26.6	63.8	64.3	21.4	62.7	52.4	26.2	53.2	46.0	31.8	45.5
Our RandForest w/ MT-baseline	**76.2**	18.3	65.9	61.9	24.6	57.6	62.7	22.6	56.1	46.0	29.0	43.6

Table 2: Results on QATS classification task. The best scores of each metric are highlighted in bold. Scores other than ours are excerpted from Štajner et al. (2016b).

Feature set	C	γ	Grammaticality	Meaning	Simplicity	Overall
ALL	1.0	0.1	76.2	65.1	57.1	57.9
-AES	1.0	0.1	76.2	65.1	57.1	57.1
-MAS(original, simple)	0.1	0.1	76.2	57.9	55.6	56.4
-MAS(simple, original)	1.0	0.1	76.2	64.3	57.1	54.8
-PAS	0.1	0.1	76.2	57.9	55.6	53.2
-DWE	0.01	1.0	76.2	57.9	55.6	51.6
-WMD	0.01	0.1	76.2	57.9	55.6	46.8
-AAS	0.1	0.1	76.2	57.9	55.6	45.2
-HAS	0.01	0.01	76.2	57.9	55.6	35.7

Table 3: Ablation analysis on accuracy. Features are in descending order of overall accuracy.

termined through 5-fold cross validation using the training data, regarding accuracy in terms of overall quality as the objective.

For the SVM classifier, we used the RBF kernel. The trinary classification was realized by means of the one-versus-the-rest strategy. For a given set of features, we examined all the combinations of hyper-parameters among $C \in \{0.01, 0.1, 1.0\}$ and $\gamma \in \{0.01, 0.1, 1.0\}$; for the full set of features, $C = 1.0$ and $\gamma = 0.1$ were chosen.

As for the MLP classifier, among 1 to 3 layers with all the combinations of dimensionality among $\{100, 200, 300, 400, 500\}$ and "ReLu" for the activation function among {Logistic, tanh, ReLu}, the 2-layer one with 200×200 dimensionality was optimal. We used Adam (Kingma and Ba, 2015) as the optimizer.

For the RandForest classifier, we examined all the combinations of the following three hyper-parameters: $\{10, 50, 100, 500, 1000\}$ for number of trees, $\{5, 10, 15, 20, \infty\}$ for the maximum depth of each tree, and $\{1, 5, 10, 15, 20\}$ for the minimum number of samples at leaves. The optimal combination for the full set of features was $(500, 15, 1)$.

3.5 Results

Experimental results are shown in Table 2. The SVM classifier based on our features greatly outperformed the state-of-the-art methods in terms of overall quality. The RandForest classifier somehow achieved the best simplicity scores ever, even though we had optimized the system with respect to the accuracy of overall quality. As we expected, MLP did not beat the other two classifiers, presumably due to the scarcity of the training data. The bottom three rows reveal that the performance in terms of overall quality was deteriorated when MT-baseline features were incorporated on top of our feature set. This suggests that word embeddings are superior to surface-level processing in finding corresponding words within sentence pairs.

Focusing on the overall quality, we conducted an ablation analysis of the SVM classifier. The analysis revealed, as shown in Table 3, that HAS, AAS, and WMD were the most important features. This can be explained by the role of word alignments during the computation. Since MT metrics, such as BLEU, rely only on surface-level matches, they are insensitive to meaning-

Original	**While** historians **concur** that the result **itself** was not **manipulated**, the voting process was neither free nor secret.
Simple	**Most** historians **agree** that the result was not **fixed**, **but** the voting process was neither free nor secret.
Hungarian Alignment	(while, but), (concur, agree), (itself, most), (manipulated, fixed), and identical word pairs.

Table 4: An example of word alignment. Differences between the original and simplified versions are presented in bold. This is a sentence pair from *good* class on overall quality. HAS using word-level similarity reaches 0.85, while BLEU is 0.54.

Feature	r_{length}	r_{label}
AES	-0.661	0.185
AAS	-0.335	0.318
MAS(original, simple)	-0.817	0.226
MAS(simple, original)	0.092	-0.090
HAS	0.061	-0.050
WMD	0.788	-0.215
PAS	-0.120	-0.039

Table 5: Correlation between each feature and the difference of sentence length and the manually-labeled quality. Note that DWE cannot be included, as it is not a scalar value but the differential vector between original and simplified sentences.

preserving rewritings from original sentence to simple one. On the other hand, as exemplified in Table 4, HAS and some other features can detect the linkages between complex words and their simpler counterparts. As a result of properly capturing the alignments between such lexical paraphrases, our system successfully classified this sentence into *good* in terms of overall quality.

We expected that AAS could yield noise, as it involves irrelevant pairs of words, but in fact, it contributed to the QATS task. We speculate that it helps to evaluate the appropriateness of substituting a word to other one considering the semantic matching with the given context, as in lexical simplification (Biran et al., 2011) and lexical substitution (Melamud et al., 2015; Roller and Erk, 2016; Apidianaki, 2016).

The contribution of WMD was expected as it was proven effective in the sentence alignment task of English Wikipedia and Simple English Wikipedia (Kajiwara and Komachi, 2016).

Table 5 shows that some of our semantic similarity features are also strongly biased by the length difference between original and simple sentences, as MT metrics (cf. Table 1). Nonetheless,

HAS was not biased by the length difference almost at all, and AAS and WMD highly correlated with the manually-labeled quality.

4 Conclusions

We presented seven types of semantic similarity features based on word alignments for quality estimation of text simplification. Unlike existing MT metrics, our features can flexibly deal with word alignments, taking deletions and paraphrases into account. Our SVM classifier based on these features achieved the best performance on the QATS dataset.

Acknowledgments

This work was carried out when the first author was taking up an internship at NICT, Japan. We are deeply grateful to the anonymous reviewers for their insightful comments and suggestions. This work was conducted under the program "Promotion of Global Communications Plan: Research, Development, and Social Demonstration of Multilingual Speech Translation Technology" of the Ministry of Internal Affairs and Communications (MIC), Japan.

References

Yosshi Adi, Einat Kermany, Yonatan Belinkov, Ofer Lavi, and Yoav Goldberg. 2017. Fine-grained Analysis of Sentence Embeddings Using Auxiliary Prediction Tasks. In *International Conference on Learning Representations*.

Eneko Agirre, Carmen Banea, Claire Cardie, Daniel Cer, Mona Diab, Aitor Gonzalez-Agirre, Weiwei Guo, Inigo Lopez-Gazpio, Montse Maritxalar, Rada Mihalcea, German Rigau, Larraitz Uria, and Janyce Wiebe. 2015. SemEval-2015 Task 2: Semantic Textual Similarity, English, Spanish and Pilot on Interpretability. In *Proceedings of the 9th International Workshop on Semantic Evaluation*. pages 252–263.

Marianna Apidianaki. 2016. Vector-space models for PPDB paraphrase ranking in context. In *Proceedings of the 2016 Conference on Empirical Methods in Natural Language Processing*. pages 2028–2034.

Jan De Belder and Marie-Francine Moens. 2010. Text Simplification for Children. In *Proceedings of the SIGIR Workshop on Accessible Search Systems*. pages 19–26.

Or Biran, Samuel Brody, and Noemie Elhadad. 2011. Putting it Simply: a Context-Aware Approach to Lexical Simplification. In *Proceedings of the 49th*

Annual Meeting of the Association for Computational Linguistics: Human Language Technologies. pages 496–501.

Marc Brysbaert and Boris New. 2009. Moving beyond Kučera and Francis: A Critical Evaluation of Current Word Frequency Norms and the Introduction of a New and Improved Word Frequency Measure for American English. *Behavior Research Methods* 41(4):977–990.

William Coster and David Kauchak. 2011. Simple English Wikipedia: A New Text Simplification Task. In *Proceedings of the 49th Annual Meeting of the Association for Computational Linguistics: Human Language Technologies.* pages 665–669.

Richard J. Evans. 2011. Comparing methods for the syntactic simplification of sentences in information extraction. *Literary and Linguistic Computing* 26(4):371–388.

William Hwang, Hannaneh Hajishirzi, Mari Ostendorf, and Wei Wu. 2015. Aligning Sentences from Standard Wikipedia to Simple Wikipedia. In *Proceedings of the 2015 Conference of the North American Chapter of the Association for Computational Linguistics: Human Language Technologies.* pages 211–217.

Tomoyuki Kajiwara and Mamoru Komachi. 2016. Building a Monolingual Parallel Corpus for Text Simplification Using Sentence Similarity Based on Alignment between Word Embeddings. In *Proceedings of the 26th International Conference on Computational Linguistics.* pages 1147–1158.

David Kauchak. 2013. Improving Text Simplification Language Modeling Using Unsimplified Text Data. In *Proceedings of the 51st Annual Meeting of the Association for Computational Linguistics.* pages 1537–1546.

Diederik P. Kingma and Jimmy Ba. 2015. Adam: A Method for Stochastic Optimization. In *Proceedings of the 3rd International Conference on Learning Representations.*

Harold W. Kuhn. 1955. The Hungarian Method for the Assignment Problem. *Naval Research Logistics Quarterly* 2:83–97.

Matt Kusner, Yu Sun, Nicholas Kolkin, and Kilian Weinberger. 2015. From Word Embeddings To Document Distances. In *Proceedings of The 32nd International Conference on Machine Learning.* pages 957–966.

Alon Lavie and Michael Denkowski. 2009. The METEOR Metric for Automatic Evaluation of Machine Translation. *Machine Translation* 23(2-3):105–115.

Vladimir Iosifovich Levenshtein. 1966. Binary Codes Capable of Correcting Deletions, Insertions and Reversals. *Soviet Physics Doklady* 10(8):707–710.

Oren Melamud, Omer Levy, and Ido Dagan. 2015. A Simple Word Embedding Model for Lexical Substitution. In *Proceedings of the 1st Workshop on Vector Space Modeling for Natural Language Processing.* pages 1–7.

Tomas Mikolov, Ilya Sutskever, Kai Chen, Greg S Corrado, and Jeff Dean. 2013. Distributed Representations of Words and Phrases and Their Compositionality. In *Advances in Neural Information Processing Systems.* pages 3111–3119.

Gustavo H. Paetzold and Lucia Specia. 2016a. SimpleNets: Evaluating Simplifiers with Resource-Light Neural Networks. In *LREC 2016 Workshop & Shared Task on Quality Assessment for Text Simplification.* pages 42–46.

Gustavo H. Paetzold and Lucia Specia. 2016b. Unsupervised Lexical Simplification for Non-Native Speakers. In *Proceedings of the Thirtieth AAAI Conference on Artificial Intelligence.* pages 3761–3767.

Kishore Papineni, Salim Roukos, Todd Ward, and Wei-Jing Zhu. 2002. BLEU: a Method for Automatic Evaluation of Machine Translation. In *Proceedings of 40th Annual Meeting of the Association for Computational Linguistics.* pages 311–318.

Ellie Pavlick, Pushpendre Rastogi, Juri Ganitkevitch, Benjamin Van Durme, and Chris Callison-Burch. 2015. PPDB 2.0: Better paraphrase ranking, fine-grained entailment relations, word embeddings, and style classification. In *Proceedings of the 53rd Annual Meeting of the Association for Computational Linguistics and the 7th International Joint Conference on Natural Language Processing.* pages 425–430.

Sarah E. Petersen and Mari Ostendorf. 2007. Text Simplification for Language Learners: A Corpus Analysis. In *Proceedings of the Speech and Language Technology in Education Workshop.* pages 69–72.

Stephen Roller and Katrin Erk. 2016. PIC a Different Word: A Simple Model for Lexical Substitution in Context. In *Proceedings of the 2016 Conference of the North American Chapter of the Association for Computational Linguistics: Human Language Technologies.* pages 1121–1126.

Yossi Rubner, Carlo Tomasi, and Leonidas J. Guibas. 1998. A Metric for Distributions with Applications to Image Databases. In *Proceedings of the Sixth International Conference on Computer Vision.* pages 59–66.

Matthew Snover, Bonnie Dorr, Richard Schwartz, Linnea Micciulla, and John Makhoul. 2006. A Study of Translation Edit Rate with Targeted Human Annotation. In *Proceedings of the 7th Conference of the Association for Machine Translation in the Americas.* pages 1–9.

Yangqiu Song and Dan Roth. 2015. Unsupervised Sparse Vector Densification for Short Text Similarity. In *Proceedings of the 2015 Conference of the North American Chapter of the Association for Computational Linguistics: Human Language Technologies*. pages 1275–1280.

Lucia Specia. 2010. Translating from Complex to Simplified Sentences. In *Proceedings of the 9th International Conference on Computational Processing of the Portuguese Language*. pages 30–39.

Lucia Specia, Dhwaj Raj, and Marco Turchi. 2010. Machine Translation Evaluation versus Quality Estimation. *Machine Translation* 24(1):39–50.

Lucia Specia, Kashif Shah, Jose G.C. de Souza, and Trevor Cohn. 2013. QuEst - A translation quality estimation framework. In *Proceedings of the 51st Annual Meeting of the Association for Computational Linguistics*. pages 79–84.

Md Arafat Sultan, Steven Bethard, and Tamara Sumner. 2014. Back to Basics for Monolingual Alignment: Exploiting Word Similarity and Contextual Evidence. *Transactions of the Association for Computational Linguistics* 2:219–230.

Md Arafat Sultan, Steven Bethard, and Tamara Sumner. 2015. DLS@CU: Sentence Similarity from Word Alignment and Semantic Vector Composition. In *Proceedings of the 9th International Workshop on Semantic Evaluation*. pages 148–153.

Sanja Štajner, Ruslan Mitkov, and Horacio Saggion. 2014. One Step Closer to Automatic Evaluation of Text Simplification Systems. In *Proceedings of the 3rd Workshop on Predicting and Improving Text Readability for Target Reader Populations*. pages 1–10.

Sanja Štajner and Maja Popović. 2016. Can Text Simplification Help Machine Translation? *Baltic Journal of Modern Computing* 4(2):230–242.

Sanja Štajner, Maja Popović, and Hanna Béchara. 2016a. Quality Estimation for Text Simplification. In *LREC 2016 Workshop & Shared Task on Quality Assessment for Text Simplification*. pages 15–21.

Sanja Štajner, Maja Popović, Horacio Saggion, Lucia Specia, and Mark Fishel. 2016b. Shared Task on Quality Assessment for Text Simplification. In *LREC 2016 Workshop & Shared Task on Quality Assessment for Text Simplification*. pages 22–31.

Sander Wubben, Antal van den Bosch, and Emiel Krahmer. 2012. Sentence Simplification by Monolingual Machine Translation. In *Proceedings of the 50th Annual Meeting of the Association for Computational Linguistics*. pages 1015–1024.

Wei Xu, Courtney Napoles, Ellie Pavlick, Quanze Chen, and Chris Callison-Burch. 2016. Optimizing Statistical Machine Translation for Text Simplification. *Transactions of the Association for Computational Linguistics* 4:401–415.

Injecting Word Embeddings with Another Language's Resource : An Application of Bilingual Embeddings

Prakhar Pandey   Vikram Pudi   Manish Shrivastava
International Institute of Information Technology
Hyderabad, Telangana, India
`prakhar.pandey@research.iiit.ac.in`
`{vikram,manish.shrivastava}@.iiit.ac.in`

Abstract

Word embeddings learned from text corpus can be improved by injecting knowledge from external resources, while at the same time also specializing them for similarity or relatedness. These knowledge resources (like WordNet, Paraphrase Database) may not exist for all languages. In this work we introduce a method to inject word embeddings of a language with knowledge resource of another language by leveraging bilingual embeddings. First we improve word embeddings of German, Italian, French and Spanish using resources of English and test them on variety of word similarity tasks. Then we demonstrate the utility of our method by creating improved embeddings for Urdu and Telugu languages using Hindi WordNet, beating the previously established baseline for Urdu.

1 Introduction

Recently fast and scalable methods to generate dense vector space models have become very popular following the works of (Collobert and Weston, 2008; Mikolov et al., 2013; Pennington et al., 2014). These methods take large amounts of text corpus to generate real valued vector representation for words (word embeddings) which carry many semantic properties.

Mikolov et al. (2013b) extended this model to two languages by introducing bilingual embeddings where word embeddings for two languages are simultaneously represented in the same vector space. The model is trained such that word embeddings capture not only semantic information of monolingual words, but also semantic relationships across different languages. A number of different methods have since been proposed to construct bilingual embeddings (Zou et al., 2013; Vulic and Moens, 2015; Coulmance et al., 2016).

A disadvantage of learning word embeddings only from text corpus is that valuable knowledge contained in knowledge resources like WordNet (Miller, 1995) is not used. Numerous methods have been proposed to incorporate knowledge from external resources into word embeddings for their refinement (Xu et al., 2014; Bian et al., 2014; Mrksic et al., 2016). (Faruqui et al., 2015) introduced *retrofitting* as a light graph based technique that improves learned word embeddings.

In this work we introduce a method to improve word embeddings of one language (target language) using knowledge resources from some other similar language (source language). To accomplish this, we represent both languages in the same vector space (bilingual embeddings) and obtain translations of source language's resources. Then we use these translations to improve the embeddings of the target language by using *retrofitting*, leveraging the information contained in bilingual space to adjust retrofitting process and handle noise. We also show why a dictionary based translation would be ineffective for this problem and how to handle situations where vocabulary of target embeddings is too big or too small compared to size of resource.

(Kiela et al., 2015) demonstrated the advantage of specializing word embeddings for either similarity or relatedness, which we also incorporate. Our method is also independent of the way bilingual embeddings were obtained. An added advantage of using bilingual embeddings is that they are better than monolingual counterparts due to incorporating multilingual evidence (Faruqui and Dyer, 2014; Mrkšić et al., 2017).

Proceedings of the The 8th International Joint Conference on Natural Language Processing, pages 116–121,
Taipei, Taiwan, November 27 – December 1, 2017 ©2017 AFNLP

2　Background

2.1　Bilingual Embeddings

Various methods have been proposed to generate bilingual embeddings. One class of methods learn mappings to transform words from one monolingual model to another, using some form of dictionary (Mikolov et al., 2013b; Faruqui and Dyer, 2014). Another class of methods jointly optimize monolingual and cross-lingual objectives using word aligned parallel corpus (Klementiev et al., 2012; Zou et al., 2013) or sentence aligned parallel corpus (Chandar A P et al., 2014; Hermann and Blunsom, 2014). Also there are other methods which use monolingual data and a smaller set of sentence aligned parallel corpus (Coulmance et al., 2016) and those which use non-parallel document aligned data (Vulic and Moens, 2015).

We experiment with *translation invariant* bilingual embeddings by (Gardner et al., 2015). We also experiment with method proposed by (Artetxe et al., 2016) where they learn a linear transform between two monolingual embeddings with *monolingual invariance preserved*. They use a small bilingual dictionary to accomplish this task. These methods are useful in our situation because they preserve the quality of original monolingual embeddings and do not require parallel text (beneficial in case of Indian languages).

2.2　Retrofitting

Retrofitting was introduced by (Faruqui et al., 2015) as a light graph based procedure for enriching word embeddings with semantic lexicons. The method operates *post processing* i.e it can be applied to word embeddings obtained from any standard technique such as Word2vec, Glove etc. The method encourages improved vectors to be similar to the vectors of *similar words* as well as similar to the original vectors. This similarity relation among words (such as synonymy, hypernymy, paraphrase) is derived from a knowledge resource such as PPDB, WordNet etc. Retrofitting works as follows:

Let matrix Q contain the word embeddings to be improved. Let $V = \{w_1, w_2...w_n\}$ be the vocabulary which is equal to number of rows in Q and d be the dimension of word vectors which is equal to number of columns. Also let Ω be the ontology that contains the intra word relations that must be injected into the embeddings. The objective of retrofitting is to find a matrix $\hat{Q}$ such that the new word vectors are close to their original vectors as well as vectors of related words. The function to be minimized to accomplish this objective is:

$$\Phi(Q) = \sum_{i=1}^{n} \left[\alpha_i \|q_i - \hat{q}_i\|^2 + \sum_{(i,j)\in E} \beta_{ij} \|q_i - q_j\|^2 \right]$$

The iterative update equation is:

$$q_i = \frac{\sum_{j:(i,j)\in E} \beta_{ij} q_j + \alpha_i \hat{q}_i}{\sum_{j:(i,j)\in E} \beta_{ij} + \alpha_i}$$

α and β are the parameters used to control the process. We discuss in Section 3.2 how we set them to adapt the process to bilingual settings.

2.3　Dictionary based approach

Before discussing our method, we would like to point that using a dictionary for translating the lexical resource and then retrofitting with this translated resource is not feasible. Firstly obtaining good quality dictionaries is a difficult and costly process[1]. Secondly it is not necessary that one would obtain translations that are within the vocabulary of the embeddings to be improved. To demonstrate this, we obtain translations for embeddings of 3 languages[2] and show the results in Table 1. In all cases the number of translations that are also present in the embedding's vocabulary are too small.

Language	Vocab	Matches
German	43,527	9,950
Italian	73,427	24,716
Spanish	41,779	16,547

Table 1: Using a dictionary based approach

3　Approach

Let S, T and R be the vocabularies of source, target and resource respectively. Size of R is always fixed while size of S and T depends on embeddings. The relation between S, T and R is shown in Figure 1. Sets S and R have one to one mapping which in not necessarily onto, while T and S have many to one mapping. Consider the ideal case where every word in R is also in S and every word in S has the exact translation from T as its nearest neighbour in the bilingual space. Then the

---

[1] eg. Google and Bing Translate APIs have become paid.
[2] using Yandex Translate API, it took around 3 days

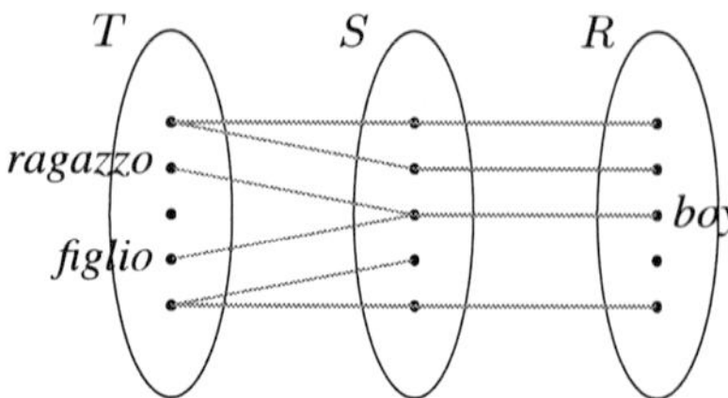

Figure 1: Relationships between Source, Target and Resource Vocabularies.

simple approach for translation would be assigning every $s_i \in S$ its nearest neighbour $t_i \in T$ as the translation.

First problem is that in practical settings these conditions are almost never satisfied. Secondly the sizes of S, T and R can be very different. Suppose the size of S, T is large compared to R or the size of T is large but size of S is comparatively smaller. In both cases size of translated resource will be too small to make impact. Thirdly words common to both R and S will be lesser than the total words in R. So the size of R accessible to T using S will be even lesser. A mechanism is therefore required to control the size of translated resource and filter incorrect translations. We accomplish this as follows:

3.1 Translating knowledge resource

For translation we adapt a dual approach that allows control over the size of the translated list. We iterate through T (not S) looking for translations in S. A translation is accepted or rejected based on whether the cosine similarity between words is above the threshold η. This method stems from the fact that mapping between T and S is many to one. So the Italian word *ragazzo* is translated to *boy*, but we can also translate (and subsequently retrofit) *figlio* to *boy* (Figure 1) in order to get a larger translated resource list with some loss in quality of list. Thus η gives us direct control over the size of translated resource list. Then to translate the list of related words, we translate normally (i.e from S to T). Algorithm 1 summarizes this process.

3.2 Retrofitting to translated resource

We modify the retrofitting procedure to accommodate noisy translations as follows:

As discussed earlier, retrofitting process controls the relative shift of vectors by two parameters α and β, where α controls the movement towards original vector and β controls movement towards vectors to be fitted with. (Faruqui et al., 2015) set α as 1 and β as $\frac{1}{\gamma}$ where γ is the number of vectors to be fitted with. Thus they give equal weights to each vector.

Cosine similarity between a word and its translation is a good measure of the confidence in its translation. We use it to set β such that different vectors get different weights. A word for which we have higher confidence in translation (i.e higher cosine similarity) is given more weight when retrofitting. Therefore w_i being the weights, α, β are set as :

$$\alpha = \sum_{i=1}^{\gamma} w_i, \quad \beta_i = w_i$$

Further reduction in weights of noisy words can be done by taking powers of cosine similarity. An example in Table 2 shows weights of similar words for Italian word *professore* derived by taking powers of cosine similarity (we refer to this power as *filter* parameter).

Words	Similarity	Weights
educatore	0.955	0.796
harvard	0.853	0.452
insegnando	0.980	0.903
insegnata	0.990	0.951

Table 2: Taking power of weights reduces weights of noisy words (here *harvard*). Here $filter = 5$.

Algorithm 1 Translating Knowledge Resource

Input : Source (S), Target (T), Resource (R), η
Output : Translated Knowledge Resource R^*

$R^* = []$
for t in T **do**
$\quad t_s \leftarrow NearestNeighbour(S)$
$\quad$**if** $similarity(t, t_s) > \eta$ **then**
$\quad\quad lexicons \leftarrow S[t_s]$
$\quad\quad$**for** l in $lexicons$ **do**
$\quad\quad\quad l_t \leftarrow NearestNeighbour(T)$
$\quad\quad\quad weight \leftarrow similarity(l, l_t)$
$\quad\quad\quad R^*[t].add(l_t, weight)$
$\quad\quad$**end for**
$\quad$**else**
$\quad\quad continue$
$\quad$**end if**
end for

Language	Vocab	TRL	Tasks	Original	Half En-riched	Full En-riched
German	43,527	18,802 37,408	MC30 RG65 WS353 (sim) Simlex999	0.631 0.503 0.600 0.333	0.643 0.531 0.631 0.356	0.662 0.600 0.635 0.373
Italian	73,427	22,022 44,309	WS353 (sim) Simlex999	0.595 0.247	0.640 0.283	0.652 0.313
Spanish	41,779	17,434 35,034	MC30 RG65	0.312 0.608	0.286 0.615	0.412 0.634
French	40,523	16,203 32,602	RG65	0.547	0.582	0.673

Table 3: Retrofitting Translation Invariant Bilingual Embeddings for German, Italian, Spanish and French using English Paraphrase Database. (TRL stands for Translated Resource Length)

4 Datasets and Benchmarks

For English as source language, we use the Paraphrase Database (Ganitkevitch et al., 2013) to specialize embeddings for similarity as it gives the best results (compared to other sources like WordNet). To specialize embeddings for relatedness, we use University of South Florida Free Association Norms (Nelson et al., 2004) as indicated by (Kiela et al., 2015). For Hindi as source language, we use Hindi WordNet (Bhattacharyya et al., 2010). Whenever the size of resource is big enough, we first inject word embeddings with half of the dataset (random selection) followed by full length dataset to demonstrate the sequential gain in performance.

Multilingual WS353 and SimLex999 datasets are by (Leviant and Reichart, 2015). We also use German RG65 (Gurevych, 2005), French RG65 (Joubarne and Inkpen, 2011) and Spanish MC30, RG65 (Hassan and Mihalcea, 2009; Camacho-Collados et al., 2015). For Indian languages we use datasets provided by (Akhtar et al., 2017).

5 Results

In this section we present the experimental results of our method.[3] Before discussing the results we explain how different parameters are chosen. We do 10 iterations of retrofitting process for all our experiments because 10 iterations are enough for convergence (Faruqui et al., 2015) and also using the same value for all experiments avoids overfitting. The value of $filter$ parameter is set as 2

---

because we believe the embeddings that we use are well trained and low in noise. This value can be increased further if word embeddings being used are very noisy but in most cases a value of 2 is enough. η value, as explained in previous sections is set such that the translated resource obtained is of sufficient length. If more lexicons in translated resource are required, relax η and vice-versa.

5.1 European Languages

Table 3 shows the result of retrofitting *translation invariant bilingual* embeddings of four European languages for similarity using English Paraphrase Database. For each language we set η as 0.70 and $filter$ as 2. The embeddings are evaluated specifically on datasets measuring similarity. All embeddings are 40 dimensional. To show that our method is effective, the embeddings are first fitted with only half of the database followed by fitting with full length database. Table 3 also contains information about the size of vocabulary and translated resource. One can compare the size of translated resource that we get using our method to the dictionary based approach.

Table 4 shows the results of specializing word embeddings for relatedness using the USF Association Norms and evaluation on WS353 relatedness task. We test only with German and Italian as only these languages had datasets to test for relatedness.

Language	Original	Fitted
German	0.461	0.520
Italian	0.460	0.523

Table 4: Specializing for relatedness

---

[3]The implementation of our method is available at https://github.com/prakhar987/InjectingBilingual

We also experiment with embeddings of large dimensions (300) and large vocabulary size (200,000) for English and Italian bilingual embeddings obtained by method described by (Artetxe et al., 2016). Table 5 shows the improvements attained for similarity task for Italian with 64,434 words in the translated resource, $\eta = 0.35$ and $filter = 2$ (notice η is much smaller since we want translated resource size to be comparable to size of vocabulary).

Task	Original	Fitted
WS353	0.648	0.680
SimLex999	0.371	0.405

Table 5: Improving large embeddings

5.2 Indian Languages

To demonstrate the utility of our method, we experiment with Indian languages, taking Hindi as the source language (which has Hindi WordNet). For target language, we take one language (Urdu) which is very similar to Hindi (belongs to same family) and one language (Telugu) which is very different from Hindi (descendants from same family). The vocabulary size of Urdu and Telugu were 129,863 and 174,008 respectively. The results are shown in Table 6. Here again we fit with half length followed by full length of Hindi WordNet. As expected, we get much higher gains for Urdu compared to Telugu.[4]

Language	Original	Half Fitted	Full Fitted
Telugu	0.427	0.436	0.440
Urdu	0.541	0.589	0.612

Table 6: Retrofitting Indian languages

6 Conclusion

In this work we introduced a method to improve word embeddings of a language using resources from another similar language. We accomplished this by translating the resource using bilingual embeddings and modifying retrofitting while handling noise. Using our method, we also created new benchmark on Urdu word similarity dataset.

---

[4]enriched embeddings and evaluation scripts can be downloaded from `https://goo.gl/tN6p3w`

References

Syed Sarfaraz Akhtar, Arihant Gupta, Avijit Vajpayee, Arjit Srivastava, and Manish Shrivastava. 2017. Word similarity datasets for indian languages: Annotation and baseline systems. In *Proceedings of the 11th Linguistic Annotation Workshop*, pages 91–94. Association for Computational Linguistics.

Mikel Artetxe, Gorka Labaka, and Eneko Agirre. 2016. Learning principled bilingual mappings of word embeddings while preserving monolingual invariance. In *Proceedings of the Conference on Empirical Methods in Natural Language Processing, EMNLP 2016*, pages 2289–2294.

Pushpak Bhattacharyya, Prabhakar Pande, and Laxmi Lupu. 2010. Hindi wordnet. Language Resources and Evaluation (LRE).

Jiang Bian, Bin Gao, and Tie-Yan Liu. 2014. Knowledge-powered deep learning for word embedding. In *Proceedings of the European Conference on Machine Learning and Knowledge Discovery in Databases - Volume 8724*, pages 132–148.

Jos Camacho-Collados, Mohammad Taher Pilehvar, and Roberto Navigli. 2015. A framework for the construction of monolingual and cross-lingualword similarity datasets. In *Proceedings of 53rd Annual Meeting of the Association for Computational Linguistics and the 7th International Joint Conference on Natural Language Processing of the Asian Federation of Natural Language Processing*, volume 2, pages 1–7.

Sarath Chandar A P, Stanislas Lauly, Hugo Larochelle, Mitesh Khapra, Balaraman Ravindran, Vikas C Raykar, and Amrita Saha. 2014. An autoencoder approach to learning bilingual word representations. In *Proceedings of Neural Information Processing Systems*, pages 1853–1861.

Ronan Collobert and Jason Weston. 2008. A unified architecture for natural language processing: Deep neural networks with multitask learning. In *Proceedings of the 25th International Conference on Machine Learning*, pages 160–167.

Jocelyn Coulmance, Jean-Marc Marty, Guillaume Wenzek, and Amine Benhalloum. 2016. Transgram, fast cross-lingual word-embeddings. *CoRR*, abs/1601.02502.

Manaal Faruqui, Jesse Dodge, Sujay K. Jauhar, Chris Dyer, Eduard Hovy, and Noah A. Smith. 2015. Retrofitting word vectors to semantic lexicons. In *Proceedings of NAACL*.

Manaal Faruqui and Chris Dyer. 2014. Improving vector space word representations using multilingual correlation. In *Proceedings of EACL*.

Juri Ganitkevitch, Benjamin Van Durme, and Chris Callison-Burch. 2013. PPDB: The paraphrase database. In *Proceedings of NAACL-HLT*, pages 758–764.

Matt Gardner, Kejun Huang, Evangelos Papalexakis, Xiao Fu, Partha Talukdar, Christos Faloutsos, Nicholas Sidiropoulos, and Tom Mitchell. 2015. Translation invariant word embeddings. In *Proceedings of EMNLP*.

Iryna Gurevych. 2005. Using the structure of a conceptual network in computing semantic relatedness. *IJCNLP 2005*, pages 767–778.

Samer Hassan and Rada Mihalcea. 2009. Cross-lingual semantic relatedness using encyclopedic knowledge. In *Proceedings of the 2009 Conference on Empirical Methods in Natural Language Processing: Volume 3*, pages 1192–1201.

Karl Moritz Hermann and Phil Blunsom. 2014. Multilingual models for compositional distributed semantics. *CoRR*, abs/1404.4641.

Colette Joubarne and Diana Inkpen. 2011. Comparison of semantic similarity for different languages using the google n-gram corpus and second- order co-occurrence measures. In *Proceedings of the 24th Canadian Conference on Advances in Artificial Intelligence*, pages 216–221.

Douwe Kiela, Felix Hill, and Stephen Clark. 2015. Specializing word embeddings for similarity or relatedness. In *Proceedings of EMNLP*.

Alexandre Klementiev, Ivan Titov, and Binod Bhattarai. 2012. Inducing crosslingual distributed representations of words. In *Proceedings COLING*, pages 1459–1474.

Ira Leviant and Roi Reichart. 2015. Judgment language matters: Multilingual vector space models for judgment language aware lexical semantics. *CoRR*, abs/1508.00106.

Tomas Mikolov, Kai Chen, Greg Corrado, and Jeffrey Dean. 2013. Efficient estimation of word representations in vector space. *CoRR*, abs/1301.3781.

Tomas Mikolov, Quoc V. Le, and Ilya Sutskever. 2013b. Exploiting similarities among languages for machine translation. *CoRR*, abs/1309.4168.

George A. Miller. 1995. Wordnet: A lexical database for english. *Communications of the ACM*, pages 39–41.

Nikola Mrksic, Diarmuid Ó Séaghdha, Blaise Thomson, Milica Gasic, Lina Maria Rojas-Barahona, Pei-Hao Su, David Vandyke, Tsung-Hsien Wen, and Steve J. Young. 2016. Counter-fitting word vectors to linguistic constraints. *In Proceedings of NAACL*, pages 142–148.

Nikola Mrkšić, Ivan Vulić, Diarmuid Ó Séaghdha, Ira Leviant, Roi Reichart, Milica Gašić, Anna Korhonen, and Steve Young. 2017. Semantic specialisation of distributional word vector spaces using monolingual and cross-lingual constraints. *Transactions of the Association for Computational Linguistics*.

Douglas L. Nelson, Cathy L. McEvoy, and Thomas A. Schreiber. 2004. The university of south florida free association, rhyme, and word fragment norms. *Behavior Research Methods, Instruments, & Computers*, 36(3):402–407.

Jeffrey Pennington, Richard Socher, and Christopher D Manning. 2014. Glove: Global vectors for word representation. In *EMNLP*, volume 12, pages 1532–1543.

Ivan Vulic and Marie-Francine Moens. 2015. Bilingual word embeddings from non-parallel document-aligned data applied to bilingual lexicon induction. In *Proceedings of the 53rd Annual Meeting of the Association for Computational Linguistics and the 7th International Joint Conference on Natural Language Processing of the Asian Federation of Natural Language Processing, Volume 2: Short Papers*, pages 719–725.

Chang Xu, Yalong Bai, Jiang Bian, Bin Gao, Gang Wang, Xiaoguang Liu, and Tie-Yan Liu. 2014. Rcnet: A general framework for incorporating knowledge into word representations. In *Proceedings of the 23rd ACM International Conference on Conference on Information and Knowledge Management*, pages 1219–1228.

Will Y. Zou, Richard Socher, Daniel Cer, and Christopher D. Manning. 2013. Bilingual word embeddings for phrase-based machine translation. In *Proceedings of EMNLP*, pages 1393–1398.

Improving Black-box Speech Recognition using Semantic Parsing

Rodolfo Corona and **Jesse Thomason** and **Raymond J. Mooney**
Department of Computer Science, University of Texas at Austin
{rcorona, jesse, mooney}@cs.utexas.edu

Abstract

Speech is a natural channel for human-computer interaction in robotics and consumer applications. Natural language understanding pipelines that start with speech can have trouble recovering from speech recognition errors. Black-box automatic speech recognition (ASR) systems, built for general purpose use, are unable to take advantage of in-domain language models that could otherwise ameliorate these errors. In this work, we present a method for re-ranking black-box ASR hypotheses using an in-domain language model and semantic parser trained for a particular task. Our re-ranking method significantly improves both transcription accuracy and semantic understanding over a state-of-the-art ASR's vanilla output.

1 Introduction

Voice control makes robotic and computer systems more accessible in consumer domains. Collecting sufficient data to train ASR systems using current state of the art methods, such as deep neural networks (Graves and Jaitly, 2014; Xiong et al., 2016), is difficult. Thus, it is common to use well-trained, cloud-based ASR systems. These systems use general language models not restricted to individual application domains. However, for an ASR in a larger pipeline, the expected words and phrases from users will be biased by the application domain. The general language model of a black-box ASR leads to more errors in transcription. These errors can cause cascading problems in a language understanding pipeline.

In this paper, we demonstrate that an in-domain language model and semantic parser can be used to improve black-box ASR transcription and downstream semantic accuracy. We consider a robotics domain, where language understanding is key for ensuring effective performance and positive user experiences (Thomason et al., 2015). We collect a dataset of spoken robot commands paired with transcriptions and semantic forms to evaluate our method.[1] Given a list of ASR hypotheses, we re-rank the list to choose the hypothesis scoring best between an in-domain trained semantic parser and language model (Figure 1). This work is inspired by other re-ranking methods which have used prosodic models (Ananthakrishnan and Narayanan, 2007), phonetic post-processing (Twiefel et al., 2014), syntactic parsing (Zechner and Waibel, 1998; Basili et al., 2013), as well as features from search engine results (Peng et al., 2013).

Other work has similarly employed semantics to improve ASR performance, for example by assigning semantic category labels to entire utterances and re-ranking the ASR n-best list (Morbini et al., 2012), jointly modeling the word and semantic tag sequence (Deoras et al., 2013), and learning a semantic grammar for use by both the ASR system and semantic parser (Gaspers et al., 2015). Closest to our work is that of Erdogan et al. (2005), which uses maximum entropy modeling to combine information from the semantic parser and ASR's language model for re-ranking. Although their method could be adapted for use with a black-box ASR, their parsing framework employs a treebanked dataset of parses (Davies et al., 1999; Jelinek et al., 1994). In contrast, the Combinatory Categorial Grammar (CCG) framework which we use in this work only requires that the root-level semantic form be given along with groundings for a small number of words (see section 2.2), significantly reducing the cost of data collection. Further, although they also experiment with an out-of-the-box language model, they only

---

[1] Our dataset will be made available upon request. Source code can be found in: `https://github.com/thomason-jesse/nlu_pipeline/tree/speech`

Proceedings of the The 8th International Joint Conference on Natural Language Processing, pages 122–127,
Taipei, Taiwan, November 27 – December 1, 2017 ©2017 AFNLP

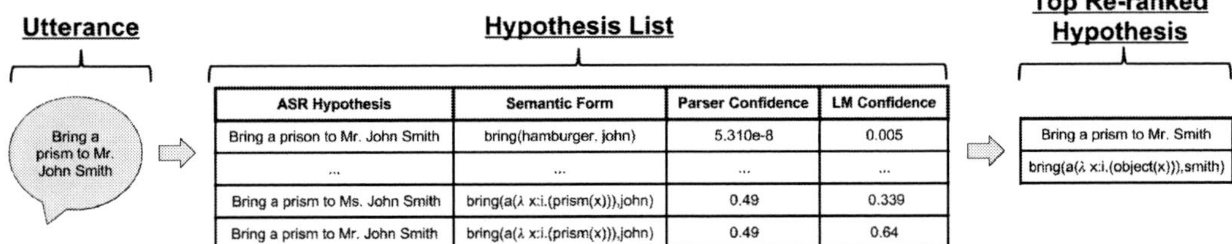

Figure 1: Our proposed methodology. The black-box ASR outputs an ordered list of its top hypotheses. Each hypothesis is given confidence scores by an in-domain semantic parser and language model, which are then used to re-rank the list. In this example, the parser has learned that "Mr." and "Ms." are functionally equivalent, while the language model has learned that "Mr." co-occurs with "John" more than "Ms." does. Together, they guide us to select the correct transcription.

measure for improvements in transcription accuracy, which may not entail improvements in language understanding (Wang et al., 2003).

To the best of our knowledge, our method is the first to improve language understanding by employing a low-cost semantic parser and language model post-hoc on a high-cost, black-box ASR system. This significantly lowers word error rate (WER) while increasing semantic accuracy.

2 Methodology

Given a user utterance U, the black-box ASR system generates a list of n-best hypotheses H. For each hypothesis $h \in H$, we produce an interpolated score[2] $S(h)$ from its language model score $S_{lm}(h)$ and semantic parser score $S_{sem}(h)$.[3] Parser confidence scores vary by orders of magnitude between hypotheses, making it difficult to find a meaningful interpolation weight α between the language model and semantic parser. We therefore normalize over the sum of scores in each hypothesis list for each model. We then choose the highest scoring hypothesis h^*:

$$h^* = \arg\max_{h \in H} \left(S(h) \right) ; \qquad (1)$$

$$S(h) = (1 - \alpha) \cdot S_{lm}(h) + \alpha \cdot S_{sem}(h). \qquad (2)$$

---

[2] In order to avoid underflow errors, all computations are done in log space.

[3] We do not assume a black-box ASR system will provide confidence scores for its n-best list. Google Speech API, for example, often only shows confidence for the top hypothesis. Preliminary experiments using proxy scores based on rank did not improve performance.

2.1 Language Model

We implement an in-domain language model using the SRI Language Modeling Toolkit (Stolcke et al., 2002). We use a trigram back-off model with Witten-Bell discounting (Witten and Bell, 1991) and an open vocabulary. We use perplexity-based, length-normalized scores to compare hypotheses with different numbers of word tokens.

2.2 Semantic Parsing Model

For semantic parsing, we used a CCG (Steedman and Baldridge, 2011) based probabilistic CKY parser.

The parser consists of a lexicon whose entries are words paired with syntactic categories and semantic forms (see Table 1 for example lexical entries). CCG categories may be atomic or func-

Surface Form	CCG Category	Semantic Form
walk	S/PP	$\lambda x.(\text{walk}(x))$
to	PP/NP	$\lambda x.(x)$
john	N	john

Table 1: Example lexical entries in our domain. Given an initial lexicon, additional entries are induced by the parser during training for use at test time.

tional, with functional categories specifying combinatory rules for adjacent categories. These may be expressed logically by representing semantic forms using a formalism such as lambda calculus. For example, consider the combination between the functional category (NP/N) and the atomic category N, along with its pertaining lambda cal-

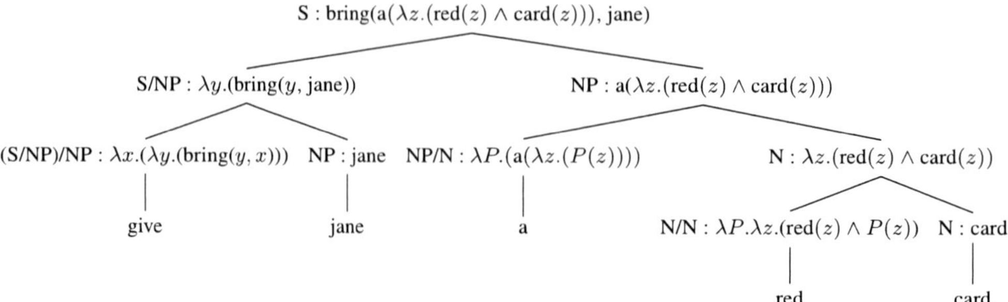

Figure 2: A parse tree of the phrase "give jane a red card." The token *give* is an imperative, taking two noun phrases on its right which represent the recipient and the patient of the action (the robot is the implicit agent in the command). *jane* immediately resolves to a noun phrase. *red* is an adjectival predicate, consuming the noun predicate *card* on its right, the result of which is consumed by the determiner *a* in order to form a complete noun phrase.

culus expression:

$$(NP/N)\ N \implies NP$$
$$(\lambda x.(x))\ y \implies y$$

The combinatory rules of a CCG implicitly define a grammar. An example CCG parse tree may be seen in Figure 2.

Following Zettlemoyer and Collins (2005), gold labels for parsing contain only root-level semantic forms, and only a small set of bootstrapping lexical entries are provided. This necessitates that latent parse trees be inferred and that additional lexical entries be induced during training.

Given a corpus of training examples T of sentences paired with their semantic forms, we follow the framework proposed by (Liang and Potts, 2015) and train a perceptron model to greedily search for the maximally scoring parse of each hypothesis. We bootstrap the parser's lexicon entries with mappings for words from 20 randomly selected examples from our validation set, which were parsed by hand to obtain the latent trees. Sample templates used to create our dataset are shown in Table 2.

To normalize likelihoods between hypotheses of different lengths, we calculate average likelihoods for CCG productions and semantic *null* nodes, then expand the semantic parse trees to accommodate the maximum token length for utterances when scoring.

Because our application is human-robot interaction, we give the parser a budget of 10 seconds

per hypothesis during the re-ranking process.[4] If a valid parse is not found in time, the hypothesis is given a confidence score of zero. If no hypotheses from a list are parsed, the re-ranking decision falls solely to the language model.

3 Experimental Evaluation

We evaluate chosen hypotheses by word error rate (WER), semantic form accuracy (whether the chosen hypothesis' semantic parse exactly matched the gold parse), and semantic form F1 score, the average harmonic mean of the precision and recall of hypotheses' semantic predicates with their corresponding gold predicates (see Table 3 for example F1 computations). In the robotic command domain, higher F1 can mean shorter clarification dialogs with users when there are misunderstandings, since the intended (gold) semantic parse's predicates are better represented for parses with higher F1. We compare the ASR's top hypothesis to re-ranking (Eq. 2) using only the language model ($\alpha = 0$), only the semantic parser ($\alpha = 1$), and a weighted combination of the two ($\alpha = 0.7$).

3.1 Dataset

We collected a corpus of speech utterances from 32 participants, consisting of both male and female, native and non-native English speakers. Participants were asked to read sentences from a computer screen for 25 minutes each, resulting in a total of 5,161 utterances. The sentences read were

---

[4] We found that hypotheses successfully parsed within the budget were parsed in 1.94 seconds on average, suggesting that a stricter budget can be used.

Template	Example Sentences	Corresponding Semantic Form
(f) (w) to (p)'s office	roll over to dr bell's office	walk(the($\lambda x.$(office(x) $\wedge$ possesses(x, tom))))
	can you please walk to john's office	walk(the($\lambda x.$(office(x) $\wedge$ possesses(x, john))))
	run over to professor smith's office	walk(the($\lambda x.$(office(x) $\wedge$ possesses(x, john))))
(f) (d) (i) to (p)	go and bring coffee to jane	bring(coffee, jane)
	please deliver a red cup to tom	bring(a($\lambda x.$(red(x) $\wedge$ cup(x))), tom)
	would you take the box to jack	bring(box, jack)
(f) (s) (p) in (l)	please look for ms. jones in the lab	searchroom(3414b, jane)
	can you find jack in room 3.512	searchroom(3512, jack)
	search for the ta in the kitchen	searchroom(kitchen, jack)

Table 2: Example templates used to generate our dataset. Our template parameterization includes items (i), people (p), locations (l), filler words (f), and actions such as walk (w), delivery(d), and search (s). Parameter instances had multiple referring expressions (e.g. "john" and "professor smith" both refer to the person *john*). Eight distinct templates were used across the 3 actions, with 70 items, 69 adjectives, over 20 referents for people, and a variety of wordings for actions and filler, resulting in over 400 million possible utterances.

generated using templates for commanding a robot in an office domain (Table 2). The use of templates allowed for the automatic generation of ground truth transcriptions and semantic forms for each spoken utterance.

3.2 Experimental Setup and Results

To test our methodology, we used the Google Speech API,[5] a state-of-the-art, black-box ASR system which has been used in recent robotics tasks (Arumugam et al., 2017; Kollar et al., 2013). For each utterance, 10 hypotheses were requested from Google Speech.[6] An average of 9.2 hypotheses were returned per utterance (the API sometimes returns fewer than requested). We held out 2 speakers from our dataset as validation for hyperparameter tuning, leaving 30 speakers for a 27/3 (90%/10%) training and test set split using 10-fold cross validation.

We set the language model and semantic parser hyperparameters using the held-out validation set. Performance of the ASR's top hypothesis (**ASR**) was tested against re-ranking solely based on semantic-parser scores (**SemP**), solely on language model scores (**LM**), and on an interpolation of these with $\alpha = 0.7$ which maximized semantic form accuracy on the validation set (**Both**).

Table 4 summarizes the results of these models on the test set. All of our model's scores are statistically significantly better than the ASR baseline ($p < 0.05$ with a Student's independent paired t-test). Additionally, **SemP** and **Both** perform sig-

nificantly better than **LM** in F1 while the **Both** condition performs significantly better than **LM** in semantic accuracy without a significant loss in WER or F1 performance against **LM** and **SemP**, respectively.

3.3 Discussion

All re-ranking conditions significantly improve word error rate, semantic parsing accuracy, and semantic form F1 scores against using the ASR's top hypothesis.

When examining the overall parsing accuracy of our models, we found that 37.5% of the ASR hypothesis lists generated for test utterances had at least 1 out of vocabulary (OOV) word per hypothesis. Our semantic parser is closed-vocabulary at test time, ignoring OOV words, which can contain valuable semantic information.

Consistent with intuition, using a language model alone decreases WER most. Semantic accuracy increases when interpolating confidences from the semantic parser and language model, meaning there are cases where the hypothesis the semantic parser most favors has an incorrect semantic form even while another hypothesis in the list gives the correct one. In this case, a lower confidence parse from a better-worded transcript is more likely to be correct, and we need both the semantic parser and the language model to select it.

There is no significant difference in semantic accuracy performance between solely using the language model or semantic parser, but interpolating the two gives a significant improvement over just using a language model. The semantic parser and interpolation conditions give significantly bet-

[5]https://cloud.google.com/speech/

[6]Preliminary experiments showed diminishing returns for hypothesis lists of size $n > 10$. Therefore, n was set to 10 for the accuracy vs. runtime tradeoff.

Semantic Form	P	R	F1
bring(cup, jane)	$\frac{3}{3}$	$\frac{3}{3}$	1.0
bring(a($\lambda x.$(red(x)$\wedge$ cup(x))), jane)	$\frac{3}{4}$	$\frac{3}{3}$	0.857
bring(jane, jane)	$\frac{3}{3}$	$\frac{2}{3}$	0.8

Table 3: Example F1 computations for the phrase "Bring Jane a cup". Here, the relevant (gold) predicates are *bring*, *cup*, and *jane*. F1 is the harmonic mean of the precision (P) and recall (R): F1$= 2 \cdot \frac{P \cdot R}{P+R}$

Model	WER	Acc	F1
Oracle	13.4 ± 4.2	27.9 ± 3.8	39.3 ± 3.9
ASR	30.8 ± 4.6	7.38 ± 1.9	15.9 ± 3.0
SemP	20.8 ± 5.3	24.8 ± 3.9	**38.3** ± 4.1
LM	**15.7** ± 4.7	22.7 ± 3.3	31.7 ± 4.1
Both	16.8 ± 4.6	**26.3** ± 3.7	**38.1** ± 4.1

Table 4: Average performance of re-ranking with standard deviation using semantic parsing (**SemP**), language model (**LM**), and **Both** against the black-box **ASR**'s top hypothesis. **Oracle** denotes the best possible performance achievable through re-ranking per metric (i.e. choosing the hypothesis from the ASR that optimizes for each metric in turn).

ter F1 performance over a language model alone. These results show that the integration of semantic information into the speech recognition pipeline can significantly improve language understanding.

4 Conclusion and Future Work

We have shown that post-hoc re-ranking of a black-box ASR's hypotheses using an in-domain language model and a semantic parser can significantly improve the accuracy of transcription *and* semantic understanding. Using both re-ranking components together improves parsing accuracy over either alone without sacrificing WER reduction.

A natural extension to this work would be to test re-ranking using a neural language model, which has been shown to encode some semantic information in addition to capturing statistical regularities in word sequences (Bengio et al., 2003).

Our approach should improve language understanding in robotics applications. The increase in F1 should help expedite dialogues because it would entail fewer predicates needing clarification from the user. Additionally, due to the large proportion of OOV words that we encountered from ASR, in the future we will use an open-vocabulary

semantic parser, perhaps through leveraging distributional semantic representations in order to induce the meaning of novel words. By adapting existing work on learning semantic parsers for robots through dialog (Thomason et al., 2015) to incorporate ASR, a robot equipped with our pipeline could iteratively learn the meaning of new words and expressions it encounters in the wild.

Acknowledgments

We thank our reviewers for their helpful feedback and requests for clarification. This work is supported by an NSF EAGER grant (IIS-1548567), an NSF NRI grant (IIS-1637736), and a National Science Foundation Graduate Research Fellowship to the second author.

References

Sankaranarayanan Ananthakrishnan and Shrikanth Narayanan. 2007. Improved speech recognition using acoustic and lexical correlates of pitch accent in a n-best rescoring framework. In *Proc. Int. Conf. Acoust., Speech, Signal Process., Honolulu, HI*, volume 4, pages 873–876. IEEE.

Dilip Arumugam, Siddharth Karamcheti, Nakul Gopalan, Lawson L. S. Wong, and Stefanie Tellex. 2017. Accurately and Efficiently Interpreting Human-Robot Instructions of Varying Granularities. In *Robotics: Science and Systems*.

Roberto Basili, Emanuele Bastianelli, Giuseppe Castellucci, Daniele Nardi, and Vittorio Perera. 2013. Kernel-based discriminative re-ranking for spoken command understanding in HRI. In *Congress of the Italian Association for Artificial Intelligence*, pages 169–180. Springer.

Yoshua Bengio, Réjean Ducharme, Pascal Vincent, and Christian Jauvin. 2003. A neural probabilistic language model. *Journal of machine learning research*, 3(Feb):1137–1155.

K. Davies, Robert E. Donovan, Mark Epstein, Martin Franz, Abraham Ittycheriah, Ea-Ee Jan, Jean-Michel LeRoux, David Lubensky, Chalapathy Neti, Mukund Padmanabhan, Kishore Papineni, Salim

Roukos, Andrej Sakrajda, Jeffrey S. Sorensen, Borivoj Tydlitát, and Todd Ward. 1999. The IBM conversational telephony system for financial applications. In *Sixth European Conference on Speech Communication and Technology, EUROSPEECH 1999, Budapest, Hungary, September 5-9, 1999*.

Anoop Deoras, Gokhan Tur, Ruhi Sarikaya, and Dilek Hakkani-Tür. 2013. Joint discriminative decoding of word and semantic tags for spoken language understanding. In *IEEE Transactions on Audio, Speech, and Language Processing*, pages 1612–1621. IEEE.

Hakan Erdogan, Ruhi Sarikaya, Stanley F Chen, Yuqing Gao, and Michael Picheny. 2005. Using semantic analysis to improve speech recognition performance. *Computer Speech & Language*, 19(3):321–343.

Judith Gaspers, Philipp Cimiano, and Britta Wrede. 2015. Semantic parsing of speech using grammars learned with weak supervision. In *HLT-NAACL*, pages 872–881.

Alex Graves and Navdeep Jaitly. 2014. Towards end-to-end speech recognition with recurrent neural networks. In *ICML*, volume 14, pages 1764–1772.

Frederick Jelinek, John Lafferty, David Magerman, Robert Mercer, Adwait Ratnaparkhi, and Salim Roukos. 1994. Decision tree parsing using a hidden derivation model. In *Proceedings of the workshop on Human Language Technology*, pages 272–277. Association for Computational Linguistics.

Thomas Kollar, Vittorio Perera, Daniele Nardi, and Manuela Veloso. 2013. Learning environmental knowledge from task-based human-robot dialog. In *Robotics and Automation (ICRA), 2013 IEEE International Conference on*, pages 4304–4309. IEEE.

Percy Liang and Christopher Potts. 2015. Bringing machine learning and compositional semantics together. *Annu. Rev. Linguist.*, 1(1):355–376.

Fabrizio Morbini, Kartik Audhkhasi, Ron Artstein, Maarten Van Segbroeck, Kenji Sagae, Panayiotis Georgiou, David R Traum, and Shri Narayanan. 2012. A reranking approach for recognition and classification of speech input in conversational dialogue systems. In *Spoken Language Technology Workshop (SLT), 2012 IEEE*, pages 49–54. IEEE.

Fuchun Peng, Scott Roy, Ben Shahshahani, and Françoise Beaufays. 2013. Search results based n-best hypothesis rescoring with maximum entropy classification. In *ASRU*, pages 422–427.

Mark Steedman and Jason Baldridge. 2011. Combinatory categorial grammar. *Non-Transformational Syntax: Formal and Explicit Models of Grammar. Wiley-Blackwell*, pages 181–224.

Andreas Stolcke et al. 2002. Srilm-an extensible language modeling toolkit. In *Intl. Conf. on Spoken Language Processing*, pages 901– 904.

Jesse Thomason, Shiqi Zhang, Raymond Mooney, and Peter Stone. 2015. Learning to interpret natural language commands through human-robot dialog. In *Proceedings of the 24th International Joint Conference on Artificial Intelligence (IJCAI)*, pages 1923–1929.

Johannes Twiefel, Timo Baumann, Stefan Heinrich, and Stefan Wermter. 2014. Improving domain-independent cloud-based speech recognition with domain-dependent phonetic post-processing. In *Twenty-Eighth AAAI Conference on Artificial Intelligence. Quebec City, Canada*, pages 1529–1536.

Ye-Yi Wang, Alex Acero, and Ciprian Chelba. 2003. Is word error rate a good indicator for spoken language understanding accuracy. In *IEEE Workshop on Automatic Speech Recognition and Understanding*, pages 577–582, St. Thomas, US Virgin Islands. Institute of Electrical and Electronics Engineers, Inc.

Ian H Witten and Timothy C Bell. 1991. The zero-frequency problem: Estimating the probabilities of novel events in adaptive text compression. *IEEE Transactions on Information Theory*, 37(4):1085–1094.

Wayne Xiong, Jasha Droppo, Xuedong Huang, Frank Seide, Mike Seltzer, Andreas Stolcke, Dong Yu, and Geoffrey Zweig. 2016. Achieving human parity in conversational speech recognition. *arXiv preprint arXiv:1610.05256*.

Klaus Zechner and Alex Waibel. 1998. Using chunk based partial parsing of spontaneous speech in unrestricted domains for reducing word error rate in speech recognition. In *Proceedings of the 36th Annual Meeting of the Association for Computational Linguistics and 17th International Conference on Computational Linguistics-Volume 2*, pages 1453–1459. Association for Computational Linguistics.

Luke S Zettlemoyer and Michael Collins. 2005. Learning to map sentences to logical form: Structured classification with probabilistic categorial grammars. In *Proceedings of the Conference on Uncertainty in Artificial Intelligence (UAI)*, pages 658–666.

Revisiting the Design Issues of Local Models for Japanese Predicate-Argument Structure Analysis

Yuichiroh Matsubayashi♠ and **Kentaro Inui**♠◇
♠Tohoku University, ◇RIKEN Center for Advanced Intelligence Project
{y-matsu, inui}@ecei.tohoku.ac.jp

Abstract

The research trend in Japanese predicate-argument structure (PAS) analysis is shifting from pointwise prediction models with local features to global models designed to search for globally optimal solutions. However, the existing global models tend to employ only relatively simple local features; therefore, the overall performance gains are rather limited. The importance of designing a local model is demonstrated in this study by showing that the performance of a sophisticated local model can be considerably improved with recent feature embedding methods and a feature combination learning based on a neural network, outperforming the state-of-the-art global models in F_1 on a common benchmark dataset.

1 Introduction

A predicate-argument structure (PAS) analysis is the task of analyzing the structural relations between a predicate and its arguments in a text and is considered as a useful sub-process for a wide range of natural language processing applications (Shen and Lapata, 2007; Kudo et al., 2014; Liu et al., 2015).

PAS analysis can be decomposed into a set of primitive subtasks that seek a filler token for each argument slot of each predicate. The existing models for PAS analysis fall into two types: local models and global models. Local models independently solve each primitive subtask in the pointwise fashion (Seki et al., 2002; Taira et al., 2008; Imamura et al., 2009; Yoshino et al., 2013). Such models tend to be easy to implement and faster compared with global models but cannot handle dependencies between primitive subtasks. Re-

cently, the research trend is shifting toward global models that search for a globally optimal solution for a given set of subtasks by extending those local models with an additional ranker or classifier that accounts for dependencies between subtasks (Iida et al., 2007a; Komachi et al., 2010; Yoshikawa et al., 2011; Hayashibe et al., 2014; Ouchi et al., 2015; Iida et al., 2015, 2016; Shibata et al., 2016).

However, even with the latest state-of-the-art global models (Ouchi et al., 2015, 2017), the best achieved F_1 remains as low as 81.4% on a commonly used benchmark dataset (Iida et al., 2007b), wherein the gain from the global scoring is only 0.3 to 1.0 point. We speculate that one reason for this slow advance is that recent studies pay too much attention to global models and thus tend to employ overly simple feature sets for their base local models.

The goal of this study is to argue the importance of designing a sophisticated local model before exploring global solution algorithms and to demonstrate its impact on the overall performance through an extensive empirical evaluation. In this evaluation, we show that a local model alone is able to significantly outperform the state-of-the-art global models by incorporating a broad range of local features proposed in the literature and training a neural network for combining them. Our best local model achieved 13% error reduction in F_1 compared with the state of the art.

2 Task and Dataset

In this study, we adopt the specifications of the NAIST Text Corpus (NTC) (Iida et al., 2007b), a commonly used benchmark corpus annotated with nominative (NOM), accusative (ACC), and dative (DAT) arguments for predicates. Given an input text and the predicate positions, the aim of the PAS analysis is to identify the head of the filler tokens

Proceedings of the The 8th International Joint Conference on Natural Language Processing, pages 128–133,
Taipei, Taiwan, November 27 – December 1, 2017 ©2017 AFNLP

for each argument slot of each predicate.

The difficulty of finding an argument tends to differ depending on the relative position of the argument filler and the predicate. In particular, if the argument is omitted and the corresponding filler appears outside the sentence, the task is much more difficult because we cannot use the syntactic relationship between the predicate and the filler in a naive way. For this reason, a large part of previous work narrowed the focus to the analysis of arguments in a target sentence (Yoshikawa et al., 2011; Ouchi et al., 2015; Iida et al., 2015), and here, we followed this setting as well.

3 Model

Given a tokenized sentence s and a target predicate p in s with the gold dependency tree t, the goal of our task is to select at most one argument token $\hat{a}$ for each case slot of the target predicate.

Taking $x_a = (a, p, s, t)$ as input, our model estimates the probability $p(c|x_a)$ of assigning a case label $c \in \{\texttt{NOM}, \texttt{ACC}, \texttt{DAT}, \texttt{NONE}\}$ for each token a in the sentence, and then selects a token with a maximum probability that exceeds the output threshold θ_c for c. The probability $p(c|x_a)$ is modeled by a neural network (NN) architecture, which is a fully connected multilayer feedforward network stacked with a softmax layer on the top (Figure 1).

$$
\begin{aligned}
g &= \text{softmax}(W_{n+1}h_n + b_{n+1}) & (1) \\
h_i &= \text{ReLU}(\text{BN}(W_i h_{i-1} + b_i)) & (2) \\
h_1 &= \text{ReLU}(\text{BN}(W_1 m + b_1)) & (3) \\
m &= [h_{\text{path}}, w_p, w_a, f(x_a)] & (4)
\end{aligned}
$$

The network outputs the probabilities g of assigning each case label for an input token a, from automatically learned combinations of feature representations in input m. Here, h_i is an i-th hidden layer and n is the number of hidden layers. We apply batch normalization (BN) and a ReLU activation function to each hidden layer.

The input layer m for the feedforward network is a concatenation of the three types of feature representations described below: a path embedding h_{path}, word embeddings of the predicate and the argument candidate w_p and w_a, and a traditional binary representation of other features $f(x_a)$.

3.1 Lexicalized path embeddings

When an argument is not a direct dependent of a predicate, the dependency path is considered as

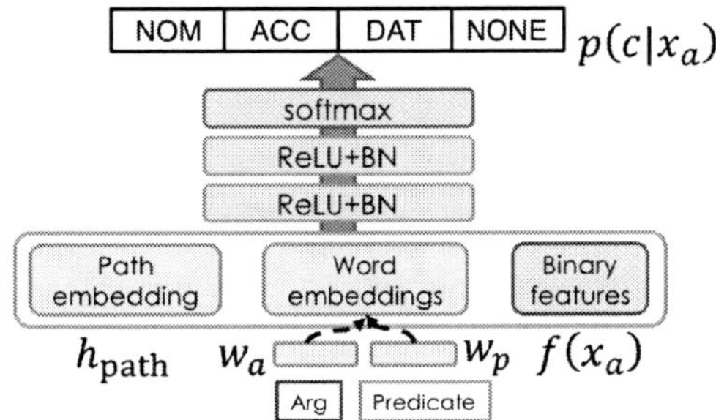

Figure 1: Network structure of our NN model

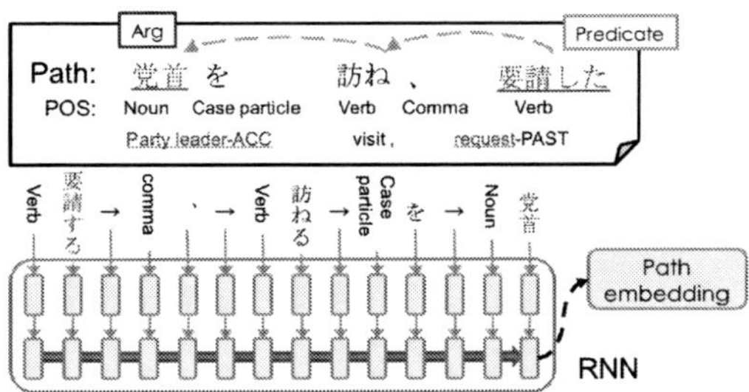

Figure 2: Path embedding

important information. Moreover, in some constructions such as raising, control, and coordination, lexical information of intermediate nodes is also beneficial although a sparsity problem occurs with a conventional binary encoding of lexicalized paths.

Roth and Lapata (2016) and Shwartz et al. (2016) recently proposed methods for embedding a lexicalized version of dependency path on a single vector using RNN. Both the methods embed words, parts-of-speech, and directions and labels of dependency in the path into a hidden unit of LSTM and output the final state of the hidden unit. We adopt these methods for Japanese PAS analysis and compare their performances.

As shown in Figure 2, given a dependency path from a predicate to an argument candidate, we first create a sequence of POS, lemma, and dependency direction for each token in this order by traversing the path.[1] Next, an embedding layer transforms the elements of this sequence into vector representations. The resulting vectors are sequentially input to RNN. Then, we use the final hidden state

---

[1] We could not use dependency labels in the path since traditional parsing framework in Japanese does not have dependency labels. However, particles in Japanese can roughly be seen as dependency relationship markers, and, therefore, we think these adaptations approximate the original methods.

For predicate p	surface, lemma, POS, type of conjugated form, nominal form of nominal verb, voice suffixes (-reru, -seru, -dekiru, -tearu)
For argument candidate a	surface, lemma, POS, NE tag, whether a is head of *bunsetsu*, particles in *bunsetsu*, right neighbor token's lemma and POS
Between predicate and argument candidate	case markers of other dependents of p, whether a precedes p, whether a and p are in the same *bunsetsu*, token- and dependency-based distances, naive dependency path sequence

Table 1: Binary features

as the path-embedding vector. We employ GRU (Cho et al., 2014) for our RNN and use two types of input vectors: the adaptations of Roth and Lapata (2016), which we described in Figure 2, and Shwartz et al. (2016), which concatenates vectors of POS, lemma and dependency direction for each token into a single vector.

3.2 Word embedding

The generalization of a word representation is one of the major issues in SRL. Fitzgerald et al. (2015) and Shibata et al. (2016) successfully improved the classification accuracy of SRL tasks by generalizing words using embedding techniques. We employ the same approach as Shibata et al. (2016), which uses the concatenation of the embedding vectors of a predicate and an argument candidate.

3.3 Binary features

Case markers of the other dependents Our model independently estimates label scores for each argument candidate. However, as argued by Toutanova et al. (2008) and Yoshikawa et al. (2011), there is a dependency between the argument labels of a predicate.

In Japanese, case markers (case particles) partially represent a semantic relationship between words in direct dependency. We thus introduce a new feature that approximates co-occurrence bias of argument labels by gathering case particles for the other direct dependents of a target predicate.

Other binary features The other binary features employed in our models have mostly been discussed in previous work (Imamura et al., 2009; Hayashibe et al., 2011). The entire list of our binary features are presented in Table 1.

4 Experiments

4.1 Experimental details

Dataset The experiments were performed on the NTC corpus v1.5, dividing it into commonly used training, development, and test divisions (Taira et al., 2008).

Hyperparameters We chose the hyperparameters of our models to obtain a maximum score in F_1 on the development data. We select $2,000$ for the dimension of the hidden layers in the feedforward network from $\{256, 512, 1000, 2000, 3000\}$, 2 for the number of hidden layers from $\{1, 2, 3, 4\}$, 192 for the dimension of the hidden unit in GRU from $\{32, 64, 128, 192\}$, 0.2 for the dropout rate of GRUs from $\{0.0, 0.1, 0.2, 0.3, 0.5\}$, and 128 for the mini-batch size on training from $\{32, 64, 128\}$.

We employed a categorical cross-entropy loss for training, and used Adam with $\beta_1 = 0.9$, $\beta_2 = 0.999$, and $\epsilon = 1e - 08$. The learning rate for each model was set to 0.0005. All the model were trained with early stopping method with a maximum epoch number of 100, and training was terminated after five epochs of unimproved loss on the development data. The output thresholds for case labels were optimized on the training data.

Initialization All the weight matrices in GRU were initialized with random orthonormal matrices. The word embedding vectors were initialized with 256-dimensional Word2Vec[2] vectors trained on the entire Japanese Wikipedia articles dumped on September 1st, 2016. We extracted the body texts using WikiExtractor,[3] and tokenized them using the CaboCha dependency parser v0.68 with JUMAN dictionary. The vectors were trained on lemmatized texts. Adjacent verbal noun and light verb were combined in advance. Low-frequent words appearing less than five times were replaced by their POS, and we used trained POS vectors for words that were not contained in a lexicon of Wikipedia word vectors in the PAS analysis task.

We used another set of word/POS embedding vectors for lexicalized path embeddings, initialized with 64-dimensional Word2Vec vectors. The embeddings for dependency directions were randomly initialized. All the pre-trained embedding vectors were fine-tuned in the PAS analysis task.

The hyperparameters for Word2Vec are "-cbow

---

[2]https://code.google.com/archive/p/Word2Vec/
[3]https://github.com/attardi/wikiextractor

Model	Binary feats.	All			F_1 in different dependency distance					
		F_1 (σ)	Prec.	Rec.	Dep	Zero	2	3	4	≥ 5
B	all	82.02 ($\pm$0.13)	83.45	80.64	89.11	49.59	57.97	47.2	37	21
B	$-$cases	81.64 ($\pm$0.19)	83.88	79.52	88.77	48.04	56.60	45.0	36	21
WB	all	82.40 ($\pm$0.20)	85.30	79.70	89.26	49.93	58.14	47.4	36	23
WBP-Roth	all	82.43 ($\pm$0.15)	84.87	80.13	89.46	50.89	58.63	49.4	39	**24**
WBP-Shwartz	all	83.26 ($\pm$0.13)	85.51	81.13	89.88	51.86	60.29	49.0	39	22
WBP-Shwartz	$-$word	83.23 ($\pm$0.11)	85.77	80.84	89.82	51.76	60.33	49.3	38	21
WBP-Shwartz	$-$\{word, path\}	83.28 ($\pm$0.16)	85.77	80.93	89.89	51.79	60.17	49.4	38	23
WBP-Shwartz (ens)	$-$\{word, path\}	**83.85**	**85.87**	**81.93**	**90.24**	**53.66**	**61.94**	**51.8**	**40**	**24**
WBP-Roth	$-$\{word, path\}	82.26 ($\pm$0.12)	84.77	79.90	89.28	50.15	57.72	49.1	38	**24**
BP-Roth	$-$\{word, path\}	82.03 ($\pm$0.19)	84.02	80.14	89.07	49.04	57.56	46.9	34	18
WB	$-$\{word, path\}	82.05 ($\pm$0.19)	85.42	78.95	89.18	47.21	55.42	43.9	34	21
B	$-$\{word, path\}	78.54 ($\pm$0.12)	79.48	77.63	85.59	40.97	49.96	36.8	22	9.1

Table 2: Impact of each feature representation. "$-$ word" indicates the removal of surface and lemma features. "$-$ cases" and "$-$ path" indicate the removal of the *case markers of other dependents* and binary path features, respectively. The task *Zero* is equivalent to the cases where the dependency distance ≥ 2.

1 -window 10 -negative 10 -hs 0 -sample 1e-5 -threads 40 -binary 0 -iter 3 -min-count 10".

Preprocessing We employed a common experimental setting that we had an access to the gold syntactic information, including morpheme segmentations, parts-of-speech, and dependency relations between *bunsetsu*s. However, instead of using the gold syntactic information in NTC, we used the output of CaboCha v0.68 as our input to produce the same word segmentations as in the processed Wikipedia articles. Note that the training data for the parser contain the same document set as in NTC v1.5, and therefore, the parsing accuracy for NTC was reasonably high.

The binary features appearing less than 10 times in the training data were discarded. For a path sequence, we skipped a middle part of intermediate tokens and inserted a special symbol in the center of the sequence if the token length exceeded 15.

4.2 Results

In the experiment, in order to examine the impact of each feature representation, we prepare arbitrary combinations of word embedding, path embedding, and binary features, and we use them as input to the feedforward network. For each model name, W, P, and B indicate the use of word embedding, path embedding, and binary features, respectively. In order to compare the performance of binary features and embedding representations, we also prepare multiple sets of binary features. The evaluations are performed by comparing precision, recall, and F_1 on the test set. These values are the means of five different models trained with

the same training data and hyperparameters.

Impact of feature representations The first row group in Table 2 shows the impact of the *case markers of the other dependents* feature. Compared with the model using all the binary features, the model without this feature drops by 0.3 point in F_1 for directly dependent arguments (*Dep*), and 1.6 points for indirectly dependent arguments (*Zero*). The result shows that this information significantly improves the prediction in both *Dep* and *Zero* cases, especially on *Zero* argument detection.

The second row group compares the impact of lexicalized path embeddings of two different types. In our setting, WBP-Roth and WB compete in overall F_1, whereas WBP-Roth is particularly effective for *Zero*. WBP-Shwartz obtains better result compared with WBP-Roth, with further 0.9 point increase in comparison to the WB model. Moreover, its performance remains without lexical and path binary features. The WBP-Shwartz (ens)$-$\{word, path\} model, which is the ensemble of the five WBP-Shwartz$-$\{word, path\} models achieves the best F_1 score of 83.85%.

To highlight the role of word embedding and path embedding, we compare B, WB, BP-Roth, and WBP-Roth models on the third row group, without using lexical and path binary features. When we respectively remove W and P-Roth from WBP-Roth, then the performance decreases by 0.23 and 0.21 in F_1. Roth and Lapata (2016) reported that F_1 decreased by 10 points or more when path embedding was excluded. However, in our models, such a big decline occurs when we

Model	ALL	Dep				Zero			
		ALL	NOM	ACC	DAT	ALL	NOM	ACC	DAT
On NTC 1.5									
WBP-Shwartz (ens) −{word, path}	**83.85**	**90.24**	**91.59**	**95.29**	62.61	**53.66**	**56.47**	**44.7**	**16**
B	82.02	89.11	90.45	94.61	60.91	49.59	52.73	38.3	11
(Ouchi et al., 2015)-local	78.15	85.06	86.50	92.84	30.97	41.65	45.56	21.4	0.8
(Ouchi et al., 2015)-global	79.23	86.07	88.13	92.74	38.39	44.09	48.11	24.4	4.8
(Ouchi et al., 2017)-multi-seq	81.42	88.17	88.75	93.68	**64.38**	47.12	50.65	32.4	7.5
Subject anaphora resolution on modified NTC, cited from (Iida et al., 2016)									
(Ouchi et al., 2015)-global							**57.3**		
(Iida et al., 2015)							41.1		
(Iida et al., 2016)							52.5		

Table 3: Comparisons to previous work in F_1

omit both path and word embeddings. This result suggests that the word inputs at both ends of the path embedding overlap with the word embedding and the additional effect of the path embedding is rather limited.

Comparison to related work Table 3 shows the comparison of F_1 with existing research. First, among our models, the B model that uses only binary features already outperforms the state-of-the-art global model on NTC 1.5 (Ouchi et al., 2017) in overall F_1 with 0.6 point of improvement. Moreover, the B model outperforms the global model of Ouchi et al. (2015) that utilizes the basic feature set hand-crafted by Imamura et al. (2009) and Hayashibe et al. (2011) and thus contains almost the same binary features as ours. These results show that fine feature combinations learned by deep NN contributes significantly to the performance. The WBP-Shwartz (ens)−{word, path} model, which has the highest performance among our models shows a further 1.8 points improvement in overall F_1, which achieves 13% error reduction compared with the state-of-the-art grobal model (81.42% of (Ouchi et al., 2017)-multi-seq).

Iida et al. (2015) and Iida et al. (2016) tackled the task of Japanese subject anaphora resolution, which roughly corresponds to the task of detecting *Zero* NOM arguments in our task. Although we cannot directly compare the results with their models due to the different experimental setup, we can indirectly see our model's superiority through the report on Iida et al. (2016), wherein the replication of Ouchi et al. (2015) showed 57.3% in F_1, whereas Iida et al. (2015) and Iida et al. (2016) gave 41.1% and 52.5%, respectively.

As a closely related work to ours, Shibata et al. (2016) adapted a NN framework to the model of Ouchi et al. (2015) using a feedforward network for calculating the score of the PAS graph. However, the model is evaluated on a dataset annotated with a different semantics; therefore, it is difficult to directly compare the results with ours.

Unfortunately, in the present situation, a comprehensive comparison with a broad range of prior studies in this field is quite difficult for many historical reasons (e.g., different datasets, annotation schemata, subtasks, and their own preprocesses or modifications to the dataset). Creating resources that would enable a fair and comprehensive comparison is one of the important issues in this field.

5   Conclusion

This study has argued the importance of designing a sophisticated local model before exploring global solution algorithms in Japanese PAS analysis and empirically demonstrated that a sophisticated local model alone can outperform the state-of-the-art global model with 13% error reduction in F_1. This should not be viewed as a matter of local models vs. global models. Instead, global models are expected to improve the performance by incorporating such a strong local model.

In addition, the local features that we employed in this paper is only a part of those proposed in the literature. For example, selectional preference between a predicate and arguments is one of the effective information (Sasano and Kurohashi, 2011; Shibata et al., 2016), and local models could further improve by combining these extra features.

Acknowledgments

This work was partially supported by JSPS KAKENHI Grant Numbers 15H01702 and 15K16045.

References

Kyunghyun Cho, Bart Van Merrienboer, Dzmitry Bahdanau, and Yoshua Bengio. 2014. On the Properties of Neural Machine Translation : Encoder Decoder Approaches. In *SSST-8*, pages 103–111.

Nicholas Fitzgerald, Oscar Täckström, Kuzman Ganchev, and Dipanjan Das. 2015. Semantic Role Labeling with Neural Network Factors. In *EMNLP*, pages 960–970.

Yuta Hayashibe, Mamoru Komachi, and Yuji Matsumoto. 2011. Japanese Predicate Argument Structure Analysis Exploiting Argument Position and Type. In *IJCNLP*, pages 201–209.

Yuta Hayashibe, Mamoru Komachi, and Yuji Matsumoto. 2014. Japanese Predicate Argument Structure Analysis by Comparing Candidates in Different Positional Relations between Predicate and Arguments. *Journal of Natural Language Processing*, 21(1):3–25.

Ryu Iida, Kentaro Inui, and Yuji Matsumoto. 2007a. Zero-anaphora resolution by learning rich syntactic pattern features. *Transactions on Asian and Low-Resource Language Information Processing*, 6(4):1–22.

Ryu Iida, Mamoru Komachi, Kentaro Inui, and Yuji Matsumoto. 2007b. Annotating a Japanese Text Corpus with Predicate-Argument and Coreference Relations. In *Linguistic Annotation Workshop*, pages 132–139.

Ryu Iida, Kentaro Torisawa, Chikara Hashimoto, Jong-Hoon Oh, and Julien Kloetzer. 2015. Intra-sentential Zero Anaphora Resolution using Subject Sharing Recognition. In *EMNLP*, pages 2179–2189.

Ryu Iida, Kentaro Torisawa, Jong-Hoon Oh, Canasai Kruengkrai, and Julien Kloetzer. 2016. Intra-Sentential Subject Zero Anaphora Resolution using Multi-Column Convolutional Neural Network. In *EMNLP*, pages 1244–1254.

Kenji Imamura, Kuniko Saito, and Tomoko Izumi. 2009. Discriminative Approach to Predicate-Argument Structure Analysis with Zero-Anaphora Resolution. In *ACL-IJCNLP*, pages 85–88.

Mamoru Komachi, Ryu Iida, Kentaro Inui, and Yuji Matsumoto. 2010. Argument structure analysis of event-nouns using lexico-syntactic patterns of noun phrases. *Journal of Natural Language Processing*, 17(1):141–159.

Taku Kudo, Hiroshi Ichikawa, and Hideto Kazawa. 2014. A Joint Inference of Deep Case Analysis and Zero Subject Generation for Japanese-to-English Statistical Machine Translation. In *ACL*, pages 557–562.

Fei Liu, Jeffrey Flanigan, Sam Thomson, Norman Sadeh, and Noah A. Smith. 2015. Toward Abstractive Summarization Using Semantic Representations. In *NAACL*, pages 1076–1085.

Hiroki Ouchi, Hiroyuki Shindo, Kevin Duh, and Yuji Matsumoto. 2015. Joint Case Argument Identification for Japanese Predicate Argument Structure Analysis. In *ACL-IJCNLP*, pages 961–970.

Hiroki Ouchi, Hiroyuki Shindo, and Yuji Matsumoto. 2017. Neural Modeling of Multi-Predicate Interactions for Japanese Predicate Argument Structure Analysis. In *ACL*, pages 1591–1600.

Michael Roth and Mirella Lapata. 2016. Neural Semantic Role Labeling with Dependency Path Embeddings. In *ACL*, pages 1192–1202.

Ryohei Sasano and Sadao Kurohashi. 2011. A Discriminative Approach to Japanese Zero Anaphora Resolution with Large-scale Lexicalized Case Frames. In *IJCNLP*, pages 758–766.

Kazuhiro Seki, Atsushi Fujii, and Tetsuya Ishikawa. 2002. A Probabilistic Method for Analyzing Japanese Anaphora Integrating Zero Pronoun Detection and Resolution. In *COLING*, pages 911–917.

Dan Shen and Mirella Lapata. 2007. Using Semantic Roles to Improve Question Answering. In *EMNLP-CoNLL*, pages 12–21.

Tomohide Shibata, Daisuke Kawahara, and Sadao Kurohashi. 2016. Neural Network-Based Model for Japanese Predicate Argument Structure Analysis. In *ACL*, pages 1235–1244.

Vered Shwartz, Yoav Goldberg, and Ido Dagan. 2016. Improving Hypernymy Detection with an Integrated Pattern-based and Distributional Method. In *ACL*, pages 2389–2398.

Hirotoshi Taira, Sanae Fujita, and Masaaki Nagata. 2008. A Japanese Predicate Argument Structure Analysis using Decision Lists. In *EMNLP*, pages 523–532.

Kristina Toutanova, Aria Haghighi, and Christopher D Manning. 2008. A Global Joint Model for Semantic Role Labeling. *Computational Linguistics*, 34(2):161–191.

Katsumasa Yoshikawa, Masayuki Asahara, and Yuji Matsumoto. 2011. Jointly Extracting Japanese Predicate-Argument Relation with Markov Logic. In *IJCNLP*, pages 1125–1133.

Koichiro Yoshino, Shinsuke Mori, and Tatsuya Kawahara. 2013. Predicate Argument Structure Analysis using Partially Annotated Corpora. In *IJCNLP*, pages 957–961.

Natural Language Informs the Interpretation of Iconic Gestures:
A Computational Approach

Ting Han and **Julian Hough** and **David Schlangen**
Dialogue Systems Group // CITEC // Faculty of Linguistics and Literary Studies
Bielefeld University
`firstname.lastname@uni-bielefeld.de`

Abstract

When giving descriptions, speakers often signify object shape or size with hand gestures. Such so-called 'iconic' gestures represent their meaning through their relevance to referents in the verbal content, rather than having a conventional form. The gesture form on its own is often ambiguous, and the aspect of the referent that it highlights is constrained by what the language makes salient. We show how the verbal content guides gesture interpretation through a computational model that frames the task as a multi-label classification task that maps multimodal utterances to semantic categories, using annotated human-human data.

1 Introduction

Besides natural language, human communication often involves other modalities such as hand gestures. As shown in Figure 1, when describing *two lanterns*, one can describe "two lanterns" verbally, while showing the **relative position** with two hands facing each other. Interestingly, when the same gesture is accompanied by the utterance "a ball", the same gesture may indicate **shape**. These gestures (referred to as 'iconic gestures' in gesture studies (McNeill, 1992)) are characterised as conveying meanings through similarity to referents in verbal content, rather than conventional forms of shape/trajectory. Hence, the interpretation of iconic gestures largely depends on verbal content.

Although this theory has been proposed and confirmed in various gesture studies (Feyereisen and De Lannoy, 1991; McNeill, 1992; Kita and Özyürek, 2003; Kita et al., 2007; Özyürek et al., 2008; Bergmann et al., 2014, 2013b), it has not

Figure 1: Speech / gesture description of a virtual scene: "... *sind halt zwei Laternen*" ("[there] are two lanterns"). Gestures indicate the **amount** (two) and **relative placement** of the two lanterns, while speech indicates the **entity** name and **amount**. From (Lücking et al., 2010).

attracted much attention from works on human-computer interfaces (HCIs), which usually assume that gestures have predefined meanings either through conventional agreements (e.g., "thumb up" for "great"), or defined by the system (e.g., "circling" for "circle") (Stiefelhagen et al., 2004; Burger et al., 2012; Lucignano et al., 2013; Rodomagoulakis et al., 2016). Hence, the systems can only interpret a limited number of gestures by classifying gestures based on the shape/trajectory of hands, then combining the information with language. We propose that, in order to incorporate iconic gestures in HCIs, natural language should be taken as an important resource to interpret iconic gestures.

The relation between speech and iconic gestures has certainly been investigated in previous work. Empirical studies such as (Kita and Özyürek, 2003; Kita et al., 2007) analysed speech and gesture semantics with statistical methods and show that the semantics of speech and gestures coordinate with each other. However, it remains unclear how to computationally derive the semantics of iconic gestures and build corresponding multimodal semantics together with the accompanying verbal content. In this paper, we address this "how" question and present a computational ap-

Proceedings of the The 8th International Joint Conference on Natural Language Processing, pages 134–139,
Taipei, Taiwan, November 27 – December 1, 2017 ©2017 AFNLP

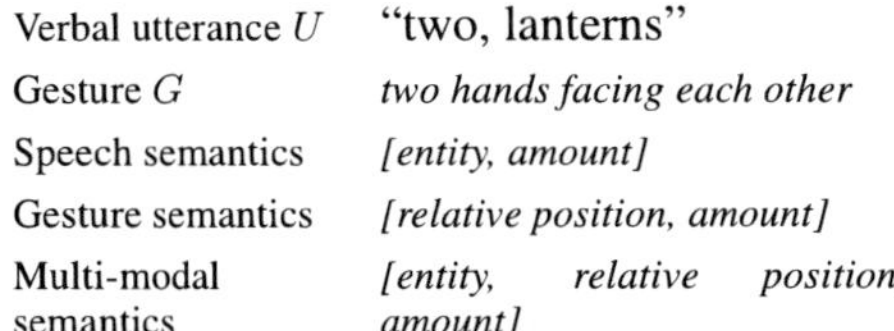

Verbal utterance U	"two, lanterns"
Gesture G	*two hands facing each other*
Speech semantics	*[entity, amount]*
Gesture semantics	*[relative position, amount]*
Multi-modal semantics	*[entity, relative position, amount]*

Figure 2: Example of a multimodal utterance, and semantic categories.

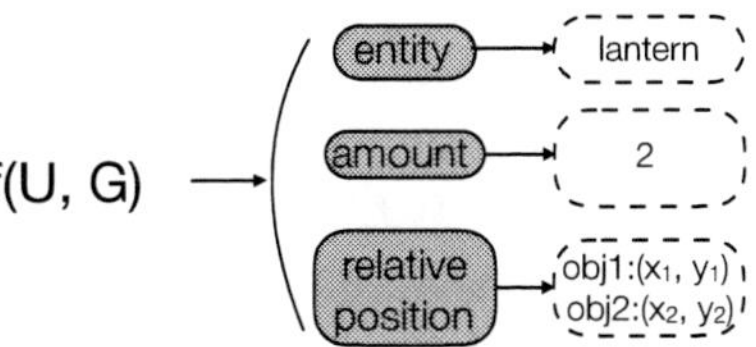

Figure 3: Mapping a speech-gesture ensemble to semantic categories in blue rectangles (U and G indicate speech and gesture). Dashed rectangles indicate the value of each semantic category, which are not included in our current work.

proach that predicts speech and gesture semantic categories using speech and gesture input as features. Speech and gesture information within the same semantic category can then be fused to form a complete multimodal meaning, where previous methods on representing multimodal semantic (Bergmann and Kopp, 2008; Bergmann et al., 2013a; Lascarides and Stone, 2009; Giorgolo, 2010) can be applied. Consequently, this enables HCIs to construct and represent multimodal semantics of natural communications involving iconic gestures.

We investigated whether language informs the interpretation of iconic gestures with the data from the SAGA corpus (Lücking et al., 2010). From the SAGA corpus, we take gesture-speech ensembles as well as semantic category annotations of speech and gestures according to the information they convey. Using words and annotations of gestures to represent verbal content and gesture information, we conducted experiments to map language and gesture inputs to semantic categories. The results show that language is more informative than gestures in terms of predicting iconic gesture semantics and multimodal semantics.

2   Task formulation

We now describe the task formally. Suppose a verbal utterance U is accompanied by a gesture G (as shown in Figure 2), we represent the speech-gesture ensemble as (U, G). The ultimate goal is to map the input information of (U, G) to a set of semantic categories according to the information they convey (as shown in Figure 3), then compose the multi-modal semantics of the ensemble with information in the same category across speech and gestures.

We define a mapping function f that takes a speech-gesture ensemble (U, G) as input, and outputs semantic categories c_i, computed by the set of features of U and G. Additionally, we assume each modality has its own meaning function $f_u(U)$ and $f_g(G)$. In this paper, we make the assumption that *multi-modal meaning* outputted by $f(U, G)$ is in fact the union of $f_u(U)$ and $f_g(G)$:

$$f_u(U) = \{c_1, c_2\}$$
$$f_g(G) = \{c_2, c_3\} \tag{1}$$
$$f(U, G) = \{c_1, c_2, c_3\}$$

Figure 3 shows an example of mapping the verbal utterance "two lanterns" to semantic categories $\{amount, entity\}$, while mapping the gesture to categories: $\{amount, relative position\}$. The semantics of the ensemble (U, G) is composed of the semantic categories and their values (in the dashed boxes). In this work we focus on predicting the semantic category rather than their value, which we leave for future work.

We derive input features for the mapping task from speech and gestures respectively:

a) Language features: The word tokens of each verbal utterance are taken as a bag-of-words to represent linguistic information. **b)** Gesture features: Hand movements and forms, including hand shape, palm direction, path of palm direction, palm movement direction, wrist distance, wrist position, path of wrist, wrist movement direction, back of hand direction and back of hand direction movement, are derived as gesture features (as there was no hand motion data, these features were manually annotated, see below for details).

Modelling the learning task   We frame the verbal utterance/gesture multimodal semantic category mapping problem as a multi-label classification task (Tsoumakas and Katakis, 2006) where several labels are predicted for an input.

Given an input feature vector X, we predict a set of semantic category labels $\{c_1, \cdots, c_i\}$, of which the length is variable. The prediction task can be further framed as multiple binary classification tasks. Technically, we trained a linear support vector classifier (SVC)[1] for each semantic label c_i (6 label classifiers in total). Given an input feature X, we apply all semantic label classifiers to the feature vector. If a semantic label classifier gives positive prediction for input X, we assign the semantic label to the input. For example, given feature vector of the input utterance "two lanterns", only the *amount* and *entiry* label classifiers give positive predictions, thus we assign *amount* and *entity* to the input utterance.

The word/gesture utterances are encoded as several-hot feature vectors as input of the classifiers, which will be explained now.

3 The SAGA corpus

We conducted the experiments with the SAGA corpus (Lücking et al., 2010), which provides fine-grained annotations for speech and gestures.
The data The corpus consists of 25 dialogues of route and sight descriptions of a virtual town. In each dialogue, a route giver gave descriptions (e.g., route directions, shape, size and location of buildings) of the virtual town to a naive route follower with speech (in German) and gestures. The dialogues were recorded with three synchronised cameras from different perspectives.

In total, 280 minutes of video and audio data were recorded. The audio was manually transcribed and aligned with videos; the gestures were manually annotated and segmented according to video and audio recordings. We selected 939 speech-gesture ensembles out of 973 annotations (Bergmann et al., 2011), omitting 34 without full annotations of speech/gesture semantic categories and gesture features. The semantic categories were annotated according to the semantic information that speech and gestures contained. In our data set, each item is a tuple of 4 elements: *(words, gesture features, speech semantic categories, gesture semantic categories)*.

There are 5 gesture semantic category labels: *shape, size, direction, relative position, amount*; the speech semantic labels consist of these and an extra label of *entity* (6 labels in total). Since there was only one gesture labeled as *direction*, we treat

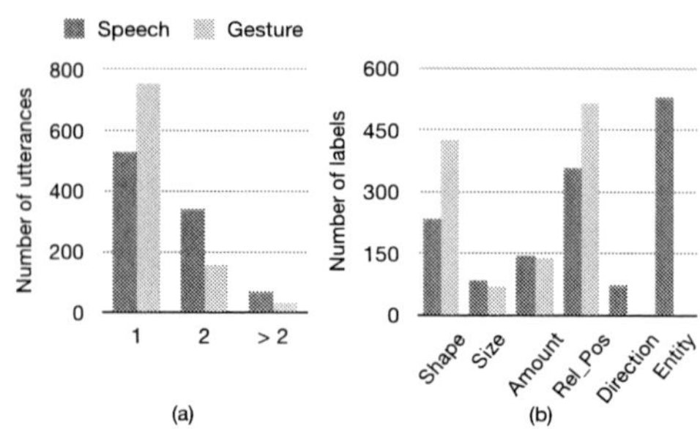

Figure 4: (a) Histogram of semantic labels per utterance/gesture. (b) Histogram of semantic labels. (Rel_Pos indicates relative position.)

it as a rare instance, and removed it from the evaluation experiments. From these the multi-modal category labels are derived as the union of those two sets for each ensemble.

Data statistics Bergmann et al. (2011) provides detailed data statistics regarding the relation of speech and gestures of the corpus. As we focus on speech and gesture semantics only here, we report statistics only for the 939 speech-gesture ensembles. On average, each verbal utterance is composed of 3.15 words. 386 gestures (41%) provide a semantic category on top of the verbal utterance (e.g., speech: {*amount, shape*}, gesture: {*relative position*}), 312 (33%) gestures convey the same amount of semantic information as the verbal utterance (e.g., speech: {*amount, shape*}, gesture: {*amount, shape*}), and 241 (26%) conveys part of the semantics of the verbal utterance (e.g., speech: {*amount, shape*}, gesture: {*amount*}).

As shown in Table 4 (a), 56% of verbal utterances and 80% of gestures are annotated with only a single label. On average, each gesture was annotated with 1.23 semantic labels and each utterance with 1.51 semantic labels. As shown in Figure 4 (b), there are many more utterances labeled with *shape*, *relative position* and *entity* than the other labels, making the data unbalanced. Moreover, there are considerably more gestures annotated with labels of *shape* and *relative position*.

Gesture features Since there is no tracked hand motion data, we used the manual annotations to represent gestures. For instance, the gesture in Figure 1 is annotated as: Left hand: [5_bent, PAB/PTR, BAB/BUP, C-LW, D-CE]; right hand: [C_small, PTL, BAB/BUP, LINE, MD, SMALL, C-LW, D-CE] in the order of hand shape, hand

---

[1]penalty: $\ell 2$, penalty parameter C=1.0, maximum iteration 1000, using an implementation in http://scikit-learn.org.

palm direction, back of hand direction, wrist position. (See (Lücking et al., 2010) for the details of the annotation scheme). Other features such as path of palm direction which are not related to this static gesture were set as 0.

We treated these annotated tokens as "words" that describe gestures. Annotations with more than 1 token were split into a sequence of tokens (e.g., BAB/BUP to BAB, BUP). Therefore, gesture feature sequences have variable lengths, in the same sense as utterances have variable amount of word tokens.

4 Experiments

We randomly selected 70% of the gesture-speech ensembles as a training set, using the rest as a test set. We designed 3 experiments to investigate whether and to what degree language and gestures inform mono-modal and multimodal semantics. Each experiment was conducted under 3 different setups, namely, using: a) only gesture features; b) only language features; c) gesture features and language features, as shown in Table 1.

Metrics We calculated **F1-score**, **precision** and **recall** for each label, and find their average, weighted by the number of true instances for each label, so that imbalanced labels are taken into account.

4.1 Results

Language semantics As shown in Table 1, the most informative features of language semantic categories are words on their own. It achieves an F1-score of 0.79 for each label, well above a chance level baseline accuracy 0.17. While as expected, gesture features are not very informative for language semantics, the gesture-only still classifier outperforms the chance level baseline with 0.38. The combination of features in the joint classifier results in slightly worse performance than language features alone, suggesting some of the gestural semantics may be complementary to, rather than identical to, the language semantics.

Gesture semantics While language features help predict the semantics of their own modality, the same is not true of gesture features. The language-only classifier achieves an F1-score of 0.78 when predicting gesture semantics, while the gesture features-only setting only achieves 0.61.

Semantics	Features	Precision	Recall	F1-score
Language	L	0.85	0.75	**0.79**
	G	0.47	0.37	0.38
	L+G	0.86	0.69	0.75
Gesture	L	0.80	0.78	**0.78**
	G	0.59	0.63	0.61
	L+G	0.82	0.77	**0.78**
Multimodal	L	0.82	0.80	**0.81**
	G	0.62	0.60	0.58
	L+G	0.83	0.80	0.80

Table 1: Evaluation results. (L and G indicates language and gesture.)

Combining language and gesture features does not improve performance, but results in a slightly higher precision score (+0.02). This is consistent with previous observations in gesture studies (Feyereisen and De Lannoy, 1991) that iconic gestures are difficult to interpret without speech. Even humans perform poorly on such a task without verbal content.

In our setup, the abstract gesture features might be one of the reasons for poor performance. Only 10 manually annotated categories were used to represent gestures, so these features might not be optimal for a computational model. It is possible that with more accurate gesture features (e.g. motion features), gestures can be better represented and more informative for interpreting gesture semantics.

Multimodal semantics As gestures can add meaningful semantic information not present in concurrent speech, we trained and evaluated classifiers on multimodal semantic categories. We assume these are the union of the gesture and language semantics for a given ensemble (as in function f in (1) above). As per the data statistics, there are the same possible 6 atomic categories as the language semantics (though they can come from the gesture as well as from the speech). As shown in Table 1, the language-only classifier performs best on this set with an F1-score of 0.81, marginally outperforming the combined language and gesture features system's 0.80. Both significantly outperform the gesture-only classifier. As with the results on gesture semantics, this suggests that multimodal meaning and meaning of iconic gesture relies heavily on speech, in accor-

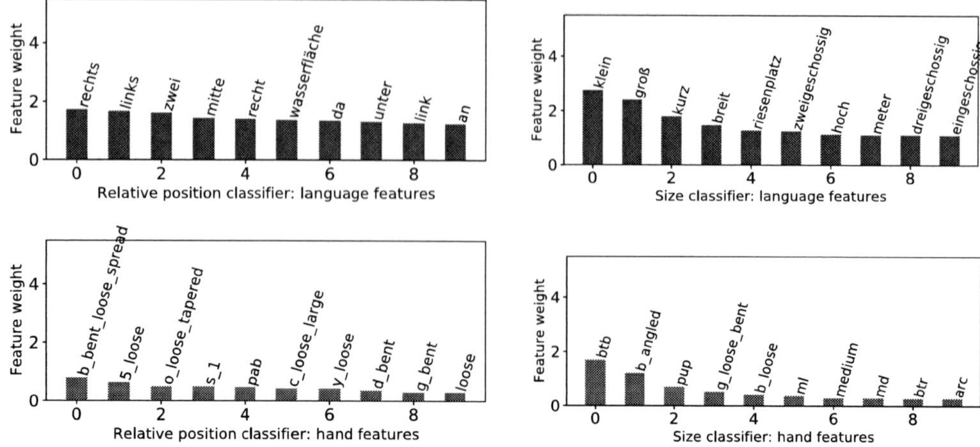

Figure 5: Featuring ranking according to coefficient values (weights assigned to the features, see (Lücking et al., 2010) for the details of the annotation scheme).

dance with the finding that the majority of gestures are inherently underspecified semantically by their physical form alone (Rieser, 2015).

Regarding individual semantic categories, we find gesture features are more informative for *shape* and *relative positions*; language is more informative for *size*, *direction* and *amount* in our dataset. Figure 5 shows the gesture and language feature ranking results for classifiers of *entity* and *relative position* accordingly. For *relative position* label prediction, the most informative language features are the words "rechts" (right) and "links" (left), while hand shape, such as b_bent_loose_spread (an open palm, thumb applied sideways, but not clearly folded and with a weak hand tension) and 5_loose (an open palm with a weak hand tension) are the two most informative gesture features. For *size* label prediction, the most informative language features are words that specify size such as "klein" (small) and "groß" (big); the most informative gesture feature is back of hand palm direction (btb, back of hand palm facing towards body).

5 Conclusion

Language and co-verbal gestures are widely accepted as an integral process of natural communication. In this paper, we have shown that natural language is informative for the interpretation of a particular kind of gesture, iconic gestures. With the task of mapping speech and gesture information to semantic categories, we show that language is more informative than gesture for interpreting not only gesture meaning, but also the overall multimodal meaning of speech and gesture. This work is a step towards HCIs which take language as an important resource for interpreting iconic gestures in more natural multimodal communication. In future work, we will predict speech/gesture semantics using raw hand motion features and investigate prediction performance in an online, continuous fashion. This forms part of our ongoing investigation into the interplay of speech and gesture semantics.

Acknowledgements

We are grateful to Kirsten Bergmann and Stefan Kopp for sharing the SAGA corpus. The first author is supported by the China Scholarship Council (CSC). This work was also supported by the Cluster of Excellence Cognitive Interaction Technology CITEC (EXC 277) at Bielefeld University, funded by the German Research Foundation (DFG).

References

Kirsten Bergmann, Volkan Aksu, and Stefan Kopp. 2011. The relation of speech and gestures: temporal synchrony follows semantic synchrony. In *Proceedings of the 2nd Workshop on Gesture and Speech in Interaction (GeSpIn 2011)*.

Kirsten Bergmann, Florian Hahn, Stefan Kopp, Hannes Rieser, and Insa Röpke. 2013a. Integrating gesture meaning and verbal meaning for german verbs of motion: Theory and simulation. In *Proceedings of the Tilburg Gesture Research Meeting (TiGeR 2013)*.

Kirsten Bergmann, Sebastian Kahl, and Stefan Kopp. 2013b. Modeling the semantic coordination of speech and gesture under cognitive and linguistic constraints. In *International Workshop on Intelligent Virtual Agents*, pages 203–216. Springer.

Kirsten Bergmann, Sebastian Kahl, and Stefan Kopp. 2014. How is information distributed across speech and gesture? a cognitive modeling approach. *Cognitive Processing, Special Issue: Proceedings of KogWis*, pages S84–S87.

Kirsten Bergmann and Stefan Kopp. 2008. Multimodal content representation for speech and gesture production. In *Proceedings of the 2nd Workshop on Multimodal Output Generation*, pages 61–68.

B. Burger, I. Ferrané, F. Lerasle, and G. Infantes. 2012. Two-handed gesture recognition and fusion with speech to command a robot. *Autonomous Robots*, 32(2):129–147.

Pierre Feyereisen and Jacques-Dominique De Lannoy. 1991. *Gestures and speech: Psychological investigations*. Cambridge University Press.

Gianluca Giorgolo. 2010. *Space and Time in Our Hands*. Ph.D. thesis, Netherlands Graduate School of Linguistics.

Sotaro Kita and Asli Özyürek. 2003. What does cross-linguistic variation in semantic coordination of speech and gesture reveal?: Evidence for an interface representation of spatial thinking and speaking. *Journal of Memory and language*, 48(1):16–32.

Sotaro Kita, Asli Özyürek, Shanley Allen, Amanda Brown, Reyhan Furman, and Tomoko Ishizuka. 2007. Relations between syntactic encoding and co-speech gestures: Implications for a model of speech and gesture production. *Language and cognitive processes*, 22(8):1212–1236.

Alex Lascarides and Matthew Stone. 2009. A formal semantic analysis of gesture. *Journal of Semantics*, 26(4):393–449.

Lorenzo Lucignano, Francesco Cutugno, Silvia Rossi, and Alberto Finzi. 2013. A dialogue system for multimodal human-robot interaction. In *Proceedings of the 15th ACM on International conference on multimodal interaction*, pages 197–204. ACM.

Andy Lücking, Kirsten Bergmann, Florian Hahn, Stefan Kopp, and Hannes Rieser. 2010. The bielefeld speech and gesture alignment corpus (saga). In *LREC 2010 workshop: Multimodal corpora–advances in capturing, coding and analyzing multimodality*.

David McNeill. 1992. Hand and Mind: What Gestures Reveal About Thought.

Asli Özyürek, Sotaro Kita, Shanley Allen, Amanda Brown, Reyhan Furman, and Tomoko Ishizuka. 2008. Development of cross-linguistic variation in speech and gesture: Motion events in english and turkish. *Developmental psychology*, 44(4):1040.

Hannes Rieser. 2015. When hands talk to mouth. gesture and speech as autonomous communicating processes. *SEMDIAL 2015 goDIAL*, page 122.

Isidoros Rodomagoulakis, Nikolaos Kardaris, Vassilis Pitsikalis, E Mavroudi, Athanasios Katsamanis, Antigoni Tsiami, and Petros Maragos. 2016. Multimodal human action recognition in assistive human-robot interaction. In *Acoustics, Speech and Signal Processing (ICASSP), 2016 IEEE International Conference on*, pages 2702–2706. IEEE.

R. Stiefelhagen, C. Fugen, R. Gieselmann, H. Holzapfel, K. Nickel, and A. Waibel. 2004. Natural human-robot interaction using speech, head pose and gestures. In *2004 IEEE/RSJ International Conference on Intelligent Robots and Systems (IROS) (IEEE Cat. No.04CH37566)*, volume 3, pages 2422–2427.

Grigorios Tsoumakas and Ioannis Katakis. 2006. Multi-label classification: An overview. *International Journal of Data Warehousing and Mining*, 3(3).

Modelling Representation Noise in Emotion Analysis using Gaussian Processes

Daniel Beck[*]

Computing and Information Systems
The University of Melbourne, Australia
`d.beck@unimelb.edu.au`

Abstract

Emotion Analysis is the task of modelling latent emotions present in natural language. Labelled datasets for this task are scarce so learning good input text representations is not trivial. Using averaged word embeddings is a simple way to leverage unlabelled corpora to build text representations but this approach can be prone to noise either coming from the embedding themselves or the averaging procedure. In this paper we propose a model for Emotion Analysis using Gaussian Processes and kernels that are better suitable for functions that exhibit noisy behaviour. Empirical evaluations in a emotion prediction task show that our model outperforms commonly used baselines for regression.

1 Introduction

The goal of Emotion Analysis is to infer latent emotions from textual data (Strapparava and Mihalcea, 2007). This problem has theoretic roots in psycholinguistics studies such as Clore et al. (1987) and Ortony et al. (1987), which aim to understand connections between emotions and words. However, Emotion Analysis also has motivations from an applied perspective, being closely related to Opinion Mining (Pang and Lee, 2008). The main difference is that the latter is usually concerned with coarse polarity predictions, while the former aims at modelling different emotional aspects in a more fine-grained level. Table 1 shows some examples taken from the "Affective Text" dataset (Strapparava and Mihalcea, 2007), in which human judges annotate news headlines according to the taxonomy proposed by Ekman (1993). Each label is a score in the $[0 - 100]$ range, where 0 means lack of the corresponding emotion and 100 corresponds to maximal emotional load.

Given the nature of the task and the available datasets, a sensible approach for Emotion Analysis is through regression models that map texts to emotion scores. This requires the choice of a suitable text representation so it can be incorporated into a model. Bag-of-words (BOW) are a common approach that works well in the presence of large amounts of data but it is unsuitable for Emotion Analysis datasets since they tend to be scarce.

An alternative is to leverage unlabelled data through the use of word embeddings (Deerwester et al., 1990; Turian et al., 2010; Mikolov et al., 2013). To obtain a fixed vector representation for a text, one can average the embeddings for each word present in the text. While this method can lose linguistic information such as word order, for some tasks it still gives good empirical performance (Hu et al., 2014; Kenter and de Rijke, 2015). However, word embeddings are known to be prone to noise due to the different contexts captured in the training procedure (Nguyen et al., 2016). This effect can be potentialised by simple averaging procedures.

In this work we propose to use Gaussian Processes (GPs) (Rasmussen and Williams, 2006) to develop Emotion Analysis models that capture noisy functions that map text representations to the emotion scores. More specifically, we propose the use of the Matèrn class of kernels to address this problem. Empirical evaluations show that our approach can outperform simpler out-of-the-box choices commonly employed in regression tasks. Overall, we show that properly motivated choices of kernels can bring benefits in prediction performance.

While the focus of this work is on Emotion Analysis, the methods proposed here are general and can be applied to other text regression settings.

2 Gaussian Process Regression

In this Section we introduce the basic concepts around GP regression. We follow closely the definition of GPs in Rasmussen and Williams (2006).

Let $\mathcal{X} = \{(\mathbf{x}_1, y_1), (\mathbf{x}_2, y_2), \ldots, (\mathbf{x}_n, y_n)\}$ be a dataset where each $\mathbf{x} \in \mathbb{R}^D$ is a D-dimensional input and $y \in \mathbb{R}$ is its corresponding response variable. A GP prior is defined as a stochastic model over the latent function f that maps the inputs in $\mathcal{X}$ to their cor-

---

[*] This work was partially done while the author was at The University of Sheffield, United Kingdom.

Proceedings of the The 8th International Joint Conference on Natural Language Processing, pages 140–145,
Taipei, Taiwan, November 27 – December 1, 2017 ©2017 AFNLP

	anger	disgust	fear	joy	sadness	surprise
Storms kill, knock out power, cancel flights	3	9	82	0	60	0
Morrissey may cheer up Eurovision	0	0	2	61	0	10
Archaeologists find signs of early chimps' tool use	0	0	2	23	0	64
Republicans plan to block Iraq debate	60	17	0	0	37	7
European Space Agency	0	0	0	2	0	0

Table 1: Emotion annotation examples, taken from the Affective Text dataset. Scores are in the $[0 - 100]$ range.

responding response variables. Formally,

$$f(\mathbf{x}) \sim \mathcal{GP}(m(\mathbf{x}), k(\mathbf{x}, \mathbf{x}')),$$

where $m(\mathbf{x})$ is the *mean* function and $k(\mathbf{x}, \mathbf{x}')$ is the kernel or *covariance* function, which describes the covariance between values of f at the different locations of $\mathbf{x}$ and $\mathbf{x}'$. For simplicity, we assume $m(\mathbf{x}) = \mathbf{0}$.

The GP prior is combined with a likelihood via Bayes' rule to obtain a posterior over the latent function:

$$p(f|\mathbf{X}, \mathbf{y}) = \frac{p(\mathbf{y}|\mathbf{X}, f)p(f)}{p(\mathbf{y}|\mathbf{X})},$$

where $\mathbf{X}$ and $\mathbf{y}$ are the training inputs and response variables, respectively. In regression, we usually assume a Gaussian likelihood for y, i.e., each $y_i = f(\mathbf{x_i}) + \eta$, where $\eta \sim \mathcal{N}(0, \sigma_n^2)$ is added white noise. This allows us to have an exact, closed formula solution for the posterior, which is itself a Gaussian $p(f|\mathbf{X}, \mathbf{y}) \sim \mathcal{N}(\mathbf{y}, \mathbf{K} + \sigma_n^2\mathbf{I})$, where $\mathbf{K}$ is the Gram matrix of kernel evaluations between inputs.

To obtain predictions for an unseen input $\mathbf{x}_*$ we integrate over all possible values of f. Since we assume a Gaussian likelihood for the unseen response variable y_*, we can obtain its distribution exactly,

$$p(y_*|\mathbf{x}_*, \mathbf{X}, \mathbf{y}) = \mathcal{N}(f_*|\mu_*, \sigma_*^2)$$
$$\mu_* = \mathbf{k}_*^T(\mathbf{K} + \sigma^2\mathbf{I}_n)^{-1}\mathbf{y}$$
$$\sigma_*^2 = k(\mathbf{x}_*, \mathbf{x}_*) - \mathbf{k}_*^T(\mathbf{K} + \sigma^2\mathbf{I}_n)^{-1}\mathbf{k}_*,$$

where $\mathbf{k}_* = [\langle\mathbf{x}_1, \mathbf{x}_*\rangle, \langle\mathbf{x}_2, \mathbf{x}_*\rangle, \ldots, \langle\mathbf{x}_n, \mathbf{x}_*\rangle]$ is the vector of kernel evaluations between the unseen input and each training input.

Choosing an appropriate kernel is a crucial step in defining a GP model. One common choice is to employ the squared exponential (SE) kernel,[1]

$$k_{\text{SE}}(\mathbf{x}, \mathbf{x}') = \sigma_v \exp(-\frac{r^2}{2}),$$
$$\text{where } r^2 = \sum_{i=1}^{D} \frac{(x_i - x_i')^2}{\ell^2}$$

is the scaled distance between the two inputs, σ_v is a scale hyperparameter and ℓ is a lengthscale hyperparameter.

The SE kernel is vastly used not only in GP models but also in Support Vector Machines (SVMs) since it is

a simple way to have a flexible non-linear model over the data. However, from a GP perspective it assumes the process is infinitely mean-square differentiable.[2] In practice, this means the resulting GP encodes functions with strong smoothness, which is not an ideal property in the presence of high amounts of noise.

2.1 Matèrn kernels

Matèrn kernels (Rasmussen and Williams, 2006, Sec. 4.2.1) are an alternative class of kernels that relax the smoothness assumptions made by the SE kernels. Formally, they define GPs which are ν-times mean-square differentiable only. Common values for ν are the half-integers ³⁄₂ and ⁵⁄₂, resulting in the following kernels:

$$k_{\text{Mat32}}(\mathbf{x}, \mathbf{x}') = \sigma_v(1 + \sqrt{3r^2}) \exp(-\sqrt{3r^2})$$
$$k_{\text{Mat52}}(\mathbf{x}, \mathbf{x}') = \sigma_v \left(1 + \sqrt{5r^2} + \frac{5r^2}{3}\right) \exp(-\sqrt{5r^2}).$$

Higher values for ν are usually not very useful since the resulting behaviour is hard to distinguish from limit case $\nu \to \infty$, which retrieves the SE kernel.

On Figure 1 we plot samples from three GP priors with Matèrn kernels with different values for ν. We can see that lower values for ν result in noisier functions. When $\nu = \frac{1}{2}$ we recover a simple exponential kernel, equivalent to Brownian motion in one dimension (Rasmussen and Williams, 2006, Sec. 4.2). The Matèrn class of kernels allows us to find a compromise between full noise behaviour and extreme smoothness, as in the case of SE.

2.2 Hyperparameter Optimisation

Most kernels rely on appropriate choices of hyperparameters, a problem of *model selection*. In non-Bayesian approaches such as SVMs, an usual approach for this is grid search, where we evaluate a set of values on a development set and choose the one with best performance. This approach can be brittle as values are constrained to the grid. It also does not scale well with the number of hyperparameters.

GPs have an elegant way to perform model selection: maximising the (log) marginal likelihood with respect

---

[1] Also known as Radial Basis Function (RBF) kernel.

[2] Mean-square differentiability is a commonly used generalisation of differentiability applied to stochastic functions. See (Rasmussen and Williams, 2006, Sec. 4.1.1) for more details.

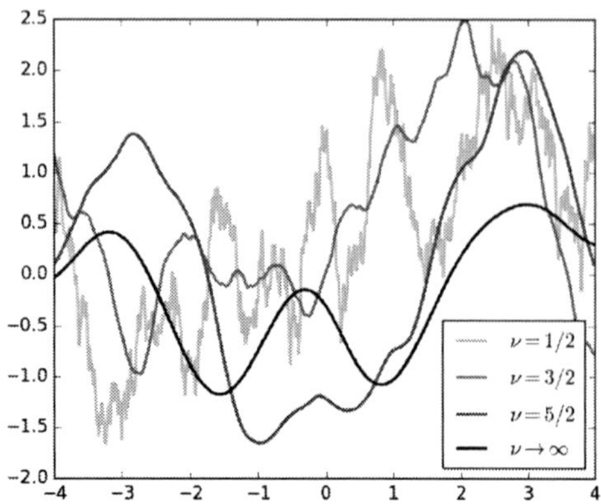

Figure 1: Sample functions from Matèrn kernels with different values for ν. The black line is equivalent to a sample from an SE kernel.

to the training data,

$$\log p(\mathbf{y}|\mathbf{X}, \boldsymbol{\theta}) = -\frac{\mathbf{y}^T \bar{\mathbf{K}}^{-1} \mathbf{y}}{2} - \frac{\log |\bar{\mathbf{K}}|}{2} - \frac{n \log 2\pi}{2},$$

where $\bar{\mathbf{K}} = \mathbf{K} + \sigma^2 \mathbf{I}_n$ and θ represents the set of hyperparameters (such as the lengthscale ℓ and the bias term b). The main advantage of this method is that we can define gradients of the marginal likelihood and employ gradient ascent optimisers, which are much faster than grid and random search.

Another advantage of this method is that it obviates the need of a validation set, making full use of the whole available training data. To understand why, we can inspect the terms of the marginal likelihood formula: the first one is the *data-fit* term and it is the only one that depends on the outputs; the second one is the *complexity penalty*, which depends only on the inputs and the third one is a normalisation constant. Intuitively, the optimisation procedure balances between complex models that highly fit the data and simple models that give a lower complexity penalty, preventing overfitting.

3 Experiments

We performed a set of experiments using two freely available datasets for Emotion Analysis, in order to assess our proposed models.[3]

3.1 Data and Preprocessing

The first dataset was employed in the SemEval2007 Affective Text shared task (Strapparava and Mihalcea, 2007) and is composed of a set of news headlines manually annotated by human judges.[4] We combined the

---

[3]Code to replicate all experiments in this section is available at `https://github.com/beckdaniel/ijcnlp17_emo`

[4]Available at `web.eecs.umich.edu/~mihalcea/downloads.html#affective`

official "dev" and "test" sets from the shared task into a single dataset containing 1,250 instances in total.

To put our models in perspective with the state-of-the-art, we also tested them in the recently released dataset for the WASSA2017 workshop shared task (Mohammad and Bravo-Marquez, 2017b).[5] The dataset is composed of tweets annotated with four of the six Ekman emotions (*anger, fear, joy* and *sadness*), with ratings originally provided by *Best-Worst Scaling* and transformed into values in the $[0 - 1]$ interval (Mohammad and Bravo-Marquez, 2017a). Unlike SemEval2007, this dataset has different instances per emotion. We combined the official "train" and "dev" sets and use that as our full training set, for each emotion.

All texts were tokenised[6], lowercased and we used 100-dimensional GloVe embeddings (Pennington et al., 2014) to represent each word[7]. To obtain a fixed vector representation for each headline we used the average of its word embeddings, ignoring out-of-vocabulary words.

3.2 Models

We compared the performance of the proposed Matèrn kernels with models based on linear and SE kernels. All GP models have hyperparameters optimised using 100 iterations of L-BFGS. Our implementation is based on the GPy toolkit.[8]

We also compared our approach with two non-Bayesian approaches commonly used in the literature, ridge regression and support vector regression (SVR) with an SE kernel. For these models we used grid search to optimise hyperparameters. The grid search procedure uses 3-fold cross-validation *within the training set*, using two folds for training and one fold as a development set. Hyperparameter values are selected by averaging the best results obtained for each fold. We use the scikit-learn toolkit (Pedregosa et al., 2011) as our underlying implementation. The hyperparameter grid for each model is shown on Table 2.

Ridge	
λ (regularisation coefficient)	$[0.01, 0.1, 1, 10, 100]$
SVR	
C (error penalty)	$[0.01, 0.1, 1, 10, 100]$
ϵ (margin size)	$[0.001, 0.01, 0.1, 1, 10]$
ℓ (SE kernel lengthscale)	$[0.01, 0.1, 1, 10, 100]$

Table 2: Hyperparameter grids for the non-Bayesian baselines.

---

[5]Availabe at `http://saifmohammad.com/WebPages/EmotionIntensity-SharedTask.html`

[6]We used the NLTK (Bird et al., 2009) PTB tokeniser.

[7]We used the GloVe version trained on a combination of Wikipedia and Gigaword, available at `nlp.stanford.edu/projects/glove`

[8]`github.com/SheffieldML/GPy`

3.3 Evaluation

We evaluated our models using Pearson's r correlation measure and Negative Log Predictive Density (NLPD) (Quiñonero-Candela et al., 2006). Pearson's r is the main metric used in previous work in Emotion Analysis and also other regression tasks. NLPD corresponds to the likelihood of the test label given the corresponding predictive distribution and it is a common way to compare GP models. It is not applicable for models that give point estimates as predictions (such as SVR) but it is useful when information about the predictive distributions is available. Higher Pearson's r and lower NLPD correspond to better performance.

For the SemEval2007 dataset we performed our experiments using 10-fold cross-validation and average the results. For the WASSA2017 dataset, we tested the performance on the official "test" sets for each emotion to make results comparable with the original shared task submissions.

3.4 Results on SemEval2007

Table 3 shows the results for all models, averaged over the emotions. We can see that both models based on Matèrn kernels outperformed the baselines. Within the Matèrn models there is a slight preference over the Matèrn ½ in terms of Pearson's r but it is not significative.

	$r\uparrow$	NLPD$\downarrow$
Baselines		
Ridge	0.547	–
SVR	0.593	–
GP Linear	0.549	4.10
GP SE	0.596	4.07
Proposed Models		
GP Matèrn ⅓	**0.616**	**4.05**
GP Matèrn ½	0.609	**4.05**

Table 3: Results on SemEval2007, averaged over all emotions and all 10 cross-validation folds.

In Table 4 we discriminate the results over each particular emotion, where we observe some interesting phenomena. For *joy* we can see that a linear GP shows higher Pearson's r compared to a GP with an SE kernel. To investigate this we inspected the individual folds for the GP SE model and we found out one of the models ended up with very low lengthscale, which resulted in an interpolation behaviour leading to overfitting. The Matèrn models did not suffer from this.

The emotion where we see the least gains from our proposed models is *fear*, which is also the one with higher absolute correlation in all models. This might be a case of diminishing returns, where we do not see much gains from using a more involved kernel because the emotion is already well explained by simpler models.

3.5 Results on WASSA2017

Table 5 shows the results for WASSA2017, averaged over all emotions/datasets. We see similar trends to the SemEval2007 results, with the Matèrn kernels outperforming the baselines and a small preference for the Matèrn ½ variant.

On Table 6 we compare our models with the official shared task baseline and the wiining submission. The Matèrn ½ model would be placed in 11th place of a total of 22 submissions, which is a promising result considering that it can be applied to other feature sets beyond word embeddings. To show this, we train another model using the 300 dimensional version of GloVe embeddings, which gives further gains in terms of Pearson's r, reaching 10th place in the official results.

The best performing submissions at this shared task used a range of other features beyond word embeddings, such as emotion lexicons and character ngrams. For future work, we plan to apply our models to these feature sets to check if they can also benefit from the flexibility coming from Matèrn kernels.

4 Related Work

Emotion Analysis has been studied in other domains beyond News headlines. Alm et al. (2005) studied emotions in the context of children's fairy tales and developed a corpus annotated at the sentence level. They use coarse-grained labels, which account for the presence or absence of emotions in each sentence. Mihalcea and Strapparava (2012) focused on analysing emotions from music, combining information from song lyrics and melody notes. They consider more fine-grained labels in this work and show promising results.

The work of Beck et al. (2014) is similar to ours, which focuses on applying multi-task GPs to encode interactions between emotions. Unlike our approach, they use a simple bag-of-words representation and an SE kernel as the underlying GP model. Compared to our model, they show much lower correlation scores (their best model achieves 0.399 Pearson's r on the SemEval2007 dataset), although these are not strictly comparable since they use different data splits and do not perform cross-validation. However, their approach is orthogonal to ours: combining the Matèrn kernels within a multi-task GP framework can be a promising avenue for future work.

Gaussian Processes have recently been proposed in a range of NLP tasks. In regression, GPs have been used to predict how long expert translators take to post-edit the output of Machine Translation systems (Cohn and Specia, 2013; Shah et al., 2013; Beck et al., 2016). GPs have also been used in social media settings, such as modelling temporal information about word usage (Preoiuc-Pietro and Cohn, 2013), user profiling (Lampos et al., 2014) and detecting rumour spreading (Lukasik et al., 2015). Many of these works rely on the ability to encode prior knowledge about the task through the use of appropriate kernels.

	Anger		Disgust		Fear		Joy		Sadness		Surprise	
	r	NLPD	r	NLPD	r	NLPD	r	NLPD	r	NLPD	r	NLPD
Baselines												
Ridge	0.584	–	0.445	–	0.680	–	0.539	–	0.636	–	0.399	–
SVR	0.632	–	0.510	–	0.732	–	0.558	–	0.687	–	0.438	–
GP Linear	0.587	3.94	0.449	3.81	0.681	4.16	0.539	4.35	0.636	4.31	0.404	4.06
GP SE	0.638	3.92	0.515	3.80	0.737	4.08	0.531	4.33	0.693	4.25	0.462	4.03
Proposed models												
GP Matèrn 3/2	**0.650**	**3.90**	**0.540**	**3.76**	**0.740**	**4.07**	**0.595**	**4.29**	**0.700**	**4.24**	**0.472**	4.03
GP Matèrn 5/2	0.647	3.91	0.533	3.78	**0.740**	4.08	0.592	**4.29**	0.698	**4.24**	0.445	**4.01**

Table 4: Emotion specific results for SemEval2007.

	$r \uparrow$	NLPD$\downarrow$
Baselines		
Ridge	0.528	–
GP Linear	0.527	-0.365
GP SE	0.551	-0.375
Proposed Models		
GP Matèrn 3/2	**0.571**	**-0.390**
GP Matèrn 5/2	0.567	-0.386

Table 5: Results for WASSA2017, using the official test set provided at the shared task.

	$r \uparrow$
Proposed Models	
GP Matèrn 3/2	0.571
GP Matèrn 3/2 + 300d embs	0.627
Shared task submissions	
Best baseline	0.660
Winning submission	0.747

Table 6: Comparison with other WASSA 2017 shared task submissions.

5 Conclusions

Emotion Analysis is a task that relies on scarce, noisy and potentially biased datasets. The use of word embeddings can help tackle sparsity problems but furthers add noise to the data being modelled. In this paper we proposed a Gaussian Process approach for Emotion Analysis that can better incorporate these aspects. Empirical findings showed that noisy behaviour can be better modelled by Matèrn kernels compared to other commonly used kernels in the literature.

An interesting avenue for future work is to address noise and bias in the response variables as well. For the kind of labels we employ in Emotion Analysis, a possible extension is to remove the Gaussian constraint and employ different likelihoods, such as a Beta distribution over the scale limits, for instance. This however makes the model intractable and approximation schemes (such as the one proposed by Opper and Archambeau (2008)) should be employed. Finally, we

also plan to apply the ideas showed here to other NLP problems with similar settings. In particular, we believe the proposed approach can be useful in any setting where (noisy) embeddings should be mapped to manually provided scores.

Acknowledgements

Daniel Beck was supported by funding from CNPq/Brazil (No. 237999/2012-9) and from the Australian Research Council (DP #160102686). The author would also like to thank the anonymous reviewers for their comments.

References

Cecilia Ovesdotter Alm, Dan Roth, and Richard Sproat. 2005. Emotions from text: machine learning for text-based emotion prediction. In *Proceedings of EMNLP*, pages 579–586.

Daniel Beck, Trevor Cohn, and Lucia Specia. 2014. Joint Emotion Analysis via Multi-task Gaussian Processes. In *Proceedings of EMNLP*, pages 1798–1803.

Daniel Beck, Lucia Specia, and Trevor Cohn. 2016. Exploring Prediction Uncertainty in Machine Translation Quality Estimation. In *Proceedings of CoNLL*.

Steven Bird, Ewan Klein, and Edward Loper. 2009. *Natural Language Processing with Python*. O'Reilly Media.

Gerald L. Clore, Andrew Ortony, and Mark A. Foss. 1987. The psychological foundations of the affective lexicon. *Journal of Personality and Social Psychology*, 53(4):751–766.

Trevor Cohn and Lucia Specia. 2013. Modelling Annotator Bias with Multi-task Gaussian Processes: An Application to Machine Translation Quality Estimation. In *Proceedings of ACL*, pages 32–42.

Scott Deerwester, Susan T. Dumais, George W. Furnas, Thomas K. Landauer, and Richard Harshman. 1990. Indexing by Latent Semantic Analysis. *Journal of the American Society For Information Science*, 41.

Paul Ekman. 1993. Facial Expression and Emotion. *American Psychologist*, 48(4):384–392.

Baotian Hu, Zhengdong Lu, Hang Li, and Qingcai Chen. 2014. Convolutional Neural Network Architectures for Matching Natural Language Sentences. In *Proceedings of NIPS*, pages 2042–2050.

Tom Kenter and Maarten de Rijke. 2015. Short Text Similarity with Word Embeddings Categories and Subject Descriptors. In *Proceedings of CIKM*, pages 1411–1420.

Vasileios Lampos, Nikolaos Aletras, Daniel Preoiuc-Pietro, and Trevor Cohn. 2014. Predicting and Characterising User Impact on Twitter. In *Proceedings of EACL*, pages 405–413.

Michal Lukasik, Trevor Cohn, and Kalina Bontcheva. 2015. Point Process Modelling of Rumour Dynamics in Social Media. In *Proceedings of ACL*, pages 518–523.

Rada Mihalcea and Carlo Strapparava. 2012. Lyrics, Music, and Emotions. In *Proceedings of the Joint Conference on Empirical Methods in Natural Language Processing and Computational Natural Language Learning*, pages 590–599.

Tomas Mikolov, Ilya Sutskever, Kai Chen, Greg Corrado, and Jeffrey Dean. 2013. Distributed Representations of Words and Phrases and their Compositionality. In *Proceedings of NIPS*, pages 1–9.

Saif M. Mohammad and Felipe Bravo-Marquez. 2017a. Emotion Intensities in Tweets. In *Proceedings of *SEM*.

Saif M. Mohammad and Felipe Bravo-Marquez. 2017b. WASSA-2017 Shared Task on Emotion Intensity. In *Proceedings of WASSA*.

Kim Anh Nguyen, Sabine Schulte im Walde, and Ngoc Thang Vu. 2016. Neural-based Noise Filtering from Word Embeddings. In *Proceedings of COLING*, pages 2699–2707.

Manfred Opper and Cédric Archambeau. 2008. The Variational Gaussian Approximation Revisited. *Neural Computation*, 21(3):786–792.

Andrew Ortony, Gerald L. Clore, and Mark A. Foss. 1987. The Referential Struture of the Affective Lexicon. *Cognitive Science*, 11:341–364.

Bo Pang and Lillian Lee. 2008. Opinion Mining and Sentiment Analysis. *Foundations and Trends in Information Retrieval*, 2(1-2):1–135.

Fabian Pedregosa, Gaël Varoquaux, Alexandre Gramfort, Vincent Michel, Bertrand Thirion, Olivier Grisel, Mathieu Blondel, Peter Prettenhofer, Ron Weiss, Vincent Duborg, Jake Vanderplas, Alexandre Passos, David Cournapeau, Matthieu Brucher, Matthieu Perrot, and Édouard Duchesnay. 2011. Scikit-learn: Machine learning in Python. *Journal of Machine Learning Research*, 12:2825–2830.

Jeffrey Pennington, Richard Socher, and Christopher D. Manning. 2014. GloVe: Global Vectors for Word Representation. In *Proceedings of EMNLP*, pages 1532–1543.

Daniel Preoiuc-Pietro and Trevor Cohn. 2013. A temporal model of text periodicities using Gaussian Processes. In *Proceedings of EMNLP*, pages 977–988.

Joaquin Quiñonero-Candela, Carl Edward Rasmussen, Fabian Sinz, Olivier Bousquet, and Bernhard Schölkopf. 2006. Evaluating Predictive Uncertainty Challenge. *MLCW 2005, Lecture Notes in Computer Science*, 3944:1–27.

Carl Edward Rasmussen and Christopher K. I. Williams. 2006. *Gaussian processes for machine learning*, volume 1. MIT Press Cambridge.

Kashif Shah, Trevor Cohn, and Lucia Specia. 2013. An Investigation on the Effectiveness of Features for Translation Quality Estimation. In *Proceedings of MT Summit XIV*.

Carlo Strapparava and Rada Mihalcea. 2007. SemEval-2007 Task 14 : Affective Text. In *Proceedings of SemEval*, pages 70–74.

Joseph Turian, Lev Ratinov, and Yoshua Bengio. 2010. Word Representations: A Simple and General Method for Semi-supervised Learning. In *Proceedings of ACL*, pages 384–394.

Are Manually Prepared Affective Lexicons Really Useful for Sentiment Analysis

Minglei Li, Qin Lu and **Yunfei Long**
{csmli,csqinlu,csylong}@comp.polyu.edu.hk

Abstract

In this paper, we investigate the effectiveness of different affective lexicons through sentiment analysis of phrases. We examine how phrases can be represented through manually prepared lexicons, extended lexicons using computational methods, or word embedding. Comparative studies clearly show that word embedding using unsupervised distributional method outperforms manually prepared lexicons no matter what affective models are used in the lexicons. Our conclusion is that although different affective lexicons are cognitively backed by theories, they do not show any advantage over the automatically obtained word embedding.

1 Introduction

Sentiment analysis aims to infer the polarity expressed in a text, which has important applications for data analysis, such as product review (Pang et al., 2008), stock market performance (Nguyen and Shirai, 2015), and crowd opinions (Rosenthal et al., 2015). Sentiment lexicons play a critical role in sentiment analysis (Hutto and Gilbert, 2014). A sentiment lexicon contains a list of words with sentiment polarity (positive or negative) or polarity intensity, such as the NRC Hashtag Lexicon (Mohammad et al., 2013) and VADER sentiment lexicon (Hutto and Gilbert, 2014). However, sentiment lexicons may fail for compositional methods to obtain sentiment of larger text units, such as phrases and sentences. For example, the phrase *avoid imprisonment* expresses positive sentiment. However, when we use sentiment lexicon, it is hard to classify this phrase because both *avoid* and *imprisonment* are nega-

tive in both VADER (Hutto and Gilbert, 2014) and NRC Hasntag (Mohammad et al., 2013) lexicons.

In addition to polarity based sentiment lexicons, which can be considered as one-dimensional affective lexicons, different multi-dimensional affect models are also proposed to represent affective information of words, such as the evaluation-potency-activity (EPA) model (Osgood, 1952) and the valence-arousal-dominance (VAD) model (Ressel, 1980). Sentiment can be seen as one of the dimensions under these affective models, such as the evaluation dimension of EPA, and the valence dimension of VAD. Aside from the EPA based lexicon (Heise, 2010), VAD based lexicons include ANEW (Bradley and Lang, 1999), extended ANEW (Warriner et al., 2013), and CVAW (Yu et al., 2016). Although multi-dimensional affective lexicons are theoretically sound, there are mainly two issues. The first one is how to obtain good coverage for affective lexicons. The second one is how to infer the representation of larger text units using word information in the affective lexicons. A previous work uses the average value of the component words as the final representation of larger texts (Yu et al., 2016).

Word embedding has recently been used to represent word semantics, such as word2vec (Mikolov et al., 2013) and Glove (Pennington et al., 2014). Word embedding represents a word as a dense vector, which can be used to measure semantic similarity of words more accurately.

To infer the representation of larger text units based on word embedding, different composition models are proposed, such as weighted addition and multiplication (Mitchell and Lapata, 2008), tensor product (Zhao et al., 2015), recursive neural network (Socher et al., 2013), recurrent neural network (Irsoy and Cardie, 2014), and convelutional neural network (Kim, 2014). Attempts have also been made to infer the affective labels

Proceedings of the The 8th International Joint Conference on Natural Language Processing, pages 146–150,
Taipei, Taiwan, November 27 – December 1, 2017 ©2017 AFNLP

of phrases based on the VAD model using compositional methods (Palogiannidi et al., 2016). However, between the VAD representation and word embedding, it is not clear which one is more effective for sentiment analysis.

Sentiment lexicons, multi-dimensional affective lexicons, and word embedding all represent a word with semantic information. Other than word embedding, all the other lexicons are specifically built for sentiment/affective analysis. Although these representations can be used for sentiment analysis of larger text units, there is no systematic comparison to test their effectiveness. In this paper, we investigate whether the manually annotated sentiment/affective lexicons have some advantage over automatically obtained word embedding on sentiment analysis tasks. Our approach is to use different word level representations to predict the sentiment of phrases to determine which representation of words is more effective. Experiments clearly show that word embedding outperforms manual affective lexicons and extended affective lexicons.

2   Related Work

To apply a sentiment lexicon in sentiment analysis, the simpliest way is to take word present in a lexicon as a simple feature (Pang et al., 2008). For intensity-based sentiment lexicons, the sentiment value can be aggregated by addition of every sentiment linked word in a sentence (Hutto and Gilbert, 2014; Vo and Zhang, 2016). Another method is to use sentiment related features, such as total count of sentiment tokens, total sentiment score, maximal sentiment score, etc.(Mohammad et al., 2013; Tang et al., 2014).

Many efforts have been made to construct multi-dimensional affective lexicons, such as ANEW for English (Bradley and Lang, 1999; Warriner et al., 2013), CVAW for Chinese (Yu et al., 2016), and other languages (Montefinese et al., 2014; Imbir, 2015). However, only few works use multi-dimensional affective lexicons for affective analysis. The work by Yu et al. (2016) uses the average VAD values of individual words as the VAD value of a sentence. In (Palogiannidi et al., 2016), affective representation of phrases is obtained through matrix-vector multiplication, where modifier words are represented by matrices and head words are represented as VAD vectors.

When word embedding is used for sentiment analysis, different composition methods are used to infer the representation of a sentence, such as simple addition, weighted addition (Mitchell and Lapata, 2008), recurrent neural networks (Irsoy and Cardie, 2014), and convolutional neural networks (Kim, 2014).

However, there is no systematic comparison between lexicon based representations and word embedding representations for sentiment analysis. This is the motivation of our work.

3   Comparison Method

Our objective is to study the effectiveness of different word representations for units longer than words for sentiment analysis. To focus more on the effectiveness of representations, we only study bigram phrases in this paper. The following is the list of lexicon resources and embeddings used for this comparative study.

1. The VADER sentiment lexicon of size 7,502, annotated through crowdsourcing (Hutto and Gilbert, 2014). Its value range is [-4, 4].

2. The NRC Hasntag sentiment lexicon (denoted as HSenti) of size 54,129, constructed automatically based on hashtags (Mohammad et al., 2013).

3. The multi-dimensional EPA lexicon of size 2,000, annotated manually (Heise, 2010) in three dimensions of evaluation, potency, activity in the range of [-4.3, 4.3].

4. The multi-dimensional VAD lexicon of size 13,915, annotated through crowdsourcing (Warriner et al., 2013). The annotation is in three dimensions of valence, arousal, dominance in the range of [1, 9].

5. Word embedding of 300 dimension with size of 2,196,017 trained by the the Glove model using unsupervised matrix factorization on a corpus of size 840 billion (Pennington et al., 2014), denoted as g300.

The manually annotated lexicons have limited sizes. For fair comparison, we use the state-of-the-art method proposed by Li et al. (2016), which train a Ridge regression model using word embedding as features to automatically extend the manually constructed lexicons so that all the vocabularies of different lexicons are the same size of g300.

Let us use the term base representations to refer to the different word representations used in this comparative study. We first construct the representation of a phrase from the base representations of its component words using some composition functions. Then, we perform sentiment prediction for phrases to evaluate which of the base representations is more effective.

In a composition model, the representation of a phrase is inferred from that of its component words. Given a phrase p with two component words w^1 and w^2 and their respective base representations $\vec{w}^1$ and $\vec{w}^2$, the representation of p, denoted by $\vec{p}$, can be constructed by a function f:

$$\vec{p} = f(\vec{w}^1, \vec{w}^2). \tag{1}$$

Different composition models are proposed for f (Mitchell and Lapata, 2008). An addition composition model can be defined as

$$\vec{p} = \vec{w}^1 + \vec{w}^2. \tag{2}$$

The multiplication composition model is defined by element-wise vector multiplication:

$$\vec{p} = \vec{w}^1 * \vec{w}^2. \tag{3}$$

The concatenation composition function that simply concatenates the two vectors:

$$\vec{p} = [\vec{w}^2, \vec{w}^1]. \tag{4}$$

A more advanced composition model is the Recurrent Neural Network (RNN). Here we use the most widely used Long Short Term Memory (LSTM) network (Hochreiter and Schmidhuber, 1997) as our composition model. It models a word sequence as:

$$\vec{i}_t = \sigma(U_i \vec{x}_t + W_i \vec{h}_{t-1} + \vec{b}_i), \tag{5}$$

$$\vec{f}_t = \sigma(U_f \vec{x}_t + W_f \vec{h}_{t-1} + \vec{b}_f), \tag{6}$$

$$\vec{o}_t = \sigma(U_o \vec{x}_t + W_o \vec{h}_{t-1} + \vec{b}_o), \tag{7}$$

$$\vec{q}_t = tanh(U_q \vec{x}_t + W_q \vec{h}_{t-1} + \vec{b}_q), \tag{8}$$

$$\vec{p}_t = \vec{f}_t * \vec{p}_{t-1} + \vec{i}_t * \vec{q}_t, \tag{9}$$

$$\vec{h}_t = \vec{o}_t * tanh(\vec{p}_t). \tag{10}$$

Here $\vec{x}_t$ is the representation of an input word representation at step t, $\vec{w}^1$ or $\vec{w}^2$. $\vec{i}_t$, $\vec{f}_t$, $\vec{h}_t$, $\vec{p}_t$, $\vec{q}_t$ are internal representations and $\vec{o}_t$ is current output representation. U_i, U_f, U_o, U_q are the model matrix parameters. Sentiment prediction is performed on the output representation the final step.

In this work, we use different composition functions to evaluate the effectiveness of different base representations.

4 Evaluation on the Comparisons

The five lexicons introduced in Section **3** are used for evaluations.

4.1 Experiment Setting

For comparison, we first extracted a set of phrases with sentiment ratings from the Stanford Sentiment Treebank (SST) (Socher et al., 2013), in which every sentence is parsed and each node in the parsed tree has a sentiment score ranging between [0, 1], and obtained by crowdsourcing. We only extract adjective-noun phrases, noun-noun phrases and verb-noun phrases, and the size of the final phrase collection in SST is 9,922. Note that only 6,736 words are used for this set of phrases and they are present in all the five lexicons used.

Based on this phrase set, we construct three sentiment analysis tasks: (1) a regression task to predict the sentiment score of phrases (labeled as **SST-R**); (2) a binary classification task by converting sentiment scores to discrete labels, where positive label is no less than 0.6 and negative label is no more than 0.4 (labeled as **SST-2c**); (3) a ternary classification task similar to SST-2C except that there is an addition of neutral label in the range of 0.4-0.6 (labeled as **SST-3c**).

Different evaluation metrics are used for the three different tasks. Mean absolute error (mae) and Kendall rank correlation coefficient (τ) are used for SST-R. Accuracy and F-score are used for SST-2c. Weighted accuracy and weighted F-score are used for SST-3c. Ridge regression and SVM with the linear kernel are used for regression and classification task, respectively[1]. For LSTM, the output layer is set differently for regression and classification tasks respectively [2]. The number of hidden dimensions in LSTM is set to 4. In all the experiments, 5-fold cross validation is used. Results are based on the best parameters we can obtain in our experiments.

4.2 Result and Analysis

Table 1 shows the result of the three tasks. Let us first take a look at the different composition functions. Multiplication performs the worst in all categories. On the other hand, LSTM, as a deep learning method, is the best performer. Addition and concatenation do have comparable performance and not too off from LSTM

---

[1]Using the scikit-learn tool: scikit-learn.org/
[2]Using the Keras tool: https://keras.io/

Feature	Comp	SST-R		SST-2c		SST-3c	
		mae	τ	acc	f	acc	f
VADER	mul	0.103	0.240	0.664	0.786	0.608	0.507
VADER	add	0.088	0.477	0.889	0.913	0.643	0.578
VADER	conc	0.086	0.482	0.888	0.912	0.655	0.591
VADER	lstm	0.086	0.487	0.894	0.917	0.667	0.655
HSenti	mul	0.110	0.060	0.636	0.777	0.573	0.418
HSenti	add	0.102	0.298	0.766	0.826	0.573	0.418
HSenti	conc	0.102	0.304	0.768	0.829	0.573	0.418
HSenti	lstm	0.100	0.307	0.770	0.825	0.610	0.556
EPA	mul	0.097	0.367	0.833	0.871	0.575	0.420
EPA	add	0.092	0.422	0.888	0.913	0.600	0.488
EPA	conc	0.092	0.427	0.887	0.912	0.602	0.493
EPA	lstm	0.091	0.438	0.893	0.915	0.633	0.605
VAD	mul	0.089	0.456	0.897	0.919	0.618	0.544
VAD	add	0.090	0.451	0.890	0.913	0.620	0.549
VAD	conc	0.089	0.459	0.894	0.917	0.625	0.557
VAD	lstm	0.090	0.466	0.891	0.915	0.635	0.602
g300	mul	0.106	0.246	0.635	0.777	0.575	0.420
g300	add	0.074	0.564	0.923	0.939	**0.755**	**0.749**
g300	conc	0.073	0.565	0.920	0.937	0.754	0.748
g300	lstm	**0.070**	**0.573**	**0.926**	**0.941**	0.751	**0.749**

Table 1: Performance of different word representations under different composition functions for SST phrase sentiment analysis. mul: multiplication composition. add: addition composition. conc: concatenation composition.

on SST-R and SST-2c. Secondly, for the two sentiment lexicons, VADER performs much better than HSenti lexicon. This may be because that VADER is manually annotated from crowdsourcing whereas HSenti is automatically obtained which contains more noise. Thirdly, for the two multi-dimensional affective lexicons, VAD performs slightly better than EPA. It is surprising that the multi-dimensional lexicons perform even worse than the sentiment lexicon VADER even though the annotated size of VAD (13,915) is much larger than VADER (7,502). This puts a question mark on the quality of annotation for multi-dimensional lexicon resources. Fourthly, word embedding[3] performs much better than all the other representations. For instance, it achieves a relative improvement of 17.7% under τ for SST-R over the secondly ranked VADER representation. Different composition functions for word embedding perform comparably. In principle, LSTM would have more benefits if the text length is longer. In this study, the performance difference is not obvious because our phrases are only bigrams.

---

[3]We also experiment on different word embedding dimensions including 50,100,200. All are better than the other lexicons.

In the first experiment, manually constructed affective lexicons are extended for comparison to be performed on the same set of word list. Since automatically extended lexicons can introduce errors, we perform the second experiment using only a manually annotated lexicon. We use the largest original VAD lexicon without extension to compare with word embedding. In this case, the intersection of VAD and word embedding has 3,908 words. The subset corpus of SST containing these words has 5,251 phrases. We perform 5-fold cross validation on this dataset. The result is shown in **Table 2**. Again, word embedding achieves much better result than manually annotated VAD lexicon. If coverage issue is considered, word embedding has even more advantages. Interestingly, comparison between **Table 1** and **Table 2** shows that the manually annotated lexicon does not perform better than its automatically extended lexicon even without considering the coverage problem.

Feature	Comp	SST-R$_s$		SST-2c$_s$		SST-3c$_s$	
		mae	τ	acc	f	acc	f
VAD	add	0.093	0.450	0.901	0.927	0.614	0.554
VAD	conc	0.092	0.465	0.905	0.931	0.624	0.568
VAD	lstm	0.093	0.471	0.885	0.916	0.620	0.594
g300	add	0.075	0.575	0.926	0.945	0.759	0.754
g300	conc	0.075	0.575	0.931	0.949	**0.762**	**0.757**
g300	lstm	**0.071**	**0.588**	**0.934**	**0.951**	0.754	0.753

Table 2: Performance of manually annotated VAD and corresponding word embedding representations under different composition functions for phrase sentiment analysis.

5 Conclusion

Automatically obtained word embedding clearly outperforms both manually and automatically obtained affective lexicons including sentiment lexicons and multi-dimensional affective lexicons. Although different affective models are backed by cognitive theories and affective lexicons are designed specifically for affective analysis, building them consumes too much resources and annotation quality may still be questioned due to added complexity. Through a downstream task of sentiment labeling of phrases, we conclude that the manually annotated affective lexicons have no advantage over word embedding under different composition models. However, affective lexicons as resources can still be used as additional features rather than being used alone.

Acknowledgments

This work is supported by HK Polytechnic University (PolyU RTVU and CERG PolyU 15211/14E).

References

Margaret M Bradley and Peter J Lang. 1999. Affective norms for english words (anew): Instruction manual and affective ratings. Technical report, Citeseer.

David R Heise. 2010. *Surveying cultures: Discovering shared conceptions and sentiments.* John Wiley & Sons.

Sepp Hochreiter and Jürgen Schmidhuber. 1997. Long short-term memory. *Neural computation*, 9(8):1735–1780.

Clayton J Hutto and Eric Gilbert. 2014. Vader: A parsimonious rule-based model for sentiment analysis of social media text. In *Eighth International AAAI Conference on Weblogs and Social Media*.

Kamil K Imbir. 2015. Affective norms for 1,586 polish words (anpw): Duality-of-mind approach. *Behavior research methods*, 47(3):860–870.

Ozan Irsoy and Claire Cardie. 2014. Modeling compositionality with multiplicative recurrent neural networks. *arXiv preprint arXiv:1412.6577.*

Yoon Kim. 2014. Convolutional neural networks for sentence classification. *arXiv preprint arXiv:1408.5882.*

Minglei Li, Yunfei Long, and Qin Lu. 2016. A regression approach to valence-arousal ratings of words from word embedding. In *International Conference on Asian Language Processing*, pages 120–123. IEEE.

Tomas Mikolov, Kai Chen, Greg Corrado, and Jeffrey Dean. 2013. Efficient estimation of word representations in vector space. *arXiv preprint arXiv:1301.3781.*

Jeff Mitchell and Mirella Lapata. 2008. Vector-based models of semantic composition. In *ACL*, pages 236–244.

Saif M Mohammad, Svetlana Kiritchenko, and Xiaodan Zhu. 2013. Nrc-canada: Building the state-of-the-art in sentiment analysis of tweets. *arXiv preprint arXiv:1308.6242.*

Maria Montefinese, Ettore Ambrosini, Beth Fairfield, and Nicola Mammarella. 2014. The adaptation of the affective norms for english words (anew) for italian. *Behavior research methods*, 46(3):887–903.

Thien Hai Nguyen and Kiyoaki Shirai. 2015. Topic modeling based sentiment analysis on social media for stock market prediction. In *ACL*, pages 1354–1364.

Charles E Osgood. 1952. The nature and measurement of meaning. *Psychological bulletin*, 49(3):197.

Elisavet Palogiannidi, Elias Iosif, Polychronis Koutsakis, and Alexandros Potamianos. 2016. A semantic-affective compositional approach for the affective labelling of adjective-noun and noun-noun pairs. In *WASSA@NAACL-HLT*.

Bo Pang, Lillian Lee, et al. 2008. Opinion mining and sentiment analysis. *Foundations and Trends® in Information Retrieval*, 2(1–2):1–135.

Jeffrey Pennington, Richard Socher, and Christopher D Manning. 2014. Glove: Global vectors for word representation. In *EMNLP*, volume 14, pages 1532–1543.

JA Ressel. 1980. A circumplex model of affect. *J. Personality and Social Psychology*, 39:1161–78.

Sara Rosenthal, Preslav Nakov, Svetlana Kiritchenko, Saif M Mohammad, Alan Ritter, and Veselin Stoyanov. 2015. Semeval-2015 task 10: Sentiment analysis in twitter. In *Proceedings of the 9th international workshop on semantic evaluation (SemEval 2015)*, pages 451–463.

Richard Socher, Alex Perelygin, Jean Y Wu, Jason Chuang, Christopher D Manning, Andrew Y Ng, Christopher Potts, et al. 2013. Recursive deep models for semantic compositionality over a sentiment treebank. In *EMNLP*, volume 1631, page 1642. Citeseer.

Duyu Tang, Furu Wei, Bing Qin, Ming Zhou, and Ting Liu. 2014. Building large-scale twitter-specific sentiment lexicon: A representation learning approach. In *COLING*, pages 172–182.

Duy Tin Vo and Yue Zhang. 2016. Dont count, predict! an automatic approach to learning sentiment lexicons for short text. In *Proceedings of ACL*, volume 2, pages 219–224.

Amy Beth Warriner, Victor Kuperman, and Marc Brysbaert. 2013. Norms of valence, arousal, and dominance for 13,915 english lemmas. *Behavior research methods*, 45(4):1191–1207.

Liang-Chih Yu, Lung-Hao Lee, Shuai Hao, Jin Wang, Yunchao He, Jun Hu, K Robert Lai, and Xuejie Zhang. 2016. Building chinese affective resources in valence-arousal dimensions. In *Proceedings of NAACL-HLT*, pages 540–545.

Yu Zhao, Zhiyuan Liu, and Maosong Sun. 2015. Phrase type sensitive tensor indexing model for semantic composition. In *AAAI*, pages 2195–2202.

MTNA: A Neural Multi-task Model for Aspect Category Classification and Aspect Term Extraction On Restaurant Reviews

Wei Xue, Wubai Zhou, Tao Li and **Qing Wang**
School of Computing and Information Sciences
Florida International University
Miami, FL, USA
`{wxue004, wzhou005, taoli, qwang028}@cs.fiu.edu`

Abstract

Online reviews are valuable resources not only for consumers to make decisions before purchase, but also for providers to get feedbacks for their services or commodities. In Aspect Based Sentiment Analysis (ABSA), it is critical to identify aspect categories and extract aspect terms from the sentences of user-generated reviews. However, the two tasks are often treated independently, even though they are closely related. Intuitively, the learned knowledge of one task should inform the other learning task. In this paper, we propose a multi-task learning model based on neural networks to solve them together. We demonstrate the improved performance of our multi-task learning model over the models trained separately on three public dataset released by SemEval workshops.

1 Introduction

Aspect Based Sentiment Analysis (ABSA) (Liu and Zhang, 2012; Pontiki et al., 2016) task is proposed to better understand rapidly-growing online reviews than traditional opinion mining (Pang and Lee, 2008). ABSA aims to extract fine-grained insights such as named entities, aspects, and sentiment polarities. We focus on two subtasks in ABSA: aspect category classification (ACC) and aspect term extraction (ATE).

Given a predefined set of aspect categories, ACC aims to identify all the aspects discussed in a given sentence, while ATE is to recognize the word terms of target entities. For example, in restaurant reviews, suppose we have two aspects `Price` and `Food`. In the sentence *"The fish is carefully selected from all over the world and taste fresh and delicious."*, the aspect category is `Food`, and the aspect term is `fish`. There could be multiple aspect categories implied in one sentence; while in other sentences, there might be even no word corresponding to the given aspect category because of noisy aspect labels or fuzzy definition of the aspect. For example, the sentence *"I had a great experience."* expresses positive attitude towards the aspect `Restaurant`, but there is no corresponding word about it.

Recognizing the commonalities between ACC and ATE task can boost the performance of both of them. The aspect information of whole sentence can make it easier to differentiate the target terms from unrelated words; while recognized target terms are the hints for predicting aspect categories. Recently, neural networks have gained tremendous popularity and success in text classification (Kim, 2014; Kalchbrenner et al., 2014) and opinion mining (Irsoy and Cardie, 2014; Liu et al., 2015). In this paper, we consider ACC and ATE task together under a multi-task setting. We conduct experiments and analysis on SemEval datasets. Our model outperforms the conventional methods and competing deep learning models that tackle two problems separately.

2 Model

In this section, we specifically define the two tasks in ABSA: aspect category classification (ACC) and aspect term extraction (ATE), then present an end-to-end model MTNA (Multi-Task neural Networks for Aspect classification and extraction) that interleaves the two tasks.

We define ACC as a supervised classification task where the sentence should be labeled according to a subset of predefined aspect labels, and ATE as a sequential labeling task where the word tokens related to the given aspects should be

Proceedings of the The 8th International Joint Conference on Natural Language Processing, pages 151–156,
Taipei, Taiwan, November 27 – December 1, 2017 ©2017 AFNLP

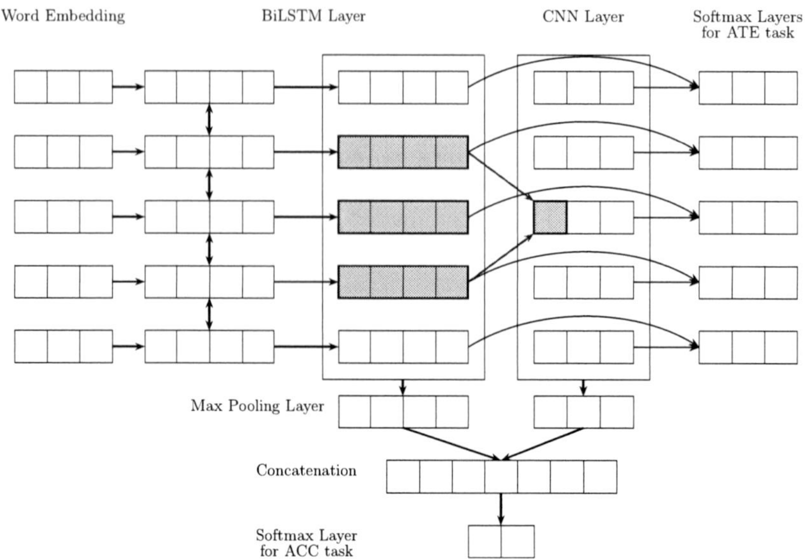

Figure 1: MTNA on a sequence of five words. The multi-task learning neural network combines BiLSTM and CNN layers together for ATE and ACC task respectively. One convolutional operation on BiLSTM layer is shown in the graph.

tagged according to a predefined tagging scheme, such as IOB (Inside, Outside, Beginning).

2.1 The Multi-task Learning Model

In this section, we describe our model MTNA.

Long Short-Term Memory (LSTM) (Hochreiter and Schmidhuber, 1997) has memory cells and a group of adaptive gates to control the information flow of the network. It has good performance in named entity recognition task (NER) to simply stack embedding layer, Bi-directional LSTM (BiLSTM) layer and softmax layer together (Lample et al., 2016). ATE task can be viewed a special case of NER (Irsoy and Cardie, 2014). Convolutional Neural Networks (CNNs) have obtained good results in text classification, which usually consist of convolutional and pooling layers (Kim, 2014; Kalchbrenner et al., 2014; Toh and Su, 2016). They can be applied on ACC task immediately.

It should be noted that ACC task and ATE task are closely related. Aspect terms often implies the related aspect category. If the names of dishes appear in a sentence, it is easy to infer that this sentence is about the aspect Food and vice-versa. Multi-task learning can help the model of each task to focus its attention to relevant features, when the other task support the features with evi-

dence (Ruder, 2017). Moreover, multi-task learning can obtain a common representation for all the tasks in the shared layers, which reduces noise in each task. We combine BiLSTM for ATE and CNN for ACC together in a multi-task framework. The parts for ACC task can utilize extra information learned in ATE task so that convolutional layers can focus on informative features. The tag prediction at each word in ATE task can also receive the distilled n-gram features of the surrounding words via convolutional operations.

The architecture of our model is shown in Figure 1. Specifically, a word embedding layer transforms indexed words to real valued vectors x_i with a pre-trained word embedding matrix (Mikolov et al., 2013; Pennington et al., 2014). Each sentence is represented by a matrix S. A BiLSTM is applied on the outputs of word embedding layer S, in which the two output vectors of the LSTMs are concatenated into a vector h_t for the t-th word. The represented features are further processed by a one-dimensional convolution layer with a set of kernels of different widths, so that the new feature maps c_t incorporate the information of words that are in the receptive field of the convolutions. For ATE task, we use softmax layer for each word in the given sentence to predict its tag. We further add skip connections between the LSTM layers to the softmax layers, since they are proved effective for training neural networks (He et al., 2016). To predict the aspect category of the sentence in ACC task, we use 1D max-over-time pooling layers (Collobert et al., 2011) which extracts maximum values from $\mathbf{h}_t$ and $\mathbf{c}_t$, a concatenation layer which joins the output vectors, and a softmax layer to output the probabilities of aspect categories. The final loss function of our model is a weighted sum of the loss functions of ACC task and ATE task. $L = L_{\mathrm{acc}} + \lambda L_{\mathrm{ate}}$, where λ is the weight parameter. L_{acc} is the cross-entropy loss function for ACC task; L_{ate} is the sentence-level log-likelihood for ATE task (Collobert et al., 2011; Lample et al., 2016).

3 Experiments

3.1 Datasets

For our experiments, we consider three data sets from SemEval workshops in recent years: SemEval 2014 Task 4 (SE14) (Pontiki et al., 2014), SemEval 2015 Task 12 (SE15) (Pontiki et al., 2015), and SemEval 2016 Task 5 (SE16) (Pontiki et al., 2016). We use the reviews in restaurant domain for all of them, and process SE14 into the same data format as the others. Each data set contains 2000 - 3000 sentences. For SE15 and SE16, an aspect label is a combination of an aspect and an attribute, like "Food#Price". There are 6 main aspects and total 12 configurations in SE15, SE16, while 5 aspects in SE14.

3.2 Experiment Setup

Following the experiment settings used by most competitors (Toh and Su, 2016; Khalil and El-Beltagy, 2016; Machacek, 2016) in SemEval 2016, we convert the multi-label aspect classification into multiple one-vs-all binary classifications. F1-score is used to measure the performance of each model for ACC task, and another F1 measure adapted for ATE task.

For MTNA model, we use the pre-trained word embedding GloVe (Pennington et al., 2014) of 200 dimensions to initialize the embedding layer. The word vectors that are out of GloVe vocabulary are randomly initialized between -0.1 and 0.1. During the training process, the embedding vectors are fine-tuned. We choose three kinds of convolution kernels which have the width of 3, 4, 5. Each of them has 100 kernels (Kim, 2014). We use tanh function as the nonlinear active function in con-

volution layers based on the results of cross validation. We train the model with Adadelta (Zeiler, 2012). For each binary classifier, a 5-fold cross validations is used to tune other hyper-parameters: mini-batch size from $\{10, 20, 50\}$, dropout rate from $\{0.1, 0.2, 0.5\}$, the dimension of LSTM cells from $\{100, 200, 500\}$, and the weight λ in the loss function from $\{0.1, 1, 10\}$.

3.3 Compared methods

Top models in SemEval. For ACC task, NRC-Can (Kiritchenko et al., 2014) and NLANGP (Toh and Su, 2015) are top models in 2014 and 2015 respectively, both of which use SVM. NLANG (Toh and Su, 2016) adopts CNN-like neural network in 2016. For ATE task, CRF (Toh and Wang, 2014; Toh and Su, 2015, 2016) is the best model on all of three data sets.

BiLSTM-CRF. To assess whether CNN can improve the performance of ATE, we use a standard Bi-directional LSTM with CRF layer (Lample et al., 2016) as the baseline to tag words.

MTNA-s. To evaluate to what extent that ATE loss function can improve the performance of the ACC task, we compare MTNA with its variance MTNA-s, the loss function of which does not include that of ATE task. However, this model keeps LSTM layer as a feature extractor before the convolution layers as MTNA does.

4 Results and Analysis

The comparison results of all methods on three datasets are shown in Table 1.

On ACC task, MTNA outperforms over other compared methods, which are proposed for a single task and cannot utilize the information from the other task. On ATE task, there are small improvement compared with conditional random field. It empirically proves that multi-task learning can benefit both tasks. MTNA has higher F1-scores compared with BiLSTM-CRF. The results confirm the effectiveness of additional convolution features for the ATE task.

MTNA-s, a smaller model without layers for ATE task, also performs better than CNN. It proves that LSTM can provide the feature engineering which captures the long-distance dependency (Zhang et al., 2016). On the aspects other than `Restaurant`, MTNA-s has slightly lower scores than MTNA, which again demonstrates the effectiveness of multi-task learning.

	SE14		SE15		SE16	
	ACC	ATE	ACC	ATE	ACC	ATE
Top models	88.57	**84.01**	62.68	67.11	73.03	72.34
BiLSTM-CRF	-	83.24	-	66.82	-	71.87
MTNA-s	87.95	-	64.32	-	75.69	-
MTNA	**88.91**	83.65	**65.97**	**67.73**	**76.42**	**72.95**

Table 1: Comparison results in F1 scores on three datasets.

Model	Aspect Category Classification			AspectTerm Extraction		
	Food	Restaurant	Service	Food	Restaurant	Service
CNN	86.29	65.27	84.02	-	-	-
Bi-LSTM-CRF	-	-	-	73.96	54.34	87.55
MTNA-s	86.41	67.89	84.93	-	-	-
MTNA	87.33	66.07	86.09	74.67	56.59	88.70
	Ambience	Drinks	Location	Ambinece	Drinks	Location
CNN	81.55	67.36	69.25	-	-	-
Bi-LSTM-CRF	-	-	-	76.23	71.38	56.77
MTNA-s	81.08	69.23	70.06	-	-	-
MTNA	83.18	68.75	71.43	77.79	72.21	60.16

Table 2: F1 scores of models on SE16 across six aspects

To access the performance of methods across different aspects, we combine all sentences labeled by the same aspect regardless of any attribute, then conduct experiments as before. We re-implement CNN model, which is used in NLANG 2016. The results are as shown in Table 2. ACC task on the aspect Restaurant is more difficult than the task on other aspects. Both CNN and MTNA have lower F1-scores on this aspect. The reason is that some sentences have restaurant names as target terms. However, there are around 40.1% sentences with Restaurant label that do not have annotated words in the training dataset, 41.2% in test dataset. Meanwhile, all methods have better results in ATE task on the aspect Service than on the other aspects, because target word tokens do not have much variety.

5 Related Work

LSTM (Hochreiter and Schmidhuber, 1997) has been applied on target extraction (Irsoy and Cardie, 2014; Liu et al., 2015). In the workshop of SemEval-2016, this sequential neural network is used to extract features for the subsequent CRF prediction (Toh and Su, 2016). In a multi-layer attention model (Wang et al., 2017), several attention subnetworks (Bahdanau et al., 2014) are used to extract aspect terms and opinion terms together without considering ACC task.

As a special case of text classification, ACC task is often treated as a supervised classification task. CNN (LeCun et al., 1998) has been used for sentiment classification (Kim, 2014; Kalchbrenner et al., 2014) and aspect classification (Toh and Su, 2016).

Collobert et al. (Collobert et al., 2011) proposed a multi-task learning system using deep learning methods for various natural language processing tasks. However, the system with window approach cannot be jointly trained with that using sentence window approach. Moreover, only embedding layer (lookup table) and linear layer are shared among tasks, which limited the utilization of shared information. On NER task, the predictions of this model depend only on the information of the current word rather than the surrounding context. The most relevant model is Dependency Sensitive Convolutional Neural Networks (DSCNN) (Zhang et al., 2016). The goal of DSCNN is solely for text classification, but our model is designed for multi-task learning of ACC and ATE.

6 Conclusion

We introduce two important tasks, e.g., aspect category classification and aspect term extraction in aspect based sentiment analysis. We propose a multi-task learning model based on recurrent neural networks and convolutional neural networks to solve the two tasks at the same time. Finally, the comparative experiments demonstrate the effectiveness of our model across three public datasets. We can utilize other linguistic information, such as POS tags and the distributional representation learned from character level convolutional neural network in the future work.

Acknowledgment

The work was supported in part by the National Science Foundation under Grant Nos. IIS-1213026 and CNS-1461926; and a FIU Dissertation Year Fellowship.

References

Dzmitry Bahdanau, Kyunghyun Cho, and Yoshua Bengio. 2014. Neural Machine Translation by Jointly Learning to Align and Translate. *arxiv* .

Ronan Collobert, Jason Weston, Léon Bottou, Michael Karlen, Koray Kavukcuoglu, and Pavel P Kuksa. 2011. Natural Language Processing (Almost) from Scratch. *Journal of Machine Learning Research* 12:2493–2537.

Kaiming He, Xiangyu Zhang, Shaoqing Ren, and Jian Sun. 2016. Deep Residual Learning for Image Recognition. In *CVPR*. pages 770–778.

Sepp Hochreiter and Jürgen Schmidhuber. 1997. Long Short-Term Memory. *Neural computation* 9(8):1735–1780.

Ozan Irsoy and Claire Cardie. 2014. Opinion Mining with Deep Recurrent Neural Networks. In *EMNLP*. pages 720–728.

Nal Kalchbrenner, Edward Grefenstette, and Phil Blunsom. 2014. A convolutional neural network for modelling sentences. In *ACL*. pages 655–665.

Talaat Khalil and Samhaa R El-Beltagy. 2016. NileTMRG at SemEval-2016 Task 5 - Deep Convolutional Neural Networks for Aspect Category and Sentiment Extraction. *SemEval@NAACL-HLT* pages 271–276.

Yoon Kim. 2014. Convolutional Neural Networks for Sentence Classification. In *EMNLP*. pages 1746–1751.

Svetlana Kiritchenko, Xiaodan Zhu, Colin Cherry, and Saif M. Mohammad. 2014. NRC-Canada-2014: Detecting aspects and sentiment in customer reviews. In *SemEval@COLING*. Association for Computational Linguistics, Stroudsburg, PA, USA, pages 437–442.

Guillaume Lample, Miguel Ballesteros, Sandeep Subramanian, Kazuya Kawakami, and Chris Dyer. 2016. Neural Architectures for Named Entity Recognition. In *NAACL-HLT*. pages 260–270.

Yann LeCun, Léon Bottou, Yoshua Bengio, and Patrick Haffner. 1998. Gradient-based learning applied to document recognition. *IEEE* 86(11):2278–2324.

Bing Liu and Lei Zhang. 2012. A Survey of Opinion Mining and Sentiment Analysis. *Mining Text Data* (Chapter 13):415–463.

Pengfei Liu, Shafiq R Joty, and Helen M Meng. 2015. Fine-grained Opinion Mining with Recurrent Neural Networks and Word Embeddings. In *EMNLP*. pages 1433–1443.

Jakub Machacek. 2016. BUTknot at SemEval-2016 Task 5 - Supervised Machine Learning with Term Substitution Approach in Aspect Category Detection. *SemEval@NAACL-HLT* pages 301–305.

Tomas Mikolov, Ilya Sutskever, Kai Chen, Greg Corrado, and Jeffrey Dean. 2013. Distributed Representations of Words and Phrases and their Compositionality. In *NIPS*. pages 3111–3119.

Bo Pang and Lillian Lee. 2008. Opinion mining and sentiment analysis. *Foundations and Trends® in Information Retrieva* 2:1–135.

Jeffrey Pennington, Richard Socher, and Christopher D Manning. 2014. Glove: Global Vectors for Word Representation. In *EMNLP*. pages 1532–1543.

Maria Pontiki, Dimitrios Galanis, Haris Papageorgiou, Suresh Manandhar, and Ion Androutsopoulos. 2015. Semeval-2015 task 12: Aspect based sentiment analysis. In *SemEval 2015*. Association for Computational Linguistics, Stroudsburg, PA, USA, pages 486–495.

Maria Pontiki, Dimitrios Galanis, John Pavlopoulos, Haris Papageorgiou, Ion Androutsopoulos, and Suresh Manandhar. 2014. Semeval-2014 task 4: Aspect based sentiment analysis. In *SemEval@COLING*. Association for Computational Linguistics, Stroudsburg, PA, USA, pages 27–35.

Maria Pontiki, Dimitris Galanis, Haris Papageorgiou, Ion Androutsopoulos, Suresh Manandhar, Mohammad AL-Smadi, Mahmoud Al-Ayyoub, Yanyan Zhao, Bing Qin, Orphee De Clercq, Veronique Hoste, Marianna Apidianaki, Xavier Tannier, Natalia Loukachevitch, Evgeniy Kotelnikov, Núria Bel, Salud María Jiménez-Zafra, and Gülşen Eryiğit. 2016. SemEval-2016 Task 5: Aspect Based Sentiment Analysis. In *SemEval@NAACL-HLT*. Association for Computational Linguistics, Stroudsburg, PA, USA, pages 19–30.

Sebastian Ruder. 2017. An Overview of Multi-Task Learning in Deep Neural Networks. *arxiv* .

Zhiqiang Toh and Jian Su. 2015. NLANGP: Supervised Machine Learning System for Aspect Category Classification and Opinion Target Extraction. In *SemEval@NAACL-HLT*. pages 496–501.

Zhiqiang Toh and Jian Su. 2016. NLANGP at SemEval-2016 Task 5: Improving Aspect Based Sentiment Analysis using Neural Network Features. In *SemEval@NAACL-HLT*. pages 282–288.

Zhiqiang Toh and Wenting Wang. 2014. DLIREC: Aspect Term Extraction and Term Polarity Classification System. In *SemEval@COLING*. Association for Computational Linguistics, Stroudsburg, PA, USA, pages 235–240.

Weya Wang, Sinno Jialin Pan, Daniel Dahlmeier, and Xiaokui Xiao. 2017. Coupled Multi-Layer Attentions for Co-Extraction of Aspect and Opinion Terms. In *AAAI*. pages 3316–3322.

Matthew D Zeiler. 2012. ADADELTA: An Adaptive Learning Rate Method. *arxiv* .

Rui Zhang, Honglak Lee, and Dragomir Radev. 2016. Dependency Sensitive Convolutional Neural Networks for Modeling Sentences and Documents. In *NAACL-HLT*. pages 1512–1521.

Can Discourse Relations be Identified Incrementally?

Frances Yung
Language Science and Technology,
Saarland University,
Saarland Informatic Campus,
66123 Saarbrücken, Germany
frances@coli.uni-saarland.de

Hiroshi Noji   Yuji Matsumoto
Information Science,
Nara Institute of Science and Technology
8916-5 Takayama, Ikoma
Nara, 630-0101, Japan
{noji,matsu}@is.naist.jp

Abstract

Humans process language word by word and construct partial linguistic structures on the fly before the end of the sentence is perceived. Inspired by this cognitive ability, incremental algorithms for natural language processing tasks have been proposed and demonstrated promising performance. For discourse relation (DR) parsing, however, it is not yet clear to what extent humans can recognize DRs incrementally, because the latent 'nodes' of discourse structure can span clauses and sentences. To answer this question, this work investigates incrementality in discourse processing based on a corpus annotated with DR signals. We find that DRs are dominantly signaled at the boundary between the two constituent discourse units. The findings complement existing psycholinguistic theories on expectation in discourse processing and provide direction for incremental discourse parsing.

1   Introduction

Incremental processing is an essential characteristic of human language comprehension, because linguistic data naturally occurs in streams. For example, during sentence comprehension, humans do not start parsing only after the whole sentence is perceived. Instead the human processor incrementally constructs a partial syntactic tree that matches the sentence prefix read so far (Tanenhaus et al., 1995). Though intuitively for parsing every word is relevant to the syntactical structure, it may not be the case for more global linguistic structures such as DRs, which may only be triggered by some informative cue words, and it is yet unclear at which point the human processor recog-

nizes a DR as the sentence is read or listened word by word.

DRs are relations between units of texts, such as clauses or sentences. For example,

1. In the first year, the bank eliminated 800 jobs. Now it says it will trim more in the next year.

the first and second sentences are connected by a *temporal* relation, as the events occur in a temporal sequence. An incremental discourse processor should predict and recognize the relation at some point before the end of the second sentence. It is useful for speech recognition and dialogue systems where real-time analysis is desirable.

Towards an incremental approach to automatic discourse parsing, this work investigates word-level incrementality in human discourse processing based on manual identification of DR cues. The point at which humans recognize a DR can provide a reference on how long an incremental discourse parser should 'wait', before there is enough input for timely yet accurate prediction of the discourse structure.

2   Related Work

This work is related to incremental approaches of natural language processing (NLP) and psycholinguistic studies on human discourse processing.

In NLP, incremental approaches are used in tasks such as syntactic parsing (Stolcke, 1995; Collins and Roark, 2004; Köhn and Menzel, 2014), semantic role labeling (Konstas et al., 2014) and other joint tasks (Hatori et al., 2012; Li and Ji, 2014; Zhou et al., 2016). These incremental systems are advantageous since they are capable of synchronous analysis by accepting sentence prefixes as inputs. On top of generating more natural and timely response in dialogue systems and improving language modeling in speech recognition,

Proceedings of the The 8th International Joint Conference on Natural Language Processing, pages 157–162,
Taipei, Taiwan, November 27 – December 1, 2017 ©2017 AFNLP

these models can also be used to reflect difficulties in human language processing (Keller, 2010; Demberg et al., 2013).

However, we are not aware of any prior work that implements a discourse processor with such a strong assumption to incrementality. Although expectation for upcoming DRs is demonstrated in various lexico-syntactic constructions in the first clause/sentence (Cristea and Webber, 1997), existing methods of discourse parsing rely on a pipeline, in which the raw text is first segmented into discourse units, mostly clauses or sentences, and the relation is predicted based on two complete discourse units. In this respect, even shift-reduce discourse parsers (Marcu, 1999; Reitter, 2003; Sagae, 2009; Ji and Eisenstein, 2014) are incremental only at discourse unit level.

In psycholinguistics, expectation in language processing is a well studied topic (e.g. Altmann (1998)). Experimental studies suggest that humans use available pragmatic cues to generate expectations and anticipate the upcoming discourse structure (Rohde, 2008), but there are diverging findings about the time-course for humans to recognize and integrate DRs. For example, Millis and Just (1994) state that integration of a *causal* relation takes place at the end of the second clause. In contrast, other experiments report that the integration already occurs in the beginning of the second clause, at least for some relation types (Traxler et al., 1997; Cozijn, 2000; Mak and Sanders, 2010, 2013; Köhne and Demberg, 2013). These experiments are, however, limited to comparison of a few relation types and mostly depend on discourse markers (e.g. *however*, *because*). We still lack an integrated picture on where humans generally recognize a DR.

3 Methodology

This study presents an off-line corpus analysis to determine when or where humans recognize a DR as they process words incrementally. To this end, we want a human subject to identify the cues within the component clauses/sentences that trigger the recognition of a given DR, such as the underlined tokens in Example (1).

Although the exact annotated resource is not yet available, we obtained such annotation by converting the annotation in the RST Signaling Corpus (Das et al., 2015).

Data The RST Signaling Corpus consists of annotation of discourse signals over the RST Discourse Treebank (Carlson et al., 2002), which is a discourse annotated resource following the Rhetorical Structure Theory (RTS) (Mann and Thompson, 1988). In the RST Discourse Treebank, a DR is annotated between two consecutive discourse units. In turn, in the RST Signaling Corpus, each DR is further labeled with one or more types of signaling strategy. These signals not only include explicit discourse markers but also other features typically used in automatic implicit relation identification and psycholinguistic research, such as reference, lexical, semantic, syntactic, graphical and genre features (Das and Taboada, 2017). For example, the *temporal* relation in Example (A) is annotated with three signal labels in the RST Signaling Corpus:[1]

(1) discourse marker (*now*)

(2) tense (*past — present, future*)

(3) lexical chain (*first year — next year*)

Only 7% of the relations are annotated as 'implicit'. Therefore, most conventionally 'implicit' relations are also annotated with explicit signals and included in the present analysis.

Locating signal positions Based on these labels, we use heuristic rules (see *appendix*) and gold syntactic annotation[2] to identify the actual cue words in the text. For example, based on the above 3 signal labels, we identify the underlined tokens in Example (1). Manual check on 200 random samples shows that all signal tokens are perfectly tagged in 95% of the samples, and the remaining 5% samples are partially correct.

We focus on relations that are signaled by surface tokens in order to examine word-level incrementality in discourse processing. Thus, we do not consider signals that are not associated with particular words, e.g. *genre*, and relations with annotations that are not specific enough. 4, 146 relations are screened[3] and 15, 977 relations are included in the analysis. The distribution of the DRs under analysis is shown in Table 1.

---

[1]The list of DR signals and the relation between the RST Treebank and the RST Signaling Corpus can be found in the *appendix*. Details can be found in the related literature.

[2]provided by the Penn Treebank, which annotates on the same text as the RST Treebank (Marcus et al., 1993)

[3]List of excluded signals are shown in the appendix.

category	relation sense	count
expansion	elaboration	7,070
	joint	1,031
	background	787
	evaluation	505
	manner-mean	197
	summary	170
	topic-comment	44
	topic-change	21
comparison	contrast	934
	comparison	243
contingency	enablement	512
	cause	499
	explanation	325
	condition	263
temporal	temporal	429
attribution	attribution	2,947
Total		**15,997**

Table 1: Sense distribution of discourse samples used in the analysis. The original RST senses are mapped to 18 conventional senses (2 screened)

Relating signal positions to incremental processing We analyze the positions of the cue tokens in relation to the DRs they signal. Each cue position is represented by its *distance* from the *boundary* of the relation's discourse units. The *boundary* is defined as the first word of the second clause/sentence in the relation, as each relation is annotated between two consecutive clauses/sentences in the RST formalism.[4] For example, the cue words *eliminated* and *now* in Example (1) have distances of -4 and 0, respectively.

Although positions of the discourse cues can be identified from the recovered annotation, it is still unclear how informative the discourse cues are. It is possible that unambiguous cues only occur at the end even though numerous cues occur in the beginning. For example, in Example 1, can people correctly anticipate the temporal relation after reading the word *now*? Or is *now* too ambiguous that it is necessary to consider all signals after reading the last word? To answer these questions, we quantify and compare the

discourse informativeness of prefixes in different sizes.

The informativeness of each prefix is calculated from the cues covered by the prefix. For each DR spanning two consecutive clauses/sentences, the prefix size ranges from the first word of the first clause/sentence to the complete first and second clauses/sentences. Consecutive cue tokens are merged as one signal and a signal is counted as being covered by a prefix only if the last token of the signal string[5] is covered by the prefix. We use majority as a baseline approach to associate the discourse signals with the relation sense. The inferred relation sense r_{p_n} based on the majority cues in discourse prefix p_n is defined as:

$$r_{p_n} = \arg \max_{r \in R} \sum_{s \in S_{p_n}} count(s, r) \qquad (1)$$

where R is the set of all relation senses; S_{p_n} is the set of signal strings covered in discourse prefix p_n; n is the *distance* of the last word of p_n; and $count(s, r)$ is the count of string s being identified as a signal for a DR of sense r in the corpus. The most frequent relation, *elaboration*, is assigned if no signals are found in the prefix.

The relation senses inferred from prefixes of various sizes are compared with the actual relation sense. Although the majority approach does not model inter-relation and ambiguity of the signals, we assume that more signals, and thus longer prefixes, give better or the same prediction[6]. Therefore, we can compare the informativeness of the prefixes with that of the whole discourse span as upper bound.

4   Results

Distribution of signal locations This analysis seeks to find out how far humans read before they recognize a DR. If DR cues are evenly distributed throughout the discourse components, partial discourse structures can plausibly be constructed on the fly. On the other hand, if the relation cues generally occur towards the end of the last clause, integration of the DR is better to be restrained until

---

[4] Some relations, e.g. *list*, have more than two consecutive units. In this case, the *distance* of the cue is the *distance* compared with the closest *boundary*.

[5] or the last token of the last span if the signal has multiple spans of strings, such as *first year – next year*

[6] Empirically, this assumption was true: in over 99% of the relation samples, majority prediction based on signals in both clauses is better or the same, as that based on the first clause alone.

all clauses are perceived, implying limited incrementality in discourse processing.

Result of the analysis reveals that it is neither of the cases. Figure 1 shows the relative *distance* of the signals with respect to the length of the discourse units. It can be observed that most signals occur at the boundary, and the further away from the boundary, the less signals are found. In fact 24% of the tagged tokens belong to the first 2 words of the second discourse unit. Note that these do not limit to explicit discourse connectives but also other lexical and semantic features.

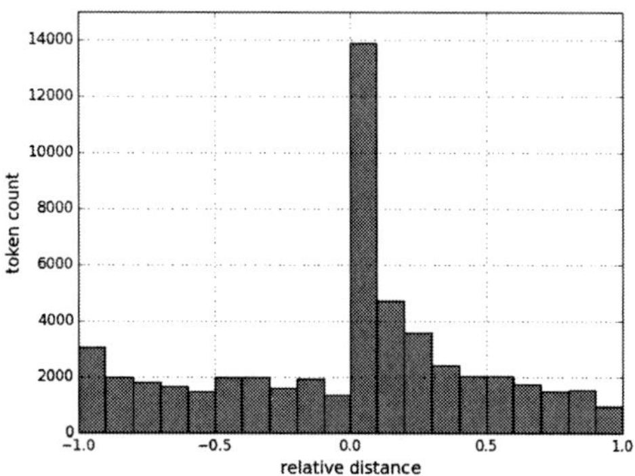

Figure 1: Distribution of the relative distances of the signal tokens.

Overall, more signal tokens locate after the boundary. Counting by relation, 52% of the relations have signals only in the second discourse unit (49% of which at the boundary), 20% have signals only in the first discourse unit, and 28% have signals in both. In other words, in 69% of the cases, all signals for the DR are covered after reading the relation boundary.

Informativeness of discourse prefixes Similarly, the informativeness of the discourse prefixes shows a leap across the *boundary*. Figure 2 illustrates the accuracy of the DR predicted by prefixes of all the relation samples collectively. *Accuracy* refers to the proportion that r_{p_n} equals the actual relation sense of the discourse sample. The upper half of Figure 2 shows that the prediction *accuracy* rises sharply after the boundary is read. According to Figure 1, more signals are detected in the first clause near the boundary, but the informativeness of the prefixes actually drops slightly, possibly due to the ambiguity of the signals. Yet the drop is reverted at the boundary and the accuracy

remains stable. This implies that the signals occurring later in the second clause do not contradict to those found at the boundary.

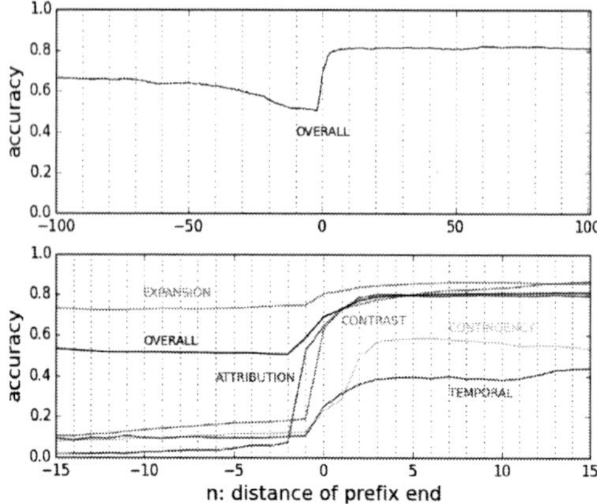

Figure 2: *'Accuracy'* of sense prediction based on oracle signals covered by discourse prefixes[8].

The lower half of Figure 2 compares the five sense categories defined in Table 1, zooming at prefixes ending near the *boundary*. It is observed that, in general, signals for *contingency* and *temporal* relations are mostly identified just after the boundary, while *expansion*, *attribution* and *contrast* relations are identified just before the boundary. The informativeness of the discourse prefixes of *expansion* relation does not rise sharply like other relations because it is the default relation when no signals are identified. Nonetheless, it still hold for all relations that predictions just after the boundary is similar to predictions at the end of the second discourse unit.

5   Conclusion

This work investigates whether DRs can be identified incrementally based on human performance. Our analysis concludes that it is possible because DR signals occur throughout the discourse. Nonetheless, the signals are not evenly distributed but concentrated on the boundary of the two discourse units. An incremental discourse parser that jointly segments discourse units and predicts DR senses can potentially output the predicted DR immediately after a *boundary* is detected, and then

---

[8]This *'accuracy'* is not comparable to the performance of automatic parsers because the signals are identified manually and the prediction is not made on a held out test set. Our focus is the comparison between the discourse prefixes.

focus on detecting *expectative* signals in the second clause/sentence for the next relation.

Results of the analysis agree with the psycholinguistics literature that DRs are integrated at the beginning of second clause/sentence of the relation, because otherwise the annotator should mostly recognize signals towards the end of the discourse. Our analysis evaluates and extends existing laboratory findings on DR processing by comparing a wide range of relations that are signaled not only by discourse markers. Expectation-focused discourse processing can also be explained by the 'good-enough' predictive approach in human language processing, which argues that humans should integrate a probabilistically 'good-enough' DR prediction at the boundary, and allocate more processing resource to predict the forth-coming DR (Ferreira and Lowder, 2016).

Nonetheless, this corpus study alone is not enough to prove the incrementality hypothesis in DR processing. As future work, we would also like to explore global signals, which are possibly recognized unconsciously and less likely to be identified. In addition, we plan to verify the cognitive reality of the signal positions by behavioral experiments with multiple subjects. Another goal is to design a word-level incremental discourse parser based on the findings of this work, taking into account global discourse flow.

Acknowledgments

This research was funded by the German Research Foundation (DFG) as part of SFB 1102 Information Density and Linguistic Encoding and the Cluster of Excellence (MMCI).

References

Gerry TM Altmann. 1998. Ambiguity in sentence processing. *Trends in cognitive sciences*, 2(4):146–152.

Lynn Carlson, Mary Ellen Okurowski, and Daniel Marcu. 2002. Ldc2002t07: Rst discourse treebank.

Michael Collins and Brian Roark. 2004. Incremental parsing with the perceptron algorithm. In *Proceedings of the Annual Meeting of the Association for Computational Linguistics*, page 111. Association for Computational Linguistics.

Reinier Cozijn. 2000. Integration and inference in understanding causal sentences. *Unpublished doctoral dissertation, Tilburg University, Tilburg, Netherlands.*

Dan Cristea and Bonnie Webber. 1997. Expectations in incremental discourse processing. In *Proceedings of the Annual Meeting of the Association for Computational Linguistics and Conference of the European Chapter of the Association for Computational Linguistics*, pages 88–95. Association for Computational Linguistics.

Debopam Das and Maite Taboada. 2017. Rst signalling corpus: a corpus of signals of coherence relations. *Language Resources and Evaluation.*

Debopam Das, Maite Taboada, and Paul McFetridge. 2015. Ldc2015t10 rst signalling corpus.

Vera Demberg, Frank Keller, and Alexander Koller. 2013. Incremental, predictive parsing with psycholinguistically motivated tree-adjoining grammar. *Computational Linguistics*, 39(4):1025–1066.

F Ferreira and MW Lowder. 2016. Prediction, information structure, and good-enough language processing. *Psychology of Learning and Motivation.*

Jun Hatori, Takuya Matsuzaki, Yusuke Miyao, and Jun'ichi Tsujii. 2012. Incremental joint approach to word segmentation, pos tagging, and dependency parsing in chinese. In *Proceedings of the Annual Meeting of the Association for Computational Linguistics*, pages 1045–1053. Association for Computational Linguistics.

Yangfeng Ji and Jacob Eisenstein. 2014. Representation learning for text-level discourse parsing. In *ACL (1)*, pages 13–24.

Frank Keller. 2010. Cognitively plausible models of human language processing. In *Proceedings of the Annual Meeting of the Association for Computational Linguistics*, pages 60–67. Association for Computational Linguistics.

Arne Köhn and Wolfgang Menzel. 2014. Incremental predictive parsing with turboparser. *Proceedings of Annual Meeting of the Association of Computational Linguistics.*

Judith Köhne and Vera Demberg. 2013. The timecourse of processing discourse connectives. In *Proceedings of the 35th Annual Meeting of the Cognitive Science Society.*

Ioannis Konstas, Frank Keller, Vera Demberg, and Mirella Lapata. 2014. Incremental semantic role labeling with tree adjoining grammar. In *Proceedings of the Conference on Empirical Methods in Natural Language Processing*, volume 301.

Qi Li and Heng Ji. 2014. Incremental joint extraction of entity mentions and relations. In *Proceedings of the Annual Meeting of the Association for Computational Linguistics*. Association for Computational Linguistics.

W Mak and T Sanders. 2010. Incremental discourse processing: How coherence relations influence the resolution of pronouns. *The linguistics enterprise: From knowledge of language to knowledge in linguistics*, pages 167–182.

Willem M Mak and Ted JM Sanders. 2013. The role of causality in discourse processing: Effects of expectation and coherence relations. *Language and Cognitive Processes*, 28(9):1414–1437.

William C Mann and Sandra A Thompson. 1988. Rhetorical structure theory: Toward a functional theory of text organization. *Text-Interdisciplinary Journal for the Study of Discourse*, 8(3):243–281.

Daniel Marcu. 1999. A decision-based approach to rhetorical parsing. In *Proceedings of the 37th annual meeting of the Association for Computational Linguistics on Computational Linguistics*, pages 365–372. Association for Computational Linguistics.

Mitchell P Marcus, Mary Ann Marcinkiewicz, and Beatrice Santorini. 1993. Building a large annotated corpus of english: The penn treebank. *Computational linguistics*, 19(2):313–330.

Keith K Millis and Marcel Adam Just. 1994. The influence of connectives on sentence comprehension. *Journal of Memory and Language*, 33(1):128.

David Reitter. 2003. Rhetorical analysis with rich-feature support vector models. *Unpublished Master's thesis, University of Potsdam, Potsdam, Germany*.

Hannah Rohde. 2008. *Coherence-Driven Effects in Sentence and Discourse Processing*. Ph.D. thesis, University of California, San Diego.

Kenji Sagae. 2009. Analysis of discourse structure with syntactic dependencies and data-driven shift-reduce parsing. In *Proceedings of the 11th International Conference on Parsing Technologies*, pages 81–84. Association for Computational Linguistics.

Andreas Stolcke. 1995. An efficient probabilistic context-free parsing algorithm that computes prefix probabilities. *Computational linguistics*, 21(2):165–201.

Michael K Tanenhaus, Michael J Spivey-Knowlton, Kathleen M Eberhard, and Julie C Sedivy. 1995. Integration of visual and linguistic information in spoken language comprehension. *Science*, 268(5217):1632.

Matthew J Traxler, Anthony J Sanford, Joy P Aked, and Linda M Moxey. 1997. Processing causal and diagnostic statements in discourse. *Journal of Experimental Psychology: Learning, Memory, and Cognition*, 23(1):88.

Junsheng Zhou, Feiyu Xu, Hans Uszkoreit, Weiguang Qu, Ran Li, and Yanhui Gu. 2016. Amr parsing with an incremental joint model. *Proceedings of SemEval*.

Speaker Role Contextual Modeling for Language Understanding and Dialogue Policy Learning

Ta-Chung Chi[*] **Po-Chun Chen**[*] **Shang-Yu Su**[†] **Yun-Nung Chen**[*]

[*]Department of Computer Science and Information Engineering
[†]Graduate Institute of Electrical Engineering
National Taiwan University
{b02902019,r06922028,r05921117}@ntu.edu.tw y.v.chen@ieee.org

Abstract

Language understanding (LU) and dialogue policy learning are two essential components in conversational systems. Human-human dialogues are not well-controlled and often random and unpredictable due to their own goals and speaking habits. This paper proposes a role-based contextual model to consider different speaker roles independently based on the various speaking patterns in the multi-turn dialogues. The experiments on the benchmark dataset show that the proposed role-based model successfully learns role-specific behavioral patterns for contextual encoding and then significantly improves language understanding and dialogue policy learning tasks[1].

1 Introduction

Spoken dialogue systems that can help users to solve complex tasks such as booking a movie ticket become an emerging research topic in the artificial intelligence and natural language processing area. With a well-designed dialogue system as an intelligent personal assistant, people can accomplish certain tasks more easily via natural language interactions. Today, there are several virtual intelligent assistants, such as Apple's Siri, Google's Home, Microsoft's Cortana, and Amazon's Echo. Recent advance of deep learning has inspired many applications of neural models to dialogue systems. Wen et al. (2017), Bordes et al. (2017), and Li et al. (2017) introduced network-based end-to-end trainable task-oriented dialogue systems.

A key component of the understanding system is a language understanding (LU) module—it parses user utterances into semantic frames that capture the core meaning, where three main tasks of LU are domain classification, intent determination, and slot filling (Tur and De Mori, 2011). A typical pipeline of LU is to first decide the domain given the input utterance, and based on the domain, to predict the intent and to fill associated slots corresponding to a domain-specific semantic template. Recent advance of deep learning has inspired many applications of neural models to natural language processing tasks. With the power of deep learning, there are emerging better approaches of LU (Hakkani-Tür et al., 2016; Chen et al., 2016b,a; Wang et al., 2016). However, most of above work focused on single-turn interactions, where each utterance is treated independently.

The contextual information has been shown useful for LU (Bhargava et al., 2013; Xu and Sarikaya, 2014; Chen et al., 2015; Sun et al., 2016). For example, the Figure 1 shows conversational utterances, where the intent of the highlighted tourist utterance is to ask about location information, but it is difficult to understand without contexts. Hence, it is more likely to estimate the location-related intent given the contextual utterance about location recommendation. Contextual information has been incorporated into the recurrent neural network (RNN) for improved domain classification, intent prediction, and slot filling (Xu and Sarikaya, 2014; Shi et al., 2015; Weston et al., 2015; Chen et al., 2016c). The LU output is semantic representations of users' behaviors, and then flows to the downstream dialogue management component in order to decide which action the system should take next, as called *dialogue policy*. It is intuitive that better understanding could improve the dialogue policy learning, so that the dialogue management can be further

---

[1]The source code is available at: https://github.com/MiuLab/Spk-Dialogue.

Proceedings of the The 8th International Joint Conference on Natural Language Processing, pages 163–168,
Taipei, Taiwan, November 27 – December 1, 2017 ©2017 AFNLP

Guide: so you of course %uh you can have dinner there and %uh of course you also can do sentosa , if you want to for the song of the sea , right ?

Tourist: yah .

Tourist: what 's the song in the sea ?

Guide: a song of the sea in fact is %uh laser show inside sentosa

Task 1: Language Understanding (User Intents)
Task 2: Dialogue Policy Learning (System Actions)

Figure 1: The human-human conversational utterances and their associated semantics from DSTC4.

boosted through interactions (Li et al., 2017).

Most of previous dialogue systems did not take speaker roles into consideration. However, we discover that different speaker roles can cause notable variance in speaking habits and later affect the system performance differently (Chen et al., 2017). From Figure 1, the benchmark dialogue dataset, Dialogue State Tracking Challenge 4 (DSTC4) (Kim et al., 2016)[2], contains two specific roles, a tourist and a guide. Under the scenario of dialogue systems and the communication patterns, we take the tourist as a user and the guide as the dialogue agent (system). During conversations, the user may focus on not only *reasoning (user history)* but also *listening (agent history)*, so different speaker roles could provide various cues for better understanding and policy learning.

This paper focuses on LU and dialogue policy learning, which targets the understanding of tourist's natural language (LU; language understanding) and the prediction of how the system should respond (SAP; system action prediction) respectively. In order to comprehend what the tourist is talking about and predict how the guide reacts to the user, this work proposes a role-based contextual model by modeling role-specific contexts differently for improving system performance.

2 Proposed Approach

The model architecture is illustrated in Figure 2. First, the previous utterances are fed into the contextual model to encode into the history summary, and then the summary vector and the current utterance are integrated for helping LU and dialogue policy learning. The whole model is trained in an end-to-end fashion, where the history summary vector is automatically learned based on two

downstream tasks. The objective of the proposed model is to optimize the conditional probability $p(\hat{\mathbf{y}} \mid \mathbf{x})$, so that the difference between the predicted distribution $q(\hat{y}_k = z \mid \mathbf{x})$ and the target distribution $q(y_k = z \mid \mathbf{x})$ can be minimized:

$$\mathcal{L} = -\sum_{k=1}^{K}\sum_{z=1}^{N} q(y_k = z \mid \mathbf{x}) \log p(\hat{y}_k = z \mid \mathbf{x}),$$

$$(1)$$

where the labels $\mathbf{y}$ can be either intent tags for understanding or system actions for dialogue policy learning.

Language Understanding (LU)   Given the current utterance $\mathbf{x} = \{w_t\}_1^T$, the goal is to predict the user intents of $\mathbf{x}$, which includes the speech acts and associated attributes shown in Figure 1; for example, QST_WHAT is composed of the speech act QST and the associated attribute WHAT. Note that we do not process the slot filling task for extracting LOC. We apply a bidirectional long short-term memory (BLSTM) model (Schuster and Paliwal, 1997) to integrate preceding and following words to learn the probability distribution of the user intents.

$$\mathbf{v}_{\text{cur}} = \text{BLSTM}(\mathbf{x}, W_{\text{his}} \cdot \mathbf{v}_{\text{his}}), \quad (2)$$

$$\mathbf{o} = \text{sigmoid}(W_{\text{LU}} \cdot \mathbf{v}_{\text{cur}}), \quad (3)$$

where W_{his} is a dense matrix and $\mathbf{v}_{\text{his}}$ is the history summary vector, $\mathbf{v}_{\text{cur}}$ is the context-aware vector of the current utterance encoded by the BLSTM, and $\mathbf{o}$ is the intent distribution. Note that this is a multi-label and multi-class classification, so the sigmoid function is employed for modeling the distribution after a dense layer. The user intent labels $\mathbf{y}$ are decided based on whether the value is higher than a threshold θ.

Dialogue Policy Learning   For system action prediction, we also perform similar multi-label

<hr>

[2] http://www.colips.org/workshop/dstc4/

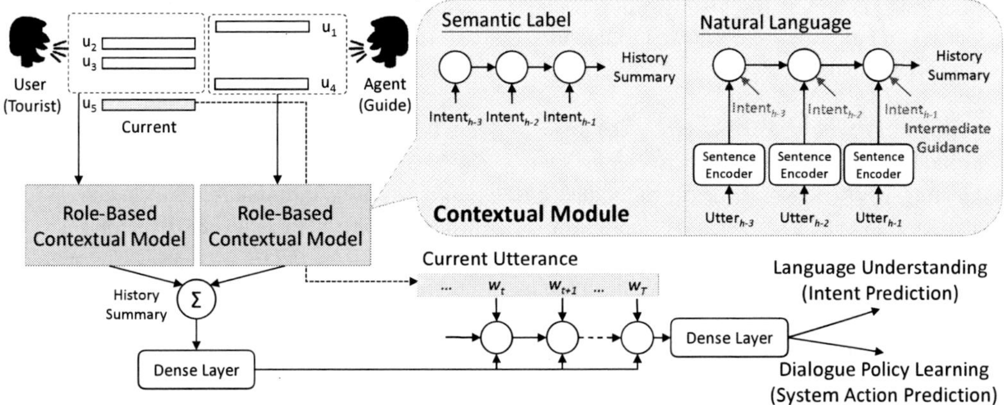

Figure 2: Illustration of the proposed role-based contextual model.

multi-class classification on the context-aware vector $\mathbf{v}_{\text{cur}}$ from (2) using `sigmoid`:

$$\mathbf{o} = \text{sigmoid}(W_\pi \cdot \mathbf{v}_{\text{cur}}), \qquad (4)$$

and then the system actions can be decided based on a threshold θ.

2.1 Contextual Module

In order to leverage the contextual information, we utilize two types of contexts: 1) semantic labels and 2) natural language, to learn history summary representations, $\mathbf{v}_{\text{his}}$ in (2). The illustration is shown in the top-right part of Figure 2.

Semantic Label Given a sequence of annotated intent tags and associated attributes for each history utterance, we employ a BLSTM to model the explicit semantics:

$$\mathbf{v}_{\text{his}} = \text{BLSTM}(\text{intent}_t), \qquad (5)$$

where intent_t is the vector after one-hot encoding for representing the annotated intent and the attribute features. Note that this model requires the ground truth annotations of history utterances for training and testing.

Natural Language (NL) Given the natural language history, a sentence encoder is applied to learn a vector representation for each prior utterance. After encoding, the feature vectors are fed into a BLSTM to capture temporal information:

$$\mathbf{v}_{\text{his}} = \text{BLSTM}(\text{CNN}(\text{utt}_t)), \qquad (6)$$

where the CNN is good at extracting the most salient features that can represent the given natural

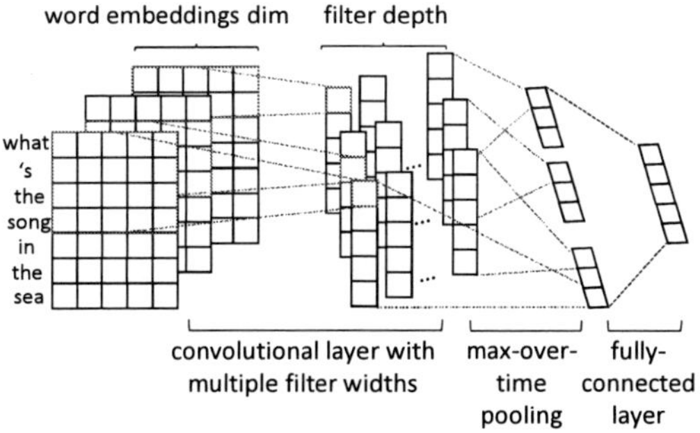

Figure 3: Illustration of the CNN sentence encoder for the example sentence *"what's the song in the sea"*.

language utterances illustrated in Figure 3. Here the sentence encoder can be replaced into different encoders[3], and the weights of all encoders are tied together.

NL with Intermediate Guidance Considering that the semantic labels may provide rich cues, the middle supervision signal is utilized as intermediate guidance for the sentence encoding module in order to guide them to project from input utterances to a more meaningful feature space. Specifically, for each utterance, we compute the cross entropy loss between the encoder outputs and corresponding intent-attributes shown in Figure 2. Assuming that l_t is the encoding loss for utt_t in the history, the final objective is to minimize $(\mathcal{L} + \sum_t l_t)$. This model does not require the

---

[3] In the experiments, CNN achieved slightly better performance with fewer parameters compared with BLSTM.

ground truth semantics for history when testing, so that it is more practical compared to the above model using semantic labels.

2.2 Speaker Role Modeling

In a dialogue, there are at least two roles communicating with each other, each individual has his/her own goal and speaking habit. For example, the tourists have their own desired touring goals and the guides are try to provide the sufficient touring information for suggestions and assistance. Prior work usually ignored the speaker role information or only modeled a single speaker's history for various tasks (Chen et al., 2016c; Yang et al., 2017). The performance may be degraded due to the possibly unstable and noisy input feature space. To address this issue, this work proposes the role-based contextual model: instead of using only a single BLSTM model for the history, we construct one individual contextual module for each speaker role. Each role-dependent recurrent unit $\text{BLSTM}_{\text{role}_x}$ receives corresponding inputs x_{i,role_x} ($i = [1, ..., N]$), which have been processed by an encoder model, we can rewrite (5) and (6) into (7) and (8) respectively:

$$\mathbf{v}_{\text{his}} = \text{BLSTM}_{\text{role}_a}(\text{intent}_{t,\text{role}_a}) \qquad (7)$$
$$+ \text{BLSTM}_{\text{role}_b}(\text{intent}_{t,\text{role}_b}).$$
$$\mathbf{v}_{\text{his}} = \text{BLSTM}_{\text{role}_a}(\text{CNN}(\text{utt}_{t,\text{role}_a})) \qquad (8)$$
$$+ \text{BLSTM}_{\text{role}_b}(\text{CNN}(\text{utt}_{t,\text{role}_b}))$$

Therefore, each role-based contextual module focuses on modeling the role-dependent goal and speaking style, and $\mathbf{v}_{\text{cur}}$ from (2) is able to carry role-based contextual information.

3 Experiments

To evaluate the effectiveness of the proposed model, we conduct the LU and dialogue policy learning experiments on human-human conversational data.

3.1 Setup

The experiments are conducted on DSTC4, which consists of 35 dialogue sessions on touristic information for Singapore collected from Skype calls between 3 tour guides and 35 tourists (Kim et al., 2016). All recorded dialogues with the total length of 21 hours have been manually transcribed and annotated with speech acts and semantic labels at each turn level. The speaker labels are also annotated. Human-human dialogues contain rich and complex human behaviors and bring much difficulty to all dialogue-related tasks. Given the fact that different speaker roles behave differently, DSTC4 is a suitable benchmark dataset for evaluation.

We choose a mini-batch `adam` as the optimizer with the batch size of 128 examples (Kingma and Ba, 2014). The size of each hidden recurrent layer is 128. We use pre-trained 200-dimensional word embeddings $GloVe$ (Pennington et al., 2014). We only apply 30 training epochs without any early stop approach. The sentence encoder is implemented using a CNN with the filters of size $[2, 3, 4]$, 128 filters each size, and max pooling over time. The idea is to capture the most important feature (the highest value) for each feature map. This pooling scheme naturally deals with variable sentence lengths. Please refer to Kim (2014) for more details.

For both tasks, we focus on predicting multiple labels including speech acts and attributes, so the evaluation metric is average F1 score for balancing recall and precision in each utterance. Note that the final prediction may contain multiple labels.

3.2 Results

The experiments are shown in Table 1, where we report the average number over five runs. The first baseline (row (a)) is the best participant of DSTC4 in IWSDS 2016 (Kim et al., 2016), the poor performance is probably because tourist intents are much more difficult than guide intents (most systems achieved higher than 60% of F1 for guide intents but lower than 50% for tourist intents). The second baseline (row (b)) models the current utterance without contexts, performing 62.6% for understanding and 63.4% for policy learning.

3.2.1 Language Understanding Results

With contextual history, using ground truth semantic labels for learning history summary vectors greatly improves the performance to 68.2% (row (c)), while using natural language slightly improves the performance to 64.2% (row (e)). The reason may be that NL utterances contain more noises and the contextual vectors are more difficult to model for LU. The proposed role-based contextual models applying on semantic labels and NL achieve 69.2% (row (d)) and 65.1% (row (f)) on F1 respectively, showing the significant improvement all model without role modeling. Fur-

Model			Language Understanding	Policy Learning
Baseline	(a)	*DSTC4-Best*	52.1	-
	(b)	BLSTM	62.6	63.4
Contextual-Sem	(c)	BLSTM	68.2	66.8
	(d)	+ Role-Based	**69.2**†	**70.1**†
Contextual-NL	(e)	BLSTM	64.2	66.3
	(f)	+ Role-Based	65.1†	66.9†
	(g)	+ Role-Based w/ Intermediate Guidance	**65.8**†	**67.4**†

Table 1: Language understanding and dialogue policy learning performance of F-measure on DSTC4 (%). † indicates the significant improvement compared to all methods without speaker role modeling.

thermore, adding the intermediate guidance acquires additional improvement (65.8% from the row (g)). It is shown that the semantic labels successfully guide the sentence encoder to obtain better sentence-level representations, and then the history summary vector carrying more accurate semantics gives better performance for understanding.

3.2.2 Dialogue Policy Learning Results

To predict the guide's next actions, the baseline utilizes intent tags of the current utterance without contexts (row (b)). Table 1 shows the similar trend as LU results, where applying either role-based contextual models or intermediate guidance brings advantages for both semantics-encoded and NL-encoded history.

3.3 Discussion

In contrast to NL, semantic labels (intent-attribute pairs) can be seen as more explicit and concise information for modeling the history, which indeed gains more in our experiments for both LU and dialogue policy learning. The results of Contextual-Sem can be treated as the upper bound performance, because they utilizes the ground truth semantics of contexts. Among the experiments of Contextual-NL, which are more practical because the annotated semantics are not required during testing, the proposed approaches achieve 5.1% and 6.3% relative improvement compared to the baseline for LU and dialogue policy learning respectively.

Between LU and dialogue policy learning tasks, most LU results are worse than dialogue policy learning results. The reason probably is that the guide has similar behavior patterns such as providing information and confirming questions etc., while the user can have more diverse interac-

tions. Therefore, understanding the user intents is slightly harder than predicting the guide policy in the DSTC4 dataset.

With the promising improvement for both LU and dialogue policy learning, the idea about modeling speaker role information can be further extended to various research topics in the future.

4 Conclusion

This paper proposes an end-to-end role-based contextual model that automatically learns speaker-specific contextual encoding. Experiments on a benchmark multi-domain human-human dialogue dataset show that our role-based model achieves impressive improvement in language understanding and dialogue policy learning, demonstrating that different speaker roles behave differently and focus on different goals.

Acknowledgements

We would like to thank reviewers for their insightful comments on the paper. The authors are supported by the Ministry of Science and Technology of Taiwan, Google Research, Microsoft Research, and MediaTek Inc..

References

Anshuman Bhargava, Asli Celikyilmaz, Dilek Hakkani-Tur, and Ruhi Sarikaya. 2013. Easy contextual intent prediction and slot detection. In *Proceedings of 2013 IEEE International Conference on Acoustics, Speech and Signal Processing*. IEEE, pages 8337–8341.

Antoine Bordes, Y-Lan Boureau, and Jason Weston. 2017. Learning end-to-end goal-oriented dialog. In *ICLR*.

Po-Chun Chen, Ta-Chung Chi, Shang-Yu Su, and Yun-Nung Chen. 2017. Dynamic time-aware attention to speaker roles and contexts for spoken language understanding. In *Proceedings of 2017 IEEE Workshop on Automatic Speech Recognition and Understanding*.

Yun-Nung Chen, Dilek Hakanni-Tür, Gokhan Tur, Asli Celikyilmaz, Jianfeng Guo, and Li Deng. 2016a. Syntax or semantics? knowledge-guided joint semantic frame parsing. In *Proceedings of 2016 IEEE Spoken Language Technology Workshop*. IEEE, pages 348–355.

Yun-Nung Chen, Dilek Hakkani-Tur, Gokhan Tur, Asli Celikyilmaz, Jianfeng Gao, and Li Deng. 2016b. Knowledge as a teacher: Knowledge-guided structural attention networks. *arXiv preprint arXiv:1609.03286* .

Yun-Nung Chen, Dilek Hakkani-Tür, Gökhan Tür, Jianfeng Gao, and Li Deng. 2016c. End-to-end memory networks with knowledge carryover for multi-turn spoken language understanding. In *Proceedings of The 17th Annual Meeting of the International Speech Communication Association*. pages 3245–3249.

Yun-Nung Chen, Ming Sun, Alexander I. Rudnicky, and Anatole Gershman. 2015. Leveraging behavioral patterns of mobile applications for personalized spoken language understanding. In *Proceedings of 17th ACM International Conference on Multimodal Interaction*. ACM, pages 83–86.

Dilek Hakkani-Tür, Gökhan Tür, Asli Celikyilmaz, Yun-Nung Chen, Jianfeng Gao, Li Deng, and Ye-Yi Wang. 2016. Multi-domain joint semantic frame parsing using bi-directional rnn-lstm. In *Proceedings of The 17th Annual Meeting of the International Speech Communication Association*. pages 715–719.

Seokhwan Kim, Luis Fernando DHaro, Rafael E Banchs, Jason D Williams, and Matthew Henderson. 2016. The fourth dialog state tracking challenge. In *Proceedings of the 7th International Workshop on Spoken Dialogue Systems*.

Yoon Kim. 2014. Convolutional neural networks for sentence classification. *arXiv preprint arXiv:1408.5882* .

Diederik Kingma and Jimmy Ba. 2014. Adam: A method for stochastic optimization. *arXiv preprint arXiv:1412.6980* .

Xuijun Li, Yun-Nung Chen, Lihong Li, Jianfeng Gao, and Asli Celikyilmaz. 2017. End-to-end task-completion neural dialogue systems. In *Proceedings of The 8th International Joint Conference on Natural Language Processing*.

Jeffrey Pennington, Richard Socher, and Christopher D Manning. 2014. Glove: Global vectors for word representation. In *Proceedings of EMNLP*. volume 14, pages 1532–1543.

Mike Schuster and Kuldip K Paliwal. 1997. Bidirectional recurrent neural networks. *IEEE Transactions on Signal Processing* 45(11):2673–2681.

Yangyang Shi, Kaisheng Yao, Hu Chen, Yi-Cheng Pan, Mei-Yuh Hwang, and Baolin Peng. 2015. Contextual spoken language understanding using recurrent neural networks. In *Proceedings of 2015 IEEE International Conference on Acoustics, Speech and Signal Processing*. IEEE, pages 5271–5275.

Ming Sun, Yun-Nung Chen, and Alexander I. Rudnicky. 2016. An intelligent assistant for high-level task understanding. In *Proceedings of The 21st Annual Meeting of the Intelligent Interfaces Community*. pages 169–174.

Gokhan Tur and Renato De Mori. 2011. *Spoken language understanding: Systems for extracting semantic information from speech*. John Wiley & Sons.

Zhangyang Wang, Yingzhen Yang, Shiyu Chang, Qing Ling, and Thomas S Huang. 2016. Learning a deep l encoder for hashing. In *Proceedings of the Twenty-Fifth International Joint Conference on Artificial Intelligence, IJCAI*. pages 2174–2180.

Tsung-Hsien Wen, Milica Gasic, Nikola Mrksic, Lina M Rojas-Barahona, Pei-Hao Su, Stefan Ultes, David Vandyke, and Steve Young. 2017. A network-based end-to-end trainable task-oriented dialogue system. In *Proceedings of EACL*.

Jason Weston, Sumit Chopra, and Antoine Bordesa. 2015. Memory networks. In *Proceedings of International Conference on Learning Representations*.

Puyang Xu and Ruhi Sarikaya. 2014. Contextual domain classification in spoken language understanding systems using recurrent neural network. In *Proceedings of 2014 IEEE International Conference on Acoustics, Speech and Signal Processing*. IEEE, pages 136–140.

Xuesong Yang, Yun-Nung Chen, Dilek Hakkani-Tür, Paul Crook, Xiujun Li, Jianfeng Gao, and Li Deng. 2017. End-to-end joint learning of natural language understanding and dialogue manager. In *Proceedings of 2017 IEEE International Conference on Acoustics, Speech and Signal Processing*. IEEE, pages 5690–5694.

Diversifying Neural Conversation Model
with Maximal Marginal Relevance

Yiping Song,[1] Zhiliang Tian,[2] Dongyan Zhao,[2] Ming Zhang,[1]* Rui Yan[2]*
Institute of Network Computing and Information Systems, Peking University, China
Institute of Computer Science and Technology, Peking University, China
`{songyiping,zhaody,mzhang_cs,ruiyan}@pku.edu.cn`
`tianzhilianghit@gmail.com` *Corresponding authors

Abstract

Neural conversation systems, typically using sequence-to-sequence (`seq2seq`) models, are showing promising progress recently. However, traditional `seq2seq` suffer from a severe weakness: during beam search decoding, they tend to rank universal replies at the top of the candidate list, resulting in the lack of diversity among candidate replies. *Maximum Marginal Relevance* (MMR) is a ranking algorithm that has been widely used for subset selection. In this paper, we propose the MMR-BS decoding method, which incorporates MMR into the beam search (BS) process of `seq2seq`. The MMR-BS method improves the diversity of generated replies without sacrificing their high relevance with the user-issued query. Experiments show that our proposed model achieves the best performance among other comparison methods.

1 Introduction

Conversation systems are of growing importance since they enable a smooth interaction interface between humans and computers: using natural language (Yan et al., 2016b). Generally speaking, there are two main categories of conversation systems: the retrieval-based (Yan et al., 2016a,b; Song et al., 2016) and the generation-based (Serban et al., 2016b; Shang et al., 2015; Serban et al., 2016a) conversation systems. In this paper, we focus on the generation-based conversation systems, which are more flexible and extensible compared with the retrieval-based ones.

The sequence-to-sequence neural network (`seq2seq`) (Sutskever et al., 2014) is a prevailing approach in generation-based conversation systems (Shang et al., 2015). It uses a recurrent neural network (RNN) to encode the source sentence into a vector, then uses another RNN to decode the target sentence word by word. Long short term memory (LSTM) (Hochreiter and Schmidhuber, 1997) and gated recurrent units (GRUs) (Cho et al., 2014) could further enhance the RNNs to model longer sentences. In the scenarios of generation-based conversation systems, the training criterion of `seq2seq` is to maximize the likelihood of the generated replies given the user-issued queries.

As is well known, the generation-based conversation systems suffer from the problem of *universally replies*, which contain less information, such as "I don't know" and "something" (Mou et al., 2016; Mrkšić et al., 2015). According to Li et al., 0.45% generated replies contain the sequence "I don't know." During the interaction between the user and the system, the user may expect more informative and diverse utterances with various expressions. The lack of diversity is one of the bottlenecks of the generation-based conversation systems. Moreover, the quality of generated replies, namely the high relevance between queries and replies, could not be obliterated when trying to improve the diversity.

In this paper, We propose the MMR-BS model to tackle the problem of diversity in the generation-based conversation systems. *Maximum Marginal Relevance* (MMR) (Jaime and Goldstein, 1998; Wang et al., 2009; Yang et al., 2007) has been widely applied in diversity modeling tasks, such as information retrieval (Stewart and Carbonell, 1998), document summarization (Zhou, 2011) and text categorization (He et al., 2012). It scores each candidate by properly measuring them in terms of quality and diversity and selects the current best candidate item at each time step. These properties make it suitable for the sub-

Proceedings of the The 8th International Joint Conference on Natural Language Processing, pages 169–174,
Taipei, Taiwan, November 27 – December 1, 2017 ©2017 AFNLP

sequences choosing in the reply generation process. Hence, we incorporate MMR into the decoding process of *Beam Search* (BS) in `seq2seq`.

To demonstrate the effectiveness of MMR-BS, we evaluate our method in terms of both *quality* and *diversity*. Enhanced with MMR, the MMR-BS model can generate more meaningful replies than other baselines, as we shall show in the experiments.

2 Preliminaries

2.1 `seq2seq` Model

`seq2seq` encodes the user-issued query q using an RNN, and decodes a corresponding reply r with another RNN. At each time step of decoding, the RNN estimates a probabilistic distribution over the vocabulary. The objective function of `seq2seq` is the log-likelihood of reply r given the query q:

$$\hat{r} = \underset{r}{\operatorname{argmax}}\{\log(p(r|q))\} \quad (1)$$

We use the attention mechanism (Bahdanau et al., 2015) to better align input and output sentences and use gated recurrent units (GRUs) to enhance RNNs' ability to handle long sentences.

2.2 Beam Search

Beam search is a prevalent decoding method in `seq2seq` (Vijayakumar et al., 2016), which maintains a set of candidate subsequences at every step of decoding process. At a time step t, we keep N subsequences based on their cumulative probabilities. At the time $t + 1$, each subsequence is appended with a word from the entire vocabulary, resulting in a larger candidate set of subsequences. Then we keep the top-N sequences in the same manner. A candidate sequence terminates when RNN predicts EOS, the special symbol indicating the end of a sequence. Let $S(y_1, \cdots, y_t|q)$ be a function that scores a subsequence $\{y_1, \cdots, y_t\}$ given a query q. The original beam search chooses N most probable replies, i.e., $S(\cdot)$ is the logarithmic probability, given by

$$S(y_t|q) = S(y_{t-1}) + \log p(y_t|q, y_1, \cdots, y_{t-1}) \quad (2)$$

3 Diverse Neural Conversation

3.1 MMR-BS Model

The beam search criterion is mainly based on the conditional probabilities of replies given the query. Universal replies, which have relatively

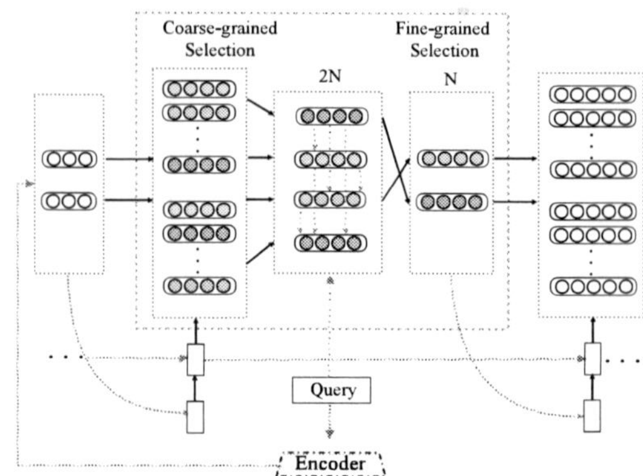

Figure 1: The architecture of MMR-BS.

higher probabilities, are likely to appear at the top of the candidate list, resulting in the lack of diversity among top replies. To handle the influence of the replies' own probabilities and address the relevance with the query at the same time, we propose MMR-BS, which applies the MMR criterion to every decoding step of beam search to upturn diverse subsequences. The whole architecture of MMR-BS is illustrated in Figure 1.

Specifically, the decoding process maintains a subsequence list S; the number of subsequences in S is N. At each time of decoding, every subsequence is appended with a word from the entire vocabulary V, resulting in $N * |V|$ subsequences. Since only N subsequences would be passed into next time step for further generation, our MMR-BS model uses two granularities of selection, which is performed in two-step strategy. We present the decoding process in Algorithm 1.

• **Coarse-grained Selection.** Coarse-grained selection follows the original scoring function in traditional beam search, which is described in equation 2. This selection strategy conditions on the probabilities of subsequences given the query, which represents the relevance between each subsequence and the query. We use coarse-grained selection to select $2N$ subsequences noted as S^{2N}.

• **Fine-grained Selection.** However, coarse-grained selection focuses on the quality of subsequences but ignores the diversity among them. The fine-grained selection adopts the MMR scoring to balance quality and diversity in the selecting process. It maintains a selected list S^s and continually adds the highest scored subsequence into S^s from the remaining candidates, i.e., $S_t^{2N} \backslash S_t^s$. This process repeats N times, resulting in N best subsequences. The scoring function of MMR con-

Algorithm 1: MMR-BS Decoding

Input: the user-issued query q, the max length of reply l, λ in MMR function

Output: generated reply set R

$R = \varnothing$;

$S_0 = \varnothing$; **for** $t = 1; t \leq l;$ **do**

   // obtain the subsequence set at time i

   $S_t = Decoding(q, S_{t-1})$;

   // coarse-grained selection

   $S_t^{2N} = Normal\ Ranking(S_t)$;

   // fine-grained selection

   $S_t^s = \varnothing$; **for** $i = 1; i \leq N;$ **do**

      $max = -\infty$;

      forall $s_j \in S_t^{2N} \setminus S_t^s$ **do**

         $score = \lambda \operatorname{sim}_{qua}(s_j, q)$
         $-(1 - \lambda)\operatorname{sim}_{div}(s_j, S_t^s)$;

         if $score > max$ **then**

            $max = score$;

            $best_s = s_j$;

      $S_t^s = S_t^s \cup best_s$;

$R = S_l^s$;

return R

---

siders the quality of a candidate as well as its diversity against previously selected ones. In particular, we have two metrics: $\operatorname{sim}_{qua}(s_i, q)$ measures the similarity of a candidate subsequence s_i with respect to the query q, indicating the quality of s_i. $\operatorname{sim}_{div}(s_i, S^s)$ measures the similarity of s_i against other replies in the selected list; $-\operatorname{sim}_{div}(\cdot)$ indicates the diversity.

MMR chooses the next candidate s^* such that

$$s^* = \operatorname*{argmax}_{s_i \in S^{2N} \setminus S^s} [\lambda \operatorname{sim}_{qua}(s_i, q) - (1-\lambda)\operatorname{sim}_{div}(s_i, S^s))] \tag{3}$$

where λ is a hyper-parameter balancing these two aspects. Thus the fine-grained selection improves the diversity and retains the quality of subsequences at each time of decoding, so the generated replies are of good quality and diversity.

3.2 Quality and Diversity Metrics

The fine-grained selection allows explicit definition of quality and diversity measurements, which are presented in this section.

Quality Metric. The semantic coherence with the query, which is based on the word-level similarity, defines the quality of each candidate subsequence. For each word in the query, we find the best match-

ing word in the subsequence using the cosine similarity of the word embeddings (Mikolov et al., 2015, 2013). Then we sum over all the similarity scores as the final quality score given by

$$\operatorname{sim}_{qua}(s_i, q) = \frac{1}{|q|} \sum_{w_i \in q} \operatorname*{argmax}_{w_j \in s_i} \cos(\boldsymbol{e}_{w_i}, \boldsymbol{e}_{w_j}) \tag{4}$$

where $\boldsymbol{e}_{w_i}$ refers to the embedding of word w_i.

Diversity Metric. The diversity score of a subsequence measures its differences against existing subsequences in the selected set S^s by the word overlapping. We represent a subsequence s_i as a vector and measure the similarity by the cosine score; the average indicates overall diversity,

$$\operatorname{sim}_{div}(s_i, S^s) = \frac{1}{|S^s|} \sum_{s_j \in S^s} \cos(\boldsymbol{s}_i, \boldsymbol{s}_j) \tag{5}$$

where $\boldsymbol{s}_i$ is a binary word vector, each element indicating if a word appears in s_i; the vector length is the number of words in s_i and s_j. Notice that, for diversity, we use binary word vectors instead of embeddings to explicitly avoid word overlap among (top-ranked) candidate subsequences.

4 Experiments

4.1 Dataset

We evaluated each approach on a massive Chinese conversation dataset crawled from Baidu Tieba[1]. There were 1,600,000 query-reply pairs for training, 2000 pairs for validation, and another unseen 2000 pairs for testing. We performed standard Chinese word segmentation.

4.2 Experimental Setups

All the methods are established on the base of the traditional `seq2seq` with same settings. In our study, word embeddings were 610d and hidden layers were 1000d, following the settings in Shang et al. We applied AdaDelta with default hyper-parameters. We kept 100k words (Chinese terms) for both queries and replies, but 30k for the decoder's output due to efficiency concerns. λ in MMR scores was empirically set to 0.5; the beam size was 30.

4.3 Algorithms for Comparison

• **Beam Search (BS).** The standard beam search in `seq2seq` which acts as the baseline.

---

[1] http://tieba.baidu.com

Method	Top-1		Top-5		Top-10		Quality
	BLEU-1	BLEU-2	BLEU-1	BLEU-2	BLEU-1	BLEU-2	
BS	0.679	0.254	1.803	0.555	2.959	0.980	0.703
DD	0.790	0.192	1.893	0.480	2.991	0.802	0.727
DBS	0.358	0.111	1.123	0.224	2.264	0.401	0.553
MMR-BS	**2.626**	**0.802**	**5.154**	**1.270**	**6.672**	**2.019**	**0.791**

Table 1: Results of quality evaluation. Inter-annotator agreement for human annotation: Fleiss' $\kappa = 0.5698$ (Fleiss, 1971), std $= 0.3453$.

Method	Top-1				Top-5				Top-10			
	distinct-1	distinct-2	distinct-3	distinct-4	distinct-1	distinct-2	distinct-3	distinct-4	distinct-1	distinct-2	distinct-3	distinct-4
BS	0.100	0.261	0.366	0.624	0.038	0.148	0.259	0.346	0.021	0.101	0.200	0.291
DD	0.130	0.333	0.489	0.623	0.047	0.191	0.334	0.448	0.027	0.134	0.263	0.377
DBS	0.113	0.321	0.495	0.649	0.056	0.206	0.371	0.524	0.036	0.171	0.334	0.487
MMR-BS	**0.152**	**0.510**	**0.725**	**0.840**	**0.063**	**0.326**	**0.600**	**0.776**	**0.037**	**0.243**	**0.517**	**0.729**

Table 2: Results of distinct scores.

Method	Top-1	Top-5	Top-10	Rates
BS	0.759	0.765	0.796	56.53%
DD	0.849	0.830	0.846	50.30%
DBS	0.901	0.897	**0.892**	45.53%
MMR-BS	**0.939**	**0.910**	0.878	**15.67%**

Table 3: Results of diverse scores and the rates of the universal replies in Top-10 reply list. Fleiss' $\kappa = 0.2540$ (Fleiss, 1971), std $= 1.563$.

- **Diverse Decoding (DD).** A work proposed by Li et al., which assigns low scores to sibling subsequences.
- **Diverse Beam Search (DBS).** A work proposed by Vijayakumar et al., which adds a similarity punishment to the scoring function.
- **MMR-BS.** The proposed model in this paper, which applies the MMR in the decoding process to select the subsequences.

4.4 Evaluation Metrics

We evaluated each method in terms of two aspects, namely the quality and the diversity. All the subjective evaluation experiments are conducted on 100 randomly sampled cases.

- **Quality Evaluation** We used BLEU scores as objective metrics to measure the coherence between the user-issued query and candidate replies, which is also used in (Li and Jurafsky, 2016; Vijayakumar et al., 2016). We calculated the BLEU scores of Top-1, Top-5 and Top-10 replies, and only display BLEU-1 and BLEU-2 scores due to the flexibility of conversation. We asked three well-educated volunteers to annotate the quality of the generated replies for each comparison method. The volunteers are asked to label each reply with a score: 0 for the improper reply, 1 for the borderline reply and 2 for the proper reply.

- **Diversity Evaluation** We used the distinct scores to measure the diversity in the generated replies, following (Li and Jurafsky, 2016; Vijayakumar et al., 2016). We also conducted the diverse scores, which is used in information retrieval to calculate the differentness between retrieved results (Zhang and Hurley, 2008),

$$\frac{2}{|R|(|R|-1)} \sum_{r_i \in R} \sum_{r_j \in R, r_i \neq r_j} (1 - \cos(\boldsymbol{r}_i, \boldsymbol{r}_j)) \tag{6}$$

where R is whole set of the generated replies and $\boldsymbol{r}_i$ is the binary word vector with same definition in Equation 5. We asked three well-educated volunteers to count the universal replies in the Top-10 reply list and calculated the rates.

4.5 Overall Performance

We presented the quality evaluation results in Table 1. DD achieves almost the same performance with the standard BS. DBS is not as good as the BS and DD. MMR-BS yields the highest BLEU scores and human annotation results, which indicates the effectiveness of the quality measurement.

We presented the diversity evaluation results in Table 2 and Table 3. BS achieves the worst performance as it does not consider about the diversity during the decoding process. DD is better than BS but not as good as DBS. DBS shows a good performance in terms of all the diversity evaluation and even outperforms MMR-BS in the Top 10 diverse score. MMR-BS outperforms all the other methods in most metrics. Compared with BS, it decreases the number of universal replies by 3 times, which is a significant improvement.

It is obvious that MMR-BS yields the highest quality and diverse scores. Compared with BS,

DD does not improve the quality very much but indeed fosters the diversity among the generated replies. DBS achieves a good diversity performance but is still worse than MMR-BS. As DBS does not perform well in quality, we can see that it sacrifices the quality to increase the diversity.

5 Related Work

To tackle diversity problem in generation-based systems, Li et al. propose a diverse decoding method[2] that avoids choosing sibling subsequences during decoding (Li and Jurafsky, 2016). Vijayakumar et al. propose a diverse beam search, which divides the subsequence into several groups during selection. These methods add a diversity punishment term to the scoring function in beam search; it is hard to balance this term with other components in the function.

MMR is widely used in information retrieval (Stewart and Carbonell, 1998), document summarization (Zhou, 2011), and text categorization (He et al., 2012). MMR allows an explicit definition of both quality and diversity, and linearly combines these two aspects. This property fits the requirements in subsequence selection in beam search where the candidate subsequences should be different from each other and retain the high coherence with the user-issued query at the same time.

6 Conclusions

In this paper, we propose an MMR-BS method to tackle the problem of diversity in generative conversation systems. MMR-BS deploys two granularities of subsequence selection during the decoding process. The first one continues to use the original scoring function, and the second one takes advantage of MMR to measure each subsequence, considering both the quality and diversity. The experimental results demonstrate the effectiveness of our method.

Acknowledgments

This paper is partially supported by the National Natural Science Foundation of China (NSFC Grant Nos. 61772039 and 91646202) and CCF-Tencent Open Research Fund.

---

[2] Originally, the approach is proposed for machine translation, but it applies to conversation systems naturally.

References

Dzmitry Bahdanau, Kyunghyun Cho, and Yoshua Bengio. 2015. Neural machine translation by jointly learning to align and translate. *ICLR*.

Kyunghyun Cho, Bart van Merrienboer, Caglar Gulcehre, Dzmitry Bahdanau, Fethi Bougares, Holger Schwenk, and Yoshua Bengio. 2014. Learning phrase representations using rnn encoder-decoder for statistical machine translation. *arXiv preprint arXiv:1406.1078*.

Joseph L Fleiss. 1971. Measuring nominal scale agreement among many raters. *Psychological Bulletin*, 76(5):378.

Liu He, Xianghong Zhang, Dayou Liu, Yanjun Li, and Lijun Yin. 2012. A feature selection method based on maximal marginal relevance. *Journal of Computer Research and Development*, pages 354–360.

Sepp Hochreiter and Jurgen Schmidhuber. 1997. Long short-term memory. *Neural computation*, 9(8):1735–1780.

Carbonell Jaime and Jade Goldstein. 1998. The use of MMR, diversity-based reranking for reordering documents and producing summaries. In *SIGIR*, pages 335–336.

Jiwei Li and Dan Jurafsky. 2016. Mutual information and diverse decoding improve neural machine translation. *arXiv preprint arXiv:1601.00372*.

Tomas Mikolov, Kai Chen, Greg Corrado, and Jeffrey Dean. 2013. Efficient estimation of word representations in vector space. *arXiv preprint arXiv:1301.3781*.

Tomas Mikolov, Ilya Sutskever, Kai Chen, Greg Corrado, and Jeffrey Dean. 2015. Distributed representations of words and phrases and their compositionality. *The Workshop on Vector Space Modeling for Natural Language Processing*, pages 8–16.

Lili Mou, Yiping Song, Rui Yan, Ge Li, Lu Zhang, and Zhi Jin. 2016. Sequence to backward and forward sequences: A content-introducing approach to generative short-text conversation. *arXiv preprint arXiv:1607.00970*.

Nikola Mrkšić, Diarmuid Ó Séaghdha, Blaise Thomson, Milica Gašić, Pei Hao Su, David Vandyke, Tsung Hsien Wen, and Steve Young. 2015. Multi-domain dialog state tracking using recurrent neural networks. In *ACL-IJCNLP*, pages 794–799.

Iulian V Serban, Alessandro Sordoni, Yoshua Bengio, Aaron Courville, and Joelle Pineau. 2016a. Building end-to-end dialogue systems using generative hierarchical neural network models. In *AAAI*, pages 3776–3783.

Iulian Vlad Serban, Alessandro Sordoni, Ryan Lowe, Laurent Charlin, Joelle Pineau, Aaron Courville, and Yoshua Bengio. 2016b. A hierarchical latent variable encoder-decoder model for generating dialogues. *arXiv preprint arXiv:1605.06069*.

Lifeng Shang, Zhengdong Lu, and Hang Li. 2015. Neural responding machine for short-text conversation. In *ACL-IJCNLP*, pages 1577–1586.

Yiping Song, Lili Mou, Rui Yan, Li Yi, Zinan Zhu, Xiaohua Hu, and Ming Zhang. 2016. Dialogue session segmentation by embedding-enhanced TextTiling. In *INTERSPEECH*, pages 2706–2710.

Jade Goldstein Stewart and Jaime G. Carbonell. 1998. The use of mmr and diversity-based reranking in document reranking and summarization. *Proceedings of the 14th Twente Workshop on Language Technology in Multimedia Information Retrieval.*, pages 335–336.

Ilya Sutskever, Oriol Vinyals, and Quoc V Le. 2014. Sequence to sequence learning with neural networks. In *NIPS*, pages 3104–3112.

Ashwin K Vijayakumar, Michael Cogswell, Ramprasath R Selvaraju, Qing Sun, Stefan Lee, David Crandall, and Dhruv Batra. 2016. Diverse beam search: Decoding diverse solutions from neural sequence models. *arXiv preprint arXiv:1610.02424*.

Baoxun Wang, Bingquan Liu, Chengjie SunXiao, and long Wang ad Bo Li. 2009. Adaptive maximum marginal relevance based multi-email summarization. *Artificial Intelligence and Computational Intelligence.*, pages 417–424.

Rui Yan, Yiping Song, and Hua Wu. 2016a. Learning to respond with deep neural networks for retrieval-based human-computer conversation system. In *SIGIR*, pages 55–64.

Rui Yan, Yiping Song, Xiangyang Zhou, and Hua Wu. 2016b. Shall I be your chat companion?: Towards an online human-computer conversation system. *ACM International on Conference on Information and Knowledge Management*, pages 649–658.

Lingpeng Yang, Donghong Ji, and Munkew Leong. 2007. Document reranking by term distribution and maximal marginal relevance for chinese information retrieval. *Information Processing and Management*, 43(2):315–326.

Mi Zhang and Neil Hurley. 2008. Avoiding monotony: Improving the diversity of recommendation lists. In *RecSys*, pages 123–130.

Zhigang Zhou. 2011. Combined features to maximal marginal relevance algorithm for multi-document summarization. *Journal of Convergence Information Technology*, pages 298–304.

Dialog for Language to Code

Shobhit Chaurasia and **Raymond J. Mooney**
Department of Computer Science
The University of Texas at Austin
shobhit@utexas.edu, mooney@cs.utexas.edu

Abstract

Generating computer code from natural language descriptions has been a long-standing problem. Prior work in this domain has restricted itself to generating code in one shot from a single description. To overcome this limitation, we propose a system that can engage users in a dialog to clarify their intent until it has all the information to produce correct code. To evaluate the efficacy of dialog in code generation, we focus on synthesizing conditional statements in the form of IFTTT recipes.

1 Introduction

Building a natural language interface for programmatic tasks has long been a goal of computational linguistics. This has been explored in a plethora of domains such as generating database queries (Zelle and Mooney, 1996; Berant et al., 2013; Yin et al., 2016), building regular expressions (Manshadi et al., 2013), commanding a robot (She et al., 2014), programming on spreadsheets (Gulwani and Marron, 2014), and event-driven automation (Quirk et al., 2015), each with its own domain-specific target language. Synthesis of computer programs in general-purpose programming languages has also been explored (Ling et al., 2016; Yin and Neubig, 2017). The existing work assumes that a working program can be generated in one shot from a single natural language description. However, in many cases, users omit important details that prevents the generation of fully executable code from their initial description.

Another line of research that has recently garnered increasing attention is that of dialog systems (Singh et al., 2002; Young et al., 2013). Dialog systems have been employed for goal-directed tasks such as providing technical support (Lowe et al., 2015) and travel information and booking (Williams et al., 2013), as well as in non-goal oriented domains such as social-media chat-bots (Ritter et al., 2011; Shang et al., 2015).

In this paper, we combine these two lines of research and propose a system that engages the user in a dialog, asking questions to elicit additional information until the system is confident that it fully understands the user's intent and has all of the details to produce correct, complete code. An added advantage of the dialog setting is the possibility of continuous improvement of the underlying semantic parser through conversations (Artzi and Zettlemoyer, 2013; Thomason et al., 2015; Weston, 2016), which could further increase success rates for code generation and result in shorter dialogs. We focus on a restrictive, yet important class of programs that deal with conditions, i.e., `if-then` statements. To this end, we use the IFTTT dataset released by Quirk et al. (2015). To the best of our knowledge, this is the first attempt to use dialog for code generation from language.

2 Task Overview

2.1 IFTTT Domain

IFTTT (if-this-then-that) is a web-service that allows users to automate simple tasks by creating short scripts, called *recipes*, through a GUI that enables them to connect web-services and smart devices. A recipe consists of a *trigger* — an event which fires the recipe — and an *action* — the task to be performed when the recipe is fired. A trigger is characterized by a *trigger channel* (the source of the event) and a *trigger function* (the nature of the event); an action is characterized by an *action channel* (the destination of the task to be performed) and an *action function* (the nature of that task). Users can share their recipes publicly with short descriptions of their functionalities.

Proceedings of the The 8th International Joint Conference on Natural Language Processing, pages 175–180,
Taipei, Taiwan, November 27 – December 1, 2017 ©2017 AFNLP

For example, a recipe with description "Text me when I am tagged in a picture on Facebook" might have trigger channel `facebook`, trigger function `you_are_tagged_in_a_photo`, action channel `sms`, and action function `send_me_an_sms`.

2.2 Problem Statement

Our goal is to synthesize IFTTT recipes from their natural language descriptions. Unlike prior work in this domain (Quirk et al., 2015; Dong and Lapata, 2016; Beltagy and Quirk, 2016; Liu et al., 2016), which restrict the system to synthesizing a recipe from a single description, we seek to enable the system to interact with users by engaging them in a dialog to clarify their intent when the system's confidence in its inference is low. This is particularly crucial when there are multiple channels or functions achieving similar goals, or when the initial recipe descriptions are vague.

3 Approach

We propose a dialog system with which users can converse using natural language to create recipes. It consists of three components: Dialog Manager, Natural Language Understanding (NLU), and Natural Language Generation (Jurafsky, 2000).

3.1 Dialog Manager

The aim of the dialog system is to determine values of channels and functions for the recipe that the user wants to create. We cast this problem as a slot-filling task, in which the system maintains a belief state — its current estimates for the slots — and follows a hand-coded policy to update its belief state until it is confident that the belief state is same as the user goal. The strategy is similar to the one used by Thomason et al. (2015).

3.1.1 Belief State

The belief state consists of four slots: `trigger_channel`, `trigger_function`, `action_channel`, and `action_function`. The slots naturally form a hierarchy: channels are above functions. Although triggers and actions are, in a loose sense, at the same level in the hierarchy[1], it is more natural to specify triggers before actions, thereby inducing a complete hierarchy over slots. This hierarchy is exploited in specifying a policy for the dialog system.

---

[1]Technically, the presence of *ingredients* — properties associated with trigger functions that can be utilized by action functions — puts triggers above actions in the hierarchy.

The system maintains a probability distribution over all possible values for each slot. After each user utterance, the probability distribution for one or more slots is updated based on the parse returned by the utterance parser (see Section 3.2). The system follows a hand-coded policy over the discrete state-space obtained from the belief state by assigning the values with highest probability (candidates with highest confidence) to each slot.

3.1.2 Static Dialog Policy

The dialog opens with an open-ended user utterance (a user-initiative) in which the user is expected to describe the recipe. Its parse is used to update all the slots in the belief state. The system moves down the slot-hierarchy, one slot at a time, and picks the next action based on the confidence of the top candidate for each slot. If the confidence is above α, the parse is accepted, and the candidate is assigned to that slot. If the confidence is below β, the parse is rejected, and the system requests information for that slot (a system-initiative). If the confidence is between α and β, the system seeks a confirmation of the candidate value for that slot; if the user affirms, the candidate is assigned to the slot, otherwise the system requests information for that slot. Value of α and β present a trade-off between dialog success and dialog length. $\alpha = 0.85$ and $\beta = 0.25$ were used in all the experiments, chosen by analyzing the performance of the dialog system on the IFTTT validation set.

3.2 Natural Language Understanding

This component is responsible for parsing user utterances. We use the model proposed by Liu et al. (2016): an LSTM-based classifier enhanced with a hierarchical, two-level attention mechanism (Bahdanau et al., 2014). In our system, the semantic parser is composed of a set of four such models, one for each slot. User-initiatives are parsed by all four models, while user responses to system-initiatives are parsed by the model corresponding to the slot under consideration.

3.3 Natural Language Generation

The dialog system uses templates and IFTTT API documentation to translate its belief state into a comprehensible utterance. For example, the confirmation request for the `blink_lights` action function of the `hue` action channel is: "Do you want to *briefly turn your hue lights off then back on* every time the applet is triggered?"

3.4 Retraining NLU using Dialog

Another advantage of using a dialog approach to recipe synthesis is that it unlocks the possibility of continuous parser improvement through conversations (Artzi and Zettlemoyer, 2013; Thomason et al., 2015; Weston, 2016). To this end, we extract training data from the dialogs. Opening user utterances and user utterances for each slot after a system-initiative in successful dialogs are paired with inferred slot values to retrain the models. Analysis of models' predictions on the validation set revealed that the attention mechanism was rather good at attending to relevant parts of an utterance; the models failed because they often couldn't pick the correct channel or function among the similar ones. Therefore, we tuned only the non-attention parameters during retraining.

4 Experiments

We trained our parser on the training set of the IFTTT corpus. Since the corpus was released, many recipes have been taken down; we could only obtain $66,588$ out of $77,495$ training recipes. We evaluated our system on the "gold" subset of the IFTTT test set created by Quirk et al. (2015) which consists of 550 recipes on which at least three humans presented with the recipe descriptions agreed with the true labels. We restricted ourselves to this subset because our experiments involved humans interacting with the dialog system to describe the recipe and answer its questions, and it was crucial that they themselves have a clear understanding of the recipe.

4.1 Experimental Setup

We used Amazon Mechanical Turk to conduct our experiments. Users were provided with recipe descriptions from the IFTTT corpus. Since descriptions could often be vague, we also explicitly provided them the details of channels and functions associated with the recipes. As noted in (Thomason et al., 2015), in which a similar interface was used to let users chat with a robot for performing navigation- and delivery-related tasks, information presented using words could linguistically prime the users. They avoided priming completely by presenting the information pictorially. Since it is unclear how to succinctly describe a recipe without using words, we, instead, used keywords for channels and functions (such as `event_starts` and `blink_lights`), which usually contain only

content words necessary to give an indication of their functionality, but are somewhat distant from natural language. Additionally, we encouraged users to use their own words based on their understanding of the recipe and restricted direct usage of these keywords. Fig. 1 shows a sample dialog.

ROBOT: Hi! Please describe the applet you want to create for automating the task you have on your mind.
YOU: Notify Glass to take and share pictures for Events.
ROBOT: Do you want an event on the Google Calendar service to trigger the applet?
YOU: yes
ROBOT: Which event on the Google Calendar service should cause the applet to run?
YOU: any event that will start
ROBOT: The applet will trigger within 15 minutes of the starting time of any event on your google calendar. It will use the Google Calendar service to look for this event. The action taken will be to send a notification to your google glass timeline. This action will be performed using the Google Glass service. Is this what you wanted?
YOU: yes
ROBOT: Ok, bye!

Figure 1: Dialog for a recipe with trigger `event_starts` on `google_calendar`, action `send_notification` on `google_glass`.

4.2 Dialog Experiments

We conducted two experiments to evaluate the efficacy of dialog in synthesizing recipes. In both the experiments, two baselines are used. First is the the best-performing model from Liu et al. (2016), currently the state-of-the-art on this task, provided only with initial recipe descriptions, as should be the case for a single-shot model. The second baseline, called "Concat," uses the same model as above, but is provided with all the user utterances from the conversation concatenated. By ensuring that both the single-shot and the dialog approach get same information, the Concat baseline provides a middle-ground between the two approaches, and is more fair to the single-shot system, but disguises its obvious deficiency: the lack of ability to ask for clarification.

4.2.1 Constrained User-Initiative

To evaluate our system directly on the test set, we constrained the users to use the original recipe descriptions as their first utterance (i.e. the user-initiative) when they were asked by the system to describe the recipe. This way, we can directly compare our results with prior work which uses this set for evaluation.

4.2.2 Free User-Initiative

To emulate a more realistic setting in which users drive the entire conversation, including the user-initiative, we allowed the users to provide the ini-

Experiment	Liu et al. (2016)	Concat Baseline	Ours	
	Accuracy	Accuracy	Accuracy	Avg. dialog length
Constrained UI	85.28^2	91.27	95.28	2.55
Free UI	66.0	77.82	81.45	4.04
After retraining	66.0	77.48	82.55	4.08

Table 1: Accuracy of recipe synthesis. Average dialog length is measured in terms of number of user utterances.

tial recipe descriptions themselves. For a fair comparison, we evaluated the Liu et al. (2016)'s baseline model on the initial descriptions provided in the conversations.

4.3 Results

The results are summarized in Table 1. The dialog approach boosts the accuracy of recipe synthesis considerably over the single-shot approach in both the experiments: 10 point increase with constrained user-initiative and over 15 point increase with free user-initiative. Even when the two approaches receive the same information (i.e., when the dialog approach is compared with the Concat baseline), the dialog approach boosts the accuracy by approximately 4 points.

Surprisingly, the accuracy of both the single-shot approach and the dialog approach fell dramatically in the experiment with free user-initiative. We contend that the reason behind this reduction is the difference between the two settings in which the recipe descriptions were created: Constrained UI experiment uses original descriptions written by the authors of the recipes with the aim of summarizing their recipes so that their functionality can be easily understood by others *without their assistance*. The descriptions used in Free UI experiment were provided by humans with the aim of describing the recipe to a system with the knowledge that the system can ask clarification questions. The former are expected to be more descriptive and self-contained than the latter. The larger average dialog length in the Free UI experiment further corroborates this point.

4.4 Parser Retraining

Parser retraining would be most helpful when the data is extracted from conversations that in-

volve channels and functions for which the existing parser's confidences are low. Therefore, we randomly sampled 100 recipes from an unused portion of the test set on which the confidence of existing parser is below β for at least two slots. About 130 data-points were extracted from conversations with humans over these recipes, and the four models were retrained.

4.4.1 Results

The accuracy of systems using retrained models is summarized in Table 1. For direct comparison, the dialog system with retrained models was evaluated using the user utterances from conversations in the Free UI experiment, except when its actions deviated from the original ones — due to an improved NLU component — in which case new user utterances were obtained. While retraining didn't improve the single-shot accuracy, there was a marginal improvement of 1.1 points in the dialog setting. Analysis of the conversations revealed that this was because the retrained models had lower confidence for some channels and functions for which it initially had high priors. On one hand, this helped the dialog system avoid getting stuck in an impasse when it assigns an incorrect value to a slot with high confidence without confirmation. On the other hand, this pessimism led to a slight increase in average dialog length.

5 Future Work

In this work, we focus only on conditionals. A natural extension would be to consider other programming constructs such as loops, procedure invocations, and sequence of execution. Dialog policy learning can be added to account for non-stationarity in the dialog environment due to parser learning (Padmakumar et al., 2017).

6 Conclusion

In this work, we demonstrated the efficacy of using dialog for mapping natural language to short, exe-

---

[2] The accuracy reported by Liu et al. (2016) is 87.5%. Our implementation of their system was able to achieve only 85.28% accuracy. The discrepancy could be because of a smaller training set (they had 68k recipes), a smaller gold test set (they had 584 recipes), or variance while training.

cutable computer code. We evaluated this idea in the domain of IFTTT recipes. The proposed system engaged the user in a dialog, asking questions to elicit additional information until it was confident in its inference, thereby increasing the accuracy on this task over the state-of-the-art models that are restricted to synthesizing recipes in one shot by $10 - 15$ points. Additionally, we demonstrated how data extracted from the conversations can be used for continuous parser learning.

Acknowledgments

We would like to thank the anonymous reviewers for their feedback, and Aishwarya Padmakumar for her ideas and insights. This work was supported by a grant from Microsoft Research.

References

Yoav Artzi and Luke Zettlemoyer. 2013. Weakly supervised learning of semantic parsers for mapping instructions to actions. *Transactions of the Association for Computational Linguistics* 1(1):49–62. https://homes.cs.washington.edu/ lsz/papers/aztacl13.pdf.

Dzmitry Bahdanau, Kyunghyun Cho, and Yoshua Bengio. 2014. Neural machine translation by jointly learning to align and translate. *CoRR* abs/1409.0473. http://arxiv.org/abs/1409.0473.

I. Beltagy and Chris Quirk. 2016. Improved semantic parsers for if-then statements. In *Proceedings of the 54th Annual Meeting of the Association for Computational Linguistics (Volume 1: Long Papers)*. Association for Computational Linguistics, pages 726–736. http://www.aclweb.org/anthology/P16-1069.

J. Berant, A. Chou, R. Frostig, and P. Liang. 2013. Semantic parsing on Freebase from question-answer pairs. In *Empirical Methods in Natural Language Processing (EMNLP)*. http://www.aclweb.org/anthology/D13-1160.

Li Dong and Mirella Lapata. 2016. Language to logical form with neural attention. In *Proceedings of the 54th Annual Meeting of the Association for Computational Linguistics (Volume 1: Long Papers)*. Association for Computational Linguistics, pages 33–43. http://www.aclweb.org/anthology/P16-1004.

Sumit Gulwani and Mark Marron. 2014. Nlyze: Interactive programming by natural language for spreadsheet data analysis and manipulation. In *Proceedings of the 2014 ACM SIGMOD International Conference on Management of Data*. ACM, SIGMOD '14, pages 803–814. http://doi.acm.org/10.1145/2588555.2612177.

Dan Jurafsky. 2000. *Speech & language processing*. Pearson Education India.

Wang Ling, Phil Blunsom, Edward Grefenstette, Karl Moritz Hermann, Tomáš Kočiský, Fumin Wang, and Andrew Senior. 2016. Latent predictor networks for code generation. In *Proceedings of the 54th Annual Meeting of the Association for Computational Linguistics (Volume 1: Long Papers)*. Association for Computational Linguistics, pages 599–609. http://www.aclweb.org/anthology/P16-1057.

Chang Liu, Xinyun Chen, Eui Chul Shin, Mingcheng Chen, and Dawn Song. 2016. Latent attention for if-then program synthesis. In *Advances in Neural Information Processing Systems 29*, Curran Associates, Inc., pages 4574–4582. http://papers.nips.cc/paper/6284-latent-attention-for-if-then-program-synthesis.pdf.

Ryan Lowe, Nissan Pow, Iulian Serban, and Joelle Pineau. 2015. The ubuntu dialogue corpus: A large dataset for research in unstructured multi-turn dialogue systems. In *Proceedings of the 16th Annual Meeting of the Special Interest Group on Discourse and Dialogue*. Association for Computational Linguistics, pages 285–294. http://aclweb.org/anthology/W15-4640.

Mehdi Manshadi, Daniel Gildea, and James Allen. 2013. Integrating programming by example and natural language programming. In *Proceedings of the Twenty-Seventh AAAI Conference on Artificial Intelligence*. AAAI Press, AAAI'13, pages 661–667. http://dl.acm.org/citation.cfm?id=2891460.2891552.

Aishwarya Padmakumar, Jesse Thomason, and Raymond J. Mooney. 2017. Integrated learning of dialog strategies and semantic parsing. In *Proceedings of the 15th Conference of the European Chapter of the Association for Computational Linguistics (EACL 2017)*. http://www.cs.utexas.edu/users/ai-lab/pub-view.php?PubID=127615.

Chris Quirk, Raymond Mooney, and Michel Galley. 2015. Language to Code: Learning Semantic Parsers for If-This-Then-That Recipes. *Proceedings of the 53rd Annual Meeting of the Association for Computational Linguistics and the 7th International Joint Conference on Natural Language Processing (Volume 1: Long Papers)* (July):878–888. http://www.aclweb.org/anthology/P15-1085.

Alan Ritter, Colin Cherry, and William B. Dolan. 2011. Data-driven response generation in social media. In *Proceedings of the Conference on Empirical Methods in Natural Language Processing*. Association for Computational Linguistics, EMNLP '11, pages 583–593. http://dl.acm.org/citation.cfm?id=2145432.2145500.

Lifeng Shang, Zhengdong Lu, and Hang Li. 2015. Neural responding machine for short-text conversation. In *Proceedings of the 53rd Annual Meeting of the Association for Computational Linguistics and the 7th International Joint Conference on Natural Language Processing (Volume 1: Long Papers)*. Association for Computational Linguistics, pages

1577–1586. http://www.aclweb.org/anthology/P15-1152.

Lanbo She, Shaohua Yang, Yu Cheng, Yunyi Jia, Joyce Chai, and Ning Xi. 2014. Back to the blocks world: Learning new actions through situated human-robot dialogue. In *Proceedings of the 15th Annual Meeting of the Special Interest Group on Discourse and Dialogue (SIGDIAL)*. Association for Computational Linguistics, pages 89–97. http://www.aclweb.org/anthology/W14-4313.

Satinder Singh, Diane Litman, Michael Kearns, and Marilyn Walker. 2002. Optimizing dialogue management with reinforcement learning: Experiments with the njfun system. *Journal of Artificial Intelligence Research* 16:105–133. https://www.jair.org/media/859/live-859-1983-jair.pdf.

Jesse Thomason, Shiqi Zhang, Raymond Mooney, and Peter Stone. 2015. Learning to interpret natural language commands through human-robot dialog. In *Proceedings of the 24th International Conference on Artificial Intelligence*. AAAI Press, IJCAI'15, pages 1923–1929. http://dl.acm.org/citation.cfm?id=2832415.2832516.

Jason E Weston. 2016. Dialog-based language learning. In *Advances in Neural Information Processing Systems 29*, Curran Associates, Inc., pages 829–837. http://papers.nips.cc/paper/6264-dialog-based-language-learning.pdf.

Jason Williams, Antoine Raux, Deepak Ramachandran, and Alan Black. 2013. The dialog state tracking challenge. In *Proceedings of the SIGDIAL 2013 Conference*. Association for Computational Linguistics, pages 404–413. http://www.aclweb.org/anthology/W13-4065.

Pengcheng Yin, Zhengdong Lu, Hang Li, and Ben Kao. 2016. Neural enquirer: Learning to query tables in natural language. In *Proceedings of the Twenty-Fifth International Joint Conference on Artificial Intelligence*. AAAI Press, IJCAI'16, pages 2308–2314. http://dl.acm.org/citation.cfm?id=3060832.3060944.

Pengcheng Yin and Graham Neubig. 2017. A syntactic neural model for general-purpose code generation. In *The 55th Annual Meeting of the Association for Computational Linguistics (ACL)*. Vancouver, Canada. https://arxiv.org/pdf/1704.01696.pdf.

Steve Young, Milica Gašić, Blaise Thomson, and Jason D Williams. 2013. Pomdp-based statistical spoken dialog systems: A review. *Proceedings of the IEEE* 101(5):1160–1179. http://ieeexplore.ieee.org/document/6407655/.

John M. Zelle and Raymond J. Mooney. 1996. Learning to parse database queries using inductive logic programming. In *AAAI/IAAI*. AAAI Press/MIT Press, Portland, OR, pages 1050–1055. http://www.cs.utexas.edu/users/ai-lab/?zelle:aaai96.

Using Analytic Scoring Rubrics in the Automatic Assessment of College-Level Summary Writing Tasks in L2

Tamara Sladoljev-Agejev[1] and **Jan Šnajder**[2]

[1] University of Zagreb, Faculty of Economics and Business, Zagreb, Croatia
[2] University of Zagreb, Faculty of Electrical Engineering and Computing,
Text Analysis and Knowledge Engineering Lab, Zagreb, Croatia
`tagejev@efzg.hr, jan.snajder@fer.hr`

Abstract

Assessing summaries is a demanding, yet useful task which provides valuable information on language competence, especially for second language learners. We consider automated scoring of college-level summary writing task in English as a second language (EL2). We adopt the Reading-for-Understanding (RU) cognitive framework, extended with the Reading-to-Write (RW) element, and use analytic scoring with six rubrics covering content and writing quality. We show that regression models with reference-based and linguistic features considerably outperform the baselines across all the rubrics. Moreover, we find interesting correlations between summary features and analytic rubrics, revealing the links between the RU and RW constructs.

1 Introduction

Writing summaries is a complex skill which relies on reading comprehension and the ability to convey the information contained in the source text(s). This makes summaries an important skill to develop for academic or professional purposes. Summary writing skills may therefore be tested in a recruitment process, or during admissions to universities, which may be particularly challenging for L2 writers who may still be struggling with lower levels of language competence such as grammar or vocabulary. This is why summary writing is sometimes used together with essays to assess university-level abilities in L2.

However, assessing L2 summaries is highly demanding, especially if analytic rubrics are involved, as they require raters' expertise and much concentration when assessing language proficiency at various levels (e.g., lexis, syntax, discourse). Moreover,

unlike in essays, in summaries raters are expected to put additional effort into checking for accuracy, relevance, completeness, and coherence of the summary against the source text. Automated scoring is thus of considerable importance to enhance assessment of summaries, especially in the context of higher education or professional environments.

This paper investigates automated scoring of summaries based on six analytic rubrics used in the assessment of college-level writing in English as a second language (EL2). The writing task assesses students' comprehension of complex texts and their ability to produce coherent writing. We build upon the Reading-for-Understanding (RU) cognitive framework (Sabatini et al., 2013) to which we add the Reading-to-Write (RW) element (e.g., Delaney (2008)) in order to analyze automated scoring both in terms of reading comprehension and writing quality.

The contribution of our work is threefold. Firstly, we experiment with regression models to predict six expert-rated analytic scores, and train models that utilize a combination of linguistic features that measure textual cohesion and coherence, as well as reference-based features that compare the summaries against the source texts and expert-compiled reference summaries. Secondly, we carry out a correlation analysis between the text features and analytic scores, discovering patterns that link the RW and RU constructs, including signals of inadequate L2 competence. Lastly, we compile and make available a dataset of expert-rated college-level summaries in EL2.[1]

2 Related Work

Automated scoring of student writing has attracted considerable attention due to the opportunity to analyze cognitive aspects of writing as well as a

---

[1] `http://takelab.fer.hr/el2-summaries`

Proceedings of the The 8th International Joint Conference on Natural Language Processing, pages 181–186,
Taipei, Taiwan, November 27 – December 1, 2017 ©2017 AFNLP

need to automate the time-consuming, cognitively demanding, and sometimes insufficiently reliable assessment process, e.g., (Burstein et al., 2013; Rahimi et al., 2015). Much has been done in the area of L1 and L2 essays, e.g., with Coh-Metrix (Crossley and McNamara, 2009; McNamara et al., 2010; Crossley and McNamara, 2011), and some studies have investigated automated scoring also in summaries, e.g., (Madnani et al., 2013). As assignments which demonstrate students' reading/writing skills and their broader academic abilities, summaries have been studied as part of university-level L2 assessment; e.g., integrated task in (Guo et al., 2013).

In such research, holistic scoring mostly supported by well-defined descriptors, e.g., (Rahimi et al., 2015), has predominantly been used to compare against automatically computed features to asses essay quality, e.g., (McNamara et al., 2010), coherence and related concepts such as comprehension in summaries, e.g., (Madnani et al., 2013; Mintz et al., 2014), ease of reading (Burstein et al., 2013) or essay organization. To the best of our knowledge, no research reports have been published on using human raters' multiple analytic scores in such studies.

From a technical perspective, the work most similar to ours is that of Madnani et al. (2013), whose model also uses reference-based features, source-copying features as well as a feature signaling text coherence for automated scoring of summaries. However, they frame the problem as a classification task and predict a single holistic score, whereas we frame the problem as a regression task and predict the scores for six rubrics.

3   Reading-for-Understanding and Reading-to-Write in L2

Summarization can be perceived as a Reading-for-Understanding (RU) task as discussed by Madnani et al. (2013) based on (Sabatini et al., 2013). In other words, summarizing includes lower- and higher-level comprehension processes leading to establishing coherence according to the most plausible intended meaning of the source text (Grosz and Sidner, 1986). Meaning is thus actively constructed by selecting and organizing the main ideas of the text into a coherent whole. When the result of comprehension processes is articulated in writing, there is a need to introduce cohesion devices which signal the rhetorical structure of the text and ensure a smooth flow of sentences. Summary writing is thus also a Reading-to-Write (RW) task (e.g., Delaney (2008)) demonstrating the ability to "convey information" as "a central component of real-world skills" (Foltz, 2016).

While there is a natural overlap between RU and RW (since RW includes and largely depends on RU), the difference between the two constructs is more prominent when summaries are written in L2. For example, a text which is mostly well understood by a non-native speaker may be poorly summarized due to insufficiently developed L2 writing leading to overreliance on bottom-up processing and lack of content integration. The RW manifestation of such problems may be "inability to paraphrase" and plagiarism, poor cohesion (Kirkland and Saunders, 1991), or weak text organization. Conversely, advanced L2 writing may sometimes combine with superficial reading (also seen in native speakers), resulting in factually inaccurate, incomplete, or incoherent summaries.

Analytic scoring based on different rubrics (e.g., accuracy, cohesion) is therefore particularly appropriate when assessing summaries in L2 as it offers more informative feedback (Bernhardt, 2010) and better captures different facets of L2 writing competence than holistic assessment (Weigle, 2002). However, analytic scoring is often exceptionally demanding for raters, especially in the case of longer texts and more than four or five scoring categories (CEFR), which motivates the use of automated assessment.

4   Data Collection

The research encompassed 114 first-year business undergraduates whose competence in English as L2 was predominantly upper intermediate and advanced. Two text-present summary writing tasks (tot. 228 summaries) were administered for two respective articles (ca. 900 words each) taken from *The Economist*, a renowned business magazine. Both times participants were required to read the article and write a summary of about 300 words. Participants were instructed that the summary should clearly present the main ideas to a third person who did not read the article.

In this work, we conceptualize RW as the ability to produce a well-organized writing with well-connected sentences (cohesion), clear paragraphing, topic sentences, and clear links between paragraphs (text organization), while RU is about covering the content of the source text accurately (factually accurate at the local level), completely (all the main ideas covered), relevantly (important ideas included), and coherently (a logical flow of ideas).

Two expert raters assessed the summaries on the 4-point analytic scales (grades 0–3) consisting of the RU content-based (accuracy/Acc, completeness/Cmp, relevance/Rev, and coherence/Chr), and RW text-based rubrics (cohesion/Chs, text organization/Org). The scales were quantified to the extent possible (e.g., by defining the number of cohesion breaks or accuracy errors for each grade). Inter-rater reliability measured by weighted kappas was as follows: accuracy 0.64, completeness 0.76, relevance 0.76, coherence 0.69, text organization 0.76, and cohesion 0.83. Despite adequate reliability, the relatively small number of summaries allowed the raters to discuss and agree all the grades.

Before automated scoring, all the summaries were checked for spelling and basic grammar (e.g., adding "s" to verbs in the present tense of the third person singular), as we were primarily interested in higher-level comprehension processes in the RU/RW construct, and not in grammar or spelling. Also, two reference summaries for each text were written by experts following the same instruction as the one given to students.

5   Automated Scoring

We frame the automated scoring as a multivariate regression task and train separate regression models for each of the six rubrics. Each regression model is trained to predict the expert-assigned score on a 0–3 scale. In using regression instead of classification, we utilize the ordinal nature of the rubric scores, but posit the equidistance of two consecutive scores.

Features.   Each of the six regression models is trained on the same set of features. The features can be grouped into reference-based features (BLEU, ROUGE, and "source-copying" features) inspired by (Madnani et al., 2013), and linguistic features derived from Coh-Metrix indices. For preprocessing (sentence segmentation and tokenization), we use the NLTK toolkit of Bird (2006).

- **BLEU** (Papineni et al., 2002) is a precision-based metric originally used for comparing machine-generated translations against reference translations. In our case, BLEU measures the n-gram overlap between the student's summary and the source text. The rationale is that a good

summary will refer to the ideas from – and hence likely reuse fragments of – the source text.

- **ROUGE** (Lin and Hovy, 2003), is a recall-oriented metric originally used for evaluating automated summarization systems. Following (Madnani et al., 2013), we use ROUGE to compare the student's summary against the two reference summaries. ROUGE is complementary to BLEU and measures to what extent the student's summary resembles the reference summaries. The intuition is that a good summary should cover all the ideas described in the reference summaries, which will be indicated by a high n-gram overlap between the two. We use five ROUGE variants: ROUGE-1, ROUGE-2, ROUGE-3, ROUGE-L, and ROUGE-SU4.

- Complementary to ROUGE, we adopt four source-copying features from (Madnani et al., 2013). **CopiedSumm** and **CopiedText** features are the sum of lengths of all the n-grams of length three or longer that are copied from the original text divided by the length of the summary and the source text, respectively. **MaxCopy** is the length of the longest n-gram copied from the source text. **FirstSent** is the number of source-text sentences that share an n-gram of length at least two with the first sentence of the summary.

- We use **Coh-Metrix** indices (Graesser et al., 2004; McNamara et al., 2014) to measure the cohesion and coherence of the summaries. The Coh-Metrix tool[2] computes a wide range of indices, from which we selected 48: 11 descriptive (DES), 12 referential cohesion (CRF) 8 LSA overlap, 9 connectives (CNC), and 8 situation model (SM) indices.

Models.   We use two regression algorithms: an L2-regularized linear regression model (Ridge regression) and a non-linear support vector regression (SVR) machine (Drucker et al., 1997) with an RBF kernel. Both algorithms rely on regularization to alleviate the problem of overfitting and multicollinearity. In addition, we experiment with feature selection based on the F-test for each feature, retaining all, 10, or 5 top-ranked features, yielding six different models. We use the sklearn implementation of the algorithms (Pedregosa et al., 2011).

Setup.   We evaluate the models using a nested 10×5 cross-validation, where the inner five folds

---

[2]http://cohmetrix.com

Model	Acc	Cmp	Rel	Chr	Org	Chs
Baseline	43.5	42.3	46.3	35.8	37.4	36.6
Ridge-all	42.2	51.6	46.8	42.3	39.3	48.1
Ridge-10	**54.1***	**54.1***	46.8	**47.7***	43.2	**55.9***
Ridge-5	**54.1***	50.2	**50.8***	47.3*	**44.5***	53.8*
SVR-all	44.8	47.2	49.4	35.8	39.7	36.6
SVR-10	30.3	37.9	41.3	35.3	28.2*	36.5
SVR-5	29.6*	39.5	35.2	34.4	36.2	37.4

Table 1: Accuracy of automated scoring across the six rubrics for the baseline and the six models using all, 10, and 5 features. Maximum scores for each rubric are shown in bold; "*" indicates statistically significant difference against baseline at p<0.05.

are used to optimize the hyperparameters via grid search. The models' performance is measured in terms of accuracy averaged over the five outer folds, by rounding the predictions to closest integers prior to computing the accuracy scores. All the features are z-scored on the train set, and the same transformation is applied on the test set. As the baseline for each rubric, we use the average expert-assigned score for that rubric. We use a two-tailed t-test to compare against the baseline, after having verified that the normality assumption is met.

Results. Table 1 shows the results. We observe that the performance varies considerably across the models and rubrics. The non-linear SVR models perform rather poorly in comparison to the baseline. On the other hand, ridge regression models with 5 or 10 features (depending on the rubric) outperform the baselines on all the six rubrics (the difference is significant at p<0.05). The improvement is most marked for cohesion and coherence (52% and 33% relative improvement, respectively), while the organization rubric appears to be the most difficult to predict. Feature selection improves the performance of ridge regression, suggesting that feature redundancy persists despite regularization.

6 Correlation Analysis

While the reference-based and linguistic features serve as good predictors for the analytic scores of college-level summaries in EL2, we expected not all the features to be equally important for all the scores. We therefore analyzed the correlations between the rubric scores and features which were ranked among the top five for any of the rubrics, plus the ROUGE-3 feature. Table 2 shows Spearman's rank correlation coefficients.

	Acc	Cmp	Rel	Chr	Org	Chs
BLEU	0.27	−0.38	−0.50	−0.51	−0.49	−0.60
CopiedOrig	0.30	−0.36	−0.48	−0.51	−0.49	−0.61
CopiedSumm	0.32	−0.35	−0.46	−0.52	−0.48	−0.59
MaxCopy	0.29	−0.35	−0.39	−0.40	−0.34	−0.38
CNCAdd		0.36	0.42		0.31	0.39
CNCAll		0.33	0.42	0.30	0.31	0.42
CNCLogic			0.39	0.34	0.40	0.46
CRFAOa			0.31	0.41	0.36	0.44
CRFCWOa			0.31	0.37	0.36	0.42
DESWLlt	0.29	0.28				
DESWLsy	0.28	0.28				
ROUGE-3			−0.30		−0.25	−0.34

Table 2: Correlations between top-ranked features and the six rubrics. Correlations of a magnitude <0.25 are omitted. All shown correlations are statistically significant at p<0.05.

The analysis reveals two correlation patterns between (1) human analytic scoring of RU (e.g., accuracy) and RW (e.g., cohesion), and (2) the computationally derived features (linguistic and reference-based). On the one side, accuracy (local, factual) is the only RU/RW dimension which correlates positively with BLEU and the three source-copying features (CopiedOrig, CopiedSumm, and MaxCopy). Moreover, accuracy and completeness are the only two dimensions positively correlating with word length features, which may also be related to the copying effort (plagiarism) when summarizing a demanding text at lower L2 competence.

On the other side, all the other RU/RW dimensions (completeness, relevance, coherence, organization, and cohesion) correlate negatively with the plagiarism-related indices, as well as with ROUGE-3. Also, positive correlations are found in all the RU/RW dimensions but accuracy with some or all of the indices relating to coherent writing (i.e., CNC connectors and CRF argument and content word overlaps). Furthermore, text organization and cohesion, the RW dimensions in our study, show the same correlation patterns as two key content-based criteria (RU): relevance and coherence.

7 Conclusion

In this paper we considered automated scoring of a college-level summary writing task in English as a second language (EL2), building on the Reading-for-Understanding (RU) cognitive framework to which we added the Reading-to-Write (RW) element. The automated scoring of the summaries was based on six analytic rubrics. A regularized regression model which uses a combination of reference-based and linguistic features outperformed the baseline model across all the six rubrics, yielding accuracies between 44.5% and 55.9% on a 4-point scale.

While this result needs to be improved to be of practical use, we discovered interesting links between RW and RU in L2 and the potential of our system to measure the construct analytically. Local accuracy found in summaries may to a large extent be related to plagiarism as a strategy demonstrating underperforming RW (rather than successful RU) as inadequate L2 and/or less developed academic ability prevent comprehension and paraphrasing. Unlike accuracy, the other dimensions (completeness, relevance, coherence, text organization and cohesion) relate to active meaning construction when building a coherent mental representation (e.g., using connectors to clarify on the links between ideas), either in reading or writing. In RU, this may mean searching for relevant information, and integrating it into a coherent whole, while in RW, coherence is possibly achieved through cohesion and text organization.

Acknowledgments

We thank Svjetlana Kolić-Vehovec for her valuable advice on the construction of the analytic scales used in this study and to Višnja Kabalin-Borenić for her assistance in the assessment of the summaries we analyzed in this work. Our thanks also go to Marin Andrijašević for his technical support.

References

Elizabeth B. Bernhardt. 2010. *Understanding Advanced Second-Language Reading*. Routledge.

Steven Bird. 2006. NLTK: the natural language toolkit. In *Proceedings of the COLING/ACL on Interactive presentation sessions*, pages 69–72. Association for Computational Linguistics.

Jill Burstein, Joel Tetreault, and Martin Chodorow. 2013. Holistic discourse coherence annotation for noisy essay writing. *Dialogue & Discourse*, 4(2):34–52.

Scott A. Crossley and Danielle S. McNamara. 2009. Computational assessment of lexical differences in L1 and L2 writing. *Journal of Second Language Writing*, 18(2):119–135.

Scott A. Crossley and Danielle S. McNamara. 2011. Understanding expert ratings of essay quality: Coh-Metrix analyses of first and second language writing. *International Journal of Continuing Engineering Education and Life Long Learning*, 21(2-3):170–191.

Yuly Asencion Delaney. 2008. Investigating the reading-to-write construct. *Journal of English for Academic Purposes*, 7(3):140–150.

Harris Drucker, Chris J.C. Burges, Linda Kaufman, Alex Smola, and Vladimir Vapnik. 1997. Support vector regression machines. In *Advances in neural information processing systems*, pages 155–161.

Peter W. Foltz. 2016. Advances in automated scoring of writing for performance assessment. In *Handbook of Research on Technology Tools for Real-World Skill Development*, pages 659–678. IGI Global.

Arthur C. Graesser, Danielle S. McNamara, Max M. Louwerse, and Zhiqiang Cai. 2004. Coh-Metrix: Analysis of text on cohesion and language. *Behavior Research Methods*, 36(2):193–202.

Barbara J. Grosz and Candace L. Sidner. 1986. Attention, intentions, and the structure of discourse. *Computational Linguistics*, 12(3):175–204.

Liang Guo, Scott A. Crossley, and Danielle S. McNamara. 2013. Predicting human judgments of essay quality in both integrated and independent second language writing samples: A somparison study. *Assessing Writing*, 18(3):218–238.

Margaret R. Kirkland and Mary Anne P. Saunders. 1991. Maximizing student performance in summary writing: Managing cognitive load. *Tesol Quarterly*, 25(1):105–121.

Chin-Yew Lin and Eduard Hovy. 2003. Automatic evaluation of summaries using n-gram co-occurrence statistics. In *Proceedings of the 2003 Conference of the North American Chapter of the Association for Computational Linguistics on Human Language Technology-Volume 1*, pages 71–78. Association for Computational Linguistics.

Nitin Madnani, Jill Burstein, John Sabatini, and Tenaha O'Reilly. 2013. Automated scoring of a summary-writing task designed to measure reading comprehension. In *Proceedings of the Eighth Workshop on Innovative Use of NLP for Building Educational Applications*, pages 163–168. Association for Computational Linguistics.

Danielle S. McNamara, Scott A. Crossley, and Philip M. McCarthy. 2010. Linguistic features of writing quality. *Written Communication*, 27(1):57–86.

Danielle S. McNamara, Arthur C. Graesser, Philip M. McCarthy, and Zhiqiang Cai. 2014. *Automated evaluation of text and discourse with Coh-Metrix*. Cambridge University Press.

Lisa Mintz, Dan Stefanescu, Shi Feng, Sidney D'Mello, and Arthur Graesser. 2014. Automatic assessment of student reading comprehension from short summaries. In *Educational Data Mining 2014*.

Kishore Papineni, Salim Roukos, Todd Ward, and Wei-Jing Zhu. 2002. BLEU: A method for automatic evaluation of machine translation. In *Proceedings of the 40th Annual Meeting on Association for Computational Linguistics*, pages 311–318. Association for Computational Linguistics.

Fabian Pedregosa, Gaël Varoquaux, Alexandre Gramfort, Vincent Michel, Bertrand Thirion, Olivier Grisel, Mathieu Blondel, Peter Prettenhofer, Ron Weiss, Vincent Dubourg, Jake Vanderplas, Alexandre Passos, David Cournapeau, Matthieu Brucher, Matthieu Perrot, and Edouard Duchesnay. 2011. Scikit-learn: Machine learning in Python. *Journal of Machine Learning Research*, 12(Oct):2825–2830.

Zahra Rahimi, Diane J Litman, Elaine Wang, and Richard Correnti. 2015. Incorporating coherence of topics as a criterion in automatic response-to-text assessment of the organization of writing. In *Proceedings of the Tenth Workshop on Innovative Use of NLP for Building Educational Applications*, pages 20–30. Association for Computational Linguistics.

John Sabatini, Tenaha O'Reilly, and Paul Deane. 2013. Preliminary reading literacy assessment framework: Foundation and rationale for assessment and system design. *ETS Research Report Series*, 2013(2).

Sara Cushing Weigle. 2002. *Assessing Writing*. Cambridge University Press.

A Statistical Framework for Product Description Generation

Jinpeng Wang[1], Yutai Hou[2,*] Jing Liu[1], Yunbo Cao[3] and Chin-Yew Lin[1]
[1] Microsoft Research Asia, {jinpwa, liudani, cyl}@microsoft.com
[2] Harbin University of Technology, ythou@ir.hit.edu.cn
[3] Tencent Corporation, Beijing, yunbocao@tencent.com

Abstract

We present in this paper a statistical framework that generates accurate and fluent product description from product attributes. Specifically, after extracting templates and learning writing knowledge from attribute-description parallel data, we use the learned knowledge to decide *what to say* and *how to say* for product description generation. To evaluate accuracy and fluency for the generated descriptions, in addition to BLEU and Recall, we propose to measure what to say (in terms of attribute coverage) and to measure how to say (by attribute-specified generation) separately. Experimental results show that our framework is effective.

1 Introduction

In this paper, we study the problem of product description generation, i.e., given attributes of a product, a system automatically generates corresponding description for this product (see Fig. 1). One application for this task is in (voice) QA systems like Amazon Echo, where reading out the attributes of a product is not desirable. We also found that only 45% of descriptions contain more than 50 words after analyzing 40 million products from Amazon. Generating descriptions for the products which do not have descriptions, and explaining complex attributes of the product for better understanding are also valuable.

Data-to-text generation renders structured records into natural language (Reiter and Dale, 2000), which is similar to this problem. Statistical approaches were employed to reduce extensive

---

Attribute Name	Attribute Value
Processor	Intel Core i3-2350M
RAM Size	6 GB
Series	Dell Inspiron
	… …
Screen Size	15.6 inches
Hard Drive Size	500 GB

(a) Product attributes

With 6 GB of memory and a Genuine Intel Core i3-2350M processor, this Dell Inspiron laptop will boost your productivity and enhance your entertainment. The bright, 15.6 inches display showcases movies and games in stunning cinema clarity. …

(b) Generated description

Figure 1: Example of generating product description from product attributes.

development time by learning rules from historical data (Langkilde and Knight, 1998; Liang et al., 2009). Duboue and McKeown (2003) proposed a statistical approach to mine content selection rules for biography descriptions; Kondadadi et al. (2013) and Howald et al. (2013) proposed a statistical approach to select appropriate templates for weather report generation.

However, product description generation is different from above work. To generating a useful product description, a system needs to be aware of the relative importance among the attributes of a product and to maintain accuracy at the same time. Successful product description generation needs to address two major challenges: (1) *What to say*: decide which attributes should be included

Proceedings of the The 8th International Joint Conference on Natural Language Processing, pages 187–192,
Taipei, Taiwan, November 27 – December 1, 2017 ©2017 AFNLP

in the description; (2) *How to say*: decide how to order selected attributes in the description.

To tackle these problems, we introduce a statistical framework. Our approach has three significant merits. (1) *Coherent with fact*: we proposed to learn structured knowledge from training dataset, and use it to choose important attributes and determine the structure of description; (2) *Fluent*: the proposed approach is template-based which guarantees grammaticality of generated descriptions, and the proposed templated knowledge help to choose semantically correct template; (3) *Highly automated*: the proposed approach required only weak human intervention.

Moreover, in addition to the standard metrics for data-to-text generation, e.g, BLEU (Konstas and Lapata, 2013; Lebret et al., 2016; Kiddon et al., 2016); to evaluate accuracy and fluency of generated descriptions, we propose to measure what to say and how to say separately.

2 Problem Definition

Fig. 2 shows the system framework of product description generation. Our system first extracts sentence level templates and learns writing knowledge from a given parallel dataset, then generates a new description for an input data at the online stage by combining sentence level templates using the learned writing knowledge. The latter step which generates document from sentences is the core component of the product description generate framework. It is called *Document Planning* and is our focus in this paper.

Document Planning as a Ranking Problem In the online stage, given the attributes of a product and the extracted templates, we first generate candidate descriptions by combining all valid templates which fit the given attributes, and then rank the candidate descriptions with the learned writing knowledge. After formulating it as a ranking problem, it is flexible to integrate all kinds of features to estimate the quality of the generated descriptions.

Sentence Level Template Extraction Given a parallel dataset, we first align descriptions and theirs corresponding attributes to extract templates. Several studies (Liang et al., 2009; Kondadadi et al., 2013; Lebret et al., 2016) can be applied to solve this problem. In this paper, we follow the approach which is proposed by Kondadadi et al. (2013). Table 1 shows some sample extracted

---

Original Text:
- The massive 8 GB of memory will allow you to have lots of files open at the same time.
- The D520 laptop installed with Windows 7.

Extracted Sentence Level Templates:
- The massive **[RAM Size]** of memory will allow you to have lots of files open at the same time.
- The <u>D520</u> laptop installed with [**Operating System**].

Table 1: Extracted template examples. Words in bracket are aligned attributes; words with underline are attributes missing in template extraction.

templates.

3 Document Planning with Writing Knowledge

Product description generation is far more than simply combining sentences level templates. As we have discussed in the introduction, there are two main challenges for this problem: *what to say* and *how to say*. To solve these problems, we propose to learn templated knowledge and structured knowledge, and use them for ranking generated candidate descriptions.

3.1 Templated Knowledge

At the first step of generating description in the online stage, we fill the extracted templates with the attributes of the input data. However, the extracted templates are with different quality or might have semantic gap with the filled values.

Value Preference For the first extracted template shown in Table 1, the context words in this template depend on value of "RAM Size" strongly. This template is more coherent with products whose "RAM Size" is "8 GB" or "16 GB" rather than that is "1 GB". To calculate the relatedness between attribute value v_a and template t, we define value preference as:

$$\text{ValPref}(v_a, t) = \sum_{v_i \in \text{V}(t)} \left(1 - \text{Dist}(v_a, v_i) \right) P(v_i),$$

$$(1)$$

where $\text{V}(t)$ is all values of an attribute which are extracted from template t in training data[1],

[1]To avoid sparseness on values, we use context words which surrounding attribute to represent template instead of using all words. In this paper, we combine the proceeding two words and the following ten words as context.

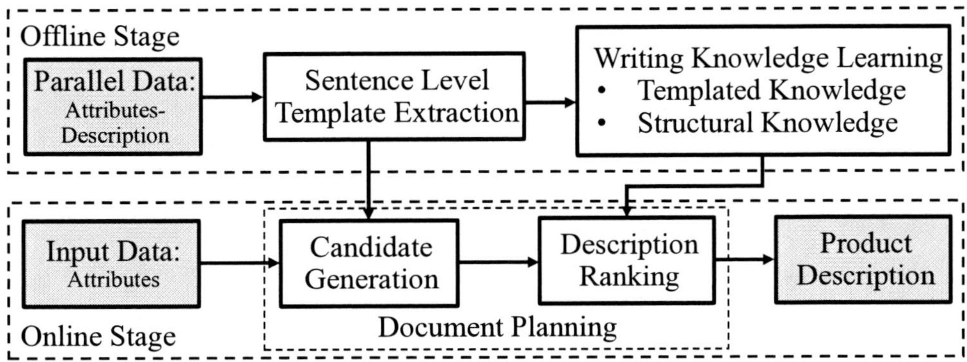

Figure 2: The system framework.

$P(v_i)$ is the probability of value v_i in $V(t)$, and $\text{Dist}(v_a, v_i)$ is defined as distance between two values. We can treat all values of attribute as string type, and use normalized editing distance to measure $\text{Dist}(v_a, v_i)$[2]. To improve accuracy for specific domain, for attributes with numerical values[3], $\text{Dist}(v_a, v_i) = \frac{|v_a - v_i|}{v_a^{(max)} - v_a^{(min)}}$, where $v_a^{(max)}$, $v_a^{(min)}$ are the upper and lower bound of attribute a in training data.

Missing Attribute For the second extracted template shown in Table 1, "D520" is an attribute value which is missing in template extraction, and such low-quality template with unaligned attribute may hurt the performance of generated description. We define *Missing Attribute* as a word that contains capital letters or numbers, and use this metric as a metric to penalize templates with potential missing attributes during template selection.

3.2 Structured Knowledge

We would also like the generated description contains the important attributes of a product and coherent in semantic. This writing knowledge can be learned from training data.

Attribute Prior Not all attributes of a product are equally important and not all of them are mentioned in a description with the same probability. To capture this information, we define the prior of an attribute a_i as $P(a_i) = \frac{\text{Mention}(a_i)}{\sum_j \text{Mention}(a_j)}$, where $\text{Mention}(a_i)$ is the number of mention of attribute a_i in the extracted templates.

Attribute Dependency It is worth noting that attributes which are mentioned in a description are interrelated. For example, in descriptions of computers, "CPU" usually mentioned in the first sentence and "RAM Speed" usually follows "RAM Size". To capture such information, the dependency between attribute a_i and a_j can be defined as $P(a_i|a_j) = \frac{\text{Co-occurrence}(a_i, a_j)}{\sum_k \text{Co-occurrence}(a_k, a_j)}$, where $\text{Co-occurrence}(a_i, a_j)$ is the count of a_i and a_j mentioned in consecutive sentences[4]. For a document d which is constructed by sentences $(s_1, ..., s_n)$, where each sentence s_i contains a set of attributes $(a_{i,1}, ...a_{i,|s_i|})$. We assume that current sentence s_i depend only on its previous sentence s_{i-1}, and the structured score for document d can be defined as

$$\text{Struct}(d) = \sum_{i=2}^{n} P(s_i|s_{i-1}) = \sum_{i=2}^{n} \frac{P(s_i, s_{i-1})}{\sum_l P(s_{(l)}, s_{i-1})},$$
(2)

where $P(s_i, s_{i-1})$ has multiple choices, e.g., $\sum_{j,k}\{P(a_{i,j}|a_{i-1,k})\}$, $\max_{j,k}\{P(a_{i,j}|a_{i-1,k})\}$ or $\min_{j,k}\{P(a_{i,j}|a_{i-1,k})\}$.

3.3 Ranking the Generated Descriptions

We first generate candidate descriptions for ranking. Given the attributes of a product, we fill the attribute values into templates which have corresponding slots, and treat all the combinations of filled templates as generated candidate descriptions. We then adopt SVM-rank (Joachims, 2002) with linear kernel to rank the candidate descriptions, and treat the top candidate as the answer. Specifically, we use BLEU score between refer-

---

[2] Normalized by the longer length of v_a and v_i.

[3] Improvement will be made even if just creating $\text{Dist}(.,.)$ for the common attributes. In our case, only "RAM Size" and "Hard Disk Size" are treated as with numerical values.

[4] For convenience, two padded sentences [Begin] and [End] are inserted to the start and the end of splited sentences.

ence description and generated description as label score and use the features shown in Table 2.

Basic knowledge:
- # words;
- # sentences;
- # mentioned attributes.

Templated knowledge:
- Value preference: is described by Eq. 1. We calculate the sum, max and min of value preferences for all attributes in candidate document, and treat them as separated features;
- # missing attribute: is described in Section 2.

Structured knowledge:
- Attribute prior: is the sum of attribute priors for attributes mentioned in candidate description.
- Attribute dependency: is described by Eq. 2. The structured scores which based on different version of $P(s_i, s_{i-1})$ are treated as separated features;

Table 2: Features of ranking model.

4 Experiments

4.1 Dataset

We collect the dataset, i.e., (description, attributes) pairs, from category "Computers & Tablets" from Amazon.com, and discard products whose description contains less than 100 words or whose attribute list contains less than five attributes. Table 3 shows the statistics[5]. This dataset has been divided into three parts to provide training (70%), validation (10%) and test sets (20%).

Parameter	Value
# (description, attribute table) pairs	25,375
Avg. # of words in description	117.4
Avg. # of sentences in description	4.7
Avg. # of attributes in attribute list	21.2

Table 3: Dataset statistics.

4.2 Compared Methods

We compare these methods in experiments: *Basic*, *+Templated*, *+Structured* and *Full* are ranked based on basic features, basic+templated features, basic+structured features and basic+templated+structured features respectively; *WordCount* and *AttriCount* are rankers which sort candidates in the descending order of word count and attribute count respectively; *OracleBLEU* is an oracle ranker which always chooses the top candidate in term of BLEU as the answer (can be seen as the upper bound of ranking).

4.3 Overall Performance

First of all, we show an example of generated description in Table 5. We adopt language similarity BLEU (Papineni et al., 2002) and retrieval accuracies top-K recall[6] as our evaluation metrics, which are widely used in related work. Table 4 shows that both of structured information and template information help improve the overall performance, and the full model achieves the best performance. Notice that the upper bound in term of BLEU is only 31.5, so the above performance is acceptable. For Recall, both Value Preference and Attribute Prior are the most useful features for retrieving the groundtruth.

Method	BLEU	Recall@3
Basic	13.2 (↑0%)	0.409 (↑0%)
+Structured	14.0 (↑6.1%)	0.795 (↑94.2%)
+Templated	15.3 (↑15.9%)	0.717 (↑75.2%)
Full	**15.4** (↑16.7%)	**0.803** (↑96.1%)
WordCount	13.1	0.255
AttriCount	11.3	0.155
OracleBLEU	31.5	1.000

Table 4: Overall performance.

4.4 Attribute Coverage

We propose to evaluate attribute coverage which is important for product description generation. For example, a product in our dataset has 21.2 attributes on average, while only 7.6 attributes are mentioned in a reference description on average. Specifically, we extract attributes which mentioned in a reference description, and compare them with those in its corresponding generated descriptions. From Table 6, we can see that by considering structured information *+Structured* is better than *+Templated* in term of attribute coverage while that is on the contrary in term of BLEU.

---

[5]The dataset will be available at `http://joopoo.github.io`

[6]The recall rate of a groundtruth (in this case the reference description) retrieval given top K candidates.

Original Description	Generated Description
Dell Inspiron 15 5000 15-5547 15.6" Touchscreen LED (In-plane Switching (IPS) Technology) Notebook - Intel Core i7 i7-4510U 2 GHz - Silver - 16 GB RAM - 1 TB HDD - Intel HD Graphics 4400 - Windows 8.1 64-bit (English) - 1920 x 1080 Display - Bluetooth - E i5547-12500sLV (Product Link: `www.amazon.com/dp/B00LGNL5S6`)	This Dell Inspiron 15-5558 laptop gives you the everyday features you need, at a great value! It runs many services simultaneously and the dynamic combination of the 2 GHz Intel Core i7 processor and 16 GB RAM enables the acute ability to focus on concurrent tasks with minimal performance degradation. It features an elegant design, includes enhancements to the apps you use most, and enables your PC and Windows 8 devices to work together in amazing ways. With flexible technology and service options, wireless connectivity, and Intel processors packed into a compact system, the Dell Inspiron 15-5558 gives you the essential mobility that will get your business going places.

Table 5: An example of generated description.

It is worth noting that *OracleBLEU* which ranks generated descriptions in term of BLEU performs fair. This is because BLEU only takes word overlap into consideration but not attributes. In other words, descriptions that share same words obtain high BLUE scores, although they are talking about different attributes. For example, descriptions about "RAM" and "Hard Disk" may share same words as "massive" or "GB". From this point, attribute coverage can be seen as complementary to BLEU.

Method	Precision	Recall	F1
Basic	0.610	0.573	0.573
+Structured	0.615	0.590	0.584
+Templated	0.612	0.580	0.577
Full	**0.623**	0.611	**0.597**
WordCount	0.623	0.543	0.557
AttriCount	0.596	**0.621**	0.589
OracleBLEU	0.605	0.592	0.577

Table 6: Performance on attribute coverage.

4.5 Attribute-Specified Generation

After evaluating attribute coverage, we move to evaluate descriptions which are generated with specific attributes. This task can help us to evaluate quality of generating description by avoiding effect due to attribute selection. In another word, we generate a product description with a given subset of attributes which have been mentioned in the reference description instead of given the whole attributes. From Table 7 we can see better performance for all methods as attributes are

specified. Our methods still outperform baselines even when part of features are weakened in this setting, e.g., the prior scores in structured feature. This means that the basic and templated features are also helpful for description generation.

Method	BLEU	
Basic	19.9	(↑0%)
+Structured	20.2	(↑1.5%)
+Templated	20.7	(↑2.0%)
Full	**20.8**	(↑4.5%)
WordCount	19.5	
AttriCount	18.8	
OracleBLEU	30.1	

Table 7: Performance on attribute-specified description generation.

4.6 Human Evaluation

In this evaluation, the following factors are evaluated: (1) Fluency; (2) Correctness: how well the generated description fits corresponding attribute values; (3) Completeness: how well the generated description mentions most of main attributes; and 4) Salient Attribute Mention: how well the generated description highlights its salient attributes. We selected 50 random test products, and for each product we used a Likert scale ($\in [1, 5]$) and report averaged ratings among two annotators.

Table 8 shows the results. The *Full* method beats *WordCount* on all metrics which means that the proposed basic, templated and structured information are helpful. Our *Full* method outperforms *Reference* in term of Completeness as the latter tends to mention fewer attributes in descriptions.

Method	Full	WordCount	Reference
Fluency	4.07	3.67	**4.62**
Correctness	4.03	3.74	**4.87**
Completeness	**4.32**	4.13	4.04
Salient Attr.	4.01	3.76	**4.33**

Table 8: Human evaluation results on the generated and reference descriptions. Score $\in [1, 5]$.

5 Conclusions

In this paper, we proposed a statistical framework for product description generation. The proposed structured information and templated information are helpful for deciding what to say and how to say for description generation. In addition, a new evaluation process is proposed to measure the generated descriptions. The experimental results show that our framework is effective in generating accurate and fluent product description.

References

Pablo A. Duboue and Kathleen R. McKeown. 2003. Statistical acquisition of content selection rules for natural language generation. In *Proceedings of the 2003 Conference on Empirical Methods in Natural Language Processing*, EMNLP '03, pages 121–128, Stroudsburg, PA, USA. Association for Computational Linguistics.

Blake Howald, Ravikumar Kondadadi, and Frank Schilder. 2013. Domain adaptable semantic clustering in statistical NLG. In *Proceedings of the 10th International Conference on Computational Semantics (IWCS 2013) – Long Papers*, pages 143–154, Potsdam, Germany. Association for Computational Linguistics.

Thorsten Joachims. 2002. Optimizing search engines using clickthrough data. In *Proceedings of the Eighth ACM SIGKDD International Conference on Knowledge Discovery and Data Mining*, KDD '02, pages 133–142, New York, NY, USA. ACM.

Chloé Kiddon, Luke Zettlemoyer, and Yejin Choi. 2016. Globally coherent text generation with neural checklist models. In *Proceedings of the 2016 Conference on Empirical Methods in Natural Language Processing, EMNLP 2016, Austin, Texas, USA, November 1-4, 2016*, pages 329–339.

Ravi Kondadadi, Blake Howald, and Frank Schilder. 2013. A statistical NLG framework for aggregated planning and realization. In *Proceedings of the 51st Annual Meeting of the Association for Computational Linguistics (Volume 1: Long Papers)*, pages 1406–1415, Sofia, Bulgaria. Association for Computational Linguistics.

Ioannis Konstas and Mirella Lapata. 2013. Inducing document plans for concept-to-text generation. In *Proceedings of the 2013 Conference on Empirical Methods in Natural Language Processing, EMNLP 2013, 18-21 October 2013, Grand Hyatt Seattle, Seattle, Washington, USA, A meeting of SIGDAT, a Special Interest Group of the ACL*, pages 1503–1514.

Irene Langkilde and Kevin Knight. 1998. Generation that exploits corpus-based statistical knowledge. In *Proceedings of the 36th Annual Meeting of the Association for Computational Linguistics and 17th International Conference on Computational Linguistics - Volume 1*, ACL '98, pages 704–710, Stroudsburg, PA, USA. Association for Computational Linguistics.

Rémi Lebret, David Grangier, and Michael Auli. 2016. Neural text generation from structured data with application to the biography domain. In *Proceedings of the 2016 Conference on Empirical Methods in Natural Language Processing, EMNLP 2016, Austin, Texas, USA, November 1-4, 2016*, pages 1203–1213.

Percy Liang, Michael I. Jordan, and Dan Klein. 2009. Learning semantic correspondences with less supervision. In *Proceedings of the Joint Conference of the 47th Annual Meeting of the ACL and the 4th International Joint Conference on Natural Language Processing of the AFNLP: Volume 1 - Volume 1*, ACL '09, pages 91–99, Stroudsburg, PA, USA. Association for Computational Linguistics.

Kishore Papineni, Salim Roukos, Todd Ward, and Wei-Jing Zhu. 2002. Bleu: A method for automatic evaluation of machine translation. In *Proceedings of the 40th Annual Meeting on Association for Computational Linguistics*, ACL '02, pages 311–318, Stroudsburg, PA, USA. Association for Computational Linguistics.

Ehud Reiter and Robert Dale. 2000. *Building Natural Language Generation Systems*. Natural Language Processing. Cambridge University Press.

Automatic Text Summarization Using Reinforcement Learning with Embedding Features

Gyoung Ho Lee, Kong Joo Lee
Information Retrieval & Knowledge Engineering Lab.,
Chungnam National University,
Daejeon, Korea
gyholee@gmail.com, kjoolee@cnu.ac.kr

Abstract

An automatic text summarization system can automatically generate a short and brief summary that contains a main concept of an original document. In this work, we explore the advantages of simple embedding features in Reinforcement leaning approach to automatic text summarization tasks. In addition, we propose a novel deep learning network for estimating Q-values used in Reinforcement learning. We evaluate our model by using ROUGE scores with DUC 2001, 2002, Wikipedia, ACL-ARC data. Evaluation results show that our model is competitive with the previous models.

1 Introduction

In this work, we present extractive text summarization for a single document based on Reinforcement leaning (RL) method. One of the advantages of the extractive approach is that a summary consists of linguistically correct sentences as long as a source document has a certain level of linguistic quality.

One of the most well-known solutions of extractive text summarization is to use maximal marginal relevance (MMR) (Goldstein et al., 2000). However, MMR cannot take into account for the quality of a whole summary because of its greediness (Ryang and Abekawa, 2012). Another solution is to use optimization techniques such as integer linear programming (ILP) to infer the scores of sentences with consideration of the quality of a whole summary (McDonald, 2007). However, these methods have a very large time complexity so they are not applicable for text summarization tasks.

A Reinforcement Learning method would be an alternative approach to optimize a score function in extractive text summarization task. Reinforcement learning is to learn how an agent in an environment behaves in order to receive optimal rewards in a given current state (Sutton, 1998).

The system learns the optimal policy that can choose a next action with the most reward value in a given state. That is to say, the system can evaluate the quality of a partial summary and determine the sentence to insert in the summary to get the most reward. It can produce a summary by inserting a sentence one by one with considering the quality of the hypothetical summary. In this work, we propose an extractive text summarization model for a single document based on a RL method.

A few researchers have proposed the RL approaches in automatic text summarization (Goldstein et al., 2000; Rioux et al. 2014; Henß et al. 2015). Previous studies mainly exploited hand-crafted complex features in RL-based automatic text summarization. However, choosing important features for a task, re-implementing the features for a new domain, and re-generating new features for a new application are very difficult and time-consuming jobs. The recent mainstream of NLP applications with Deep Learning is to reduce the burden of hand-crafted features. Embedding is one of the simplest deep learning techniques to build features that represent words, sentences, or documents. It has already shown state-of-the art performance in many NLP applications.

The main contributions of our work are as follows: first, we explore the advantages of simple embedding features in RL approach to automatic text summarization tasks. Content embeddings vector and position embeddings vector are only

Proceedings of the The 8th International Joint Conference on Natural Language Processing, pages 193–197,
Taipei, Taiwan, November 27 – December 1, 2017 ©2017 AFNLP

features that our system adopts. Second, we propose a novel deep learning network for estimating Q-values used in RL. This network is devised to consider the relevance of a candidate sentence for an entire document as well as the naturalness of a generated summary.

We evaluate our model by using ROUGE scores (Lin, 2004) and show that the performance of our model is comparable to that of the previous studies which rely on as many features as possible.

2   Related Work

As far as we know, Ryang and Abekawa (2012) have so far been the first ones who applied RL to the text summarization. The authors regard the extractive summarization task as a search problem. In their work, a state is a subset of sentences and actions are transitions from one state to the next state. They only consider the final score of the whole summary as reward and use TD(λ) as RL framework. Rioux et al. (2014) extended this approach by using TD. They employed ROUGE as part of their reward function and used bi-grams instead of tf $*$ idf as features. Henß and Mieskes (2015) introduced Q-learning to text summarization. They suggest RL-based features that describe a sentence in the context of the previously selected sentences and how adding this sentence changes hypothetical summary. Our work extends previous work using DQN based algorithm and embedding features.

3   Model for Automatic text summarization

In this work, we apply the Deep Q-Networks (DQN)-based model (Volodymyr et al. 2015) to automatic text summarization tasks. In the case of text summarization, the state denotes a summary which can still be incomplete and the action denotes the addition of a sentence to this summary. For using RL method in text summarization, there are two parameters that should be predefined. One is a length limitation of a summary. The other parameter is a reward value for a partial summary. In this work, we use the same length limitation and reward function used in Henß et al., (2015). The reward function is defined as:

$$Reward(\text{state}_t, \text{state}_{t+1}) =$$
$$Score(\text{state}_{t+1}, \text{Hd}) - Score(\text{State}_t, \text{Hd}) \quad (1)$$

In the above equation, *Score* measures the quality of the partial summary (state) by comparing it with the corresponding human reference summary **Hd**. We use the ROUGE-2 score for the measurement.

3.1   Q-Network

Q-learning models the value $Q(s_t; a_t)$ of performing an action a_t in the current state s_t. We use a deep neural network model with a regression function to compute the Q-values.

The model can calculate a Q-value based on a partial summary (current state) and a candidate sentence (action). The output Q-value indicates the expectation value that the agent can get when it selects the candidate sentence as a part of the summary. Figure 1 shows the Q-network model we propose in this work.

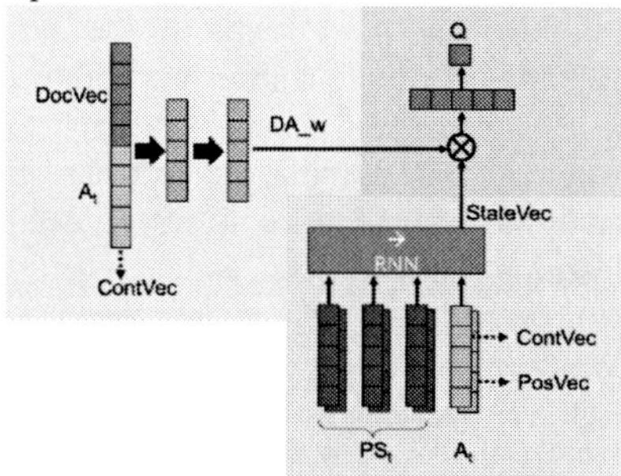

Figure 1: Architecture of our Q-network

The Q-network model consists of three modules shown in Figure 1. First module (upper left in the figure) is to represent that a semantic relationship between the input document and the candidate sentence (A_t). The input document is provided as DocVec in which the whole meaning of the document is embedded. The candidate sentence is represented as a sentence embedding vector ContVec. The vector DocVec and ContVec are the inputs to this module. The output of the module is vector DA_w, which is calculated as :

$$DA\_w = sigmoid\left(W_{da_{out}}, \text{hidden}_{da}\right) \quad (2)$$
$$\text{hidden}_{da} = \tanh\left(w_{da_{hidden}}, Input_{da}\right) \quad (3)$$
$$input_{da} = Concat(DocVec, ContVec \ of \ A_t) \quad (4)$$

For simplicity, the biases are all omitted in the equations. The active function of the output layer is sigmoid function so that each element in DA_w has a value between 0~1.

The second module (bottom right in the figure) is to represent the relationship between the partial summary and the candidate sentence. The module is constructed as a RNN (Recurrent Neural Network), in which the candidate sentence appears in the given partial summary(PS) as a history. Each sentence is represented as the two vectors which contain the content information(ContVec) and the position information(PosVec), respectively. Through the RNN, the partial summary and the candidate sentence are transformed into the final state vector (StateVec). We implement the RNN which uses GRU unit and tanh activation function, and outputs 50-dimensional state vector.

The third module (upper center in the figure) takes the DA_w and StateVec as the input, and calculates the Q-value as the output. It combines the two vectors into element-wise dots and converts them into Q-value through a linear regression function. The output Q-value is the expected value that can be obtained when a new summary is generated by inserting a candidate sentence into a partial summary.

3.2 Reinforcement Learning in Text Summarization

The agent of the text summarization in this work has a sentence *Selector* and three memories. The role of the agent is to generate a summary for an input document by using the sentence *Selector*. The agent has the following three memories. 1) D memory contains information about sentences in an input document. 2) PS memory contains information about sentences in a partial summary generated so far. 3) C memory contains information about the sentences that have not yet been selected in the summary.

After the *Selector* calculates Q-values for each sentence in C memory based on information of D and PS memory, it moves the sentence with the largest Q-value from C Memory to PS Memory. RL method enables the *Selector* to select an appropriate sentence for generating the best summary.

Our Q-Learning algorithm is similar to DQN. Please refer the Volodymyr et al. (2015) for a more detailed explanation about the algorithm. The difference between DQN and our model is table 1 and equation (5)

$$a_t = argmax_{c \in C_t} Q(D, PS_t, c; \theta) \qquad (5)$$

Initial state	Next state
$D = \{s_1, s_2, ..., s_n\}$, $C_0 = \{s_1, s_2, ..., s_n\}$ $PS_0 = \{s_0\}$ $S_0 = \{D, C_0, PS_0\}$	$C_{t+1} \leftarrow C_t - \{a_t\}$ $PS_{t+1} \leftarrow PS_t + \{a_t\}$ $S_{t+1} \leftarrow \{D, C_{t+1}, PS_{t+1}\}$

Table 1. Definition of State0 and Next state in our Q-Learning algorithm

4 Experiments

4.1 Experimental data

In order to evaluate our method, we use DUC 2001, DUC 2002 datasets, Anthology Reference Corpus (ACL-ARC) (Bird, 2008), and WIKI data which have been used in the previous studies Henß et al, (2015).

The numbers of training data and testing data are shown in Table 2.

	DUC 2001	DUC 2002	ACL-ARC	WIKI
#-TR	299	-	5500	1936
#-TE	306	562	613	900

Table 2: Number of each data
#-TR=The number of documents in training data
#-TE=The number of document in testing data

4.2 Features

In this work, a sentence is the unit of summarization. A sentence is represented by both a content vector and a position vector. A content vector(ContVec) represents the meaning of a sentence, and a position vector (PosVec) indicates the position of a sentence in a document. ContVec is estimated by the average of word embeddings in a sentence. We use pre-trained 50-dimensional word embeddings vector from GloVe (Pennington et al., 2014). Due to the lack of training data, word embeddings vector are not updated during the training.

The position of a sentence in a document is useful information for summarization. For example, important sentences are likely to appear in front of a newspaper article. Therefore, we adopt positional information as a main feature.

The positional information has three views.

1) An absolute position of the sentence (PosSent) within a paragraph

2) An absolute position of the paragraph (PosPara) in which the sentence belongs within a section
3) An absolute position of the section (PosSect) in which the sentence belongs in a document.

Each position is encoded as a 50-dimensional vector (PosSentVec, PosParaVec, PosSectVec). The vector PosVec denotes a sentence position and is calculated as:

$$PosVec = Element\text{-}wise\ sum\ of \\ (PosSectVec, PosParaVec, PosSentVec) \tag{6}$$

In Figure 1, each sentence in RNN is represented as the element-wise sum of ContVec and PosVec to take into account the meaning of the sentence as well as its position. For calculating DA_w in Figure 1, a candidate sentence A_t is represented as a ContVec only. DocVec is estimated as the average of embeddings vector of words that occur in the document.

4.3 Experimental Results

Figure 2 shows the training progress on WIKI's validation data. We use ROUGE-2 scores for evaluation. The y-axis of the graph is the ROUGE-2 score for the validation data and the x-axis is the number of validation steps. One single evaluation is performed after every 200 times of mini-batch training.

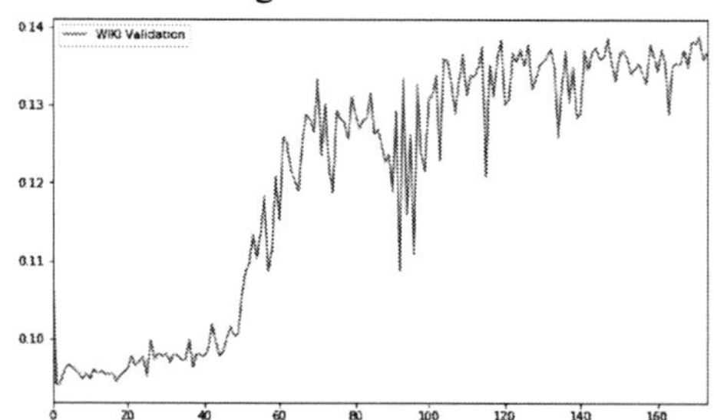

Figure 2: Training progress on WIKI's training and validation data

In Figure 2, the ROUGE-2 scores rarely change until the first 50 steps. We infer that the agent tries various combinations of sentences during this period. However, the ROUGE-2 score surges rapidly between 50 and 60 steps. At this step, the agent comes to know which sentence to choose to generate the best summary. After 120 steps, the model reaches a stable status.

Table 3 shows the first two sentences of the summary results for the Wikipedia article 'Banded sugar ant'. The number '#/#' in Table 3 indi-

cates the positional information. In the third row of table 3, 1/7 means that it was extracted from the first section of the seven sections of the source text. This section has 3 paragraphs, and the first paragraph out of 3 paragraphs, which has 4 sentences. 1/3 and 1/4 mean that the system summary sentence is extracted from this position.

Document Title: Banded sugar ant		
System Summary		
1	1/7	The banded sugar ant was first described by German entomologist Wilhelm Ferdinand Erichson, who named it "Formica consobrina" in 1842.
	1/3	
	1/4	
2	3/7	It occurs along the north-east coast of Queensland, from Charters Towers in the north to Brisbane in the south.
	1/2	
	2/7	
Human Summary		
1		The banded sugar ant ("Camponotus consobrinus"), also known as the sugar ant, is a species of ant endemic to Australia.
2		A member of the genus "Camponotus" in the subfamily Formicinae, it was described by German entomologist Wilhelm Ferdinand Erichson in 1842.

Table 3: Example of system summary

Table 4 shows the comparison experiments in terms of ROUGE-2.

	ACL-ARC	WIKI	DUC 2001	DUC 2002
TextRank	0.0844	0.1256	0.1866	0.2240
L2R	0.1052	0.1276	0.1934	0.2181
Regression	0.0883	0.1261	**0.1942**	0.2187
RL-full	0.1102	0.1321	0.1993	**0.2252**
Our work	**0.1158**	**0.1398**	0.1832	0.2163

Table 4: Rouge-2 of our work and previous studies

Our method outperforms the previous studies (TextRank(Mihalcea and Tarau, 2005), L2R(Henß et al, 2015), Regression(Henß et al, 2015), RL-full (Henß et al, 2015)) on ACL-ARC and WIKI data but achieves lower performance than the previous studies on DUCs. However, the differences of ROUGE scores between the models are relatively small. These experimental results show that our model is competitive with the previous models. Also, the embedding features have proven to be useful in RL method.

5 Conclusion

In this work, we propose an extractive text summarization model for a single document based on RL method. We use only embedding features that convey meaning and position of a sentence. We also extend the previous study by introducing DQN-based algorithms to train Q-network efficiently and effectively. Evaluation results show that our model is promising for text summarization even though it uses only simple features. Finally, we would like to apply our method to more complex summarization tasks such as multi-document or query focus summarization.

Acknowledgments

This research was supported by Basic Science Research Program through the National Research Foundation of Korea(NRF) funded by the Ministry of Science, ICT & Future Planning(NRF-2015R1C1A2A01051685)

References

Seonggi Ryang and Takeshi Abekawa. 2012. Framework of automatic text summarization using reinforcement learning. In Joint Conference on Empirical Methods in Natural Language Processing and Computational Natural Language Learning Seattle, Washington, USA, October 2013, pages 256–265. Association of Computational Linguistics.

R. McDonald. 2007. A study of global inference algorithms in multi-document summarization. Advances in Information Retrieval, pages 557–564.

Cody Rioux, Sadid A. Hasan, and Yllias Chali. 2014. Fear the reaper: A system for automatic multidocument summarization with reinforcement learning. In Proceedings of the 2014 Conference on Empirical Methods in Natural Language Processing (EMNLP), October 25-29, 2014, Doha, Qatar., pages 681–690.

HENß, Stefan; MIESKES, Margot; GUREVYCH, Iryna. 2015. A Reinforcement Learning Approach for Adaptive Single-and Multi-Document Summarization. In: GSCL.. pages. 3-12.

MNIH, Volodymyr, et al. 2015. Human-level control through deep reinforcement learning. Nature, 518.7540: 529-533.

Chin-Yew Lin. 2004. ROUGE: A Package for Automatic Evaluation of Summaries. In Proceedings of the Workshop on Text Summarization Branches Out at ACL 2004, Barcelona, Spain, 25–26 July, 2006, pages 74–81.

Steven Bird, Robert Dale, Bonnie Dorr, Bryan Gibson, Mark Joseph, Min-Yen Kan, Dongwon Lee, Brett Powley, Dragomir Radev, and Yee Fan Tan. 2008. The ACL anthology reference corpus: A reference dataset for bibliographic research in computational linguistics. In Proceedings of the 6th International Conference on Language Resources and Evaluation (LREC), Marrakech, Morocco, 26 May – 1 June 2008.

Rada Mihalcea and Paul Tarau. 2005. A language independent algorithm for single and multiple document summarization. In Proceedings of the 2nd International Joint Conference on Natural Language Processing, Jeju Island, South Korea, 11–13 October 2005, pages 19–24.

Pennington, J., Socher, R., & Manning, C. D. (2014, October). Glove: Global vectors for word representation. In EMNLP. Vol. 14, pages. 1532-1543.

Sutton, R. S., & Barto, A. G. 1998. Reinforcement learning: An introduction(Vol. 1, No. 1). Cambridge: MIT press.

Goldstein, J., Mittal, V., Carbonell, J., & Kantrowitz, M. (2000, April). Multi-document summarization by sentence extraction. In Proceedings of the 2000 NAACL-ANLPWorkshop on Automatic summarization-Volume 4 (pp. 40-48). Association for Computational Linguistics.

SSAS: Semantic Similarity for Abstractive Summarization

Raghuram Vadapalli   **Litton J Kurisinkel**   **Manish Gupta**[*]   **Vasudeva Varma**
International Institute of Information Technology – Hyderabad
Hyderabad India
{raghuram.vadapalli, litton.jkurisinkel}@research.iiit.ac.in
{manish.gupta, vv}@iiit.ac.in

Abstract

Ideally a metric evaluating an abstract system summary should represent the extent to which the system-generated summary approximates the semantic inference conceived by the reader using a human-written reference summary. Most of the previous approaches relied upon word or syntactic sub-sequence overlap to evaluate system-generated summaries. Such metrics cannot evaluate the summary at semantic inference level. Through this work we introduce the metric of Semantic Similarity for Abstractive Summarization (**SSAS**)[1], which leverages natural language inference and paraphrasing techniques to frame a novel approach to evaluate system summaries at semantic inference level. SSAS is based upon a weighted composition of quantities representing the level of agreement, contradiction, topical neutrality, paraphrasing, and optionally ROUGE score between a system-generated and a human-written summary.

1 Introduction

Abstractive summarization techniques try to mimic human expert's capabilities of inference making and producing a summary in her own writing style. Automated abstractive summarization techniques are highly desirable since one needs a lot of effort and language skills for generating summaries from varying information sources such as social media, databases, web articles etc. It is crucial for a constructive evolution of research on abstractive summarization, to establish a metric which can judge the quality of a system-generated abstractive summary. An ideal metric should be able to represent the similarity of *semantic inference* perceived by a reader from system-generated summary to that from a human-written reference summary.

Most of the existing summarization metrics are well-suited for extractive summaries, and are directly or indirectly based upon word or syntactic substructure overlap (Lin, 2004). Evaluation of abstractive summarization needs a semantic overlap based method. Although there are some metrics which attempt to evaluate the summary at semantic level (Nenkova and Passonneau, 2004; Passonneau et al., 2013; Yang et al., 2016), they either demand high level of human involvement or rely on external discrete vocabulary information (Miller et al., 1990). Also they are less equipped to conceive the accurate semantic inference from long sequences of summary text.

For instance, consider the following statements.
A: Mary lived through an era of liberating reform for women.
B: Mary's life spanned years of incredible change for women.
C: Mary lived through an era of suppression of women.

Considering *A* as the reference summary element, most of the previous metrics give higher score to *C* than *B* even when *C* is clearly contradicting *A*. Actual scores for above samples are shown in Table 1.

Bowman et al. (2015) mention that understanding entailment and contradiction is fundamental to understanding natural language. The lack of consideration of semantics when evaluating summarization automatically, motivates us to propose a new metric focused on semantic matching between system and human summaries.

---

[*] The author is also a Principal Applied Scientist at Microsoft (gmanish@microsoft.com).

[1] Data and code are shared at `http://somewhereonweb.com`.

Proceedings of the The 8th International Joint Conference on Natural Language Processing, pages 198–203,
Taipei, Taiwan, November 27 – December 1, 2017 ©2017 AFNLP

Method	B	C
ROUGE-1	0.33	0.66
ROUGE-2	0.0	0.4
ROUGE-L	0.33	0.66
ROUGE-SU4	0.05	0.45
PEAK	0.45	0.33
SSAS	0.65	0.48

Table 1: Scores given to Samples B and C by Various Metrics

Our main contributions are as follows.

- We propose a novel metric SSAS for semantic assessment of abstractive summaries.

- The method includes computing various semantic and lexical similarity measures between reference summary and system summary, and learning a weight vector to combine these measures into a single score such that the score maximally correlates with human evaluation of summaries.

- We experimentally show the robustness and effectiveness of SSAS.

The rest of the paper is organized as follows. Section 2 describes previous attempts at evaluating summarization systems. Section 3 describes our approach in detail. We discuss our experimental results in Section 4. We conclude with a summary in Section 5.

2 Related Work

The following are two broad approaches popular for evaluation of summaries proposed in the past.

2.1 ROUGE Based Approaches

ROUGE-n measures evaluate the system summary on the basis of n-gram overlap. ROUGE-SU and ROUGE-L evaluate content overlap in a more sophisticated manner. But they still cannot reliably capture semantic overlap or semantic contradiction. Recently Ng and Abrecht (2015) tried to enhance ROUGE using word embeddings, but word embeddings cannot grasp the semantic inference induced by a sequence of words.

2.2 Pyramid Based Approaches

In pyramid evaluation (Nenkova and Passonneau, 2004), Summarization Content Units (SCUs) are extracted from model summaries and they are given weights which are equal to the number of reference summaries they occur in. After this, a generated summary is given a score which is equal to the normalized sum of the weights of the overlapping SCUs. Pyramid score does not evaluate the semantic overlap in a continuous space, and also requires manual efforts when performing evaluation.

Autopyramid (Passonneau et al., 2013) automates a part of the pyramid based evaluation which checks whether an SCU is present in the generated summary. Though they use various generic dense representations (Guo and Diab, 2012) for estimating semantic similarity between SCUs, Autopyramid cannot explicitly quantify the quality of a summary based on its agreement or contradiction with a reference summary.

The PEAK (Yang et al., 2016) method for evaluation automates the extraction part of the SCUs, and they use the ADW (Align, Disambiguate and Walk) algorithm (Pilehvar et al., 2013) to compute semantic similarity. However, their approach fails to model contradiction, paraphrase identification and other features like natural language inference.

3 Approach for SSAS Computation

We first extract SCUs using the automatic SCU extraction scheme introduced by PEAK model I, which in turn relies on Open Information Extraction (OpenIE) (Angeli et al., 2015) for the extraction process. Given a reference summary R and a system summary S, we obtain SCU sets $SCUs(R)$ and $SCUs(S)$ with cardinality n and m respectively. Next, we derive a set of natural language inference and paraphrasing features from the text pieces. Computation of these features is explained in Section 3.1. After that, we use a ranking model to learn the weights for combining these features to obtain a score. Finally, we normalize the obtained score. Ranking and Normalization are discussed in detail in Section 3.2.

3.1 Features for SSAS

SSAS uses natural language inference (NLI) features, paraphrase features and ROUGE-SU4 as features. We discuss these in detail below.

3.1.1 NLI Features

In this subsection, we consider features that capture natural language inference-based similarity between text pieces. We leverage the neural attention model, proposed by Cheng et al. (2016)

for this purpose. Let $E(a,b), C(a,b)$ and $N(a,b)$ be the entailment, contradiction and topic neutrality probabilities respectively between two SCUs a and b such that $E(a,b) + C(a,b) + N(a,b) = 1$. Based on these probability scores, we compute values for the following features from sets $SCUs(R)$ and $SCUs(S)$.

Combined Entailment Scores: We compute two features F_{e1} and F_{e2} which quantify the combined entailment score between reference summary and system summary. F_{e1} (Eq. 1) finds the SCU $b \in SCUs(S)$ that is best entailed by each SCU $a \in SCUs(R)$, and then computes average entailment score across all $a \in SCUs(R)$. F_{e2} (Eq. 2) is defined similarly, but aggregates scores across all $a \in SCUs(S)$ and considers entailment of an SCU $b \in SCUs(R)$ by an SCU $a \in SCUs(S)$.

$$F_{e1} = \frac{1}{n} \sum_{a \, \epsilon \, SCUs(R)} \max_{b \epsilon SCUs(S)} E(a,b) \qquad (1)$$

$$F_{e2} = \frac{1}{m} \sum_{a \, \epsilon \, SCUs(S)} \max_{b \epsilon SCUs(R)} E(a,b) \qquad (2)$$

Combined Contradiction Scores: Similar to entailment scores, two features F_{c1} and F_{c2} quantify the combined contradiction score as shown in Eqs. 3 and 4 respectively.

$$F_{c1} = \frac{1}{n} \sum_{a \, \epsilon \, SCUs(R)} \max_{b \epsilon SCUs(S)} C(a,b) \qquad (3)$$

$$F_{c2} = \frac{1}{m} \sum_{a \, \epsilon \, SCUs(S)} \max_{b \epsilon SCUs(R)} C(a,b) \qquad (4)$$

Combined Topic Neutrality Scores: Finally, two features F_{n1} and F_{n2} are computed to quantify the combined topical neutrality score as shown in Eqs. 5 and 6 respectively.

$$F_{n1} = \frac{1}{n} \sum_{a \, \epsilon \, SCUs(R)} \max_{b \epsilon SCUs(S)} N(a,b) \qquad (5)$$

$$F_{n2} = \frac{1}{m} \sum_{a \, \epsilon \, SCUs(S)} \max_{b \epsilon SCUs(R)} N(a,b) \qquad (6)$$

3.1.2 Paraphrase Features

We compute the paraphrasing probability $P(a,b)$ for two SCUs a and b using the model proposed by Kiros et al. (2015) which is trained on MSRP corpus (Bouamor et al., 2012). The combined paraphrase scores F_{p1} and F_{p2} are given by Eqs. 7 and 8 respectively.

$$F_{p1} = \frac{1}{n} \sum_{a \, \epsilon \, SCUs(R)} \max_{b \epsilon SCUs(S)} P(a,b) \qquad (7)$$

$$F_{p2} = \frac{1}{m} \sum_{a \, \epsilon \, SCUs(S)} \max_{b \epsilon SCUs(R)} P(a,b) \qquad (8)$$

3.1.3 ROUGE-SU4 Feature

Along with other dense semantic level features, n-gram overlap can also be indicative to evaluate the summary quality. Following this intuition, we include ROUGE score between the system summary S and the reference summary R as one of the features.

$$F_R = \text{ROUGE-SU4}(S, R) \qquad (9)$$

3.2 Computing SSAS

For every pair (R, S), we concatenate the extracted features to form the feature vector $\vec{f}$.

$$\vec{f} = [F_{e1}, F_{e2}, F_{c1}, F_{c2}, F_{n1}, F_{n2}, F_{p1}, F_{p2}, F_R]$$

We estimate a score for S with respect to R as shown in Eq. 10.

$$score(S, R) = \vec{\lambda} \cdot [\vec{f}, 1] \qquad (10)$$

where $\vec{\lambda}$ is a learned 10 dimensional parameter vector (9 for features + 1 for bias). The value of $\vec{\lambda}$ is optimized so that the score as computed using Eq. 10 matches human assigned score. Finally, we compute the normalized SSAS score for a system summary with respect to the reference summary using min-max normalization as shown in Eq. 11.

$$SSAS(S, R) = \frac{\vec{\lambda} \cdot ([\vec{f}, 1] - [\vec{f_{min}}, 1])}{\vec{\lambda} \cdot ([\vec{f_{max}}, 1] - [\vec{f_{min}}, 1])} \qquad (11)$$

where $\vec{f_{max}}$ is the feature vector of an ideal summary obtained by setting values for entailment, paraphrase and ROUGE features to 1, and rest all to 0. $\vec{f_{min}}$ is the feature vector of an extremely bad summary obtained by setting values for contradiction features to 1, and rest all to 0. Overall, SSAS scores lie between 0 and 1. The higher the SSAS score, the better is the system summary S.

4 Experiments and Results

In this section, we discuss details of our dataset, comparison of multiple ranking models, and comparison of SSAS with other metrics for summarization.

4.1 Dataset

We obtained DUC[2] 2002, 2003, 2004 datasets and the TAC[3] dataset which contain triplets (D, HS, LS) where D denotes the document/corpus to be summarized, HS denotes the human-written summary of D, and LS denotes the list of system summaries with their corresponding human evaluation scores.

In total, we collected approximately 250 (D, HS, LS) triplets from these datasets. Since SSAS is framed to evaluate abstractive summary, we constructed a test set comprising strictly abstractive summaries for 30 documents in DUC 2002 dataset separate from the training and development sets. Although we perform experiments by taking single human-written summary, extension to use multiple reference summaries is straightforward. Using multiple references also aligns with the notion that there is no single best summary.

4.2 Learning to Rank by Optimizing $\vec{\lambda}$

The value of $\vec{\lambda}$ is optimized by applying 'Learning To Rank' (LTR) techniques over training data comprising of (D, HS, LS) triplets. The optimization is performed such that the ranking order obtained by Eq. 10 maximally correlates with ranking order obtained by human scores. We executed development experiments with the three different LTR techniques (Burges et al., 2005; Cao et al., 2007): Pairwise, Listwise and Regression.

The results on the development dataset in terms of Pearson correlation and Spearman rank correlation are shown in Table 2. As the table shows, Listwise comparison gained better results though the results are not significantly different from others.

4.3 Evaluating SSAS

As mentioned earlier, to create the test dataset we chose 30 document-reference summary pairs from DUC 2002 and asked two human annotators to read each of the reference summary and to

[2]http://duc.nist.gov/data.html
[3]http://tac.nist.gov/data/past/2011/Summ11.html

Method	Pearson Correlation	Spearman Rho
Pairwise	0.970	0.975
Listwise	0.978	0.979
Regression	0.964	0.967

Table 2: Pearson Correlation and Spearman Rho for the Three Ranking Models

Method	Accuracy	σ
ROUGE-1	0.810	NA
ROUGE-2	0.782	NA
ROUGE-L	0.825	NA
ROUGE-SU4	0.839	NA
PEAK	0.861	NA
SSAS without F_{e1}, F_{e2}	0.854	5.44e-6
SSAS without F_{c1}, F_{c2}	0.893	4.38e-6
SSAS without F_{n1}, F_{n2}	0.862	6.12e-6
SSAS without F_{p1}, F_{p2}	0.845	4.1e-6
SSAS without F_R	0.882	5.64e-6
SSAS with all features	**0.913**	6.22e-6
Human	1.000	NA

Table 3: Results on the Custom Dataset

reproduce the content in their own writing style with full freedom to choose the convenient vocabulary. The human summarizers are post-graduate students in computational linguistics and we call the summary written by them as abstract summary $AbSum$. For each document in the test set a random subset of sentences are chosen to form a random summary $RandSum$ of the document. We use SSAS to score $AbSum$ and $RandSum$ with respect to the reference summary. The reliability of the metric is proportional to the number of times $AbSum$ is scored better than $RandSum$.

For the metric to be reliable, it is important to show that it produces consistent results even if the training and test data are from different types of data. For this purpose, we trained the model on the following three different subsets and recorded

Method	Execution Time (sec)
ROUGE	4
PEAK	10
SSAS	200

Table 4: Approximate Execution Times of Various Metrics on Test Data

standard deviation of accuracy: a subset of 80 triples from DUC, a subset of 80 triples from TAC, a subset of 40 triples each from DUC and TAC.

Table 3 shows the mean results obtained by repeatedly selecting sentences for random summary 10 times over each of the above training subsets and the standard deviation obtained on changing training subset. The insignificance of standard deviation shows that the metric produces consistent results as long as training data is reliable.

4.4 Analysis of Results

From Table 3, we see that excluding contradiction does not have much impact on results. This is not surprising as we trained the data on DUC and TAC datasets which have very few contradictory sentences as they are extractive summaries. Nonetheless, we propose incorporating contradiction as abstractive summaries have a good chance of producing contradictory sentences. We can address this problem by training on human-evaluated abstractive summaries which we leave as future work.

We also see that F_{p1} and F_{p2} (features corresponding to paraphrasing) are important features since excluding them has a significant impact on the results.

Table 4 shows the approximate execution times for various methods. Since SSAS performs similarity assessment using deep semantic analysis, it does take significantly large amount of execution time compared to other methods. However, SSAS computations for multiple summaries can be easily parallelized.

5 Conclusions

In this work, we proposed a novel metric SSAS for semantic assessment of abstractive summaries. Our experiments show that SSAS outperforms previously proposed metrics. While the metric shows a very strong correlation with human judgments, it is computationally very intensive because of the deep semantic models which are used to compute various features. In the future, we plan to explore more efficient ways to obtain the feature vectors for SSAS computation.

References

Gabor Angeli, Melvin Jose Johnson Premkumar, and Christopher D. Manning. 2015. Leveraging Linguistic Structure For Open Domain Information Extraction. In *Proc. of the 53rd Annual Meeting of the Association for Computational Linguistics (ACL).* pages 344–354.

Houda Bouamor, Aurélien Max, and Anne Vilnat. 2012. Automatic Acquisition and Validation of Subsentential Paraphrases: A Bilingual Study. *Journal of the Association pour le Traitement Automatique des Langues (TAL)* 53(1):11–37.

Samuel R. Bowman, Gabor Angeli, Christopher Potts, and Christopher D. Manning. 2015. A Large Annotated Corpus for Learning Natural Language Inference. In *Proc. of the 2015 Conf. on Empirical Methods in Natural Language Processing (EMNLP).*

Chris Burges, Tal Shaked, Erin Renshaw, Ari Lazier, Matt Deeds, Nicole Hamilton, and Greg Hullender. 2005. Learning to Rank using Gradient Descent. In *Proc. of the 22nd Intl. Conf. on Machine learning (ICML).* pages 89–96.

Zhe Cao, Tao Qin, Tie-Yan Liu, Ming-Feng Tsai, and Hang Li. 2007. Learning to Rank: From Pairwise Approach to Listwise Approach. In *Proc. of the 24th Intl. Conf. on Machine learning (ICML).* pages 129–136.

Jianpeng Cheng, Li Dong, and Mirella Lapata. 2016. Long Short-Term Memory Networks for Machine Reading. *Proc. of the 2016 Conf. on Empirical Methods in Natural Language Processing (EMNLP)* pages 551–562.

Weiwei Guo and Mona T. Diab. 2012. Modeling Sentences in the Latent Space. In *Proc. of the 50th Annual Meeting of the Association for Computational Linguistics (ACL).* pages 864–872.

Ryan Kiros, Yukun Zhu, Ruslan R Salakhutdinov, Richard Zemel, Raquel Urtasun, Antonio Torralba, and Sanja Fidler. 2015. Skip-Thought Vectors. In *Proc. of the 2015 Conf. on Advances in Neural Information Processing Systems (NIPS).* pages 3294–3302.

Chin-Yew Lin. 2004. ROUGE: A Package for Automatic Evaluation of Summaries. In *Proc. of the Workshop on Text Summarization Branches Out (WAS).* pages 74–81.

G. A. Miller, C. Fellbaum, D. Gross, and K. J. Miller. 1990. Introduction to WordNet: An On-Line Lexical Database. *Intl. Journal of Lexicography (IJL)* 3(4):235–244.

Ani Nenkova and Rebecca J. Passonneau. 2004. Evaluating Content Selection in Summarization: The Pyramid Method. In *Proc. of the 2004 Human Language Technology Conf. of the North American Chapter of the Association for Computational Linguistics (HLT-NAACL).* pages 145–152.

Jun-Ping Ng and Viktoria Abrecht. 2015. Better Summarization Evaluation with Word Embeddings for

ROUGE. In *Proc. of the 2015 Conf. on Empirical Methods in Natural Language Processing (EMNLP)*. pages 1925–1930.

Rebecca J Passonneau, Emily Chen, Weiwei Guo, and Dolores Perin. 2013. Automated Pyramid Scoring of Summaries using Distributional Semantics. In *Proc. of the 51st Annual Meeting of the Association for Computational Linguistics (ACL)*. pages 143–147.

Mohammad Taher Pilehvar, David Jurgens, and Roberto Navigli. 2013. Align, Disambiguate and Walk: A Unified Approach for Measuring Semantic Similarity. In *Proc. of the 51st Annual Meeting of the Association for Computational Linguistics (ACL)*. pages 1341–1351.

Qian Yang, Rebecca J Passonneau, and Gerard de Melo. 2016. PEAK: Pyramid Evaluation via Automated Knowledge Extraction. In *Proc. of the 13th AAAI Conf. on Artificial Intelligence (AAAI)*. pages 2673–2680.

Taking into account Inter-sentence Similarity for Update Summarization

Maâli Mnasri
CEA, LIST,
Univ. Paris-Sud,
Université Paris-Saclay.
maali.mnasri@cea.fr

Gaël de Chalendar
CEA, LIST,
Gif-sur-Yvette,
F-91191 France.
gael.de-chalendar@cea.fr

Olivier Ferret
CEA, LIST,
Gif-sur-Yvette,
F-91191 France.
olivier.ferret@cea.fr

Abstract

Following Gillick and Favre (2009), a lot of work about extractive summarization has modeled this task by associating two contrary constraints: one aims at maximizing the coverage of the summary with respect to its information content while the other represents its size limit. In this context, the notion of redundancy is only implicitly taken into account. In this article, we extend the framework defined by Gillick and Favre (2009) by examining how and to what extent integrating semantic sentence similarity into an update summarization system can improve its results. We show more precisely the impact of this strategy through evaluations performed on DUC 2007 and TAC 2008 and 2009 datasets.

1 Introduction

As recently shown by Hirao et al. (2017) from a theoretical viewpoint, there is still room for improvements in the extractive approach of Automatic Summarization (AS), which is the framework in which our work takes place. In this context, many methods have been developed for selecting sentences according to various features and aggregating the results of this selection for building summaries. All these methods aim at selecting the most informative sentences and minimizing their redundancy while not exceeding a maximum length.

In this article, we focus on Multi-Document Summarization (MDS) and more particularly on its update variant. Having two or more sets of documents ordered chronologically, the update summarization task consists in summarizing the newer documents under the assumption that a user has already read the older documents. Hence, the work done for tackling this task has mainly extended the work done for MDS by taking into account the notion of novelty through different means. Wan (2012) integrates this notion in the framework of graph-based methods for computing the salience of sentences while Delort and Alfonseca (2012) achieve this integration in the context of hierarchical topic models. Li et al. (2012) go one step further in hierarchical Bayesian models by applying the paradigm of Hierarchical Dirichlet Processes to the update task.

Another interesting way to consider the problem of AS is to formalize it as a constraint optimization problem based on Integer Linear Programming (ILP). ILP-based approaches are very flexible as they allow to jointly optimize several constraints and were found very successful for MDS, as illustrated by the ICSISumm system of Gillick and Favre (2009). They have also been developed for the update summarization task, with work such as (Li et al., 2015) about the weighting of concepts.

However, the most obvious weakness of such methods, particularly the one proposed by Gillick and Favre (2009), is their implicit way of modeling information redundancy. This prevents them from exploiting work about textual entailment or paraphrase detection, which could be especially relevant in the context of MDS. In this article, we aim at extending the update summarization frame-

Proceedings of the The 8th International Joint Conference on Natural Language Processing, pages 204–209,
Taipei, Taiwan, November 27 – December 1, 2017 ©2017 AFNLP

work of Gillick and Favre (2009) by integrating non-redundancy features in a more explicit way through sentences semantic similarities.

2 Summarization framework

For performing MDS with update, the approach we propose includes two main steps. First, we perform a semantic clustering over the input documents sentences, including the old and the new document sets. Then, we select a subset of sentences for the summary while considering the semantic information resulting from the clustering step. We detail each of these two steps hereafter.

2.1 Semantic clustering

As in basic MDS, update MDS aims to optimize the content relevance, the information redundancy within a document set and the final summary length. The additional constraint is to detect information novelty in the new documents in order to avoid repeating what has already been read.

Since emphasizing information novelty in the update summary is equivalent to penalizing old information in the new document set, we should start by identifying sentences from the new set that are equivalent to sentences from the old set. One way to achieve such identification is to perform semantic clustering over all the sentences, whatever their source. The aim of semantic clustering here is to group sentences conveying the same information, even when they are expressed in different ways. In addition to detecting redundancy over time, this filtering step allows to decrease the sentence selection cost by reducing the number of possible combinations of sentences. Furthermore, considering similarity at the sentence level rather than the sub-sentence level is more efficient since the number of sentences is much lower, which ensures less calculations of pairwise similarities.

Clustering method For performing the semantic clustering of sentences, we need a clustering algorithm that uses semantic similarity as a major feature with a low computing time. Partitioning algorithms like *k-means* require the number of clusters to be set in advance, which is inconsistent with our main need. Moreover, setting up a similarity threshold is less dependent on the size of the considered data than setting up the number of clusters. While the latter depends on the test data size and the content diversity, the former depends on the similarity measure itself and could be set up on large annotated corpora. Among the clustering methods relying on a similarity matrix as input, we chose the Markov Cluster Algorithm (MCL), a network-based clustering algorithm simulating the flow in graphs, known to be fast and scalable (van Dongen, 2000). It assumes that "a random walk on a network that visits a dense cluster will likely not leave it until many of its vertices have been visited". In our case, it turns the adjacency matrix of sentences into a transition matrix. Since our goal is to build small and tight clusters, we removed pairwise similarities under a given threshold. Finally, as MCL performs hard clustering, each sentence belongs to one cluster only.

Semantic similarity measure Sentence semantic similarity has gained a lot of interest recently, especially in the context of SemEval evaluations (Agirre et al., 2016). However, in practice, most proposed similarity measures for AS are subject to a time efficiency problem which tends to increase with the quality of the similarity measure. This is the case of the lexical word alignment based similarity that won the SemEval 2014 sentence similarity task (Sultan et al., 2014). We found it unusable in our set-up due to its computational complexity as we calculate about 5 million sentence pair similarities for some datasets while the SemEval 2014 corpus, for instance, gathers only 3,750 sentence pairs. Given this constraint, we chose a similarity measure relying on low dimensional word vectors from word embeddings. In fact, simply averaging word embeddings of all words in a sentence has proven to produce a sentence vector encoding its meaning and has shown a good performance in multiple tasks and particularly in text similarity tasks (Das et al., 2016; White et al., 2015; Gershman and Tenenbaum, 2015; Hill et al., 2016). We adopted this method to represent sentences and used only the embeddings of unigrams since bigrams and phrases are generally not well covered by the existing pre-trained embeddings[1]. Before building the sentence vectors, we did not perform any normalization of the words in documents (unigrams) as words in pre-trained embeddings are not normalized. Finally, we classically defined the similarity of two sentences as the cosine similarity of their vectors.

---

[1] Only 0.08% of TAC 2008 dataset bigrams are covered by the Glove840B embeddings.

2.2 Sentence selection

Extracting one sentence per cluster to generate summaries as in (Zopf et al., 2016) leads to poor results for update MDS. We have rather added the information brought by our semantic clustering to an ILP model for selecting sentences. This model is the ICSISumm model proposed by Gillick and Favre (2009). It is a maximum coverage model operating at the concept level where concepts are word bigrams. The score of a summary is the sum of its bigram weights. Each bigram is credited only once in the summary score to favor diversity at the lexical level. Thus, redundancy is globally and implicitly minimized. To address the update task, the value of concepts appearing in first sentences are up-weighted by a factor of 3 as in (Gillick and Favre, 2009). The ILP problem is formalized as follows:

$$\text{Maximize} : \sum_i w_i.c_i$$

$$\text{Subject to} : \sum_j s_j.l_j \leq L \tag{1}$$

$$s_j.Occ_{ij} \leq c_i, \forall i, j \tag{2}$$

$$\sum_j s_j.Occ_{ij} \geq c_i, \forall i \tag{3}$$

$$c_i \in \{0,1\} \, \forall i \text{ and } s_j \in \{0,1\} \, \forall j$$

where c_i is a variable indicating the presence of the concept i in the summary; w_i refers to the weight of the concept i, which is its document frequency; l_j represents the length of the sentence j while L is a constant representing the summary maximum length; s_j is the variable that indicates the presence of the sentence j in the summary and finally, Occ_{ij} is a constant parameter indicating the presence of concept i in sentence j. While the constraint (1) prevents the whole summary from exceeding the maximum length limit, constraints (2) and (3) ensure its consistency.

To take into account the semantic clustering of sentences in the ILP model, we focused on the weighting of bigrams since in such models, the concept weighting method is a key factor in the performance of the system (Li et al., 2015). As our aim is to reduce redundancy with the old information, we chose to penalize the weights of bigrams occurring in both old and new documents. If a bigram appears in a cluster including sentences from both old and new document sets, its weight is penalized by an α parameter as follows: $w_i' = \frac{w_i}{\alpha}$. The value of α is determined on a development set. As in (Gillick and Favre, 2009), bigrams whose weights are lower than a fixed threshold are pruned before solving the ILP problem for computational efficiency. However, since this pruning can have a negative impact results if it is too restrictive (Boudin et al., 2015), we carried out the penalization process after the bigram pruning step.

3 Experiments

3.1 Evaluation Setup

For our experiments, we used the DUC 2007 update corpus and TAC 2008 and 2009 update corpora. The 3 datasets are composed respectively of 10, 48 and 44 topics. They gather respectively about 25, 20 and 20 news articles per topic. The articles are ordered chronologically and partitioned into 3 sets, A to C, for DUC 2007 and two sets, A to B, for both TAC 2008 and 2009. We only considered sets A and B for all the datasets.

To evaluate our approach, we classically adopted the ROUGE[2] framework (Lin, 2004), which estimates a summary score by its n-gram overlap with several reference summaries (Rn). Although our method is unsupervised, we had to tune two parameters: the similarity threshold in the clustering step (for sparcifying the input similarity matrix) and the penalization factor α in the sentence selection. As training data, we used for each dataset the two other datasets. To set up these parameters, we followed a greedy sequential approach for optimizing ROUGE on each training set. We maximized the ROUGE-2 recall score (bigrams overlap) particularly since it has shown the best agreement with manual evaluations (Hong et al., 2014). Yet, we report in what follows three variants of ROUGE: ROUGE-1, which computes the overlap with reference summaries in terms of unigrams, ROUGE-2, described previously and ROUGE-SU4, which computes the overlap of skip-grams with a skip distance of 4 words at most. Again following (Hong et al., 2014), we only report the recall values of the ROUGE metrics because their precision and f-measure values are very close to them.

---

[2]ROUGE parameters: -n 2 -2 4 -m -l 100 -u -c 95 -p 0.5 -f A -r 1000

System/dataset	DUC 2007			TAC 2008			TAC 2009		
	R1	R2	RSU4	R1	R2	RSU4	R1	R2	R4
Baseline systems									
ICSISumm 2009	33.73	7.59	11.23	38.28	11.19	14.46	37.40	10.37	13.86
ICSISumm-BG-DOWN-1	34.46	7.91	11.74	36.99	10.15	13.66	37.39	10.25	13.87
ICSISumm-BG-DOWN-2	33.71	7.55	11.22	38.02	11.05	14.18	37.27	9.91	13.62
State-of-the-art systems									
Supervised ILP	-	-	-	-	9.99	13.61	-	9.61	13.77
Topic Modeling	-	-	-	36,73	10.41	13.79	36.42	9.58	13.53
CorrRank	-	-	-	36.71	9.70	13.19	36.87	9.73	13.59
Proposed systems									
MCL-W2V-ICSISumm	34.99	8.14	11.79	38.52	11.49	14.68	37.50	10.48	13.98
MCL-GLOVE-ICSISumm	**36.08**	**9.46**	**12.96**	**38.62**	**11.57**	**14.75**	**37.53**	**10.60**	**14.08**
MCL-ConceptNet-ICSISumm	35.23	8.30	11.98	38.28	11.21	14.49	**37.53**	10.38	13.91

Table 1: Average ROUGE recall scores on DUC 2007, TAC 2008 and TAC 2009 datasets

3.2 Results

We compare our system to three baselines and three high-level state-of-the-art references.

Baseline systems

- ICSISumm 2009. This is the system described in Section 2.2, on which we built our contribution. We report here the version with no sentence compression. It is worth noting that ICSISumm was still found the best performing system in (Hong et al., 2014).

- ICSISumm-BG-DOWN-1. This baseline is an adaptation of the ICSISumm 2009 system in which we down-weight the bigrams occurring in the chronologically first set of documents (A).

- ICSISumm-BG-DOWN-2. In this modified version of the ICSISumm 2009 system, we down-weight the bigrams whose frequency in the chronologically first set of documents (A) is greater than their frequency in the more recent document set (B).

The last two baselines, which do not include our semantic clustering of sentences, are tested to check how effective is this clustering and to what extent it is needed.

State-of-the-art systems

- Topic Modeling. This system uses topic probability distributions for salience determination and a dynamic modeling approach for redundancy control (Wang and Zhou, 2012).

- CorrRank. This algorithm selects sentences using a topic evolution pattern by filtering sentences from particular topic evolution categories (Lei and Yanxiang, 2010).

- Supervised ILP. This system predicts the bigrams weights by means of a supervised model using salience and novelty features at the sentence and bigram level. Sentence selection is done by an ILP model and a regression model for sentence reranking (Li et al., 2015).

Proposed systems We present the results of our system with different pre-trained word embeddings for evaluating sentence similarities. All the considered training sets showed that the optimal performance is reached when the penalization factor α is set to 3. No similarity threshold is set lower than 0.95, which guarantees a precision level for the similarity measure at least equal to the precisions reported in Table 2.

- MCL-W2V-ICSISumm. This version relies on 3 million vectors (300 dimensions) trained with the CBOW model of Word2Vec (Mikolov et al., 2013) on 100 billion words from a Google News dataset.

- MCL-GLOVE-ICSISumm. In this run, we used 2.2 million word vectors (300 dimensions) trained with GloVe (Pennington et al., 2014) on the 840 billion tokens from the Common Crawl repository.

- MCL-ConceptNet-ICSISumm. This version computes similarities with the ConceptNet

Dataset	Precision	Recall
MSRpara	91.44	17.69
SemEvaL STS 2014	88.00	14.17
SemEvaL STS 2015	90.60	11.46
SemEvaL STS 2016	88.28	25.98

Table 2: Results of our sentence semantic similarity with the minimum threshold value of 0.95

Vector Ensemble embeddings (Speer and Chin, 2016), which is a combination of GloVe and Word2Vec embeddings enriched with knowledge from the ConceptNet semantic network and PPDB.

Table 1 shows that for all the different word embeddings, our system outperforms all our references. The improvement is observed for the three ROUGE measures we used. The improvement over ICSISumm 2009, which has the same settings as our system, confirms the interest of handling redundancy explicitly in the update summarization task. However, the improvement over ICSISumm-BG-DOWN-1&2 also shows that basic methods for performing this handling are not efficient in ILP models, contrary to our sentence semantic clustering approach. Our second version using Glove pre-trained vectors reports higher results than those using Word2Vec or Concept-Net Ensemble word vectors. This could be explained by the size of the training sets for building the word vectors as the Common Crawl dataset is much larger than the Google News dataset. Moreover, the impact of the quality of the vectors on our results indirectly confirms the interest of our proposal.

Since the semantic similarity of sentences is central in our approach, we have tried to characterize *a posteriori* the similarity corresponding to the value of our similarity threshold as it was optimized on our development sets. We have applied our semantic similarity measure to reference evaluation datasets for sentence similarity[3]: the MSR Paraphrase Corpus (Dolan et al., 2004) and the SemEval STS datasets (Agirre et al., 2016). In order to calculate precision and recall scores on the SemEval datasets, we consider a result as a true positive if our similarity is higher than 0.95 and

the gold standard similarity is higher than 3^4. We present in Table 2, the evaluation of our similarity measure using the Google's pre-trained word vectors. On all datasets, our similarity shows a high precision but a weak recall. This trend is particularly noticeable on the MSR Paraphrase Corpus: when our system regroups two sentences, they are paraphrases in 91.44% of the cases, which fits our initial hypotheses and illustrates their validity.

4   Conclusion and Perspectives

For concluding, we showed that taking into account the semantic similarity of sentences for discarding redundancy in a maximal bigram coverage problem improves the update summarization performance and can be done by modifying the weights of bigrams in an ILP model according to the results of the semantic clustering of sentences.

The most direct perspective we will follow for extending this work is to improve the recall of the semantic similarity measure to increase the ability of our system to detect redundancy. In a more global extension, we will associate this criterion about redundancy with criteria more focused on information salience based on the discourse structure of documents.

References

Eneko Agirre, Carmen Banea, Daniel Cer, Mona Diab, Aitor Gonzalez-Agirre, Rada Mihalcea, German Rigau, and Janyce Wiebe. 2016. SemEval-2016 Task 1: Semantic Textual Similarity, Monolingual and Cross-Lingual Evaluation. In *Proceedings of the 10th International Workshop on Semantic Evaluation (SemEval-2016)*, pages 497–511, San Diego, California.

Florian Boudin, Hugo Mougard, and Benot Favre. 2015. Concept-based Summarization using Integer Linear Programming: From Concept Pruning to Multiple Optimal Solutions. In *2015 Conference on Empirical Methods in Natural Language Processing (EMNLP 2015)*, pages 1914–1918, Lisbon, Portugal.

Arpita Das, Harish Yenala, Manoj Chinnakotla, and Manish Shrivastava. 2016. Together we stand: Siamese Networks for Similar Question Retrieval. In *Proceedings of the 54th Annual Meeting of the Association for Computational Linguistics (ACL 2016)*, pages 378–387, Berlin, Germany.

Jean-Yves Delort and Enrique Alfonseca. 2012. DualSum: a Topic-Model based approach for update

---

[3]To our knowledge, the only dataset specifically dedicated to the evaluation of sentence clustering in the context of MDS is described in (Geiss, 2009) but it is not publicly available.

[4]Starting from 3, two sentences are considered as equivalent in the SemEval gold standard.

summarization. In *13th Conference of the European Chapter of the Association for Computational Linguistics (EACL 2012)*, pages 214–223, Avignon, France.

Bill Dolan, Chris Quirk, and Chris Brockett. 2004. Unsupervised construction of large paraphrase corpora: exploiting massively parallel news sources. In *Proceedings of the 20th international conference on Computational Linguistics (COLING 2004)*, pages 350–356.

Stijn van Dongen. 2000. *Graph Clustering by Flow Simulation*. Ph.D. thesis, University of Utrecht.

Johanna Geiss. 2009. Creating a Gold Standard for Sentence Clustering in Multi-Document Summarization. In *47th Annual Meeting of the Association for Computational Linguistics and 4th International Joint Conference on Natural Language Processing of the AFNLP (ACL-IJCNLP 2009), Student Research Workshop*, pages 96–104, Singapore.

S.J. Gershman and J.B. Tenenbaum. 2015. Phrase similarity in humans and machines. In *Proceedings of the 37th Annual Conference of the Cognitive Science Society*.

Dan Gillick and Benoit Favre. 2009. A Scalable Global Model for Summarization. In *Workshop on Integer Linear Programming for Natural Language Processing (ILP'09)*, pages 10–18, Boulder, Colorado.

Felix Hill, Kyunghyun Cho, and Anna Korhonen. 2016. Learning Distributed Representations of Sentences from Unlabelled Data. In *2016 Conference of the North American Chapter of the Association for Computational Linguistics: Human Language Technologies (HLT-NAACL 2016)*, pages 1367–1377, San Diego, California.

Tsutomu Hirao, Masaaki Nishino, Jun Suzuki, and Masaaki Nagata. 2017. Enumeration of Extractive Oracle Summaries. In *15th Conference of the European Chapter of the Association for Computational Linguistics (EACL 2017)*, pages 386–396, Valencia, Spain.

Kai Hong, John Conroy, Benoit Favre, Alex Kulesza, Hui Lin, and Ani Nenkova. 2014. A Repository of State of the Art and Competitive Baseline Summaries for Generic News Summarization. In *Ninth International Conference on Language Resources and Evaluation (LREC'14)*, pages 1608–1616, Reykjavik, Iceland. ELRA.

Huang Lei and He Yanxiang. 2010. CorrRank: Update Summarization Based on Topic Correlation Analysis. In *Advanced Intelligent Computing Theories and Applications. With Aspects of Artificial Intelligence. 6th International Conference on Intelligent Computing (ICIC 2010)*, pages 641–648, Changsha, China.

Chen Li, Yang Liu, and Lin Zhao. 2015. Improving Update Summarization via Supervised ILP and Sentence Reranking. In *Proceedings of the 2015 Conference of the North American Chapter of the Association for Computational Linguistics: Human Language Technologies*, pages 1317–1322, Denver, Colorado.

Jiwei Li, Sujian Li, Xun Wang, Ye Tian, and Baobao Chang. 2012. Update Summarization using a Multi-level Hierarchical Dirichlet Process Model. In *COLING 2012*, pages 1603–1618, Mumbai, India.

Chin-Yew Lin. 2004. ROUGE: A Package for Automatic Evaluation of Summaries. In *ACL-04 Workshop Text Summarization Branches Out*, pages 74–81, Barcelona, Spain.

Tomas Mikolov, Kai Chen, Greg Corrado, and Jeffrey Dean. 2013. Efficient estimation of word representations in vector space. In *International Conference on Learning Representations 2013 (ICLR 2013), workshop track*.

Jeffrey Pennington, Richard Socher, and Christopher D. Manning. 2014. GloVe: Global Vectors for Word Representation. In *2014 Empirical Methods in Natural Language Processing (EMNLP 2014)*, pages 1532–1543.

Robert Speer and Joshua Chin. 2016. An Ensemble Method to Produce High-Quality Word Embeddings. *CoRR*, abs/1604.01692.

Md Arafat Sultan, Steven Bethard, and Tamara Sumner. 2014. DLS@CU: Sentence Similarity from Word Alignment. In *8th International Workshop on Semantic Evaluation (SemEval 2014)*, pages 241–246, Dublin, Ireland.

Xiaojun Wan. 2012. Update Summarization Based on Co-Ranking with Constraints. In *COLING 2012*, pages 1291–1300, Mumbai, India.

Hongling Wang and Guodong Zhou. 2012. Toward a Unified Framework for Standard and Update Multi-Document Summarization. *ACM Transactions on Asian Language Information Processing (TALIP)*, 11(2):1–18.

Lyndon White, Roberto Togneri, Wei Liu, and Mohammed Bennamoun. 2015. How Well Sentence Embeddings Capture Meaning. In *Proceedings of the 20th Australasian Document Computing Symposium (ADCS'15)*, pages 1–8, New York, NY, USA. ACM.

Markus Zopf, Eneldo Loza Mencía, and Johannes Fürnkranz. 2016. Sequential Clustering and Contextual Importance Measures for Incremental Update Summarization. In *26th International Conference on Computational Linguistics (COLING 2016)*, pages 1071–1082.

Hyperspherical Query Likelihood Models with Word Embeddings

Ryo Masumura[†]   **Taichi Asami**[†]   **Hirokazu Masataki**[†]
Kugatsu Sadamitsu[‡]   **Kyosuke Nishida**[†]   **Ryuichiro Higashinaka**[†]
NTT Media Intelligence Laboratories, NTT Corporation,
1-1, Hikarinooka, Yokosuka-shi, Kanagawa, 239-0847, Japan
[†]{masumura.ryo, asami.taichi, masataki.hirokazu
nishida.kyosuke, higashinaka.ryuichiro}@lab.ntt.co.jp
[‡]k.sadamitsu.ic@future.co.jp

Abstract

This paper presents an initial study on hyperspherical query likelihood models (QLMs) for information retrieval (IR). Our motivation is to naturally utilize pretrained word embeddings for probabilistic IR. To this end, key idea is to directly leverage the word embeddings as random variables for directional probabilistic models based on von Mises-Fisher distributions that are familiar to cosine distances. The proposed method enables us to theoretically take semantic similarities between document and target queries into consideration without introducing heuristic expansion techniques. In addition, this paper reveals relationships between hyperspherical QLMs and conventional QLMs. Experiments show document retrieval evaluation results in which a hyperspherical QLM is compared to conventional QLMs and document distance metrics using word or document embeddings.

1 Introduction

In information retrieval (IR), language modeling is known to be one of the most successful techniques (Ponte and Croft, 1998). A typical usage is query likelihood models (QLMs), in which language models are constructed from each retrieved document. In QLM-based probabilistic IR, the documents are ranked by probabilities for which a query can be generated by the document language model.

In this field, categorical QLMs which model generative probability of words using categorical distributions are fundamental models (Ponte and Croft, 1998; Zhai and Lafferty, 2001). It is known that the categorical QLMs do not perform well for vocabulary mismatches because categorical distribution cannot consider semantic relationships between words. Therefore, several expansion techniques such as query expansion (Bai et al., 2005), translation QLMs (Berger and Lafferty, 1999), and latent variable models (Wei and Croft, 2006) have been proposed in order to take semantic relationships between document and target query into account.

Recently, word embeddings, which are continuous vector representations embedding word semantic information, have been utilized for enhancing the previous expansion techniques (Zhang et al., 2016; Mitra and Craswell, 2017). The word embeddings can be easily acquired in an unsupervised manner from large scale text sets based on embedding modeling, i.e., skip-gram, continuous bag-of-words (CBOW) (Mikolov et al., 2013) or GloVe (Pennington et al., 2014). Zuccon et al. (2015); Ganguly et al. (2015); Zamani and Croft (2016a) used the word embeddings in order to assist translation QLMs. Zamani and Croft (2016b); Kuzi et al. (2016) used the word embeddings in order to perform query expansion. However, previous word embedding-based probabilistic IR methods have no theoretical validity since the word embeddings were heuristically introduced.

In order to perform more natural word embedding based probabilistic IR, our key idea is to directly leverage word embeddings rather than words as random variables for language models. In fact, the word embeddings can capture semantic similarity of words using directional information based on cosine distance (Mnih and Kavukcuglu, 2013). This motivates us to introduce directional probabilistic models based on von Mises-Fisher distributions which are familiar to the cosine distance (Banerjee et al., 2005; Sra, 2016).

This paper proposes a hyperspherical QLMs in which random variables are modeled by a mix-

Proceedings of the The 8th International Joint Conference on Natural Language Processing, pages 210–216,
Taipei, Taiwan, November 27 – December 1, 2017 ©2017 AFNLP

ture of von Mises-Fisher distributions. The hyperspherical QLMs can theoretically utilize word embeddings for probabilistic IR without introducing heuristic formulations. Main contributions are summarized as follows.

- This paper formulates hyperspherical QLMs based on both a maximum likelihood estimation and a maximum a posteriori estimation.
- This paper reveals that hyperspherical QLMs can be represented as an extended form of categorical QLMs and a theoretical form of translation QLMs.
- This paper shows document retrieval evaluation results in which a hyperspherical QLM is compared with conventional QLMs and document distance metrics with word or document embeddings.

2 Related Work

This paper is closely related to document distance metrics using word or document embeddings. One major distance metric is the cosine distance between two document vectors that are composed by averaging word embeddings (Vulic and Moens, 2015; Brokos et al., 2016) or document embeddings called paragraph vectors (PVs) (Le and Mikolov, 2014). Another highly efficient distance metric is word mover's distance (WMD), which leverages word embeddings (Kusner et al., 2015). In this work, we also examined these distance metrics in a document retrieval evaluation.

Generative models of word embeddings have recently been proposed in topic modeling in order to capture the semantic structure of words and documents (Das et al., 2015; Batmanghelich et al., 2016). To the best of our knowledge, this paper is the first work on language modeling that handles word embeddings as random variables.

3 IR based on QLMs

IR based on probabilistic modeling uses the probability of a document D given a query Q. One of the most famous approaches is QLM-based IR in which documents are ranked by the probabilities that a query can be generated by the document language model (Ponte and Croft, 1998). Given a query $Q = \{w_1, \cdots, w_T\}$, IR based on QLMs ranks documents as

$$P(D|Q) \overset{\text{rank}}{\propto} \prod_{t=1}^{T} P(w_t|\Theta_D), \qquad (1)$$

where Θ_D denotes a parameter of QLM for D.

3.1 Categorical QLMs

Categorical QLMs model $P(w|\Theta_D)$ using a categorical distribution. In a maximum likelihood (ML) estimation for the categorical QLM, a generative probability of a word w is defined as

$$P(w|\Theta_D^{\text{ML}}) = \frac{c(w, D)}{|D|}, \qquad (2)$$

where $c(w, D)$ is the word count of w in D, and $|D|$ is the number of all words in D.

In a maximum a posteriori (MAP) estimation, a document collection C in which all of the retrieved documents are included is used for a prior (Zhai and Lafferty, 2001). MAP estimated generative probability of a word w is defined as

$$P(w|\Theta_D^{\text{MAP}}) = \frac{c(w, D) + \tau \frac{c(w, C)}{|C|}}{|D| + \tau}, \qquad (3)$$

where $c(w, D)$ is the word count of w in C, and $|C|$ is the number of all words in C. τ is a hyper parameter for adjusting smoothing.

3.2 Translation QLMs

Translation QLMs were introduced for expanding categorical QLMs (Berger and Lafferty, 1999). The translation QLMs are usually used together with the categorical QLMs, and enable us to take into account relationships between a word in the query and semantically related words in the document. A generative probability of a word w is defined as

$$P(w|\Theta_D^{\text{TR}}) = \sum_{v \in \mathcal{V}} P(v|\Theta_D)P(w|v), \qquad (4)$$

where $\mathcal{V}$ is the vocabulary. $P(v|\Theta_D)$ is the generative probability of a word v, which is also calculated by Eq. (2) or (3). $P(w|v)$ represents the probability of translating word v into word w. $P(w|v)$ is heuristically calculated as

$$P(w|v) = \frac{\text{sim}(w, v)}{\sum_{w \in \mathcal{V}} \text{sim}(w, v)}, \qquad (5)$$

where $\text{sim}(w, v)$ is the word similarity between w and v. In order to calculate $P(w|v)$, cosine distances between pre-trained word embeddings were recently utilized (Zuccon et al., 2015; Ganguly et al., 2015). Thus, the word similarity is calculated as

$$\text{sim}(w, v) = \boldsymbol{w}^{\top}\boldsymbol{v}, \qquad (6)$$

where $\boldsymbol{w}$ is the word embedding normalized to a unit length for w.

4 IR based on Hyperspherical QLMs

This paper proposes a novel probabilistic IR method based on hyperspherical QLM that leverages pre-trained word embeddings as random variables for directional probabilistic models. The pre-trained word embeddings can capture semantic similarity of words on a unit hypersphere, so we deal with normalized word embeddings to unit length. Given a query $Q = \{w_1, \cdots, w_T\}$, normalized word embeddings $\{w_1, \cdots, w_T\}$ can be acquired using embedding models. IR based on hyperspherical QLMs ranks documents as

$$P(D|Q) \overset{\text{rank}}{\propto} \prod_{t=1}^{T} p(w_t|\Lambda_D), \qquad (7)$$

where p means a probability density and Λ_D denotes a parameter of a hyperspherical QLM for D.

4.1 Formulation

The hyperspherical QLMs are formulated by a mixture of von Mises-Fisher distributions which are familiar to cosine distances (Banerjee et al., 2005; Sra, 2016). The von Mises-Fisher distribution defines a probability density over points on a unit hypersphere. A probability density based on the mixture of von Mises-Fisher distributions is formulated as

$$p(w|\Lambda) = \sum_{m=1}^{M} \alpha_m f(w|\mu_m), \qquad (8)$$

$$f(w|\mu_m) = C_d(\kappa) \exp(\kappa w^\top \mu_m), \qquad (9)$$

where M is the number of mixtures. The parameter Λ corresponds to $\{\alpha_m, \mu_m\}$. α_m means a mixture weight, and μ_m means a directional mean of the m-th von Mises-Fisher distribution. κ is a concentration parameter that is treated as a smoothing parameter. $C_d(\kappa)$ is a normalized parameter that depends on κ and the number of dimensions of word embeddings d. Note that $w^\top \mu_m$ is the cosine distance between w and μ_m.

4.2 ML and MAP Estimation for Mixture of von Mises-Fisher Distributions

ML estimation for a mixture of von Mises-Fisher distributions given normalized word embeddings $D = \{w_1, \cdots, w_{|D|}\}$ determines model parameters Λ_D^{ML} as

$$\Lambda_D^{\text{ML}} = \underset{\Lambda}{\arg\max}\, P(D|\Lambda). \qquad (10)$$

The ML estimation is based on the expectation maximization algorithm. ML estimated parameters $\Lambda_D^{\text{ML}} = \{\hat{\alpha}_m\}, \{\hat{\mu}_m\}$ are recursively calculated as

$$\hat{\alpha}_m = \frac{1}{|D|} \sum_{t=1}^{|D|} q(m|w_t, \Lambda), \qquad (11)$$

$$\hat{r}_m = \sum_{t=1}^{|D|} w_t q(m|w_t, \Lambda), \qquad (12)$$

$$\hat{\mu}_m = \frac{\hat{r}_m}{||\hat{r}_m||}, \qquad (13)$$

where $q(m|w_t, \Lambda)$ is a load factor of the m-th distribution for the t-th word embedding.

MAP estimation for a mixture of von Mises-Fisher distributions given normalized word embeddings $D = \{w_1, \cdots, w_{|D|}\}$ determines model parameters Λ_D^{ML} as

$$\Lambda_D^{\text{MAP}} = \underset{\Lambda}{\arg\max}\, P(D|\Lambda)P(\Lambda). \qquad (14)$$

Given pre-trained parameters $\bar{\Lambda} = \{\bar{\alpha}_m, \bar{r}_m\}$, MAP-estimated parameters $\Lambda_D^{\text{MAP}} = \{\hat{\alpha}_m, \hat{\mu}_m\}$ are calculated as

$$\hat{\alpha}_m = \frac{\tau}{|D| + \tau} \bar{\alpha}_m + \frac{|D|}{|D| + \tau} \frac{1}{|D|} \sum_{t=1}^{|D|} q(m|w_t, \bar{\Lambda}), \qquad (15)$$

$$\hat{r}_m = \frac{\tau}{|D| + \tau} \bar{r}_m + \frac{|D|}{|D| + \tau} \sum_{t=1}^{|D|} w_t q(m|w_t, \bar{\Lambda}), \qquad (16)$$

$$\hat{\mu}_m = \frac{\hat{r}_m}{||\hat{r}_m||}, \qquad (17)$$

where τ is a hyper parameter for adjusting smoothing.

For computation of load factors, both the soft-assignment rule and the hard-assignment rule can be used. Both computations are defined as

$$q_{\text{s}}(m|w_t, \Lambda) = \frac{\alpha_m f(w_t|\mu_m)}{\sum_{l=1}^{M} \alpha_l f(w_t|\mu_l)}, \qquad (18)$$

$$q_{\text{h}}(m|w_t, \Lambda) = \begin{cases} 1 & m = \underset{l}{\arg\max}\, \alpha_l f(w_t|\mu_l), \\ 0 & \text{otherwise}, \end{cases} \qquad (19)$$

where q_{s} is the load factor using the soft-assignment rule and q_{h} is the load factor using the hard-assignment rule.

4.3 Training of Hyperspherical QLMs

In order to introduce a mixture of von Mises-Fisher distributions to hyperspherical QLMs, unified assumptions are essential for each document modeling because the hyperspherical QLMs are utilized for IR. Therefore, we introduce the following assumptions.

- The number of mixtures corresponds to vocabulary size.

$$M = |\mathcal{V}|. \tag{20}$$

- The mean direction of each von Mises-Fisher distribution is fixed to normalized word embeddings of each word in the vocabulary.

$$\hat{\boldsymbol{\mu}}_m = \boldsymbol{v}_m, \tag{21}$$

where $v_m \in \mathcal{V}$.

- For computation of load factors in document modeling, a hard-assignment rule is used.

To summarize the above, the hyperspherical QLMs can be theoretically estimated as simple forms using ML or MAP estimation. In fact, mixture weights are estimated as ML or MAP estimated values in categorical QLMs. In ML estimation, $\hat{\alpha}_m$ estimated from document D is determined as

$$\hat{\alpha}_m = \frac{c(v_m, D)}{|D|}. \tag{22}$$

Thus, ML estimated generative probability of $\boldsymbol{w}$ in the hyperspherical QLMs is formulated as

$$p(\boldsymbol{w}|\boldsymbol{\Lambda}_D^{\text{ML}}) = \sum_{v \in \mathcal{V}} \frac{c(v, D)}{|D|} f(\boldsymbol{w}|\boldsymbol{v}), \tag{23}$$

where $\boldsymbol{v}$ is a normalized word embedding of v.

In MAP estimation, $\hat{\alpha}_m$ estimated from document D is determined as

$$\hat{\alpha}_m = \frac{c(v_m, D) + \tau \frac{c(v_m, C)}{|C|}}{|D| + \tau}, \tag{24}$$

where C is document collection in which all retrieved documents are included. Thus, MAP estimated generative probability of $\boldsymbol{w}$ in the hyspherical QLMs is formulated as

$$p(\boldsymbol{w}|\boldsymbol{\Lambda}_D^{\text{MAP}}) = \sum_{v \in \mathcal{V}} \frac{c(v, D) + \tau \frac{c(v, C)}{|C|}}{|D| + \tau} f(\boldsymbol{w}|\boldsymbol{v}). \tag{25}$$

4.4 Relationships

The hyperspherical QLMs can be interpreted as an extended form of categorical QLMs. Eq. (23) includes the ML estimated term presented in Eq. (2), and Eq. (25) includes the MAP estimated term presented in Eq. (3). In fact, hyperspherical QLMs can be converted into categorical QLMs by

$$\lim_{\kappa \to \infty} p(\boldsymbol{w}|\boldsymbol{\Theta}_D) = P(w|\boldsymbol{\Lambda}_D). \tag{26}$$

In addition, hyperspherical QLMs can be regarded as a theoretical form of translation QLMs. Eqs. (23) and (25) are similar to Eq. (4). In fact, hyperspherical QLMs are almost the same as translation QLMs by defining a word similarity as

$$\text{sim}(w, v) = \exp(\kappa \boldsymbol{w}^\top \boldsymbol{v}). \tag{27}$$

While Eq. (6) is heuristically formulated, Eq. (27) is theoretically formulated as a log-linear form based on the directional probabilistic modeling.

5 Experiments

5.1 Setups

We performed an experiment on a document retrieval task, in which we used 20 news group datasets[1] for evaluation. The datasets were formally split into 11,314 training and 7,531 test articles. The training articles were used for collecting documents and the test articles were used for queries. Label information about news groups was only utilized for deciding whether a retrieved document is relevant to the query in evaluation. These setups are equivalent to the evaluation in Salakhutdinov and Hinton (2009); Larochelle and Lauly (2012). We removed common stop words, and the 5,000 most frequent words in the training articles were used for the vocabulary.

In order to utilize word embeddings, data sets in a one billion word language modeling benchmark[2] were prepared. We constructed CBOW and PV with distributed BOW (PV-DBOW). These pretrained embedding models were utilized for IR-methods. The dimension of the word and document embeddings was set to 200.

For evaluation, the following IR methods were used. **TFIDF** used cosine distance between two document vectors composed by word TF-IDF values. **CWV** used cosine distance between two

---

[1] http://qwone.com/~jason/20Newsgroups/20news-bydate.tar.gz

[2] http://github.com/ciprian-chelba/1-billion-word-language-modeling-benchmark

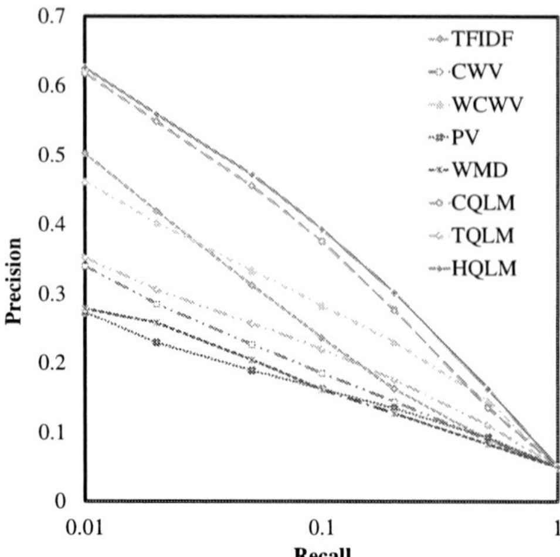

Figure 1: Precision-recall curves results.

Table 1: `mAP` and `P@10` results.

IR methods	Embeddings	mAP	P@10
TFIDF		0.123	0.478
CWV	✓	0.109	0.321
WCWV	✓	0.165	0.438
PV	✓	0.105	0.284
WMD	✓	0.103	0.287
CQLM		0.182	0.586
TQLM	✓	0.126	0.343
HQLM	✓	**0.198**	**0.594**

document vectors composed by averaging word embeddings (Vulic and Moens, 2015). **WCWV** used cosine distance between two document vectors composed by adding word embeddings with IDF weights (Brokos et al., 2016). **PV** used cosine distance of two document vectors composed by PV-DBOW (Le and Mikolov, 2014). **WMD** used WMD using word embeddings (Kusner et al., 2015). **CQLM** used discrete QLMs estimated by Eq. (4) where τ was set to 2,000 (Zhai and Lafferty, 2001). **TQLM** used translation QLMs where word similarity was calculated by Eq. (6) using word embeddings, and Eq. (3) was used for calculating generative probability (Ganguly et al., 2015). **HQLM** used hyperspherical QLMs estimated by Eq. (11) using word embeddings, in which τ and κ were respectively set to 2,000 and 20.

5.2 Results

We assessed the performance of each IR-method with precision-recall curves, mean average precision (`mAP`), and precision at 10 (`P@10`). Figure 1 shows the precision-recall curve results and Table 1 shows the `mAP` and `P@10` results. The results are averaged over all possible queries.

The results show that CQLM and HQLM clearly outperformed document distance metric-based IR methods with word or document embeddings. This confirms that QLM-based IR is a helpful approach for document retrieval. Although word or document embeddings trained from a lot

of text sets can efficiently capture semantic information in continuous space, the document distance metrics using the embeddings were insufficient for document retrieval. In addition, we attained superior performance only introducing HQLM compared to CQLM while single use of TQLM did not perform well. In fact, previous work attained performance improvements by combining TQLM with CQLM. These results confirm that HQLM can effectively utilize word embeddings for document retrieval. Furthermore, we analyzed that relevant documents ranked low in CQLM were moved up by HQLM. This indicates HQLM can robustly calculate generative probabilities of words that were not included in a target query. We also verified that HQLM showed similar results to CQLM when κ was set to a large value ($\kappa = 500$). This confirms that Eq. (12), which insists HQLM can be represented as CQLM, is a proper theory.

6 Conclusions

In this paper, we proposed a word embedding-based probabilistic IR method based on hyperspherical QLMs that are modeled by a mixture of von Mises-Fisher distributions. We found the hyperspherical QLMs could theoretically utilize word embeddings for IR without introducing heuristic formulations. We found that the hyperspherical QLMs can be represented as an extended form of categorical QLMs and a theoretical form of translation QLMs. Our experiments on a document retrieval task showed hyperspherical QLM outperformed previous QLMs and document distance metrics with word or document embeddings. In the future, we will examine large scale document retrieval evaluation.

References

Jing Bai, Dawei Song, Peter Bruza, Jian-Yun Nie, and Guihong Cao. 2005. Query expansion using term relationships in language models for information retrieval. *In Proc. Conference on Information and Knowledge Management (CIKM)* pages 688–695.

Arindam Banerjee, Inderjit S. Dhillon, Joydeep Ghosh, and Suvrit Sra. 2005. Clustering on the unit hypersphere using von mises-fisher distribution. *Journal of Machine Learning Research* 6:1345–1382.

Nematollah Kayhan Batmanghelich, Ardavan Saeedi, Karthik R. Narasimhan, and Samuel J. Gershman. 2016. Nonparametric spherical topic modeling with word embeddings. *In Proc. Annual Meeting of the Association for Computational Linguistics (ACL)* pages 537–542.

Adam Berger and John Lafferty. 1999. Information retrieval as statistical translation. *In Proc. Annual International ACM Conference on Research and Development in Information Retrieval (SIGIR)* pages 222–229.

Georgios-Ioannis Brokos, Prodromos Malakasiotis, and Ion Androutsopoulos. 2016. Using centroids of word embeddings and word mover's distance for biomedical document retrieval in question answering. *In Proc. Workshop on Biomedical Natural Language Processing (BioNLP)* pages 114–118.

Rajarshi Das, Manzil Zaheer, and Chris Dyer. 2015. Gaussian LDA for topic models with word embeddings. *In Proc. Annual Meeting of the Association for Computational Linguistics (ACL)* pages 795–804.

Debasis Ganguly, Dwaipayan Roy, Mandar Mitra, and Gareth J.F. Jones. 2015. A word embedding based generalized language model for information retrieval. *In Proc. Annual International ACM Conference on Research and Development in Information Retrieval (SIGIR)* pages 795–798.

Matt J. Kusner, Yu Sun, Nicholas I. Kolkin, and Kilian Q. Weinberger. 2015. From word embeddings to document distances. *In Proc. International Conference on Machine Learning (ICML)* .

Saar Kuzi, Anna Shtok, and Oren Kurland. 2016. Query expansion using word embeddings. *In Proc. Conference on Information and Knowledge Management (CIKM)* pages 1929–1932.

Hugo Larochelle and Stanislas Lauly. 2012. A neural autoregressive topic model. *In Proc. Advances in Neural Infomation Processing Systems (NIPS)* pages 2708–2716.

Quoc Le and Tomas Mikolov. 2014. Distributed representations of sentences and documents. *In Proc. International Conference on Machine Learning (ICML)* pages 1188–1196.

Tomas Mikolov, Ilya Sutskever, Kai Chen, Ggeg Corrado, and Jeffrey Dean. 2013. Distributed representation of words and phrases and their compositionality. *In Proc. Advances in Neural Information Processing Systems (NIPS)* pages 3111–3119.

Bhaskar Mitra and Nick Craswell. 2017. Neural text embeddings for information retrieval. *In Proc. ACM International Conference on Web Search and Data Mining (WSDM)* pages 813–814.

Andriy Mnih and Koray Kavukcuglu. 2013. Learning word embeddings efficiently with noise-contrastive estimation. *In Proc. Advances in Neural Information Processing Systems (NIPS)* pages 2265–2273.

Jeffrey Pennington, Richard Socher, and Christopher D Manning. 2014. Glove: Global vectors for word representation. *In Proc. Empirical Methods in Natural Language Processing (EMNLP)* pages 1532–1543.

Jay M. Ponte and W. Bruce Croft. 1998. A language modeling approach to information retrieval. *In Proc. Annual International ACM Conference on Research and Development in Information Retrieval (SIGIR)* pages 275–281.

Ruslan Salakhutdinov and Geoffrey Hinton. 2009. Replicated softmax: an undirected topic model. *In Proc. Advances in Neural Information Processing Systems (NIPS)* pages 1607–1614.

Suvrit Sra. 2016. Directional statistics in machine learning: a brief review. *arXiv prerint arXiv:1605.00316* .

Ivan Vulic and Marie-Francine Moens. 2015. Monolingual and cross-lingual information retrieval models based on (bilingual) word embeddings. *In Proc. Annual International ACM Conference on Research and Development in Information Retrieval (SIGIR)* pages 363–372.

Xing Wei and W. Bruce Croft. 2006. LDA-based document models for ad-hoc retrieval. *In Proc. Annual International ACM Conference on Research and Development in Information Retrieval (SIGIR)* pages 178–185.

Hamed Zamani and W. Bruce Croft. 2016a. Embedding-based query language models. *In Proc. ACM International Conference on the Theory of Information Retrieval (ICTIR)* pages 147–156.

Hamed Zamani and W. Bruce Croft. 2016b. Estimating embedding vectors for queries. *In Proc. ACM International Conference on the Theory of Information Retrieval (ICTIR)* pages 123–132.

Chengxiang Zhai and John Lafferty. 2001. A study of smoothing methods for language models applied to ad hoc information retrieval. *In Proc. Annual International ACM Conference on Research and Development in Information Retrieval (SIGIR)* pages 334–342.

Ye Zhang, Md Mustafizur Rahman, Alex Braylan, Brandon Dang, Heng-Lu Chang, Henna Kim, Quinten McNamara, Aaron Angert, Edward Banner, Vivek Khetan, Tyler McDonnell, An Thanh Nguyen, Dan Xu, Byron C. Wallace, and Matthew Lease. 2016. Neural information retrieval: A literature review. *arXiv prerint arXiv:1611.06792* .

Guido Zuccon, Bevan Koopman, Peter Bruza, and Leif Azzopardi. 2015. Integrating and evaluating neural word embeddings in information retrieval. *In Proc. Australasian Document Computing Symposium (ADCS)* 12:1–8.

Dual Constrained Question Embeddings with Relational Knowledge Bases for Simple Question Answering

Kaustubh Kulkarni and **Riku Togashi** and **Hideyuki Maeda** and **Sumio Fujita**
Yahoo Japan Corporation,
Tokyo, Japan
{kkulkarn,rtogashi,hidmaeda,sufujita}@yahoo-corp.jp

Abstract

Embedding based approaches are shown to be effective for solving simple Question Answering (QA) problems in recent works. The major drawback of current approaches is that they look only at the similarity (constraint) between a question and a head, relation pair. Due to the absence of tail (answer) in the questions, these models often require paraphrase datasets to obtain adequate embeddings. In this paper, we propose a dual constraint model which exploits the embeddings obtained by Trans* family of algorithms to solve the simple QA problem without using any additional resources such as paraphrase datasets. The results obtained prove that the embeddings learned using dual constraints are better than those with single constraint models having similar architecture.

1 Introduction

Recent progress in Knowledge Bases (KB) related technologies enable us to enhance an atomic fact repository of inter-entity relationship. For example KB completion aims to infer unknown entities in atomic facts, which is represented in the form of triplets (h, r, t) where h, r, t represent a head entity, relationship and a tail entity respectively, e.g. (*Barack Obama, Nationality, USA*) which corresponds to the factual knowledge that "the nationality of Barack Obama is USA". Freebase[1] and DBPedia[2] contain such atomic facts about entities in the real world. However, the real challenge for leveraging such knowledge in practical applications consists of mapping natural language questions to their corresponding entries in thus enhanced KBs.

Current embedding based QA models such as (Bordes et al., 2014a,b, 2015; Golub and He, 2016) are focusing on a sequential inference of predicting the pair of (h, r) from the given question (q), then inferring (t) corresponding to the predicted pair (h, r) using any KB completion models e.g. Trans* family models. This is a reasonable approach since such a type of questions contain information about both the head entity and the relation. However, once the first step of inference fails to match the correct (h, r) pair, it is hopeless for the second step to answer the correct entity. In order to avoid this problem, they use additional resources such as question paraphrases or entity aliases.

In this paper, we propose a completely different approach which uses a Trans* family based scoring function to predict the pair of (h, r) from q, and also maps q to t simultaneously. We learn embeddings for question words, entities and relations from the KB simultaneously bringing them into an euclidean space. Proposed dual constraint concurrent inference achieved better performance on a standard dataset than single constraint sequential inference methods without using any additional resources.

2 Related Work

Our work is inspired by the recent advances in solving simple QA problems using embedding approaches such as (Bordes et al., 2014a,b, 2015) which show that these approaches are very effective in mapping natural language questions to the corresponding triplet in a KB. They learn the embeddings for each question by a Bag Of Words (BOW) representation. (Jain, 2016) focuses on the positions of the question words and

---

[1]https://developers.google.com/freebase/
[2]http://wiki.dbpedia.org/

Proceedings of the The 8th International Joint Conference on Natural Language Processing, pages 217–221,
Taipei, Taiwan, November 27 – December 1, 2017 ©2017 AFNLP

incorporate them into the model. Some models such as (Yih et al., 2015; Dai et al., 2016) focus on deep networks to encode question words and KB constituents. (Dai et al., 2016) have modeled the probability of predicting head and relation jointly, proposing two neural networks for learning the embeddings. (Golub and He, 2016) introduced attention mechanism for character level LSTM encoding of questions and entities for embedding question words and KB constituents. (Yin et al., 2016) proposed to use char-CNN to encode the entities and word-CNN with maxpooling to encode relations. (Yu et al., 2017) focused on the different granularity of relation representation. (Lukovnikov et al., 2017) have used rich entity information to get more powerful KB constituents encodings. Note that all these models focused on a single constraint sequential inference that uses similarities between q and (h,r) pairs to learn embeddings. Our method applies a dual constrained concurrent inference that uses similarities between q and t on top of (h,r) pairs while leveraging embeddings pre-trained by the Trans* family of algorithms.

Various Trans* family models such as **TransE** (Bordes et al., 2013),**TransH**(Wang et al., 2014),**TransR** (Lin et al., 2015) are proposed to learn low dimension embeddings of KB constituents using relations in KB as translations over entity embedding space.

3   Proposed Method

We propose an embedding based approach where both question words and KB constituents are mapped into a common low dimensional embedding space.

Single Constrained Sequential Inference: In the common euclidean space of question and KB constituents embeddings, assume d_1 to be euclidean distance between question embedding (**q**) and additive vector of head entity and relation (**h+r**). As shown in Figure 1[a] current QA models try to minimize d_1 so as to predict head entity and relation pair (h,r) from the question(q), consequently they have a single constraint such that corresponding **q** and **h+r** should be closer to each other. Assume d_2 to be an euclidean distance between tail entity embedding (**t**) and (**h+r**). Trans* family of algorithms try to minimize d_2 so as to predict tail entity (t) from a pair of (h,r). Current models minimize d_1 and d_2 in the two distinct

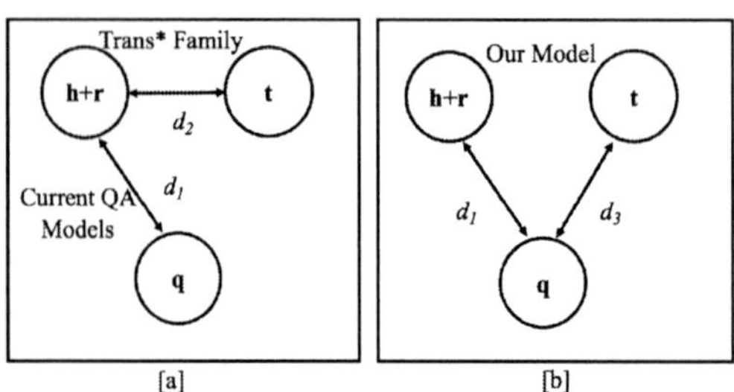

Figure 1: **[a]** Single constrained QA models minimize the distance (d_1) between Question Embeddings (q) and head entity, relation pair (h,r) and Trans* family of algorithms minimize distance (d_2) between tail entity (t) and (h,r). **[b]** Our model minimize the distance (d_3) between q and t along with d_1 thus applying the second constraint on q.

steps, indirectly bringing **q** closer to **t**.

Dual Constrained Concurrent Inference: A QA system is preferably able to directly retrieve an answer entity upon a submission of a question. The problem here is that a simple factoid question does not contain sufficient information of the answer entity by definition. Thus our model should learn question embeddings such that **q** should be closer to **t** as well as (**h+r**). Assume d_3 to be an euclidean distance between (**q**) and (**t**) in the same vector space as earlier model, as can be seen in Figure 1[b], our model minimizes $d_1 + d_3$ i.e. bringing **q** closer to both **h+r** and **t**. This is implemented as a dual constraint in objective function when learning **q**, which reduces the degree of freedom of **q**, resulting in a better euclidean space in comparison with single constrained models. Thanks to these constraints we do not need any additional resources such as question paraphrase datasets while achieving on a par performance with the current models.

3.1   TransR

TransR (Lin et al., 2015) is an algorithm to learn low dimensional vector representations of entities and relations in the Knowledge Base. TransR adopts a score function f_r to measure the credibility of a KB triplet $(h,\ r,\ t)$ such that the score is low when $(h,\ r,\ t)$ is likely to be true and high otherwise.

TransR represents entities and relations in distinct vector spaces i.e. *entity space* and *relation space*. For each triplet, let $\mathbf{h} \in \mathbb{R}^k, \mathbf{t} \in \mathbb{R}^k$ be an entity embedding of either head or tail respec-

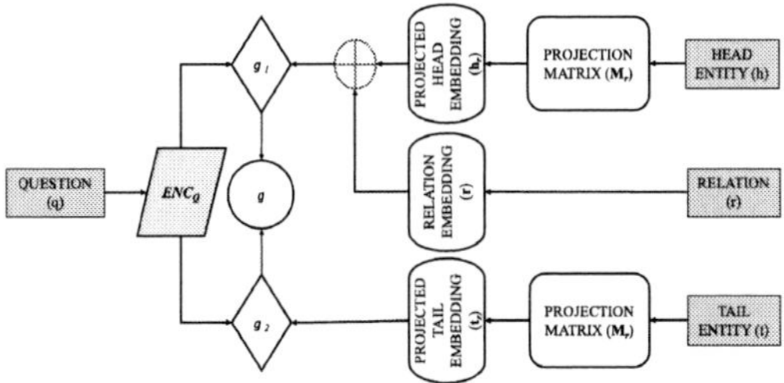

Figure 2: Overview of our learning diagram

tively and $\mathbf{r} \in \mathbb{R}^d$ be a relation embedding, where k and d are the dimensions of embeddings of entities and relations respectively. It also trains a relation specific projection Matrix $\mathbf{M}_r \in \mathbb{R}^{k \times d}$, which projects entities from the entity space to a corresponding relation space. With this projection matrix, projected vectors of entities are defined as,

$$\mathbf{h}_r = \mathbf{hM}_r, \ \mathbf{t}_r = \mathbf{tM}_r.$$

The score function is defined as:

$$f_r = \|\mathbf{h}_r + \mathbf{r} - \mathbf{t}_r\|_2^2.$$

Constraints are enforced on the norms of embeddings h, r, t and projection matrices, i.e. $\forall \ \mathbf{h}, \mathbf{r}, \mathbf{t}$ we have $\|\mathbf{h}\|_2 \leq 1, \|\mathbf{r}\|_2 \leq 1, \|\mathbf{t}\|_2 \leq 1, \|\mathbf{hM}_r\|_2 \leq 1, \|\mathbf{tM}_r\|_2 \leq 1$.

Margin based score function is defined as objective for training purpose which is as follows:

$$C = \sum_{(h,\, r,\, t) \in S} \sum_{(h',\, r,\, t') \in S'} max(0, f_r(h,t) + \gamma - f_r(h',t'))$$

where $max(x,y)$ returns the larger value between x and y, γ is the margin parameter, S is the set of correct triplets from dataset and S' is the set of corrupted triplets generated by using various negative sampling methods for training purpose.

3.2 Model

As shown in Figure 2, our model pre-trains the entity (**h,t**) and relation (**r**) embeddings with TransR, whereas encoding questions into $\mathbf{q} \in \mathbb{R}^d$ where d is the size of question embedding. Questions should be closer to the sum of (h) and (r) of the corresponding triplet in the KB, similarly the answer of the question should be closer to the vector of tail entity (t). We propose a score function $g(h, r, t, q)$ such that the score is low if (h, r, t) is the triplet corresponding to the question (q) and high otherwise. Scores of the question embedding are defined as:

1. This indicates how close a question is to the combination of head entity (h) and relation (r) embeddings in TransR relation space

$$g_1 = \|\mathbf{h}_r + \mathbf{r} - \mathbf{q}\|_2^2$$

2. This indicates how close a question is to the tail entity (t) embedding in a TransR relation space.

$$g_2 = \|\mathbf{t}_r - \mathbf{q}\|_2^2$$

Then the final score of the question is defined as:

$$g = g_1 + g_2.$$

Additional constraints are enforced on norms of embeddings such that $\|\mathbf{q}\|_2 \leq 1$. Due to a dual constraint mentioned above on the question embedding (**q**), the degree of freedom is reduced considerably, which leads to fast training.

3.3 Training

Similar to previous studies involving embedding models (Bordes et al., 2014a,b, 2015), our model is trained with a ranking criterion. The objective of the learning is that the positive triplet should be closer to the natural language question than any other negative triplet by a certain margin γ in the embedding space. Thus we adopt a margin-based objective function for training purpose as follows:

$$L = \sum_{(h,\, r,\, t,\, q) \in S} \sum_{(h',\, r',\, t',q) \in S'} max(0, g_1(h, r, q) +$$
$$\gamma - g_1(h',r',q)) + max(0, g_2(t,q) + \gamma - g_2(t',q))$$

where $max(x,y)$ and γ are same as defined earlier. S is the set of correct pairs of a triplet and a question from the dataset and S' is the set of pairs of a negative triplet and a question as S.

3.4 Negative Triplet generation

For generating negative triplets we use a method known as *candidates as negatives*, which is proposed by (Bordes et al., 2015). In this method, non-supported triplets are chosen randomly from the set of candidate triplets.

4 Experiments

4.1 Knowledge Base and Dataset

We use FB2M as our base KB which is an extract of the Freebase with about 2M entities and

5k relations. We use **SimpleQuestions**[3] dataset introduced by (Bordes et al., 2015) for training and testing purposes. This dataset consists of a total of 108,442 natural language questions in English written by human English speaking annotators each paired with a corresponding triplet from FB2M that provides the answer. Out of whole data 75,910 data points were used for Training, 10,845 for validation and 21,687 for testing purpose.

4.2 Experimental Setup

TransR embeddings TransR embeddings of size 64 initialized randomly with uniform distribution were pre-trained with Probabilistic Negative Sampling method proposed by (Kanojia et al., 2017). **Question Encoding** Question is represented as sequence of words $(x_1, x_1, ..., x_{|q|})$. Low dimension vectors for each word in vocabulary are learnt and each word x_i is mapped to its vector. Word embedding size was set at 64 and initialized with random uniform distribution. We experimented with two methods to encode questions from individual question word embeddings:

Bag-of-Words (BOW) : It is a sum of individual word embeddings i.e.

$$\mathbf{q} = \sum_{i=1}^{|q|} x_i$$

Long Short Term Memory (LSTM)(Hochreiter and Schmidhuber, 1997): Each question is encoded using LSTM with dynamic RNN units with hidden layer size of 64 and forget bias as 1.0. Output of the last LSTM unit was taken as the question encoding.

We experimented with Batch size as 512, margin (γ) at 0.1 and Adam optimizer with learning rate of 0.001.

Candidate Pruning: Calculation of score for all triplets from the dataset is an memory and time wise prohibitive operation. Thus, at first we prune the facts to generate candidate facts similar to (Jain, 2016). Then only these candidate facts are scored by feeding them as input to our network. To generate these candidate facts, we match all possible n-grams of words of the question to Freebase entities and discard all n-grams (and their matched entities) that are a subsequence of another n-gram. All facts having one of the remaining entities as subject are added to candidate fact list. Facts with lowest score (g) out of candidates is retrieved as answer to the question. We evaluate our model based on

Setup	Path-level Accuracy(%)
Random Guess	4.9
Word Position(Jain, 2016)	59.7
Memory NW (Bordes et al., 2015)	62.7
Dual constrained BOW encoding	61.03
Dual constrained LSTM encoding	**64.05**

Table 1: Experimental Results on SimpleQuestion dataset for FB2M settings.

path-level accuracy in which prediction is correct if the head entity (h) and relation (r) of retrieved triplet are correct.

5 Results

The results of our experiments are shown in Table 1. We observe that our model gains 2-5% improvement in the path level accuracy than single constrained word level embeddings approaches by (Bordes et al., 2015; Jain, 2016) who have similar architecture to ours. Note that they use additional resources such as question paraphrase dataset and entity aliases while our model uses original dataset only. There are recent studies such as (Yin et al., 2016; Lukovnikov et al., 2017; Yu et al., 2017) which reported better accuracies on the same test set, by adopting either char-level CNNs or richer representations of entities/relations. Note that our dual constraint concurrent inference can be easily incorporated into such methods thus our method is complementary to their methods. We also report comparisons between different question encoding methods of our model. LSTM encoding outperforms BOW as it captures syntactic clues to map question onto the KB.

6 Conclusion and Future Work

In this work we show that Translation Embeddings learned using Trans* family of algorithms enable our model to learn the latent relationships between question and triplet using a unique score function. This results in a better performance in contrast with single constrained models as the essence of the triplet is inherently passed to the model in the form of embeddings. It also eliminates the need to use additional datasets to achieve good performance. The added dual constraint enforces the model to reduce the dual euclidean distance between question and triplet pairs, thereby generating adequate embeddings. Note that the dual constrained method can be extended to recent state of the art systems which use rich networks to obtain

---

[3]https://research.fb.com/downloads/babi/

better results.

In future, we hope to apply this method to richer embeddings obtained using deep networks. As shown in (Golub and He, 2016) character level encodings based models have been proven to be more precise compared to word level models for a simple QA task. We hope to extend our model to character level ones. Also the entity accuracy is comparatively lower than the relation accuracy which can be improved by using better entity linkers in questions.

References

Antoine Bordes, Sumit Chopra, and Jason Weston. 2014a. Question answering with subgraph embeddings. In *EMNLP*, pages 615–620. ACL.

Antoine Bordes, Nicolas Usunier, Sumit Chopra, and Jason Weston. 2015. Large-scale simple question answering with memory networks. *CoRR*, abs/1506.02075.

Antoine Bordes, Nicolas Usunier, Alberto Garcia-Duran, Jason Weston, and Oksana Yakhnenko. 2013. Translating embeddings for modeling multi-relational data. In *Advances in Neural Information Processing Systems 26*, pages 2787–2795.

Antoine Bordes, Jason Weston, and Nicolas Usunier. 2014b. Open question answering with weakly supervised embedding models. In *ECML/PKDD (1)*, volume 8724 of *Lecture Notes in Computer Science*, pages 165–180. Springer.

Zihang Dai, Lei Li, and Wei Xu. 2016. CFO: conditional focused neural question answering with large-scale knowledge bases. *CoRR*, abs/1606.01994.

David Golub and Xiaodong He. 2016. Character-level question answering with attention. *CoRR*, abs/1604.00727.

Sepp Hochreiter and Jürgen Schmidhuber. 1997. Long short-term memory. *Neural Comput.*, 9(8):1735–1780.

Sarthak Jain. 2016. Question answering over knowledge base using factual memory networks. In *Proceedings of NAACL-HLT*, pages 109–115.

Vibhor Kanojia, Hideyuki Maeda, Riku Togashi, and Sumio Fujita. 2017. Enhancing knowledge graph embedding with probabilistic negative sampling. In *Proceedings of the 26th International Conference Companion on World Wide Web*, WWW '17 Companion, pages 801–802. International World Wide Web Conferences Steering Committee.

Yankai Lin, Zhiyuan Liu, Maosong Sun, Yang Liu, and Xuan Zhu. 2015. Learning entity and relation embeddings for knowledge graph completion. In *Proceedings of the Twenty-Ninth AAAI Conference on Artificial Intelligence*, AAAI'15, pages 2181–2187. AAAI Press.

Denis Lukovnikov, Asja Fischer, Soeren Auer, and Jens Lehmann. 2017. Neural network-based question answering over knowledge graphs on word and character level. In *Proceedings of the 26th international conference on World Wide Web*.

Zhen Wang, Jianwen Zhang, Jianlin Feng, and Zheng Chen. 2014. Knowledge graph embedding by translating on hyperplanes. In *AAAI*, pages 1112–1119. AAAI Press.

Scott Wen-tau Yih, Ming-Wei Chang, Xiaodong He, and Jianfeng Gao. 2015. Semantic parsing via staged query graph generation: Question answering with knowledge base. ACL Association for Computational Linguistics.

Wenpeng Yin, Mo Yu, Bing Xiang, Bowen Zhou, and Hinrich Schütze. 2016. Simple question answering by attentive convolutional neural network. *CoRR*, abs/1606.03391.

Mo Yu, Wenpeng Yin, Kazi Saidul Hasan, Cícero Nogueira dos Santos, Bing Xiang, and Bowen Zhou. 2017. Improved neural relation detection for knowledge base question answering. *CoRR*, abs/1704.06194.

Efficiency-aware Answering of Compositional Questions using Answer Type Prediction

David Ziegler, Abdalghani Abujabal, Rishiraj Saha Roy and Gerhard Weikum
Max Planck Institute for Informatics
Saarland Informatics Campus, Germany
`{daziegler, abujabal, rishiraj, weikum}@mpi-inf.mpg.de`

Abstract

This paper investigates the problem of answering compositional factoid questions over knowledge bases (KB) under efficiency constraints. The method, called TIPI, (i) decomposes compositional questions, (ii) predicts answer types for individual sub-questions, (iii) reasons over the compatibility of joint types, and finally, (iv) formulates compositional SPARQL queries respecting type constraints. TIPI's answer type predictor is trained using distant supervision, and exploits lexical, syntactic and embedding-based features to compute context- and hierarchy-aware candidate answer types for an input question. Experiments on a recent benchmark show that TIPI results in state-of-the-art performance under the real-world assumption that only a single SPARQL query can be executed over the KB, and substantial reduction in the number of queries in the more general case.

1 Introduction

Motivation. Question answering over knowledge bases (KB-QA) has gained attention, facilitated by the rise of large-scale knowledge bases such as Freebase (Bollacker et al., 2007), DBPedia (Auer et al., 2007) and YAGO (Suchanek et al., 2007). The key challenge for KB-QA is to align mentions and relational phrases in a natural language question to semantic items in the KB (entities and predicates), and to construct a valid SPARQL query that is then executed over the KB to retrieve crisp answers (Abujabal et al., 2017; Bast and Haussmann, 2015; Yahya et al., 2013; Yih et al., 2015).

Questions going beyond simple factoid questions (like *"Who won a Nobel Prize in Physics?"*) that are prevalent in popular KB-QA benchmarks are generally out of scope for most state-of-the-art KB-QA systems (Yih et al., 2015; Dong et al., 2015; Berant and Liang, 2015). However, questions like *"Who won a Nobel Prize in Physics and was born in Bavaria?"*, can be decomposed into a set of simpler questions *"Who won a Nobel Prize in Physics?"* and *"Who was born in Bavaria?"*. We refer to such questions as *compositional questions*, and these are the focus of this work.

Limitations of state-of-the-art. A few past approaches that can handle such compositional questions (Bao et al., 2016; Xu et al., 2016; Abujabal et al., 2017) generate and execute candidate SPARQL queries for each sub-question separately and/or use the intersection as the final answer (*Werner Heisenberg*, among others). This creates the challenge of deciding which queries from the different sub-questions fit together. Past efforts use information about answers to all generated SPARQL queries, and retrospectively choose a query pair from among these whose answer intersection is non-empty. However, this mode of operation is highly inefficient, since it necessitates execution of all generated queries, followed by a ranking or aggregation phase. We aim to address this concern, leveraging the compatibility of expected *answer types*. Such compatibility, as we show, has the potential to prune the search space of candidate SPARQL queries.

Approach. Given a complex question, our proposed method TIPI first decomposes it into simple sub-questions. Next, it predicts a ranked list of fine-grained answer types for each sub-question, respecting a type hierarchy. TIPI then seeks candidate SPARQL queries corresponding to these sub-questions as input from an underlying KB-QA model, and finds pairs of compatible queries from among these using hierarchy-based reasoning. Finally, it scores these pairs and finds the best

222

Proceedings of the The 8th International Joint Conference on Natural Language Processing, pages 222–227,
Taipei, Taiwan, November 27 – December 1, 2017 ©2017 AFNLP

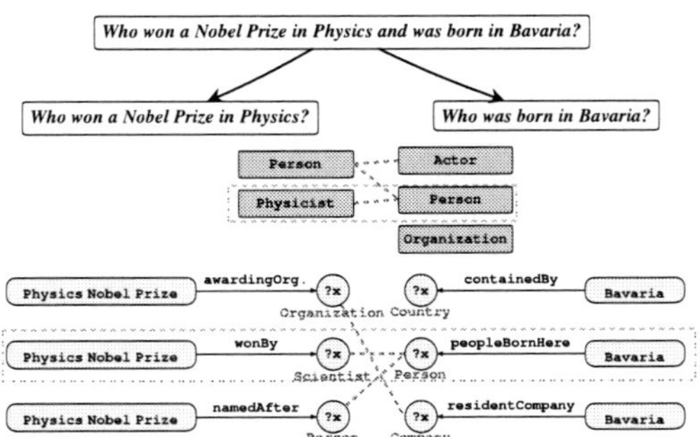

Figure 1: A toy example showing how TIPI works. Top: Decompose question. Middle: Determine compatible types among answer types of the two sub-questions. Bottom: Stitch compatible queries together and prune queries by answer type. This is followed by scoring and ranking of the query pairs to formulate the best compositional query.

pair to formulate a compositional query, to be executed over the KB. The final two steps contribute towards TIPI's efficiency-aware perspective.

Contributions. The paper makes the following three contributions:

- We are the first to exploit answer types for handling compositional questions in KB-QA;

- Experiments show state-of-the-art performance under practical efficiency constraints;

- Finally, TIPI contains a hierarchy- and context-aware fine-grained answer typing module that can be used as a plug-in by any KB-QA system.

2   Answering Compositional Questions

We now explain the steps by which TIPI handles the answering of a compositional question, taking the running example of *"Who won a Nobel Prize in Physics and was born in Bavaria?"*. A simplified workflow is shown in Figure 1.

Question decomposition. Given a compositional question, TIPI first decomposes it into simple sub-questions *"Who won a Nobel Prize in Physics?"* and *"Who was born in Bavaria?"*, using dependency parse patterns (Xu et al., 2016; Bao et al., 2014). These patterns can handle several kinds of compositional questions with multiple entities or relations (e.g., questions with relative clauses and coordinating conjunctions). Question decomposition has also been applied to the IBM Watson system (Boguraev et al., 2014),

where the authors separated cases as being either *parallel* or *nested*. This work deals with parallel decomposition, and handling nesting like *"which daughter of john f. kennedy studied at radcliffe college?"* is future work.

Answer Type prediction. Next, we predict a set of *expected answer types* for each sub-question using an answer type predictor, described in the next section. The typing module is a context-aware hierarchical classifier that takes a question as input and produces a set of answer types along with confidence scores as output (like `Person`: 0.8, `Actor`: 0.3, `Scientist`: 0.6; scores need not add up to one).

Type compatibility scoring. We define two types to be *compatible* whenever they are the same, or one is an ancestor of the other, according to some type system. For example, `Scientist` and `Person` are compatible, as the former is a descendant of the latter. Now, let T_1 and T_2 be a pair of predicted types for the first and second sub-questions, respectively. We score each such pair with a linear combination of *granularity* and *confidence* as follows:

$$score(T_1, T_2) = \gamma \cdot max(level(T_1), level(T_2))$$
$$+ (1 - \gamma) \cdot avg(conf(T_1), conf(T_2))$$

if T_1 and T_2 are compatible, else zero. Here, $level(T_i)$ and $conf(T_i)$ refer to the level of T_i in the type system, and the classifier prediction confidence for T_i, respectively. We take the root to be at level zero, with finer types having higher levels. Thus, pairs with fine-grained types (like `Physicist`), and with high prediction confidences, accumulate higher scores. Mixing parameter γ is chosen to be 0.5. We take the highest scoring type pair, and then take the finer of the two types as the final prediction (`Physicist` in this example). The intuition here is that one sub-question might reveal more typing information (*"Who won a Nobel Prize in Physics?"* gives `Physicist`) than the other (*"Who was born in Bavaria?"* only gives `Person`).

Compositional query formulation. We now let a KB-QA system generate a ranked list of SPARQL queries for each sub-question. In past work, all query pairs (one from each sub-question) are combined to create numerous compositional queries. Our goal is to stitch only type-compatible queries, which is achieved as follows. Each query predicate has a *type signature* from the KB, which states the expected types for the pred-

[.*]* [*which*|*what*] [lemma: be]? [det]? [adj|adv]* [noun]+ [.*]*
(*E.g.: What is the current currency in Germany?*)

[.*]* [*which*|*what*] [lemma: be]? [det]? [adj|adv]* [noun] [*of*] [det]?
[adj|adv]* [noun]+ [.*]* (*E.g.: What kind of currency does Germany have?*)

[.*]* [*which*|*what*] [lemma: be] [det]? [noun]+ [poss] [adj|adv]*
[noun]+ [.*]* (*E.g.: What is Germany's currency?*)

Table 1: Patterns to extract lexical answer types (underlined). Symbols are borrowed from standard regular expression conventions.

icate. We use our final predicted type to remove all queries from either sub-question whose type signatures are not compatible to it. Thus, queries like `PhysicsNobelPrize wonBy x?` and `Bavaria peopleBornHere x?`, with compatible type signatures `Physicist` and `Person` are retained, while `Bavaria containedBy x?` and `PhysicsNobelPrize awardingOrg x?` with signatures `Country` and `Organization` are removed. All surviving query pairs are combined, and are then scored by the sum of the inverses of the ranks they had from the underlying KB-QA model. The pair that maximizes this rank inversion score is finally chosen for execution by the system: `PhysicsNobelPrize wonBy x?` . `Bavaria peopleBornHere x?` for our example.

3 Predicting Answer Types

Our strategy for answer type prediction is to harness explicit clues available in the question, and to resort to more implicit ones only when such signals are not present. We thus use a two-stage approach, inspired by work on named entity typing (Del Corro et al., 2015; Yosef et al., 2012)[1]: (1) candidate collection, using lexico-syntactic patterns to identify lexical types which can be mapped to a set of semantic types using lexicons; (2) type selection, using a hierarchical classifier to disambiguate among the candidates. *Note that in absence of explicit clues for candidates in the question, our method proceeds directly to the second stage.*

Candidate Collection. To extract the lexical answer type from a question, we use simple POS patterns (examples in Table 1), utilizing Stanford CoreNLP for tokenization and POS-tagging (Manning et al., 2014). In a second step, the lexical type extracted from the question is mapped

to a set of semantic types (KB-types) using lexicons (Berant et al., 2013). Such lexicons can be constructed by mining entity-annotated relational phrases in CLUEWEB09 (Lin et al., 2012). For example, the lexical type *'physicist'* may map to the semantic types `Scientist`, `Theoretical physicist` and `Quantum physicist`.

Type Selection. From the candidate collection phase, we receive a set of candidate types, for each of which we run a binary classifier to get a confidence score. If no lexical answer type could be found in the question (like *"Where did Einstein study?"*) or there were no lexicon entries, the classifier makes predictions on all types from our type system. The hierarchical classifier works as follows: starting at the root of the type system we predict probabilities for its children that are candidates, using per-type binary classifiers. Iteratively, this process is repeated for sub-trees whose root has a confidence score above a global threshold α.

Training. We start with a dataset where each question is labeled with a set of expected answer types. We use the *siblings strategy* (Silla and Freitas, 2011) to train a classifier for each type: we use all questions labeled with `T` as positive instances for a type `T`; we use *only* those questions as negative instances that are labeled with some sibling of `T` according to the type system. We use four sets of *features*: (i) *Surface features:* n-grams of length up to three from the question; (ii) *Dependency parse features:* n-grams constructed by hops over relations in the dependency tree to capture long-range dependencies; (iii) *Word2vec features:* Per question, we add ten words most similar to the question words (except for stopwords and entities) using a pre-trained model of word2vec (Mikolov et al., 2013); and (iv) *Question length:* The number of tokens in the question. To reduce data sparsity, we replace all question entities by a wildcard for pattern generalization, before computing the features.

4 Experiments

4.1 Setup

Dataset. We use the very recent dataset of 150 compositional questions[2] created by Abujabal et al. (2017) which were sampled from the 2013

---

[1] While the task in named entity typing is somewhat similar to answer typing, the crucial difference is that in the latter the entity (answer) itself is missing.

[2] Available for download at `http://people.mpi-inf.mpg.de/~abujabal/publications/quint/complex-questions-wikiasnwers-150.json`, Accessed 22 September 2017.

WikiAnswers resource (Fader et al., 2013). Every question in this dataset was constrained to have more than one named entity or relational phrase (e.g., *"Who directed Braveheart and Paparazzi?"* and *"Who directed Braveheart and played in Mad Max?"*). We use Freebase as the underlying KB.

Baselines. We use the following baselines: the open-source AQQU system (Bast and Haussmann, 2015) (best performing public KB-QA system on the popular WebQuestions benchmark (Berant et al., 2013)), and reimplemented versions of the answer stitching mechanism (ANSSTITCH) in Abujabal et al. (2017), and the query stitching mechanism (QUERYSTITCH) in Bao et al. (2016). As mentioned in Section 2, TIPI acts as a plug-in for KB-QA systems, and hence needs an underlying model to generate queries. To this end, we build and evaluate AQQU+TIPI and QUERYS-TITCH+TIPI. If question decomposition fails, or if TIPI prunes away all queries with a non-empty answer set, we *back off* to the original model. Abujabal et al. (2017) use an alternative approach of stitching answers for sub-questions instead of queries, and hence it is not meaningful to have a comparable ANSSTITCH+TIPI system.

Training the type predictor. We use the 1000 most frequent types from Freebase as our type system. Since there is no dataset directly containing questions and answer types, we resort to *distant supervision* as follows: for each gold answer to a question in WebQuestions (WQ) (Berant et al., 2013) and SimpleQuestions (SQ) (Bordes et al., 2015), we look up its *notable types* from Freebase. This is often a large set, agnostic to the context of the specific question at hand: e.g. Germany, the answer to *"What is Albert Einstein's nationality?"*, has 53 notable types, including context-irrelevant ones like Filming Location and Treaty Signatory. We prune this set in two ways: (1) keep only those types that are in our type system, and (2) retrieve *expected types* of Freebase predicates corresponding to relations in the question (e.g. hasNationality has the expected object type Country) and only retain types compatible to these. This is possible via gold SPARQL queries available in WQ and SQ. We then train the hierarchical classifier on a total of $10k$ questions ($3k$ from WQ, $6.4k$ from SQ, and $0.6k$ Freebase type descriptions). Threshold α was tuned to 0.6 on a development set of $2k$ questions ($0.8k$ from WQ and $1.2k$ from SQ) by optimizing on F1.

Feature Sets	Prec (Auto)	Prec (Human)
Surface	71.9	65.6
Surface + DP	72.2	65.9
Surface + DP + w2v	73.2	67.1
Surface + DP + w2v + QLen	**73.9**	**67.3**

Table 2: Intrinsic evaluation of type prediction, showing effects of feature ablation.

4.2 Results

Intrinsic evaluation of type predictor. We evaluate our type predictor intrinsically in two ways: (i) automatic evaluation, treating the labels generated by distant supervision as gold labels, and (ii) human evaluation. Three human annotators marked, for each prediction, whether it is correct and context-aware: e.g. for *"Who developed the theory of relativity?"*, they would mark Scientist and Person as correct but not NobelPrizeWinner or Teacher. Note that in the automatic evaluation, the context-oblivious types might be deemed as correct. Table 2 shows the results of automatic evaluation in the left column and human evaluation in the right column. The predictions are of high precision, even under human evaluation which only considers context-aware predictions as correct. Mean Cohen's κ (Cohen, 1960) is 0.743, showing good inter-annotator agreement. Feature ablation shows that each of the four feature sets is useful.

Answering performance. Since each question potentially has a set of correct answers, we compute precision, recall and F-score for each question, and then average it over all 150 questions. We evaluate two setups: (i) when only the top-ranking compositional query is executed, and (ii) when the rank-based query scoring component is disabled and all surviving compositional queries (combinations of type-compatible queries) are executed. Results are presented in Table 3, where we make the following key observations:

TIPI results in state-of-the-art performance. In the case of best query execution, we find that TIPI's preferential scoring system for fine-grained types proves highly effective: QUERYS-TITCH+TIPI achieves the highest F1 on the dataset (0.367). It also has the best overall recall (0.469), and is in the top-2 for precision. Thus, TIPI helps attain the best performance under the practical constraint of executing only a single query and eliminating the overhead of answer aggregation.

TIPI improves efficiency while maintaining

Approach	Only best query executed over KB			All queries executed over KB			
Metric	Precision	Recall	F1-Score	#Queries	Precision	Recall	F1-Score
ANSSTITCH (Abujabal et al., 2017)	0.345	0.409	0.344	97.4	**0.495**	**0.556**	**0.485**
AQQU (Bast and Haussmann, 2015)	0.245	0.466	0.253	54.5	0.245	0.466	0.253
AQQU+**TIPI**	0.209	**0.515**	0.231	**35.7**	0.209	0.515	0.231
QUERYSTITCH (Bao et al., 2016)	**0.358**	0.428	**0.360**	57.5	0.459	0.544	0.456
QUERYSTITCH+**TIPI**	**0.356**	0.469	**0.367**	**36.0**	0.439	**0.566**	0.445

Table 3: Answering performance on 150 compositional questions from Abujabal et al. (2017). The two best (*minimum* for #Queries, *maximum* for all other columns) values in every column are marked in **bold**.

comparable performance. In the unconstrained scenario, by reasoning over type compatibility, TIPI substantially reduces the number of queries that the KB-QA system executes (35.7 from 54.5 (AQQU), and 36.0 from 57.5 (QUERYSTITCH)). This is achieved while maintaining comparable F1 performance. Moreover, note that the best performing method with TIPI (QUERYSTITCH+TIPI) improves efficiency by a factor of 2.71 on the overall best performing ANSSTITCH (97.4 queries to 36.0). The generally lower values corresponding to the AQQU rows is because AQQU was originally designed for single-relation KB-QA.

Analysis. Question decomposition failures are the primary cause of error. TIPI's success hinges on the triggering of question decomposition rules adapted from Xu et al. (2016); it is worthwhile to note that results were even more encouraging when the 43 questions for which the rules did not fire were excluded from the analysis. Results averaged over the remaining 107 questions show that QUERYSTITCH+TIPI performs the best on all three metrics (F1 = 0.372, Prec = 0.365, Rec = 0.402) under best-query execution. In the all-queries case, QUERYSTITCH+TIPI reduces the number of queries by an even greater factor of 3.13 (w.r.t. ANSSTITCH) with only a 0.02 drop in F1. This error analysis suggests that better question decomposition, going beyond simple syntactic rules, will improve overall performance. Finally, representative questions that could only be answered when TIPI was used as plug-in, are shown in Table 4.

5 Related Work

Answer typing has proved effective both for text-based QA (Ravichandran and Hovy, 2002) and KB-QA (Bast and Haussmann, 2015; Savenkov and Agichtein, 2016), for example, in ranking of answers (Murdock et al., 2012) or queries (Yavuz

---

"who is the president of the us who played in bedtime for bonzo?"
"who played for ac milan and inter milan?"
"what movie did russell crowe and denzel washington work on together?"
"which country were the adidas and puma footwear founded?"

Table 4: Questions that could be answered only when TIPI was used as a plug-in.

et al., 2016). Answer typing was mostly limited to considering coarse-grained types (Bast and Haussmann, 2015; Lally et al., 2012) and lexical answer types (Berant and Liang, 2015; Abujabal et al., 2017). Both such modes fail when the answer type is not explicit. More recently, Yavuz et al. (2016) exploit more implicit type cues for KB-QA: but their method of creating training data is context-agnostic, which we remedy in our work. An early line of work deals with *question classification* (Li and Roth, 2002; Blunsom et al., 2006; Huang et al., 2008), but they were designed for a handful of TREC types and is not really relevant for KB-QA with thousands of distinct classes. Finally, this work is the first to harness answer types for compositional KB-QA.

6 Conclusion

We presented TIPI, a mechanism for enabling KB-QA systems to answer compositional questions using answer type prediction. TIPI relies on a fine-grained answer typing module, that respects question context and type hierarchy. Experiments on a recent benchmark show that TIPI achieves state-of-the-art performance under single-query execution, and substantial query reduction when the top-1 query constraint is relaxed to admit more queries. Improving question decomposition, and handling more implicit forms of question compositionality, are promising future directions.

References

Abdalghani Abujabal, Mohamed Yahya, Mirek Riedewald, and Gerhard Weikum. 2017. Automated template generation for question answering over knowledge graphs. In *WWW*.

Sören Auer, Christian Bizer, Georgi Kobilarov, Jens Lehmann, Richard Cyganiak, and Zachary Ives. 2007. Dbpedia: A nucleus for a web of open data. *The Semantic Web*.

Junwei Bao, Nan Duan, Zhao Yan, Ming Zhou, and Tiejun Zhao. 2016. Constraint-based question answering with knowledge graph. In *COLING*.

Junwei Bao, Nan Duan, Ming Zhou, and Tiejun Zhao. 2014. Knowledge-based question answering as machine translation. In *ACL*.

Hannah Bast and Elmar Haussmann. 2015. More accurate question answering on freebase. In *CIKM*.

Jonathan Berant, Andrew Chou, Roy Frostig, and Percy Liang. 2013. Semantic parsing on Freebase from question-answer pairs. In *EMNLP*.

Jonathan Berant and Percy Liang. 2015. Imitation learning of agenda-based semantic parsers. *TACL*.

Phil Blunsom, Krystle Kocik, and James R. Curran. 2006. Question classification with log-linear models. In *SIGIR*.

Branimir Boguraev, Siddharth Patwardhan, Aditya Kalyanpur, Jennifer Chu-Carroll, and Adam Lally. 2014. Parallel and nested decomposition for factoid questions. *Natural Language Engineering*, 20(4).

Kurt Bollacker, Patrick Tufts, Tomi Pierce, and Robert Cook. 2007. A platform for scalable, collaborative, structured information integration. In *Intl. Workshop on Information Integration on the Web*.

Antoine Bordes, Nicolas Usunier, Sumit Chopra, and Jason Weston. 2015. Large-scale simple question answering with memory networks. In *arXiv*.

Jacob Cohen. 1960. A coefficient of agreement for nominal scales. *Educational and psychological measurement*, 20(1).

Luciano Del Corro, Abdalghani Abujabal, Rainer Gemulla, and Gerhard Weikum. 2015. FINET: Context-aware fine-grained named entity typing. In *EMNLP*.

Li Dong, Furu Wei, Ming Zhou, and Ke Xu. 2015. Question answering over freebase with multi-column convolutional neural networks. In *ACL*.

Anthony Fader, Luke Zettlemoyer, and Oren Etzioni. 2013. Paraphrase-driven learning for open question answering. In *ACL*.

Zhiheng Huang, Marcus Thint, and Zengchang Qin. 2008. Question classification using head words and their hypernyms. In *EMNLP*.

Adam Lally, John M Prager, Michael C McCord, Branimir K Boguraev, Siddharth Patwardhan, James Fan, Paul Fodor, and Jennifer Chu-Carroll. 2012. Question analysis: How Watson reads a clue. *IBM Journal of Research and Development*.

Xin Li and Dan Roth. 2002. Learning question classifiers. In *COLING*.

Thomas Lin, Mausam, and Oren Etzioni. 2012. Entity linking at web scale. In *Joint Workshop on Automatic Knowledge Base Construction and Web-scale Knowledge Extraction*.

Christopher D. Manning, Mihai Surdeanu, John Bauer, Jenny Finkel, Steven J. Bethard, and David McClosky. 2014. The Stanford CoreNLP natural language processing toolkit. In *ACL*.

Tomas Mikolov, Kai Chen, Greg Corrado, and Jeffrey Dean. 2013. Efficient estimation of word representations in vector space. In *arXiv*.

J. William Murdock, Aditya Kalyanpur, Chris Welty, James Fan, David A Ferrucci, DC Gondek, Lei Zhang, and Hiroshi Kanayama. 2012. Typing candidate answers using type coercion. *IBM Journal of Research and Development*.

Deepak Ravichandran and Eduard Hovy. 2002. Learning surface text patterns for a question answering system. In *ACL*.

Denis Savenkov and Eugene Agichtein. 2016. When a Knowledge Base Is Not Enough: Question Answering over Knowledge Bases with External Text Data. In *SIGIR*.

Carlos Nascimento Silla and Alex Alves Freitas. 2011. A survey of hierarchical classification across different application domains. *Data Mining and Knowledge Discovery*.

Fabian M Suchanek, Gjergji Kasneci, and Gerhard Weikum. 2007. YAGO: A core of semantic knowledge. In *WWW*.

Kun Xu, Siva Reddy, Yansong Feng, Songfang Huang, and Dongyan Zhao. 2016. Question answering on freebase via relation extraction and textual evidence. In *ACL*.

Mohamed Yahya, Klaus Berberich, Shady Elbassuoni, and Gerhard Weikum. 2013. Robust question answering over the Web of linked data. In *CIKM*.

Semih Yavuz, Izzeddin Gur, Yu Su, Mudhakar Srivatsa, and Xifeng Yan. 2016. Improving semantic parsing via answer type inference. In *EMNLP*.

Wen-tau Yih, Ming-Wei Chang, Xiaodong He, and Jianfeng Gao. 2015. Semantic parsing via staged query graph generation: Question answering with knowledge base. In *ACL*.

Mohamed Amir Yosef, Sandro Bauer, Johannes Hoffart, Marc Spaniol, and Gerhard Weikum. 2012. HYENA: Hierarchical Type Classification for Entity Names. In *COLING*.

High Recall Open IE for Relation Discovery

Hady Elsahar, Christophe Gravier, Frederique Laforest
Université de Lyon, Laboratoire Hubert Curien, Saint-Étienne, France
`hady.elsahar@univ-st-etienne.fr`
`christophe.gravier@univ-st-etienne.fr`
`frederique.laforest@univ-st-etienne.fr`

Abstract

Relation Discovery discovers predicates (relation types) from a text corpus relying on the co-occurrence of two named entities in the same sentence. This is a very narrowing constraint: it represents only a small fraction of all relation mentions in practice. In this paper we propose a high recall approach for predicate extraction which enables covering up to 16 times more sentences in a large corpus. Comparison against OpenIE systems shows that our proposed approach achieves 28% improvement over the highest recall OpenIE system and 6% improvement in precision over the same system.

1 Introduction

The recent years have shown a large number of knowledge bases such as YAGO (Suchanek et al., 2007), Wikidata (Vrandečić and Krötzsch, 2014) and Freebase (Bollacker et al., 2008). These knowledge bases contain information about world entities (e.g. countries, people...) using a set of predefined predicates (e.g. birth place, profession...) that comes from a fixed ontology. The number of predicates can vary according to the KB ontology. For example there are 6,1047 DB-pedia unique predicates compared to only 2,569 in Wikidata. This has led to an emergence of unsupervised approaches for relation extraction which can scale to open relations that are not predefined in a KB ontology.

1.1 Open Information Extraction

Open information extraction (Open IE) systems extract linguistic relations in the form of tuples from text through a single data-driven pass over a large text corpus. Many Open IE systems have been proposed in the literature, some of them are based on patterns over shallow syntactic representations such as TEXTRUNNER (Banko et al., 2007) and REVERB (Fader et al., 2011), pattern learning in OLLIE (Mausam et al., 2012), Tree Kernels (Xu et al., 2013) or logic inference in STANFORD OPEN IE (Angeli et al., 2015).

Open IE has demonstrated an ability to scale to a non-predefined set of target predicates over a large corpus. However extracting new predicates (relation types) using Open IE systems and merging to existing knowledge bases is not a straightforward process, as the output of Open IE systems contains redundant facts with different lexical forms e.g. *(David Bowie, was born in, London)* and *(David bowie, place of birth, London)*.

1.2 Relation Discovery and Clustering

Relation clustering and relation discovery techniques try to alleviate this problem by grouping surface forms between each pair of entities in a large corpus of text. A large body of work has been done in that direction, through: clustering of OpenIE extractions (Mohamed et al., 2011; Nakashole et al., 2012a,b), topic modeling (Yao et al., 2011, 2012), matrix factorization (Takamatsu et al., 2011) and variational autoencoders (Marcheggiani and Titov, 2016). These approaches are successful to group and discover relation types from a large text corpus for the aim of later on adding them as knowledge base predicates.

1.3 Relation Discovery with a Single Entity Mention

Previously described relation discovery techniques discover relations between a detected pair of named entities. They usually use a preprocessing step to select only sentences with the mention of a pair of named entities (Figure 1 ex-

Proceedings of the The 8th International Joint Conference on Natural Language Processing, pages 228–233,
Taipei, Taiwan, November 27 – December 1, 2017 ©2017 AFNLP

ample 1). This step skips many sentences in which only one entity is detected. These sentences potentially contain important predicates that can be extracted and added to a KB ontology.

Figure 1 illustrates different examples of these sentences, such as: When the object is not mentioned (example 2), Questions where the object is not mentioned (example 3) or when one of the entities is hard to detect because of coreferencing or errors in NER tagging (example 4). By analysing

1. The ***official currency*** of the **U.K.** is the **Pound sterling**.

2. The **U.K.** ***official currency*** is down 16 percent since June 23.

3. What is the ***official currency*** of **U.K.** ?

4. .. which is considered the ***official currency*** of **U.K.**

Figure 1: Examples of textual representations mentioning the predicate "official currency".

630K documents from the NYT corpus (Sandhaus, 2008) as illustrated in Figure 2, the number of sentences with two 2 detected named entities is only **1.8M sentences**. Meanwhile, there are almost **30M sentences** with one entity (16 times more), which can be explored for predicate mentions. As the set of covered sentences is limited, so is the number of possibly discovered predicates.

In this paper we propose a predicate-centric method to extract relation types from such sentences while relying on only one entity mention. For relation clustering, we leverage various features from relations, including linguistic and semantic features, and pre-trained word embeddings. We explore various ways of re-weighting and fusing these features for enhancing the clustering results. Our predicate-centric method achieves 28% enhancement in recall over the top Open IE system and with a very comparable precision scores over an OpenIE benchmark (Stanovsky and Dagan, 2016). It demonstrates its superiority for the discovery of relation types.

2 Our Approach

2.1 Extraction of Predicates

Banko et.al (Banko and Etzioni, 2008) show that the majority of relations in free text can be represented using a certain type of Part of Speech (POS) patterns (e.g. "VB", "VB IN", "NN IN"). Ad-

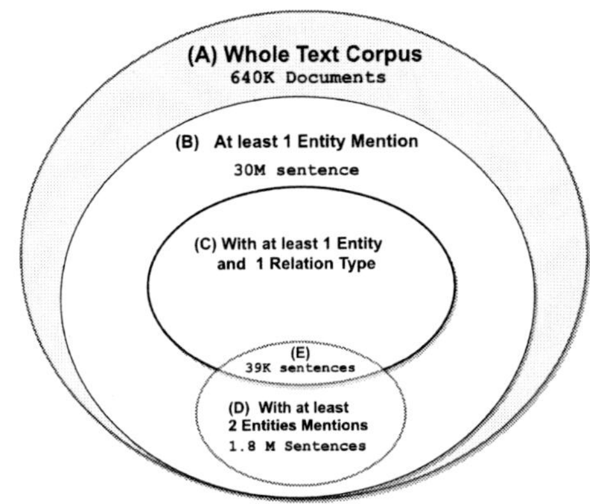

Figure 2: Distribution of sentences in the NYT corpus (A), which have: (B) at least 1 entity mention, (C) at least 1 entity and a predicate attached to it, (D) at least 2 entities mentions, (E) at least 2 entities and a relation in between in Freebase.

ditionally Riedel et al. (Riedel et al., 2013) propose the Universal Schemas model in which the lexicalized dependency path between two named entities in the same sentence is used to represented the relation in between. We follow a similar approach to extract lexical forms of predicates in sentences and connect them to named entities in the sentences.

First to expand the set of predicate patterns proposed by Banko et al., we collect labels and aliases for 2,405 Wikidata (Vrandečić and Krötzsch, 2014) predicates, align them with sentences from Wikipedia, and run the CoreNLP POS tagger (Manning et al., 2014) on them. This results in a set of 212 unique patterns $POS = \{pos_i, ..., pos_n\}$ [1].

Second, for each sentence in the corpus we do the following:

(i) extract the linguistic surface forms of predicate candidates P_c by matching the POS tagging of the sentence with the set of POS patterns POS.

(ii) extract candidate named entities E_c using the CoreNLP NER tagger (Manning et al., 2014).

(iii) extract the lexicalized dependency path dp_i and its direction between every named entity $e_i \in E_c$ and candidate relation predicates $p_i \in P_c$ (if exist). The direction of the dependency path highly correlates with the entity

---

[1] http://bit.ly/2obhbyF

229

being subject or object of the candidate predicate (Roth and Lapata, 2016).

The result of this process is a set of extractions $Ext = \{(p_i, e_i, dp_i)...(p_n, e_n, dp_n)\}$, in which a predicate p_i is connected to a named entitiy e_i through a directed dependency paths dp_i. We ignore all the candidate predicates that are not connected to a named entity though a dependency path. The confidence for each extraction is calculated according to the rank of its dependency path dp_i and its POS pattern.

2.2 Predicates Representation and Clustering

For each predicate in Ext, there are predicates though having different surface forms, express the same semantic relationship (e.g. "was born in", "birth place"). Following (Mohamed et al., 2011), we treat predicates with the same surface form as one input to the clustering approach. A feature representation vector for each unique predicate is built from multiple sentences across the text corpus. In the literature, this approach is referred to as the macro scenario, in contrast to the micro scenario (Yao et al., 2011; Marcheggiani and Titov, 2016) where every sentence in the corpus is treated individually. The input to the clustering process in the macro scenario is very small in comparison to the micro scenario, which makes the macro scenario more scalable.

For each unique predicate $p_i \in P$ we built a feature vector that consists of the following set of features:

1. Sum of TF-IDF re-weighted word embeddings for each word in p_i.

2. Count vector of each entity appearing as subject and as an object to p_i

3. Count vector of entity types appearing as subject and as an object to p_i

4. Count vector of each unique dependency path p_i that extracted p_i

5. The POS pattern of p_i encoded as a vector containing counts of each POS tag.

The previous features are not equally dense – concatenating all of them as a single feature vector for each relation is expected to skew the clustering algorithm. In supervised relation extraction, this is not an issue as the learning algorithm is expected to do feature selection automatically using training data. Here, it is not the case. In order to circumvent the sparse features bias, we apply individual feature reduction of the sparse features before merging them to the rest of the feature vectors. For feature reduction, we use Principal Component Analysis (PCA) (Jolliffe, 2011). Once this reduction is applied, we apply a K-Means clustering (Hartigan and Wong, 1979) algorithm over the relations feature vectors in order to group relations into k clusters.

3 Experiments and Evaluation

3.1 Predicates Extraction

In this section we demonstrate the effectiveness of using the proposed predicate-centric approach for relation discovery. For that we use a large scale dataset that was used for benchmarking Open IE (Stanovsky and Dagan, 2016). The dataset is comprised of 10,359 Open IE gold standard extractions over 3,200 sentences. Extractions are evaluated against the gold standard using a matching function between the extracted predicate and candidate predicates from Open IE systems. Extracted predicates that do not exist in the gold standard are calculated as false positives. We compare our predicate extraction method with a set of 6 Open IE systems, which are: REVERB, OLLIE, STANFORD-OPENIE, CLAUSIE (Corro and Gemulla, 2013), OPENIE4.0 an extension of SRL-based IE (Christensen et al., 2011) and noun phrase processing (Pal and Mausam, 2016) , and PROPS (Stanovsky et al., 2016).

Figure 3 shows that our proposed approach scores the highest recall amongst all the Open IE systems with 89% of predicates being extracted, achieving 28% improvement over CLAUSIE, the Open IE system with the highest recall and 6% improvement in precision over the same system. This shows that our approach is more useful when the target application is relation discovery, as it is able to extract predicates in the long tail with comparable precision, as shown in Figure 4. Table 2 shows a set of example sentences in the evaluation dataset in which none of the existing Open Information Extraction systems where able to extract, while they are correctly extracted by our approach.

3.2 Quality of Relation Clustering

To the best of our knowledge, the literature does not provide datasets for evaluating Relation Dis-

Sentence	Target predicate	Predicate-Centric	Extraction
Nicephorus Xiphias , who had conquered the old Bulgarian capitals.	conquered	conquered $\rightarrow$	$dobj \rightarrow MISC$
Muncy Creek then turns northeast , crossing Pennsylvania Route 405	crossing	crossing $\rightarrow$	$dobj \rightarrow LOCATION$
This was replaced by a Town Hall	replaced by	replaced by $\rightarrow nmod \rightarrow LOCATION$	
Starting in 2009 , Akita began experiencing ...	Starting in	Starting in $\rightarrow nmod \rightarrow DATE$	

Table 1: Example of sentences where all OpenIE systems failed to extract target relations, and their corresponding Predicate-Centric extractions.

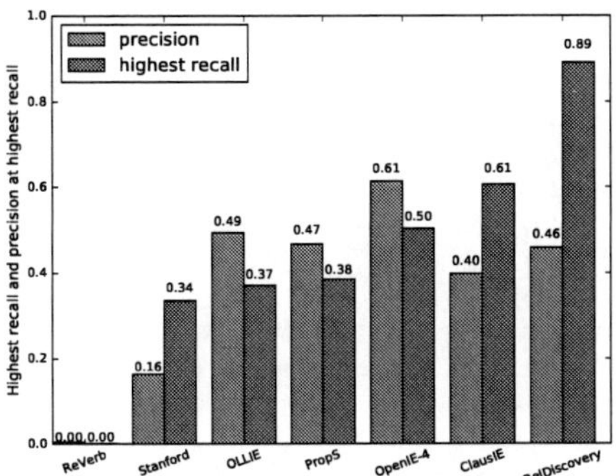

Figure 3: Maximum recall of top Open IE systems and their corresponding precisions in comparison with our approach **RelDiscovery** on (Stanovsky and Dagan, 2016) evaluation dataset.

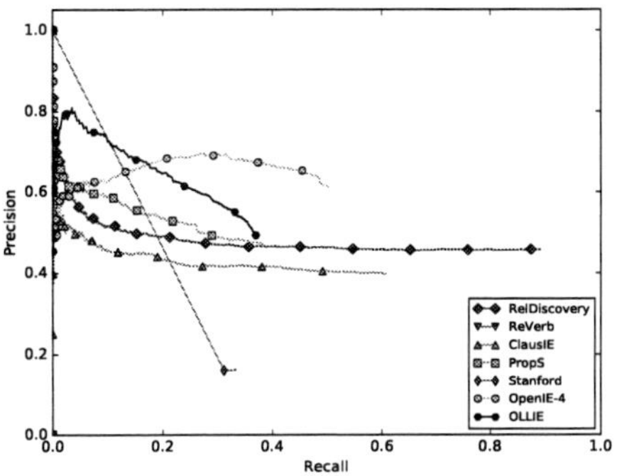

Figure 4: Precision and recall curve of our relation discovery method **RelDiscovery** with different OpenIE systems.

Em-Ft	wEm-Ft	wEm-Ft-PCA	ALL
0.41	0.50	0.55	**0.58**

Table 2: pairwise F1 scores using word embeddings and sparse features (Em-Ft), after re-weighting word embeddings (wEm-Ft), after doing feature reduction (wEm-Ft-PCA), and combining all features (ALL).

covery methods on the macro scenario. So we use GOOGLE-RE[2], a high quality dataset, that consists of sentences manually annotated with triples from Freebase (Bollacker et al., 2008). The dataset consists of 34,741 labeled sentences, for 5 Freebase relations: "institution", "place of birth", "place of death", "date of birth" and "education degree". We run our predicate extraction approach on the dataset and manually label the most frequent 2K extracted relations into 6 classes: the 5 target semantic relations in GOOGLE-RE and an additional class "OTHER" for other relations. We then divide them to 80-20% test-validation splits. For feature building, we use word2vec pre-trained word embeddings (Mikolov et al., 2013). We tune the PCA using the validation dataset. Results in Table 2 show that the re-weighting of Word embedding using TF-IDF had a significant improvement over only summing word embeddings. This opens the door for exploring more common unsupervised representations for short texts. Additionally, individual feature reduction on the sparse features has significantly enhanced the pairwise F1 score of the clustering algorithm.

4 Conclusion

We introduce a high recall approach for predicate extraction. It covers up to 16 times more sentences in a large corpus. Our approach is predicate-centric and learns surface patterns to directly extract lexical forms representing predicates and attach them to named entities. Evaluation on an OpenIE benchmark show that our system was able to achieve a significantly high recall (89%) with 28% improvement over the CLAUSIE, the Open IE system with the highest recall. It shows also a with very comparable precision with the rest of the OpenIE systems. Additionally, we introduce a baseline for comparing similar predicates. We show that re-weighting word embeddings and performing PCA for sparse features before fusing them significantly enhances the clustering perfor-

---

[2] http://bit.ly/2oyGBcZ

mance, reaching up to 0.58 pairwise F1 score.

References

Gabor Angeli, Melvin Johnson Premkumar, and Christopher D Manning. 2015. Leveraging linguistic structure for open domain information extraction. In *Proceedings of the 53rd Annual Meeting of the Association for Computational Linguistics and the 7th International Joint Conference on Natural Language Processing of the Asian Federation of Natural Language Processing, ACL*, pages 26–31.

Michele Banko, Michael J Cafarella, Stephen Soderland, Matt Broadhead, and Oren Etzioni. 2007. Open Information Extraction from the Web. In *The twentieth international joint conference on artificial intelligence, IJCAI 2007*, pages 2670—-2676, Hyderabad, India.

Michele Banko and Oren Etzioni. 2008. The tradeoffs between open and traditional relation extraction. In *ACL 2008, Proceedings of the 46th Annual Meeting of the Association for Computational Linguistics, June 15-20, 2008, Columbus, Ohio, USA*, pages 28–36.

Kurt Bollacker, Colin Evans, Praveen Paritosh, Tim Sturge, and Jamie Taylor. 2008. Freebase: a collaboratively created graph database for structuring human knowledge. In *Proceedings of the 2008 ACM SIGMOD international conference on Management of data*, pages 1247–1250. ACM.

Janara Christensen, Mausam, Stephen Soderland, and Oren Etzioni. 2011. An analysis of open information extraction based on semantic role labeling. In *Proceedings of the 6th International Conference on Knowledge Capture (K-CAP 2011), June 26-29, 2011, Banff, Alberta, Canada*, pages 113–120.

Luciano Del Corro and Rainer Gemulla. 2013. Clausie: clause-based open information extraction. In *22nd International World Wide Web Conference, WWW '13, Rio de Janeiro, Brazil, May 13-17, 2013*, pages 355–366.

Anthony Fader, Stephen Soderland, and Oren Etzioni. 2011. Identifying relations for open information extraction. In *Proceedings of the Conference on Empirical Methods in Natural Language Processing*, pages 1535–1545. Association for Computational Linguistics.

John A Hartigan and Manchek A Wong. 1979. Algorithm as 136: A k-means clustering algorithm. *Journal of the Royal Statistical Society. Series C (Applied Statistics)*, 28(1):100–108.

Ian T. Jolliffe. 2011. Principal component analysis. In *International Encyclopedia of Statistical Science*, pages 1094–1096.

Christopher D Manning, Mihai Surdeanu, John Bauer, Jenny Rose Finkel, Steven Bethard, and David Mc-Closky. 2014. The stanford corenlp natural language processing toolkit. In *ACL (System Demonstrations)*, pages 55–60.

Diego Marcheggiani and Ivan Titov. 2016. Discrete-state variational autoencoders for joint discovery and factorization of relations. *Transactions of the Association for Computational Linguistics*, 4.

Mausam, Michael Schmitz, Robert Bart, Stephen Soderland, and Oren Etzioni. 2012. Open Language Learning for Information Extraction. In *Proceedings of the 2012 Joint Conference on Empirical Methods in Natural Language Processing and Computational Natural Language Learning, EMNLP 2012*, pages 523—-534. Association for Computational Linguistics.

Tomas Mikolov, Ilya Sutskever, Kai Chen, Gregory S. Corrado, and Jeffrey Dean. 2013. Distributed representations of words and phrases and their compositionality. In *Advances in Neural Information Processing Systems 26: 27th Annual Conference on Neural Information Processing Systems 2013. Proceedings of a meeting held December 5-8, 2013, Lake Tahoe, Nevada, United States.*, pages 3111–3119.

Thahir Mohamed, Estevam R. Hruschka Jr., and Tom M. Mitchell. 2011. Discovering relations between noun categories. In *Proceedings of the 2011 Conference on Empirical Methods in Natural Language Processing, EMNLP 2011, 27-31 July 2011, John McIntyre Conference Centre, Edinburgh, UK, A meeting of SIGDAT, a Special Interest Group of the ACL*, pages 1447–1455.

Ndapandula Nakashole, Gerhard Weikum, and Fabian M. Suchanek. 2012a. Discovering and exploring relations on the web. *PVLDB*, 5(12):1982–1985.

Ndapandula Nakashole, Gerhard Weikum, and Fabian M. Suchanek. 2012b. PATTY: A taxonomy of relational patterns with semantic types. In *Proceedings of the 2012 Joint Conference on Empirical Methods in Natural Language Processing and Computational Natural Language Learning, EMNLP-CoNLL 2012, July 12-14, 2012, Jeju Island, Korea*, pages 1135–1145.

Harinder Pal and Mausam. 2016. Demonyms and compound relational nouns in nominal open IE. In *Proceedings of the 5th Workshop on Automated Knowledge Base Construction, AKBC@NAACL-HLT 2016, San Diego, CA, USA, June 17, 2016*, pages 35–39.

Sebastian Riedel, Limin Yao, Benjamin M. Marlin, and Andrew McCallum. 2013. Relation extraction with matrix factorization and universal schemas. In *Joint Human Language Technology Conference/Annual*

Meeting of the North American Chapter of the Association for Computational Linguistics (HLT-NAACL '13).

Michael Roth and Mirella Lapata. 2016. Neural semantic role labeling with dependency path embeddings. In *Proceedings of the 54th Annual Meeting of the Association for Computational Linguistics, ACL 2016, August 7-12, 2016, Berlin, Germany, Volume 1: Long Papers*.

Evan Sandhaus. 2008. The new york times annotated corpus. *Linguistic Data Consortium, Philadelphia*, 6(12):e26752.

Gabriel Stanovsky and Ido Dagan. 2016. Creating a large benchmark for open information extraction. In *Proceedings of the 2016 Conference on Empirical Methods in Natural Language Processing, EMNLP 2016, Austin, Texas, USA, November 1-4, 2016*, pages 2300–2305.

Gabriel Stanovsky, Jessica Ficler, Ido Dagan, and Yoav Goldberg. 2016. Getting more out of syntax with props. *CoRR*, abs/1603.01648.

Fabian M Suchanek, Gjergji Kasneci, and Gerhard Weikum. 2007. Yago: a core of semantic knowledge. In *Proceedings of the 16th international conference on World Wide Web*, pages 697–706. ACM.

Shingo Takamatsu, Issei Sato, and Hiroshi Nakagawa. 2011. Probabilistic matrix factorization leveraging contexts for unsupervised relation extraction. In *Advances in Knowledge Discovery and Data Mining - 15th Pacific-Asia Conference, PAKDD 2011, Shenzhen, China, May 24-27, 2011, Proceedings, Part I*, pages 87–99.

Denny Vrandečić and Markus Krötzsch. 2014. Wikidata: a free collaborative knowledgebase. *Communications of the ACM*, 57(10):78–85.

Ying Xu, Mi-Young Kim, Kevin Quinn, Randy Goebel, and Denilson Barbosa. 2013. Open Information Extraction with Tree Kernels. In *The 2013 Conference of the North American Chapter of the Association for Computational Linguistics: Human Language Technologies, HLT-NAACL 2013*, pages 868–877, Atlanta, Georgia.

Limin Yao, Aria Haghighi, Sebastian Riedel, and Andrew McCallum. 2011. Structured relation discovery using generative models. In *Proceedings of the Conference on Empirical Methods in Natural Language Processing*, pages 1456–1466. Association for Computational Linguistics.

Limin Yao, Sebastian Riedel, and Andrew McCallum. 2012. Unsupervised relation discovery with sense disambiguation. In *Proceedings of the 50th Annual Meeting of the Association for Computational Linguistics: Long Papers-Volume 1*, pages 712–720. Association for Computational Linguistics.

Using Context Events in Neural Network Models for Event Temporal Status Identification

Zeyu Dai, Wenlin Yao, Ruihong Huang
Department of Computer Science and Engineering
Texas A&M University
{jzdaizeyu, wenlinyao, huangrh}@tamu.edu

Abstract

Focusing on the task of identifying event temporal status, we find that events directly or indirectly governing the target event in a dependency tree are most important contexts. Therefore, we extract dependency chains containing context events and use them as input in neural network models, which consistently outperform previous models using local context words as input. Visualization verifies that the dependency chain representation can effectively capture the context events which are closely related to the target event and play key roles in predicting event temporal status.

1 Introduction

Event temporal status identification aims to recognize whether an event has happened (PAST), is currently happening (ON-GOING) or has not happened yet (FUTURE), which can be crucial for event prediction, timeline generation and news summarization.

Our prior work (Huang et al., 2016) showed that linguistic features, such as tense, aspect and time expressions, are insufficient for this challenging task, which instead requires accurate understanding of composite meanings from wide sentential contexts. However surprisingly, the best performance for event temporal status identification was achieved by a Convolutional Neural Network (CNN) running on local contexts (seven words to each side) surrounding the target event (Huang et al., 2016).

Considering the following sentence with a future event "protest":

(1) *Climate activists from around the world will launch a hunger strike here on Friday, describing their **protest (FU)** as a "moral reaction to an immoral situation" in the face of environmental catastrophe.*

The local context "describing" may mislead the classifier that this is an on-going event, while the actual future temporal status indicative words, "will launch", appear nine words away from the target event mention "protest". Clearly, the local window of contexts is filled with irrelevant words, meanwhile, it fails to capture important temporal status indicators. However, as shown in figure 1, the event "launch" is actually a high order indirect governor word of the target event word "protest" and is only two words away from the target event in the dependency tree. Indeed, we observed that the temporal status indicators are often words that syntactically govern or depend on the event mention at all levels of a dependency tree. Furthermore, we observed that higher level governing words in dependency trees frequently refer to events as well, which are closely related to the target event and useful to predict its temporal status.

Following these observations, we form a dependency chain of relevant contexts by extracting words that appear between an event mention and the root of a dependency parse tree as well as words that are governed by the event mention. Then we use the extracted dependency chain as input for neural network classifiers. This is an elegant method to capture long-distance dependency between events within a sentence. It is known that a verb and its direct or indirect governor can be far away in a word sequence if modifiers such as adjectives or clauses lie in between, but they are adjacent in the parse tree.

Experimental results using two neural network models (i.e., LSTMs and CNNs) show that classifiers with dependency chains as input can better capture temporal status indicative contexts and

Proceedings of the The 8th International Joint Conference on Natural Language Processing, pages 234–239,
Taipei, Taiwan, November 27 – December 1, 2017 ©2017 AFNLP

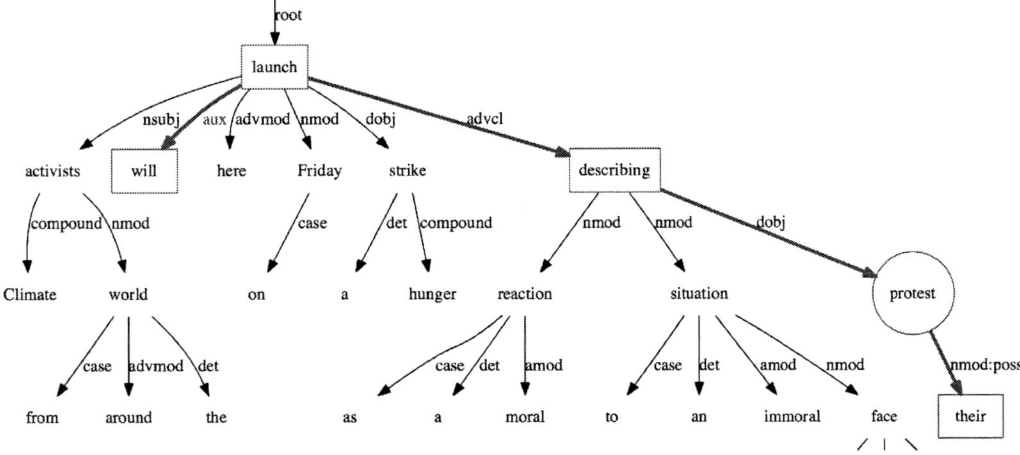

Figure 1: The dependency parse tree for the example (1). The blue and bold edges show the extracted dependency chain for the target event "protest" (in circle).

clearly outperform the ones with local contexts. Furthermore, the models with dependency chains as input outperform a tree-LSTM model in which the full dependency trees are used as input. Visualization reveals that it is much easier for neural net models to identify and concentrate on the relevant regions of contexts using the dependency chain representation, which further verifies that additional event words in a sentential context are crucial to predict target event temporal status.

2 Related Work

Constituency-based and dependency-based parse trees have been explored and applied to improve performance of neural nets for the task of sentiment analysis and semantic relation extraction (Socher et al., 2013; Bowman and Potts, 2015; Tai et al., 2015). The focus of these prior studies is on designing new neural network architectures (e.g., tree-structured LSTMs) corresponding to the parse tree structure. In contrast, our method aims at extracting appropriate event-centered data representations from dependency trees so that the neural net models can effectively concentrate on relevant regions of contexts.

Similar to our dependency chains, dependency paths between two nodes in a dependency tree have been widely used as features for various NLP tasks and applications, including relation extraction (Bunescu and Mooney, 2005), temporal relation identification (Choubey and Huang, 2017) semantic parsing (Moschitti, 2004) and question

answering (Cui et al., 2005). Differently, our dependency chains are generated with respect to an event word and include words that govern or depend on the event, which therefore are not bounded by two pre-identified nodes in a dependency tree.

3 Dependency Chain Extraction

Figure 1 shows the dependency parse tree[1] for the example (1). To extract the dependency chain for the target event, we have used a two-stage approach to create the chain. In the first stage, we start from the target event, traverse the dependency parse tree, identify all its direct or indirect governors and dependents and include these words in the chain. For the example (1), a list of words [launch, describing, protest, their] are included in the dependency chain after the first stage.

Then in the second stage, we apply one heuristic rule to extract extra words from the dependency tree. Specifically, if a word is in a particular dependency relation[2], *aux*, *auxpass* or *cop*, with a word that is already in the chain after the first stage, then we include this word in the chain as well. For the example (1), the word "will" is inserted into the dependency chain in the second stage. The reason we perform this additional step is that context words identified with one of the above three dependency relations usually indicate

---

[1]We used the Stanford CoreNLP to generate dependency parse trees.

[2]http://nlp.stanford.edu/software/dependencies_manual.pdf

Model	PA	OG	FU	Macro	Micro
Local Contexts					
CNN (Huang et al., 2016)	91/83/87	46/57/51	49/67/57	62/69/65	77/77/76.9
LSTM	88/83/85	47/54/51	52/62/57	63/66/64	75/75/75.5
Dependency Chains					
CNN	91/84/87	49/63/55	60/65/62	67/71/68	79/79/78.6
LSTM	92/85/**88**	49/63/**55**	63/71/**67**	68/73/**70**	80/80/**79.6**
Full Dependency Trees					
tree-LSTM	92/80/86	47/59/53	30/58/40	56/66/60	75/75/75.1

Table 1: Classification results on the test set. Each cell shows Recall/Precision/F1 score.

tense, aspect or mood of a context event, which are useful in determining the target event's temporal status.

For each extracted dependency chain, we sort the words in the chain according to their textual order in the original sentence. Then the ordered sequence of words will be used as the input for LSTMs and CNNs.

4 Experiments

4.1 The EventStatus Corpus

We experiment on the EventStatus corpus (Huang et al., 2016), which contains 4500 English and Spanish news articles about civil unrest events (e.g., protest and march), where each civil unrest event mention has been annotated with three categories, **Past (PA)**, **On-Going (OG)** and **Future (FU)**, to indicate if the event has concluded, is currently ongoing or has not happened yet.

We only use the English portion of the corpus which include 2364 documents because our previous work (Huang et al., 2016) has reported that the quality of dependency parse trees generated for Spanish articles is poor and our approach heavily rely on dependency trees. Furthermore, we randomly split the data into tuning (20%) and test (80%) set, and conduct the final evaluation using 10-fold cross-validation on the test set, following the prior work (Huang et al., 2016). Table 2 shows the distribution of each event temporal status category in the dataset.

	PA	**OG**	**FU**
Test	1406(67%)	429(21%)	254(12%)
Tuning	354(61%)	157(27%)	66(12%)

Table 2: Temporal Status Label Distribution

4.2 Neural Network Models

In our experiments, we applied three types of neural network models including CNNs (Collobert et al., 2011; Kim, 2014), LSTMs (Schmidhuber and Hochreiter, 1997), and tree-LSTMs (Tai et al., 2015). For CNNs, we used the same architecture and parameter settings as (Huang et al., 2016) with a filter size of 5. For LSTMs, we implemented a simple architecture that consists of one LSTM layer and one output layer with softmax function. For tree-LSTMs, we replicated the Dependency tree-LSTMs[3] from (Tai et al., 2015) and added an output layer on top of it. Both of the two latter neural nets used the same number (300) of hidden units as CNNs. Note that we have also experimented with complex LSTM models, including the ones with multiple layers, with bidirectional inferencing (Schuster and Paliwal, 1997) as well as with attention mechanism (Bahdanau et al., 2015; Wang et al., 2016), however none of these complex models improve the event temporal status prediction performance.

All the models were trained using RMSProp optimizer with the initial learning rate 0.001 and the same random seed. In addition, we used the pre-trained 300-dimension English word2vec[4] embeddings (Mikolov et al., 2013b,a). The training epochs and dropout (Hinton et al., 2012) ratio for neural net layers were treated as hyperparameters and were tuned using the tuning set. The best LSTM model ran for 50 training epochs and used a dropout ratio of 0.5.

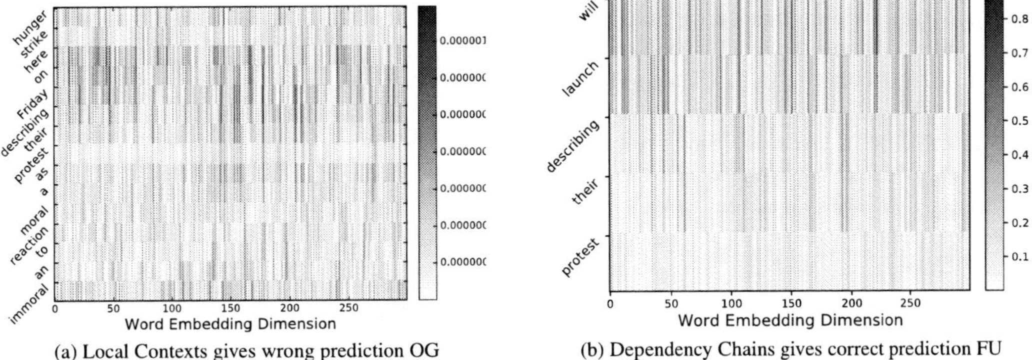

(a) Local Contexts gives wrong prediction OG

(b) Dependency Chains gives correct prediction FU

Figure 2: Saliency heatmaps for the example (1). Local Context Input: *hunger strike here on Friday, describing their protest as a moral reaction to an immoral*; Dependency Chain Input: *will launch describing their protest*. A deeper color indicates that the corresponding word has a higher weight and contributes more to the prediction.

4.3 Classification Result

Table 1 shows the new experimental results on the test set as well as our prior results (Huang et al., 2016). For models using local contexts as input, the context window size of 7 (7 words preceding and following the target event mention, therefore, 15 words in total) yields the best result, as reported in our prior paper (Huang et al., 2016). Note that dependency chains we generated have an average length of 7.4 words in total, which are much shorter than 15 words of local contexts as used before.

From Table 1, we can see that both LSTM and CNN models using dependency chains as input consistently outperform the corresponding models using local contexts. Especially, the LSTM model running on dependency chains achieves the best performance of 70.0% Macro and 79.6% Micro F1-score, which outperforms the previous local context based CNN model (Huang et al., 2016) by a large margin. Statistical significance testing shows that the improvements are significant at the $p < 0.01$ level (t-test). In particular for on-going and future events, the dependency chain based LSTM model improves the temporal status classification F-scores by 4 and 10 percentages respectively. In addition, the tree-LSTM model taking account of full dependency trees achieves a comparable result with local context based neural network models, but performs worse than dependency chain based models. The reason why the tree-LSTM model does not work well is that irrel-

evant words, including adjective modifiers and irrelevant clauses forming branches of dependency trees, may distract the classifier and have negative effect in predicting the temporal status of an event.

5 Visualizing LSTM

Following the approach used in (Li et al., 2016), we drew salience heatmaps[5] in order to understand contributions of individual words in a dependency chain to event temporal status identification. Figure 2 shows heatmaps of LSTM models when applied to example (1) using its different data representations as input. We can clearly see that the dependency chain input effectively retains contexts that are relevant for predicting event temporal status. Specifically, as shown in Figure 2(b), the context event "launch" that indirectly governs the target event "protest" in the dependency chain together with the auxiliary verb "will" have received the highest weights and are most useful in predicting the correct temporal status.

6 Error Analysis

More than 40% of errors on the tuning set produced by our best LSTM model are due to the *"Past or On-going ambiguity"*, which usually happen when there are few signals within a sentence that can indicate whether an event has concluded or not. In such scenarios, the classifier tends to predict the temporal status as *Past* since this event

---

[5]Illustrate absolute values of derivatives of the loss function to each input dimension.

temporal status is majority in the dataset, which explains the low performance on predicting on-going events. To resolve such difficult cases, even wider contexts beyond one sentence should be considered.

Around 10% of errors are time expression related. The neural net models seem not be able to wisely use time expressions (e.g., "in 1986", "on Wednesday") without knowing the exact document creation time and their temporal relations. In addition, some mislabelings occur because neural nets are unable to capture compositionality of multi-word expressions or phrasal verbs that alone can directly determine the temporal status of their following event, such as "on eve of" and "go on".

7 Conclusion

We presented a novel dependency chain based approach for event temporal status identification which can better capture relevant regions of contexts containing other events that directly or indirectly govern the target event. Experimental results showed that dependency chain based neural net models consistently outperform commonly used local context based models in predicting event temporal status, as well as a tree-structured neural network model taking account of complete dependency trees. To further improve the performance of event temporal status identification, we believe that wider contexts beyond the current sentence containing an event should be exploited.

Acknowledgments

We acknowledge the support of NVIDIA Corporation for their donation of one GeForce GTX TITAN X GPU used for this research.

References

Dzmitry Bahdanau, Kyunghyun Cho, and Yoshua Bengio. 2015. Neural machine translation by jointly learning to align and translate. In *Proc. ICLR*.

Samuel R Bowman and Christopher Potts. 2015. Recursive neural networks can learn logical semantics. *ACL-IJCNLP 2015*, page 12.

Razvan C Bunescu and Raymond J Mooney. 2005. A shortest path dependency kernel for relation extraction. In *Proceedings of the conference on human language technology and empirical methods in natural language processing*, pages 724–731. Association for Computational Linguistics.

Prafulla Kumar Choubey and Ruihong Huang. 2017. A sequential model for classifying temporal relations between intra-sentence events. *Proceedings of the 2017 Conference on Empirical Methods in Natural Language Processing, Short Papers*.

Ronan Collobert, Jason Weston, Léon Bottou, Michael Karlen, Koray Kavukcuoglu, and Pavel Kuksa. 2011. Natural language processing (almost) from scratch. *Journal of Machine Learning Research*, 12(Aug):2493–2537.

Hang Cui, Renxu Sun, Keya Li, Min-Yen Kan, and Tat-Seng Chua. 2005. Question answering passage retrieval using dependency relations. In *Proceedings of the 28th annual international ACM SIGIR conference on Research and development in information retrieval*, pages 400–407. ACM.

Geoffrey E Hinton, Nitish Srivastava, Alex Krizhevsky, Ilya Sutskever, and Ruslan R Salakhutdinov. 2012. Improving neural networks by preventing co-adaptation of feature detectors. *arXiv preprint arXiv:1207.0580*.

Ruihong Huang, Ignacio Cases, Dan Jurafsky, Cleo Condoravdi, and Ellen Riloff. 2016. Distinguishing past, on-going, and future events: The eventstatus corpus. In *Proceedings of the 2016 Conference on Empirical Methods in Natural Language Processing*, pages 44–54, Austin, Texas. Association for Computational Linguistics.

Yoon Kim. 2014. Convolutional neural networks for sentence classification. *arXiv preprint arXiv:1408.5882*.

Jiwei Li, Xinlei Chen, Eduard Hovy, and Dan Jurafsky. 2016. Visualizing and understanding neural models in nlp. In *Proceedings of NAACL-HLT*, pages 681–691.

Tomas Mikolov, Kai Chen, Greg Corrado, and Jeffrey Dean. 2013a. Efficient estimation of word representations in vector space. *ICLR Workshop*.

Tomas Mikolov, Ilya Sutskever, Kai Chen, Greg S Corrado, and Jeff Dean. 2013b. Distributed representations of words and phrases and their compositionality. In *Advances in neural information processing systems*, pages 3111–3119.

Alessandro Moschitti. 2004. A study on convolution kernels for shallow semantic parsing. In *Proceedings of the 42nd Annual Meeting on Association for Computational Linguistics*, page 335. Association for Computational Linguistics.

Jürgen Schmidhuber and Sepp Hochreiter. 1997. Long short-term memory. *Neural Comput*, 9(8):1735–1780.

Mike Schuster and Kuldip K Paliwal. 1997. Bidirectional recurrent neural networks. *IEEE Transactions on Signal Processing*, 45(11):2673–2681.

Richard Socher, Alex Perelygin, Jean Wu, Jason Chuang, Christopher D. Manning, Andrew Ng, and Christopher Potts. 2013. Recursive deep models for semantic compositionality over a sentiment treebank. In *Proceedings of the 2013 Conference on Empirical Methods in Natural Language Processing*, pages 1631–1642, Seattle, Washington, USA. Association for Computational Linguistics.

Kai Sheng Tai, Richard Socher, and Christopher D. Manning. 2015. Improved semantic representations from tree-structured long short-term memory networks. In *ACL*.

Yequan Wang, Minlie Huang, Xiaoyan Zhu, and Li Zhao. 2016. Attention-based LSTM for aspect-level sentiment classification. In *Proceedings of the 2016 Conference on Empirical Methods in Natural Language Processing, EMNLP 2016, Austin, Texas, USA, November 1-4, 2016*, pages 606–615.

Identifying Protein-protein Interactions in Biomedical Literature using Recurrent Neural Networks with Long Short-Term Memory

Yu-Lun Hsieh
SNHCC, TIGP, Academia Sinica, and
National Cheng Chi University, Taiwan
morphe@iis.sinica.edu.tw

Yung-Chun Chang
Graduate Institute of Data Science,
Taipei Medical University, Taiwan
changyc@tmu.edu.tw

Nai-Wen Chang and **Wen-Lian Hsu**
IIS, Academia Sinica, Taiwan
{nwchang,hsu}@iis.sinica.edu.tw

Abstract

Accurate identification of protein-protein interaction (PPI) helps biomedical researchers to quickly capture crucial information in literatures. This work proposes a recurrent neural network (RNN) model to identify PPIs. Experiments on two largest public benchmark datasets, AIMed and BioInfer, demonstrate that RNN outperforms state-of-the-art methods with relative improvements of 10% and 18%, respectively. Cross-corpus evaluation also indicates that RNN is robust even when trained on data from different domains. These results suggest that RNN effectively captures semantic relationships among proteins without any feature engineering.

1 Introduction

In systematic biology, protein-protein interaction (PPI) is an important subject that aims at exploring the role of intermolecular interactions, which is crucial for reconstructing molecular networks in cells (Mori, 2004). A widely-used information source regarding PPI is PubMed, which contains over 27 million research papers and continues to grow at a rate of 1.5 million per year. Given the vast amount of papers published, collecting PPI information manually is time-consuming. Thus, a major research question in biomedical text-mining is to efficiently identify the sentences that contain PPIs. Although certain PPI may span across multiple sentences, existing work mostly focus on those PPIs existing within a single sentence (Tikk et al., 2010). For instance, given the sentence "STAT3 selectively interacts with Smad3 to antagonize TGF-β signaling," a model should correctly identify that proteins *STAT3*, *Smad3*, and *TGF-β*

have interactions with one another. More specifically, there are $\binom{3}{2} = 3$ pairs of proteins in the sentence, and there are PPIs in all three pairs. Note that the exact type of interaction is not in the scope of this task.

Recent breakthrough in neural network (NN) led to increasing amount of work that apply NN on various text-mining tasks. Specifically, convolutional neural networks (CNN) (Lecun et al., 1998) have been most commonly adapted for PPI. Compared with traditional machine learning (ML) methods such as SVM (Cortes and Vapnik, 1995), CNN models do not require tedious feature engineering and domain knowledge. However, how to best incorporate linguistic and semantic information into the CNN model remains an active research topic, since previous CNN-based methods have not achieved state-of-the-art performance in PPI identification task (Peng and Lu, 2017).

This paper proposes a novel approach based on recurrent neural networks (RNNs) to capture the long-term relationships among words in order to identify PPIs. The proposed model is evaluated on two largest PPI corpora, *i.e.*, AIMed (Bunescu et al., 2005) and BioInfer (Pyysalo et al., 2007) using cross-validation (CV) and cross-corpus (CC) settings. Experimental results from CV show that RNN outperforms state-of-the-art methods by relative improvements of 10% and 18% on AIMed and BioInfer, respectively. Furthermore, RNN remains effective even when trained on a different domain in the CC setting.

The rest of this paper is organized as follows. Sec. 2 provides important previous work related to PPI and NN. Sec. 3 describes the architecture of the proposed model. Sec. 4 details the experimental procedure and Sec. 5 presents experimental results and findings. Finally, Sec. 6 concludes this paper and points to the directions for future work.

Proceedings of the The 8th International Joint Conference on Natural Language Processing, pages 240–245,
Taipei, Taiwan, November 27 – December 1, 2017 ©2017 AFNLP

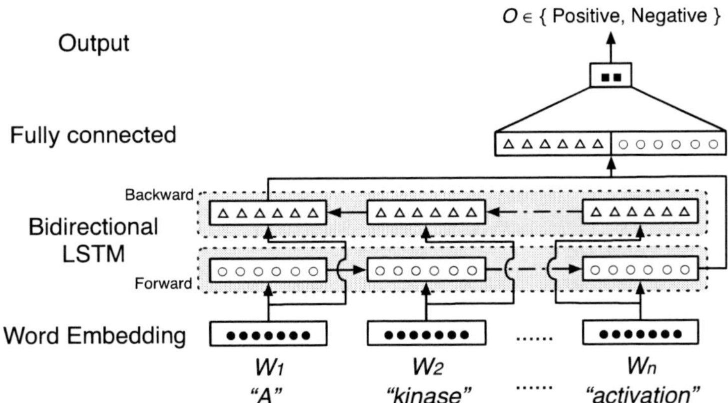

Figure 1: Overview of the proposed model. The first layer transforms words into corresponding embeddings and feeds them sequentially to the bi-directional RNN. The forward and backward output vectors are concatenated as the new "feature vector" and sent to the fully connected layer for final classification. For simplicity w/o losing details, dropout layers are omitted.

2 Related work

PPI identification can be cast as a binary classification problem where discriminative classifiers are trained with a set of positive and negative instances. Two major categories of approaches are proposed, *i.e.*, manual rule-based systems and ML approaches (Bunescu et al., 2005). The former approach is intuitive but time-consuming and requires intensive labor, while the latter are more common and primarily "kernel-based". Kernel-based methods usually take advantage of the syntactic or semantic structure of a sentence. For example, Qian and Zhou (2012) includes shortest dependency path (sdp) with tree-kernel classifier, and Chang et al. (2016) integrate knowledge base with a tree kernel to strengthen PPI identification. Other approaches include shortest path kernels (Bunescu and Mooney, 2005), graph kernel (Airola et al., 2008), composite kernel (Miwa et al., 2009), subsequence kernels (Kim et al., 2010), and tree kernels (Eom et al., 2006; Qian and Zhou, 2012). However, engineering features from different sources may not lead to optimal results.

Recent advances in NN research have been applied to PPI identification as well. Zhao et al. (2016) used an auto-encoder for feature extraction from words and a logistic regression for classification. Li et al. (2015) proposed a hybrid of kernel- and NN-based model and examined the strength of integrating NN-extracted features into kernels. They conclude that NNs can automatically extract discriminative features and aid kernels in PPI identification. Furthermore, Peng and Lu (2017) integrated dependency graph information into a CNN and improved performances on AIMed and BioInfer over kernel-based methods, with F-scores 63.5% and 65.3%, respectively. Hua and Quan (2016) used shortest dependency path feature to simplify the input and avoid bias from feature selection. Their method achieved 66.6% F-score on AIMed and 75.3% on BioInfer dataset. Alternatively, RNN with Long Short-Term Memory (LSTM) (Hochreiter and Schmidhuber, 1997) have been shown to possess outstanding abilities when modeling sequential data with long-term dependency (Greff et al., 2017). Majority of previous work that use LSTM focused on machine translation (Sutskever et al., 2014), named-entity recognition (Lample et al., 2016), or classification of a sequence, *e.g.*, the sentiment of a piece of movie review (Tai et al., 2015). Recently, LSTMs have been utilized to perform relation extraction and classification on general texts (Miwa and Bansal, 2016).

3 Method

We propose a novel approach for identifying PPI using bi-directional RNN with LSTM. Figure 1 illustrates the overview of our model, which takes a sentence containing protein entities as input and outputs a probability distribution (Bernoulli distribution) corresponding to whether there exists a PPI or not. There are three types of layers: an embedding layer, a recurrent layer, and a fully connected layer, which are described as follows.

Embedding Layer transforms words into embeddings (Mikolov et al., 2013), which are dense, low-dimensional, and real-valued vectors. They capture syntactic and semantic information provided by its neighboring words. In this work, we examine the effect of pre-training embeddings by comparing randomly initialized and pre-trained ones from Chiu et al. (2016), which was trained on over 25 million PubMed records.

Recurrent Layer is constructed using LSTM cells, as illustrated in Fig. 2. An LSTM cell contains a "memory" cell and three "gates", *i.e.*, input, forget, and output. The input gate modulates the current input and previous output. The forget gate tunes the content from previous memory to the current. Finally, the output gate regulates the output from the memory.

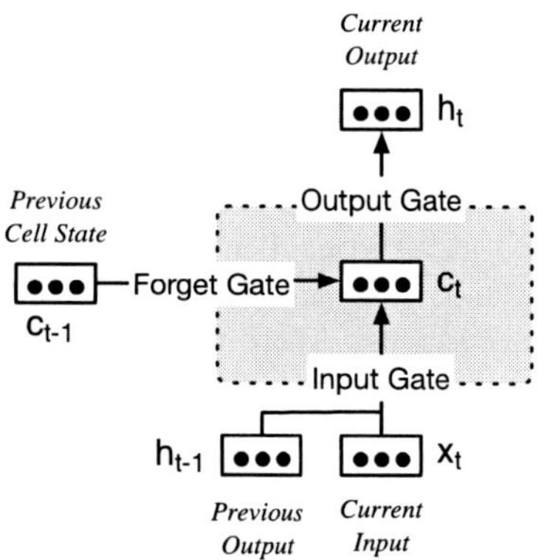

Figure 2: Simplified illustration of an LSTM cell. The input gate and forget gate jointly control the content of the memory c_t, and the output gate regulates output from c_t.

Specifically, let $\mathbf{x}_t$ be the input at time t, and $\mathbf{i}_t, \mathbf{f}_t, \mathbf{o}_t$ correspond to input, forget, and output gates, respectively. $\mathbf{c}_t$ denotes the memory cell and $\mathbf{h}_t$ is the output. The learnable parameters include $W_{i,f,o,c}$ and $U_{i,f,o,c}$. They are defined as:

$$\mathbf{i}_t = \sigma(W_i\mathbf{x}_t + U_i\mathbf{h}_{t-1})$$
$$\mathbf{f}_t = \sigma(W_f\mathbf{x}_t + U_f\mathbf{h}_{t-1})$$
$$\mathbf{o}_t = \sigma(W_o\mathbf{x}_t + U_o\mathbf{h}_{t-1})$$
$$\tilde{\mathbf{c}}_t = \tanh(W_c\mathbf{x}_t + U_c\mathbf{h}_{t-1})$$
$$\mathbf{c}_t = \mathbf{f}_t \circ \mathbf{c}_{t-1} + \mathbf{i}_t \circ \tilde{\mathbf{c}}_t$$
$$\mathbf{h}_t = \mathbf{o}_t \circ \tanh(\mathbf{c}_t)$$

where "∘" denotes the element-wise product of vectors and σ represents the sigmoid function.

We use a bi-directional RNN to encode a sequence in forward and backward directions, which has been proven effective in sequence modeling tasks (Dyer et al., 2015). In essence, it uses two cells, one to encode the input sequence in its original order and the other in reverse. Subsequently, the two outputs are concatenated and fed to the **Fully Connected Layer**. It serves as a classifier where the output represents class probabilities.

4 Experiments

We evaluate the proposed method with two largest publicly available PPI corpora: AIMed and BioInfer. Distribution of the corpora is shown in Table 1. We adopt 10-fold cross-validation (CV)

Table 1: Statistics of AIMed and BioInfer.

Corpus	Total # of Sentences	# of Positive/Negative Protein Pairs
AIMed	1,955	1,000/4,834
BioInfer	1,100	2,534/7,132

and cross-corpus (CC) testing scheme. The evaluation metrics are the precision, recall, and F1-score for both schemes. Compared methods include the shortest dependency path-directed constituent parse tree (SDP-CPT) method (Qian and Zhou, 2012), in which the tree representation generated from a syntactic parser is refined by using the shortest dependency path between two entity mentions derived from a dependency parser; A knowledge-based approach PIPE (Chang et al., 2016) that extracts linguistic interaction patterns and learned by a convolution tree kernel; A composite kernel approach (CK) (Miwa et al., 2009) which combines several different layers of information from a sentence with its syntactic structure by using several parsers; and a graph kernel method (GK) (Airola et al., 2008) that integrates parse structure sub-graph and a linear order sub-graph. We further compare with recent NN-based approaches: sdpCNN (Hua and Quan, 2016) which combines CNN with shortest dependency path features; McDepCNN (Peng and Lu, 2017) that uses positional embeddings along with word embeddings as the input, and a tree kernel using various word embeddings labeled as TK+WE (Li et al., 2015). We also evaluate the effect of pre-training of word embeddings by comparing ran-

Table 2: Results (in %) from 10-fold cross-validation on AIMed and BioInfer corpora. Bold font indicates the best performance in a column. Standard deviations are enclosed in parentheses.

Method	AIMed			BioInfer		
	Precision	**Recall**	**F-score**	**Precision**	**Recall**	**F-score**
GK	52.9	61.8	56.4	56.7	67.2	61.3
SDP-CPT	59.1	57.6	58.1	-	-	62.4
CK	55.0	68.8	60.8	65.7	71.1	68.1
PIPE	57.2	64.5	60.6	68.6	70.3	69.4
McDepCNN	67.3	60.1	63.5	62.7	68.2	65.3
sdpCNN	64.8	67.8	66.0	73.4	77.0	75.2
TK+WE	-	-	69.7	-	-	74.0
$LSTM_{rand}$	70.1 (6.5)	70.4 (6.4)	70.1 (5.5)	83.6 (2.4)	83.3 (2.7)	83.4 (2.3)
$LSTM_{pre}$	**78.8** (5.6)	**75.2** (5.0)	**76.9** (4.9)	**87.0** (2.3)	**87.4** (2.3)	**87.2** (1.9)

domly initialized and pre-trained embeddings, labeled as $LSTM_{rand}$ and $LSTM_{pre}$, respectively.

4.1 Experimental Setup

To ensure the generalization of the learned model, the protein names recognized in the text are replaced with "PROTEIN1", "PROTEIN2", or "PROTEIN", where "PROTEIN1" and "PROTEIN2" are the pair of interest, and other non-participating proteins are marked as "PROTEIN". An example is given as follows. The sentence "Thymocyte activation induces the association of phosphatidylinositol 3-kinase and pp120 with CD5" contains three proteins, namely, "phosphatidylinositol 3-kinase", "pp120", and "CD5". In the three possible pairs of proteins, two of them are in interaction relations. Therefore, there are three variants of this sentence with proteins being replaced by the special labels in the data, and two of them are marked as "positive" while the other one as "negative". During testing, all the variants will be scored. The maximum sentence length is set to 100, where longer sentences are truncated and shorter sentences padded with zeros. We use 200-dimension embeddings and 400-dimension LSTM cells. The dropout rate is set to 0.5. `RMSProp` optimizer (Tieleman and Hinton, 2012) with default learning rate settings are applied[1]. With a batch size of 16, training one epoch on one Titan X GPU takes approximately one minute. The throughput of the inference stage is around 130KB of text per second.

---

[1]We implement the model using Keras with tensorflow (Abadi et al., 2015) backend. Code can be downloaded from `https://github.com/ylhsieh/ppi_lstm_rnn_keras`

5 Results and Discussion

Ten-fold cross-validation results on AIMed and BioInfer are listed in Table 2. Kernel-based methods can achieve decent F-scores of 61% and 69%. All NN-based methods outperform kernel-based ones by up to 10% on AIMed and 5% on BioInfer. When using randomly initialized embeddings, RNN exhibits similar performance as other NN models. However, by taking advantage of pre-trained embeddings, RNN further advances F-scores by 7% and 13% on AIMed and BioInfer, respectively. In other words, pre-training contribute to relative improvements of 10% and 18%. These results demonstrate that, even though kernel-based methods all include syntactic or semantic structures and carefully crafted features, neural networks are capable of automatically capturing contextual information that is crucial for identifying PPIs. Moreover, we can see that the standard deviations of the performance by RNN on the larger corpus, *i.e.*, BioInfer, is much lower than that of the smaller corpus (5 vs. 2). Besides, the relative improvement of RNN over compared methods on BioInfer is greater as well (10% and 18%). This suggests that richer context information in a larger corpus may be difficult to be manually modeled via feature engineering or rule creation, but is a well-suited learning source for neural networks.

Table 3 shows the cross-corpus results, in which different methods are trained on one corpus and tested on the other. We observe that, although RNN performs slightly better than McDepCNN, CK and PIPE methods are much more robust when learning on different corpora. We postulate that knowledge may play an important role in this scenario, and effective incorporation of such information into RNN can be a promising direction for future research.

Table 3: Cross-corpus results (in %) of two corpora. Bold font indicates the best performance in a column.

Method	Train Test AIMed BioInfer		Train Test BioInfer AIMed	
GK	47.1		47.2	
CK	53.1		49.6	
PIPE	**58.2**		**52.1**	
McDepCNN	48.0		49.9	
Proposed	*49.3*		*50.7*	

6 Conclusion

We propose an end-to-end RNN-based model to identify PPIs in biological literature. Cross-validation results demonstrate that it outperforms existing methods in the two largest corpora, BioInfer and AIMed. Potential directions for future work include integrating features that have been proven useful in identifying PPIs, and conduct extensive experiments under the cross-learning scheme. Also, we will explore networks with different architectures in order to further advance the current model.

Acknowledgments

We are grateful for the constructive comments from three anonymous reviewers. This work was supported by grant MOST105-2221-E-001-008-MY3 from the Ministry of Science and Technology, Taiwan.

References

Martín Abadi, Ashish Agarwal, Paul Barham, Eugene Brevdo, Zhifeng Chen, Craig Citro, Greg S. Corrado, Andy Davis, Jeffrey Dean, Matthieu Devin, Sanjay Ghemawat, Ian Goodfellow, Andrew Harp, Geoffrey Irving, Michael Isard, Yangqing Jia, Rafal Jozefowicz, Lukasz Kaiser, Manjunath Kudlur, Josh Levenberg, Dan Mané, Rajat Monga, Sherry Moore, Derek Murray, Chris Olah, Mike Schuster, Jonathon Shlens, Benoit Steiner, Ilya Sutskever, Kunal Talwar, Paul Tucker, Vincent Vanhoucke, Vijay Vasudevan, Fernanda Viégas, Oriol Vinyals, Pete Warden, Martin Wattenberg, Martin Wicke, Yuan Yu, and Xiaoqiang Zheng. 2015. TensorFlow: Large-scale machine learning on heterogeneous systems. Software available from tensorflow.org. http://tensorflow.org/.

Antti Airola, Sampo Pyysalo, Jari Björne, Tapio Pahikkala, Filip Ginter, and Tapio Salakoski. 2008. All-paths graph kernel for protein-protein interaction extraction with evaluation of cross-corpus learning. *BMC bioinformatics* 9(11):S2.

R. C. Bunescu and R. J. Mooney. 2005. A shortest path dependency kernel for relation extraction. *Proceedings of the Conference on Human Language Technology and Empirical Methods in Natural Language Processing* pages 724–731.

Razvan Bunescu, Ruifang Ge, Rohit J Kate, Edward M Marcotte, Raymond J Mooney, Arun K Ramani, and Yuk Wah Wong. 2005. Comparative experiments on learning information extractors for proteins and their interactions. *Artificial intelligence in medicine* 33(2):139–155.

Y. C. Chang, C. H. Chu, Y. C. Su, C. C. Chen, and W. L. Hsu. 2016. PIPE: a protein-protein interaction passage extraction module for BioCreative challenge. *Database (Oxford)* 2016. https://doi.org/10.1093/database/baw101.

Billy Chiu, Gamal Crichton, Anna Korhonen, and Sampo Pyysalo. 2016. How to train good word embeddings for biomedical NLP. In *Proceedings of the 15th Workshop on Biomedical Natural Language Processing*. Association for Computational Linguistics, Berlin, Germany, pages 166–174.

Corinna Cortes and Vladimir Vapnik. 1995. Support-vector networks. *Machine learning* 20(3):273–297.

Chris Dyer, Miguel Ballesteros, Wang Ling, Austin Matthews, and Noah A. Smith. 2015. Transition-based dependency parsing with stack long short-term memory. In *Proceedings of the 53rd Annual Meeting of the Association for Computational Linguistics and the 7th International Joint Conference on Natural Language Processing (Volume 1: Long Papers)*. Association for Computational Linguistics, Beijing, China, pages 334–343. http://www.aclweb.org/anthology/P15-1033.

J. H. Eom, S. Kim, S. H. Kim, and B. T. Zhang. 2006. A tree kernel-based method for protein-protein interaction mining from biomedical literature. *Knowledge Discovery in Life Science Literature, Proceedings* 3886:42–52.

Klaus Greff, Rupesh K Srivastava, Jan Koutník, Bas R Steunebrink, and Jürgen Schmidhuber. 2017. LSTM: A search space odyssey. *IEEE transactions on neural networks and learning systems* PP(99):1–11.

Sepp Hochreiter and Jürgen Schmidhuber. 1997. LSTM can solve hard long time lag problems. In *Advances in Neural Information Processing Systems*. pages 473–479.

Lei Hua and Chanqin Quan. 2016. A shortest dependency path based convolutional neural network for protein-protein relation extraction. *BioMed Research International* 2016.

Seonho Kim, Juntae Yoon, Jihoon Yang, and Seog Park. 2010. Walk-weighted subsequence kernels for protein-protein interaction extraction. *BMC bioinformatics* 11(1):107.

Guillaume Lample, Miguel Ballesteros, Sandeep Subramanian, Kazuya Kawakami, and Chris Dyer. 2016. Neural architectures for named entity recognition. In *Proceedings of NAACL-HLT*. pages 260–270.

Y. Lecun, L. Bottou, Y. Bengio, and P. Haffner. 1998. Gradient-based learning applied to document recognition. *Proceedings of the Ieee* 86(11):2278–2324. https://doi.org/Doi 10.1109/5.726791.

Lishuang Li, Rui Guo, Zhenchao Jiang, and Degen Huang. 2015. An approach to improve kernel-based protein-protein interaction extraction by learning from large-scale network data. *Methods* 83:44 – 50.

Tomas Mikolov, Ilya Sutskever, Kai Chen, Greg S Corrado, and Jeff Dean. 2013. Distributed representations of words and phrases and their compositionality. In *Advances in neural information processing systems*. pages 3111–3119.

Makoto Miwa and Mohit Bansal. 2016. End-to-end relation extraction using lstms on sequences and tree structures. In *Proceedings of the 54th Annual Meeting of the Association for Computational Linguistics (Volume 1: Long Papers)*. Association for Computational Linguistics, Berlin, Germany, pages 1105–1116.

Makoto Miwa, Rune Sætre, Yusuke Miyao, and Jun'ichi Tsujii. 2009. Protein–protein interaction extraction by leveraging multiple kernels and parsers. *International journal of medical informatics* 78(12):e39–e46.

Hirotada Mori. 2004. From the sequence to cell modeling: comprehensive functional genomics in escherichia coli. *BMB Reports* 37(1):83–92.

Yifan Peng and Zhiyong Lu. 2017. Deep learning for extracting protein-protein interactions from biomedical literature. In *Proceedings of the 2017 Workshop on Biomedical Natural Language Processing*. To appear.

Sampo Pyysalo, Filip Ginter, Juho Heimonen, Jari Björne, Jorma Boberg, Jouni Järvinen, and Tapio Salakoski. 2007. Bioinfer: a corpus for information extraction in the biomedical domain. *BMC bioinformatics* 8(1):50.

L. H. Qian and G. D. Zhou. 2012. Tree kernel-based protein–protein interaction extraction from biomedical literature. *Journal of Biomedical Informatics* 45(3):535 – 543.

Ilya Sutskever, Oriol Vinyals, and Quoc V Le. 2014. Sequence to sequence learning with neural networks. In *Advances in neural information processing systems*. pages 3104–3112.

Kai Sheng Tai, Richard Socher, and Christopher D. Manning. 2015. Improved semantic representations from tree-structured long short-term memory networks. In *Proceedings of the 53rd Annual Meeting of the ACL and the 7th IJCNLP*. Association for Computational Linguistics, Beijing, China, pages 1556–1566.

Tijmen Tieleman and Geoffrey Hinton. 2012. Lecture 6.5-rmsprop: Divide the gradient by a running average of its recent magnitude. *COURSERA: Neural networks for machine learning* 4(2).

Domonkos Tikk, Philippe Thomas, Peter Palaga, Jörg Hakenberg, and Ulf Leser. 2010. A comprehensive benchmark of kernel methods to extract protein–protein interactions from literature. *PLoS Comput Biol* 6(7):e1000837.

Zhehuan Zhao, Zhihao Yang, Hongfei Lin, Jian Wang, and Song Gao. 2016. A protein-protein interaction extraction approach based on deep neural network. *International Journal of Data Mining and Bioinformatics* 15(2):145–164.

Identifying Empathetic Messages in Online Health Communities

Hamed Khanpour
Computer Science and Engineering
University of North Texas
Hamedkhanpour@my.unt.edu

Cornelia Caragea
Computer Science
Kansas State University
ccaragea@k-state.edu

Prakhar Biyani
Yahoo Research
pxb5080@yahoo-inc.com

Abstract

Empathy captures one's ability to correlate with and understand others' emotional states and experiences. Messages with empathetic content are considered as one of the main advantages for joining online health communities due to their potential to improve people's moods. Unfortunately, to this date, no computational studies exist that automatically identify empathetic messages in online health communities. We propose a combination of Convolutional Neural Networks (CNN) and Long Short Term Memory (LSTM) networks, and show that the proposed model outperforms each individual model (CNN and LSTM) as well as several baselines.

1 Introduction

Empathy captures the ability of an individual to correlate with and gain an accurate understanding of other individuals' emotional states by putting oneself in their situations with appropriate reactions (Batson, 2009; Launay et al., 2015). Empathy is shown to have a fundamental role in connecting people in a community together (Davis et al., 2004). Recently, many studies in social and psychological sciences have investigated the correlation between the empathetic capability of users in a social network and their characteristics and behavioral patterns. For example, Kardos et al. (2017) analyzed social networks and found that higher empathetic abilities in social network users result in a bigger size of close friends' lists and vice versa. Medeiros and Bosse (2016) and Coursaris and Liu (2009) also expressed that empathetic abilities account for social support in social media, and Mayshak et al. (2017) showed that the level of user engagement with social networking websites has a direct correlation with empathetic abilities. Finally, Del Rey et al. (2016) suggested that empathy negatively predicts traditional bullying and cyber-bullying perpetration.

In a health domain, recent studies show that empathy is one of the main advantages of using online health communities (OHCs) (Medeiros and Bosse, 2016; Nambisan, 2011; Malik and Coulson, 2010), which potentially fosters the healing process by decreasing distress and increasing optimism (Goubert et al., 2005; Olson, 1995). Table 1 shows an example from a cancer community, illustrating the function of empathetic messages.

The above studies, in social sciences and psychology, are based upon questionnaires, direct interviews, or at most hundreds of samples from manually collected data. These studies, however, suffer from several issues including scalability, biased data usage (Qiu et al., 2011), and high reliance on human memory that might not remember details accurately (Redelmeier and Kahneman, 1996; Litwin and McGuigan, 1999).

In the context of general social media, several computational studies started to analyze empathetic messages. However, these studies are contextually different from our study, which is focused on the health domain. For example, Rao et al. (2014) considered empathy as one of the eight classes of emotions in their classification task. In another work, Alam et al. (2017) annotated and modeled empathy in spoken conversations, based on multi-modal features extracted from conversations (such as acoustic features and video frames). As mentioned above, this is different from our work contextually and in terms of the applied methods. We use only textual comments.

Despite the importance of empathy in augmenting patients' positive feelings (Goubert et al., 2005; Olson, 1995), to our knowledge, there has not been any computational approaches proposed

Proceedings of the The 8th International Joint Conference on Natural Language Processing, pages 246–251,
Taipei, Taiwan, November 27 – December 1, 2017 ©2017 AFNLP

–Patient: Hi all sense being on chemo (5 down 1 to tch) with the last two really I have had a problem with my BP being high. I am having a problem with my heart racing. At rest it may get down to 86. When my oncologist did the muga scan it went from 68 to 63. I have never had a problem with my heart at all. I'm Very nervous.
–Commentator: I had much the same problem while doing chemo, the last 2 or 3 rounds were the worst. Try not to worry to much! By the way I am the proud owner of 3 chihuahuas. Blessings to you...Alison
–Patient: Thanks so much I feel allot better now. I did talk to my Dr and he is giving me meds to lower the rate. I feel like I spend my time fighting side affects LOL. Thanks sisters. Take care all

Table 1: A sample of an empathetic message and its impact on patient's emotion

for identifying and analyzing empathetic messages in OHCs. Computational studies that analyzed OHCs data, have focused on analyzing emotional and informational support in patients' messages (Biyani et al., 2014; Wang et al., 2014; Qiu et al., 2011). Zhao et al. (2014, 2011) used the result of analyzing social support in OHCs for identifying influential users. However, these works address emotional support in general and do not focus on identifying empathetic messages.

In this paper, we propose a computational approach to analyzing large amounts of messages in OHCs and to automatically identifying messages that contain empathy. This first study on identifying empathetic messages in OHCs aims to make an appropriate foundation for further, deeper, and scalable studies and developing applications. Automatic empathetic message identifier can be used by OHCs' moderators for monitoring communities mental health, cyber-bullying and cyber-stalking detection, measuring the level of users engagement in communities (Mayshak et al., 2017), predicting users' position in online communities (Kardos et al., 2017), as well as the loneliness of users (Pamukçu and Meydan, 2010). Furthermore, such an application can be employed in measuring nursing skills (Yu and Kirk, 2008), measuring the quality of online counseling sessions, and assessing the quality of human-robot interactions (Fung et al., 2016; Leite et al., 2013).

Our contributions in this work are as follows:

1. We propose a machine learning model for identifying empathetic messages in OHCs. To our knowledge, this is the first work on automatically detecting empathy in OHCs.

2. We experimentally validate our empathy identification model on a manually annotated dataset generated from the Cancer Survivors' Network of the American Cancer Society.

3. We show that in general empathetic messages are correlated with a positive change in participants' sentiments.

2   Data Collection and Annotation

We randomly selected 225 comments from 21 discussion threads in the Lung Cancer discussion board in a Cancer Survivor' Network (CSN)[1]. Following Biyani et al. (2014), we selected messages (i.e., sentences in comments) with length greater than four words. We ended up with 1041 messages in total. We integrated our collected data with 1066 messages extracted from the breast cancer discussion board in CSN that was provided by Biyani et al. (2014).

The purpose of the annotation was to tag empathetic messages through which the message providers intended to show their empathy towards other people. Two annotators (graduate students) contributed to the task. They were asked to get familiarized with the concept of empathy by reading two studies (i.e., Collins (2014) and Decety and Jackson (2004)) during a week. After a group meeting between annotators and researchers to share and discuss their understanding of empathetic messages in the presence of two psychologists, the annotation task began in an iterative fashion similar to prior studies and guidelines (DMello, 2016; Fort et al., 2016; Shanahan et al., 2006) . In each round, 200 messages were assigned and annotators discussed disagreements with researchers; 100% inter-annotator agreement (IAA) was achieved after each round of discussions. We used Cohen's kappa for measuring IAA. After three initial rounds of annotations, the remaining data (1507 messages) were assigned to the annotators where they achieved 87% IAA. The last round of the assigned data was adjudicated by one of the authors. Table 3 provides the distribution of empathetic messages in the two datasets (breast cancer (B-dataset) and lung cancer (L-dataset)). As can be seen, B-dataset has significantly more empathetic messages than the L-dataset.

---

[1]https://csn.cancer.org

247

Hyper-parameter Settings
–LSTM: W2vec-S=150, LR= 0.001, L2reg=1$E-5$, Decay rate=0.7, Dropout=0.5, Layer=5, 1-Max pooling, Order= 3
–ConvLST:W2vec-S=150, LR= 0.01, L2reg=1$E-5$, Decay rate=0.7, Dropout=0.5, Layer=2, 1-Max pooling, Order= 2
–CNN: W2vec-S=150, LR= 0.1, L2reg=1$E-5$, Decay rate=0.5, Dropout=0.5, Layer=2, 1-Max pooling, FRS=(1,2,3), NF=64

Table 2: Hyperparameter settings for each model.

3 Model

Dataset	Empathetic msgs.	Percentage(%)
B-dataset	494 out of 1066	46.3
L-dataset	295 out of 1041	28.3

Table 3: Statistics from the data collections.

In this section, we describe our proposed model for empathetic messages identification in OHCs.

Problem Statement: Given a message (i.e., a sentence in a comment) in an OHC, $S = \{W_1, W_2, \cdots, W_i, \cdots, W_n\}$ containing n words, the task is to classify it as empathetic or not.

3.1 Word Representations

We use word embeddings with an embedding matrix $E_w \in R^{d_w \times V_m}$ where d_w is the embedding dimension and V_m is the word vocabulary size. We generate word embedding matrices by using the whole CSN collected data (i.e., users' comments from June 2000 to June 2012) of three different dimensions (i.e., 75, 150, 300). We use W2vector module in Gensim (Řehůřek and Sojka, 2010).

3.2 Model Description

The proposed model for classifying empathetic messages combines convolutional and LSTM (long short-term memory) networks (which we call ConvLSTM). Our ConvLSTM network takes word embeddings as input and creates a sequence of dense, real-valued vectors: $E = (e_1, e_2, \cdots, e_T)$. By applying multiple convolutional layers to E and using pooling, we obtain a dynamic sequence of feature vectors: $F = (f_1, f_2, \cdots, f_n)$, which is fed into the LSTM. The output of the LSTM network is given to a softmax function to compute the predictive probabilities, $p(y = k|S)$, of each of the classes given a message S (see Figure 1).

4 Experiments

In this section, we present our optimization process and the results of our model. We report precision, recall, and F-1 score, all macro-averaged across 10 folds in a cross-validation setting.

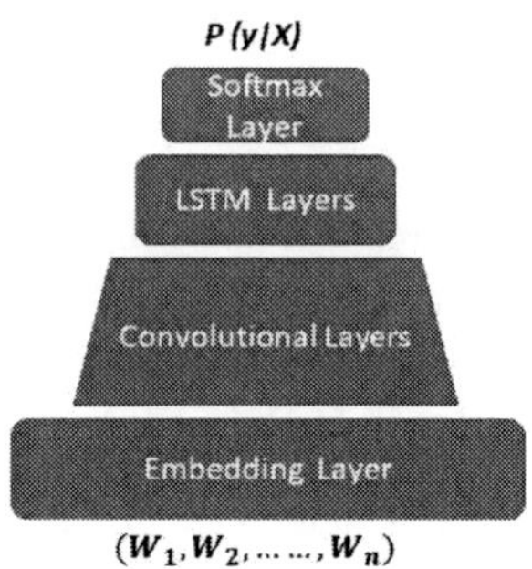

Figure 1: ConvLSTM structure for empathetic message identification.

Hyperparameters settings: We optimized hyper-parameter values by performing a grid search on a development set, which consisted of 15% of instances in the training set in 10-fold cross validation experiments. We optimized hyperparameters of ConvLSTM and each of embedded models (i.e., CNN and LSTM) to compare their performances with ConvLSTM. We used a range of values for the following hyperparameters: word embedding vector size (i.e., $75, 150$, and 300), learning rate (LR) $[0.1, 0.001]$, l_2 regularization (L2reg) $[0.0, 5E-5, 1E-5]$, decay rate $[0.0, 0.1, \cdots, 0.8]$, dropout $[0.0, 0.1, \cdots, 0.6]$, number of layers $[1, 2, \cdots, 10]$, pooling methods [1-Max, Mean, Last state], order size in LSTM {unigram, bigram, trigram}, filter region sizes (FRS) $[(1,2,3), (2,3,4), (3,4,5), (4,5,6)]$ and number of feature maps (NF) in CNN $[32, 64, \cdots, 256]$. Table 2 shows the best hyperparameters' settings by which each model achieved the best F-1 score on the development set.

Baselines: We compare our models with the following baselines:

1. **Bag-of-words and POS tags:** Word frequencies and their part-of-speech tags show the primary property of the text and has been used in studies on OHCs' message processing (Biyani et al., 2014, 2012b,a). We used both words and their POS tags' frequencies as features. We obtained the best performance using term-frequency encoding

Method	P(%)	R(%)	F-1 (%)
ConvLST	78.61	**78.12**	**78.36**
LSTM	**79.47**	75.00	77.17
CNN	76.20	77.00	76.60
BoW+POS	71.8	68.2	69.90
Lexical-based	54.5	46.9	50.4

Table 4: Empathetic message identification.

and document frequencies between 2 and 95% of the total documents. Multinomial Naïve Bayes achieved the best results among all evaluated classifiers (e.g., Support Vector Machines and Random Forest).

2. **Lexicon-based model:** Lexicon-based approaches have been used in many studies related to emotion detection (Strapparava and Mihalcea, 2007; Strapparava et al., 2004) and sentiment analysis tasks (Mohammad, 2012; Liu, 2012; Biyani et al., 2013). Following Biyani et al. (2014), we used the same lexicons. These lexicons include: weak and strong subjective words, cancer drugs, side-effects, and therapeutic procedures, for building our baseline's feature set.

Empathetic Message Identification: Table 4 compares the performance of our proposed model (ConvLSTM) with CNN, LSTM, and the baselines. As can be seen, our model achieves the best F-1 score, which is 8.46% higher than the F-1 score of the best baseline (i.e., 69.90%). Also, we can see that the combination of CNN and LSTM (ConvLSTM), which employs the sequences of important features extracted by CNN, achieves better performance than each of the individual CNN and LSTM models.

While LSTM achieved the best precision, ConvLSTM obtained the highest F-1 score and recall. Table 4 shows that Lexical-based baseline resulted in the lowest F-1 score. The lexicon-based baseline uses two types of features: subjectivity-related and informational-related features. After removing subjectivity features, the F-1 score drops to 15.7% and after removing informational features, the F-1 score drops to 47.3%. These results suggest that the subjectivity features are more effective than the informational-related ones, as expected, in identifying empathetic messages.

Sentiment Dynamics with Empathetic Messages: In this section, we conduct an experiment to investigate the potential of empathetic messages for changing the thread originator's feelings. We used the data extracted from CSN, which include

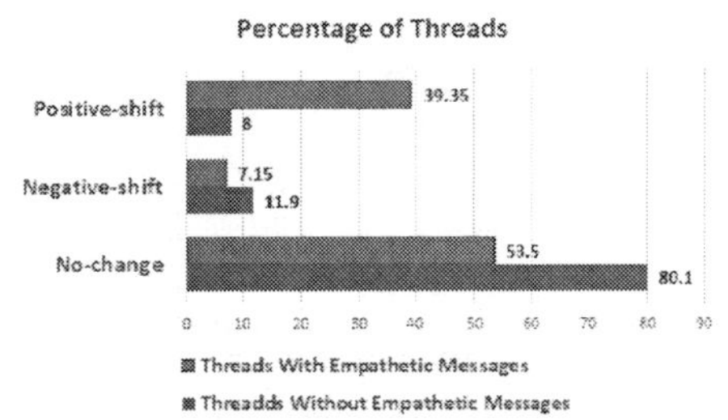

Figure 2: Thread-initiator's feeling transformation as a result of empathetic messages in a thread.

users' comments from June 2000 to June 2012. We extracted all threads where the originator of a thread replied (at least) once after an empathetic comment was posted from other users (responders). We followed the same experimental setting presented in Qiu et al. (2011). In total, 12915 discussion threads were extracted for analysis.

We ran our ConvLSTM model for empathetic message identification on all responders' messages, which were posted between two posts of the originator (e.g., the **Commentator**'s post in Table 1). We also discarded messages in which an initiator simply thanks a fellow member and used a threshold of four on the number of words (Biyani et al., 2014). We ran Stanford sentiment toolkit (Manning et al., 2014) on the originators' posts (e.g., the **Patient**'s posts in Table 1) to identify their sentiment. In this way, it is possible to determine whether the empathetic messages provided by responders who replied to the thread, are able to change the sentiment of the thread originator. To better understand any changes in feelings, we categorized changes in three groups, i.e., Positive-shift, Negative-shift, and No-change. Positive-shift represents any positive change in the sentiment of the thread initiator such as negative-to-positive, neutral-to-positive, negative-to-neutral. Negative-shift has a converse settings compared with the Positive-shift and No-change represents a state that originator's second post reflects the same sentiment as the initial one.

These results are shown in Figure 2 (the red bars). As can be seen from the figure, in 39.35% of the threads, empathetic messages bring a positive-shift in originators' feelings as opposed to only 7.15% negative-shift. We can also observe that in 53.5% of the threads, the originators' feelings do not change. Thus, we can conclude that empathetic messages play a major role in improving participants' feelings in OHCs.

We also contrasted the positive-shift, negative-shift, and no-change in the threads with empathetic messages (the red bars in Figure 2) with those in the threads without empathetic messages (the blue bars in Figure 2) to better understand the impact of empathy on people's moods. More precisely, we ran the sentiment tool over the threads with no empathetic messages and found that only 8% positive shift, 11.9% negative shift and 80.1% no-change occurred. These results suggest that positive sentiment changes occur more prominently in threads containing empathetic messages compared to those with no empathetic messages.

5 Conclusion and Future Work

In this paper, we presented a machine learning model for identifying empathetic messages in online health communities. Our model is based on a combination of Convolutional Neural Networks and Long Short Term Memory networks, called ConvLSTM. We showed that ConvLSTM outperforms strong baselines. Moreover, we showed that empathetic messages do cause positive shifts in patients' sentiments in OHCs. In future, it would be interesting to investigate empathy identification in other sub-forums and the relation between the number of empathetic messages in a thread and the change in thread originators' emotional states.

Acknowledgments

We are grateful to the American Cancer Society for making the Cancer Survivors' Network available to us. We would like to thank Iulia Bivolaru and Manoj Panchagnula for their help with data preparation. We also thank Kenneth Portier and Greta Greer from ACS for their contributions to various discussions related to this work.

References

Firoj Alam, Morena Danieli, and Giuseppe Riccardi. 2017. Annotating and modeling empathy in spoken conversations. *arXiv preprint arXiv:1705.04839*.

C Daniel Batson. 2009. These things called empathy: eight related but distinct phenomena.

Prakhar Biyani, Sumit Bhatia, Cornelia Caragea, and Prasenjit Mitra. 2012a. Thread specific features are helpful for identifying subjectivity orientation of online forum threads. In *COLING*, pages 295–310.

Prakhar Biyani, Cornelia Caragea, Prasenjit Mitra, and John Yen. 2014. Identifying emotional and informational support in online health communities. In *COLING*, pages 827–836.

Prakhar Biyani, Cornelia Caragea, Prasenjit Mitra, Chong Zhou, John Yen, Greta E Greer, and Kenneth Portier. 2013. Co-training over domain-independent and domain-dependent features for sentiment analysis of an online cancer support community. In *Proc. of the 2013 IEEE/ACM ASONAM*, pages 413–417.

Prakhar Biyani, Cornelia Caragea, Amit Singh, and Prasenjit Mitra. 2012b. I want what i need!: analyzing subjectivity of online forum threads. In *Proc. of the 21st ACM CIKM*, pages 2495–2498. ACM.

Franklin M Collins. 2014. The relationship between social media and empathy.

Constantinos K Coursaris and Ming Liu. 2009. An analysis of social support exchanges in online hiv/aids self-help groups. *Computers in Human Behavior*, 25(4):911–918.

M Davis, L Tiedens, and C Leach. 2004. Negotiating the border between self and other. *The social life of emotions*, pages 19–42.

Jean Decety and Philip L Jackson. 2004. The functional architecture of human empathy. *Behavioral and cognitive neuroscience reviews*, 3(2):71–100.

Rosario Del Rey, Lambros Lazuras, José A Casas, Vassilis Barkoukis, Rosario Ortega-Ruiz, and Haralambos Tsorbatzoudis. 2016. Does empathy predict (cyber) bullying perpetration, and how do age, gender and nationality affect this relationship? *Learning and Individual Differences*, 45:275–281.

Sidney K DMello. 2016. On the influence of an iterative affect annotation approach on inter-observer and self-observer reliability. *IEEE Transactions on Affective Computing*, 7(2):136–149.

Karën Fort et al. 2016. *Collaborative Annotation for Reliable Natural Language Processing: Technical and Sociological Aspects*. Wiley Online Library.

Pascale Fung, Dario Bertero, Yan Wan, Anik Dey, Ricky Ho Yin Chan, Farhad Bin Siddique, Yang Yang, Chien-Sheng Wu, and Ruixi Lin. 2016. Towards empathetic human-robot interactions. *arXiv preprint arXiv:1605.04072*.

Liesbet Goubert, Kenneth D Craig, Tine Vervoort, Stephen Morley, MJL Sullivan, Williams de CAC, A Cano, and Geert Crombez. 2005. Facing others in pain: the effects of empathy. *Pain*, 118(3):285–288.

Peter Kardos, Bernhard Leidner, Csaba Pléh, Péter Soltész, and Zsolt Unoka. 2017. Empathic people have more friends: Empathic abilities predict social network size and position in social network predicts empathic efforts. *Social Networks*, 50:1–5.

Jacques Launay, Eiluned Pearce, Rafael Wlodarski, Max van Duijn, James Carney, and Robin IM Dunbar. 2015. Higher-order mentalising and executive functioning. *Personality and individual differences*, 86:6–14.

Iolanda Leite, André Pereira, Samuel Mascarenhas, Carlos Martinho, Rui Prada, and Ana Paiva. 2013. The influence of empathy in human–robot relations. *International journal of human-computer studies*, 71(3):250–260.

Mark S Litwin and Kimberly A McGuigan. 1999. Accuracy of recall in health-related quality-of-life assessment among men treated for prostate cancer. *Journal of Clinical Oncology*, 17(9):2882–2882.

Bing Liu. 2012. Sentiment analysis and opinion mining. *Synthesis lectures on human language technologies*, 5(1):1–167.

Sumaira H Malik and Neil S Coulson. 2010. Coping with infertility online: an examination of self-help mechanisms in an online infertility support group. *Patient education and counseling*, 81(2):315–318.

Christopher D Manning, Mihai Surdeanu, John Bauer, Jenny Rose Finkel, Steven Bethard, and David McClosky. 2014. The stanford corenlp natural language processing toolkit. In *ACL (System Demonstrations)*, pages 55–60.

Richelle Mayshak, Stefanie J Sharman, Lucy Zinkiewicz, and Alexa Hayley. 2017. The influence of empathy and self-presentation on engagement with social networking website posts. *Computers in Human Behavior*, 71:362–377.

Lenin Medeiros and Tibor Bosse. 2016. Empirical analysis of social support provided via social media. In *International Conference on Social Informatics*, pages 439–453. Springer.

Saif M Mohammad. 2012. # emotional tweets. In *Sixth International Workshop on Semantic Evaluation*, pages 246–255.

Priya Nambisan. 2011. Information seeking and social support in online health communities: impact on patients' perceived empathy. *Journal of the American Medical Informatics Association*, 18(3):298–304.

Joanne K Olson. 1995. Relationships between nurse-expressed empathy, patient-perceived empathy and patient distress. *Journal of Nursing Scholarship*, 27(4):317–322.

Burcu Pamukçu and Betül Meydan. 2010. The role of empathic tendency and perceived social support in predicting loneliness levels of college students. *Procedia-Social and Behavioral Sciences*, 5:905–909.

Baojun Qiu, Kang Zhao, Prasenjit Mitra, Dinghao Wu, Cornelia Caragea, John Yen, Greta E Greer, and Kenneth Portier. 2011. Get online support, feel better–sentiment analysis and dynamics in an online cancer survivor community. In *PASSAT and SocialCom*, pages 274–281. IEEE.

Yanghui Rao, Qing Li, Liu Wenyin, Qingyuan Wu, and Xiaojun Quan. 2014. Affective topic model for social emotion detection. *Neural Networks*, 58:29–37.

Donald A Redelmeier and Daniel Kahneman. 1996. Patients' memories of painful medical treatments: Real-time and retrospective evaluations of two minimally invasive procedures. *Pain*, 66(1):3–8.

Radim Řehůřek and Petr Sojka. 2010. Software Framework for Topic Modelling with Large Corpora. In *Proceedings of the LREC 2010 Workshop on New Challenges for NLP Frameworks*, pages 45–50.

James G Shanahan, Yan Qu, and Janyce Wiebe. 2006. *Computing attitude and affect in text: Theory and applications*, volume 20. Springer.

Carlo Strapparava and Rada Mihalcea. 2007. Semeval-2007 task 14: Affective text. In *4th Semantic Evaluations*, pages 70–74.

Carlo Strapparava, Alessandro Valitutti, et al. 2004. Wordnet affect: an affective extension of wordnet. In *LREC*, volume 4, pages 1083–1086.

Xi Wang, Kang Zhao, and Nick Street. 2014. Social support and user engagement in online health communities. In *Smart Health*, pages 97–110. Springer.

Juping Yu and Maggie Kirk. 2008. Measurement of empathy in nursing research: systematic review. *Journal of Advanced Nursing*, 64(5):440–454.

Kang Zhao, Baojun Qiu, Cornelia Caragea, Dinghao Wu, Prasenjit Mitra, John Yen, Greta E. Greer, and Kenneth Portier. 2011. Identifying leaders in an online cancer survivor community. In *Proceedings of the 21st Annual Workshop on Information Technologies and Systems (WITS 2011)*.

Kang Zhao, John Yen, Greta Greer, Baojun Qiu, Prasenjit Mitra, and Kenneth Portier. 2014. Finding influential users of online health communities: a new metric based on sentiment influence. *Journal of the American Medical Informatics Association*, 21(e2):e212–e218.

Fake News Detection Through Multi-Perspective Speaker Profiles

Yunfei Long[1], Qin Lu[1], Rong Xiang[2], Minglei Li[1] and Chu-Ren Huang[3]
[1]Department of Computing, The Hong Kong Polytechnic University
csylong,csluqin,csmli@comp.polyu.edu.hk
[2]Advanced Micro Devices, Inc.(Shanghai)
Rong.Xiang@amd.com
[3]Department of Chinese and Bilingual Studies, The Hong Kong Polytechnic University
churen.huang@polyu.edu.hk

Abstract

Automatic fake news detection is an important, yet very challenging topic. Traditional methods using lexical features have only very limited success. This paper proposes a novel method to incorporate speaker profiles into an attention based LSTM model for fake news detection. Speaker profiles contribute to the model in two ways. One is to include them in the attention model. The other includes them as additional input data. By adding speaker profiles such as party affiliation, speaker title, location and credit history, our model outperforms the state-of-the-art method by 14.5% in accuracy using a benchmark fake news detection dataset. This proves that speaker profiles provide valuable information to validate the credibility of news articles.

1 Introduction

Fake news is written and published with the intent to mislead its readers in order to gain financially or politically, often with sensationalist, exaggerated, or patently false headlines attract readers' attention [1]. Fake news is more dangerous than newspaper gaffes, especially in social media. One of the worst effect of fake news in China is an incidence after the Fukushima Daiichi nuclear disaster in 2011. A fake news in microbiology claims that salt can prevent radiation, but the nuclear disaster makes salt contaminated. This fake news triggered people stockpiling table salt in China, resulted in a huge market disorder. [2]

Fake news detection is defined as the task of categorizing news along a continuum of veracity with an associated measure of certainty (Conroy et al., 2015). Detecting fake news in social media has been an extremely important, yet technically very challenging problem. The difficulty comes partly from the fact that even human beings may have difficulty identifying between real news and fake news. In one study, human judges, by a rough measure of comparison, achieved only 50-63 % success rates in identifying fake news (Rubin, 2017).

The most of fake news detection algorithms try to linguistic cues (Feng and Hirst, 2013; Markowitz and Hancock, 2014; Ruchansky et al., 2017). Several successful studies on fake news detection have demonstrated the effectiveness of linguistic cue identification, as the language of truth news is known to differ from that of fake news (Bachenko et al., 2008; Larcker and Zakolyukina, 2012). For example, deceivers are likely to use more sentiment words, more sense-based words (e.g., seeing, touching), and other-oriented pronouns, but less self-oriented pronouns. Compared to real news, fake news shows lower cognitive complexity and uses more negative emotion words. However, the linguistic indicators of fake news across different topics and media platforms are not well understood. Rubin (2015) points out that there are many types of fake news, each with different potential textual indicators. This indicates that using linguistic features is not only laborious but also topic/media dependent domain knowledge, thus limiting the scalability of these solutions.

In addition to lexical features, speaker profile information can be useful (Gottipati et al., 2013; Long et al., 2016). Speaker profiles, including party affiliations, job title of speaker, as well as topical information which can also be used to in-

---

[1]$https://en.wikipedia.org/wiki/Fake_news$
[2]https://blogs.wsj.com/chinarealtime/2011/03/17/fearing-radiation-chinese-rush-to-buy-table-salt/

Proceedings of the The 8th International Joint Conference on Natural Language Processing, pages 252–256,
Taipei, Taiwan, November 27 – December 1, 2017 ©2017 AFNLP

dicate the credibility of a piece of news. For example, a conservative might neglect the impact of climate change, while a progressive might exaggerate inequality. On some occasions, it is hard to make fake claims like congressional inquiry. But in other cases, the speaker tend to exaggerate facts like the campaign rally. For the study use profile information, Wang (2017) proposes a hybrid CNN model to detect fake news, which uses speaker profiles as a part of the input data. Wang (2017) also made the first large scale fake news detection benchmark dataset with speaker information such as party affiliation, location of speech, job title, credit history as well as topic.

The Long-Short memory network (LSTM), as a neural network model, is proven to work better for long sentences (Tang et al., 2015). Attention models are also proposed to weigh the importance of different words in their context. Current attention models are either based on local semantic attentions (Yang et al., 2016) or user attentions(Chen et al., 2016).

In this paper, we propose a model to incorporate speaker profile into fake news detection. Profile information is used in two ways. The first way includes profiles as an attention factor while the second one includes profiles as additional input data. Evaluations are conducted using the dataset provided by Wang (2017). Experimental results show that incorporating speaker profile can improve performance dramatically. Our accuracy can reach 0.415 in the benchmark dataset, about 14.5% higher than state-of-the-art hybrid CNN model.

2   Proposed Model

Our proposed model uses LSTM model (Gers, 2001) as the basic classifier. The attention models and speaker profile information are added into LSTM to form a hybrid model.

Figure 1 shows the hybrid LSTM. Note that the first LSTM is for obtaining the representation of news articles. The speaker profile is used to construct two attention factors. One uses only the speaker profile and the other uses topic information of the news articles. The second LSTM simply uses speaker profiles to obtain the vector presentations of speakers. The two representations are then concatenated in the soft-max function for classification.

Let D be a collection of news and P be a collection of profiles. A piece of news, d_k, $d_k \in D$, includes both its text as a sentence, denoted by s_k, and a speaker profile , denoted by p_k, $p_k \in P$. A sentence s_k is formed by a sequence of words $s_k = w_{k1}w_{k2}...w_{kl_k}$, where l_k is the length of s_k. The features of a word $w_i \in S_k$ form a word vector $\vec{v}^{w_i}$ with length N, $\vec{v}^{w_i} = [F_1{}^{w_i}, F_2{}^{w_i}....F_N{}^{w_i}]$. Every $w_k \in s_k$ and $p_k \in P$ are fed into the first LSTM. The speaker based profile vector $\vec{s}$ and the topic based profile vector $\vec{t}$ serve as the two attention factors for s_k. The output of the two LSTM models are $\vec{s_k}$ and $\vec{p_k}$. Finally, $\vec{s_k}$ and $\vec{p_k}$ are concatenated to form the representation $\vec{d_k}$. The final layer projects $\vec{d_k}$ onto the target space of L class labels though a soft-max layer.

A LSTM model has five types of gates in each node i represented by five vectors including an input gate $\vec{i_i}$, a forget gate $\vec{f_i}$, an output gate $\vec{o_i}$, a candidate memory cell gate $\vec{c}'_i$, and a memory cell gate $\vec{c_i}$. $\vec{f_i}$ and $\vec{o_i}$ are used to indicate which values will be updated, either to forget or to keep. $\vec{c}'_i$ and $\vec{c_i}$ are used to keep the candidate features and the actual accepted features, respectively.

Each node i corresponds to each word w_i in a given sentence S_k, represented by its word embedding $\vec{w_i}$. The LSTM cell state $\vec{c_i}$ and the hidden state $\vec{h}_{S_k:w_i}$ can be updated in two steps. In the first step, the previous hidden state $\vec{h}_{S_k:w_{i-1}}$ uses a hyperbolic function to form $\vec{c}'_i$ as defined below.

$$\vec{c}'_i = tanh(\hat{W}_c * [\vec{h}_{S_k:w_{i-1}} * \vec{w_i}] + \hat{b}), \quad (1)$$

where $\hat{W}_c$ is a parameter matrix, $\vec{h}_{S_k:w_{i-1}}$ is the previous hidden state and $\vec{w_i}$ is the word vector. $\hat{b}$ is the regularization parameter matrix. In the second step, $\vec{c_i}$ is updated by $\vec{c}'_i$ and its previous state $\vec{c}_{i-1}$ according to the below formula:

$$\vec{c_i} = \vec{f_i} \odot \vec{c}_{i-1} + \vec{i_i} \odot \vec{c}'_i. \quad (2)$$

The hidden state of w_i can be obtained by

$$\vec{h}_{S:w_i} = \vec{o_i}tanh(\vec{f_i} \odot \vec{c_i}). \quad (3)$$

The forget gate $\vec{f_i}$ is for keeping the long term memory. A series of hidden states $\vec{h_1}\vec{h_2}...\vec{h_i}$ can serve as input to the average pooling layer to obtain the representation $\vec{s_k}$. $\vec{p_k}$, the representation of p_k, can be obtained similarly through the same LSTM model. Details will not be repeated here.

Similar to other attention models, speaker profile based attention factors are included in the first LSTM for each text, s_k. Rather than feeding speaker profiles as hidden states to an average pooling layer, we use attention mechanism which uses a weighting scheme to indicate importance of different words to the meaning of the news.

We use speaker profile and topic information for weight training, which are represented by continuous and real-valued vectors $\vec{s}$ and $\vec{t}$, respectively. Let α_{w_i} denote the weight to measure the importance of w_i in s_k. The attention weight α_{w_i} for each hidden state can be defined as:

$$\alpha_{w_i} = \frac{exp(e(\vec{h}_{S_k:w_i}, \vec{s}, \vec{t}))}{\sum_{k=1}^{l_i} exp(e(\vec{h}_{S_k:w_i}, \vec{s}, \vec{t}))} \tag{4}$$

where e is score function to indicate the importance of words defined by:

$$exp(e(\vec{h}_{S_k:w_i}, \vec{s}, \vec{t}) = v^T tanh(\hat{W}_H \vec{h}_{S_k:w_i} + \hat{W}_s \vec{s} + \hat{W}_t \vec{t} + \vec{b}) \tag{5}$$

where W_H, W_S, W_T are weight matrices, v is weight vector and v^T denotes its transpose. This model can train speaker vector $\vec{s}$ and topic vector $\vec{t}$ at the same time.

Formally, the enhanced sentence representation $\vec{s_k}$ is a weighted sum of hidden states as Formula 6

$$\vec{s_k} = \sum_t \alpha_{w_i} \vec{h}_{S_k:w_i}. \tag{6}$$

Similarly, we use the second LSTM model to get the representation of profile $\vec{p_k}$. The final news representation $\vec{d_k}$ is computed by concatenating $\vec{p_k}$ and $\vec{s_k}$, represented in Formula 7:

$$\vec{d_k} = \vec{s_k} \oplus \vec{p_k}. \tag{7}$$

In LSTM model, we use a hidden layer to project the final news vector $\vec{d_k^f}$ through a hyperbolic function.

$$\vec{d_k^f} = tanh(\hat{W}_h \vec{d_k} + \hat{b}_h), \tag{8}$$

where $\hat{W}_h$ is the weight matrix of the hidden layer and $\hat{b}_h$ is the regularization matrix.

Finally, prediction for any label $l \epsilon L$ obtained by the soft-max function is defined as:

$$P(y = l | \vec{d_k^f}) = \frac{e^{\vec{d_k^f}^T \vec{W}_l}}{\sum_{l=1}^{L} e^{\vec{d_k^f}^T \vec{W}_l}} \tag{9}$$

where $\vec{W}_l$ is the soft-max weight for each label.

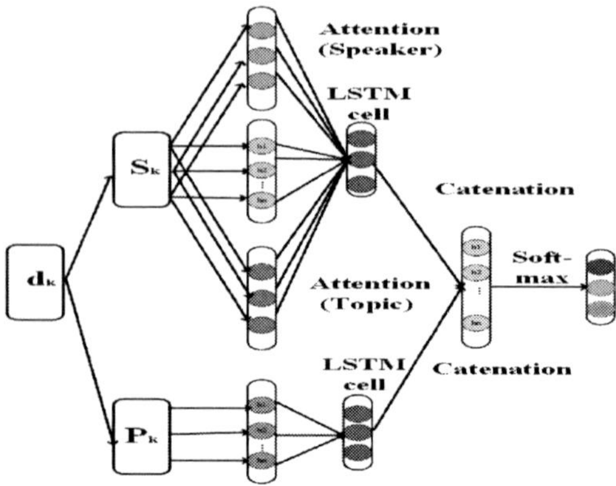

Figure 1: Hybrid fake news detection model with attention mechanism

Statistics	Num	Labels	Num
Training Set	10,269	Pants on fire	1,050
Develop Set	1,284	False	2,511
Testing Size	1,283	Barely-true	2,108
Democrats	4,150	Half-true	2,638
Republicans	5,687	Mostly-true	2,466
Others	2,185	True	2,063

Table 1: The statistics of the LIAR data set

3 Performance Evaluation

Evaluations are performed using the LIAR dataset by Wang (2017). The dataset contains 12,836 short statements from 3,341 speakers covering 141 topics in POLITIFACT.COM[3]. Each news includes text content, topic, and speaker profile. Speaker profiles include speaker name, title, party affiliation, current job, location of speech, and credit history. The credit history includes the historical records of inaccurate statements for each speaker. Annotation is based on evaluations by professional editors. The labels take discrete values from 1 to 6 corresponding to *pants-fire, false, barely-true, half-true, mostly-true,* and *true*. The statistics are listed in the Table 1.

Models	Dev.	Test
Majority	0.204	0.208
LSTM	0.241	0.245
CNN-Wang	0.247	0.247
CNN-WangP	**0.247**	**0.270**

Table 2: The results for baseline models

---

[3] http://www.politifact.com/truth-o-meter/

The performance of four baseline models are shown in Table 2 including a simple majority model, the LSTM model without using profile information, the hybrid CNN model proposed by Wang (2017) without profile information(CNN-Wang), and the hybrid CNN model by Wang with profile information(CNN-WangP).

Note that firstly, LSTM without profile does not perform better than CNN-Wang. However, other studies show that when attention model is incorporated, LSTM generally outperforms that of CNN model (Chen et al., 2016; Yang et al., 2016) which will be shown later. Secondly, CNN-WangP, which uses speaker profiles has the best performance. For word representation, we train the skip-gram word embedding (Mikolov et al., 2013) on each dataset separately to initialize the word vectors. All embedding sizes on the model are set to $N = 200$, a commonly used size.

In speaker profiles, there are four basic attributes: *party affiliation(Pa)*, *location of speech(La)*, *job title of speaker(Ti)*, and *credit history(Ch)* which counts the inaccurate statements for speaker in past speeches. Note that *credit history* is not a commonly available data. It is included here for comparison to CNN-Wang(P). We conduct experiment on using these attributes individually and in combinations.

	Without Att		With Att	
Profile	Dev	Test	Dev	Test
CNN-Wang	0.247	0.247	N/A	N/A
CNN-WangP	0.247	0.274	N/A	N/A
Base LSTM	0.241	0.245	0.250	0.255
Pa	0.247	0.246	0.253	0.257
La	0.243	0.245	<u>0.266</u>	<u>0.268</u>
Ti	0.241	0.247	0.258	0.257
Ch	0.363	0.368	**0.378**	**0.385**
Pa+La	0.250	0.252	0.255	0.261
Pa+Ti	0.261	0.264	0.267	0.265
La+Ti	0.267	0.264	<u>0.268</u>	<u>0.271</u>
Ti+Ch	0.378	0.380	**0.381**	**0.387**
Pa+Ti+Ch	0.385	0.387	0.397	0.395
Pa+La+Ti	0.270	0.275	<u>0.274</u>	<u>0.279</u>
La+Ti+Ch	0.388	0.401	**0.398**	**0.405**
Pa+La+Ti+Ch	0.392	0.399	**0.407**	**0.415**

Table 3: Evaluation on accuracy using different combinations of profile attributes

Table 3 shows the performance of our proposed model with the top performers of the baseline systems put in the first two lines. The basic LSTM model shown as Base-LSTM in Table 3 performs less than CNN-WangP and similar to CNN-Wang without profile information. In other words, LSTM has no obvious model advantage in this set of training data. We may also infer that the lexicon and style differences between fake news and true news are not large enough for detection. And, the difference in the choice of deep neural network models are also not significant if profile information is not supplied.

Table 3 also shows that speaker profile information can improve fake news detection significantly. Besides *credit history*, which gives the largest improvement of 3%, *location of speaker* gives more improvements than *part affiliation* and *job title* with improvement of 2.3%. When all attributes are included in detection, the performance surge to over 40% in accuracy. Obviously, if *credit history* of a speaker is available, it is not hard to see how useful it is for fake new detection. In practice, however, we cannot expect the credit history information to be available all the time for fake news detection. Therefore, it is more important to observe those combinations without *Ch* for *credit history*. The best performers without *Ch* are marked with underlines. The combination of using all three attributes still outperforms CNN-WangP by 16.7% even though CNN-WangP has *credit history* included. This further proves the effectiveness of our proposed method.

4 Conclusion

This paper proposes a hybrid attention-based LSTM model for fake news detection. In our model, speaker profiles can contribute to fake news detection in two ways: One is to include them as attention factors for the learning of news text; and the other is to use them as additional inputs to provide more information. Experimental results show that both methods of using speaker profiles can contribute to the improvement of fake news detection. This can be interpreted as speaker's intention to speak the truth or fake it largely depends on his/her, profiles, especially his/hers credit history. Adopting speaker profiles into an attention based LSTM detection model can reach over 41.5% in accuracy with net increase of 14.5% in accuracy compared to the state-of-the-art model. Even without the use of credit history, the performance net increase is still by 0.5%.

Acknowledgments

The work is partially supported by the research grants from Hong Kong Polytechnic University (PolyU RTVU) and GRF grant(CERG PolyU 15211/14E).

References

Joan Bachenko, Eileen Fitzpatrick, and Michael Schonwetter. 2008. Verification and implementation of language-based deception indicators in civil and criminal narratives. In *Proceedings of the 22nd International Conference on Computational Linguistics-Volume 1*, pages 41–48. Association for Computational Linguistics.

Huimin Chen, Maosong Sun, Cunchao Tu, Yankai Lin, and Zhiyuan Liu. 2016. Neural sentiment classification with user and product attention. EMNLP.

Niall J Conroy, Victoria L Rubin, and Yimin Chen. 2015. Automatic deception detection: methods for finding fake news. *Proceedings of the Association for Information Science and Technology*, 52(1):1–4.

Vanessa Wei Feng and Graeme Hirst. 2013. Detecting deceptive opinions with profile compatibility. In *IJCNLP*, pages 338–346.

Felix Gers. 2001. *Long short-term memory in recurrent neural networks*. Ph.D. thesis, Universität Hannover.

Swapna Gottipati, Minghui Qiu, Liu Yang, Feida Zhu, and Jing Jiang. 2013. Predicting users political party using ideological stances. In *International Conference on Social Informatics*, pages 177–191. Springer.

David F Larcker and Anastasia A Zakolyukina. 2012. Detecting deceptive discussions in conference calls. *Journal of Accounting Research*, 50(2):495–540.

Yunfei Long, Qin Lu, Yue Xiao, MingLei Li, and Chu-Ren Huang. 2016. Domain-specific user preference prediction based on multiple user activities. In *Big Data (Big Data), 2016 IEEE International Conference on*, pages 3913–3921. IEEE.

David M Markowitz and Jeffrey T Hancock. 2014. Linguistic traces of a scientific fraud: The case of diederik stapel. *PloS one*, 9(8):e105937.

Tomas Mikolov, Kai Chen, Greg Corrado, and Jeffrey Dean. 2013. Efficient estimation of word representations in vector space. *arXiv preprint arXiv:1301.3781*.

Victoria L Rubin. 2017. Deception detection and rumor debunking for social media.

Victoria L Rubin, Yimin Chen, and Niall J Conroy. 2015. Deception detection for news: three types of fakes. *Proceedings of the Association for Information Science and Technology*, 52(1):1–4.

Natali Ruchansky, Sungyong Seo, and Yan Liu. 2017. Csi: A hybrid deep model for fake news. *arXiv preprint arXiv:1703.06959*.

Duyu Tang, Bing Qin, and Ting Liu. 2015. Document modeling with gated recurrent neural network for sentiment classification. In *Proceedings of the 2015 Conference on Empirical Methods in Natural Language Processing*, pages 1422–1432.

William Yang Wang. 2017. ” liar, liar pants on fire”: A new benchmark dataset for fake news detection. *arXiv preprint arXiv:1705.00648*.

Zichao Yang, Diyi Yang, Chris Dyer, Xiaodong He, Alex Smola, and Eduard Hovy. 2016. Hierarchical attention networks for document classification. In *Proceedings of the 2016 Conference of the North American Chapter of the Association for Computational Linguistics: Human Language Technologies*.

Improving Neural Text Normalization with Data Augmentation at Character- and Morphological Levels

Itsumi Saito[1] **Jun Suzuki**[2] **Kyosuke Nishida**[1] **Kugatsu Sadamitsu**[1*]
Satoshi Kobashikawa[1] **Ryo Masumura**[1] **Yuji Matsumoto**[3] **Junji Tomita**[1]
[1]NTT Media Intelligence Laboratories, [2]NTT Communication Science Laboratories
[3]Nara Institute of Science and Technology
{saito.itsumi, suzuki.jun, nishida.kyosuke}@lab.ntt.co.jp,
{masumura.ryo, kobashikawa.satoshi, tomita.junji}@lab.ntt.co.jp
matsu@is.naist.jp, k.sadamitsu.ic@future.co.jp

Abstract

In this study, we investigated the effectiveness of augmented data for encoder-decoder-based neural normalization models. Attention based encoder-decoder models are greatly effective in generating many natural languages. In general, we have to prepare for a large amount of training data to train an encoder-decoder model. Unlike machine translation, there are few training data for text-normalization tasks. In this paper, we propose two methods for generating augmented data. The experimental results with Japanese dialect normalization indicate that our methods are effective for an encoder-decoder model and achieve higher BLEU score than that of baselines. We also investigated the oracle performance and revealed that there is sufficient room for improving an encoder-decoder model.

1 Introduction

Text normalization is an important fundamental technology in actual natural language processing (NLP) systems to appropriately handle texts such as those for social media. This is because social media texts contain non-standard texts, such as typos, dialects, chat abbreviations[1], and emoticons; thus, current NLP systems often fail to correctly analyze such texts (Huang, 2015; Sajjad et al., 2013; Han et al., 2013). Normalization can help correctly analyze and understand these texts.

One of the most promising conventional approaches for tackling text normalizing tasks is using statistical machine translation (SMT) techniques (Junczys-Dowmunt and Grundkiewicz, 2016; Yuan and Briscoe, 2016), in particular, utilizing the Moses toolkit (Koehn et al., 2007). In recent years, encoder-decoder models with an attention mechanism (Bahdanau et al., 2014) have made great progress regarding many NLP tasks, including machine translation (Luong et al., 2015; Sennrich et al., 2016), text summarization (Rush et al., 2015) and text normalization (Xie et al., 2016; Yuan and Briscoe, 2016; Ikeda et al., 2017). We can also simply apply an encoder-decoder model to text normalization tasks. However, it is well-known that encoder-decoder models often fail to perform better than conventional methods when the availability of training data is insufficient. Unfortunately, the amount of training data for text normalization tasks is generally relatively small to sufficiently train encoder-decoder models. Therefore, data utilization and augmentation are important to take full advantage of encoder-decoder models. Xie et al. (2016) and Ikeda et al. (2017) reported on improvements of data augmentation in error correction and variant normalization tasks, respectively.

Following these studies, we investigated data-augmentation methods for neural normalization. The main difference between the previous studies and this study is the method of generating augmentation data. Xie et al. (2016) and Ikeda et al. (2017) used simple morphological-level or character-level hand-crafted rules to generate augmented data. These predefined rules work well if we have sufficient prior knowledge about the target text-normalization task. However, it is difficult to cover all error patterns by simple rules and predefine the error patterns with certain text normalization tasks, such as dialect normalization whose error pattern varies from region to

---

Present affiliation: Future Architect,Inc.

[1]short forms of words or phrases such as "4u" to represent "for you"

Proceedings of the The 8th International Joint Conference on Natural Language Processing, pages 257–262,
Taipei, Taiwan, November 27 – December 1, 2017 ©2017 AFNLP

region. We propose two-level data-augmentation methods that do not use prior knowledge.

The contributions of this study are summarized as follows: (1) We propose two data-augmentation methods that generate synthetic data at character and morphological levels. (2) The experimental results with Japanese dialect text normalization demonstrate that our methods enable an encoder-decoder model, which performs poorly without data augmentation, to perform better than Moses, which is a strong baseline method when there is a small number of training examples.

2 Text Normalization using Encoder-Decoder Model

In this study, we focus on the dialect-normalization task as a text-normalization task. The input of this task is a dialect sentence, and the output is a "standard sentence" that corresponds to the given input dialect sentence. A "standard sentence" is written in normal form.

We model our dialect-normalization task by using a character-based attentional encoder-decoder model. More precisely, we use a single layer long short-term memory (LSTM) for both the encoder and decoder, where the encoder is bi-directional LSTM. Let $s = (s_1, s_2, \ldots, s_n)$ be the character sequence of the (input) dialect sentence. Similarly, let $t = (t_1, t_2, \ldots, t_m)$ be the character sequence of the (output) standard sentence. The notations n and m are the total lengths of the characters in s and t, respectively. Then, the (normalization) probability of t given dialect sentence s can be written as

$$p(t|s, \theta) = \prod_{j=1}^{m} p(t_j|t_{<j}, s), \qquad (1)$$

where θ represents a set of all model parameters in the encoder-decoder model, which are determined by the parameter-estimation process of a standard softmax cross-entropy loss minimization using training data. Therefore, given θ and s, our dialect normalization task is defined as finding t with maximum probability:

$$\hat{t} = \operatorname{argmax}_t\{p(t|s, \theta)\}, \qquad (2)$$

where $\hat{t}$ represents the solution.

3 Proposed Methods

This section describes our proposed methods for generating augmented-data. The goal with aug-

standard morphs (m_t)	dialect morphs (m_s)	$p(m_s|m_t)$
し/ない (*shinai*)	せん (*sen*)	0.767
の/です/が (*nodesuga*)	ん/じゃ/けど (*njyakedo*)	0.553
ください (*kudasai*)	つか/あ/さい (*tukasai*)	0.517

Table 1: Examples of extracted morphological conversion patterns

mented data generation is to generate a large amount of corresponding standard and dialect sentence pairs, which are then used as additional training data of encoder-decoder models. To generate augmented data, we construct a model that converts standard sentences to dialect sentences since we can easily get a lot of standard sentences. Our methods are designed based on different perspectives, namely, morphological- and character-levels.

3.1 Generating Augmented Data using Morphological-level Conversion

Suppose we have a small set of standard and dialect sentence pairs and a large standard sentences. First, we extract morphological conversion patterns from a (small) set of standard and dialect sentence pairs. Second, we generate the augmented data using extracted conversion patterns.

Extracting Morphological Conversion Patterns For this step, both standard and dialect sentences, which are basically identical to the training data, are parsed using a pre-trained morphological analyzer. Then, the longest difference subsequences are extracted using dynamic programming (DP) matching. We also calculate the conditional generative probabilities $p(m_s|m_t)$ for all extracted morphological conversion patterns, where m_s is a dialect morphological sequence and m_t is a standard morphological sequence. We set $p(m_s|m_t) = F_{m_s,m_t}/F_{m_t}$, where F_{m_s,m_t} is the joint frequency of (m_s, m_t) and F_{m_t} is the frequency of m_t in the extracted morphological conversion patterns of training data. Table 1 gives examples of extracted patterns from Japanese standard and dialect sentence pairs, which we discuss in the experimental section.

Generating Augmented Data using Extracted Morphological Conversion Patterns After we obtain morphological conversion patterns, we generate a corresponding synthesized dialect sentence of each given standard sentence by using the ex-

Algorithm 1 Generating Augmented Data using Morphological Conversion Patterns

---

morphlist ← MorphAnalyse(standardsent)
newmorphlist ← []
for $i = 0 \ldots len(morphlist)$ **do**
    sent ← CONCAT(mrphlist[i:])
    MatchedList ← CommonPrefixSearch(PatternDict, sent)
    m_{si} ← SAMPLE(MatchedList, $P(m_s|m_t)$)
    newmorphlist ← APPEND(newmorphlist, m_{si})
end for
synthesizedsent ← CONCAT(newmrphlist)

return synthesizedsent

---

input (standard sentence): インストールしなかった
morph sequence: インストール/し/なかっ/た/
matched conversion pattern:
(m_t, m_s) = (し/なかっ/た, せん/かった)
replaced morph sequence: インストール/せん/かった
output (augmented sentence): インストールせんかった

Table 2: Example of generated augmentation data using morphological conversion patterns

tracted morphological conversion patterns. Algorithm 1 shows the detailed procedure of generating augmented data.

More precisely, we first analyze the standard sentences with the morphological analyzer. We then look up the extracted patterns for the segmented corpus from left to right and replace the characters according to probability $p(m_s|m_t)$. Table 2 shows an example of generated augmentation data. When we sample dialect pattern m_s from MatchedList, we use two types of $p(m_s|m_t)$. The first type is fixed probability. We set $p(m_s|m_t)$ = 1/len(MatchedList) for all matched patterns. The second type is generative probability, which is calculated from the training data (see the previous subsection). The comparison of these two types of probabilities is discussed in the experimental section.

3.2 Generating Augmented Data using Character-level Conversion

For our character-level method, we take advantage of the phrase-based SMT toolkit Moses for generating augmented data. The idea is simple and straightforward; we train a 'standard-to-dialect' sentence SMT model at a character-level and apply it to a large non-annotated standard sentences. This model converts the sentence by using character phrase units. Thus, we call this method "character-level conversion".

3.3 Training Procedure

We use the following two-step training procedure. (1) We train model parameters by using both human-annotated and augmented data. (2) We then retrain the model parameters only with the human-annotated data, while the model parameters obtained in the first step are used as initial values of the model parameters in this (second) step. We refer to these first and second steps as "pre-training" and "fine-tuning", respectively. Obviously, the augmented data are less reliable than human-annotated data. Thus, we can expect to improve the performance of the normalization model by ignoring the less reliable augmented data in the last-mile decision of model parameter training.

4 Experiments

4.1 Data

The dialect data we used were crowdsourced data. We first prepared the standard seed sentences, and crowd workers (dialect natives) rewrote the seed sentences as dialects. The target areas of the dialects were Nagoya (NAG), Hiroshima (HIR), and Sendai (SEN), which are major cities in Japan. Each region's data consists of 22,020 sentence pairs, and we randomly split the data into training (80%), development (10%), and test (10%). For augmented data, we used the data of Yahoo chiebukuro, which contains community QA data. Since the human-annotated data are spoken language text, we used the community QA data as close-domain data.

4.2 Settings

For the baseline model other than encoder-decoder models, we used Moses. Moses is a tool of training statistical machine translation and a strong baseline for the text-normalization task (Junczys-Dowmunt and Grundkiewicz, 2016). For such a task, we can ignore the word reordering; therefore, we set the distortion limit to 0. We used MERT on the development set for tuning. We confirmed that using both manually annotated and augmented data for building LM greatly degraded its final BLUE score in our preliminary experiments and used only manually annotated data as the training data of LM.

We used beam search for the encoder-decoder model (EncDec) and set the beam size to 10. When in the n beam search step, we used length normalized score $S(t, s)$, where

method	BLEU		
	NAG	HIR	SEN
No-transformation	72.4	63.9	57.3
Moses (train)	**80.1**	72.3	67.1
Moses (train + mr:R)	75.4	71.0	64.9
Moses (train + mr:W)	80.0	73.7	67.7
Moses (train + mo)	79.9	74.3	66.9
Moses (train + mo + mr:W)	80.0	73.3	67.8
EncDec (train)	43.3	33.9	27.6
EncDec (train + mr:R)	75.3 / 63.5	69.0 / 67.3	64.2 / 58.8
EncDec (train + mr:W)	78.6 / 78.2	74.9 / 73.5	68.0 / 67.6
EncDec (train + mo)	79.1 / 79.1	74.2 / 72.9	66.9 / 65.6
EncDec (train + mo+mr:W)	**80.1** / 79.5	**75.5** / 74.6	**68.2** / 68.1

Table 3: BLEU scores of normalization. "/" indicates with (left) and without (right) fine tuning. 200,000 pairs of augmented data were used.

method	BLEU		
	NAG	HIR	SEN
Moses (oracle)	80.2	75.7	68.3
Moses (best)	80.1	74.3	67.8
EncDec (oracle)	84.8	81.6	73.1
EncDec (best)	80.1	75.5	68.2

Table 4: Evaluation of oracle sentences

$S(t, s) = \log(p(t|s, \theta))/|t|$. We maximize $S(t, s)$ to find normalized sentence. We set the embedding size of the character and hidden layer to 300 and 256, respectively. We used "mrphaug (mr)" as the augmented data generated from morphological-level conversion and "mosesaug (mo)" as augmented data generated from character-level conversion (Moses). The "mr:R" and "mr:W" represent the difference in generative probability $p(m_s|m_t)$, which is used when generating augmented data; "mr:R" indicates fixed generative probability and "mr:W" indicates weighted generative probability. For the evaluation, we used BLEU (Papineni et al., 2002), which is widely used for machine translation.

4.3 Results

Table 3 lists the normalization results. No-transformation indicates the result of evaluating input sentences without transformation. Moses achieved a reasonable BLEU score with a small amount of human-annotated data. However, the improvement of adding augmented data was limited. On the other hand, the encoder-decoder model showed a very low BLEU score with a small amount of human-annotated data. With this amount of data, the encoder-decoder model generated a sentence that was quite different from the reference. When adding augmented data, the BLEU score improved, and fine tuning was effective for all cases.

When comparing our augmented-data-generation methods, generating data according to fixed probability (mr:R) degraded the BLEU score both for Moses and the encoder-decoder model. When generating data with fixed probability, the quality of augmented data becomes quite low. However, by generating data according to generative probability (mr:W), which is estimated with training data, the BLEU score improved. This indicates that when generating data using morphological-level Conversion, it is important to take into account the generative probability. Combining "mr:W" and "mo" (train+mo+mr:W) achieves higher BLEU scores than that of other methods. This suggests that combining different types of data will have a positive effect on normalization accuracy.

When comparing three difference regions, the BLUE scores of Moses (train) and EncDec (train+mo+mr:W) for NAG (Nagoya) were the same score, while there were improvements for HIR (Hiroshima) and SEN (Sendai). It is inferred that the effect of the proposed methods for NAG were limited because the difference between input (dialect) sentences and correct (standard) sentences was small.

5 Discussion

Oracle Analysis To investigate the further improvement on normalization accuracy, we analyzed oracle performance. We enumerated the top 10 candidates of normalized sentences from Moses and proposed method, extracted the candidates that were the most similar to the reference, and calculated the BLEU scores. Table 4 shows the results of oracle performance. Interestingly, the oracle performances of the encoder-decoder model with augmented data was quite high, while that of Moses was almost the same as the best score. This implies that there is room for improvement for the encoder-decoder model by just improving the decoding or ranking function.

Other text normalization task In this study, we evaluated our methods with Japanese dialect data. However, these methods are not limited to Japanese dialects because they do not use dialog-specific information. If there is prior knowledge, the combination of them will be more promising for improve normalization performance. We will investigate the effectiveness of our methods for other normalization tasks for future work.

Limitation Since our data-augmentation methods are based on human-annotated training data, the variations in the generated data depend on the amount of training data. The variations in augmented data generated with our data-augmentation methods are strictly limited within those appearing in the human-annotated training data. This essentially means that the quality of augmented data deeply relies on the amount of (human-annotated) training data. We plan to develop more general methods that do not deeply depend on the amount of training data.

6 Conclusion

We investigated the effectiveness of our augmented-data-generation methods for neural text normalization. From the experiments, the quality of augmented data greatly affected the BLEU score. Moreover, a two-step training strategy and fine tuning with human-annotated data improved this score. From these results, there is possibility to improve the accuracy of normalization if we can generate higher quality data. For future work, we will explore a more advanced method for generating augmented data.

References

Dzmitry Bahdanau, Kyunghyun Cho, and Yoshua Bengio. 2014. Neural machine translation by jointly learning to align and translate. *CoRR*.

Bo Han, Paul Cook, and Timothy Baldwin. 2013. Lexical normalization for social media text. *ACM Trans. Intell. Syst. Technol.*, pages 5:1–5:27.

Fei Huang. 2015. Improved arabic dialect classification with social media data. In *Proceedings of the 2015 Conference on Empirical Methods in Natural Language Processing*, pages 2118–2126, Lisbon, Portugal. Association for Computational Linguistics.

Taishi Ikeda, Hiroyuki Shindo, and Yuji Matsumoto. 2017. Japanese text normalization with encoder-decoder model. In *Proceedings of the 2nd Workshop on Noisy User-generated Text (WNUT)*.

Marcin Junczys-Dowmunt and Roman Grundkiewicz. 2016. Phrase-based machine translation is state-of-the-art for automatic grammatical error correction. In *Proceedings of the 2016 Conference on Empirical Methods in Natural Language Processing*.

Philipp Koehn, Hieu Hoang, Alexandra Birch, Chris Callison-Burch, Marcello Federico, Nicola Bertoldi, Brooke Cowan, Wade Shen, Christine Moran, Richard Zens, Chris Dyer, Ondrej Bojar, Alexandra Constantin, and Evan Herbst. 2007. Moses: Open source toolkit for statistical machine translation. In *Proceedings of the 45th Annual Meeting of the ACL on Interactive Poster and Demonstration Sessions*.

Thang Luong, Hieu Pham, and Christopher D. Manning. 2015. Effective approaches to attention-based neural machine translation. In *Proceedings of the 2015 Conference on EMNLP*.

Kishore Papineni, Salim Roukos, Todd Ward, and Wei-Jing Zhu. 2002. Bleu: A method for automatic evaluation of machine translation. In *Proceedings of the 40th Annual Meeting on Association for Computational Linguistics*.

Alexander M. Rush, Sumit Chopra, and Jason Weston. 2015. A neural attention model for abstractive sentence summarization. In *Proceedings of the 2015 Conference on Empirical Methods in Natural Language Processing*.

Hassan Sajjad, Kareem Darwish, and Yonatan Belinkov. 2013. Translating dialectal arabic to english. In *Proceedings of the 51st Annual Meeting of the Association for Computational Linguistics (Volume 2: Short Papers)*, pages 1–6, Sofia, Bulgaria. Association for Computational Linguistics.

Rico Sennrich, Barry Haddow, and Alexandra Birch. 2016. Improving neural machine translation models with monolingual data. In *Proceedings of the 54th Annual Meeting of the Association for Computational Linguistics (Volume 1: Long Papers)*.

Ziang Xie, Anand Avati, Naveen Arivazhagan, and Andrew Y. Ng. 2016. Neural language correction with character-based attention. *CoRR*.

Zheng Yuan and Ted Briscoe. 2016. Grammatical error correction using neural machine translation. In *Proceedings of the 2016 Conference of the North American Chapter of the Association for Computational Linguistics: Human Language Technologies*.

Using Social Networks to Improve
Language Variety Identification with Neural Networks

Yasuhide Miura[†,‡]

yasuhide.miura
@fujixerox.co.jp

Tomoki Taniguchi[†]

taniguchi.tomoki
@fujixerox.co.jp

Motoki Taniguchi[†]

motoki.taniguchi
@fujixerox.co.jp

Shotaro Misawa[†]

misawa.shotaro
@fujixerox.co.jp

Tomoko Ohkuma[†]

ohkuma.tomoko
@fujixerox.co.jp

[†]Fuji Xerox Co., Ltd.
[‡]Tokyo Institute of Technology

Abstract

We propose a hierarchical neural network model for language variety identification that integrates information from a social network. Recently, language variety identification has enjoyed heightened popularity as an advanced task of language identification. The proposed model uses additional texts from a social network to improve language variety identification from two perspectives. First, they are used to introduce the effects of homophily. Secondly, they are used as expanded training data for shared layers of the proposed model. By introducing information from social networks, the model improved its accuracy by 1.67–5.56. Compared to state-of-the-art baselines, these improved performances are better in English and comparable in Spanish. Furthermore, we analyzed the cases of Portuguese and Arabic when the model showed weak performances, and found that the effect of homophily is likely to be weak due to sparsity and noises compared to languages with the strong performances.

1 Introduction

Language identification is a fundamentally important natural language processing (NLP) task that is usually applied before more sophisticated grammatical or semantic analyses. It is especially important in cases when analyzing user generated contents such as social media, which include various languages often, without accurate language information. General purpose language identification tools such as *TextCat* (Cavnar and Trenkle,

1994) and *langid.py* (Lui and Baldwin, 2012) can identify 50–100 languages with accuracy of 86–99%. However, these tools have not considered discrimination between closely related language varieties.

Recently, language identification among similar languages or language varieties has been studied actively to realize more advanced language identification (Goutte et al., 2016). Since 2014, VarDial workshops, which specifically examine linguistic variation, have organized shared tasks of discriminating between similar languages (Zampieri et al., 2014). More recently, language variety analysis has attracted an author profiling community to include it in a PAN shared task that targets social media (Rangel Pardo et al., 2017). A language variety that a person uses often depends on his or her regional and cultural backgrounds. The identification of language variety can enhance a social media analysis by providing such background information.

We tackle this language variety identification in Twitter with a hierarchical neural network model (Lin et al., 2015; Yang et al., 2016b) integrating information from a social network. The use of social network information has shown effectiveness in analyzing various user attributes (Wang et al., 2014; Li et al., 2014, 2015; Rahimi et al., 2015a,b) where homophily (McPherson et al., 2001) exists. Neural networks have recently shown superior performance for solving a variety of problems in NLP. However, for language variety identification, sparse traditional models have shown stronger performance than deep neural models (Medvedeva et al., 2017). Numerous parameters in neural network models make it difficult to apply to language variety identification where the training data are

Proceedings of the The 8th International Joint Conference on Natural Language Processing, pages 263–270,
Taipei, Taiwan, November 27 – December 1, 2017 ©2017 AFNLP

limited to a maximum number of several thousands.

We expect to obtain two effects by introducing additional texts from a social network into our model. First, we introduce additional texts that are likely to share the same language variety by homophily. Secondly, we let several layers of our model be trained with more texts by sharing several layers of the model among the processes of a target user and its linked users with a social network. The contributions of this paper are the following:

1. We propose a novel neural network model that uses social network information for language variety identification in Twitter.

2. We show that additional texts of linked users can improve language variety identification.

3. We reveal that a neural network model can be efficiently trained by sharing layers within the processes of a target user and its linked users.

2 Related Works

2.1 Language Variety Identification

The increase of web documents in various languages has raised interest in identifying language varieties automatically. Inspired by some early works in Malay and Indonesian (Ranaivo-Malançon, 2006), south Slavic languages (Ljubešić et al., 2007), and Chinese varieties (Huang and Lee, 2008), studies of language varieties, similar languages, or dialects have expanded to examine numerous languages. The recent expansion of language variety identification has been well surveyed in works by Goutte et al. (2016) and Zampieri et al. (2017). As in other NLP tasks, various neural network models have been applied recently to language variety identification (Belinkov and Glass, 2016; Bjerva, 2016; Cianflone and Kosseim, 2016; Criscuolo and Aluisio, 2017; Medvedeva et al., 2017). However, these neural network models have shown inferior performance compared to sparse traditional models in comparisons (Malmasi et al., 2016; Zampieri et al., 2017).

2.2 NLP with Social Network Information

Social media have attracted numerous NLP studies to analyze its texts. Social media contain interactions among users such as follow, hashtag, mention, reply, and retweet. Many studies have exploited such social network information to enhance NLP models. The use of social networks has shown effectiveness for strengthening NLP tasks such as sentiment analysis (Speriosu et al., 2011; Tan et al., 2011; Vanzo et al., 2014; Ren et al., 2016; Yang and Eisenstein, 2017), skill inference (Wang et al., 2014), user attribute extraction (Li et al., 2014, 2015), geolocation prediction (Rahimi et al., 2015a,b), and entity linking (Yang et al., 2016a).

Integration of social network information into neural network models is accomplished in these studies through joint training (Li et al., 2015), context-based sub-networks (Ren et al., 2016), embedding of social network components (Yang et al., 2016a), and social attention (Yang and Eisenstein, 2017). These are effective approaches in terms of accuracy but they make models more difficult to train with additional parameters. We designed our model to share layers among different processes to facilitate training of the neural network model.

3 Models

3.1 NN-HIER

We prepare a basic neural network model NN-HIER, which is a variant of known hierarchical models (Lin et al., 2015; Yang et al., 2016b). NN-HIER in Figure 1 portays the architecture of this model. For each user, the model accepts the words of user tweets. The words are embedded with a word embedding layer and are processed with a recurrent neural network (RNN) layer, a max-pooling layer, an attention mechanism (Bahdanau et al., 2014) layer, and fully connected (FC) layers. As an implementation of RNN, we used Gated Recurrent Unit (GRU) (Cho et al., 2014) with a bi-directional setting.

The bi-directional GRU outputs $\overrightarrow{h}$ and $\overleftarrow{h}$ are concatenated to form g *where* $g_t = \overrightarrow{h_t} \| \overleftarrow{h_t}$. g is further processed with a max-over time process in MaxPooling to obtain a tweet representation m. Attention$_U$ computes a user representation o as a weighted sum of m_n with weight α_n:

$$o = \sum_n \alpha_n m_n$$

$$\alpha_n = \frac{\exp\left(v_\alpha^T u_n\right)}{\sum_l \exp\left(v_\alpha^T u_l\right)} \quad (1)$$

$$u_n = \tanh\left(W_\alpha m_n + b_\alpha\right) \quad (2)$$

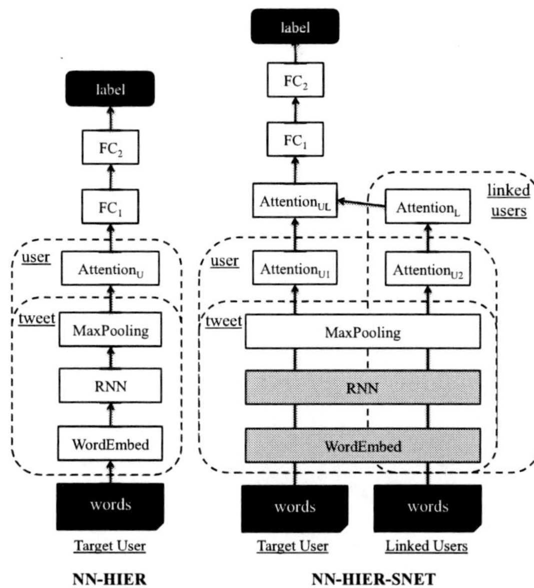

	en	es	pt	ar
$\#train_8$	2,880	3,360	960	1,920
$\#dev_1$	360	420	120	240
$\#test_1$	360	420	120	240
#total	3,600	4,200	1,200	2,400
#langvar	6	7	2	4
#mention	73,897	59,685	11,541	20,287

Table 1: Numbers of training data, development data, test data, entire data (total), language varieties (langvar), and mentioned users (mention).

	en	es	pt	ar
#node	77,497	63,885	12,741	22,687
avg degree	3.12	3.45	2.26	2.59
isolated nodes	3.92%	5.83%	6.33%	28.88%

Table 2: Characteristics of nodes in mention networks for each language. Avg degree is an average node degree and isolated nodes are the percentage of labeled nodes that are not connected to other labeled nodes.

Figure 1: Architectures of NN-HIER and NN-HIER-SNET. tweet represents tweet-level processes, user represents user-level processes, and linked users represents linked-users-level processes. Shaded layers are layers with shared weights over the target user process and the linked users process.

where v_α is a weight vector, W_α is a weight matrix, and b_α a bias vector. u_n is an attention context vector calculated from m_n with a single FC layer (Eq. 2). u_n is normalized with softmax to obtain α_n as a probability (Eq. 1). Finally, the user representation is passed respectively to FC_1 and FC_2.

3.2 NN-HIER-SNET

We extend NN-HIER by adding an additional level of hierarchy to process linked users of a target user. This extension is intended to introduce effects of homophily into our model. NN-HIER-SNET in Figure 1 presents this extended model. NN-HIER-SNET includes additional attention layers $Attention_L$ and $Attention_{UL}$ to process linked users. $Attention_L$ accepts multiple user representations and combined them as in $Attention_U$ to form a linked users representation. $Attention_{UL}$ further merges a target user representation (an output of $Attention_{U1}$) and $Attention_L$ to obtain an updated target user representation.

An important characteristic of NN-HIER-SNET is that the weights of WordEmbed and RNN are shared across the target user process and the linked users process. This sharing allows the weights to be trained with more texts than those of NN-HIER. Attention processes over tweets are separated ($Attention_{U1}$ and $Attention_{U2}$) so that the target user process and the linked users process can pick tweets differently between the two kinds of user processes.

4 Data

We used PAN@CLEF 2017 Author Profiling Training Corpus[1] to train the proposed models. The dataset consists of 11,400 Twitter users labeled with language variety of English (en), Spanish (es), Portuguese (pt), and Arabic (ar). Because the proposed model of Section 3.2 integrates texts of linked users, we additionally collected timelines of mentioned users in this dataset as linked users using Twitter REST APIs. #mention in Table 1 are the numbers of users mentioned for each language.

We divided this dataset into $train_8$, dev_1, and $test_1$ using a stratified sampling with a ratio of 8:1:1. Table 1 presents statistics of these divisions and Table 2 shows characteristics of nodes in the mention networks of each language. $test_1$ differs from the test data of PAN@CLEF 2017 Author Profiling Task. We chose to use a subset of the training data as test data because the true test data can not be accessed publicly (Potthast et al., 2014).

---

[1] http://pan.webis.de/clef17/pan17-web/author-profiling.html

Model	en	es	pt	ar
SVM-W2	83.06	95.74	98.61	80.00
SVM-W2C6	85.56	95.71	98.99	82.08
SVM-W2C6-SNET	82.69	92.86	99.17	80.42
SVM-W2C6-SNET-R	86.11	93.33	99.17	82.71
NN-HIER	85.83	93.57	99.17	78.75
NN-HIER-SNET	91.39	95.48	93.33	80.42

Table 3: Accuracies of the proposed models and the baselines. Underlined values represent the best values for each language.

5 Experiment

5.1 Baselines

We prepared four support vector machine based baselines: SVM-W2, SVM-W2C6, SVM-W2C6-SNET, and SVM-W2C6-SNET-R.

SVM-W2

A support vector machine model with tf-idf weighted word 1–2 grams. We prepared SVM-W2 with a soft margin setting and configured parameter $C \in \{0.1, 0.5, 1.0, 5.0, 1e^2, 5e^2, 1e^3\}$ using the development sets. For multi-class classification, we used an one-vs.-the-rest scheme.

SVM-W2C6

An extended model of SVM-W2 which additionally uses tf-idf weighted character 1–6 grams. This setting is simple, but similar models have shown state-of-the-art performance in past Var-Dial tasks (Malmasi et al., 2016; Zampieri et al., 2017).

SVM-W2C6-SNET

An extension of SVM-W2C6 with features of linked users. tf-idf weighted word 1–2 grams and tf-idf weighted character 1–6 grams of linked users were added to SVM-W2C6 with a feature space separated from other SVM-W2C6 features.

SVM-W2C6-SNET-R

A variant of SVM-W2C6-SNET with a restricted feature space for linked users. The size of feature space for linked users are restricted to be equal to the size of feature space for target users in this model. Since, in general, there are more texts of linked users than that of target users, this restriction suppresses the effect of social network information.

5.2 Model Configurations

We trained our model by stochastic gradient descent over shuffled mini-batches with cross-entropy loss as an objective function. Word embeddings were pre-training using streaming tweets

Model	en	es	pt	ar
Majority Baseline	16.67	14.29	50.00	25.00
NN-HIER	85.83	93.57	99.17	78.75
Label Propagation	75.28	78.81	83.33	60.42

Table 4: Accuracies of the label propagation approach and the comparison approaches.

by fastText (Bojanowski et al., 2016) using the skip-gram algorithm. The details of the model configurations including a text processor and layer unit sizes are described in Appendix A.

5.3 Result

We evaluated NN-HIER, NN-HIER-SNET, and the baseline models using $train_8$, dev_1, and $test_1$ for each language. Table 3 presents the model accuracies. By introducing additional texts of linked users, the accuracy of the proposed model improved by 1.67–5.56, except for Portuguese. Even compared to the best performing baselines, the model performed better in English and comparably in Spanish. Compared to the improvements obtained in NN-HIER-SNET, the expansion texts of linked users in the baseline models has shown only slight improvements in English, Portuguese, and Arabic with SVM-W2C6-SNET-R.

6 Discussions

6.1 Effects of Homophily

The experiment revealed the effectiveness of combining texts of a target user with social network information for language variety identification. For comparison, we additionally performed a label propagation experiment to observe performances of language variety identification without texts. Following the approaches by Rahimi et al. (2015a) and Rahimi et al. (2015b), we extracted an undirected graph of the social network from target users and their linked users. The labels of training users were propagated to test users using the algorithm of Zhou et al. (2004) with $\alpha = 0.99$.

Table 4 presents the performance of this label propagation approach. The performance are better than the majority baseline but are substantially lower than those from our text model (NN-HIER). Especially, the performance of Arabic is weak compared to other languages since the percentage of isolated nodes is high in Arabic (Table 2). The result suggests that social network information without texts is ineffective for language variety identification, at least in a dataset of several thousand users.

Model	en	es	pt	ar
NN-HIER-SNET	91.39	95.48	93.33	80.42
NN-HIER-SNET-NS	75.56	84.76	93.33	80.00

Table 5: Accuracies of NN-HIER-SNET with non-shared (NS) layers.

6.2 Effects of Shared Layers

NN-HIER-SNET includes shared layers to suppress the increase of neural networks parameters. To ascertain the effects of these shared layers, we additionally evaluated NN-HIER-SNET with non-shared layers. NN-HIER-SNET-NS in Table 5 presents performances of this setting. As expected, the performances were fundamentally inferior to the shared layers architecture. They performed especially badly in English and Spanish, for which the numbers of mentioned users were high (Table 1). The result shows that the shared layer architecture is effective for language variety identification.

6.3 Social Network Characteristics and Performances of Proposed Model

NN-HIER-SNET showed improvements over the baseline models in English and Spanish. These two languages are more dense than Portuguese and Arabic in terms of average node degree (Table 2), and are likely to obtain richer information from social networks. We further investigated the languages of tweets in linked users to capture additional characteristics of social networks for each language. Table 6 shows the summary of this investigation. In all four languages, the top linked language is same as a target language. However, their percentages vary from 78.08–94.26%, indicating differences in the amount of texts in different languages. These texts with different languages will likely to be noises in the texts of linked users for language variety identification. As in average node degree, English and Spanish are in better conditions compared to Portuguese and Arabic with smaller noises. Sparsity and noises in social networks will likely to weaken the effect of homophily, resulting to small or negative improvements in performances.

7 Conclusion

We proposed a neural network model that integrates information from a social network for language variety identification. The model showed 1.67–5.56 improvements in accuracy from introducing additional texts with shared layers. Fur-

Target Language	Linked Language		
	1st	2nd	3rd
en	en: 94.26%	und: 3.50%	fr: 0.39%
es	es: 87.09%	en: 6.67%	und: 4.22%
pt	pt: 78.08%	en: 9.48%	und: 7.14%
ar	ar: 82.07%	en: 9.39%	und: 6.77%

Table 6: Top 3 languages and their percentages in tweets of linked users. Language und is given in a case when the automatic language detection of a tweet has failed.

thermore, compared to the performance of a state-of-the-art baseline model, the model performed better in English and comparably well in Spanish. In Portuguese and Arabic, the model performed weakly compared to the baseline models. We analyzed characteristic of social network in these languages and found that their sparsity and noises have possibly weakened the effect of homophily. The result underscores the promising future of applying neural network models to language variety identification.

As future works of this study, we plan to expand the use of the proposed models for application to other user attributes. We expect that a user attribute having a tendency for homophily is likely to benefit from the proposed model as in language variety identification. Additionally, we plan to perform a comparison of the model against an alternative approach to introduce social network information. Recently, neural network models like Graph Convolutional Networks (Kipf and Welling, 2016) are proposed to process graph data. We would like to observe the differences between a hierarchal approach and a graph process approach in a utilization of social network information.

Acknowledgments

We would like to thank the members of Okumura–Takamura Group at Tokyo Institute of Technology for having fruitful discussions about social media analysis. We would also like to thank the anonymous reviewer for their comments to improve this paper.

References

Dzmitry Bahdanau, Kyunghyun Cho, and Yoshua Bengio. 2014. Neural machine translation by jointly learning to align and translate. *arXiv preprint arXiv:1409.0473*.

Yonatan Belinkov and James Glass. 2016. A character-level convolutional neural network for distinguishing similar languages and dialects. In *Proceedings of the Third Workshop on NLP for Similar Languages, Varieties and Dialects (VarDial3)*, pages 145–152.

Johannes Bjerva. 2016. Byte-based language identification with deep convolutional networks. In *Proceedings of the Third Workshop on NLP for Similar Languages, Varieties and Dialects (VarDial3)*, pages 119–125.

Piotr Bojanowski, Edouard Grave, Armand Joulin, and Tomas Mikolov. 2016. Enriching word vectors with subword information. *arXiv preprint arXiv:1607.04606*.

William B. Cavnar and John M. Trenkle. 1994. Ngram-based text categorization. In *Proceedings of the Third Symposium on Document Analysis and Information Retrieval*, pages 161–175.

Kyunghyun Cho, Bart van Merrienboer, Caglar Gulcehre, Dzmitry Bahdanau, Fethi Bougares, Holger Schwenk, and Yoshua Bengio. 2014. Learning phrase representations using RNN encoder–decoder for statistical machine translation. In *Proceedings of the 2014 Conference on Empirical Methods in Natural Language Processing (EMNLP)*, pages 1724–1734.

Andre Cianflone and Leila Kosseim. 2016. N-gram and neural language models for discriminating similar languages. In *Proceedings of the Third Workshop on NLP for Similar Languages, Varieties and Dialects (VarDial3)*, pages 243–250.

Marcelo Criscuolo and Sandra Maria Aluisio. 2017. Discriminating between similar languages with word-level convolutional neural networks. In *Proceedings of the Fourth Workshop on NLP for Similar Languages, Varieties and Dialects (VarDial)*, pages 124–130.

Cyril Goutte, Serge Léger, Shervin Malmasi, and Marcos Zampieri. 2016. Discriminating similar languages: Evaluations and explorations. In *Proceedings of the Tenth International Conference on Language Resources and Evaluation (LREC 2016)*.

Chu-Ren Huang and Lung-Hao Lee. 2008. Contrastive approach towards text source classification based on top-bag-of-word similarity. In *Proceedings of the 22nd Pacific Asia Conference on Language, Information and Computation*, pages 404–410.

Thomas N. Kipf and Max Welling. 2016. Semi-supervised classification with graph convolutional networks. *arXiv preprint arXiv:1609.02907*.

Jiwei Li, Alan Ritter, and Eduard Hovy. 2014. Weakly supervised user profile extraction from Twitter. In *Proceedings of the 52nd Annual Meeting of the Association for Computational Linguistics*, pages 165–174.

Jiwei Li, Alan Ritter, and Dan Jurafsky. 2015. Learning multi-faceted representations of individuals from heterogeneous evidence using neural networks. *arXiv preprint arXiv:1510.05198*, abs/1510.05198.

Rui Lin, Shujie Liu, Muyun Yang, Mu Li, Ming Zhou, and Sheng Li. 2015. Hierarchical recurrent neural network for document modeling. In *Proceedings of the 2015 Conference on Empirical Methods in Natural Language Processing*, pages 899–907.

Nikola Ljubešić, Nives Mikelić, and Damir Boras. 2007. Language identification: how to distinguish similar languages? In *Proceedings of the 29th International Conference on Information Technology Interfaces*, pages 541–546.

Marco Lui and Timothy Baldwin. 2012. langid.py: An off-the-shelf language identification tool. In *Proceedings of the ACL 2012 System Demonstrations*, pages 25–30.

Shervin Malmasi, Marcos Zampieri, Nikola Ljubešić, Preslav Nakov, Ahmed Ali, and Jörg Tiedemann. 2016. Discriminating between similar languages and arabic dialect identification: A report on the third DSL shared task. In *Proceedings of the Third Workshop on NLP for Similar Languages, Varieties and Dialects (VarDial3)*, pages 1–14.

Miller McPherson, Lynn Smith-Lovin, and James M Cook. 2001. Birds of a feather: Homophily in social networks. *Annual Review of Sociology*, 27(1):415–444.

Maria Medvedeva, Martin Kroon, and Barbara Plank. 2017. When sparse traditional models outperform dense neural networks: the curious case of discriminating between similar languages. In *Proceedings of the Fourth Workshop on NLP for Similar Languages, Varieties and Dialects (VarDial)*, pages 156–163.

Martin Potthast, Tim Gollub, Francisco Rangel, Paolo Rosso, Efstathios Stamatatos, and Benno Stein. 2014. Improving the reproducibility of PAN's shared tasks: Plagiarism detection, author identification, and author profiling. In *Information Access Evaluation meets Multilinguality, Multimodality, and Visualization. 5th International Conference of the CLEF Initiative (CLEF 14)*, pages 268–299.

Afshin Rahimi, Trevor Cohn, and Timothy Baldwin. 2015a. Twitter user geolocation using a unified text and network prediction model. In *Proceedings of the 53rd Annual Meeting of the Association for Computational Linguistics and the 7th International Joint Conference on Natural Language Processing*, pages 630–636.

Afshin Rahimi, Duy Vu, Trevor Cohn, and Timothy Baldwin. 2015b. Exploiting text and network context for geolocation of social media users. In *Proceedings of the 2015 Conference of the North American Chapter of the Association for Computational Linguistics: Human Language Technologies*, pages 1362–1367.

Bali Ranaivo-Malançon. 2006. Automatic identification of close languages – case study: Malay and indonesian. *ECTI Transaction on Computer and Information Technology*, 2(2):126–133.

Francisco Manuel Rangel Pardo, Paolo Rosso, Martin Potthast, and Benno Stein. 2017. Overview of the 5th Author Profiling Task at PAN 2017: Gender and Language Variety Identification in Twitter. In *Working Notes Papers of the CLEF 2017 Evaluation Labs*, volume 1866.

Yafeng Ren, Yue Zhang, Meishan Zhang, and Donghong Ji. 2016. Context-sensitive Twitter sentiment classification using neural network. In *Proceedings of Thirtieth AAAI Conference on Artificial Intelligence*.

Michael Speriosu, Nikita Sudan, Sid Upadhyay, and Jason Baldridge. 2011. Twitter polarity classification with label propagation over lexical links and the follower graph. In *Proceedings of the First Workshop on Unsupervised Learning in NLP*, pages 53–63.

Chenhao Tan, Lillian Lee, Jie Tang, Long Jiang, Ming Zhou, and Ping Li. 2011. User-level sentiment analysis incorporating social networks. In *Proceedings of the 17th ACM SIGKDD International Conference on Knowledge Discovery and Data Mining*, pages 1397–1405.

Andrea Vanzo, Danilo Croce, and Roberto Basili. 2014. A context-based model for sentiment analysis in Twitter. In *Proceedings of COLING 2014, the 25th International Conference on Computational Linguistics*, pages 2345–2354.

Zhongqing Wang, Shoushan Li, Hanxiao Shi, and Guodong Zhou. 2014. Skill inference with personal and skill connections. In *Proceedings of COLING 2014, the 25th International Conference on Computational Linguistics*, pages 520–529.

Yi Yang, Ming-Wei Chang, and Jacob Eisenstein. 2016a. Toward socially-infused information extraction: Embedding authors, mentions, and entities. In *Proceedings of the 2016 Conference on Empirical Methods in Natural Language Processing*, pages 1452–1461.

Yi Yang and Jacob Eisenstein. 2017. Overcoming language variation in sentiment analysis with social attention. *Transactions of the Association for Computational Linguistics*, 5:295–307.

Zichao Yang, Diyi Yang, Chris Dyer, Xiaodong He, Alex Smola, and Eduard Hovy. 2016b. Hierarchical attention networks for document classification. In *Proceedings of the 2016 Conference of the North American Chapter of the Association for Computational Linguistics: Human Language Technologies*, pages 1480–1489.

Marcos Zampieri, Shervin Malmasi, Nikola Ljubešić, Preslav Nakov, Ahmed Ali, Jörg Tiedemann, Yves Scherrer, and Noëmi Aepli. 2017. Findings of the VarDial evaluation campaign 2017. In *Proceedings of the Fourth Workshop on NLP for Similar Languages, Varieties and Dialects (VarDial)*, pages 1–15.

Marcos Zampieri, Liling Tan, Nikola Ljubešić, and Jörg Tiedemann. 2014. A report on the DSL shared task 2014. In *Proceedings of the First Workshop on Applying NLP Tools to Similar Languages, Varieties and Dialects*, pages 58–67.

Denny Zhou, Olivier Bousquet, Thomas N. Lal, Jason Weston, and Bernhard Schölkopf. 2004. Learning with local and global consistency. In *Advances in Neural Information Processing Systems 16*, pages 321–328.

A Supplemental Materials

Text Processor We applied unicode normalization, Twitter user name normalization, and URL normalization for text pre-processing. Preprocessed texts were tokenized with Twokenize[2] for English and NLTK[3] WordPunctTokenizer for three other languages. Words are converted to lower case form, with ignored capitalization.

Pre-training of Embeddings

We collected tweets using Twitter Streaming APIs to pre-train the word embedding matrix of the models. Neural network models are known to perform better when word embeddings are pre-trained by a large-scale dataset. The following steps describe details of the collection process.

1. Tweets with lang metadata of en, es, pt, and ar were collected via Twitter Streaming APIs during March–May 2017.

2. Retweets are removed from the collected tweets.

3. Tweets posted by bots[4] are deleted from the collected tweets.

Table 7 presents the number of resulting tweets. We pre-trained word embeddings with these tweets by fastText using the skip-gram algorithm. The pre-training parameters are dimension=100, learning rate=0.025, window size=5, negative sample size=5, and epoch=5.

Layer Unit Sizes & Maximum Linked Users

We set the following unit size of RNN $= 100$, unit size of $FC_1 = 100$, and the unit size of FC_2 to the number of labels. The context vector sizes of attention layers were set to $\text{Attention}_U = 200$, $\text{Attention}_{U1} = 200$, $\text{Attention}_{U2} = 200$, and $\text{Attention}_{UL} = 200$. To make our model tractable, we limited the maximum number of linked users to 3.

Optimization Strategy

We used cross-entropy loss as an objective function of the proposed models. The objective function was minimized through stochastic gradient descent over shuffled mini-batches with a learning rate of 0.01, momentum of 0.9, and gradient

	en	es	pt	ar
#tweet	12.39M	3.71M	3.16M	2.87M

Table 7: Number of tweets collected for each language with Twitter Streaming APIs.

clipping of 3.0. The model parameters were set to the best performing parameters in terms of loss in the development data.

---

[2]https://github.com/myleott/ark-twokenize-py

[3]http://www.nltk.org/

[4]We assembled a Twitter client list consisting of 80 clients that are used for manual postings.

Boosting Neural Machine Translation

Dakun Zhang and **Jungi Kim** and **Josep Crego** and **Jean Senellart**

`firstname.lastname@systrangroup.com`

SYSTRAN / 5 rue Feydeau, 75002 Paris, France

Abstract

Training efficiency is one of the main problems for Neural Machine Translation (NMT). Deep networks need for very large data as well as many training iterations to achieve state-of-the-art performance. This results in very high computation cost, slowing down research and industrialisation. In this paper, we propose to alleviate this problem with several training methods based on data boosting and bootstrap with no modifications to the neural network. It imitates the learning process of humans, which typically spend more time when learning "difficult" concepts than easier ones. We experiment on an English-French translation task showing accuracy improvements of up to 1.63 BLEU while saving 20% of training time.

1 Introduction

With the rapid development of research on Neural Machine Translation (NMT), translation quality has been improved significantly compared with traditional statistical based method (Bahdanau et al., 2014; Cho et al., 2015; Zhou et al., 2016; Sennrich et al., 2015). However, training efficiency is one of the main challenges for both academia and industry. A huge amount of training data is still necessary to make the translation acceptable (Koehn and Knowles, 2017). Though new techniques have recently been proposed (Vaswani et al., 2017; Gehring et al., 2017), fully trained NMT models still need for long training periods (sometimes by weeks) even using cutting-edge hardware.

NMT system directly models the mappings between source sentence $x_1^n = (x_1, ..., x_n)$ and target sentence $y_1^m = (y_1, ..., y_m)$, with n and m

words respectively (Sutskever et al., 2014). Usually, such system is based on an encoder-decoder-attention framework, in which the source sentence is fed into an encoder word by word to form a fixed length representation vector, with a forward sequence of hidden states $(\overrightarrow{h_1}, ..., \overrightarrow{h_n})$ and a backward sequence $(\overleftarrow{h_1}, ..., \overleftarrow{h_n})$. With the attention mechanism (Bahdanau et al., 2014), a decoder is used to decide which part of the source sentence to pay attention to and predict corresponding word representation at time t together with history predictions before time t. Then, a softmax is used to restore the word representation to natural target words. During the training process, the parameter Θ is optimized:

$$p(y_1^m | x_1^n; \Theta) = \prod_{t=1}^m p(y_t | y_{<t}, x_1^n; \Theta)$$

The amount of parameters which is proportional to the network size and the size of training corpora both decide the cost of training for NMT systems. In order to achieve an acceptable performance on systems, deep networks (up to 8 layers) and more iterations (10-18 epochs) are necessary with a certain amount of data (Wu et al., 2016; Crego et al., 2016). Since several weeks are needed to generate results, it is difficult to experiment with several different meta-parameters, hence slowing down innovation.

While Wu et al. (2016) proposes a brute-force approach with massive data and model parallelism as a way to accelerate training, in this paper, we focus on a different approach based on ranking training sentence pairs by "difficulty". We aim at boosting the optimisation problem through targeting difficult training instances rather than spending time on easier ones.

Every several epochs, we re-select 80% of the data from the corpus with the highest perplexity (ppl.) to use for training. There is no extra calculation cost since we get these ppl. loss

Proceedings of the The 8th International Joint Conference on Natural Language Processing, pages 271–276,
Taipei, Taiwan, November 27 – December 1, 2017 ©2017 AFNLP

from the previous epoch. Finally, we achieve a 1.63 BLEU points improvement while saving 20% training cost at the same time, which is quite a stable improvement compared with our baseline system on English-French translations.

2 Related Work

Training efficiency has been a main concern by many researchers in the field of NMT. Data parallelism and model parallelism are two commonly used techniques to improve the speed of training (Wu et al., 2016). As a result, multiple GPUs or T-PUs[1] are needed which requires additional replication and combination costs. Data parallelism does not reduce the actual cost of computation, it only saves time by using additional computational power.

Chen et al. (2016b) proposed a modified RN-N structure with a full output layer to facilitate the training when using a large amount of data. Kalchbrenner et al. (2016) proposed ByteNet with two networks to encode the source and decode the target at the same time. Gehring et al. (2017) use convolutional neural networks to build the system with a nature of parallelization. Kuchaiev and Ginsburg (2017) focus on how to reduce the computational cost through patitioning or factorizing LSTM matrix. To compare, our method does not modify the network itself and can be used in any NMT framework.

Other methods focus on how to reduce the parameters trained by the model (See et al., 2016). They show that with a pruning technique, 40-60% of the parameters can be pruned out. Similar methods are proposed to reduce the hidden units with knowledge distillation (Crego et al., 2016; Kim and Rush, 2016). They re-train a smaller student model using text translated from teacher models. They report a 70% reduction on the number of parameters and a 30% increase in decoding speed. Hubara et al. (2016) proposed to reduce the precision of model parameters during training and network activations, which can also bring benefits to training efficiency.

To the best of our knowledge the closest idea to our work is instance weighting (Jiang and Zhai, 2007), which is often used for domain adaptation. They add instance dependent weights to the loss function to help improving the performance. As a comparison, we focus on using "difficult" in-

stances in training rather than spending training time on easier ones. We improve the accuracy while simultaneously reducing the cost of training.

3 Training Policies

To train a NMT system, we first design a neural network with some fixed meta-parameters (e.g. number of neurons, LSTM layers, etc.). Then, we feed the network with training instances (in a way of mini-batch) (Ioffe and Szegedy, 2015) until all instances of a training set are consumed. The operation is repeated until the model converges. Parameters of the network turn to an optimum status and as a consequence, the system reaches best performance.

During this process, there is no distinction between training instances. That is, all the instances are regarded as equal and used to train the NMT model equally. However, some instances are relatively easy for the model to learn (e.g. shorter or frequently used sentences). To use them repeatedly results in a waste of time. Moreover, to avoid overfitting and to help convergence, training instances are often randomly shuffled before used to train a model, hence, introducing un-certainty to the final status of the system.

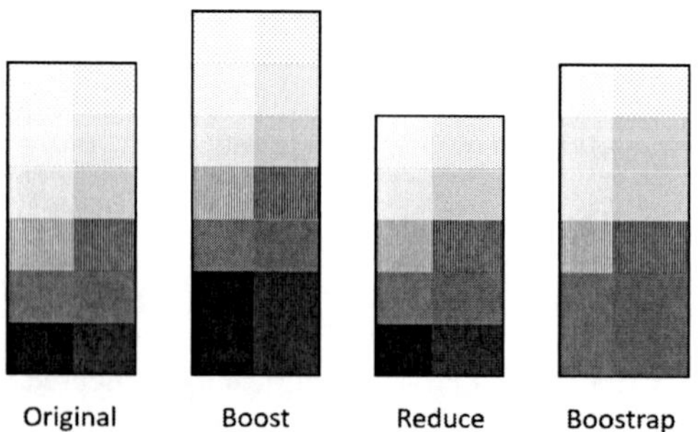

Figure 1: Training data selection. Levels of grey are used to indicate perplexity ranges. Darker/lighter indicate higher/lower perplexity.

Inspired by machine learning algorithms (e.g. boosting, bootstrap, etc.), which are widely used to improve the stability and accuracy especially in the field of text classification, we force the neural network to pay closer attention to "difficult" training examples. To our knowledge, this is the first approach that integrates such meta-algorithms within NMT training. Figure 1 illustrates different methods to select training instances. Instances are

---

[1]Google's Tensor Processing Unit (Wu et al., 2016).

initially sorted based on their translation perplexities (Original) to be finally duplicated (Boost), reduced (Reduce), or just re-sampled (Bootstrap). Such adjustment is applied during each training epoch, thus results in different cost and accuracy.

To be specific, at each training epoch we extend the training set with sentence pairs that the translation model finds "difficult" to translate (**Boost**). We approximate this procedure by choosing sentences with a high perplexity score. In Figure 1, the block with higher perplexity sentences (darker) is repeated in the Boosting set when compared to the Original set. The process has no additional computational cost since perplexity is already computed in a previous iteration.

To put it further, we may focus on "difficult" sentences by removing "easy" ones from the training set (**Reduce**). In Figure 1, the block with lower perplexity sentences (lighter) is missing in the Reduction set when compared to the Original set.

Finally, we randomly sample 100% of the sentences from the corpus as a comparison to the baseline system (**Bootstrap**). In Figure 1, some blocks of the Original set appear repeated in the Bootstrap set while some others are missing, due to a random re-sampling.

4 Experiments

In this section we report on the experiments conducted to evaluate the suitability of the proposed methods. We begin with details of the NMT system parameters as well as the corpora employed.

4.1 System Description

We build our NMT system based on an open-source project OpenNMT[2]. We use a bidirectional RNN encoder with 4 LSTM layers with each containing $1,000$ nodes. Word embeddings are sized of 500 cells and we set the dropout probability to 0.3. Batch size is set to 64. The maximum length of both source and target sentences is set to 80 and we limit the vocabulary size to $50K$ words for both source and target languages.

The default optimiser is SGD with starting learning rate 1.0. We start to decay the learning rate from epoch 10, or when we find a perplexity increasing compared with the previous epoch on a validation set. Evaluation is performed on a held-out testset with BLEU score (Papineni et al., 2002).

---

[2]http://opennmt.net

4.2 Corpora

We used an in-house generic corpus built as mix from several client data consisting of French-English sentences pairs. We split the corpus into three sets: training, validation and a held-out test set. Table 1 shows statistics of the data used in our experiments.

	#sents	#tok (EN)	#tok (FR)
Train	1M	24M	26M
Valid	2,000	48K	55K
Test	2,000	48K	54K

Table 1: Statistics of the data used in our experiments. M stands for millions and K for thousands.

4.3 Results

We train four systems corresponding to the different training policies considered in this paper following the system configuration detailed in Section 4.1. During each training epoch:

- **default** uses the entire original data.

- **boost** extends 10% the original data with the most difficult sentence pairs (following perplexity).

- **reduce** keeps 80% the most difficult instances of the previous epochs, discarding the remaining 20%. Note that the procedure restarts using the entire training set every 3 epochs. That is it uses 100%, 80%, 64%, 100%, 80%, 64%, ... of the training data.

- **bootstrap** re-samples 100% the training set. Hence allowing for repeated and missing sentences of the original training set.

All systems are trained up to 18 epochs[3]. Evaluation results are shown in Figure 2 and Table 2. Each result is averaged from two systems initialised with different random seeds to alleviate the influence of randomisation.

As it can be seen, **boost** outperforms the default method by $+1.49$ (BLEU) at the cost of using 10% of additional training data. However, the system converges faster than any other system as best performance is achieved at epoch 14, while others need to achieve the best after epoch 16.

---

[3]For some experiments, we continue to train until 22 epochs. However, there is no further improvement.

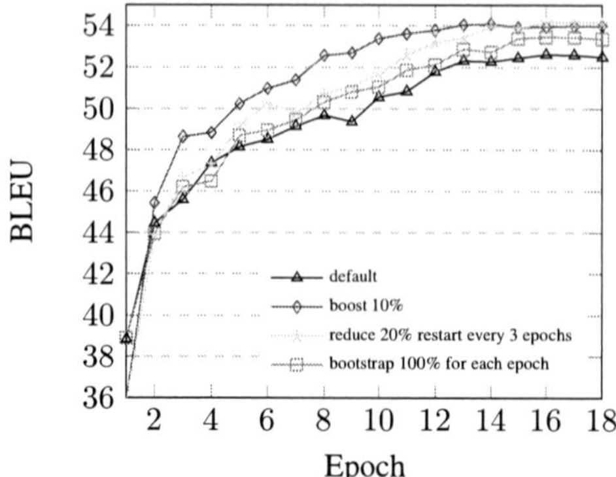

Figure 2: Effect of data boosting during training for English-French translation.

The **reduce** system finally obtains the highest accuracy scores, outperforming the default method by +1.63 (BLEU). In addition to accuracy, the system performing the **reduce** method needed only 80% less data than the default. It shows that this policy is promising.

Considering **boostrap**, the score steadily improves. Though not so significantly, it outperforms also the default method by +0.87 (BLEU) with better stability. Finally, we ensemble the 4 best systems (epoch 18) generated by each method, getting an additional +0.92 BLEU improvement.

	BLEU	Data
default	52.49	100%
boost	53.98	110%
reduce	**54.12**	**80%**
boostrap	53.36	100%
Ensemble	55.04	-

Table 2: BLEU score, and data size conditions for different training policies.

4.3.1 Perplexity Normalisation

In this work we use perplexity as the measure for translation "difficulty", computed over each training batch. We distinguish instances between "difficult" ones and "easy" ones in order to save time during system training. Since perplexity will always increase when the sentences are long, a normalisation method is typically needed. We test several normalisation strategies:

- by batch size (number of training instances)

- by (target) sentence length

- without normalisation (longer sentences were always assigned a higher perplexity)

Experimental results show no significant performance differences for any of the strategies. An explanation for such behaviour may be found on the fact that long sentences are also difficult translations. Thus, the selected subsets (by any normalisation strategy) are very similar.

4.4 Analysis

We propose a simple data manipulation technique to help improving efficiency and performance of NMT models during training. The idea imitates the human learning process. Typically, humans need to spend more time to learn "difficult" concepts and less time for easier ones . As a consequence, we force the NMT system to spend more time on more "difficult" instances, while "skipping" easier examples at the same time. Thus, We emulate a human spending additional energy on learning complex concepts.

We inspect the selected "difficult" examples according to perplexity. We find that almost all such examples containing complex structures, thus being difficult to be translated. To force the system to pay much attention on them can adjust it towards "mastering" more information for these sentences.

An interesting conclusion is that, we can train the NMT system with 80% of the most complex sentences. That is to say, when training examples with smaller perplexity are removed and those with larger ones are emphasised, the system performs better in terms of accuracy and efficiency.

Further experiments need to be conducted for a detailed insight of the methods presented. Like measuring the impact of using several ratios of training data boosted/reduced. As well as studying the impact of the methods on different language pairs and data size conditions.

5 Conclusions

For NMT, training cost is a big problem for even a medium-sized corpus with cutting-edge hardware. At the same time, the trained model is apt to converge to a local optima, which makes the training more instable. In this paper, we proposed a data boosting method for NMT to help improving stability and efficiency. Experiments show that the improvement is quite stable during almost all training iterations. By adding 10% training corpus, translation score is improved by 1.49 BLEU scores and by reducing the size of the corpus by 20%, translation performance improved by 1.63.

The method we proposed focuses on training process only. There is no restriction for the neural network structure. It can be used in any data parallelism framework and then distributed onto multi-GPUs. Also, corpus pre-processing like tokenization (e.g. using sub-word unit (Sennrich et al., 2015)) and other techniques like guided training (Shen et al., 2016; Chen et al., 2016a) can be freely added based on the method we proposed. In the future, we plan to investigate more on the influence of training data especially in the later phase of training.

Acknowledgments

We thank the anonymous reviewers for their insightful comments.

References

Dzmitry Bahdanau, Kyunghyun Cho, and Yoshua Bengio. 2014. Neural machine translation by jointly learning to align and translate. *arXiv preprint arXiv:1409.0473*.

Wenhu Chen, Evgeny Matusov, Shahram Khadivi, and Jan-Thorsten Peter. 2016a. Guided alignment training for topic-aware neural machine translation. *arXiv preprint arXiv:1607.01628*.

Xie Chen, Xunying Liu, Yongqiang Wang, Mark JF Gales, and Philip C Woodland. 2016b. Efficient training and evaluation of recurrent neural network language models for automatic speech recognition. *IEEE/ACM Transactions on Audio, Speech, and Language Processing*, 24(11):2146–2157.

Sébastien Jean Kyunghyun Cho, Roland Memisevic, and Yoshua Bengio. 2015. On using very large target vocabulary for neural machine translation.

Josep Maria Crego, Jungi Kim, Guillaume Klein, Anabel Rebollo, Kathy Yang, Jean Senellart, Egor Akhanov, Patrice Brunelle, Aurelien Coquard, Yongchao Deng, Satoshi Enoue, Chiyo Geiss, Joshua Johanson, Ardas Khalsa, Raoum Khiari, Byeongil Ko, Catherine Kobus, Jean Lorieux, Leidiana Martins, Dang-Chuan Nguyen, Alexandra Priori, Thomas Riccardi, Natalia Segal, Christophe Servan, Cyril Tiquet, Bo Wang, Jin Yang, Dakun Zhang, Jing Zhou, and Peter Zoldan. 2016. Systran's pure neural machine translation systems. *CoRR*, abs/1610.05540.

Jonas Gehring, Michael Auli, David Grangier, Denis Yarats, and Yann N Dauphin. 2017. Convolutional sequence to sequence learning. *arXiv preprint arXiv:1705.03122*.

Itay Hubara, Matthieu Courbariaux, Daniel Soudry, Ran El-Yaniv, and Yoshua Bengio. 2016. Quantized neural networks: Training neural networks with low precision weights and activations. *arXiv preprint arXiv:1609.07061*.

Sergey Ioffe and Christian Szegedy. 2015. Batch normalization: Accelerating deep network training by reducing internal covariate shift. In *Proceedings of the 32nd International Conference on Machine Learning*, volume 37 of *Proceedings of Machine Learning Research*, pages 448–456, Lille, France. PMLR.

Jing Jiang and ChengXiang Zhai. 2007. Instance weighting for domain adaptation in nlp. In *ACL*, volume 7, pages 264–271.

Nal Kalchbrenner, Lasse Espeholt, Karen Simonyan, Aaron van den Oord, Alex Graves, and Koray Kavukcuoglu. 2016. Neural machine translation in linear time. *arXiv preprint arXiv:1610.10099*.

Yoon Kim and Alexander M Rush. 2016. Sequence-level knowledge distillation. *arXiv preprint arXiv:1606.07947*.

Philipp Koehn and Rebecca Knowles. 2017. Six challenges for neural machine translation. *arXiv preprint arXiv:1706.03872*.

Oleksii Kuchaiev and Boris Ginsburg. 2017. Factorization tricks for lstm networks. *arXiv preprint arXiv:1703.10722*.

Kishore Papineni, Salim Roukos, Todd Ward, and Wei-Jing Zhu. 2002. Bleu: a method for automatic evaluation of machine translation. In *Proceedings of the 40th annual meeting on association for computational linguistics*, pages 311–318. Association for Computational Linguistics.

Abigail See, Minh-Thang Luong, and Christopher D Manning. 2016. Compression of neural machine translation models via pruning. *arXiv preprint arXiv:1606.09274*.

Rico Sennrich, Barry Haddow, and Alexandra Birch. 2015. Neural machine translation of rare words with subword units. *arXiv preprint arXiv:1508.07909*.

Shiqi Shen, Yong Cheng, Zhongjun He, Wei He, Hua Wu, Maosong Sun, and Yang Liu. 2016. Minimum risk training for neural machine translation. In *Proceedings of the 54th Annual Meeting of the Association for Computational Linguistics (Volume 1: Long Papers)*, pages 1683–1692, Berlin, Germany. Association for Computational Linguistics.

Ilya Sutskever, Oriol Vinyals, and Quoc V Le. 2014. Sequence to sequence learning with neural networks. In *Advances in neural information processing systems*, pages 3104–3112.

Ashish Vaswani, Noam Shazeer, Niki Parmar, Jakob Uszkoreit, Llion Jones, Aidan N. Gomez, Lukasz Kaiser, and Illia Polosukhin. 2017. Attention is all you need.

Yonghui Wu, Mike Schuster, Zhifeng Chen, Quoc V Le, Mohammad Norouzi, Wolfgang Macherey, Maxim Krikun, Yuan Cao, Qin Gao, Klaus Macherey, et al. 2016. Google's neural machine translation system: Bridging the gap between human and machine translation. *arXiv preprint arXiv:1609.08144*.

Jie Zhou, Ying Cao, Xuguang Wang, Peng Li, and Wei Xu. 2016. Deep recurrent models with fast-forward connections for neural machine translatin. *arXiv preprint arXiv:1606.04199*.

Improving Japanese-to-English Neural Machine Translation by Voice Prediction

Hayahide Yamagishi, **Shin Kanouchi**, **Takayuki Sato**, and **Mamoru Komachi**

Tokyo Metropolitan University
{yamagishi-hayahide, kanouchi-shin, sato-takayuki} at ed.tmu.ac.jp,
komachi at tmu.ac.jp

Abstract

This study reports an attempt to predict the voice of reference using the information from the input sentences or previous input/output sentences. Our previous study presented a voice controlling method to generate sentences for neural machine translation, wherein it was demonstrated that the BLEU score improved when the voice of generated sentence was controlled relative to that of the reference. However, it is impractical to use the reference information because we cannot discern the voice of the correct translation in advance. Thus, this study presents a voice prediction method for generated sentences for neural machine translation. While evaluating on Japanese-to-English translation, we obtain a 0.70-improvement in the BLEU using the predicted voice.

1 Introduction

Recently, recurrent neural networks such as encoder-decoder models have gained increasing attention in machine translation owing their ability to generate fluent sentences. Controlling the output of the encoder-decoder model is difficult; however, several control mechanisms have been developed. For example, Sennrich et al. (2016) attempted to control honorifics in English-German neural machine translation (NMT). They trained an attentional encoder-decoder model (Bahdanau et al., 2015) using source data wherein the honorific information of a target sentence was represented by an additional word. They obtained a 3.2-point improvement in the BLEU score when the sentence was controlled to the same honorifics as the reference.

Similar to the research of Sennrich et al. (2016),

Yamagishi et al. (2016) reported an attempt to control the voice of a generated sentence using an attentional encoder-decoder model. They added a label to the end of the source sentence using the voice information of the target sentence during training. Subsequently, they translated the source sentences with a specified voice by appending the voice information. As a result, 0.73-point improvement in BLEU was achieved if the reference information was used.

Although Yamagishi et al. (2016) showed the upper bound for the improvement, it is impractical to use the reference information in the test phase. Therefore, in this study, we develop a voice classifier using a logistic regression model with simple context features. Note that our previous experiments did not exclude intransitive verb from the training and testing process, which may result in over-estimation of the active voice. Thus, for fair comparison, our test data constructed in this paper only contain transitive verbs. Our results demonstrate 67.7% and 66.0% voice prediction accuracies for the target sentence translated from Japanese to English on Asian Scientific Paper Excerpt Corpus (ASPEC, Nakazawa et al. (2016)) and NTCIR PatentMT Parallel Corpus (NTCIR, Goto et al. (2013)), respectively. An evaluation of the translation shows the statistically significant improvements in the BLEU score when using the predicted voice. In addition, a manual inspection shows that the voice-controlled translation clearly produces more fluent translation than the baseline.

2 Voice Prediction

Our previous study (Yamagishi et al., 2016) did not build a voice classifier for voice control; we used the majority of voice for each verb in the training corpus. We reported that the majority vote did not consistently improve the BLEU score. In

Proceedings of the The 8th International Joint Conference on Natural Language Processing, pages 277–282,
Taipei, Taiwan, November 27 – December 1, 2017 ©2017 AFNLP

contrast, this study develops a voice classifier using the following seven features. In this way, we can consider the context information of the source and target languages when predicting the voice of generated sentences. Note that we expect not only the quality of the voice prediction but also the quality of the translation to improve. These features are concatenated as a vector used to train a logistic regression model.

SrcSubj: Phrase embedding of the subject in a source sentence[1].

SrcPred: Phrase embedding of the predicate in a source sentence.

SrcPrevPred: Phrase embedding of the predicate in the previous source sentence.

SrcVoice: Voice of the source sentence.

TrgPrevObj: Word embedding of the objects in the previous target sentence.

TrgPrevVoice: Voice of the output sentences from previous three sentences.

TrgVoicePrior: The majority of target voice of each predicate phrase in a source sentence.

The phrase embeddings are the average of the all the word embeddings, except for alphabets, numerals, and punctuation marks in the phrase. All features are calculated from the information obtained from the main clauses. "Previous sentence" is flagged when an input sentence is not the first sentence in a document. We use SrcPrevPred, TrgPrevObj, and TrgPrevVoice to consider the information structure of a document.

TrgPrevVoice and TrgVoicePrior accept only three values, i.e., "Active," "Passive," and "No information." TrgVoicePrior represents the relation between the predicate of a source sentence and the voice of a target sentence. If the predicate of a test sentence is included in the training data, we obtain the majority of the voice distribution each predicate phrase in the training data. It can be noted that only the value of TrgVoicePrior was directly used as a label by Yamagishi et al. (2016); TrgVoicePrior was not used as a feature in the logistic regression model.

SrcVoice represents the voice of the source side. However, unlike English, it is difficult to formulate simple rules to obtain the voice of Japanese

sentences[2]. Thus, this feature shows whether the sentence has an auxiliary verb of representing passive voice.

3 Experiments

3.1 The Control Framework

Here we explain the voice controlling method proposed by Yamagishi et al. (2016) for Japanese-to-English NMT. We parse the target sentence and then evaluate the result to determine whether the ROOT is a past participle and whether it has a be-verb in the children. If both the conditions are satisfied, the target sentence is considered "passive." Otherwise, it is considered "active." The voice information is added to the end of the source sentence as a word. Finally, we create a new training corpus using labeled sentences. In the test phase, an `<Active>` or `<Passive>` label is added to the end of the source sentences to generate sentences in the desired voice.

3.2 Settings

We experimented with four labeling patterns.

ALL_ACTIVE: All sentences to active voice.

ALL_PASSIVE: All sentences to passive voice.

REFERENCE: Each sentence to the same voice as that of the reference sentence.

PREDICT: Each sentence to the predicted voice.

We mainly use the ASPEC (Nakazawa et al., 2016) in this experiment. The ASPEC comprises abstracts from scientific papers. We reconstructed the ASPEC as a document-level bilingual corpus. Sentences with more than 50 words from the training data are deleted, and the parallel documents that comprise continuous sentences are collected. As a result, the number of sentences in the training data is 1,103,336 (329,025 documents; the average number of sentences per document is 3.35). The original test data comprises 453 documents (four sentences in each document). Thus, it has 1,812 sentences in total. To evaluate voice control accuracy, we select 100 active sentences and 100 passive sentences from the top of the original test data. As stated in Section 1, sentence pairs whose ROOT of the reference is an intransitive verb are

---

[1] We extract the NP with the nominative case particle.

[2] In Japanese, the auxiliary verbs "れる (*reru*)" or "られる (*rareru*)" are typically used in the passive voice. However, they are also used to represent possibility or honorifics. It is difficult to apply simple rule to distinguish their usage.

omitted from the test data because it may not be possible to generate the passive sentences.

We also use the NTCIR Corpus (Goto et al., 2013) to investigate the corpus-specific tendencies. As a result of the preprocessing used with the NTCIR, the number of sentences in this training data is 1,169,201. The NTCIR10 development data and test data are used, which include 2,741 and 2,300 sentences, respectively. Note that we could not reconstruct this corpus at a document-level one. Therefore, our voice classifier only uses the sentence-level features in the experiments of voice prediction experiments.

The experimental results are based on accuracy, BLEU scores (Papineni et al., 2002), and human evaluation. Two types of accuracy were considered, i.e., voice accuracy and control accuracy. Voice accuracy is calculated as the agreement between the voice of the reference and that of the generated sentence. Control accuracy is calculated as the agreement between the label and the voice of the generated sentence. Note that only one evaluator performs annotation. We do not consider subject and object alternation because this evaluation only focuses on the voice of the sentence. We show two BLEU scores, i.e., BLEUall and BLEU200. BLEUall represents the score evaluated using all official test data, and BLEU200 represent the score evaluated using arranged test data described earlier. We statistically evaluate the BLEU scores using the bootstrap resampling implemented in Travatar[3]. The human evaluation involves pairwise comparison between the baseline results and the REFERENCE results (Base:REF) or between the baseline results and the PREDICT results (Base:PRED). The evaluator of this comparison is only one. Note that the evaluator differs from the voice label annotator.

We use CaboCha[4] (Ver. 0.68) to parse the Japanese sentences, and the Stanford Parser[5] (Ver. 3.5.2) to parse the English sentences. Scikit-learn (Ver. 0.18) is used to implement logistic regression. The word embeddings[6] (Mikolov et al., 2013) that we use as the features for voice prediction are trained using the source side of training corpus of ASPEC with 100 dimensions. The voice-labeling performance is 95%.

We obtain two NMT models, one trained using

the original corpus and the other trained using the labeled corpus. The former model is the baseline. These models are optimized by Adagrad (learning rate: 0.01). The vocabulary size is 30,000, the dimensions of the embeddings and hidden units are 512, and the batch size during training is 64. We train both the models for 15 epochs. We use Chainer (Ver. 1.18; Tokui et al. (2015)) to implement NMT models proposed by Bahdanau et al. (2015). We train Word2Vec with all 3,008,500 sentences in the ASPEC original training data for initializing the word vectors. Likewise, we use the source side of the training corpus of NTCIR to train Word2Vec for the experiments of NTCIR.

4 Results and Discussion

4.1 Voice Classifier Result

Table 1 summarizes the results of label prediction and an ablation test for feature selection. Yamagishi et al. (2016) reported that the accuracy of the majority voice was 63.7% on the ASPEC. Therefore, we obtained slight improvements in those scores by using the regression model with several features.

First, we discuss the result using ASPEC. The model using SrcPred, TrgPrevVoice, and TrgVoicePrior obtains the highest accuracy. The most important feature is SrcPred. The words included in the predicate phrase have some tendencies in each voice. TrgVoicePrior comprises the majority of the information in the training data. It is possible that this feature is inaccurate for verbs having no voice skewness tendency. TrgPrevVoice is also a useful feature to predict the voice, except for the first sentence in each document. SrcVoice is not a useful feature because the voice of the source sentence is not always the same as that of the target sentence. The voice concordance rate between languages is 53.5% on ASPEC.

Accuracy decreases using the other features. SrcSubj and TrgPrevObj are useless because many source sentences do not contain any subject and many target sentences do not contain any object. SrcPrevPred is ineffective because the voice seems to be determined by the discourse structure of the target sentences. We consider that the voice of output sentence is influenced by the words included in the previous outputs. However, our classifier only requires the voice information for the previous outputs.

Second, we discuss the result obtained using the

---

[3]http://www.phontron.com/travatar/index.html
[4]https://taku910.github.io/cabocha/
[5]http://nlp.stanford.edu/software/lex-parser.shtml
[6]https://radimrehurek.com/gensim/models/word2vec.html

Feature \ Corpus	ASPEC										NTCIR				
SrcSubj	✓		✓	✓	✓	✓	✓	✓			✓		✓	✓	✓
SrcPred	✓	✓		✓	✓	✓	✓	✓	✓	✓	✓	✓		✓	✓
SrcPrevPred	✓	✓	✓		✓	✓	✓	✓			—	—	—	—	—
SrcVoice	✓	✓	✓	✓		✓	✓	✓	✓		✓	✓	✓		✓
TrgPrevObj	✓	✓	✓	✓	✓		✓	✓			—	—	—	—	—
TrgPrevVoice	✓	✓	✓	✓	✓	✓		✓	✓	✓	—	—	—	—	—
TrgVoicePrior	✓	✓	✓	✓	✓	✓	✓		✓	✓	✓	✓	✓	✓	
Accuracy (%)	67.2	67.3	65.2	67.2	66.9	67.3	65.9	65.4	67.5	**67.7**	65.7	65.9	65.9	65.8	**66.0**

Table 1: Results of label prediction and ablation test for feature selection. "✓" represents "used", and "—" represents "cannot be used" in each column.

NTCIR corpus. Herein, the highest accuracy is 66.0%, which is obtained by the model using three features, i.e., SrcSubj, SrcPred, and SrcVoice. SrcVoice is the best predictive feature because the voice concordance rate is 63.3% on NTCIR. When we examine the top 50 most frequent predicates in both corpora, auxiliary verbs that represent passiveness are found in five predicates in the AS-PEC, while auxiliary verbs are found in 17 predicates in the NTCIR. If a source sentence includes those 17 predicates, the generated sentence tends to be a passive sentence. It is not clear why the effective features for voice prediction differ in these corpora because the percentages of sentences that do not have the subject are quite similar.

4.2 Translation Result

Table 2 shows the voice controlling results. "Other" indicates that the generated sentence is unreadable and that it does not include a verb.

Table 2(a) shows the result using ASPEC. The baseline model tends to generate a passive sentence, although the number of active sentences is greater than that of the passive sentences in the training data. This occurs because the generated sentence using a transitive verb tends to be a passive sentence under the general condition due to the fact that active sentences in the training data may contain an intransitive verb. We perform Base:REF comparison in which a human evaluator assessed that REFERENCE is better than the baseline model. We can obtain further improvement if we can appropriately change the voice of the generated sentence to that of the reference. With PREDICT, we obtain a 0.70-point improvement in the BLEUall score. The score of Base:PRED is close to that of Base:REF. Although we do not use the reference information in PREDICT, we obtain a promising result in human evaluations using the proposed method.

We observe the same tendencies when using the NTCIR, as shown in Table 2(b). The improve-ment to the BLEUall score between Baseline and REFERENCE is less than that in the ASPEC experiment. If an NMT model tends to generate sentences in a particular voice, the voice control method fixes this tendency. We can observe this tendency in the voice accuracy of Baseline; however, this is not observable in the training data. Thus, the voice control method becomes more effective when voice accuracy is low.

4.3 Discussion of Translation

Table 2 shows that it was difficult to generate active sentences. It is difficult for the model to generate an appropriate subject when a sentence is forced to become an active sentence despite it should be a passive sentence. The model tends to generate appropriate subjects only if a high-frequency verb is included in the generated sentence. In the NTCIR experiment, the model tends to generate the passive sentences, even though it is forced to produce active sentences when the source sentence has an auxiliary verb which represents passiveness. This tendency is not observed with the ASPEC because this corpus includes fewer sentences with such auxiliary verbs than the NTCIR. The reasons why ALL_PASSIVE obtains high accuracy is that these problems do not occur when generating the passive sentences.

Table 3 summarizes the examples of the generated sentences on the experiment using ASPEC. Example 1 shows that the voice of the generated sentence was appropriately controlled in the case of a single sentence. The voice controlling method only annotates voice information for the main clause; however, some input sentences are complex sentences. Examples 2 and 3 show the results of the subordinate clause and coordinate clause, respectively. The voice of the main clause is different from that of the subordinate clause at "to be Passive" in Example 2, although the voice of the main clause is the same as that of the coordinate clause in Example 3.

Experiment	# Active	# Passive	# Other	Voice acc.	Control acc.	BLEU200	BLEUall	Base:REF	Base:PRED
Reference	100	100	—	—	—	—	—	—	—
Baseline	31	163	6	60.5%	—	20.60	17.16	80	76
ALL_ACTIVE	147	44	9	57.5%	73.5%	20.22	—	—	—
ALL_PASSIVE	6	189	5	51.0%	94.5%	20.18	—	—	—
REFERENCE	82	113	5	89.0%		**22.47	**18.78	120	—
PREDICT	74	118	8	64.0%	89.0%	21.05	*17.86	—	124

(a) Experiments using ASPEC.

Experiment	# Active	# Passive	# Other	Voice acc.	Control acc.	BLEU200	BLEUall
Reference	100	100	—	—	—	—	—
Baseline	69	127	3	66.0%	—	31.80	29.29
ALL_ACTIVE	127	69	4	71.0%	63.5%	31.91	—
ALL_PASSIVE	17	186	3	55.0%	93.0%	32.32	—
REFERENCE	80	116	4	89.5%		**33.90	*29.80
PREDICT	73	122	5	69.5%	83.0%	33.16	29.59

(b) Experiments using NTCIR.

Table 2: Performance of voice control, BLEU score, and the result of the human evaluations in each corpus. These scores are calculated by original test data except for BLEUall. * represents the p-value < 0.05, and ** represents the p-value < 0.01 over the baseline.

Example 1	Source	リサイクルに関する最近の話題を紹介した．
	Reference	recent topics on recycling are introduced .
	To be Active	this paper introduces recent topics on the recycling .
	To be Passive	recent topics on the recycling are presented .
Example 2	Source	また，ドットの形状及び結晶性は温度に依存することも分かった．
	Reference	it was also proven that the shape and crystallinity of the dots were dependent on temperatures .
	To be Active	the morphology and the crystallinity of the dots depended on the temperature .
	To be Passive	it was also found that the shape and the crystallinity of the dots depend on the temperatures .
Example 3	Source	超電導材料開発のためのデータベースを構築し，材料設計用演えきシステムの開発を行った。
	Reference	a database for development of superconducting material was constructed , and deduction system for material design was developed .
	To be Active	we constructed a database for the development of superconducting materials and developed a deduction system for material design .
	To be Passive	a database for the development of superconducting materials was constructed , and the <unk> system for material design was developed .

Table 3: Examples of the generated sentences on the experiment using ASPEC.

Clause type		ALL_ACTIVE	ALL_PASSIVE
Coordinate	# Active	22	8
	# Passive	19	40
	# Total	41	48
	Agreement	63.4%	77.1%
Subordinate	# Active	29	21
	# Passive	15	13
	# Total	44	34
	Agreement	55.5%	38.2%

Table 4: The number of coordinate or subordinate clause in each voice on ASPEC.

Table 4 summarizes the results of the coordinate and subordinate clauses on the experiment of ASPEC. "Agreement" in this table represents the concordance rate between the voice of the main clause and that of each clause. If this rate is high, the voice of all clauses in a sentence is controlled to the same voice as the added label. The voices of the dependent clauses are not controlled, although the voice of the main clause can be controlled at high accuracy. As mentioned previously, the translation model tends to generate a passive sentence when it is expected to generate a transitive verb. We recognize the same tendency in the generation of the voice of the coordinate clause. Conversely, the voice of the subordinate clause tends to be active because the "be-verb + adjective" structure or "be-verb + noun" structure tends to be used in the subordinate clause, as in the abovementioned example. Hence, the proposed method greatly influences the main clause to which the voice information is added, although it also affects the dependent clauses.

5 Conclusion

This paper reported an attempt to predict the voice of reference sentence to improve the translation quality using the voice controlling method. We used simple features to train the logistic regression model. As a result, we predicted the voice of the reference sentences at 67.7% accuracy on ASPEC and at 66.0% on NTCIR, respectively. We observed difference of important features between the corpora. Certain improvement in BLEU score was achieved using the voice classifier results to output generated sentences in Japanese-to-English NMT. We will attempt to improve the quality of machine translation using context information of a document, including the voice information.

References

Dzmitry Bahdanau, Kyunghyun Cho, and Yoshua Bengio. 2015. Neural machine translation by jointly learning to align and translate. In *Proceedings of the International Conference on Learning Representations (ICLR)*.

Isao Goto, Bin Lu, and Benjamin K Tsou. 2013. Overview of the Patent Machine Translation Task at the NTCIR-10 Workshop. In *Proceedings of the 10th NII Testbeds and Community for Information access Research Conference (NTCIR)*.

Tomas Mikolov, Ilya Sutskever, Kai Chen, Greg S Corrado, and Jeff Dean. 2013. Distributed representations of words and phrases and their compositionality. In *Advances in Neural Information Processing Systems 26*, pages 3111–3119.

Toshiaki Nakazawa, Manabu Yaguchi, Kiyotaka Uchimoto, Masao Utiyama, Eiichiro Sumita, Sadao Kurohashi, and Hitoshi Isahara. 2016. ASPEC: Asian scientific paper excerpt corpus. In *Proceedings of the Ninth International Conference on Language Resources and Evaluation (LREC 2016)*, pages 2204–2208.

Kishore Papineni, Salim Roukos, Todd Ward, and Wei-Jing Zhu. 2002. BLEU: a method for automatic evaluation of machine translation. In *Proceedings of the 40th annual meeting on Association for Computational Linguistics (ACL)*, pages 311–318.

Rico Sennrich, Barry Haddow, and Alexandra Birch. 2016. Controlling politeness in neural machine translation via side constraints. In *Proceedings of the 2016 Conference of the North American Chapter of the Association for Computational Linguistics: Human Language Technologies (NAACL-HLT)*, pages 35–40.

Seiya Tokui, Kenta Oono, Shohei Hido, and Justin Clayton. 2015. Chainer: a next-generation open source framework for deep learning. In *Proceedings of Workshop on Machine Learning Systems (LearningSys) in the 2015 Conference on Neural Information Processing Systems (NIPS)*.

Hayahide Yamagishi, Shin Kanouchi, Takayuki Sato, and Mamoru Komachi. 2016. Controlling the voice of a sentence in Japanese-to-English neural machine translation. In *Proceedings of the 3rd Workshop on Asian Translation (WAT2016)*, pages 203–210.

Utilizing Lexical Similarity between Related, Low-resource Languages for Pivot-based SMT

Anoop Kunchukuttan, Maulik Shah
Pradyot Prakash, Pushpak Bhattacharyya
Department of Computer Science and Engineering
Indian Institute of Technology Bombay
{anoopk,maulik.shah,pradyot,pb}@cse.iitb.ac.in

Abstract

We investigate pivot-based translation between related languages in a low resource, phrase-based SMT setting. We show that a subword-level pivot-based SMT model using a related pivot language is substantially better than word and morpheme-level pivot models. It is also highly competitive with the best direct translation model, which is encouraging as no direct source-target training corpus is used. We also show that combining multiple related language pivot models can rival a direct translation model. Thus, *the use of subwords as translation units coupled with multiple related pivot languages can compensate for the lack of a direct parallel corpus.*

1 Introduction

Related languages are those that exhibit lexical and structural similarities on account of sharing a **common ancestry** or being in **contact for a long period of time** (Bhattacharyya et al., 2016). Machine Translation between related languages is a major requirement since there is substantial government, commercial and cultural communication among people speaking related languages *e.g.*, Europe, India and South-East Asia. These constitute some of the most widely spoken languages in the world, but many of these language pairs have few or no parallel corpora. We address the scenario when no direct corpus exists between related source and target languages, but they share limited parallel corpora with a third related language.

Modelling **lexical similarity** among related languages is the key to building good-quality SMT systems with limited parallel corpora. *Lexical similarity* means that the languages share many words

with similar form (spelling and pronunciation) and meaning *viz.* cognates, lateral borrowings or loan words from other languages *e.g.*, `blindness` is `andhapana` in Hindi, `aandhaLepaNaa` in Marathi.

For translation, lexical similarity can be utilized by transliteration of untranslated words while decoding (Durrani et al., 2010) or post-processing (Nakov and Tiedemann, 2012; Kunchukuttan et al., 2014). An alternative approach involves the use of subwords as basic translation units. Subword units like character (Vilar et al., 2007; Tiedemann, 2009), orthographic syllables (Kunchukuttan and Bhattacharyya, 2016b) and byte pair encoded units (Kunchukuttan and Bhattacharyya, 2017) have been used with varying degrees of success.

On the other hand, if no parallel corpus is available between two languages, pivot-based SMT (Gispert and Marino, 2006; Utiyama and Isahara, 2007) provides a systematic way of using an intermediate language, called the *pivot language*, to build the source-target translation system. The pivot approach makes no assumptions about source, pivot, and target language relatedness.

Our work **brings together subword-level translation and pivot-based SMT in low resource scenarios**. We refer to orthographic syllables and byte pair encoded units as subwords. We show that using a pivot language related to both the source and target languages along with subword-level translation (i) significantly outperforms morpheme and word-level pivot translation, and (ii) is very competitive with subword-level direct translation. We also show that combining multiple pivot models using different related pivot languages can rival a direct parallel corpora trained model. To the best of our knowledge, ours is the first work that shows that **a pivot system can be very competitive with a direct system (in**

Proceedings of the The 8th International Joint Conference on Natural Language Processing, pages 283–289,
Taipei, Taiwan, November 27 – December 1, 2017 ©2017 AFNLP

the restricted case of related languages). Previous work on morpheme and word-level pivot models with multiple pivot languages have reported lower translation scores than the direct model (More et al., 2015; Dabre et al., 2015). Tiedemann (2012)'s work uses a character-level model in just one language pair of the triple (source-pivot or pivot-target) when the pivot is related to either the source or target (but not both).

2 Proposed Solution

We first train phrase-based SMT models between source-pivot (S-P) and pivot-target (P-T) language pairs using subword units, where the pivot is related to the source and target. We create a pivot translation system by combining the S-P and P-T models. If multiple pivot languages are available, linear interpolation is used to combine pivot translation models. In this section, we describe each component of our system and the design choices.

Subword translation units: We explore *orthographic syllable (OS)* and *Byte Pair Encoded unit (BPE)* as subword units.

The *orthographic syllable*, a **linguistically motivated unit**, is a sequence of one or more consonants followed by a vowel, *i.e.* a C^+V unit (*e.g. spacious* would be segmented as *spa ciou s*). Note that the vowel character sequence *iou* represents a single vowel.

On the other hand, the *BPE unit* is motivated by **statistical properties of text** and represents stable, frequent character sequences in the text (possibly linguistic units like syllables, morphemes, affixes). Given monolingual corpora, BPE units can be learnt using the Byte Pair Encoding text compression algorithm (Gage, 1994).

Both OS and BPE units are variable length units which provide appropriate context for translation between related languages. Since their vocabularies are much smaller than the morpheme and word-level models, data sparsity is not a problem. OS and BPE units have outperformed character n-gram, word and morpheme-level models for SMT between related languages (Kunchukuttan and Bhattacharyya, 2016b, 2017).

While OS units are approximate syllables, BPE units are highly frequent character sequences, some of them representing different linguistic units like syllables, morphemes and affixes. While orthographic syllabification applies to writing systems which represent vowels (alphabets and

abugidas), BPE can be applied to text in any writing system.

Training subword-level models: We segment the data into subwords during pre-processing and indicate word boundaries by a boundary marker (_) as shown in the example for OS below:

word: `Childhood means simplicity .`

subword: `Chi ldhoo d _ mea ns _ si mpli ci ty _ .`

For building subword-level phrase-based models, we use (a) monotonic decoding since related languages have similar word order, (b) higher order language models (10-gram) since data sparsity is a lesser concern due to small vocabulary size (Vilar et al., 2007), and (c) word-level tuning (by post-processing the decoder output during tuning) to optimize the correct translation metric (Nakov and Tiedemann, 2012). After decoding, we regenerate words from subwords (desegmentation) by concatenating subwords between consecutive occurrences of the boundary markers.

Pivoting using related language: We use a language related to both the source and target language as the pivot language. We explore two widely used pivoting techniques: phrase-table triangulation and pipelining.

Triangulation (Utiyama and Isahara, 2007; Wu and Wang, 2007; Cohn and Lapata, 2007) "joins" the source-pivot and pivot-target subword-level phrase-tables on the common phrases in the pivot columns, generating the pivot model's phrasetable. It recomputes the probabilities in the new source-target phrase-table, after making a few independence assumptions, as shown below:

$$P(\bar{t}|\bar{s}) = \sum_{\bar{p}} P(\bar{t}|\bar{p})P(\bar{p}|\bar{s}) \qquad (1)$$

where, $\bar{s}, \bar{p}$ and $\bar{t}$ are source, pivot and target phrases respectively.

In the **pipelining/transfer** approach (Utiyama and Isahara, 2007), a source sentence is first translated into the pivot language, and the pivot language translation is further translated into the target language using the S-P and P-T translation models respectively. To reduce cascading errors due to pipelining, we consider the top-k source-pivot translations in the second stage of the pipeline (an approximation to expectation over all translation candidates). We used $k = 20$ in our experiments. The translation candidates are scored as shown below:

$$P(\mathbf{t}|\mathbf{s}) = \sum_{i=1}^{k} P(\mathbf{t}|\mathbf{p}^i)P(\mathbf{p}^i|\mathbf{s}) \qquad (2)$$

where, $\mathbf{s}, \mathbf{p}^i$ and $\mathbf{t}$ are the source, i^{th} best source-pivot translation and target sentence respectively.

Using Multiple Pivot Languages : We use multiple pivot languages by combining triangulated models corresponding to different pivot languages. Linear interpolation is used (Bisazza et al., 2011) for model combination. Interpolation weights are assigned to each phrase-table and the feature values for each phrase pair are interpolated using these weights as shown below:

$$f^j(\bar{s}, \bar{t}) = \sum_i \alpha_i f_i^j(\bar{s}, \bar{t}) \qquad (3)$$

$$\text{s.t} \quad \sum_i \alpha_i = 1, \quad \alpha_i \geq 0$$

where, f^j is feature j defined on the phrase pair $(\bar{s}, \bar{t})$, α_i is the interpolation weight for phrase-table i. Phrase-table i corresponds to the triangulated phrase-table using language i as a pivot.

3   Experimental Setup

Languages: We experimented with multiple languages from the two major language families of the Indian subcontinent: *Indo-Aryan* branch of the Indo-European language family (Bengali, Gujarati, Hindi, Marathi, Urdu) and *Dravidian* (Malayalam, Telugu, Tamil). These languages have a substantial overlap between their vocabularies due to contact over a long period (Emeneau, 1956; Subbarao, 2012).

Dataset: We used the *Indian Language Corpora Initiative (ILCI) corpus*[1] for our experiments (Jha, 2012). The data split is as follows – **training: 44,777, tuning: 1K, test: 2K** sentences. Language models for word-level systems were trained on the target side of training corpora plus monolingual corpora from various sources [hin: 10M (Bojar et al., 2014), urd: 5M (Jawaid et al., 2014), tam: 1M (Ramasamy et al., 2012), mar: 1.8M (news websites), mal: 200K, ben: 400K, pan: 100K, guj:400K, tel: 600K (Quasthoff et al., 2006) sentences]. We used the target side of parallel corpora for morpheme, OS, BPE and character-level LMs.
System details: We trained PBSMT systems for all translation units using *Moses* (Koehn

---

[1]available on request from tdil-dc.in

et al., 2007) with *grow-diag-final-and* heuristic for symmetrization of alignments, and Batch MIRA (Cherry and Foster, 2012) for tuning. Subword-level representation of sentences is long, hence we speed up decoding by using cube pruning with a smaller beam size (pop-limit=1000) for OS and BPE-level models. This setting has been shown to have minimal impact on translation quality (Kunchukuttan and Bhattacharyya, 2016a).

We trained 5-gram LMs with Kneser-Ney smoothing for word and morpheme-level models, and 10-gram LMs for OS, BPE, character-level models. We used the *Indic NLP library*[2] for orthographic syllabification, the *subword-nmt library*[3] for training BPE models and *Morfessor* (Virpioja et al., 2013) for morphological segmentation. These unsupervised morphological analyzers for Indian languages, described in Kunchukuttan et al. (2014), are trained on the ILCI corpus and the Leipzig corpus (Quasthoff et al., 2006). The BPE vocabulary size was chosen to match OS vocab size. We use *tmtriangulate*[4] for phrase-table triangulation and *combine-ptables* (Bisazza et al., 2011) for linear interpolation of phrase-tables.
Evaluation: The primary evaluation metric is word-level BLEU (Papineni et al., 2002). We also report LeBLEU (Virpioja and Grönroos, 2015) scores in the appendix. LeBLEU is a variant of BLEU that does soft-matching of words and has been shown to be better for morphologically rich languages. We use bootstrap resampling for testing statistical significance (Koehn, 2004).

4   Results and Discussion

In this section, we discuss and analyze the results of our experiments.

4.1   Comparison of Different Subword Units

Table 1 compares pivot-based SMT systems built with different units. We observe that *the OS and BPE-level pivot models significantly outperform word, morpheme and character-level pivot models* (average improvements above 55% over word-level and 14% over morpheme-level). The greatest improvement is observed when the source and target languages belong to different families (though they have a contact relationship), showing that subword-level models can utilize the lex-

---

[2]http://anoopkunchukuttan.github.io/indic_nlp_library
[3]https://github.com/rsennrich/subword-nmt
[4]github.com/tamhd/MultiMT

Lang Triple	Word	Morph	BPE	OS	Char
mar-guj-hin	30.23	36.49	39.05	**39.81**[†]	34.32
mar-hin-ben	16.63	21.04	22.46	**22.92**[†]	17.00
mal-tel-tam	4.55	6.19	**7.69**[†]	7.19	3.51
tel-mal-tam	5.13	8.29	**9.84**[†]	8.39	4.26
hin-tel-mal	5.29	8.32	9.57	**9.67**	6.24
mal-tel-hin	10.03	13.06	**17.68**	17.26	9.12
mal-urd-hin	7.70	11.29	**16.40**	NA	7.46
urd-hin-mal	5.58	6.64	**7.58**	NA	4.07
average % change w.r.t (BPE,OS)	*(+66,+57)%*	*(+21,+14)%*			*(+81,+66)%*

Table 1: Comparison of triangulation for various translation units (BLEU). Lang triple refers to the source-pivot-target languages. Scores in **bold** indicate highest values for the language triple. † means difference between OS and BPE scores is statistically significant ($p < 0.05$). NA: OS segmentations cannot be done for Urdu. The last row shows average change in BLEU scores for word, morpheme and character-level model compared to the OS and BPE-level models.

Lang Triple	BPE		OS	
	pip	*tri*	*pip*	*tri*
mar-guj-hin	38.25	**39.05**[†]	38.11	**39.81**[†]
mar-hin-ben	**22.50**	22.46	22.83	**22.92**
mal-tel-tam	**7.84**	7.69	6.94	**7.19**
tel-mal-tam	8.47	**9.84**[†]	7.96	**8.39**[†]
hin-tel-mal	9.31	**9.57**	9.31	**9.67**[†]
mal-tel-hin	17.39	**17.68**	16.96	**17.26**
mal-urd-hin	**16.93**[†]	16.40	NA	NA
urd-hin-mal	**8.83**[†]	7.58	NA	NA

Table 2: Comparison of pipelining (*pip*) and triangulation (*tri*) approaches for OS and BPE (BLEU). † means difference between *pip* and *tri* is statistically significant ($p < 0.05$)

ical similarity between languages. Translation between agglutinative Dravidian languages also shows a major improvement. The OS and BPE models are comparable in performance. However, unlike OS, BPE segmentation can also be applied to translations involving languages with non-alphabetic scripts (like Urdu) and show significant improvement in those cases also. Evaluation with LeBLEU (Virpioja and Grönroos, 2015), a metric suited for morphologically rich languages, shows similar trends (results in Appendix A). For brevity, we report BLEU scores in subsequent experiments.

Subword-level models outperform other units for the pipelining approach to pivoting too. Triangulation and pipelining approaches are comparable for BPE and OS models (See Table 2). Hence,

Lang Triple	Word	Morph	BPE	OS	Char
mar-guj-hin	0.64	1.39	1.74	2.33	3.04
mar-hin-ben	0.58	1.36	1.71	2.6	3.47
mal-tel-tam	0.61	2.32	3.27	4.19	2.58
tel-mal-tam	0.75	2.82	4.09	2.76	2.42
hin-tel-mal	0.56	2.08	2.86	2.97	2.25
mal-tel-hin	0.55	2.28	2.85	3.56	2.57
mal-urd-hin	0.25	1.16	1.84	NA	2.05
urd-hin-mal	0.42	0.79	1.62	NA	1.47

Table 3: Ratio of triangulated to component phrase-table sizes. We use the size of larger of the component phrase-tables to compute the ratio.

Lang Triple	Pivot	Direct				Pivot
	BPE	BPE	Word	Morph	OS	OS
mar-guj-hin	39.05	43.19	38.87	42.81	43.69	39.81
mar-hin-ben	22.46	24.13	21.13	23.96	23.53	22.92
mal-tel-tam	7.69	8.67	6.38	7.61	7.84	7.19
tel-mal-tam	9.84	11.61	9.58	10.61	10.52	8.39
hin-tel-mal	9.57	10.73	8.55	9.23	10.46	9.67
mal-tel-hin	17.68	20.54	15.18	17.08	18.44	17.26
mal-urd-hin	16.4	20.54	15.18	17.08	18.44	NA
urd-hin-mal	7.58	8.44	6.49	7.05	NA	NA

Table 4: Pivot *vs.* Direct translation (BLEU)

we report results for only the triangulation approach in subsequent experiments.

4.2 Why is Subword-level Pivot SMT better?

Subword-level pivot models are better than other units for two reasons. One, *the underlying S-P and P-T translation models are better* (*e.g.* 16% and 3% average improvement over word and morpheme-level models for OS). Two, the triangulation process involves an *inner join* on pivot language phrases common to the S-P and P-T phrase-tables. This causes data sparsity issues due to the large word and morpheme phrase-table vocabulary (Dabre et al., 2015; More et al., 2015). On the other hand, *the OS and BPE phrase-table vocabularies are smaller, so the impact of sparsity is limited*. This effect can be observed by comparing the ratio of the triangulated phrase-table (S-P-T) with the component phrase-tables (S-P and P-T). The size of the triangulated phrase-table is less than the size of the underlying tables at the word-level, while it increases by a few multiples for subword-level models (see Table 3).

4.3 Comparison of Pivot & Direct Models

We compared the OS and BPE-level models with direct models trained on different translation units

Model	mar-ben		mal-hin	
	OS	BPE	OS	BPE
best pivot	22.92 *(hin)*	22.46 *(hin)*	17.52 *(tel)*	18.47 *(guj)*
direct	23.53	24.13	18.44	20.54
all pivots	23.69	23.20†	19.12†	20.28
direct+all pivots	24.41‡	**24.49‡**	19.44‡	**20.93‡**

Table 5: Combination of multiple pivots (BLEU). **Pivots used for** (i) mar-ben: guj, hin, pan (ii) mal-hin: tel, mar, guj. Best pivot language indicated in brackets. Statistically significant difference from *direct* is indicated for: *all pivots*(†) and *direct+all pivots*(‡) ($p < 0.05$).

Lang Triple	Pivot			Direct		
	Morph	OS	BPE	Morph	OS	BPE
hin-tel-mal	4.72	5.96	6.00	5.99	6.26	6.37
mal-tel-hin	8.29	11.33	10.94	11.12	13.32	14.45
mal-tel-tam	4.41	5.82	5.85	5.84	5.88	6.75

Table 6: Cross domain translation (BLEU)

(see Table 4). These subword-level pivot models outperform word-level direct models by 5-10%, which is encouraging. Remarkably, the subword-level pivot model is competitive with the morpheme-level models (about 95% of the morpheme BLEU score). The subword-level pivot models are competitive with the best performing direct counterparts too (about 90% of the direct system BLEU score). To put this fact in perspective, the BLEU scores of morpheme and word-level pivot systems are far below their corresponding direct systems (about 15% and 35% respectively). *These observations strongly suggest that pivoting at the subword-level can better reconstruct the direct translation system than word and morpheme-level pivot systems.*

4.4 Multiple Pivot Languages

We investigated if combining multiple pivot translation models can be a substitute for the direct translation model. *Direct model* refers to translation system built using the source-target parallel corpus. Using linear interpolation with *equal weights*, we combined pivot translation models trained on different pivot languages. Table 5 shows that *the combination of multiple pivot language models outperformed the individual pivot models, and is comparable to the direct translation system.* Previous studies have shown that word and morpheme-level multiple pivot systems were not competitive with the direct system, possibly due to the effect of sparsity on triangulation (More et al., 2015; Dabre et al., 2015). Our results show that once the ill-effects of data sparsity are reduced due to the use of subword models, multiple pivot languages can maximize translation performance because: (i) they bring in more translation options, and (ii) they improve the estimates of feature values with evidence from multiple languages. Linear interpolation of the direct system with all the pivot systems with equal interpolation weights also benefitted the translation system. Thus, *multilinguality helps overcome the lack of parallel corpora between the two languages.*

4.5 Cross-Domain Translation

We also investigated if the OS and BPE-level pivot models are robust to domain change by evaluating the pivot and direct translation models trained on tourism and health domains on an agriculture domain test set of 1000 sentences (results in Table 6). For cross-domain translation too, the subword-level pivot models outperform morpheme-level pivot models and are comparable to a direct morpheme-level model. The OS and BPE-level models systems experience much lesser drop in BLEU scores *vis-a-vis* direct models, in contrast to the morpheme-level models. Since morpheme-level pivot models encounter unknown vocabulary in a new domain, they are less resistant to domain change than subword-level models.

5 Conclusion and Future Work

We show that pivot translation between related languages can be competitive with direct translation if a *related pivot language* is used and *subword units* are used to represent the data. Subword units make pivot models competitive by (i) utilizing lexical similarity to improve the underlying S-P and P-T translation models, and (ii) reducing losses in pivoting (owing to small vocabulary). Combining multiple related pivot models can further improve translation. Our SMT pivot translation work is useful for low resource settings, while current NMT systems require large-scale resources for good performance. We plan to explore multilingual NMT in conjunction with subword representation between related languages with a focus on reducing corpus requirements. Currently, these ideas are being actively explored in the research community in a general setting.

References

Pushpak Bhattacharyya, Mitesh Khapra, and Anoop Kunchukuttan. 2016. Statistical Machine Translation Between Related Languages. `www.cfilt.iitb.ac.in/publications/naacl-2016-tutorial.pdf`. Annual Conference of the North American Chapter of the Association for Computational Linguistics: Tutorials.

Arianna Bisazza, Nick Ruiz, Marcello Federico, and Bruno Kessler. 2011. Fill-up versus interpolation methods for phrase-based SMT adaptation. In *International Workshop on Spoken Language Translation*.

Ondřej Bojar, Vojtěch Diatka, Pavel Rychlý, Pavel Straňák, Vít Suchomel, Aleš Tamchyna, and Daniel Zeman. 2014. HindEnCorp – Hindi-English and Hindi-only Corpus for Machine Translation. In *Proceedings of the 9th International Conference on Language Resources and Evaluation*.

Colin Cherry and George Foster. 2012. Batch tuning strategies for Statistical Machine Translation. In *Proceedings of the 2012 Conference of the North American Chapter of the Association for Computational Linguistics: Human Language Technologies*.

Trevor Cohn and Mirella Lapata. 2007. Machine translation by triangulation: Making effective use of multi-parallel corpora. In *Proceedings of the Annual Meeting on Association for Computational Linguistics*.

Raj Dabre, Fabien Cromieres, Sadao Kurohashi, and Pushpak Bhattacharyya. 2015. Leveraging Small Multilingual Corpora for SMT Using Many Pivot Languages. In *Annual Conference of the North American Chapter of the Association for Computational Linguistics*.

Nadir Durrani, Hassan Sajjad, Alexander Fraser, and Helmut Schmid. 2010. Hindi-to-Urdu machine translation through transliteration. In *Proceedings of the 48th Annual Meeting of the Association for Computational Linguistics*.

Murray B Emeneau. 1956. India as a lingustic area. *Language* .

Philip Gage. 1994. A New Algorithm for Data Compression. *The C Users Journal* .

Adri'a De Gispert and Jose B Marino. 2006. Catalan-English Statistical Machine Translation without parallel corpus: Bridging through Spanish. In *In Proc. of 5th International Conference on Language Resources and Evaluation (LREC)*.

Bushra Jawaid, Amir Kamran, and Ondřej Bojar. 2014. Urdu monolingual corpus. LINDAT/CLARIN digital library at the Institute of Formal and Applied Linguistics, Charles University in Prague. http://hdl.handle.net/11858/00-097C-0000-0023-65A9-5.

Girish Nath Jha. 2012. The TDIL program and the Indian Language Corpora Initiative. In *Language Resources and Evaluation Conference*.

Philipp Koehn. 2004. Statistical Significance Tests for Machine Translation Evaluation. In *Conference on Empirical Methods in Natural Language Processing*.

Philipp Koehn, Hieu Hoang, Alexandra Birch, Chris Callison-Burch, Marcello Federico, Nicola Bertoldi, Brooke Cowan, Wade Shen, Christine Moran, Richard Zens, et al. 2007. Moses: Open source toolkit for Statistical Machine Translation. In *Proceedings of the 45th Annual Meeting of the ACL on Interactive Poster and Demonstration Sessions*.

Anoop Kunchukuttan and Pushpak Bhattacharyya. 2016a. Faster decoding for subword level Phrase-based SMT between related languages. In *Third Workshop on NLP for Similar Languages, Varieties and Dialects*.

Anoop Kunchukuttan and Pushpak Bhattacharyya. 2016b. Orthographic Syllable as basic unit for SMT between Related Languages. In *Empirical Methods in Natural Language Processing*.

Anoop Kunchukuttan and Pushpak Bhattacharyya. 2017. Learning variable length units for SMT between related languages via Byte Pair Encoding. In *First Workshop on Subword and Character level models in NLP*.

Anoop Kunchukuttan, Ratish Pudupully, Rajen Chatterjee, Abhijit Mishra, and Pushpak Bhattacharyya. 2014. The IIT Bombay SMT System for ICON 2014 Tools Contest. In *NLP Tools Contest at ICON 2014*.

Rohit More, Anoop Kunchukuttan, Raj Dabre, and Pushpak Bhattacharyya. 2015. Augmenting Pivot based SMT with word segmentation. In *International Conference on Natural Language Processing*.

Preslav Nakov and Jörg Tiedemann. 2012. Combining word-level and character-level models for machine translation between closely-related languages. In *Proceedings of the 50th Annual Meeting of the Association for Computational Linguistics: Short Papers-Volume 2*.

Kishore Papineni, Salim Roukos, Todd Ward, and Wei-Jing Zhu. 2002. BLEU: A method for automatic evaluation of machine translation. In *Association for Computational Linguistics*.

Uwe Quasthoff, Matthias Richter, and Christian Biemann. 2006. Corpus portal for search in monolingual corpora. In *Proceedings of the fifth international conference on language resources and evaluation*.

Loganathan Ramasamy, Ondřej Bojar, and Zdeněk Žabokrtský. 2012. Morphological Processing for English-Tamil Statistical Machine Translation. In *Proceedings of the Workshop on Machine Translation and Parsing in Indian Languages*.

Karumuri Subbarao. 2012. *South Asian Languages: A Syntactic Typology*. Cambridge University Press.

Jörg Tiedemann. 2009. Character-based PBSMT for closely related languages. In *Proceedings of the 13th Conference of the European Association for Machine Translation*.

Jörg Tiedemann. 2012. Character-based pivot translation for under-resourced languages and domains. In *Proceedings of the Conference of the European Chapter of the Association for Computational Linguistics*.

Masao Utiyama and Hitoshi Isahara. 2007. A Comparison of Pivot Methods for Phrase-Based Statistical Machine Translation. In *Annual Conference of the North American Chapter of the Association for Computational Linguistics*.

David Vilar, Jan-T Peter, and Hermann Ney. 2007. Can we translate letters? In *Proceedings of the Second Workshop on Statistical Machine Translation*.

Sami Virpioja and Stig-Arne Grönroos. 2015. LeBLEU: N-gram-based Translation Evaluation Score for Morphologically Complex Languages. In *Workshop on Machine Translation*.

Sami Virpioja, Peter Smit, Stig-Arne Grönroos, Mikko Kurimo, et al. 2013. Morfessor 2.0: Python implementation and extensions for Morfessor Baseline. Technical report, Aalto University.

Hua Wu and Haifeng Wang. 2007. Pivot language approach for phrase-based Statistical Machine Translation. *Machine Translation* .

A LeBLEU Scores

Table 7 shows LeBLEU scores for the experiments using phrase-triangulation. We observe that the same trends hold as with BLEU scores.

Lang Triple	Word	Morph	BPE	OS	Char
mar-guj-hin	0.692	0.725	0.737	**0.747**	0.713
mar-hin-ben	0.505	0.616	0.638	**0.646**	0.577
mal-tel-tam	0.247	0.364	**0.426**	0.407	0.213
tel-mal-tam	0.242	0.433	**0.485**	0.441	0.392
hin-tel-mal	0.291	0.376	0.420	**0.432**	0.306
mal-tel-hin	0.247	0.364	**0.426**	0.404	0.213
mal-urd-hin	0.328	0.436	**0.501**	NA	0.377
urd-hin-mal	0.313	0.353	**0.420**	NA	0.323
average % change w.r.t (BPE,OS)	*(+51,+49)%*	*(+12,+8)%*			*(+42,+42)%*

(a) Comparison of phrase-triangulation for various subwords

Lang Triple	Pivot	Direct				Pivot
	BPE	BPE	Word	Morph	OS	OS
mar-guj-hin	0.737	0.766	0.746	0.767	0.766	0.747
mar-hin-ben	0.638	0.653	0.568	0.645	0.656	0.646
mal-tel-tam	0.426	0.465	0.314	0.409	0.447	0.407
tel-mal-tam	0.485	0.530	0.410	0.511	0.534	0.441
hin-tel-mal	0.420	0.468	0.393	0.436	0.477	0.432
mal-tel-hin	0.426	0.565	0.460	0.528	0.551	0.404
mal-urd-hin	0.501	0.565	0.460	0.528	0.551	NA
urd-hin-mal	0.420	0.416	0.350	0.379	NA	NA

(b) Pivot *vs.* direct translation

Table 7: LeBLEU Scores

Key-value Attention Mechanism for Neural Machine Translation

Hideya Mino [1,2]*   **Masao Utiyama** [3]   **Eiichiro Sumita** [3]   **Takenobu Tokunaga** [2]
[1]NHK Science & Technology Research Laboratories
[2]Tokyo Institute of Technology
[3]National Institute of Information and Communication Technology
mino.h-gq@nhk.or.jp {mutiyama, eiichiro.sumita}@nict.go.jp
take@c.titech.ac.jp

Abstract

In this paper, we propose a neural machine translation (NMT) with a key-value attention mechanism on the source-side encoder. The key-value attention mechanism separates the source-side content vector into two types of memory known as the key and the value. The key is used for calculating the attention distribution, and the value is used for encoding the context representation. Experiments on three different tasks indicate that our model outperforms an NMT model with a conventional attention mechanism. Furthermore, we perform experiments with a conventional NMT framework, in which a part of the initial value of a weight matrix is set to zero so that the matrix is at the same initial-state as the key-value attention mechanism. As a result, we obtain comparable results with the key-value attention mechanism without changing the network structure.

1 Introduction

Recently, neural machine translation (NMT) (Sutskever et al., 2014; Cho et al., 2014) has achieved impressive results owing to its capacity to model the translation process end-to-end within a single probabilistic model. The unique features of the most popular approaches to NMT comprise a encoder-decoder architecture comprising recurrent neural networks (RNNs) and an attention mechanism, whereby the decoder can attend directly to localized information from source sequence tokens for generating a target sequence

---

* This work was performed while the first author was affiliated with National Institute of Information and Communication Technology, Kyoto, Japan.

(Bahdanau et al., 2015; Luong et al., 2015). The encoder-decoder architecture predicts the target word with a target hidden-state and a context vector. This context vector is calculated as a weighted average over all source hidden-states. The weight of a source hidden-state is calculated as the inner product of the source hidden-state and the target word hidden-state. Note that the source hidden-state acts as the key to weight itself. It also acts as the value to predict the target word through the context vector. Daniluk et al. (2017) suppose that the dual use of a single vector makes training the model difficult and propose the use of a key-value paired structure, which is a generalized way of storing content in the vector.

In this paper, we propose splitting the matrix of the source hidden-states into two parts, an approach suggested by Daniluk et al. (2017) and Miller et al. (2016). The first part refers to the key used to calculate the attention distribution or weights. The second part refers to the value for the source-side context representation.

We empirically demonstrate that the separation of the source-side context vector into the key and value significantly improves the performance of an NMT using three different English-to-Japanese translation tasks.

2 Related Work

A significant amount of research has been performed on the use of memory within neural networks. For instance, an RNN features an implicit memory in the form of recurring hidden states. However, a vanilla RNN is known to have difficulties in storing information for long time-spans (Bengio et al., 1994). To overcome this problem, LSTM (Hochreiter and Schmidhuber, 1997), or GRU (Cho et al., 2014), which contain memory cells with a recurrently self-connected linear unit

Proceedings of the The 8th International Joint Conference on Natural Language Processing, pages 290–295,
Taipei, Taiwan, November 27 – December 1, 2017 ©2017 AFNLP

have been proposed.

Attention-based neural networks with soft or hard attention over an input have shown successful results in a wide range of tasks including machine translation (Bahdanau et al., 2015), sentence summarization (Rush et al., 2015), and image captioning (Xu et al., 2015). These attention-based networks use an encoded memory for both as the key and value as described in the Introduction to calculate the output.

In contrast to the dual use of a single memory vector, Miller et al. (2016) have proposed key-value memory networks with key- and value-memory vectors to solve question-answering tasks, which use a generalized approach to store content in the memory. The key-memory vectors are used to calculate the attention weights, which address relevant memories with respect to the question, whereas the value-memory vectors are used to calculate the contextual representation to predict the answer. Daniluk et al. (2017) introduce a key-value attention model for neural language modeling that separates output vectors into keys to calculate the attention distribution and values for encoding the next-word distribution and context representation. We also focus on the key-value attention model. Our approach differs from the approach of Daniluk et al. (2017) in that they use it for the language model only; in contrast we use the key-value attention to encode the source-side context and predict the target-side word for translation.

3 Method

3.1 NMT with Attention

Our work is based on an attention-based NMT (Luong et al., 2015), which generates a target sentence $\boldsymbol{y} = (y_1, ..., y_N) \in \mathbb{R}^{V_t \times N}$ from the source sentence $\boldsymbol{x} = (x_1, ..., x_M) \in \mathbb{R}^{V_s \times M}$. V_s and V_t denote the vocabulary size of the source and target side, respectively. The attention-based model comprises two components, an encoder and a decoder. The encoder embeds the source sentence $\boldsymbol{x}$ into vectors through an embedding matrix and produces the hidden states using a bidirectional RNN, which represents a forward and a backward sequence. Thus, we have

$$\overrightarrow{h}_i = \text{enc}_1(\boldsymbol{W}_s x_i, \overrightarrow{h}_{i-1}), \tag{1}$$

$$\overleftarrow{h}_i = \text{enc}_2(\boldsymbol{W}_s x_i, \overleftarrow{h}_{i+1}). \tag{2}$$

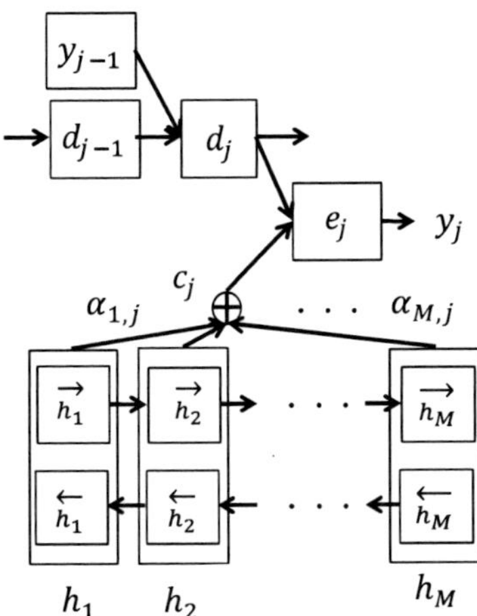

Figure 1: Encoder-decoder NMT architecture

$\boldsymbol{W}_s \in \mathbb{R}^{K \times V_s}$ is an embedding matrix where K is the word embedding size, and enc_1 and enc_2 are nonlinear functions as in LSTM. Then, as illustrated in Figure 1, the forward and backward hidden states $\overrightarrow{h}$ and $\overleftarrow{h}$ are concatenated into the hidden states $\boldsymbol{h} = (h_1, ..., h_M) \in \mathbb{R}^{K \times M}$ as

$$h_i = \boldsymbol{W}_e[\overrightarrow{h}_i^\top; \overleftarrow{h}_i^\top]^\top, \tag{3}$$

where $\boldsymbol{W}_e \in \mathbb{R}^{K \times 2K}$ is a matrix for the affine transform. Each hidden state, represented as a single vector, can be seen a memory vector that includes not only the lexical information at its source position, but also information about the left and right contexts. Then, the decoder predicts the target sentence $\boldsymbol{y}$ using a conditional probability calculated as bellow:

$$p(y_j|\boldsymbol{y}_{1,j-1}, \boldsymbol{x}) = \text{softmax}(\boldsymbol{W}_o e_j + b_o), \tag{4}$$

where $\boldsymbol{W}_o \in \mathbb{R}^{V_t \times K}$ and $b_o \in \mathbb{R}^{V_t}$ are implemented as a matrix and a bias of a feedforward neural network with a softmax output layer. $e_j \in \mathbb{R}^K$ is calculated by concatenating a hidden state with a context vector, and performing an affine transform with tanh function as

$$e_j = \tanh(\boldsymbol{W}_d[d_j; c_j]^\top), \tag{5}$$

where $\boldsymbol{W}_d \in \mathbb{R}^{K \times 2K}$ is a matrix for the affine transform; $d_j \in \mathbb{R}^K$ is the hidden state of the decoder RNN; and $c_j \in \mathbb{R}^K$ is the context vector derived from the source sentence. d_j is a fixed-length continuous vector computed by

$$d_j = \text{dec}(d_{j-1}, y_{j-1}). \tag{6}$$

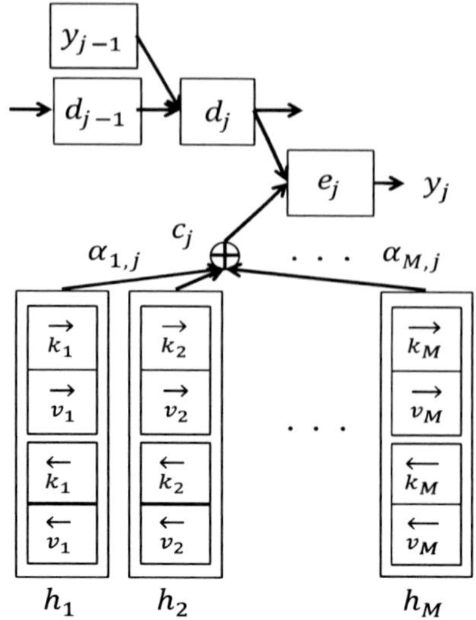

Figure 2: Encoder-decoder NMT architecture with key-value attention

Here dec is a nonlinear function analogous to enc1 or enc2; d_1 is set to a matrix of an affine transformation of the last hidden state h_M. The context vector c_j is computed as a convex sum of the hidden states h_i of Equation (3):

$$c_j = \sum_{i=1}^{M} \alpha_{i,j} h_i, \qquad (7)$$

where $\alpha_{i,j}$, known as the attention weight, is a scalar weight computed by

$$\alpha_{i,j} = \frac{\exp\{\text{score}(d_{j-1}, h_i)\}}{\sum_{l=1}^{M} \exp\{\text{score}(d_{j-1}, h_l)\}}, \qquad (8)$$

where the score function is referred as a content-based function and can be an arbitrary similarity function. We use the dot product, following Luong et al. (2015).

3.2 NMT with Key-value Attention

Attention-based NMT encodes an arbitrary sequence of source-side words into fixed-length dense vectors as in h in Eq. (3), which are used to calculate the attention weights and the context vectors as in Equations 8 and (7). However, the requirement to compress all necessary information into a single memory vector in each memory slot is likely to cause performance deficiencies. Therefore, to alleviate this problem, Miller et al. (2016)

and Daniluk et al. (2017) propose the use of a separate vector depending on the purpose. Inspired by them, we introduce a key-value attention mechanism into NMT to calculate the context vector with explicit separate vectors as shown in Figure 2. The encoder embeds the source sentence x and produces hidden states $\overrightarrow{h_i}$ and $\overleftarrow{h_i}$ as in Equations (1) and (2). Then, the two hidden states are decomposed into two respective parts, which are a key and a value, as

$$\overrightarrow{h_i} = \begin{bmatrix} \overrightarrow{k}_i \\ \overrightarrow{v}_i \end{bmatrix}, \overleftarrow{h_i} = \begin{bmatrix} \overleftarrow{k}_i \\ \overleftarrow{v}_i \end{bmatrix}, \qquad (9)$$

where the number of dimensions of the keys $\overrightarrow{k}_i$ and $\overleftarrow{k}_j$ and the values $\overrightarrow{v}_i$ and $\overleftarrow{v}_i$ is $K/2$. The forward and backward hidden-states $\overrightarrow{k}$ $\overleftarrow{k}$ $\overrightarrow{v}$ and $\overleftarrow{v}$ are concatenated into the hidden states h as

$$h_i = \begin{bmatrix} k_i \\ v_i \end{bmatrix} = \begin{bmatrix} W_f \begin{bmatrix} \overrightarrow{k}_i \\ \overleftarrow{k}_i \end{bmatrix} \\ W_g \begin{bmatrix} \overrightarrow{v}_i \\ \overleftarrow{v}_i \end{bmatrix} \end{bmatrix}, \qquad (10)$$

where $W_f \in \mathbb{R}^{K/2 \times K}$ and $W_g \in \mathbb{R}^{K/2 \times K}$ are matrices for the affine transform. The hidden states k and v indicate the key- and value-memory vector, respectively. Then, the decoder predicts the target sentence y using a conditional probability calculated as in Equations (4), (5), and (6). The context vector c_j in Eq. (5) is computed as a convex sum of the value memory v in Equation (10):

$$c_j = \sum_{i=1}^{M} \alpha_{i,j} v_i \qquad (11)$$

where $\alpha_{i,j}$ is calculated with the key memory k_i as

$$\alpha_{i,j} = \frac{\exp\{\text{score}(d_{j-1}, k_i)\}}{\sum_{l=1}^{M} \exp\{\text{score}(d_{j-1}, k_l)\}}. \qquad (12)$$

We also use the dot product for the score.

3.3 NMT Modifying Initial Weight

Another approach to alleviating this problem is modifying the score function in Eq. (8) and the initial value of the weight W_d in Eq. (5) of Section 3.1. The benefit of this approach is that the modification to the source code is minimal and the W_d may be tuned for better values. We suppose

Corpus		Training				Development			Test		
	Sents.	Word types		Avg. length		Sents.	Word types		Sents.	Word types	
		en	ja	en	ja		en	ja		en	ja
IWSLT'07	40K	9K	10K	9.3	12.7	0.5K	1.2K	1.3K	0.5K	0.8K	0.9K
NTCIR-10	717K	105K	79K	23.3	27.7	2.0K	5.0K	4.4K	0.5K	2.4K	2.1K
ASPEC	843K	288K	143K	22.1	23.9	1.8K	7.1K	6.3K	1.8K	7.0K	6.4K

Table 1: Datasets

that the upper half of the hidden states h in Eq. (3) produced by the encoder is used to calculate the alignment weight and the lower half of h is used to encode the source-side context vector. Then, we present two modifications. Firstly, since the score function in Eq. (8) calculates the alignment weight, we modify Eq. (8) to be zero for the lower half of the output of the score function as

$$\alpha_{i,j} = \frac{\exp\{\mathrm{score}(d_{j-1}, h_i \odot u)\}}{\sum_{l=1}^{M} \exp\{\mathrm{score}(d_{j-1}, h_l \odot u)\}}, \quad (13)$$

where $u \in \mathbb{R}^K$ is a vector for masking of which the upper half is one and the lower half is zero, and $\odot$ denotes the element-wise multiplication operation of the two vectors. Secondly, e_j in Eq. (5) is calculated with the context vector c_j, of which the upper half should not be used hereafter. Therefore, we set the initial weight of W_d to

$$\begin{bmatrix} w_{1,1} & \cdots & w_{1,k} & 0 & \cdots & 0 & w_{1,3K/2} & \cdots & w_{1,2K} \\ & & & & \vdots & & & & \\ w_{K/2,1} & \cdots & \cdots & \cdots & \cdots & \cdots & \cdots & \cdots & w_{K/2,2K} \\ & & & & \vdots & & & & \\ w_{K,1} & \cdots & \cdots & \cdots & \cdots & \cdots & \cdots & \cdots & w_{K,2K} \end{bmatrix} .$$

The particular concern is that, unlike Section 3.2, the upper and lower halves of h in the model are not completely independent though the upper and lower halves of the initial state are independently used to train the model.

The objective of the three methods in this section is to jointly maximize the conditional probability for each generated target word as

$$\theta^* = \arg\max_{\theta} \sum_{t=1}^{T} \sum_{j=1}^{L_t} \log p(y_j^t | \mathbf{y}_{1,j-1}^t, \mathbf{x}^t, \theta), \quad (14)$$

where $(\mathbf{x}^t, \mathbf{y}^t)$ is the t-th training pair of sentences, and L_t is the length of the t-th target sentence $\mathbf{y}^t$.

4 Experiments

We evaluate the proposed method using three different English-to-Japanese translation tasks.

4.1 Data and Model Parameters

The corpora used were IWSLT'07 (Fordyce, 2007), NTCIR-10 (Goto et al., 2013), and AS-PEC (Nakazawa et al., 2016) shown in Table 1. We constrained training sentences to a maximum length of 40 words to speed up the training. Each test sentence had a single reference translation.

4.2 Settings

The inputs and outputs of our model are sequences of one-hot vectors with dimensionality corresponding to the sizes of the source and target vocabularies. For NTCIR-10 and ASPEC, we replaced words with frequencies less than 3 with the [UNK] symbol and excluded them from the vocabularies. Each source and target word was projected into a 540-dimensional continuous Euclidean space to reduce the dimensionality. The depth of the stacking LSTMs was 2 and the hidden-layer size was set to 540. Each model was optimized using Adam (Kingma and Ba, 2014) with the following parameters: $\alpha = 1e - 3$, $\beta_1 = 0.9$, $\beta_2 = 0.999$, and $\epsilon = 1e - 8$. To prevent overfitting we used dropout (Srivastava et al., 2014) with a drop rate of $r = 0.5$ to the last layer of each stacking LSTM. All weight matrices of each model were initialized by sampling from a normal distribution of 0 mean and 0.05 standard deviation. The gradient at each update was calculated using a minibatch of at most 64 sentence pairs which was run for a maximum of 20 iterations for the entire training data. Training was early-stopped to maximize the performance on the development set measured by BLEU. We used a single Tesla K80 GPU with 12 GB memory for training. For decoding, we used a beam search with a beam size of 10. The beam search was terminated when an end-of-sentence [EOS] symbol was generated. We used Chainer 1.21.0 (Tokui et al., 2015) to implement all the models.

System	
source	This makes it difficult to reproduce by a thin film multi-reproducing head .
reference	この ため 薄膜 マルチ 再生 ヘッド (**a thin film multi-reproducing head**) に よ る 再生 が 困難 と な る 。
attn	これ に より 、 薄 い (**a thin**) 薄膜 磁気 ヘッド (**thin film reproducing head**) に よ る 再生 が 困難 に な る 。
key-value	これ に より 、 薄膜 磁気 ヘッド (**a thin film reproducing head**) に よ る 再生 は 困難 で あ る 。
modifying-IW	よ っ て 、 薄膜 磁気 ヘッド (**a thin film reproducing head**) に よ る 再生 が 困難 で あ る 。

Figure 3: Examples of the outputs

System	IWSLT'07	NTCIR-10	ASPEC
attn	49.1	31.1	29.6
key-value	49.3	33.8 †	30.7 †
modifying-IW	49.6	32.6 †	30.0

Table 2: BLEU scores for the attention-based NMT (*attn*), NMT with the key-value attention (*key-value*), and NMT modifying initial weight (*modifying-IW*) (†: significantly better than *attn* ($p < 0.05$).

5 Results

Table 2 summarizes the results for all the three tasks. NMT with the key-value attention achieved statistically significant results for the experiments with NTCIR-10 and ASPEC, though the experiments with IWSLT07 showed no such statistically significant results. The reason for our model's small difference in BLEU for IWSLT07 is likely due to the low number of word types used. The number of word types used in IWSLT07 was much lower than in the others, as presented in Table 1. Our model can be considered to be more effective for tasks with a vast vocabulary size. The results with NMT modifying initial weight are almost comparable to NMT with the key-value attention. Figure 3 shows the example of the outputs with each model. Though the attention-based NMT translates the same part of the sentence ("thin") twice, the NMT with the key-value attention and the NMT modifying initial weight translate correctly. These results show that the use of the separate memories for every different purpose improve the NMT translation quality and the initial weights of the hidden layers are likely to be able to control a single memory to keep dealing with the key and the value as separate as possible. For the training and translation speed, we did not observe large difference between these three models, since the three models have almost same number of parameters.

6 Conclusion

We propose a new method with the key-value attention mechanism in order to make the attention mechanism simpler. Our empirical evaluation shows that the proposed method is effective in achieving substantial improvements in terms of translation quality consistently across three different tasks.

Acknowledgments

This work was partially supported by the program "Promotion of Global Communications Plan: Research, Development, and Social Demonstration of Multilingual Speech Translation Technology" of MIC, Japan.

References

Dzmitry Bahdanau, Kyunghyun Cho, and Yoshua Bengio. 2015. Neural machine translation by jointly learning to align and translate. In *ICLR*.

Yoshua Bengio, Patrice Simard, and Paolo Frasconi. 1994. Learning long-term dependencies with gradient descent is difficult. *IEEE Transactions on Neural Networks* 5(2):157–166.

Kyunghyun Cho, Bart van Merrienboer, Caglar Gulcehre, Dzmitry Bahdanau, Fethi Bougares, Holger Schwenk, and Yoshua Bengio. 2014. Learning phrase representations using rnn encoder–decoder for statistical machine translation. In *Proceedings of the 2014 Conference on Empirical Methods in Natural Language Processing (EMNLP)*. Association for Computational Linguistics, Doha, Qatar, pages 1724–1734.

Michal Daniluk, Tim Rocktäschel, Johannes Welbl, and Sebastian Riedel. 2017. Frustratingly short attention spans in neural language modeling. *CoRR* abs/1702.04521.

Cameron Shaw Fordyce. 2007. Overview of the 4th international workshop on spoken language translation iwslt 2007 evaluation campaign. In *In Proceedings of IWSLT 2007*. Trento, Italy, pages 1–12.

Isao Goto, Ka-Po Chow, Bin Lu, Eiichiro Sumita, and Benjamin K. Tsou. 2013. Overview of the patent machine translation task at the NTCIR-10 workshop. In *Proceedings of the 10th NTCIR Conference on Evaluation of Information Access Technologies, NTCIR-10, National Center of Sciences, Tokyo, Japan, June 18-21, 2013*.

Sepp Hochreiter and Jürgen Schmidhuber. 1997. Long short-term memory. *Neural Comput.* 9(8):1735–1780.

Diederik P. Kingma and Jimmy Ba. 2014. Adam: A method for stochastic optimization. *CoRR* abs/1412.6980.

Thang Luong, Hieu Pham, and Christopher D. Manning. 2015. Effective approaches to attention-based neural machine translation. In *Proceedings of the 2015 Conference on Empirical Methods in Natural Language Processing*. Association for Computational Linguistics, Lisbon, Portugal, pages 1412–1421.

Alexander H. Miller, Adam Fisch, Jesse Dodge, Amir-Hossein Karimi, Antoine Bordes, and Jason Weston. 2016. Key-value memory networks for directly reading documents. In *Proceedings of the 2016 Conference on Empirical Methods in Natural Language Processing, EMNLP 2016, Austin, Texas, USA, November 1-4, 2016*. pages 1400–1409.

Toshiaki Nakazawa, Manabu Yaguchi, Kiyotaka Uchimoto, Masao Utiyama, Eiichiro Sumita, Sadao Kurohashi, and Hitoshi Isahara. 2016. Aspec: Asian scientific paper excerpt corpus. In Nicoletta Calzolari (Conference Chair), Khalid Choukri, Thierry Declerck, Marko Grobelnik, Bente Maegaard, Joseph Mariani, Asuncion Moreno, Jan Odijk, and Stelios Piperidis, editors, *Proceedings of the Ninth International Conference on Language Resources and Evaluation (LREC 2016)*. European Language Resources Association (ELRA), Portoro, Slovenia, pages 2204–2208.

Alexander M. Rush, Sumit Chopra, and Jason Weston. 2015. A neural attention model for abstractive sentence summarization. In *Proceedings of the 2015 Conference on Empirical Methods in Natural Language Processing*. Association for Computational Linguistics, Lisbon, Portugal, pages 379–389.

Nitish Srivastava, Geoffrey Hinton, Alex Krizhevsky, Ilya Sutskever, and Ruslan Salakhutdinov. 2014. Dropout: A simple way to prevent neural networks from overfitting. *Journal of Machine Learning Research* 15:1929–1958.

Ilya Sutskever, Oriol Vinyals, and Quoc V. V Le. 2014. Sequence to sequence learning with neural networks. In Z. Ghahramani, M. Welling, C. Cortes, N.D. Lawrence, and K.Q. Weinberger, editors, *Advances in Neural Information Processing Systems 27*, Curran Associates, Inc., pages 3104–3112.

Seiya Tokui, Kenta Oono, Shohei Hido, and Justin Clayton. 2015. Chainer: a next-generation open source framework for deep learning. In *Proceedings of Workshop on Machine Learning Systems (LearningSys) in The Twenty-ninth Annual Conference on Neural Information Processing Systems (NIPS)*.

Kelvin Xu, Jimmy Ba, Ryan Kiros, Kyunghyun Cho, Aaron C. Courville, Ruslan Salakhutdinov, Richard S. Zemel, and Yoshua Bengio. 2015. Show, attend and tell: Neural image caption generation with visual attention. In *Proceedings of the 32nd International Conference on Machine Learning, ICML 2015, Lille, France, 6-11 July 2015*. pages 2048–2057.

Transfer Learning across Low-Resource, Related Languages for Neural Machine Translation

Toan Q. Nguyen and **David Chiang**
Department of Computer Science and Engineeering
University of Notre Dame
{tnguye28,dchiang}@nd.edu

Abstract

We present a simple method to improve neural translation of a low-resource language pair using parallel data from a related, also low-resource, language pair. The method is based on the transfer method of Zoph et al., but whereas their method ignores any source vocabulary overlap, ours exploits it. First, we split words using Byte Pair Encoding (BPE) to increase vocabulary overlap. Then, we train a model on the first language pair and transfer its parameters, including its source word embeddings, to another model and continue training on the second language pair. Our experiments show that transfer learning helps word-based translation only slightly, but when used on top of a much stronger BPE baseline, it yields larger improvements of up to 4.3 BLEU.

1 Introduction

Neural machine translation (NMT) (Sutskever et al., 2014; Bahdanau et al., 2015) is rapidly proving itself to be a strong competitor to other statistical machine translation methods. However, it still lags behind other statistical methods on very low-resource language pairs (Zoph et al., 2016; Koehn and Knowles, 2017).

A common strategy to improve learning of low-resource languages is to use resources from related languages (Nakov and Ng, 2009). However, adapting these resources is not trivial. NMT offers some simple ways of doing this. For example, Zoph et al. (2016) train a *parent* model on a (possibly unrelated) high-resource language pair, then use this model to initialize a *child* model which is further trained on a low-resource language pair. In particular, they showed that a French-English model could be used to improve translation on a wide range of low-resource language pairs such as Hausa-, Turkish-, and Uzbek-English.

In this paper, we explore the opposite scenario, where the parent language pair is also low-resource, but related to the child language pair. We show that, at least in the case of three Turkic languages (Turkish, Uzbek, and Uyghur), the original method of Zoph et al. (2016) does not always work, but it is still possible to use the parent model to considerably improve the child model.

The basic idea is to exploit the relationship between the parent and child language lexicons. Zoph et al.'s original method makes no assumption about the relatedness of the parent and child languages, so it effectively makes a random assignment of the parent-language word embeddings to child-language words. But if we assume that the parent and child lexicons are related, it should be beneficial to transfer source word embeddings from parent-language words to their child-language equivalents.

Thus, the problem amounts to finding a representation of the data that ensures a sufficient overlap between the vocabularies of the languages. To do this, we map the source languages to a common alphabet and use Byte Pair Encoding (BPE) (Sennrich et al., 2016) on the union of the vocabularies to increase the number of common subwords.

In our experiments, we show that transfer learning helps word-based translation, but not always significantly. But when used on top of a much stronger BPE baseline, it yields larger and statistically significant improvements. Using Uzbek as a parent language and Turkish and Uyghur as child languages, we obtain improvements over BPE of 0.8 and 4.3 BLEU, respectively.

Proceedings of the The 8th International Joint Conference on Natural Language Processing, pages 296–301,
Taipei, Taiwan, November 27 – December 1, 2017 ©2017 AFNLP

English	Turkish	Uzbek
clinic	poliklinikte, poliklinie, polikliniine	poliklinikasi, poliklinikaga, poliklinikalar
parliament	parlamentosuna, parlamentosundan, parlamentosu	parlamentning, parlamentini, parlamentiga
meningococcus	meningokokuna, meningokosemi, meningokoklar	meningokokk, meningokokkli, meningokokkning

Table 1: Some examples of similar words in Turkish and Uzbek that share the same root.

2 Background

2.1 Attentional Model

We use the 2-layer, 512-hidden-unit *global* attentional model with *general* scoring function and *input feeding* by Luong et al. (2015). For the purposes of this paper, the most important detail of the model is that (as in many other models) the word types of both the source and target languages are mapped to vector representations called *word embeddings*, which are learned automatically with the rest of the model.

2.2 Language transfer

We follow the transfer learning approach proposed by Zoph et al. (2016). In their work, a parent model is first trained on a high-resource language pair. Then the child model's parameter values are copied from the parent's and are fine-tuned on its low-resource data.

The source word embeddings are copied with the rest of the model, with the ith parent-language word embedding being assigned to the ith child-language word. Because the parent and child source languages have different vocabularies, this amounts to randomly assigning parent source word embeddings to child source words. In other words, even if a word exists in both the parent and child vocabularies, it's extremely unlikely that it will be assigned the same embedding in both models.

By contrast, because the target language is the same in both the parent and child models, the target word embeddings are frozen during fine-tuning.

2.3 Related languages

The experiments described below are on translation from three Turkic languages to English. The Turkic language family is a group of related lan-

model	word-based		BPE 5k		BPE 60k	
	toks $\times 10^6$	sents $\times 10^3$	toks $\times 10^6$	sents $\times 10^3$	toks $\times 10^6$	sents $\times 10^3$
Uzb par	1.5	102	2.4	92	1.9	103
Tur chd	0.9	56	1.5	50	1.2	57
Uzb par	1.5	102	2.4	90	2.0	103
Uyg chd	1.7	82	2.1	77	2.0	88

Table 2: Number of tokens and sentences in our training data.

guages with a very wide geographic distribution, from Turkey to northeastern Siberia. Turkic languages are morphologically rich, and have similarities in phonology, morphology, and syntax. For instance, in our analysis of the training data, we find many Turkish and Uzbek words sharing the same root and meaning. Some examples are shown in Table 1.

2.4 Byte Pair Encoding

BPE (Sennrich et al., 2016) is an efficient word segmentation algorithm. It initially treats the words as sequences of character tokens, then iteratively finds and merges the most common token pair into one. The algorithm stops after a controllable number of operations, or when no token pair appears more than once. At test time, the learned merge operations are applied to merge the character sequences in test data into larger symbols.

3 Method

The basic idea of our method is to extend the transfer method of Zoph et al. (2016) to share the parent and child's source vocabularies, so that when source word embeddings are transferred, a word that appears in both vocabularies keeps its embedding. In order for this to work, it must be the case that the parent and child languages have considerable vocabulary overlap, and that when a word occurs in both languages, it often has a similar meaning in both languages. Thus, we need to process the data to make these two assumptions hold as much as possible.

3.1 Transliteration

If the parent and child language have different orthographies, it should help to map them into a common orthography. Even if the two use the same script, some transformation could be applied; for example, we might change French *-eur* endings to Spanish *-or*. Here, we take a minimalist approach. Turkish and Uzbek are both written using Latin script, and we did not apply any transformations to them. Our Uyghur data is written in Arabic script, so we transliterated it to Latin script using an off-the-shelf transliterator.[1] The transliteration is a string homomorphism, replacing Arabic letters with English letters or consonant clusters independent of context.

3.2 Segmentation

To increase the overlap between the parent and child vocabularies, we use BPE to break words into subwords. For the BPE merge rules to not only find the common subwords between two source languages but also ensure consistency between source and target segmentation among each language pair, we learn the rules from the union of source and target data of both the parent and child models. The rules are then used to segment the corpora. It is important to note that this results in a single vocabulary, used for both the source and target languages in both models.

4 Experiments

We used Turkish-, Uzbek-, and Uyghur-English parallel texts from the LORELEI program. We tokenized all data using the Moses toolkit (Koehn et al., 2007); for Turkish-English experiments, we also truecased the data. For Uyghur-English, the word-based models were trained in the original Uyghur data written in Arabic script; for BPE-based systems, we transliterated it to Latin script as described above.

For the word-based systems, we fixed the vocabulary size and replaced out-of-vocabulary

words with _UNK. We tried different sizes for each language pair; however, each word-based system's target vocabulary size is limited by that of the child, so we could only use up to 45,000 word types for Turkish-English and 20,000 for Uyghur-English.

The BPE-based systems could make use of bigger vocabulary size thanks to the combination of both parent and child source and target vocabularies. We varied the number of BPE merge operations from 5,000 to 60,000. Instead of using a fixed vocabulary cutoff, we used the full vocabulary; to ensure the model still learns how to deal with unknown words, we trained on two copies of the training data: one unchanged, and one in which all rare words (whose frequency is less than 5) were replaced with _UNK. Accordingly, the number of epochs was halved.

Following common practice, we fixed an upper limit on training sentence length (discarding longer sentences). Because the BPE-based systems have shorter tokens and therefore longer sentences, we set this upper limit differently for the word-based and BPE-based systems to approximately equalize the total size of the training data. This led to a limit of 50 tokens for word-based models and 60 tokens for BPE-based models. See Table 2 for statistics of the resulting datasets.

We trained using Adadelta (Zeiler, 2012), with a minibatch size of 32 and dropout with a dropout rate of 0.2. We rescaled the gradient when its norm exceeded 5. For the Uzbek-English to Turkish-English experiment, the parent and child models were trained for 100 and 50 epochs, respectively. For the Uzbek-English to Uyghur-English experiment, the parent and child models were trained for 50 and 200, respectively. As mentioned above, the BPE models were trained for half as many epochs because their data is duplicated.

We used beam search for translation on the dev and test sets. Since NMT tends to favor short translations (Cho et al., 2014), we use the length normalization approach of Wu et al. (2016) which uses a different score $s(e \mid f)$ instead of log-probability:

$$s(e \mid f) = \frac{\log p(e \mid f)}{lp(e)}$$

$$lp(e) = \frac{(5 + |e|)^\alpha}{(5 + 1)^\alpha}.$$

We set $\alpha = 0.8$ for all of our experiments.

---

[1] https://cis.temple.edu/~anwar/code/latin2uyghur.html

		baseline		transfer		transfer+freeze	
		BLEU	size	BLEU	size	BLEU	size
Tur-Eng	word-based	8.1	30k	8.5*	30k	8.6*	30k
	BPE	12.4	10k	13.2†	20k	—	—
Uyg-Eng	word-based	8.5	15k	10.6†	15k	8.8*	15k
	BPE	11.1	10k	15.4‡	8k	—	—

Table 3: Whereas transfer learning at word-level does not always help, our method consistently yields a significant improvement over the stronger BPE systems. Scores are case-sensitive **test** BLEU. Key: `size` = vocabulary size (word-based) or number of BPE operations (BPE). The symbols † and ‡ indicate statistically significant improvements with $p < 0.05$ and $p < 0.01$, respectively, while $*$ indicates a statistically insignificant improvement ($p > 0.05$).

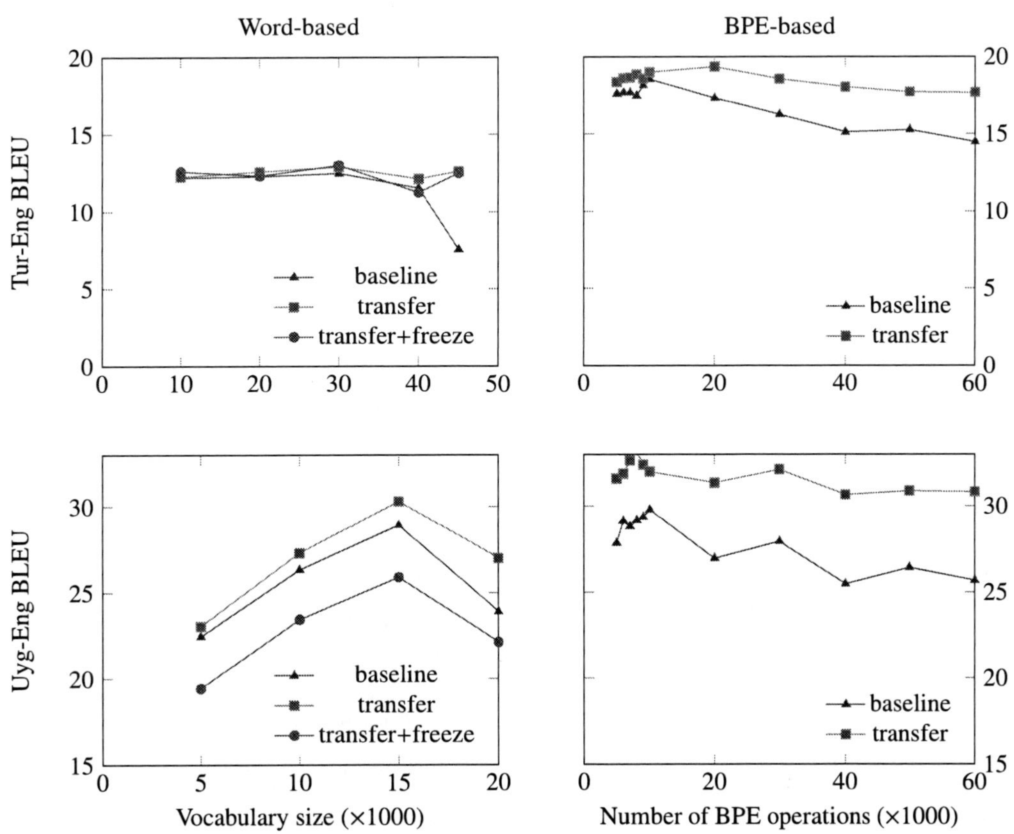

Figure 1: Tokenized **dev** BLEU scores for various settings as a function of the number of word/subword types. Key: baseline = train child model only; transfer = train parent, then child model; +freeze = freeze target word embeddings in child model.

task	settings	train	dev
Tur-Eng	word-based 30k	3.9%	3.6%
	BPE 20k	58.8%	25.0%
Uyg-Eng	word-based 15k	0.5%	1.7%
	BPE 8k	57.2%	48.5%

Table 4: Amount of child's source types that appear in parent.

We stopped training when the tokenized BLEU score was maximized on the development set. We also optimized the vocabulary size and the number of BPE operations for the word-based and BPE-based systems, respectively, to maximize the tokenized BLEU on the development set.

After translation at test time, we rejoined BPE segments, recased, and detokenized. Finally, we evaluated using case-sensitive BLEU.

As a baseline, we trained a child model using BPE but without transfer (that is, with weights randomly initialized). We also compared against a word-based baseline (without transfer) and two word-based systems using transfer without vocabulary-sharing, corresponding with the method of Zoph et al. (2016) (§2.2): one where the target word embeddings are fine-tuned, and one where they are frozen.

5 Results and Analysis

Our results are shown in Table 3. In this low-resource setting, we find that transferring word-based models does not consistently help. On Turkish-English, both transfer methods give only a statistically insignificant improvement ($p > 0.05$); on Uyghur-English, transfer without freezing target embeddings helps somewhat, but transfer with freezing helps only insignificantly.

In both language pairs, the models that use BPE perform much better than their word-based counterparts. When we apply transfer learning to this much stronger baseline, we find that the relative improvements actually increase; that is, the combined effect of BPE and transfer learning is more than additive. On Turkish-English, the improvement is +0.8 BLEU over the BPE baseline; on Uyghur-English, a healthy +4.3 over the BPE baseline.

A similar pattern emerges when we examine the best BLEU scores on the development set (Figure 1). Whereas word-based transfer methods help very little for Turkish-English, and help or hurt slightly for Uyghur-English, our BPE-based transfer approach consistently improves over both the baseline and transfer word-based models. We surmise that the improvement is primarily due to the vocabulary overlap created by BPE (see Table 4).

6 Conclusion

In this paper, we have shown that the transfer learning method of Zoph et al. (2016), while appealing, might not always work in a low-resource context. However, by combining it with BPE, we can improve NMT performance on a low-resource language pair by exploiting its lexical similarity with another related, low-resource language. Our results show consistent improvement in two Turkic languages. Our approach, which relies on segmenting words into subwords, seems well suited to agglutinative languages; further investigation would be needed to confirm whether our method works on other types of languages.

7 Acknowledgements

This research was supported in part by University of Southern California subcontract 67108176 under DARPA contract HR0011-15-C-0115. Nguyen was supported by a fellowship from the Vietnam Education Foundation. We would like to express our great appreciation to Dr. Sharon Hu for letting us use her group's GPU cluster (supported by NSF award 1629914), and to NVIDIA corporation for the donation of a Titan X GPU.

References

Dzmitry Bahdanau, Kyunghyun Cho, and Yoshua Bengio. 2015. Neural machine translation by jointly learning to align and translate. In *Proc. ICLR*.

Kyunghyun Cho, Bart van Merriënboer, Dzmitry Bahdanau, and Yoshua Bengio. 2014. On the properties of neural machine translation: Encoder–decoder approaches. In *Proc. Workshop on Syntax, Semantics and Structure in Statistical Translation*.

Philipp Koehn, Hieu Hoang, Alexandra Birch, Chris Callison-Burch, Marcello Federico, Nicola Bertoldi, Brooke Cowan, Wade Shen, Christine Moran, Richard Zens, et al. 2007. Moses: Open source toolkit for statistical machine translation. In *Proc. ACL*.

Philipp Koehn and Rebecca Knowles. 2017. Six challenges for neural machine translation. In *Proc. First Workshop on Neural Machine Translation*. Association for Computational Linguistics.

Thang Luong, Hieu Pham, and Christopher D. Manning. 2015. Effective approaches to attention-based neural machine translation. In *Proc. EMNLP*.

Preslav Nakov and Hwee Tou Ng. 2009. Improved statistical machine translation for resource-poor languages using related resource-rich languages. In *Proc. EMNLP*.

Rico Sennrich, Barry Haddow, and Alexandra Birch. 2016. Neural machine translation of rare words with subword units. In *Proc. ACL*.

Ilya Sutskever, Oriol Vinyals, and Quoc V Le. 2014. Sequence to sequence learning with neural networks. In *Advances in Neural Information Processing Systems 27*.

Yonghui Wu, Mike Schuster, Zhifeng Chen, Quoc V Le, Mohammad Norouzi, Wolfgang Macherey, Maxim Krikun, Yuan Cao, Qin Gao, Klaus Macherey, et al. 2016. Google's neural machine translation system: Bridging the gap between human and machine translation. arXiv:1609.08144.

Matthew D. Zeiler. 2012. ADADELTA: An adaptive learning rate method. arXiv:1212.5701v1.

Barret Zoph, Deniz Yuret, Jonathan May, and Kevin Knight. 2016. Transfer learning for low-resource neural machine translation. In *Proc. EMNLP*.

Concept Equalization to Guide Correct Training of Neural Machine Translation

Kangil Kim
Konkuk University
Republic of Korea

Jong-Hun Shin
ETRI
Republic of Korea

Seung-Hoon Na[*]
Chonbuk National University
Republic of Korea

SangKeun Jung
SK Telecom
Republic of Korea

Abstract

Neural machine translation decoders are usually conditional language models to sequentially generate words for target sentences. This approach is limited to find the best word composition and requires help of explicit methods as beam search. To help learning correct compositional mechanisms in NMTs, we propose concept equalization using direct mapping distributed representations of source and target sentences. In a translation experiment from English to French, the concept equalization significantly improved translation quality by 3.00 BLEU points compared to a state-of-the-art NMT model.

1 Introduction with Related Works

After the possibility of learning end-to-end translation model (Sutskever et al., 2014) was reported, there has been a surge of research to apply recurrent neural networks (RNN) with long short term memory (LSTM) (Hochreiter and Schmidhuber, 1997) to machine translation. After intensive developments, this approach becomes the state-of-the-art of machine translation called as neural machine translation (NMT). Remarkable approaches are bidirectional LSTM using both forward and backward sequences (Sutskever et al., 2014), attention model to learn explicit alignment models (Bahdanau et al., 2014; Luong et al., 2015a), rare word modeling to estimate unknown word through alignment information (Luong et al., 2014). Many other detailed following techniques improved the performance such as batch normalization (Ioffe and Szegedy, 2015), ensembles, beam search, input feature specialization,

---

[*]corresponding author: nash@jbnu.ac.kr

and input feeding, which are all aggregated into Google's NMT report (Wu et al., 2016).

Most decoders of NMTs are conditional language models, which sequentially generate target words and its proceeding correct target words in the condition of a given source sentence. This approach is a greedy algorithm, so dependency of selected words to subsequent words may restrict selecting the best target word composition. Beam search is a promising method to approximate the correct compositions. However, inversely, promising results imply that NMTs are still weak to learn the dependency between words in a target sentence. This limitation in training process creates fundamental barrier of representing correct translation process in a neural network. In (Ranzato et al., 2015), this issue was discussed as a problem of maximum likelihood estimation ignoring the dependency between selected target words and an approach penalizing the likelihood with sentence-level distance has been proposed (Shen et al., 2015).

Beyond correct target word generation, translation may be regarded as a subproblem to find mapping of sentence-level semantics between two languages. Accuracy of this mapping is often limited because of ambiguity caused by many-to-many mapping relations. It is difficult to find exact mapping with simple and direct mapping models as the reported difficult in mapping simpler word-level semantics (AP et al., 2014; Luong et al., 2015b; Upadhyay et al., 2016).The framework of NMTs is the most successful model to find an exact mapping of sentence-level semantics so far. However, its huge expression power leads to inefficiency in training which requires addition connections to transfer related information such as attention or input feeding models (Bahdanau et al., 2014; Wu et al., 2016). This inefficiency may be removed by using simple di-

Proceedings of the The 8th International Joint Conference on Natural Language Processing, pages 302–307,
Taipei, Taiwan, November 27 – December 1, 2017 ©2017 AFNLP

rect models to restrict unnecessary area to search in training step.

In this paper, we propose *concept equalization* method to apply the direct semantic-mapping model to existing NMT frameworks for guiding training of model parameters. Distinguished contributions of this method are to introduce 1) an effective penalty function and 2) a plug-in framework to transfer the constraint information of the penalty to LSTM stacks. In practical translation tasks from English to French, this method improves translation quality and convergence speed to local optima. Extra benefit is easy adaptation to any type of NMT frameworks.

Paper structure is as follows. Section 2 explains motivations and details of concept equalization. Section 3 shows experimental configurations on data, model, and runs and Section 4 interprets the results. Section 5 is conclusion and future work.

2 Concept Equalization

2.1 Limit of Learning Target Composition

Beam search is a promising method for NMTs by overcoming the problem of greedy search in sequential target word generation. On the other hand, the impact of beam search inversely implies that the sequential decisions by the model are likely to be incorrect to select the best sentences in many cases. There are many possible causes for the inaccurate prediction of composition of target words such as inaccurate model representation, complex parameter landscapes, and noise data.

A possible cause is the simple representation of the correctness of target words. In current NMTs, cross-entropy is the most popular cost function composed of probabilities of selecting each correct word of a target sequence. Therefore, only one variable is responsible for representing whether the selected target word is correct. Using only one variable may be risky because the second probable word and its highly probable following sequences may give higher cross-entropy than any sequences derived from the correct word selection. This case is a deceptive example of restricting accurate word composition in decoders.

Another cause is slow parameter update in NMT structures. In LSTMs, the gradient vanishing (Bengio et al., 1994) over time steps is resolved by using memory cells and over vertical structures by addition input feeding

or multidimensional memories (Wu et al., 2016; Kalchbrenner et al., 2015). They are applied to the encoder and decoder, but the interface part is often a feedforward layer suffering from the gradient vanishing. This vanishing limits the achievable translation quality in general and may restrict learning the correct composition.

2.2 Motivation: Concept Equalization

To resolve the limited target word composition, two approaches are proposed: 1) direct linking the interface vector to the cost function and 2) increasing the dimension for representing correctness of target words. The first approach defines a cost function to directly use the transferred interface vector, so that the depth from the cost the interface vector decreases and reduce the effect of gradient vanishing. In the second approach, if we train NMT to select a correct word only if its all variables are the most probable, then the deception of selecting the second probable word in one perspective is easily excluded. This second approach is somewhat new in NMT literature, because the dimension of probability vectors is already so high that increasing the dimension becomes serious burden.

To use the two approaches without problems, we introduce a *concept equalization* for training NMT where the concept indicates the semantics of source and target sentences and represented as two vectors. A expected role of this approach is to guide NMTs not to train obviously wrong sentences in explicit direct mapping models. The method is illustrated in Fig. 1 and described in the following sections.

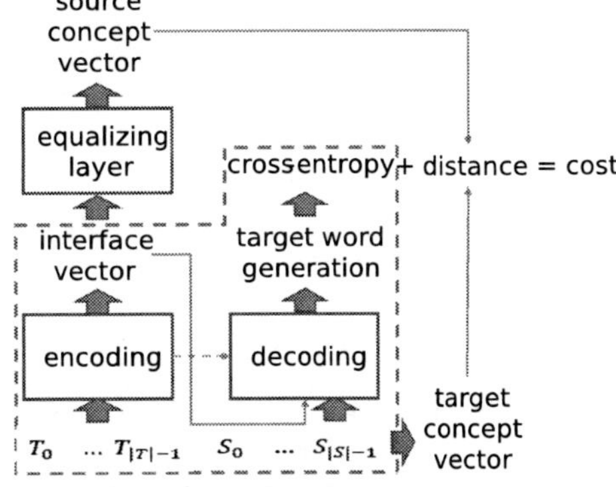

Figure 1: Concept Equalization Model Plugged In to Typical Neural Machine Translation (red and dashed line: typical model)

2.3 Concept Equalization Model

We newly propose the following three parts compared to typical NMT frameworks.

Raw Concept Vector Representation Representing a target word as a vector, concept equalization assigns many variables to indicate the correctness of target word without increasing the dimension of existing probability vectors for calculating cross-entropy. The concept vector $\mathbf{c}_S$ of source sentence S and $\mathbf{c}_T$ of target sentence T are defined as

$$\mathbf{c}_S = \sum_{t=1}^{|S|} \mathbf{h}_t \quad , \quad \mathbf{c}_T = \sum_{t=1}^{|T|} \mathbf{w}_t$$

where $\mathbf{h}_t$ is the hidden vector generated from the top LSTM stacks at time step t in a NMT encoder and $\mathbf{w}_t$ is the word vector at time t in a decoder. This raw vector generation process can be easily extended to existing NMTs. For example, in bidirectional models, $\mathbf{h}_t$ is replaced by $\mathbf{h}_t^f \| \mathbf{h}_t^b$. In bidirectional attention models, interface vectors are transformed vectors of $\mathbf{h}_t$ with alignment model and target word, but we can still use $\mathbf{h}_t^f \| \mathbf{h}_t^b$.

Equalizing Layer In equalization, the biggest risk is the conflict of vector distribution of $\mathbf{h}_t$ desirable for minimizing cross-entropy and for concept distance because of quality decrease of local optima. From the definition, many sentences can be mapped to a concept vector in both sides, which increases ambiguity and their average distances as well. If the average is relatively larger than cross-entropy, distance-cost dominates the parameter updates. If this phenomenon is maintained near optimal, the converged model will be far from the true optimal. Pros of this mapping is restricting generation of undesirable sentences using many variables and potential cons is the accuracy decrease by the conflict. To reduce the negative, we use one more linear combination layer for more flexible mapping, which will reduce average distance between the concepts.

$$\mathbf{v}_S = \mathbf{W}_e \mathbf{c}_S + \mathbf{b}_e \quad , \quad \mathbf{v}_T = \mathbf{c}_T \qquad (1)$$

The equalizing layer is composed of parameters $\mathbf{W}_e$ and $\mathbf{b}_e$ and the concept vector $\mathbf{v}_S$ is the output vector of the layer from the given raw concept vector $\mathbf{r}_S$.

Cost Function In sentence-level translation, underlying assumption is that the semantics of matching sentences are so equal that any distributed representation of two sentences in a vector space should be equal. In the assumption, reducing the distance of the concepts is a perfect goal for maintaining the same true optimal of NMT and therefore we can directly use it as a cost function. To use it, we set a cost function as following equation.

$$\text{new cost}(\theta, D) = \text{cost}(\theta, D) + ||\mathbf{v}_S - \mathbf{v}_T||_2 \qquad (2)$$

which uses Euclidean distance of the concept vectors as a penalty. θ is a parameter set to represent a model and D is a given training data set. This method adds cost and distance without any scaling factors because the equalizing layer implicitly adapts its scale in updates. In early stages of the updates, the layer gives large distance for all vectors by random initialization but the large distance dominates updates and makes NMTs rapidly converge to a model to generate small distance over all vectors. Then, the impact of cross-entropy increases and the model moves to the true optimal determined by the entropy. Therefore, if the optimal distance is sufficiently small, then this method will guide the training in early updates and preserve the true optimal with respect to cross entropy with restriction of generating negative sentences.

3 Experiment Setting

We performed translation experiments from English to French to evaluate the impact of concept equalization in a state-of-the-art NMT.

3.1 Data Preparation

We used WMT14 Europarl parallel corpus for training [1] and applied tokenizing, lowercasing, and limiting token numbers by 40 in a sentence through using scripts provided by a machine translation package, MOSES (Koehn et al., 2007) [2]. Starting and ending symbol are attached to each source sentence. Test set is the first 10,000 sentences of the news-commentary set released with the Europarl corpus. Data statistics are shown in Table 1. We extracted word vectors from the training set using a neural network language model implemented in word2vec [3] for English and French. Extracted word vector dictionaries are imported in training phases.

---

[1] http://www.statmt.org/wmt14/
[2] http://www.statmt.org/moses/
[3] https://code.google.com/archive/p/word2vec/

Table 1: Data Statistics

	training		test	
	En	Fr	En	Fr
tokens	30.7M	34.2M	0.2M	0.2M
sentences	1.5M		10,000	

3.2 Neural Network Structure

Because of the lack of space, we drop full mathematical description of our model. We built bidirection model and passed the **h** and **c** from the forward to backward pass of the encoder. Then the $\mathbf{h}_t$ of forward and $\mathbf{h}_{|S|-t}$ are concatenated to derive $\mathbf{r}_s$. Attention model is equal to (Bahdanau et al., 2014) except additionally passing **c** for initialization of the decoder. The input word vectors are fed on to the second shallowest LSTM stack of the encoder. To boost converging speed, we applied batch normalization through weighted average of original and normalized vectors. The weight is decayed by multiplying 0.8 at each epoch, which becomes almost 0 after 16 epochs. The concept equalization is only applied to the training phase. Sample phase is equal to typical NMTs.

Table 2: Detailed Model and Run Settings

LSTM stacks	4	parameter	
cells per stacks	250	encoder	3.05M
dim. of word	50	decoder	3.10M
dim. of attention	250	output	11M
dim. of equalizer	50	interface	0.19M
batch size	128	epochs	50

4 Results and Discussions

We evaluated BLEU and NIST (Papineni et al., 2002; Doddington, 2002) score as shown in Table 3. In the table, we can confirm that applying

Table 3: Translation Quality of NMT with and without Applying Concept Equalization

	equalized NMT		NMT	
epoch	NIST	BLEU	NIST	BLEU
11	5.7682	22.78	5.3333	20.89
14	6.2776	25.48	5.6247	21.70
17	6.2786	25.31	5.9214	23.98
30	6.5775	26.68	5.9941	23.86
38	6.6466	27.08	6.0282	24.08

concept equalization improves translation quality by 3 BLEU and 0.6186 NIST after 38 epochs

compared to a typical state-of-the-art NMT. The baseline BLEU is 24.08 similar to or smaller than the results of (Bahdanau et al., 2014), but the used training sentences are 8 million in the paper while we used 1.5 million, which may be the reason of the baseline gape.

Fig. 2 shows the training accuracy change by epochs. The accuracy is the portion of correctly selected words in the training set through applying argmax to probability vectors generated by the decoder. Applying the concept equalization shows faster convergence before 5 epochs, but converges to lower optimal points after 50 epochs compared to the normal NMT. From this result,

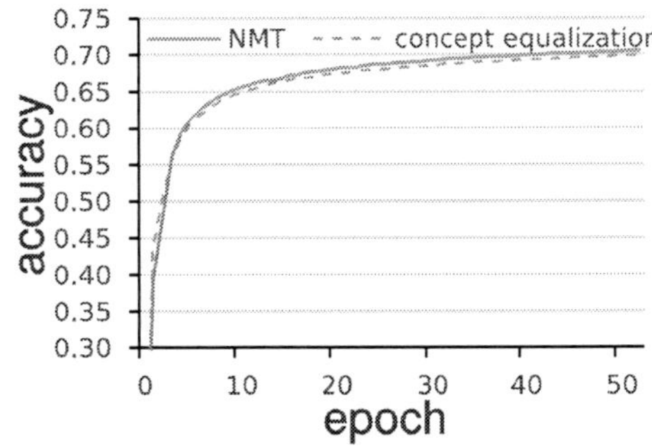

Figure 2: Training Accuracy by Epoch (accuracy: correctly selected token rate in training)

we can confirm the equalization boost the speed of convergence, but the conflict limits the accuracy near optimals. This is consistent behavior to the properties of the method. A notable point is that the translation quality is significantly improved. We guess the cause is the different underlying assumptions in decoding. In the case of training accuracy, the decoder assumes receiving correct input at every time step while it uses previously selected word in actual decoding. Therefore, in actual decoding to generate translation for the test set, a selected wrong word in an intermediate step may cause subsequent errors by strange context generation. Overall, the two results imply that the equalization guides the model to be robust to the unseen errors by restricting generation of strange sequences without any regularization techniques as randomized distortions on some parts of models.

5 Conclusion

In this paper, we raised the issue of limit in learning correct target word composition of current

NMTs. To resolve it, we introduced concept equalization to learn direct mapping of source and target sentences for guiding the NMT training. In the result, translation quality is significantly improved and training speed becomes slightly faster in early epochs. This method is expected to effectively discard wrong target composition from the observations.

6 Future Work

We will generalize this work for various direct mapping models and wider empirical tasks. Impact of concept equalization to cost landscape in parameter optimization will be more rigorously analyzed.

Acknowledgement

This work was partly supported by Institute for Information & communications Technology Promotion(IITP) grant funded by the Korea government(MSIT) (R7119-16-1001, Core technology development of the real-time simultaneous speech translation based on knowledge enhancement) and the MSIT(Ministry of Science and ICT), Korea, under the ITRC(Information Technology Research Center) support program(IITP-2017-2016-0-00465) supervised by the IITP(Institute for Information & communications Technology Promotion).

References

Sarath Chandar AP, Stanislas Lauly, Hugo Larochelle, Mitesh Khapra, Balaraman Ravindran, Vikas C Raykar, and Amrita Saha. 2014. An autoencoder approach to learning bilingual word representations. In *Advances in Neural Information Processing Systems*, pages 1853–1861.

Dzmitry Bahdanau, Kyunghyun Cho, and Yoshua Bengio. 2014. Neural machine translation by jointly learning to align and translate. *arXiv preprint arXiv:1409.0473*.

Yoshua Bengio, Patrice Simard, and Paolo Frasconi. 1994. Learning long-term dependencies with gradient descent is difficult. *IEEE transactions on neural networks*, 5(2):157–166.

George Doddington. 2002. Automatic evaluation of machine translation quality using n-gram co-occurrence statistics. In *Proceedings of the second international conference on Human Language Technology Research*, pages 138–145. Morgan Kaufmann Publishers Incorporation.

Sepp Hochreiter and Jürgen Schmidhuber. 1997. Long short-term memory. *Neural computation*, 9(8):1735–1780.

Sergey Ioffe and Christian Szegedy. 2015. Batch normalization: Accelerating deep network training by reducing internal covariate shift. In *International Conference on Machine Learning*, pages 448–456.

Nal Kalchbrenner, Ivo Danihelka, and Alex Graves. 2015. Grid long short-term memory. *arXiv preprint arXiv:1507.01526*.

Philipp Koehn, Hieu Hoang, Alexandra Birch, Chris Callison-Burch, Marcello Federico, Nicola Bertoldi, Brooke Cowan, Wade Shen, Christine Moran, Richard Zens, et al. 2007. Moses: Open source toolkit for statistical machine translation. In *Proceedings of the 45th Annual Meeting of the ACL on Interactive Poster and Demonstration Sessions*, pages 177–180. Association for Computational Linguistics.

Minh-Thang Luong, Hieu Pham, and Christopher D Manning. 2015a. Effective approaches to attention-based neural machine translation. *arXiv preprint arXiv:1508.04025*.

Minh-Thang Luong, Ilya Sutskever, Quoc V Le, Oriol Vinyals, and Wojciech Zaremba. 2014. Addressing the rare word problem in neural machine translation. *arXiv preprint arXiv:1410.8206*.

Thang Luong, Hieu Pham, and Christopher D Manning. 2015b. Bilingual word representations with monolingual quality in mind. In *VS@ HLT-NAACL*, pages 151–159.

Kishore Papineni, Salim Roukos, Todd Ward, and Wei-Jing Zhu. 2002. Bleu: a method for automatic evaluation of machine translation. In *Proceedings of the 40th annual meeting on association for computational linguistics*, pages 311–318. Association for Computational Linguistics.

Marc'Aurelio Ranzato, Sumit Chopra, Michael Auli, and Wojciech Zaremba. 2015. Sequence level training with recurrent neural networks. *arXiv preprint arXiv:1511.06732*.

Shiqi Shen, Yong Cheng, Zhongjun He, Wei He, Hua Wu, Maosong Sun, and Yang Liu. 2015. Minimum risk training for neural machine translation. *arXiv preprint arXiv:1512.02433*.

Ilya Sutskever, Oriol Vinyals, and Quoc V Le. 2014. Sequence to sequence learning with neural networks. In *Advances in neural information processing systems*, pages 3104–3112.

Shyam Upadhyay, Manaal Faruqui, Chris Dyer, and Dan Roth. 2016. Cross-lingual models of word embeddings: An empirical comparison. *arXiv preprint arXiv:1604.00425*.

Yonghui Wu, Mike Schuster, Zhifeng Chen, Quoc V Le, Mohammad Norouzi, Wolfgang Macherey, Maxim Krikun, Yuan Cao, Qin Gao, Klaus Macherey, et al. 2016. Google's neural machine translation system: Bridging the gap between human and machine translation. *arXiv preprint arXiv:1609.08144.*

PubMed 200k RCT:
a Dataset for Sequential Sentence Classification in Medical Abstracts

Franck Dernoncourt*
Adobe Research
dernonco@adobe.com

Ji Young Lee*
MIT
jjylee@mit.edu

Abstract

We present PubMed 200k RCT[1], a new dataset based on PubMed for sequential sentence classification. The dataset consists of approximately 200,000 abstracts of randomized controlled trials, totaling 2.3 million sentences. Each sentence of each abstract is labeled with their role in the abstract using one of the following classes: background, objective, method, result, or conclusion. The purpose of releasing this dataset is twofold. First, the majority of datasets for sequential short-text classification (i.e., classification of short texts that appear in sequences) are small: we hope that releasing a new large dataset will help develop more accurate algorithms for this task. Second, from an application perspective, researchers need better tools to efficiently skim through the literature. Automatically classifying each sentence in an abstract would help researchers read abstracts more efficiently, especially in fields where abstracts may be long, such as the medical field.

1 Introduction

Short-text classification is an important task in many areas of natural language processing, such as sentiment analysis, question answering, or dialog management. For example, in a dialog management system, one might want to classify each utterance into dialog acts (Stolcke et al., 2000).

In the dataset we present in this paper, PubMed 200k RCT, each short text we consider is one sentence. We focus on classifying sentences in medical abstracts, and particularly in randomized controlled trials (RCTs), as they are commonly considered to be the best source of medical evidence (Tianjing Li, 2015). Since sentences in an abstract appear in a sequence, we call this task the *sequential sentence classification* task, in order to distinguish it from general text or sentence classification that does not have any context.

The number of RCTs published every year is steadily increasing, as Figure 1 illustrates. Over 1 million RCTs have been published so far and around half of them are in PubMed (Mavergames, 2013), which makes it challenging for medical investigators to pinpoint the information they are looking for. When researchers search for previous literature, e.g., to write systematic reviews, they often skim through abstracts in order to quickly check whether the papers match the criteria of interest. This process is easier when abstracts are *structured*, i.e., the text in an abstract is divided into semantic headings such as objective, method, result, and conclusion. However, over half of published RCT abstracts are *unstructured*, as shown in Figure 2, which makes it more difficult to quickly access the information of interest.

Consequently, classifying each sentence of an abstract to an appropriate heading can significantly reduce time to locate the desired information, as Figure 3 illustrates. Besides assisting humans, this task may also be useful for a variety of downstream applications such as automatic text summarization, information extraction, and information retrieval. In addition to the medical applications, we hope that the release of this dataset will help the development of algorithms for sequential sentence classification.

---

* These authors contributed equally to this work.
[1] The dataset is freely available at https://github.com/Franck-Dernoncourt/pubmed-rct

Proceedings of the The 8th International Joint Conference on Natural Language Processing, pages 308–313,
Taipei, Taiwan, November 27 – December 1, 2017 ©2017 AFNLP

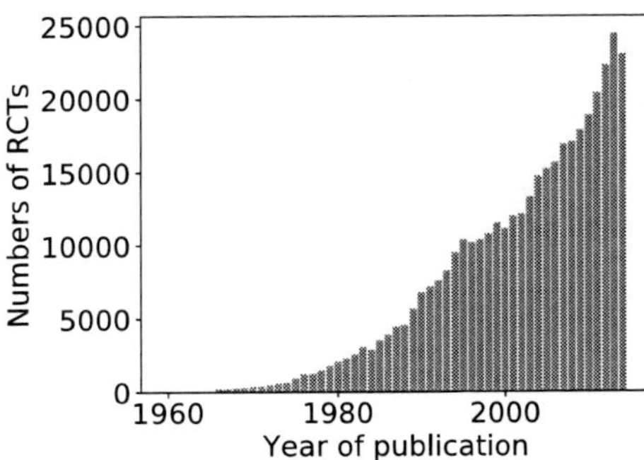

Figure 1: Number of RCTs present in PubMed published yearly between 1960 and 2014 (inclusive). The first documented controlled trial dates back 1747 (Dunn, 1997), but the scientific value of RCTs became widely recognized only by the late 20th century as the standard method for medical evidence (Meldrum, 2000).

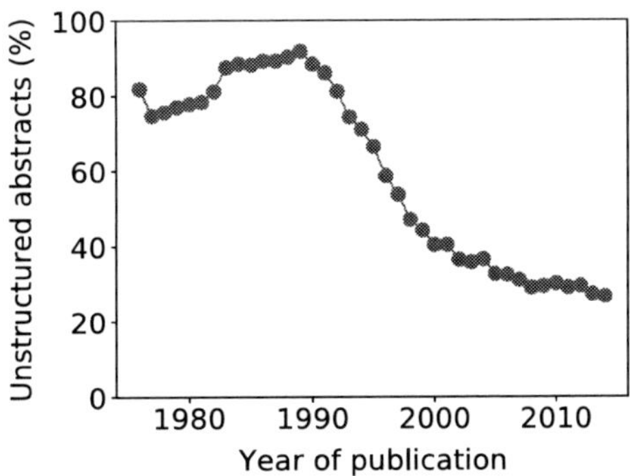

Figure 2: Evolution of the percentage of RCT abstracts present in PubMed that are unstructured between 1975 and 2014 (inclusive). The years before 1975 were omitted due to the low number of RCTs. Overall, approximately half of the RCT abstracts are unstructured. An RCT abstract is considered as unstructured if and only if at least one of its section is labeled as "None".

2 Related Work

Existing datasets for classifying sentences in medical abstracts are either small, not publicly available, or do not focus on RCTs. Table 1 presents an overview of existing datasets.

The most studied dataset to our knowledge is the NICTA-PIBOSO corpus published by Kim et al. (2011). This dataset was the basis of the ALTA 2012 Shared Task (Amini et al., 2012), in which 8 competing research teams participated.

Achilles tendinopathy (AT) is a common and difficult to treat musculoskeletal disorder. The purpose of this study is to examine whether 1 injection of platelet-rich plasma (PRP) would improve outcomes more effectively than placebo (saline) after 3 months when used to treat AT. A total of 24 male patients with chronic AT (median disease duration, 33 months) were randomized (1:1) to receive either a blinded injection of PRP (n = 12) or saline (n = 12). Patients were informed that they could drop out after 3 months if they were dissatisfied with the treatment. After 3 months, all patients were reassessed (no dropouts). No difference between the PRP and the saline group could be observed with regard to the primary outcome (VISA-A score: mean difference [MD], -1.3; 95% CI, -17.8 to 15.2; P = .868), Secondary outcomes were pain at rest (MD, 1.6; 95% CI, -0.5 to 3.7; P = .137), pain while walking (MD, 0.8; 95% CI, -1.8 to 3.3; P = .544), pain when tendon was squeezed (MD, 0.3; 95% CI, -0.2 to 0.9; P = .208). PRP injection did not result in an improved VISA-A score over a 3-month period compared with placebo. The conclusions are limited to the 3 months after treatment owing to the large dropout rate.

Figure 3: Example of abstract with the method section highlighted. Abstracts in the medical field can be long. This abstract was taken from (Krogh et al., 2016) and several sentences have been removed for the sake of conciseness. Providing clinical researchers and practitioners a tool that would allow them to highlight the section(s) that they are interested in would help them explore the literature more efficiently.

Only the dataset published in (Davis-Desmond and Mollá, 2012) is publicly available: two datasets can only be obtained via email inquiries, and the other datasets are not accessible (unanswered email requests or negative replies). The only public dataset is also the smallest one.

3 Dataset Construction

3.1 Abstract Selection

Our dataset is constructed upon the MEDLINE/PubMed Baseline Database published in 2016, which we will refer to as PubMed in this paper. PubMed can be accessed online by anyone, free of charge and without having to go through any registration. It contains 24,358,442 records. A record typically consists of metadata on one article, as well as the article's title and in many cases its abstract.

We use the following information from each PubMed record of an article to build our dataset: the PubMed ID (PMID), the abstract and its structure if available, and the Medical Subject Head-

Dataset	Size	Manual	RCT	Available
Hara et al. (2007)	200	y	y	email
Hirohata et al. (2008)	104k	n	n	no
Chung (2009)	327	y	y	no
Boudin et al. (2010)	29k	n	n	no
Kim et al. (2011)	1k	y	n	email
Huang et al. (2011)	23k	n	n	no
Robinson (2012)	1k	n	y	no
Zhao et al. (2012)	20k	y	n	no
Davis et al. (2012)	194	n	y	public
Huang et al. (2013)	20k	n	y	no
PubMed 200k RCT	196k	n	y	no

Table 1: Overview of existing datasets for sentence classification in medical abstracts. The size is expressed in terms of number of abstracts.

ings (MeSH) terms. MeSH is the NLM controlled vocabulary thesaurus used for indexing articles for PubMed.

We select abstracts from PubMed based on the two following criteria:

- the abstract must belong to an RCT. We rely on the article's MeSH terms only to select RCTs. Specifically, only the articles with the MeSH term D016449, which corresponds to an RCT, are included in our dataset. 399,254 abstracts fit this criterion.

- the abstract must be structured. In order to qualify as structured, it has to contain between 3 and 9 sections (inclusive), and it should not contain any section labeled as "None", "Unassigned", or "" (empty string). Only 0.5% of abstracts have fewer than 3 sections or more than 9 sections: we chose to discard these outliers. The label of each section was originally given by the authors of the articles, typically following the guidelines given by journals: as many labels exist, PubMed maps them into a smaller set of standardized labels: background, objective, methods, results, conclusions, "None", "Unassigned", or "" (empty string).

195,654 abstracts fit these two criteria, i.e., belong to RCTs and are structured.

3.2 Dataset Split

The dataset contains 195,654 abstracts and is randomly split into three sets: a validation set containing 2500 abstracts, a test set containing 2500

Dataset	$|V|$	Train	Validation	Test
PubMed 20k	68k	15k (180k)	2.5k (30k)	2.5k (30k)
PubMed 200k	331k	190k (2.2M)	2.5k (29k)	200 (29k)

Table 2: Dataset overview. $|V|$ denotes the vocabulary size. For the train, validation and test sets, we indicate the number of abstracts followed by the number of sentences in parentheses.

abstracts, and a training set containing the remaining 190,654 abstracts. Since 200k abstracts may be too many for some applications, we also provide a smaller dataset, PubMed 20k RCT, which contains 15000 abstracts for the training set, 2500 abstracts for the validation set, and 2500 abstracts for the test set. The 20k abstracts were chosen from the 200k abstracts by taking the most recently published ones. Table 2 presents the number of abstracts and sentences for both PubMed 20k RCT and PubMed 200k RCT, for each split of the data set.

3.3 Dataset Format

The dataset is provided as three text files: one for the training set, one for the validation set, and one for the test set. Each file has the same format: each line corresponds to either a PMID or a sentence with its capitalized label at the beginning. Each token is separated by a space. Listing 1 shows an excerpt from these files.

For each abstract, sentence and token boundaries are detected using the Stanford CoreNLP toolkit (Manning et al., 2014). We provide two versions of the dataset: one with the original text, and one where digits are replaced by the character @ (at sign).

```
###9813759
OBJECTIVE This study evaluated an   [...]
OBJECTIVE It was hypothesized that  [...]
METHODS Participants were @ men     [...]
METHODS Psychological functioning   [...]
RESULTS Intervention group subject  [...]
RESULTS Compared to the control     [...]
CONCLUSIONS This study has shown    [...]
```

Listing 1: Example of one abstract as formatted in the PubMed 200k RCT dataset set. The PMID of the corresponding article is 9813759; the article can be found that https://www.ncbi.nlm.nih.gov/pubmed/9813759.

4 Dataset Analysis

Figure 4 counts the number of sentences per label: the least common label (objective) is approximately four times less frequent than the most common label (results), which indicates that the dataset is not excessively unbalanced. Figure 5 shows the distribution of the number of tokens the sentence. Figure 6 shows the distribution of the number of sentences per abstract. Figures 4, 5 and 6 are based on PubMed 200k RCT.

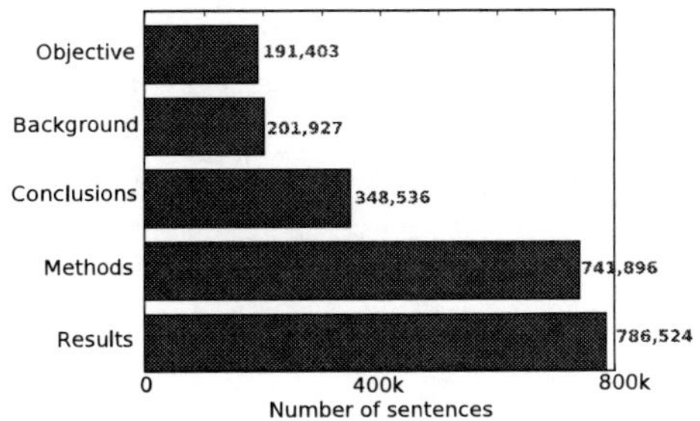

Figure 4: Number of sentences per label

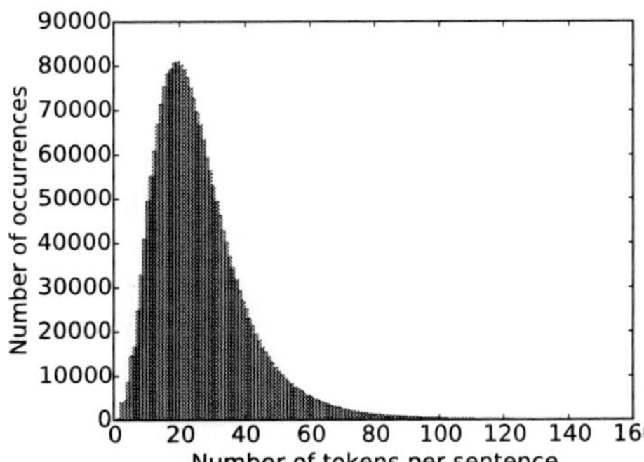

Figure 5: Distribution of the number of tokens the sentence. Minimum: 1; mean: 26.2; maximum: 338; variance: 227.6; skewness: 2.0; kurtosis: 8.7.

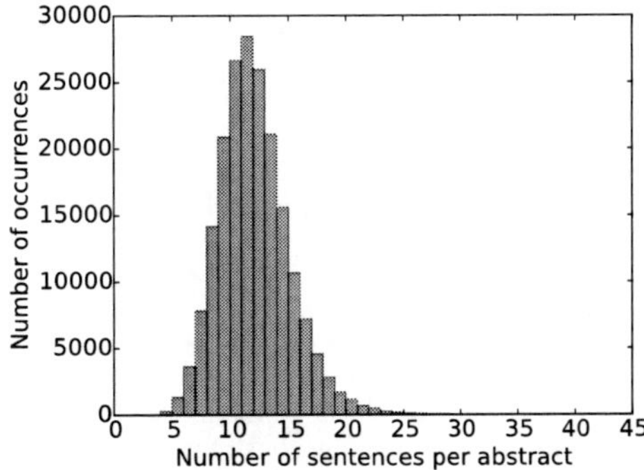

Figure 6: Distribution of the number of sentences per abstract. Minimum: 3; mean: 11.6; maximum: 51; variance: 9.5; skewness: 0.9; kurtosis: 2.6.

5 Performance Benchmarks

We report the performance of several systems to characterize our dataset. The first baseline is a classifier based on logistic regression (LR) using n-gram features extracted from the current sentence: it does not use any information from the surrounding sentences. This baseline was implemented with scikit-learn (Pedregosa et al., 2011).

The second baseline (Forward ANN) uses the artificial neural network (ANN) model presented in (Lee and Dernoncourt, 2016): it computes sentence embeddings for each sentence, then classifies the current sentence given a few preceding sentence embeddings as well as the current sentence embedding.

The third baseline is a conditional random field (CRF) that uses n-grams as features: each output variable of the CRF corresponds to a label for a sentence, and the sequence the CRF considers is the entire abstract. The CRF baseline therefore uses both preceding and succeeding sentences when classifying the current sentence. CRFs have been shown to give strong performances for sequential sentence classification (Amini et al., 2012). This baseline was implemented with CRFsuite (Okazaki, 2007).

The fourth baseline (bi-ANN) is an ANN consisting of three components: a token embedding layer (bi-LSTM), a sentence label prediction layer (bi-LSTM), and a label sequence optimization layer (CRF). The architecture is described in (Dernoncourt et al., 2016) and has been demonstrated to yield state-of-the-art results for sequential sentence classification.

Table 3 compares the four baselines. As expected, LR performs the worst, followed by the Forward ANN. The bi-ANN outperforms the CRF, but as the data set becomes larger the difference of performances diminishes.

Table 4 presents the precision, recall, F1-score and support for each class with the bi-ANN. Accurately classifying the background and objective classes is the most challenging. The confusion matrix in Table 5 shows that background sentences are often confused with objective sentences, and vice versa.

Table 6 gives more details on the LR baseline, and illustrates the impact of the choice of the n-gram size on the performance. By the same token, Table 7 shows the impact of the choice of the window size on the performance of the CRF.

Model	PubMed 20k	PubMed 200k
LR	83.1	85.9
Forward ANN	86.1	88.4
CRF	89.5	91.5
bi-ANN	**90.0**	**91.6**

Table 3: F1-scores on the test set of several baselines. The presented results for the ANN-based models are the F1-scores on the test set of the run with the highest F1-score on the validation set.

	Precision	Recall	F1-score	Support
Background	70.7	81.1	75.6	2663
Conclusions	94.6	93.7	94.2	4426
Methods	95.5	96.5	96.0	9751
Objective	77.1	65.3	70.7	2377
Results	95.6	94.8	95.2	10276
Total	91.7	91.6	91.6	29493

Table 4: Results for each class obtained by the bi-ANN model on the PubMed 200k RCT test set. The total support is 29493, i.e. the number of sentences in the test set.

	Backg.	Concl.	Methods	Obj.	Res.
Background	2760	12	62	424	5
Conclusions	41	4149	9	0	227
Methods	82	17	9409	31	212
Objective	757	0	69	1551	0
Results	14	208	303	5	9746

Table 5: Confusion matrix on the PubMed 200k RCT test set obtained with the bi-ANN model. Rows correspond to actual labels, and columns correspond to predicted labels. For example, 62 background sentences were predicted as method.

6 Conclusion

In this article we have presented PubMed 200k RCT, a dataset for sequential sentence classification. It is the largest such dataset that we are aware of. We have evaluated the performance of several baselines so that researchers may directly compare their algorithms against them without having to develop their own baselines. We hope that the release of this dataset will accelerate the development of algorithms for sequential sentence classification and increase the interest of the text mining community in the study of RCTs.

N-gram size	Precision	Recall	F1-score	Runtime
1	82.3	82.7	82.4	4406
2	85.1	85.4	85.2	13237
3	85.5	85.8	85.6	20618
4	85.7	86.0	85.8	25553
5	**85.8**	**86.1**	**85.9**	35006

Table 6: Results obtained on the PubMed 200k RCT test set by the LR model with different size of n-grams as features. The n-gram size indicates the size of the largest n-grams: For example, if the n-gram size is 3, it means unigrams, bigrams and trigrams are extracted as features. The maximum n-gram size in our experiments is 5 due to RAM limitation. The runtime is expressed in seconds and comprises both training and testing times.

Window size	Precision	Recall	F1-score	Runtime
1	90.6	90.6	90.6	1565
2	91.0	91.0	91.0	2490
3	91.1	91.1	91.1	3908
4	**91.5**	**91.5**	**91.5**	4867
5	90.9	91.0	90.9	6424
6	91.4	91.4	91.4	7649
7	91.3	91.3	91.3	7929
8	90.9	90.9	90.9	7644
9	91.2	91.3	91.2	7891

Table 7: Results obtained on the PubMed 200k RCT test set by the CRF model with different window sizes. A window of size k means that for each token, features are extracted from the current token, the k preceding tokens as well as the k succeeding tokens. The runtime is expressed in seconds and comprises both training and testing times.

References

Iman Amini, David Martinez, and Diego Molla. 2012. Overview of the ALTA 2012 Shared Task. In *Australasian Language Technology Association Workshop 2012*. volume 7, page 124.

Florian Boudin, Jian-Yun Nie, Joan C Bartlett, Roland Grad, Pierre Pluye, and Martin Dawes. 2010. Combining classifiers for robust PICO element detection. *BMC medical informatics and decision making* 10(1):29.

Grace Yuet-Chee Chung. 2009. Towards identifying intervention arms in randomized controlled trials: extracting coordinating constructions. *Journal of biomedical informatics* 42(5):790–800.

Patrick Davis-Desmond and Diego Mollá. 2012. Detection of evidence in clinical research papers. In

Proceedings of the Fifth Australasian Workshop on Health Informatics and Knowledge Management-Volume 129. Australian Computer Society, Inc., pages 13–20.

Franck Dernoncourt, Ji Young Lee, and Peter Szolovits. 2016. Neural networks for joint sentence classification in medical paper abstracts. *European Chapter of the Association for Computational Linguistics (EACL) 2017* .

Peter M Dunn. 1997. James lind (1716-94) of edinburgh and the treatment of scurvy. *Archives of Disease in Childhood-Fetal and Neonatal Edition* 76(1):F64–F65.

Kazuo Hara and Yuji Matsumoto. 2007. Extracting clinical trial design information from medline abstracts. *New Generation Computing* 25(3):263–275.

Kenji Hirohata, Naoaki Okazaki, Sophia Ananiadou, and Mitsuru Ishizuka. 2008. Identifying sections in scientific abstracts using conditional random fields. In *Proceedings of the Third International Joint Conference on Natural Language Processing: Volume-I*.

Ke-Chun Huang, I-Jen Chiang, Furen Xiao, Chun-Chih Liao, Charles Chih-Ho Liu, and Jau-Min Wong. 2013. Pico element detection in medical text without metadata: Are first sentences enough? *Journal of biomedical informatics* 46(5):940–946.

Ke-Chun Huang, Charles Chih-Ho Liu, Shung-Shiang Yang, Furen Xiao, Jau-Min Wong, Chun-Chih Liao, and I-Jen Chiang. 2011. Classification of pico elements by text features systematically extracted from pubmed abstracts. In *Granular Computing (GrC), 2011 IEEE International Conference on*. IEEE, pages 279–283.

Su Nam Kim, David Martinez, Lawrence Cavedon, and Lars Yencken. 2011. Automatic classification of sentences to support evidence based medicine. *BMC bioinformatics* 12(2):S5.

Thøger P Krogh, Torkell Ellingsen, Robin Christensen, Pia Jensen, and Ulrich Fredberg. 2016. Ultrasound-guided injection therapy of achilles tendinopathy with platelet-rich plasma or saline a randomized, blinded, placebo-controlled trial. *The American journal of sports medicine* .

Ji Young Lee and Franck Dernoncourt. 2016. Sequential short-text classification with recurrent and convolutional neural networks. In *Human Language Technologies 2016: The Conference of the North American Chapter of the Association for Computational Linguistics, NAACL HLT* .

Christopher D. Manning, Mihai Surdeanu, John Bauer, Jenny Finkel, Steven J. Bethard, and David McClosky. 2014. The Stanford CoreNLP natural language processing toolkit. In *Association for Computational Linguistics (ACL) System Demonstrations*. pages 55–60.

Chris Mavergames. 2013. The future of knowledge: Cochranetech to 2020 (and beyond). 21st Cochrane Colloquium. http://mavergames.info/.

Marcia L Meldrum. 2000. A brief history of the randomized controlled trial: From oranges and lemons to the gold standard. *Hematology/oncology clinics of North America* 14(4):745–760.

Naoaki Okazaki. 2007. Crfsuite: a fast implementation of conditional random fields (CRFs). http://www.chokkan.org/software/crfsuite/.

Fabian Pedregosa, Gaël Varoquaux, Alexandre Gramfort, Vincent Michel, Bertrand Thirion, Olivier Grisel, Mathieu Blondel, Peter Prettenhofer, Ron Weiss, Vincent Dubourg, et al. 2011. Scikit-learn: Machine learning in python. *Journal of Machine Learning Research* 12(Oct):2825–2830.

David Alexander Robinson. 2012. Finding patient-oriented evidence in pubmed abstracts. *Athens: University of Georgia* .

Andreas Stolcke, Klaus Ries, Noah Coccaro, Elizabeth Shriberg, Rebecca Bates, Daniel Jurafsky, Paul Taylor, Rachel Martin, Carol Van Ess-Dykema, and Marie Meteer. 2000. Dialogue act modeling for automatic tagging and recognition of conversational speech. *Computational linguistics* 26(3):339–373.

Kay Dickersin Tianjing Li. 2015. Introduction to systematic review and meta-analysis. *Coursera* .

Jin Zhao, Praveen Bysani, and Min-Yen Kan. 2012. Exploiting classification correlations for the extraction of evidence-based practice information. In *AMIA*.

A Parallel Corpus of Python Functions and Documentation Strings for Automated Code Documentation and Code Generation

Antonio Valerio Miceli Barone and **Rico Sennrich**
School of Informatics, The University of Edinburgh
`amiceli@inf.ed.ac.uk`
`rico.sennrich@ed.ac.uk`

Abstract

Automated documentation of programming source code and automated code generation from natural language are challenging tasks of both practical and scientific interest. Progress in these areas has been limited by the low availability of parallel corpora of code and natural language descriptions, which tend to be small and constrained to specific domains.

In this work we introduce a large and diverse parallel corpus of a hundred thousands Python functions with their documentation strings ("docstrings") generated by scraping open source repositories on GitHub. We describe baseline results for the code documentation and code generation tasks obtained by neural machine translation. We also experiment with data augmentation techniques to further increase the amount of training data. We release our datasets and processing scripts in order to stimulate research in these areas.

1 Introduction

Joint processing of natural languages and programming languages is a research area concerned with tasks such as automated source code documentation, automated code generation from natural language descriptions and code search by natural language queries. These tasks are of great practical interest, since they could increase the productivity of programmers, and also of scientific interest due to their difficulty and the conjectured connections between natural language, computation and reasoning (Chomsky, 1956; Miller, 2003; Graves et al., 2014).

1.1 Existing corpora

Major breakthroughs have been recently achieved in machine translation and other hard natural language processing tasks by using neural networks, such as sequence-to-sequence transducers (Bahdanau et al., 2014). In order to properly generalize, neural networks need to be trained on large and diverse datasets.

These techniques have also been applied with some success to code documentation (Iyer et al., 2016) and code generation (Ling et al., 2016; Yin and Neubig, 2017), but these works trained and evaluated their models on datasets which are small or limited to restricted domains, in some cases single software projects.

Source code can be collected by scraping open source repositories from code hosting services such as GitHub[1] (Allamanis and Sutton, 2013; Bhoopchand et al., 2016), but the main difficulty is finding natural language annotations that document the code in sufficient detail.

Some existing corpora, such as the the DJANGO dataset and the Project Euler dataset (Oda et al., 2015) have been created by human annotators, who can produce high accuracy examples, but this annotation process is expensive and relatively slow, resulting in small (from a few hundreds to less than 20,000 examples) and homogeneous datasets. Other corpora have been assembled from user-generated descriptions matched to code fragments mined from public websites such as StackOverflow[2] (Allamanis et al., 2015b; Iyer et al., 2016) or IFTTT[3] (Quirk et al., 2015). These datasets can be large ($> 100,000$ examples) but often very noisy. Another approach is to target a very specific domain, namely trading card

---

[1] `github.com`
[2] `stackoverflow.com`
[3] `ifttt.com`

Proceedings of the The 8th International Joint Conference on Natural Language Processing, pages 314–319,
Taipei, Taiwan, November 27 – December 1, 2017 ©2017 AFNLP

games (Magic the Gathering and Hearthstone) (Ling et al., 2016), where code is very repetitive and contains a natural language description (the card text) that can be extracted using simple hand-coded rules. Like the human-annotated corpora, these corpora have high accuracy but are small and very domain-specific.

In practice the existing low-noise corpora seem to have drawbacks which cause them to be unusually easy. The published evaluation scores on these dataset are are surprisingly high even for baseline systems (Oda et al., 2015; Yin and Neubig, 2017), with BLEU scores more than twice those of machine translation between natural languages (Cettolo et al., 2016), a task that we would expect to be no more difficult than code documentation or code generation, especially given the much larger amount of available data.

The DJANGO and and Project Euler corpora use pseudo-code rather than true natural language as a code description, resulting in code fragments and descriptions being similar and easy to align. The Magic the Gathering and Hearthstone code fragments are repetitive, with most code of an example being either boilerplate or varying in a limited number of ways that correspond to specific keywords in the description. We conjecture that, as a consequence of these structural properties, these corpora don't fully represent the complexity of code documentation and code generation as typically done by human programmers, and may be thus of limited use in practical applications.

Therefore we identify the need for a more challenging corpus that better represents code and documentation as they occur in the wild.

1.2 Our proposal

In this work we seek to address these limitations by introducing a parallel corpus of over a hundred thousands diverse Python code fragments with descriptions written by their own programmers.

The Python programming language allows each source code object to contain a "docstring" (documentation string), which is retained at runtime as metadata. Programmers use docstrings to describe the functionality and interface of code objects, and sometimes also usage examples. Docstrings can be extracted by automatic tools to generate, for instance, HTML documentation or they can be accessed at runtime when running Python in interactive mode.

We propose the use of docstrings as natural language descriptions for code documentation and code generation tasks. As the main contribution of this work, we release **code-docstring-corpus**: a parallel corpus of Python function declarations, bodies and descriptions collected from publicly available open source repositories on GitHub.

Current approaches to sequence transduction work best on short and ideally independent fragments, while source code can have complex dependencies between functions and classes. Therefore we only extract top-level functions since they are usually small and relatively self-contained, thus we conjecture that they constitute meaningful units as individual training examples. However, in order to support research on project-level code documentation and code generation, we annotate each sample with metadata (repository owner, repository name, file name and line number), enabling users to reconstruct dependency graphs and exploit contextual information.

Class definitions and class methods are not included in our main corpus but will be released in an extended version of the corpus, which will also include the commit hash metadata for all the collected repositories.

We train and evaluate baseline neural machine translation systems for the code documentation and the code generation tasks. In order to support comparisons using different evaluation metrics, we also release the test and validation outputs of these systems.

We additionally release a corpus of Python functions without docstrings which we automatically annotated with synthetic docstrings created by our code documentation system. The corpora, extraction scripts and baseline system configurations are available online at `https://github.com/EdinburghNLP/code-docstring-corpus`.

2 Dataset

2.1 Extraction and preparation

We used the GitHub scraper[4] by Bhoopchand et al. (2016) with default settings to download source code from repositories on GitHub, retaining Python 2.7 code.

We split each top-level function in a declaration (decorators, name and parameters), a docstring (if

---

[4] `https://github.com/uclmr/pycodesuggest`

Dataset	Examples	Tokens	LoCs
Parallel decl.	150,370	556,461	167,344
Parallel bodies	150,370	12,601,929	1,680,176
Parallel docstrings	150,370	5,789,741	-
Code-only decl.	161,630	538,303	183,935
Code-only bodies	161,630	13,009,544	1,696,594

Table 1: Number of examples, tokens and lines of code in the corpora.

Corpus	Element	Mean	Std.	Median
Parallel	Declarations	3.70	7.62	3
Parallel	Bodies	83.81	254.47	40
Parallel	Docstrings	38.50	71.87	16
Code-only	Declarations	3.33	5.04	2
Code-only	Bodies	80.49	332.75	37

Table 2: Tokens per example statistics.

present) and the rest of the function body. If the docstring is present, the function is included in the main parallel corpus, otherwise it is included in the "monolingual" code-only corpus for which we later generate synthetic docstrings.

We further process the the data by removing the comments, normalizing the code syntax by parsing and unparsing, removing semantically irrelevant spaces and newlines and escaping the rest and removing empty or non-alphanumeric lines from the docstrings. Preprocessing removes empty lines and decorative elements from the docstrings but it is functionally reversible on the code[5].

An example of an extracted function based on scikit-learn (Pedregosa et al., 2011) (with docstring shortened for brevity) is provided in fig. 1.

2.2 Dataset description

The extraction process resulted in a main parallel corpus of 150,370 triples of function declarations, docstrings and bodies.

We partition the main parallel corpus in a training/validation/test split, consisting of 109,108 training examples, 2,000 validation examples and 2,000 test examples (the total size is smaller than the full corpus due to duplicate example removal).

The code-only corpus consists of 161,630 pairs of function declarations and bodies. The synthetic docstring corpus consists of docstrings generated using from the code-only corpus using our NMT code documentation model, described in the next section.

We report corpora summary statistics in tables 1 and 2.

---

[5]except in the rare cases where the code accesses its own docstring or source code string

3 Baseline results

Since we are releasing a novel dataset, it is useful to assess its difficulty by providing baseline results for other researchers to compare to and hopefully improve upon.

3.1 Setup

In order to obtain these baseline results, we train Neural Machine Translation (NMT) models in both direction using Nematus[6] (Sennrich et al., 2017). Our objective here is not to compete with syntax-aware techniques such as Yin and Neubig (2017) but to assess a lower bound on the task performance on this dataset without using knowledge of the structure of the programming language.

We prepare our datasets considering the function declarations as part of the input for both the documentation and generation tasks. In order to reduce data sparsity, we sub-tokenize with the Moses (Koehn et al., 2007) tokenization script (which splits some source code identifiers that contain punctuation) followed by Byte-Pair Encoding (BPE) (Sennrich et al., 2016b). BPE sub-tokenization has been shown to be effective for natural language processing, and for code processing it can be considered a data-driven alternative to the heuristic identifier sub-tokenization of Allamanis et al. (2015a). We train our models with the Adam optimizer (Kingma and Ba, 2015) with learning rate 10^{-4}, batch size 20. We use a vocabulary size of 89500 tokens and we cap training sequence length to 300 tokens for both the source side and the target side. We apply "Bayesian" recurrent dropout (Gal and Ghahramani, 2016) with drop probability 0.2 and word drop probability 0.1. We perform early stopping by computing the likelihood every 10000 on the validation set and terminating when no improvement is made for more than 10 times. For the code documentation task, we use word embedding size 500, state size 500 and no backpropagation-through-time gradient truncation. For the code generation task, we use word embedding size 400, state size 800 and BPTT gradient truncation at 200 steps. These differences are motivated by GPU memory considerations.

After training the code documentation model, we apply it to the corpus-only datasets to generate synthetic docstrings. We then combine this

---

[6]https://github.com/EdinburghNLP/
nematus

```
def _intercept_dot (w, X, y):
    """Computes y * np.dot(X, w).
    It takes into consideration if the intercept should be fit or not.
    Parameters
    ----------
    w : ndarray, ndarray, shape (n_features,) or (n_features + 1,)
        Coefficient vector.
    [...]
    """
    c = 0.
    if w.size == X.shape[1] + 1:
        c = w[-1]
        w = w[:-1]
    z = safe_sparse_dot(X, w) + c
    yz = y * z
    return w, c, yz
```

```
def _intercept_dot (w, X, y):
```

```
'Computes y * np.dot(X, w). DCNL It takes into consideration if the intercept should
    be fit or not. DCNL Parameters DCNL w : ndarray, shape (n_features,) or (
    n_features + 1,) DCNL Coefficient vector. DCNL [...]'
```

```
DCSP c = 0.0 DCNL DCSP if (w.size == (X.shape[1] + 1)): DCNL DCSP  DCSP c = w[(-1)]
    DCNL DCSP  DCSP w = w[:(-1)] DCNL DCSP z = (safe_sparse_dot(X, w) + c) DCNL
    DCSP yz = (y * z) DCNL DCSP return (w, c, yz)
```

```
github/scikit-learn/scikit-learn/sklearn/linear_model/logistic.py 39
```

Figure 1: A Python function with its extracted declaration, docstring, body and repository metadata.

System	BLEU	
	valid.	test
Code-to-docstring	14.03	13.84
Docstring-to-code (base)	10.32	10.24
Docstring-to-code (backtransl.)	10.85	10.90

Table 3: Code documentation and code generation accuracy (`multi-bleu.perl`).

semi-synthetic corpus to the main parallel corpus to train another code generation model, with the same hyperparameters as above, according to the backtranslation approach of Sennrich et al. (2016a).

3.2 Results

We report BLEU scores for our models in table 3. Backtranslation provides a moderate improvement of $0.5 - 0.6$ BLEU points over the base model.

Both tasks on this dataset appear to be very challenging, in comparison with the previously published results in the $60 - 85$ BLEU range by Oda et al. (2015) and Yin and Neubig (2017) on other Python corpora (DJANGO and Hearthstone), which are unusually high compared to machine translation between natural languages, where reaching 40 BLEU points is challenging. While BLEU is only a shallow approximation of model accuracy, these large differences are suffi-

cient to demonstrate the challenging nature of our dataset compared to the existing datasets. We conjecture that this indicative of the strength of our dataset at representing the true complexity of the tasks.

4 Conclusions

We argue that the challenging nature of code documentation and code generation is not well represented by the existing corpora because of their drawbacks in terms of noise, size and structural properties.

We introduce a large and diverse parallel corpus of Python functions with their docstrings scraped from public repositories. We report baseline results on this dataset using Neural Machine Translation, noting that it is much more challenging than previously published corpora as evidenced by translation scores. We argue that our corpus better captures the complexity of code documentation and code generation as done by human programmers and may enable practical applications.

We believe that our contribution may stimulate research in this area by promoting the development of more advanced models that can fully tackle the complexity of these tasks. Such models could be, for instance, integrated into IDEs to provide documentation stubs given the code, code stubs given the documentation or context-aware autocomplete suggestions. As future work, we encourage the creation of similar corpora for other programming languages which support standardized code documentation, such as Java.

Finally, we hope that this research area eventually improves the understanding and possible replication of the human ability to reason about algorithms.

References

Miltiadis Allamanis, Earl T Barr, Christian Bird, and Charles Sutton. 2015a. Suggesting accurate method and class names. In *Proceedings of the 2015 10th Joint Meeting on Foundations of Software Engineering*, pages 38–49. ACM.

Miltos Allamanis and Charles Sutton. 2013. Mining source code repositories at massive scale using language modeling. In *Working Conference on Mining Software Repositories (MSR)*.

Miltos Allamanis, Daniel Tarlow, Andrew Gordon, and Yi Wei. 2015b. Bimodal modelling of source code and natural language. In *Proceedings of the 32nd International Conference on Machine Learning*, pages 2123–2132, Lille, France. PMLR.

Dzmitry Bahdanau, Kyunghyun Cho, and Yoshua Bengio. 2014. Neural machine translation by jointly learning to align and translate. *arXiv preprint arXiv:1409.0473*.

Avishkar Bhoopchand, Tim Rocktäschel, Earl Barr, and Sebastian Riedel. 2016. Learning python code suggestion with a sparse pointer network. *arXiv preprint arXiv:1611.08307*.

Mauro Cettolo, Jan Niehues, Sebastian Stüker, Luisa Bentivogli, and Marcello Federico. 2016. Report on the 13th IWSLT Evaluation Campaign. In *IWSLT 2016*, Seattle, USA.

Noam Chomsky. 1956. Three models for the description of language. *IRE Transactions on information theory*, 2(3):113–124.

Yarin Gal and Zoubin Ghahramani. 2016. A Theoretically Grounded Application of Dropout in Recurrent Neural Networks. In *Advances in Neural Information Processing Systems 29 (NIPS)*.

Alex Graves, Greg Wayne, and Ivo Danihelka. 2014. Neural turing machines. *arXiv preprint arXiv:1410.5401*.

Srinivasan Iyer, Ioannis Konstas, Alvin Cheung, and Luke Zettlemoyer. 2016. Summarizing source code using a neural attention model. In *Proceedings of the 54th Annual Meeting of the Association for Computational Linguistics*, pages 2073–2083.

Diederik P. Kingma and Jimmy Ba. 2015. Adam: A Method for Stochastic Optimization. In *The International Conference on Learning Representations*, San Diego, California, USA.

Philipp Koehn, Hieu Hoang, Alexandra Birch, Chris Callison-Burch, Marcello Federico, Nicola Bertoldi, Brooke Cowan, Wade Shen, Christine Moran, Richard Zens, et al. 2007. Moses: Open source toolkit for statistical machine translation. In *Proceedings of the 45th annual meeting of the ACL on interactive poster and demonstration sessions*, pages 177–180.

Wang Ling, Edward Grefenstette, Karl Moritz Hermann, Tomáš Kočiský, Andrew Senior, Fumin Wang, and Phil Blunsom. 2016. Latent predictor networks for code generation. *arXiv preprint arXiv:1603.06744*.

George A Miller. 2003. The cognitive revolution: a historical perspective. *Trends in cognitive sciences*, 7(3):141–144.

Yusuke Oda, Hiroyuki Fudaba, Graham Neubig, Hideaki Hata, Sakriani Sakti, Tomoki Toda, and Satoshi Nakamura. 2015. Learning to generate pseudo-code from source code using statistical machine translation (t). In *Automated Software Engineering (ASE), 2015 30th IEEE/ACM International Conference on*, pages 574–584. IEEE.

F. Pedregosa, G. Varoquaux, A. Gramfort, V. Michel, B. Thirion, O. Grisel, M. Blondel, P. Prettenhofer, R. Weiss, V. Dubourg, J. Vanderplas, A. Passos, D. Cournapeau, M. Brucher, M. Perrot, and E. Duchesnay. 2011. Scikit-learn: Machine learning in Python. *Journal of Machine Learning Research*, 12:2825–2830.

Chris Quirk, Raymond Mooney, and Michel Galley. 2015. Language to code: Learning semantic parsers for if-this-then-that recipes. In *Proceedings of the 53rd Annual Meeting of the Association for Computational Linguistics and the 7th International Joint Conference on Natural Language Processing*, pages 878–888, Beijing, China.

Rico Sennrich, Orhan Firat, Kyunghyun Cho, Alexandra Birch, Barry Haddow, Julian Hitschler, Marcin Junczys-Dowmunt, Samuel Läubli, Antonio Valerio Miceli Barone, Jozef Mokry, and Maria Nadejde. 2017. Nematus: a Toolkit for Neural Machine Translation. In *Proceedings of the Demonstrations at the 15th Conference of the European Chapter of the Association for Computational Linguistics*, Valencia, Spain.

Rico Sennrich, Barry Haddow, and Alexandra Birch. 2016a. Improving Neural Machine Translation Models with Monolingual Data. In *Proceedings of the 54th Annual Meeting of the Association for Computational Linguistics*, pages 86–96, Berlin, Germany.

Rico Sennrich, Barry Haddow, and Alexandra Birch. 2016b. Neural Machine Translation of Rare Words with Subword Units. In *Proceedings of the 54th Annual Meeting of the Association for Computational Linguistics*, pages 1715–1725, Berlin, Germany.

Pengcheng Yin and Graham Neubig. 2017. A syntactic neural model for general-purpose code generation. In *The 55th Annual Meeting of the Association for Computational Linguistics (ACL)*, Vancouver, Canada.

Building Large Chinese Corpus for Spoken Dialogue Research in Specific Domains

Changliang Li, Xiuying Wang
Institute of Automation, Chinese Academy of Sciences
{changliang.li,xiuying.wang}@ia.ac.cn

Abstract

Corpus is a valuable resource for information retrieval and data-driven natural language processing systems, especially for spoken dialogue research in specific domains. However, there is little non-English corpora, particular for ones in Chinese. Spoken by the nation with the largest population in the world, Chinese become increasingly prevalent and popular among millions of people worldwide. In this paper, we build a large-scale and high-quality Chinese corpus, called CSDC (Chinese Spoken Dialogue Corpus). It contains five domains and more than 140 thousand dialogues in all. Each sentence in this corpus is annotated with slot information additionally compared to other corpora. To our best knowledge, this is the largest Chinese spoken dialogue corpus, as well as the first one with slot information. With this corpus, we proposed a method and did a well-designed experiment. The indicative result is reported at last.

1 Introduction

Spoken dialogue system is regarded as the original form of the famous Turing test, as well as a long goal in artificial intelligence and natural language processing field. Though much progress has achieved, the research for spoken dialogue in specific domains faces many challenges, such as query understanding and the response generation and so on. Large-scale conversation corpus with rich annotation will offer great support to the research.

With the development of network and communication technology, there is a vast amount of data available documenting human communication. Much of them could be used, perhaps after some preprocessing, to train a dialogue system. English receives much more research attention than any other languages. In the last few decades, several English conversation corpora have been published, such as Carnegie Mellon Communicator Corpus (Bennett and Rudnicky,2002), Dialog State Tracking Challenge (DSTC) (Williams et al.,2013) and DIALOG mathematical proof dataset (Wolska et al., 2004). However, little research on other language discourse have been reported, which limits the growing research interest in these languages.

In this paper, we mainly focus on Chinese corpus creation for its wide range of use and its popularity. To overcome this problem, we build a large-scale corpus of spoken dialogue system, which consists of five domains and more than 140 thousand dialogues. To our best knowledge, it is the largest scale Chinese spoken dialogue corpus. Moreover, different to all other corpora including ones in English and any other languages, each sentence in our corpus is annotated with rich slot information. It is the first corpus annotated with this kind of information, which will play a major role in building spoken dialogue system.

The structure of the paper is as follows. Section 2 introduces some related works on spoken dialogue corpus. Section 3 lays out the process of corpus construction and the statistics about our corpus. Section 4 proposes a method combination

320

with the constructed corpus and presents the result. Section 5 gives the conclusions to end the paper.

2   Related word

In this section, we review some English corpus and some related efforts for building Chinese corpus. Since there are many English corpora, we just list some examples.

1)   Switchboard dataset (Godfrey et al.,1992)

One popular corpus is Switchboard dataset (Godfrey et al.,1992). It consists of approximately 2,500 dialogues over the phone from 500 speakers, along with word-by-word transcriptions. About 70 casual topics were provided, of which about 50 were frequently used. The corpus has been used for a wide variety of other tasks, including the modeling of dialogue acts such as 'statement', 'question', and 'agreement' (Stolcke et al., 2000).

2)   The Ritel corpus (Rosset and Petel, 2006)

It is a small dataset of 528 spoken questions and answers in a conversational format. The purpose of the project was to integrate spoken language dialogue systems with open domain information retrieval systems, with the end goal of allowing humans to ask general questions and iteratively refine their search. The questions in the corpus mostly revolve around politics and the economy, along with some conversations about arts and science-related topics.

3)   The DIALOG mathematical proof dataset (Wolska et al., 2004)

It is a Wizard-of-Oz dataset involving an automated tutoring system that attempts to advise students on proving mathematical theorems. The system is completed by using a hinting algorithm that provides clues when students come up with an incorrect answer. At only 66 dialogues, the dataset is tiny and consists of a conglomeration of text-based interactions with the system, as well as think-aloud audio and video footage recorded by the users as they interacted with the system.

Chinese corpus is few, and we list two relatively popular ones.

4)   CASIA-CASSIL(Zhou)

It is a large-scale corpus of Chinese casual telephone conversations in tourism domain. The source data is collected from a large number of spontaneous telephone recordings up to the present. After a strict selection, only a minority of dialogs remains, which are with good voice quality, enough turns and strictly belong to required domains.

5)   Lancaster Los Angeles Spoken Chinese Corpus (LLSCC)

It is a corpus of spoken Mandarin Chinese. The corpus is composed of 1,002,151 words of dialogues and monologs, both spontaneous and scripted, in 73,976 sentences and 49,670 utterance units (paragraphs). LLSCC has seven sub-corpora, Conversations: Telephone Calls Play & Movie Transcripts, TV Talk Show Transcripts: Debate Transcripts Oral Narratives and Edited Oral Narratives.

Both Chinese corpora cannot fulfill the demand for Chinese spoken dialogue system research. So we built a larger and richer corpus in this paper.

3   Corpus Creation

In this section, we describe the steps we took in the construction of our corpus. Figure 1 gives an overview of the main workflow of our corpus creation. We will illustrate the details in the following subsections.

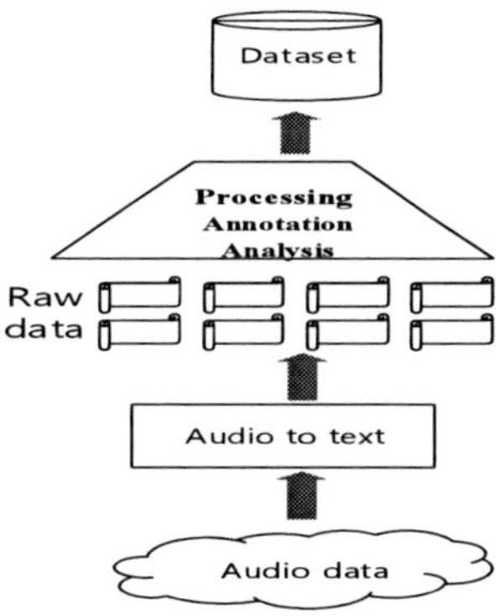

Figure 1 Overview of the main workflow of our corpus creation

3.1   Collection

The source of the corpus is very crucial to determine the quality of corpus. The dialogue data in a specific domain in real life is often combined with commercial secrets as well as with peoples' private information. For example, when a person books ticket through phone, he/she has to offer private information. So it is hard to obtain such data from a website or by some free methods. That is why there is a little corresponding corpus of dialogue in particular domains.

While collecting original data, we are assisted by volunteers, who offer the data from their real life for research purpose. The data consists of their audio data (phone recorders) while they call for some service, such as booking restaurant or hotel.

Since we have got the original data, we then employ speech recognition technology to transfer audio to text.

3.2 Data Processing and Annotation

Since we have the real data, we make two steps following. Firstly, for protecting the privacy right, we remove the private information. We used the encoded token to replace any information which may release private information such as name, phone number and so on.

Second, after analyzing the data, we find that there is much rough data, due to either the error of transferring audio to text or meaningless sentences caused by the bad habits of oral communication. Furthermore, many people are hired as expert assisted roles to select high-quality data and make the text more formal.

Slot information is required in specific domains. We manually extracted the slot as attachment information of dialogues. The slot number is limited in one specific area, for example in the domain of weather querying there are only two slots, time and location. Table 1 gives the example of the final version in booking hotel domain.

q: 您要什么房间，要几间？　　　{What type room will you book, and how many rooms do you want?} [0] [0] [0] [0] [0] [0]
a: 我想订三间总统套间。　　　{ I'd like to reserve three presidential suites } [0] [0] [0] [0] [0] [0]
q: 住几天您？　　　{ How long are you going to stay? }
[总统套间] [三] [0] [0] [0] [0]
a: 就住一天就行。　　　{ one day is ok}
[总统套间] [三] [0] [0] [0] [0]
q: 您贵姓啊？　　　{would you like to offer you name ,sir?}
[总统套间] [三] [0] [一天] [0] [0]
U: 我的称呼是吴佳。　{My name is wujia}
[总统套间] [三] [0] [一天] [0] [0]
M: 什么时候来？　　　{ When would you like to check in? }
[总统套间] [三] [0] [一天] [吴佳] [0]
U: 大概五月八号下午五点吧。　　{ At about five p.m. on May 8th }
[总统套间] [三] [0] [一天] [吴佳] [0]
M: 你给我您的电话。{ sir, please tell my your phone number }
[总统套间] [三] [五月八号下午五点] [一天] [吴佳] [0]
U: 联系号码是 012321322。　　　{it's 012321322 }
[总统套间] [三] [五月八号下午五点] [一天] [吴佳] [0]
M: 好的，吴佳，为您预订了五月八号下午五点总统套间三间。{ ok, sir, we reserve three presidential suites for you at five p.m. on May 8 }
[总统套间] [三] [五月八号下午五点] [一天] [吴佳] [012321322]

Table 1: dialogue example in booking hotel domain.

The content in braces is the corresponding English version for better understanding. The content in brackets is corresponding slots information. 0 means the slot is empty at present. In this example, the slots are room type, number of rooms, the data check in, stay time, customer name and phone number.

3.3 Analysis

As a result, we have got the final version corpus of 5 domains. The detailed statistics are summarized in this subsection.

Table 2 gives the slot distribution in each domain.

Domain	slot	num
Booking restaurant	Time/number of people/name	3
Booking hotel	Room type/number of rooms/time to check in/stay time/name/phone number	6
Weather query	Time/location	2
Ordering taxi	Destination/departure/name/phone number	5
Top up	Phone number/ Amount of money	2

Table 2: slot distribution in each domain

We can see that booking hotel domain has the most slots. Weather query and top up has only two slots.

Figure 2 gives the dialogue distribution in each domain.

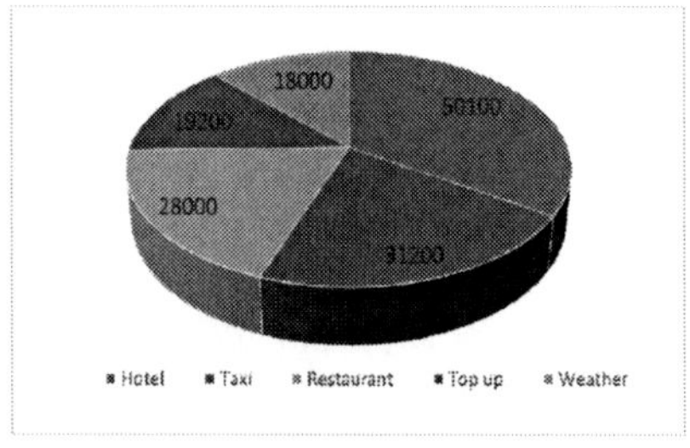

Figure 2: The dialogue distribution in each domain

From Figure 2, we know that booking hotel domain has the most dialogues, and weather query domain has the least dialogues. This distribution relates closely to the slot distribution.

Figure 3 gives the sentence length distribution of each domain.

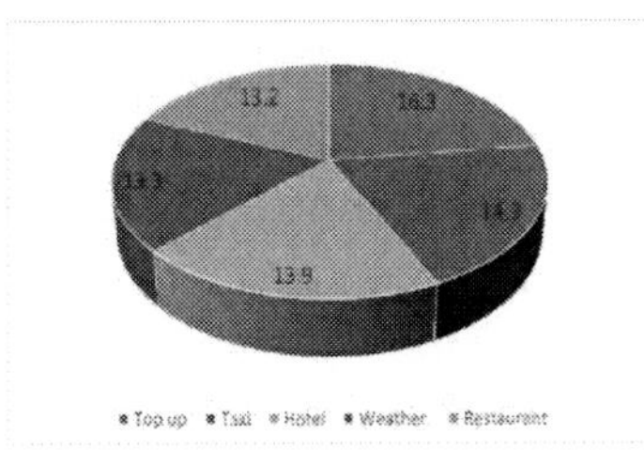

Figure 3: The sentence length distribution

From Figure 3, we know that the average length of sentences in each domain is similar.

Figure 4 gives the Dialogue turn distribution in each domain.

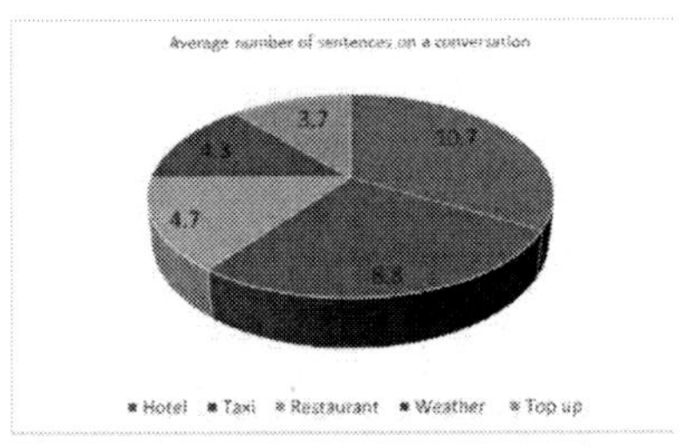

Figure 4: The Dialogue turn distribution

From Figure 4, we can see booking hotel and ordering taxi needs more turns to finish the dialogue. This distribution relates closely to the slot distribution. It is easy to understand that more slots, more turns required to obtain all information.

Figure 5 gives the word distribution in the sentences.

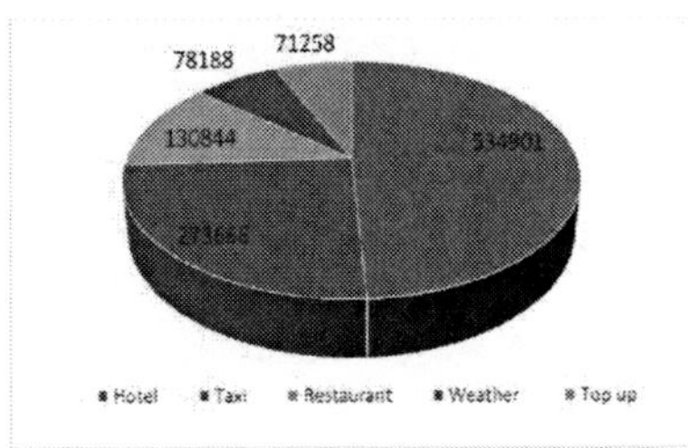

Figure 5: The word distribution in sentence

From Figure 5, we know that average length of sentences in each domain is similar.

From the statistics, we can see that the distribution of our corpus is relatively stable.

4 Method Based on the Corpus

Based on the corpus, we develop a model for spoken dialogue research in specific domains. The basic idea of the method is to introduce slot information in the corpus into the sequence-to-sequence framework.

After a query is given, the first slot is set as zero as there is no slot information at the beginning. Slot information is extracted at next turn, so the slot state is changed by fulfilling the corresponding information. The dialogue system works gradually like this and as a result, finish the dialogue when all the slot information received.

Evaluation metrics for dialogue is still an open problem. At present, the popular metric is the turns that the model needs to fulfill all the slots and finish the process. The experiment result shows that combination with the created corpus, it requires almost the same turn as used in real life. However, there are still many open problems worthy researching.

5 Conclusion

In this paper, we introduce a high-quality and large corpus for spoken dialogue research in specific domains. The corpus consists of five different domains and more than 140 thousand dialogues. All the data are created based on real life data. As our best knowledge, this is the largest Chinese spoken dialogue corpus, as well as the first one with rich slot information. We believe that the corpus will greatly support the spoken dialogue system research.

References

C. Bennett and A. I Rudnicky. 2002.The Carnegie Mellon communicator corpus.

J. Williams, A. Raux, D. Ramachandran, and A. Black. 2013. The dialog state tracking challenge. In Special

Interest Group on Discourse and Dialogue (SIGDI-AL).

M. Wolska, Q. B. Vo, D. Tsovaltzi, I. Kruijff-Korbayová, E. Karagjosova, H. Horacek, A. Fiedler, and C. 2004. Benzmüller. Anannotated corpus of tutorial dialogs on mathematical theorem proving. In The International Conference on LanguageResources and Evaluation (LREC).

Godfrey J J, Holliman E C, McDaniel J. 1992. SWITCHBOARD: Telephone speech corpus for research and development. Acoustics, Speech, and

Signal Processing, 1992. ICASSP-92., 1992 IEEE International Conference on. IEEE, 1992, 1: 517-520.

A. Stolcke, K. Ries, N. Coccaro, E. Shriberg, R. Bates, D. Jurafsky, P. Taylor, R. Martin, C. Van Ess-Dykema, and M. Meteer. 2000. Dialogue act modeling for automatic tagging and recognition of conversational speech. Computational linguistics(2000), 26(3):339–373.

S. Rosset and S. Petel. 2006. The ritel corpus-an annotated human-machine open-domain question answering spoken dialog corpus. In The International Conference on Language Resources and Evaluation (LREC).

Zhou K, Li A, Zong C. Dialogue-Act Analysis with a Conversational Telephone Speech Corpus Recorded in Real Scenarios.

Identifying Speakers and Listeners of Quoted Speech in Literary Works

Chak Yan Yeung and **John Lee**
Department of Linguistics and Translation
City University of Hong Kong
chak.yeung@my.cityu.edu.hk, jsylee@cityu.edu.hk

Abstract

We present the first study that evaluates both speaker and listener identification for direct speech in literary texts. Our approach consists of two steps: identification of speakers and listeners near the quotes, and dialogue chain segmentation. Evaluation results show that this approach outperforms a rule-based approach that is state-of-the-art on a corpus of literary texts.

1 Introduction

A literary work can be analysed in terms of its conversational network, often encoded as a graph whose nodes represent characters, and whose edges indicate dialogue interactions between characters. Such a network has been drawn for *Hamlet* (Moretti, 2011), Classical Greek tragedies (Rydberg-Cox, 2011), as well as a set of British novels (Elson et al., 2010).

To automatically construct these networks, it is necessary to identify the speakers and listeners of quoted speech. Past research on quote attribution has mostly focused on speaker identification (O'Keefe et al., 2012; He et al., 2013). In the only previous study that attempts both speaker and listener identification (Elson et al., 2010), there was no formal evaluation on the listeners. Listener identification can be expected to be challenging, since they are more often implicit.

This paper presents the first evaluation on both speaker and listener identification, with two main contributions. First, we present a new model that incorporates dialogue chain segmentation. We show that it outperforms a rule-based approach that is state-of-the-art on a corpus of literary texts. Second, training data from the same author, or even from the same literary genre, cannot be assumed in a realistic scenario. We investigate the amount of training data that is required for our statistical model to outperform the rule-based approach.

2 Previous Work

Among rule-based approaches on speaker identification, most rely on speech verbs to locate the speakers (Pouliquen et al., 2007; Glass and Bangay, 2007; Liang et al., 2010; Ruppenhofer et al., 2010).

For machine learning approaches, Elson and McKeown (2010) treated the task as classification, using features such as the distance between quotes and speakers, the presence of punctuation marks, etc. O'Keefe et al. (2012) reformulated the task as a sequence labelling task. In the news domain, their statistical model outperformed a rule-basd approach; in the literary domain, however, the rule-based approach achieved the best performance. This rule-based approach will be compared with our proposed approach in our experiments. Similar to our approach, He et al. (2013) parsed the sentences near the quotation. Their method, however, includes a manual preprocessing step that extracts all name mentions in the text and clusters them into character aliases, and so cannot be directly compared with our approach, which does not require preprocessing and thus can be more easily applied to larger datasets.

3 Approach

Our task is to identify the speakers and listeners of the quotes in a text. We count the system output as correct if it identifies the specific text spans that indicate the speakers and listeners of the quote. When the text only implicitly identifies the speakers and listeners, the mentions of these characters that are closest to the quote are considered the gold answer.

Proceedings of the The 8th International Joint Conference on Natural Language Processing, pages 325–329,
Taipei, Taiwan, November 27 – December 1, 2017 ©2017 AFNLP

We use a simple rule-based method to extract all direct quotes. We then perform quote attribution in a two-step process: speaker and listener identification from context, and dialogue chain segmentation.

3.1 Speaker and listener identification from context

The system first identifies the speakers and listeners in the context around the quote. We extract two sentences before and two sentences after each quote for tagging, excluding the words within the quote. We adopt a sequence labelling approach, using a CRF model (Lafferty et al., 2001) to tag each word as one of 'speaker', 'listener', or 'neither'. For each word, we extract the following features:

Word identity: The word itself.

POS: The POS tag is useful, for example, in capturing the text spans that indicate possible entities.

Head: The head of the word, extracted from the dependency tree, can captue verbs that indicate direct speech.

Dependency relation: The grammatical relation between the word and its head. As shown by He et al. (2013), dependency relations of reported speech verbs are useful in extracting speakers, with 'nsubj' usually suggesting a speaker, and 'nmod' or 'dobj' favoring a listener.

Sentence distance: The location of the sentence in relation to the quote (-1, -2, +1, or +2).

Paragraph distance: The number of paragraphs that separate the word and the quote. This captures the observation that a new paragraph usually signifies a change of speaker and listener.

Matching word in quote: A binary feature of whether the word can be found within the quote. As pointed out by He et al. (2013), the speaker name is rarely found within the quote while the reverse is true for the listener.

Initial word and POS: The first word in the sentence and its POS tag are useful in capturing the pattern of "[speech verb] [speaker]" that is often found after a quote (e.g. "..." said Peter.).

3.2 Dialogue chain segmentation

In this step, we segment the quotes in a text into dialogue chains. Each quote can be a continuation of a dialogue, i.e., its speaker (listener) is the listener (speaker) of the preceding quote; otherwise, it is the beginning of a new chain. As shown in Table 1, we label each quote either as B(egin) or C(ontinue).

Sentence	Tag
(1) *A centurion came to him, asking for help: "..."*	B
(2) *Jesus said to him, "..."*	C
(3) *But the centurion replied, "..."*	C
(4) *When Jesus heard this he was amazed and said to those who followed him, "..."*	B

Table 1: Quotes (1) to (3) form a dialogue chain; (4) starts a new one.

Similar to the first step, we use a sequence labelling approach with a CRF model (Lafferty et al., 2001). The quotes in the whole document are seen as one single sequence. For each quote, we extract the following features:

Distance: The number of sentences separating the current quote from the preceding one. The closer the two quotes are, the more likely it is for them to be in the same dialogue chain.

Speaker/Listener identity: Within a dialogue chain, the speaker and listener of the nth quote are the same as those in the $(n + 2)^{\text{th}}$ quote; their identities are reversed, however, in the $(n + 1)^{\text{th}}$ quote. To capture these patterns, we include eight binary features that compare the predicted speakers and listeners of the current quote with those of the $(n \pm 1)^{\text{th}}$ quote and the $(n \pm 2)^{\text{th}}$ quotes.

Implicit: Two binary features — no extracted speakers and listeners — capture the observation that from the third quote in a dialogue chain, the speakers and listeners can sometimes be omitted.

Pronoun: Two binary features — the extracted speakers and listeners being pronouns — capture the observation that from the third quote in a dialogue chain, the speakers and listeners can be referred to as pronouns.

After tagging (Table 1), the system fills in any missing speakers and listeners. If two consecutive quotes belong to the same chain, the system will infer the speaker (listener) of one quote to be the listener (speaker) of the other.

4 Baselines

4.1 Speaker and listener identification

Distance baseline. We re-implemented the rule-based approach that was state-of-the-art for literary texts (O'Keefe et al., 2012), achieving the best performance on a re-annotated version of the Elson et al. (2010) dataset. We take as entities all pronouns and all words tagged as person and organization by the Stanford NER tagger (Finkel et al., 2005). We compiled a list of quotative verbs by retrieving the verbs closest to the quotes in the training set.[1]

Dependency baseline (Dep). We parsed the sentence that contains the quote, excluding the words within the quote and replacing the trailing comma, if any, with a full-stop. If a quotative verb is modified by a word with the dependency relation 'nsubj', that word is extracted as the speaker; if it is modified by a word with 'dobj' or 'nmod', that word is extracted as the listener.

4.2 Dialogue chain segmentation

Elson et al. (2010) used the distance between two quotes to determine whether they belong to the same chain. We use the same feature to train a CRF model for chain segmentation.

5 Data

We tested our approach on two datasets: the novel *Emma* and the *New Testament*.

The *Emma* set was taken from the corpus of 19th-century British novels compiled by Elson and McKeown (2010). Since the original annotations did not annotate listeners and did not indicate the text span of the speaker that is connected with the quotation, we performed re-annotation on the *Emma* portion of the corpus.[2] This dataset contains 737 quotes; 63% of the quotes belong to dialogue chains of length two or more. We performed a four-fold cross validation on this set since each fold cannot have too few dialogue chains for meaningful evaluation on chain segmentation.

The *New Testament* (NT) set contains a total of 1628 quotes[3]; 43% of the quotes belong to dialogue chains of length two or more. We divided the text into seven folds following a natural division of the books.

6 Experimental results

We used the Stanford parser (Manning et al., 2014) for POS tagging and dependency parsing, and CRF++ (Kudo, 2005) for training CRF models.

6.1 In-domain

As shown in Tables 2 and 3, for *Emma*, our approach achieved an average accuracy of 52.46/28.46 for speakers/listeners. For the NT, the average accuracies for speakers and listeners are 66.09 and 56.97.[4] For both datasets, our approach significantly outperformed[5] both baselines.

Dataset →	*Emma*		*NT*	
↓ Model	no seg	w/ seg	no seg	w/ seg
Distance	40.06	43.73	45.39	45.61
Dep	8.98	10.20	56.63	56.63
Proposed	42.11	**52.46**	66.05	**66.09**

Table 2: Speaker identification accuracy, before and after dialogue chain segmentation (Section 3.2).

Dataset →	*Emma*		*NT*	
↓ Model	no seg	w/ seg	no seg	w/ seg
Distance	6.95	13.62	24.91	26.92
Dep	5.31	6.53	25.29	29.83
Proposed	17.99	**28.46**	52.94	**56.97**

Table 3: Listener identification accuracy, before and after dialogue chain segmentation (Section 3.2).

As shown in Table 4, our dialogue chain segmentation achieved 89.8 precision and 78.3 recall for *Emma*, and 90.2 precision and 89.5 recall for the NT. It significantly improved[6] the F-measure over the distance baseline.

The segmentation step yielded a higher degree of improvement in accuracy for *Emma* than for the NT, due to differences in literary style. The system was often able to extract speakers and listeners in the NT from the context around the quote, and so did not benefit much from dialogue chain boundary. In novels such as *Emma*, however, the listeners were often not specified in the context around

---

[1]We require each verb to be attested at least two times in the training set.

[2]Two annotators re-annotate the first 100 quotes. The kappa was 0.89/0.83 for speakers/listeners. Most disagreements involved conversations with three or more characters, where the identity of the listener was often unclear. One of the annotators completed the rest of the re-annotation.

[3]Please see Lee and Yeung (2016) for details of this dataset. The paragraph distance feature was omitted since the corpus did not contain information on paragraphs.

[4]Among utterances with no speaker/listener, the system correctly output "no speaker" at 60% (out of 10) in Emma and 29% (out of 7) in NT, and correctly output "no listener" at 73% (out of 42) in Emma and 80% (out of 195) in NT.

[5]At $p \leq 0.001$ by McNemar's test for all cases.

[6]At $p \leq 0.001$ by McNemar's test.

Figure 1: Accuracy of the proposed approach and distance baseline on training sets of different sizes for *Emma* (left) and the *New Testament* (right).

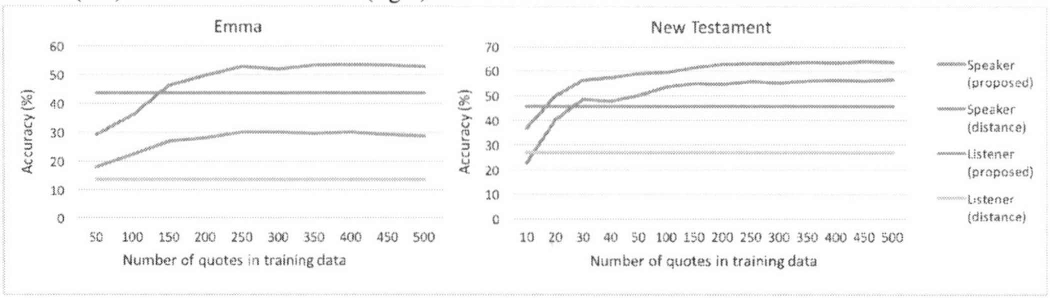

the quote and the speakers were sometimes omitted. This led to lower performance in the first identification step, which only considered the context around the quote, but greater improvement with the segmentation step.

Most errors involved speakers embedded within a long description, where the act of speaking was not explicitly stated. Consider "... and Harriet then came running... which Miss Woodhouse hoped very soon to compose.", which serves as the description of a quote. Harriet's role as the speaker was only implied and could not be captured by the system. Another source of error was the verb "hear", which reversed the usual pattern of the subject being the speakers and the object being the listeners. For example, in the sentence "They were only hearing, '...'", the system tagged the word "they" as the speaker instead of as the listener. Overall, listener identification is less accurate than speaker, because listeners were less often explicitly stated. It is particularly challenging in single-quote chains, where the preceding and following quotes cannot provide hints.

Dataset →	*Emma*	*NT*
↓ **Model**	P/R/F	P/R/F
Elson et al.	91.2/54.2/67.9	90.3/66.4/76.5
Proposed	**89.8/78.3/83.7**	**90.2/89.5/89.9**

Table 4: Precision/recall/F-measure for our dialogue chain segmentation (Section 3.2), and that of Elson et al. (2010).

6.2 Out-of-domain

One advantage of the distance-based baseline is lesser reliance on in-domain training data. Indeed, our statistical approach benefits from learning the names of the frequent speakers and listeners, as well as the speech-reporting style, from the same text. In practice, however, one may not assume the availability of a large amount of training data from the same text or author, or even from the same literary genre. We therefore re-investigate the performance of our approach when it has no access to the character names, and when it has mismatched, or limited in-domain training data.

Frequent speakers/listeners. To eliminate knowledge of the frequent speakers and listeners gained by our proposed model, we replaced all words tagged as entities with "PERSON". In this setting, the speaker and listener identification accuracy of our proposed approach decreased to 51.22/27.78 for *Emma* and 65.97/57.15 for the NT. These results, however, are still significantly better than both baselines.[7]

Limited training data. The accuracy dropped to below 25% for all cases with mismatched training data. When trained on the NT, the system failed to capture speakers that appear after the quote (e.g. "..." said her father.), a pattern common in *Emma* but rare in the NT. Inversely, when trained on *Emma*, the system could not recognize the frequent NT pattern "[speaker] said to [listener]".

As an alternative solution, we investigated how much in-domain data would be needed for our statistical model to outperform the distance-based baseline. As shown in Figure 1, relatively little annotation effort would be sufficient: our model significantly outperformed all baselines with a training set of 200 quotes for *Emma*, and a training set of 20 quotes for the NT.[8]

---

[7] p ≤ 0.001 by McNemar's test.
[8] p ≤ 0.001 by McNemar's test for all cases.

7 Conclusion

We have proposed a novel approach for quote attribution that incorporates dialogue chain segmentation. We report the first evaluation on listener identification. For speaker identification, we show that our approach outperforms the state-of-the-art rule-based approach for literary texts (O'Keefe et al., 2012). Further, we show that our results can be generalized to out-of-domain literary texts with a modest amount of training data annotation.

Acknowledgments

The authors gratefully acknowledge support from the CityU Internal Funds for ITF Projects (no. 9678104).

References

D. K. Elson, N. Dames, and K. R. McKeown. 2010. Extracting social networks from literary fiction. In *Proc. Association for Computational Linguistics (ACL)*.

David Elson and Kathleen McKeown. 2010. Automatic Attribution of Quoted Speech in Literary Narrative. In *Proc. AAAI*.

Jenny Rose Finkel, Trond Grenager, and Christopher Manning. 2005. Incorporating non-local information into information extraction systems by gibbs sampling. In *Proceedings of the 43rd annual meeting on association for computational linguistics*. Association for Computational Linguistics, pages 363–370.

Kevin Glass and Shaun Bangay. 2007. A Naive Salience-based Method for Speaker Identification in Fiction Books. In *Proc. 18th Annual Symposium of Pattern Recognition*.

Hua He, Denilson Barbosa, and Grzegorz Kondrak. 2013. Identification of Speakers in Novels. In *Proc. ACL*.

Taku Kudo. 2005. *CRF++: Yet Another CRF Toolkit*. http://taku910.github.io/crfpp/.

John Lafferty, Andrew McCallum, and Fernando Pereira. 2001. Conditional random fields: Probabilistic models for segmenting and labelling sequence data. In *Proc. International Conference on Machine Learning*.

John Lee and Chak Yan Yeung. 2016. An annotated corpus of direct speech. In *Proc. LREC*.

J. Liang, N. Dhillon, and K. Koperski. 2010. A large-scale system for annotating and querying quotations in news feeds. In *Proceedings of the 3rd International Semantic Search Workshop*. pages 1–5.

Christopher D. Manning, Mihai Surdeanu, John Bauer, Jenny Finkel, Steven J. Bethard, and David Mc-Closky. 2014. The Stanford CoreNLP Natural Language Processing Toolkit. In *Proc. ACL System Demonstrations*. pages 55–60.

F. Moretti. 2011. Network theory, plot analysis. *New Left Review* 68.

Tim O'Keefe, Silvia Pareti, James R. Curran, Irena Koprinska, and Matthew Honnibal. 2012. A Sequence Labelling Approach to Quote Attribution. In *Proc. EMNLP*.

B. Pouliquen, R. Steinberger, and C. Best. 2007. Automatic detection of quotations in multilingual news. In *Proc. Recent Advances in Natural Language Processing*. pages 487–492.

Josef Ruppenhofer, Caroline Sporleder, and Fabian Shirokov. 2010. Speaker Attribution in Cabinet Protocols. In *Proc. LREC*.

J. Rydberg-Cox. 2011. Social networks and the language of greek tragedy. *Journal of the Chicago Colloquium on Digital Humanities and Computer Science* 1(3).

Language-Independent Prediction of Psycholinguistic Properties of Words

Yo Ehara

y-ehara@aist.go.jp http://yoehara.com/
Artificial Intelligence Research Center (AIRC),
National Institute of Advanced Industrial Science and Technology (AIST)
2-4-7 Aomi, Koto-ku, Tokyo, Japan

Abstract

The psycholinguistic properties of words, namely, word familiarity, age of acquisition, concreteness, and imagery, have been reported to be effective for educational natural language-processing tasks. Previous studies on predicting the values of these properties rely on language-dependent features. This paper is the first to propose a practical language-independent method for predicting such values by using only a large raw corpus in a language. Through experiments, our method successfully predicted the values of these properties in two languages. The results for English were competitive with the reported accuracy achieved using features specific to English.

1 Introduction

The psycholinguistic properties of words, namely, word familiarity, age of acquisition, concreteness, and imagery, are measured real values of human responses in cognitive experiments in which participants are presented with the written or spoken form of words (Coltheart, 1981). They are not only important for psycholinguistics but for natural language processing (NLP) because they are effective features for educational applications such as lexical simplification (Jauhar and Specia, 2012). In spite of their importance, dictionaries describing them are rare and small. To enlarge these dictionaries, previous methods have been used to predict the values of these properties using supervision from a small dictionary and features from other language resources. The predicted values can be further used as features for other NLP tasks and provide excellent results (Mohler et al., 2014; Köper and Im Walde, 2016; Paetzold and Specia, 2016).

However, all previous studies relied on language-specific features; thus, their methods cannot be applied to other languages. When predicting the psycholinguistic properties, considering the word *domains* is quite effective. For example, "bread" and "onion" have high concreteness values of 622 and 632, respectively, while those of "economy" and "finance" are low, i.e., 284 and 371, respectively[1]. Evidently, capturing word domains, such as "food" and "economics", is effective for roughly predicting the range of values. To capture word domains, previous studies used combinations of semantic features, such as WordNet (Miller, 1995), and word frequencies from corpora in various domains. Since both are language-specific, previously proposed methods are language-dependent.

In this study, we propose a simple but practical language-independent method for predicting the psycholinguistic properties of words. It involves using only a large raw corpus of the target language. Our key idea is two-fold. First, instead of using the combination of semantic features and word frequencies, we first decompose the raw corpus by using latent Dirichlet allocation (LDA) and use the probability of words given each topic to capture the word domains. Second, we apply a multi-task Gaussian process regression (GPR), which enables the joint prediction of these properties. This captures the relations among the properties and can improve predictive accuracy. Our experimental results are competitive with those in which language-dependent features are used.

Our method is also useful with linear models for analyzing the obtained prediction models. The

---

[1]The values are taken from (Coltheart, 1981), which encodes all properties within fixed ranges. The larger values indicate the more concrete, or physical, what the word signifies is.

Proceedings of the The 8th International Joint Conference on Natural Language Processing, pages 330–336,
Taipei, Taiwan, November 27 – December 1, 2017 ©2017 AFNLP

weight of each topic indicates how well the obtained prediction models capture domains. This characteristic is useful for error analysis and further improving the prediction models.

2 Task Setting

2.1 Dataset

First, we briefly introduce the available psycholinguistic databases. The Machine Readable Dictionary (MRC) psycholinguistic database (Coltheart, 1981) is one of the largest for English and also used in psycholinguistic social studies (Schwartz et al., 2013). The 27 psycholinguistic properties of words in the database also contain easily obtainable lexical properties[2]. By excluding these properties, 4 of the 27 properties are considered important for NLP applications: familiarity, age of acquisition, concreteness, and imagery. Each property is available for a different set of vocabulary. Familiarity is the frequency with which a word is seen, heard, or used daily and available for 9,392 words. Age of acquisition is the age at which a word is learned and available for 3,503 words. Concreteness is the degree of how palpable the object to which the word refers is and available for 8,228 words. Imagery is the intensity with which a word arouses images and available for 9,240 words.

These properties are measured through questionnaires given to adult native speakers of the language. For Japanese, we can use a word familiarity and imagery database for Japanese (Amano and Kondo, 1998).

2.2 Formalization

Let T be the number of psycholinguistic properties, e.g., the MRC database has $T = 4$ properties. Let V be the set of all the vocabulary. We have supervision for some words in V. Let $S \subset V$ be the set of words with supervision. Then, we have training data $\mathcal{D} = \{(\mathbf{y}_v, \mathbf{x}_v)|v \in S\}$, in which $\mathbf{y}_v$ is a T-dimensional vector filled with the values of the T properties of word v, and $\mathbf{x}$ is a K-dimensional feature vector where K is the number of features. Then, the goal of the task is, given new word $v' \in V \setminus S$, to predict the vector of its properties, namely $\mathbf{y}_{v'}$.

For $\mathbf{x}$, the choice of features to use has been extensively studied for predicting familiarity. Tanaka-Ishii and Terada (2011) investigated the relation between corpus frequency and familiarity and found that high correlation can be achieved using the logarithm of frequencies of various corpora because each corpus is focused on different domains. Unlike their study, we have only one large raw corpus for each language.

3 Proposed Method

As mentioned above, the key idea of our method is two-fold. First, we use LDA (Blei et al., 2003) to calculate the $p(word|topic)$ probability from a large raw corpus. The number of topics K is a hyper-parameter of LDA. This probability can be regarded as (and used as) a substitute of word frequencies from various corpora. Although we have only one raw corpus, LDA enables us to use K probabilities. These enriched features enable us to effectively capture domains of words.

Second, we use multi-task GPR (Bonilla et al., 2008) with which we can predict $\mathbf{y}$ jointly. Previous studies built a predictor for each element of $\mathbf{y}$, i.e., each property, independently. Joint prediction can capture the relations among the psycholinguistic properties. This enables us to take the values of easy-to-predict properties into account when predicting the values of difficult-to-predict properties. Thus, joint prediction can boost predictive accuracy.

4 Experiments

We conducted experiments on English and Japanese. The proposed method requires only one large raw corpus for each language. Wikipedia (**Wiki**) can be used for this thanks to its availability in many languages. For comparison, we used general corpora, i.e., British National Corpus (**BNC**) by The BNC Consortium (2007) for English, and **BCCWJ** (Maekawa, 2007) for Japanese. In each language, we extracted the top 100,000 words in frequency on Wikipedia and ignored other words in the experiment using **gensim** [3]. For Japanese word segmentation and lemmatization, we used (Kudo, 2005).

We used the datasets described in §2 as the psycholinguistic database. For each property from the word set of these candidates, we chose words that

---

[2]The full list of the 27 properties can be found in `http://websites.psychology.uwa.edu.au/school/MRCDatabase/uwa_mrc.htm`

[3]`https://radimrehurek.com/gensim/wiki.html`

Model	Feature set	Familiarity		Age of Acquisition		Concreteness		Imagery	
-	-	ρ	r	ρ	r	ρ	r	ρ	r
FREQ(Wiki)		0.681	0.667	0.391	0.412	0.041	0.049	0.215	0.244
SVR-RBF	LDA(Wiki)	0.814	0.804	0.750	0.754	0.766	0.760	0.737	0.726
SVR-RBF	w2v(Wiki)	0.692	0.659	0.562	0.563	0.819	0.818	0.693	0.689
SVR-RBF	All	0.838	0.821	0.774	0.776	0.823	0.820	0.762	0.752
Ridge	LDA(Wiki)	0.836	0.820	0.763	0.759	0.773	0.766	0.741	0.722
Ridge	w2v(Wiki)	0.660	0.635	0.550	0.547	0.833	0.830	0.702	0.697
Ridge	All	0.849	0.823	0.770	0.772	**0.843**	**0.837**	0.767	0.757
GPR-RBF	LDA(Wiki)	0.829	0.820	0.766	0.764	0.777	0.771	0.747	0.735
GPR-RBF	w2v(Wiki)	0.683	0.653	0.557	0.555	0.827	0.826	0.692	0.687
GPR-RBF	All	0.845	0.829	0.781	0.782	0.819	0.818	0.769	0.759
JGPR-RBF	All	**0.854**	**0.838**	**0.793**	**0.789**	0.818	0.814	**0.772**	**0.762**
FREQ(BNC)		0.777	0.749	0.339	0.365	0.062	0.062	0.045	0.050
SVR-RBF	LDA(BNC)	0.860	0.840	0.754	0.767	0.610	0.602	0.648	0.646
SVR-RBF	w2v(BNC)	0.697	0.683	0.641	0.631	0.858	0.857	0.796	0.786
SVR-RBF	All	**0.874**	**0.860**	0.807	0.809	0.862	0.859	0.817	0.807
GPR-RBF	LDA(BNC)	0.855	0.836	0.757	0.770	0.601	0.589	0.648	0.646
GPR-RBF	w2v(BNC)	0.698	0.687	0.657	0.650	0.850	0.846	0.785	0.777
GPR-RBF	All	0.869	0.856	0.824	0.825	0.871	**0.866**	0.826	0.816
JGPR-RBF	All	0.867	0.852	**0.833**	**0.839**	**0.871**	0.865	**0.831**	**0.820**
(Paetzold and Specia, 2016)		0.863	0.846	0.871	0.862	0.876	0.869	0.835	0.823

Table 1: Prediction Results of English. Larger values imply better predictive accuracy.

completely matched the spelling of those that appear in the database and used these words as the vocabulary set. As a result, we obtained $|V| = 1,842$ words for the MRC database [4].

From the $1,842$ words, we took 500 for the test data. We used the other $1,342$ words for training and development, over which the parameters of methods are tuned using 5-fold cross validation.

We compared the following feature sets. **FREQ(corpus name)** is the log of word frequency in the *corpus name*, and **LDA(corpus name)** is the log of word probability given each topic calculated by applying LDA to *corpus name*. We used the **gensim** implementation and fixed the number of topics to 150 for both English and Japanese. For all 150 topics, we calculated $\log p(word|topic)$ and used all the 150 log-probabilities as features. **w2v(corpus name)** are word-embedding features obtained using the Word2Vec toolkit (Mikolov et al., 2013) trained on *corpus name*. We used the Word2Vec setting for

each property according to p. 438 of Paetzold and Specia (2016). **All** is the concatenated features of FREQ, LDA, and w2v.

We compared the following regression models[5]. Two are linear models: support vector regression (SVR) (Smola and Vapnik, 1997) with a linear kernel and Ridge regression (Tikhonov, 1963), denoted as **Ridge**, a linear regression with penalties (regularization) added to keep parameters from taking extreme values. They have a weight for each feature; thus, each feature's importance can be obtained from its weight. In contrast, methods using radial-basis function (RBF) kernels do not provide weight vectors, via which we cannot obtain each feature's importance. However, we used **SVR-RBF**, SVR with a radial-basis function (RBF) kernel, **GPR-RBF**, GPR with an RBF kernel, and **JGPR-RBF**, GPR with an RBF kernel and joint prediction (§3) since these models can take into account combinations of features using the RBF kernels, which are useful for combining

---

[4]The number of these target words was lower than that given in Paetzold and Specia (2016) because 1) we only used the words that had all four properties, and 2) many words that share the same spelling are doubly registered for verbs and nouns in the MRC database.

[5]The results of SVR with a linear kernel and Ridge in BNC were lower than the other models and were omitted from Table 1 due to space limitations. We used scikit-learn (http://scikit-learn.org/) to implement all models and will release them after acceptance.

both domain and semantic features.

4.1 Quantitative Results

For evaluation measures, as done by Paetzold and Specia (2016), we used Pearson's correlation coefficient (r) and Spearman's rank correlation coefficient (ρ) between the predicted and target properties of a word in the test set. Intuitively, the former shows accurateness in predicting the values of the target property, and the latter shows that of predicting the ranking of that property.

The experimental results are listed in Table 1. The bold values are the largest in each column in a section. When predicting familiarity and age of acquisition, we can see that **LDA** consistently outperformed **w2v**. This suggests that domains are more informative than semantic features for predicting these two properties. In contrast, when predicting concreteness and imagery, **w2v** performed better than **LDA** except when predicting imagery with **Wiki** features. This suggests that semantics is more important than domains for predicting these. This matches our intuition of psycholinguistic properties because familiarity and age of acquisition mainly reflect the difficulty of words, while concreteness and imagery have little to do with difficulty and more to do with the semantic aspects of words.

We can also see that **BNC** roughly performed better than **Wiki**. This shows that BNC, a general corpus, is better for predicting psycholinguistic properties than Wikipedia. One possible explanation for this phenomena could be that BNC is manually tuned to be general and to include typical usage of the language, while Wikipedia, a collection of user content, is noisy.

All performed consistently better than **LDA** and **w2v**. Thanks to joint prediction, **JGPR-RBF** performed better than **GPR-RBF** in almost all cases and performed the best out of the all models in most cases, especially when used for **Wiki**. This suggests that joint prediction is robust against the noise in Wikipedia. At the bottom of Table 1, we cite the results by Paetzold and Specia (2016)[6],

---

[6]Their results are not directly comparable to ours because their test set used in the experiments was not known; thus, different from ours. We are also interested in the difference of verbs and nouns with the same spelling. We also re-implemented and applied their bootstrapping method to our language-independent features. This re-implementation slightly (below 0.01) outperformed the Ridge regression, on which their method is based, but performed worse than **JGPR-RBF**.

Model	Feature set	Familiarity		Imagery	
-	-	ρ	r	ρ	r
FREQ(Wiki)		0.225	0.224	0.119	0.076
GPR-RBF	LDA(Wiki)	0.512	0.492	0.554	0.643
GPR-RBF	w2v(Wiki)	0.576	0.576	0.600	0.682
GPR-RBF	All	0.607	0.610	0.650	0.727
JGPR-RBF	All	**0.609**	**0.612**	**0.650**	**0.727**
FREQ(BCCWJ)		0.272	0.234	0.187	0.120
GPR-RBF	LDA(BCCWJ)	0.477	0.485	0.517	0.539
GPR-RBF	w2v(BCCWJ)	0.592	0.608	0.624	0.700
GPR-RBF	All	0.620	0.623	**0.662**	0.727
JGPR-RBF	All	**0.626**	**0.624**	0.659	**0.727**

Table 2: Prediction Results for Japanese

Weight	Top words	Interpretation
2.387	the, he, and, in, his, to, of, was, as, at	General topic
1.851	food, rice, restaurant, fruit, sugar, beer, milk, meat, tea	Food
0.919	john, st, william, sir, american, de, thomas, bishop, henry, charles	Peoplefs names

Table 3: Top 3 highly weighted topics

who used language-dependent features. Our results were competitive with theirs, although our method uses features obtained only from the raw corpus, i.e., language independent.

4.1.1 Prediction Results for Japanese

In Japanese, only familiarity and imagery are available (Amano and Kondo, 1998). The number of words whose familiarity and imagery were annotated was $2,475$. Among those, we used $2,030$ words for training and development. A disjoint set of 445 words were used for test.

For simplicity, we show the results of the best two models, **GPR-RBF** and **JGPR-RBF** in Table 2. We can first see that frequencies of Japanese corpora have lower correlation values with familiarity and imagery in Japanese compared with English. This implies that, overall, in this experimental setting, Japanese psycholinguistic properties were more difficult to predict than those of English. We discuss this reason in §5. Similar to English, **All** consistently performed the best in each corpus, and the general corpus (**BCCWJ**) performed better than Wikipedia. We can also see that **JGPR-RBF** outperformed **GPR-RBF** in almost all cases, presumably thanks to joint prediction.

4.2 Qualitative Results

Table 3 lists the top 3 topics highly weighted using **Ridge** with **LDA(Wiki)** in Table 1 and words in the topics when predicting word familiarity. The most weighted topics are called "general" topics and contain words that appear in most of the documents in the dataset. Since words that appear in every document tend to have high frequency, this result is also consistent with that by Tanaka-Ishii and Terada (2011), in which word familiarity roughly correlates with word frequencies.

The next weighted topics are those related to food and peoplefs names. This also matches our intuition of "familiarity" because we use these words in daily life, and they usually do not have negative connotations. In Table 3, stop words are omitted from these topics' top-word lists except for the general topic.

5 Discussion

Frequency is a good estimator for difficulty-related properties, namely familiarity and age of acquisition. Specifically, familiarity was previously reported to be one (Tanaka-Ishii and Terada, 2011). Since $p(word|topic)$ is the frequency of words in the topic except for the normalizing constant, it can naturally be a good estimator for the properties for which frequency is a good estimator. A corpus is a collection of documents in various domains, and the proportion of the domains of the collected documents varies corpus to corpus. By directly using $p(word|topic)$ as features, we can adjust the proportion of the domains of the given corpus to the proportion to which the target psycholinguistic property tends to correlate. Also, $p(word|topic)$ is practically easy to use: preparing 150 different corpora to use their frequencies is impractical, whereas preparing 150 different $p(word|topic)$ probabilities is easy.

Removing the stop words before applying LDA would be appropriate if we do not need to predict psycholinguistic properties for stop words. However, both English and Japanese psycholinguistic databases include the properties for words usually considered as stop words. Thus, we included these words when we ran LDA so that we could obtain p(word—topic) for stop words.

English and Japanese correlation values differ greatly. This difference may be explained by the difference in the original psychological experimental settings or the difference in writing systems for English and Japanese. We focused on predicting word properties when participants respond for written language. The Japanese writing system involves Chinese characters, in which many characters are ideographic. This may have resulted in the difference.

Our experimental results shown in Table 1 and Table 2 indicate the predictive performance of each model under a fixed training-data size. We also conducted experiments on smaller training-data sizes, for example, half the experiments in §4. Overall, the **JGPR-RBF** produced the best or competitive results when compared to other models for smaller sizes as well. For example, with half the training size, **JGPR-RBF** performed the best among the models listed in Table 1 for familiarity and age of acquisition and both types of correlation coefficients.

6 Conclusion

We proposed a language-independent method for predicting the psycholinguistic-property values of words. It involves using only a large raw corpus for a language. To predict these properties, capturing the word domains is important. We capture them with word probability given each topic obtained by applying LDA to the raw corpus. Jointly predicting multiple properties also leads to better prediction. Experiments showed that our method improves predictive performance by joint prediction and is competitive when language-dependent features are used. When used with linear models, our method provided interesting insights between word familiarity and daily life, which can be used for further error analysis.

Predicting psycholinguistic properties of words has broad application: other than lexical simplification, which we mainly focused on, as mentioned in §1, we can use word familiarity and age of acquisition as features indicating word difficulty. Such features are valuable for the vocabulary-prediction task in which learners' vocabulary knowledge is predicted (Ehara et al., 2010, 2012, 2013, 2016). We focused on lexical simplification as the direct application of predicting the pscyholinguistic properties of words. Future work includes leveraging confidence values that GPR can produce for graph-based weakly supervised learning, as in (Ehara et al., 2014).

Acknowledgments

This work was supported by JSPS KAKENHI Grant Number 15K16059.

References

Shigeaki Amano and Tadahisa Kondo. 1998. Estimation of mental lexicon size with word familiarity database. In *Proceedings of the 5th International Conference on Spoken Language Processing (ICSLP)*.

David M. Blei, Andrew Y. Ng, and Michael I. Jordan. 2003. Latent dirichlet allocation. *Journal of machine Learning research*, 3(Jan):993–1022.

Edwin V Bonilla, Kian M. Chai, and Christopher Williams. 2008. Multi-task gaussian process prediction. In *Advances in Neural Information Processing Systems 20 (NIPS)*, pages 153–160.

Max Coltheart. 1981. The mrc psycholinguistic database. *The Quarterly Journal of Experimental Psychology*, 33(4):497–505.

Yo Ehara, Yukino Baba, Masao Utiyama, and Eiichiro Sumita. 2016. Assessing translation ability through vocabulary ability assessment. In *Proceedings of the Twenty-Fifth International Joint Conference on Artificial Intelligence (IJCAI)*, pages 3712–3718.

Yo Ehara, Yusuke Miyao, Hidekazu Oiwa, Issei Sato, and Hiroshi Nakagawa. 2014. Formalizing word sampling for vocabulary prediction as graph-based active learning. In *Proceedings of the 2014 Conference on Empirical Methods in Natural Language Processing (EMNLP)*, pages 1374–1384, Doha, Qatar. Association for Computational Linguistics.

Yo Ehara, Issei Sato, Hidekazu Oiwa, and Hiroshi Nakagawa. 2012. Mining words in the minds of second language learners: learner-specific word difficulty. In *Proceedings of the 24th International Conference on Computational Linguistics (COLING 2012)*, Mumbai, India.

Yo Ehara, Nobuyuki Shimizu, Takashi Ninomiya, and Hiroshi Nakagawa. 2010. Personalized reading support for second-language web documents by collective intelligence. In *Proceedings of the 15th international conference on Intelligent user interfaces (IUI 2010)*, pages 51–60, Hong Kong, China. ACM.

Yo Ehara, Nobuyuki Shimizu, Takashi Ninomiya, and Hiroshi Nakagawa. 2013. Personalized reading support for second-language web documents. *ACM Transactions on Intelligent Systems and Technology*, 4(2).

Sujay K. Jauhar and Lucia Specia. 2012. Uow-shef: Simplex – lexical simplicity ranking based on contextual and psycholinguistic features. In **SEM 2012: The First Joint Conference on Lexical and Computational Semantics – Volume 1: Proceedings of the main conference and the shared task, and Volume 2: Proceedings of the Sixth International Workshop on Semantic Evaluation (SemEval 2012)*, pages 477–481.

Maximilian Köper and Sabine Schulte Im Walde. 2016. Automatically generated affective norms of abstractness, arousal, imageability and valence for 350 000 german lemmas. In *Proceedings of the 10th International Conference on Language Resources and Evaluation (LREC)*.

Taku Kudo. 2005. Mecab: Yet another part-of-speech and morphological analyzer. *http://mecab. sourceforge. net/*.

Kikuo Maekawa. 2007. Kotonoha and bccwj: development of a balanced corpus of contemporary written japanese. In *Corpora and Language Research: Proceedings of the First International Conference on Korean Language, Literature, and Culture*, pages 158–177.

Tomas Mikolov, Ilya Sutskever, Kai Chen, Greg S Corrado, and Jeff Dean. 2013. Distributed representations of words and phrases and their compositionality. In *Advances in Neural Information Processing Systems (NIPS)*, pages 3111–3119.

George Armitage Miller. 1995. Wordnet: a lexical database for english. *Communications of the ACM*, 38(11):39–41.

Michael Mohler, Marc Tomlinson, David Bracewell, and Bryan Rink. 2014. Semi-supervised methods for expanding psycholinguistics norms by integrating distributional similarity with the structure of wordnet. In *Proceedings of the Ninth International Conference on Language Resources and Evaluation (LREC)*, pages 3020–3026.

Gustavo Paetzold and Lucia Specia. 2016. Inferring psycholinguistic properties of words. In *Proceedings of the 2016 Conference of the North American Chapter of the Association for Computational Linguistics: Human Language Technologies (NAACL-HLT)*, pages 435–440.

H. Andrew Schwartz, Johannes C. Eichstaedt, Margaret L. Kern, Lukasz Dziurzynski, Stephanie M. Ramones, Megha Agrawal, Achal Shah, Michal Kosinski, David Stillwell, Martin E. P. Seligman, and Lyle H. Ungar. 2013. Personality, gender, and age in the language of social media: The open-vocabulary approach. *PLOS ONE*, 8(9):1–16.

Alex Smola and Vladimir Vapnik. 1997. Support vector regression machines. In *Advances in neural information processing systems (NIPS)*, volume 9, pages 155–161.

Kumiko Tanaka-Ishii and Hiroshi Terada. 2011. Word familiarity and frequency. *Studia Linguistica*, 65(1):96–116.

The BNC Consortium. 2007. The british national corpus, version 3 (bnc xml edition). Distributed by Oxford University Computing Services on behalf of the BNC Consortium. URL: `http://www.natcorp.ox.ac.uk/`.

Andrey Tikhonov. 1963. Solution of incorrectly formulated problems and the regularization method.
Soviet Math. Dokl., 5:1035–1038.

Correlation Analysis of Chronic Obstructive Pulmonary Disease (COPD) and its Biomarkers Using Word Embeddings

Byeong-Hun Yoon and Yu-Seop Kim

Hallym University, South Korea
yqudgns1222@gmail.com and yskim01@hallym.ac.kr

Abstract

It is very costly and time consuming to find new biomarkers for specific diseases in clinical laboratories. In this study, to find new biomarkers most closely related to Chronic Obstructive Pulmonary Disease (COPD), which is widely known as respiratory disease, biomarkers known to be associated with respiratory diseases and COPD itself were converted into word embedding. And their similarities were measured. We used Word2Vec, Canonical Correlation Analysis (CCA), and Global Vector (GloVe) for word embedding. In order to replace the clinical evaluation, the titles and abstracts of papers retrieved from Google Scholars were analyzed and quantified to estimate the performance of the word embedding models.

1   Introduction

Chronic Obstructive Pulmonary Disease (COPD) is the fourth leading cause of mortality in the world and the seventh in Korea. It is one of the most respiratory diseases in the elderly, and is known to be a very dangerous disease. Similar to asthma, COPD has symptoms of airway disorders such as dyspnea, cough, and sputum. COPD mainly exacerbates pulmonary function, leading to death. (Vestbo et al., 2013)

Accordingly, research on bio-markers, which serve as an index for predicting the disease and detecting changes in the body, is underway (Aronson et al., 2005). A biomarker is an index that can detect changes in the body using DNA, RNA, metabolites, proteins, and protein fragments. Therefore, many researchers are working hard to find new biomarkers that are deeply related to

specific diseases. Recently there have been several attempts to extract such information from documents (Poon et al., 2014) (Poon et al., 2015). (Youn et al., 2016) tried to find biomarkers related to ovarian cancer by using word embeddings. The research is the base step of this paper.

In this study, 26 respiratory-related biomarkers recommended by Chuncheon Kangwon National University Hospital[1] were selected for the first time in order to search for bio-markers related to COPD. We also extracted 800,000 titles and abstracts from Pubmed[2] to construct word embedding. Canonical Correlation Analysis (CCA) (Stratos et al., 2015), Word2vec (Mikolov et al., 2013), and Global Vector (GloVe) (Pennington et al., 2014) were used as word embedding models. With these models, word-embeddings of COPD and respiratory bio-makers are acquired. The word embeddings of COPD and the bio-markers are mapped in two dimensions using t-SNE (t-Distributed Stochastic Neighbor Embedding) (Maaten et al., 2008) and the result is visualized. The relationship between COPD and biomarkers are examined by measuring and comparing the similarity of COPD with biomarkers using cosine similarity.

Clinical trials should follow to validate the methodology presented in this study. However, since this is very difficult in practice, we intend to test this indirectly by analyzing the results of Google Scholars[3]. In other words we analyzed the Google Scholars' search results and compare the pairs with high scores to those with low scores to verify the validity of the proposed methodology.

This paper is composed as follows. Section 2 explains the biomarkers considered in this study. Section 3 explains the models used for word embedding in this study. Section 4 explains the over-

---

[1] https://www.knuh.or.kr/eng/main/index.asp
[2] https://www.ncbi.nlm.nih.gov/pubmed/
[3] https://scholar.google.co.kr/

Proceedings of the The 8th International Joint Conference on Natural Language Processing, pages 337–342,
Taipei, Taiwan, November 27 – December 1, 2017 ©2017 AFNLP

all flow of this study. Section 5 discusses the experiment and its results. Finally, Chapter 6 discusses conclusions and future research.

2 Bio-markers for COPD

A biomarker is an index that can detect changes in the body using DNA, RNA, metabolites, proteins, and protein fragments. In addition, biomarkers can be used to effectively diagnose various diseases.

The biomarkers listed in table 1 are known to be related to respiratory diseases and are included in the 26 markers recommended by Kangwon National University Hospital.

Table 1 : Bio-marker 26

Bio-marker	SP-D, CC-16, IP-10, IL-2, Eotaxin-1, Leptin Adiponectin, Ghrelin, PAI-1, IL-10, LDL, PON-1 SAA, C9, IGFBP-2, CD105, NF-kB, NSE CYFRA21-1, CEA, TRAIL, DR5, Angiostatin, Endostatin, Calprotectin, rbp

Surfactant, pulmonary-associated protein D, also known as SFTPD or SP-D (Lahti et al., 2008), is a lung-related protein. In addition, SP-D plays an important role in lung immunity and is known to regulate the function of many immune cells.

Clara Cell Secretory Protein (CC-16) (Broeckaert and Bernard, 2000) is known to be a protein distributed in the endocardium and the respiratory bronchus of the lungs and has immunomodulatory and anti-inflammatory effects.

Interferon gamma-induced protein 10 (IP-10) (Dufour et al., 2002) is also known to be CXCL10 or B10. It is involved in the Th1 immune response and is known to be increased in infectious diseases including inflammation of the respiratory tract, immune disorders, and tumors.

Interleukin 2 (IL-2) (Koreth et al., 2011) is an immunoreactive substance involved in anti-inflammatory immune responses, macrophage function to damaged cells, and restoration of the original state. IL-2 plays a major role in the immune system, and if production is reduced, immune defense can be seriously compromised.

In this study, 22 respiratory markers were also recommended and analyzed for their association with COPD.

3 Word-embeddings

Word-embedding is a technique that learns the vector representation of every word in a given Corpus. We can measure the similarity between several words, and perform vector computation with vectorized semantics to enable additional inference. In this paper, we investigate the relationship between COPD and its bio-markers using the following word-embedding models: CCA, Word2vec, and GloVe.

3.1 CCA

CCA (Hotelling and Harold, 1936) is a technique known by Hotelling (1936), which is a technique for examining the correlation of variables. CCA is a statistical method used to investigate the relationship between two words, and it is a technique that simultaneously examines the correlation between variables in a set and variables in another set. In other words, it is a useful tool to grasp the correlation of variable group (X, Y) and to grasp the relationship between two features (Jang et al., 2013).

3.2 Word2vec

Word2vec is a Google-released model in 2013. Word2vec has the premise that words with the same context have close meanings. It is also most commonly used to understand sentences in text. There are CBOW (Continuous Bag of Words) and Skip-grams in the learning method of the word2vec model. The CBOW method predicts the target word using the context that the surrounding word makes. On the other hand, skip-gram (Mikolov et al., 2013) predicts words that can come around in one word. In addition, Skip-grams are known to be more accurate in large datasets. Therefore, we use Skip-gram method in this paper.

3.3 GloVe

GloVe (Pennington et al., 2014) stands for Global Vector, and it is a method of expressing a word as a vector using a non-local learning algorithm. In addition, it is a hybrid model that considers not only the global context but also the local context of the word.

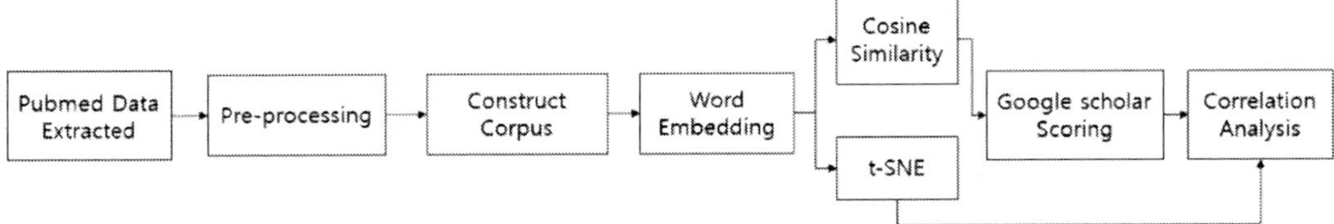

Figure 1 The whole process of proposed research

4 Methodology

In this paper, about 800,000 papers are download-ed from the PubMed site, and word embeddings are applied to only the title and abstract part of each paper. Since there are various expressions for each biomarker in the bio documents, in the pre-processing process, called normalization, the cor-pus is newly constructed by replacing these vari-ous forms into a single form. To do this, various forms of markers, including COPD, must be con-structed in dictionary form first. Three word em-bedding models are used for this corpus to con-struct two-, five-, ten-, and hundred-dimension lexical vectors. Among them, 100-dimensional vectors are reduced to two dimensions using t-SNE and the result is mapped to a two-dimensional graph. The t-SNE is used to directly look up biomarkers closely related to COPD through the visualization process. Also, the origi-nal vectors that are not reduced are also analyzed to calculate the similarity with COPD. By calcu-lating the similarity between the original vectors, we try to more precisely find the related markers.

The process of analyzing the relationship with the last stage, Google Scholars, is for analyzing the validity of the methodology rather than ana-lyzing the relationship between COPD and bi-omarkers. Figure 1 shows this whole process.

5 Experiment

In this paper, we construct new corpus with nxml documents downloaded from PubMed site. As a result of extracting the nxml document, a total of 807,821 papers were extracted, and the titles and abstracts were collected separately and used as a corpus for word embedding. More than two mil-lion words are represented by word embedding. Table 2 shows the most similar words to COPD.

Table 2 The most similar words to *'COPD.'*

Rank	token	similarity
1	exacerbation	0.851586342
2	spirometry	0.819786787
3	obstructive	0.812012613
4	asthma	0.803823590
5	ipf	0.798491836
6	aecopd	0.783644378
7	bronchodilators	0.779349267
8	asthmatics	0.774952054
9	hyperinflation	0.752177000
10	BHR	0.750948250

A word *'exacerbation'* may refer to an increase in the severity of a disease or its signs and symp-toms[4]. *'Spirometry'* is the most common of the pulmonary function tests[5]. And doctors may clas-sify lung conditions as *'obstructive'* lung disease or restrictive lung disease[6].

Among two millions word vectors, biomarkers related to pulmonary diseases such as metabolic syndrome and lung cancer are extracted separately to reveal their relationship with COPD. The mark-ers listed in table 1 are recommended by Ka-ngwon National University Hospital.

Twenty six biomarkers are embedded in four cases such as 2-dimensional, 5-dimensional, 10-dimensional, and 100-dimensional. In the case of a high-dimensional vector, the value of a certain element is excessively large, which may interfere with accurate similarity calculation. To solve this problem, a 100-dimensional vector value is re-duced to two dimensions using t-SNE and the re-sult is mapped to a two-dimensional space. [Fig-ure 2] shows the results of visualizing two-dimensional mapping of 100-dimensional vectors

---

[4] http://www.medicinenet.com

[5] https://en.wikipedia.org/wiki/Spirometry

[6] http://www.webmd.com/lung/obstructive-and-restrictive-lung-disease#1

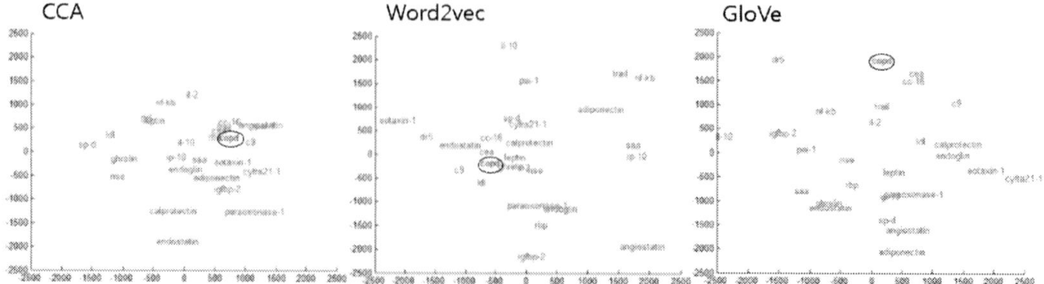

Figure 2 Mapping results of COPD and biomarkers in two-dimensional space.

embedded in CCA, word2vec, and GloVe. In figure 2, all but the COPD are biomarkers.

As shown in figure 2, in the case of CCA and Word2vec, bio-markers are distributed evenly around COPD. However, in the case of GloVe, COPD is found to be far apart. However, in all three models, bio-markers located close to COPD are CC-16 and CEA. In addition, we can see that rbp, ghrelin, and trail are close to COPD on the t-SNE.

Then, the degree of similarity is calculated by applying the cosine similarity to the two-, five-, ten- or 100-dimensional vectors embedded in three ways. Here, it is assumed that the markers with high similarity values are more closely related to COPD. Clinical trials must be conducted to verify the validity of this assumption. However, in reality, clinical trials are very difficult, so this study tries indirect verification through Google Scholars.

Table 3 shows the results for all experiments with 5 markers of the highest similarities and 5 markers of the lowest similarities through Google Scholars. For an indirect evaluation via Google Scholars, we first attempt to search for the keyword "COPD marker_name" pairs. The titles and abstracts of the top 20 papers presented in the search results were analyzed and quantified. Where title_both is the average number of articles having both keywords in the titles and abs_both is the average number of articles having both keywords in the abstracts.

Table 3 shows how well each algorithm discriminates between good markers and bad mark-

Table 3. The average number of articles having both COPD and the biomarker. 'BEST' means the most similar pairs and 'WORST' means the least similar pairs.

algorithm	dimension	BEST		WORST	
		title_both	abs_both	title_both	abs_both
CCA	2	3.8	7.6	5.2	7.4
	5	1.4	5.4	5.4	7.4
	10	0.4	3.6	3.2	6
	100	1.4	3.8	2.2	5.2
	t-SNE	0.2	2	3.6	7.2
Word2vec	2	4.4	7.8	3.4	4.6
	5	5.4	8.8	1.2	1.8
	10	6.8	9.8	3.2	5.6
	100	4.6	8	1	1.4
	t-SNE	2.6	6.2	3.8	7.2
GloVe	2	3.8	7.4	5.8	10.2
	5	0.6	4.2	4.6	8
	10	4	8.4	3.4	5.4
	100	6	10.8	1.2	2
	t-SNE	3.4	6.6	5	8.2

Table 4. Biomarkers with the highest similarities with COPD

Word2Vec				
biomarker	Similarity	title_both	abs_both	words
cc-16	0.57279	11	15	1
eotaxin-1	0.48002	1	3	4
sp-d	0.45937	7	8	2
cyfra21-1	0.40179	0	4	8
ip-10	0.35346	4	10	5
average		4.6	8	4
GloVe				
biomarker	Similarity	title_both	abs_both	words
adiponectin	0.15436	11	17	1
cea	0.14091	1	8	1
pai-1	0.11407	1	5	1
saa	0.10816	4	7	1
leptin	0.10062	13	17	1
average		6	10.8	1

ers. In other words, the larger the difference between the values of BEST and WORST, the more favorable it is. As a result, the BEST marker values of CCA were lower than those of the WORST markers. This shows that the CCA does not play a significant role in this problem. On the other hand, Word2vec is a very stable methodology because all the BEST marker values show higher values than the WORST cases, unless the dimension is reduced by t-SNE. However, GloVe showed a stable appearance as the number of dimensions increased, while it didn't in case of 2- and 5-dimension. In the 100 dimension, it showed a bigger difference than word2vec.

Table 4 shows the similarities with the markers analyzed as having the highest correlation values with COPD in Wor2Vec 100 dimension and GloVe 100 dimension. It shows that cc-16 recommended by Word2Vec and adiponectin and leptin recommended by GloVe have already undergone much research on COPD. On the other hand, Word2Vec's eotaxin-1 cyfra21-1 and GloVe's cea and saa have not. This provides a direction for new clinical studies. In other words, among the markers with a high degree of similarity, the markers that are searched with a low frequency in the Google Scholar will be subject to various clinical studies in the future. And if you expand it further, it will help you to find new markers for specific diseases.

In fact, it has been found that cyfra21-1, which has been shown to have a high similarity, not having much research interest so far, to COPD, was found to have a significant correlation with the phenotype of COPD in clinical trial. Currently, Kangwon National University Hospital is conducting experiments to obtain more reliable clinical results.

Table 5. Comparison to Human Selection

Rank (Word2vec)	marker	Rank (Human)
1	CC-16	2
2	Eotaxin-1	9
3	SP-D	1
4	Cyfra21-1	13
5	IP-10	13

Rank (Human)	marker	Rank (Word2vec)
1	SP-D	3
2	CC-16	1
3	Leptin	9
4	Ghrelin	21
5	PAI-1	14

Finally, we compare the most closely related markers recommended by word2vec (100 dimension) to the score made by human researchers. Table 5 shows the rankings that markers recommended by Word2Vec have been given by human researchers. For 26 markers, the rank correlation coefficient value between word2vec and human is 0.44.

Three clinical specialists participated in this experiment. These are professors who have been engaged in research for a long time in university hospitals, but the number of specialists involved should be increased. They are all respiratory medicine specialists, but they are not familiar with all biomarkers used in this research. Therefore, the comparison with the specialists should be seen not only from the performance evaluation of this study but also from the perspective of supplementing the specialists.

6   Conclusion

In this paper, we use word embedding to find markers that are closely related to COPD. For word embedding, we used CCA, Word2Vec, and GloVe. Experimental results show that Word2Vec and GloVe have the best performance when they are 100 dimensions.

In the future, based on this research, we seek to find new markers that are closely related to specific diseases. To do this, it is necessary to construct a corpus that summarizes the various forms of expression that a disease or a marker has. Also, it is necessary to develop various processing algorithms for expressions composed of words. In addition, we will conduct further research on the value of similarity itself as well as the relative ranking of biomarkers.

In this paper, the word embedding is performed in a given corpus, and similarity is calculated by fixed embedding. Later, we will express this problem as deep neural network and develop a model that can learn and predict based on this.

Acknowledgments

This work was supported by a National Research Foundation of Korea grant funded by the Ministry of Science and ICT of the Korea Government (No. 2015R1A2A2A01007333) and by Hallym University Research Fund, 2017 (HRF-201704-013).

References

Jeffrey K. Aronson. 2005. Biomarkers and surrogate endpoints. *British journal of clinical pharmacology*, 59(5):491-494.

Bernard Broeckaert. 2000. Clara cell secretory protein (CC16): characteristics and perspectives as lung peripheral biomarker. *Clinical and Experimental Allergy*, 30(4):469–475.

Jennifer H. Dufour, Michelle Dziejman, Michael T. Liu, Josephine H. Leung, Thomas E. Lane, and Andrew D. Luster. 2002. IFN-gamma-inducible protein 10 (IP-10; CXCL10)-deficient mice reveal a role for IP-10 in effector T cell generation and trafficking, *Journal of Immunology*. 168 (7), 3195–3204.

Harold Hotelling. 1936. Relations between two sets of variates, *Biometrika*, 283(3/4): 321-377.

Min-Ki Jang, Yu-Seop Kim, Chan-Young Park, Hye-Jeong Song and Jong-Dae. Kim. 2013. Integration of Menopausal Information into the Multiple Biomarker Diagnosis for Early Diagnosis of Ovarian Cancer. *International Journal of Bio-Science and Bio-Technology*, 5(4):215-222.

John Koreth, Ken-ichi Matsuoka, Haesook T. Kim, Sean M. McDonough, Bhavjot Bindra, Edwin P. Alyea, Philippe Armand, Corey Cutler, Vincent T. Ho, Nathaniel S. Treister, Don C. Bienfang, Sashank Prasad, Dmitrios Tzachanis, Robin M. Joyce, David E. Avigan, Joseph H. Antin, Jerone Ritz, and Robert J. Soiffer. 2011. Interleukin-2 and Regulatory T Cells in Graft-versus-Host Disease. *New England Journal of Medicine*, 365(22):2055-2066.

Meri Lahti, Johan Löfgren, Riita Marttila, Marjo Renko, Tuula Klaavuniemi, Ritva Haataja, Mika Ramet and Mikko Hallman. 2002. Surfactant protein D gene polymorphism associated with severe respiratory syncytial virus infection. *Pediatric research*, 51(6):696-699.

Laurens van der Maaten and Geoffrey Hinton. 2008. Visualizing data using t-SNE. *Journal of Machine Learning Research*, 9:2579-2605.

Tomas Mikolov, Kai Chen, Greg Corrado and Jeffrey Dean. 2013. Efficient Estimation of Word Representations in Vector Space. *arXiv preprint* arXiv:1301.3781.

Tomas Mikolov, Ilya Sutskever, Kai Chen, Greg S. Corrado and Jeff Dean. 2013. Distributed Representations of Words and Phrases and their Compositionality. *In Advances in neural information processing systems (NIPS2013)*, 3111-3119.

Jeffrey Pennington, Richard. Socher and Christopher D. Manning. 2014. Glove: Global vectors for word representation. *In Proceedings of the Empirical Methods in Natural Language Processing (EMNLP 2014)*, 1532-1543.

Hoifung Poon, Chris Quirk, Charlie DeZiel, and David Heckerman. 2014. Literone: PubMed-scale Genomic Knowledge Base in the Cloud. *Bioinformatics*, 30(19):2840-2842.

Hoifung Poon, Kristina Toutanova, and Chris Quirk. 2015. Distant Supervision for Cancer Pathway Extraction from Text. *In Proceedings of the Pacific Symposium, Biocomputing 2015*, 120-131.

Karl Stratos, Michael Collins, and Daniel Hsu. 2015. Model-based word embeddings from decompositions of count matrices. *In Proceedings of the Annual Meeting of the Association for Computational Linguistics (ACL 2015)*, 1282 – 1291.

Jorgen Vestbo, Suzanne S. Hurd, Alvar G. Agustí, Paul W. Jones, Claus Vogelmeier, Antonio Anzueto, Peter J. Barnes, Leonardo M. Fabbri, Fernando J. Martinez, Masaharu Nishimura, Robert A. Stockley, Don D. Sin, and Roberto Rodriguez-Roisin. 2013. Global strategy for the diagnosis, management, and prevention of chronic obstructive pulmonary disease: GOLD executive summary. *American journal of respiratory and critical care medicine*, 187 (4):347-365.

Young-Shin Youn, Chan-Young Park, Jong-Dae Kim, Hye-Jeong Song, and Yu-Seop Kim. 2016. Finding a New Bio-Markers of a Specific Disease using Word Embeddings. *In Proceedings of the fifth International Multi-Conference on Engineering and Technology Innovation 2016 (IMETI-2016)*.

Reference-based Metrics can be Replaced with Reference-less Metrics in Evaluating Grammatical Error Correction Systems

Hiroki Asano[12], **Tomoya Mizumoto**[2], and **Kentaro Inui**[12]
[1] Graduate School of Information Sciences, Tohoku University
[2] RIKEN Center for Advanced Intelligence Project
`asano@ecei.tohoku.ac.jp,tomoya.mizumoto@riken.jp`
`inui@ecei.tohoku.ac.jp`

Abstract

In grammatical error correction (GEC), automatically evaluating system outputs requires gold-standard references, which must be created manually and thus tend to be both expensive and limited in coverage. To address this problem, a reference-less approach has recently emerged; however, previous reference-less metrics that only consider the criterion of grammaticality, have not worked as well as reference-based metrics. This study explores the potential of extending a prior grammaticality-based method to establish a reference-less evaluation method for GEC systems. Further, we empirically show that a reference-less metric that combines fluency and meaning preservation with grammaticality provides a better estimate of manual scores than that of commonly used reference-based metrics. To our knowledge, this is the first study that provides empirical evidence that a reference-less metric can replace reference-based metrics in evaluating GEC systems.

1 Introduction

Grammatical error correction (GEC) has been an active research area since a series of shared tasks was launched at CoNLL (Ng et al., 2013, 2014). The GEC mainly constitutes a generative task, i.e., a task that produces a grammatically correct sentence from a given original sentence whereby multiple distinct outputs can be judged "correct" for a single input. Therefore, automatically evaluating the performance is not straightforward and is considered as an important issue as in the fields of translation and summarization.

A common approach to automatically evaluating GEC systems involves reference-based evaluation, where gold-standard references are manually created for a given test set of original sentences and each system output is scored by comparing it with corresponding gold-standard references with some metrics (referenced-based metric) (Dahlmeier and Ng, 2012; Felice and Briscoe, 2015; Napoles et al., 2015), analogous to BLEU (Papineni et al., 2002) in machine translation. Reference-based evaluation, however, has a severe drawback. In GEC, multiple outputs can be a right answer for a single input sentence. If the gold-standard references at hand lack coverage, reference-based metrics may unfairly underestimate system performance. One way to cope with this problem is to exhaustively collect potential corrections; however, this is not straightforward and can be of immense cost.

As an alternative approach to this problem, Napoles et al. (2016) proposed a new method that does not require gold-standard references (i.e., *reference-less* metric). Their idea is to evaluate GEC system performance by assessing the grammaticality of system outputs without gold-standard references. This approach is advantageous in that it does not require manual creation of references. The results of the experiments reported in (Napoles et al., 2016), however, reveal that their reference-less metric cannot evaluate GEC systems as well as a reference-based metric, GLEU+ (Napoles et al., 2015).

Given the above, we explore the potential capabilities of reference-less evaluation by extending grammaticality-based method of Napoles et al. (2016) with other assessment criteria. More specifically, we consider the criteria of fluency and meaning preservation as additions to grammaticality and empirically show that a reference-less metric that combining these three criteria can evaluate

Proceedings of the The 8th International Joint Conference on Natural Language Processing, pages 343–348,
Taipei, Taiwan, November 27 – December 1, 2017 ©2017 AFNLP

GEC systems better than reference-based metrics. To our best knowledge, this is the first study that provides such empirical evidence to show that a reference-less metric can replace reference-based metrics in evaluating GEC systems.

2 Reference-less GEC assessment

There are two key ideas behind our reference-less approach to GEC assessment. First, we explore a range of criteria for assessing grammatical corrections that are considered important in the GEC literature and can be automated without reference data. Second, we identify a system that combines the aforementioned criteria to provide a better estimate of manual scores as compared with reference-based metrics. Given these two key ideas, we consider the following three criteria: grammaticality, fluency, and meaning preservation.

Grammaticality The criterion of grammaticality in the metric defined by Napoles et al. (2016) is modeled on the linguistic-feature-based model originally proposed by Heilman et al. (2014). We also use a similar method. More specifically, for a hypothesis h, the grammaticality score $S_G(h)$ is determined by a logistic regression with linguistic features, including the number of misspellings, language model scores, out-of-vocabulary counts, and PCFG and link grammar features. We extend this model by incorporating the number of errors detected by the Language Tool[1]. Further, we trained our model using the GUG dataset (Heilman et al., 2014) and the implementation provided by Napoles et al. (2016).[2] In addition, we used Gigaword (Parker et al., 2011) and TOEFL11 (Blanchard et al., 2013) to train the language model. The resulting grammaticality model achieved an accuracy of 78.9%, slightly higher than the original model (77.2%), in the binary prediction of grammaticality on the GUG dataset.

Fluency The importance of fluency in GEC has been shown by Sakaguchi et al. (2016) and Napoles et al. (2017), however there are no evaluation metrics that consider fluency. Fluency can be captured by statistical language modeling (Lau et al., 2015). More specifically, for a hypothesis h,

fluency score $S_F(h)$ is calculated as follows:[3]

$$S_F(h) = \frac{\log P_m(h) - \log P_u(h)}{|h|}, \quad (1)$$

where $|h|$ denotes the sentence length, $P_m(h)$ denotes the probability of the sentence given by a language model, and $P_u(h)$ denotes the unigram probability of the sentence. In our study, we adopted Recurrent Neural Network Language Models implemented via faster-rnnlm.[4] Further, we used 10 million sentences from the British National Corpus (BNC Consortium, 2007) and Wikipedia. Given these datasets, we found the fluency scored by our model to have a correlation coefficient (Pearson's r) of 0.395 with acceptability scored by humans in the same setting described by Lau et al. (2015).

Meaning preservation In GEC, the meaning of original sentences should be preserved. As an example, consider sentence (1a) below being revised to form sentence (1b).

(1) a. *It is unfair to release a law only point to the genetic disorder.* (original)

    b. *It is unfair to pass a law.* (revised)

Sentence (1b) is grammatically correct, but does not preserve the meaning of sentence (1a), and thus sentence (1b) should be considered as inappropriate. To assess how much of the meaning of an original sentence is preserved in a revision, one can consider the use of an evaluation metric devised in the MT field. In this study, we adopt METEOR (Denkowski and Lavie, 2014) because it focuses on semantic similarity much more so than other common metrics, such as BLEU. Meaning score $S_M(h, s)$ for input of a source sentence s and a hypothesis h is calculated as follows:

$$S_M(h, s) = \frac{P \cdot R}{t \cdot P + (1 - t) \cdot R}, \quad (2)$$

where $P = \frac{m(h_c, s_c)}{|h_c|}$ and $R = \frac{m(h_c, s_c)}{|s_c|}$. h_c denotes content words in the hypothesis h, s_c denotes content words in the source sentence s, and $m(h_c, s_c)$ denotes the number of matched content words between the output and the original sentence, and

---

[1] https://languagetool.org
[2] https://github.com/cnap/
grammaticality-metrics/tree/master/
heilman-et-al

[3] In many cases $S_F(h)$ is more than 0 and less than 1. When it is less than 0, $S_F(h) = 0$, and when it is more than 1, $S_F(h) = 1$
[4] https://github.com/yandex/
faster-rnnlm

is calculated considering inflection, synonyms and misspellings[5]. Note that we use $t = 0.85$, which is a default value provided of METEOR.

The above three criteria are combined as follows:

$$\text{Score}(h, s) = \alpha \text{S}_\text{G}(h) + \beta \text{S}_\text{F}(h) + \gamma \text{S}_\text{M}(h, s), \quad (3)$$

where the ranges of S_G, S_F, and S_M are [0, 1] and $\alpha + \beta + \gamma = 1$. We choose these weights empirically with a development dataset.

3 Experiments

We conducted two experiments to investigate the extent to which our reference-less metric is close to human evaluation compared with baseline reference-based metrics. We used two commonly used reference-based metrics M^2 (Dahlmeier and Ng, 2012) and GLEU+ (Sakaguchi et al., 2016; Napoles et al., 2016) (A modified version of GLEU (Napoles et al., 2015)).

3.1 Automatic ranking of GEC systems

We first compare the proposed reference-less metric with respect to how closely each metric correlates with human ratings.

For this experiment, we used the CoNLL-2014 Shared Task (CoNLL) dataset (Ng et al., 2014). The CoNLL dataset is a collection of the outputs produced by the 12 participant GEC systems submitted to the CoNLL-2014 Shared Task, where the 12 GEC systems' outputs to each input student sentence are ranked by multiple human raters (Grundkiewicz et al., 2015). An advantage of using this dataset is that it includes an extensive set of references for each input student sentence: two references originally provided in the CoNLL-2014 Shared Task, eight references provided by Bryant and Ng (2015), and eight references provided by Sakaguchi et al. (2016). In the experiment, we used all the 18 references for the baseline reference-based metrics in order to bring out the maximal potential of those metrics.

For tuning the weights, α, β and γ, of our metric, we used another distinct dataset, the JHU FLuency-Extended GUG (henceforth, JF-LEG) dataset (Napoles et al., 2017). This dataset

is a collection of tuples of an input student sentence, four GEC system outputs, and a human rating. We selected weights with the highest correlation on the JFLEG dataset, obtaining $\alpha = 0.07$, $\beta = 0.83$, and $\gamma = 0.10$. Note that these optimized weights should not be interpreted as the relative importance of the subcomponents because outputs of those subcomponents differ in variance.

For testing, following the experiments reported in (Napoles et al., 2016), the 12 system outputs for each input student sentence were scored with each metric, and next for each metric, the 12 systems were ranked according to their averaged scores. Each metric's ranking was then compared to the human ranking of Grundkiewicz et al. (2015, Table 3c[6]) to compute the correlation coefficients, Spearman's ρ and Pearson's r.

The results are shown in Table 1. Many interesting findings can be drawn. The grammaticality metric alone, which corresponds to (Napoles et al., 2016), outperformed M^2 but did not perform as well as GLEU+. The meaning preservation metric exhibited poor correlation with human ranking; however, when combining meaning preservation with fluency, the prediction capability boosted, prevailing over GLEU+. We believe this result makes good sense because the meaning preservation metric, i.e. METEOR, relies mostly on shallow similarity (although it partially considers paraphrases) and tends to prefer system outputs with fewer corrections; nevertheless, it plays a significant role when balanced with fluency. Combining all the three subcomponents even further improved Spearman's ρ ($\rho = 0.874$), significantly outperforming both M^2 and GLEU+. To our knowledge, this is the first study that provides empirical evidence that a reference-less metric can correlate better with human ratings compared with the state-of-the-art reference-based metrics in evaluating GEC systems.

3.2 Minimal edits vs. fluent edits

According to recent work by Sakaguchi et al. (2016), the aspect of fluency is potentially even further important than ever considered in the GEC literature. We expect that this emphasis on fluency might bring further advantages to reference-less metrics as opposed to reference-based metrics.

---

[5]In order to handle misspellings, we first ran a spell checker on a given input sentence to obtain candidate corrections and then put them into METEOR to find the maximum score.

[6]We used the TrueSkill ranking simply because (i) we wanted to compare our results with those reported in Napoles et al. (2016), where only TrueSkill was used, and (ii) system outputs in the JFLEG are also ranked with TrueSkill.

Metric	Spearman's ρ	Pearson's r
M^2	0.648	0.632
GLEU+	0.857	0.843
Grammar	0.835	0.759
Meaning	-0.192	0.198
Fluency	0.819	0.864
Grammar+Meaning	0.813	0.794
Meaning+Fluency	0.868	0.876
Fluency+Grammar	0.819	0.864
Combination (proposed)	**0.874**	**0.878**

Table 1: Correlation between human and metric rankings.

In their recent work, Sakaguchi et al. (2016) created an interesting dataset by asking four human editors to produce one *minimal edit* (minimal grammatical error corrections) and one *fluent edit* (extended corrections with maximal fluency) for each original student sentence in the aforementioned CoNLL dataset (corresponding to the "eight references provided by Sakaguchi et al. (2016)" referred to in 3.1). Using this dataset, Sakaguchi et al. showed that human raters clearly prefer fluency edits to minimal edits.

An intriguing question here is whether our reference-less metric (the combination of grammaticality, fluency and meaning-preservation) is indeed capable of preferring fluent edits to minimal edits despite that fluent edits are less similar to their original sentences than minimal edits. We therefore conducted a supplemental experiment as follows.

We chose two editors out of the four editors employed for Sakaguchi et al. (2016)'s dataset and extracted the four edits by these two editors (Editor A and Editor B) for each original student sentence, fluent edits by Editor A (Flu-A), minimal edits by Editor A (Min-A), fluent edits by Editor B (Flu-B), minimal edits by Editor B (Min-B), as the test set. We then applied our metric and the two baseline metrics to this test set to rank the four sets of edits, where the reference-based metrics used the remaining references (the 14 references for each original sentence).

The results are shown in Table 2. While the proposed metric (Combination) consistently prefers fluent edits, the reference-based metrics seriously underestimate fluent edits. GLEU+ consistently preferred the minimal edits. This is somewhat an expected result because the majority of the reference data consists of "minimal edits" reflecting the nature of the GEC task and GLEU+ tends to lean towards the majority of the references. One

rank	Combination (proposed)	M^2	GLEU+
1	Flu-A (0.865)	Min-B (0.641)	Min-B (0.628)
2	Flu-B (0.854)	Flu-A (0.634)	Flu-B (0.607)
3	Min-B (0.848)	Flu-B (0.626)	Min-A (0.606)
4	Min-A (0.844)	Min-A (0.590)	Flu-A (0.563)

Table 2: Rankings of the four reference sets with each metric. Scores assigned by the GEC metrics are shown in parentheses.

Sentence	Comb.	M^2	GLEU+
From this scope, social media has shortened our distance. (minimal)	0.541	1.00	0.575
From this perspective, social media has made the world smaller. (fluent)	0.688	0.277	0.251

Table 3: An example that the reference-less metric works well and the sentence-level scores by GEC metrics.

straightforward way to cope with this problem is to collect as many diverse fluent edits as possible, which would be prohibitively costly though. M^2 may not suffer the same problem; however, as revealed by our first experiment, M^2 can be far less appropriate as a metric for GEC assessment compared with GLEU+ (see Table 1). In contrast, the proposed reference-less approach has good potential for this issue. Table 3 shows an example where the proposed metric preferred a fluent edit but the reference-based metrics preferred a minimal edit. The reference-based metrics gave low scores to the fluent edit because the human references did not cover the correction "made the world smaller".

4 Discussion and Conclusions

In this paper, we have presented a reference-less approach to automatic assessment of GEC systems and have empirically shown that combining the three criteria of grammaticality, fluency, and meaning preservation can boost the correlation with human ratings. To our best knowledge, the paper has provided the first empirical evidence supporting the hypothesis that a reference-less metric can outperform and thus potentially replace the state-of-the-art reference-based metrics in this research field.

Our error analysis has revealed that the proposed metric still has room for improvement. One obvious point of improvement is around meaning preservation. The present choice for this component, METEOR, does not allow us to take nearly synonymous phrases into account. For example, METEOR wrongly votes for an original sentence *our family and relatives grew us up* against a correctly revised sentence *our family and relatives brought us up*. Recent advances in computational modeling of sentence similarity (He and Lin, 2016; Rychalska et al., 2016, etc.) should be worthwhile to incorporated.

It has also turned out that the present fluency metric is undesirably affected by misspelled words. As in Equation 1, the unigram probability regularizes the sentence probability so that the score of fluency will not be underestimated by rare words. However, with misspelled words, the normalization works excessively as they are treated as rare words. This newly provides an interesting issue of how to estimate the fluency of student sentences.

Another direction for improvement is to explore methods for combining grammaticality, fluency and meaning preservation. For example, the oracle combination[7] of the three components exhibited a significantly high correlation with the human ranking ($\rho = 0.951$, $r = 0.923$). This also indicates further room for improvement.

References

Daniel Blanchard, Joel Tetreault, Derrick Higgins, Aoife Cahill, and Martin Chodorow. 2013. *TOEFL11: A Corpus of Non-Native English*. Technical report, Educational Testing Service.

BNC Consortium. 2007. *The British National Corpus*. version 3 (BNC XML Edition). Distributed by Oxford University Computing Services on behalf of the BNC Consortium.

Christopher Bryant and Hwee Tou Ng. 2015. How Far are We from Fully Automatic High Quality Grammatical Error Correction? In *Proceedings of the 53rd Annual Meeting of the Association for Computational Linguistics and the 7th International Joint Conference on Natural Language Processing (Volume 1: Long Paper*, pages 697–707.

Daniel Dahlmeier and Hwee Tou Ng. 2012. Better evaluation for grammatical error correction. In *Proceedings of the 2012 Conference of the North American Chapter of the Association for Computational Linguistics: Human Language Technologies*, pages 568–572.

Michael Denkowski and Alon Lavie. 2014. Meteor Universal: Language Specific Translation Evaluation for Any Target Language. In *Proceedings of the Ninth Workshop on Statistical Machine Translation*, pages 376–380.

Mariano Felice and Ted Briscoe. 2015. Towards a standard evaluation method for grammatical error detection and correction. In *Proceedings of the 2015 Conference of the North American Chapter of the Association for Computational Linguistics: Human Language Technologies*, pages 578–587.

Roman Grundkiewicz, Marcin Junczys-Dowmunt, and Edward Gillian. 2015. Human Evaluation of Grammatical Error Correction Systems. In *Proceedings of the 2015 Conference on Empirical Methods in Natural Language Processing*, pages 461–470.

Hua He and Jimmy J Lin. 2016. Pairwise Word Interaction Modeling with Deep Neural Networks for Semantic Similarity Measurement. In *Proceedings of the 2016 Conference of the North American Chapter of the Association for Computational Linguistics: Human Language Technologies*, pages 937–948.

Michael Heilman, Aoife Cahill, Nitin Madnani, Melissa Lopez, Matthew Mulholland, and Joel Tetreault. 2014. Predicting Grammaticality on an Ordinal Scale. In *Proceedings of the 52nd Annual Meeting of the Association for Computational Linguistics (Volume 2: Short Papers)*, pages 174–180.

Jey Han Lau, Alexander Clark, and Shalom Lappin. 2015. Unsupervised Prediction of Acceptability Judgements. In *Proceedings of the 53rd Annual Meeting of the Association for Computational Linguistics and the 7th International Joint Conference on Natural Language Processing (Volume 1: Long Papers)*, pages 1618–1628.

Courtney Napoles, Keisuke Sakaguchi, Matt Post, and Joel Tetreault. 2015. Ground Truth for Grammatical Error Correction Metrics. In *Proceedings of the 53rd Annual Meeting of the Association for Computational Linguistics and the 7th International Joint Conference on Natural Language Processing (Volume 2: Short Papers)*, pages 588–593.

Courtney Napoles, Keisuke Sakaguchi, and Joel Tetreault. 2016. There's No Comparison: Reference-less Evaluation Metrics in Grammatical Error Correction. In *Proceedings of the 2016 Conference on Empirical Methods in Natural Language Processing*, pages 2109–2115.

Courtney Napoles, Keisuke Sakaguchi, and Joel Tetreault. 2017. JFLEG: A Fluency Corpus and B enchmark for Grammatical Error Correction. In *Proceedings of the 15th Conference of the European Chapter of the Association for Computational Linguistics: Volume 2, Short Papers*, pages 229–234.

Hwee Tou Ng, Siew Mei Wu, Ted Briscoe, Christian Hadiwinoto, Raymond Hendy Susanto, and Christopher Bryant. 2014. The CoNLL-2014 Shared Task on Grammatical Error Correction. In *Proceedings of the Eighteenth Conference on Computational Natural Language Learning: Shared Task*, pages 1–14.

---

[7]The weights were set to a value that achieves the highest correlation on the CoNLL dataset.

Hwee Tou Ng, Siew Mei Wu, Yuanbin Wu, Christian Hadiwinoto, and Joel Tetreault. 2013. The CoNLL-2013 Shared Task on Grammatical Error Correction. In *Proceedings of the Seventeenth Conference on Computational Natural Language Learning: Shared Task*, pages 1–12.

Kishore Papineni, Salim Roukos, Todd Ward, and Wei-Jing Zhu. 2002. BLEU: a Method for Automatic Evaluation of Machine Translation. In *Proceedings of 40th Annual Meeting of the Association for Computational Linguistics*, pages 311–318.

Robert Parker, David Graff, Junbo Kong, Ke Chen, and Kazuaki Maeda. 2011. *English Gigaword Fifth Edition LDC2011T07*. Philadelphia: Linguistic Data Consortium.

Barbara Rychalska, Katarzyna Pakulska, Krystyna Chodorowska, Wojciech Walczak, and Piotr Andruszkiewicz. 2016. Samsung Poland NLP Team at SemEval-2016 Task 1: Necessity for diversity; combining recursive autoencoders, WordNet and ensemble methods to measure semantic similarity. In *Proceedings of the 10th International Workshop on Semantic Evaluation*, pages 602–608.

Keisuke Sakaguchi, Courtney Napoles, Matt Post, and Joel Tetreault. 2016. Reassessing the Goals of Grammatical Error Correction: Fluency Instead of Grammaticality. *Transactions of the Association for Computational Linguistics*, 4:169–182.

CVBed: Structuring CVs using Word Embeddings

Shweta Garg

Delhi Technological University
New Delhi, India
shweta_bt2k14@dtu.ac.in

Sudhanshu S Singh and **Abhijit Mishra** and **Kuntal Dey**
IBM Research, New Delhi and Bangalore, India
{sudsing3, abhijimi, kuntadey}@in.ibm.com

Abstract

Automatic analysis of curriculum vitae (CVs) of applicants is of tremendous importance in recruitment scenarios. The semi-structuredness of CVs, however, makes CV processing a challenging task. We propose a solution towards transforming CVs to follow a unified structure, thereby, paving ways for smoother CV analysis. The problem of restructuring is posed as a *section relabeling problem*, where each section of a given CV gets reassigned to a predefined label. Our relabeling method relies on *semantic relatedness* computed between section header, content and labels, based on *phrase-embeddings* learned from a large pool of CVs. We follow different heuristics to measure semantic relatedness. Our best heuristic achieves an F-score of 93.17% on a test dataset with gold-standard labels obtained using manual annotation.

1 Introduction

Automatic processing of curriculum vitae (CVs) is important in multiple real-life scenarios. This includes analyzing, organizing and deriving actionable business intelligence from CVs. For corporates, such processing is interesting in scenarios such as hiring applicants as employees, promoting and transitioning employees to new roles *etc*. For individuals, it is possible to add value by designing CV improvement and organization tools, enabling them to create more effective CVs specific to their career objectives as well as maintain the CVs easily over time. Hence, it is important to transform CVs to follow a unified structure, thereby, paving ways for smoother and more ·

effective manual/automated CV analysis.

The semi-structuredness of CVs, with the diversity that different CVs exhibit, however, makes CV processing a challenging task. For example, a first CV could have sections *personal details, education, technical skills, project experience, managerial skills, others* and a second CV, equivalent to the first one, could have sections *about me, career objective, work experience, academic background, proficiency, professional interests*, in that order. Note that, some sections are equivalent (e.g., *personal details* and *about me*) in the two CVs, some sections are simply absent in some CVs (e.g., any equivalent of *others* that is present in the first CV, is missing in the second CV) and some sections in one CV is a composition of multiple sections in another CV (e.g., *proficiency* in the second CV is a combination of *technical skills* and *managerial skills* of the first). In real-life, the variations are high, and the solutions available today are far from perfect. Clearly, the problem at hand requires attention.

Multiple industrial solutions, such as Text Kernel[1], Burning Glass[2] and Sovren[3], have attempted to solve the problem at hand, and are offered as commercial products. Several researchers have also investigated the problem. Yu et al. (2005) proposed a hybrid (multipass) information extraction model to assign labels to block of CVs. Subsequent works, such as Chuang et al. (2009) and Maheshwari et al. (2010), also used multipass approaches, and feature-based machine learning techniques. Kopparapu (2010) suggested a knowledge-based approach, using section-specific keywords and n-grams. Tosik et al. (2015) found word embeddings to be more effective compared to word types and other features for CRF mod-

---

[1]https://www.textkernel.com
[2]http://burning-glass.com
[3]https://www.sovren.com

349

Proceedings of the The 8th International Joint Conference on Natural Language Processing, pages 349–354,
Taipei, Taiwan, November 27 – December 1, 2017 ©2017 AFNLP

els. Singh et al. (2010) and Marjit et al. (2012), amongst others, also proposed different solutions.

We use a phrase-embedding based approach to identify and label sections, as well as investigate the usefulness of traditional language resources such as WordNet (Miller, 1995) and ConceptNet (Liu and Singh, 2004). Empirically, our approach significantly outperforms other approaches.

2 Central Idea

As discussed earlier, CVs generally do not follow any predefined structure, and hence it would be hard to propose a deterministic (rule-based) solution for parsing and categorizing the sections of CV. This necessitates the application of statistical classification to map each section of the CV to section-labels chosen from an exhaustive list of predefined labels. Now, applying supervised classification for this task would require a large amount of manually labeled training data which is extremely time consuming. Our approach, on the other hand, is based on unsupervised learning where each label is chosen based on the *semantic relatedness* between the label and the section content (in terms of section-header and section-body). For example, a section titled "Academic qualifications" could be semantically closer to a predefined label "Education" than "Skills"; the section would thus be categorized under "Education". We propose two schemes for obtaining the semantic relatedness between section headers, bodies and the predefined labels (discussed in Section 3.2).

2.1 Scheme 1: Exhaustive Comparison

In the first scheme, we perform an exhaustive similarity comparison of all the words that appear in the given section of the test CV, with the label set. In this scheme, for each section extracted from the CVs, content words from the section headers and bodies are extracted and combined. A *lexical similarity* measure is computed, between each label in the label-set and each word extracted from the section. The average lexical similarity score for each label, with all the words in the section, is then computed. The label with the highest average similarity score is selected as the winner label. The intuition behind this scheme is that, labels that share maximum lexical similarity with section have the maximum semantic relatedness with the section, hence, most appropriate.

Formally, let $L = \{l_1, l_2, ..., l_n\}$ be the set of available labels. Let $W = \{w_1, w_2, ..., w_m\}$ be the set of words present in a given section. Let $\sigma(w_i, l_j)$ represent the semantic similarity of word w_i with the label l_j. The average similarity $\lambda(l_j, W)$ of label l_j with the set of words W is computed as:

$$\lambda(l_j, W) = \frac{\sum\limits_{i=1}^{m} \sigma(w_i, l_j)}{|W|} \tag{1}$$

The label selected as the winner, $\Lambda(L, W)$, is:

$$\Lambda(L, W) = \forall(j) max(\lambda(l_j, W)) \tag{2}$$

For computing semantic similarity σ, we use WordNet (Miller, 1995) *path* similarity (Leacock and Chodorow, 1998) and *Wu-Palmer* similarity (Wu and Palmer, 1994) and ConceptNet (Liu and Singh, 2004; Havasi et al., 2007) based similarity (Spagnola and Lagoze, 2011). The systems variants for these three similarity measures are, henceforth, referred to as PATH, WUP, CONCEPT. As expected, WordNet and ConceptNet offer limited coverage, resulting in many of the similarity scores as 0. We therefore propose another variant (referred to as EMBEDDING) where lexical similarity is the cosine similarity between the embeddings of the two input words. The word embeddings are learned using the training data consisting of 1179 CVs (detailed in Section 3.1) using the skip-gram approach (Mikolov et al., 2013a,b), implemented with the help of `gensim` package in python (Řehůřek and Sojka, 2010). The embedding dimension, min count, and window size were empirically set to 100, 5 and 4 respectively, and the vocabulary size turned out to be 7970.

2.2 Scheme 2: MultiEmbedding

In the second scheme, we employ MULTIEM-BEDDING, a *representative word-cluster similarity based* approach. Here, instead of directly comparing the words appearing in the test data, we do the following. First, content words from section header and body are extracted and combined to form the set of words $W = \{w_1, w_2, ..., w_m\}$, as discussed earlier. Their embeddings $\epsilon(W) = \{\epsilon(w_1), \epsilon(w_2), ..., \epsilon(w_m)\}$ are then extracted. The embeddings are averaged, to find the average embedding of the section, as:

$$E(W) = \frac{\sum\limits_{i=1}^{m} \epsilon(w_i)}{|W|} \tag{3}$$

	#CVs	#Sections	$\frac{\#Sections}{\#CVs}$
Train	1179	6085	5.2
Test	130	747	5.7

Table 1: Dataset statistics

We then extract the top M words, W', from the training-data vocabulary, based on the cosine similarity between the averaged embedding $E(W')$ and the vocabulary words W. Intuitively, these words act as the representative cluster of words, semantically most similar to the section content. The embeddings of these top M words in the vocabulary are then obtained as $\epsilon(W') = \{\epsilon(w_{1'}), \epsilon(w_{2'}), ..., \epsilon(w_{m'})\}$ and averaged in a manner similar to Equation 3, to obtain E(W'). Then, for each label $l_j \in L$, the cosine similarity of l_j and the averaged embedding $E(W')$ is calculated. The winner label is the one that shows up the maximum cosine similarity.

2.3 Split Section Approach

One of the main drawbacks of the schemes proposed is that they do not treat section headers and body-content separately. In practice, however, section headers can sometimes play a crucial role in determining the category that the section should belong to. This motivated us to propose other set of variants, in which section header and body-content are treated as two separate entities. The steps in the schemes proposed are carried independently on header and body-content. After lexical similarity with labels for both body and header are computed separately, the winner label is selected through voting. This idea lead to 5 more model variants such as SPLIT-PATH, SPLITWUP, SPLITCONCEPT, SPLITEM-BEDDING, SPLITMULTIEMBEDDING.

We also implemented other variants such as: (a) averaging embeddings of words in the test data and then comparing the cosine similarity between the averaged resultant embedding with label embeddings (b) getting the top M words using Word-Net and ConceptNet similarities. But these methods did not perform well, hence, results are not reported for these methods.

3 Experimental Setup

3.1 Dataset Creation and Preprocessing

Since, there is no publicly available standard CV dataset, we randomly pulled out 1309 number of CVs by requesting the recruitment division of a multinational organization (anonymized in this version). Since CVs can come up with different file formats (such as pdf, html *etc.*), we converted every CV to docx format using the abiword application[4], thereby preserving meta information about sections. The docx files are then processed using the docx package in python to separate out section headers and bodies for each CV. Textual noise in the form of non-Unicode characters and escape characters are then removed. Table 1 presents a detailed statistics about the number of CVs and number sections thus obtained.

3.2 Defining Labels

Our task intends to eventually help in analysis of CV by categorizing them, making it necessary for us to define a label-set that ensures decent coverage while maintaining a proper level of granularity. If the labels are too coarse or too fine, it will considerably increase the effort of analyzing the CVs and our task will be ineffective. We, thus, carefully chose 30 labels from the Text Kernel[5] platform, which provides a considerable coverage while balancing the granularity. The labels are shared in the supplementary material. In future, we plan to include important multi-word labels in our label set.

3.3 Test Data Annotation

To evaluate our methods against ground truth, we employed two software professionals (with acceptable working proficiency in English) to annotate the sections in the test data. The inter-annotator agreement between the annotators turns out to be 669 out of the 747 sections (89.56%), with 78 non-agreements. We manually inspect all the cases of non-agreement, and find that these are very similar. Some examples of such confusion pairs are *skills* vs. *interests*, *training* vs. *internship*, etc. In order to resolve, in a label pre-processing step, we randomly choose one of the non-agreeing two labels and assign the chosen label to the test instances, before we perform ground

---

[4]https://www.abisource.com
[5]https://www.textkernel.com

truth validation. The labels provided by the annotators are compared with the output generated by our system, to obtain precision, recall, accuracy and F-score measures.

4 Results and Insights

We present the results and insights obtained from the experiments in this section.

4.1 Results

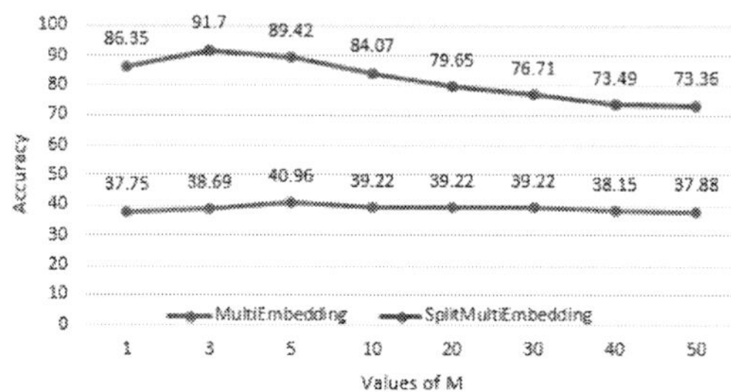

Figure 1: Variation of accuracy with M, the number of representative words chosen

From Table 2, we observe that the SPLITEM-BEDDING method, which is the embodiment of Scheme 1 (given in Section 2.1) where $\sigma(w_i, l_j)$, the semantic similarity of word w_i with the label l_j, is computed using embedding, yields the highest precision across all the methods. However, SPLITMULTIEMBEDDING, a variant of Scheme 2 (given in Section 2.2) where the embeddings of section header and body are independently computed, and a weighted combination of the embeddings is used to retrieve the representative words of the section to compare with the embeddings of the labels, delivers the highest recall and F-score values, as well as, the highest overall accuracy. Thus, the SPLITMULTIEMBEDDING approach with $M = 3$ empirically turns out to be the most effective approach. Overall, 4 of the approaches deliver strong performances (F-score > 80%): SPLITMULTIEMBEDDING, SPLITEMBEDDING, SPLITPATH and SPLITWUP.

Figure 1 shows the impact of varying M, on the system accuracy, for the MULTIEMBEDDING and SPLITMULTIEMBEDDING approaches. It is evident from the figure that for SPLITMULTIEM-BEDDING, the most effective value is $M = 3$, while for SPLITEMBEDDING the value is $M = 5$. Beyond these values of M, too many words get chosen, which in turn confuses the system.

4.2 Error Analysis

We investigate the errors that our system makes, by comparing the section headers we obtain, with ground truth. Table 3 captures a random sample of the classifications made by our system. Note that, CVs that contain Personal sections (including name, email and other details inside the section), have always been classified with 100% accuracy. This also applies for CVs that have separate section headers for identification, such as Name, Email *etc*. On the other hand, for sections that are intuitively more complex, show some (meaningful) confusions across classes. For example, one would naturally assume Activities to have semantic overlaps with Skill, and similarly Work with Internship, and Project with Publications, among others. A few confusions are more intriguing, such as Project with Country (1 instance), and Education with City (1 instance). These confusions are rare although existent, showing the effectiveness of our system in general though there are perhaps some corner cases that can potentially be improved in the future.

5 Discussion

One aspect to note is that the approaches where the CV section header and body content are split, and the embeddings are subsequently combined in a weighted manner, outperform the approaches where the section header and body are given equal weightage. This conforms to the intuition that section headers bear a higher significance, compared to words that tend to appear in section bodies.

Further, we observe that the word embedding based approaches consistently and significantly outperform the WordNet and ConceptNet based approaches. While WordNet and Concept-Net are valuable lexical resources on their own, but clearly a predefined knowledge representation proves to be inadequate to capture the intricacies that CVs tend to present in real life. This highlights (a) the inherent challenge in dealing with the semi-structured and heterogeneous data that CVs present to computational systems, as well as (b) the importance of learning the lexical characteristics from the core application domain.

6 Conclusion

In this paper, we posed the restructuring of CVs as a section relabeling problem. We proposed a methodology to reassign a predefined label to each

Approach	Precision	Recall	F-Score	Accuracy
PATH	79.224	50.870	61.96	50.870
SPLITPATH	92.367	83.936	87.95	83.936
WUP	48.838	30.656	37.67	30.656
SPLITWUP	92.223	83.936	87.88	83.936
CONCEPT	58.241	43.507	49.81	43.507
SPLITCONCEPT	77.054	72.155	74.52	72.155
EMBEDDING	79.277	30.522	44.07	30.522
SPLITEMBEDDING	**95.029**	86.613	90.63	86.613
MULTIEMBEDDING ($M = 3$)	77.183	38.688	51.54	38.688
SPLITMULTIEMBEDDING ($M = 3$)	94.687	**91.700**	**93.17**	**91.700**

Table 2: Results for relabeling task for multiple approaches, numbers are shown in %

Ground Truth	Total	Correct	List of Confusions
PROJECT	110	99	Publication: 8, Training: 1, Activities: 1, Country: 1
EDUCATION	102	101	City: 1
ACTIVITIES	36	28	Skill: 3, Interest: 1, Work: 1, Hobby: 1, Publication: 1, Country: 1
PUBLICATION	30	26	Reference: 4
WORK	32	23	Inernship: 5, Reference: 2, Interest: 2
SKILL	87	84	Interest: 1, Education: 1, Objective: 1
PERSONAL	61	61	—
NAME	57	57	—
EMAIL	9	9	—

Table 3: Confusion matrix, showing some randomly chosen ground truth classes from actual CV section headers, and our system predictions in the form of <incorrect class: incorrect classification count of our system for that class>

section of given CVs, learning phrase embeddings from a pool of training CVs, and exploring several heuristics to compute the semantic relatedness between section headers, section contents and available labels. Our best heuristic achieves an F-score of 93.17% on a test dataset, with gold-standard labels obtained using manual annotation. Our system is useful in practical scenarios such as applicant management for recruitments, employee career management, and automated CV creation and maintenance for individuals.

References

Zhang Chuang, Wu Ming, Li Chun Guang, Xiao Bo, and Lin Zhi-qing. 2009. Resume parser: Semi-structured chinese document analysis. In *Computer Science and Information Engineering, 2009 WRI World Congress on*. IEEE, volume 5, pages 12–16.

Catherine Havasi, Robert Speer, and Jason Alonso. 2007. Conceptnet 3: a flexible, multilingual semantic network for common sense knowledge. In *Recent advances in natural language processing*. John Benjamins Philadelphia, PA, pages 27–29.

Sunil Kumar Kopparapu. 2010. Automatic extraction of usable information from unstructured resumes to aid search. In *Progress in Informatics and Computing (PIC), 2010 IEEE International Conference on*. IEEE, volume 1, pages 99–103.

Claudia Leacock and Martin Chodorow. 1998. Combining local context and wordnet similarity for word sense identification. *WordNet: An electronic lexical database* 49(2):265–283.

Hugo Liu and Push Singh. 2004. Conceptneta practical commonsense reasoning tool-kit. *BT technology journal* 22(4):211–226.

Sumit Maheshwari, Abhishek Sainani, and P Reddy. 2010. An approach to extract special skills to improve the performance of resume selection. *Databases in Networked Information Systems* pages 256–273.

Ujjal Marjit, Kumar Sharma, and Utpal Biswas. 2012. Discovering resume information using linked data.

International Journal of Web & Semantic Technology 3(2):51.

Tomas Mikolov, Kai Chen, Greg Corrado, and Jeffrey Dean. 2013a. Efficient estimation of word representations in vector space. *arXiv preprint arXiv:1301.3781* .

Tomas Mikolov, Ilya Sutskever, Kai Chen, Greg S Corrado, and Jeff Dean. 2013b. Distributed representations of words and phrases and their compositionality. In *Advances in neural information processing systems*. pages 3111–3119.

George A Miller. 1995. Wordnet: a lexical database for english. *Communications of the ACM* 38(11):39–41.

Radim Řehůřek and Petr Sojka. 2010. Software Framework for Topic Modelling with Large Corpora. In *Proceedings of the LREC 2010 Workshop on New Challenges for NLP Frameworks*. ELRA, Valletta, Malta, pages 45–50. `http://is.muni.cz/publication/884893/en`.

Amit Singh, Catherine Rose, Karthik Visweswariah, Vijil Chenthamarakshan, and Nandakishore Kambhatla. 2010. Prospect: a system for screening candidates for recruitment. In *Proceedings of the 19th ACM international conference on Information and knowledge management*. ACM, pages 659–668.

Steve Spagnola and Carl Lagoze. 2011. Edge dependent pathway scoring for calculating semantic similarity in conceptnet. In *Proceedings of the Ninth International Conference on Computational Semantics*. Association for Computational Linguistics, pages 385–389.

Melanie Tosik, Carsten Lygteskov Hansen, Gerard Goossen, and Mihai Rotaru. 2015. Word embeddings vs word types for sequence labeling: the curious case of cv parsing. In *VS@ HLT-NAACL*. pages 123–128.

Zhibiao Wu and Martha Palmer. 1994. Verbs semantics and lexical selection. In *Proceedings of the 32nd annual meeting on Association for Computational Linguistics*. Association for Computational Linguistics, pages 133–138.

Kun Yu, Gang Guan, and Ming Zhou. 2005. Resume information extraction with cascaded hybrid model. In *Proceedings of the 43rd Annual Meeting on Association for Computational Linguistics*. Association for Computational Linguistics, pages 499–506.

Leveraging Diverse Lexical Chains to Construct Essays
for Chinese College Entrance Examination

Liunian Li Xiaojun Wan Jin-ge Yao Siming Yan
Institute of Computer Science and Technology, Peking University, Beijing 100871, China
The MOE Key Laboratory of Computational Linguistics, Peking University
{liliunian, wanxiaojun, yaojinge, dantes}@pku.edu.cn

Abstract

In this work we study the challenging task of automatically constructing essays for Chinese college entrance examination where the topic is specified in advance. We explore a sentence extraction framework based on diversified lexical chains to capture coherence and richness. Experimental analysis shows the effectiveness of our approach and reveals the importance of information richness in essay writing.

1 Introduction

Chinese National Higher Education Entrance Examination, a.k.a. Gaokao ("高考") in Chinese, has a similar format to the American SAT, except that it lasts more than twice as long. The nine-hour test is offered just once a year and is the sole determinant for admission to virtually all Chinese colleges and universities. It emphasizes several subjects including math and science, but also measures knowledge of written Chinese and English. It includes various types of questions such as multiple-choice questions, short-answer questions and essays. In this work, we focus on the Chinese essay writing questions, typically in the format of writing a topically rich but coherent essay when specified a topical word or title. Developing a system that can construct essays in the context of exams is not for mimicking or surpassing human writing, but to provide analytical assistance for students and high school teachers to improve essay writing. The task is challenging as it requires analyzing of the given topic and the ability to organize coherent descriptions in sentences and paragraphs, while the content should cover rich aspects and discussions but still conforms to the given topic. As a preliminary study we only explore sentence extraction to get a sense of how well automatic approaches could achieve when evaluated by professional evaluators.

We explore an approach based on lexical chains, i.e., sequences of words containing a series of conceptually related words in a discourse. Lexical chains could be useful to assist analyzing topical coherence and we will show their effectiveness in essay construction. For a given topic, we first retrieve a few topically relevant documents, from which the lexical chains will be built. Each lexical chain corresponds to a subtopic. We would like to have each subtopic representative, while the overall subtopics are diverse enough to cover as many topically related aspects as possible. We leverage a diversified ranking algorithm to calculate the importance weights for different lexical chains, then form the essay by selecting and organizing sentences to cover the important chains.

In this paper we provide a focused study on a specific topic. Our contributions can be summarized as follows:

- To the best of our knowledge, we are the first study Chinese essay generation for Chinese college entrance exams. We utilize sentence extraction as a viable step towards essay generation for exams.

- Considering the nature of the problem, we propose a framework based on diversified selection of lexical chains, to cover rich and diverse aspects of the given topical word.

- Manual evaluation from experienced high school teachers shows the feasibility for automatic essay generation, as well as the effectiveness and the potential of our approach, revealing the importance of information richness and diversity for essay writing in the context of Chinese college entrance exams.

Proceedings of the The 8th International Joint Conference on Natural Language Processing, pages 355–360,
Taipei, Taiwan, November 27 – December 1, 2017 ©2017 AFNLP

2 Approach

In this preliminary study, we directly use sentences from a large source corpus to construct the final essay. This can be treated as a viable intermediate step towards full generation. We design a framework that consists of article retrieval, lexical chain construction, sentence extraction and information ordering. Note that in this study the specified topic for essay writing is in the form of one single topical word while our approach relies on vectorial representations. Nevertheless, our solution can naturally generalize to sentential inputs, since we could use sentence embedding models (e.g. RNNs, skip-thought vectors) to get a vectorized representaion.

2.1 Article Retrieval

In this study we find that a simple retrieval model based on latent semantic analysis (Deerwester et al., 1990, LSA) works relatively well. Specifically, we get semantic vector representations for each document and the given topical word by performing singular value decomposition on the term-document matrix, where each element corresponds to the tf-idf value for a particular word in the document. Articles with the highest similarity scores with the given topic word will be retrieved for the next steps. We also tried an even simpler approach to directly use averaged word vectors to represent a document and search for the documents that lead to the largest cosine similarity values with the given topical word. This approach turns out to prefer shorter articles and yields less accurate performance compared with LSA.

2.2 Building Lexical Chains

The main task studied in this paper is to construct an essay for a˙ specified topic word. A lexical chain (Morris and Hirst, 1991) is a sequence of words that consists of a series of conceptually related words in a discourse. A lexical chain can be used to model topical contexts as well as text coherence. In our study, we adapt the calculation method used by Barzilay and Elhadad (1999) for our purpose. Due to the shortage of high-coverage thesaurus, we utilize vector semantics to capture lexical relationships, and find that pairwise similarities defined by word vectors can be used to build reliable lexical chains while being more flexible.

We treat each retrieved article as a list of words.

For the purpose of this study, we only consider adjectives and nouns when constructing the chains. Since in Chinese articles, most frequently used adverbs (such as "那么"-*so*) and verbs (such as "成为"-*becomes*, "有"-*exist*) are used for syntactic integrity and do not contain topically related information.

Given an article, we take out each word one by one and check whether and where it should be placed. If this word has not been included in any chain, we treat it as a candidate and traverse all current chains to calculate the similarity between the candidate and the chain. The candidate word will be attached to the chain with the highest similarity value if it surpasses a threshold. Here the similarity between a candidate word w and a chain C is defined as the similarity between w and the last word in C. [1]

2.3 Importance Estimation for Chains

Not all of the constructed lexical chains should be used for further processing, as some may not cover important aspects of the given topic. There could be many ways for estimating the importance of different lexical chains. In this work we model the problem using graph-based ranking, treating each candidate chain as a node in a graph. The edge weight is assigned to be pairwise similarity between two chains C_1 and C_2, defined as $cos(\frac{1}{\#C_1} \sum_{w \in C_1} vec(w),)$, i.e. the similarity between their average word vectors.

In order to cover more aspects about the topic and to avoid redundancy, we would like to assign high important scores on more diverse chains. Therefore we utilize DivRank (Mei et al., 2010), a well-known diversified ranking algorithm, for calculating the ranking scores for different chains. Specifically, we utilize the pointwise variant of DivRank. At time T, the transition probability from node u to node v is defined as follows:

$$p_T(u, v) = (1 - \lambda)p^*(v) + \lambda \frac{p_0(u, v)p_T(v)}{D_T(u)} \quad (1)$$

where $p^*(v)$ is a distribution which represents the prior preference of visiting vertex v, $p_0(u, v)$ is the initialized transition matrix estimated from a regular time-homogenous random walk, and

---

[1] We find a more straightforward definition $\max_{t \in C} sim(w, t)$ less effective as it encourages a rich-gets-richer effect which leads to long chains but incoherent thematic meanings.

$D_T(u) = \sum_{v \in V} p_0(u,v) p_T(v)$ is a normalizing factor for the second term. The weights for each node are initialized to be the cosine similarity between the corresponding chain and the topic, which can in some sense reflect the prior relevance. After the algorithm converges, i.e. $p_T(v) \approx p_{T-1}(u) p_{T-1}(u,v)$, we can select the top-ranking chains as subtopics for essay construction according to the values of $p_T(v)$.

2.4 Sentence Selection

We now have our subtopics, i.e. important lexical chains, prepared. The next step is to select sentences to cover those subtopics. For each candidate sentence, we use the average vector of nouns and adjectives as its vectorial representation, denoted as $\mathbf{s}$. Let $\mathbf{c}$ and $\mathbf{t}$ be the average word vector of the current lexical chain and the vector of the topical word, respectively. We define the weight for sentence $\mathbf{s}$ to be a linear combination of chain similarity and topical word similarity:

$$weight(\mathbf{s}) = \frac{\cos(\mathbf{s},\mathbf{t}) + \rho \cdot \cos(\mathbf{s},\mathbf{c})}{1+\rho} \quad (2)$$

We empirically set the ratio parameter ρ to be 0.8 and observe that the selected sentences can cover the subtopic well while being coherent with the topical word.

An essay in Chinese college entrance exams normally has a length between 800 and 1,200 Chinese characters. The most typical essays contain around 1,000 characters. We find that taking seven top-ranking subtopics (chains) can lead to a good coverage of the given topic, and selecting four sentences for each subtopic to form a paragraph will make the overall length just around 1,000. Therefore we limit the numbers for subtopic and sentence selection as such.

2.5 Sentence Ordering

After selecting sentences for each subtopic, we need to order them to form paragraphs and order the paragraphs to construct the full essay. A straightforward way is to greedily select elements based on similarity between each candidate and the previously selected sentence or paragraph. Preliminary experiments suggest that most elements share high similarity values due to our selection criteria in previous steps, causing simple greedy selection strategy to fail. Therefore, we consider a different method: ordering sentences and paragraphs according to its position in the

original article. The position of each candidate can be represented as a rational number, dividing the current position number by the total number of sentences in that paragraph. We find readability within a paragraph largely increased after such strategy for sentence ordering. The intuition is that sentences in the front or at the end typically contain more general discussion while sentences in the middle tend to describe specific details or expansive contents. For paragraph ordering, we take a similar approach by calculating relative positions in the original document.

3 Experimental Study

3.1 Settings

3.1.1 Data

Since we study approaches based on sentence extraction in this preliminary work, We collected a source corpus that contains 800 articles in Chinese, with the overall size around 800,000 Chinese characters. The source corpus consists of essays written by various authors, discussing relatively diverse topics. [2]

Since the similarity calculations in our framework involves vectorial representations for each word, we trained 300 dimensional GloVe vectors (Pennington et al., 2014) on the Chinese Gigaword corpus (Graff and Chen, 2005). We used the Stanford Chinese Segmenter for word segmentation (Tseng et al., 2005).

For evaluation, 10 topics which have once appeared in previous Chinese college entrance exams will be provided for all the experimented essay construction systems. We have manually checked that there indeed exists several sentences in the source corpus that are relevant to the given topic. A good system should detect such sentences and use them to generate the essay that well responds to the specified topic.

3.1.2 Evaluation

Given a topical word, every student will write a completely different essay. The diversity of possible essays makes automatic evaluation metrics that count on content overlaps impossible since system outputs can then only be compared with rather limited references. Therefore we leave proper design of automatic metrics as future work and only

---

[2] To promote related experimental and educational studies, we have attached the corpus in the supplementary materials which could be found in the ACL Anthology.

perform manual evaluation in this study.

We conduct manual ratings on a few important metrics (in a 1-10 rating system, the higher the better) in generic generation systems that also should be emphasized in this study, including

- **Topical consistency (const.)**: on how much is the output consistent with the given topic.

- **Overall readability (read.)**: overall readability of the essay in terms of text coherence.

- **Content diversity (div.)**: whether the essay covering multiple aspects of the topic or just repeating the same argument.

For the purpose of this study, we also evaluate the output essays using the evaluation criteria for the Chinese college entrance exams. The total rating score is 60 points, assigned for the *basic level* and the *advanced level* respectively. The basic level (40 points in total) considers whether the most basic requirements have been fulfilled, such as whether the essay conforms to the given topic, describing with structural integrity and using correct punctuation. The advanced level (20 points in total) measures how much depth, richness, literary grace and novelty there exist in the content of the essay. We ask 10 high school teachers who are experienced in such essay evaluation settings to conduct manual scoring. Note that in evaluations of the exams, the above points will not be strictly assigned one by one, only an overall score will be seen. We conform with this scoring approach in this study.

3.1.3 Baselines

To verify the effectiveness of our proposed approach, we compare with two baseline systems: The system (**Baseline1**) that utilizes topically related words and clusters rather than our proposed diversified lexical chains for subtopic representation, and a more straightforward baseline (**Baseline2**) that select sentences which have the most similar vectorial representations with the given topical word. The former baseline can be treated as a reimplementation of the very recent Chinese essay generating system proposed by Qin et al. (2015). All systems are evaluated on the given 10 topics, producing 30 essays in total.

3.2 Results

Table 1 lists the manual rating scores (average and standard deviation [3] of the scores from the 10 high school teachers) for the outputs from different systems. The differences between systems are statistically significant in Bonferroni adjusted pairwise-t testing with $p < 0.01$. We can see that our proposed framework outperforms the baseline systems in all evaluation criteria. We also provide the example outputs in the appendix.

	Baseline1	Baseline2	Proposed
Basic (40)	29.42±4.43	32.75±1.84	34.82±1.50
Adv (20)	11.65±2.53	13.1±1.79	14.97±1.23
Score (60)	41.07±6.22	45.85±3.51	49.78±2.65
const. (10)	5.38±0.98	6.47±0.84	6.90±0.76
read. (10)	5.23±0.81	6.27±0.75	6.78±0.68
div. (10)	5.15±0.74	5.8±0.87	6.92±0.75

Table 1: Evaluation results for different systems. Each cell contains the average and standard deviation of the ten scores assigned to an output.

3.3 Discussion

Here we provide some qualitative analysis for our use of lexical chains and diversified importance ranking. Given the topic word "挫折"(*setback*), we can find 40 chains in total. the top-ranking chains from diversified ranking are displayed in Figure 1a, along with the top-ranking subchains produced by the PageRank algorithm (Page et al., 1999) in Figure 1b. We can observe that chains in (1a) contain direct explanations as well as consequential attitudes and related association of words, while most chains in (1b) only cover the literal meaning of the word "挫折"(*setback*), without extensions in depth.

We also made some statistics to make sure that all systems are not directly using the original source documents. All systems produced essays using sentences from multiple articles between 9 and 21, with the overlapping proportion for single source document no more than 15%. This is intuitively a side evidence on that if a student wants to write a good essay, he or she may have to read a lot of good materials for preparation of expressions, wording choices as well as ideas.

4 Related Work

To the best of our knowledge, there exist few studies on automatically challenging the Chinese

---

[3]The standard deviation reflects the variance of different evaluators on each output, therefore also reflects agreements.

曲折(intricate) - 坎坷(bumpy) - 漫长(long-term) - 艰辛(hardship) - 历程(progress)
勇敢(brave) - 毅力(determination) - 勇气(courage) - 坚强(adamancy) - 坚韧(tenacity)
    - 自信(confident) - 信心(confidence)
意志(willpower) - 斗志(fighting will) - 顽强(indomitable) - 艰难(tough) - 困苦(tribulation)
可怕(dreadful) - 悲剧(tragedy) - 灾难(disaster) - 灾害(calamity) - 严峻(rigorous)
    - 因素(factors)
特殊(special) - 困难(difficulty) - 困境(straits) - 低谷(trough)
人生(life) - 理想(cause) - 精神(spirit) - 理念(ethic) - 思维(thinking) -观念(concept)
态度(attitude) - 理性(rational) - 冷静(calm) - 理智(wise)

(a)

曲折(intricate) - 坎坷(bumpy) - 漫长(long-term) - 艰辛(hardship) - 历程(progress)
可怕(dreadful) - 悲剧(tragedy) - 灾难(disaster) - 灾害(calamity) - 严峻(rigorous)
    - 因素(factors)
特殊(extraordinary) - 困难(difficulty) - 困境(straits) - 低谷(trough)
意志(willpower) - 斗志(fighting will) - 顽强(indomitable) - 艰难(tough) - 困苦(tribulation)
痛苦(suffering) - 悲伤(sorrow) - 伤痛(pain) - 痛楚(agony)
悲哀(grieve) - 难过(sad) - 失望(disappointed) - 绝望(despair) - 无助(helpless)
    - 孤独(loneliness)
茫然(at a loss) - 迷茫(confused) - 困惑(puzzled) - 尴尬(embarrassed)

(b)

Figure 1: Lexical chains formulated by (a) DivRank and (b) PageRank

college entrance tests. One recent work focuses on multiple choice questions in that context (Guo et al., 2017).

The approach of selecting sentence for constructing essays share similar methodological nature with extractive summarization, where classic graph-based ranking has been shown useful (Erkan and Radev, 2004). Diversified selection could further improve information coverage (Mei et al., 2010; Lin and Bilmes, 2011; Hong et al., 2014). Note that the goal of essay writing is different with summarization. The task in this study is to generate a rich but coherent article, and every student or system could write a very different essay, while the goal of summarization is to condense documents, in which case the output results should be similar in content, covering the same important facts.

The closest study with the main theme of this paper is perhaps the recent work by Qin et al. (2015) on essay generation, which directly utilizes words as subtopic representations rather than our proposed usage of diversified lexical chains.

5   Conclusion and Future Work

In this paper, we study the challenging task of essay construction for Chinese college entrance exams, propose a framework based on diversified lexical chains and show its effectiveness.

Our framework is simple in nature and is by no means perfect. For example, structural coherence is not explicitly modeled in our method since lexical chains could only capture topical coherence. We leave more elaborated strategies for content planning as future work. Also, we would like to extend the framework for more difficult titles or topics by exploring proper vectorial representations, and to collect manual data for supervised learning. Methods beyond sentence extraction should also be explored to utilize more elaborative syntactic and discursive structures.

Acknowledgments

This work was supported by 863 Program of China (2015AA015403), NSFC (61331011), and Key Laboratory of Science, Technology and Standard in Press Industry (Key Laboratory of Intelligent Press Media Technology). We thank the anonymous reviewers for helpful comments. Xiaojun Wan is the corresponding author.

References

Regina Barzilay and Michael Elhadad. 1999. Using lexical chains for text summarization. *Advances in automatic text summarization*, pages 111–121.

Scott Deerwester, Susan T Dumais, George W Furnas, Thomas K Landauer, and Richard Harshman. 1990. Indexing by latent semantic analysis. *Journal of the American society for information science*, 41(6):391.

Günes Erkan and Dragomir R. Radev. 2004. Lexrank: Graph-based lexical centrality as salience in text summarization. *Journal of Artifitial Intelligence Research (JAIR)*, 22:457–479.

David Graff and Ke Chen. 2005. Chinese gigaword. *LDC Catalog No.: LDC2003T09, ISBN*, 1:58563–58230.

Shangmin Guo, Xiangrong Zeng, Shizhu He, Kang Liu, and Jun Zhao. 2017. Which is the effective way for gaokao: Information retrieval or neural networks? In *Proceedings of the 15th Conference of the European Chapter of the Association for Computational Linguistics: Volume 1, Long Papers*, pages 111–120, Valencia, Spain. Association for Computational Linguistics.

Kai Hong, John Conroy, Benoit Favre, Alex Kulesza, Hui Lin, and Ani Nenkova. 2014. A repository of state of the art and competitive baseline summaries for generic news summarization. In *Proceedings of the Ninth International Conference on Language Resources and Evaluation (LREC'14)*, pages 1608–1616, Reykjavik, Iceland.

Hui Lin and Jeff Bilmes. 2011. A class of submodular functions for document summarization. In *Proceedings of the 49th Annual Meeting of the Association for Computational Linguistics: Human Language Technologies*, pages 510–520, Portland, Oregon, USA. Association for Computational Linguistics.

Qiaozhu Mei, Jian Guo, and Dragomir Radev. 2010. Divrank: the interplay of prestige and diversity in information networks. In *Proceedings of the 16th ACM SIGKDD international conference on Knowledge discovery and data mining*, pages 1009–1018. Acm.

Jane Morris and Graeme Hirst. 1991. Lexical cohesion computed by thesaural relations as an indicator of the structure of text. *Computational linguistics*, 17(1):21–48.

Lawrence Page, Sergey Brin, Rajeev Motwani, and Terry Winograd. 1999. The pagerank citation ranking: Bringing order to the web. Technical report, Stanford InfoLab.

Jeffrey Pennington, Richard Socher, and Christopher Manning. 2014. Glove: Global vectors for word representation. In *Proceedings of the 2014 Conference on Empirical Methods in Natural Language Processing (EMNLP)*, pages 1532–1543, Doha, Qatar. Association for Computational Linguistics.

Bing Qin, Duyu Tang, Xinwei Geng, Dandan Ning, Jiahao Liu, and Ting Liu. 2015. A planning based framework for essay generation. *arXiv preprint arXiv:1512.05919*.

Huihsin Tseng, Pichuan Chang, Galen Andrew, Daniel Jurafsky, and Christopher Manning. 2005. A conditional random field word segmenter for sighan bakeoff 2005. In *Proceedings of the fourth SIGHAN workshop on Chinese language Processing*, volume 171. Citeseer.

Draw and Tell: Multimodal Descriptions Outperform Verbal- or Sketch-Only Descriptions in an Image Retrieval Task

Ting Han and **David Schlangen**
Dialogue Systems Group // CITEC // Faculty of Linguistics and Literary Studies
Bielefeld University
`firstname.lastname@uni-bielefeld.de`

Abstract

While language conveys meaning largely symbolically, actual communication acts typically contain iconic elements as well: People gesture while they speak, or may even draw sketches while explaining something. Image retrieval *prima facie* seems like a task that could profit from combined symbolic and iconic reference, but it is typically set up to work either from language only, or via (iconic) sketches with no verbal contribution. Using a model of grounded language semantics and a model of sketch-to-image mapping, we show that adding even very reduced iconic information to a verbal image description improves recall. Verbal descriptions paired with fully detailed sketches still perform better than these sketches alone. We see these results as supporting the assumption that natural user interfaces should respond to multimodal input, where possible, rather than just language alone.

1 Introduction

In natural interactions, descriptions are typically multimodal: Someone explaining a route might point at visible landmarks while talking, or gesture them into the air, or may sketch a route on a piece of paper, if they have one handy (Emmorey et al., 2000; Tversky et al., 2009).

Especially descriptions of visual objects or situations can be supported by the iconic mode of reference provided by gestures or sketches, that is, reference via similarity rather than via symbolic convention (Pierce, 1867; Kendon, 1980; McNeill, 1992; Beattie and Shovelton, 1999). A technical task that is a direct, but controlled model of this is

Figure 1: A photograph; a verbal description of its content; and a sketch.

the task of *image retrieval*, that is, the task of retrieving one out of many photographs, based on a description of it.[1] In current work, these descriptions are typically 'monomodal', either purely verbal descriptions (Schuster et al., 2015; Hu et al., 2016),[2] or via hand-drawn sketches (Sangkloy et al., 2016; Qian et al., 2016; Yu et al., 2016).

In this work, we were interested in combining these modalities for image retrieval. We collected verbal descriptions of images (as shown in Figure 1), where the images were taken from an existing collection that provides for each image a matching sketch (Sangkloy et al., 2016). We trained "words-as-classifiers" models (Kennington and Schlangen, 2015; Schlangen et al., 2016) on the verbal descriptions to match these with images, and used the "triplet network" introduced by Sangkloy et al. (2016) to extract embeddings for the sketches. These models provide comparison scores for descriptions and candidate images, and can be combined into a joint score for a multimodal description (Section 3). We experiment with reduced sketches containing only a certain amount of the strokes from the full sketch, and

---

[1] Note that we use *strict retrieval* here, where a single, known image is to be retrieved, rather than an arbitrary one that fits a general description.

[2] As implemented and in commercial use on popular internet search engines.

Proceedings of the The 8th International Joint Conference on Natural Language Processing, pages 361–365,
Taipei, Taiwan, November 27 – December 1, 2017 ©2017 AFNLP

Figure 2: Example of the crowd-worker task. *Provide a description that identifies the left-most image within this set:* [the elephant] facing right, trunk coiled toward mouth

show that adding even very reduced iconic information to the verbal image description improves recall (Section 4). Verbal descriptions paired with fully detailed sketches still perform better than these sketches alone. Using reduced sketches allows us to quantify redundancy between modalities, and it also makes it possible to explore how information becomes available incrementally, as sketch and utterance progress. We see our results as supporting the claim that natural user interfaces should respond to multimodal input—sketches, or, going beyond that, iconic gestures—, where possible, rather than just language alone.

2 Data

Collecting verbal descriptions of images The starting point is a collection of 10,805 real-life photographs taken from ImageNet (Russakovsky et al., 2015), as selected by the Sketchy corpus of sketches (see next section; we sampled from all categories). We collected a verbal description for each photograph from English speakers using the Crowdflower service.[3] Workers were asked to list attributes of the target object so that another person would be able distinguish the described photograph from 6 distractors from the same image category. (See example in Figure 2.) Using attributes such as orientation, colour or shape was suggested, however, workers were encouraged to list any attribute values that might help, separating them with commas. As the image category was already known, workers were only asked to provide attributes.

To evaluate the quality of the descriptions, we randomly selected 100 descriptions and conducted an image selection task. A different set of workers was presented with 7 images in the same category, one target and 6 distractors. Workers correctly selected 71% of the photographs, which shows that some of the collected verbal descriptions did not refer unambiguously.

In total, we collected 10,805 object descriptions (100,620 tokens altogether). After spell checking, the vocabulary size is 4,982 (type/token ratio of 0.5). On average, each object was annotated with 3 attributes, while each attribute on average spans over 4.6 words. There were 29,234 different types of (potentially multi-word) attributes. To reduce this variability and ease the learning (described below), we devised a rule-based normalisation that mapped constructions such as "facing to the left", "facing left", "looking to the left" to the same attribute type (*facing-left*), leaving us with 18,673 different attribute types.

The Sketchy Corpus We profited from the availability of a dataset that pairs individual images (from ImageNet, using 100 images each from 125 different categories) with sketch representations of their content, the *sketchy database* (Sangkloy et al., 2016). These sketches were drawn from memory, but were validated to represent specifically the given image and not just its semantic category. Figure 1 above gave an example of such a sketch.

The sketches are stored as SVG files containing the start and end times of strokes, which allowed us to construct reduced versions containing only the first $n\%$ of strokes. Figure 3 shows some examples of such reductions. This gives us a rough approximation to an importance ordering of details in the sketch, under the assumption that the most salient features of the image might be drawn first. (We will further explore this assumption in future work.)

In the experiments reported below, we follow the training/test split used by Sangkloy et al. (2016). As we used the pre-trained sketch-image retrieval model from the Sketchy Database, we follow the train-test split setup of the corpus. In total, there are 9,734 unique photographs in our training set, and 1,071 photographs and 5,371 sketches in the test set (that is, for most images there are 5 different sketches). That is, there are

---

[3] http://www.crowdflower.com

5371 sketch/photograph ensembles in our image retrieval evaluations. Chance level recall of the image retrieval task @K=1 is 0.093% (@K=10: 0.93%).

3 Models

The retrieval combines separate word/image and sketch/image models, which will be described here.

Grounding verbal descriptions to images To judge how well a verbal description fits with a photograph, we trained logistic regression classifiers for all category words and attribute types (following the "words-as-classifiers" (WAC) approach, (Kennington and Schlangen, 2015; Schlangen et al., 2016)).[4] The classifiers take a feature representation of an image (extracted by the convolutional neural-network described below) and produce for each word an "appropriateness score". To train for example the classifier for the word "elephant", we selected all photographs which were annotated with the category word "elephant" as positive training examples, then randomly selected the same amount of photographs that are not annotated as elephant as negative examples. (Similarly for the attribute types.) We trained classifiers for words or (normalised) attribute types which occurred more than 10 times in the corpus.

Given an image description D : $w_{a_1}, \cdots, w_{a_n}, w_c$, where w_{a_i} indicates an attribute word, and w_c indicates a category word, we compute a score for a given photograph $\mathbf{P}$ and using the word/image classifiers $s_w(\cdot)$ as follows:

$$s_D(D, \mathbf{P}) = s_{w_c}(\mathbf{P}) \times \sum_{i=1}^{n} s_{w_{a_i}}(\mathbf{P}) \qquad (1)$$

(That is, attribute contributions are combined additively and then multiplicatively with the category. Attributes for which no classifier could be trained were left out of the composition.)

Comparing Sketches with Images For the comparison of the sketches with the images, and the extraction of image features, we used the "tripled network" model devised and trained by (Sangkloy et al., 2016). This model is composed of two GoogLeNet networks (Szegedy et al., 2015), one for sketches and one for images. It

---

[4]Using $\ell 2$ regularisation, liblinear optimizer, regularisation strength 1.0.

is trained with a ranking loss function, with input tuples of the form (S, I+, I-) corresponding to a sketch, a matching image and a non-matching image. As a result, the network has a set of parameters for the sketch-network and a set of parameters for the photo-network. It learns a joint 1024 dimensional embedding space of sketches and photographs. The vector distance between a sketch and an image indicates their visual similarity (please refer to the original paper for more details for model structures). We used the reciprocal of the distance as the score to measure the fitness between a sketch and a photograph:

$$s_{sk}(\mathbf{S}, \mathbf{P}) = d(\mathbf{S}, \mathbf{P})^{-1} \qquad (2)$$

where $\mathbf{P}$ indicates the feature vector of the photograph, derived with the image network, while $\mathbf{S}$ indicates the feature vector of the sketch, derived with the sketch network.

Multimodal Fusion We adopt a late fusion approach, and combine the scores as follows:

$$s_{sk+cat+att} = s_{sk}(\mathbf{P}, \mathbf{S}) \times s_d(\mathbf{P}, \mathbf{d}) \qquad (3)$$

4 Results

We evaluate the performance of verbal descriptions alone, and verbal descriptions with various levels of sketch detail added, with the results shown in Table 1, and procedures explained in the following.

Metric Following the convention of image retrieval tasks evaluation, we measure the photograph retrieval performances by average recall @K. For a given photo query, recall @ K is 1 if the corresponding photograph is among the top K retrieved results and 0 otherwise. We average over all test queries to produce average recalls. We report the average recall @K=1 and @K=10.

Mono-modal descriptions First of all, we evaluated the image retrieval performance only with verbal descriptions. Using just attributes (*att*), we achieve an average recall (@1) of 0.03, which is not surprising, given that attributes such as "facing left" can potentially describe many images. Giving the category alone (*cat*) gives an average recall of 0.12 (@1) and 0.9 (@10), respectively. This shows that the category classifiers perform well in detecting the right category (there are 8.57 images on average from each category in the test

| Sketch Detail | 10% | | 30% | | 50% | | 70% | | 90% | | 100% | |
Recall	@1	@10	@1	@10	@1	@10	@1	@10	@1	@10	@1	@10
sk	0.01	0.06	0.07	0.27	0.17	0.55	0.25	0.70	0.31	0.79	0.35	0.84
att	0.03	0.23	0.03	0.23	0.03	0.23	0.03	0.23	0.03	0.23	0.03	0.23
cat	0.12	**0.90**	0.12	**0.90**	0.12	0.90	0.12	0.90	0.12	0.90	0.12	0.90
cat+att	0.14	0.83	0.14	0.83	0.14	0.83	0.14	0.83	0.14	0.83	0.14	0.83
sk+att	0.03	0.16	0.09	0.39	0.20	0.64	0.28	0.76	0.33	0.83	0.37	0.87
sk+cat	0.12	0.76	0.20	0.85	0.28	**0.92**	0.34	**0.94**	**0.38**	**0.96**	**0.41**	**0.96**
sk+cat+att	**0.15**	0.81	**0.21**	0.87	**0.30**	**0.92**	**0.35**	**0.94**	**0.38**	0.95	**0.41**	**0.96**

Table 1: Average recall at K=1 and 10, at different levels of sketch detail. Highest number in column in bold. Numbers for language-only conditions do not change with level of sketch detail.

set). Combining *cat* and *att* improves performance somewhat @1, but even has a negative impact @10, indicating that the attributes can "override" the category and push images that are appropriate for the attributes, but not the category, into the top 10.

We also show results for the sketches alone, at various levels of detail of the sketch. (E.g., "10%" only contains the first 10% of strokes, etc. The 100% condition is the one reported by (Sangkloy et al., 2016), our results are within 0.01 of the ones reported there.)

cat+att	30% *sk+* *cat+att*	30% *sk*	100% *sk*
chicken, can see head only, head is mainly red skin			
Rank=1	Rank=1	Rank=27	Rank=1
camel, light brown, laying down, head on right, has blanket to ride on			
Rank=3	Rank=1	Rank=29	Rank=1
butterfly, facing left, white			
Rank=3	Rank=1	Rank=32	Rank=1

Figure 3: Retrieval with verbal description only (1st column), verbal description plus 30% sketch (2nd column), 30% sketch (3rd column) and 100% sketch (4th column).

Multimodal descriptions As Table 1 (first column) shows, combining even the very reduced sketch information at a 10% detail level improves results @1 compared to language-only (if only marginally). The improvement increases with the level of sketch detail, and reaches at 70% sketch detail a level at which the multimodal ensemble performs as well as the full sketch (0.35 @1), improving 0.16 points over the language-only baseline. The fullest combination (full utterance, 100% sketch) improves over the full sketch by 0.06 points (0.41 vs. 0.35).

Figure 3 shows some selected examples with sketches at various detail settings.

5 Conclusions

This paper introduced a corpus of natural language attribute descriptions of images taken from a corpus that paired these images with sketches. We showed that a model of grounded word meaning trained on these data can be combined with an existing model of sketch/image relation, where the combination improves retrieval performance relative to the separate models. Specifically, the model profited even from small amounts of iconic information (sketches reduced to 30% of their strokes). We draw from these results the tentative conclusion that it can be advantageous to add modalities other than language (and hence allow reference other than through symbols, namely through iconic similarity relations) for certain tasks.

In future work, we plan to directly train a joint model that directly processes language and iconic input. Our ultimate goal is to allow *gestural* iconic input, which can be expected to also provide only a reduced level of detail, in a setting where real-world locations (rather than images of objects) are to be described. How comparable this is to the reduced sketches used here is an exciting question to explore next.

We have made the image descriptions of the corpus publicly available in Bielefeld University PUB system (Han and Schlangen, 2017). The code of the image retrieval models is available on GitHub `https://github.com/TINGH/multimodal-object-description`

Acknowledgments

This work was supported by the Cluster of Excellence Cognitive Interaction Technology CITEC (EXC 277) at Bielefeld University, which is funded by the German Research Foundation (DFG). The first author would like to acknowledge the support from the China Scholarship Council (CSC).

References

Geoffrey Beattie and Heather Shovelton. 1999. Mapping the range of information contained in the iconic hand gestures that accompany spontaneous speech. *Journal of language and social psychology*, 18(4):438–462.

Karen Emmorey, Barbara Tversky, and Holly a. Taylor. 2000. Using space to describe space: Perspective in speech, sign, and gesture. *Spatial Cognition and Computation*, 2(3):157–180.

Ting Han and David Schlangen. 2017. Draw and Tell: a Corpus of Multimodal Object Descriptions.

Ronghang Hu, Huazhe Xu, Marcus Rohrbach, Jiashi Feng, Kate Saenko, and Trevor Darrell. 2016. Natural language object retrieval. In *Proceedings of the IEEE Conference on Computer Vision and Pattern Recognition*, pages 4555–4564.

Adam Kendon. 1980. Gesticulation and speech: Two aspects of the process of utterance. *The relationship of verbal and nonverbal communication*, 25(1980):207–227.

Casey Kennington and David Schlangen. 2015. Simple learning and compositional application of perceptually grounded word meanings for incremental reference resolution. In *Proceedings of the Conference for the Association for Computational Linguistics (ACL)*.

D McNeill. 1992. Hand and Mind: What Gestures Reveal About Thought. *What gestures reveal about*, pages 1–15.

Charles Sanders Pierce. 1867. On a new list of categories. In Charles Hartshorne and Paul Weiss, editors, *C.S. Pierce: The Collected Papers*. Harvard University Press, Cambridge, M.A., USA.

Xueming Qian, Xianglong Tan, Yuting Zhang, Richang Hong, and Meng Wang. 2016. Enhancing sketch-based image retrieval by re-ranking and relevance feedback. *IEEE Transactions on Image Processing*, 25(1):195–208.

Olga Russakovsky, Jia Deng, Hao Su, Jonathan Krause, Sanjeev Satheesh, Sean Ma, Zhiheng Huang, Andrej Karpathy, Aditya Khosla, Michael Bernstein, Alexander C. Berg, and Li Fei-Fei. 2015. ImageNet Large Scale Visual Recognition Challenge. *International Journal of Computer Vision (IJCV)*, 115(3):211–252.

Patsorn Sangkloy, Nathan Burnell, Cusuh Ham, and James Hays. 2016. The sketchy database: learning to retrieve badly drawn bunnies. *ACM Transactions on Graphics (TOG)*, 35(4):119.

David Schlangen, Sina Zarrieß, and Casey Kennington. 2016. Resolving references to objects in photographs using the words-as-classifiers model. In *Proceedings of ACL 2016*, Berlin, Germany.

Sebastian Schuster, Ranjay Krishna, Angel Chang, Li Fei-Fei, and Christopher D Manning. 2015. Generating semantically precise scene graphs from textual descriptions for improved image retrieval. In *Proceedings of the fourth workshop on vision and language*, volume 2.

Christian Szegedy, Wei Liu, Yangqing Jia, Pierre Sermanet, Scott Reed, Dragomir Anguelov, Dumitru Erhan, Vincent Vanhoucke, and Andrew Rabinovich. 2015. Going deeper with convolutions. In *Proceedings of the IEEE conference on computer vision and pattern recognition*, pages 1–9.

Barbara Tversky, Julie Heiser, Paul Lee, and MariePaule Daniel. 2009. Explanations in Gesture, Diagram, and Word. In Kenny R. Coventry, Thora Tenbrink, and John Bateman, editors, *Spatial Language and Dialogue*, pages 119–131. Oxford University Press.

Qian Yu, Feng Liu, Yi-Zhe Song, Tao Xiang, Timothy M Hospedales, and Chen-Change Loy. 2016. Sketch me that shoe. In *Proceedings of the IEEE Conference on Computer Vision and Pattern Recognition*, pages 799–807.

Grammatical Error Correction with Neural Reinforcement Learning

Keisuke Sakaguchi[†] and **Matt Post**[‡] and **Benjamin Van Durme**[†‡]

[†]Center for Language and Speech Processing, Johns Hopkins University
[‡]Human Language Technology Center of Excellence, Johns Hopkins University
{keisuke,post,vandurme}@cs.jhu.edu

Abstract

We propose a neural encoder-decoder model with reinforcement learning (NRL) for grammatical error correction (GEC). Unlike conventional maximum likelihood estimation (MLE), the model directly optimizes towards an objective that considers a *sentence-level*, task-specific evaluation metric, avoiding the exposure bias issue in MLE. We demonstrate that NRL outperforms MLE both in human and automated evaluation metrics, achieving the state-of-the-art on a fluency-oriented GEC corpus.

1 Introduction

Research in automated Grammatical Error Correction (GEC) has expanded from token-level, closed class corrections (e.g., determiners, prepositions, verb forms) to phrase-level, open class issues that consider fluency (e.g., content word choice, idiomatic collocation, word order, etc.).

The expanded goals of GEC have led to new proposed models deriving from techniques in data-driven machine translation, including phrase-based MT (PBMT) (Felice et al., 2014; Chollampatt et al., 2016; Junczys-Dowmunt and Grundkiewicz, 2016) and neural encoder-decoder models (Yuan and Briscoe, 2016). Napoles et al. (2017) recently showed that a neural encoder-decoder can outperform PBMT on a fluency-oriented GEC data and metric.

We investigate training methodologies in the neural encoder-decoder for GEC. To train the neural encoder-decoder models, maximum likelihood estimation (MLE) has been used, where the objective is to maximize the (log) likelihood of the parameters for a given training data.

As Ranzato et al. (2015) indicates, however, MLE has drawbacks. The MLE objective is based

---

Algorithm 1: Reinforcement learning for neural encoder-decoder model.

Input: Pairs of source (X) and target (Y)
Output: Model parameter $\hat{\theta}$

1   initialize($\hat{\theta}$)
2   **for** $(x, y) \in (X, Y)$ **do**
3     $(\hat{y}_1, ...\hat{y}_k), (p(\hat{y}_1), ...p(\hat{y}_k)) = $ sample($x, k, \hat{\theta}$)
4     $p(\hat{y}) = $ normalize($p(\hat{y})$)
5     $\bar{r}(\hat{y}) = 0$ // expected reward
6   **for** $\hat{y}_i \in \hat{y}$ **do**
7       $\bar{r}(\hat{y}) + = p(\hat{y}_i) \cdot$ score($\hat{y}_i, y$)
8   backprop($\hat{\theta}, \bar{r}$) // policy gradient $\frac{\partial}{\partial \hat{\theta}}$
9   **return** $\hat{\theta}$

---

on *word-level* accuracy against the reference, and the model is not exposed to the predicted output during training (exposure bias). This becomes problematic, because once the model fails to predict a correct word, it falls off the right track and does not come back to it easily.

To address the issues, we employ a neural encoder-decoder GEC model with a reinforcement learning approach in which we directly optimize the model toward our final objective (i.e., evaluation metric). The objective of the neural reinforcement learning model (NRL) is to maximize the expected reward on the training data. The model updates the parameters through back-propagation according to the reward from predicted outputs. The high-level description of the training procedure is shown in Algorithm 1, and more details are elaborated in §2. To our knowledge, this is the first attempt to employ reinforcement learning for directly optimizing the encoder-decoder model for GEC task.

We run GEC experiments on a fluency-oriented GEC corpus (§3), demonstrating that NRL outperforms the MLE baseline both in human and automated evaluation metrics.

Proceedings of the The 8th International Joint Conference on Natural Language Processing, pages 366–372,
Taipei, Taiwan, November 27 – December 1, 2017 ©2017 AFNLP

2 Model and Optimization

We use the *attentional neural encoder-decoder* model (Bahdanau et al., 2014) as a basis for both NRL and MLE. The model takes (possibly ungrammatical) source sentences $x \in X$ as an input, and predicts grammatical and fluent output sentences $y \in Y$ according to the model parameter θ. The model consists of two sub-modules, *encoder* and *decoder*. The encoder transforms x into a sequence of vector representations (hidden states) using a bidirectional gated recurrent neural network (GRU) (Chung et al., 2014). The decoder predicts a word y_t at a time, using previous token y_{t-1} and linear combination of encoder information as attention.

2.1 Maximum Likelihood Estimation

Maximum Likelihood Estimation training (MLE) is a standard optimization method for encoder-decoder models. In MLE, the objective is to maximize the log likelihood of the correct sequence for a given sequence for the entire training data.

$$L(\theta) = \sum_{\langle X,Y \rangle} \sum_{t=1}^{T} \log p(y_t|x, y_1^{t-1}; \theta) \qquad (1)$$

The gradient of $L(\theta)$ is as follows:

$$\frac{\partial L(\theta)}{\partial \theta} = \sum_{\langle X,Y \rangle} \sum_{t=1}^{T} \frac{\nabla p(y_t|x, y_1^{t-1}; \theta)}{p(y_t|x, y_1^{t-1}; \theta)} \qquad (2)$$

One drawback of MLE is the *exposure bias* (Ranzato et al., 2015). The decoder predicts a word conditioned on the correct word sequence (y_1^{t-1}) during training, whereas it does with the predicted word sequence ($\hat{y}_1^{t-1}$) at test time. Namely, the model is not exposed to the predicted words in training time. This is problematic, because once the model fails to predict a correct word at test time, it falls off the right track and does not come back to it easily. Furthermore, in most sentence generation tasks, the MLE objective does not necessarily correlate with our final evaluation metrics, such as BLEU (Papineni et al., 2002) in machine translation and ROUGE (Lin, 2004) in summarization. This is because MLE optimizes word level predictions at each time step instead of evaluating sentences as a whole.

GEC is no exception. It depends on sentence-level evaluation that considers grammaticality and fluency. For this purpose, it is natural to use GLEU (Napoles et al., 2015), which has been used as a fluency-oriented GEC metric. We explain more details of this metric in §2.3.

2.2 Neural Reinforcement Learning

To address the issues in MLE, we directly optimize the neural encoder-decoder model toward our final objective for GEC using reinforcement learning. In reinforcement learning, *agents* aim to maximize expected *rewards* by taking *actions* and updating the *policy* under a given *state*. In the neural encoder-decoder model, we treat the encoder-decoder as an agent which predicts a word from a fixed vocabulary at each time step (the action), given the hidden states of the neural encoder-decoder representation. The key difference from MLE is that the reward is not restricted to token-level accuracy. Namely, any arbitrary metric is applicable as the reward.[1]

Since we use GLEU as the final evaluation metric, the objective of NRL is to maximize the expected GLEU by learning the model parameter.

$$\begin{aligned} J(\theta) &= \mathbb{E}[r(\hat{y}, y)] \\ &= \sum_{\hat{y} \in S(x)} p(\hat{y}|x; \theta) r(\hat{y}, y) \end{aligned} \qquad (3)$$

where $S(x)$ is a sampling function that produces k samples $\hat{y}_1, ... \hat{y}_k$, $p(\hat{y}|x; \theta)$ is a probability of the output sentence, and $r(\hat{y}, y)$ is the reward for $\hat{y}_k$ given a reference set y. As described in Algorithm 1, given a pair of source sentence and the reference (x, y), NRL takes k sample outputs $\hat{y}_1, ... \hat{y}_k$ and their probabilities $p(\hat{y}_1), ... p(\hat{y}_k)$ (line 3).[2] Then, the expected reward is computed by multiplying the probability and metric score for each sample $\hat{y}_i$ (line 7).

In the encoder-decoder model, the parameters θ are updated through back-propagation and the number of parameter updates is determined by the partial derivative of $J(\theta)$, called the *policy gradient* (Williams, 1992; Sutton et al., 1999) in reinforcement learning:

$$\frac{\partial J(\theta)}{\partial \theta} = \alpha \mathbb{E}\left[\nabla \log p(\hat{y})\{r(\hat{y}, y) - b\}\right] \qquad (4)$$

where α is a learning rate and b is an arbitrary baseline reward to reduce the variance. The sample mean reward is often used for b (Williams, 1992), and we follow it in NRL.

It is reasonable to compare NRL to minimum risk training (MRT) (Shen et al., 2016). In fact,

---

[1] The reward is given at the end of the decoder output (i.e., delayed reward).

[2] We sampled sentences from softmax distribution.

Corpus	# sents.	mean chars per sent.	# sents. edited
NUCLE	57k	115	38%
FCE	34k	74	62%
Lang-8	1M	56	35%

Table 1: Statistics of training corpora

NRL with a *negative expected reward* can be regarded as MRT. The gradient of MRT objective is a special case of *policy gradient* in NRL. We show mathematical details about the relevance between NRL and MRT in the supplemental material (Appendix A).

2.3 Reward in Grammatical Error Correction

To capture fluency as well as grammaticality in evaluation on such references, we use GLEU as the reward. We have shown GLEU to be more strongly preferred than other GEC metrics by native speakers (Sakaguchi et al., 2016). Similar to BLEU in machine translation, GLEU computes n-gram precision between the system hypothesis (H) and the reference (R). In GLEU, however, n-grams in source (S) are also considered. The precision is penalized when the n-gram in H overlaps with the source and not with the reference.

$$\text{GLEU} = \text{BP} \cdot \exp \left(\sum_{n=1}^{4} \frac{1}{n} \log p'_n \right)$$

$$p'_n = \frac{N(H, R) - [N(H, S) - N(H, S, R)]}{N(H)}$$

$$\text{BP} = \begin{cases} 1 & \text{if } h > r \\ \exp(1 - r/h) & \text{if } h \leq r \end{cases}$$

where $N(A, B, C, ...)$ is the number of overlapped n-grams among the sets, and BP *brevity penalty* is compute based on token length in the system hypothesis (h) and the reference (r).

3 Experiments

Data For training the models (MLE and NRL), we use the following corpora: the NUS Corpus of Learner English (NUCLE) (Dahlmeier et al., 2013), the Cambridge Learner Corpus First Certificate English (FCE) (Yannakoudakis et al., 2011), and the Lang-8 Corpus of learner English (Tajiri et al., 2012). The basic statistics are shown in Table 1.[3] We exclude some unreasonable edits (comments by editors, incomplete sentences such

Models	Methods	# sents. (corpora)
CAMB14	Hybrid (rule + PBMT)	155k (NUCLE, FCE, in-house)
AMU	PBMT + GEC-feat.	2.3M (NUCLE, Lang8)
NUS	PBMT + Neural feat.	2.1M (NUCLE, Lang8)
CAMB16	enc-dec (MLE) + unk alignment	1.96M (non-public CLC)
MLE/NRL	enc-dec (MLE/NRL)	720k (NUCLE, Lang8, FCE)

Table 2: Summary of baselines, MLE and NRL models.

as URLs, etc.) using regular expressions and setting a maximum token edit distance within 50% of the original length. We also ignore sentences that are longer than 50 tokens or sentences where more than 5% of tokens are out-of-vocabulary (the vocabulary size is 35k). In total, we use 720k pairs of sentences for training (21k from NUCLE, 32k from FCE, and 667k from Lang-8). Spelling errors are corrected in preprocessing with the Enchant open-source spell checking library.[4]

Hyperparameters For both MLE and NRL, we set the vocabulary size to be 35k for both source and target. Words are represented by a vector with 512 dimensions. Maximum output token length is 50. The size of hidden layer units is 1,000. Gradients are clipped at 1, and beam size during decoding is 5. We regularize the GRU layer with a dropout probability of 0.2.

For MLE we use mini-batches of size 40, and the ADAM optimizer with a learning rate of 10^{-4}. We train the encoder-decoder with MLE for 900k updates, selecting the best model according to the development set evaluation.

For NRL we set the sample size to be 20. We use the SGD optimizer with a learning rate of 10^{-4}. For the *baseline reward*, we use average of sampled reward following Williams (1992). The sentence GLEU score is used as the reward $r(\hat{y}, y)$. Following a similar (but not the same) strategy of the Mixed Incremental Cross-Entropy Reinforce (MIXER) algorithm (Ranzato et al., 2015), we initialize the model by MLE for 600k updates, followed by another 600k updates using NRL, and select the best model according to the development set evaluation. Our NRL is implemented by extending the Nematus toolkit (Sennrich et al., 2017).[5]

---

[3]All the datasets are publicly available, for purposes of reproducibility. For more details about each dataset, refer to Sakaguchi et al. (2017).

[4]https://github.com/AbiWord/enchant

[5]NRL code is available at https://github.com/keisks/nematus/tree/nrl-gleu

	dev set		test set	
Models	Human	GLEU	Human	GLEU
Original	-1.072	38.21	-0.760	40.54
AMU	-0.405	41.74	-0.168	44.85
CAMB14	-0.160	42.81	-0.225	46.04
NUS	-0.131	46.27	-0.249	50.13
CAMB16	-0.117	47.20	-0.164	52.05
MLE	-0.052	48.24	-0.110	52.75
NRL	0.169	**49.82**	0.111	**53.98**
Reference	1.769	55.26	1.565	62.37

Table 3: Human (TrueSkill) and GLEU evaluation of system outputs on the development and test set.

Baselines In addition to our MLE baseline, we compare four leading GEC systems. All the systems are based on SMT, but they take different approaches. The first model, proposed by Felice et al. (2014), uses a combination of a rule-based system and PBMT with language model reranking (referring as CAMB14). Junczys-Dowmunt and Grundkiewicz (2016) proposed a PBMT model that incorporates linguistic and GEC-oriented sparse features (AMU). Another PBMT model, proposed by Chollampatt et al. (2016), is integrated with neural contextual features (NUS). Finally, Yuan and Briscoe (2016) proposed a neural encoder-decoder model with MLE training (CAMB16). This model is similar to our MLE model, but CAMB16 additionally trains an unsupervised alignment model to handle spelling errors as well as unknown words, and it uses 1.96M sentence pairs extracted from the non-public Cambridge Learner Corpus (CLC). The summary of baselines is shown in Table 2.[6]

Evaluation For evaluation, we use the JFLEG corpus (Heilman et al., 2014; Napoles et al., 2017), which consists of 1501 sentences (754: dev, 747: test) with four fluency-oriented references.

In addition to the automated metric (GLEU), we run a human evaluation using Amazon Mechanical Turk (MTurk). We randomly select 200 sentences each from the dev and test set. For each sentence, two turkers are repeatedly asked to rank five systems randomly selected from all eight: the four baseline models, MLE, NRL, one randomly selected human correction, and the original sentence. We infer the evaluation scores by comparing pairwise rankings with the TrueSkill algorithm (Herbrich et al., 2006; Sakaguchi et al., 2014).

---

[6]The four baselines are not tuned toward the same dev set as MLE and NRL. Also, they use different training set (Table 2). We compare them just for reference.

Models	Precision	Recall	M2 ($F_{0.5}$)
AMU	69.95	18.81	45.32
CAMB14	65.09	22.84	47.51
NUS	69.59	29.19	54.50
CAMB16	64.35	32.26	53.67
MLE	66.00	34.62	55.87
NRL	65.93	37.28	**57.15**

Table 4: M2 ($F_{0.5}$) scores on the dev set.

Models	Precision	Recall	M2 ($F_{0.5}$)
AMU	69.39	20.79	47.29
CAMB14	63.52	23.44	47.33
NUS	68.08	32.30	55.73
CAMB16	65.66	35.93	56.34
MLE	65.19	37.66	56.88
NRL	65.80	40.96	**58.68**

Table 5: M2 ($F_{0.5}$) scores on the test set.

	NRL > MLE	NRL = MLE	NRL < MLE
Dev	33%	45%	22%
Test	30%	57%	13%

Table 6: Ratio of pairwise (preference) judgments between NRL and MLE. NRL >MLE: NRL correction is preferred over MLE. NRL <MLE: MLE is preferred over NRL. NRL =MLE: NRL and MLE are tied.

Results Table 3 shows the human evaluation by TrueSkill and automated metric (GLEU). In both dev and test set, NRL outperforms MLE and other baselines in both the human and automatic evaluations. Human evaluation and GLEU scores correlate highly, corroborating the reliability of GLEU. With respect to inter-annotator agreement, Spearman's rank correlation between Turkers is 55.6 for the dev set and 49.2 for the test set. The correlations are sufficiently high to show the agreement between Turkers, considering the low chance level (i.e., ranking five randomly selected systems consistently between two Turkers).

Table 4 and 5 show the M2 ($F_{0.5}$) scores (Dahlmeier and Ng, 2012), which compute phrase-level edits between the system hypothesis and source and compare them with the oracle edits. Although this metric has several drawbacks such as underestimation of system performance and indiscrimination between "no change" and "wrong edits" (Felice et al., 2014), we see that the correlation between the M2 scores and human evaluation is still high in the result.

Finally, Table 6 shows the percentages of preference in the pairwise comparisons between NRL and MLE. In both the dev and test sets, around 30% of NRL corrections are preferred over MLE and approximately 50% are tied.

Orig.	but found that successful people use the people money and use there idea for a way to success .
Ref.	But it was found that successful people use other people 's money and use their ideas as a way to success .
MLE	But found that successful people use the people money and use it for a way to success .
NRL	But found that successful people use the people 's money and use their idea for a way to success .
Orig.	Fish firming uses the lots of special products such as fish meal .
Ref.	Fish firming uses a lot of special products such as fish meal .
MLE	Fish contains a lot of special products such as fish meals .
NRL	Fish shops use the lots of special products such as fish meal .

Table 7: Example outputs by MLE and NRL

Analysis Table 7 presents example outputs from MLE and NRL. In the first example, both MLE and NRL successfully corrected the homophone error (*there vs. their*), but MLE changed the meaning of the original sentence by replacing *their idea* to *it*. Meanwhile, NRL made the sentence more grammatical by adding a possessive *'s*. The second example demonstrates challenging issues for future work in GEC. The correction by MLE looks fairly fluent as well as grammatical, but it is semantically nonsense. The correction by NRL is also fairly fluent and makes sense, but the meaning has been changed too much. For further improvement, better GEC models that are aware of the context or possess world knowledge are needed.

4 Conclusions

We have presented a neural encoder-decoder model with reinforcement learning for GEC. To alleviate the MLE issues (exposure bias and token-level optimization), NRL learns the policy (model parameters) by directly optimizing toward the final objective by treating the final objective as the reward for the encoder-decoder agent. Using a GEC-specific metric, GLEU, we have demonstrated that NRL outperforms the MLE baseline on the fluency-oriented GEC corpus both in human and automated evaluation metrics. As a supplement, we have explained the relevance between minimum risk training (MRT) and NRL, claiming that MRT is a special case of NRL.

Acknowledgments

This work was supported in part by the JHU Human Language Technology Center of Excellence (HLTCOE), and DARPA LORELEI. The U.S. Government is authorized to reproduce and distribute reprints for Governmental purposes. The views and conclusions contained in this publication are those of the authors and should not be interpreted as representing official policies or endorsements of DARPA or the U.S. Government.

References

Dzmitry Bahdanau, Kyunghyun Cho, and Yoshua Bengio. 2014. Neural machine translation by jointly learning to align and translate. *arXiv:1409.0473*.

Shamil Chollampatt, Duc Tam Hoang, and Hwee Tou Ng. 2016. Adapting grammatical error correction based on the native language of writers with neural network joint models. In *Proceedings of the 2016 Conference on Empirical Methods in Natural Language Processing*, pages 1901–1911, Austin, Texas. Association for Computational Linguistics.

Junyoung Chung, Caglar Gulcehre, KyungHyun Cho, and Yoshua Bengio. 2014. Empirical evaluation of gated recurrent neural networks on sequence modeling. *arXiv:1412.3555*.

Daniel Dahlmeier and Hwee Tou Ng. 2012. Better evaluation for grammatical error correction. In *Proceedings of the 2012 Conference of the North American Chapter of the Association for Computational Linguistics: Human Language Technologies*, pages 568–572, Montréal, Canada. Association for Computational Linguistics.

Daniel Dahlmeier, Hwee Tou Ng, and Siew Mei Wu. 2013. Building a large annotated corpus of learner english: The NUS Corpus of Learner English. In *Proceedings of the Eighth Workshop on Innovative Use of NLP for Building Educational Applications*, pages 22–31, Atlanta, Georgia. Association for Computational Linguistics.

Mariano Felice, Zheng Yuan, Øistein E. Andersen, Helen Yannakoudakis, and Ekaterina Kochmar. 2014. Grammatical error correction using hybrid systems and type filtering. In *Proceedings of the Eighteenth Conference on Computational Natural Language Learning: Shared Task*, pages 15–24, Baltimore, Maryland. Association for Computational Linguistics.

Michael Heilman, Aoife Cahill, Nitin Madnani, Melissa Lopez, Matthew Mulholland, and Joel Tetreault. 2014. Predicting grammaticality on an ordinal scale. In *Proceedings of the 52nd Annual Meeting of the Association for Computational Linguistics*, pages 174–180, Baltimore, Maryland. Association for Computational Linguistics.

Ralf Herbrich, Tom Minka, and Thore Graepel. 2006. TrueSkill™: A Bayesian skill rating system. In

Proceedings of the Twentieth Annual Conference on Neural Information Processing Systems, pages 569–576, Vancouver, British Columbia, Canada. MIT Press.

Marcin Junczys-Dowmunt and Roman Grundkiewicz. 2016. Phrase-based machine translation is state-of-the-art for automatic grammatical error correction. In *Proceedings of the 2016 Conference on Empirical Methods in Natural Language Processing*, pages 1546–1556, Austin, Texas. Association for Computational Linguistics.

Chin-Yew Lin. 2004. Rouge: A package for automatic evaluation of summaries. In *Text Summarization Branches Out: Proceedings of the ACL-04 Workshop*, pages 74–81, Barcelona, Spain. Association for Computational Linguistics.

Courtney Napoles, Keisuke Sakaguchi, Matt Post, and Joel Tetreault. 2015. Ground truth for grammatical error correction metrics. In *Proceedings of the 53rd Annual Meeting of the Association for Computational Linguistics and the 7th International Joint Conference on Natural Language Processing*, pages 588–593, Beijing, China. Association for Computational Linguistics.

Courtney Napoles, Keisuke Sakaguchi, and Joel Tetreault. 2017. JFLEG: A fluency corpus and benchmark for grammatical error correction. In *Proceedings of the 15th Conference of the European Chapter of the Association for Computational Linguistics*, pages 229–234, Valencia, Spain. Association for Computational Linguistics.

Franz Josef Och. 2003. Minimum error rate training in statistical machine translation. In *Proceedings of the 41st Annual Meeting of the Association for Computational Linguistics*, pages 160–167, Sapporo, Japan. Association for Computational Linguistics.

Kishore Papineni, Salim Roukos, Todd Ward, and Wei-Jing Zhu. 2002. Bleu: a method for automatic evaluation of machine translation. In *Proceedings of 40th Annual Meeting of the Association for Computational Linguistics*, pages 311–318, Philadelphia, Pennsylvania. Association for Computational Linguistics.

Marc'Aurelio Ranzato, Sumit Chopra, Michael Auli, and Wojciech Zaremba. 2015. Sequence level training with recurrent neural networks. *arXiv:1511.06732*.

Keisuke Sakaguchi, Courtney Napoles, Matt Post, and Joel Tetreault. 2016. Reassessing the goals of grammatical error correction: Fluency instead of grammaticality. *Transactions of the Association for Computational Linguistics*, 4:169–182.

Keisuke Sakaguchi, Courtney Napoles, and Joel Tetreault. 2017. GEC into the future: Where are we going and how do we get there? In *Proceedings of the 12th Workshop on Innovative Use of NLP*

for Building Educational Applications, pages 180–187, Copenhagen, Denmark. Association for Computational Linguistics.

Keisuke Sakaguchi, Matt Post, and Benjamin Van Durme. 2014. Efficient elicitation of annotations for human evaluation of machine translation. In *Proceedings of the Ninth Workshop on Statistical Machine Translation*, pages 1–11, Baltimore, Maryland. Association for Computational Linguistics.

Rico Sennrich, Orhan Firat, Kyunghyun Cho, Alexandra Birch, Barry Haddow, Julian Hitschler, Marcin Junczys-Dowmunt, Samuel Läubli, Antonio Valerio Miceli Barone, Jozef Mokry, and Maria Nadejde. 2017. Nematus: a toolkit for neural machine translation. In *Proceedings of the Software Demonstrations of the 15th Conference of the European Chapter of the Association for Computational Linguistics*, pages 65–68, Valencia, Spain. Association for Computational Linguistics.

Shiqi Shen, Yong Cheng, Zhongjun He, Wei He, Hua Wu, Maosong Sun, and Yang Liu. 2016. Minimum risk training for neural machine translation. In *Proceedings of the 54th Annual Meeting of the Association for Computational Linguistics*, pages 1683–1692, Berlin, Germany. Association for Computational Linguistics.

Richard S Sutton, David A McAllester, Satinder P Singh, Yishay Mansour, et al. 1999. Policy gradient methods for reinforcement learning with function approximation. In *NIPS*, volume 99, pages 1057–1063.

Toshikazu Tajiri, Mamoru Komachi, and Yuji Matsumoto. 2012. Tense and aspect error correction for ESL learners using global context. In *Proceedings of the 50th Annual Meeting of the Association for Computational Linguistics*, pages 198–202, Jeju Island, Korea. Association for Computational Linguistics.

Ronald J Williams. 1992. Simple statistical gradient-following algorithms for connectionist reinforcement learning. *Machine learning*, 8(3-4):229–256.

Helen Yannakoudakis, Ted Briscoe, and Ben Medlock. 2011. A new dataset and method for automatically grading ESOL texts. In *Proceedings of the 49th Annual Meeting of the Association for Computational Linguistics: Human Language Technologies*, pages 180–189, Portland, Oregon. Association for Computational Linguistics.

Zheng Yuan and Ted Briscoe. 2016. Grammatical error correction using neural machine translation. In *Proceedings of the 2016 Conference of the North American Chapter of the Association for Computational Linguistics: Human Language Technologies*, pages 380–386, San Diego, California. Association for Computational Linguistics.

A Minimum Risk Training and Policy Gradient in Reinforcement Learning

We explain the relevance between minimum risk training (MRT) (Shen et al., 2016) and neural reinforcement learning (NRL) for training neural encoder-decoder models. We describe the detailed derivation of gradient in MRT, and show that MRT is a special case of NRL.

As introduced in §2, the model takes ungrammatical source sentences $x \in X$ as an input, and predicts grammatical and fluent output sentences $y \in Y$. The objective function in NRL and MRT are written as follows.

$$J(\theta) = \mathbb{E}[r(\hat{y}, y)] \tag{5}$$

$$R(\theta) = \sum_{(X,Y)} \mathbb{E}[\Delta(\hat{y}, y)] \tag{6}$$

where $r(\hat{y}, y)$ is the *reward* and $\Delta(\hat{y}, y)$ is the *risk* for an output $(\hat{y})$.

For the sake of simplicity, we consider expected loss in MRT for a single training pair:

$$\tilde{R}(\theta) = \mathbb{E}[\Delta(\hat{y}, y)]$$

$$= \sum_{\hat{y} \in S(x)} q(\hat{y}|x; \theta, \alpha) \Delta(\hat{y}, y) \tag{7}$$

where

$$q(\hat{y}|x; \theta, \alpha) = \frac{p(\hat{y}|x; \theta)^\alpha}{\sum_{\hat{y}' \in S(x)} p(\hat{y}'|x; \theta)^\alpha} \tag{8}$$

$S(x)$ is a sampling function that produces k samples $\hat{y}_1, ... \hat{y}_k$, and α is a smoothing parameter for the samples (Och, 2003). Although the direction to optimize (i.e., minimizing or maximizing) is different, we see the similarity between $J(\theta)$ and $\tilde{R}(\theta)$ in the sense that they both optimize models directly towards evaluation metrics.

The partial derivative of $\tilde{R}(\theta)$ with respect to the model parameter θ is derived as follows.

$$\frac{\partial \tilde{R}(\theta)}{\partial \theta} = \frac{\partial}{\partial \theta} \sum_{\hat{y} \in S(x)} q(\hat{y}|x; \theta, \alpha) \Delta(\hat{y}, y)$$

$$= \sum_{\hat{y} \in S(x)} \Delta(\hat{y}, y) \frac{\partial}{\partial \theta} q(\hat{y}|x; \theta, \alpha) \tag{9}$$

We need $\frac{\partial}{\partial \theta} q(\hat{y}|x; \theta, \alpha)$ in (9). For space efficiency, we use $q(\hat{y})$ as $q(\hat{y}|x; \theta, \alpha)$ and $p(\hat{y})$ as $p(\hat{y}|x; \theta)$ below.

$$\frac{\partial}{\partial \theta} q(\hat{y}) = \frac{\partial q(\hat{y})}{\partial p(\hat{y})} \frac{\partial p(\hat{y})}{\partial \theta} \quad (\because \text{chain rule})$$

$$= \frac{\partial q(\hat{y})}{\partial p(\hat{y})} \nabla p(\hat{y}) \tag{10}$$

For $\frac{\partial q(\hat{y})}{\partial p(\hat{y})}$, by applying the quotient rule to (8),

$$\frac{\partial q(\hat{y})}{\partial p(\hat{y})} = \frac{\{\sum_{\hat{y}'} p(\hat{y}')^\alpha\} \frac{\partial}{\partial p(\hat{y})} p(\hat{y})^\alpha - p(\hat{y})^\alpha \frac{\partial}{\partial p(\hat{y})} \sum_{\hat{y}'} p(\hat{y}')^\alpha}{\{\sum_{\hat{y}'} p(\hat{y}')^\alpha\}^2}$$

$$= \frac{\alpha p(\hat{y})^{\alpha-1}}{\sum_{\hat{y}'} p(\hat{y}')^\alpha} - \frac{\alpha p(\hat{y})^\alpha p(\hat{y})^{\alpha-1}}{\{\sum_{\hat{y}'} p(\hat{y}')^\alpha\}^2}$$

$$= \alpha \frac{p(\hat{y})^{\alpha-1}}{\sum_{\hat{y}'} p(\hat{y}')^\alpha} \left\{ 1 - \frac{p(\hat{y})^\alpha}{\sum_{\hat{y}'} p(\hat{y}')^\alpha} \right\}$$

$$= \alpha \frac{p(\hat{y})^\alpha}{\sum_{\hat{y}'} p(\hat{y}')^\alpha} \frac{1}{p(\hat{y})} \left\{ 1 - \frac{p(\hat{y})^\alpha}{\sum_{\hat{y}'} p(\hat{y}')^\alpha} \right\} \tag{11}$$

Thus, from (10) and (11), (9) is

$$\frac{\partial \tilde{R}(\theta)}{\partial \theta} = \sum_{\hat{y} \in S(x)} \Delta(\hat{y}, y) \nabla p(\hat{y})$$

$$\left[\alpha \frac{p(\hat{y})^\alpha}{\sum_{\hat{y}'} p(\hat{y}')^\alpha} \frac{1}{p(\hat{y})} \left\{ 1 - \frac{p(\hat{y})^\alpha}{\sum_{\hat{y}'} p(\hat{y}')^\alpha} \right\} \right]$$

$$= \alpha \mathbb{E} \left[\nabla p(\hat{y}) \cdot \frac{1}{p(\hat{y})} \left\{ \Delta(\hat{y}, y) - \mathbb{E}[\Delta(\hat{y}, y)] \right\} \right]$$

$$= \alpha \mathbb{E} \left[\nabla \log p(\hat{y}) \left\{ \Delta(\hat{y}, y) - \mathbb{E}[\Delta(\hat{y}, y)] \right\} \right] \tag{12}$$

According to the policy gradient theorem for REINFORCE (Williams, 1992; Sutton et al., 1999), the partial derivative of (5) is given as follows:

$$\frac{\partial J(\theta)}{\partial \theta} = \tilde{\alpha} \mathbb{E} \left[\nabla \log p(\hat{y}) \{ r(\hat{y}, y) - b \} \right] \tag{13}$$

where $\tilde{\alpha}$ is a *learning rate*[7] and b is arbitrary *baseline reward* to reduce the variance of gradients. Finally, we see that the gradient of MRT (12) is a special case of policy gradient in REINFORCE (13) with $b = \mathbb{E}[\Delta(\hat{y}, y)]$. It is also interesting to see that the smoothing parameter α works as a part of learning rate ($\tilde{\alpha}$) in NRL.

---

[7]In this appendix, we use $\tilde{\alpha}$ to distinguish it from smoothing parameter α in MRT.

Coreference Resolution on Math Problem Text in Japanese

Takumi Ito and **Takuya Matsuzaki** and **Satoshi Sato**
Graduate School of Engineering, Nagoya University, Japan
{takumi_i,matuzaki,ssato}@nuee.nagoya-u.ac.jp

Abstract

This paper describes a coreference resolution system for math problem text. Case frame dictionaries and a math taxonomy are utilized for supplying domain knowledge. The system deals with various anaphoric phenomena beyond well-studied entity coreferences.

1 Introduction

There is a growing interest in the natural language processing of mathematical problem text (e.g., Mitra and Baral, 2016; Upadhyay et al., 2016; Matsuzaki et al., 2017) because it serves as a prototypical example of a natural language interface for intelligent systems. In this paper, we describe a coreference resolution system for math problem text. In order to solve a math problem, all the anaphoric expressions including those referring to a proposition, as well as those referring to an entity, must be correctly analyzed. Although much research has been done on coreference resolution for texts such as newspaper, few researches have been done on math problems text.

Previous studies mainly focused on the relation between pronouns or definite noun phrases and their antecedents, and the resolution of zero (i.e., omitted) arguments of verbs. For instance, Iida et al. (2016) investigated zero anaphoric resolution on news text in Japanese and they considered only the zero arguments of a predicate.

On the other hand, in math problems, the arguments of unsaturated nouns are often omitted. This phenomenon is called bridging anaphora (Clark, 1975). For instance, in the following passage:

> There is a right triangle ABC with $\angle C = 90°$.
> Let the length of the hypotenuse (of ϕ) be c.

the argument of "hypotenuse" is omitted and

has to be identified as "triangle ABC". There are studies that focus on such phenomena in Japanese (Sasano and Kurohashi, 2009) and English (Gerber and Chai, 2010). Our task includes theirs, but we need to consider issues peculiar to math problems. For example, we need to be stricter in detecting a zero pronoun, as in:

> $x^2 = 1$ has a positive <u>solution</u> *(of ϕ).

One may be tempted to posit the existence of a zero argument of "a positive solution" that refers to "$x^2 = 1$". The principle of compositionality suggests that "a positive solution of $x^2 = 1$" has "1" as its denotation, but "$x^2 = 1$ has 1" does not make sense. That is, we must *not* supply the "omitted" argument to "a solution" in this sentence to derive a correct semantic representation, e.g., $\exists x(x^2 = 1 \land x > 0)$. No previous work, including Iida et al's, has dealt with such "syntactically determined" zero arguments as far as we are aware of. It is partly because most previous work has focused on the resolution of zero arguments of a predicate and there is no Japanese predicate that syntactically determines the antecedent of its zero argument.

Table 1 shows the types and the numbers of anaphoric expressions in math problems. For the survey, we randomly chose 100 problems from the entrance exam problems of seven top-ranked national universities in Japan from 1990 to 2014 (EEP) and 88 problems from the national standardized test for university admission in the even years from 1998 to 2014 (NST).

Table 1 reveals that there are few cases where (definite) common nouns are used anaphorically. One reason is that a symbol is often assigned to an entity as soon as it is introduced in a problem, such as in: "Let C be the circle that is ..." and the entity is thereafter referred to by the symbol but not by

Proceedings of the The 8th International Joint Conference on Natural Language Processing, pages 373–377,
Taipei, Taiwan, November 27 – December 1, 2017 ©2017 AFNLP

Table 1: Type of Anaphoric Expression

Type		Example	Count	
			NST	EEP
Demonstrative	Pronoun	*sore* "it", *sorera* "they"	3	2
	Determiner	*kono* "this", *korerano* "these"	28	14
Zero pronoun as argument of unsaturated noun		$(\phi\text{-}no)$ *hankei* "radius (of ϕ)"	121	61
Common Noun		*houteishiki* "(the) equation"	1	5
Conditional Demonstrative		*konotoki* "for this case"	57	33
Others		*ippou* "one", *tahou* "the other"	29	16

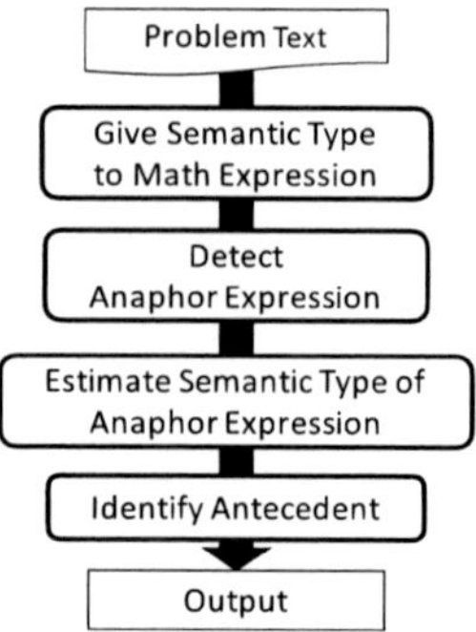

Figure 1: Overview of System

a definite noun. On the other hand, the number of occurrences of zero pronouns is very large. However, in 69% of them, the antecedents are syntactically determined. We need to discern them from the others so that heuristics-based antecedent determination is *not* applied to them. We can also see there are many conditional demonstratives, which refer not to entities but to propositions. There are several previous works that address them, such as Bejan and Harabagiu (2014), but it is much less studied compared to entity coreference resolution.

In the rest of the paper, we describe our coreference resolution system (§2) and provide some experimental results (§3). We then explain typical remaining errors (§4).

2 Methods

Our system handles four types of anaphoric expressions: pronouns, demonstrative determiner + nouns, zero pronouns, and conditional demonstratives. The first two types are analyzed according to a basic processing flow (§2.1). Zero pronouns are handled by slightly modifying the basic flow (§2.2). Conditional demonstratives are processed differently than the others since they refer to a proposition but not to an entity (§2.3).

2.1 Basic Processing Flow

An overview of the coreference resolution system is shown in Fig. 1. The input is a math problem in which math expressions are encoded in MathML[1]. The system first tags each math expression with a label indicating its semantic type based on the syntactic pattern of the MathML expression. The semantic types are categories of mathematical objects such as "integer", "real number", "circle", "ellipse", etc. We currently have 543 semantic

---

[1]https://www.w3.org/TR/MathML3/

types. The distribution is very long-tailed and we observed only 106 of these types in the experiment presented in the current paper. For example, if the math expression is $\triangle ABC$, a label "triangle" is given. If the math expression is $y = 2x$, three labels, "function", "equation", and "line", are given.

Next, anaphoric expressions are detected by a regular expression and the semantic types and the number of their antecedents are determined. If a noun appears immediately after a demonstrative such as in "this function", the semantic type is determined by the noun. Otherwise, it is determined using a case frame dictionary. For example, in the case of "it intersects with the circle", we know the semantic type of "it" is a type of "Shape" by the case frame of the predicate "intersect".

The antecedents are then identified among the nouns, math expressions, and symbols that match the semantic type and are closest to the anaphoric expression. When a plural anaphoric expression includes a specific number (e.g., "these two triangles"), we identify as many antecedents as specified in all the preceding context from the closest to the anaphor. In contrast, for a plural anaphora including no specific number (e.g.,"these triangles"), if we consider all the candidates in all the preceding context, there would be many false-positives. We thus need to limit the range of the context in which we identify the antecedents. Based on observation, we chose the window of two sentences as the range.

The case frame dictionary includes two sub-dictionaries, one for verbs and the other for unsaturated nouns. The verb case frame dictionary consists of 1858 frames and the unsaturated noun dictionary consists of 195 frames. They specify the semantic type and the number of arguments (sg: singular or pl: plural). An excerpt of each is shown in Fig. 2. The first example means "a

374

(Shape,sg-ga) (Point,sg-o) tooru
[Shape-NOM Point-ACC pass]

(Vec,sg-to) (Vec,sg-ga) chokkou-suru
[Vec-COM Vec-NOM perpendicular]

(Circle,sg-no) hankei
[Circle,sg-GEN radius]

(Integer,pl-no) kobaisu
[Integer,pl-GEN common multiple]

Figure 2: Case Frame Dictionary (top: verbs, bottom: unsaturated nouns)

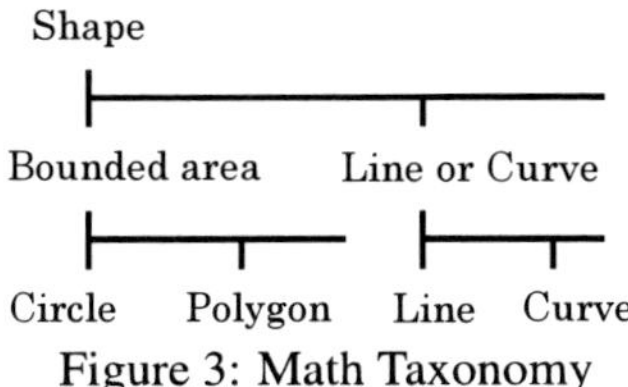

Figure 3: Math Taxonomy

planar figure passes through a point", for instance.

We also use a math taxonomy to test if the type of an antecedent candidate is compatible with an anaphoric expression. A small part of the math taxonomy is shown in Fig. 3. The number of nodes of the taxonomy is 130.

2.2 Zero Pronoun

Processing of zero pronouns is almost the same as the basic processing flow. However, the detection of anaphoric expressions and the determination of their semantic types and plurality are done differently. In the detection of anaphoric expressions, firstly all the words in the dictionary of unsaturated nouns are extracted from a problem. The system judges that there is a zero argument of an unsaturated noun if none of the following conditions are met:

1. There is an overt genitive argument of the unsaturated noun that matches the semantic type of the argument (e.g., radius of a circle)
2. The unsaturated noun is in a relative clause and the noun modified by the relative clause matches the semantic type of the argument of the unsaturated noun
3. The unsaturated noun is an argument of a prescribed set of predicates, such as *motsu* "have" and *toru* "take".

Case 2 and 3 exclude the cases where the antecedent of the zero argument is syntactically determined. A typical example of case 2 is *hankei-ga 3-no en* "a circle whose radius is 3". In En-

glish, the relativizer "whose" specifies the genitive relation between "circle" and "radius" but in Japanese no such grammatical relations are specified by the (zero) relativizer. Therefore, the detection rule becomes complicated. Case 3 excludes the cases such as "$f(x) = 0$ has a real solution (of ϕ)", where the coreferential relation is controlled by the head verb (e.g., "has") and hence the resolution is done in syntactic/semantic parsing stage.

Next, the semantic type and the number of the antecedent(s) are determined using the case frame dictionary. For example, when the unsaturated noun is "initial term (of ϕ)", the type of the zero argument is assumed to be "number sequence" and the number is singular.

2.3 Conditional Demonstrative

In math problems, coreferential expressions such as "for this case", "in case of (1)", and "the following condition" refer to propositions. We call them *conditional demonstratives* in this paper. Our system handles three types of such expressions as described below.

First type is *kono/sono-toki* "for this/that case". There are two usages of it. One indicates that all the previous conditions given in a problem are effective, and the other refers to a specific proposition, as in:

> 1. There is $\triangle ABC$ with $AB = BC = CA = 1$.
> <u>Kono-toki,</u> $\triangle ABC$-no menseki-o motomeyo.
> <u>For this case</u> $\triangle ABC$-GEN area-ACC calculate.
> *For this case, calculate the area of $\triangle ABC$.*
> 2. $f(x)$-no saidaichi-to <u>sono-toki</u>-no x-o
> $f(x)$-GEN maximum-and <u>for that case</u> x-ACC
> motomeyo.
> find.
> *Find the maximum value of $f(x)$ and the value of x that gives the maximum*

The underlined part, *Kono-toki* "for this case", in the problem 1 indicates all the conditions given so far for $\triangle ABC$ have to be taken into consideration in solving it. As the English translation suggests, *Kono-toki* (and *Sono-toki*) in this usage can be omitted without changing the meaning of the problem. On the other hand, the underlined part *Sono-toki* "for that case" in the problem 2 points to a specific condition "$f(x)$ becomes maximum" and cannot be omitted. We discriminate these two cases using regular expression patterns and rewrite the conditional demonstrative in the latter usage with the proposition it refers to (underlined in the example below):

375

$f(x)$-no saidaichi-to $f(x)$-ga saidai-ni
$f(x)$-GEN maximum-COM $f(x)$-NOM maximum
naru toki-no x-o motomeyo.
become when x-ACC find.
Find the maximum value of $f(x)$ and the value of x that gives the maximum

To identify what is referred to by a phrase such as "in the case of (1)", we have to extract a proposition or a condition from the sub-problem designated by the problem number. To that end, we seek for a key phrase in the sub-problem that typically marks such a proposition. For example, *P-youna* "such that P", *P-tame-no* "so that P", *P-toki* "when P" and *P-to-suru* "assume that P" (P : proposition) are such key phrases. We rewrite the referring expression with the proposition identified by the key phrase as in:

(1) $f(x)$-no saidaichi-ga 3-ni naru you-ni a-o sadameyo.
(1) Determine the value of a so that the maximum value of $f(x)$ is 3.
(2) (1)-no baai-ni $f(x)$-no saisyouchi-o motomeyo.
(2) In the case of (1), find the minimum value of $f(x)$.
After rewriting (2)
(2) $f(x)$-no saidaichi-ga 3-ni naru-toki $f(x)$-no saisyouchi-o motomeyo.
(2) When the maximum value of $f(x)$ is 3, find the minimum value of $f(x)$.

For a referring expression such as *tsugino-shiki/joken* "the following formula/condition", the referents are searched from the succeeding context. Specifically, the sentence or math expression just after the sentence including "the following condition" is identified as the referent and the referring expression is rewritten as follows:

Tsugi-no houteishiki-o mitasu $\triangle ABC$-o kangaeru :
$\sin A = \sin B$
Consider $\triangle ABC$ which satisfies the following equation : $\sin A = \sin B$
After rewriting
$\sin A = \sin B$-o mitasu $\triangle ABC$-o kangaeru.
Consider $\triangle ABC$ which satisfies $\sin A = \sin B$

3 Evaluation

We evaluated the system performance using three data sets. The first is 20 mock tests of Japanese national standardized test for university admission (MockNST) that consists of 74 problems. MockNST was also used for the system test while the development; hence it is a closed test data. The

Table 2: Accuracy of Zero Pronoun Detection

	Precision	Recall	F1
MockNST	74% (32/43)	84% (32/38)	79%
MockUT	89% (8/9)	100% (8/8)	93%

Table 3: Accuracy of antecedent identification

	Demons-trative	Zero Pronoun	Condi-tional	Total
MockNST	12/20	31/32	3/5	46/57 (81%)
MockUT	2/3	6/8	2/4	10/15 (67%)

second is 20 mock tests of the entrance exam of the University of Tokyo (MockUT) that consists of 41 problems. MockUT was kept unseen while the system development. We additionally used EEP data (see §1) for the evaluation of the resolution of conditional demonstratives.

Table 2 shows the accuracy of zero pronoun detection. The low precision means that unnecessary zero pronoun detection was performed. There were in total twelve such cases on MockNST and MockUT. Two thirds of them were due to an error in syntactic dependency analysis, which resulted in a failure in the recognition of the construction that determines the zero arguments of the unsaturated noun syntactically (§2.2). Table 3 shows the accuracy of the identification of antecedents.

Table 4 presents the accuracy at the problem level (i.e., perfect match) on MockUT. Approximately one third of the problems in MockUT include at least one coreference. About half of them could be completely resolved.

We also evaluated the accuracy of the resolution of conditional demonstratives on the 100 problems of EEP data set because conditional demonstratives were not frequently used in MockUT. In EEP, ten problems required coreference resolution of conditional demonstratives. Table 5 provides the details.

4 Remaining Problems

We found three types of frequent errors in the output of the current system. The first is due to an error in the dependency analysis, such as in:

$x^4 - ax - a = 0$-ga, kyojiku-jou-no fukusosuu-o kai-ni motsu youna jissuu a-o subete motomeyo.
Find all real numbers a such that $x^4 - ax - a = 0$ has a solution on the imaginary axis of the complex plane.

In this problem, the dependency parser selected *motomeyo* "find" as the head of "$x^2 - ax - a = 0$" but it should be *motsu* "has". Due to this error,

Table 4: Evaluation at Problem level

#Coreferences	%Problems	Correct
≥ 1	32% (13/41)	54% (7/13)
None	68% (28/41)	—

Table 5: Evaluation of Conditional Demonstrative

	"for this case"	"in case of (1)"	Total
Accuracy	8/8	1/2	9/10 (90%)

the system cannot detect the pattern *X-ga Y-o kaini motsu* "X has a solution in Y" and unnecessary zero anaphora resolution was done.

The second is due to a kind of polymorphism in the natural language:

> $\triangle ABC$-no   menseki-o $S(a)$-de   arawasu-toki kono-kansuu-no gurafu-o kake.
> *Letting S(a) be the area of $\triangle ABC$, draw the graph of this function.*

In this problem, $S(a)$ is first defined as a real number (area) but later referred to as a function. Due to this type mismatch, antecedent detection for *kono-kansuu* "this function" was failed.

The third is due to a failure in the recognition of the plurality of the zero pronoun.

> En O-to   houbutsusen C-ga   ten $P(\sqrt{3},0)$-o kyouyuu-shi, sarani P-ni okeru (ϕ-no) sessen-ga icchi-siteiru.
> *Circle O and parabola C share the point $P(\sqrt{3},0)$ and the tangent lines (of ϕ) at P coincide.*

In this problem, a zero argument of *sessen* "tangent line" was successfully detected but it was wrongly interpreted as singular while it actually refers to "*O* and *C*". Thus only *C* was identified as the antecedent. This is because there is no morphological indication of the number of a noun (such as -s in English) in Japanese. To solve this problem, we could utilize the case frame of *icchisuru* "coincide", which specifies a plural noun phrase as its subject. By this, we know *sessen* "tangent line(s)" actually signifies more than one entities and so is its zero argument.

5 Conclusion

This paper described a coreference resolution system for math problem text. The system deals with various anaphoric phenomena such as conditional demonstratives referring to propositions and syntactically controlled zero arguments. Evaluation showed the accuracy of the coreference resolution at the problem level was 54%. Our future work includes accurate recognition of the plurality of the

zero pronouns and fixing the error of the dependency analysis.

Acknowledgments

This research was supported by Todai Robot Project at National Institute of Informatics. We are gratefully acknowledge Gakko Hojin Takamiya Gakuen Yoyogi Seminar, Benesse Co., and Suken Shuppan Co., Ltd. for the math problem text data.

References

Cosmin Adrian Bejan and Sanda Harabagiu. 2014. Unsupervised event coreference resolution. *Computational Linguistics* 40(2):311–347.

Herbert H Clark. 1975. Bridging. In *Proceedings of the 1975 workshop on Theoretical issues in natural language processing*. Association for Computational Linguistics, pages 169–174.

Matthew Gerber and Joyce Y Chai. 2010. Beyond nombank: A study of implicit arguments for nominal predicates. In *Proceedings of the 48th Annual Meeting of the Association for Computational Linguistics*. Association for Computational Linguistics, pages 1583–1592.

Ryu Iida, Kentaro Torisawa, Jong-Hoon Oh, Canasai Kruengkrai, and Julien Kloetzer. 2016. Intrasentential subject zero anaphora resolution using multi-column convolutional neural network. In *Proceedings of the 2016 Conference on Empirical Methods in Natural Language Processing*. pages 1244–1254.

Takuya Matsuzaki, Takumi Ito, Hidenao Iwane, Hirokazu Anai, and Noriko H. Arai. 2017. Semantic parsing of pre-university math problems. In *Proceedings of the 55th Annual Meeting of the Association for Computational Linguistics*. Association for Computational Linguistics, pages 2131–2141.

Arindam Mitra and Chitta Baral. 2016. Learning to use formulas to solve simple arithmetic problems. In *Proceedings of the 54th Annual Meeting of the Association for Computational Linguistics*. pages 2144–2153.

Ryohei Sasano and Sadao Kurohashi. 2009. A probabilistic model for associative anaphora resolution. In *Proceedings of the 2009 Conference on Empirical Methods in Natural Language Processing: Volume 3-Volume 3*. Association for Computational Linguistics, pages 1455–1464.

Shyam Upadhyay, Ming-Wei Chang, Kai-Wei Chang, and Wen-tau Yih. 2016. Learning from explicit and implicit supervision jointly for algebra word problems. In *Proceedings of the 2016 Conference on Empirical Methods in Natural Language Processing*. pages 297–306.

Utilizing Visual Forms of Japanese Characters for Neural Review Classification

Yota Toyama   **Makoto Miwa**   **Yutaka Sasaki**

Toyota Technological Institute

2-12-1 Hisakata, Tempaku-ku, Nagoya, Aichi, 468-8511, Japan

{sd16423, miwa-makoto, yutaka.sasaki}@toyota-ti.ac.jp

Abstract

We propose a novel method that exploits visual information of ideograms and logograms in analyzing Japanese review documents. Our method first converts font images of Japanese characters into character embeddings using convolutional neural networks. It then constructs document embeddings from the character embeddings based on Hierarchical Attention Networks, which represent the documents based on attention mechanisms from a character level to a sentence level. The document embeddings are finally used to predict the labels of documents. Our method provides a way to exploit visual features of characters in languages with ideograms and logograms. In the experiments, our method achieved an accuracy comparable to a character embedding-based model while our method has much fewer parameters since it does not need to keep embeddings of thousands of characters.

1 Introduction

Some languages like Japanese and Chinese have ideograms and logograms that are characters representing words or phrases by themselves. In these languages, such kinds of characters usually have the same visual (surface) components (radicals) when they have similar semantic or phonetic features. Figure 1 illustrates three Japanese *Kanji* characters related to fish. These Kanji characters share the same visual components unlike English characters or words. This kind of shared components often appears in the Kanji characters as shown in Table 1. Most natural languages methods, however, ignore the visual information since they often treat texts as sequences of symbolic val-

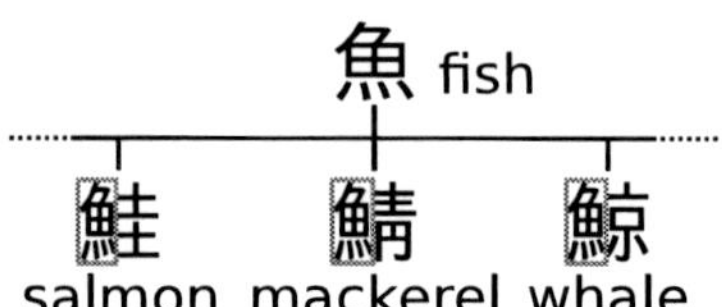

Figure 1: Kanji characters relevant to fish and their sharing components (radicals)

Component	Kanji characters
食 (eat)	飯 (food), 飲 (drink), 餐 (meal)
土 (soil)	地 (earth), 場 (field), 坂 (slope)

Table 1: Kanji characters with shared components

ues like integer indices. They therefore lose significant useful information in processing texts in such languages. Furthermore, these languages usually contain many kinds of characters. For example, a typical Japanese character set JIS X 0213 contains 11,233 different characters including Hiraganas, Katakanas, and Kanjis. This large number of characters often makes it difficult to apply recent character embedding models to such languages, and this fact prompts us to reduce the number of parameters used to store information for characters.

We propose a novel method to analyze Japanese review documents with exploiting the visual information of ideograms and logograms. Our method extends character-based Hierarchical Attention Networks (HAN) (Yang et al., 2016) by incorporating visual information of characters. The method first builds character embeddings from their font images and then feeds them as inputs into the character-based HAN.

Our main contribution is to show the usability of font images as potential character representation not to use them as additional information but to substitute for integer indices. Our method represents documents without the need for external

Proceedings of the The 8th International Joint Conference on Natural Language Processing, pages 378–382,
Taipei, Taiwan, November 27 – December 1, 2017 ©2017 AFNLP

character dictionaries like radical dictionaries and without depending on the characters such as Hiraganas, Katakanas, and Kanjis. Additionally, we show our method can simplify a baseline model with reducing the number of parameters by adopting a convolutional neural network (CNN) to extract character features from font images.

2 Baseline model

Our method is based on a review classification model named Hierarchical Attention Networks (HAN) (Yang et al., 2016). We employ this method since this is one of the state-of-the-art methods in sentiment classification on English datasets of Yelp, IMDB, Yahoo Answer, and Amazon reviews, and we aim to evaluate the visual information on the state-of-the-art model. The HAN model is composed of bidirectional Recurrent Neural Networks of Gated Recurrent Units (GRU-RNNs). The RNNs are stacked hierarchically from a word level to a sentence level. The model encodes a sequence of lower-level embeddings to an upper-level embedding in a bottom up manner with attention mechanisms. For example, a sentence embedding is calculated from the word embeddings in a sentence, and a document embedding is calculated from the sentence embeddings in a document. The attentions are calculated using the outputs of lower-level RNNs and then applied to the outputs to calculate the embedding of each upper-level element as follows:

$$\mathbf{h}_i = \tanh(W_w \mathbf{l}_i + \mathbf{b}_w)$$
$$\mathbf{u} = \sum_i \alpha_i \mathbf{h}_i, \; \alpha_i = \frac{\exp(\mathbf{h}_i^\top \mathbf{c})}{\sum_i \exp(\mathbf{h}_i^\top \mathbf{c})} \quad (1)$$

where $\mathbf{l}_i$ is the embedding of a i-th lower-level element in a sequence and $\mathbf{u}$ is the embedding of an upper-level element. W_w, $\mathbf{b}_w$ and $\mathbf{c}$ are parameters to be tuned during training. $\mathbf{c}$ also provides a way to investigate the grounds of predictions with attention mechanisms. This hierarchical architecture allows to suppress the effects of gradient vanishing when RNNs are applied to long sequences.

3 Proposed method

We propose a novel model that utilizes visual font image information of characters to represent characters. Using font images for Japanese has several merits compared with symbolic features of characters. First, font images are available to any characters unlike some character-specific features that

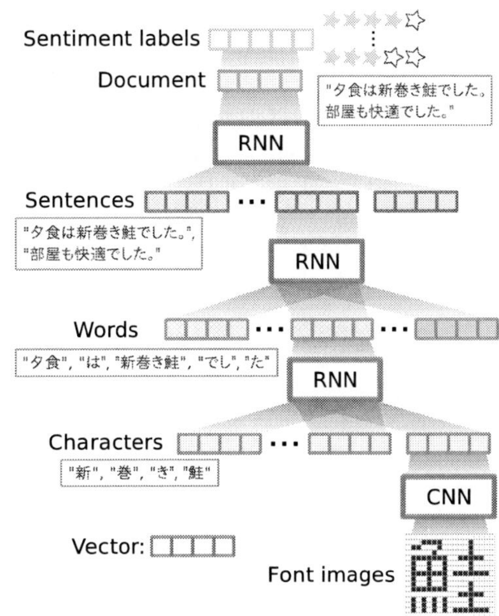

Figure 2: Proposed model for a review document "夕食は新巻き鮭でした。部屋も快適でした。" "The dinner was a lightly salted salmon. The room was comfortable too."

need to be treated differently. For instance, radicals are specific to Kanjis, and dictionaries are required to extract such features. Second, we should be able to find proper font images for characters in some way most of the time. That is because most datasets are composed of documents written on some computers and people should not use characters that do not have proper font images as they cannot be rendered on their systems. Third, we can reduce the number of parameters.

We convert each font image into its corresponding character embedding with CNN and incorporate them into a character-based HAN model, which is a straight-forward extension of the HAN model with character-level RNNs[1].

Font images are extracted as fixed-size images, and they are used statically throughout training and evaluation. All the pixel values in the font images, which are originally with a range of $[0, 255)$ of integers, are normalized into real values with a range of $[0, 1)$. The CNN consists of five convolutional layers interleaved by pooling layers[2]. We

---

[1]Yang et al. (2016) mentioned the possibility of character-based HAN in their paper, but they did not evaluate it.

[2]We empirically chose this number of layers. We also tried to use VGG (Simonyan and Zisserman, 2015) with Xavier initialization (Glorot and Bengio, 2010) to convert

stack the character-based HAN on the top of the CNN to hierarchically structure documents from characters to words, sentences, and documents. The final document embeddings are passed to softmax functions through a hidden layer to predict sentiment labels. Since our task consists of multiple classification tasks, we prepare an individual softmax function for each classification task in the output layer with sharing the hidden layer.

4 Experiments

4.1 Dataset

We used 320,000 reviews in the dataset of Rakuten Travel review[3]. We split them into training, development, and test data with 300,000, 10,000, and 10,000 reviews respectively. The task is multi-category sentiment classification; the task consists of 6-class (0 (no rating) and 1 (bad) to 5 (good)) sentiment classifications for seven categories (location, room, food, bath, service, facility, and overall). All documents were normalized by NFKC Unicode normalization and then by a Japanese text normalizer `neologdn`[4]. The documents were segmented into sentences by a regular expression, and every sentence was segmented into words by a Japanese morphological analyzer MeCab (Kudo et al., 2004).

Character and word vocabularies were constructed from those appeared more than nine times in training and development datasets[5]. As a result, we chose 2,709 characters from 3,630 characters. We employed the IPA Gothic TrueType font[6] to represent characters.

4.2 Experimental settings

We compared our font-based model with the character-based HAN. We used Python and TensorFlow to implement the models, and ran them on an NVidia GeForce GTX TITAN X. We reimplemented the HAN model from scratch and extended it to implement our model.

We optimized all the models by Adam with suggested parameters on the paper (Kingma and Ba, 2015). We employed mini-batch training and

---

font images without pre-training, but it did not work well even after many training epochs.

[3] `http://www.nii.ac.jp/dsc/idr/en/rakuten/rakuten.html`

[4] `https://github.com/ikegami-yukino/neologdn`

[5] We empirically chose this threshold. We got lower score when we used all the characters.

[6] `http://ipafont.ipa.go.jp/`

batch sizes were fixed to 16. For the character-based HAN, character, word, sentence and document embedding sizes were set to 100, 150, 100 and 50 respectively. Note that the embedding sizes for the inputs of upper layer (RNN or hidden layer) were doubled before they were fed to the upper layer since GRU-RNNs were bidirectional and embeddings of outputs from lower forward and backward RNNs were concatenated. For example, the size of the last hidden layer was set to 100. We tuned the other hyper-parameters in a greedy strategy. As for regularization, we applied L2 regularization with a scale of 1e-8 and did not use dropout. The model was updated in 66,348 times.

As for our font-based model, the font images were represented as 2-dimensional matrices of 64×64 single-channel images with 8-bit depth. Each hidden image from each pooling layer in the CNN part of our model had 32 channels. The resulting hidden images were 2x2 32-channel images, which were then flatten as character embeddings before they were fed to the RNN that converted character embeddings into word embeddings. The sizes of word, sentence, and document embeddings were set to 150, 100 and 50 respectively. We updated the model in 206,230 times from scratch without any regularization or any pre-training of the CNN.

4.3 Results

We show the numbers of parameters for character embeddings in Table 2. This table shows that our model needs less parameters than the character embedding-based model since the number of parameters in our model does not depend on the number of character types. This table indicates that character-based HAN can keep only 374 characters with the similar model size to ours.

The accuracies of the models on the Rakuten Travel dataset are shown in Table 3. We show the results with an embeddings-based classification method by Toyama et al. (2016) for reference. As the table shows, the plain HAN works better than the existing method and our method achieved an accuracy comparable to a plain HAN. The result indicates two insights. First, our model extracted character features successfully from font images in spite of the complexity of images, deep CNN architecture and less parameters, and the font images can be an alternative for symbolic character

Method	#parameters
character-based HAN	270,900
Our method	37,312

Table 2: Comparison of the numbers of parameters related to character embeddings

Method	Accuracy (%)
Toyama et al. (2016)	50.2
character-based HAN	53.4
Our method	53.3

Table 3: Accuracies of methods on the Rakuten Travel dataset

indices in representing characters. Second, the use of font images to represent characters is reasonable for the multi-category sentiment classification.

5   Related work

Many deep learning models have been proposed for sentiment classification and have achieved the state-of-the-art performance. These models grasp and utilize dynamics in natural languages, such as negation and emphasis relations among words and sentences. Yang et al. (2016) proposed Hierarchical Attention Networks (HAN), which are composed of hierarchically stacked RNNs, and each RNN captures dynamics of words or sentences. Our model extends this model by incorporating visual information of characters.

Some shallow models are still comparable with the deep learning models. FastText (Joulin et al., 2016) employs a multi-layer perceptron, which constructs a hidden document embedding from unigram and bigram embeddings and classifies the document using the document embedding. Our CNN model can be used to incorporate visual features of characters into these models.

The most similar work to ours is the work by Costa-juss et al. (2017) since they used font images in their method, although their target task is not review classification but neural machine translation. They initialized embeddings with bitmap fonts, and they achieved a better BLEU score than a baseline method without bitmap fonts of Chinese characters. They, however, did not directly incorporated the font images into their models unlike ours and they used the font information as additional information, so the parameters were increased by using font images in their model.

Several other related work has exploited processing the character components, mostly radicals, in Japanese (Yencken and Baldwin, 2008) and Chinese (Jin et al., 2012; Lepage, 2014; Shi et al., 2015; Li et al., 2015; Dong et al., 2016). Sun et al. (2014) proposed radical-enhanced Chinese character embeddings for word segmentation in Chinese. They utilized radical information of Chinese characters using a radical-mapping dictionary. Their model consists of two models for words segmentation and radical prediction with sharing parameters of character embeddings. They incorporate the radical information into character embeddings by this radical prediction. Their method was tailored for Chinese where all the characters have radicals as character components. Some kinds of Japanese characters like Hiraganas and Katakanas are syllabograms that do not represent words, so their method is not directly applicable to Japanese. Also, most of the existing work depends on dictionaries. Our method models the visual character information directly, so our method is applicable to Chinese or any other languages without any dictionary.

6   Conclusion

We proposed a method for a multi-category sentiment classification that exploits font images as potential representation of documents. The experimental results showed that our method performs as well as the plain character-based HAN on a dataset of Rakuten Travel reviews with reducing the number of parameters. The results suggest that our method can utilize visual features of font images successfully to represent characters and such visual information works well for multi-category sentiment classification.

As future work, we would like to investigate the better modeling of the font images by incorporating an attention mechanism to represent the locations of font images. This will enable us to investigate how our model works on the task by checking whether the visual attentions are paid on character components like radicals in Kanji characters. We would also like to compare and/or combine our method with its variants with more symbolic character features like radial information from Kanji dictionaries. That should help existing methods to run on test datasets with the existence of unknown characters since our method does depend not on artificial hand-crafted features of characters extracted from dictionaries that may lack some rare characters but only on visual information of characters.

Acknowledgments

This work was supported by the TOYOAKI Scholarship Foundation.

References

Marta R. Costa-juss, David Aldn, and Jos A. R. Fonollosa. 2017. Chinese - spanish neural machine translation enhanced with character and word bitmap fonts. In *Machine Translation*, page 1 - 13, Barcelona, Spain.

Chuanhai Dong, Jiajun Zhang, Chengqing Zong, Masanori Hattori, and Hui Di. 2016. Character-based LSTM-CRF with radical-level features for chinese named entity recognition. In *The Fifth Conference on Natural Language Processing and Chinese Computing & The Twenty Fourth International Conference on Computer Processing of Oriental Languages(NLPCC-ICCPOL 2016)*, pages 239–250, Kunming, China.

Xavier Glorot and Yoshua Bengio. 2010. Understanding the difficulty of training deep feedforward neural networks. In *Proceedings of the International Conference on Artificial Intelligence and Statistics (AISTATS' 10)*. Society for Artificial Intelligence and Statistics.

Peng Jin, John Carroll, Yunfang Wu, and Diana McCarthy. 2012. Distributional similarity for chinese: Exploiting characters and radicals. *Mathematical Problems in Engineering*, 2012.

Armand Joulin, Edouard Grave, Piotr Bojanowski, and Tomas Mikolov. 2016. Bag of tricks for efficient text classification. *arXiv preprint*, abs/1607.01759.

Diederik Kingma and Jimmy Ba. 2015. Adam: A method for stochastic optimization. In *Proceedings of the 3rd International Conference on Learning Representations (ICLR2015)*, San Diego, CA.

Taku Kudo, Kaoru Yamamoto, and Yuji Matsumoto. 2004. Applying conditional random fields to japanese morphological analysis. In *Proceedings of EMNLP 2004*, pages 230–237, Barcelona, Spain. ACL.

Yves Lepage. 2014. Analogies between binary images: Application to chinese characters. In *Computational Approaches to Analogical Reasoning: Current Trends*, pages 25–57. Springer.

Yanran Li, Wenjie Li, Fei Sun, and Sujian Li. 2015. Component-enhanced chinese character embeddings. In *Proceedings of the 2015 Conference on Empirical Methods in Natural Language Processing*, pages 829–834, Lisbon, Portugal. ACL.

Xinlei Shi, Junjie Zhai, Xudong Yang, Zehua Xie, and Chao Liu. 2015. Radical embedding: Delving deeper to chinese radicals. In *Proceedings of the 53rd Annual Meeting of the Association for Computational Linguistics and the 7th International Joint Conference on Natural Language Processing (Volume 2: Short Papers)*, pages 594–598, Beijing, China. Association for Computational Linguistics.

Karen Simonyan and Andrew Zisserman. 2015. Very deep convolutional networks for large-scale image recognition. In *Proceedings of the 3rd International Conference on Learning Representations (ICLR2015)*, San Diego, CA.

Yaming Sun, Lei Lin, Nan Yang, Zhenzhou Ji, and Xiaolong Wang. 2014. Radical-enhanced chinese character embedding. In *International Conference on Neural Information Processing*, pages 279–286. Springer.

Yota Toyama, Makoto Miwa, and Yutaka Sasaki. 2016. Rating prediction by considering relations among documents and sentences and among categories. In *Proceedings of the Twenty-second Annual Meeting of the Association for Natural Language Processing*, pages 158–161. (In Japanese).

Zichao Yang, Diyi Yang, Chris Dyer, Xiaodong He, Alex Smola, and Eduard Hovy. 2016. Hierarchical attention networks for document classification. In *Proceedings of NAACL-HLT*, pages 1480–1489, San Diego, CA. ACL.

Lars Yencken and Timothy Baldwin. 2008. Measuring and predicting orthographic associations: Modelling the similarity of japanese kanji. In *Proceedings of the 22nd International Conference on Computational Linguistics (Coling 2008)*, pages 1041–1048, Manchester, UK. Coling 2008 Organizing Committee.

A Multi-task Learning Approach to Adapting Bilingual Word Embeddings for Cross-lingual Named Entity Recognition

Dingquan Wang[1]   **Nanyun Peng**[3]*   **Kevin Duh**[12]

[1] Center for Language and Speech Processing, Johns Hopkins University
[2] Human Language Technology Center of Excellence, Johns Hopkins University
[3] Information Sciences Institute, University of Southern California
wdd@cs.jhu.edu, npeng@isi.edu, kevinduh@cs.jhu.edu

Abstract

We show how to adapt bilingual word embeddings (BWE's) to bootstrap a cross-lingual name-entity recognition (NER) system in a language with no labeled data. We assume a setting where we are given a comparable corpus with NER labels for the source language only; our goal is to build a NER model for the target language. The proposed multi-task model jointly trains bilingual word embeddings while optimizing a NER objective. This creates word embeddings that are both shared between languages and fine-tuned for the NER task. As a proof of concept, we demonstrate this model on English-to-Chinese transfer using Wikipedia.

1 Introduction

Cross-lingual transfer is an important technique for building natural language processing (NLP) systems for *low-resource* languages, where labeled examples are scarce. The main idea is to transfer labels or models from *high-resource* languages. Representative techniques include (a) projecting labels (or information derived from labels) across parallel corpora (Yarowsky et al., 2011; Das and Petrov, 2011; Che et al., 2013; Zhang et al., 2016), and (b) training universal models using unlexicalized features (McDonald et al., 2011; Täckström et al., 2012; Zirikly and Hagiwara, 2015) or bilingual word embeddings (Xiao and Guo, 2014; Gouws and Søgaard, 2015).

Here, we focus on the bilingual word embedding (BWE) approach. In particular, we are interested in leveraging recent advances in learning BWE from comparable corpora (Hermann and

---

*This research was majorly conducted when the author was at Johns Hopkins University.

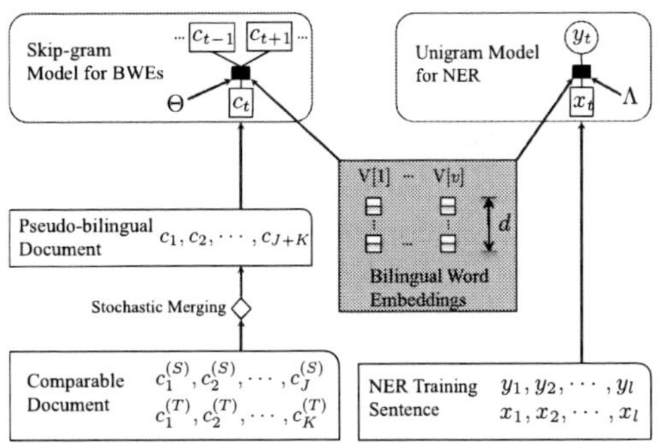

Figure 1: Our multi-task framework, which trains bilingual word embeddings from comparable corpora while optimizing an NER objective on the high-resource language. The NER part of the model is then tested on a low-resource language.

Blunsom, 2014; Vulic and Moens, 2015; Gouws and Søgaard, 2015). A comparable corpus is a collection of document pairs written in different languages but talking about the same topic (e.g. interconnected Wikipedia articles). The advantage of comparable corpora is that they may be more easily acquired in the language and domain of interest. However, cross-lingual transfer on comparable corpora is more difficult than on parallel corpora, due to the difficulty in finding high-quality word translation equivalences.

Our contributions are two-fold: First, we investigate cross-lingual transfer on an NER task, and found that pre-trained BWE's do not necessarily help out-of-the-box. This corroborates results in the monolingual setting, where it is widely recognized that training task-specific embeddings is helpful for the downstream tasks like NER (Peng and Dredze, 2015; Ma and Hovy, 2016).

Second, we propose a multi-task learning framework that utilizes comparable corpora to jointly train BWE's and the downstream NER task (Figure 1). We experimented with a Wikipedia

Proceedings of the The 8th International Joint Conference on Natural Language Processing, pages 383–388,
Taipei, Taiwan, November 27 – December 1, 2017 ©2017 AFNLP

corpus, training a NER model from labeled English articles (high-resource) and testing it on Chinese articles (low-resource)[1]. The challenge with training task-specific embeddings in cross-lingual transfer is that the task in which we have labels (English NER) is not equivalent to the task we care about (Chinese NER). Despite this, we demonstrate improvements on NER F-scores with our multi-task model.

2 The Multi-task Framework

Assumptions : We assume two resources: First is a comparable corpus where S ("source") refers to the high-resource language and T ("target") refers to the low-resource language. The comparable corpus is denoted as $\mathcal{C} = \{(\mathbf{c}_i^{(S)}, \mathbf{c}_i^{(T)}) \mid i \in [1, M]\}$, where each $(\mathbf{c}_i^{(S)}, \mathbf{c}_i^{(T)})$ is a tuple of comparable documents written in S and T, and M is the size (total number of tuples) of $\mathcal{C}$.

We also assume a labeled NER corpus on the high-resource language, which may be disjoint from $\mathcal{C}$. Let $X^{(S)} = \{\mathbf{x}_i^{(S)} \mid i \in [1, N^{(S)}]\}$ and $Y^{(S)} = \{\mathbf{y}_i^{(S)} \mid i \in [1, N^{(S)}]\}$ together form the NER training examples of S, where each $\mathbf{y}_i^{(S)}$ is the gold tag sequence of sentence $\mathbf{x}_i^{(S)}$, and $N^{(S)}$ is the number of training examples.

Training : Given $X^{(S)}$ and $Y^{(S)}$ and $\mathcal{C}$ the training objective (loss) L is:

$$\alpha \underset{X^{(S)},Y^{(S)}}{\text{Ln}} (V, \Lambda) + (1 - \alpha)\underset{\mathcal{C}}{\text{Lm}}(V, \Theta) \quad (1)$$

Ln is the loss for training the NER tagger in S, Lm is the loss for training the BWE's, and $\alpha \in [0, 1]$ is coefficient for balancing these two losses. Λ, V and Θ are the model parameters, where Λ is Ln-specific parameter, Θ is the Lm-specific parameter and V is the $d \times v$-shape BWE's that shared are by both Ln and Lm. v is the size of the joint vocabulary $\mathcal{V}$ and $\mathcal{V}$ is formed by *concatenating*[2] the vocabulary of S and T, d is the dimension of the word embedding. Figure 1 gives a visualization of the framework.

Evaluation : At test time, given $X^{(T)}$ – the raw sentences of T, we evaluate the F1 score of $\bar{Y}^{(T)}$ predicted by the trained model $\{V^*, \Lambda^*\}$ against the true label $Y^{(T)}$. Note that this model is trained on NER labels in S only, so it is imperative for the learned BWE's to map S and T words with the same NER label into nearby spaces.

Our framework (Equation 1) is flexible to different definitions of Ln and Lm objectives. Below, we describe a specific instantiation that fits well with cross-lingual NER.

2.1 Design of Ln

Given the labeled training data $X^{(S)}, Y^{(S)}$ of S, we optimize the conditional log-likelihood as Ln (superscripts S are suppressed for readability):

$$\underset{X,Y}{\text{Ln}} (V, \Lambda) = \frac{1}{N} \sum_{i=1}^{N} \log p_{V,\Lambda}(\mathbf{y}_i \mid \mathbf{x}_i) \quad (2)$$

$p_{V,\Lambda}(\mathbf{y} \mid \mathbf{x})$ is the conditional probability of $\mathbf{y}$ given $\mathbf{x}$ parameterized by V and Λ such that

$$p_{V,\Lambda}(\mathbf{y} \mid \mathbf{x}) = \frac{\exp(s_{V,\Lambda}(\mathbf{x}, \mathbf{y}))}{\sum_{\mathbf{y}' \in \mathcal{Y}} \exp(s_{V,\Lambda}(\mathbf{x}, \mathbf{y}'))} \quad (3)$$

. $s_{V,\Lambda}(\dots)$ is a score function of a sentence and its possible NER-tag sequence. $\mathcal{Y}$ is the set of all possible NER-tag sequences.

Unigram Model : Given a sentence $\mathbf{x} \in X$ with length l and its label $\mathbf{y} \in Y$, the score function of unigram model is simply:

$$s_{V,\Lambda}(\mathbf{x}, \mathbf{y}) = \sum_{t \in [1,l]} V[x_t]^\top \cdot W[y_t] + \mathbf{b}[y_t] \quad (4)$$

where $\Lambda \overset{\text{def}}{=} \{W, b\}$, W is a $d \times n$-shape matrix that maps the word vector $V[x_t]$ into the NER-tag space, n is the number of NER-tag types, which is 7 as will be explained in §3.1. $\mathbf{b}$ is the bias vector with size n. The reason why we call this model unigram is it only looks at the word itself without its context.[3]

2.2 Design of Lm

Here we adopt the method of Vulic and Moens (2015), which is the only mechanism for training on comparable documents as far as we know: First we transform $\mathcal{C}$ into a *pseudo-bilingual* corpora $\mathcal{C}'$ by a stochastic merging process of two documents as shown in Alg. 1. The idea is to mix together the two documents in different languages into a single document (where S and T words are interspersed), then apply a standard monolingual word embedding algorithm.

---

[1]Chinese can be considered a high-resource language for NER, but we use it as a proof-of-concept and do not use any existing Chinese resources.

[2]Same word in different languages is treated separately.

[3]Besides unigram, we also tried LSTM+CRF (Lample et al., 2016) for longer context. Despite good results in monolingual NER, it did poorly in our cross-lingual experiments.

Algorithm 1 Stochastic merging of two documents, where len(**c**) returns the number of tokens of document **c**, **c**$[i]$ is the ith token of document **c**.

Input: Comparable Document: $\mathbf{c}^{(S)}, \mathbf{c}^{(T)}$
Output: Pseudo-bilingual Document: **c**
1: $\mathbf{c} \leftarrow []; i_1 \leftarrow 0; i_2 \leftarrow 0$
2: $r \leftarrow \dfrac{\text{len}(\mathbf{c}^{(S)})}{\text{len}(\mathbf{c}^{(S)})+\text{len}(\mathbf{c}^{(T)})}$
3: **while** $i_1 < \text{len}(\mathbf{c}^{(S)})$ **and** $i_2 < \text{len}(\mathbf{c}^{(T)})$ **do**
4:     $p \sim \text{Uniform}[0,1]$
5:     **if** $i_2 == \text{len}(\mathbf{c}^{(T)})$ **or** $p < r$ **then**
6:         $\mathbf{c}.\text{append}(\mathbf{c}^{(S)}[i_1])$
7:         $i_1 \leftarrow i_1 + 1$
8:     **else**
9:         $\mathbf{c}.\text{append}(\mathbf{c}^{(T)}[i_2])$
10:         $i_2 \leftarrow i_2 + 1$
    return c

We use the standard skip-gram objective (Mikolov et al., 2013) by considering each pseudo-bilingual document as a single sentence. $\text{Lm}_{\mathcal{C}}(V, \Theta)$ is given by:

$$\underset{\mathbf{c}\in\mathcal{C}'}{\text{mean}} \ \underset{t\in[1,\text{len}(\mathbf{c})]}{\text{mean}} \sum_{\substack{-w\leq j\leq w \\ j\neq 0}} \log p_{V,\Theta}(c_{t+j}|c_t) \quad (5)$$

, where w is the word window, c_t is the tth token of **c**. $p_{V,\Theta}(\dots)$ is the standard context probability parameterized by V and Θ such that

$$p_{V,\Theta}(c_O|c_I) = \frac{V[c_I]^\top \cdot V'[c_O]}{\sum_{c'_O\in\mathcal{V}} V[c_I]^\top \cdot V'[c'_O]} \quad (6)$$

$\Theta \overset{\text{def}}{=} \{V'\}$, where V' is the context embedding with size $d \times v$. In the implementation, we use negative sampling to save the computation, since we desire using a large vocabulary to handle as many words as possible for cross-lingual transfer.

2.3 Optimization

Full Joint (FJ) Training : First optimize Ln by updating V and Λ. Then optimize Lm by updating V, Θ. Repeat.

Half-fixed Joint (HFJ) Training : Same as FJ Training, except in the Lm optimization step, the English word embeddings are fixed and only the Chinese word embeddings are updated. The motivation is to anchor the English embeddings to fit the NER objective Ln, and encourage the Chinese embedding (of comparable documents) to move towards this anchor.

Inspired by Lample et al. (2016), for both approaches, words with frequency 1 in the NER data are replaced by OOV with probability 0.5 to so that embedding OOV could be optimized.

3 Experiments

3.1 Data

We use the EN-ZH portion of the Wikipedia Comparable Corpora[4]. For experiment purposes, we sampled 19K document pairs[5] as our comparable corpora $\mathcal{C}$. The NER labeled data on English (S) is obtained by collecting the first **paragraph** of each English document in $\mathcal{C}$ as $X^{(S)}$, and labeling it with Stanford NER tagger (Finkel et al., 2005) to generate $Y^{(S)}$.[6]

For the NER test data in Chinese (T), we separately sampled 1K documents and collected the first sentence as $X^{(T)}$. We ran automatic word segmentation[7] and manually labeled $X^{(T)}$ to generate $Y^{(T)}$. The English side of these 1K tuple is treated as held-out data for tuning NER hyperparameters, and is labeled with the same Stanford NER tagger. We use the BIO tagging scheme for 3 basic named-entity types ("LOC" for location, "ORG" for organization and "PER" for person), so the output space is 7 tags. The data statistics are shown in Table 1. The size of BWE's is about 1M with 514K being Chinese words.

	$\mathcal{C}$	$X^{(S)}$	$X^{(T)}$
#Document Tuple	19K	-	-
#Sentence	1.8M	45K	1K
#Token	24M	994K	20K

Table 1: Data statistics.

3.2 Results

We compare our multi-task model with FJ and HFJ alternate training[8] against a baseline where BWE's

---

[4] http://linguatools.org/tools/corpora/wikipedia-comparable-corpora/

[5] We started from 20K pairs in totall, then we first sampled out 1K from the Chinese side for the final evaluation and left 19K for training. We consider it as a reasonable number compared to Vulic and Moens (2015), which used 14K pairs for Spanish-English and 19K for Italian-English.

[6] We treat these automatic NER tags as "gold" labels to simulate a scenario where we want cross-lingual transfer on T to do at least as well as on S. But naturally our model can also use human annotations if available.

[7] https://github.com/fxsjy/jieba

[8] For training the BWE's, we borrow the same hyperparameters as Vulic and Moens (2015) – learning rate of **0.025**,

---

385

d	Baseline	HFJ	FJ
64	6.54	**13.5**	7.01
128	14.95	**20.27**	17.14
256	13.69	**24.29**	16.53
512	**21.23**	17.7	20.14

Table 2: The F1 scores on the Chinese held-out data averaged over multiple restarts. d is the dimension of the BWE's. All the BWE's are initialized by the output of Vulic and Moens (2015) trained on $\mathcal{C}$. "Baseline" fixes the BWE's and only trains Λ, "HFJ" and "FJ" are proposed joint training methods described in §2.3

are pre-trained on $\mathcal{C}$, then held fixed when training a NER tagger. This baseline corresponds to a two-step procedure where word embeddings pre-trained on comparable corpora is used as features when training an NER.[9]

Table 2 shows the F1 scores. We observe the joint training methods (HFJ & FJ) outperform the baseline method with embedding size 64, 128, and 256. For example, for $d = 256$, HFJ achieves an F1 score of 24%, compared to the baseline of 13%, implying that jointly tuning the embedding on both comparable corpora and NER objectives (HFJ) is better than fine-tuning only NER objective after training on comparable corpora (baseline). Further, HFJ results are better than FJ, implying when optimizing Lm, it is better to tune the Chinese embedding toward an anchored English embedding, rather than allow both to be updated.

We note that the trend is different for $d = 512$: it might be that as the NER model grows larger, there is a risk of overfitting[10] the English NER data and losing generality on Chinese NER. We observe similar trends when we replaced the uni-

gram model with a LSTM+CRF (see §2.1) in Ln. This degraded results for all systems, e.g. with $d = 256$, "Baseline" F1 dropped from 13.69 to 6.07, and "FJ" dropped from 16.53 to 8.62.

It is interesting to see the impact of joint training on BWE's. In Table 3, given a Chinese query, we show the most similar words in English returned by computing the Euclidean distance between BWE's ($d = 256$). While both pre-trained and jointly-trained BWE's retrieve correct English translations, jointly-trained BWE's retrieves more words with the same NER type. For example, "Spanish", and "Greek" – the adjective forms of "Spain" and "Greece", rank highly with the pre-trained BWE's due to semantic similarity. But these may degrade NER since these adjectives are not labeled "LOC". Our multi-task model mitigates this confusion.

4   Conclusion & Future Work

We show how a multi-task learning approach can help adapt bilingual word embeddings (BWE's) to improve cross-lingual transfer. Joint training of BWE's encourages the BWE's to be task-specific, and outperforms the baseline of using pre-trained BWE's. We showed promising results on the challenging task of cross-lingual NER on comparable corpora, where the target language has no labels. Future work will aim to improve the absolute F1 scores by combining limited labels in the low-resource languages, via exploiting document structure in Wikipedia (Richman and Schone, 2008; Steinberger et al., 2011; Tsai et al., 2016; Ni and Florian, 2016; Pan et al., 2017). While we only focus on the most difficult case where the source language and target languages are not in the same family, and a bilingual dictionary is not available in this paper, it is interesting to study how this technique could be applied when the different levels of supervision are available on various language pairs in the future.

Acknowledgment

We thank Mark Dredze and Mo Yu for the useful discussion and Jason Eisner for the suggestion of some relevant previous work. Finally, we thank the anonymous reviewers for the high-quality suggestions.

---

negative sampling with **25** samples and subsampling rate of value **1e-4**. The dropout rate of **0.3** is decided by the best F1 score of the language-specific NER tagger on the English held-out data. The coefficient α for balancing two Ln and Lm should presumably be chosen by tuning on the labelled data for Chinese, which is not available in our setting. So we heuristically set it to **0.5** by assuming they are equally helpful. Our fully unsupervised setting has no NER training data available on the Chinese side for tuning. To prevent the training from overfitting to the English data, we heuristically early stop after **10000** pairs of alternating updates of Lm and Ln.

[9]Another possible baseline is using only Ln for training, this will not work because Ln only consists of English data, so the Chinese embeddings will stay random when English embedding are optimized, resulting random outputs on the Chinese side.

[10]When training with $d = 512$, the F1 on training data is consistently > 60 for the last epochs, which is about 50 with $d = 256$.

Query	Type	Top 8 results in English
NBA	ORG	**NBA**, rebounds, **Knicks**, **Lakers**, Lewiston-Porter, **76ers**, guard-forward, **Celtics**
NBA		**NBA**, **Lakers**, Gervin, rebounds, **Celtics**, **Cavaliers**, **Knicks**, **All-Defensive**
西班牙	LOC	**Spain**, Spanish, **Nogueruelas**, Rosanes, **Mazarete**, **Ólvega**, Marquesado, **Montija**
Spain		**Spain**, Rosanes, **Cenicientos**, **Madrid**, Sorita, **Alcahozo**, **Nogueruelas**, **Villaralto**
希腊	LOC	**Greece**, Greek, **Achaia**, annalistic, heroized, Gigantomachy, Hecabe, river-god
Greece		Hachadoor, **Greece**, Demoorjian, **Safranbolu**, **Scicli**, **Holasovice**, **Sighisoara**, **Litomysl**
卡卡	PER	**Kakashi**, **Moure**, Uzumaki, cosplayed, **Uchiha**, humanizing, **Yens**, hilarious
Kaka		**Kakashi**, **Kaka**, **Moure**, **Nedved**, **Suazo**, **Batistuta**, Uzumaki, **Quagliarella**

Table 3: Top similar words in the English given a Chinese query. "Type" is the gold named-entity type of the query. For each query, the upper row is calculated with the baseline BWE's, and the lower row is calculated with HFJ BWE's. The words with the same type as the query are bold-faced, and we observe more of these cases with HFJ.

References

Wanxiang Che, Mengqiu Wang, Christopher D. Manning, and Ting Liu. 2013. Named entity recognition with bilingual constraints. In *Proceedings of the 2013 Conference of the North American Chapter of the Association for Computational Linguistics: Human Language Technologies*, pages 52–62, Atlanta, Georgia. Association for Computational Linguistics.

Dipanjan Das and Slav Petrov. 2011. Unsupervised part-of-speech tagging with bilingual graph-based projections. In *Proceedings of the 49th Annual Meeting of the Association for Computational Linguistics: Human Language Technologies - Volume 1*, HLT '11, pages 600–609, Stroudsburg, PA, USA. Association for Computational Linguistics.

Rose Jenny Finkel, Trond Grenager, and Christopher Manning. 2005. Incorporating non-local information into information extraction systems by gibbs sampling. In *Proceedings of the 43rd Annual Meeting of the Association for Computational Linguistics (ACL'05)*, pages 363–370. Association for Computational Linguistics.

Stephan Gouws and Anders Søgaard. 2015. Simple task-specific bilingual word embeddings. In *Proceedings of the 2015 Conference of the North American Chapter of the Association for Computational Linguistics: Human Language Technologies*, pages 1386–1390, Denver, Colorado. Association for Computational Linguistics.

Karl Moritz Hermann and Phil Blunsom. 2014. Multilingual Distributed Representations without Word Alignment. In *Proceedings of ICLR*.

Guillaume Lample, Miguel Ballesteros, Sandeep Subramanian, Kazuya Kawakami, and Chris Dyer. 2016. Neural architectures for named entity recognition. In *Proceedings of the 2016 Conference of the North American Chapter of the Association for Computational Linguistics: Human Language Technologies*, pages 260–270. Association for Computational Linguistics.

Xuezhe Ma and Eduard H. Hovy. 2016. End-to-end sequence labeling via bi-directional lstm-cnns-crf. *CoRR*, abs/1603.01354.

Ryan McDonald, Slav Petrov, and Keith Hall. 2011. Multi-source transfer of delexicalized dependency parsers. In *Proceedings of the 2011 Conference on Empirical Methods in Natural Language Processing*, pages 62–72, Edinburgh, Scotland, UK. Association for Computational Linguistics.

Tomas Mikolov, Ilya Sutskever, Kai Chen, Greg S Corrado, and Jeff Dean. 2013. Distributed representations of words and phrases and their compositionality. In C. J. C. Burges, L. Bottou, M. Welling, Z. Ghahramani, and K. Q. Weinberger, editors, *Advances in Neural Information Processing Systems 26*, pages 3111–3119. Curran Associates, Inc.

Jian Ni and Radu Florian. 2016. Improving multilingual named entity recognition with wikipedia entity type mapping. pages 1275—1284.

Xiaoman Pan, Boliang Zhang, Jonathan May, Joel Nothman, Kevin Knight, and Heng Ji. 2017. Cross-lingual name tagging and linking for 282 languages. In *Proceedings of the 55th Annual Meeting of the Association for Computational Linguistics (Volume 1: Long Papers)*. Association for Computational Linguistics.

Nanyun Peng and Mark Dredze. 2015. Named entity recognition for chinese social media with jointly trained embeddings. In *Proceedings of the Conference on Empirical Methods in Natural Language Processing (EMNLP)*.

Alexander E Richman and Patrick Schone. 2008. Mining wiki resources for multilingual named entity recognition. In *ACL*, pages 1–9.

Ralf Steinberger, Bruno Pouliquen, Mijail Kabadjov, Jenya Belyaeva, and Erik van der Goot. 2011. Jrc-names: A freely available, highly multilingual named entity resource. *RECENT ADVANCES IN*, page 104.

Oscar Täckström, Ryan McDonald, and Jakob Uszkoreit. 2012. Cross-lingual word clusters for direct transfer of linguistic structure. In *Proceedings of the 2012 conference of the North American chapter of the association for computational linguistics: Human language technologies*, pages 477–487. Association for Computational Linguistics.

Chen-Tse Tsai, Stephen Mayhew, and Dan Roth. 2016. Cross-lingual named entity recognition via wikification. In *Proceedings of The 20th SIGNLL Conference on Computational Natural Language Learning*, pages 219–228, Berlin, Germany. Association for Computational Linguistics.

Ivan Vulic and Marie-Francine Moens. 2015. Bilingual word embeddings from non-parallel document-aligned data applied to bilingual lexicon induction. In *Proceedings of the 53rd Annual Meeting of the Association for Computational Linguistics (ACL 2015)*. ACL.

Min Xiao and Yuhong Guo. 2014. Distributed word representation learning for cross-lingual dependency parsing. In *Proceedings of the Eighteenth Conference on Computational Natural Language Learning*, pages 119–129, Ann Arbor, Michigan. Association for Computational Linguistics.

D. Yarowsky, G. Ngai, and R. Wicentowski. 2011. Inducing multilingual text analysis tools via robust projection across aligned corpora. In *Proceedings of the First International Conference on Human Language Technology Research*.

Dongxu Zhang, Boliang Zhang, Xiaoman Pan, Xiaocheng Feng, Heng Ji, and Weiran Xu. 2016. Bitext name tagging for cross-lingual entity annotation projection. page 461–470.

Ayah Zirikly and Masato Hagiwara. 2015. Cross-lingual transfer of named entity recognizers without parallel corpora. In *Proceedings of the 53rd Annual Meeting of the Association for Computational Linguistics and the 7th International Joint Conference on Natural Language Processing (Volume 2: Short Papers)*, pages 390–396, Beijing, China. Association for Computational Linguistics.

Investigating the Effect of Conveying Understanding Results in Chat-Oriented Dialogue Systems

Koh Mitsuda   Ryuichiro Higashinaka   Junji Tomita
NTT Media Intelligence Laboratories, Nippon Telegraph and Telephone Corporation
`{mitsuda.ko,higashinaka.ryuichiro,tomita.junji}@lab.ntt.co.jp`

Abstract

In dialogue systems, conveying understanding results of user utterances is important because it enables users to feel understood by the system. However, it is not clear what types of understanding results should be conveyed to users; some utterances may be offensive and some may be too commonsensical. In this paper, we explored the effect of conveying understanding results of user utterances in a chat-oriented dialogue system by an experiment using human subjects. As a result, we found that only certain types of understanding results, such as those related to a user's permanent state, are effective to improve user satisfaction. This paper clarifies the types of understanding results that can be safely uttered by a system.

1 Introduction

Current dialogue systems often convey the understanding results of user utterances for confirmation and for showing understanding. Task-oriented dialogue systems repeat information provided by users by using understanding results of user utterances to confirm the content of user utterances (Litman and Silliman, 2004; Raux et al., 2005). Chat-oriented dialogue systems also need to confirm the content of user utterances and to show understanding so that the systems can be more affective.

However, some of the understanding results should not be conveyed to users. For instance, some utterances (e.g. "You are stubborn.") may be offensive and some (e.g. "It is summer.") may be too commonsensical. To create a dialogue system which conveys one's understanding results, we need to know what types of the results can be used as system utterances.

In this paper, focusing on chat-oriented dialogue systems, we investigate the effects of conveying understanding results of user utterances. Specifically, we investigate the types of results that can be conveyed to users without lowering user satisfaction. For this purpose, we first prepared various types of understanding results. Then, by a subjective experiment, we examined their individual effects on user satisfaction. Note that, in this paper, we focus on the effects of system utterances that convey understanding results "as they are"; that is, utterances are literally the same as understanding results.

As a result of the experiment, we found that user's temporary states during dialogue should not be conveyed and user's permanent states and information irrelevant to users themselves can be conveyed safely as system utterances. Our results are useful for creating a dialogue system that conveys understanding results.

2 Data of Understanding Results

For our investigation, we need to prepare understanding results categorized by their types. For this purpose, we use a corpus of *PerceivedInfo* collected in our previous work (Mitsuda et al., 2017). In this corpus, user utterances in chat-oriented dialogue are associated with the information that can be perceived/inferred by humans from these utterances. Such information is called *PerceivedInfo* (perceived information).

Figure 1 shows an example of a chat-oriented dialogue and their *PerceivedInfo* in the corpus. As stimuli for collecting *PerceivedInfo*, a Japanese chat-oriented dialogue corpus (Higashinaka et al., 2014) was used. *PerceivedInfo* was written by multiple annotators using natural sentences with

Proceedings of the The 8th International Joint Conference on Natural Language Processing, pages 389–394,
Taipei, Taiwan, November 27 – December 1, 2017 ©2017 AFNLP

	Chat-oriented dialogue		Perceived information for U_{13}
U_i	*Speaker*: utterance		**B** doesn't mind going a long way.
U_1	**A**: Hello, nice to meet you!		**B** drives a car.
U_2	**B**: Nice to meet you too.		**B** is active.
U_3	**A**: I feel autumn coming, how about you?		**B** likes going on pleasure trips.
U_4	**B**: I think so too.		**B** likes mountains.
U_5	**B**: The cicadas have gotten quiet recently.		**B** likes Mt. Fuji.
			B likes autumn leaves around Mt. Fuji.
...			**B** likes the outdoors.
U_{12}	**B**: Do you go anywhere interesting in autumn?		**B** lives in Kanto prefecture.
U_{13}	**B**: I'll visit Mt. Fuji if I feel up to it.		**B** lives near Mt. Fuji.
...			**B** would like **A** to be surprised.
U_{36}	**A**: Let's talk about this next time.		Mt. Fuji is famous for autumn leaves.
U_{37}	**B**: Okay.		

Figure 1: Example of chat-oriented dialogue and perceived information in *PerceivedInfo* corpus. **A** and **B** correspond to speakers.

Level 1	Level 2	Level 3	Description	Example
Thought (55.1%)	Thought (35.8%)	Belief self (30.7%)	Speaker's belief for him/herself	**A** likes watching TV.
		Belief other (5.1%)	Speaker's belief toward listener	**A** agrees with **B**.
	Desire (19.3%)	Desire (9.9%)	Speaker's desire relative to him/herself	**A** wants to talk about Mt. Fuji.
		Request (9.4%)	Speaker's request to listener	**A** wants to be praised by **B**.
Fact (44.9%)	A's fact (37.9%)	Attribute (20.2%)	User-modeling information of speaker	**A** is married., **A** can drink.
		Behavior (14.4%)	Speaker's action	**A** drives a car., **A** is thinking.
		Circumstance (3.3%)	Background around speaker	**A** is close with friends.
	Other fact (7.0%)	Certain fact (3.9%)	Certain fact irrelevant to speaker	Mt. Fuji is famous for red leaves.
		Uncertain fact (3.1%)	Uncertain fact irrelevant to speaker	A rice crop may fail.

Table 1: Classification of perceived information used for investigation. **A** and **B** correspond to speakers.

regard to each utterance in the dialogue.

Table 1 shows the classification of *Perceived-Info* created in our previous work. These types were determined by manual clustering. The classification was evaluated by inter-annotator agreement among three annotators using 3,000 instances of *PerceivedInfo* with "Level 3" types. Fleiss' κ showed substantial agreement (0.69), indicating the validity of the classification.

In this work, we use the *PerceivedInfo* in this corpus as understanding results and investigate the effects of system utterances that convey *Perceived-Info*. We also investigate how the effects are different depending on the types of *PerceivedInfo* in the classification.

3 Experiment

Using *PerceivedInfo*, we evaluated the effects of system utterances conveying the understanding results in an experiment. Below, we explain the procedure to create the utterances for the experiment and how we evaluate them.

Figure 2 shows the flow of preparation and evaluation. We first select pairs of *PerceivedInfo* and a user utterance used for writing that *Perceived-Info* from the corpus. The writers rewrite or refer

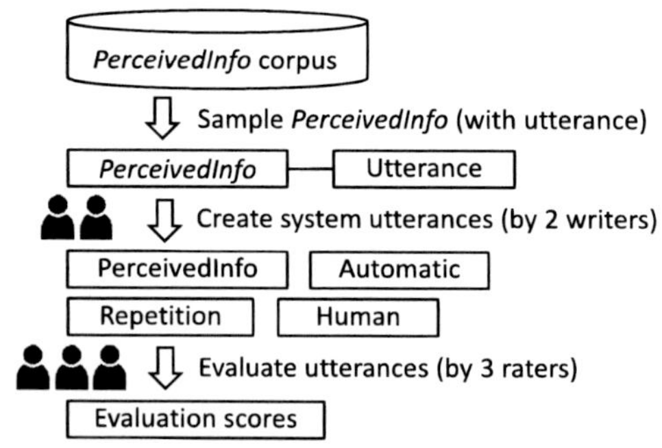

Figure 2: Preparation and evaluation of system utterances

to the *PerceivedInfo* and utterance to create system utterances. Finally, raters evaluate them by questionnaire, giving a score to each utterance.

3.1 Types of System Utterances

Table 2 shows the four types of system utterances prepared for evaluation. Utterances from *PerceivedInfo* are compared with those of three other types; namely, "Automatic," "Repetition," and "Human." "PerceivedInfo" is described below.

System utterance	Description	Example
PerceivedInfo	Confirmation of perceived information	You are active, aren't you?
Automatic	Response generated by a chat-oriented dialogue system	Do you work at Mt. Fuji?
Repetition	Repetition of user utterance in tag question form	You will visit Mt. Fuji, won't you?
Human	Response created by writer using keyword in user utterance	Mt. Fuji is a good place, isn't it?

Table 2: Types of system utterances prepared for evaluation. "Example" column shows system utterance when user utterance is "I'll visit Mt. Fuji if I feel up to it." (utterance U_{13} in Figure 1).

PerceivedInfo This utterance simply conveys *PerceivedInfo* in the form of confirmation. The utterance ends with a tag question form to confirm the content of *PerceivedInfo*. Rewriting *PerceivedInfo* is done manually. The symbols A and B that indicate speakers are changed to "You" or "I".

3.2 Types of Utterances for Comparison

We prepared three other types of system utterances for comparison. "Automatic" emulates the utterance of a chat-oriented dialogue system that is currently available. "Repetition" represents a simple repetition of the content of a user utterance. "Human" is an utterance conceived by human.

Automatic This utterance is an automatic response from a chat-oriented dialogue system that generates an utterance on the basis of keywords extracted from user utterances. To prepare responses, we use a Japanese chat-oriented dialogue system by NTT DOCOMO (Onishi and Yoshimura, 2014).

Repetition This utterance is a repetition of a predicate argument structure in a user utterance (Higashinaka et al., 2014). It ends with a tag question form (in Japanese, "*desu ne*") to show that the system understands the content of a user utterance. The utterance is manually created by extracting and rewriting a predicate argument structure from the user utterance.

Human This utterance is a human-level utterance (i.e., upper bound). We prepare it by having writers manually write an appropriate response to a keyword in the user utterance. Writers are instructed to select their favorite keyword in the utterance and use it to create a response that would satisfy users.

3.3 Preparation and Evaluation of Utterances

To clarify the difference of effects caused by the types of *PerceivedInfo*, we randomly selected approximately the same number of *PerceivedInfo* from each type in "Level 3" shown in Table 1. In total, we prepared 500 instances of *PerceivedInfo*; that is, 500 *PerceivedInfo* and user utterances associated with *PerceivedInfo*.

Using the 500 *PerceivedInfo* and utterances, "PerceivedInfo" and "Repetition" were written by a single writer and two versions of "Human" were written by two writers (Writer$_1$ and Writer$_2$) independently. We evaluated both utterances of "Human" written by the writers, because the quality of "Human" may depend on the writer. "Automatic" were generated from the chat-oriented dialogue system by NTT DOCOMO using the utterance as an input to the system. Following this experimental set-up, we prepared five types of utterances (including two versions of "Human") for each pair of *PerceivedInfo* and a user utterance, totalling 2,500 utterances, for evaluation.

To evaluate how each utterance is usable as a system utterance in dialogue, we annotated "naturalness" to the utterances. Raters were instructed to evaluate how natural the response was in the chat-oriented dialogue and to annotate an absolute score for each utterance in one of seven grades from one (very unnatural) to seven (very natural). They evaluated the five types of utterances at the same time. They could see not only a user utterance and system utterance but also the context before the user utterance. Three raters worked independently.

3.4 Results of Subjective Evaluation

Table 3 shows the results of the evaluation, where the average scores annotated by three raters to the five types of utterances are listed. The results show that "Human by Writer$_1$" and "Human by Writer$_2$" were ranked the highest by all raters, with "Automatic" ranked as the lowest. The order of the evaluated scores tended to be consistent in all raters ("Human by Writer$_1$," "Human by Writer$_2$," "Repetition," "PerceivedInfo," and "Automatic"). Spearman's rank correlation coefficient between two annotators averages at 0.56. "Per-

System utterance	Rater$_1$	Rater$_2$	Rater$_3$	Average
PerceivedInfo	2.7	3.1	3.1	3.0
Automatic	2.1	2.3	2.2	2.2
Repetition	3.7	4.0	4.6	4.1
Human by Writer$_1$	4.5	5.4	5.5	5.1
Human by Writer$_2$	4.5	5.1	5.5	5.0

Table 3: Naturalness scores of system utterances annotated by three raters

ceivedInfo" was evaluated as being more natural than "Automatic," but less natural than "Repetition."

From this result, we can say that using only *PerceivedInfo* as system utterances is not an effective method. However, since there may be a difference among the types of *PerceivedInfo*, we further investigated the evaluation scores in each type of *PerceivedInfo*.

Figure 3 shows the averaged naturalness scores annotated for each type of "PerceivedInfo." The scores were clearly divided into three ranges: 1–2, 2–4, and 4–5, and defined as **Low-rate type**, **Mid-rate type**, and **High-rate type**, respectively. We investigated what *PerceivedInfo* exist in each type and the reasons for their high or low rating. For reference, we list examples and scores of *PerceivedInfo* in each type in Table 4.

Low-rate type An utterance in the Low-rate type mainly refers to user's temporary states, such as thoughts, emotion, or behavior during dialogue (e.g., "You want me to agree, don't you?"). Even an utterance that includes a positive expression (e.g., "You like me, don't you?") tends to be evaluated as unnatural. This can be partly explained by the politeness theory (Brown and Levinson, 1987). Utterances in the Low-rate type that mention a user's temporary state would create the need for the user to explain. Thus, a user's negative face, the desire to be left free to act as he or she chooses, can be threatened.

Mid-rate type An utterance in the Mid-rate type generally refers to user's permanent states, such as favorites, experience, or profiles (e.g., "You like cool cars, don't you?"). Such an utterance tends to be evaluated as natural as "Repetition." However, an utterance including a negative expression (e.g., "You are stubborn, aren't you?") or a part of profiles (e.g. "You are a woman, aren't you?") tends to be evaluated as unnatural.

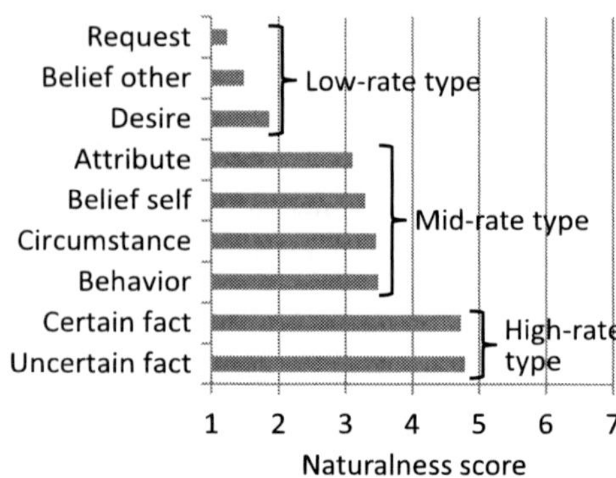

Figure 3: Naturalness scores of system utterances conveying perceived information on each type in Table 1

This means that a mention of something negative or private about the user is not a good option. This can also be explained by the politeness theory as a violation of a user's positive face; that is a desire to keep self-image approved.

High-rate type An utterance in the High-rate type generally refers to the content that does not directly relate to users, such as general facts (e.g., "A trip abroad is expensive, isn't it?"). Many utterances are evaluated as more natural than "Repetition" and as natural as "Human." This may be because the utterances in the High-rate type do not threaten a user's face because the content of the utterances has no direct relation to users.

From the experiment, we found that utterances created from specific types of *PerceivedInfo* are evaluated as more natural than others. Our results conform to the politeness theory and further provide quantitative evaluation of utterances that convey *PerceivedInfo*. One interesting thing is that the violation of the negative face has more impact on the naturalness when compared to that of the positive face. It is of great interest that, although much *PerceivedInfo* occurs during a dialogue, only a part of it can be uttered.

Although further investigation is needed, our results are useful for providing a guideline for creating system utterances that convey understanding results.

Rate	PerceivedInfo	Worst utterance	Score	Best utterance	Score
Low	Request	You want me to agree, don't you?	1.0 (1,1,1)	You want to talk about China, don't you?	2.0 (1,2,3)
		You want to talk, don't you?	1.0 (1,1,1)	You want me to go to a gym, don't you?	1.7 (1,3,1)
		You want me to know about you, don't you?	1.0 (1,1,1)	You want to talk ordinarily, don't you?	1.7 (1,3,1)
	Belief other	You trust me, don't you?	1.0 (1,1,1)	You agree with me, don't you?	2.7 (3,3,2)
		You like me, don't you?	1.0 (1,1,1)	You are interested in my topic, aren't you?	2.3 (3,3,1)
		You misunderstand me, don't you?	1.0 (1,1,1)	My impression is changing, isn't it?	2.0 (3,2,1)
	Desire	You want to change the topic, don't you?	1.0 (1,1,1)	You long for nomadic life, don't you?	4.7 (5,2,7)
		You want to boast of your partner, don't you?	1.0 (1,1,1)	You want to go to Germany, don't you?	4.3 (4,4,5)
		You want to sympathize with me, don't you?	1.0 (1,1,1)	You want to live in cool place, don't you?	4.3 (4,5,4)
Mid	Attribute	You are a woman, aren't you?	1.0 (1,1,1)	You are sociable, aren't you?	6.3 (5,7,7)
		You are easygoing, aren't you?	1.0 (1,1,1)	You are willing to go out, aren't you?	6.3 (5,7,7)
		You are weak, aren't you?	1.0 (1,1,1)	You are kind, aren't you?	5.7 (3,7,7)
	Belief self	You are boastful, aren't you?	1.0 (1,1,1)	You like cool cars, don't you?	6.3 (5,7,7)
		You are a little embarrassed, aren't you?	1.3 (1,2,1)	You like Mt. Fuji, don't you?	6.0 (5,6,7)
		You are uninterested in agriculture, aren't you?	1.7 (1,3,1)	You like the outdoors, don't you?	5.3 (5,4,7)
	Circumstance	There is a computer in your home, isn't there?	1.7 (2,2,1)	You belong to the soccer team, don't you?	6.0 (5,6,7)
		You live on your husband's earnings, don't you?	1.7 (2,2,1)	It is sunny around you, isn't it?	5.3 (3,6,7)
		Your parents are well, aren't they?	2.0 (2,3,1)	Your relatives like celebrations, don't they?	5.0 (4,4,7)
	Behavior	You think about what to say, don't you?	1.3 (2,1,1)	You went out this summer, didn't you?	5.3 (3,6,7)
		You show me interests, don't you?	1.3 (1,2,1)	You lost your appetite due to how the food looks.	5.3 (4,5,7)
		You think what to say next,don't you?	1.3 (2,1,1)	You drink herb tee, don't you?	5.0 (2,7,6)
High	Certain fact	It is September, isn't it?	3.0 (3,5,1)	Wheels are expensive, aren't they?	6.7 (7,6,7)
		Bikes have various price ranges, don't they?	3.3 (3,3,4)	It is humid, isn't it?	6.3 (7,5,7)
		Road bikes and bicycles are different, aren't they?	3.7 (3,4,4)	Curved handlebars are special, aren't they?	6.3 (6,6,7)
	Uncertain fact	Using computers takes a lot of time, doesn't it?	2.0 (1,4,1)	A trip abroad is expensive, isn't they?	6.7 (7,6,7)
		That is a bad restaurant, isn't it?	3.3 (2,3,5)	Nagatomo showed great activity, didn't he?	6.3 (7,5,7)
		Muscle pain arises the next day, doesn't it?	3.7 (4,4,3)	Germany is safe, isn't it?	6.3 (6,5,7)

Table 4: Best and worst three utterances conveying perceived information on each type in Table 1. "Score" column shows average score and each score annotated by three raters.

4 Related Work

Although there has been no studies that explored the effect of utterances conveying system's understanding results to users, there have been several that have explored what linguistic behavior can be used or how to utter contents in dialogue systems from the viewpoints of social aspects (especially on the politeness theory).

For example, Gupta et al. constructed a task-oriented dialogue system in the cooking domain in which utterance generation is performed on the basis of the politeness theory (Gupta et al., 2007). Wang et al. estimated the politeness of each utterance in a task-oriented dialogue system by using various features, such as insults or criticisms (Wang et al., 2012). Danescu et al. constructed a corpus in which politeness is annotated in online community data and constructed a model for estimating politeness using linguistic features, such as gratitude expressions or positive and negative lexicons (Danescu-Niculescu-Mizil et al., 2013).

5 Conclusion

In this paper, we investigated what types of understanding results can be used as system utterances. Using the corpus of *PerceivedInfo* (perceived information), we manually created and evaluated the utterances that convey *PerceivedInfo*. We found that certain types of *PerceivedInfo*, especially those related to a user's permanent state and information irrelevant to users themselves, are usable.

For future work, we want to construct a dialogue system that conveys the understanding results in the way we proposed. For this purpose, we need to create an automatic estimator of *PerceivedInfo*. In this work, we used the understanding results as they were; however, we can create various system utterances from *PerceivedInfo*, and, in such a case, other types of *PerceivedInfo* can be effectively used. We want to further pursue how we can make use of *PerceivedInfo* in dialogue systems.

References

Penelope Brown and Stephen C. Levinson. 1987. *Politeness: Some universals in language usage*, volume 4. Cambridge university press.

Cristian Danescu-Niculescu-Mizil, Moritz Sudhof, Dan Jurafsky, Jure Leskovec, and Christopher Potts. 2013. A computational approach to politeness with application to social factors. In *Proc. ACL*. pages 250–259.

Swati Gupta, Marilyn A. Walker, and Daniela M. Romano. 2007. How rude are you?: Evaluating politeness and affect in interaction. In *Proc. International Conference on Affective Computing and Intelligent Interaction*. pages 203–217.

Ryuichiro Higashinaka, Kenji Imamura, Toyomi Meguro, Chiaki Miyazaki, Nozomi Kobayashi, Hiroaki

Sugiyama, Toru Hirano, Toshiro Makino, and Yoshihiro Matsuo. 2014. Towards an open domain conversational system fully based on natural language processing. In *Proc. COLING*. pages 928–939.

Diane J Litman and Scott Silliman. 2004. ITSPOKE: An intelligent tutoring spoken dialogue system. In *Proc. NAACL-HLT*. pages 5–8.

Koh Mitsuda, Ryuichiro Higashinaka, and Yoshihiro Matsuo. 2017. What information should a dialogue system understand?: Collection and analysis of perceived information in chat-oriented dialogue. In *Proc. IWSDS*.

Kanako Onishi and Takeshi Yoshimura. 2014. Casual conversation technology achieving natural dialog with computers. *NTT DOCOMO Technical Journal* 15(4):16–21.

Antonie Raux, Brian Langner, Dan Bohus, and Alan W Black Maxine Eskenazi. 2005. Let's Go Public! taking a spoken dialogue system to the real world. In *Proc. Interspeech*. pages 885–888.

William Yang Wang, Samantha Finkelstein, Amy Ogan, Alan W Black, and Justine Cassell. 2012. "love ya, jerkface": Using sparse log-linear models to build positive and impolite relationships with teens. In *Proc. SIGDIAL*. pages 20–29.

Extracting and Understanding Contrastive Opinion through Topic Relevant Sentences

Ebuka Ibeke and **Chenghua Lin** and **Adam Wyner** and **Mohamad Hardyman Barawi**
Department of Computing Science
University of Aberdeen, UK
{e.e.ibeke,chenghua.lin,azwyner,r01mhbb}@abdn.ac.uk

Abstract

Contrastive opinion mining is essential in identifying, extracting and organising opinions from user generated texts. Most existing studies separate input data into respective collections. In addition, the relationships between the topics extracted and the sentences in the corpus which express the topics are opaque, hindering our understanding of the opinions expressed in the corpus. We propose a novel unified latent variable model (contraLDA) which addresses the above matters. Experimental results show the effectiveness of our model in mining contrasted opinions, outperforming our baselines.

1 Introduction

Recent text mining applications have uncovered public opinions and social trends. This is partially driven by large corpora of opinionated documents in the web. Contrastive opinion mining is the discovery of opposing opinions and sentiments held by individuals or groups about a given topic. The usefulness of contrastive opinion mining spans across many applications such as discovering the public's stand on major socio-political events (Fang et al., 2012), observing heated debates over controversial issues (Lippi and Torroni, 2016), and product review sites (Lerman and McDonald, 2009). Considering the volume of reviews, it is highly desirable to acquire an overview of the major viewpoints from large amounts of text data automatically, allowing one to convert data into actionable knowledge for timely decision-making.

Recently, there have been some studies on mining contrastive viewpoints or opinions from text (Paul and Girju, 2009; Fang et al., 2012; Elahi and Monachesi, 2012; Gutiérrez et al., 2016). However, these studies assume that input data are separated into different collections beforehand, e.g., news articles from CNN vs. those from Fox News about the same set of events. While this assumption might hold for some practical scenarios, one quite often needs to analyse contrastive opinions contained in a single collection such as an open-ended discussion about government policy or commercial products in order to understand the viewpoints and their connections across the collection.

In addition, it is natural that debates on some topics are more prominent, indicating the importance of the topic. Therefore, being able to understand the prominence of a topic and the levels of contrastive sentiment will help one to prioritise actions. Finally, existing models generally interpret contrastive opinions solely in terms of the extracted topic words, which are not adequate to help us accurately understand the opinions presented in the corpus since the topic words only express shallow semantics. Understanding the dependency between the sentences in the corpus and the topic of discussion would be illuminating. The representative sentences also help to clarify the coherence of the extracted topics.

In this paper, we address the aforementioned issues by proposing a novel unified latent variable model (contraLDA) for mining contrastive opinion from text collections. The proposed model contributes the following: (1) automatically discovers contrastive opinion from both single and multiple text collections; (2) quantifies the strength of opinion contrastiveness towards the topic of interest, which could allow one to swiftly flag issues that require immediate attention; and (3) adopts the sentence extraction approach in (Barawi et al., 2017) to extract relevant sentences related to topics, making sentiment-bearing top-

395

Proceedings of the The 8th International Joint Conference on Natural Language Processing, pages 395–400,
Taipei, Taiwan, November 27 – December 1, 2017 ©2017 AFNLP

ics clearer to users. Experimental results show that our model outperforms several baseline models in terms of extracting coherent and distinctive sentiment-bearing topics which express contrastive opinions. The topic relevant sentences extracted by our approach further help us effectively understand and interpret sentiment-bearing topics.

2 Methodology

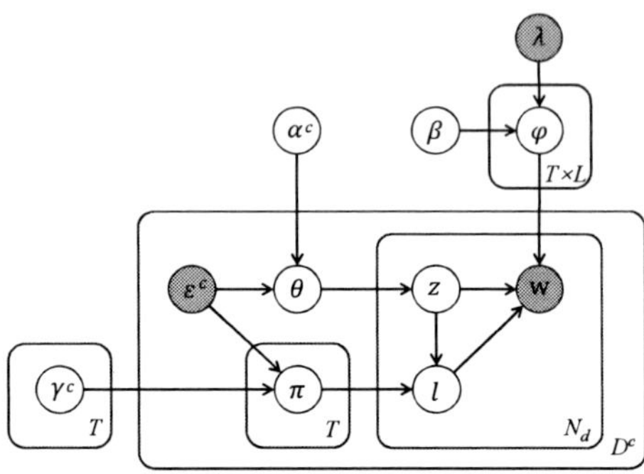

Figure 1: The contraLDA Model.

We propose a model called contraLDA which offers a unified framework for mining contrastive opinions from text, where the source of text could be either a single collection or multiple collection of text. The graphical model of contraLDA is shown in Figure 1. Given a collection of documents D, assume that D can be divided in to C classes: $D = \{D^c\}_{c=1}^{C}$ with D^c documents per class, each document d in class c is a sequence of N_d words, each word in the document is an item from a vocabulary with V distinct terms, and c is the class index. Also assuming that L and T are the total number of sentiment labels and topics, respectively, the complete procedure for generating a word w_n in contraLDA is as follows: first, one draws a topic z from the class-constrained topic distribution θ_d^c. Following that, one draws a sentiment label l from the topic specific, class-constrained sentiment distribution $\pi_{d,z}^c$. Finally, one draws a word from the per-corpus word distribution $\varphi_{z,l}$ conditioned on both topic z and sentiment label l. Note that documents of all collections share the same φ, and we can fully keep track of which collection a document belongs to based on its class index c. It is also important to note that the number of classes C plays a key role in controlling the operation mode of contraLDA. That is when $C = 1$, contraLDA is essentially modelling a single collection of text without any class membership information. In the scenario where $C > 1$, contraLDA will be switching to model multiple collections of text, e.g., documents annotated with class labels, or articles from New York Times and Xinhua News about the same set of events. We summarise the generative process of contraLDA as follows:

- For each topic $z \in \{1, \cdots, T\}$
    - For each sentiment label $l \in \{1, \cdots, S\}$
        * Draw $\varphi_{z,l} \sim \mathrm{Dir}(\beta_{z,l})$.

- For each document $d \in D$
    - choose a distribution $\theta_d^c \sim \mathrm{Dir}(\epsilon_z^c \cdot \alpha)$.
    - For each sentiment label l under document d,
        * Choose a distribution $\pi_{d,z}^c \sim \mathrm{Dir}(\epsilon_l^c \cdot \gamma)$.
    - For each word $n \in \{1, \cdots, N_d^c\}$ in document d
        * Choose a topic $z_n \sim \mathrm{Mult}(\theta_d^c)$,
        * Choose a sentiment label $l_n \sim \mathrm{Mult}(\pi_{d,z_n}^c)$,
        * Choose a word $w_n \sim \mathrm{Mult}(\varphi_{z_n,l_n})$.

2.1 Incorporating Supervised Information.

The contraLDA model can be trained flexibly depending on the type of supervision information available. Specifically, if there are only labelled features available (e.g., sentiment lexicon, or topic seed words), our model will incorporate the labelled features to constrain the Dirichlet prior of topic-word distributions, which essentially plays a role in governing the model inference. If there is fully labelled data available, e.g., labelled documents, our model will account for the full supervision from document labels during the generative process, where each document can associate with a single class label or multiple class labels. However, if the dataset contains both labelled and unlabelled data, our model will account for the available labels during the generative process as well as incorporate the labelled features as above to constrain the Dirichlet prior.

When labelled data is available, contraLDA incorporates supervised information by constraining that a training document can only be generated from the topic set with class labels corresponding to the document's observed label set. This is achieved by introducing a dependency link from the document label matrix ϵ to the Dirichlet priors α and γ. Suppose a corpus has three topical labels denoted by $Z = \{z_1, z_2, z_3\}$ and for each label z_k there are two sentiment labels denoted by $l = \{l_1, l_2\}$. Given observed label matrix $\epsilon_c = \{\epsilon_z^c, \epsilon_l^c\} = \{(1, 0, 1), (1, 0)\}$ which indicates that d is associated with topic labels z_1, z_3 as well as sentiment label l_1, we can encode the label information into contraLDA as

$$\boldsymbol{\alpha}_d^c = \boldsymbol{\epsilon}_z^c \cdot \boldsymbol{\alpha} \qquad (1)$$

$$\boldsymbol{\gamma}_d^c = \boldsymbol{\epsilon}_l^c \cdot \boldsymbol{\gamma} \qquad (2)$$

This ensures that d can only be generated from topics associated with observed class labels from ϵ. If there are no labelled documents available, contraLDA will incorporate labelled features from $\boldsymbol{\lambda}$ (e.g., sentiment lexicons) for constraining the Dirichlet priors $\boldsymbol{\beta}$ using the same strategy described in (Lin and He, 2009; Lin et al., 2012a).

2.2 Inference.

From the contraLDA graphical model depicted in Figure 1, we can write the joint distribution of all observed and hidden variables which can be factored into three terms:

$$P(\mathbf{w}, \mathbf{z}, \mathbf{l}|\boldsymbol{\alpha}, \boldsymbol{\beta}, \boldsymbol{\gamma}, \mathbf{c}) =$$
$$P(\mathbf{w}|\mathbf{z}, \mathbf{l}, \boldsymbol{\beta})P(\mathbf{l}|\mathbf{z}, \boldsymbol{\gamma}, \mathbf{c})P(\mathbf{z}|\boldsymbol{\alpha}, \mathbf{c}) \qquad (3)$$

The main objective of inference in contraLDA is then to find a set of model parameters that can best explain the observed data, namely, the class-constrained topic proportion $\boldsymbol{\theta}^c$, the class-constrained topic label specific sentiment proportion $\boldsymbol{\pi}^c$, and the per-corpus word distribution $\boldsymbol{\varphi}$. To compute these target distributions, we need to calculate the posterior distribution of the model. As the posterior is intractable, we use a collapsed Gibbs sampler to approximate the posterior based on the full conditional distribution for each word token in position t. By evaluating the model joint distribution in Eq. 3, we can yield the full conditional distribution as follows

$$P(z_t = k, l_t = j|\mathbf{w}, \mathbf{z}^{-t}, \mathbf{l}^{-t}, \boldsymbol{\alpha}, \boldsymbol{\beta}, \boldsymbol{\gamma}, \mathbf{c}) \propto$$
$$\frac{N_{k,j,w_t}^{-t} + \beta_{k,j,i}}{N_{k,j}^{-t} + \sum_i \beta_{k,j,i}} \cdot \frac{N_{d,k}^{-t} + \alpha_{d,k}^c}{N_d^{-t} + \sum_k \alpha_{d,k}^c}$$
$$\cdot \frac{N_{d,k,j}^{-t} + \gamma_{d,k,j}^c}{N_{d,k}^{-t} + \sum_j \gamma_{d,k,j}^c}. \qquad (4)$$

where the superscript $-t$ denotes a quantity that excludes data from tth position, $N_{k,j,w}$ is the number of times word w appeared in topic k with sentiment label j, $N_{k,j}$ is the number of times words are assigned to topic k and sentiment label j, $N_{d,k}$

is the number of times topic k is assigned to some word tokens in document d, N_d is the total number of words in document d, $N_{d,k,j}$ is the number of times a word from document d is associated with topic k and sentiment label j.

Using Eq. 4, we can obtain sampling assignments for contraLDA model, based on which model parameters can be estimated as

$$\varphi_{k,j,i} = \frac{N_{k,j,i} + \beta_{k,j,i}}{N_{k,j} + \sum_i \beta_{k,j,i}}, \quad \theta_{d,k,j}^c = \frac{N_{d,k} + \alpha_{k,j}^c}{N_d + \sum_k \alpha_{d,k}^c}$$
and
$$\pi_{d,k}^c = \frac{N_{d,k,j} + \gamma_{d,k,j}^c}{N_{d,k} + \sum_j \gamma_{d,k,j}^c}.$$

2.3 Modelling the associations between sentiment-bearing topics and sentences.

Our model adopts a computational mechanism (Barawi et al., 2017) that can uncover the association between an opinionated (or sentiment-bearing) topic and the underlying sentences of a corpus. First, we preserve the sentential structure of each document during the corpus preprocessing step (see §3 for more details). Second, modelling topic-sentence relevance is essentially equivalent to calculating the probability of a sentence given a sentiment-bearing topic $p(\text{sent}|z, l)$. The posterior inference of our model, based on Gibbs sampling, can recover the hidden sentiment label and topic label assignments for each word in the corpus. Such label-word assignment information provides a means for re-assembling the relevance between a word and a sentiment-bearing topic. By leveraging the sentential structure information and gathering the label assignment statistics for each word of a sentence, we can derive the probability of a sentence given a sentiment-bearing topic as

$$p(\text{sent}|z, l) = \frac{p(z, l|\text{sent}) \cdot p(\text{sent})}{p(z, l)}$$
$$\propto p(z, l|\text{sent}) \cdot p(\text{sent}) \qquad (5)$$

where

$$p(z, l|\text{sent}) = \frac{\sum_{w,z',l'} \varphi_{z',l',w}}{\sum_{w \in \text{sent}} \varphi_{z',l',w}}, \qquad (6)$$

$$p(\text{sent}) = \sum_z \sum_l \prod_{w \in \text{sent}} \varphi_{z,l,w}. \qquad (7)$$

Also $p(l, z)$ is discounted as it is a constant when comparing sentential labels for the same sentiment-bearing topic. The extracted sentences for each sentiment-bearing topic are ranked based on their probability scores.

3 Experimental Setup

Dataset. We evaluate the performance of our model[1] for contrastive opinion mining on the El Capitan dataset[2] (Ibeke et al., 2016) which consists of reviews manually annotated (with 18 topic labels and 3 sentiment labels in total) for various opinion mining tasks. The dataset consists of 2,232 customer reviews, with topic and sentiment annotations at both the review and sentence levels. For the sentiment labels, we only concentrate on positive and negative sentiment labels with the 2.3% of neutral reviews being ignored, since the aim of this study is to mine contrastive opinion from text. The dataset has 10,348 sentences with an average length of 17.3 words.

Preprocessing. We preprocessed the experimental dataset by first performing automatic sentence segmentation[3] in order to preserve the sentential structure information of each document. We then remove punctuation, numbers, non-alphabet characters, stop words, lowercase all words, and perform stemming.

4 Experimental Results

Topic coherence. We first quantitatively measure the coherence of the extracted topics by our model and compare the results with a number of baselines, namely, LDA (Blei et al., 2003), ccLDA (Paul and Girju, 2009), TAM (Paul and Girju, 2010), and VODUM (Thonet et al., 2016). We employ normalised pointwise mutual information (NPMI) (Bouma, 2009) which outperforms other metrics in measuring topic coherence (Newman et al., 2010; Aletras and Stevenson, 2013). We run our model and the baseline models with two sentiment labels (i.e., positive and negative), and vary the topic number setting $T \in \{5, 10, 20, 30, 40, 50\}$, setting $\beta = 0.01$ (Steyvers and Griffiths, 2007) and $\alpha = 0.1$. Our model learns α directly from data using maximum-likelihood estimation (Lin et al., 2012b).

As can be seen from Figure 2a, there is a general pattern for all tested models, where the coherence score of the extracted topics decreases as a larger number of topics K being modelled. This is inline with the observations of (Mimno et al.,

---

[1]While our model can be applied to both single and multiple data collections, due to page limits, we only show the experimental results on a single dataset.

[2]https://github.com/eibeke/El-Capitan-Dataset

[3]http://www.nltk.org/

2011; Gutiérrez et al., 2016), who discovered that as the number of topics increases, lower-likelihood topics tend to be more incoherent, resulting in lower coherence score for topics. In terms of individual models, our model consistently achieves a higher coherent score than all baseline models. For instance, when compared with the best baseline VODUM, our model gives over 8% averaged improvement. This demonstrates the capability of the proposed contraLDA in extracting coherent and meaningful topics.

Analysis of opinion contrastiveness. We further study the problem of quantifying the strength of opinion contrastiveness towards the topic of interest, which allows one to swiftly flag topics or issues that require immediate attention. We approach this by computing the prominence score for each sentiment-bearing topic extracted by contraLDA given a corpus c using

$$P(z, l|\boldsymbol{c}) = \frac{1}{|D|} \sum_{d=1}^{D} P(l|z, d) P(z|d)$$

$$= \frac{1}{|D|} \sum_{d=1}^{D} \theta_{d,z} \cdot \pi_{d,z,l}, \qquad (8)$$

where D is the total number of documents in the corpus. Thus the prominence for topic z in a corpus can be derived as

$$P(z) = \sum_{l} P(z, l). \qquad (9)$$

Figure 2b shows some contrastive opinion topic pairs ordered by their prominence in the corpus. Modelling topic prominence and sentiment contrastiveness provides a quick overview of the notable topics and the sentiments towards them. We can easily identify that the most heated topics are `update` and `performance`. In terms of opinion contrastiveness, we see that `Speed` received quite balanced positive and negative sentiment magnitude. `Performance` and `Update` are skewed towards the negative sentiment, indicating that a majority of customers experienced a performance drop after upgrading to El Capitan.

Contrastive opinion topic analysis. In this experiment, we qualitatively evaluate our model in the task of discovering contrastive opinions.

The top panel of Table 1 shows contrastive opinion topic pairs extracted by our model. Note that `Performance`, `Office` and `Yosemite` are label information from the El Capitan

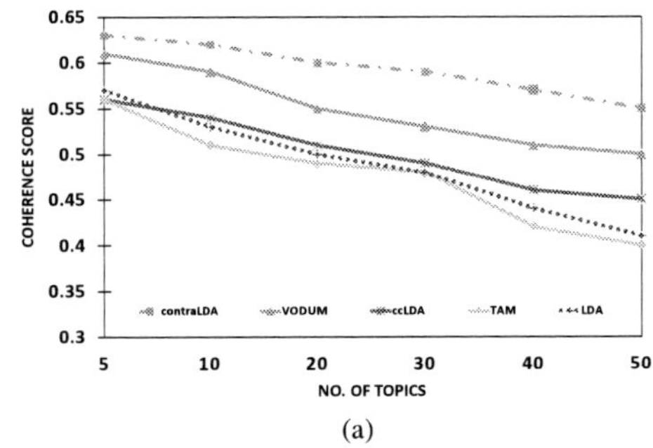
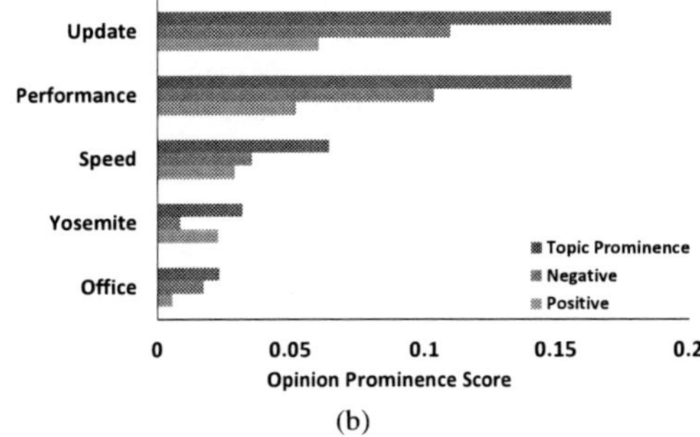

Figure 2: Topic coherence analysis using NPMI (a); Analysis of topic prominence and sentiment contrastiveness (b). NB: blue bar indicates the overall prominence of contrastive topic pair; green bar indicates the strength of a positive sentiment topic, and red bar for negative sentiment topic.

Performance		Office		Yosemite	
+	-	+	-	+	-
work	crash	offic	offic	yosemit	yosemit
run	work	microsoft	use	work	upgrad
perform	time	compat	work	time	destroy
faster	app	quick	microsoft	downgrade	slow
app	use	fine	ms	restor	work
smooth	slow	work	crash	issu	mac
new	mac	updat	issu	instal	bad
pro	open	upgrad	word	machin	problem
macbook	freez	new	excel	macbook	maverick
better	just	didn	appl	revert	appl

Performance +	So much better than before, and apps run faster too.
Performance -	Computer slows down dramatically, programs freeze.
Office +	Office 2016 opens quickly with no issues.
Office -	Update:Office apps tend to crash after the update!
Yosemite +	So I downgraded back to Yosemite and - hey presto!
Yosemite -	My 2010 iMac was destroyed by Yosemite.

Table 1: Contrastive opinion topic examples and the top rated sentence for each topic.

dataset. A topic pair, e.g., (Performance+, Performance-), expresses contrastive opinions towards the same topic Performance, with '+' and '-' indicating the topic sentiment orientation. For instance, the two topics under Performance+ suggests that some people feel the system *performs better* and *app runs faster*, whereas Performance- seems to show highly contrastive opinion that people have bad experience after upgrade, e.g., *app crashes* or *freezes*, *mac* becomes *slow*. However, it is still impossible to accurately interpret the extracted topics solely based on its multinomial distribution, especially when one is unfamiliar with the topic domain. We bridge this gap by extracting the most relevant sentences for a given topic, which can greatly facilitate sentiment-bearing topic interpretation (as described in § 2.3).

The bottom panel of Table 1 shows the extracted top sentences (ranked based on Eq. 5) for each topic. For instance, the extracted top sentences for the Office topic show that some customers recorded an improvement with their office app (e.g., "*Office* 2016 opens *quickly* with no issues"), while others are unhappy with the office app (e.g., "Update: *Office* apps tend to *crash* after the update"). We see that the top sentences can effectively bridge the gap between the topic word distributions and the opinion encoded within the topic, and hence can greatly help facilitate sentiment-bearing topic understanding and interpretation.

5   Conclusion

We presented the contraLDA model which detects contrastive opinions both in single and multiple data collections, and determines the sentiments of the extracted opinions. Our model effectively mines coherent topics and contrastive opinions from text. Experimental results show that our model outperforms baselines in extracting coherent topics. In addition, we presented a mechanism for extracting sentences from corpus that are relevant to sentiment-bearing topics, which helps understanding and interpretation of the topics discovered. We plan to further investigate our approach on datasets from more domains.

Acknowledgments

This work is supported by the awards made by the UK Engineering and Physical Sciences Research Council (Grant number: EP/P005810/1).

References

Nikolaos Aletras and Mark Stevenson. 2013. Evaluating topic coherence using distributional semantics. In *Proceedings of the 10th International Conference on Computational Semantics (IWCS)*. pages 13–22.

Mohamad H. Barawi, Chenghua Lin, and Advaith Siddharthan. 2017. Automatically labelling sentiment-bearing topics with descriptive sentence labels. In *In Proceedings of the 22nd International Conference on Natural Language and Information Systems (NLDB)*. pages 299–312.

David M. Blei, Andrew Y. Ng, and Michael I. Jordan. 2003. Latent dirichlet allocation. *The Journal of Machine Learning Research* 3:993–1022.

Gerlof Bouma. 2009. Normalized (pointwise) mutual information in collocation extraction. *In The German Society for Computational Linguistics and Language Technology (GSCL)* pages 31–40.

Mohammad F. Elahi and Paola Monachesi. 2012. An examination of cross-cultural similarities and differences from social media data with respect to language use. In *The Emotion and Sentiment Analysis Workshop in the 10th Language Resources and Evaluation Conference (LREC)*. pages 4080–4086.

Yi Fang, Luo Si, Naveen Somasundaram, and Zhengtao Yu. 2012. Mining contrastive opinions on political texts using cross-perspective topic model. In *Proceedings of the International Conference on Web Search and Data Mining (WSDM)*. pages 63–72.

ED Gutiérrez, Ekaterina Shutova, Patricia Lichtenstein, Gerard de Melo, and Luca Gilardi. 2016. Detecting cross-cultural differences using a multilingual topic model. *Transactions of the Association for Computational Linguistics (TACL)* 4:47–60.

Ebuka Ibeke, Chenghua Lin, Chris Coe, Adam Wyner, Dong Liu, Mohamad H. Barawi, and Noor F.A. Yusof. 2016. A curated corpus for sentiment-topic analysis. In *The Emotion and Sentiment Analysis Workshop in the 10th Language Resources and Evaluation Conference (LREC), Slovenia*.

Kevin Lerman and Ryan McDonald. 2009. Contrastive summarization: an experiment with consumer reviews. In *Proceedings of human language technologies: The Annual Conference of the North American Chapter of the Association for Computational Linguistics (ACL)*. pages 113–116.

Chenghua Lin and Yulan He. 2009. Joint sentiment/topic model for sentiment analysis. In *Proceedings of the 18th ACM conference on Information and knowledge management*. ACM, pages 375–384.

Chenghua Lin, Yulan He, Richard Everson, and Stefan Ruger. 2012a. Weakly supervised joint sentiment-topic detection from text. *IEEE Transactions on Knowledge and Data Engineering* 24(6):1134–1145.

Chenghua Lin, Yulan He, Carlos Pedrinaci, and John Domingue. 2012b. Feature lda: a supervised topic model for automatic detection of web api documentations from the web. In *International Semantic Web Conference (ISWC)*. Springer, pages 328–343.

Marco Lippi and Paolo Torroni. 2016. Argument mining from speech: Detecting claims in political debates. In *In Association for the Advancement of Artificial Intelligence (AAAI)*. pages 2979–2985.

David Mimno, Hanna M. Wallach, Edmund Talley, Miriam Leenders, and Andrew McCallum. 2011. Optimizing semantic coherence in topic models. In *Proceedings of the Conference on Empirical Methods in Natural Language Processing (EMNLP)*. pages 262–272.

David Newman, Jey H. Lau, Karl Grieser, and Timothy Baldwin. 2010. Automatic evaluation of topic coherence. In *Human Language Technologies: The Annual Conference of the North American Chapter of the Association for Computational Linguistics (ACL)*. pages 100–108.

Michael Paul and Roxana Girju. 2009. Cross-cultural analysis of blogs and forums with mixed-collection topic models. In *Proceedings of the Conference on Empirical Methods on Natural Language Processing (EMNLP)*. pages 1408–1417.

Michael Paul and Roxana Girju. 2010. A two-dimensional topic-aspect model for discovering multi-faceted topics. *In Association for the Advancement of Artificial Intelligence (AAAI)* .

Mark Steyvers and Tom Griffiths. 2007. Probabilistic topic models pages 424–440.

Thibaut Thonet, Guillaume Cabanac, Mohand Boughanem, and Karen Pinel-Sauvagnat. 2016. Vodum: a topic model unifying viewpoint, topic and opinion discovery. In *European Conference on Information Retrieval*. Springer, pages 533–545.

CWIG3G2 – Complex Word Identification Task across Three Text Genres and Two User Groups

Seid Muhie Yimam[†], Sanja Štajner[‡], Martin Riedl[†], and Chris Biemann[†]

[†]Language Technology Group, Department of Informatics, Universität Hamburg, Germany
[‡]Data and Web Science Group, University of Mannheim, Germany
{yimam, riedl, biemann}@informatik.uni-hamburg.de
sanja@informatik.uni-mannheim.de

Abstract

Complex word identification (CWI) is an important task in text accessibility. However, due to the scarcity of CWI datasets, previous studies have only addressed this problem on Wikipedia sentences and have solely taken into account the needs of non-native English speakers. We collect a new CWI dataset (CWIG3G2) covering three text genres (NEWS, WIKINEWS, and WIKIPEDIA) annotated by both native and non-native English speakers. Unlike previous datasets, we cover single words, as well as complex phrases, and present them for judgment in a paragraph context. We present the first study on cross-genre and cross-group CWI, showing measurable influences in native language and genre types.

1 Introduction

Complex word identification (CWI) is a sub-task of lexical simplification (LS), which identifies difficult words or phrases in a text. Lexically and semantically complex words and phrases can pose difficulties to text understanding for many people, e.g. non-native speakers (Petersen and Ostendorf, 2007; Aluísio et al., 2008), children (De Belder and Moens, 2010), and people with various cognitive or reading impairments (Feng et al., 2009; Rello et al., 2013; Saggion et al., 2015). It has been shown that people with dyslexia read faster and understand texts better when short and frequent words are used (Rello et al., 2013), whilst the non-native English speakers need to be familiar with about 95% of text vocabulary for a basic text comprehension (Nation, 2001), and even 98% of text vocabulary for enjoying (unsimplified) leisure texts (Hirsh and Nation, 1992).

Many published guidelines cover recommendations of how to write texts which are easy-to-understand for various target populations, e.g. (Mencap, 2002; PlainLanguage, 2011; Freyhoff et al., 1998). However, manual production of texts from scratch for each target population separately cannot keep up with the amount of information which should be accessible for everyone. Therefore, many systems for automatic lexical simplification (LS) of texts have been proposed. LS systems take as input a text of a certain level of difficulty and output a text in a simplified form without changing its meaning. Most LS systems have the functionality of replacing potentially complex words with synonyms or related words that are easier to understand and yet still fit into context. Some of these systems treat all content words in a text as potentially difficult words, e.g. (Horn et al., 2014; Glavaš and Štajner, 2015). Other systems try to detect complex words first and then perform the replacement with simpler words, e.g. (Paetzold and Specia, 2016b), which seems to significantly improve the results (Paetzold and Specia, 2015).

Most LS systems focus on simplifying news articles (Aluísio et al., 2008; Carroll et al., 1999; Saggion et al., 2015; Glavaš and Štajner, 2015). However, only small amounts of newswire texts are available that contain annotations for manual simplifications. Most LS systems rely on sentence alignments between English Wikipedia and English Simple Wikipedia (Coster and Kauchak, 2011). Thus, existing CWI datasets cover mostly the Wikipedia Genre (Shardlow, 2013; Horn et al., 2014; Paetzold and Specia, 2016a).

We collect a new CWI dataset (CWIG3G2) covering three genres: professionally written news articles, amateurishly written news articles (WikiNews), and Wikipedia articles. Then, we test whether or not the complex word (CW) annotations collected on one genre can be used for

Proceedings of the The 8th International Joint Conference on Natural Language Processing, pages 401–407,
Taipei, Taiwan, November 27 – December 1, 2017 ©2017 AFNLP

predicting CWs on another genre and also explore if the native and non-native user groups share the same lexical-semantic simplification needs.

2 Related Work

Previous datasets relied on Simple Wikipedia and edit histories as a 'gold standard' annotation of CWs, despite the fact that the use of Simple Wikipedia as a 'gold standard' for text simplification has been disputed (Amancio and Specia, 2014; Xu et al., 2015). Currently, the largest CWI dataset is the SemEval-2016 (Task 11) dataset (Paetzold and Specia, 2016a). It consists of 9,200 sentences collected from previous datasets (Shardlow, 2013; Horn et al., 2014; Kauchak, 2013). For the creation of the SemEval-2016 CWI dataset, annotators were asked to annotate (only) one word within a given sentence as complex or not. In the training set (200 sentences), each target word was annotated by 20 people, whilst in the test set (9,000 sentences) each target word was annotated by a single annotator from a pool of 400 annotators. The goal of the shared task was to predict the complexity of a word for a non-native speaker based on the annotations of a larger group of non-native speakers. This introduced strong biases and inconsistencies in the test set, resulting in very low F-scores across all systems (Paetzold and Specia, 2016a; Wróbel, 2016).

The systems of the SemEval-2016 shared task were ranked based on their F-scores (the standard F_1-measure) and the newly introduced G-scores (the harmonic mean between accuracy and recall). When performing a Spearman correlation between F-score and G-scores considering all systems of the SemEval-2016 task, we obtain a reasonable correlation value of 0.69. However, considering the correlation between the 10 best G-scoring systems a negative correlation of -0.34 is achieved. A similar trend is obtained for the 10 best F-scoring systems resulting in a correlation score of -0.74. The best system with respect to the G-score (77.4%), but at the cost of F-score being as low as 24.60%, uses a combination of threshold-based, lexicon-based and machine learning approaches with minimalistic voting techniques (Paetzold and Specia, 2016a). The highest scoring system with respect to the F-score (35.30%), which obtained a G-score of 60.80%, uses threshold-based document frequencies on Simple Wikipedia (Wróbel, 2016). Focusing on the standard F_1-score as the main evaluation measure in our experiments, we replicate this system on a recent Simple Wikipedia dump, and consider it as our baseline system.

There are very few works on non-English CWI; the only dataset we are aware of, containing annotations for English, German and Spanish, is described in our previous paper (Yimam et al., 2017).

3 Collection of the New CWI Dataset

We collect complex word and phrase annotations (sequences of words, up to maximum 50 characters), using the Amazon Mechanical Turk (MTurk) crowdsourcing platform, from native and non-native English speakers. We ask participants if they are native or non-native English speakers, and collect proficiency levels (beginner, intermediate, advanced) for non-native speakers.

Data Selection: CWIG3G2 comprises of texts from three different genres: professionally written news, WikiNews (news written by amateurs), and Wikipedia articles. For the NEWS dataset, we used 100 news stories from the EMM News-Brief compiled by Glavaš and Štajner (2013) for their event-centered simplification task. For the *WikiNews*, we collected 42 articles from the Wikipedia news. To resemble the existing CW resources (Shardlow, 2013; Paetzold and Specia, 2016a; Kauchak, 2013), we collected 500 sentences from Wikipedia.

Annotation Procedure: Using MTurk, we create paragraph-level HIT (Human Intelligence Task). In order to control the annotation process, we do not allow users to select words like determiners, numbers and phrases of more than 50 characters in length. To encourage annotators to carefully read the text and to only highlight complex words, we offer a bonus that doubles the original reward if at least half of their selections match selections from other workers. To discourage arbitrarily larger annotations, we limit the maximum number of selections that annotators can highlight to 10. If an annotator cannot find any complex word, we ask them to provide a comment. The collection is being conducted until we find at least 10 native and 10 non-native annotators per HIT. Figure 1 shows the instruction given to the workers with example sentences where possible complex phrases are highlighted in yellow.

Differences to Previous CWI Datasets: Our annotation procedure differs from others in several ways. First, we did not limit our task on collecting

-----INSTRUCTIONS----

Assume the texts are meant for non-native language learners, children, or people with disabilities. Using your mouse pointer, highlight words or phrases which you think are hard to understand. You can select at most ten and at least three words or phrases in this HIT. Highlight again if you want to remove them. Highlighting parts of a word IS NOT accepted. Highlighting the whole sentence IS NOT accepted. If you believe that there are NO hard words or phrases to highlight in this HIT, tell us why in the comment box below. If you have any comment about this HIT, tell us also in the comment box.

Bonus: If your highlighting matches with 60% of the other worker's highlighting, the reward of the HIT will be doubled! The bonus is calculated after the HITs are completed by other workers and might take more than TWO days to be paid.

Examples:

The Israeli official said the new ambassador to Cairo, Yaakov Amitai, was expected to travel to the Egyptian capital in December to present his **credentials**, but the embassy would not be **staffed** or resume normal activity until acceptable **security arrangements** were in place.
Many Egyptians view Israel, which signed a **peace treaty** with Egypt in 1979 after four wars between the two countries, with **hostility**.

Figure 1: Complex word identification instruction with examples.

Dataset	All		Native		Non-native		Both
	Sing.	Mult.	Sing.	Mult.	Sing.	Mult.	
NEWS	8.10	91.90	13.87	86.13	14.47	85.53	70.47
WIKINEWS	10.16	89.84	16.15	83.85	17.15	82.85	76.75
WIKIPEDIA	8.92	91.08	15.06	84.94	15.94	84.06	77.06

Table 1: Distributions of selected CPs (in %) across all annotators (*All*), native and non-native annotators, and CPs selected by at least one native and one non-native annotator (*Both*). The *Sing.* column stands for annotations selected by only one annotator while the *Mult.* column stands for annotations selected by at least two annotators.

complex words in isolation, but we also allowed marking multi-word expressions and sequences of words as complex. This allowed for collecting a richer dataset (of complex words and phrases). Secondly, to make the process closer to a real-world application, we showed longer text passages (5–10 sentences) and asked the annotators to mark 10 complex words or phrases at the most. The former allows to take into account larger contexts both during the annotation and later during feature extraction in classification experiments, while the latter shaped our task slightly different than in previous CWI datasets. By not preselecting the target words (as it was the case in collection of the previous CWI datasets), we did not bias and limit selections of the human annotators. Finally, we have created balanced annotations from 10 native and 10 non-native speakers.

4 Analysis of Collected Annotations

A total of 183 workers (134 native and 49 non-native) participated in the annotation task and a total of 76,785 complex phrase (CP) annotations have been collected from all genres, out of which 10,006 are unique CPs. In total, 30 workers have been participated on each HIT where on average 15 assignments are completed by native and non-native speakers. We have selected only the top 10 assignments per HIT for each group (native and non-native), after sorting them based on the work-

ers inter-annotator agreement scores, to build the balanced datasets used in this study. The balanced datasets comprise a total of 62,991 CPs.

Around 90% of CPs have been selected by at least two annotators (see Table 1). However, when we separate the selections made by native and non-native speakers, we see that: (1) the percentage of multiple selected CPs by native speakers and non-native speakers decreases; (2) the percentage of multiply selected CPs by non-native speakers is always lower (83%–85%) than the percentage of multiply selected CPs by native speakers (84%–86%), regardless of the text genre; and (3) the percentage of CPs selected by at least one native and one non-native annotator is lower for the NEWS genre (70%) than for the WIKINEWS and WIKE-PEDIA genres (77%).

From these results, we can see that there is a quantifiable difference in the annotation agreements by the native and non-native speakers. The low IAA between native and non-native speakers (column *Both*) indicates that the lexical simplification needs might be different for those two groups.

5 Classification Experiments

We developed a binary classification CWI system, with performances comparable to the state-of-the-art results of the SemEval-2016 shared task.

5.1 Features

We use four different categories of features.

Frequency and length features: Due to the common use of these features in selecting the most simple lexical substitution candidate (Bott et al., 2012; Glavaš and Štajner, 2015), we use three length features: the number of vowels (vow), syllables (syl), and characters (len) and three frequency features: the frequency of the word in Simple Wikipedia (sim), the frequency of the word in the paragraph (of HIT) (wfp), and the frequency of the word in the Google Web 1T 5-Grams (wbt).

Syntactic features: Based on the work of Davoodi and Kosseim (2016), the part of speech (POS) tag influences the complexity of the word. We used POS tags (pos) predicted by the Stanford POS tagger (Toutanova et al., 2003).

Word embeddings features: Following the work of Glavaš and Štajner (2015), as well as Paetzold and Specia (2016b), we train a word2vec model (Mikolov et al., 2013) using English Wikipedia and the AQUAINT corpus of English news texts (Graff, 2002). We train 200-dimensional embeddings using skip-gram training and a window size of 5. We use the word2vec representations of CPs as a feature (emb), and also compute the cosine similarities between the vector representations of CP and the paragraph ($cosP$) and the sentence which contains it ($cosS$). The paragraph and sentence representations are computed by averaging the vector representations of the content words.

Topic Features: We use topic features that are extracted based on an LDA (Blei et al., 2003) model that was trained on English Wikipedia using 100 topics. The first feature is the topic distribution of the word (lda). The second feature captures the topic-relatedness for a word within its context. For this we compute the cosine similarity between the word-topic vector and the sentence ($ldcS$) and paragraph ($ldcP$) vector.

5.2 Experimental setups

We use different machine learning algorithms from the scikit-learn machine learning framework. In this paper, we report only the results of the best classifiers based on NearestCentroid (NC).

We produce six new datasets (three different genres times two different groups of annotators) using the balanced datasets. We first partition the balanced datasets of each genre into training, development and test (80:10:10) sets, while ensur-

System	G-score	F-score
Our system	**75.51**	**35.44**
Best (G-score) system	77.40	24.60
Best (F-score) system	60.80	35.50

Table 2: Results on the SemEval-2016 shared task.

Dataset	F-score		G-score	
	Our	BL	Our	BL
NEWS	**70.86**	59.72	**80.16**	69.87
WIKINEWS	**66.67**	58.62	**73.16**	66.65
WIKIPEDIA	**71.14**	67.20	**71.85**	67.47

(a) Native datasets

Dataset	F-score		G-score	
	Our	BL	Our	BL
NEWS	**66.30**	58.75	**74.78**	67.79
WIKINEWS	**68.13**	59.13	**75.96**	67.97
WIKIPEDIA	**70.34**	62.28	**74.49**	67.01

(b) Non-native datasets

Table 3: Results of our CWI system (*Our*) and the baseline system (BL) on our six new datasets.

ing that we do not having the same sentences in training, development and test sets. The best performing feature set, consisting of pos, len, sim, wfp, vow, and cos, is used to build our CWI systems. We discuss the results of different experimental setups using these best features in Section 6. We have combined the training and development sets for the final experiments. The baseline is based on frequency thresholds using the Simple English Wikipedia as a corpus (Wróbel, 2016).

6 Results and Discussion

Results for different combinations of datasets, including baselines, cross-genre, cross-group and cross-group-genre, are shown in Tables 2–6.

Shared Task Results (Table 2): On the shared task dataset, our system reaches almost the same F-score (35.44) as the best F-scored system (35.30), but at the same time achieves a significantly better G-score (75.51) than the same system (60.80). On CWIG3G2 datasets, the F-scores are significantly higher than on the shared task dataset both for the baseline and NC-classifier (Table 3). This is probably due to the unbalanced distribution of *complex* words in the shared task training and test sets or the fact that their test set instances were annotated by a single annotator only.

Within-group-genre Results (Table 3): Our system outperforms the baseline for all datasets. Even if non-native annotators have marked more *complex* phrases than the native annotators, the CWI

Training on	Testing on		
	NEWS	WIKINEWS	WIKIPEDIA
NEWS	**70.86**	66.48	**71.43**
WIKINEWS	67.41	**66.67**	68.35
WIKIPEDIA	64.24	64.18	71.14

(a) Native datasets

Training on	Testing on		
	NEWS	WIKINEWS	WIKIPEDIA
NEWS	**66.30**	70.79	**69.15**
WIKINEWS	66.43	68.13	69.70
WIKIPEDIA	66.97	68.29	70.34

(b) Non-native datasets

Table 4: Results of the cross-genre experiments.

Test	Training on native		Training on non-native	
	Native	Non-Native	Native	Non-native
NEWS	**70.86**	67.10	**69.85**	66.30
WIKINEWS	**66.67**	64.51	**65.58**	68.13
WIKIPEDIA	71.14	64.85	**72.95**	70.34

Table 5: Results of the cross-group experiments.

system performs well on the native datasets, except for the case of WIKINEWS dataset. The drop in the F-scores of the NEWS and WIKIPEDIA systems when moving from native to non-native datasets, could probably be attributed to a slightly lower inter-annotator agreement among non-native than native annotators.

Cross-genre Results (Table 4): When applying the CWI system on the NEWS test set and training it with the other genres, we observe performance drops for the native group and performance improvements for the non-native group. For the WIKINEWS test set, there is a slight decrease in performance when the CWI systems are trained with NEWS and WIKIPEDIA datasets of the native groups while there is an increase in performance when the CWI system is trained on the non-native groups. For the WIKIPEDIA genre test set, there is a drop in performance when the CWI system is trained on both NEWS and WIKINEWS genres of the non-native groups while there is an increase in performance when the CWI system is trained on the NEWS training set and decrease for the WIKINEWS training set of the native groups.

Cross-group Results (Table 5): When training our CWI systems on the datasets annotated by the native speakers, we obtain significantly higher F-scores when testing on the datasets annotated by the same group (native speakers), as it was expected. In the case of training on the datasets annotated by the non-native speakers, however, the results are the opposite of what we expected; we

Training on	Testing on		
	NEWS	WIKINEWS	WIKIPEDIA
NEWS	**67.10**	**68.53**	**68.22**
WIKINEWS	63.74	64.51	64.03
WIKIPEDIA	61.72	63.17	64.85

(a) Using NATIVE training sets and NON-NATIVE test sets

Training on	Testing on		
	NEWS	WIKINEWS	WIKIPEDIA
NEWS	**69.85**	65.93	71.17
WIKINEWS	68.64	65.58	70.29
WIKIPEDIA	68.80	**66.58**	**72.95**

(b) Using NON-NATIVE training sets and NATIVE test sets

Table 6: Cross-genre and cross-group results.

obtain significantly higher F-scores when testing on the datasets annotated by the other group (native speakers). These results imply that the inter-annotator agreement (IAA) on the test set might impact the results more than the type of the annotator group does (Table 1 shows much higher IAA among native than non-native English speakers, which holds both for the training and test datasets). **Cross-group-genre Results (Table 6)**: Similar to the the cross-group experiments, the best results are achieved when tested on the datasets annotated by native speakers, indicating once again that the F-score is highly influenced by the inter-annotator agreement on the test set.

7 Conclusions

To enable building of generalisable and more reliable CWI systems, we collected new complex phrase identification datasets (CWIG3G2) across three text genres, annotated both by native and non-native English speakers.[1] The analysis of our crowdsourced data showed that native speakers have higher inter-annotator agreement than the non-native speakers regardless of the text genre.

We built CWI systems comparable to the state of the art and showed that predicting the CWs for native speakers is an easier task than predicting the CWs for non-native speakers. Furthermore, we showed that within-genre CWI indeed leads to better classification performances, albeit with a small margin over cross-genre CWI. Finally, we showed that CWI systems trained on native datasets can be used to predict CWs for non-native speakers and vice versa. For future CWI tasks, we recommend to take language proficiency levels into account.

---

[1]Datasets available at: `https://lt.informatik.uni-hamburg.de/resources/data/complex-word-identification-dataset.html`

Acknowledgements

This work has been partially supported by the SEMSCH project at the University of Hamburg, and partially supported by the SFB 884 on the Political Economy of Reforms at the University of Mannheim (project C4), both funded by the German Research Foundation (DFG).

References

Sandra M. Aluísio, Lucia Specia, Thiago A.S. Pardo, Erick G. Maziero, and Renata P.M. Fortes. 2008. Towards Brazilian Portuguese automatic text simplification systems. In *Proceedings of the eighth ACM symposium on Document engineering*, DocEng '08, pages 240–248, New York, USA.

Marcelo A. Amancio and Lucia Specia. 2014. An Analysis of Crowdsourced Text Simplifications . In *Proceedings of the 3rd Workshop on Predicting and Improving Text Readability for Target Reader Populations (PITR)*, pages 123–130, Gothenburg, Sweden.

David M. Blei, Andrew Y. Ng, and Michael I. Jordan. 2003. Latent dirichlet allocation. *Journal of Machine Learning Research (JMLR)*, 3:993–1022.

Stefan Bott, Luz Rello, Biljana Drndarevic, and Horacio Saggion. 2012. Can Spanish be simpler? LexSiS: Lexical simplification for Spanish. In *Proceedings of COLING 2012*, pages 357–374, Mumbai, India.

John Carroll, Guido Minnen, Darren Pearce, Yvonne Canning, Siobhan Devlin, and John Tait. 1999. Simplifying text for language-impaired readers. In *Proceedings of EACL 1999*, pages 269–270, Bergen, Norway.

William Coster and David Kauchak. 2011. Simple English Wikipedia: a new text simplification task. In *Proceedings of ACL&HLT*, pages 665–669, Portland, Oregon, USA.

Elnaz Davoodi and Leila Kosseim. 2016. CLaC at SemEval-2016 Task 11: Exploring linguistic and psycho-linguistic Features for Complex Word Identification. In *Proceedings of the 10th International Workshop on Semantic Evaluation (SemEval-2016)*, pages 982–985, San Diego, California, USA.

Jan De Belder and Marie-Francine Moens. 2010. Text simplification for children. In *Proceedings of the SIGIR workshop on accessible search systems*, pages 19–26, Geneva, Switzerland.

Lijun Feng, Noémie Elhadad, and Matt Huenerfauth. 2009. Cognitively motivated features for readability assessment. In *Proceedings of the 12th Conference of the European Chapter of the Association for Computational Linguistics*, EACL '09, pages 229–237, Athens, Greece.

Geert Freyhoff, Gerhard Hess, Linda Kerr, Bror Tronbacke, and Kathy Van Der Veken. 1998. *Make it Simple, European Guidelines for the Production of Easy-to-Read Information for People with Learning Disability*. ILSMH European Association, Brussels, Belgium.

Goran Glavaš and Sanja Štajner. 2013. Event-centered simplification of news stories. In *Proceedings of the Student Research Workshop at the International Conference on Recent Advances in Natural Language Processing*, pages 71–78, Hissar, Bulgaria.

Goran Glavaš and Sanja Štajner. 2015. Simplifying Lexical Simplification: Do We Need Simplified Corpora? In *Proceedings of the 53rd Annual Meeting of the Association for Computational Linguistics and the 7th International Joint Conference on Natural Language Processing (Volume 2: Short Papers)*, pages 63–68, Beijing, China.

David Graff. 2002. The AQUAINT Corpus of English News Text LDC2002T31. In *Web Download. Philadelphia: Linguistic Data Consortium*.

David Hirsh and Paul Nation. 1992. What vocabulary size is needed to read unsimplified texts for pleasure? *Reading in a Foreign Language*, 8(2):689–696.

Colby Horn, Cathryn Manduca, and David Kauchak. 2014. A Lexical Simplifier Using Wikipedia. In *Proceedings of the 52nd Annual Meeting of the Association for Computational Linguistics (Volume 2: Short Papers)*, pages 458–463, Baltimore, Maryland, USA.

David Kauchak. 2013. Improving Text Simplification Language Modeling Using Unsimplified Text Data. In *Proceedings of the 51st Annual Meeting of the Association for Computational Linguistics (Volume 1: Long Papers)*, pages 1537–1546, Sofia, Bulgaria.

Mencap. 2002. Am I making myself clear? Mencap's guidelines for accessible writing.

Tomas Mikolov, Ilya Sutskever, Kai Chen, Gregory S. Corrado, and Jeffrey Dean. 2013. Distributed Representations of Words and Phrases and their Compositionality. In *Advances in Neural Information Processing Systems 26: 27th Annual Conference on Neural Information Processing Systems 2013*, pages 3111–3119, Stateline, Nevada, USA.

Paul I. S. Nation. 2001. *Learning vocabulary in another language*. Ernst Klett Sprachen.

Gustavo H. Paetzold and Lucia Specia. 2015. LEXenstein: A Framework for Lexical Simplification. In *Proceedings of ACL-IJCNLP 2015 System Demonstrations*, pages 85–90, Beijing, China.

Gustavo H. Paetzold and Lucia Specia. 2016a. SemEval 2016 Task 11: Complex Word Identification. In *Proceedings of the 10th International Workshop on Semantic Evaluation (SemEval-2016)*, pages 560–569, San Diego, California, USA.

Gustavo H. Paetzold and Lucia Specia. 2016b. Unsupervised Lexical Simplification for Non-native Speakers. In *Proceedings of the Thirtieth AAAI Conference on Artificial Intelligence*, pages 3761–3767, Phoenix, Arizona, USA.

Sarah E. Petersen and Mari Ostendorf. 2007. Text Simplification for Language Learners: A Corpus Analysis. In *Proceedings of Workshop on Speech and Language Technology for Education*, pages 69–72, Farmington, Pennsylvania, USA.

PlainLanguage. 2011. Federal plain language guidelines.

Luz Rello, Ricardo Baeza-Yates, Laura Dempere-Marco, and Horacio Saggion. 2013. Frequent words improve readability and short words improve understandability for people with dyslexia. In *Proceedings of the 14th International Conference on Human-Computer Interaction (INTERACT)*, pages 203–219, Cape Town, South Africa.

Horacio Saggion, Sanja Štajner, Stefan Bott, Simon Mille, Luz Rello, and Biljana Drndarevic. 2015. Making It Simplext: Implementation and Evaluation of a Text Simplification System for Spanish. *ACM Transactions on Accessible Computing*, 6(4):14:1–14:36.

Matthew Shardlow. 2013. The CW Corpus: A New Resource for Evaluating the Identification of Complex Words. In *Proceedings of the Second Workshop on Predicting and Improving Text Readability for Target Reader Populations*, pages 69–77, Sofia, Bulgaria.

Kristina Toutanova, Dan Klein, Christopher Manning, and Yoram Singer. 2003. Feature-Rich Part-of-Speech Tagging with a Cyclic Dependency Network. In *North American Chapter of the Association for Computational Linguistics - Human Language Technologies (NAACL HLT 2003)*, pages 982–985, Edmonton, Canada.

Krzysztof Wróbel. 2016. PLUJAGH at SemEval-2016 Task 11: Simple System for Complex Word Identification. In *Proceedings of the 10th International Workshop on Semantic Evaluation (SemEval-2016)*, pages 953–957, San Diego, California, USA.

Wei Xu, Chris Callison-Burch, and Courtney Napoles. 2015. Problems in current text simplification research: New data can help. *Transactions of the Association for Computational Linguistics*, 3:283–297.

Seid Muhie Yimam, Sanja Štajner, Martin Riedl, and Chris Biemann. 2017. Multilingual and Cross-Lingual Complex Word Identification. In *Proceedings of RANLP*, pages 813–822, Varna, Bulgaria.

Generating Stylistically Consistent Dialog Responses
with Transfer Learning

Reina Akama[†1], **Kazuaki Inada**[†2], **Naoya Inoue**[†3], **Sosuke Kobayashi**[‡4], **Kentaro Inui**[†*5]

[†]Graduate School of Information Sciences, Tohoku University

[‡]Preferred Networks, Inc.

[*]RIKEN Center for Advanced Intelligence Project

{[1]reina.a,[2]kazuaki.inada,[3]naoya-i,[5]inui}@ecei.tohoku.ac.jp,
[4]sosk@preferred.jp

Abstract

We propose a novel, data-driven, and stylistically consistent dialog response-generation system. To create a user-friendly system, it is crucial to make generated responses not only appropriate but also stylistically consistent. For leaning both the properties effectively, our proposed framework has two training stages inspired by transfer learning. First, we train the model to generate appropriate responses, and then we ensure that the responses have a specific style. Experimental results demonstrate that the proposed method produces stylistically consistent responses while maintaining the appropriateness of the responses learned in a general domain.

1 Introduction

Dialog response-generation (DRG) systems have been studied extensively over the decades. In the recent years, there is a growing interest in a data-driven DRG system leveraging a large amount of conversational texts in social networking services (SNSs) such as Twitter. One successful approach is to train a neural sequence-to-sequence model (seq2seq) (Sutskever et al., 2014) on conversations from SNS, where the seq2seq learns a mapping from a user utterance to the appropriate response with recurrent neural networks (RNNs) (Shang et al., 2015; Li et al., 2016; Serban et al., 2017).

The prior data-driven approach, however, suffers a major drawback. Since a wide variety of users, ranging from young to old, and from female to male, participates in an SNS, the learned responses are not guaranteed to be stylistically consistent (e.g. in terms of politeness). For example, we show actual responses generated by

1a)	*User:*	こんにちは (konnichiha . / Hello.)
1b)	*System:*	今日も元気いっぱいでいこうな
		(kyou mo genki ippai de iko u na . / Yo, man! How ya doing today?)
2a)	*User:*	今日は雪です
		(kyou ha yuki desu . / It is snowing today.)
2b)	*System:*	雪降ってるんですか
		(yuki ga hu tte iru n desu ka . / Is it?)
3a)	*User:*	寒いです (samui desu . / It's cold.)
3b)	*System:*	よしよし手をつないであげますわ
		(yoshi yoshi , te wo tsunai de age masu wa . / Oh, dear. I'm gonna hold your lovely hands.)

Table 1: Example of stylistically inconsistent responses generated by a vanilla seq2seq trained on our Twitter dialog corpus.

a vanilla seq2seq-based DRG system trained on Twitter conversations in Table 1. The responses have inconsistent style as if the system had multiple personalities; the responses are friendly (1b), polite (2b), or feminine (3b). To create a user-friendly DRG system, it is crucial to generate responses that are stylistically consistent.

This paper proposes a novel, data-driven, and stylistically consistent DRG model. A vanilla seq2seq cannot generate stylistically consistent responses without training on a large amount of stylistically consistent dialog responses, which is prohibitively costly. To address this issue, we apply transfer learning, namely transferring knowledge about response generation in a general domain into the task of stylistically consistent response generation.

In the literature, little attention has been paid to the stylistic consistency of the generated responses. There are some previous attempts on transforming a style of dialog utterances into a specified one (Walker et al., 2012; Miyazaki et al., 2015). Their approaches assume that original utterances are given by a separate independent system and need some manual annotations. Li et al.

Proceedings of the The 8th International Joint Conference on Natural Language Processing, pages 408–412,
Taipei, Taiwan, November 27 – December 1, 2017 ©2017 AFNLP

(2016) aim for response generation with a consistent "persona" by conditioning a seq2seq on a specific Twitter user ID embedding. However, their work focuses on the consistency in the content of the generated responses and they did not directly evaluate the stylistic consistency of their system.

This is the first study that focuses on building a stylistically consistent end-to-end and data-driven DRG model and empirically evaluates the stylistic consistency of generated responses in single-turn dialogs. Our experiments demonstrate that the proposed method produces stylistically consistent responses while maintaining the appropriateness of responses learned from a general domain.

2 Related Work

The literature includes some prior studies that aim for transforming a style of dialog utterances into a specified one (Walker et al., 2012; Miyazaki et al., 2015). Walker et al. (2012) extract rules representing characters from their annotated movie subtitle corpora. Miyazaki et al. (2015) propose a method of converting utterances using rewriting rules automatically derived from a Twitter corpus. These approaches have a fundamental problem to need some manual annotations, which is a main issue to be solved in this work. We propose an end-to-end and data-driven framework which addresses both response generation and stylistic transformation.

Transfer learning is a machine learning technique effective for many NLP tasks (Pan and Yang, 2010), which effectively trains a machine learning model by transferring knowledge about a general domain into a target domain. By applying transfer learning to a stylistically consistent DRG system, once we build a DRG system without stylistic consistency, it is easy to change its style by adding a small stylistically consistent corpus.

3 Generating Stylistically Consistent Responses with Transfer Learning

Given an utterance style, our goal is to create a DRG system that can keep producing utterances with the specified style. Inspired by the success of the data-driven approach, one can prepare a corpus of conversations for every possible style and feed it to a seq2seq. However, in order to obtain a stylistically consistent DRG system through a vanilla seq2seq, this method requires millions of training instances for each target style, which is prohibitively expensive.

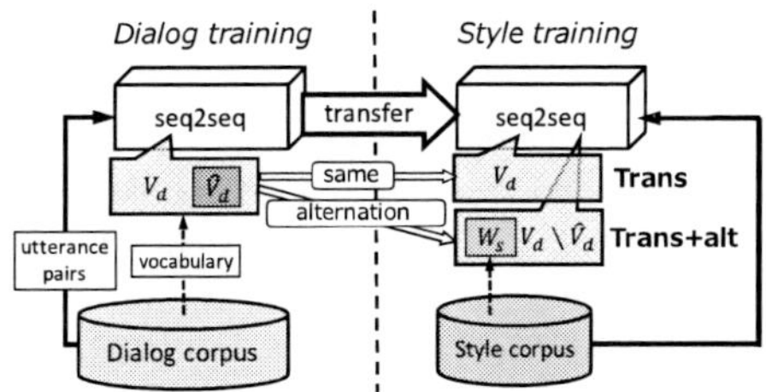

Figure 1: Overview of our framework. Trans shares the same vocabulary in dialog and style training. Trans+alt alters a vocabulary to consider expressions specific in a style corpus.

3.1 General Framework

To address this issue, we propose a novel two-staged training framework for building a stylistically consistent response-generation model, as depicted in Figure 1. The core idea is as follows. A stylistically consistent response generation model has to learn at least three aspects of responses: *content, fluency* and *style*. We hypothesize that learning the content and fluency requires a large amount of training instances, whereas learning the style requires far less training instances. Inspired by transfer learning, our training strategy is divided into two steps (henceforth, dialog training and style training). We thus assume two types of corpora as training data: (i) *dialog corpus*, a large conversational corpus *without* stylistic consistency, and (ii) *style corpus*, a small conversational corpus *with* stylistic consistency.

In our experiments, we used single-turn dialog (i.e. utterance pairs) as training data. However, the proposed framework is applicable to multi-turn dialog as long as we have a response-generation model.

First, in dialog training, we train a seq2seq response generation model on a dialog corpus to learn the content and fluency of responses, namely how to generate responses without taking into account stylistic consistency. Seq2seq (Sutskever et al., 2014) is an RNN-based approach effective for response generation (Shang et al., 2015; Li et al., 2016; Serban et al., 2017). A typical seq2seq has a vocabulary of a limited size (e.g., tens of thousands) to speed up the training process, reduce the computational memory usage and prevent overfitting. Following a typical practice in seq2seq, we use the top N_d most frequent words in a dialog corpus as the seq2seq vocabulary (henceforth, V_d) and convert the other infrequent words into a special symbol UNK.

Second, in style training, we use a style corpus to fine-tune the seq2seq that is already trained with a dialog corpus to ensure that the generated responses are stylistically consistent. The model inherits all the model parameters (i.e. word embeddings and weight matrices in the RNNs) and the seq2seq vocabulary (henceforth, V_s) from dialog training.

Note that obtaining a large-scale dialog corpus is relatively easy. For example, one can simply use the whole Twitter conversations as a dialog corpus. As for a style corpus, one can extract utterances made by a specific character from a movie script as in (Walker et al., 2012). One advantage of our framework is that once a large-scale dialog corpus is obtained and dialog training is done, it is easy to change its style by adding a small style corpus.

3.2 Vocabulary in Transferred Model

When applying transfer learning to a seq2seq, creating a vocabulary for style training is not a trivial job. In our experiments, we explore two strategies. In Trans, our first strategy, we simply use the same vocabulary for dialog training and style training (i.e. $V_s = V_d$). However, this may not be a good strategy, because the top N_d most frequent words in a dialog corpus do not necessarily include words that are potentially useful for generating stylistically consistent responses.

To remedy this, in Trans+alt, our second strategy, we alter the seq2seq vocabulary V_s that is used for dialog training before style training (henceforth, *vocabulary alternation*). Let W_s be a set of the top N_s most frequent words which are only included in a style corpus, and $\hat{V}_d$ be a set of the top N_s most *infrequent* words in V_d. Instead of simply setting $V_s = V_d$, we set $V_s = V_d \setminus \hat{V}_d \cup W_s$ (i.e. the top $N_d - N_s$ most frequent words in a dialog corpus plus the N_s most frequent words in a style corpus). Intuitively, we basically employ V_d as V_s, but replace infrequent words from the dialog corpus with frequent words in the style corpus.

4 Experiments

4.1 Setups

Datasets A summary of our corpora is shown in Table 2. The dialog corpus contains approximately 3.7 M Japanese utterance pairs extracted from tweet-reply chains on Twitter.[1] The style

---

	Utterance pairs	Vocabulary	Overlap (%)
Dialog corpus	3,688,162	591,880	-
Tetsuko corpus	12,564	12,102	7,230 (59.7)
Oja corpus	1,476	2,137	1,532 (71.7)

Table 2: Dialog corpus and style corpora used in our experiments. 'Overlap' represents the number of overlap words between a dialog corpus and style corpus.

Model	Transfer learning	Dialog corpus	Style corpus	Vocabulary alternation
Base		✓		
Mix		✓	✓	✓
Trans	✓	✓	✓	
Trans+alt	✓	✓	✓	✓

Table 3: Four models for our experiments

corpus contains pairs of utterances extracted from subtitles of a Japanese TV show. We prepare two instances of style corpus: (i) *Tetsuko corpus*, where all the responses are made by Tetusko Kuroyanagi, an elderly, polite, and female TV personality, and (ii) *Oja corpus*, where all the responses are made by Ojarumaru, a five-year-old kids' cartoon character who uses classical Japanese expressions (e.g., see Appendix A, Table 5). We use 95 % of the corpora for training and 5 % for validation.

Baselines We prepare two baseline models without transfer learning: (i) Base, a vanilla seq2seq trained on the dialog corpus only, and (ii) Mix, a vanilla seq2seq trained on the mixture of a dialog corpus and style corpus, where Mix is applied to the vocabulary alternation as well as Trans+alt. We summarize the baseline models and proposed models in Table 3.

Settings All the four models use the following settings. The seq2seq encoder and decoder are two-layer LSTMs with 2048 units using 1024-dimensional word embeddings. The vocabulary size (N_d) is $25,000$. We train the models using Adam (Kingma and Ba, 2015) with mini-batch size 64 and performed early stopping for perplexity using the validation data. For the vocabulary alternation in Mix and Trans+alt, we use $N_s = 1,000$ for Tetsuko corpus and $N_s = 500$ for Oja corpus.[2]

4.2 Evaluation Method

Conventionally, DRG systems are evaluated through reference-based evaluation (e.g. BLEU

---

[1] Noisy sentences (e.g., URLs) are filtered out.

[2] We decide the values of Ns with reference to Table 2.

Style		Base	Mix	Trans	Trans+alt
Tetsuko	AR	49.0	50.0	53.0	$60.0^{\dagger B, \dagger M}$
	SC	19.5	22.5	$30.5^{\ddagger B, \dagger M}$	$34.0^{\ddagger B, \ddagger M}$
Oja	AR	50.0	46.5	49.0	$57.0^{\ddagger B, \ddagger M, \dagger T}$
	SC	2.5	26.5	$72.0^{\ddagger B, \ddagger M}$	$82.5^{\ddagger B, \ddagger M, \dagger T}$

Table 4: Results of human evaluation. AR and SC denotes the appropriateness of response and stylistic consistency, respectively. Superscripts $^{\dagger B, \dagger M, \dagger T}$ (and $^{\ddagger B, \ddagger M, \ddagger T}$) indicate the statistical significance against Base, Mix and Trans (sign test, $p < 0.05$ for †, $p < 0.01$ for ‡), respectively.

(Papineni et al., 2002; Sordoni et al., 2015; Li et al., 2016)) or subjective human evaluation (Walker et al., 2012; Vinyals and Le, 2015; Shang et al., 2015). We employ human evaluation, because human evaluation captures more stylistic consistency than reference-based evaluation, and word-overlap similarity metrics such as BLEU correlates weakly with human judgments (Liu et al., 2016).

For query utterances, we randomly extract 50 sentences from Twitter. There is no overlap between these query utterances, and the training and validation data. Each model generates four responses from one query utterance by beam sampling (beam width 3) using four different random seeds. Therefore, the total number of responses generated by one model is 200.

We use Yahoo! Crowd Sourcing[3] for human evaluation. Given (i) a query utterance Q, (ii) the response R generated by a model, and (iii) a style description S that the model are trying to generate with, the workers are independently asked to answer the following two questions:

- Whether R is a grammatically and semantically appropriate response to Q.

- Whether the style of R matches S.

Note that the workers were given only a style description S with several example utterances but not the specific name of individual target character. Each response is judged by five workers, who do not know which model generated each response. The final answer is determined by majority vote.

4.3 Results

Table 4 shows the percentage of responses judged as 'appropriate response' (AR) and 'stylistically

consistent' (SC).[4] Base indicates that the dialog corpus's style only matches 19.5% in Tetsuko corpus and 2.5% in Oja corpus. Trans and Trans+alt, the proposed transfer learning frameworks, successfully generate more stylistically consistent responses while maintaining the appropriateness of generated responses learned from a dialog corpus (Base v.s. Trans, Trans+alt). In addition, transfer learning is more effective than simply mixing a dialog corpus and style corpus (Mix v.s. Trans+alt). Recall that the difference between Mix and Trans+alt is whether transfer learning is applied, namely the two models are trained on the same corpora and seq2seq vocabulary. Furthermore, the vocabulary alternation in style training (see Sec. 3.2) helps to make the generated responses more stylistically consistent (Trans v.s. Trans+alt). Overall, the improvement on Oja corpus is more salient than that on Tetsuko corpus. We attribute this to the fact that Tetsuko corpus is closer to the original dialog corpus.

Moreover, Trans+alt improves the appropriateness of the responses. On both style corpora, Trans+alt achieves the best result among the four models. Table 6 in Appendix B and Table 7 in Appendix C show actual responses generated by Trans+alt. By analyzing the generated responses, we find that inappropriate responses such as dull responses (e.g., I don't know) and Internet slangs are relatively fewer, even though we did not make any special treatment. We attribute this to the fact that Trans+alt is additionally trained on less noisy real conversations (i.e., TV subtitles) with a better vocabulary, where new frequent words in a less noisy style corpus are pushed.

The overall results support our assumption that style training requires far less training data than dialog training (see Sec. 3.1). We speculate that styles of utterances are characterized by a smaller variety of lexical choices such as sentence-final auxiliary expressions and personal pronouns. For Japanese, in fact, it is shown that sentence-final auxiliary expressions are an important factor for changing the character of a dialog system (Miyazaki et al., 2015).

---

[3]https://crowdsourcing.yahoo.co.jp/

[4]The percentage of judgments agreed by the workers, where the number of votes to *yes* or *no* is more than 3, is 72.4 (AR) and 70.1 (SC) on Tetsuko corpus, and 68.0 (AR) and 82.0 (SC) on Oja corpus.

5 Conclusion

We have presented a novel end-to-end framework to build a stylistically consistent dialog response-generation system, leveraging transfer learning. We have demonstrated that we are able to produce stylistically consistent responses by transfer learning while maintaining the appropriateness of responses learned from a general domain. The proposed framework allows us to train a response generation model on a large-scale, and easily-obtainable dialog corpus without stylistic consistency and then on a small-scale stylistically consistent corpus. This is the first work to focus on creating a stylistically consistent end-to-end DRG system and evaluating stylistic consistency in neural dialog response generation studies.

In future work, we plan to improve style training so that it can learn only the style of responses. We will assign a weight indicating the degree of stylistic peculiarity to each word in a style corpus, which controls the aggressiveness of style training. Another future work includes exploring an effective way of creating a style corpus, e.g. automatically collecting polite utterances from a large Twitter corpus with a filter, or generating stylistically consistent responses with a smaller or even no specific style corpus.

Acknowledgments

This work was supported by JSPS KAKENHI Grant Number 15H01702.

References

Diederik Kingma and Jimmy Ba. 2015. Adam: A method for stochastic optimization. In *The International Conference on Learning Representations (ICLR)*.

Jiwei Li, Michel Galley, Chris Brockett, Georgios Spithourakis, Jianfeng Gao, and Bill Dolan. 2016. A persona-based neural conversation model. In *Proceedings of the 54th Annual Meeting of the Association for Computational Linguistics*, pages 994–1003.

Chia-Wei Liu, Ryan Lowe, Iulian Serban, Mike Noseworthy, Laurent Charlin, and Joelle Pineau. 2016. How not to evaluate your dialogue system: An empirical study of unsupervised evaluation metrics for dialogue response generation. In *Proceedings of the 2016 Conference on Empirical Methods in Natural Language Processing*, pages 2122–2132. Association for Computational Linguistics.

Chiaki Miyazaki, Toru Hirano, Ryuichiro Higashinaka, Toshiro Makino, and Yoshihiro Matsuo. 2015. Automatic conversion of sentence-end expressions for utterance characterization of dialogue systems. In *Proceedings of the 29th Pacific Asia Conference on Language, Information and Computation (PACLIC)*, pages 307–314.

Sinno Jialin Pan and Qiang Yang. 2010. A survey on transfer learning. *IEEE Transactions on knowledge and data engineering*, 22(10):1345–1359.

Kishore Papineni, Salim Roukos, Todd Ward, and Wei-Jing Zhu. 2002. Bleu: a method for automatic evaluation of machine translation. In *Proceedings of the 40th annual meeting on association for computational linguistics*, pages 311–318. Association for Computational Linguistics.

Iulian Vlad Serban, Alessandro Sordoni, Ryan Lowe, Laurent Charlin, Joelle Pineau, Aaron Courville, and Yoshua Bengio. 2017. A hierarchical latent variable encoder-decoder model for generating dialogues. In *Thirty-First AAAI Conference on Artificial Intelligence*, pages 3295–3301.

Lifeng Shang, Zhengdong Lu, and Hang Li. 2015. Neural responding machine for short-text conversation. In *Proceedings of the 53rd Annual Meeting of the Association for Computational Linguistics and the 7th International Joint Conference on Natural Language Processing (Volume 1: Long Papers)*, pages 1577–1586. Association for Computational Linguistics.

Alessandro Sordoni, Michel Galley, Michael Auli, Chris Brockett, Yangfeng Ji, Margaret Mitchell, Jian-Yun Nie, Jianfeng Gao, and Bill Dolan. 2015. A neural network approach to context-sensitive generation of conversational responses. In *Proceedings of the 2015 Conference of the North American Chapter of the Association for Computational Linguistics: Human Language Technologies*, pages 196–205. Association for Computational Linguistics.

Ilya Sutskever, Oriol Vinyals, and Quoc V Le. 2014. Sequence to sequence learning with neural networks. In *Advances in neural information processing systems*, pages 3104–3112.

Oriol Vinyals and Quoc Le. 2015. A neural conversational model. In *International Conference on Machine Learning(ICML) Deep Learning Workshop 2015*.

Marilyn A Walker, Grace I Lin, and Jennifer Sawyer. 2012. An annotated corpus of film dialogue for learning and characterizing character style. In *LREC*, pages 1373–1378.

Learning to Explain Non-Standard English Words and Phrases

Ke Ni and **William Yang Wang**
Department of Computer Science
University of California, Santa Barbara
Santa Barbara, CA 93106 USA
{ke00@umail},{william@cs}.ucsb.edu

Abstract

We describe a data-driven approach for automatically explaining new, non-standard English expressions in a given sentence, building on a large dataset that includes 15 years of crowdsourced examples from *UrbanDictionary.com*. Unlike prior studies that focus on matching keywords from a slang dictionary, we investigate the possibility of learning a neural sequence-to-sequence model that generates explanations of unseen non-standard English expressions given context. We propose a dual encoder approach—a word-level encoder learns the representation of context, and a second character-level encoder to learn the hidden representation of the target non-standard expression. Our model can produce reasonable definitions of new non-standard English expressions given their context with certain confidence.

1 Introduction

In the past two decades, the majority of NLP research focused on developing tools for the Standard English on newswire data. However, the non-standard part of the language is not well-studied in the community, even though it becomes more and more important in the era of social media. While we agree that one must take a cautious approach to automatic generation of non-standard language (Hickman, 2013), but for many practical purposes, it is also of crucial importance for machines to be able to *understand* and *explain* this important subversion of the language.

In the NLP community, using dictionaries of non-standard language as an external knowledge source is useful for many tasks. For example, Burfoot and Baldwin (2009) consult the slang defini-

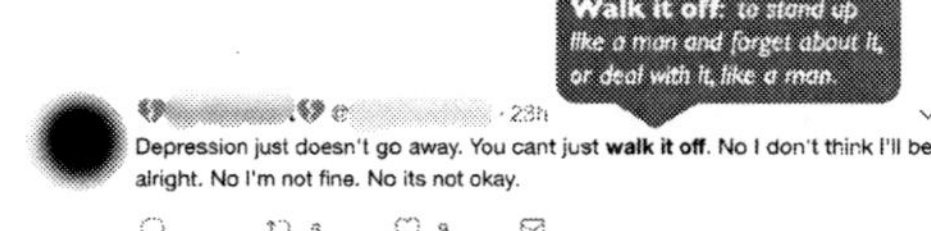

Figure 1: An example Tweet with a non-standard English expression. Our model aims at automatically explaining any newly emerged, non-standard expressions (generating the blue box).

tions from Wiktionary to detect satirical news articles. Wang and McKeown (2010) show that using a slang dictionary of 5K terms can help detecting vandalism of Wikipedia edits. Han and Baldwin (2011) make use of the same slang dictionary, and achieve the best performance by combining the dictionary lookup approach with word similarity and context for Twitter and SMS text normalization. However, using a 5K slang dictionary may suffer from the coverage issue, since slang is evolving rapidly in the social media age[1]. Recently, Thanapon Noraset (2016) shows that it is possible to use word embeddings to generate plausible definitions. Nonetheless, one weakness is that definition of a word may change within different contexts.

In contrast, we take a more radical approach: we aim at building a general purpose sequence-to-sequence neural network model (Sutskever et al., 2014) to explain any non-standard English expression, which can be used in many NLP and social media applications. More specifically, given a sentence that includes a non-standard English expression, we aim at automatically generating the translation of the target expression. Previously, this is not possible because the resources of labeled

---

[1] For example, more than 2K entries are submitted daily to Urban Dictionary (Kolt and Lazier, 2009), the largest online slang resource.

Proceedings of the The 8th International Joint Conference on Natural Language Processing, pages 413–417,
Taipei, Taiwan, November 27 – December 1, 2017 ©2017 AFNLP

non-standard expressions are not available. In this paper, we collect a large corpus of 15 years of crowdsourced examples, and formulate the task as a sequence-to-sequence generation problem. Using a word-level model, we show that it is possible to build a general purpose non-standard English words and phrases explainer using neural sequence learning techniques. To summarize our contributions:

- We present a large, publicly available corpus of non-standard English words and phrases, including 15 years of definitions and examples for each entry via crowdsourcing;

- We present a hybrid word-character sequence-to-sequence model that directly explains unseen non-standard expressions from social media;

- Our novel dual encoder LSTM model outperforms a standard attentive LSTM baseline, and it is capable of generative plausible explanation for unseen non-standard words and phrases.

In the next section, we outline related work on non-standard expressions and social media text processing. We will then introduce our dual encoder based attentive sequence-to-sequence model for explaining non-standard expressions in Section 3. Experimental results are shown in Section 4. And finally, we conclude in Section 5.

2 Related Work

The study of non-standard language is of interests to many researchers in the social media and NLP communities. For example, Eisenstein et al. (2010) propose a latent variable model to study the lexical variation of the language on Twitter, where many regional slang words are discovered. Zappavigna (2012) identifies the Internet slang as an important component in the discourse of Twitter and social media. Gouws et al. (2011) provide a contextual analysis of how social media users shorten their messages. Notably, a study on Tweet normalization (Han and Baldwin, 2011) finds that, even when using a small slang dictionary of 5K words, Slang makes up 12% of the ill-formed words in a Twitter corpus of 449 posts. In the NLP community, slang dictionary is widely used in many tasks and applications (Burfoot and Baldwin, 2009; Wang and McKeown, 2010; Rosenthal

and McKeown, 2011). However, we argue that using a small, fixed-size dictionary approach may be suboptimal: it suffers from the low coverage problem, and to keep the dictionary up to date, maintaining such dictionary is also expensive and time-consuming. To the best of our knowledge, our work is the first to build a general purpose machine learning model for explaining non-standard English terms, using a large crowdsourced dataset.

3 Our Approach

3.1 Sequence-to-Sequence Model

Since our goal is to automatically generate explanations for any non-standard English expressions, we select sequence-to-sequence models with attention mechanisms as our fundamental framework (Bahdanau et al., 2014), which can produce abstractive explanations, and assign different weights to different parts of a sentence. To model both the context words and the non-standard expression, we propose a hybrid word-character dual encoder. An overview of our model is shown in Figure 2.

3.2 Context Encoder

Our context encoder is basically a recurrent neural network with long-short term memory (LSTM) (Hochreiter and Schmidhuber, 1997). LSTM consists of input gates, forget gates and output gates, together with hidden units as its internal memory. Here, i controls the impact of new input, while f is a forget gate, and o is an output gate. $\tilde{C}_t$ is the candidate new value. h is the hidden state, and m is the cell memory state. "$\odot$" means element-wise vector product. The definition of the gates, memory, and hidden state is:

$$i_t = \sigma(W_i[x_t, h_{t-1}])$$

$$f_t = \sigma(W_f[x_t, h_{t-1}])$$

$$o_t = \sigma(W_o[x_t, h_{t-1}])$$

$$\tilde{C}_t = \tanh(W_c[x_t, h_{t-1}])$$

$$m_t = m_{t-1} \odot f_t + i_t \odot \tilde{C}_t$$

$$h_t = m_t \odot o_t$$

At each step, RNN is given a vector as input, changes its hidden states and produces outputs from its last layer. Hidden states and outputs are stored and later passed to a decoder, which produces final outputs based on hidden states, outputs,

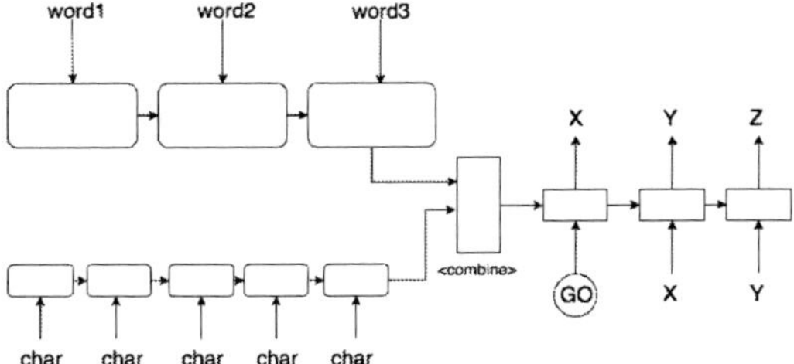

Figure 2: Dual Encoder Structure. *Top left: a word-level LSTM encoder for modeling context. Bottom left: a character-level LSTM encoder for modeling target non-standard expression. Right: an LSTM decoder for generating explanations.*

and the decoder's own parameters. The context encoder learns and encodes sentence-level information for the decoder to generate explanations.

3.3 Attention Mechanism

The idea of designing an attention mechanism is to select key focuses in the sentence. More specifically, we would like to pay attention to specific parts of encoder outputs and states. We follow a recent study (Vinyals et al., 2015) to setup an attention mechanism. We have a separate LSTM for decoding.

Here we briefly explain the method. When the decoder starts its decoding process, it has all hidden units from the encoder, denoted as $(h_1..h_{T_1})$. Also we denote the hidden state of the decoder as $(d_1..d_{T_2})$. T_1 and T_2 are input and output lengths. At each time step, the model computes new weighted hidden states based on encoder states and three learnable components: v, W_1' and W_2'.

$$u_i^t = v^T tanh(W_1'h_i + W_2'd_t)$$

$$a_i^t = softmax(u_i^t)$$

$$d_t' = \sum_{i=1}^{T_1} a_i^t h_i$$

Here a denotes the attention weights. u^t has length T_1. After the model computes d_t', it concatenates d_t' and d_t as new hidden states used for prediction and next update.

3.4 Dual Encoder Structure

Given a single context encoder, it is challenging for any decoder to generate explanation in the instance. The reason is that there could be multiple non-standard expressions in the sentence, and

it confuses the decoder on which one it should explain. In practice, the user can often pin point to the exact expression she or he does not know, so in this work, we design a second encoder to learn the representation of the target non-standard expression.

Since our goal is to explain any non-standard English words and phrases, we consider a character-level encoder for this purpose. This second encoder reads the embedding vector of each character at each time step, and produces an output vector, and hidden states. Our dual encoder model linearly combines the hidden states of the character-level target expression encoder with the hidden states of the word-level encoder with the following equation:

$$h_{new} = h_1W_1 + h_2W_2 + B$$

Here, h_1 is the context representation, and h_2 is the target expression representation. The Bias B and the combination weights W_1 and W_2 are learnable.

4 Experiment

4.1 Dataset

We collect the non-standard English corpus[2] from Urban Dictionary (UD)[3]—the largest online slang dictionary, where terms, definitions and examples are submitted by the crowd. UD is made a reliable resource, due to the quality control of its publishing procedure. To prevent vandalism, a user must have a Facebook or Gmail account, and when each user submits an entry, the UD editors will vote "Publish" or "Don't Publish" (Lloyd, 2011). Each editor is also distinguished by IP addresses, and HTTP cookies are used to prevent each editor from cheating. In recent years, United States Federal government has consulted UD for the definition of "murk" in a threat case (Jackson, 2011), whereas UD is also referred in a financial restitution case in Wisconsin (Kaufman, 2013), as well as determining appropriate license plates in Las Vegas (Davis, 2011).

A total of 421K entries (words and phrases) from the period of 1999-2014 are collected. Each entry includes a list of candidate definitions and examples, as well as the surface form of the target

---

Instance: *"dude taht roflcopter was pretty loltastic!!1!"*
Target: loltastic
Reference: something funnyishly fantastic.
Generated Explanation (Single): a really cool , amazing , and good looking .
Generated Explanation (Dual): a word that is extremely awesome .
Instance: *"danny is so jelouse of my work!"*
Target: jelouse
Reference: how unintelligent people who think they are better than someone spells "jealous".
Generated Explanation (Single): your friend ' s way of saying "
Generated Explanation (Dual): a word used to describe a situation , or a person who is a complete idiot .
Instance: *"that sir right there, is being quite adoucheous"*
Target: adoucheous
Reference: a person acting in a conformative manner that causes social upset and violence.
Generated Explanation (Single): when a male is being a male and a male .
Generated Explanation (Dual): the act of being a douchebag .

Figure 3: Some generated explanations from our system.

term. Using the UD API, we can pinpoint the token positions of the words/phrases, and obtain the ground truth labels for tagging.

Our training and testing data use all the examples in an entry (a non-standard expression). We randomly select 371,028 entries for training, resulting in 907,624 sequence pairs of instance and reference explanation. The test set includes 50,000 entries, and 61,330 sentences. Note that all testing target non-standard expressions, instances and examples do not overlap with those in the training dataset.

4.2 Experimental Settings

Our implementation is based on Tensorflow[4]. For input embeddings, we randomly initialize the word vectors. We use stochastic gradient descent with adaptive learning rate to optimize the cross entropy function. We use BLEU scores (Papineni et al., 2002) for the evaluation.

4.3 Quantitative and Qualitative Results

Quantitative experimental results are showed in Table 1. Here we compare the performance of our proposed large dual encoder model to a single

[4]www.tensorflow.org

Model (w. attention)	hidden units	B1	B2
single encoder	1024	21.06	2.1
small dual encoder	512	21.84	2.2
large dual encoder	1024	**24.58**	**2.37**
full char-level model	256	21.13	1.8

Table 1: BLEU scores for explaining non-standard English words and phrases in test dataset.

context encoder, word-level attentive sequence-to-sequence, as well as a full character-level context encoder model. We use 256 hidden units for this full character-level, because it is the largest setting that fits our Titan X Pascale GPU. Character-level model has longer sequence, which becomes one of its shortages compared with word-level model.

We see that the single encoder and full character level context models do not offer the best empirical performances on this dataset. Our novel dual encoder method, which combines the strengths of word-level and character-level sequence-to-sequence models, obtained the best performance.

For qualitative analysis, we provide some generated explanations in Figure 3. For example, the first target non-standard expression is the word "loltastic", which is a combination of the words "lol" and "fantastic". To explain this composite non-standard expression, a character-level encoder is needed. The generated explanation from our dual encoder approach clearly makes more sense than the single decoder result.

Overall, dual encoder can explain words with more confidence partly because it knows which words it needs to explain, especially for sentences containing multiple non-standard English words and phrases. Our model can also accurately explain many known acronyms. We also notice that LSTM cells outperform gated recurrent units (GRUs) (Cho et al., 2014), and attention mechanism improves the performance.

5 Conclusion

In this paper, we introduce a new task of learning to explain newly emerged, non-standard English words and phrases. To do this, we collected 15-year of UrbanDictionary data, and designed a dual encoder attentive sequence-to-sequence model to learn the hidden context representation and the hidden non-standard expression embedding. We showed that combining word-level and character-level models improved the performance for this task

References

Dzmitry Bahdanau, Kyunghyun Cho, and Yoshua Bengio. 2014. Neural machine translation by jointly learning to align and translate. *arXiv preprint arXiv:1409.0473* .

Clint Burfoot and Timothy Baldwin. 2009. Automatic satire detection: Are you having a laugh? In *Proceedings of the ACL-IJCNLP 2009 conference short papers*. Association for Computational Linguistics, pages 161–164.

Kyunghyun Cho, Bart van Merriënboer, Dzmitry Bahdanau, and Yoshua Bengio. 2014. On the properties of neural machine translation: Encoder–decoder approaches. *Syntax, Semantics and Structure in Statistical Translation* page 103.

Johnny Davis. 2011. *In praise of urban dictionaries.* The Guardian.

Jacob Eisenstein, Brendan O'Connor, Noah A Smith, and Eric P Xing. 2010. A latent variable model for geographic lexical variation. In *Proceedings of the 2010 Conference on Empirical Methods in Natural Language Processing*. Association for Computational Linguistics, pages 1277–1287.

Stephan Gouws, Donald Metzler, Congxing Cai, and Eduard Hovy. 2011. Contextual bearing on linguistic variation in social media. In *Proceedings of the Workshop on Languages in Social Media*. Association for Computational Linguistics, pages 20–29.

Bo Han and Timothy Baldwin. 2011. Lexical normalisation of short text messages: Makn sens a# twitter. In *Proceedings of the 49th Annual Meeting of the Association for Computational Linguistics: Human Language Technologies-Volume 1*. Association for Computational Linguistics, pages 368–378.

Leo Hickman. 2013. *Why IBM's Watson supercomputer can't speak slang.* The Guardian.

Sepp Hochreiter and Jürgen Schmidhuber. 1997. Long short-term memory. *Neural computation* 9(8):1735–1780.

Joe Jackson. 2011. *Feds Check Urban Dictionary to Crack Gun-Store Death Threat.* TIME.

Leslie Kaufman. 2013. *For the Word on the Street, Courts Call Up an Online Witness.* The New York Times.

Leah Kolt and Matt Lazier. 2009. *Alumni in the News: Summer & Fall 2009.* Cal Poly Magazine.

JoAnn Lloyd. 2011. *Alum Aaron Peckham's Urban Dictionary Redefines Language.* Cal Poly Magazine.

Thanapon Noraset, Liang Chen, Larry Birnbaum, and Doug Downey. 2016. Definition modeling: Learning to define word embeddings in natural language. In *AAAI*. pages 3259–3266.

Kishore Papineni, Salim Roukos, Todd Ward, and Wei-Jing Zhu. 2002. Bleu: a method for automatic evaluation of machine translation. In *Proceedings of the 40th annual meeting on association for computational linguistics*. Association for Computational Linguistics, pages 311–318.

Sara Rosenthal and Kathleen McKeown. 2011. Age prediction in blogs: A study of style, content, and online behavior in pre-and post-social media generations. In *Proceedings of the 49th Annual Meeting of the Association for Computational Linguistics: Human Language Technologies-Volume 1*. Association for Computational Linguistics, pages 763–772.

Ilya Sutskever, Oriol Vinyals, and Quoc V Le. 2014. Sequence to sequence learning with neural networks. In *Advances in neural information processing systems*. pages 3104–3112.

Oriol Vinyals, Łukasz Kaiser, Terry Koo, Slav Petrov, Ilya Sutskever, and Geoffrey Hinton. 2015. Grammar as a foreign language. In *Advances in Neural Information Processing Systems*. pages 2773–2781.

William Yang Wang and Kathleen McKeown. 2010. "got you!": Automatic vandalism detection in wikipedia with web-based shallow syntactic-semantic modeling. In *Proceedings of the 23rd International Conference on Computational Linguistics (Coling 2010)*.

Michele Zappavigna. 2012. *Discourse of Twitter and social media: How we use language to create affiliation on the web.* A&C Black.

Towards Abstractive Multi-Document Summarization Using Submodular Function-Based Framework, Sentence Compression and Merging

Yllias Chali
University of Lethbridge
Lethbridge, Alberta, Canada
chali@cs.uleth.ca

Moin Tanvee
University of Lethbridge
Lethbridge, Alberta, Canada
tanvee@uleth.ca

Mir Tafseer Nayeem
University of Lethbridge
Lethbridge, Alberta, Canada
mir.nayeem@uleth.ca

Abstract

We propose a submodular function-based summarization system which integrates three important measures namely importance, coverage, and non-redundancy to detect the important sentences for the summary. We design monotone and submodular functions which allow us to apply an efficient and scalable greedy algorithm to obtain informative and well-covered summaries. In addition, we integrate two abstraction-based methods namely sentence compression and merging for generating an abstractive sentence set. We design our summarization models for both generic and query-focused summarization. Experimental results on DUC-2004 and DUC-2007 datasets show that our generic and query-focused summarizers have outperformed the state-of-the-art summarization systems in terms of ROUGE-1 and ROUGE-2 recall and F-measure.

1 Introduction

Existing multi-document summarization techniques mainly fall into two categories: extractive and abstractive. Extractive approach selects important source sentences to cover the overall concepts of the document set (Erkan and Radev, 2004; Lin and Bilmes, 2010; Boudin et al., 2015; Parveen and Strube, 2015; Parveen et al., 2015; Cheng and Lapata, 2016; Nallapati et al., 2017). This method is very popular because of its simplicity and speed. But it mostly generates less condensed summaries with redundant information. On the other hand, abstractive summarization is a way of natural language generation and using this approach, it is possible to produce human-like summaries (Rush et al., 2015; Chopra et al., 2016; Wang and Ling, 2016). It requires deep language understanding. Though this technique is complex and less popular than the extractive approach, it is possible to produce more informative and fluent summary. For generating abstractive summaries, researchers often try to modify the candidate sentences by either shortening and compressing it (Knight and Marcu, 2000; Berg-Kirkpatrick et al., 2011; Filippova et al., 2015) or by merging several sentences which is called sentence fusion (Barzilay and McKeown, 2005; Cheung and Penn, 2014; Bing et al., 2015).

In this paper, we divide the whole task of summarization in two main phases: document shrinking and summarization. In the first phase, we apply sentence compression and merging to produce concise and new candidate sentences for the summary. In the second phase, we represent summarization as a submodular function maximization problem under budgeted constraints. While generating summaries, our system considers three important measures namely importance, coverage, and non-redundancy to ensure summary quality. We design three submodular functions for each these measures. The importance property of the summary considers how much relevant information present in a summary. The coverage measure ranks the sentences based on the fact of how representative they are of the document cluster. The third objective function is designed for measuring non-redundancy of the summaries. This metric assigns a score to a sentence based on how many distinct concepts it contains and how dissimilar it is with the other summary sentences. We design the summarization model for both generic and query-focused summarization. Finally, a modified greedy algorithm is applied which obtains near optimal summaries guaranteed to be within $(1 - 1/\sqrt{e})$ of the optimal solution.

Proceedings of the The 8th International Joint Conference on Natural Language Processing, pages 418–424,
Taipei, Taiwan, November 27 – December 1, 2017 ©2017 AFNLP

2   Related Work

Most of the research on document summarization are extractive which principally based on two important objectives, namely maximizing the relevance and minimizing the redundancy (Carbonell and Goldstein, 1998; Erkan and Radev, 2004). Besides, formulation of summarization as a maximum coverage problem with knapsack constraint (MCKP) (Takamura and Okumura, 2009; Morita et al., 2011) have been used. Recently, summarization has also been considered as a submodular function maximization (Lin and Bilmes, 2010, 2011; Dasgupta et al., 2013) where greedy algorithms were adopted to achieve near optimal summaries. However, the main drawback of all the extractive approaches is that they can not avoid the inclusion of insignificant information which degrades the summary quality.

On the other hand, the abstractive approach in a multi-document setting aims at generating summaries by deeply understanding the contents of the document set and rewriting the most relevant information in natural language. Two recent abstractive techniques are most commonly used to accomplish the task: sentence compression (Knight and Marcu, 2000) and sentence fusion (Barzilay and McKeown, 2005). In the recent years, sentence compression is jointly used with the extractive system to improve summary quality (Berg-Kirkpatrick et al., 2011; Martins and Smith, 2009). In addition, sentence fusion-based models have also been proposed where sentence fragments from multiple sentences are combined to cover more information in a concise manner (Barzilay and McKeown, 2005; Filippova et al., 2015; Ganesan et al., 2010; Thadani and McKeown, 2013; Cheung and Penn, 2014; Bing et al., 2015).

3   Document Shrinking

In this phase, we used sentence compression and sentence merging to prepare a better and more concise document set before approaching the actual summarization task.

3.1   Sentence Compression

Sentence compression is a technique of shortening sentences which can be used with the extractive system to improve summary quality. Consider the following example sentence as a candidate sentence of the summary:

"*According to a newspaper report*, a total of 4,299 political opponents died or disappeared during Pinochet's term."

In this sentence, we can see the part shown in the italic font is not carrying much significance and can be removed. We removed these sort of insignificant sub-parts of sentences following Berg-Kirkpatrick et al., (2011)'s compression technique.

In addition, we removed the sub-clauses related to the reporting verbs from sentences following (Chali and Uddin, 2016), like in the following example sentence:

Cambodian parties agreed to a Coalition government led by Hun Sen, the official said.

We considered mostly used reporting verbs such as *said, told, reported,* and *announced* to find out subclause. It is known that the sentence which contains a reporting verb is always the 'root' of the dependency tree. Following this rule, we traversed the tree to find out the subclause related to the reporting verb and removed it from the sentence.

3.2   Sentence Merging

Sentence merging is a technique to create a more informative sentence by merging the information from different source sentences. According to Bing et al., (2015), human summary writers usually merge the important facts in different verb phrases (VPs) about the same entity into a single sentence. Based on this assumption, we design a sentence merging technique. While Bing et al., (2015), took phrases as the basic linguistic unit and merge phrases to produce a summary, we take sentences as the basic linguistic units and merge them to generate new sentences for the summary. For example, the following sentences: (1) *Cambodian prime minister Hun Sen has ruled through violence*, (2) *Hun Sen threatened to eliminate opponents* can be merged as (3) *Hun Sen has ruled through violence and threatened to eliminate opponents*. For merging two sentences, we identify the sentences which start with a coreferent subject in order to preserve the gramaticality of the newly generated sentence, which is a key challenge in abstractive summarization.

Our system first applies Stanford Coreference Resolution engine (Lee et al., 2013) on each sentence of a document. From this step, we obtain a set of clusters containing the noun phrases that refer to the same entity in a document. A new sentence is generated from two sentences if they share a coreferent NP as the subject but have different VPs. We picked the sentences closest to each other for merging and produced the new sentences. The natural order of the sentences has thus been preserved.

After this phase, we obtain a cluster of documents containing concise sentences. Now, this document set is the input of our document summarization phase.

4   Document Summarization

We consider text summarization as a budgeted submodular function maximization problem similar to the recent works of (Lin and Bilmes, 2011), but our proposed monotone submodular objective function is significantly different from their work, which is discussed in this section.

4.1   Problem Definition

Suppose U be the finite set of all textual-units (sentence) in the documents. Our task of summarization is to select a subset $S \subseteq U$ that maximizes the submodular function. Since there is a length constraint in standard summarization tasks (e.g., DUC[1] evaluations), we consider the problem as a submodular function maximization with budgeted constraints:

$$\max_{S \subseteq U} \left\{ f(S) : \sum_{i \in S} cost_i \leq B_{max} \right\} \quad (1)$$

where, $cost_i$ is the non-negative cost of selecting the textual-unit i and B_{max} is the budget. The value of B_{max} could be the number of words or bytes in the summary. $f(S)$ is the submodular objective function that scores the summary quality.

4.1.1   Generic Summarization

We design a monotone submodular objective function composed of three important objectives for document summarization. These objectives are responsible for measuring summary's importance, coverage and non-redundancy property. The proposed objective function is:

$$f(S) = \alpha r(S) + \beta c(S) + \Lambda h(S) \quad (2)$$

where, $r(S)$ measures summary's importance quality, $c(S)$ measures summary's coverage quality, $h(S)$ measures summary's non-redundancy

quality and α, β, and Λ are non-negative trade-off coefficients which can be tuned empirically[2].

As we know, the linear combination of the submodular functions is submodular (Lin and Bilmes, 2011) and all the proposed subparts of our objective function are submodular, the function $f(S)$ is also submodular.

One of the basic requirements of a good summary is that it should contain the most important information across multiple documents. To model this property, we introduce a new monotone nondecreasing submodular function based on the *atomic concept*. In our definition, atomic concepts are the atomic terms that bear significance in a sentence. Our system, therefore, considers only verbs, named-entities, and adjectives as atomic concepts (excluding the stop words). Our proposed submodular function is:

$$r(S) = \sum_{i=1}^{N} \frac{1}{pos(S_i)} \Omega_i . \lambda_{S_i} \quad (3)$$

where, $\lambda_{S_i} \in \{0, 1\}$, $\lambda_{S_i} = 1$ if sentence S_i is in the summary, otherwise $\lambda_{S_i} = 0$. Ω_i is the importance score of sentence S_i and $pos(S_i)$ denotes the position of sentence S_i in the document.

We consider the relevance of the summary as the summation of the importance scores of the sentences in it. First, we utilize the Markov random walk model used by (Hong and Nenkova, 2014; Mihalcea and Tarau, 2004) to score each concept from the document set. Then we score every sentence based on the weight of the constituent words in the sentence. We only decrease the weight of the constituent concepts when it appears in multiple sentences in the summary. While sentence similarity-based approaches (Lin and Bilmes, 2011) do not consider the individual word's importance to model the importance property, our proposed submodular function is based on the atomic concept and this model encourages coverage of most of the important concepts across the documents.

A good summary has the capability to cover most of the important aspects of a document set. To formulate this, we consider a submodular objective function which utilizes the following 'sentence similarity-based approach' based on "facil-

---

[1]http://www-nlpir.nist.gov/projects/duc/index.html

[2]The values for the coefficients are 1.0, 1.0 and 5.0 for α, β, and Λ respectively, as found empirically using DUC-2003 development set during the experiments.

ity location objective" (Cornuejols et al., 1977).

$$d(S) = \sum_{i \in V} max_{j \in S} sim(i,j) \qquad (4)$$

where, $sim(i,j)$ denotes the deep semantic sentence similarity between sentence i and j. For measuring the similarity between sentences, we used the Word2Vec sentence similarity measure (Mikolov et al., 2013). We first remove all the stop words[3] which do not add much meaning to the sentence and then run Word2Vec[4] on the words in both sentences. We calculate the average vector for all words in both sentences and use cosine similarity between vectors to find the semantic similarity between sentences. Finally, following equation (4), a sentence's eligibility to be included in the summary depends on how similar it is with all the other sentences in the document cluster.

Minimizing redundant information in the summary is handled by the following submodular function:

$$h(S) = \sum_{C_k \in \eta(S)} \sigma(C_k) - \sum_{i,j \in S, i \neq j} sim(i,j) \quad (5)$$

where, $sim(i,j)$ is the deep semantic sentence similarity between summary sentence i and j, $\sigma(C_k)$ is the weight of k-th concept term, and $\eta(S)$ is the set of all distinct terms in the summary.

The first part of the function $h(S)$ is based on atomic-concept which scores the summary by measuring the weighted sum of the unique concept terms in the summary. In the second part, we penalize the summary redundancy by measuring semantic similarity among the summary sentences. Finally, our task is to maximize the proposed submodular function $f(S)$ to produce a relevant, well-covered, and non-redundant summary using the modified greedy algorithm for submodular function (Lin and Bilmes, 2010).

The reason behind choosing this algorithm is that a solution is guaranteed to be within a constant factor $(1 - 1/\sqrt{e})$ of the optimal solution when the objective function is monotone submodular. Since the scoring function $f(s)$ of our proposed summarizer is non-decreasing monotone submodular, we thus use the following greedy algorithm to obtain the near optimal solution.

Algorithm 1 A Greedy algorithm for maximizing the objective function

---

Require: A minimization LP in standard form.
Ensure: Integral solution, IR1 to the LP.
1: $S \leftarrow \emptyset, M \leftarrow \{1, ..., N\}$
2: **while** $M \neq 0$ **do**
3: $\quad q \leftarrow argmax_{p \in M} \frac{f(S \cup \{p\}) - f(S)}{(c_p)^r}$
4: $\quad$ **if** $\sum_{j \in S} C_j + C_q \leq B_{max}$ and $f(S \cup \{q\}) - f(S) \geq 0$ **then**
5: $\quad\quad S \leftarrow S \cup \{q\}$
6: $\quad$ **end if**
7: $\quad M \leftarrow M \setminus \{q\}$
8: **end while**
9: $t^* \leftarrow argmax_{t \in \{1,...,N\}, c_t \leq B_{max}} f(\{t\})$
10: **if** $f(t^*) > f(S)$ **then**
11: $\quad$ **return** t^*
12: **else return** S
13: **end if**

4.2 Query-focused Summarization

For the query-focused summarization phase, we propose the following objective function:

$$f(S) = \alpha r(S) + \Upsilon q(S) + \Lambda h(S) \qquad (6)$$

where, $r(S)$ measures summary's importance quality, $q(S)$ measures summary's query relevance quality, $h(S)$ measures summary's non-redundancy quality and α, Υ, and Λ are non-negative trade-off coefficients which can be tuned empirically[5].

We keep the importance and non-redundancy reward function similar to the generic summarizer described in the previous section. In addition, we design a query relevance objective function which considers the two important aspects: (1) how related summary sentences are with the query?, and (2) how much query dependent information is covered in the summary?

$$q(S) = \psi . \sum_{j \in S} Sim(q, s_j) + \theta . n_{j,q} \qquad (7)$$

where, $Sim(i,j)$ is the similarity between summary sentence j and query q, here similarity means the cosine similarity of the average word vectors obtained from Word2Vec (Mikolov et al., 2013) for the query and the summary sentence. $n_{j,q}$ is the number of query terms present in the

---

[3]http://jmlr.org/papers/volume5/lewis04a/a11-smart-stop-list/english.stop
[4]https://code.google.com/archive/p/word2vec/

[5]The values for the coefficients are 1.0, 10.0, and 5.0 for α, Υ, and Λ respectively, as found empirically using the development set DUC-2006 during the experiments.

summary sentence j. ψ, and θ are non-negative trade-off coefficients which have been tuned empirically during the experiments[6].

5 Experiments

To evaluate our generic and query-focused summaries, we use DUC-2004 and DUC-2007 datasets, respectively. We perform some basic preprocessing on all the documents such as tokenization, part-of-speech tagging and document coreference resolution using Stanford CoreNLP (Manning et al., 2014). We also use Porter's stemmer (Porter, 1999) for stemming all the words and remove all the stop words from the smart stop words list[7]. For query-focused summarization, we use word vectors from Word2Vec (Mikolov et al., 2013) which allows us to obtain better similarity scores between the sentences and the queries. We evaluate our system generated summaries using the automatic evaluation toolkit ROUGE version 1.5.5 (Lin, 2004).

We compare the results of our systems (i.e., document shrinking + summarization or document summarization + shrinking) with other state-of-the-art generic summarization methods. The comparison is shown in Table 1 where we report the values of ROUGE-1 recall and F-1 measure[8] of different approaches. From the table, we can see that our generic multi-document summarizer (document shrinking + summarization) significantly outperforms those systems in all measures. This result suggests the effectiveness of sentence compression and merging phase in our system. It also shows the effectiveness of using semantic similarity measures to select important sentences in the summary. Moreover, our system also uses a separate redundancy function which also helps to generate summaries with less redundancy compared to the systems which only concentrate on summary's coverage and relevance. These results also confirm that the proposed strategy can improve summary quality.

We compare our query-focused summarizer with other state-of-the-art query summarization methods. Table 2 shows the comparison in terms

Systems	R-1	F-1
Best system in DUC-04 (peer 65)	0.3828	0.3794
(Takamura and Okumura, 2009)	0.385	-
(Lin and Bilmes, 2011)	0.3935	0.389
(McDonald, 2007)	0.362	0.338
(Wang et al., 2009)	0.3907	-
Document Shrinking + Summarization	**0.4127**	**0.4133**
Document Summarization + Shrinking	0.3874	0.3882

Table 1: Results on DUC-2004 Datasets

Systems	R-2	F-2
Best system in DUC-07 (peer 15)	0.1245	0.1229
(Lin and Bilmes, 2011)	0.1238	0.1233
(Toutanova et al., 2007)	0.1189	0.1189
(Haghighi and Vanderwende, 2009)	0.118	-
Document Shrinking + Summarization	**0.1258**	**0.1264**
Document Summarization + Shrinking	0.1133	0.1149

Table 2: Results on DUC-2007 Datasets

of ROUGE scores[9] between our system and the best performing systems. From the table, we can say that our query-focused multi-document summarizer (document shrinking + summarization) outperforms the best-known systems in DUC-2007. It is notable that the best system in DUC-2007 takes the topic title as a query and uses Yahoo search engine to get a ranked set of retrieved documents which were used later to calculate the query relevance score (Pingali et al., 2007). However, our system is totally unsupervised and does not use any external source for the summary generation.

6 Conclusion

In this paper, we proposed a new summarization framework using different submodular functions with deep semantic features and abstraction-based methods. Abstraction-based methods help the system to obtain concise and more informative candidate summary sentences. We selected the best sentences for the summary by maximizing the submodular objective function. The empirical results show that our generic and query-focused summarization model outperform the state-of-the-art systems.

Acknowledgments

This research was supported by the Natural Sciences and Engineering Research Council (NSERC) of Canada and the University of Lethbridge.

---

[6]The values for the query relevance coefficients are 4.0 and 2.0 for ψ and θ respectively, as found empirically using the development set DUC-2006 during the experiments.

[7]http://jmlr.org/papers/volume5/lewis04a/a11-smart-stop-list/english.stop

[8]ROUGE runtime arguments for DUC-2004: ROUGE -a -c 95 -b 665 -m -n 4 -w 1.2

[9]ROUGE runtime arguments for DUC-2007: ROUGE -n 2 -x -m -2 4 -u -c 95 -r 1000 -f A-p 0.5-t 0-d

References

R. Barzilay and K. R. McKeown. 2005. Sentence fusion for multidocument news summarization. *Computational Linguistics*, 31(3):297–328.

T. Berg-Kirkpatrick, D. Gillick, and D. Klein. 2011. Jointly learning to extract and compress. In *Proceedings of the 49th Annual Meeting of the Association for Computational Linguistics: Human Language Technologies-Volume 1*, pages 481–490. Association for Computational Linguistics.

L. Bing, P. Li, Y. Liao, W. Lam, W. Guo, and R. J. Passonneau. 2015. Abstractive multi-document summarization via phrase selection and merging. *Proceedings of the 53rd Annual Meeting of the Association for Computational Linguistics and the 7th International Joint Conference on Natural Language Processing*.

F. Boudin, H. Mougard, and B. Favre. 2015. Concept-based summarization using integer linear programming: From concept pruning to multiple optimal solutions. In *Proceedings of the 2015 Conference on Empirical Methods in Natural Language Processing*, pages 1914–1918. Association for Computational Linguistics.

J. Carbonell and J. Goldstein. 1998. The use of mmr, diversity-based reranking for reordering documents and producing summaries. In *Proceedings of the 21st annual international ACM SIGIR conference on Research and development in information retrieval*, pages 335–336. ACM.

Y. Chali and M. Uddin. 2016. Multi-document summarization based on atomic semantic events and their temporal relationships. In *Advances in Information Retrieval*, pages 366–377. Springer.

J. Cheng and M. Lapata. 2016. Neural summarization by extracting sentences and words. In *Proceedings of the 54th Annual Meeting of the Association for Computational Linguistics (Volume 1: Long Papers)*, pages 484–494, Berlin, Germany. Association for Computational Linguistics.

J. C. Cheung and G. Penn. 2014. Unsupervised sentence enhancement for automatic summarization. In *Proceedings of the 2014 Conference on Empirical Methods in Natural Language Processing (EMNLP)*, pages 775–786. Association for Computational Linguistics.

S. Chopra, M. Auli, A. M. Rush, and S. Harvard. 2016. Abstractive sentence summarization with attentive recurrent neural networks. *Proceedings of NAACL-HLT16*, pages 93–98.

G. Cornuejols, M. L. Fischer, and G. L. Nemhauser. 1977. Location of bank accounts to optimize float: An analytic study of exact and approximate algorithms. *Management Science*, 23(8):789–810.

A. Dasgupta, R. Kumar, and S. Ravi. 2013. Summarization through submodularity and dispersion. In *Proceedings of the 51st Annual Meeting of the Association for Computational Linguistics ACL*, pages 1014–1022.

G. Erkan and D. R. Radev. 2004. Lexrank: graph-based lexical centrality as salience in text summarization. *Journal of Artificial Intelligence Research*, pages 457–479.

C. Fellbaum, editor. 1998. *Wordnet: An Electronic Database*. MIT Press.

K. Filippova, E. Alfonseca, C. A. Colmenares, L. Kaiser, and O. Vinyals. 2015. Sentence compression by deletion with lstms. In *Proceedings of the 2015 Conference on Empirical Methods in Natural Language Processing*, pages 360–368.

K. Ganesan, C. Zhai, and J. Han. 2010. Opinosis: a graph-based approach to abstractive summarization of highly redundant opinions. In *Proceedings of the 23rd international conference on computational linguistics*, pages 340–348. Association for Computational Linguistics.

A. Haghighi and L. Vanderwende. 2009. Exploring content models for multi-document summarization. In *Proceedings of Human Language Technologies: The 2009 Annual Conference of the North American Chapter of the Association for Computational Linguistics*, pages 362–370. Association for Computational Linguistics.

K. Hong and A. Nenkova. 2014. Improving the estimation of word importance for news multi-document summarization. In *Proceedings of the 14th Conference of the European Chapter of the Association for Computational Linguistics*, pages 712–721. Association for Computational Linguistics.

K. Knight and D. Marcu. 2000. Statistics-based summarization - step one: Sentence compression. In *Proceedings of the 17th National Conference on Artificial Intelligence*, Austin.

H. Lee, A. Chang, Y. Peirsman, N. Chambers, M. Surdeanu, and D. Jurafsky. 2013. Deterministic coreference resolution based on entity-centric, precision-ranked rules. *Computational Linguistics*, 39(4):885–916.

C.-Y. Lin. 2004. Rouge: A package for automatic evaluation of summaries. In *Proceedings of the 42nd Annual Meeting of the Association for Computational Linguistics, Workshop on Text Summarization Branches Out*.

H. Lin and J. Bilmes. 2010. Multi-document summarization via budgeted maximization of submodular functions. In *Proceedings of the 2010 Conference of the North American Chapter of the Association for Computational Linguistics*, pages 912–920. Association for Computational Linguistics.

H. Lin and J. Bilmes. 2011. A class of submodular functions for document summarization. In *Proceedings of the 49th Annual Meeting of the Association for Computational Linguistics: Human Language Technologies-Volume 1*. Association for Computational Linguistics.

C. D. Manning, M. Surdeanu, J. Bauer, J. Finkel, S. J. Bethard, and D. McClosky. 2014. The stanford corenlp natural language processing toolkit. In *Proceedings of the 52nd Annual Meeting of the Association for Computational Linguistics System Demonstrations*.

A. Martins and N. A. Smith. 2009. Summarization with a joint model for sentence extraction and compression. In *Proceedings of the Workshop on Integer Linear Programming for Natural Language Processing*, pages 1–9. Association for Computational Linguistics.

R. McDonald. 2007. A study of global inference algorithms in multi-document summarization. In *European Conference on Information Retrieval*, pages 557–564. Springer.

R. Mihalcea and P. Tarau. 2004. Textrank: Bringing order into texts. In *Proceedings of EMNLP 2004*, pages 404–411, Barcelona, Spain. Association for Computational Linguistics.

T. Mikolov, I. Sutskever, K. Chen, G. S. Corrado, and J. Dean. 2013. Distributed representations of words and phrases and their compositionality. In *In Advances in neural information processing systems*, pages 3111–3119.

H. Morita, T. Sakai, and M. Okumura. 2011. Query snowball: a co-occurrence-based approach to multi-document summarization for question answering. In *Proceedings of the 49th Annual Meeting of the Association for Computational Linguistics: Human Language Technologies: short papers-Volume 2*, pages 223–229. Association for Computational Linguistics.

R. Nallapati, F. Zhai, and B. Zhou. 2017. Summarunner: An interpretable recurrent neural network model for extractive summarization. In *Proceedings of the 31st AAAI Conference on Artificial Intelligence*, San Francisco. AAAAI Press.

D. Parveen, H. M. Ramsl, and M. Strube. 2015. Topical coherence for graph-based extractive summarization. In *Proceedings of the 2015 Conference on Empirical Methods in Natural Language Processing*, pages 1949–1954. Association for Computational Linguistics.

D. Parveen and M. Strube. 2015. Integrating importance, non-redundancy and coherence in graph-based extractive summarization. In *Proceedings of the 24th International Joint Conference on Artificial Intelligence*, page 12981304.

P. Pingali, K. Rahul, and V. Varma. 2007. Iiit hyderabad at duc 2007. In *Proceedings of the Document Understanding Conference*.

M.F. Porter. 1999. An algorithm for suffix stripping. *Program*, 14(3):130–137.

M. A. Rush, S. Chopra, and J. Weston. 2015. A neural attention model for abstractive sentence summarization. In *Proceedings of the 2015 Conference on Empirical Methods in Natural Language Processing*, pages 379–389. Association for Computational Linguistics.

H. Takamura and M. Okumura. 2009. Text summarization model based on maximum coverage problem and its variant. In *Proceedings of the 12th Conference of the European Chapter of the Association for Computational Linguistics*, pages 781–789. Association for Computational Linguistics.

K. Thadani and K. McKeown. 2013. Supervised sentence fusion with single-stage inference. In *Proceedings of the International Joint Conference on Natural Language Processing*, pages 1410–1418.

K. Toutanova, C. Brockett, M. Gamon, J. Jagarlamudi, H. Suzuki, and L. Vanderwende. 2007. The pythy summarization system: Microsoft research at duc 2007. In *Proceedings of the Document Understanding Conference*.

D. Wang, S. Zhu, T. Li, and Y. Gong. 2009. Multi-document summarization using sentence-based topic models. In *Proceedings of the ACL-IJCNLP 2009 Conference*, pages 297–300. Association for Computational Linguistics.

L. Wang and W. Ling. 2016. Neural network-based abstract generation for opinions and arguments. In *Proceedings of the 2016 Conference of the North American Chapter of the Association for Computational Linguistics: Human Language Technologies*, pages 47–57, San Diego, California. Association for Computational Linguistics.

Domain Adaptation for Relation Extraction with Domain Adversarial Neural Network

Lisheng Fu Thien Huu Nguyen* Bonan Min[†] Ralph Grishman
New York University, New York, NY, USA
{lisheng, grishman}@cs.nyu.edu
* University of Oregon, Eugene, OR, USA
thien@cs.uoregon.edu
[†] Raytheon BBN Technologies, Cambridge, MA, USA
bonan.min@raytheon.com

Abstract

Relations are expressed in many domains such as newswire, weblogs and phone conversations. Trained on a source domain, a relation extractor's performance degrades when applied to target domains other than the source. A common yet labor-intensive method for domain adaptation is to construct a target-domain-specific labeled dataset for adapting the extractor. In response, we present an unsupervised domain adaptation method which only requires labels from the source domain. Our method is a joint model consisting of a CNN-based relation classifier and a domain-adversarial classifier. The two components are optimized jointly to learn a domain-independent representation for prediction on the target domain. Our model outperforms the state-of-the-art on all three test domains of ACE 2005.

1 Introduction

Relation Extraction (RE) captures the semantic relation between two entities within a sentence, such as the Located relation between e1 and e2 in the sentence: "in the <e2>West Bank</e2>, a <e1>passenger </e1>was wounded when an Israeli bus came under fire." The same relation might be expressed differently across diverse documents, topics and genres. We often observed that a relation extractor's performance degrades when applied to a domain other than the domain it is trained on.

A simple method for domain adaptation (Blitzer et al., 2006; Daume, 2007; Jing and Zhai, 2007) is to construct a labeled dataset for the target domain, and then adjust a trained model with it. This is inefficient for relations - annotation is laborious to obtain, not to mention that relation mentions are sparse in the text. Take ACE 2004 as an example, Personal/Social relations appear only once on average per document. Such a method will not scale to the open-ended set of possible domains.

Among the features (Zhou et al., 2005) used for relation extraction, shortest dependency path can be applied cross-domain while argument-specific features (e.g., entity types, lexical forms) are likely to be more domain-specific. We hypothesize that it is possible to learn both domain-invariant and domain-specific representations with neural networks, and use the domain-invariant representation for many new domains.

In this paper, we propose to use a Domain Adversarial Neural Network (DANN) (Ganin and Lempitsky, 2015; Ajakan et al., 2014) to learn a domain-invariant representation for relations. Our contributions are twofold:

- We propose a novel domain adaptation approach for relation extraction that learns cross-domain features by itself and that requires no labels in targets.

- Experiments on the ACE domains show that our approach improves on the state-of-the-art across all domains.

In the rest of the paper, we will first briefly summarize related work, then describe the model (Section 3). We will present experimental results and conclusion at the end.

2 Related Work

There has been a lot of research on domain adaptation in natural language processing (Blitzer et al., 2006; Daume, 2007; Jing and Zhai, 2007; Glorot et al., 2011; Ajakan et al., 2014;

Proceedings of the The 8th International Joint Conference on Natural Language Processing, pages 425–429,
Taipei, Taiwan, November 27 – December 1, 2017 ©2017 AFNLP

Ganin and Lempitsky, 2015). Most of the existing domain adaptation methods are based on discrete feature representations and linear classifiers. There is also recent work on domain adaptation for relation extraction including feature-based systems (Nguyen and Grishman, 2014; Nguyen et al., 2014) and kernel-based system (Plank and Moschitti, 2013). Nguyen and Grishman (2014) and Nguyen et al. (2014) both require a few labels in the target domain. Our proposed method can perform domain adaptation without target labels.

Some other methods also do not have such requirement. Plank and Moschitti (2013) designed the semantic syntactic tree kernel (SSTK) to learn cross-domain patterns. Nguyen et al. (2015b) constructed a case study comparing feature-based methods and kernel-based models. They presented some effective features and kernels (e.g. word embedding).We share the same intuition of finding those cross-domain features, but our work differs from such previous work in that they manually designed those features and kernels while we automatically learn cross-domain features from unlabeled target-domain examples with neural networks. To our best knowledge, this is the first work on neural networks for domain adaptation of relation extraction.

3 Model

We formulate the relation extraction task as a classification problem over all entity pairs (relation candidates) in a sentence. The overall structure of the model is shown in Figure 1. The model will first convert a relation candidate into a fixed-length matrix, then uses a single-layer Convolutional Neural Network (CNN) with dropout to learn its hidden representation $repr$. On top of $repr$, it uses two decoders: a fully-connected layer with dropout for predicting the relation type (Zeng et al., 2014) (Section 3.1), and another decoder with domain adversarial neural network(Ganin and Lempitsky, 2015) to predict its domain. The additional domain-adversarial decoder is used to enforce the feature layer to be domain-invariant (Section 3.2).

3.1 CNN-based Encoder-Decoder Model for Relations

Each sentence is truncated or padded to a fixed length (l_s) of tokens. Each token of the text is then

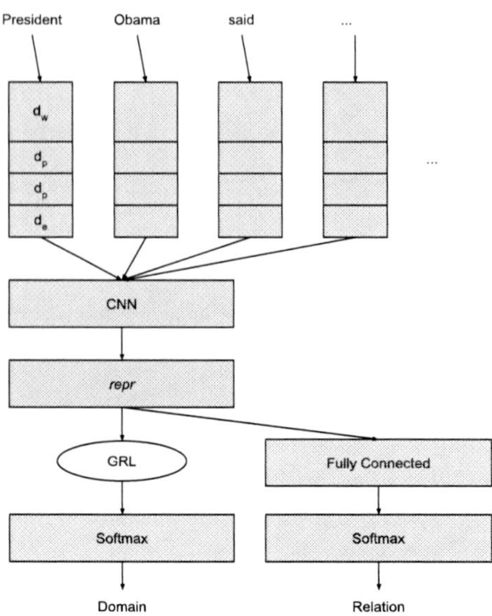

Figure 1: Model architecture

represented as the concatenation of its word embedding, its position embedding and its entity type embedding. They form the input layer:

Word embedding: We use pre-trained word embedding from word2vec (Mikolov et al., 2013). The size of the embedding is $|V| \cdot d_w$, where $|V|$ is the vocabulary size, and d_w is the embedding dimension.

Position embedding: For each token, we look up its two position embeddings from the two position embedding tables (randomly initialized) with its relative distances to the two arguments, respectively. The final embedding is the concatenation of the two. The size of one embedding table is $(2 \cdot l_s - 1) \cdot d_p$, where l_s is the sentence length, and d_p is the embedding dimension.

Entity type embedding: For each token, we look up its entity-type embedding from the entity-type embedding table. Tokens outside the two entity spans will be randomly initialized to the same non-entity vector. Tokens within the two arguments will be converted to the vector of the argument's entity type. The size of the embedding table is $(|E| + 1) * d_e$, where $|E|$ is the number of entity types, and d_e is the embedding dimension.

Chunk embedding: Similar to entity type, we have chunk embedding according to each token's chunk type. The size of embedding table is $(|C| + 1) * d_c$, where $|C|$ is the number of chunk types, and d_c is the embedding dimension.

On dep path embedding: For each token, we have a vector to indicate whether the token is on the dependency path between the two entities. The vector size is d_d.

The input layer is a matrix with size $(d_w + 2 \cdot d_p + d_e + d_c + d_d) \cdot l_s$. A standard convolution layer with variable window sizes (feature maps) is applied on this, following by max-pooling and dropout. Each filter with the same window size has the same filter size. The output is the feature representation layer ($repr$) of size $d_f \cdot |W|$, where d_f is the filter size, and $|W|$ is the size of the set of window sizes. We add fully connected layers to this feature representation with softmax to predict the relation type. The model is similar to that in (Nguyen and Grishman, 2016), but with fewer features.

3.2 Domain Adversarial Neural Network

How does domain adaptation work without any labeled examples for the target domain? Following Ganin and Lempitsky (2015) and Ajakan et al. (2014), we use DANN to learn a representation that is more general across domains and eliminating source-only distinctive features that are easily learned with labeled source data.

It learns domain invariant features by jointly optimizing the underlying feature layer from the main learning task and the domain label predictor. In this case, the main learning task is the relation type prediction in Section 3.1. The domain label predictor is a binary classifier that discriminates whether the example is from source or target. The domain classifier consists of the gradient reversal layer (GRL) and a few fully connected layers. The GRL is defined as an identity function with reversed gradient for backpropagation. For input layer x:

$$GRL(x) = x, \frac{d}{dx}GRL(x) = -I$$

where I is the identity matrix.

We use a binary cross-entropy loss for the domain classifier:

$$L_{domain} = \sum_{i=0}^{N_s+N_t} \{d_i log(\hat{d_i}) + (1 - d_i)log(1 - \hat{d_i})\}$$

where $d_i \epsilon \{0, 1\}$ is the domain label $\{source, target\}$, and N_s, N_t stand for the number of examples in source and target.

The loss of the whole model is the linear combination of the task loss and the domain loss:

$$L = L_{relation} + \lambda \cdot L_{domain}$$

where λ is the adaptation weight, and $L_{relation}$ is the loss of the relation classifier.

During the training, half of the examples comes from the source and half of them comes from the target in a single batch. Only examples from source have relation labels, while both source and target examples have domain labels. As the result, the source part is used to calculate the relation loss $L_{relation}$. The whole batch is used to calculate the domain loss L_{domain}

We choose the feature representation layer ($repr$) from the relation model (Section 3.1) as the input to GRL. During the training, while the parameters of the relation and domain decoders are both optimized to *minimize* their errors, the parameters of $repr$ are optimized to *minimize* the loss of the relation decoder and to *maximize* (due to GRL) the loss of the domain classifier. The latter encourages domain-invariant features to emerge for domain adaptation.

In feature-based models, lexicon-level features are often domain-specific such as a person's name. e.g. word-level features that contain *Obama* and *US* can be indicators for employment relation. It is true in many news articles, but not in general. Instead of manually deciding whether to use the feature or not, we can use DANN to read the target domain text to make the decision depending on the domain.

4 Experiments

4.1 Dataset

We use the ACE 2005 dataset to evaluate domain adaptation by dividing its articles from its six genres into respective domains: broadcast conversation (*bc*), broadcast news (*bn*), telephone conversation (*cts*), newswire (*nw*), usenet (*un*) and weblogs (*wl*). Previous work (Gormley et al., 2015; Nguyen and Grishman, 2016) uses newswire (*bn* & *nw*) as the training set, half of *bc* as the development set, the other half of *bc*, *cts* and *wl* as the test sets. We use the same data split. Our model requires unlabeled target domain instances. To meet this requirement and avoid train-on-test, we also split *cts* and *wl* when adapting to them. For all three test domains, we use half of the dataset as the development set, and the other half as the test set (Table 1). We use the same training set and the same preprocessing. This results in 43,497 entity pairs for training. We also use the same label set which is expanded by creating two relation types for each asymmetric relation.

Split	bc†	wl	cts
train	nw & bn	nw & bn	nw & bn
dev	half of bc	half of wl	half of cts
test	half of bc	half of wl	half of cts

Table 1: Data split for the experiments. †This data split is the same as several previous work

4.2 Configuration and Hyperparameters

We use word embedding pre-trained on newswire with 300 dimensions from word2vec (Mikolov et al. 2013). We fix the word embeddings during the training because tuning did not show improvement. We follow Nguyen and Grishman (2016) to set the hyperparameters for CNN: the embedding sizes (Section 3.1) d_e, d_p, d_d, d_c, d_d, = 50, the max sentence length l_s = 50, the set of filter window sizes W = 2, 3, 4, 5, the number of filters for each window size d_f = 150, and the dropout rate to be 0.5. We use one fully connected layer with 300 dimensions for the relation decoder before the softmax layer. We only use a softmax layer for domain decoder. The learning rate is 0.001. We halve the learning rate every two epoches. We use Adam as the optimization method. The adaptation weight is tuned to be 0.1 using the dev set. For all scores, we run experiments 10 times and take the average.

4.3 Evaluation

Method	bc	wl	cts	avg
Gormley 2015	61.90	N/A	N/A	N/A
Nguyen 2016	63.26	N/A	N/A	N/A
CNN	64.44	54.58	57.02	58.64
CNN + DANN	**65.16**	**55.55**	**57.19**	**59.30**

Table 2: Adaptation to the *bc* domain. F1 scores are reported on test sets with same splits. *p-value* < 0.01 for bc CNN vs. CNN+DANN.

Our baseline CNN model achieved comparable performance to the state-of-the-art relation extraction methods (Table 2). Compared to (Gormley et al., 2015; Nguyen and Grishman, 2016), our baseline model already obtained higher score on *bc*. They also reported higher scores by ensemble with other models (feature-based or multiple neural net models) which is not directly comparable to a single model. Essentially, our model can also serve as one of the base models in the ensemble.

We trained DANN to read the development set of *bc* to adapt to this domain. Although the gain seems to be small, the improvement is statistically significant (*p-value* < 0.01). We ran an instance-based sign test on the combination of the output of 10 experiments. We have 10 observations of each instance in the original dataset. we treat them as different examples when calculating the significance. While DANN improves *bc* significantly, we also want to find out how it works on other domains. In the original split used by previous work, *wl* and *cts* do not have dev and test split. We, therefore, created the data split by ourselves and compare the results to our own baseline model. We observe similar improvement on *wl*, but not on *cts*. By doing some feature engineering on the embedding layer, we found that the Chunk embedding and On dep path embedding improves the *cts* a lot. The model obtains 52.96 (without) and 57.02 (with) these embeddings. With DANN, it obtains 53.74 (+0.78) and 57.19 (+0.17). The effective hand-designed cross-domain features from the embedding layer could make the room for improvement smaller.

Given a group of documents, our approach is to let the DANN read more unlabeled documents from the same domain and train the relation decoder along with it. Then, we obtain a better model for this domain. This also means that we will have to train different models for different domains. Ideally, we would like to have a model that can work on all domains at the same time. To test this, we try to adapt to the three domains in the dataset at the same time. Under this setting, DANN reads unlabeled data from all three domains along with the supervised relation model. As the result (Table 3), the model tends to learn something in between. It performs better on *bc* and *wl*, but worse on *cts*. It is not very surprising since DANN will force the representation layer to be domain-invariant. To really lift the performance of all the domains with a single model, the model needs to capture some domain-specific representation as well. This would be hard to achieve without labels from the target domains, but still an interesting direction to investigate. Under the current situation, it would be better to train separate models that are adapted to each domain.

Method	bc	wl	cts	avg
CNN	64.33	54.58	57.02	58.64
+ DANN (all)	64.94	55.17	56.08	58.73
+ DANN (each)	**65.16**	**55.55**	**57.19**	**59.30**

Table 3: F1 scores on adaptation to all three domains at the same time and adaptation to each domain individually.

5 Conclusion

Our model successfully obtains improvement on all three test domains of relations at ACE 2005. It uses a domain adversarial neural network to learn cross-domain features. It does not require hand-crafted features for domain adaptation. It can be a useful tool for relation extraction since labeled data is always hard to acquire.

References

Hana Ajakan, Pascal Germain, Hugo Larochelle, Franois Laviolette, and Mario Marchand. 2014. Domain-adversarial neural networks. In *arXiv*.

John Blitzer, Ryan McDonald, and Fernando Pereira. 2006. Domain adaptation with structural correspondence learning. In *EMNLP*.

Hal Daume. 2007. Frustratingly easy domain adaptation. In *ACL*.

Yaroslav Ganin and Victor Lempitsky. 2015. Unsupervised domain adaptation by backpropagation. In *ICML*.

Xavier Glorot, Antoine Bordes, and Yoshua Bengio. 2011. Domain adaptation for large-scale sentiment classification: A deep learning approach. In *ICML*.

Matthew R. Gormley, Mo Yu, and Mark Dredze. 2015. Improved relation extraction with feature-rich compositional embedding models. In *EMNLP*.

Jiang Jing and ChengXiang Zhai. 2007. Instance weighting for domain adaptation in nlp. In *ACL*.

Tomas Mikolov, Kai Chen, Greg Corrado, and Jeffrey Dean. 2013. Efficient estimation of word representations in vector space. In *ICLR*.

Minh Luan Nguyen, Ivor W. Tsang, Kian Ming Adam Chai, and Hai Leong Chieu. 2014. Robust domain adaptation for relation extraction via clustering consistency. In *ACL*.

Thien Huu Nguyen and Ralph Grishman. 2014. Employing word representations and regularization for domain adaptation of relation extraction. In *ACL*.

Thien Huu Nguyen and Ralph Grishman. 2016. Combining neural networks and log-linear models to improve relation extraction. In *Proceedings of IJCAI Workshop on Deep Learning for Artificial Intelligence (DLAI)*.

Thien Huu Nguyen, Barbara Plank, and Ralph Grishman. 2015b. Semantic representations for domain adaptation: A case study on the tree kernel-based method for relation extraction. In *ACL-IJCNLP*.

Barbara Plank and Alessandro Moschitti. 2013. Embedding semantic similarity in tree kernels for domain adaptation of relation extraction. In *ACL*.

Daojian Zeng, Kang Liu, Siwei Lai, Guangyou Zhou, and Jun Zhao. 2014. Relation classification via convolutional deep neural network. In *COLING*.

GuoDong Zhou, Jian Su, Jie Zhang, and Min Zhang. 2005. Exploring various knowledge in relation extraction. In *ACL*.

Lexical Simplification with the Deep Structured Similarity Model

Lis Pereira[1,3] *   Xiaodong Liu[2]   John Lee[3]

[1]Weathernews Inc., Nakase 1-3 Mihama-ku, Chiba-shi, 261-0023 Chiba, Japan
[2]Microsoft Research, One Microsoft Way, Redmond, WA 98052, USA
[3] Department of Linguistics and Translation, City University of Hong Kong
kanash@wni.com, xiaodl@microsoft.com, jsylee@cityu.edu.hk

Abstract

We explore the application of a Deep Structured Similarity Model (DSSM) to ranking in lexical simplification. Our results show that the DSSM can effectively capture fine-grained features to perform semantic matching when ranking substitution candidates, outperforming the state-of-the-art on two standard datasets used for the task.

1 Introduction

Lexical simplification is the task of automatically rewriting a text by substituting words or phrases with simpler variants, while retaining its meaning and grammaticality. The goal is to make the text easier to understand for children, language learners, people with cognitive disabilities and even machines. Approaches to lexical simplification generally follow a standard pipeline consisting of two main steps: *generation* and *ranking*. In the generation step, a set of possible substitutions for the target word is commonly created by querying semantic databases such as Wordnet (Devlin and Tait, 1998), learning substitution rules from sentence-aligned parallel corpora of complex-simple texts (Horn et al., 2014; Paetzold and Specia, 2017), and learning word embeddings from a large corpora to obtain similar words of the complex word (Glavaš and Štajner, 2015; Kim et al., 2016; Paetzold and Specia, 2016a, 2017). In the ranking step, features that discriminate a substitution candidate from other substitution candidates are leveraged and the candidates are ranked with respect to their simplicity and contextual fitness.

The ranking step is challenging because the substitution candidates usually have similar meaning to the target word, and thus share similar context features. State-of-the-art approaches to ranking in lexical simplification exploit supervised machine learning-based methods that rely mostly on surface features, such as word frequency, word length and n-gram probability, for training the model (Horn et al., 2014; Bingel and Søgaard, 2016; Paetzold and Specia, 2016a, 2017). Moreover, deep architectures are not explored in these models. Surface features and shallow architectures might not be able to explore the features at different levels of abstractions that capture nuances that discriminate the candidates.

In this paper, we propose to use a Deep Structured Similarity Model (DSSM) (Huang et al., 2013) to rank substitution candidates. The DSSM exploits a deep architecture by using a deep neural network (DNN), that can effectively capture contextual features to perform semantic matching between two sentences. It has been successfully applied to several natural language processing (NLP) tasks, such as machine translation (Gao et al., 2014), web search ranking (Huang et al., 2013; Shen et al., 2014; Liu et al., 2015), question answering (Yih et al., 2014), and image captioning (Fang et al., 2015). To the best of our knowledge, this is the first time this model is applied to lexical simplification. We adapt the original DSSM architecture and objective function to our specific task. Our evaluation on two standard datasets for lexical simplification shows that this method outperforms state-of-the-art approaches that use supervised machine learning-based methods.

2 Method

2.1 Task Definition

We focus on the ranking step of the standard lexical simplification pipeline. Given a dataset of tar-

---

*This research was conducted while the first author was a Post Doctoral Fellow at the City University of Hong Kong.

Proceedings of the The 8th International Joint Conference on Natural Language Processing, pages 430–435,
Taipei, Taiwan, November 27 – December 1, 2017 ©2017 AFNLP

get words, their sentential contexts and substitution candidates for the target words, the goal is to train a model that accurately ranks the candidates based on their simplicity and semantic matching.

For generating substitution candidates, we utilize the method proposed by Paetzold and Specia (2017), which was recently shown to be the state-of-art method for generating substitution candidates. They exploit a hybrid substitution generation approach where candidates are first extracted from 550,644 simple-complex aligned sentences from the Newsela corpus (Xu et al., 2015). Then, these candidates are complemented with candidates generated with a retrofitted word embedding model. The word embedding model is retrofitted over WordNet's synonym pairs (for details, please refer to Paetzold and Specia (2017)).

For ranking substitution candidates, we use a DSSM, which we elaborate in the next section.

2.2 DSSM for Ranking Substitution Candidates

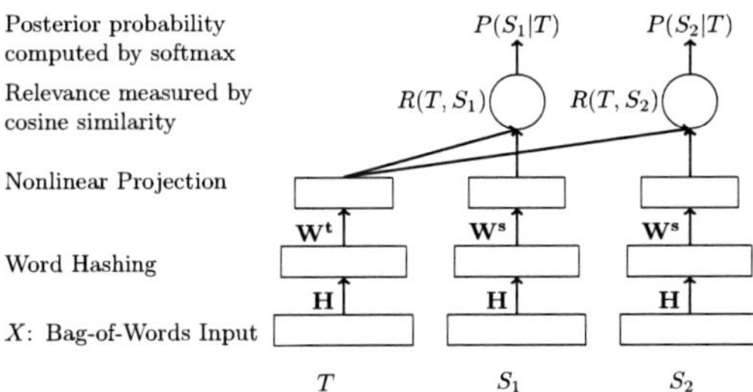

Figure 1: **Architecture of the Deep Structured Similarity Model (DSSM):** The input X (either a target word or a substitute candidate and their sentential contexts, T and S, respectively) is first represented as a bag of words, then hashed into letter 3-grams H. Non-linear projection W_t generates the semantic representation of T and non-linear projection W^s constructs the semantic representation of S. Finally, the cosine similarity is adopted to measure the relevance between the T and S. At last, the posterior probabilities over all candidates are computed.

Compared to other latent semantic models, such as Latent Semantic Analysis (Deerwester et al., 1990) and its extensions, Deep Structured Similarity Model (also called Deep Semantic Similarity Model) or DSSM (Huang et al., 2013) can capture fine-grained local and global contextual features more effectively. The DSSM is trained by optimizing a similarity-driven objective, by projecting the whole sentence to a continuous semantic space. In addition, it is is built upon characters (rather than words) for scalability and generalizability (He, 2016). Figure 1 shows the architecture of the model used in this work. It consists of a typical DNN with a word hashing layer, a nonlinear projection layer, and an output layer. Each component is described in the following:

Word Hashing Layer: the input is first mapped from a high-dimensional one-hot word vector into a low-dimentional letter-trigram space (with the dimentionality as low as 5k), a method called *word hashing* (Huang et al., 2013). For example, the word *cat* is hashed as the bag of letter trigram *#-c-a, c-a-t, a-t-#*, where # is a boundary symbol (Liu et al., 2015). The word hashing helps the model generalize better for out-of-vocabulary words and for spelling variants of the same word (Liu et al., 2015).

Nonlinear Projection Layer: This layers maps the substitution candidate and the target word in their sentential contexts, S and T respectively, which are represented as letter tri-grams, into d-dimension semantic representations, S^{S_q} and T^{S_q} respectively:

$$l = tanh(Wx) \tag{1}$$

where the nonlinear activation $tanh$ is defined as: $tanh(z) = \frac{1-e^{-2z}}{1+e^{-2z}}$.

Output Layer: This layer computes the semantic relevance score between S and T as:

$$R(T, S) = cosine(T^{S_q}, S^{S_q}) = \frac{T^{S_q T} S^{S_q}}{\|T^{S_q}\|\|S^{S_q}\|} \tag{2}$$

2.3 Features for DSSM

As baseline features, we use the same n-gram probability features as in Paetzold and Specia (2017), who also employ a neural network to rank substitution candidates. As in Paetzold and Specia (2017), the features were extracted using the SubIMDB corpus (Paetzold and Specia, 2015). We also experiment with additional features that have been reported as useful in this task. For each target word and a substitution candidate word we also compute: cosine similarity, word length, and alignment probability in the sentence-aligned Normal-Simple Wikipedia corpus (Kauchak, 2013). The cosine similarity feature is computed using the SubIMDB corpus.

2.4 Implementation Details and Training Procedure of the DSSM

Following previous works that used supervised machine learning for ranking in lexical simplification (Horn et al., 2014; Paetzold and Specia, 2017), we train the DSSM using the LexMTurk dataset (Horn et al., 2014), which contains 500 instances composed of a sentence, a target word and substitution candidates ranked by simplicity (Paetzold and Specia, 2017). In order to learn the parameters W^t and W^s (Figure 1) of the DSSM, we use the standard backpropagation algorithm (Rumelhart et al., 1988). The objective used in this paper follows the pair-wise learning-to-rank paradigm outlined in (Burges et al., 2005).

Given a target word and its sentential context T, we obtain a list of candidates **L**. We set different positive values to the candidates based on their simplicity rankings. E.g., if the list of the candidates is ordered by simplificity as, $L = \{A^+ > B^+ > C^+\}$, the labels are first constructed as $L = \{y_{A^+} = 3, y_{B^+} = 2, y_{C^+} = 1\}$. The values are then normalized by dividing by the maximum value in the list: $L = \{y_{A^+} = 1, y_{B^+} = 0.667, y_{C^+} = 0.333\}$. If the target word was not originally in **L**, we add it with label 0. This enables the model to reflect the label information in the similarity scores. We minimize the Bayesian expected loss as: $\sum_{l=1}^{L} \ell(S_l, T)$, where $\ell(S_l, T)$ is defined as:

$$-\{y_l ln P(S_l|T) + (1 - y_l)ln(1 - P(S_l|T))\} \quad (3)$$

Note that $P(S_l|T)$ is computed as:

$$P(S_l|T) = \frac{exp(\gamma R(S_l, T))}{\sum_{S_i \in L} exp(\gamma R(S_i, T))} \quad (4)$$

here, γ is a tuning factor.

We used 5-cross validation approach to select hyper-parameters, such as number of hidden nodes. We set the gamma factor as 10 as per Huang et al. (2013). The selected hyper-parameters were used to train the model in the whole LexMTurk dataset. We employ early-stopping and select the model whose change of the average loss in each epoch was smaller than 1.0e-3. Since the training data is small (only 500 samples) we use a smaller number of hidden nodes,

$d = 32$, in the nonlinear projection layer and adopt a higher dropout rate (0.4). The model is optimized using Adam (Kingma and Ba, 2014) with the learning rate fixed at 0.001, and is trained for 30 epochs. The mini-batch is set to 16 during training.

3 Experiments

3.1 Datasets and Evaluation Metrics

To evaluate the proposed model, we conduct experiments on two common datasets for lexical simplification: BenchLS (Paetzold and Specia, 2016b), which contains 929 instances, and NN-SEval (Paetzold and Specia, 2016a), which contains 239 instances. Each instance is composed of a sentence, a target word, and a set of gold candidates ranked by simplicity (Paetzold and Specia, 2017). Since both datasets contain instances from the LexMturk dataset (Horn et al., 2014), which we use for training the DNN, we remove the overlap instances between training and test datasets [1]. We finally obtain 429 remaining instances in the BenchLS dataset, and 78 instances in the NNEval dataset, which are used in our evaluation.

We adopt the same evaluation metrics featured in Glavaš and Štajner (2015) and Horn et al. (2014): 1) **precision**: ratio of correct simplifications out of all the simplifications made by the system; 2) **accuracy**: ratio of correct simplifications out of all words that should have been simplified; and 3) **changed**: ratio of target words changed by the system.

3.2 Baselines

We compared the proposed model (DSSM Ranking) to two state-of-the-art approaches to ranking in lexical simplification that exploit supervised machine learning-based methods. The first baseline is the Neural Substitution Ranking (NSR) approach described in (Paetzold and Specia, 2017), which employs a multi-layer perceptron neural network. We reimplement their model as part of the LEXenstein toolkit (Paetzold and Specia, 2015). The network has 3 hidden layers with 8 nodes each. Unlike the proposed model, they treat ranking in lexical simplification as a standard classification problem. The second baseline is SVM^{rank} (Joachims, 2006) (linear kernel

---

[1] Running on the original test datasets leads our system to obtain higher results than the ones reported here. Therefore, in order to avoid bias, we removed the overlap instances from both test datasets.

Substitution Candidates Ranking	Features	BenchLS			NNSEval		
		Prec.	Acc.	Changed	Prec.	Acc.	Changed
NSR	n-gram probs.	0.313	0.233	0.743	0.153	0.102	0.666
SVM^{rank}	n-gram probs.	0.354	0.261	0.736	0.166	0.102	0.615
DSSM Ranking	n-gram probs.	0.337	0.284	0.841	0.216	0.166	0.769
DSSM Ranking	all	**0.375**	**0.319**	**0.850**	**0.306**	**0.243**	**0.794**
Selection Step + Substitution Candidates Ranking	Features	BenchLS			NNSEval		
		Prec.	Acc.	Changed	Prec.	Acc.	Changed
NSR	n-gram probs.	0.304	0.214	0.703	0.204	0.102	0.500
SVM^{rank}	n-gram probs.	0.357	0.263	0.736	0.187	0.115	0.615
DSSM Ranking	n-gram probs.	0.355	0.286	0.806	0.259	0.179	0.692
DSSM Ranking	all	**0.383**	**0.328**	**0.857**	**0.333**	**0.269**	**0.807**

Table 1: Substitution candidates ranking results. *n-gram probs.* denotes the n-gram probability features described in Paetzold and Specia (2017), and *all* denotes all features described in Section 2.3. All values marked in bold are significantly higher compared to the best baseline, SVM^{rank}, measured by t-test at p-value of 0.05.

with default parameters) for ranking substitution candidates, similar to the method described in (Horn et al., 2014). All the three models employ the n-gram probability features extracted from the SubIMDB corpus (Paetzold and Specia, 2015), as described in (Paetzold and Specia, 2017), and are trained using the LexMTurk dataset.

3.3 Results

The top part of table 1 (Substitution Candidates Ranking) summarizes the results of all three systems. Overall, both SVM^{rank} and DSSM Ranking outperform the NSR Baseline. The DSSM Ranking performs comparably to SVM^{rank} when using only n-gram probabilities as features, and consistently leverages all features described in Section 2.3, outperforming all systems in accuracy, precision and changed ratio. We experimented with adding all features described in Section 2.3 to the baselines as well, however, we obtained no improvements compared to using only n-gram probability features.

We also tried running all ranking systems on selected candidates that best replace the target word in the input sentence. We follow the Unsupervised Boundary Ranking Substitution Selection method described in Paetzold and Specia (2017), which ranks candidates according to how well they fit the context of the target word, and discards 50% of the worst ranking candidates. The bottom part of the table 1 (Selection Step + Substitution Candidates Ranking) summarizes the results of all ranking systems after performing the selection step on generated substitution candidates. We obtain similar tendency in the results, with the DSSM Ranking outperforming both baselines. The results indicate the advantage of using a deep architecture,

and of building a semantic representation of the whole sentence on top of the characters. To illustrate by examples, Table 2 lists the top candidate ranked by the systems for different input sentences. In the examples, the DSSM Ranking correctly ranked a substitute for the target word, while the two baselines either left the target word unchanged, or ranked an incorrect substitute.

Input = "things continued on an **informal**, personal basis, by phone, I [remained] close friends with two of them, but Izzat al Gazawi died last year."	
NSR	informal
SVM^{rank}	cozy
DSSM Ranking	**casual**
Input = "perhaps the effect of West Nile Virus is sufficient to extinguish endemic birds already **severely** stressed by habitat losses."	
NSR	severely
SVM^{rank}	severely
DSSM Ranking	**seriously**

Table 2: Top candidate ranked by the systems for different input sentences. The word in bold is the word to be simplified. The word highlighted denotes a correct answer.

4 Conclusions

We presented an effective method for ranking in lexical simplification. We explored the application of a DSSM that builds a semantic representation of the whole sentence on top of characters. The DSSM can effectively capture fine-grained features to perform semantic matching when ranking substitution candidates, outperforming state-of-art approaches that use supervised machine learning to ranking in lexical simplification. For future work, we plan to examine and incorporate a larger feature set to the DSSM, as well as try other DSSM architectures, such as the Convolutional DSSM (C-DSSM) (Shen et al., 2014).

Acknowledgments

We thank Gustavo Paetzold and Kevin Duh for valuable help.

This work was supported by the Innovation and Technology Fund (Ref: ITS/132/15) of the Innovation and Technology Commission, the Government of the Hong Kong Special Administrative Region; and by CityU Internal Funds for ITF Projects (no. 9678104).

References

Joachim Bingel and Anders Søgaard. 2016. Text simplification as tree labeling. In *The 54th Annual Meeting of the Association for Computational Linguistics*, page 337.

Chris Burges, Tal Shaked, Erin Renshaw, Ari Lazier, Matt Deeds, Nicole Hamilton, and Greg Hullender. 2005. Learning to rank using gradient descent. In *Proceedings of the 22nd international conference on Machine learning*, pages 89–96. ACM.

Scott Deerwester, Susan T Dumais, George W Furnas, Thomas K Landauer, and Richard Harshman. 1990. Indexing by latent semantic analysis. *Journal of the American society for information science*, 41(6):391.

Siobhan Devlin and John Tait. 1998. The use of a psycholinguistic database in the simplification of text for aphasic readers. *Linguistic databases*, pages 161–173.

Hao Fang, Saurabh Gupta, Forrest Iandola, Rupesh K Srivastava, Li Deng, Piotr Dollár, Jianfeng Gao, Xiaodong He, Margaret Mitchell, John C Platt, et al. 2015. From captions to visual concepts and back. In *Proceedings of the IEEE Conference on Computer Vision and Pattern Recognition*, pages 1473–1482.

Jianfeng Gao, Xiaodong He, Wen-tau Yih, and Li Deng. 2014. Learning continuous phrase representations for translation modeling. In *ACL*. Citeseer.

Goran Glavaš and Sanja Štajner. 2015. Simplifying lexical simplification: Do we need simplified corpora? In *Proceedings of the 53rd Annual Meeting of the Association for Computational Linguistics and the 7th International Joint Conference on Natural Language Processing*, volume 2, pages 63–68.

Xiaodong He. 2016. Deep learning for natural language processing machine learning. In *"Machine Learning Summer School"*.

Colby Horn, Cathryn Manduca, and David Kauchak. 2014. Learning a lexical simplifier using wikipedia. In *ACL (2)*, pages 458–463.

Po-Sen Huang, Xiaodong He, Jianfeng Gao, Li Deng, Alex Acero, and Larry Heck. 2013. Learning deep structured semantic models for web search using clickthrough data. In *Proceedings of the 22nd ACM international conference on Conference on information & knowledge management*, pages 2333–2338. ACM.

Thorsten Joachims. 2006. Training linear svms in linear time. In *Proceedings of the 12th ACM SIGKDD international conference on Knowledge discovery and data mining*, pages 217–226. ACM.

David Kauchak. 2013. Improving text simplification language modeling using unsimplified text data. In *ACL (1)*, pages 1537–1546.

Yea-Seul Kim, Jessica Hullman, Matthew Burgess, and Eytan Adar. 2016. Simplescience: Lexical simplification of scientific terminology. In *Proceedings of the 2016 Conference on Empirical Methods in Natural Language Processing*, pages 1066–1071.

Diederik Kingma and Jimmy Ba. 2014. Adam: A method for stochastic optimization. *arXiv preprint arXiv:1412.6980*.

Xiaodong Liu, Jianfeng Gao, Xiaodong He, Li Deng, Kevin Duh, and Ye-Yi Wang. 2015. Representation learning using multi-task deep neural networks for semantic classification and information retrieval. In *HLT-NAACL*, pages 912–921.

G.H. Paetzold and Lucia Specia. 2017. Lexical simplification with neural ranking. In *EACL*, pages 34–40.

Gustavo Paetzold and Lucia Specia. 2015. Lexenstein: A framework for lexical simplification. In *ACL (System Demonstrations)*, pages 85–90.

Gustavo H Paetzold and Lucia Specia. 2016a. Unsupervised lexical simplification for non-native speakers. In *Proceedings of the Thirtieth AAAI Conference on Artificial Intelligence*, pages 3761–3767. AAAI Press.

Gustavo Henrique Paetzold and Lucia Specia. 2016b. Benchmarking lexical simplification systems. *Proceedings of the 10th LREC*.

David E Rumelhart, Geoffrey E Hinton, and Ronald J Williams. 1988. Learning representations by back-propagating errors. *Cognitive modeling*, 5(3):1.

Yelong Shen, Xiaodong He, Jianfeng Gao, Li Deng, and Grégoire Mesnil. 2014. "learning semantic representations using convolutional neural networks for web search". In *"Proceedings of the 23rd International Conference on World Wide Web"*, pages "373–374". "ACM".

Wei Xu, Chris Callison-Burch, and Courtney Napoles. 2015. Problems in current text simplification research: New data can help. *Transactions of the Association for Computational Linguistics*, 3:283–297.

Wen-tau Yih, Xiaodong He, and Christopher Meek.
2014. Semantic parsing for single-relation question
answering. In *ACL (2)*, pages 643–648. Citeseer.

Proofread Sentence Generation as Multi-Task Learning with Editing Operation Prediction

Yuta Hitomi[1]   Hideaki Tamori[1]   Naoaki Okazaki[2]   Kentaro Inui[3]
[1] Media Lab, The Asahi Shimbun Company
[2] Tokyo Institute of Technology
[3] Tohoku University, RIKEN Center Advanced Intelligence Project
{hitomi-y1, tamori-h}@asahi.com, okazaki@c.titech.ac.jp
inui@ecei.tohoku.ac.jp

Abstract

This paper explores the idea of *robot editors*, automated proofreaders that enable journalists to improve the quality of their articles. We propose a novel neural model of multi-task learning that both generates proofread sentences and predicts the editing operations required to rewrite the source sentences and create the proofread ones. The model is trained using logs of the revisions made professional editors revising draft newspaper articles written by journalists. Experiments demonstrate the effectiveness of our multi-task learning approach and the potential value of using revision logs for this task.

1 Introduction

There is growing research interest in automatic sentence generation (Vinyals et al., 2015; Rush et al., 2015; Sordoni et al., 2015). Coincidentally (or inevitably), media companies have increasingly attempted to create *robot journalists* that can automatically generate content, mostly using data from limited domains (e.g., earthquakes, sports and stockmarkets) (Clerwall, 2014; Carlson, 2015; Dorr, 2016). In this paper, we explore the idea of *robot editors*, i.e., automated proofreaders that enable journalists to improve the quality of their articles.

The most closely related field to the topic of this paper is grammatical error correction (Dale and Kilgarriff, 2011; Dale et al., 2012; Ng et al., 2013, 2014). However, this task handles only grammatical errors, whereas proofreading encompasses a variety of tasks:grammatical error correction (GEC), spell checks, simplification, fact checking, standardization, compression, paraphrasing, etc. Another task, the automated evaluation of sci-entific writing shared task (Daudaravicius et al., 2016), has the goal of automatically evaluating scientific writing. The focus of this shared task was the binary classification problem of detecting sentences that need improvement. Although the corpus used contained qualitative improvements, the shared task did not tackle high-quality sentence generation.

This paper investigates the task of proofread sentence generation (PSG) using logs of the revisions made by professional editors to draft newspaper articles written by journalists. The goal of this research is to explore a computational model for improving text quality. To this end, we propose a novel multi-task learning approach that both generates proofread sentences and predicts the editing operations involved in rewriting the source sentences to create the proofread ones.

The contributions of this research are three-folds: (i) This is the first study to explore an encoderdecoder architecture for PSG. (ii) We show that our proposed multi-task learning method can outperform a state-of-the-art baseline method for GEC. (iii) We also examine the benefits and issues of using revision logs for PSG.

2 Method

Given a source sentence (sequence of words) $x_1, \cdots, x_m$, this study addresses the task of generating the proofread sentence $y_1, \cdots, y_n$, where m and n denote the number of words in the source and proofread sentences, respectively. Usually, proofreading does not change the content of the input text significantly, and changes only small parts of the text. Thus, detecting source sentence spans that require revision is an important PSG sub-task. This paper explores a multi-task learning approach that both generates proofread sentences and predicts the editing operations required.

Proceedings of the The 8th International Joint Conference on Natural Language Processing, pages 436–441,
Taipei, Taiwan, November 27 – December 1, 2017 ©2017 AFNLP

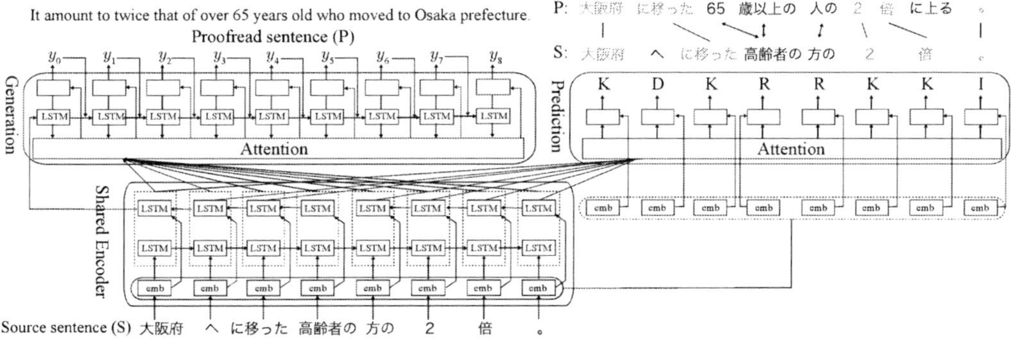

Figure 1: Overview of the neural network model for generating proofread sentences and predicting editing operations via multi-task learning. Boxes labeled 'emb' denote word embeddings.

Inspired by work on multi-task learning in neural networks, we implement multi-task learning as an end-to-end neural network with a shared source sentence encoder (Figure 1). The network generates proofread sentences and predicts editing operations.Although these two tasks solve the same problem, we believe that these two neural network models focus on different aspects of the data. The generation model considers the source sentence as a whole (although it may also include an attention mechanism), whereas the prediction model looks at the local contexts of words in order to correct functional word usage, incorrect spellings, and so on. This is why we have designed the proposed method using a multi-task learning approach.

2.1 Generating proofread sentences using an encoderdecoder model with attention

Following recent work on GEC (Yuan and Briscoe, 2016), we use an encoder-decoder model with global attention (Luong et al., 2015) to generate proofread sentences. We use bi-directional Long Short-Term Memory (LSTM) to encode the source sentences. LSTMs recurrently compute the memory and hidden vectors at time step $s \in \{1, \cdots, m\}$ using those at time step $s - 1$ or $s + 1$ and the word x_s in the source sentence, as follows:

$$[\overrightarrow{h}_s; \overrightarrow{c}_s] = \overrightarrow{\mathrm{LSTM}}(x_s, [\overrightarrow{h}_{s-1}; \overrightarrow{c}_{s-1}]), \quad (1)$$

$$[\overleftarrow{h}_s; \overleftarrow{c}_s] = \overleftarrow{\mathrm{LSTM}}(x_s, [\overleftarrow{h}_{s+1}; \overleftarrow{c}_{s+1}]). \quad (2)$$

Here, c_s and h_s represent the memory and hidden vectors, respectively, at time step s. The encoder output is a concatenation of the hidden vectors:

$$\widetilde{h}_s = [\overrightarrow{h}_s; \overleftarrow{h}_s]. \quad (3)$$

The decoder computes the memory and hidden vectors at time step $t \in \{1, \cdots, n\}$ using those at time step $t - 1$ and the (predicted) word w_t as follows:

$$[h_t; c_t] = \overrightarrow{\mathrm{LSTM}}(w_t, [h_{t-1}; c_{t-1}]). \quad (4)$$

Here, we set $h_0 = \overleftarrow{h}_1$ and $c_0 = 0^1$. For $t > 1$, we feed the y_{t-1} predicted at the previous time step back as the input word w_t of the decoder.

The decoder predicts the word y_t at time step t using a softmax layer on top of the vector $\bar{h}_t$ with an integrated attention mechanism:

$$\log p(y|x) = \sum_{n=1}^{t} \log p(y_t|y_{<t}, \boldsymbol{x}), \quad (5)$$

$$p(y_t|\boldsymbol{y}_{<t}, \boldsymbol{x}) = \mathrm{softmax}(\boldsymbol{W}_o\bar{h}_t), \quad (6)$$

$$\bar{h}_t = \tanh(\boldsymbol{W}_r[\boldsymbol{v}_t; h_t]), \quad (7)$$

$$\boldsymbol{v}_t = \sum_s \alpha_t(s)\widetilde{h}_s, \quad (8)$$

$$\alpha_t(s) = \frac{\exp(h_t^\intercal \boldsymbol{W}_a \widetilde{h}_s)}{\sum_{s'} \exp(h_t^\intercal \boldsymbol{W}_a \widetilde{h}_{s'})}. \quad (9)$$

Here, $\boldsymbol{v}_t$ represents a vector computed by the attention mechanism at time step t, and $\alpha_t(s)$ is an attention score computed at decoding time step t by looking at the source word at encoding time step s.

---

[1] The reason for using $\overleftarrow{h}_1$ instead of $\widetilde{h}_1$ is to speed up training by reducing the dimensionality of the vectors in the decoder.

2.2 Editing-operation prediction as a sequential labeling task

In addition to performing sentence revision, we propose to simultaneously undertake an additional task: *editing-operation prediction*. Formally, given a source sentence $x_1, \cdots, x_m$, this task predicts the sequence of editing operations $z_1, \cdots, z_m$ required to obtain the revised sentence $y_1, \cdots, y_n$, where each editing operation z_i keeps (K), deletes (D), inserts (I), or replaces (R) the word x_i. This task resembles grammatical error detection.

As explained in Section 3.1, the revision logs do not provide supervised training data for the editing operations, only pairs of source and proofread sentences. We therefore created pseudo supervised training data by running the `diff` program on the word sequences of the source and proofread sentences. There are cases where multiple sequences of primitive editing-operations can be derived from a pair of sentences. The performance may be improved if the best operation sequence. However, we leave this direction out of scope of this paper. To obtain an editing-operation sequence that was the same length as the source sentence (m), we labeled I labels to the words immediately following the positions where the actual insert operations were required.

We reuse the vector $\tilde{h}_s$ for word x_s in the source sentence (Equation 3) to predict z_s:

$$\log p(z|x) = \sum_{s=1}^{m} \log p(z_s|z_{<s}, \boldsymbol{x}), \qquad (10)$$

$$p(z_s|\boldsymbol{z}_{<s}, \boldsymbol{x}) = \text{softmax}(\boldsymbol{W}_l \tanh(\tilde{\boldsymbol{h}}_i)). \quad (11)$$

Liu and Liu (2016) proposed a grammatical error detection method that considers intra-attention. We also explored this approach by replacing the softmax function in Equation 11 with the following one:

$$p(z_s|\boldsymbol{z}_{<s}, \boldsymbol{x}) = \text{softmax}(\boldsymbol{W}_l \bar{\boldsymbol{u}}_t) \quad (12)$$

$$\bar{\boldsymbol{u}}_t = \tanh(\boldsymbol{W}_s[\boldsymbol{x}_t; \boldsymbol{u}_t]) \quad (13)$$

$$\boldsymbol{u}_s = \sum_i \beta_s(i)\tilde{\boldsymbol{h}}_s \quad (14)$$

$$\beta_s(i) = \frac{\exp(\tilde{\boldsymbol{h}}_s^{\mathsf{T}}\tilde{\boldsymbol{h}}_i)}{\sum_{i'} \exp(\tilde{\boldsymbol{h}}_s^{\mathsf{T}}\tilde{\boldsymbol{h}}_{i'})} \quad (15)$$

Here, $\boldsymbol{u}_s$ represents a vector computed by the attention mechanism at time step s, and $\beta_s(i)$ is an attention score computed at time step s by looking at the source word at time step $i \in \{1, \cdots, m\}$.

Dataset	# changed	# unchanged	# total
Train	710,540	1,317,260	2,027,800
Validation	63,062	96,938	160,000
Test	458	642	1,100

Table 1: The Numbers of instances in each dataset.

2.3 Training

Given a training dataset $\mathcal{D}$, we minimize the following multi-task learning loss function:

$$-\sum_{(x,y,z)\in\mathcal{D}} \{\log p(y|x) + \log p(z|x)\}. \quad (16)$$

We also consider a loss function that weights the sub-task loss (Zhang et al., 2014):

$$-\sum_{(x,y,z)\in\mathcal{D}} \{\log p(y|x) + \lambda \log p(z|x)\}. \quad (17)$$

Here, λ ($0 \leq \lambda \leq 1$) denotes the weight given to the editing-operation prediction errors, learned through gradient descent. In contrast to conventional multi-task learning, which maximizes performance for all tasks, our primary goal is to optimize the main task which is why we have created a loss function that weights the sub-task differently.

3 Experiments

3.1 Dataset

We used a corpus of Japanese newspaper articles where professional editors at a media company had rewritten draft articles (written by journalists) to create proofread (published) (Tamori et al., 2017). The dataset consists of 2,209,249 sentence pairs in total: 810,227 pairs were changed during the revision process, and 1,399,022 pairs were left unchanged. To focus on revisions within sentence boundaries, we excluded revisions involving sentence splitting or merging. This dataset reflects the real work done by the company to improve the quality of its newspaper articles. The revisions came in a variety of forms, from syntactic changes, such as GEC and spelling normalization to content-level changes, such as elaboration and fact checking. Table 1 shows the number of instances in the training, validation, and test sets.

We split the sentences into words using SentencePiece[2] to efficiently reduce the vocabulary

---

[2] https://github.com/google/sentencepiece
SentencePiece is an unsupervised text tokenizer.

Dataset	Model	GLEU	Prec	Recall	$F_{0.5}(M^2)$	WER	BLEU
All pairs	Gen	70.14	*	*	*	24.90	74.02
	Gen + Pred	70.47	*	*	*	24.23	**75.37**
	Gen + Pred Attn	**70.68**	*	*	*	**23.90**	74.48
	Gen + Pred Attn + W	70.57	*	*	*	37.24	54.76
Changed pairs	Gen	67.74	22.27	6.12	14.23	36.74	64.23
	Gen + Pred	68.10	23.14	5.59	13.37	35.67	**66.29**
	Gen + Pred Attn	**68.63**	24.89	6.28	14.84	**35.55**	65.31
	Gen + Pred Attn + W	67.01	**36.59**	**13.30**	**26.59**	48.91	45.82
Unchanged pairs	Gen	86.72	*	*	*	16.47	82.69
	Gen + Pred	87.34	*	*	*	**15.51**	**83.33**
	Gen + Pred Attn	**87.44**	*	*	*	16.17	82.51
	Gen + Pred Attn + W	87.27	*	*	*	28.94	62.66

Table 2: Performance of the proposed and baseline methods. The asterisks '*' indicate performance values that are unavailable because the precision and recall for unchanged pairs are always 0 and 100.

size. We used proofread sentences (published newspaper articles) to train SentencePiece. Vocabulary sizes for the input and output layers were 32,661 and 32,630, respectively. Our model can be trained without unknown words.

3.2 Experimental setup

The batch size was set to 100 and, improve computational efficiency, each batch consisted of sentences of the same length. The dimensionality of the distributed representations (word embeddings and hidden states) to was 300. The model parameters were trained using Adam. Following Jozefowicz et al. (2015), forget gate bias was initialized to 1.0, and the other gate biases were initialized to 0. In addition, we used dropout (at a rate of 0.2) for the LSTMs. Breadth-first search was used for decoding, with a beam width of 10 (Yuan, 2017).

Six measures were utilized to evaluate the performance of the PSG model: GLEU (Napoles et al., 2015)[3], precision, recall, M^2 score (Dahlmeier and Ng, 2012), Word Error Rate (WER) (Jurafsky and Martin, 2008), and BLEU (Papineni et al., 2002). These measures are often used in GEC and machine translation research. Note that the precision, recall, and M^2 score measures excluded words appearing in both the source and proofread sentences from evaluation (Dahlmeier and Ng, 2012).

3.3 Results

Table 2 shows the performance of the proposed method according to the above metrics. Two vari-

ants of the proposed method were used: "Gen + Pred" used Equation 11 (without the attention mechanism for predicting edit operations), whereas "Gen + Pred Attn" used Equation 12 (with the attention mechanism), and "Gen + Pred Attn + W" used Equations 12 and 17 (weighting the sub-task losses). For comparison, we also report the performance of a baseline method "Gen" used only an encoder-decoder model (described in Section 2.1) without multi-task learning.

The multi-task learning models outperformed the baseline encoder-decoder model for all metrics. The use of intra-attention for predicting editing-operations was also effective, except for the BLEU metric and the WER for unchanged pairs. Unlike BLEU, GLEU includes a mechanism for penalizing incorrect 'reluctant' revisions (copying words from the source sentences) and rewarding correct 'aggressive' revision (adding words that do not appear in the source sentences). We can therefore infer that "Gen + Pred with Attn" model was more aggressive in changing words in the source sentences than "Gen + Pred" model.

The table also shows the models' performances for changed/unchanged sentence pairs. As expected, the performance metrics for unchanged pairs are higher than those for changed pairs. The low recall values for changed pairs indicate that it is difficult to predict words that do not appear in the source sentences.

However, we can see that weighting sub-task losses improved precision, recall, and M^2 score performance. We believe that active proofreading performance improved because of not over-

---

[3]The hyperparameter λ of GLEU was set to 1.

learning the sub-task. That said, the other metrics decreased because the model made changes in many places where no editing was required.

3.4 Discussion

In this section, we discuss issues with the presented method and dataset. The presented method was not good at inserting words, particularly when the editor had appended new information to the sentence, as in the following example.

- **Source**: Soon it will have been six months since the law was established.

- **Proofread**: *On the 19th,* it will have been six months since the law was established *last September.*

It is difficult for a computational model to insert the phrases "on the 19th" and "last September". We found that 132 of the 366 changed pairs (28.8%) in the test set included new information. Although this kind of editing improves the quality of the article, it is unrealistic to handle this situation using an encoder-decoder model. It may be useful to separate these pairs from the dataset in future.

We also observed instances in which editors merged pieces of information from multiple sentences, particularly so as to yield more concise sentences, as in the following example.

- **Source**: A meeting where people who heve lost their families to cancer discuss ... .There are ten members in their 30s to 70s *who have lost their families to cancer.*

- **Proofread**: A meeting where people who have lost their families to cancer discuss ... .There are ten members in their 30s to 70s.

As a result, it may be worth exploring not only discarding instances where additional information has been added to the proofread sentences but also building a model that considers other sentences appearing near the source sentence.

We also noticed cases where the sentences output by the model provide good revisions but did not match to the reference sentences, such as the following.

- **Source**: The reserve players tackle it frantically *so they won't* miss the chance.

- **Proofread**: The reserve players tackle it frantically *so as not to* miss *the* opportunity.

- **System output**: The reserve players tackle it frantically *so as not to* miss *the chance.*

As has often been discussed in the literature on machine translation, summarization, and GEC, establishing a good evaluation metric is an ongoing research issue.

4 Conclusion

In this paper, we have presented a novel multi-task learning approach for combined PGS and editing-operation prediction. Experimental results show that our approach was able to outperform the baseline for all metrics. The experiments also show that newspaper article revision logs can provide promising supervised training data for the model. We plan to continue exploring ways of creating good-quality articles in the future.

Acknowledgments

We thank the anonymous reviewers for their suggestions. We also thank Takafumi Ochiai and Yosuke Fukada for their contribution to storing the dataset.

References

Matt Carlson. The robotic reporter. *Digital Journalism*, 3(3):416–431, 2015.

Christer Clerwall. Enter the robot journalist. *Journalism Practice*, 8(5):519–531, 2014.

Daniel Dahlmeier and Hwee Tou Ng. Better evaluation for grammatical error correction. In *Proceedings of the 2012 Conference of the North American Chapter of the Association for Computational Linguistics: Human Language Technologies (NAACL 2012)*, pages 568–572, 2012.

Robert Dale and Adam Kilgarriff. Helping our own: The HOO 2011 pilot shared task. In *Proceedings of the 13th European Workshop on Natural Language Generation (ENLG 2011)*, pages 242–249, 2011.

Robert Dale, Ilya Anisimoff, and George Narroway. HOO 2012: A report on the preposition and determiner error correction shared task. In *Proceedings of the Seventh Workshop on Building Educational Applications Using NLP*, pages 54–62, 2012.

Vidas Daudaravicius, Rafael E Banchs, Elena Volodina, and Courtney Napoles. A report on the automatic evaluation of scientific writing shared task. In *Proceedings of the 11th Workshop on Innovative*

Use of NLP for Building Educational Applications, pages 53–62, 2016.

Konstantin Nicholas Dorr. Mapping the field of algorithmic journalism. *Digital Journalism*, 4(6):700–722, 2016.

Rafal Jozefowicz, Wojciech Zaremba, and Ilya Sutskever. An empirical exploration of recurrent network architectures. In *Proceedings of the 32nd International Conference on Machine Learning (ICML-15)*, pages 2342–2350, 2015.

Daniel Jurafsky and James H. Martin. *Speech and Language Processing : an introduction to natural language processing, computational linguistics, and speech recognition*. Prentice Hall, 2008.

Zhuoran Liu and Yang Liu. Exploiting unlabeled data for neural grammatical error detection. *CoRR*, abs/1611.08987, 2016.

Minh-Thang Luong, Hieu Pham, and Christopher D. Manning. Effective approaches to attention-based neural machine translation. In *Proceedings of the 2015 Conference on Empirical Methods in Natural Language Processing (EMNLP 2015)*, pages 1412–1421, 2015.

Courtney Napoles, Keisuke Sakaguchi, Matt Post, and Joel Tetreault. Ground truth for grammatical error correction metrics. In *Proceedings of the 53rd Annual Meeting of the Association for Computational Linguistics and the 7th International Joint Conference on Natural Language Processing (ACL-IJCNLP 2015)*, pages 588–593, 2015.

Hwee Tou Ng, Yuanbin Wu, and Christian Hadiwinoto. The CoNLL-2013 shared task on grammatical error correction. In *Proceedings of the Seventeenth Conference on Computational Natural Language Learning: Shared Task (CoNLL Shared Task 2013)*, pages 1–12, 2013.

Hwee Tou Ng, Siew Mei Wu, Ted Briscoe, Christian Hadiwinoto, Raymond Hendy Susanto, and Christopher Bryant. The CoNLL-2014 shared task on grammatical error correction. In *Proceedings of the Eighteenth Conference on Computational Natural Language Learning: Shared Task (CoNLL Shared Task 2014)*, pages 1–14, 2014.

Kishore Papineni, Salim Roukos, Todd Ward, and Wei-Jing Zhu. BLEU: a method for automatic evaluation of machine translation. In *Proceedings of 40th Annual Meeting of the Association for Computational Linguistics (ACL 2002)*, pages 311–318, 2002.

Alexander M. Rush, Sumit Chopra, and Jason Weston. A neural attention model for abstractive sentence summarization. In *Proceedings of the 2015 Conference on Empirical Methods in Natural Language Processing (EMNLP 2015)*, pages 379–389, 2015.

Alessandro Sordoni, Michel Galley, Michael Auli, Chris Brockett, Yangfeng Ji, Margaret Mitchell, Jian-Yun Nie, Jianfeng Gao, and Bill Dolan. A neural network approach to context-sensitive generation of conversational responses. In *Proceedings of the 2015 Conference of the North American Chapter of the Association for Computational Linguistics: Human Language Technologies*, pages 196–205, Denver, Colorado, May–June 2015. Association for Computational Linguistics.

Hideaki Tamori, Yuta Hitomi, Naoaki Okazaki, and Kentaro Inui. Analyzing the revision logs of a japanese newspaper for article quality assessment. In *Proceedings of the 2017 EMNLP Workshop: Natural Language Processing meets Journalism*, pages 46–50, Copenhagen, Denmark, September 2017. Association for Computational Linguistics.

Oriol Vinyals, Alexander Toshev, Samy Bengio, and Dumitru Erhan. Show and tell: A neural image caption generator. In *the IEEE Conference on Computer Vision and Pattern Recognition (CVPR 2015)*, 2015.

Zheng Yuan. Grammatical error correction in nonnative English. Technical Report 904, University of Cambridge, Computer Laboratory, 2017.

Zheng Yuan and Ted Briscoe. Grammatical error correction using neural machine translation. In *Proceedings of the 2016 Conference of the North American Chapter of the Association for Computational Linguistics: Human Language Technologies (NAACL-HLT 2016)*, pages 380–386, 2016.

Zhanpeng Zhang, Ping Luo, Chen Change Loy, and Xiaoou Tang. Facial landmark detection by deep multi-task learning. In *European Conference on Computer Vision*, pages 94–108. Springer, 2014.

An Exploration of Data Augmentation and RNN Architectures for Question Ranking in Community Question Answering

Charles Chen
School of EECS
Ohio University
Athens, OH 45701
lc971015@ohio.edu

Razvan Bunescu
School of EECS
Ohio University
Athens, OH 45701
bunescu@ohio.edu

Abstract

The automation of tasks in community question answering (cQA) is dominated by machine learning approaches, whose performance is often limited by the number of training examples. Starting from a neural sequence learning approach with attention, we explore the impact of two data augmentation techniques on question ranking performance: a method that swaps reference questions with their paraphrases, and training on examples automatically selected from external datasets. Both methods are shown to lead to substantial gains in accuracy over a strong baseline. Further improvements are obtained by changing the model architecture to mirror the structure seen in the data.

1 Introduction

Community question answering (cQA) is an information seeking paradigm in which users ask questions and contribute answers on a dedicated website that facilitates quality-based ranking and retrieval of contributed content. The questions posted on a QA website range from very general (e.g. Yahoo! Answers), to topic-specific, such as programming languages (e.g. Stack Overflow) or relevant for a geographical area (e.g. Qatar Living). An important task in cQA is that of question retrieval, wherein questions that have already been answered on the website are ranked with respect to how well their answers match the information need expressed in a new question. Numerous approaches to question retrieval, question ranking, or question-question similarity have been proposed over the last decade, of which (Xue et al., 2008; Bernhard and Gurevych, 2008; Duan et al., 2008; Cao et al., 2009; Wang et al., 2009; Bunescu

and Huang, 2010; Zhou et al., 2011) are just a few. Very recently, question-question similarity has received renewed interest as a subtask in the SemEval cQA evaluation exercise (Nakov et al., 2016). In this paper, we approach question ranking in a context where the input is restricted to the question text and describe data augmentation methods and RNN architectures that are empirically shown to improve ranking performance. We expect these ideas to also benefit more comprehensive approaches, such as the SemEval cQA exercise, which exploit answers and comments associated with previously answered questions.

2 Ranking Model with Attention

Following the notation of Bunescu and Huang (2010), we use $\langle Q_i \succ Q_j | Q_r \rangle$ to denote that the answer to question Q_i is expected to be more useful than the answer to Q_j in terms of satisfying the information need expressed in Q_r. If $\langle Q_i \succ Q_j | Q_r \rangle$, then the question ranking system is expected to rank Q_i higher than Q_j, through a scoring function $s(Q_r, Q)$ that is trained to capture how relevant Q is to Q_r. Training and evaluating the scoring function requires a dataset of ranking triples $\langle Q_i \succ Q_j | Q_r \rangle$. Ranking triples are usually introduced implicitly by annotating questions into 3 major categories: paraphrases ($\mathcal{P}$), useful ($\mathcal{U}$), and neutral ($\mathcal{N}$). A paraphrasing question $Q_p \in \mathcal{P}$ is semantically equivalent with or very close to the reference question. A question $Q_u \in \mathcal{U}$ is deemed useful or relevant if its answer is expected to overlap in information content with the answer of the reference question, whereas the answer of a neutral or irrelevant question $Q_n \in \mathcal{N}$ should be irrelevant for the reference question. Correspondingly, the following relations are assumed to hold: $\langle Q_p \succ Q_u | Q_r \rangle$, i.e. a *paraphrasing* question is more useful than a *useful* question;

Proceedings of the The 8th International Joint Conference on Natural Language Processing, pages 442–447,
Taipei, Taiwan, November 27 – December 1, 2017 ©2017 AFNLP

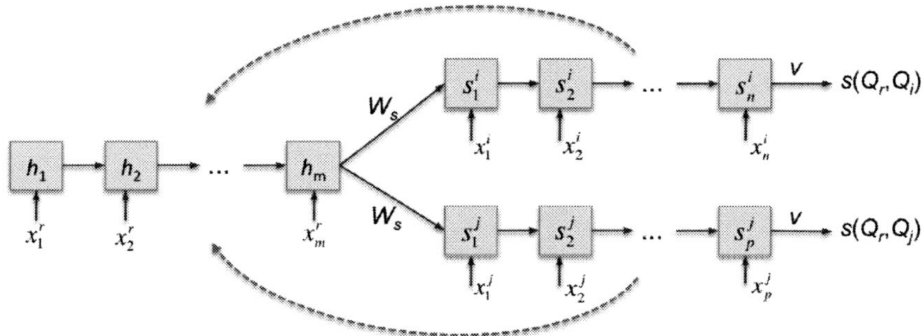

Figure 1: Neural sequence learning with attention (SLA) model for question ranking.

$\langle Q_u \succ Q_n | Q_r \rangle$, i.e. a *useful* question is more useful than a *neutral* question; and by transitivity $\langle Q_p \succ Q_n | Q_r \rangle$. The resulting triples can be used for training and evaluating the scoring function $s(Q_r, Q)$ using a ranking objective, which is the approach taken in this paper. An alternative is to use a binary classification objective by considering only two categories of questions, e.g. relevant ($P \cup U$) and irrelevant (N), as was done in SemEval. However, by ignoring the difference in utility between paraphrases and useful questions during training, a binary classification approach is likely to underperform a ranking approach that is trained on all the ranking triples implied by the original 3 categories of questions.

To compute the ranking function $s(Q_r, Q)$, we use neural sequence learning with attention (SLA), as illustrated in Figure 1. Neural networks with attention have been successful used in a wide variety of tasks, ranging from image classification and dynamic visual control (Mnih et al., 2014), to machine translation (Bahdanau et al., 2015) and image caption generation (Xu et al., 2015). Very recently, the SLA approach was used for semantic entailment (Rocktschel et al., 2015) and cQA tasks (Mohtarami et al., 2016), although still with an objective (e.g., cross entropy) aimed at classification. The questions Q_r and Q are processed sequentially, using for each a separate RNN with gated recurrent units (GRU) (Cho et al., 2014). Following the notation of Bahdanau et al. (2015), the states s_t corresponding to positions t in question Q are computed recursively as follows:

$$s_t = (1 - z_t) \circ s_{t-1} + z_t \circ \hat{s}_t \tag{1}$$
$$\hat{s}_t = \tanh(Wx_t + U(r_t \circ s_{t-1}) + [Cc_t])$$
$$r_t = \sigma(W_r x_t + U_r s_{t-1} + [C_r c_t])$$
$$z_t = \sigma(W_z x_t + U_z s_{t-1} + [C_z c_t])$$

The states h_t for the reference question Q_r are computed using the same equations, but with different parameters and without the attention terms shown between brackets. The initial state $h_0 = 0$, whereas $s_0 = \tanh(W_s h_m)$ is computed as a normalized linear transformation of the last state h_m. Words are mapped to their word2vec embeddings x_t, pre-trained on Google News (Mikolov et al., 2013). States s_t require a context vector c_t, to be computed with the attention model below:

$$c_t = \sum_{j=1}^{m} \alpha_{tj} * h_j \,, \text{ where } \alpha_{tj} = \frac{exp(e_{tj})}{\sum_{k=1}^{m} exp(e_{tk})} \tag{2}$$
$$e_{tj} = a(s_{t-1}, h_j) = v_a^T \tanh(W_a s_{t-1} + U_a h_j)$$

The score $s(Q_r, Q) = v^T s_n$ is computed as a linear combination of the RNN state corresponding to the last word in Q. Given a set of training triples $\langle Q_i, Q_j | Q_r \rangle$, the model parameters are trained to optimize the margin-based ranking criterion shown in Equation 3.

$$J(\theta) = \sum_{Q_i > Q_j | Q_r} max \{0, \gamma - s(Q_r, Q_i) + s(Q_r, Q_j)\} \tag{3}$$

3 Data Augmentation

Supervised ML approaches are often limited by the number of available training examples. Using the SLA approach described in Section 2, we explore the impact of two data augmentation techniques for question ranking: a novel method that swaps reference questions with their paraphrases, and training on examples from external datasets.

3.1 Question Swapping

Since paraphrases are semantically equivalent with or very close to the reference questions, during *training* we swap each paraphrase question with the reference question, and generate additional ranking triples of the type $\langle Q_r \succ Q_u | Q_p \rangle$, $\langle Q_u \succ Q_n | Q_p \rangle$, and $\langle Q_r \succ Q_n | Q_p \rangle$. We emphasize that question swapping is done only for the groups of questions used for training; the development and test triples are kept the same. Paraphrase questions are seldom entirely equivalent with the reference question. Consequently, when question swapping is used to augment the training examples, it will inevitably introduce some noise.

3.2 External Datasets

Another approach to increasing the size of the training set is by adding examples from other datasets. Table 1 shows the datasets used in the experiments in this paper, together with statistics such as the number of questions groups and the total number of questions in each category. The DRLM dataset was introduced by Zhang et al. (2016) and, like Complex, contains questions posted on Yahoo! Answers. However it does not contain paraphrases and thus cannot benefit from question swapping. The SemEval dataset (Nakov et al., 2016) was created from questions posted on the Qatar Living forum and has a different distribution and structure. In particular, a question has two fields: a body containing the actual question and a subject. The body field often contains multiple sentences. In the experiments reported in Sec-

Dataset	Groups	$\mathcal{P}$	$\mathcal{U}$	$\mathcal{N}$	Triples
Complex	60	89	730	714	9979
Simple	60	134	778	621	10436
SemEval	387	372	1148	2333	7247
– Train	267	232	841	1581	4984
– Devel	50	59	155	285	1002
– Test	70	81	152	467	1261
DRLM	1478	0	6434	7747	27111

Table 1: Datasets & Statistics.

tion 4, DRLM is used as an external dataset for training Complex and SemEval question ranking models.

3.2.1 Weighted External Data

External triples can be very different from target triples in terms of vocabulary, syntactic structure, or length. As such, considering external triples as being equally important as target triples during training can be detrimental to the target performance. To alleviate this effect, we introduce a tunable weight hyperparameter $\alpha \in [0, 1]$ such that target triples get a weight of α in the objective

function, whereas external triples are assigned a weight of $1 - \alpha$, both normalized by the number of training triples in the target ($\mathcal{T}$) and external ($\mathcal{E}$) datasets, respectively.

$$J(\theta) = \frac{\alpha}{|\mathcal{T}|} J_\mathcal{T}(\theta) + \frac{(1 - \alpha)}{|\mathcal{E}|} J_\mathcal{E}(\theta) \tag{4}$$

The overall objective function is shown in Equation 4, where $J_\mathcal{T}$ and $J_\mathcal{E}$ are defined using the margin-based ranking criterion from Equation 3 on the corresponding dataset.

3.2.2 Selection with Language Models

To further alleviate the potential detrimental effects due to possibly significant lexical and syntactic differences between external and target triples, we train a character-aware neural language model (LM) (Kim et al., 2016) on the set of questions from the target question groups used for training and rank all external questions in ascending order, based on the perplexity computed by the target LM. We introduce a tunable proportion hyperparameter γ and select to add only the $\gamma|\mathcal{T}|$ triples that can be obtained from the top ranked external questions. This procedure enables the selection of triples with external questions that are most LM-similar with the target training questions, akin to the approach proposed by Moore and Lewis (2010) for selecting external text segments for training language models. LM-based data augmentation was also shown to benefit domain adaptation for tasks such as temporal expression recognition (Kolomiyets et al., 2011) and semantic role labeling (Ngoc Do et al., 2015).

4 Experimental Evaluation

We evaluate the baseline SLA approach on the Simple and Complex datasets introduced in (Bunescu and Huang, 2010) and compare against their SVM approach which uses a number of manually engineered features, such as similarities between focus words (tagged by another SVM), similarities between main verbs, and matchings between dependency graphs anchored at focus words. The 60 groups of questions in each dataset are partitioned into 12 folds and at each cross-validation iteration 10 folds are used for training, 1 for development and 1 for testing. This is repeated 12 times such that each fold gets to be used for testing, and the results are pooled over all folds. The SLA model is trained with AdaDelta using minibatches of size 256, and regularized using early stopping on the validation fold. Table 2 shows the triple-level accuracies i.e. the percentage of ranking triples $\langle Q_i \succ Q_j | Q_r \rangle$ for which $s(Q_r, Q_i) > s(Q_r, Q_j)$. The results show that the

Complex		Simple	
SVM	SLA	SVM	SLA
82.5	**85.6**	82.1	**85.8**

Table 2: SLA baseline accuracy vs. SVM.

SLA model is a strong baseline, as it outperforms the SVM approach of Bunescu and Huang (2010) that uses explicit syntactic and focus information.

Dataset	Triples	Accuracy
Complex	9979	85.6
+ swaps	23296	**86.5**
SemEval	4984	87.6
+ swaps	8606	**89.1**

Table 3: Accuracy, w/ or w/o swaps in training.

Table 3 shows the impact of question swapping on the Complex and SemEval datasets, following the official training vs. test split for SemEval. Table 4 shows the impact of adding the entire external dataset DRLM to the Complex and SemEval training examples, with and without swaps. Due to the time consuming nature of cross-validation, for the Complex dataset we chose to test only on 1 fold, using 10 folds as training and 1 fold as validation. Since 10 training folds amount to 50 groups of questions, we call it Complex$_{50}$. We also evaluated the impact of adding examples from Simple when training on Complex. The test and validation datasets are never augmented with examples generated from swaps or external datasets. External examples helped substantially on Complex, which benefited from DRLM more than from Simple, likely because DRLM's question groups are many and diverse, whereas Simple contains the same groups as Complex, but with different questions selected as reference. Combining the two augmentation methods resulted in further improvements for Complex.

However, using all DRLM examples hurt SemEval performance, which was not surprising given the substantial difference between SemEval and DRLM questions. Consequently, we ran an additional evaluation in which we combined the weighted scheme from Section 3.2.1 with the LM-based selection from Section 3.2.2. To tune the

Dataset	Triples	Accuracy
Complex$_{50}$	8387	80.9
+ Simple	17084	**86.8**
+ DRLM	35498	**88.9**
+ swaps	19278	84.6
+ Simple + swaps	43891	**87.3**
+ DRLM + swaps	46389	**92.1**
SemEval	4984	87.6
+ DRLM	32137	86.2
+ swaps	8606	**89.1**

Table 4: Accuracy on Complex and SemEval, w/ and w/o training on external examples or swaps.

weight α and the proportion γ we used grid search on the development data, where α was selected from $\{0.50, 0.70, 0.85, 1.0\}$ and γ was selected from consecutive powers of 2 starting from 0.5 until the proportion exhausted all external triples. Table 5 shows the result of using weighted and LM-selected external triples, on both small (10 groups for Complex, 50 groups for SemEval) and big (all 50 groups for Complex, all 267 groups for SemEval) target datasets. The results now show

Dataset	Triples	Accuracy
Complex$_{10}$	1562	73.1
+ DRLM ($\alpha = 0.85, \gamma = 16$)	26554	**87.8**
Complex$_{50}$	8387	80.9
+ DRLM ($\alpha = 0.70, \gamma = 2$)	25161	**85.7**
SemEval$_{50}$	845	80.2
+ DRLM ($\alpha = 0.50, \gamma = 32$)	27885	**85.6**
SemEval$_{267}$	4984	87.6
+ DRLM ($\alpha = 0.85, \gamma = 0.5$)	7490	**88.0**

Table 5: Results w/ and w/o training on weighted external triples using LM-based selection.

consistent improvements from using external data on both Complex and SemEval, with more marked improvements when the target dataset is small.

4.1 Multiple Sequence Structures

So far, the SemEval experiments used only the question body (*Body*). To also use the subject, one could simply concatenate the subject and the body (*Body + Subj*) and apply the same SLA architecture from Figure 1. However, as shown in Table 6, this actually hurt performance, likely because the system did not know where the question body started in each input sequence. To capture the SemEval question structure, we experimented with the architecture shown in Figure 2, in which different RNNs are used for the subject and the body (*Body & Subj*). Given that subjects are supposed to be short, we implemented attention only

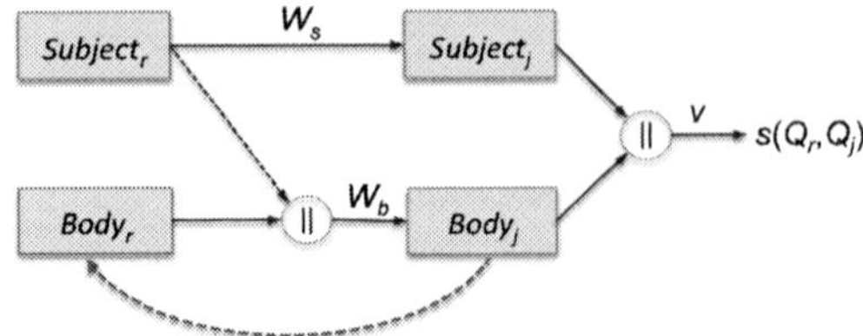

Figure 2: Subject-Body RNN architecture.

for the body sequence. In a second version, the output from the reference subject is concatenated to the output from the reference body, and used to initialize the RNN for the body of the second question (*Body || Subj*). The results in Table 6 show that the new architecture improves accuracy substantially, especially the second version with concatenated outputs.

Body	Body + Subj	Body & Subj	Body || Subj
87.6	87.3	91.8	**92.7**

Table 6: SemEval accuracy, using Body & Subj.

5 Conclusion and Future Work

We explored data augmentation methods and RNN architectures that were shown to improve question ranking performance. We expect these ideas to benefit more comprehensive approaches that also exploit answers and comments associated with previously answered questions, as was done in the SemEval cQA evaluation exercise (Nakov et al., 2016). The number and breadth of some experiments were limited by the available computational power, which we hope to address in future work.

Acknowledgments

We would like to thank the anonymous reviewers for their helpful comments. This work was supported by an allocation of computing time from the Ohio Supercomputer Center.

References

Dzmitry Bahdanau, Kyunghyun Cho, and Yoshua Bengio. 2015. Neural machine translation by jointly learning to align and translate. In *International Conference on Learning Representations (ICLR)*, pages 1–15.

Delphine Bernhard and Iryna Gurevych. 2008. Answering learners' questions by retrieving question paraphrases from social Q&A sites. In *EANL '08: Proceedings of the Third Workshop on Innovative Use of NLP for Building Educational Applications*, pages 44–52, Morristown, NJ, USA. Association for Computational Linguistics.

Razvan Bunescu and Yunfeng Huang. 2010. Learning the relative usefulness of questions in community QA. In *Proceedings of the 2010 Conference on Empirical Methods in Natural Language Processing*, pages 97–107. Association for Computational Linguistics.

Xin Cao, Gao Cong, Bin Cui, Christian Søndergaard Jensen, and Ce Zhang. 2009. The use of categorization information in language models for question retrieval. In *Proceedings of the 18th ACM Conference on Information and Knowledge Management*, pages 265–274, New York, NY, USA. ACM.

Kyunghyun Cho, Bart van Merriënboer, Çalar Gülçehre, Dzmitry Bahdanau, Fethi Bougares, Holger Schwenk, and Yoshua Bengio. 2014. Learning phrase representations using RNN encoder–decoder for statistical machine translation. In *Proceedings of the 2014 Conference on Empirical Methods in Natural Language Processing (EMNLP)*, pages 1724–1734, Doha, Qatar. Association for Computational Linguistics.

Huizhong Duan, Yunbo Cao, Chin-Yew Lin, and Yong Yu. 2008. Searching questions by identifying question topic and question focus. In *Proceedings of ACL-08: HLT*, pages 156–164, Columbus, Ohio.

Yoon Kim, Yacine Jernite, David Sontag, and Alexander M. Rush. 2016. Character-aware neural language models. In *Proceedings of the Thirtieth AAAI Conference on Artificial Intelligence*, AAAI'16, pages 2741–2749. AAAI Press.

Oleksandr Kolomiyets, Steven Bethard, and Marie-Francine Moens. 2011. Model-portability experiments for textual temporal analysis. In *Proceedings of the 49th Annual Meeting of the Association for Computational Linguistics: Human Language Technologies: Short Papers - Volume 2*, HLT '11, pages 271–276, Stroudsburg, PA, USA. Association for Computational Linguistics.

Tomas Mikolov, Ilya Sutskever, Kai Chen, Greg S. Corrado, and Jeff Dean. 2013. Distributed representations of words and phrases and their compositionality. In *Proceedings of NIPS 26*, pages 3111–3119.

Volodymyr Mnih, Nicolas Heess, Alex Graves, and Koray Kavukcuoglu. 2014. Recurrent models of visual attention. In *Advances in Neural Information Processing Systems 27*, pages 2204–2212.

Mitra Mohtarami, Yonatan Belinkov, Wei-Ning Hsu, Kfir Bar Yu Zhang Tao Lei, Scott Cyphers, and James Glass. 2016. SLS at SemEval-2016 Task 3: Neural-based approaches for ranking in community question answering. In *Proceedings of SemEval*, pages 828–835.

Robert C. Moore and William Lewis. 2010. Intelligent selection of language model training data. In *Proceedings of the ACL 2010 Conference Short Papers*, ACLShort '10, pages 220–224, Stroudsburg, PA, USA. Association for Computational Linguistics.

Preslav Nakov, Lluís Màrquez, Alessandro Moschitti, Walid Magdy, Hamdy Mubarak, abed Alhakim Freihat, Jim Glass, and Bilal Randeree. 2016. SemEval-2016 Task 3: Community question answering. *Proceedings of SemEval*, pages 525–545.

Quynh Thi Ngoc Do, Steven Bethard, and Marie-Francine Moens. 2015. Domain adaptation in semantic role labeling using a neural language model and linguistic resources. *IEEE/ACM Transactions on Audio, Speech and Language Processing*, 23(11):1812–1823.

Tim Rocktschel, Edward Grefenstette, Karl Moritz Hermann, Tom Koisk, and Phil Blunsom. 2015. Reasoning about entailment with neural attention. In *International Conference on Learning Representations (ICLR)*, pages 1–15.

Kai Wang, Zhaoyan Ming, and Tat-Seng Chua. 2009. A syntactic tree matching approach to finding similar questions in community-based QA services. In *Proceedings of the 32nd International ACM SIGIR Conference on Research and Development in Information Retrieval*, pages 187–194, New York, NY, USA. ACM.

Kelvin Xu, Jimmy Lei Ba, Ryan Kiros, Kyunghyun Cho, Aaron Courville, Ruslan Salakhutdinov, Richard S. Zemel, and Yoshua Bengio. 2015. Show, attend and tell: Neural image caption generation with visual attention. In *32nd International Conference on Machine Learning, ICML 2015*, pages 2048–2057.

Xiaobing Xue, Jiwoon Jeon, and W. Bruce Croft. 2008. Retrieval models for question and answer archives. In *Proceedings of the 31st Annual International ACM SIGIR Conference on Research and Development in Information Retrieval*, pages 475–482, New York, NY, USA. ACM.

Kai Zhang, Wei Wu, Fang Wang, Ming Zhou, and Zhoujun Li. 2016. Learning distributed representations of data in community question answering for question retrieval. In *Proceedings of the 9th ACM International Conference on Web Search and Data Mining*, pages 533–542. ACM.

Guangyou Zhou, Li Cai, Jun Zhao, and Kang Liu. 2011. Phrase-based translation model for question retrieval in community question answer archives. In *Proceedings of the 49th Annual Meeting of the Association for Computational Linguistics: Human Language Technologies - Volume 1*, pages 653–662, Stroudsburg, PA, USA. Association for Computational Linguistics.

Deriving Consensus for Multi-Parallel Corpora: an English Bible Study

Patrick Xia and **David Yarowsky**
Center for Language and Speech Processing, Johns Hopkins University
{paxia, yarowsky}@jhu.edu

Abstract

What can you do with multiple noisy versions of the same text? We present a method which generates a single consensus between multi-parallel corpora. By maximizing a function of linguistic features between word pairs, we jointly learn a single corpus-wide multiway alignment: a consensus between 27 versions of the English Bible. We additionally produce English paraphrases, word-level distributions of tags, and consensus dependency parses. Our method is language independent and applicable to any multi-parallel corpora. Given the Bible's unique role as alignable bitext for over 800 of the world's languages, this consensus alignment and resulting resources offer value for multilingual annotation projection, and also shed potential insights into the Bible itself.

1 Introduction

Noisy or heterogeneous copies of the same text are prevalent in religious and literary texts (Resnik et al., 1999; Koppel et al., 2016), machine translation n-best lists (Kumar and Byrne, 2004; Papineni et al., 2002), comparable corpora (Barzilay and Lee, 2003), and social media (Xu et al., 2015). While copies can be analyzed independently or together in a pairwise manner, information can be lost by not using them all jointly.

We view these copies of text as **multi-parallel corpora**, which consist of multiple sets of comparable or partially aligned documents. This contrasts with parallel corpora, which are usually between only two. The goal of this work is to produce word alignments for multi-parallel corpora (Fig. 1).

We approach this problem by tying the multi-parallel corpora together using features such as

Consensus	newsimplified	montgomery	lexham
Then	(Then, 0)	(Thereupon, 0)	(Then, 0)
Herod	(Herod, 1)	(Herod, 1)	(Herod, 1)
secretly	(secretly, 2)	(secretly, 3)	(secretly, 2)
called	(called, 3)	(sent, 2)	(summoned, 3)
for		(for, 4)	
the	(the, 4)	(the, 5)	(the, 4)
wise		(wise, 5)	
men	(astrologers, 5)	(Magi, 6)	(men, 6)

Figure 1: A sample of Fig. 3, in which different words with a similar meaning are aligned. Each entry contains the word and its index in the original sentence.

pairwise word alignments, dependency parses, and POS tags. Our method jointly learns word alignments and annotations for these features in the English Biblical multi-parallel corpora. We produce multiway word alignments, complete dependency parses, and POS tag annotations for the English Bible. While our resources and choice of features are catered for our specific domain, the method can be applied more broadly for aligning and establishing consensus in any domain.

The English Bible is a literary religious text with multiple authors, disputed authorship structure, and multiple revisions for language modernization.[1] While there is existing computational work in Biblical analysis (Lee, 2007), our contribution of automatically generated consensus annotations for all verses allows future research to efficiently investigate across all English Bibles. As the Bible is available in electronic form in over 800 of the world's languages (Mayer and Cysouw, 2014), the Bible may be the only parallel corpus for low-resource languages, and our in-domain resources can be a valuable reference.[2]

---

[1] The unresolved Synoptic Problem questions the order and dependencies of the the Synoptic Gospels.

[2] Available at github.com/pitrack/monolign.

Proceedings of the The 8th International Joint Conference on Natural Language Processing, pages 448–453,
Taipei, Taiwan, November 27 – December 1, 2017 ©2017 AFNLP

2 Method

The consensus consists of aligned tokens between the corpora. Assuming each corpus consists of partially aligned documents (e.g. verses of the Bible), we first target the word alignments at the document level. We then use a bootstrapping approach to produce the final corpus-wide alignment. By using a majority vote, the final alignments can produce additional consensus resources.

2.1 Document-level alignment

To create document-level alignments, documents from each corpus are processed sequentially. Suppose $L = \{D_1, D_2, ..., D_k\}$ is a set of parallel documents where $d_{i,j}$ is the jth token in D_i. A matching $\mathcal{M}_L$ is a document-level alignment which consists of a set of relations, $R_1, ..., R_r$. For example, if $|L| = 2$, then $\mathcal{M}_L$ is a one-to-one word alignment between two lines of text. Its relations are either an aligned pair of tokens or an unaligned singleton token.

In Algorithm 1, $\mathcal{M}_L$ is generated by adding the next document to an existing matching and weighing the edges between tokens and relations according to Equation 1. Edges are pruned to both speed up the solver and avoid conflating separate or weakly related tokens. The maximum weighted matching is then used to decide which relations are expanded.

$$W(d_{i,j}, R_k) = \sum_{d \in R_k} f(d, d_{i,j}). \qquad (1)$$

Algorithm 1 Document-level alignment

```
function ALIGNDOCUMENTS(L)
    L = D₁, D₂, ..., Dₖ        ▷ Assume fixed ordering
    M = {{d₁,ⱼ} : d₁,ⱼ ∈ D₁}
                    ▷ Initialize matching with singletons relations
    for Dᵢ = D₂, ..., Dₖ do
        (V, E) = (Dᵢ ∪ M, Dᵢ × M)
        G = (V, E, W(E))       ▷ W is defined by Eqn. 1
        G' = PRUNE(G)          ▷ Remove small edges
        A = MAXWEIGHTMATCHING(G')
        for (d, R) ∈ A do
            R ← R ∪ {d}
        M ← M ∪ {{dᵢ,ⱼ} : dᵢ,ⱼ ∈ Dᵢ \ A}
                    ▷ Update existing relations or create new singletons
    return M
```

The scoring function, f, is a weighted sum of the features described in Table 1. While a feasible weight function could be normalized by $|R_k|$, we instead choose to sum. If two different relations have a similar meaning but are not initially placed

Feature	Values	Description
IDENTITY	Binary	$d = e$
PAIRWISE	Binary	Aligned(d, e)
LEMMA	Binary	Lemma$(d) = $ Lemma(e)
POS	Binary	POS$(d) = $ POS(e)
PARENT	Binary	Parent$(d) = $ Parent(e)
NEIGHBORS	Integer	$|L^+(d) \cap L^+(e)|$, $L^+(d)$ is the multiset of outgoing edge labels from d in the dependency parse.
CHILDREN	Integer	The number of children u, v of d, e where the edges (d, u) and (e, v) have the same label and Aligned(u, v).
PARENT(V)	Real	Relates a child v of e to d by considering the set U that aligns to v. For each $u \in U$, we increment the score if its parent is d and give additional points if the parent's POS tag and edge label is the same as those of e. However, these are normalized by $|U|$.

Table 1: These specific features are used in $f(d, e)$. Aligned(d, e) is determined by the bitext aligner, and PARENT(V) is a feature for each child v of e. All features have weight 1, except for IDENTITY, which has weight 3. The pruning threshold is 4. These values could be further tuned.

together, both will grow as tokens from new tokens would have a similar score to both. By using total score, the bigger relation will dominate. On the other hand, taking the sum could lead large relations matching with unrelated tokens. For ease of future analysis, errors of this type were preferred.

$$F(\mathcal{M}) = \sum_{R_i \in \mathcal{M}} \sum_{d, e \in R_i} f(d, e) \qquad (2)$$

A matching is scored by summing pairwise scores in all of its relations (Equation 2). Ideally, we would directly maximize $F(\mathcal{M})$, but that is NP-hard.[3] Instead, we match each document greedily.

2.2 Creating a corpus alignment

Suppose the documents in the multi-parallel corpora $\mathcal{C} = C_1, C_2, \ldots, C_c$ are already aligned, so for any document, we can find its counterpart in each C_i, if it exists. This is the case for the Biblical data since the verse numbers act as document labels.

Given an existing document-level alignment, we can improve the accuracy of individual features. For example, tokens within the same relation are synonymous, and so they are used to recompute the PAIRWISE feature. Algorithm 1 depends on the initial ordering of L. This motivates Algorithm 2,

---

[3]With just three documents, this is a weighted variant of the 3-dimensional matching problem.

which both recomputes the feature values and shuffles the documents between each of the $T = 10$ iterations.

Algorithm 2 Corpus alignment

Input: Multi-parallel corpora $\mathcal{C} = C_1, C_2, ...C_c$
Parse and tag each $C_i \in \mathcal{C}$ [4]
for $t = 1 ... T$ **do**
    Recompute corpus statistics
    Align every pair $C_i, C_j \in \mathcal{C}$
    $\mathcal{C}$.shuffle()   ▷ Choose a new order for the documents
    for all documents $L \in \mathcal{C}$ **do**
        $\mathcal{M}_{L,t} = \text{ALIGNDOCUMENTS}(L)$
Output: $\{\text{argmax}_{\mathcal{M}_{L,t}} F(\mathcal{M}_{L,t}) : L \in \mathcal{C}\}$

2.3 Dataset and tools

The corpus of Bibles were collected by Mayer and Cysouw (2014) and contains 27 English versions. 23 contain just the New Testament (~8K verses, ~200K words), while four also include the Old Testament (~31K verses, ~900K words).

We use `fast_align` (Dyer et al., 2013), a greedy, transition-based dependency parser (Honnibal and Johnson, 2015), and an averaged perceptron POS tagger with Brown cluster features (Collins, 2002; Koo et al., 2008) for feature computation.[5]

3 Results

3.1 Analysis of alignments

Fig. 3 shows an example of an alignment produced by our system.[6] There are a few misalignments due to both literary divergence and our design choices, such as the sum in Equation 1 and targeting one-to-one alignments.

The visualization of the matchings simplifies analysis of literary variation. Relations with only a few or different members are easy to spot. These anomalies can be indicators of different choices in translation, unclean source text, or use of older language. For example, unlike "wise men" and "magi," "astrologers" only appears once across the rows **wise men** in Fig. 3, so the word choice may be a deliberate. Small or singleton relations prompt further investigation into the source.[7] Since some of our features are independent of meaning, we correctly align non-English (e.g. Hebrew) words.

---

[4]If parsing or tagging is improved by the alignments from the previous iteration, it could be rerun every iteration.
[5]Implemented by `https//spacy.io`.
[6]More examples in Appendix Tables 7 and 8
[7]In Matthew 8:22 (diaglot version), an error in the source was discovered by an extraneous singleton relation: {"The"}.

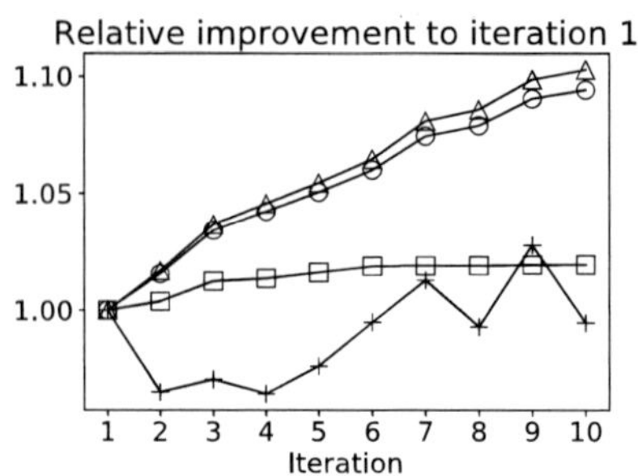

Figure 2: Relative change in total score with respect to the first iteration: Entire text ($\bigcirc$); Old Testament ($\square$); New Testament ($\triangle$); per iteration ($+$). Since the feature weights are fixed, the absolute score is not meaningful.

Word indices in each of the columns also show the degree of reordering, which itself is a measure of divergence.

3.2 Improvements across iterations

Fig. 2 tracks the relative change in total score summed across all the documents. The Old Testament plateaus early, possibly because there are only four sources. The high variance in per iteration score shows the large effect of the ordering.

3.3 Limitations

Since there are no gold-standard annotations for this task, it is difficult to perform a meaningful quantitative evaluation on the alignments directly. Empirical evaluation is also challenging due to the scale of even a single multiway alignment.

Because the tools used are not trained specifically for historical English religious texts, it is possible for the features themselves to be imprecise or noisy. For this predominantly modern English corpora, tokens with incorrectly preprocessed features can still be placed in the correct relation due to the correct features. For an even better alignment, additional features or a looser definition of IDENTITY would encourage improved alignments.

The proposed method assumes a one-to-one mapping between tokens and relations. Multi-word expressions in the consensus, like **wise men**, can be viewed as a multi-relation expression. It is challenging to generalize our method to many-to-many alignments.

4 Additional Biblical Resources

For a given relation, a consensus annotation can be derived by taking the majority annotation of the

Figure 3: A matching for document D = Matthew 2:7. For space reasons, nine versions are shown in the same order they were aligned. Each row is a relation; the row header is its most common word. Each cell (r, c) is a member of the relation R_r and contains a token and an index from document D_c. The relations are arranged by the consensus index. Consensus POS tags and edges to the head token are shown in the analysis column. For presentation purposes, row headers are **bolded** if the majority of the documents in this table had a word in the relation. * indicates that there existed an equally competitive tag. Misalignments are *italicized*.

tokens in that relation. This can be extended on the corpus-level to word types by considering all relations represented by or containing that type.

4.1 In-domain paraphrases

We create a Bible-specific set of paraphrases. To obtain a distribution of similar words to a specific type w, we consider either all tokens in all relations that contain w (finer) or just the majority type of relations containing w (coarser) (Fig. 4).

```
Fine-grained paraphrases:
HEROD: Herod (0.90), Herodes (0.04), he (0.01) ...
SECRET: secret (0.59), mystery (0.19), private
(0.04) ...
Coarse-grained paraphrases:
HEROD: Herod (0.95), Herods (0.05)
SECRET: secret (1.00)
```

Figure 4: Each word is followed by possible paraphrases and their proportions, which are computed from the consensus.

The domain specific paraphrases demonstrate the linguistic variation across the Bible, which can be further analyzed. Fig. 5 explores some of the variations that occur in our specific domain.

4.2 Consensus distributions

We can compute both the majority values (Fig. 3) and the entire distributions (Fig. 6) of specific features such as POS tags and head words. Aggregating each corpus independently before alignment,

```
HYMENAEUS: Hymenaeus (0.82), Hymenius (0.04),
Hymeneus (0.04), Humenaios (0.04) ...
BLAZES: burns (0.48), burning (0.33) burneth
(0.10), blazes (0.04) ...
CHALLENGED: said (0.15), opposed (0.13), urged
(0.12), tested (0.10), tempted (0.06), tried (0.05),
asked (0.04).
```

Figure 5: These examples demonstrate spelling variation, language modernization, and unexpected domain-specific distributions.

we can compute the possible tags for a word type. By using the alignments, the distribution of tags is softer. This could be useful as a prior in cross-lingual tag projection, since bitexts in the Bible are often not exact translations.

For each possible head of a token, we compute consensus edge labels. By taking the most frequent edges, this results in a consensus dependency parse. If the proportions are used instead of the consensus, the result is a distribution over possible parses.

5 Discussion and Related Work

While monolingual insights like paraphrases have potential applications in semantic textual similarity (Agirre et al., 2012), there exist bigger corpora for those tasks, such as PPDB (Ganitkevitch et al., 2013). However, as the Bible is often the only significant parallel text for many of the world's languages, improved 27-way consensus English

POS tags
Before corpus alignments:
TIME: NN (1.00)
SECRET: NN (0.54), JJ (0.46)
With corpus alignments:
TIME: NN (0.94), NNS (0.05) ...
SECRET: JJ (0.51), NN (0.47), NNS (0.01) ...

Head words
Before corpus alignments:
TIME: `at` (0.23), `for` (0.09), `in` (0.07), `is` (0.06) ...
SECRET: `in` (0.28), `is` (0.06) `kept` (0.04) `places` (0.04) ...
With corpus alignments:
TIME: `at` (0.17), `in` (0.09), `for` (0.09), `is` (0.05) ...
SECRET: `in` (0.32), `place` (0.05), `mystery` (0.04), `is` (0.04) ...

Figure 6: A comparison of the POS tags (above) and head words (below) distributions for *time* and *secret* with and without the consensus alignment.

resources created here have value for annotation projection to low-resource languages.

The Bible has been productively used as a key resource for cross-lingual knowledge transfer (Yarowsky et al., 2001; Agić et al., 2015). Specifically, Johannsen et al. (2016) suggests a method for projecting POS tags and dependency parses onto a target language. Our approach can be modified in a similar way. By restricting the scoring function to use entirely language-independent features (e.g. pairwise alignments), our algorithm still maximizes the score of the matching by relearning an improved dictionary between iterations. The corpus alignment may also be desirable over separate alignments for multi-source projection tasks in noisier data because a word or phrase may only align with only a subset of the sources.

By generating resources specifically for the Bible, we hope to foster future computational methods for studying religious texts. Current Biblical visualization (Zhang et al., 2016) and authorship (Moritz et al., 2016) works use a small subset of the translations to perform their analysis. Our resources would encourage analysis across all versions of the Bible, which would be less biased than picking a small set. By weighing the votes cast by each token in a relation, it is even possible to emphasize a specific corpus.

The algorithms described in Section 2 can be applied to any parallel corpora. The scoring function is simple and accommodates arbitrary features. While our approach specifically assumes the documents (verses) within the corpora are already aligned, knowing which documents are similar (e.g. through clustering) is sufficient – perhaps

at the cost of quality – to align and generate the subsequent resources.

6 Conclusion

We present a method for analyzing noisy multi-parallel text on significant multi-parallel corpora: 27 versions of the English Bible. The algorithm maximizes a flexible heuristic scoring function, so it is language-independent and applicable to any multi-parallel corpora. We produce a corpus-wide word alignment and use its consensus to create additional in-domain resources.

Given the Bible's unique role as the primary or only significant bitext for many of the world's languages, the robustly induced consensus analyses and associated alignments offer particular value to annotation projection in low-resource languages. In addition, these results shed insight into the underlying semantics of very widely studied source texts via both consensus and divergence of their multiple distinct translations.

Acknowledgments

This material is based upon work supported in part by DARPA LORELEI. Any opinions, findings and conclusions or recommendations expressed in this material are those of the authors and do not necessarily reflect the views of DARPA.

References

Željko Agić, Dirk Hovy, and Anders Søgaard. 2015. If all you have is a bit of the Bible: Learning POS taggers for truly low-resource languages. In *Proceedings of the 53rd Annual Meeting of the Association for Computational Linguistics and the 7th International Joint Conference on Natural Language Processing (Volume 2: Short Papers)*, pages 268–272, Beijing, China. Association for Computational Linguistics.

Eneko Agirre, Daniel Cer, Mona Diab, and Aitor Gonzalez-Agirre. 2012. SemEval-2012 task 6: A pilot on semantic textual similarity. In **SEM 2012: The First Joint Conference on Lexical and Computational Semantics – Volume 1: Proceedings of the main conference and the shared task, and Volume 2: Proceedings of the Sixth International Workshop on Semantic Evaluation (SemEval 2012)*, pages 385–393, Montréal, Canada. Association for Computational Linguistics.

Regina Barzilay and Lillian Lee. 2003. Learning to paraphrase: An unsupervised approach using multiple-sequence alignment. In *Proceedings of the 2003 Conference of the North American Chapter of the Association for Computational Linguistics on Human Language Technology - Volume 1*, pages 16–23.

Michael Collins. 2002. Discriminative training methods for hidden Markov models: Theory and experiments with perceptron algorithms. In *Proceedings of the 2002 Conference on Empirical Methods in Natural Language Processing*, pages 1–8.

Chris Dyer, Victor Chahuneau, and Noah A. Smith. 2013. A simple, fast, and effective reparameterization of IBM model 2. In *Proceedings of the 2013 Conference of the North American Chapter of the Association for Computational Linguistics: Human Language Technologies*, pages 644–648, Atlanta, Georgia. Association for Computational Linguistics.

Juri Ganitkevitch, Benjamin Van Durme, and Chris Callison-Burch. 2013. PPDB: The paraphrase database. In *Proceedings of the 2013 Conference of the North American Chapter of the Association for Computational Linguistics: Human Language Technologies*, pages 758–764, Atlanta, Georgia. Association for Computational Linguistics.

Matthew Honnibal and Mark Johnson. 2015. An improved non-monotonic transition system for dependency parsing. In *Proceedings of the 2015 Conference on Empirical Methods in Natural Language Processing*, pages 1373–1378, Lisbon, Portugal. Association for Computational Linguistics.

Anders Johannsen, Željko Agić, and Anders Søgaard. 2016. Joint part-of-speech and dependency projection from multiple sources. In *Proceedings of the 54th Annual Meeting of the Association for Computational Linguistics (Volume 2: Short Papers)*, pages 561–566, Berlin, Germany. Association for Computational Linguistics.

Terry Koo, Xavier Carreras, and Michael Collins. 2008. Simple semi-supervised dependency parsing. In *Proceedings of ACL-08: HLT*, pages 595–603, Columbus, Ohio. Association for Computational Linguistics.

Moshe Koppel, Moty Michaely, and Alex Tal. 2016. Reconstructing ancient literary texts from noisy manuscripts. In *Proceedings of the Fifth Workshop on Computational Linguistics for Literature*, pages 40–46.

Shankar Kumar and William Byrne. 2004. Minimum bayes-risk decoding for statistical machine translation. In *In Proceedings of the NAACL 2004*, pages 169–176.

John Lee. 2007. A computational model of text reuse in ancient literary texts. In *Proceedings of the 45th Annual Meeting of the Association of Computational Linguistics*, pages 472–479.

Thomas Mayer and Michael Cysouw. 2014. Creating a massively parallel Bible corpus. In *Proceedings of the Ninth International Conference on Language Resources and Evaluation (LREC'14)*.

Maria Moritz, Andreas Wiederhold, Barbara Pavlek, Yuri Bizzoni, and Marco Büchler. 2016. Non-literal text reuse in historical texts: An approach to identify reuse transformations and its application to Bible reuse. In *Proceedings of the 2016 Conference on Empirical Methods in Natural Language Processing*, pages 1849–1859, Austin, Texas. Association for Computational Linguistics.

Kishore Papineni, Salim Roukos, Todd Ward, and Wei-Jing Zhu. 2002. BLEU: A method for automatic evaluation of machine translation. In *Proceedings of the 40th Annual Meeting on Association for Computational Linguistics*, ACL '02, pages 311–318.

Philip Resnik, Mari Broman Olsen, and Mona Diab. 1999. The Bible as a parallel corpus: Annotating the 'Book of 2000 Tongues'. *Computers and the Humanities*, 33(1):129–153.

Wei Xu, Chris Callison-Burch, and Bill Dolan. 2015. Semeval-2015 task 1: Paraphrase and semantic similarity in twitter (pit). In *Proceedings of the 9th International Workshop on Semantic Evaluation (SemEval 2015)*, pages 1–11, Denver, Colorado. Association for Computational Linguistics.

David Yarowsky, Grace Ngai, and Richard Wicentowski. 2001. Inducing multilingual text analysis tools via robust projection across aligned corpora. In *Proceedings of the First International Conference on Human Language Technology Research*, pages 1–8, San Diego. Association for Computational Linguistics.

Ken Zhang, Carlos Folgar, and Jess McCuan. 2016. Decoding the Bible. `https://quid.com/feed/decoding-the-bible`.

Author Index

Association for Computational Linguistics
209 N. Eighth Street
Stroudsburg, Pennsylvania 18360

ISBN 978-1-5108-5293-8